THE VICTORIA HISTORY
OF THE
COUNTIES OF ENGLAND

A HISTORY OF
WILTSHIRE
VOLUME XV

Oxford University Press, Walton Street, Oxford OX2 6DP
Oxford New York
Athens Auckland Bangkok Bombay
Calcutta Cape Town Dar es Salaam Delhi
Florence Hong Kong Istanbul Karachi
Kuala Lumpur Madras Madrid Melbourne
Mexico City Nairobi Paris Singapore
Taipei Tokyo Toronto

and associated companies in
Berlin Ibadan

Oxford is a trade mark of Oxford University Press

Published in the United States
by Oxford University Press Inc., New York

British Library Cataloguing in Publication Data
A catalogue record for this book is available
from the British Library

ISBN 0 19 722785 6

Typeset at the University of London Computer Centre
Printed in Great Britain
on acid-free paper by
Butler and Tanner Ltd, Frome

THE VICTORIA HISTORY
OF THE
COUNTIES OF ENGLAND

EDITED BY C. R. J. CURRIE

THE UNIVERSITY OF LONDON
INSTITUTE OF
HISTORICAL RESEARCH

INSCRIBED TO THE

MEMORY OF HER LATE MAJESTY

QUEEN VICTORIA

WHO GRACIOUSLY GAVE THE TITLE TO

AND ACCEPTED THE DEDICATION

OF THIS HISTORY

A HISTORY OF

WILTSHIRE

EDITED BY D. A. CROWLEY

VOLUME XV

AMESBURY HUNDRED

BRANCH AND DOLE HUNDRED

PUBLISHED FOR

THE INSTITUTE OF HISTORICAL RESEARCH

BY

OXFORD UNIVERSITY PRESS

1995

CONTENTS OF VOLUME FIFTEEN

LIST OF ILLUSTRATIONS

Thanks are rendered to the following for permission to reproduce material: the British Library, the British Museum, the Courtauld Institute of Art (photographs of paintings by John Buckler in Devizes Museum), Elisabeth, Lady Moyne, and Mrs. Janet Stone (engraving of Biddesden House), the Royal Commission on the Historical Monuments of England, Salisbury and South Wiltshire Museum, Wiltshire Archaeological and Natural History Society, and Wiltshire Library and Museum Service.

LIST OF ILLUSTRATIONS

LIST OF ILLUSTRATIONS

LIST OF MAPS

The maps listed below were drawn by K. J. Wass from drafts prepared by D. A. Crowley, Jane Freeman, and Janet H. Stevenson. The parish and other boundaries are taken from inclosure award and tithe award maps and from Ordnance Survey maps of the later 19th century.

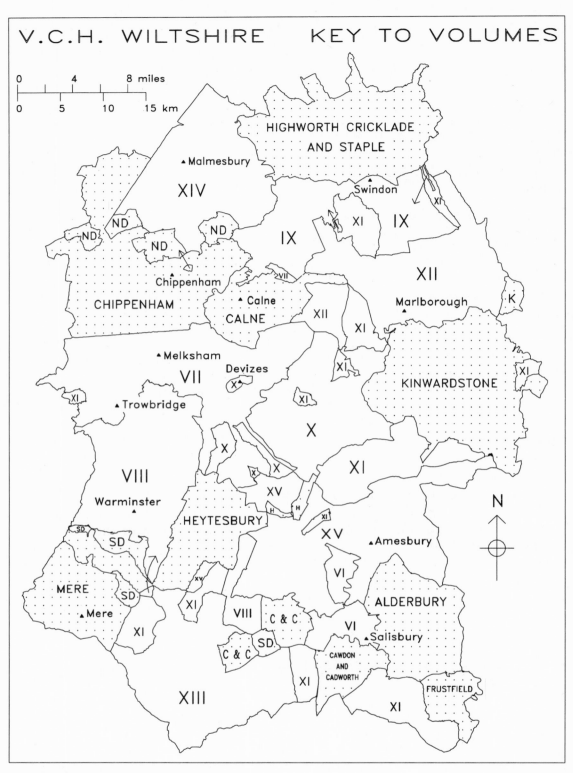

V.C.H. WILTSHIRE KEY TO VOLUMES

Detached parts of hundreds:

C & C Cawdon and Cadworth **SD** South Damerham **K** Kinwardstone
ND North Damerham **H** Heytesbury

Contents of volumes:

I-V General chapters
VI Wilton, Salisbury; Underditch hundred; part of Branch and Dole hundred
VII Bradford, Melksham, and Potterne and Cannings hundreds

VIII Warminster, Westbury, and Whorwellsdown hundreds
IX Kingsbridge hundred
X Swanborough hundred; Devizes
XI Downton hundred and Elstub and Everleigh hundred

XII Ramsbury and Selkley hundreds; Marlborough
XIII Chalke and Dunworth hundreds
XIV Malmesbury hundred
XV Amesbury hundred; part of Branch and Dole hundred

EDITORIAL NOTE

LIKE the fifteen earlier volumes of the *Victoria History of Wiltshire*, this volume has been prepared under the supervision of the Wiltshire Victoria County History Committee. The origin and early constitution of that Committee are described in the Editorial Note to Volume VII, the first to be published. New arrangements introduced in 1975 are outlined in the Editorial Note to Volume XI, and a further modification in 1990 is described in the Editorial Note to Volume XIV. In 1991 Thamesdown Borough Council, which with its predecessor Swindon Borough Council had met more than a fifth of the cumulative costs of the research for, and writing of, the Wiltshire *History*, gave notice of withdrawal from the Committee, and it made its last contribution in 1993. The Local Authorities retaining representation on the Committee were thus Wiltshire County Council and the District Councils of Kennet, Salisbury, North Wiltshire, and West Wiltshire. To them the University of London again offers its profound thanks for their continued support of the Wiltshire V.C.H. Committee, whose collaboration in the enterprise is once more warmly acknowledged.

In 1992 Mr. D. M. Kent resigned as Honorary Secretary of the Committee, and was succeeded by Mr. M. O. Holder. At the same time Mr. E. J. P. Thornton resigned as Honorary Treasurer and was succeeded by Mr. F. R. Marshall. Grateful thanks are owed to Mr. Kent and Mr. Thornton for their eighteen years' helpful service to the Committee. The origins of that service are recorded in the Editorial Note to Volume X.

Thanks are also offered to the many people who have helped in the compilation of this volume by granting access to documents and buildings in their ownership or care, by providing information, or by giving advice. Most of them are named in the footnotes to the articles with which they helped. Special mention must be made of the assistance given by the County Archivist (Mr. S. D. Hobbs) and his staff and by the Local Studies Librarian of Wiltshire County Council (Mr. M. J. Marshman) and his assistants, of the access provided by the Government Property Lawyers and the Treasury Solicitor to records in their keeping, and of information provided by the Defence Land Agent.

The *General Introduction* to the *Victoria County History*, published in 1970, and its *Supplement* published in 1990 give an outline of the structure and aims of the series as a whole, with an account of its progress.

WILTSHIRE
VICTORIA COUNTY HISTORY COMMITTEE

As at 5 July 1994

COUNCILLOR MRS. V. C. S. LANDELL MILLS,   *Representing the Wiltshire County Council*
    Chairman
COUNCILLOR D. M. FIRMAGER
COUNCILLOR A. J. MASTERS
COUNCILLOR MRS. P. RUGG

COUNCILLOR MISS P. E. G. COURTMAN   *Representing the Kennet District Council*

COUNCILLOR S. R. FEAR   *Representing the Salisbury District Council*
COUNCILLOR MRS. J. M. LONGDEN

COUNCILLOR MRS. L. BENNETT   *Representing the North Wiltshire District*
COUNCILLOR MISS D. J. MATTHEWS   *Council*

COUNCILLOR MRS. J. L. REPTON   *Representing the West Wiltshire District Council*
COUNCILLOR J. E. SYME

PROFESSOR C. R. ELRINGTON   *Representing the Central Committee of the*
     Victoria County History

MR. G. G. BROWN   *Representing the Wiltshire Archaeological and*
     Natural History Society

Co-opted Members

DR. J. H. BETTEY   MISS SUSAN REYNOLDS
MR. D. F. HODSON   MR. K. H. ROGERS
DR. R. F. HUNNISETT   MR. BONAR SYKES
MR. M. J. LANSDOWN

MR. M. O. HOLDER, *Hon. Secretary*
MR. F. R. MARSHALL, *Hon. Treasurer*

LIST OF CLASSES OF DOCUMENTS
IN THE PUBLIC RECORD OFFICE
USED IN THIS VOLUME
WITH THEIR CLASS NUMBERS

Clerks of Assize
          Western Circuit
  ASSI 21   Crown Minute Books
  ASSI 25   Indictment Files

Chancery
          Proceedings
  C 1   Early
  C 2   Series I
  C 3   Series II
          Six Clerks Series
  C 5   Bridges
  C 11   Various Six Clerks, Series I
  C 44   Judicial Proceedings (Common Law
              Side), Tower Series
  C 54   Close Rolls
  C 60   Fine Rolls
  C 66   Patent Rolls
  C 78   Decree Rolls
  C 81   Warrants for the Great Seal,
              Series I
  C 88   Files (Tower and Rolls Chapel),
              Records upon Outlawries
  C 113   Judicial Proceedings (Equity
              Side), Masters' Exhibits,
              Kindersley
          Inquisitions post mortem
  C 134   Series I, Edward II
  C 138   Henry V
  C 139   Henry VI
  C 140   Edward IV and V
  C 142   Series II
  C 143   Inquisitions ad quod damnum
  C 146   Ancient Deeds, Series C
  C 260   Files (Tower and Rolls Chapel),
              Recorda

Court of Common Pleas
          Feet of Fines
  CP 25/1   Series I
  CP 25/2   Series II
  CP 40   Plea Rolls
  CP 43   Recovery Rolls

Duchy of Lancaster
  DL 7   Inquisitions post mortem
          Deeds
  DL 25   Series L
  DL 27   Series LS
  DL 29   Ministers' Accounts
  DL 42   Miscellaneous Books

DL 43   Rentals and Surveys

Exchequer, King's Remembrancer
  E 126   Entry Books of Decrees and Orders,
              Series IV
  E 134   Depositions taken by Commission
  E 136   Escheators' Accounts
  E 150   Inquisitions post mortem,
              Series II
  E 159   Memoranda Rolls
  E 178   Special Commissions of Inquiry
  E 179   Subsidy Rolls, etc.
  E 210   Ancient Deeds, Series D

Exchequer, Augmentation Office
  E 301   Certificates of Colleges and Chan-
              tries
  E 305   Deeds of Purchase and Exchange
  E 309   Enrolments of Leases
  E 310   Particulars for Leases
  E 317   Parliamentary Surveys
  E 318   Particulars for Grants of Crown
              Lands
          Ancient Deeds
  E 326   Series B
  E 328   Series BB

Exchequer, First Fruits and Tenths Office
  E 331   Bishops' Certificates of Institu-
              tions to Benefices

Exchequer, Lord Treasurer's Remembrancer's
and Pipe Offices
  E 368   Memoranda Rolls
  E 372   Pipe Rolls

Ministry of Education
  ED 2   Parish Files
  ED 7   Public Elementary Schools, Pre-
              liminary Statements
  ED 21   Public Elementary School Files

Registry of Friendly Societies
  FS 4   Rules and Amendments, Indexes,
              Series II

Home Office
  HO 52   Correspondence and Papers,
              Municipal and Provincial,
              Counties: Correspondence
  HO 107   Census Returns, 1841
  HO 129   Ecclesiastical Returns

LIST OF CLASSES OF DOCUMENTS

NOTE ON ABBREVIATIONS

Among the abbreviations and short titles used are the following:

Abbrev. Plac.	*Placitorum Abbreviatio*, ed. W. Illingworth (Record Commission, 1811)
Abbrev. Rot. Orig.	*Rotulorum Originalium in Curia Scaccarii Abbreviatio* (Record Commission, 1805)
Acct. of Wilts. Schs.	*An Account of Schools for the Children of the Labouring Classes in the County of Wiltshire,* H.C. 27 (1859 Sess. 1), xxi (2)
Alnwick Castle Mun.	Muniments at Alnwick Castle, Northumb.
Alum. Cantab.	*Alumni Cantabrigienses,* ed. J. and J. A. Venn
Alum. Oxon.	*Alumni Oxonienses,* ed. J. Foster
Ann. Mon.	*Annales Monastici,* ed. H. R. Luard (Rolls Series, 1864–9)
Arch. Jnl.	*Archaeological Journal*
Aubrey, *Nat. Hist. Wilts.* ed. Britton	John Aubrey, *Natural History of Wiltshire,* ed. John Britton (London, 1847)
Aubrey, *Topog. Coll.* ed. Jackson	*The Topographical Collections of John Aubrey,* ed. J. E. Jackson (Devizes, 1862)
B.L.	British Library
Add. Ch.	Additional Charter
Add. MS.	Additional Manuscript
Cott. MS.	Cottonian Manuscript
Eg. Ch.	Egerton Charter
Harl. Ch.	Harleian Charter
Harl. MS.	Harleian Manuscript
Lansd. Ch.	Lansdowne Charter
Bk. of Fees	*The Book of Fees* (H.M.S.O. 1920–31)
Boyton Manor Archive	Muniments of the Fane family, formerly at Boyton Manor, now in the Wiltshire Record Office
Bracton's Note Bk.	H. de Bracton, *Note Book,* ed. F. W. Maitland (London, 1887)
Burke, *Commoners*	J. Burke and others, *A History of the Commoners* (London, 1833–8)
Burke, *Ext. & Dorm. Baronetcies*	J. Burke and others, *Extinct and Dormant Baronetcies*
Burke, *Land. Gent.*	J. Burke and others, *Landed Gentry*
Burke, *Land. Gent. of Ireland*	B. Burke and others, *Landed Gentry of Ireland*
Burke, *Peerage*	J. Burke and others, *A Dictionary of the Peerage*
Cal. Chanc. Wts.	*Calendar of Chancery Warrants preserved in the Public Record Office* (H.M.S.O. 1927)
Cal. Chart. R.	*Calendar of the Charter Rolls preserved in the Public Record Office* (H.M.S.O. 1903–27)
Cal. Close	*Calendar of the Close Rolls preserved in the Public Record Office* (H.M.S.O. 1892–1963)
Cal. Cttee. for Compounding	*Calendar of the Proceedings of the Committee for Compounding, etc. 1643–1660* (H.M.S.O. 1889–92)
Cal. Cttee. for Money	*Calendar of the Proceedings of the Committee for the Advance of Money, 1642–1646* (H.M.S.O. 1888)
Cal. Fine R.	*Calendar of the Fine Rolls preserved in the Public Record Office* (H.M.S.O. 1911–62)
Cal. Inq. Misc.	*Calendar of Inquisitions Miscellaneous (Chancery) preserved in the Public Record Office* (H.M.S.O. 1916–68)
Cal. Inq. p.m.	*Calendar of Inquisitions post mortem preserved in the Public Record Office* (H.M.S.O. 1904–92)
Cal. Inq. p.m. Hen. VII	*Calendar of Inquisitions post mortem, Henry VII* (H.M.S.O. 1898–1955)
Cal. Lib.	*Calendar of the Liberate Rolls preserved in the Public Record Office* (H.M.S.O. 1916–64)

NOTE ON ABBREVIATIONS

Cal. Papal Reg.	*Calendar of Papal Registers: Papal Letters* (H.M.S.O. and Irish Manuscripts Commission, 1893–1986)
Cal. Pat.	*Calendar of the Patent Rolls preserved in the Public Record Office* (H.M.S.O. 1891–1986)
Cal. S.P. Dom.	*Calendar of State Papers, Domestic Series* (H.M.S.O. 1856–1972)
Calamy Revised, ed. Matthews	*Calamy Revised: being a Revision of Edmund Calamy's Account of the Ministers and others Ejected and Silenced, 1660–2*, by A. G. Matthews (1934)
Camden, *Brit.* (1806)	W. Camden, *Britannia*, with additions by R. Gough (1806)
Cart. Sax. ed. Birch	*Cartularium Saxonicum*, ed. W. de G. Birch (1885–93)
Cat. Anct. D.	*Descriptive Catalogue of Ancient Deeds in the Public Record Office* (H.M.S.O. 1890–1915)
Cath. Dir.	*Catholic Directory of England and Wales*
Ch. Com.	Church Commissioners
Char. Com.	Charity Commission
Chron. Rog. de Houedene	*Chronica Rogeri de Houedene*, ed. W. Stubbs (Rolls Series, 1868–71)
Churches of SE. Wilts.	*Churches of South-East Wiltshire* (Royal Commission on the Historical Monuments of England, 1987)
Close R.	*Close Rolls of the Reign of Henry III preserved in the Public Record Office* (H.M.S.O. 1902–75)
Complete Peerage	G. E. C[ockayne] and others, *The Complete Peerage* (2nd edn. 1910–59)
Compton Census	*The Compton Census of 1676: a critical edition*, ed. A. Whiteman (British Academy Records of Social and Economic History, N.S. x)
T. Cox, *Magna Brit.*	T. Cox, *Magna Britannia Antiqua et Nova* (London, 1738)
Crockford	*Crockford's Clerical Directory*
Cur. Reg. R.	*Curia Regis Rolls preserved in the Public Record Office* (H.M.S.O. 1922–79)
D. & C. Sar.	Dean and chapter of Salisbury
D. & C. Windsor Mun.	Muniments of the dean and canons of St. George's chapel, Windsor
D. & C. Winton. Mun.	Muniments of the dean and chapter of Winchester
D.N.B.	*Dictionary of National Biography*
Dugdale, *Mon.*	W. Dugdale, *Monasticon Anglicanum*, ed. J. Caley and others (1817–30)
Educ. Enq. Abstract	*Abstract of Returns relative to the State of Education in England*, H.C. 62 (1835), xliii
Educ. of Poor Digest	*Digest of Returns to the Select Committee on the Education of the Poor*, H.C. 224 (1819), ix (2)
Ekwall, *Eng. Place-Names*	E. Ekwall, *The Concise Oxford Dictionary of English Place-Names* (4th edn. 1960)
Endowed Char. Wilts.	*Endowed Charities of Wiltshire*, H.C. 273 (1908), lxxx (northern division); H.C. 273-i (1908), lxxxi (southern division)
Eton Coll. Mun.	Muniments of Eton College, Bucks.
Ex. e Rot. Fin.	*Excerpta e Rotulis Finium in Turri Londinensi asservati*, ed. Charles Roberts (Record Commission, 1835)
Feud. Aids	*Inquisitions and Assessments relating to Feudal Aids preserved in the Public Record Office* (H.M.S.O. 1899–1920)
Finberg, *Early Wessex Chart.*	H. P. R. Finberg, *Early Charters of Wessex* (Leicester, 1964)
First Pembroke Survey, ed. Straton	*Survey of the Lands of William, First Earl of Pembroke*, ed. C. R. Straton (Roxburghe Club, 1909)
G.E.C. Baronetage	G. E. C[ockayne], *Complete Baronetage* (1900–9)
G.P.L., Treas. Solicitor	Government Property Lawyers, records of the Treasury Solicitor, Taunton
G.R.O.	General Register Office
Gent. Mag.	*Gentleman's Magazine* (1731–1867)
Geol. Surv.	Geological Survey
H.C.	House of Commons
H.M.S.O.	Her (His) Majesty's Stationery Office

NOTE ON ABBREVIATIONS

Harl. Soc.	Harleian Society
Hist. MSS. Com.	Royal Commission on Historical Manuscripts
Hist. Parl.	*The History of Parliament*
Hoare, *Mod. Wilts.*	Sir Richard Colt Hoare and others, *The History of Modern Wiltshire* (London, 1822–43)
Inq. Non.	*Nonarum Inquisitiones in Curia Scaccarii*, ed. G. Vandersee (Record Commission, 1807)
Kelly's Handbk.	*Kelly's Handbook to the Titled, Landed and Official Classes*
L.J.	*Journals of the House of Lords*
L. & P. Hen. VIII	*Letters and Papers, Foreign and Domestic, of the Reign of Henry VIII* (H.M.S.O. 1864–1932)
Lamb. Palace Libr.	Lambeth Palace Library
Land Util. Surv.	Land Utilisation Survey
Lewis, *Topog. Dict. Eng.*	S. Lewis, *Topographical Dictionary of England*
Lond. Gaz.	*London Gazette*
Longleat Mun.	Longleat House Muniments
Misc. Herald. et Geneal.	*Miscellanea Genealogica et Heraldica*
N.S.	New Series
Nat. Soc. *Inquiry, 1846–7*	*Result of the Returns made to the General Inquiry made by the National Society, 1846–7* (1849)
Nightingale, *Wilts. Plate*	J. E. Nightingale, *Church Plate of Wiltshire* (Salisbury, 1891)
O.S.	Ordnance Survey
J. Ogilby, *Brit.*	J. Ogilby, *Britannia* (1675)
Orig. Rec. ed. G. L. Turner	*Original Records of Early Nonconformity under Persecution and Indulgence*, ed. G. L. Turner (1911–14)
P.N. Wilts. (E.P.N.S.)	J. E. B. Gover, Allen Mawer, and F. M. Stenton, Place-Names of Wiltshire (English Place-Name Society, xvi)
P.R.O.	Public Record Office (see above, p. xv)
P.R.S., Pipe R. Soc.	Pipe Roll Society
Pat. R.	*Patent Rolls of the Reign of Henry III preserved in the Public Record Office* (H.M.S.O. 1901–3)
Pevsner, *Wilts.* (2nd edn.)	Nikolaus Pevsner, *Buildings of England: Wiltshire*, revised by Bridget Cherry (1975)
Phillipps, *Wilts. Inst.*	*Institutiones Clericorum in Comitatu Wiltoniae*, ed. Sir Thomas Phillipps (priv. print. 1825)
Pigot, *Nat. Com. Dir.*	Pigot, *National Commercial Directory*
Plac. de Quo Warr.	*Placita de Quo Warranto*, ed. W. Illingworth and J. Caley (Record Commission, 1818)
Poor Law Abstract, 1804	*Abstract of Returns relative to the Expense and Maintenance of the Poor* (printed by order of the House of Commons, 1804)
Poor Law Abstract, 1818	*Abstract of Returns relative to the Expense and Maintenance of the Poor*, H.C. 82 (1818), xix
Poor Law Com. 1st Rep.	*First Annual Report of the Poor Law Commissioners for England and Wales*, H.C. 500 (1835), xxxv
Poor Law Com. 2nd Rep.	*Second Annual Report of the Poor Law Commissioners for England and Wales*, H.C. 595 (1836), xxix (1)
Poor Rate Returns, 1816–21	*Poor Rate Returns, 1816–21*, H.C. 556, Supplementary Appendix (1822), v
Poor Rate Returns, 1822–4	*Poor Rate Returns, 1822–4*, H.C. 334, Supplementary Appendix (1825), iv
Poor Rate Returns, 1825–9	*Poor Rate Returns, 1825–9*, H.C. 83 (1830–1), xi
Poor Rate Returns, 1830–4	*Poor Rate Returns, 1830–4*, H.C. 444 (1835), xlvii
Princ. Regy. Fam. Div.	Principal Registry of the Family Division, Somerset House
Proc. before the Justices	*Proceedings before the Justices of the Peace in the 14th and 15th centuries*, ed. B. H. Putnam (Ames Foundation, 1938)
R.O.	Record Office
Rec. Com.	Record Commission

NOTE ON ABBREVIATIONS

Red Bk. Exch.	*The Red Book of the Exchequer*, ed. H. Hall (Rolls Series, 1896)
Reg.	Register
Reg. Chichele	*The Register of Henry Chichele, Archbishop of Canterbury*, ed. E. F. Jacob (Canterbury and York Society, 1934–47)
Reg. Ghent	*Registrum Simonis de Gandavo, Diocesis Saresbiriensis*, ed. C. T. Flower and M. C. B. Dawes (Canterbury and York Society, 1934)
Reg. Hallum	*The Register of Robert Hallum, Bishop of Salisbury*, ed. J. Horn (Canterbury and York Society, 1982)
Reg. Martival	*The Registers of Roger Martival, Bishop of Salisbury*, ed. K. Edwards and others (Canterbury and York Society, 1959–75)
Reg. Regum Anglo-Norm.	*Regesta Regum Anglo-Normannorum, 1066–1154*, ed. H. W. C. Davis and others (1913–69)
Reg. St. Osmund	*Vetus Registrum Sarisberiense alias Dictum Registrum Sancti Osmund Episcopi*, ed. W. H. R. Jones (Rolls Series, 1883–4)
Rep. Com. Eccl. Revenues	*Report of the Commissioners appointed to Inquire into the Ecclesiastical Revenues of England and Wales* [67], H.C. (1835), xxii
Return of Non-Provided Schs.	*Return of Schools Recognised as Voluntary Public Elementary Schools*, H.C. 178–xxxi (1906), lxxxviii
Returns relating to Elem. Educ.	*Returns relating to Elementary Education*, H.C. 201 (1871), lv
Rot. Chart.	*Rotuli Chartarum*, ed. T. D. Hardy (Record Commission, 1837)
Rot. Cur. Reg.	*Rotuli Curiae Regis, 6 Richard I to 1 John*, ed. F. Palgrave (Record Commission, 1835)
Rot. de Ob. et Fin.	*Rotuli de Oblatis et Finibus in Turri Londinensi asservati*, ed. T. D. Hardy (Record Commission, 1835)
Rot. Hund.	*Rotuli Hundredorum temp. Hen. III & Edw. I*, ed. W. Illingworth and J. Caley (Record Commission, 1812–18)
Rot. Lib.	*Rotuli de Liberate ac de Misis et Praestitis regnante Johanne*, ed. T. D. Hardy (Record Commission, 1844)
Rot. Litt. Claus.	*Rotuli Litterarum Clausarum*, ed. T. D. Hardy (Record Commission, 1833–44)
Rot. Litt. Pat.	*Rotuli Litterarum Patentium*, ed. T. D. Hardy (Record Commission, 1835)
Rot. Normanniae	*Rotuli Normanniae in Turri Londinensi asservati*, ed. T. D. Hardy (Record Commission, 1835)
Rot. Parl.	*Rotuli Parliamentorum* [1783]
Sar. Chart. and Doc.	*Charters and Documents illustrating the History of the Cathedral, City, and Diocese of Salisbury, in the Twelfth and Thirteenth Centuries, etc.* ed. W. Dunn Macray (Rolls Series, 1891)
Soc. Antiq.	Society of Antiquaries of London
Tax. Eccl.	*Taxatio Ecclesiastica Angliae et Walliae auctoritate P. Nicholai IV circa A.D. 1291*, ed. S. Ayscough and J. Caley (Record Commission, 1802)
Treas. Solicitor	Records of the Treasury Solicitor, Queen Anne's Chambers, 28 Broadway, London
Univ. Brit. Dir.	*Universal British Directory of Trade, Commerce, and Manufacture*, ed. P. Barfoot and J. Wilkes (1791–8)
V.C.H.	*Victoria County History*
Valor Eccl.	*Valor Ecclesiasticus temp. Henr. VIII*, ed. J. Caley and J. Hunter (Record Commission, 1810–34)
W.A.M.	*Wiltshire Archaeological and Natural History Magazine*
W.A.S. (Libr.)	Wiltshire Archaeological and Natural History Society (Library in the Museum, Long Street, Devizes)
W.N. & Q.	*Wiltshire Notes and Queries* (Devizes, 1896–1917)
W.R.O.	Wiltshire Record Office

Principal classes used:
A   Quarter Sessions records
D   Salisbury Diocesan records
EA   Enclosure Awards
F   County Council records

NOTE ON ABBREVIATIONS

G	Rural District and Borough Council records
L	Charity Commission records
W.R.S.	Wiltshire Record Society (*formerly* Records Branch of W.A.S.)
Walker Revised, ed. Matthews	*Walker Revised; being a Revision of John Walker's Sufferings of the Clergy during the Grand Rebellion, 1642–60*, ed. A. G. Matthews
Walters, *Wilts. Bells*	H. B. Walters, *Church Bells of Wiltshire* (Devizes, 1927–9)
Williams, *Cath. Recusancy*	J. A. Williams, *Catholic Recusancy in Wiltshire, 1660–1791* (Catholic Record Society, 1968)
Williamstrip Mun.	Muniments of Earl St. Aldwyn at Williamstrip House, Coln St. Aldwyns, Glos.
Wilts. Cuttings	Volumes of newspaper and other cuttings in W.A.S. Libr.
Wilts. Inq. p.m. 1242–1326	*Abstracts of Wiltshire Inquisitiones post mortem in the reigns of Henry III, Edward I, and Edward II, 1242–1326*, ed. E. A. Fry (Index Library, xxxvii)
Wilts. Inq. p.m. 1327–77	*Abstracts of Wiltshire Inquisitiones post mortem in the reign of Edward III, 1327–77*, ed. Ethel Stokes (Index Library, xlviii)
Wilts. Inq. p.m. 1625–49	*Abstracts of Wiltshire Inquisitiones post mortem in the reign of Charles I, 1625–49*, ed. G. S. and E. A. Fry (Index Library, xxiii)
Wilts. Tracts	Collections of tracts in W.A.S. Libr.
Winch. Coll. Mun.	Muniments of Winchester College, Hants

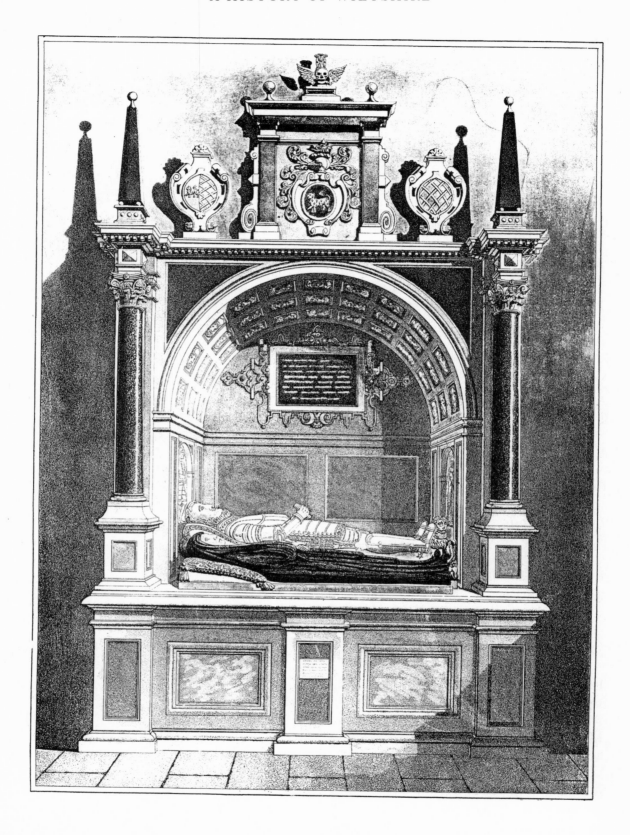

GREAT WISHFORD: MONUMENT IN CHURCH COMMEMORATING SIR RICHARD GROBHAM

INTRODUCTION

THE 25 parishes of Amesbury hundred and Branch and Dole hundred lie on chalk, mostly on the south-east part of Salisbury Plain, and their downland bears many marks of prehistoric settlement, cultivation, and ceremony. Stonehenge, in Amesbury parish, was in 1984 with its hinterland designated a World Heritage Site. Between the downs the villages lie, sometimes several to a parish, close together beside rivers converging on Salisbury, those of Amesbury hundred beside the Christchurch Avon and the Bourne, those of the old Branch hundred beside the Wylye, and those of the old Dole hundred beside the Till. Most had a strip of land, stretching from the river to the downs, on which open-field husbandry was practised. A straight line dividing Amesbury and Dole hundreds may have been drawn at a formal partition.

Until the 20th century no landowner was pre-eminent in the two hundreds. In the Middle Ages the largest estates were those of Amesbury abbey and Wilton abbey. Amesbury then had some urban characteristics, and Ludgershall, where the king had a small castle, became a parliamentary borough, but in neither hundred was there a substantial town, and in neither has any trade or industry become prominent. The villages were numerous and small, the churches likewise. There were evidently two fortified houses in the 12th century, the Giffards' at Sherrington and the Husseys' at Stapleford. They have not survived, and the only manor house of more than local importance was that called Amesbury Abbey. The area depended on sheep-and-corn husbandry and its main markets were Wilton and Salisbury. From the 17th century meadows were watered; open-field cultivation continued until the 19th century in many of the parishes, and in the 18th new areas of open field were laid out in some. After inclosure farmsteads were erected on the downs in every parish. Until coverts were planted in the 19th and 20th centuries the area contained very little woodland. It was poorly served by railways in the 19th century, the opportunity for dairy farming was thus restricted, and large flocks of sheep were kept on the downs until c. 1900.

From 1897 the War Department bought estates on Salisbury Plain to provide land for military training. In 1994 the Ministry of Defence owned c. 26,000 a. of the two hundreds. Tidworth, Bulford, and Larkhill army camps were built and Amesbury and Ludgershall, each of which had a railway station, and later Durrington grew to serve them. About 1900 roads across the downs were closed and firing ranges were set up, and later much downland was rough grassland given over to training in the use of tanks. Boscombe Down airfield is centred in Amesbury parish, and in Allington and Boscombe there are land and buildings of the Chemical and Biological Defence Establishment based at Porton down. To the south-west, especially in the Wylye valley, the villages remain rural and the land agricultural.

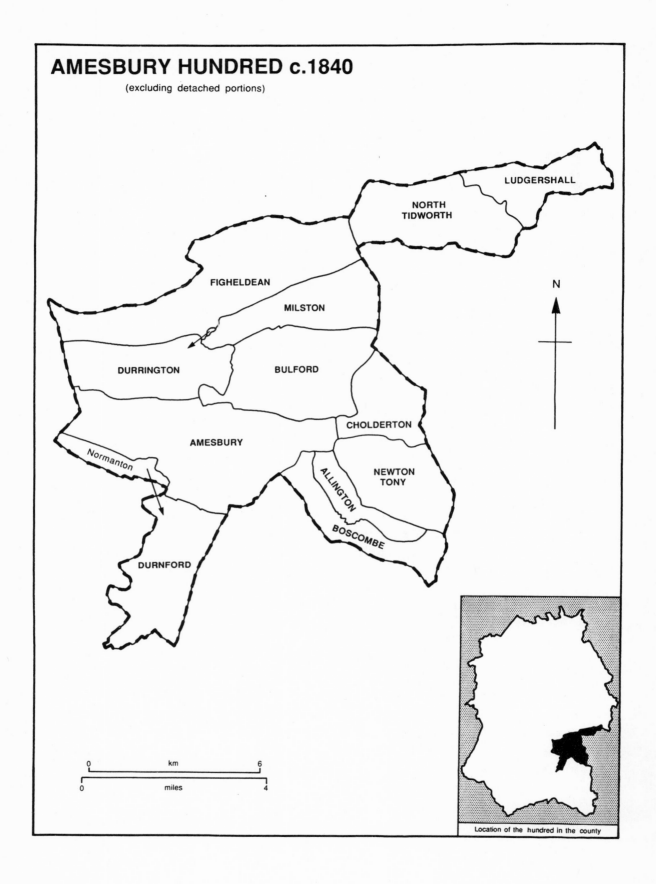

AMESBURY HUNDRED c.1840

(excluding detached portions)

LUDGERSHALL

NORTH TIDWORTH

N

FIGHELDEAN

MILSTON

DURRINGTON

BULFORD

CHOLDERTON

AMESBURY

Normanton

NEWTON TONY

ALLINGTON

BOSCOMBE

DURNFORD

0   km   6

0   miles   4

Location of the hundred in the county

AMESBURY HUNDRED

AMESBURY, held by the royal house of Wessex and the site of a wealthy nunnery, was locally important in the Anglo-Saxon period,[1] and by 1084 had given its name to a hundred.[2] Both the hundred and Amesbury manor passed with the Crown until the manor was granted away, probably in the 1140s. The hundred remained in the king's hands until, between 1189 and 1249, it was acquired by the lord of Amesbury manor.[3] Thereafter the hundred descended with the manor and met at Amesbury.[4]

In 1084 the hundred included lands in the valley of the Christchurch Avon, evidently all those in the parishes of Amesbury, Bulford, Durrington, Milston, and Figheldean, and, east and north-east of Amesbury, lands mainly in the valley of the Bourne, evidently all those in the parishes of Allington, Boscombe, Cholderton, Ludgershall, Newton Tony, and North Tidworth.[5] One of two estates at Kingston Deverill was, like Durrington, an appurtenance of Amesbury manor,[6] was almost certainly part of the hundred in 1084, and was so in 1332;[7] an estate called Shaw, later in Chute parish, was possibly part of the hundred in 1084 but is not known to have been afterwards. Compton, in Enford, and East Winterslow, in Winterslow, were among estates held until c. 1080 by Aubrey de Couci, others of which were in the hundred in 1084,[8] and had become part of the hundred by 1249.[9] In the Avon valley south of Amesbury, Durnford parish, or at least the main part of it, was transferred from Underditch hundred to Amesbury hundred between 1249 and 1281,[10] and Normanton, its detached part, was in Amesbury hundred by 1268.[11] West Wellow in East Wellow (Hants), where the lord of the hundred was overlord, had also been added to Amesbury hundred by 1268.[12] An estate in West Tytherley (Hants) was held in the later 13th century and earlier 14th by the owners of estates in Durnford and was considered part of Amesbury hundred in 1332 and 1334,[13] as, for reasons that are obscure, was land at Burghfield (Berks.).[14] By the early 14th century estates east of Reading and owned by the lord of Amesbury manor had been annexed to Amesbury hundred and to Wiltshire: they were at Broad Hinton, Hinton Odes, Hinton Pipard, Hinton Hatch, and Twyford (all in Hurst), Diddenham (in Shinfield), Farley, Great Sheepbridge, and Little Sheepbridge (all in Swallowfield), and Ashridge, Beaches, and Buckhurst (all in Wokingham).[15]

Amesbury hundred was evidently at its most extensive in the early 14th century, although by then the moiety of Compton which was in the honor of Leicester had been withdrawn to become part of Everleigh liberty, later part of Elstub and Everleigh hundred.[16] By c. 1400 the lands east of Reading had been detached from Amesbury hundred and organized as Ashridge, otherwise Hertoke, hundred:[17] they

---

[1] Below, Amesbury, intro. (the town to c. 1540); manors (preamble). [2] *V.C.H. Wilts*. ii, p. 194.
[3] Ibid. v. 49; below, Amesbury, manors (Amesbury).
[4] e.g. *Cal. Inq. p.m*. xvii, p. 316; Longleat Mun., Seymour papers, xii, ff. 256v.–257; Alnwick Castle Mun. X.II.11, box 6, survey, 1634, pp. 249–50; W.R.O. 283/202; for the meeting place, e.g. P.R.O., E 317/Wilts. no. 2.
[5] *V.C.H. Wilts*. ii, pp. 194–5.
[6] Ibid. p. 132; *W.A.M*. lii. 75–7.
[7] *Tax List, 1332* (W.R.S. xlv), 113.
[8] *V.C.H. Wilts*. ii, pp. 134, 195.
[9] *Crown Pleas, 1249* (W.R.S. xvi), pp. 182–3.

[10] *V.C.H. Wilts*. vi. 195; P.R.O., JUST 1/1001, rot. 18d.
[11] P.R.O., JUST 1/998A, rot. 24d.
[12] *V.C.H. Hants*, iv. 536; cf. below, Amesbury, manors (Amesbury).
[13] *Rot. Hund*. (Rec. Com.), ii (1), 237; *Cal. Inq. p.m*. viii, p. 16; *V.C.H. Wilts*. iv. 297; *Tax List, 1332* (W.R.S. xlv), 112; cf. below, Durnford, manors (Southend; Little Durnford).
[14] *V.C.H. Wilts*. iv. 297; *Tax List, 1332* (W.R.S. xlv), 113.
[15] *Tax List, 1332* (W.R.S. xlv), 114–15; *V.C.H. Wilts*. v. 1–2; *V.C.H. Berks*. iii. 228, 247, 253–4, 263, 267, 271.
[16] *V.C.H. Wilts*. iv. 297, 299; xi. 106–7, 120; *Tax List, 1332* (W.R.S. xlv), 114.
[17] *V.C.H. Wilts*. v. 2.

were transferred to Berkshire in 1844.[18] The estate in West Tytherley and the land at Burghfield are not known to have been part of Amesbury hundred after 1334. From *c.* 1400 the composition of the hundred was not changed: in the early 19th century it included 12 parishes, Allington, Amesbury, Boscombe, Bulford, Cholderton, Durnford, Durrington, Figheldean, Ludgershall, Milston, Newton Tony, and North Tidworth,[19] and West Wellow, East Winterslow, part of Compton, and part of Kingston Deverill.[20] The histories of the parishes are related below; that of Compton was given with Enford[21] and that of West Wellow with East Wellow;[22] those of Kingston Deverill and East Winterslow are reserved for volumes relating to Mere and Alderbury hundreds respectively.

There were many exemptions from the jurisdiction of Amesbury hundred courts. As lord of Amesbury manor the lord of the hundred withdrew his own men from it; in the later 13th century he claimed return of writs, view of frankpledge, and other liberties in respect of the manor,[23] and later is known to have held a view for it.[24] In 1179 quittance from the hundred court was among liberties confirmed to Amesbury priory,[25] which, in Amesbury hundred, held Bulford, West Boscombe in Boscombe, Alton Parva and Choulston in Figheldean, Biddesden in Ludgershall, and an estate in Amesbury.[26] A similar liberty was granted between 1189 and 1199 to Geoffrey Hussey[27] (fl. 1198), who held Figheldean manor and Ablington, Knighton, and possibly Syrencot, all in Figheldean.[28] From 1347 the men of Newton Tony were exempted by a grant of view of frankpledge to their lord.[29] Ludgershall borough, governed in the earlier Middle Ages by the bailiff of Ludgershall castle, who returned royal writs direct to Westminster and held view of frankpledge, was already exempt[30] when in 1449 the Crown included leet jurisdiction in a grant of the manor.[31] Ratfyn manor in Amesbury, the Rectory manor in Durnford, East End manor in Durrington, and part of Knighton were all held by Salisbury cathedral in the Middle Ages and, presumably under a grant of freedom from suit of hundreds made to the cathedral in 1158, were evidently exempt.[32] Also exempt from the jurisdiction of the hundred court was the part of Kingston Deverill in the hundred:[33] the exemption may have arisen from a privilege enjoyed by the canons of Le Mans (Sarthe), its owners in the earlier Middle Ages.[34] One estate may have been withdrawn without a grant. In 1281 Gilbert de Neville, lord of West End manor in Durrington, claimed to hold the assize of bread and of ale,[35] and in the earlier 14th century view of frankpledge was held for the manor;[36] in the earlier 15th century attempts to enforce the jurisdiction of Amesbury hundred court over the manor were unsuccessful.[37] Other attempts to withdraw failed. By 1268 William of Durnford, lord of Southend and Little Durnford manors in Durnford, and John son of Aucher, lord of Normanton manor, had for three years prevented the sheriff from levying aid from their estates,[38] and in 1275 the overlord of Normanton claimed gallows and the assize

[18] *V.C.H. Wilts.* iv. 339 n.   [19] Ibid. 326.
[20] Hoare, *Mod. Wilts.* Mere, 138; W.R.O. 283/202.
[21] *V.C.H. Wilts.* xi. 115–34.
[22] *V.C.H. Hants.* iv. 535–40.
[23] P.R.O., JUST 1/1001, rot. 19d.
[24] Below, Amesbury, local govt. (Amesbury).
[25] *Cal. Chart. R.* 1257–1300, 157–9.
[26] Below, manors sections of par. hists.
[27] *Cal. Chart. R.* 1226–57, 394.
[28] Below, Figheldean, manors.
[29] *Cal. Chart. R.* 1341–1417, 64–5.
[30] Below, Ludgershall, local govt.

[31] *Cal. Pat.* 1446–52, 247.
[32] *V.C.H. Wilts.* iii. 159; below, Amesbury, manors (Ratfyn); local govt. (Amesbury); Durnford, manors (Rectory); local govt.; Durrington, manors (E. End); local govt.; Figheldean, manors (Knighton); local govt.
[33] e.g. Longleat Mun., Seymour papers, xii, ff. 256v.–257.   [34] *W.A.M.* lii. 74–7.
[35] P.R.O., JUST 1/1001, rot. 19d.; below, Durrington, manors (W. End).
[36] Below, Durrington, local govt.
[37] *V.C.H. Wilts.* v. 68.
[38] P.R.O., JUST 1/998A, rot. 24d.; below, Durnford, manors.

of bread and of ale there;[39] later, however, all the men of Durnford, presumably except those of the Rectory manor, were represented at the hundred courts.[40]

Records of the hundred courts survive for 1534, 1547–58, 1576, 1578–1614, 1632–3, 1725–35, and 1743–71.[41] The places not exempt from their jurisdiction were in tithings called Biddesden, Tidworth Zouche, Tidworth Moels, Cholderton, West Wellow, East Winterslow, Milston and Brigmerston, Great Durnford, Little Durnford, Compton and Alton, Allington, and West Amesbury and Wilsford. It is not clear why Biddesden attended the courts.[42] The two tithings of Tidworth bore the names of manors in the parish in the Middle Ages;[43] Cholderton tithing included East Boscombe in Boscombe; Brigmerston is in Milston parish. The whole of the main part of Durnford parish, including Netton, Newtown, and Salterton, was probably in the two tithings bearing its name; Alton, constituting a tithing with a moiety of Compton, was Alton Magna, the only part of Figheldean parish to attend.[44] West Amesbury manor in Amesbury evolved in the Middle Ages, evidently free from the jurisdiction of Amesbury manor and Amesbury priory courts:[45] despite the name of the tithing its partner was Normanton,[46] not Normanton's larger neighbour Wilsford, which was in Underditch hundred.[47] The records of 1547–8 are of a court held every three weeks and doing very little business; some meetings were attended by an officer called the bailiff of Amesbury borough. Other records are of the court at which leet jurisdiction was exercised: in the 16th and 17th centuries the court was held twice a year, in spring and autumn, and called a view of frankpledge, in the 18th century once a year, in October, and called a court leet. At that court in the 16th century the assize of bread and of ale was sometimes enforced, waifs and strays were reported, and orders were occasionally made to remedy public nuisances. Later, little more was done than to appoint tithingmen and to record the making of small customary payments, and, possibly because the tithings had little cohesion as a group, the court was of little importance.

The hundred was worth £15 2s. 10d. in 1364,[48] £13 5s. 4d. in 1651.[49] Later the value was only that of cert money twice a year, a tithing fine once a year in autumn, and suitors' fines. It was £8 2s. in 1707, £7 7s. 1d. in the early 19th century, when West Wellow tithing and West Amesbury and Wilsford tithing paid nothing.[50]

The officers of the hundred were the bailiff or high constable and two constables.[51] Members of the Goion family, lords of Coombes Court manor in Amesbury, were bailiffs in the late 13th century and early 14th. Robert Goion, bailiff in 1289, was accused of unlawfully levying money for scotales.[52] It became customary for the owner of Coombes Court manor to be the bailiff and to appoint a salaried deputy to collect the cert money and fines and to summon men to serve on grand and hundred juries.[53]

39 *Rot. Hund.* (Rec. Com.), ii (1), 265.
40 Below, this section.
41 Para. based on Longleat Mun., Seymour papers, xii, ff. 256v.–257; W.R.O. 192/24A; 283/2, bk. M; 283/2, views 1576; ct. bks. 1585–98; 1598–1608; 1608–14; 283/7; 283/14, ct. bk. 1725–35; 283/15, ct. bk. 1743–71.
42 Cf. above, this section.
43 Below, N. Tidworth, manors (Moels; Zouche).
44 Cf. above, this section; below, Figheldean, intro.
45 Below, Amesbury, manors (W. Amesbury); local govt. (W. Amesbury).
46 e.g. W.R.O. 283/2, ct. bk. 1608–14, ct. 5 Oct. 1608.
47 *V.C.H. Wilts.* vi. 195.

48 P.R.O., DL 43/9/25.
49 Ibid. E 317/Wilts. no. 2.
50 Longleat Mun., Seymour papers, xii, ff. 256v.–257; Alnwick Castle Mun. X.II.11, box 6, survey, 1634, pp. 249–50; W.R.O. 283/62, chief rents, 1707; 283/202; 490/1116.
51 *V.C.H. Wilts.* v. 68; *Sess. Mins.* (W.R.S. iv), 72; *Cal. S.P. Dom.* 1603–10, 147; P.R.O., JUST 1/1001, rot. 1; W.R.O. 192/24A.
52 *Antrobus D.* (W.R.S. iii), pp. 5–6; P.R.O., JUST 1/1001, rot. 1; JUST 1/1006, rot. 58d.; below, Amesbury, manors (Coombes Ct.).
53 W.R.O. 283/23, summons, 1735; 283/62, chief rents, 1707.

ALLINGTON[1] lies in the Bourne valley 12 km. north-east of Salisbury.[2] Boscombe parish was in 1934 added to Allington,[3] which until then was a long and narrow parish of 957 a. (387 ha.) with the river Bourne flowing across the middle. Few natural features mark the parish boundary. The boundary with Boscombe, more than half the total length, was marked in the extreme north-west by mounds visible in the later 19th century,[4] and both north-west and south-east of Allington village by a road. Near the Bourne a zigzag on the Boscombe boundary suggests a late division of pasture, some of which may have been marshy.

Upper Chalk outcrops over the whole parish. The Bourne, which meanders across the parish, flows intermittently in winter and spring and is dry in summer and autumn: it has deposited gravel but no alluvium, and there is gravel in a dry tributary valley north of the church. The downland, highest at 155 m. in the extreme south-east, is generally flat although from both sides the land falls steeply to the river, which is at *c.* 75 m.[5] There were meadows beside the Bourne, open fields on the chalk higher up on each side, and rough pasture on the downs at each end of the parish.[6] Apart from orchards in the village there was no woodland in the parish until, between 1899 and 1923, a small area west of the church was planted with trees.[7] The south-east end of the parish was part of a military training area from the earlier 20th century.[8]

Portway, the Roman road from Silchester to Old Salisbury, crosses the south-east part of the parish and apparently remained in use as a local route until the 20th century.[9] In the 17th century the main Oxford–Salisbury road via Hungerford (Berks.) crossed the north-western tip of the parish. Between 1675 and 1773 a new course further west was adopted for it;[10] the road across Allington parish declined in importance and was a rough track in 1993. Allington village is on the road linking the villages of the Bourne valley to Salisbury. When that road was turnpiked in 1835, to complete a Swindon–Salisbury turnpike road via Marlborough, a new section was made south to Allington village from the western edge of the park of Wilbury House in Newton Tony. The road, disturnpiked in 1876,[11] remained the main Swindon–Salisbury road in 1993, when the old section between Allington and Newton Tony villages was a minor road. Two roads, one from Winterslow along parts of the parish boundary and one from Newton Tony, crossed the parish,

converged west of it, and led to Amesbury.[12] South-east of the village the Winterslow road was diverted away from the boundary to serve a new farmstead in the mid 19th century,[13] was closed south-east of the farmstead when military training began, and was not tarmacadamed. The development of Boscombe Down airfield west of the parish caused the Amesbury road to be diverted along a route, called the Allington track, improved in the 1950s and leading to Amesbury by the main London–Exeter road.[14]

The London–Salisbury railway line, built by the L. & S.W.R. along the south-east side of Portway, was opened in 1857[15] and remained a main line in 1993. A light railway from Grateley (Hants) to Amesbury, diverging from the main line in Newton Tony parish, was opened across the north-west part of Allington parish in 1902[16] and closed in 1963.[17]

The parish is not known to be rich in prehistoric remains. A Bronze-Age brooch was found near Portway, and Romano-British sherds were found both near the village and north-west of Portway. Parts of three ditches, all possibly associated with animal husbandry, cross the parish, two in the south-east and one in the north-west.[18]

Allington may have been a small village in the 14th century[19] and had only 35 poll-tax payers in 1377.[20] With only 75 inhabitants in the parish in 1801, 64 in 1821, and never more than 94, the village was very small in the 19th century and may have shrunk since the 14th. Between 1891 and 1911, when it was 207, the population trebled, and there was evidently some new housing: the reasons for the rapidity of the increase are obscure. There were 175 inhabitants in 1931. The population of the enlarged parish increased after the Second World War mainly because of new housing in Allington, and of the 469 inhabitants in 1991[21] about three quarters lived at Allington.

Allington village[22] grew up on the right bank of the Bourne where the old road to Salisbury beside the river is crossed by the Winterslow road, which fords the river. In the 20th century the old Salisbury road was called Newton Tony Road, the north-west part of the Winterslow road Wyndham Lane. South-west of the ford an open space on low ground formed a green, west of which stands the church and south stood the rectory house. There were six farmsteads and little else in the village in 1840: three farmsteads stood around the green, two in Wyndham Lane, and one east of the crossroads in Newton Tony

1   This article was written in 1993.
2   Maps used include O.S. Maps 6", Wilts. LXI (1883 and later edns.); 1/25,000, 41/13, 41/23 (1948 and later edns.); 1/50,000, sheet 184 (1988 edn.); 1", sheet 14 (1817 edn.).   3   *Census*, 1931.
4   O.S. Map 6", Wilts. LXI (1883 edn.).
5   Geol. Surv. Map 1/50,000, drift, sheet 298 (1976 edn.).
6   Below, econ. hist.
7   O.S. Maps 6", Wilts. LXI (1883 and later edns.).
8   Below, this section.
9   *V.C.H. Wilts.* i (1), 25; O.S. Maps 6", Wilts. LXI (1883 and later edns.).
10   J. Ogilby, *Brit.* (1675), pl. 83; *Andrews and Dury, Map* (W.R.S. viii), pl. 6; O.S. Map 1", sheet 14 (1817 edn.); below, N. Tidworth, intro. [roads].

11   *V.C.H. Wilts.* iv. 257, 262, 266, 270; O.S. Map 1", sheet 14 (1817 edn.); P.R.O., IR 30/38/6; below, Newton Tony, intro. [roads].
12   O.S. Map 1", sheet 14 (1817 edn.).
13   Ibid. 6", Wilts. LXI (1883 edn.); P.R.O., IR 30/38/6.
14   O.S. Map 1", sheet 167 (1960 edn.); W.R.O., G 1/132/51; below, Amesbury, intro. (roads).
15   *V.C.H. Wilts.* iv. 286.   16   Ibid. 291.
17   P. A. Harding, *Bulford Branch Line*, 3, 7–8, 27–8.
18   *V.C.H. Wilts.* i (1), 26, 249–50; i (2), 403.
19   *Tax List, 1332* (W.R.S. xlv), 112.
20   *V.C.H. Wilts.* iv. 306.
21   Ibid. 339; *Census*, 1991; O.S. Maps 6", Wilts. LXI (1883 and later edns.).
22   See plate facing p. 250.

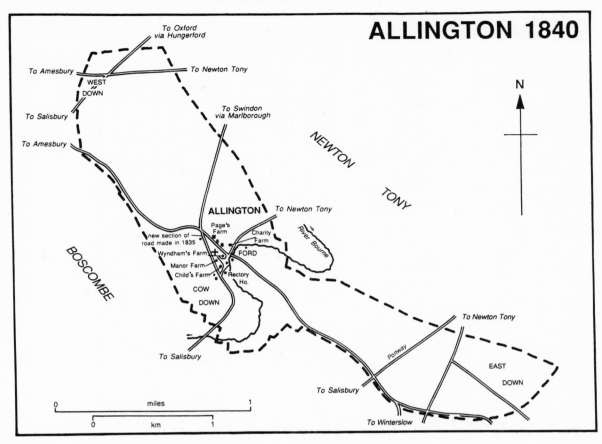

ALLINGTON 1840

To Oxford
via Hungerford

To Amesbury
To Newton Tony
WEST
DOWN

To Swindon
via Marlborough

To Salisbury

To Amesbury

N

NEWTON

TONY

ALLINGTON
To Newton Tony

Page's
Farm
Charity
Farm
new section of
road made in 1835
Wyndham's Farm
FORD
Manor Farm
Child's Farm
Rectory
Ho.

River Bourne

BOSCOMBE

COW

DOWN

To Salisbury

To Newton Tony

Portway

EAST

DOWN

To Salisbury

To Winterslow

0   miles   1

0   km   1

Road.[23] A farmhouse and two cottages had been burned down in 1788.[24] Of the farmhouses standing in 1840 Manor Farm, that nearest the church, was standing in the 17th century and was destroyed by fire in 1860.[25] South-east of it Child's Farm, called Kea Cottage in 1993, was built in the 17th century as a three-bayed timber-framed house with a thatched roof. At the crossroads Wyndham's Farm was also built in the 17th century as a timber-framed house of three bays. It was rebuilt in brick and rubble, and the inside refitted, in the 18th century, and extended southwards and again refitted in the 19th; a two-storeyed brick bay was built at the south end c. 1900. In Wyndham Lane on the north-east side Bishop's Cottage was built, of flint with brick quoins and a thatched roof, for Richard Bishop c. 1789.[26] North-west of it on the same side Page's Farm was standing in 1795 and was demolished between 1961 and 1977.[27] On the north-west side of Newton Tony Road Charity Farm was built in 1780–1[28] and rebuilt in 1893–4 as a red-brick house.[29] A pair of cottages had been built on the east side of the green by 1840;[30] adjoining it and later part of a terrace of three buildings a nonconformist

chapel incorporating a cottage was built c. 1843.[31] The rectory house was demolished in the later 19th century.[32]

The village was bypassed by the new section of the Swindon–Salisbury road made in 1835.[33] In the 20th century the old section south of the village and the new section were together called Tidworth Road, along which several buildings were erected in the 19th century and early 20th. On the west side at the junction of the old and new sections the New Inn, on the site of a building standing in 1795, was open in 1848.[34] Its name was changed to the Old Inn in the later 19th century, it was rebuilt in the earlier 20th,[35] and it was open in 1993. A house standing south of it in 1993 may incorporate parts of one standing in 1795.[36] The Flint House was built on the west side of the road between 1840 and c. 1875,[37] and a group of buildings including a farmstead on the west side and a range of three cottages on the east side was erected north of the junction of Tidworth Road and Wyndham Lane in the later 19th century and earlier 20th. On the east side three thatched cottages built between 1899 and 1923 were replaced by a commercial garage in the later 20th century.[38] South of the

23 P.R.O., IR 29/38/6; IR 30/38/6.
24 Wilts. Cuttings, xxvi. 51.
25 Ibid. xvi. 23; W.R.O. 885/2/1, deed, 26 Feb. 1685.
26 W.R.O., A 1/345/5.
27 Ibid. EA/157; O.S. Maps 6", Wilts. SU 23 NW. (1961 edn.); 1/10,000, SU 23 NW. (1977 edn.).
28 W.R.O., A 1/345/5.
29 Endowed Char. Wilts. (S. Div.), 32.
30 P.R.O., IR 29/38/6; IR 30/38/6.

31 Below, nonconf.   32 Ibid. church.
33 Above, this section [roads].
34 Kelly's Dir. Wilts. (1848); W.R.O., EA/157.
35 O.S. Maps 6", Wilts. LXI (1883 and later edns.).
36 W.R.O., EA/157.
37 O.S. Map 6", Wilts. LXI (1883 edn.); P.R.O., IR 30/38/6.
38 O.S. Maps 6", Wilts. LXI (1883 and later edns.); W.A.S. Libr., sale cat. xxi, no. 3.

village a new rectory house was built on the east side in 1877,[39] and a new farmstead, Cloudlands Farm, on the west side between 1899 and 1923.[40]

On rising ground east of the village Allington House, a large house of stone, was built in 1923;[41] beside Tidworth Road at the north end of the village four council houses were built in 1929[42] and four private houses in the 1930s;[43] south of the village, on what until 1934 was the boundary with Boscombe, an estate of 20 houses, 4 flats, and 3 bungalows was built as Bourne View by the local authority from c. 1948.[44] After c. 1960 houses and bungalows were also built in the old part of the village: Wyndham Lane was built up on both sides, eight red-brick houses, including two altered 19th-century cottages, were built on the site of Manor Farm, and there was some infilling. Also after c. 1960 houses and bungalows were built round the junction of Wyndham Lane and Tidworth Road.[45]

On the south-east downs Allington Farm was built immediately south-east of the railway c. 1867.[46] From 1916 it was within the military training area and not used much for agriculture; by the Second World War and in 1993 the site was used for breeding animals for what is now the Chemical and Biological Defence Establishment, based at Porton down in Idmiston,[47] and many new buildings have been erected. On the north-west downs Arundel Farm was evidently built by the state c. 1917 and was used for several years as an animal farm for the Experimental Station, Porton.[48] A new house was built in the late 20th century, when few, if any, of the original farm buildings survived.

MANORS AND OTHER ESTATES. Before 1066 Amesbury abbey was unlawfully dispossessed of 4 hides at Allington by Earl Harold but by 1086 had recovered them. Earl Harold held another 4-hide estate at Allington in 1066; it was afterwards held and forfeited by Aubrey de Couci, and in 1086 was held by the king.[49] The later descent of each estate is obscure.

In 1285 Ralph de la Stane and his wife Agnes settled *ALLINGTON* manor for life on William of Draycot and his wife Susan.[50] In 1312 Agnes, then Agnes de Percy, may have been disputing the manor, as she was the advowson of the

church, with Sir John Dun.[51] The manor belonged to William Buckland and his wife Joan in 1330,[52] evidently to Buckland in 1348 and to Sir Thomas Hungerford (d. 1397) in 1379,[53] and to John Wallop in 1428.[54] From John it descended in the direct line to Thomas, John (d. 1486), and Richard[55] (d. 1503). It was held by Richard's relict Elizabeth (d. 1505), reverted to his brother Robert[56] (d. 1535), and was apparently held by Robert's relict Rose.[57] On Rose's death the manor passed to Robert's nephew (Sir) John Wallop (d. 1551), who was succeeded by his brother Sir Oliver[58] (d. 1566). It descended, again in the direct line, to Sir Henry[59] (d. 1599), Henry[60] (d. 1642),[61] and Robert (d. 1667), a regicide. Robert's estates were confiscated at the Restoration, and in 1661 granted to his brother-in-law Thomas Wriothesley, earl of Southampton,[62] who in 1666 sold Allington manor to William Craven, earl of Craven. In 1680 Craven sold it in portions.[63]

The demesne, *MANOR* farm, was bought by Edward Miller (d. 1712), who in 1685 gave a third of it to his son Nicholas (d. 1711) and Nicholas's wife Denise (d. 1717).[64] Edward sold his two thirds in 1708 to his grandson William Carpenter,[65] who sold them in 1722 to Henry Hyde.[66] In 1724 Hyde sold them to John Baker,[67] to whom Nicholas's son John sold his third in 1727.[68] Baker sold the whole estate in 1737 to Joseph Earle's trustees.[69] In 1762 the trustees sold it to Edward Hearst[70] (d. 1767),[71] who already owned land in the parish.[72]

Hearst's composite estate, reputed *ALLINGTON* manor,[73] descended to his daughter Caroline, wife of H. P. Wyndham[74] (d. 1819), and to her son Wadham Wyndham (d. 1843), who owned 546 a. in the parish in 1840.[75] Wadham was succeeded by his sister Caroline (d. 1845), wife of John Campbell, from 1844 John Campbell-Wyndham. Under the terms of Wadham's will the manor passed from Caroline to her son J. H. Campbell-Wyndham (d. 1868) and successively to her daughters Julia (d. 1869), wife of Edward Thornton (later Thornton-Wyndham), and Ellen (d. 1890), wife of Richard King (later King-Wyndham). Ellen's successor was her niece Caroline Hetley (d. 1908), wife of Philip Pleydell-Bouverie (from 1868 Pleydell-Bouverie-Campbell, from 1890 Pleydell-Bouverie-Campbell-Wyndham).

39 Below, church.
40 O.S. Maps 6", Wilts. LXI. NW. (1901, 1926 edns.).
41 Ibid.; W.R.O. 1807/7; ibid. G 1/500/2.
42 W.R.O., G 1/600/1.
43 Cf. O.S. Map 1/2,500, Wilts. LXI. 2 (1939 edn.).
44 W.R.O., A 1/355/336; A 1/355/341; A 1/355/351; G 1/505/1; G 1/516/3; G 1/602/2–3.
45 O.S. Maps 6", Wilts. SU 23 NW. (1961 edn.); 1/10,000, SU 23 NW. (1977 edn.).
46 W.A.S. Libr., J. Wilkinson, par. hist. collns. no. 158.
47 G. B. Carter, *Porton Down*, 2–4; inf. from Defence Land Agent, Durrington.
48 Carter, *Porton Down*, 15.
49 *V.C.H. Wilts.* ii, pp. 98–9, 131, 134.
50 *Feet of F.* 1272–1327 (W.R.S. i), p. 27.
51 *Reg. Ghent* (Cant. & York Soc.), ii. 783; below, church.
52 *Feet of F.* 1327–77 (W.R.S. xxix), p. 25.
53 Phillipps, *Wilts. Inst.* i. 44, 63; *Complete Peerage*, vi. 613.
54 *Feud. Aids*, v. 241.
55 *Cal. Inq. p.m. Hen. VII*, i, p. 84; for the Wallop fam., *Hants Pedigrees* (Harl. Soc. lxiv), 25–6.
56 *Cal. Inq. p.m. Hen. VII*, ii, pp. 463, 476; *Testamenta Vetusta*, ed. N. H. Nicolas, ii. 473.
57 Phillipps, *Wilts. Inst.* i. 205; *Testamenta Vetusta*, ii. 631.
58 P.R.O., C 142/94, no. 46.
59 Ibid. C 142/143, no. 26, where Allington is not expressly mentioned.
60 Ibid. C 142/256, no. 6.
61 *Hist. Parl., Commons*, 1558–1603, iii. 567.
62 *D.N.B.* (s.v. Rob. Wallop); P.R.O., C 66/2975, no. 10.
63 W.R.O. 885/2/1, deeds, Southampton to Craven, 1666; Craven to Miller, 1680.
64 Ibid. 885/2/1, deeds, Craven to Miller, 1680; 26 Feb. 1685; 1068/2.
65 Ibid. 885/2/2, deed, Miller to Carpenter, 1708.
66 Ibid. 885/2/2, deed, Carpenter to Hyde, 1722.
67 Ibid. 885/2/1, deed, Hyde to Baker, 1724.
68 Ibid. 885/2/1, deed, Miller to Baker, 1727.
69 Ibid. 885/2/2, deed, Baker to Earle's trustees, 1737.
70 Ibid. 885/2/2, deed, Earle's trustees to Hearst, 1762.
71 *Musgrave's Obit.* iii (Harl. Soc. xlvi), 184.
72 Below, this section (Thorp's; Goodall's).
73 Hoare, *Mod. Wilts.* Amesbury, 108.
74 For the Wyndhams, Burke, *Land. Gent.* (1937), 2509.
75 W.R.O., A 1/345/5; P.R.O., IR 29/38/6.

Caroline was succeeded by her son Richard Campbell-Wyndham (d. 1909), whose heir was his sister Mary, wife of Walter Long (from 1909 Walter Campbell-Wyndham).[76] Between 1840 and 1910 Page's farm[77] was added to the manor, presumably by purchase.[78] From 1916 the War Department occupied the land south-east of the London–Salisbury railway line, 173 a., and in 1925 bought it; the Ministry of Defence owned it in 1993.[79] The Campbell-Wyndhams sold the remainder of the manor in portions in 1923.[80] The largest farm, Wyndham's, 242 a., was bought by A. A. Curtis (d. 1952),[81] and in 1993, then 161 a. between the village and the London–Salisbury railway, belonged to Mr. and Mrs. M. Snell.[82] In 1993 Mr. M. Rowland owned c. 300 a. north-west of the village.[83]

William, earl of Craven, sold what was later called CHILD'S farm in 1680 to William Child[84] (d. 1688), and the land descended in turn to Child's son William[85] (d. 1728) and grandson William Child.[86] In 1795 it belonged to W. B. Child (d. 1798), whose son W. B. Child[87] sold it c. 1806 to a Mr. Horne, presumably Roger Horne (d. 1845), the owner in 1832.[88] James Horne owned the farm, 172 a. north-west of the village, in 1840 and 1865.[89] It was sold c. 1895 in portions.[90]

Richard Scotney in 1388[91] and Isabel Scotney in 1401–2[92] were overlords of THORP'S estate. Catherine, relict of Sir John Thorp (d. 1386), held the estate until her death in 1388. It passed to Sir John's son Edward, to Henry Thorp (d. 1416) and his wife Cicely (fl. 1419),[93] and to Henry's son Ralph. It evidently descended in the Thorp and Clifford families with East Boscombe manor,[94] and in 1598 Henry Clifford sold it to John Hatchman.[95] In 1618 Hatchman sold the estate, then 3 yardlands, to John Poncherdon,[96] the owner in 1630.[97] It belonged to William Hearst in 1705 and passed to his sons William (d. 1724 or 1725) and Edward in turn.[98] From 1762 it was part of Edward's reputed manor of Allington.[99]

Stephen Cox (d. 1608) devised 1½ yardland to his kinsman John Goodall,[1] possibly him who

died c. 1621.[2] John Goodall (d. 1639) devised GOODALL'S to his son John,[3] and the estate descended to John Goodall (d. 1719), whose son John[4] sold it in 1721 to William Hearst, probably the younger.[5] It passed with Thorp's and in 1762 became part of the reputed manor of Allington.[6]

Thomas Mackerell (d. 1627) owned 2 yardlands, most of what was later called PAGE'S farm. His daughter Anne and her husband John Swayne[7] sold the estate in 1655 to James Barbon,[8] and in 1668 Henry Edmonds sold it to Samuel Heskins[9] (d. 1709), rector of Cholderton.[10] It passed to Heskins's son the Revd. Samuel Heskins (d. 1733),[11] and later belonged to Robert Bunny (will proved 1771). It passed to Bunny's brother Thomas[12] (will proved 1785) and to Thomas's son Robert[13] (will proved 1799).[14] In 1840 the farm, 144 a. north-west of the village, belonged to Jane Mayhew,[15] and by 1910 had been added to Allington manor.[16]

John Miles sold a small farm in 1780–1 to Richard Harrison's charity for Amesbury.[17] CHARITY farm, 21 a. in 1840,[18] was sold by the charity between 1910 and 1925.[19]

In 1179 Henry II confirmed to Amesbury priory 4 a. of wheat in Allington, possibly representing an estate of tithes held until 1177 by Amesbury abbey.[20] A small portion of tithes from Allington evidently became part of West Boscombe manor, which the priory held until the Dissolution.[21] The tithes of oats from 4 yardlands belonged to Robert Waters with West Boscombe manor[22] in 1839, when they were valued at £2 5s. and commuted.[23]

ECONOMIC HISTORY. There was land at Allington for 4 ploughteams in 1086. Of the 8 hides 5¼ were demesne on which there were 2 teams and 6 servi. On the other land 4 villani, 9 coscets, and 1 cottar had 2 teams. There were 13 a. of meadow; the pasture measured 1 league by 1 furlong and 3 square furlongs. The lands were in two estates[24] but there is no evidence

76 W. P. W. Phillimore and E. A. Fry, Changes of Name, 33, 52, 256; Burke, Land. Gent. (1937), 2509, corrected by V.C.H. Hants, iii. 247–8; P.R.O., PROB 11/1990, ff. 364v.–370v. 77 Below, this section (Page's).
78 P.R.O., IR 29/38/6; IR 30/38/6; W.R.O., Inland Revenue, val. reg. 148 and map 61.
79 Carter, Porton Down, 4; inf. from Defence Land Agent.
80 W.R.O. 1807/6.
81 Ibid. G 1/500/2; ibid. TS. of Allington par. reg.
82 Inf. from Mr. M. Snell, Old Hall, Durnford.
83 Inf. from Mr. P. J. Rowland, Ratfyn Farm, Amesbury.
84 W.R.O. 885/2/1, deed, Craven to Miller, 1680.
85 Ibid. wills, archd. Sar., Wm. Child, 1688.
86 Ibid. wills, cons. Sar., reg. 3, f. 353; ibid. 1068/2.
87 Ibid. EA/157; P.R.O., PROB 11/1316, ff. 21–2.
88 W.R.O., A 1/345/5; ibid. TS. of Allington par. reg.
89 Harrod's Dir. Wilts. (1865); P.R.O., IR 29/38/6; IR 30/38/6. 90 Wilts. Cuttings, v. 280.
91 Cal. Inq. p.m. xvi, pp. 244–5.
92 Feud. Aids, vi. 627.
93 Cal. Inq. p.m. xvi, pp. 244–5; Cal. Close, 1419–22, 9; P.R.O., PROB 11/2B, f. 63 and v.
94 Below, Boscombe, manors (E. Boscombe).
95 W.R.O. 885/1/1, final concord, 1598.
96 Ibid. 885/1/1, deed, Hatchman to Poncherdon, 1618.
97 Ibid. 885/1/1, deed, Poncherdon to Brownjohn, 1630.
98 Ibid. 885/1/2, deed, Hearst to Noyes, 1731; P.R.O., PROB 11/605, ff. 99–100. 99 Above, this section.

1 W.R.O. 885/1/1, will of Steph. Cox, 1608.
2 Ibid. wills, archd. Sar., John Goodall, 1621.
3 Ibid. wills, archd. Sar., John Goodall, 1639.
4 Ibid. 885/1/2, deed, Goodall to Goodall, 1700; ibid. 1068/2.
5 Ibid. 885/1/2, deed, Goodall to Hearst, 1721.
6 Above, this section (Thorp's).
7 Wilts. Inq. p.m. 1625–49 (Index Libr.), 140–1.
8 W.R.O. 130/2, deed, Swayne to Barbon, 1655.
9 Ibid. 130/2, deed, Edmonds to Heskins.
10 Ibid. 1293/1; below, Cholderton, church.
11 Alum. Oxon. 1500–1714, ii. 699; W.R.O. 130/2, deeds, Heskins to Webb, 1717; Heskins to Bevis, 1724.
12 W.R.O. 130/2, deeds, Bunny to Bunny, 1777–8; 212A/27/3, terrier, 1774; P.R.O., PROB 11/968, ff. 111v.–112. 13 P.R.O., PROB 11/1126, ff. 117v.–118v.
14 Ibid. PROB 11/1326, ff. 305–11; W.R.O., EA/157.
15 P.R.O., IR 29/38/6; IR 30/38/6.
16 W.R.O., Inland Revenue, val. reg. 148 and map 61; above, this section.
17 W.R.O., A 1/345/5. 18 P.R.O., IR 29/38/6.
19 W.R.O., Inland Revenue, val. reg. 148; ibid. G 1/500/2.
20 Cal. Chart. R. 1257–1300, 157–9; for the hist. of the abbey and priory, V.C.H. Wilts. iii. 242–59.
21 e.g. Tax. Eccl. (Rec. Com.), 180; Feud. Aids, v. 289.
22 Cf. below, Boscombe, manors (W. Boscombe).
23 P.R.O., IR 29/38/6.
24 V.C.H. Wilts. ii, pp. 131, 134.

that each was restricted to either the south-east or north-west side of the Bourne.

There were open fields in each half of the parish, common pasture for sheep on the downland at each end, and meadow land on both sides of the river, but there is evidence of only one common pasture for cattle. In the 18th century there were *c*. 410 a. of arable and upland pasture in the south-east half, *c*. 435 a. in the north-west: in each *c*. 150 a. were pasture. There were three open fields in each half, the meadows included a commonable one in which shares were assigned by lot, and there was a cow down of 60 a. west of the river south of the village. Land in each set of open fields carried with it the right to feed sheep only on the adjoining down. In the 17th century sheep were stinted at 50 to 1 yardland.[25] By 1674 part of the north-west down had been burnbaked,[26] and in 1731 a tenant was permitted to plough 20 a. of old lains or downland provided that after three years the land was reseeded with rye grass or sainfoin.[27] In the later 18th century the stints were 60 sheep to 1 yardland in the south-east, 50 to 1 yardland in the north-west.[28] Apart from the home closes all the land remained commonable.[29]

In the Middle Ages each demesne or customary holding may have been restricted to one half of the parish, as some later holdings were. In 1661 the demesne of Allington manor, nominally *c*. 237 a., was in the south-east; three other holdings of the manor, nominally of *c*. 58 a., *c*. 47 a., and *c*. 28 a., were wholly in the north-west; of two other 28-a. holdings one was in the south-east and one included land in both halves.[30] The rector had land in both halves, most in the north-west.[31] In 1774 the estate later called Page's farm, 79 a., included 3 yardlands, *c*. 57 a., in the north-west and ½ yardland, *c*. 15 a., in the south-east; the farm included 3 a. of inclosed pasture and 1 a. of common meadow.[32]

All the commonable land of Allington was inclosed in 1795 by Act. Thereafter there were apparently seven farms. All the south-east half of the parish, *c*. 410 a., was evidently in Manor farm. In the north-west half there were farms of 171 a. and 136 a., four, including the glebe as one, of less than 35 a., and possibly one of *c*. 110 a.[33] Between 1795 and 1840 all the north-west down except 20 a. was converted to arable, as were 23 a. of the cow down. In 1840 there were *c*. 668 a. of arable and 181 a. of downland pasture. The arable in the south-east was in a single field of 220 a., and there were fields of 142

a. and 102 a. in the north-west. Manor farm was 546 a. including *c*. 140 a. in the north-west half; Child's, 172 a., and Page's, 144 a., were the other principal farms.[34]

Sheep-and-corn husbandry continued on the large farms in the parish until *c*. 1900; dairying increased in the earlier 20th century.[35] Manor, 679 a. in 1910 when it included Page's,[36] remained the principal farm until it was broken up 1916 × 1923. In 1916 the 173 a. south-east of the railway line, and Allington Farm, erected there *c*. 1867, largely went out of agricultural use; some land on that side of the railway in Allington, Boscombe, and Newton Tony parishes was cultivated from Allington Farm for the Chemical and Biological Defence Establishment in 1993, but most of the 173 a. was then rough grass.[37] From 1923 the rest of the land in the south-east half of the parish was in Wyndham's farm, *c*. 242 a. in 1925,[38] and in the 1930s it was about half arable and half pasture.[39] In 1993 Wyndham's farm, 161 a., included *c*. 129 a. of arable and, near the Bourne, *c*. 32 a. of pasture; the remaining land in the south-east was worked as part of Manor farm, Newton Tony, and was mainly arable.[40] In the north-west half of the parish much arable was laid to pasture between 1840 and the early 20th century.[41] In the late 19th century Child's farm was fragmented, as the north-west part of Manor farm was in 1923,[42] and from then there were several small farms[43] probably devoted to dairying. In the 1930s only about a third of the north-west was arable.[44] Arundel Farm was in the 1930s the base of a small dairy farm.[45] Cloudlands farm, *c*. 56 a. in 1993, was a small farm consisting of most of the former cow down.[46] Charity farm, 21 a. in 1910, had been increased to 107 a. by 1925[47] and was all permanent pasture in 1993.[48] In the north-west part of the parish in 1993 *c*. 300 a. of arable were worked from Ratfyn Farm, Amesbury.[49]

There was a mill at Allington in 1086[50] but no evidence of one later.

LOCAL GOVERNMENT. About £20 a year was spent on poor relief in the 1770s and 1780s. In 1802–3 £73 was spent on regular relief for 5 adults and 11 children and on occasional relief for 5 people, in all nearly a third of the inhabitants.[51] An average of £95 was spent 1812–15 on 12 adults, of whom about half were relieved regularly 1812–14, about a quarter in 1814–15.[52] The amounts spent 1816–34, highest at £110 in

25 W.R.O., D 1/24/3/1–3; ibid. EA/157; ibid. 212A/27/3, terrier, 1774; P.R.O., IR 29/38/6; IR 30/38/6.
26 W.R.O., wills, archd. Sar., John Miller, 1680.
27 Ibid. 885/1/2, deed, Hearst to Noyes, 1731.
28 Ibid. 212A/27/3, terrier, 1774.   29 Ibid. EA/157.
30 Ibid. 885/2/1, deed, Southampton to Craven, 1666.
31 Ibid. D 1/24/3/1–3.
32 Ibid. 212A/27/3, terrier, 1774.
33 Ibid. EA/157.
34 P.R.O., IR 29/38/6; IR 30/38/6.
35 Ibid. MAF 68/151, sheet 13; MAF 68/493, sheet 9; MAF 68/1063, sheet 9; MAF 68/1633, sheet 16; MAF 68/2203, sheet 9; MAF 68/2773, sheet 15; MAF 68/3319, sheet 6.
36 W.R.O., Inland Revenue, val. reg. 148 and map 61; cf. P.R.O., IR 29/38/6; IR 30/38/6.
37 Above, intro.; inf. from Defence Land Agent.
38 W.R.O., G 1/500/2.
39 [1st] Land Util. Surv. Map, sheet 122.
40 Inf. from Mr. M. Snell, Old Hall, Durnford.
41 [1st] Land Util. Surv. Map, sheet 122; P.R.O., IR 29/38/6; IR 30/38/6.
42 Above, manors.
43 W.R.O., G 1/500/2.
44 [1st] Land Util. Surv. Map, sheet 122.
45 Kelly's Dir. Wilts. (1931, 1939).
46 Local inf.
47 W.R.O., Inland Revenue, val. reg. 148; ibid. G 1/500/2.
48 Inf. from Mr. C. R. White, Treetops, Newton Tony Road.
49 Inf. from Mr. P. J. Rowland, Ratfyn Farm, Amesbury.
50 V.C.H. Wilts. ii, p. 134.
51 Ibid. iv. 339; Poor Law Abstract, 1804, 558–9.
52 Poor Law Abstract, 1818, 492–3.

1830 and lowest at £45 in 1833, were among the smallest in Amesbury hundred.[53] The parish became part of Amesbury poor-law union in 1835.[54] It was included in Salisbury district in 1974.[55]

CHURCH. Allington church was evidently standing in the 12th century.[56] In 1650 it was proposed to add the parish to Boscombe, but the proposal was not implemented then.[57] The rectory was united with that of Boscombe in 1924,[58] and in 1970 the parishes were united.[59] The united benefice became part of Bourne Valley benefice in 1973.[60]

Ralph de la Stane and his wife Agnes, lords of Allington manor, held the advowson of the rectory in 1285.[61] The right to present was disputed in 1312 between Agnes, then Agnes de Percy, and Sir John Dun, who each presented: neither candidate was admitted and the bishop collated by lapse.[62] John Etton presented in 1338, possibly by grant of a turn; William Buckland, lord of the manor, presented in 1348, Sir Thomas Hungerford, probably lord of the manor, presented in 1379, and for a reason which is obscure the bishop collated in 1381. From then until the mid 17th century the lord of the manor presented,[63] except in 1577 when, again for a reason now unknown, the king presented.[64] The advowson was retained by William, earl of Craven (d. 1697), when he sold the manor in 1680. It passed to his cousin William Craven, Lord Craven (d. 1711), and in turn to that William's sons William, Lord Craven (d. 1739), and Fulwar, Lord Craven (d. 1764). Fulwar was succeeded by his cousin William Craven, Lord Craven (d. 1769), he by his nephew William, Lord Craven (d. 1791), and he by his son William, Lord Craven (cr. earl of Craven 1801, d. 1825).[65] The advowson descended in the direct line to William (d. 1866), George (d. 1883), and William (d. 1921), whose relict Cornelia (d. 1961) had the right to present for the united benefice alternately from 1924.[66] The bishop collated by lapse in 1933. In 1964 William, earl of Craven, the grandson of William (d. 1921), transferred the right to the bishop of Salisbury, who in 1973 became chairman of the Bourne Valley patronage board.[67]

The rectory was not taxed in the Middle Ages, presumably because it was too poor.[68] It was worth £14 13s. 4d. in 1535,[69] £60 in 1650.[70] With an average yearly value of £236 c. 1830 it was one of the poorer livings in Amesbury deanery.[71] The rector took all tithes from the parish except the small portion taken by the successors of Amesbury abbey. The rector's were valued at £230 in 1839 and commuted.[72] The glebe consisted of nominally c. 44 a. with pasture rights,[73] 35 a. from inclosure in 1795.[74] In 1929 the rector sold 30 a.;[75] c. 4 a. remained in 1993.[76] The rectory house may have been rebuilt or altered by Stephen Templer, rector from 1536 to c. 1559.[77] It needed repair in the later 16th century and in the 1660s,[78] was in poor condition in the earlier 19th century,[79] and was demolished between 1877 and 1899.[80] A large new rectory house of red brick built in 1877[81] was sold in 1974.[82] A new house in the village was built c. 1974 for a team vicar.

In the Middle Ages a cow and a few sheep were given to pay for a candle in the church.[83] Robert Thatcham, rector 1474–81, Stephen Templer, rector from 1536 to c. 1559 and vicar of Idmiston from 1542, and Nicholas Fuller, rector 1590–1623 and rector of Bishop's Waltham (Hants) from 1620, was each a canon of Salisbury.[84] Templer may have lived sometimes at Allington and preached there regularly.[85] In 1577 services were infrequent and held by a curate.[86] Fuller sometimes resided, and completed his *Theological Miscellanies* at Allington in 1616.[87] John South, rector 1623–4, was regius professor of Greek at Oxford.[88] Nathaniel Forster, rector from c. 1642 to 1698, had been sequestered by 1650 when the intruder, Peter Titley, preached twice each Sunday.[89] Forster administered the sacrament quarterly in 1662.[90] Henry Lewis, curate of Allington and assistant curate of Amesbury in 1783, held a service at Allington every Sunday, alternately morning and afternoon. He held services on Christmas day and Good Friday and on fasts and festivals, and administered the sacrament at Christmas, Easter, and Whitsun to 4–5 communicants.[91]

53 *Poor Rate Returns, 1816–21*, 185; *1822–4*, 225; *1825–9*, 215; *1830–4*, 209.
54 *Poor Law Com. 2nd Rep.* App. D, 558.
55 O.S. Map 1/100,000, admin. areas, Wilts. (1974 edn.).
56 Below, this section [architecture].
57 *W.A.M.* xl. 259–60.
58 Ch. Com. file 89944.
59 *Lond. Gaz.* 2 Oct. 1970, p. 10764.
60 Inf. from Ch. Com.
61 *Feet of F.* 1272–1327 (W.R.S. i), p. 27.
62 *Reg. Ghent* (Cant. & York Soc.), ii. 783, 800.
63 Phillipps, *Wilts. Inst.* (index in *W.A.M.* xxviii. 211).
64 *Cal. Pat.* 1575–8, p. 250.
65 Phillipps, *Wilts. Inst.* ii. 45, 55, 59, 61, 83, 88, 97, 99, 105; for the Cravens, *Complete Peerage*, iii. 500–6; Burke, *Peerage* (1963), 614–15.
66 *Crockford* (1907 and later edns.); Ch. Com. file, NB 34/32B/2; ibid. 89944.
67 Ch. Com. file 52099; W.R.O. 1807/6; inf. from Ch. Com.
68 *Tax. Eccl.* (Rec. Com.), 180.
69 *Valor Eccl.* (Rec. Com.), ii. 91.
70 *W.A.M.* xl. 259.
71 *Rep. Com. Eccl. Revenues*, 822–3.
72 P.R.O., IR 29/38/6; above, manors [tithes].
73 W.R.O., D 1/24/3/1–3.

74 Ibid. EA/157; P.R.O., IR 29/38/6; IR 30/38/6.
75 Ch. Com. file 89944.
76 Inf. from Ch. Com.
77 Phillipps, *Wilts. Inst.* i. 205, 220; W.A.S. Libr., Wilkinson, par. hist. collns. no. 158.
78 W.R.O., D 1/43/4, f. 2; D 1/43/5, f. 35v.; D 1/43/6, f. 4; D 1/54/1/3, no. 51; D 1/54/3/2, no. 10.
79 Ibid. 1068/1; W.A.S. Libr., Wilkinson, par. hist. collns. no. 158.
80 O.S. Maps 6", Wilts. LXI (1883 edn.); LXI. NW. (1901 edn.).
81 W.R.O., D 1/11/240; ibid. 1807/2.
82 Wilts. Cuttings, xxvii. 230.
83 P.R.O., E 318/31/1729.
84 Le Neve, *Fasti, 1300–1541, Salisbury*, 81; *Alum. Oxon. 1500–1714*, ii. 539; iv. 1466; Phillipps, *Wilts. Inst.* i. 205, 220.
85 W.R.O., D 1/43/1, f. 109v.; above, this section.
86 *V.C.H. Wilts.* iii. 33.
87 W.R.O. 1068/9; 1807/2B.
88 Phillipps, *Wilts. Inst.* ii. 12; *Alum. Oxon. 1500–1714*, iv. 1391.
89 *Walker Revised*, ed. Matthews, 372; *W.A.M.* xl. 259.
90 *V.C.H. Wilts.* iii. 45 n.
91 *Vis. Queries, 1783* (W.R.S. xxvii), pp. 21–2, 24.

F. W. Fowle, rector 1816–76, was also perpetual curate of Amesbury, where he lived, and from 1841 a canon of Salisbury.[92] He usually employed a curate to serve Allington.[93] A service each Sunday was still held alternately morning and afternoon in 1832[94] and 1850–1, when c. 20 attended in the morning and c. 35 in the afternoon.[95] In 1863 the curate, A. Child, instituted a harvest festival. In 1864 he held and preached at two services each Sunday, held services on Christmas day, Ash Wednesday, Good Friday, and Wednesdays in Lent, and administered the sacrament at Christmas and Easter and on either Whit Sunday or Trinity Sunday to c. 9 communicants.[96] H. W. Barclay, rector of Boscombe from 1891 and of Allington from 1895, was the first resident incumbent for many years and became the first incumbent of the united benefice in 1924.[97]

The church was rebuilt 1848–51 and dedicated in 1851 to *ST. JOHN THE BAPTIST*.[98] The old church, of unknown invocation,[99] was standing, to judge from the incorporation of parts of a 12th-century chancel arch in the new, in the 12th century. It comprised a chancel and a nave with south porch surmounted by a low tower of which the upper stage was weatherboarded. The chancel was altered or rebuilt in the 13th century; the porch and the tower were built then or in the early 14th century. The east window and a south window in the nave were enlarged in the 15th century or early 16th.[1] Inside the church there was a painting of St. Christopher on the north wall of the nave.[2] The new church was built of flint with freestone dressings. The plans, inspired by the curate William Grey and drawn by F. R. Fisher, reproduced the design of the old church except for the upper stage of its tower, and provided for several old features besides the chancel arch to be incorporated.[3] The upper stage of the tower was given an embattled parapet and a pyramidal roof. The 12th-century font was buried beneath a replica.[4] The chancel was painted and its floor tiled c. 1877 to commemorate F. W. Fowle.[5]

The king's commissioners took 2½ oz. of plate in 1553 and left a chalice of 9½ oz. A chalice hallmarked for 1576, a paten hallmarked for 1848, and a flagon given in 1851 were held in 1891 and 1993.[6] There were three bells in 1553 and 1993. The present tenor was cast c. 1350, probably at Salisbury; the present second was cast by John Wallis in 1613, the treble by C. & G. Mears in 1849.[7] Births were registered 1655–9. Registrations of baptisms from 1660 and of marriages from 1664 are complete. Those of burials, which begin in 1656, are lacking for 1678–94.[8]

NONCONFORMITY.
Several people from Allington attended a Presbyterian conventicle at Newton Tony.[9] There were 4 nonconformists at Allington in 1668, 11 in 1674,[10] and 17 in 1676.[11] In 1669 four houses at Allington were used for meetings.[12] One of the preachers was John Crofts, ejected rector of Mottisfont (Hants), who was buried at Allington in 1695.[13]

A house at Allington was certified for Primitive Methodists in 1833 and 1838, and a chapel certified for the same congregation in 1843[14] was possibly built to adjoin it.[15] In 1850–1 congregations in the chapel were much larger than in the church: in 1851 on Census Sunday 41 attended morning service, 46 the afternoon one.[16] Although they occasionally attended church, half of the inhabitants of Allington were Primitive Methodists in 1864.[17] The chapel remained open in 1993.

Dissenters held open-air meetings on the south-east downs of Allington each year in the 1860s.[18]

EDUCATION.
The c. 12 children at Allington in 1858 attended schools at Cholderton, Newton Tony, and Idmiston.[19] From 1902 they went to school at Boscombe and from 1972 at Idmiston.[20]

CHARITIES FOR THE POOR.
From c. 1793 or earlier to 1876 the rectors gave bread, cheese, and beer to paupers on Christmas day. By will proved 1899 Ellen Meyrick gave the income from £200 for old paupers at Christmas. Two received £1 each in 1900.[21] In 1949–50 the income, £5, was shared by 5–6 old people,[22] and from 1973 was allowed to accumulate.[23]

92 *Alum. Oxon. 1715–1886*, ii. 485; Le Neve, *Fasti, 1541–1857, Salisbury*, 36; Ch. Com. file, NB 34/32B/2.
93 W.A.S. Libr., Wilkinson, par. hist. collns. no. 158; W.R.O. 1068/1.
94 Ch. Com. file, NB 34/32B/2.
95 P.R.O., HO 129/262/3/3/3.
96 W.R.O., D 1/56/7.
97 *Crockford* (1926); Ch. Com. file 89944.
98 *Churches of SE. Wilts.* (R.C.H.M.), 102; W.R.O., D 1/61/6/22.
99 e.g. J. Ecton, *Thesaurus* (1763), 391.
1 Hoare, *Mod. Wilts.* Amesbury, 108; J. Buckler, watercolour in W.A.S. Libr., vol. i. 4.
2 W.A.S. Libr., Wilkinson, par. hist. collns. no. 158.
3 *Churches of SE. Wilts.* 102; W.R.O., D 1/61/6/22.
4 W.A.S. Libr., Wilkinson, par. hist. collns. no. 158.
5 Inscription in chancel; above, this section.
6 Nightingale, *Wilts. Plate*, 36; inf. from the vicar, Allington.
7 Walters, *Wilts. Bells*, 10; *Church Guide*; inf. from the vicar.
8 W.R.O. 1068/2–5; bishop's transcripts for 1608–37 and later are ibid.; marriages are printed in *Wilts. Par. Reg. (Mar)*, ed. W. P. W. Phillimore and J. Sadler, iii. 143–6.
9 *Orig. Rec.* ed. G. L. Turner, ii, p. 1071; below, Newton Tony, nonconf.
10 W.R.O., D 1/54/3/2, no. 10; D 1/54/6/4, no. 32.
11 *V.C.H. Wilts.* iii. 106.
12 *Orig. Rec.* ii, p. 1071.
13 *Calamy Revised*, ed. Matthews, 145; W.R.O. 1807/6.
14 *Meeting Ho. Certs.* (W.R.S. xl), pp. 133, 145, 157.
15 W.R.O. 1807/7; above, intro.
16 P.R.O., HO 129/262/3/3/6; above, church.
17 W.R.O., D 1/56/7.
18 W.A.S. Libr., Wilkinson, par. hist. collns. no. 158.
19 *Acct. of Wilts. Schs.* 3.
20 Below, Boscombe, educ.
21 *Endowed Char. Wilts.* (S. Div.), 18–20.
22 W.R.O., L 2, Allington.
23 Inf. from the vicar.

AMESBURY

AMESBURY is a small town 12 km. north of Salisbury[24] at the centre of the eponymous parish, in which Stonehenge stands.[25] In the Middle Ages it had a wealthy nunnery;[26] in the 20th century it grew, stimulated by nearby military camps, a railway, and an increase of road traffic through it.[27] The parish is large, extending 10.5 km. east–west and measuring 2,402 ha. (5,936 a.), and the Christchurch Avon meanders north–south across the middle of it. In the Middle Ages there were four settlements, Amesbury town and Ratfyn hamlet east of the river, and the hamlet now called Countess and the small village of West Amesbury west of it: Amesbury's lands were in the south and east parts of the parish, those of the other settlements in the north-east, north-west, and south-west parts respectively.[28] In 1086 Ratfyn was not in the large estate called Amesbury, as the other parts of the present parish almost certainly were,[29] and later had its own chapel, but by the early 15th century, when its inhabitants lacked rights of burial and baptism in their chapel,[30] it had evidently been added to Amesbury parish.

The parish boundary crosses gently sloping downland for much of its length, in few places corresponds with the relief, and is nowhere intricate. It follows the Avon for short distances north and south. On the downs some prehistoric features were adopted as boundaries: a barrow marks the south-west corner of the parish, another is at the elbow in the west boundary, a ditch marks the boundary in the south-east, and barrows, a ditch, and the north bank of the earthwork called the Cursus[31] mark parts of the long north boundary. By the early 17th century boundary mounds had been made in many places[32] and one, on the south-east, was visible in the 19th and 20th centuries;[33] by the 20th century stones had been set up along the west part of the northern boundary.[34] In the north-west the boundary was marked by a road which disappeared in the 18th century.[35] To east and west the straightness of the boundaries with Cholderton and Winterbourne Stoke suggest formal divisions of the downland: the north section of the Winterbourne Stoke boundary is the south end of a line which divides several other pairs of parishes. To the south-east the use of downland was disputed between Amesbury and

Boscombe in the 16th and 17th centuries;[36] by 1726, evidently to end the dispute, 36 a. had been designated as common to both places;[37] and in 1866 the boundary between the two parishes was defined by a line bisecting the common plot.[38]

Chalk outcrops over the whole parish. The Avon has deposited alluvium and gravel on each bank, and a tributary now dry has deposited a tongue of gravel east of it in the coomb of which part is called Folly bottom. A large area of gravel on the left bank of the Avon provides the site for the town.[39] The relief is gentle almost throughout the parish. The highest point, a little over 165 m., is in the north-east on the slopes of Beacon Hill, the summit of which is in Bulford. The lowest point, where the Avon leaves the parish, is a little below 75 m. There are some steep slopes near the river on its right bank, and the largest expanse of level ground in the parish is at c. 100 m. west of Stonehenge.

From the Middle Ages to the 20th century sheep-and-corn husbandry predominated throughout the parish. Amesbury and West Amesbury each had open fields and common pastures, and Countess Court manor and Ratfyn almost certainly had. In each case the arable was on the chalkland nearest to the settlement, with extensive downland pasture further east or west and meadows beside the Avon. Large areas of the downland pasture had been ploughed by the early 18th century; more was ploughed in the late 18th century or early 19th and in the mid 20th.[40] A small park between the river and the town, encompassing the site of the nunnery, was greatly extended west of the river in the 18th century.[41] In the early 20th century the flat downland west of Stonehenge was used as an airfield, as then and later was downland in the south-east.[42]

In 1086 the large estate called Amesbury included 24 square leagues of woodland.[43] Almost certainly the woodland lay east of Salisbury near West Dean, where woods called Bentley and Ramshill were for long parts of Amesbury manor,[44] or near Hurst (Berks.), where extensive woodland was considered part of the manor in the 14th and 15th centuries.[45] There was very little woodland in Amesbury parish in the 18th century. Some was in the small park in 1726, more was planted in the western extension of the park between 1735 and 1773.[46] Trees were

---

[24] This article was written in 1992–3. Maps used include O.S. Maps 6", Wilts. LIV–LV, LX–LXI (1883–7 and later edns.); 1/25,000, SU 13 (1961 edn.); SU 14, SU 24 (1958 edns.); 1/50,000, sheet 184 (1974 edn.); 1", sheet 14 (1817 edn.).

[25] Below, this section (Stonehenge).

[26] V.C.H. Wilts. iii. 242–59.

[27] Below, this section (railways; military activity; the town from c. 1900); Bulford, intro.; Durrington, intro.

[28] Ibid. this section; agric. (in each case s.vv. Amesbury; W. Amesbury; Countess (Ct.); Ratfyn).

[29] Ibid. manors (Amesbury; Ratfyn).

[30] Chandler's Reg. (W.R.S. xxxix), p. 31.

[31] Below, this section (other prehist. remains).

[32] Alnwick Castle Mun. X.II.11, box 6, survey, 1634, pp. 169–70, 183: 'cumulus' is translated to 'mound'.

[33] O.S. Maps 6", Wilts. LX (1887 and later edns.).

[34] Ibid. 1/2,500, Wilts. LIV. 10–11 (1924 edn.).

[35] Alnwick Castle Mun. X.II.11, box 6, survey, 1634, p. 170; below, this section (roads).

[36] e.g. W.R.O. 283/6, bk. O, ct. 16 Dec. 1566; Alnwick Castle Mun. X.II.11, box 6, survey, 1634, p. 179.

[37] W.R.O. 944/2.   [38] Ibid. EA/185.

[39] Geol. Surv. Maps 1", drift, sheet 282 (1967 edn.); 1/50,000, drift, sheet 298 (1976 edn.).

[40] Below, agric.; inf. from Mr. C. H. Crook, Mallards, Blackhorse Lane, Hurdcott.

[41] Below, manors (Priory).

[42] Ibid. this section (military activity).

[43] V.C.H. Wilts. ii, p. 116.

[44] e.g. P.R.O., DL 29/1/1, rot. 12; DL 43/9/25; W.R.O. 944/1.

[45] e.g. Cal. Inq. p.m. xvii, p. 316; Cal. Fine R. 1422–30, 321.

[46] Andrews and Dury, Map (W.R.S. viii), pls. 5–6, 8–9; W.R.O. 944/1–2; for the date 1735, cf. below, manors (W. Amesbury).

AMESBURY c. 1815

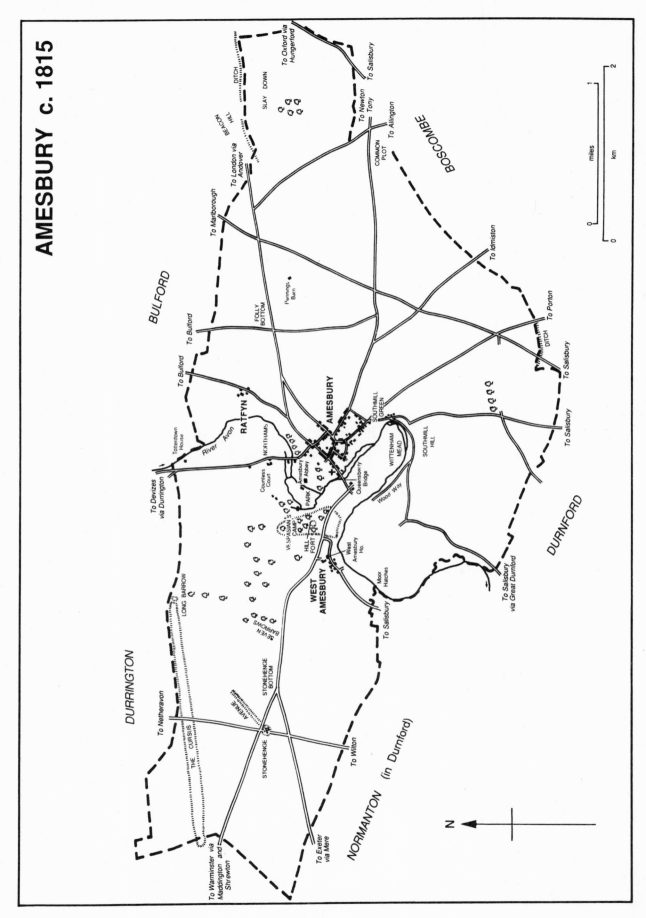

planted in various coppices after 1825, and in 1846 there were c. 150 a. of woodland. There were 161 a. of woodland in 1910, about the same in 1993: the largest areas were in the north-west corner of the parish, Fargo plantation (50 a.) planted 1825 × 1846, in part of the large park, Vespasian's camp (49 a.) mostly planted 1735 × 1773, and in the east on Slay down, 18 a. formerly furze or gorse.[47] The suggestion that clumps of trees apparently standing in 1825 represented the disposition of ships at the battle of the Nile (1798)[48] is implausible, since they are likely to have been planted in the western extension of the park before 1778.[49]

At its greatest extent Chute forest reached west to the Avon, and the eastern part of Amesbury parish was subject to the forest law in the late 12th century. By the mid 13th century the forest had been restricted and excluded Amesbury, and when its boundary was redefined in 1300 Amesbury was outside it.[50]

Roads. Amesbury is on a main road leading south-west from London via Andover (Hants). The road crossed the Avon in the town, turned north-westwards, passed through the prehistoric remains called Seven Barrows and along a section of the north-west boundary of the parish, crossed Shrewton village north of its church, and led via Warminster to Bridgwater (Som.) and Barnstaple (Devon). A little west of the town a road diverged from it and led west and south-west via Mere towards Exeter.[51] A road from Chipping Campden (Glos.) via Marlborough to Salisbury crossed the east part of the parish and the London road on the downs, and an Oxford–Salisbury road via Hungerford (Berks.) crossed the tip of the parish south-east of Beacon Hill.[52] Between 1675 and 1773 a more westerly course was adopted for the road from Hungerford, which subsequently merged with the Marlborough road north of the parish:[53] its old course across the parish remained a track in 1993. Other roads led north and south from the town to link the villages on each bank of the Avon, north towards Marlborough and Devizes, south towards Salisbury.[54] That linking those on the west bank crosses the river twice at Amesbury: it is likely that soon after 1177 it was diverted south-eastwards between the crossings to follow the course of the London road through the town.[55]

The Warminster and Barnstaple road was imparked and closed when the park was extended westwards, possibly soon after 1735 but much more likely c. 1761,[56] and its course to Shrewton via Seven Barrows and the parish boundary has disappeared.[57] The Amesbury turnpike trust was created in 1761. In that year the London road via Andover was turnpiked from Thruxton (Hants) across Amesbury parish as far as the town, west of the town the Mere road was turnpiked as a continuation of it, and about then construction of a new straight road from the south end of Seven Barrows towards Warminster via Shrewton was begun. The new road was not finished, and by 1773 a new straight turnpike road towards Warminster via Maddington (now part of an enlarged Shrewton village) had been made: it diverged from the Mere road in the dry valley called Stonehenge bottom and ran, where almost certainly no road had existed before, very close to the north part of Stonehenge. The roads were disturnpiked in 1871.[58] The Andover–Mere road increased in importance in the 20th century, and as part of the main London–Exeter road was designated a trunk road in 1958;[59] a new section to bypass the town to the north was opened in 1970.[60]

Two other roads were turnpiked in 1761 and disturnpiked in 1871. One, that later called Countess Road and likely to have been diverted soon after 1177, led on the west bank northwards from the town as far as the boundary with Durrington. The other led north from the London road at Folly bottom to Bulford and other villages on the east bank,[61] and replaced a direct lane to Bulford nearer the river and through Ratfyn:[62] parts of the old lane were in use in 1993. The Marlborough road across the downs declined in importance from 1835 when a Marlborough–Salisbury road further east was turnpiked:[63] in the 20th century two military camps were built[64] on its line, and two parts of it in Amesbury parish were tarmacadamed, that linking Bulford camp to the London road, and that serving Boscombe Down airfield from the south. As that downland route declined in the 19th century a north–south route through the town became more important. An Amesbury to Old Salisbury road, consisting of a road leading south from the town to the downs of Great Durnford (in Durnford) and thence the old Marlborough road, was turnpiked in 1835, and in 1840 the road on the west bank of the Avon was turnpiked from the Durrington boundary northwards. Salisbury could thus be reached from Devizes, Swindon, and Marlborough on a turnpike road through Amesbury, where it crossed the river and the London road: in Amesbury parish the road was disturnpiked north of the river in 1871, south of it in 1876.[65] At the south edge of the town a short eastwards diver-

47 *Andrews and Dury, Map* (W.R.S. viii), pl. 5; W.R.O. 283/202; 944/1–2; ibid. tithe award; ibid. Inland Revenue, val. reg. 147; for the name Vespasian's camp, below, this section (other prehist. remains).
48 Wilts. Cuttings, xxviii. 217; xxix. 197; W.R.O. 283/202.
49 W.R.O. 490/1116; below, manors (Priory); agric. (W. Amesbury); cf. *Univ. Brit. Dir.* ii (1793), 44.
50 *V.C.H. Wilts.* iv. 424–5, 453.
51 J. Ogilby, *Brit.* (1675), pl. 32; *W.A.M.* x. 68–9; Alnwick Castle Mun. X.II.11, box 6, survey, 1634, pp. 170, 183.   52 Ogilby, *Brit.* pls. 83, 85.
53 Below, Bulford, intro. [roads]; N. Tidworth, intro. [roads].
54 *Andrews and Dury, Map* (W.R.S. viii), pls. 5, 8–9.

55 Below, this section (the town to c. 1540).
56 Ibid. manors (Priory; W. Amesbury; Countess Ct.).
57 Cf. W.R.O. 490/1116.
58 J. H. Chandler, *Amesbury Turnpike Trust* (S. Wilts. Ind. Arch. Soc. iv); *Andrews and Dury, Map* (W.R.S. viii), pls. 5, 8; *V.C.H. Wilts.* iv. 270; *W.A.M.* lxi. 93; C. Chippindale, *Stonehenge Complete*, 212–13.
59 W.R.O., F 4/200/21.
60 *Rep. Co. Surveyor, 1969–70* (Wilts. co. council); J. Chandler and P. Goodhugh, *Amesbury* (1989), 75.
61 Chandler, *Amesbury Turnpike*; *V.C.H. Wilts.* iv. 270.
62 Cf. O.S. Map 6", Wilts. LIV (1887 edn.); below, Bulford, intro. [roads].   63 *V.C.H. Wilts.* iv. 262, 270.
64 Below, this section (military activity); Bulford, intro.
65 *V.C.H. Wilts.* iv. 262, 264, 270–1.

sion in a cutting was made for it in 1837[66] and, to avoid a bend, a short new section was made there in 1974–5;[67] a new section through the town was made in 1964–5.[68] South of Amesbury the road to Salisbury on the west bank of the Avon through West Amesbury was tarmacadamed and in 1993 remained in use. That on the east bank went out of use between Amesbury and Great Durnford after the road to Old Salisbury was turnpiked in 1835.[69]

In the 17th and 18th centuries roads led from the town east and south-east to Newton Tony, Idmiston, and Porton (in Idmiston), each in the Bourne valley.[70] Part of the Idmiston road survives as Allington Way, and parts of the others survive as tracks or footpaths. In the mid 20th century all three roads were blocked by Boscombe Down airfield, a track across the east part of the parish was improved as a road to link Allington to the London road, and north to the Bulford road, which had been turnpiked as far as Folly bottom, Porton Road was improved to link the airfield to the London road.[71] Also in the mid 20th century a track across the south part of the parish was improved as a road to divert traffic between the airfield and Salisbury westwards off the old Marlborough road and away from the runways.[72]

A road called the Wiltway in 1428 and crossing arable west of the Avon[73] was almost certainly a north–south road leading towards Wilton and was evidently closed when the park was extended soon after 1760. Further west Stonehenge was on the line of a Netheravon–Wilton road which may have been well used in the 18th century[74] but was never tarmacadamed: it was diverted west of Stonehenge in 1923.[75]

A road on the left bank of the Avon linking the south end of the town to West Amesbury was called the Wood way in 1502 and later,[76] and part of it was a track in 1993, but an early 18th-century road from West Amesbury across downland to Berwick St. James disappeared, evidently before 1773.[77]

Railways. The Amesbury and Military Camp Light Railway was built as a branch of the London & South Western Railway from Grateley (Hants) to Amesbury in 1902, diverging from the main line in Newton Tony parish. A station and sidings were built east of the town immediately south of the London road. The line was extended under the road and via Ratfyn to Bulford and Bulford camp in 1906.[78] A short spur served Boscombe Down airfield from *c.* 1918 to 1920. From a junction at Ratfyn to Druid's Head in Wilsford, via Larkhill army camp in Durrington and across the north-west tip of Amesbury parish, the Larkhill light military railway was opened in 1914–15: spurs were made *c.* 1917 to serve Stonehenge airfield. The

railway was run from a camp in Countess Road. Although military, it was available for some public use. The spurs had evidently been dismantled by 1923 and the whole line had been closed by 1928. The Newton Tony to Bulford line was closed to passengers in 1952 and to goods in 1963; the track was lifted in 1965.[79]

Stonehenge. On the downs west of the Avon Stonehenge was constructed in phases in the period *c.* 3100 B.C. to *c.* 1100 B.C. In the first a roughly circular bank and ditch, 56 holes arranged in a circle within and near the ditch, and a cremation cemetery were dug, and outside the circle several posts and stones were erected; one of the stones, an undressed sarsen, is now called the Heel stone. In the second phase unworked bluestones brought from Wales were set up as two unfinished circles within, and concentric with, the bank and ditch, and an avenue was made from a new entrance to the circle: a line along the avenue connected the centre of the circles to the point on the horizon where the sun rises at the summer solstice. The same line is the axis of the building constructed in the third phase: the bluestones were removed, five trilithons arranged on the plan of a horseshoe were erected, and, within and concentric with the bank and encircling the trilithons, a peristyle of 30 upright stones and 30 lintels was built. The peristyle is exactly circular, *c.* 100 ft. in diameter, and the upper surface of the lintels is level. The stones are sarsens probably brought from the downs near Avebury. At the junction of the avenue and the bank two stones were set up, a fallen one of which is now called the Slaughter stone. Either in the second phase or the third four sarsens were set up within and near the bank on diameters intersecting at the centre of the circle: the two to survive are now called the Station stones. After the trilithons and peristyle were built some of the bluestones were arranged within the horseshoe to mark out an oval which included trilithons; later they were reset as a shadow of the main building, as a horseshoe within the horseshoe of sarsen trilithons, and as a circle between that and the peristyle. Within both horseshoes a single dressed sarsen was set up and, fallen, is now called the Altar stone. The purpose of the building is most likely to have been ceremonial, but 20th-century students have shown it to be capable of use in astronomy. Of *c.* 162 stones forming part of the building when the final phase was completed *c.* 60 were *in situ* in 1993, and some fallen stones survived in whole or in part. Among known historical monuments the use of materials brought from far away and the size and sophistication of the trilithons and peristyle make Stonehenge unique.[80]

66 W.R.O., D 1/21/5/2.
67 *Rep. Co. Surveyor, 1974–5* (Wilts. co. council).
68 Ibid. *1965.*
69 Cf. below, Durnford, intro. [roads].
70 *Andrews and Dury, Map* (W.R.S. viii), pls. 5–6; Alnwick Castle Mun. X.II.11, box 6, survey, 1634, pp. 185, 204, 210.   71 W.R.O., F 4/500/41; F 4/500/44.
72 O.S. Map 6", Wilts. LX (1887 and later edns.).
73 *Antrobus D.* (W.R.S. iii), p. 19; cf. below, Durrington, intro. [roads].
74 *Andrews and Dury, Map* (W.R.S. viii), pls. 5, 8; for the

park, below, manors (Priory).   75 W.R.O., G 1/132/7.
76 Ibid. 944/1; *Antrobus D.* (W.R.S. iii), p. 35.
77 *Andrews and Dury, Map* (W.R.S. viii), pl. 5; W.R.O. 944/1.
78 *V.C.H. Wilts.* iv. 291; P. A. Harding, *Bulford Branch Line,* 3.
79 N. D. G. James, *Plain Soldiering,* 198, 203, 206–7; Harding, op. cit. 3, 10, 28; O.S. Map 6", Wilts. LIV. SW. (1925 edn.).
80 Chippindale, *Stonehenge Complete,* 10, 12–15, 266–71; *V.C.H. Wilts.* i (2), 321–4, 326–8; see below, plate facing p. 26.

Henry of Huntingdon mentioned Stonehenge *c.* 1130,[81] and by the 16th century it was widely known as an historical monument. It was visited by James I in 1620, and about then George Villiers, marquess of Buckingham, had an exploratory hole dug in the middle of it.[82] Inigo Jones (d. 1652) investigated the architecture of the building, John Aubrey's account was published in 1695, and William Stukeley made a systematic study in the 1720s. The main archaeological excavations have been by William Cunnington in the early 19th century, William Gowland in 1901, William Hawley 1919–26, and R. J. C. Atkinson, Stuart Piggott, and J. F. S. Stone in the 1950s.[83]

The more widely knowledge of Stonehenge's existence was disseminated the more it was visited. The downland on which it stands was open, although privately owned, and access was unrestricted.[84] In 1770 the Amesbury turnpike trust advertized its roads as good for viewing Stonehenge,[85] and in the 19th century the monument became a destination of outings and a venue of social events.[86] In 1901 the landowner, Sir Edmund Antrobus, Bt., inclosed *c.* 20 a. around it and began to charge for admission: his right to do so was confirmed by the High Court in 1905. Stonehenge was protected under the Ancient Monuments Act from 1913.[87] Cecil Chubb (cr. baronet 1919) bought it with 31 a. in 1915 and gave it to the nation in 1918.[88] In 1919–20 stones in danger of falling were secured, in 1958 stones which had fallen in 1797 and 1900 were re-erected, and later other stones were secured in their positions.[89] To avoid the monument the Netheravon–Wilton road was diverted westwards in 1923,[90] and to preserve the monument's environment the National Trust in 1927 and 1929 bought most of the west half of Amesbury parish.[91] In 1984 Stonehenge and its hinterland were designated a World Heritage Site.[92]

The numbers of paying visitors grew from 38,000 in 1922,[93] to 124,000 in 1951, 666,000 in 1975,[94] and 650,000 in 1992–3.[95] Since 1978 visitors have not been allowed to go among the stones.[96] Soon after 1918 a pair of cottages south-east of the stones was built for the custodians,[97] and in 1927 a privately owned café was built nearby.[98] In the 1930s both were demolished and a pair of thatched cottages, Stonehenge Cottages, was built 1 km. east beside the Exeter road. On the north side of the Shrewton road a car park was opened in 1935[99] and extended in 1966; for access to the monument, which is on the south side, an underpass was built in 1968.[1]

From *c.* 1822 to *c.* 1880 Henry Browne and his son Joseph, both of Amesbury, each acted as a guide to Stonehenge and sold models and paintings of it.[2] In the later 18th century and early 19th visitors to the monument were thought to be important to Amesbury's prosperity,[3] but later in the 19th most organized excursions, including those by rail from London, were evidently via Salisbury.[4] In the 20th century most visitors used motor vehicles, and many also visited the town even after the London–Exeter road bypassed it in 1970. There were festivities in the town and at the monument about the time of the summer solstice in the later 19th century;[5] at the monument such festivities increased in the 20th century, and at the same time quasi-religious ceremonies organized by the Ancient Druid Order were held there.[6] The festivities had become notorious by the 1980s when the government (from 1984 English Heritage), as custodian of the monument, the National Trust, as owner of the land on which they took place, and the police combined to prevent them.[7]

Other prehistoric remains. The western downs of Amesbury parish are rich in prehistoric remains,[8] some older than Stonehenge.[9] The site of a second henge monument 1 km. ESE. of Stonehenge was identified in the 1950s and partly excavated in 1980.[10] North of Stonehenge the Cursus is an east–west earthwork enclosure nearly 3 km. long and less than 150 m. broad: it is thought to be late-Neolithic. A north–south long barrow at the east end of the Cursus is unusually large.[11] There are many other barrows. Notable groups are formed by those in a line near the south side of the Cursus at its west end, those in a line south of the east end of the Cursus, and those south-west of Stonehenge.[12] The southern part of the second group, where seven barrows are close together, was called Seven Barrows in the early 15th century[13] and until *c.* 1900;[14] the whole line is now called King

81   Hen. of Huntingdon, *Hist. Angl.* (Rolls Ser.), 12.
82   Chippindale, op. cit. 47; *W.A.M.* xlii. 611.
83   Chippindale, op. cit. 48, 57, 66, 68–72, 74–9, 81, 113–14, 117, 122, 124, 167–72, 180–4, 201–4.
84   Ibid. *passim.*
86   Chippindale, op. cit. 153, where the ref. to the fair at Stonehenge seems incorrect: cf. below, fairs.
87   *W.A.M.* lxx/lxxi. 112–20.
88   Ibid. xl. 366–8; Burke, *Peerage* (1924), 515; W.R.O. 1619, box 6, deed, Antrobus to Chubb, 1915.
89   Chippindale, op. cit. 179–80, 205.
90   W.R.O., G 1/132/7.
91   Below, manors (W. Amesbury; Countess Ct.).
92   *Stonehenge* (Eng. Heritage leaflet).
93   *W.A.M.* xlii. 405; cf. below, plate facing p. 26.
94   Chippindale, op. cit. 253, 260.
95   Inf. from Eng. Heritage, Stonehenge.
96   *Stonehenge* (Eng. Heritage leaflet).
97   Chippindale, op. cit. 192; O.S. Map 6", Wilts. LIV. SW. (1925 edn.).
98   W.R.O. 1821/32.
99   Chippindale, op. cit. 192, 194–5; O.S. Maps 1/2,500,

Wilts. LIV. 14 (1939 edn.); LIV. 15 (1937 edn.).
1   Chippindale, op. cit. 259; *W.A.M.* lxviii. 57.
2   Chippindale, op. cit. 143, 146–7.
3   *Univ. Brit. Dir.* ii (1793), 38; J. Britton, *Beauties of Wilts.* ii. 153.
4   Chippindale, op. cit. 148, 159; *Devizes Gaz.* 24 Aug. 1899.
5   Chippindale, op. cit. 156; W.R.O., F 8/500, Amesbury, Rose's sch.
6   Chippindale, op. cit. 172–3, 255–7, 259–63; L. V. Grinsell, *Druids and Stonehenge* (W. Country Folklore, xi), 13.
7   C. Chippindale and others, *Who Owns Stonehenge?* 29–31.
8   J. Richards, *Stonehenge Environs Project*, pp. 2–3.
9   Chippindale, *Stonehenge Complete*, 265.
10   Richards, op. cit. pp. 123–58.
11   *V.C.H. Wilts.* i (2), 305, 320, 327, 332.
12   Ibid. i (1), 137, 149–52, 205, 207, 213, 216, 222; Richards, op. cit. pp. 2–3.
13   *Antrobus D.* (W.R.S. iii), pp. 18–19.
14   O.S. Maps 6", Wilts. LIV. SE. (1901, 1926 edns.).

Barrows.[15] A barrow called Luxen 1 km. south-east of Stonehenge seems to have been particularly prominent in the 18th century.[16] Prehistoric field systems have been recognized west of Stonehenge.[17]

On the eastern downs of the parish there are also many barrows;[18] one near the Allington track was constructed c. 2020 B.C. and was altered several times.[19] Six prehistoric ditches cross that part of the parish or mark its boundary,[20] and there is evidence of three prehistoric field systems, in the south along the boundary with and extending into Durnford, in the east corner, and in Folly bottom.[21]

Only one pre-Roman inhabited site in the parish is known. On a hill on the right bank of the Avon and near the town an Iron-Age hill fort covers 37 a.;[22] the sides of the hill were called the Walls in the 16th century and later,[23] the whole hill Vespasian's camp from the 18th century or earlier.[24] A Romano-British settlement site 1.5 km. east of Amesbury church was found c. 1990.[25]

Population. The parish may have had c. 375 poll-tax payers in 1377: with Normanton in Durnford parish it had 391.[26] The population in 1676 may have been c. 850.[27] In 1801, when it was 721, the number of inhabitants may have been at or near its lowest since the earlier Middle Ages. It rose from 723 in 1811 to 944 in 1831. The increase to 1,171 in 1841 was caused partly by the opening of Amesbury union workhouse in the parish in 1837–8; 106 lived in the workhouse in 1841. The population remained between 1,100 and 1,200 from 1841 to 1881, but had fallen to 981 by 1891. As the town grew from c. 1900 the population of the parish increased from 1,143 in 1901 to 1,253 in 1911; it doubled between 1911 and 1931, and more than doubled between 1931[28] and 1961, when it was 5,611. It was 5,684 in 1971, 6,656 in 1991.[29]

Military activity. Stonehenge airfield, with a landing ground between the Shrewton and Exeter roads west of Stonehenge, was opened in 1917 for training bomber pilots, and hangars and other buildings were erected north and south of the Exeter road. The airfield was closed in 1920. Some of the buildings were used for farming in the 1920s but all had been demolished by the 1930s.[30]

On Blackcross down south-east of the town

Boscombe Down (initially Red House Farm) airfield was opened in 1917 for training pilots. Buildings had been erected by 1918 and were extended in 1919, but the airfield was closed in 1920. It was reopened in 1930 with c. 283 a. in Amesbury, additional land in Boscombe and Idmiston, and buildings on which work was begun in 1927. It was used mainly by bomber squadrons until 1939, when the Aeroplane and Armament Experimental Establishment moved there. The buildings and landing ground were in Amesbury parish but later the runways, of which the first was started in 1944, were in Boscombe and Idmiston. The Evaluation (formerly Experimental) Establishment was still at Boscombe Down in 1992, and its main work was still to test aeroplanes and weapons. The airfield was greatly expanded after the Second World War. Many new buildings were erected, especially in the 1950s, and adjoining land in Amesbury and other parishes was acquired. By 1937 nine houses in Allington Way had been erected for commissioned officers, four in Main Road for warrant officers, and 33 in Imber Road and Main Road for airmen,[31] and after the Second World War several housing estates were built on the west side of the airfield.[32] The built-up area has acquired the name Boscombe Down. A church was built but, unlike Bulford, Larkhill, and Tidworth army camps,[33] Boscombe Down has been provided with few commercial or social facilities.

Sport. The Avon at Amesbury was evidently much used for fishing and fowling in the 16th century.[34] Parts of the river were several to the lord of the Earldom manor and the Priory manor, to his tenants, and to the lords of other manors.[35] In the 1580s dace were netted at certain times of the year.[36] Trout, crayfish, and loach were caught in the 17th century,[37] and trout from Amesbury were sold at Salisbury market in the 18th.[38]

In the early 17th century the earl of Hertford may have hunted deer from his house at Amesbury,[39] and Philip Herbert, earl of Pembroke and of Montgomery, or his son Philip, Lord Herbert, was among those hawking at Amesbury in 1640.[40] The fishing, fowling, hunting, and hawking were leased with the house in the late 17th century and early 18th.[41] Kennels had been built at the house by 1726.[42] In 1800 sporting rights

15 Richards, op. cit. p. 2.
16 W.R.O. 944/1.
17 Richards, op. cit. pp. 2–3.
18 *V.C.H. Wilts.* i (1), 151–2, 207, 214–16, 222, 225.
19 Ibid. i (2), 347, 354–6, 381.
20 Ibid. i (1), 250–1.
21 Ibid. 272; O.S. Map 1/50,000, sheet 184 (1974 edn.).
22 *V.C.H. Wilts.* i (1), 261–2.
23 *Antrobus D.* (W.R.S. iii), pp. 34–6; W.R.O. 944/1.
24 *V.C.H. Wilts.* i (1), 261; W.R.O. 776/6.
25 *W.A.M.* lxxxv. 156.
26 *V.C.H. Wilts.* iv. 306.
27 *Compton Census*, ed. Whiteman, 124.
28 *V.C.H. Wilts.* iv. 318, 339; P. Goodhugh, 'Poor Law in Amesbury', *Wilts. Ind. Arch.* ii. 9.
29 *Census*, 1961; 1971; 1991.
30 James, *Plain Soldiering*, 170–1; C. Ashworth, *Action Stations*, v (1990), 254; N. C. Parker, *Aviation in Wilts.* (S. Wilts. Ind. Arch. Soc. v); O.S. Map 6", Wilts. LIV. SW. (1925 edn.).
31 Ashworth, *Action Stations*, 43–6; *Boscombe Bulletin*

(Aircraft and Armament Evaluation Establishment, ix), *passim* (copy in Wilts. Libr. headquarters, Trowbridge); *Boscombe Down: Record Site Plan* (pub. *After the Battle* mag.; copy ibid.); for acquisition of land, below, manors (Earldom).
32 Below this section (the town from c. 1900).
33 Ibid. church; Bulford, intro.; Durrington, intro.; N. Tidworth, intro.
34 W.R.O. 283/5, ct. bk. 1586–98, view 12 Mar. 31 Eliz. I.
35 Alnwick Castle Mun. X.II.11, box 6, survey, 1634, pp. 179, 183.
36 W.R.O. 283/4, ct. bk. 1583–90, view 24 Mar. 27 Eliz. I.
37 *W.A.M.* lii. 14.
38 *Topog. Hist. Wilts.* (Gent. Mag. Libr.), 200.
39 *Antrobus D.* (W.R.S. iii), pp. 77, 82; for successive hos., below, manors (Priory).
40 *Cal. S.P. Dom.* 1640–1, 183.
41 W.R.O. 283/44.
42 Ibid. 944/1–2.

and the kennels, but not Amesbury Abbey, were held on lease by Sir James Mansfield, a lawyer and keen sportsman.[43] Hawking continued at Amesbury until 1903 or later: the Old Hawking club, formed in 1864, transferred its headquarters from Amesbury to Shrewton in 1903.[44]

Hares were coursed on the downs in the later 16th century.[45] Sir Elijah Impey, lessee of Amesbury Abbey 1792–4, was said to have favoured coursing,[46] and in 1803 meetings for coursing were held at Amesbury.[47] In the early 19th century hares were said to be numerous[48] and the coursing excellent.[49] The Amesbury coursing club was formed in 1822, the owner of the land allowed hares to be preserved, and downland near Stonehenge and elsewhere in the parish was regularly used for coursing. The Altcar (Lancs.) club held a seven-day meeting at Amesbury in 1864,[50] and the South of England club later met at Stonehenge.[51]

Two cricket matches were played near Stonehenge in 1781, and in the early 19th century the Stonehenge cricket ground was described as beautiful and famous. Wiltshire played Hampshire on it in 1835. Amesbury had a cricket team, and possibly a cricket club, in 1826.[52]

In 1728 the lord of West Amesbury manor reserved the right to set up posts on a racecourse near Stonehenge,[53] but there is no direct evidence of horseracing in the parish.

AMESBURY. Its name suggests that Amesbury was a stronghold of Ambrosius Aurelianus, a leader of resistance against Saxon settlers in the later 5th century.[54] It has been suggested that the fort on the hill later called Vespasian's camp was such a stronghold and that after c. 500 A.D., setting a precedent for Salisbury, settlement and the name transferred themselves from the hilltop to the present lowland site of the town. There is, however, no archaeological evidence that the hill fort was used for settlement as late as the 5th century.[55] It was believed in the late Middle Ages, when an inscription in a book described Amesbury priory as the monastery 'Ambrosii burgi', that there was a link between Ambrosius and Amesbury:[56] if the link existed, it is most likely that Ambrosius's stronghold was where the town is now.

The town to c. 1540. Amesbury, so called and almost certainly on its present site, was a notable settlement in the 10th century. The witan met there in 932 and 995,[57] and Amesbury abbey was founded c. 979. It is very likely that the abbey was built on the site of the present parish church

and that, when the abbey was closed in 1177, its church became the parish church.[58] The abbey was replaced in 1177 by a priory belonging to the order of Fontevrault, for which a new house and a new church were built between then and 1186. The new buildings, grand enough for some of the Angevin kings of England and their close relatives to lodge and worship in,[59] were on and around the site, north of the parish church, now occupied by the house called Amesbury Abbey.[60] To the north and west the site was bounded by the Avon; to the north-east and south-east it was evidently enclosed by a wall.[61]

Amesbury is at a crossing of the Avon by a main road leading south-west from London[62] and had become a small town, with a market and with tenements called burgages, by the 13th century.[63] The road evidently marked the south-eastern boundary of the priory's precinct. When the priory was built the north–south road linking the villages on the west bank of the Avon, which apparently led across what became the precinct to the river crossing near the parish church, was diverted to the north-east side of the precinct and joined the main road at the east corner.[64] From that corner to the river crossing the main road was called High Street in 1364,[65] Marlborough Street in the 15th and 16th centuries, High Street again later.[66] It was narrowed when, presumably soon after 1177, buildings were erected in the north-west half of it along the line of the precinct boundary: the obstruction caused by the buildings on the north-west side was still apparent in the 18th century when the entrances to High Street both from the London road and from the river crossing were offset to the south-east. The main entrance to the precinct was halfway along High Street on the north-west side and, when that side of High Street was built up, was approached between the buildings and along what was later called Abbey Lane.[67] There was apparently a second entrance immediately west of the parish church.[68] Opposite Abbey Lane, and opening from High Street, land was used as a market place, evidently from the earlier 13th century, and by the 1540s a market house, presumably the building which in the early 19th century was open on the ground floor with a room above, had been erected in the opening.[69] The market place was evidently a long and narrow triangle, with the market house at the apex and the town pound at the centre of the base; the line of the south side continued as the west side of Southmill Lane (now Salisbury Road), and the line of the north side remains as

43 Ibid. 212B/89; 377/3, rent r. 1800; *D.N.B.*
44 *V.C.H. Wilts.* iv. 362; *W.A.M.* xxxiii. 82.
45 W.R.O. 283/5, ct. bk. 1586–98, view 12 Mar. 31 Eliz. I.
46 *D.N.B.*; J. Soul, *Amesbury Hist. and Prehist.* 17–18.
47 Wilts. Cuttings, i. 19.
48 Aubrey, *Nat. Hist. Wilts.* ed. Britton, 108.
49 W.R.O. 283/202.
50 *V.C.H. Wilts.* iv. 383.
51 *W.A.M.* xxxix. 424.
52 *V.C.H. Wilts.* iv. 377–8.
53 W.R.O. 283/132, lease, Hayward to Biggs, 1728.
54 Ekwall, *Eng. Place-Names* (1960), 9; *Eng. Place-Name Elements* (E.P.N.S.), i. 61–2; *V.C.H. Wilts.* i (2), 467–8.
55 Chandler and Goodhugh, *Amesbury*, 5–6.
56 B.L. Add. MS. 18632.
57 *V.C.H. Wilts.* ii, p. 9.

58 Ibid. iii. 242–3; below, churches.
59 *V.C.H. Wilts.* iii. 243–5, 247, 256–7.
60 Ibid. 257; Wilts. Cuttings, x. 283.
61 *V.C.H. Wilts.* iii. 257; Alnwick Castle Mun. X.II.11, box 6, survey, 1634, p. 183.
62 For the road, above, this section (roads).
63 *Cur. Reg. R.* xvi, p. 471; below, mkts.
64 The old line of the road is suggested by W.R.O. 944/1.
65 P.R.O., DL 43/9/25.
66 Ibid. C 142/274, no. 65; Chandler and Goodhugh, *Amesbury*, 23; W.R.O. 906/W/5; 944/1.
67 W.R.O. 944/1.
68 Below, church [architecture].
69 W.R.O. 944/1; Wilts. Cuttings, vii. 225; P.R.O., SC 6/Hen. VIII/3986, rot. 73d.; Alnwick Castle Mun. X.II.11, box 6, survey, 1634, pp. 175, 183; below, mkts.

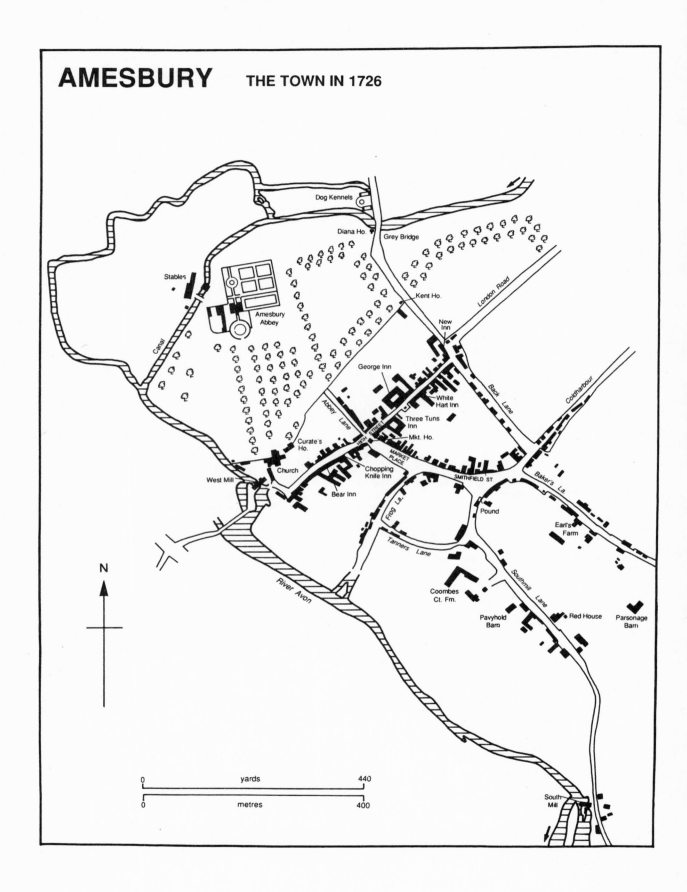

AMESBURY   THE TOWN IN 1726

Dog Kennels

Diana Ho.   Grey Bridge

Stables   Kent Ho.   London Road

New Inn

Amesbury Abbey   George Inn   Back Lane   Coldharbour

White Hart Inn

Three Tuns Inn

Abbey Lane   Mkt. Ho.

Curate's Ho.   HIGH STREET   MARKET PLACE

Church   Chopping Knife Inn   SMITHFIELD ST.   Baker's La.

West Mill   Bear Inn   Pound   Earl's Farm

Frog La.

Tanners Lane   Southmill Lane

Coombes Ct. Fm.   Red House   Parsonage Barn

River Avon   Pavyhold Barn

N

| 0 | yards | 440 |
| 0 | metres | 400 |

Canal

South Mill

the north side of Salisbury Street (formerly Smithfield Street).[70] In the Middle Ages other streets in the town were called Carpenter Street (1321–1450), Pauncet Street (1332–8),[71] possibly named after the Pauncefoot family which owned West Amesbury manor,[72] and Frog Lane (from 1463).[73] The shops and shambles mentioned in the 14th century, the 22 burgages held of Amesbury manor in 1364, the *c.* 50 cottages belonging to the priory at the Dissolution, and the inns mentioned in the early 16th century[74] are likely to have stood in High Street and streets close to it.

In the 18th century the principal farmsteads in Amesbury stood away from High Street and the market place along roads called Baker's Lane (later Bakehouse Lane, later Earls Court Road) and Southmill Lane.[75] Before the market place was narrowed[76] the two roads were extensions of its two long sides, and it is possible that the farmsteads were built in each as a result of late 12th- or early 13th-century planning. The demesne farm buildings of Amesbury manor, possibly on the site in Earls Court Road later occupied by Earls Farm, included a long house with hall, a gatehouse, and a large barn in 1364.[77]

The priory gave Amesbury most of its fame in the Middle Ages. It was visited several times by Henry III and frequently by Edward I whose mother, daughter, and niece were each a nun there.[78] Catherine of Aragon lodged there on her journey to London in 1501.[79] The town itself was a minor administrative centre. Hundred courts were held there,[80] in 1491 a forest eyre was held there,[81] and in 1537 Fisherton gaol was delivered there.[82]

Except for the church no medieval building is known to survive in the town.

The town c. 1540 to c. 1900. Most buildings of Amesbury priory were demolished or unroofed in 1541–2. The prioress's house with its service buildings, a stable, two barns, and two gatehouses were spared.[83] The reference in a lease of 1560 to dilapidated buildings and to stone and lead in or around the walls of the conventual church is likely to repeat the words of a lease of 1542 and not to indicate, as has been suggested, that demolition was postponed.[84] The receiver's house, however, and a lodging for five chaplains of the priory, both proscribed in 1539,[85] were among several other priory buildings standing *c.* 1574.[86] The receiver's house stood in 1590.[87] Between 1595 and 1601 a new mansion house was built on the site of the

priory,[88] and more of the old buildings are likely to have been demolished: the lodging and possibly a gatehouse in Abbey Lane survived.[89] The precincts of the new house were apparently those of the priory, except that the south-east boundary was evidently set further back from High Street:[90] Diana House and Kent House were built at the north-east and east corners respectively, and as an access Abbey Lane may have been closed.[91]

In the early 17th century there may not have been many buildings between High Street, which was probably built up on both sides, and the principal farmsteads to the south-east. A reference to the 'south place' at the north end of Frog Lane suggests that building on the land bounded on the west by Frog Lane and on the south by Tanners Lane had by then not intruded on the south-east part of the market place to break the line to Southmill Lane. The Avon was bridged at the south end of Frog Lane.[92] There were many cottages in the town in 1635.[93] Some may have been in Frog Lane, in Coldharbour, so called in 1660,[94] and Back Lane, so called in 1678,[95] but only two apparently 17th-century cottages, one in Frog Lane and one at the south-west end of Coldharbour, survive as evidence. Dark Lane, referred to in 1676,[96] has not been located.

Its position on a main route brought troops to Amesbury in the Civil War and possibly in 1685 and 1688, but there was no fighting. In 1644 Robert Devereux, earl of Essex, was there with a troop of 100 parliamentarians,[97] and in 1646 troops were apparently quartered at Countess Court.[98] In 1685 Henry Mordaunt, earl of Peterborough, a supporter of James II, and in 1688 Major-Gen. Percy Kirk, then supporting William of Orange, may have had troops at Amesbury.[99]

In 1726 there were buildings all along High Street on both sides except where the graveyard adjoined it.[1] Many of them standing *c.* 1735 were of three storeys.[2] In 1726 the market place remained wide at its west end and trees grew in the middle of it. The south-east part had been inclosed, reducing the east end to what was called Smithfield Street. A smaller triangle of open space remained where Baker's Lane and Southmill Lane led from Smithfield Street. Tanners Lane linked Southmill Lane and Frog Lane. An almost unbroken line of houses, some of them farmhouses, on the north side of the market place and of Smithfield Street linked the

70 Cf. W.R.O. 944/1–2.
71 *Antrobus D.* (W.R.S. iii), pp. 5, 7–8, 23.
72 Below, manors (W. Amesbury).
73 *Antrobus D.* (W.R.S. iii), p. 26.
74 Ibid. p. 13; P.R.O., DL 43/9/25; ibid. SC 6/Hen. VIII/3986, rot. 73 and d.; below, this section (inns).
75 W.R.O. 944/1–2.
76 Below, this section (the town *c.* 1540 to *c.* 1900).
77 P.R.O., DL 43/9/25.
78 *V.C.H. Wilts.* iii. 245, 247.   79 *W.A.M.* x. 68–9.
80 P.R.O., CP 25/1/251/21, no. 6.
81 *W.A.M.* xlix. 397.
82 *L. & P. Hen. VIII*, xii (2), p. 472.
83 *W.A.M.* x. 74–82; xii. 357; *V.C.H. Wilts.* iii. 257.
84 *V.C.H. Wilts.* iii. 257; *Antrobus D.* (W.R.S. iii), pp. 47–9.   85 *W.A.M.* xii. 357.
86 W.R.O. 283/6, bk. of surveys and leases, 1574.

87 Ibid. 283/24.   88 Below, manors (Priory).
89 *Antrobus D.* (W.R.S. iii), p. 76; Alnwick Castle Mun. X.II.11, box 6, survey, 1634, p. 222.
90 Alnwick Castle Mun. X.II.11, box 6, survey, 1634, p. 183; W.R.O. 944/1.
91 Below, manors (Priory); see plates facing p. 43.
92 Alnwick Castle Mun. X.II.11, box 6, survey, 1634, p. 170.   93 Ibid. pp. 194–207, 213, 233–42.
94 W.R.O. 283/4, ct. bk. 1658–60, ct. 11 Apr. 1660.
95 Ibid. 283/6, ct. papers 1676–80, view 18 Sept. 1678.
96 Ibid. 283/6, ct. papers 1676–80, view 22 Apr. 1676.
97 Hist. MSS. Com. 3, *4th Rep., De la Warr*, p. 296; D.N.B.
98 *W.A.M.* xxvi. 371.
99 *Cal. S.P. Dom.* 1685, p. 250; Hist. MSS. Com. 21, *Hamilton*, suppl. p. 111; D.N.B.
1   W.R.O. 944/1.
2   Ibid. 283/6, survey, *c.* 1741.

houses and inns in High Street to the principal farmsteads in Baker's Lane and Southmill Lane. Only one house stood on the south side of the market place, two on the south side of Smithfield Street. There were 66 houses and cottages on the waste, 16 in Frog Lane (most on the west side), 15 in Back Lane (most on the west side), 18 in Coldharbour (most on the south side), 12 in Baker's Lane, and 5 near the river at Southmill Green. There was also a group of buildings, including one where Comilla House later stood, outside High Street at its junction with Back Lane and the London road.[3]

Between 1725 and 1778 the occupation by Charles Douglas, duke of Queensberry, and his wife Catherine of the mansion,[4] in which at one time 49 servants were resident,[5] may have increased the prosperity of the town. In the same period, however, the number of farmsteads was much reduced,[6] and in 1751 a fire destroyed or damaged c. 25 buildings, most of which seem to have been in High Street.[7] In the late 18th century and early 19th the town was evidently in decline,[8] and in the later 19th road traffic through it was reduced as railways were made elsewhere. In 1809 the market house, also called the guildhall, town hall, or court house, was taken down,[9] and in 1812 there were vacant sites on both sides of High Street towards the north-east end,[10] presumably where buildings destroyed by fire in 1751 had not been replaced.

The south-west end of High Street was renamed Church Street between 1851 and 1878.[11] Buildings of before c. 1800 to survive in High Street include four or five houses of the 17th or 18th century, most with shops on the ground floor, and the George and the New Inn. Those of before c. 1800 in Church Street include two apparently 18th-century houses, another possibly 17th-century, and the King's Arms.[12] Comilla House is of the mid 18th century and was possibly built c. 1761 when the London road was turnpiked; in the 1980s it was extended and converted to a nursing home.[13] On the north side of the market place a house with a shop on the ground floor is apparently 17th-century, and two houses are apparently 18th-century; a small house on the north side of what was Smithfield Street may also be 18th-century. The former line of the south side of the market place is still marked by a house apparently built in the later 18th century to replace that standing in 1726. In the earlier 19th century a terrace with a school at each end was built in front of that line, and the market place was thus narrowed.[14] In the 20th century a new building replaced the school

at the west end, and in 1993 five shops occupied the remainder of the terrace. Between 1851 and 1878 the market place and most of Smithfield Street were renamed Salisbury Street.[15]

In Earls Court Road (formerly Baker's Lane) Earls Court (formerly Earl's) Farm was altered and made smaller in the 20th century: its rear wing, in which 16th-century timber was re-used, is a fragment of an 18th-century house, and its main range, facing the road, was built in the 19th century. In Salisbury Road (formerly Southmill Lane) Viney's (formerly Coombes Court) Farm has a main north-west range with a south-east cross wing and is apparently of the 16th century, and the Red House is an early 18th-century red-brick farmhouse with a principal five-bayed west front to which a porch was added in the 19th century. Of the many cottages in Frog Lane, Back Lane, Coldharbour, and Baker's Lane and at Southmill Green c. 1800[16] only the apparently 17th-century cottages in Frog Lane and Coldharbour, the Greyhound in Coldharbour, and a small thatched cottage in Earls Court Road (Baker's Lane) survive. All the cottages on the west side of Back Lane had been demolished by 1851.[17]

Several large houses were built in the 19th century. On the south-east side of High (Church) Street Wyndersham House was built in 1848. At both ends its street frontage incorporates 18th-century parts of the four tenements which the house replaced:[18] between them a substantial five-bayed house with a central staircase hall and large rooms on the garden side was built. The hall and the rear south-western room were later extended into the garden, and to the north-east the open space between the house and its stables was roofed. In the later 19th century the house was used as a school and a vicarage house.[19] By 1923 it had been converted to a hotel, the Avon;[20] the hotel was renamed the Avon Arms and c. 1962 the Antrobus Arms.[21] In the angle of Smithfield Street and Back Lane the Cottage, later called Amesbury House, was apparently built in the early 19th century and had a principal front of five bays; it was demolished in the late 1960s.[22] Its stables, of red brick and contemporary with the house, survive. The Amesbury union workhouse was built in Salisbury Road, which was diverted east of it, in 1837: it was of flint and red brick to designs of W. B. Moffatt, an associate of Sir Gilbert Scott.[23] On the south-east side of High Street towards the north-east end a house, in 1993 the Fairlawn hotel, was built between 1825 and 1851 for G. B. Batho,[24] and, in the angle of Frog Lane and

3 W.R.O. 944/1–2.
4 Below, manors (Priory).   5 W.R.O. 283/203.
6 Below, agric. (Amesbury).
7 W. A. Bewes, *Church Briefs*, 325; Wilts. Cuttings, vii. 224; W.R.O. 283/177.
8 Above, this section (population).
9 Wilts. Cuttings, vii. 225; P.R.O., SC 6/Hen. VIII/3986, rot. 73d.; W.R.O. 283/15, ct. 25 Oct. 1750; 377/1, letter received 6 Mar. 1809.
10 W.R.O. 490/1116.
11 Ibid. 1550/48; O.S. Map 6″, Wilts. LIV (1887 edn.); for the two streets, see below, plates facing p. 27.
12 For the three inns, below, this section (inns).
13 Chandler and Goodhugh, *Amesbury*, 72; local inf.; above, this section (roads); below, this section (inns).

14 W.R.O. 1550/48; below, educ.
15 O.S. Map 6″, Wilts. LIV (1887 edn.); W.R.O. 1550/48.
16 Cf. W.R.O. 490/1116; 944/1.   17 Ibid. 1550/48.
18 Ibid.; notes by W. C. Kemm (collated by P. Dyke; copy in Wilts. Libr. headquarters, Trowbridge); see below, plate facing p. 27.
19 Below, churches; educ.
20 W.R.O., G 1/500/1.
21 Ibid. 2357/6.
22 Chandler and Goodhugh, *Amesbury*, 142.
23 Goodhugh, 'Poor Law in Amesbury', *Wilts. Ind. Arch.* ii. 7–9; above, this section (roads).
24 Chandler and Goodhugh, *Amesbury*, 130; W.R.O. 283/202; 1550/48.

Tanners Lane, Redworth House, large and of red brick, was built c. 1888 for W. Q. Cole.[25]

A toll house, of coursed flint with brick dressings, was built c. 1835 where, north of the workhouse, the new section of the Salisbury road diverged from the old,[26] which retained the name Southmill Lane. Two pairs of cottages incorporating flint and stone chequerwork and with cast-iron window frames were built on the north side of Tanners Lane between 1825 and 1851.[27] Also in the 19th century several cottages were built in Coldharbour, a terrace of six cottages was built in Parsonage Road, which linked Earls Court Road and Salisbury Road, and two houses were built at Southmill Green. Frog Lane and Tanners Lane were together renamed Flower Lane between c. 1877 and 1899.[28]

On farmland worked from the town several farmsteads were built between 1825 and the late 1870s. Those called the Pennings and Stockport, respectively east and south of the town, had been built by 1851 and included cottages. New Barn and Olddown Barn were built south-west of the town, and Beacon Hill Barn, near which two houses were built between 1923 and 1939, was built in the east corner of the parish.[29]

The town from c. 1900. Although small, Amesbury was the town nearest and most accessible to the military camps set up in Bulford and Durrington parishes c. 1899.[30] They, with later military camps in Amesbury parish, the railway opened in 1902,[31] and the increase in road traffic, evidently stimulated business in the town. When in 1915 most of the land in the parish was offered for sale much became available for building and was highly valued.[32] To accommodate those employed in businesses in the town and the civilians working at the camps, the town grew much after 1918, mainly eastwards.

Between 1900 and 1914 a new school in Back Lane, which was later renamed School Road, replaced the schools on the south side of Salisbury Street. A police station, of red brick with textured ashlar dressings, was also built in Back Lane.[33] Between Redworth House and the east side of Frog Lane two terraces of cottages, of 4 and of 8, were built,[34] and soon after 1911 a new street, Edwards Road, was made between Earls Court Road and Salisbury Road[35] and two trios of cottages were built in it. Other new cottages included three terraces of four in Earls Court Road.[36] For railway workers a house and a pair of cottages had been built at the site of the station

by 1899, and two pairs of cottages were built there soon afterwards.[37]

Between 1918 and 1939 houses were built by the government, by Amesbury rural district council, and by private speculators. After the First World War the Board of Agriculture and Fisheries set up a farm colony east of the town on Earls Court farm for former soldiers.[38] In 1919 Holders Road was made north–south from where the London road crossed the railway to Earls Court Road, and beside it c. 30 cottages were built 1920–1 for the smallholders. The Building Research Board of the Department of Scientific and Industrial Research designed and built three of the cottages there, and two in Ratfyn Road, to test new methods of construction and old methods which had fallen into disuse:[39] four of the five were standing in 1993. Council houses were built in the south-east angle of Parsonage Road and Salisbury Road from c. 1920; 82 had been built by 1932.[40] In the late 1930s 11 council houses were built in Coldharbour and 12 in James Road near the station.[41] There were three main ribbons of speculative building in the 1920s and 1930s. To the east the whole of London Road, called Station Road until the mid 1930s, was built up between the station and the north-east end of High Street: the buildings included four concrete bungalows with flat roofs and arcaded fronts.[42] To the north houses were built along Countess Road,[43] and to the west along the south side of the Exeter road, there called Stonehenge Road.[44] Between 1923 and 1937 on the west side of Salisbury Road seven cottages were built south of the workhouse and six pairs of houses nearer the town.[45] From c. 1929 house building began beside a track, later Kitchener Road, south-east of and parallel to London Road, and apparently in the 1930s three pairs of bungalows were built in a new street, Church Lane, off the south-west end of Church Street.[46] East of the town married quarters were built in Allington Way, Main Road, and Imber Avenue, all on the west side of Boscombe Down airfield, between 1927 and 1937.[47] Between the two world wars new buildings were also erected in the old part of the town. The British Legion club in Church Street, Lloyds Bank at the junction of Church Street and Salisbury Street on or near the site of the market house, and the Midland Bank in High Street had all been built by 1923. A large furniture warehouse was built on the east side of Salisbury Road, commercial

25   O.S. Maps 6", Wilts. LIV (1887 edn.); LIV. SE. (1901 edn.); W.R.O. 2132/2.   26   Above, this section (roads).
27   W.R.O. 283/202; 1550/48.
28   O.S. Maps 1/2,500, Wilts. LIV. 16 (1887, 1901 edns.).
29   Ibid. 6", Wilts. LIV, LX (1887 edns.); LV (1883 and later edns.); 1/2,500, Wilts. LV. 13 (1939 edn.).
30   Below, Bulford, intro.; Durrington, intro.
31   Above, this section (railways; military activity).
32   Wilts. Cuttings, xiv. 186–7; W.R.O. 776/6.
33   O.S. Maps 1/2,500, Wilts. LIV. 16 (1901 and later edns.); below, this section (public services); educ.
34   W.A.S. Libr., sale cat. xxi, no. 3; O.S. Map 1/2,500, Wilts. LIV. 16 (1924 edn.).
35   O.S. Maps 1/2,500, Wilts. LIV. 16 (1901, 1924 edns.); W.R.O. 776/5.
36   O.S. Map 1/2,500, Wilts. LIV. 16 (1901 edn.); W.R.O. 776/6.
37   O.S. Maps 1/2,500, Wilts. LIV. 16 (1901, 1924 edns.).

38   Below, agric. (Amesbury).
39   W. R. Jaggard, *Experimental Cottages* (H.M.S.O.), *passim.*
40   O.S. Map 1/2,500, Wilts. LX. 4 (1937 edn.); W.R.O., G 1/603/1.
41   W.R.O., G 1/501/1; G 1/602/2.
42   Ibid. G 1/501/1; G 1/760, *passim; Kelly's Dir. Sar.* (1935–6 and later edns.); Chandler and Goodhugh, *Amesbury,* 83–5; O.S. Maps 1/2,500, Wilts. LIV. 16 (1901 and later edns.).
43   Below, this section (Countess).
44   Ibid. this section (W. Amesbury).
45   O.S. Maps 1/2,500, Wilts. LX. 4 (1925, 1937 edns.); W.R.O., G 1/760/47.
46   O.S. Maps 1/2,500, Wilts. LIV. 16 (1924, 1937 edns.); W.R.O. G 1/760/75.
47   *Boscombe Down: Record Site Plan* (pub. *After the Battle* mag.); above, this section (military activity).

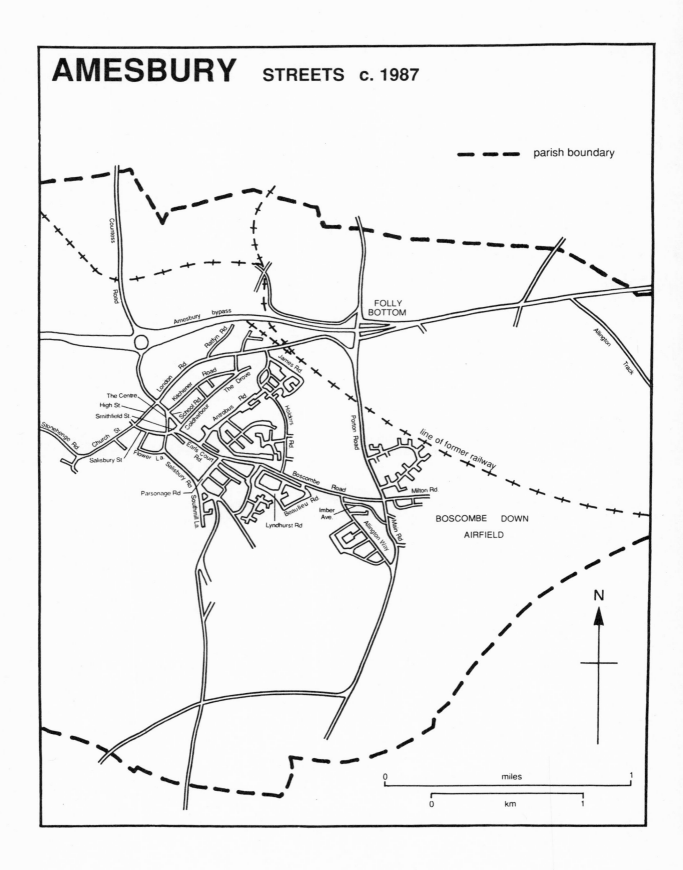

AMESBURY STREETS c. 1987

- - - parish boundary

Countess Road

FOLLY BOTTOM

Amesbury bypass

Allington Track

Raflyn Rd.

James Rd

London Rd.

Kitchener Road

The Drove

The Centre

School Rd

Coldharbour

Antrobus Rd

Holders Rd

Parton Road

line of former railway

High St.

Smithfield St.

Stonehenge Rd

Church St.

Salisbury St.

Flower La

Earls Court Rd

Salisbury Rd.

Boscombe Road

Milton Rd.

BOSCOMBE DOWN AIRFIELD

Parsonage Rd

Southmill La.

Beaulieu Rd.

Imber Ave.

Lyndhurst Rd

Allington Way

Main Rd.

N

| miles | | |
| 0 | | 1 |

| km | | |
| 0 | | 1 |

garages were built in High Street and elsewhere, and a school, a Roman Catholic church, a cinema, a bus station, a museum, and other buildings to provide public services were erected.[48]

After the Second World War many civilians were employed at Boscombe Down and the other military camps nearby,[49] and many new houses were built at Amesbury. In James Road 32 council houses were built in the period 1947–9.[50] About 1950 a new road, Antrobus Road, was made to link Earls Court Road and the north end of Holders Road, and in the triangle bounded by the three roads c. 314 council houses were built between 1950 and 1961.[51] About another 48 council houses were built in the angle of Holders Road and James Road in the 1960s,[52] 64 in the angle of Holders Road and Earls Court Road in 1973,[53] and after 1975 some east of Holders Road and some south of Boscombe Road (the extension of Earls Court Road).[54] In the 1950s Coldharbour was extended north- eastwards as the Drove,[55] and a school built between it and Antrobus Road[56] separated areas of council and private housing. In the Drove, in and off Kitchener Road, and in Beacon Close in an angle of London Road and the railway, private housing, mainly bungalows, was built between 1957 and 1975. South-east of the town new housing was built for military personnel: by 1957 c. 45 houses had been built in Imber Avenue and Ashley Walk, 36 south-west of Allington Way, and c. 60 in Lyndhurst Road near the town; in Beaulieu Road, off Lyndhurst Road, c. 56 houses were built in the early 1960s; and in the 1970s more houses were built at Boscombe Down, mainly south-west of Allington Way and on both sides of Milton Road. A large estate of private houses was built on high ground in the south-east part of the town between 1975 and 1985,[57] and in the early 1990s numerous private houses were being built on the remaining open space, bounded by Holders Road, Boscombe Road, and the line of the railway, between the town and Boscombe Down.

In the old part of the town Redworth House was bought by Amesbury rural district council in 1949 for use as offices:[58] in 1993 it was so used by Salisbury district council and Wiltshire county council. The Centre, a new road to divert north and south traffic from High Street and School Road, was made across the garden of Amesbury House in 1964–5:[59] on the east side of the new road the house was replaced by a health centre opened in 1970[60] and a new public

library opened in 1973;[61] on the west side the garden was converted to a public car park in 1973.[62] The library is octagonal with walls of chequered flint and ashlar and a pyramidal roof of sheeted metal. The old workhouse was demolished in 1967;[63] houses were built on its site. A small group of shops in Abbey Square off the north-west side of Church Street was built in 1971;[64] a supermarket on the north side of Salisbury Street and new shops on the corner of Salisbury Street and Flower Lane were built in 1984.[65] Accommodation for old people built in the 1970s and 1980s includes 50 rooms at Buckland Court in Salisbury Road, 35 flats in the grounds of Amesbury Abbey,[66] and c. 26 flats in London Road. At the west end of London Road 31 houses were built c. 1985, and the farmyard of Red House farm in Salisbury Road was used for housing c. 1990. In the later 20th century there has been infilling in most parts of the town, and in the early 1990s an estate of c. 30 houses was built behind buildings on the north-west side of High Street. Church Street, High Street, and Salisbury Street are in a conservation area designated in 1980.[67]

Bridges. At the south-west end of High Street, part of the London–Bridgwater road,[68] there was a bridge across a course of the Avon in the late 16th century. The bridge was of several arches and was called West bridge in 1578.[69] There were two bridges in 1593,[70] in 1675 there was a stone bridge over an east course and a wooden bridge over a west course,[71] and in 1726 the river was apparently crossed by a ford below West Mill and by the two bridges. The crossing remained north-west of the south-west end of High Street in 1726.[72] A new crossing in a straight line with High Street was made before 1773,[73] presumably soon after the turnpiking of the road in 1761.[74] Queensberry bridge was built on that line in 1775 to replace an existing stone bridge[75] over the western and main course; it is of ashlar and has five segmental rusticated arches and a solid parapet. A small stone bridge over the east course is apparently also 18th-century.

The north–south road likely to have been diverted to the north-east side of the priory precinct soon after 1177[76] crossed the Avon at the north-east corner of the precinct on Grey bridge, so called in 1540.[77] In the later 16th century there were two bridges,[78] presumably one over a north course and one over a south course, and there were two such bridges in 1636 and later. Only the southern, over the main

48 O.S. Maps 1/2,500, Wilts. LIV. 16 (1924, 1937 edns.); below, this section (public services; recreation).
49 W.R.O., G 1/132/105.   50 Ibid. G 1/600/1.
51 Ibid. G 1/602/2; O.S. Maps 1/25,000, 41/14 (1948 edn.); SU 14 (1958 edn.).
52 W.R.O., G 1/602/4.   53 Ibid. G 1/132/124.
54 Cf. O.S. Map 1/10,000, SU 14 SE. (1976 edn.).
55 Ibid. 1/25,000, 41/14 (1948 edn.); SU 14 (1958 edn.).
56 Below, educ.
57 O.S. Maps 1/50,000, sheet 184 (1974 edn.); 1/25,000, SU 14 (1958 edn.); SU 04/14 (1987 edn.); 1/10,000, SU 14 SE. (1976 edn.); G.P.L., Treas. Solicitor, 365/74; 638/75.
58 W.R.O., G 1/132/68.
59 *Rep. Co. Surveyor, 1965* (Wilts. co. council).
60 *Rep. Medical Off. of Health, 1971* (Wilts. co. council).
61 W.R.O., F 1/250/47.   62 Ibid. G 1/132/130.
63 Wilts. Cuttings, xxiii. 34.

64 Pevsner, *Wilts.* (2nd edn.), 93.
65 Inf. from Mr. P. S. Goodhugh, 34 Countess Road.
66 Inf. from Housing and Health Off., Salisbury district council, 26 Endless Street, Salisbury; Mr. J. V. Cornelius-Reid, Cholderton Ho.
67 Inf. from Co. Planning Officer, Co. Hall, Trowbridge.
68 Above, this section (roads).
69 W.R.O. 283/7, views 14 Oct. 20 Eliz. I; 20 Oct. 21 Eliz. I.
70 Ibid. 283/5, ct. bk. 1586–98, view 24 Apr. 1593.
71 Ogilby, *Brit.* pl. 32.   72 W.R.O. 944/1.
73 *Andrews and Dury, Map* (W.R.S. viii), pl. 5.
74 Above, this section (roads).
75 W.R.O. 283/188; date on bridge.
76 Above, this section (the town to c. 1540).
77 Longleat Mun., Seymour papers, xii, f. 250v.
78 W.R.O. 283/4, ct. bk. 1583–90, view 28 Mar. 29 Eliz. I.

course, bore the name Grey bridge in the 18th century.[79] It was replaced by a new bridge built *c.* 1970.[80] The northern, built in the 18th century and widened in 1910,[81] is of two arches and of ashlar.

At the south end of Frog Lane the Avon was crossed by Broad bridge, so called in 1566. The bridge was standing in 1635,[82] but in 1726 the river was forded at its site.[83]

Inns. Amesbury, a market town on a main road, has had many inns. It had four or five in the early 16th century, one of which, the George, first mentioned in 1522,[84] bore the same name in 1993 and, on the north-west side of High Street,[85] almost certainly occupied the same site. The timber-framed range adjoining the street had a jettied upper floor and was evidently built *c.* 1560, shortly after the inn was damaged by fire.[86] The north-eastern end was raised, a carriageway made through the centre, and the jetty underbuilt with stone in the 18th century, evidently soon after the inn was damaged in the fire of 1751.[87] About 1908 a back range which formed the north-west side of a courtyard was demolished and a brick wing was built at the south-west end.[88] Sir George Rodney committed suicide at the George in 1601.[89] The inn had a cockpit and a skittle alley *c.* 1735.[90] Three other early 16th-century inns, the Three Cups, the Swan, and the Crown may all have ceased to be inns in the early 18th century: the Three Cups and the Swan were in High Street.[91]

In 1620 there were six innkeepers and three alehouse keepers in Amesbury.[92] Of the inns in 1635 the Chopping Knife, in High Street, bore its name until 1800 or later, the Falcon until 1717 or later. The White Hart in High Street, an inn in 1700 and 1726, was later called the Jockey: it remained open until *c.* 1800. In addition to the George, the Chopping Knife, and the White Hart, the Bear, on the south-east side near the south-west end, and the Three Tuns, on the same side near the middle, were in High Street in 1726. The New Inn, open in 1726[93] and until the 1780s, was rebuilt, possibly *c.* 1761, and was later called Comilla House.[94] The Bear is last known to have been an inn in 1770,[95] the Three Tuns in 1771.[96] Several new inns were evidently opened in the earlier 18th century, the Angel and the Ship (each mentioned only in 1717),[97] the

King's Arms and the Greyhound (each in High Street and first mentioned in 1735),[98] and the Red Lion, which had been renamed the Fox by 1750.[99] The Greyhound, near the George, was damaged by the fire of 1751 and had been closed by 1771;[1] the Fox was damaged by fire in 1803[2] and is not known to have been open later.

The closure of several inns in the late 18th century and early 19th was evidently at a time of diminished prosperity in Amesbury. There were almost certainly fewer inns in the town in 1822 than at any time since the Middle Ages: there were then four, the George, the King's Arms, the New Inn, and the Bell Tap.[3] The King's Arms and the New Inn were presumably the houses, in Church Street and on the south-east side of High Street respectively, bearing those names in 1993; the house in High Street was formerly the Three Tuns.[4] The King's Arms is a brick house of the 18th century. The New Inn, timber-framed and of the late 16th century or early 17th, has a large central room, a north-east parlour, and a south-west cross wing; a carriageway, cut through the south-west end of the central room when the house was converted to an inn, was later taken back into the room. The Bell Tap was presumably on the site of the Bell, so called in 1880,[5] on the north side of Salisbury Street: the Bell was rebuilt in 1908.[6] A fifth inn, an 18th-century house of banded chalk and brick at the corner of Cold-harbour and Earls Court Road, was opened as the Greyhound in the 1930s[7] and remained open in 1993.

Public services. In 1827 a lockup with a curved west wall was built in the north-east angle of High Street and the market place.[8] No constable was appointed by a court at Amesbury after the county police force was formed in 1839.[9] There was a police station in Salisbury Street in the 1880s;[10] that and the lockup presumably remained in use until a new police station was built in School Road in 1912. The lockup was standing in 1993, when it was a shop. The police station in School Road had four cells, and living accommodation for a superintendent, a sergeant, and four unmarried constables.[11] It was converted for private residence after a new police station was opened in Salisbury Road in 1976.[12]

Amesbury had a fire engine from 1771 or

79 *Andrews and Dury, Map* (W.R.S. viii), pl. 5; Alnwick Castle Mun. X.II.11, box 6, survey, 1634, p. 183.
80 Chandler and Goodhugh, *Amesbury*, 70–1.
81 Date on bridge.
82 Alnwick Castle Mun. X.II.11, box 6, survey, 1634, p. 170; W.R.O. 283/6, bk. O, ct. 2 Apr. 1566.
83 W.R.O. 944/1.
84 Ibid. 283/8, acct. 7 Hen. VII; *W.N. & Q.* iii. 296; *Antrobus D.* (W.R.S. iii), p. 76; P.R.O., C 1/259, no. 18; C 1/1211, no. 42; ibid. SC 6/Hen. VIII/3986, rot. 74.
85 See plate facing p. 27.
86 *Antrobus D.* (W.R.S. iii), p. 51.
87 W.R.O. 283/177.
88 Ibid. 776/119.
89 P.R.O., E 134/44 Eliz. I Hil./9.
90 W.R.O. 283/6, survey, *c.* 1741.
91 Ibid.; 283/16; 283/81, lease, Queensberry to Sturges, 1730; 944/1–2; *Antrobus D.* (W.R.S. iii), p. 44.
92 *Early-Stuart Tradesmen* (W.R.S. xv), pp. 12–14.
93 Alnwick Castle Mun. X.II.11, box 6, survey, 1634, pp. 175, 213; *Endowed Char. Wilts.* (S. Div.), 23; W.R.O. 283/63, deed, Viner to Blackman, 1700; 334/22; 377/6;

944/1–2; 1619, box 8, abstr. of Douglas's title.
94 W.R.O. 377/1, memo. 1788; 944/3; above, this section (the town *c.* 1540 to *c.* 1900).
95 W.R.O. 283/168, 1770, f. 45.
96 Ibid. 944/3.   97 Ibid. 334/22.
98 Ibid. 283/6, survey, *c.* 1741.
99 Ibid. 283/76, lease, Queensberry to Henesey, 1750.
1 Ibid. 283/177; 944/3.
2 Ibid. D 1/21/5/2.
3 Ibid. 944/1–2.
4 Ibid. 944/1–2.
5 *Kelly's Dir. Wilts.* (1880).
6 Chandler and Goodhugh, *Amesbury*, 151.
7 *Kelly's Dir. Wilts.* (1935, 1939).
8 Chandler and Goodhugh, *Amesbury*, 123; cf. W.R.O. 283/202; 1550/48.
9 W. C. Kemm, *Amesbury Church and Abbey*, 25; *V.C.H. Wilts.* v. 243; cf. below, local govt. (Amesbury).
10 Chandler and Goodhugh, *Amesbury*, 137; *Kelly's Dir. Wilts.* (1885).
11 *Wilts. Gaz.* 10 Apr. 1913; date on bldg.
12 W.R.O., F 1/250/4.

From the east

Visitors *c.* 1925

AMESBURY: STONEHENGE

Church Street from the south-west

High Street from the north-east

AMESBURY

earlier. In 1771 it was housed on the south side of Smithfield Street or in Frog Lane or Tanners Lane,[13] presumably at the angle of Frog Lane and the market place as it was in 1812[14] and 1823.[15] About 1920 a motorized fire engine was bought and a new building at the angle of Earls Court Road and Salisbury Road erected to house it.[16] In 1954–5 a new fire station was built at the junction of Salisbury Road and Flower Lane.[17]

A gasworks had been built north of the town and on the south bank of the Avon by 1878.[18] Electricity was generated by the Amesbury Electric Light Company at South Mill from 1922:[19] the gasworks was removed between 1899 and 1923,[20] presumably c. 1922. Electricity mains were laid from 1927.[21] Electricity was later supplied from other sources, substations were constructed at Ratfyn,[22] and in 1948 South Mill was closed as a power station.[23] Public sewers were laid, disposal works were built south of the town, and a pumping station was built in Flower Lane, all c. 1905. The disposal works were rebuilt in 1931 and the new works were later extended. Between 1937 and 1948 the War Department built disposal works at Ratfyn to serve Boscombe Down and other military camps. The sewerage systems were integrated after the Second World War.[24] Water mains were laid in the town c. 1926.[25]

A cemetery and mortuary chapel south-west of the town were consecrated in 1860.[26] The cemetery was enlarged in 1918, the chapel demolished in 1972.[27]

Wilts. & Dorset Motor Services had a garage in Amesbury in 1923,[28] built a bus station at the junction of Salisbury Road and Salisbury Street in the mid 1930s,[29] and built a new garage c. 1937.[30] The bus depot was closed c. 1971.[31]

There was a public reading room in Church Street in 1910 and 1923:[32] it was presumably closed in 1925 when Antrobus House was opened.[33] A branch of the county library was opened in the town in 1950–1, was in the former fire station at the angle of Earls Court Road and Salisbury Road from 1959 to 1973, and in 1973 was moved to the new library building.[34]

Recreation. Amesbury had several bands in the late 19th century and early 20th. A town brass band formed c. 1878 was re-formed after the First World War, acquired new silver-plated instruments in 1930, and continued until the mid 1960s. In 1969 it was re-formed as Amesbury Town Silver Band,[35] which, as Amesbury Town Band, still gave performances in the 1990s.[36]

A bioscope was set up at the junction of Earls Court Road and Salisbury Road in 1911 or soon after, and a wooden cinema was built there. A new cinema, the Plaza, was opened in 1936[37] and demolished in 1993.[38] The New Theatre Ballroom in High Street was open in the 1940s and 1950s.[39]

Antrobus House in Salisbury Road[40] was opened in 1925. It was built for public use by a trust endowed by members of the Antrobus family, who until 1915 owned most of the land in the parish, and contained on the first floor a museum and a library and on the ground floor a hall to be used as a reading room and for social functions. The two-storeyed building, designed by Geoffrey Fildes, is of red brick with stone dressings, is in neo-Wren style, and has a tall central block surmounted by a cupola; it is flanked by a curator's house and a caretaker's house, each in similar style, one to the north and one to the south. Also for public use tennis courts and a bowling green were made in its garden c. 1925.[41] In the later 20th century there were few artefacts in the museum and both the upper room and the lower were available for meetings: Amesbury town council met in the upper.[42] The caretaker lived in one of the houses, the other having been converted to service rooms.[43]

A recreation ground south-west of the town was opened in the 1920s: it has been used for team sports, carnivals, and flower shows.[44] In 1974 a sports hall and youth centre was opened near the school off Antrobus Road.[45]

WEST AMESBURY. In the Middle Ages the village evidently consisted of a line of farmsteads on the north side of the road following the right bank of the Avon.[46] So called in 1205,[47] and with its own open fields and common pastures in the 13th century,[48] it may represent planned colonization on Amesbury manor. In the 17th century the road was called a street where it passed

13   Ibid. 944/3.
14   Ibid. 490/1116.
15   Ibid. 283/202.
16   Chandler and Goodhugh, *Amesbury*, 137, 147; O.S. Maps 1/2,500, Wilts. LIV. 16 (1901 and later edns.).
17   *Rep. Chief Fire Officer, 1954* (Wilts. co. council); *1955*.
18   O.S. Map 6", Wilts. LIV (1887 edn.).
19   Chandler and Goodhugh, *Amesbury*, 63.
20   O.S. Maps 6", Wilts. LIV. SE. (1901, 1926 edns.).
21   W.R.O., A 1/373/21.
22   Chandler and Goodhugh, *Amesbury*, 63–5; O.S. Map 1/10,000, SU 14 SE. (1976 edn.).
23   D. A. E. Cross, 'Hydro-Electricity on Rivers of Avon Basin' (TS. in Co. Libr. headquarters, Trowbridge), 4.
24   O.S. Maps 1/2,500, Wilts. LIV. 16 (1937 edn.); 1/25,000, 41/14 (1948 edn.); W.R.O., G 1/132/22; ibid. 1340/45; Wilts. co. council, Control Map, Amesbury, 1957.
25   W.R.O., G 1/132/12.
26   Ibid. D 1/60/7/7.
27   Ibid. 2357/7.
28   Ibid. G 1/500/1.
29   Ibid. G 1/760/98; O.S. Maps 1/2,500, Wilts. LIV. 16 (1924, 1937 edns.).
30   W.R.O., G 1/760/265.

31   Ibid. G 1/132/135.
32   Ibid. Inland Revenue, val. reg. 147; ibid. G 1/500/1.
33   Below, this section (recreation).
34   W.R.O., F 1/250/47; inf. from Wilts. Libr. and Mus. Service, Co. Hall, Trowbridge.
35   Chandler and Goodhugh, *Amesbury*, 109–10.
36   Inf. from Mr. Goodhugh.
37   Chandler and Goodhugh, *Amesbury*, 139–40, 143.
38   Personal observation.
39   Chandler and Goodhugh, *Amesbury*, 130; W.R.O., G 1/516/1.
40   See plate facing p. 59.
41   Pevsner, *Wilts.* (2nd edn.), 93; Wilts. Cuttings, x. 259, 269; W.R.O., L 2, Amesbury, Antrobus trust; below, manors.
42   Chandler and Goodhugh, *Amesbury*, 65.
43   Inf. from Mr. N. Morrison, Countess Farm.
44   Chandler and Goodhugh, *Amesbury*, 108–9; W.R.O., L 2, Amesbury, Antrobus trust.
45   Inf. from Mr. Goodhugh.
46   See plate facing p. 59.
47   *Rot. Chart.* (Rec. Com.), 155.
48   Below, agric. (W. Amesbury).

through the village,[49] which was often called Little Amesbury.[50] Taxation assessments of the 14th century suggest that the village was small,[51] and it is likely never to have contained as many as 10 farmsteads. It had *c.* 60 inhabitants in 1841[52] and contained 2 houses and 12 cottages in 1910.[53]

In the mid 16th century a new house was built on the north side of the street at the east end; from 1618 or earlier, possibly until 1628, it was apparently lived in by the lord of West Amesbury manor,[54] and it survives as the west range of West Amesbury House. It has thick walls of rubble and a five-bayed roof with arch-braced collar trusses and curved wind braces. The ground floor has two rooms separated by an east–west cross passage, and the moulded timber screen to the north survives. The first floor, which is entered from the east through a stone doorway with a two-centred head, was originally a single room open to the roof. The house was altered in the early 17th century, the date of two walls of panelling. It seems to have been a farmhouse from 1628[55] until the early 18th century, when it was enlarged; the enlargement is most likely to have been soon after 1735, the year in which the house was bought by Charles, duke of Queensberry.[56] A large eastern extension was built and the original house was partly refitted; the original staircase does not survive and was presumably removed then. The gabled south front of the old house was rebuilt as the west end of a symmetrical front in which stands a slightly recessed entrance. The whole front was built of chequered stone and flint, with mullioned windows and tall gables, probably as a deliberate attempt to give the house an appearance of antiquity. In the 19th century a range of building to the east was demolished, part of it between 1812 and 1825,[57] and minor additions were made to the north and east parts of the house. West of the house stands an 18th- century red-brick stable. By 1773 a small formal garden had been made east of the house and, south of the house, an avenue had been planted between the street and the river;[58] opposite the entrance to the house rusticated gate piers apparently of the 18th century stand at the entrance to the avenue. West Amesbury House was a farmhouse in the mid 19th century[59] but not in the 20th.[60]

A farmhouse described in 1728 as new[61] is evidently the house called Moor Hatches in 1993. It is the only house known to have been built on the south side of the street. Adjoining it a farm building bears a date stone apparently of the 1720s: that, other farm buildings, and a new building to link them,[62] were adapted to form a single house in the 20th century. Also in the street in 1993 stood a thatched 18th-century farmhouse and a thatched, apparently 17th-century, cottage, each much enlarged in its own style, two large thatched barns converted for residence, and a thatched range of several cottages each of a single storey and attic. A little west of the village Coneybury House, in vernacular style and thatched, was built between 1923 and 1939.[63] Farm buildings in the street went out of use in the 20th century,[64] and the village was designated a conservation area in 1980.[65]

On the downs west of the village a farmstead, called Fargo or Virgo and incorporating a pair of cottages, was built between 1825 and 1851[66] and demolished *c.* 1917.[67] Beside the Exeter road a pair of cottages was built between 1825 and 1846;[68] a house stood on the site in 1993. Stonehenge Cottages beside it were built in the 1930s.[69]

In the 20th century, mostly in the 1920s and 1930s, *c.* 25 private houses were built on the south side of Stonehenge Road east of the village and 5 in Riverside Avenue south of the road at its east end. A thatched 18th-century cottage stands at that end; near it a toll house demolished in the earlier 20th century[70] was similar to that at Countess.[71]

COUNTESS. If there were open fields in the north-west corner of the parish[72] they may have been worked from a settlement of several farmsteads, but there is evidence of only one from 1364, when it was called Countess Court,[73] to 1993, when it was called Countess Farm. The name Countess was evidently taken from either Rametta (fl. 1248), a daughter of John Viscount and called the Viscountess, Joan, countess of Lincoln (d. by 1322), or Alice, countess of Lincoln and of Salisbury (d. 1348), each of whom held the land.[74] Countess Farm, beside the road leading south to Amesbury on the west bank of the Avon, is likely to be on the site of Countess Court. The farmhouse consists of two ranges: the west is a 17th-century timber-framed block which was extended northwards and encased in brick in the 18th century; the east, with a principal east front, was added in the early

49 Alnwick Castle Mun. X.II.11, box 6, survey, 1634, p. 229.
50 e.g. *Antrobus D.* (W.R.S. iii), *passim.*
51 *Tax List, 1332* (W.R.S. xlv), 109; *V.C.H. Wilts.* iv. 306.
52 P.R.O., HO 107/1165.
53 W.R.O., Inland Revenue, val. reg. 147.
54 *Antrobus D.* (W.R.S. iii), p. 105; below, manors (W. Amesbury); cf. W.R.O. 283/136, lease, Washington to Trotman, 1628.
55 W.R.O. 283/136, lease, Washington to Trotman, 1628.
56 Below, manors (W. Amesbury).
57 W.R.O. 283/202; 490/1116.
58 *Andrews and Dury, Map* (W.R.S. viii), pl. 5.
59 *Kelly's Dir. Wilts.* (1848); W.R.O. 1550/48.
60 e.g. *Kelly's Dir. Wilts.* (1903 and later edns.); W.R.O. 776/6.
61 W.R.O. 283/132, lease, Hayward to Biggs, 1728.
62 Ibid. 283/202; 776/6; O.S. Maps 1/2,500, Wilts. LIV.

15 (1901 and later edns.).
63 O.S. Maps 1/2,500, Wilts. LX. 3 (1925, 1939 edns.).
64 cf. W.R.O. 776/6.
65 Inf. from Co. Planning Officer, Co. Hall, Trowbridge.
66 W.R.O. 283/202; 1550/48; Soul, *Amesbury Hist. and Prehist.* 23, dates it 1840, but it was not marked on a map of 1846: W.R.O., tithe award.
67 O.S. Maps 1/2,500, Wilts. LIV. 14 (1901, 1924 edns.); cf. above, this section (military activity).
68 W.R.O. 283/202; ibid. tithe award.
69 Above, this section (Stonehenge).
70 O.S. Maps 1/2,500, Wilts. LIV. 15 (1901 and later edns.); LX. 3 (1925, 1939 edns.).
71 Chandler and Goodhugh, *Amesbury*, 89; below, this section (Countess). 72 Below, agric. (Countess Ct.).
73 P.R.O., DL 43/9/25.
74 *Hist. Northumb.* (Northumb. Co. Hist. Cttee.), ii. 11, 15; below, manors (Countess Ct.).

19th. The course of the road was apparently moved a little east from the house,[75] presumably when the east range was built. Among modern farm buildings stand four weatherboarded barns, two of 5 bays, one of 7, and one of 3: two are dated 1772 and the others are apparently contemporary with them.

Several cottages were built near the farmstead in the 19th and 20th centuries, on the west side of the road a pair between 1812 and 1825, a pair between 1825 and 1846,[76] and a trio between 1899 and 1915, and on the east side a pair between 1915 and 1923.[77] On the west side and c. 250 m. north of the farmstead stands a toll house, of red brick with a pyramidal roof, evidently of c. 1761.[78] On the east side and beside the boundary with Durrington a house called Totterdown was standing in 1773.[79] It was demolished between 1812 and 1825.[80]

The road, from the north-east end of High Street to the parish boundary, was called Countess Road from the mid 20th century.[81] A new Totterdown House was built near the site of the old c. 1927,[82] and both sides of Countess Road were built up with private houses southwards from the Durrington boundary from c. 1926.[83] By 1993 c. 116 had been built between the boundary and Countess Farm. In the north-east angle of Countess Road and the Amesbury bypass a hotel, a restaurant, and a filling station were built in 1989 for motorists.[84]

On the downs west of Countess a farmstead called Seven Barrows, incorporating a pair of cottages, was built between 1846 and 1876.[85] It was demolished c. 1977.[86]

RATFYN. In the 14th and 15th centuries Ratfyn was a settlement of several farmsteads and cottages on the east bank of the Avon and had a chapel.[87] It had 17 poll-tax payers in 1377,[88] fewer than 10 households in 1428.[89] In the 16th century it may have been the site of only a single farmstead,[90] as it was in the 19th. A farmhouse and two pairs of cottages stood there in 1846[91] and two more cottages were built between 1923 and 1937. In the 20th century Ratfyn has been the site of a railway junction and siding, two railway-engine sheds, a sewage disposal works, and two electricity substations.[92]

The present farmhouse was built in the later 18th century and was L-shaped. Its main fronts,

south and east, are of red brick, the others of chequered chalk and flint. The angle was filled by a block built in the early 19th century, and later in that century a north service wing was built. The two pairs of cottages had been converted to a terrace by 1876;[93] part of it is apparently 18th-century, the rest 19th-century. There are two groups of farm buildings, one mainly and one wholly 20th-century.

On the downs east of the hamlet New Barn was built beside the London road between 1846 and 1876. Three cottages were built beside it in the early 20th century.[94]

MANORS AND OTHER ESTATES. King Alfred (d. 899) devised Amesbury to his son Aethelweard.[95] The estate may have belonged to rulers of the region for many centuries: Stonehenge is likely to have been built and developed by such rulers,[96] and the legend that Ambrosius Aurelianus was active locally and gave his name to Amesbury may have a basis in fact.[97] On Aethelweard's death in 922 Amesbury presumably reverted to Alfred's son King Edward the Elder (d. 924)[98] and apparently descended with the crowns of Wessex and of England.[99] Edward the Elder's son King Eadred (d. 955) devised it to his mother Eadgifu;[1] she possibly held it for life, and c. 979 it may have been held by Aelfthryth, who was the relict of King Edgar, Eadgifu's grandson.[2] Amesbury continued to pass with the Crown and was one of King Edward the Confessor's estates held, after the Conquest, by William I, who took from it yearly only the cost of keeping his household for one night.[3]

In 1086 the king's Amesbury estate included land away from Amesbury itself,[4] and nearly all of what became Amesbury parish belonged to him. Before the Conquest part of the estate, probably land at Amesbury, was held by three thegns, but between 1067 and 1071 it was acquired by William FitzOsbern, earl of Hereford, and given to the king in an exchange;[5] King Edward (d. 1066) gave 2 hides of the estate to Wilton abbey,[6] but in 1086 the abbey held nothing at Amesbury. Two other estates at Amesbury in 1066 were not the king's: Ulmer held 1 hide, and Alric and Cole between them held 3 yardlands. Edward of Salisbury, sheriff of Wiltshire, held both estates in 1086, when

75 cf. O.S. Map 1/2,500, Wilts. LIV. 16 (1887 edn.).
76 W.R.O. 283/202; 490/1116; ibid. tithe award.
77 Ibid. 776/6; O.S. Maps 1/2,500, Wilts. LIV. 16 (1901, 1924 edns.).
78 Cf. above, this section (roads).
79 *Andrews and Dury, Map* (W.R.S. viii), pl. 8.
80 W.R.O. 283/202; 490/1116.
81 Ibid. G 1/701/1.
82 Ibid. G 1/760/60. 83 Ibid. G 1/132/12.
84 Plaque on bldg.
85 O.S. Map 6", Wilts. LIV (1887 edn.); W.R.O., tithe award.
86 Inf. from Mr. Morrison.
87 *Chandler's Reg.* (W.R.S. xxxix), p. 31; *Tax List, 1332* (W.R.S. xlv), 109.
88 *V.C.H. Wilts.* iv. 306. 89 Ibid. 314.
90 P.R.O., E 318/37/2027.
91 W.R.O. 1550/48; ibid. tithe award.
92 O.S. Maps 6", Wilts. LIV. SE. (1901 and later edns.).
93 Ibid. 1/2,500, Wilts. LIV. 16 (1887 edn.).
94 Ibid. 1/2,500, Wilts. LIV. 16 (1887 and later edns.);

W.R.O., tithe award.
95 *Eng. Hist. Doc. c. 500–1042*, ed. D. Whitelock (1979), p. 535.
96 Above, intro. (Stonehenge).
97 *V.C.H. Wilts.* i (2), 467–8; Ekwall, *Eng. Place-Names* (1960), 9; for the legend, Camden, *Brit.* (1806), i. 134–6; above, intro. (Amesbury).
98 *Handbk. Brit. Chronology*, ed. E. B. Fryde, D. E. Greenway, S. Porter, and I. Roy (1986), 23–4.
99 *V.C.H. Wilts.* ii, p. 9.
1 *Eng. Hist. Doc. c. 500–1042*, p. 555; *Handbk. Brit. Chronology*, 26.
2 *V.C.H. Wilts.* iii. 242; *Handbk. Brit. Chronology*, 26–7.
3 *V.C.H. Wilts.* ii, p. 116.
4 e.g. Durrington (below, Durrington, manors), land at Kingston Deverill (*W.A.M.* lii. 76), and land at Lyndhurst (Hants) and in the Isle of Wight (*V.C.H. Wilts.* ii, pp. 61, 116).
5 *V.C.H. Wilts.* ii, p. 116. A different interpretation of the evidence is ibid. pp. 60–1; *W.A.M.* lii. 70.
6 *V.C.H. Wilts.* ii, p. 116.

Osmund held them of him, and an Englishman held of Osmund 1½ of the 3 yardlands;[7] both presumably passed to Edward's son Walter (d. 1147) and grandson Patrick, earl of Salisbury,[8] and presumably were part of Amesbury manor from the mid 12th century.[9] Ratfyn, however, was not part of the king's Amesbury estate in 1086 and did not belong to a lord of Amesbury manor until 1841.[10]

The Amesbury estate which William I held apparently passed with the Crown until the 1140s. It is likely to have been granted, without most of the land away from Amesbury, by the Empress Maud to Patrick of Salisbury when, between 1142 and 1147, she created him earl of Salisbury, and Patrick held it in 1155.[11] By the earlier 13th century parts of Amesbury parish had been subinfeudated;[12] Bentley wood in West Dean, almost certainly part of the estate in 1086,[13] was evidently not subinfeudated and remained part of Amesbury manor until the 19th century.[14]

AMESBURY manor descended with the earldom of Salisbury from Patrick[15] (d. 1168) to his son William[16] (d. 1196) and William Longespée[17] (d. 1226), the husband of William's daughter and heir Ela (d. 1261): Longespée's lands were forfeited in 1216, for his support of Louis of France, and restored in 1217.[18] Ela, who took the veil in 1238, held the manor from 1226,[19] and in 1236–7 it passed to her son William Longespée (d. 1250), styled earl of Salisbury.[20] It descended to that William's son Sir William (d. 1257), who was granted free warren in his demesne land in 1252.[21] Sir William's daughter and heir Margaret was a minor,[22] and Queen Eleanor held the manor from 1257 to 1268 when Margaret, from 1261 countess of Salisbury (d. 1306 × 1310), and her husband Henry de Lacy, earl of Lincoln (d. 1311), entered on it.[23] On Lacy's death it passed to his and Margaret's daughter Alice, countess of Lincoln and of Salisbury (d. 1348), wife of Thomas, earl of Lancaster (d. 1322).[24]

A dispute whether Alice was lawfully married to Thomas or to Richard de St. Martin, a knight of John de Warenne, earl of Surrey, led to armed conflict between Thomas and John in 1317–18: when they made peace in 1319 part of Alice's inheritance, including Amesbury manor, was

granted to John for life.[25] In 1322, after Thomas was judged a traitor and executed, Alice, later wife of Ebles Lestrange, Lord Strange, granted the reversion of the manor to Edward II[26] who, also in 1322, granted it to the younger Hugh le Despenser, Lord le Despenser;[27] the king resumed it on Despenser's execution in 1326, and in 1327 granted the manor to Joan, wife of John, earl of Surrey, for life from her husband's death.[28] John died seised in 1347;[29] Joan granted her life interest to Edward, prince of Wales, in 1348[30] and died in 1361.[31]

In 1337 Edward III created William de Montagu earl of Salisbury and granted to him the reversion of Amesbury manor in tail male.[32] The reversion passed on William's death in 1344 to his son William, earl of Salisbury (d. 1397),[33] who entered on the manor in 1361.[34] In 1365 John of Gaunt, duke of Lancaster, and his wife Blanche claimed Amesbury and other manors from William on the apparently spurious grounds that the manors were part of the inheritance of Thomas, earl of Lancaster, which passed to his brother Henry, earl of Lancaster (d. 1345), when the judgement against Thomas was reversed in 1327, and which descended to Blanche as Henry's granddaughter. The dispute was referred to the king,[35] and by a compromise William, earl of Salisbury, retained Amesbury manor.[36] At William's death in 1397 the manor passed with the earldom to his nephew John de Montagu (d. 1400), on whose attainder in 1401[37] it was forfeited to Henry IV. The king, as heir of Thomas, earl of Lancaster, claimed to hold it as part of the duchy of Lancaster,[38] but restored it to John's son Thomas, earl of Salisbury, in 1409.[39] At Thomas's death in 1428 Amesbury manor, which was held in tail male, was separated from the earldom of Salisbury, which was limited to heirs of the body, and passed to his uncle Richard de Montagu (d. *s.p.m.* 1429). On Richard's death the manor escheated to Henry VI subject to the dower of Thomas's relict Alice, from 1430 wife of William de la Pole, earl of Suffolk, in a third.[40]

In 1433 the king granted the manor to his uncle John, duke of Bedford (d. 1435), whose heir he was.[41] It was held as dower by John's relict Jacquette (d. 1472) in 1436–7,[42] but in 1438–9 was again the king's.[43] In 1439 the king sold it

7 *V.C.H. Wilts.* ii, p. 136.
8 *Complete Peerage*, xi. 373–5.
9 Below, this section.   10 Ibid. (Ratfyn).
11 *Pipe R.* 1156–8 (Rec. Com.), 57; *Complete Peerage*, xi. 376.   12 Below, this section.
13 *V.C.H. Wilts.* ii, p. 116; above, intro.
14 Hoare, *Mod. Wilts.* Amesbury, 82.
15 For the earldom, and Patrick's descendants, *Complete Peerage*, xi. 375–84.
16 *Pipe R.* 1168 (P.R.S. xii), 157.
17 Ibid. 1197 (P.R.S. N.S. viii), 208.
18 *Complete Peerage*, xi. 380–1.
19 P.R.O., E 372/71, rot. 9.
20 Ibid. E 372/80, rot. 5; E 372/81, rot. 12d.; E 372/82, rot. 10.
21 *Cal. Chart. R.* 1226–57, 413.
22 For Marg., her husband, and daughter, *Complete Peerage*, vii. 681–8.
23 *W.A.M.* lii. 82; *Cal. Pat.* 1258–66, 419; *Close R.* 1264–8, 464.   24 *Cal. Inq. p.m.* v, p. 157.
25 *Complete Peerage*, vii. 392–3; P.R.O., DL 42/11, f. 55 and v.

26 *Complete Peerage*, vii. 395–6; *Cal. Close*, 1318–23, 574; *D.N.B.* (s.v. Thomas).
27 *Cal. Chart. R.* 1300–26, 450.
28 *Complete Peerage*, iv. 270; *Cal. Pat.* 1327–30, 21.
29 *Cal. Inq. p.m.* ix, pp. 45–6.   30 *Cal. Pat.* 1348–50, 93.
31 *Cal. Inq. p.m.* xi, p. 185.   32 *Cal. Pat.* 1334–8, 426.
33 *Complete Peerage*, xi. 388.
34 *Cal. Close*, 1360–4, 220–1.
35 Ibid. 1364–8, 112–13; *Complete Peerage*, iv. 204; vii. 399.
36 *Feet of F.* 1327–77 (W.R.S. xxix), p. 129; cf. *V.C.H. Wilts.* vii. 129.
37 *Cal. Inq. p.m.* xvii, pp. 314, 316; *Complete Peerage*, xi. 391–2.
38 *Cal. Pat.* 1399–1401, 426; *Cal. Close*, 1399–1402, 60.
39 *Cal. Close*, 1405–9, 445; *Complete Peerage*, xi. 393.
40 *Complete Peerage*, xi. 395; *W.A.M.* lxxii/lxxiii, 141–2; *Cal. Fine R.* 1430–7, 64–5; P.R.O., C 139/41, no. 57, rot. 39; C 139/45, no. 39, rot. 4.
41 *Cal. Pat.* 1429–36, 296–7; P.R.O., C 139/77, no. 36, rot. 29.
42 *Complete Peerage*, ii. 72; P.R.O., SC 6/1062/4.
43 *Cal. Pat.* 1436–41, 162; P.R.O., SC 6/1114/14.

to his granduncle Cardinal Henry Beaufort, bishop of Winchester,[44] to whom in 1441 Alice, countess of Suffolk, and her husband, on receipt of compensation from the king, surrendered her third.[45] Cardinal Beaufort granted the whole manor of Amesbury to the hospital of Holy Cross, Winchester, in 1446.[46]

After the victory of Edward IV, supported by Richard Nevill, earl of Warwick, over Henry VI, in 1461 parliament restored to Richard's mother Alice, countess of Salisbury, daughter of Thomas, earl of Salisbury (d. 1428), Amesbury manor and other lands which John, earl of Salisbury, held at his death opposing Henry IV in 1400: that the manor had been restored in 1409 and, held in tail male, had escheated to Henry VI in 1429 was ignored,[47] and the hospital of Holy Cross was deprived of it.[48] On Alice's death in 1462 Amesbury manor passed to Warwick (d. 1471), at the partition of whose lands it was allotted to his daughter Isabel (d. 1476), wife of George Plantagenet, duke of Clarence (d. 1478). From 1478 it was held by Isabel's son Edward Plantagenet, earl of Warwick, a minor,[49] but in 1492 Margaret, countess of Richmond (d. 1509), the mother of Henry VII and grandniece of Cardinal Beaufort, petitioned parliament for it: she referred to the earlier tenure in tail male, by which it escheated to Henry VI, claimed it as Beaufort's heir, ignored Beaufort's gift of it to Holy Cross, and succeeded in her petition.[50] The manor was apparently held in 1501 by Henry VII,[51] and descended to Henry VIII.[52] In 1513 Margaret Pole, from then countess of Salisbury, was given the lands held by her brother Edward, earl of Warwick, at his execution in 1499:[53] Amesbury manor was not among them,[54] but she may nevertheless have held it between 1513 and 1515. Thereafter, however, it was the king's[55] and in 1536 he granted it to Sir Edward Seymour, Viscount Beauchamp,[56] from 1537 earl of Hertford, from 1547 duke of Somerset.[57] By Act of 1540 the manor was settled on Seymour for life, and after on his son Edward by his wife Anne Stanhope.[58]

In 1541 Seymour acquired other land in the parish,[59] and thereafter Amesbury manor came to be called the *EARLDOM* or Earl's manor of Amesbury. Seymour held it until he was executed and attainted in 1552. An Act of that year confirmed the Act of 1540, and the manor was appointed to Edward[60] (a minor until 1558, cr. earl of Hertford 1559, d. 1621); it descended with the earldom to that Edward's grandson William Seymour (cr. marquess of Hertford 1641, duke of Somerset 1660, d. 1660), to William's grandson William Seymour, duke of Somerset (d. 1671), and to that William's uncle John Seymour, duke of Somerset (d. 1675). On John's death the manor passed to the younger William's sister Elizabeth (d. 1697), from 1676 wife of Thomas Bruce (d. 1741), earl of Ailesbury from 1685. Elizabeth's heir, her son Charles Bruce,[61] in 1720 sold it to his cousin once removed Henry Boyle, Lord Carleton (d. 1725),[62] who devised it to his nephew Charles Douglas, duke of Queensberry (d. 1778), the husband of Catherine Hyde (d. 1777), reputedly Henry's natural daughter.[63] The manor passed in 1778 with the dukedom to Charles's cousin once removed William Douglas; at William's death in 1820 it passed to his kinsman Archibald Douglas, Lord Douglas; and in 1825 Lord Douglas sold it to Sir Edmund Antrobus, Bt. (d. 1826).[64] It descended with the baronetcy to Sir Edmund's nephew Sir Edmund Antrobus (d. 1870), to that Sir Edmund's son Sir Edmund (d. 1899), and in turn to that Sir Edmund's sons Sir Edmund (d. 1915) and Sir Cosmo.[65] Other manors and estates in the parish were added to the Earldom manor, principally the Priory manor in 1541, West Amesbury in 1735, Coombes Court and Countess Court in 1760, and Ratfyn in 1841,[66] and from 1841 the Antrobuses owned nearly all the parish. Sir Cosmo offered the estate for sale in 1915, when most land of the Earldom manor was in Earls Court, Ratfyn, and Red House farms.[67]

A. C. Young bought Earls Court and Ratfyn farms, 1,613 a., in 1916, and in 1919 sold them to the Board of Agriculture and Fisheries.[68] Earls Court farm, 236 a., was immediately fragmented as smallholdings.[69] Ratfyn farm was divided by the Ministry of Agriculture into three farms. Beacon Hill farm, 451 a., was bought c. 1955 by Mr. C. H. Crook, the owner in 1993; Pennings farm, 262 a., was bought in 1960 by E. C. Sandell, whose son Mr. I. F. Sandell owned it in 1993.[70] Red House farm, 964 a., was bought in 1916 by John Wort (d. 1921), George Way (d. 1939), and J. H. Wort (d. 1960),[71] in business together as Wort & Way, builders, of Salis-

44 *Cal. Pat.* 1436–41, 311; *D.N.B.*
45 *Cal. Pat.* 1436–41, 480; *Feet of F. 1377–1509* (W.R.S. xli), p. 115; *Cal. Close,* 1441–7, 9.
46 *Cal. Pat.* 1452–61, 233–4.
47 *Rot. Parl.* v. 484–5; *Complete Peerage,* xi. 392, 395–8; xii (2), 385–93; above, this section.
48 *W.A.M.* lxxii/lxxiii. 145.
49 *Complete Peerage,* xi. 398; xii (2), 392; P.R.O., C 140/68, no. 47, rot. 21; ibid. E 136/155, pp. 7–8; ibid. SC 6/1118/4.
50 *Rot. Parl.* vi. 446–8; *Complete Peerage,* x. 827; above, this section.   51 P.R.O., SC 6/Hen. VII/1364.
52 Ibid. SC 6/Hen. VIII/7019.
53 *Complete Peerage,* xi. 399–400; 5 Hen. VIII, c. 12.
54 Above, this section.
55 P.R.O., SC 6/Hen. VIII/3822–3.
56 *L. & P. Hen. VIII,* x, p. 526.
57 *Complete Peerage,* vi. 504.
58 P.R.O., E 328/117; D. & C. Windsor Mun. XV. 8. 8.
59 Below, this section (Priory).   60 P.R.O., E 328/117.
61 *Complete Peerage,* i. 59–61; vi. 505–7; xii (1), 69–76;

W.R.O. 283/24; 283/80, lease, Som. to Hearst, 1675.
62 *Complete Peerage,* iii. 26–7; xii (1), 69–75; W.R.O. 1619, box 5, deed, Bruce to Carleton, 1720.
63 *Complete Peerage,* iii. 26–7; x. 694–700; P.R.O., PROB 11/602, f. 94.
64 *Complete Peerage,* iv. 441–2; x. 701–4; W.R.O. 1619, box 4, deed, Douglas to Antrobus, 1825; box 8, abstr. of Douglas's title.   65 Burke, *Peerage* (1959), 80.
66 Below, this section.
67 Alnwick Castle Mun. X.II.11, box 6, survey, 1634, pp. 169–70; W.R.O. 776/6.
68 Wilts. Cuttings, xv. 216; G.P.L., Treas. Solicitor, 1136/75.
69 Above, intro. (the town from c. 1900); below, agric. (Amesbury).
70 Deed in possession of Dr. C. Goodson-Wickes, Watergate Ho., Bulford; inf. from Mr. I. F. Sandell, Pikes Cottage, W. Amesbury; Mr. C. H. Crook, Mallards, Blackhorse Lane, Hurdcott; for Ratfyn farm, below, this section (Ratfyn).
71 G.P.L., Treas. Solicitor, 365/74; 1684/65.

bury.[72] Wort & Way sold 283 a. in 1925, c. 50 a. in 1947, further land in 1949, and 53 a. in 1960, all to the state for Boscombe Down airfield and housing associated with it.[73] The firm was dissolved in 1967.[74] The remainder of Red House farm was sold in 1982 by H. G. Way to Mr. J. C. Salvidge, the owner of 300 a. of it in 1993. In the later 1980s Mr. Salvidge sold c. 150 a. as Stockport farm to Mr. I. F. Sandell, the owner of that land in 1993, and 56 a. in 1990 to the Ministry of Defence.[75]

Amesbury abbey is unlikely to have owned any land in the parish apart from its own site, and in 1179 Amesbury priory, which replaced the abbey in 1177, was endowed with none outside the site.[76] What became the *PRIORY* manor was built up piecemeal: the priory acquired 1 yardland in Amesbury in 1237,[77] presumably the land which it held in 1242,[78] and 105 a. in West Amesbury from Roger Convers in 1268,[79] presumably the land which it held there in 1275.[80] The priory was granted free warren in its demesne land in the parish in 1286.[81] Other land may have been added to the estate by 1291 when the priory's temporalities in the parish were worth £7 a year,[82] and in 1315 Walter Lovel gave 6 bovates in West Amesbury, an estate in which the priory had held Walter Aleyn's life interest since 1309.[83] At the Dissolution[84] it held its own site, mills, 37 a. of meadow, pasture, and parkland, a nominal 290 a. of arable, feeding for 374 sheep, c. 50 cottages and houses in the town, including two inns, and a further c. 10 a.:[85] some of its agricultural land was in Amesbury, some in West Amesbury.[86] In an exchange the Crown granted that estate in 1541 to Edward, earl of Hertford,[87] later duke of Somerset, on whose attainder in 1552 it was forfeited. In 1553, under the Act of 1552, it was assigned to Edward's son Edward, from 1559 earl of Hertford, in recompense for lands settled on the younger Edward in 1540 and alienated before 1552.[88] Later called Amesbury Priory manor it descended with the Earldom manor.[89] In 1915 it was represented by an estate which, including the site of the priory and some of its lands, consisted of Amesbury Abbey, its park, and land adjoining the park to the west, a total of 264 a.[90] That estate passed

from Sir Cosmo Antrobus, Bt. (d. 1939), with the baronetcy to his cousin Sir Philip Antrobus (d. 1968) and his second cousin once removed Sir Philip Antrobus.[91] In 1979–80 the house and c. 20 a. were sold to Mr. J. V. Cornelius-Reid, the owner in 1992.[92] Of the rest c. 200 a. belonged to Sir Philip in 1992.[93]

There is no evidence that the prioress's house was lived in after the Dissolution, and what is likely to have been a smaller house stood on its site c. 1574.[94] A new mansion house[95] on the site of the priory was built for Edward, earl of Hertford, between 1595, when he brought the site in hand,[96] and 1601, when he lived at Amesbury.[97] It may have been completed by 1599, when Hertford was seeking to exclude a yearly fair from what had been the priory's precinct.[98] In 1600 a gatehouse, Diana House, was built at the north-east corner of the precinct; also in 1600 an ornamental tower was built, evidently within or overlooking the precinct; and in 1607 a gatehouse, Kent House, was built at the east corner of the precinct. Both Diana House and Kent House are of flint with slated ogee roofs and of two storeys; each has no more than a single pentagonal room to each storey and has an adjoining three-storeyed hexagonal stair turret. Kent House was enlarged, possibly c. 1761 to designs by Henry Flitcroft,[99] and was a farmhouse in the later 18th century.[1] The tower, which may have been of similar style, was evidently re-erected as a feature of the landscape around Wilbury House in Newton Tony in the 18th century.[2] The precincts of the priory, of which the Avon and a wall were boundaries, formed a park around the house,[3] except that the south-east boundary was evidently moved north-west away from the backs of the buildings in High Street;[4] the main entrances to the priory, along Abbey Lane[5] and apparently west of the parish church,[6] may have been replaced by a main entrance near Kent House and a service entrance near Diana House. There was a bowling green in the park in 1635.[7] The mansion was lived in by Robert Devereux, earl of Essex, in 1636,[8] in 1640 visited by Philip, earl of Pembroke, or by Lord Herbert,[9] and in the Interregnum lived in by William, marquess of

[72] *Kelly's Dir. Wilts.* (1915 and later edns.).
[73] G.P.L., Treas. Solicitor, 365/74; 1511/65; 1605/65; 2274/76.   [74] *Wilts. Cuttings,* xxiii. 63.
[75] Inf. from Mr. J. C. Salvidge, Home Farm, S. Tidworth; Mr. Sandell; Defence Land Agent, Durrington.
[76] *Cal. Chart. R.* 1257–1300, 157–8.
[77] P.R.O., CP 25/1/250/11, no. 2; ibid. DL 43/9/25.
[78] *Cur. Reg. R.* xvi, p. 471.
[79] P.R.O., CP 25/1/251/21, no. 38.
[80] Ibid. KB 27/15, rot. 4d.
[81] *Cal. Chart. R.* 1257–1300, 336.
[82] *Tax. Eccl.* (Rec. Com.), 185.
[83] *Cal. Pat.* 1307–13, 203; *Feet of F. 1272–1327* (W.R.S. i), p. 92.
[84] For the priory's hist. as a cell of an alien ho., *V.C.H. Wilts.* iii. 248–53.
[85] *Valor Eccl.* (Rec. Com.), ii. 93; P.R.O., SC 6/Hen. VIII/3986, rott. 73–4.
[86] Below, econ. hist. (Amesbury; W. Amesbury).
[87] P.R.O., E 305/4/C 18.
[88] Ibid. E 328/117; D. & C. Windsor Mun. XV. 8. 8.
[89] Above, this section.
[90] Alnwick Castle Mun. X.II.11, box 6, survey, 1634, p. 183; W.R.O. 776/6.
[91] Burke, *Peerage* (1959), 80; *Who Was Who, 1961–70,*

2; *Who's Who,* 1991, 43.
[92] Inf. from Mr. J. V. Cornelius-Reid, Cholderton Ho.
[93] Inf. from Sir Phil. Antrobus, Bt., W. Amesbury Ho.
[94] W.R.O. 283/6, bk. of surveys and leases, 1574.
[95] Cf. *Antrobus D.* (W.R.S. iii), p. 76.
[96] W.R.O. 283/6, bk. D, agreement, Hertford and Poore, 1595.
[97] e.g. *V.C.H. Wilts.* v. 124 n.; P.R.O., E 134/44 Eliz. I Hil./9.
[98] Hist. MSS. Com. 43, *15th Rep. VII, Ailesbury,* p. 155.
[99] J. Bold, *Wilton Ho. and Eng. Palladianism* (R.C.H.M), 118–19, 133, 135; for the tower, cf. W.R.O. 283/44, lease, Ailesbury to Shannon, 1686; for the two hos., see below, plate facing p. 43.
[1] Below, agric. (Amesbury; W. Amesbury).
[2] Bold, *Eng. Palladianism,* 133, 135; below, Newton Tony, manors (Newton Tony).
[3] W.R.O. 283/6, bk. D, agreement, Hertford and Poore, 1595; 283/44, lease, Ailesbury to Shannon, 1686; Alnwick Castle Mun. X.II.11, box 6, survey, 1634, p. 183.
[4] Cf. W.R.O. 944/1; above, intro. (the town to c. 1540).
[5] Alnwick Castle Mun. X.II.11, box 6, survey, 1634, p. 183.   [6] Below, church [architecture].
[7] Alnwick Castle Mun. X.II.11, box 6, survey, 1634, p. 222.   [8] *Cal. S.P. Dom.* 1636–7, 196.
[9] Ibid. 1640–1, 183; cf. above, intro. (sport).

Hertford, on the order of parliament.[10] Nothing remains of it, except perhaps the four-centred doorway incorporated in the basement of the present Amesbury Abbey.

A new house[11] was evidently designed for Lord Hertford (d. 1660) by John Webb and had been built for him or his successor William, duke of Somerset, by the early 1660s.[12] Called the Abbey in the mid 18th century,[13] it was in the style associated with Inigo Jones and innovative in both plan and appearance. The south front was of nine bays and was rusticated on the ground and first floor; in the centre a portico rose through the first and second storeys. The principal rooms were on the first floor and were wrapped around three sides of the main staircase, which was lit from a central recess in the north elevation: although the south front was c. 75 ft. long those rooms were neither numerous nor large. There was a low third storey below the cornice.[14] In the late 17th century and early 18th the house was leased,[15] but for most of the period 1725–78 was lived in by Charles and Catherine, duke and duchess of Queensberry.[16] To provide a new dining room, a new drawing room, and an additional staircase Queensberry added a symmetrical block to each of the east and west sides of the house in the late 1740s and the 1750s, and about then attic dormers were added to the old part of the house. The design of the new blocks has been attributed to Flitcroft.[17]

In the early 18th century, and almost certainly from when it was built, the house stood within walled enclosures: that on the north-east contained gardens, and on the south there was a forecourt with a semicircular south perimeter from gates in which a double avenue led to the church. A little west of the house stood an irregular group of buildings, probably used as stables,[18] which was demolished in the early 19th century: some of the buildings, which evidently incorporated round-headed windows,[19] may have been erected in the 16th century or earlier. Kennels stood north of Diana House in the north-east corner of the park. North and west of the house a canal cut across a meander of the Avon, presumably to serve the priory, divided the park from meadows between the watercourses. In much of the park east and south of the house there were plantations, the geometrical patterns of which were unrelated to the house. Almost certainly between 1720 and 1725 new gates were erected near Kent House. To provide access to the mansion from the London road without entering the town, an entrance avenue, later called Lord's Walk, was then planted east of the gates; within the gates an avenue along

the south-east boundary and, from near the church, the south avenue formed a long and dramatic approach to the main front of the house.[20] In 1733 the walled enclosures were replaced by a smaller forecourt and a haha was made around the house.[21] After the duke of Queensberry bought West Amesbury manor in 1735[22] the formal landscaping was extended west of the Avon. A design of 1738 by Charles Bridgeman included geometrically arranged avenues and paths through plantations on Vespasian's camp. Clearings where the avenues crossed were intended to be the sites of pavilions, and at the centre of the side of the hill facing the house a clearing was to be crossed by a terrace. A large kite-shaped kitchen garden was to be made west of the house, and east a great lawn with a pavilion at its east end. The gardens were unfinished in 1748, and some of Bridgeman's designs, almost certainly including the kitchen garden, were not executed. Plantations, paths, and the terrace on Vespasian's camp were completed, and a vaulted cave was built from the west side of the terrace, to designs attributed to Flitcroft, and was later named after the dramatist John Gay. Access to Vespasian's camp, as proposed by Bridgeman, was along an avenue leading north-west from the house and over the Avon,[23] and a bridge had been built by 1773:[24] the present bridge, three-arched and of stone, bears the inscription 1777.[25] West of the bridge a smaller bridge over an inlet in a marshy area is surmounted by a Chinese pavilion; the pavilion had been built by 1748, was evidently altered or decorated with the advice of Sir William Chambers c. 1772, and was restored in 1986.[26] The park was enlarged north-westwards after 1760, the year in which the duke of Queensberry bought Countess Court manor, and in 1773 was c. 360 a.[27] By 1787 the forecourt south of the house had been removed and the park extended to the portico.[28] By the early 19th century a gateway west of the church had become the principal access to the park, and a drive led from it to the house.[29] The 17th-century piers of the gateway are presumably those formerly in the forecourt.[30] The house was not lived in by William, duke of Queensberry,[31] and in the period 1778–1825 was sometimes leased; land was disparked c. 1778.[32]

In 1834 Sir Edmund Antrobus began to rebuild Amesbury Abbey to designs by Thomas Hopper.[33] Although the lower part of the rusticated south wall and some of the foundations of the old house were re-used, the new house, taller by the equivalent of one storey and with a taller and wider portico, differs much from the old. On the first floor of the original block the central

10 Cal. S.P. Dom. 1651, 91.
11 See plate facing p. 42.
12 Bold, Eng. Palladianism, 96, 99–100.
13 W.R.O. 283/168, 1759–60, f. 1.
14 Bold, Eng. Palladianism, 94, 97–105.
15 W.R.O. 283/44.   16 D.N.B.
17 Bold, Eng. Palladianism, 98, 108.
18 W.R.O. 944/1; for the gate piers, below, this section.
19 Kemm, Amesbury Church and Abbey, 19.
20 W.R.O. 944/1.
21 Hoare, Mod. Wilts. Amesbury, 79.
22 Below, this section (W. Amesbury).

23 Bold, Eng. Palladianism, 106, 108, 120.
24 Andrews and Dury, Map (W.R.S. viii), pl. 5.
25 See plate facing p. 58.
26 Bold, Eng. Palladianism, 122; see below, plate facing p. 58.
27 Andrews and Dury, Map (W.R.S. viii), pls. 5, 8; W.R.O. 944/3; below, this section (Countess Ct.).
28 Bold, Eng. Palladianism, 107.
29 O.S. Map 1", sheet 14 (1817 edn.).
30 See plate facing p. 43.   31 D.N.B.
32 V.C.H. Wilts. iii. 94; W.R.O. 377/1.
33 See plate facing p. 42.

saloon was lengthened by having the other rooms on the south front thrown into it, and the staircase, which was moved northwards, was surrounded by an arcaded gallery or landing. The mid 18th-century blocks were demolished, and new larger side blocks were built each with a projecting centre of four bays with attached Corinthian three-quarter columns: behind one projection was a new dining room, behind the other a new drawing room. A small service block, with its own symmetrical elevations, was built to the north and partially separated from the house by a small court; it was enlarged in 1860. In 1904, to designs by Detmar Blow, the saloon was refitted and the main staircase from the ground floor to the first was altered from three flights around a square well to a broad stair rising directly from the entrance hall. The house was converted to flats c. 1960, when some of the larger rooms were subdivided,[34] and to a nursing home c. 1980, when lifts were installed.[35]

Manors and other estates in the parish evolved from lands of Amesbury manor held by free tenure in the Middle Ages. What became COOMBES COURT manor was held in the 12th and 13th centuries by members of the Everard and Goion families. A little of the land was in West Amesbury.[36] William, earl of Salisbury (d. 1226), confirmed to Geoffrey Goion 1 yardland in Amesbury, held by serjeanty, which Geoffrey's forebears had held of William's,[37] and before 1229 Roger son of Everard and Robert Goion held land in West Amesbury.[38] Geoffrey Goion held estates in the parish reckoned as ¼ and ⅕ knight's fee in 1242–3.[39] In 1272 John Goion may have held some or all of the lands,[40] which are likely to have passed to his son Robert (fl. 1289).[41] In 1312 John Goion, presumably another, and his wife Alice settled an estate in the parish on themselves and the heirs of John's body with remainder to William Everard and his wife Agnes.[42] Later Agnes married a John Goion[43] (perhaps him who fl. 1312), who may have held the estate in 1340.[44] By 1364 the estate had passed to Agnes's and John's daughter Edith, wife of Walter of Coombe, and it was held by Edith's son Walter of Coombe in 1382.[45] From then to 1538 it descended with Moels manor in North Tidworth.[46] It was held from

1407 or earlier by the younger Walter's son or nephew Robert of Coombe;[47] it passed from Robert (d. by 1416) to his son John,[48] before 1454 to John's son Richard[49] (d. by 1460), and from Richard to his brother John.[50] That John of Coombe's heir was his daughter Joan, wife of Ralph Bannister (d. 1492), and Joan's was her daughter Joan Bannister, who married Thomas Dauntsey[51] and William Walwyn.

About 1540 Coombes Court manor passed to Edmund Walwyn,[52] who in 1546–7 sold it to Michael Scot[53] (d. 1553). Scot devised it to his son Thomas in tail with remainder to his son William (d. 1605), who had entered on it by 1576. William's heir, his son John,[54] in 1611 sold the manor to Henry Sherfield[55] (d. 1634), the puritan recorder of, and M.P. for, Salisbury,[56] whose relict Rebecca Sherfield held it after his death.[57] By order of Chancery, Sherfield's trustees conveyed it in 1638, subject to Rebecca's jointure, to his principal creditor Sir Thomas Jervoise.[58] It was held by Sir Thomas's sons Thomas and Henry in 1656 and was apparently settled on Henry in 1664.[59] In 1668 Henry sold it to William Viner (d. 1680 × 1683).[60] It passed to William's relict Elizabeth Viner (d. 1697 or 1698)[61] and to his son William, who in 1701 sold it to Francis Kenton (d. 1719 or 1720). Kenton's heir was his grandson Francis Kenton[62] (d. 1755), M.P. for Salisbury 1722–7,[63] who devised it to his cousin Henry Dawson. In 1760 Dawson sold the manor to Charles, duke of Queensberry.[64]

Coombes Court manor was represented by Viney's farm, 744 a., sold by Sir Cosmo Antrobus with West Amesbury farm to I. C. Crook in 1916.[65] In 1943 Crook sold it to his son N. C. Crook (d. 1946), whose relict Mrs. M. J. Crook owned it in 1993.[66]

An estate called PAVYHOLD, nominally 190 a. in Amesbury with pasture rights there,[67] belonged to the lord of Countess Court manor in 1584[68] and probably much earlier. It descended with the manor and was bought in 1760 by Charles, duke of Queensberry.[69]

Land possibly acquired from the lord of Countess Court manor in the later 14th century by Robert Saucer, was held in 1428 by his sons-in-law Thomas Hobbes and Walter Mes-

34 Bold, *Eng. Palladianism*, 110–17.
35 Inf. from Mr. Cornelius-Reid.
36 e.g. W.R.O. 944/2; Alnwick Castle Mun. X.II.11, box 6, survey, 1634, p. 187.
37 P.R.O., DL 43/9/25.
38 Ibid. CP 25/1/250/8, no. 11.
39 *Bk. of Fees*, ii. 709, 744.
40 Hist. MSS. Com. 55, *Var. Colln.* iv, p. 151.
41 *Antrobus D.* (W.R.S. iii), p. 3; P.R.O., JUST 1/1006, rot. 58d.   42 *Feet of F.* 1272–1327 (W.R.S. i), p. 82.
43 *W.N. & Q.* vii. 501; W.R.O. 283/59, deed, Coombe to Upton, 1382.   44 *Cal. Close*, 1339–41, 341.
45 P.R.O., DL 43/9/25; W.R.O. 283/59, deed, Coombe to Upton, 1382.   46 Below, N. Tidworth, manors (Moels).
47 W.R.O. 283/59, deed, Upton to Coombe, 1407.
48 P.R.O., CP 40/637, rot. 319.
49 W.R.O. 283/59, deed, Messinger to Coombe, 1454.
50 P.R.O., C 1/26, no. 453.
51 *Cal. Inq. p.m. Hen. VII*, i, pp. 349–50.
52 Longleat Mun., Seymour papers, xii, f. 253v.; W.R.O. 283/59, deed, Bundy to Hippisley, 1560.
53 P.R.O., CP 25/2/46/324, no. 39; W.R.O. 283/59, deed, Walwyn to Scot, 1546.

54 P.R.O., C 142/274, no. 65; C 142/291, no. 57; W.R.O. 283/6, view 21 Mar. 1576.
55 P.R.O., CP 25/2/370/9 Jas. I Mich.; W.R.O. 283/59, deed, Scot to Sherfield, 1611.
56 Hoare, *Mod. Wilts.* Salisbury, 374; *V.C.H. Wilts.* v. 132.
57 Alnwick Castle Mun. X.II.11, box 6, survey, 1634, p. 187.
58 W.R.O. 283/59, deed, Maydwell to Jervoise, 1639.
59 Ibid. 283/59, deeds, Sherfield to Jervoise, 1639; Jervoise to Cole, 1664; 283/64.
60 Ibid. 283/6, ct. papers 1676–80, view 3 May 1680; 1619, box 7, deeds, Jervoise to Viner, 1668; mortgage, 1683.
61 Ibid. 283/63, deed, Viner to Smith, 1687; ibid. wills, subdean Sar., Eliz. Viner, 1697.
62 Ibid. 1619, box 7, deed, Viner to Kenton, 1701; copy will of Francis Kenton, 1719; deed, Kenton to Kenton, 1720.
63 *Hist. Parl., Commons*, 1715–54, ii. 187.
64 W.R.O. 1619, box 7, copy will of Francis Kenton, 1754; deed, Dawson to Queensberry, 1760.
65 Ibid. 776/6; 944/1–2; 1260/5.
66 Inf. from Mr. R. C. Crook, 11 Salisbury Road.
67 Alnwick Castle Mun. X.II.11, box 6, survey, 1634, p. 185.
68 W.R.O. 283/4, ct. bk. 1583–90, view 31 May 26 Eliz. I.
69 Below, this section (Countess Ct.).

sager,[70] and may have been *SAUCER'S* yard-land in Amesbury, which descended with a holding mainly in West Amesbury.[71] The yardland was sold by Thomas Hayward to trustees of Henry Spratt in 1718, and given to Spratt's school in Amesbury in 1719.[72] The school owned it until 1900.[73]

In 1743 Anne Wormstall *alias* Tyler gave 57 a. in Amesbury with pasture rights there to support a General Baptist congregation in Rushall. In 1771 the estate was acquired by Charles, duke of Queensberry, in exchange for £30 a year and added to his Amesbury estate.[74]

The land of West Amesbury, apparently all part of the king's Amesbury estate in 1086 and subinfeudated later, was in several freeholds in the 13th century. Some land was acquired by Amesbury priory and became part of the Priory manor.[75]

What became *WEST AMESBURY* manor was held of William, styled earl of Salisbury, by Patrick de Montfort as mesne lord in 1242–3.[76] The manor apparently evolved from the carucate conveyed by Reynold of Bungay and his wife Philippe to John son of Warin in 1236.[77] The Bungays may have retained an interest in that land: in 1242–3 Rayner of Bungay, probably Reynold, was said to hold land in West Amesbury of Patrick,[78] and in 1249 John son of Warin disputed the carucate with Philippe's daughters Petra, wife of John of Lincoln, and Pauline.[79] The carucate may have been that held, apparently *c.* 1260, by John Renger[80] (d. by 1270), whose heirs were his sisters Idony, wife of Richard of Hadstock, Cecily, wife of Roger le Gras, and Margery, relict of John Veel: the heirs conveyed that land to Richard le Gras who in 1270 conveyed it to Nicholas, son of Ellis, and his wife Alice.[81] It may also have been the land held, possibly as early as 1275, by John of Monmouth[82] who conveyed that land, or a large part of it, to William de Forstel in 1308.[83] William's relict Eleanor, wife of Ralph of Coulston, made an unsuccessful claim for dower in 1328, and about then the land apparently passed from Monmouth to John Pauncefoot and his wife Maud.[84] What became West Amesbury manor descended in the Pauncefoot family:[85] it

was held in 1379 by Richard Pauncefoot,[86] possibly John's grandson, in 1412 by Richard's son Thomas,[87] and in 1428, when it was said to have been earlier Patrick de Montfort's, by Thomas's son Walter.[88] In 1429 Walter conveyed it to his brother Robert,[89] whose heir was his daughter Elizabeth (d. 1528), wife of James Daubeney.[90] The Daubeneys held the manor in 1510[91] and it descended with the manor of Wayford (Som.) to their son Giles (d. 1559), who in 1546 settled it on his son Hugh (d. 1565), and to Hugh's son Giles (d. 1630), who in 1607 settled it on his son James (d. *s.p.* 1613).[92] About 1615 James's feoffees sold the manor to Robert Newdick, who added it to South's estate, bought in 1614, and was much impleaded by his creditors;[93] in 1628 Newdick sold the enlarged manor to Sir Laurence Washington[94] (d. 1643). West Amesbury manor, together with 2 yardlands in Amesbury, descended with Garsdon manor to Sir Laurence's son Laurence (d. 1661) and to Laurence's daughter Elizabeth, from 1671 wife of Sir Robert Shirley, Bt. (from 1677 Baron Ferrers, from 1711 Earl Ferrers).[95] Elizabeth and Sir Robert sold it to Thomas Hayward in 1677.[96] Hayward (d. 1724)[97] was succeeded by his son Philip, rector of Ham, who sold the manor to Charles, duke of Queensberry, in 1735.[98]

Most of the land of the manor was in an estate of 843 a., consisting of West Amesbury farm, land and a farmstead called Fargo, and 51 a. in Normanton, which was sold with Viney's farm in 1916 by Sir Cosmo Antrobus to I. C. Crook.[99] Crook sold to the National Trust 389 a. in 1927 and 396 a. in 1929: the trust owned the land in 1993.[1]

Several freeholds, mostly in West Amesbury, were merged as an estate called *SOUTH'S*.[2] An estate in West Amesbury apparently descended in the Saucer family: lands there were held in 1242–3 by John Saucer, of Patrick de Montfort as mesne lord,[3] in the later 13th century by the same or another John Saucer,[4] by Robert Saucer (d. by 1393) and his relict Alice,[5] and by Thomas Saucer (d. by 1428). Robert's and Thomas's lands passed to Robert's daughters Isabel, wife of Walter Messager (fl. 1428), and Anne, wife of Thomas Hobbes (fl. 1428),[6] and to his grandsons John Messager (fl. 1483), a priest, and Thomas

70 *Feud. Aids*, v. 240; *Antrobus D.* (W.R.S. iii), p. 32; for the manor, below, this section (Countess Ct.).
71 e.g. Alnwick Castle Mun. X.II.11, box 6, survey, 1634, p. 188; below, this section (South's).
72 W.R.O. 1619, box 4, deeds, Hayward to Hilliard, 1718; Hilliard to Holland, 1719.
73 *Endowed Char. Wilts.* (S. Div.), 30.
74 *V.C.H. Wilts.* x. 146.
75 Above and below, this section.   76 *Bk. of Fees*, ii. 744.
77 P.R.O., CP 25/1/250/9, no. 26.
78 *Bk. of Fees*, ii. 744; *Bradenstoke Cart.* (W.R.S. xxxv), p. 103.   79 *Civil Pleas, 1249* (W.R.S. xxvi), p. 119.
80 *Close R. 1259–61*, 160.
81 *Antrobus D.* (W.R.S. iii), pp. 3–4; P.R.O., CP 25/1/283/17, no. 480.   82 P.R.O., KB 27/15, rot. 4d.
83 *Feet of F. 1272–1327* (W.R.S. i), p. 73.
84 P.R.O., CP 40/273, rot. 30d.; CP 40/274, rott. 59d., 63; CP 40/275, rot. 258d.
85 For the Pauncefoots, F. W. Weaver, *Visit. Som.* 58.
86 *Antrobus D.* (W.R.S. iii), p. 12.
87 *Feud. Aids*, vi. 539.
88 Ibid. v. 242.   89 *Antrobus D.* (W.R.S. iii), pp. 20–1.
90 P.R.O., C 142/80, no. 159.

91 *Antrobus D.* (W.R.S. iii), pp. 36–7.
92 Ibid. pp. 43, 84–7; *V.C.H. Som.* iv. 70, where the date of the younger Jas.'s d. is misprinted (cf. P.R.O., C 142/663, no. 197).
93 *Antrobus D.* (W.R.S. iii), pp. xvi–xix, 102–3, 114–17; below, this section.
94 *Antrobus D.* (W.R.S. iii), pp. xix–xx; P.R.O., CP 25/2/508/4 Chas. I Trin.
95 *V.C.H. Wilts.* xiv. 90; Alnwick Castle Mun. X.II.11, box 6, survey, 1634, p. 188.
96 W.R.O. 1619, box 5, deed, Ferrers to Hayward, 1677.
97 Ibid. 283/141, deed, Lade and Hayward, 1731.
98 Ibid. 1619, box 7, deed, Hayward to Queensberry, 1735; box 8, abstr. of Douglas's title; Phillipps, *Wilts. Inst.* ii. 55, 71.
99 W.R.O. 490/1116; 1260/5; above, this section (Coombes Ct.).
1 Inf. from Nat. Trust, Wessex Regional Off., Bishopstrow; Mr. C. H. Crook, Mallards, Blackhorse Lane, Hurdcott.
2 Alnwick Castle Mun. X.II.11, box 6, survey, 1634, pp. 188, 213.   3 *Bk. of Fees*, ii. 744.
4 *Antrobus D.* (W.R.S. iii), p. 3.
5 Ibid. pp. 14–15.   6 Ibid. pp. 18–19.

Hobbes.[7] John Messager's lands may have passed to Hobbes, most of whose estate was bought from his descendants by William South (d. 1552) in the period 1523–8.[8] South's estate descended to his son Thomas, who in 1577 settled it on his son Thomas (d. 1606), and to the younger Thomas's son Edward.[9] The first three Souths added to it,[10] and in 1614 Edward sold it to Robert Newdick:[11] from c. 1615 South's descended with West Amesbury manor.[12]

Part of the younger Thomas Hobbes's estate was acquired from his grandson William Silverthorn by Gilbert Beckington in 1517. At Gilbert's death in 1527–8 *BECKINGTON'S* estate passed to his son John[13] (fl. 1581).[14] In 1568 John conveyed it to his son Mellor,[15] whose son Gilbert held it in 1581.[16] Gilbert was succeeded c. 1615[17] by his son Gilbert (fl. 1654), whose son Gilbert sold the estate, 1½ yardland, to Simon Shepherd 1662–4. In 1678 Shepherd sold it to Thomas Hayward,[18] and it was merged with West Amesbury manor.[19]

An estate in West Amesbury, *LAMBERT'S*, descended with Langford Dangers manor in Little Langford from the mid 13th century to the mid 14th.[20] Ralph Dangers held it in the mid 13th century,[21] John Dangers in 1309,[22] John Dangers in 1364, when it was 2 yardlands,[23] and William Dangers in 1397.[24] William's heir was his son Richard whose relict Christine, wife of John Kaynell, sold it to Edmund Lambert c. 1482.[25] Lambert (d. 1493) was succeeded by his sons William[26] (d. 1504) and Thomas[27] (d. 1509) in turn and by Thomas's son William (born c. 1508),[28] who was presumably the William Lambert who in 1569 sold the land to the elder Thomas South.[29]

From 1409 or earlier a small estate in West Amesbury descended with Normanton manor.[30] It was bought from William Trenchard by the younger Thomas South in 1584.[31]

Land in West Amesbury given in 1452 by Thomas Saucer and his wife Christine to Robert Saucer (fl. 1476)[32] was apparently that held at his death in 1502 by Giles Saucer, whose heir

was his son Thomas, a minor.[33] Its later descent is obscure.

In the later 12th century Bradenstoke priory was given rents of 12d. from Amesbury and 12s. from West Amesbury, and c. 1200 was given 1 yardland.[34] The yardland had apparently been alienated by 1205,[35] as the 12s. rent was in the mid 13th century.[36] The priory had land in the parish in 1232,[37] temporalities worth 9s. 2d. in 1291,[38] and ½ yardland in 1364:[39] no later reference to its estate there has been found.

Maud Everard gave land in Amesbury to Lacock abbey,[40] and in 1241 Ela Longespée, abbess of Lacock and previously lord of Amesbury manor, gave 40s. rent from West Amesbury.[41] The abbey was entitled to the rent, due from Amesbury priory, until the Dissolution,[42] but there is no evidence that it kept the land.

The land in Amesbury held by Saier de Quency, earl of Winchester (d. 1219), his wife Margaret (d. 1235), and his son Roger, earl of Winchester (d. 1264),[43] may have been the later *COUNTESS COURT* manor, also called the Conyger manor.[44] What did become the manor was held in 1242–3 of the lord of Amesbury manor by Everard Tyes as ¼ knight's fee.[45] Everard's relict Rametta held it as dower. In 1248 she leased it for 15 years to Sir William Longespée,[46] either him who was lord of Amesbury manor and died in 1250 or his son, namesake, and heir; by 1253, when the younger Sir William (d. 1257) leased it for life with reversion to himself or his heirs, he had apparently acquired the inheritance.[47] The estate presumably passed with Amesbury manor to the younger Sir William's daughter and heir Margaret, but the later claim, probably mistaken, that her husband Henry, earl of Lincoln (d. 1311), lord of Amesbury manor in her right, acquired it from what would have been another Everard Tyes[48] was accepted, and from 1311 to her death by 1322 the estate was held as dower by Henry's relict Joan.[49] Henry's heir was his and Margaret's daughter Alice (d. 1348) who married Thomas, earl of Lancaster, and in 1322

7 *Antrobus D.* (W.R.S. iii), pp. 31–2.
8 Ibid. pp. xv, 39–40; W.R.O. 283/123, deeds, Silverthorn to South, 1523; Balet to South, 1525.
9 *Antrobus D.* (W.R.S. iii), pp. xv, 55–7; P.R.O., C 142/291, no. 144.
10 *Antrobus D.* (W.R.S. iii), p. 42; W.R.O. 283/123, deeds, Lister to South, 1541; Harrison to South, 1557; below, this section.
11 *Antrobus D.* (W.R.S. iii), p. xv; P.R.O., CP 25/2/370/12 Jas. I Trin.
12 Above, this section (W. Amesbury).
13 *Antrobus D.* (W.R.S. iii), pp. 37, 39–41; W.R.O. 283/8, ct. 5 Nov. 24 Hen. VIII.   14 P.R.O., REQ 2/88/26.
15 *Antrobus D.* (W.R.S. iii), pp. 52–3.
16 W.R.O. 283/5, ct. bk. 1581–2, view 3 Mar. 23 Eliz. I.
17 Ibid. 283/8, ct. Mar. 13 Jas. I.
18 Ibid. 283/137, deed, Juniper to Shepherd, 1664; 283/138, deeds, Beckington to Tildsley, 1654; Beckington to Salmon, 1662; 283/139, deed, Shepherd to Hayward, 1678.
19 Above, this section (W. Amesbury).
20 Below, Little Langford, manors (Langford Dangers).
21 *Bradenstoke Cart.* (W.R.S. xxxv), p. 103; P.R.O., CP 25/1/251/16, no. 81; CP 25/1/251/17, no. 8.
22 *Feet of F.* 1272–1327 (W.R.S. i), p. 123.
23 P.R.O., DL 43/9/25.
24 *Antrobus D.* (W.R.S. iii), pp. 15–16.
25 Ibid. pp. 30–1.

26 *Cal. Inq. p.m. Hen. VII*, i, p. 404.
27 Ibid. ii, p. 541.   28 P.R.O., C 142/25, no. 4.
29 Ibid. CP 25/2/239/11 Eliz. I East.
30 *Feet of F.* 1377–1509 (W.R.S. xli), pp. 63–4; below, Durnford, manors (Normanton).
31 *Antrobus D.* (W.R.S. iii), pp. 61–2.
32 Ibid. pp. 23, 28–9.
33 *Cal. Inq. p.m. Hen. VII*, ii, p. 508.
34 *Bradenstoke Cart.* (W.R.S. xxxv), pp. 94–5.
35 *Rot. Chart.* (Rec. Com.), 155.
36 *Bradenstoke Cart.* (W.R.S. xxxv), p. 103.
37 Ibid. p. 197.
38 *Tax. Eccl.* (Rec. Com.), 185, 193.
39 P.R.O., DL 43/9/25.
40 *Cat. Anct. D.* iv, A 10230.
41 *Lacock Chart.* (W.R.S. xxxiv), p. 83; P.R.O., CP 25/1/251/13, no. 51.
42 *Valor Eccl.* (Rec. Com.), ii. 93, 116.
43 *Complete Peerage*, xii (2), 748–54; P.R.O., DL 25/2336.
44 For the alternative name, *Feet of F.* 1377–1509 (W.R.S. xli), p. 137.   45 *Bk. of Fees*, ii. 709.
46 *Hist. Northumb.* ii. 11, 15; P.R.O., DL 27/56.
47 P.R.O., CP 25/1/251/17, no. 24; for Amesbury manor, above, this section.
48 *Wilts. Inq. p.m.* 1242–1326 (Index Libr.), 385–6.
49 *Cal. Close*, 1307–13, 314; *Cal. Inq. p.m.* vi, p. 220.

the estate was claimed by the king because Thomas's lands had been forfeited:[50] the claim was evidently unjustified and the estate was restored to Alice. In 1326 she and her husband Ebles Lestrange, from 1327 Lord Strange (d. 1335), were licensed to settle it on themselves for life with remainder to the younger Hugh le Despenser, Lord le Despenser, but may not have done so before Despenser was executed in that year.[51] They later settled it on themselves and their heirs, and between 1335 and 1341 Alice and Ebles's nephew and heir Roger Lestrange, Lord Strange (d. 1349), conveyed it, presumably by sale, to Nicholas de Cauntelo, Lord Cauntelo (d. 1355). The estate was given before 1341 to Nicholas's son William[52] (d. 1375), from 1355 Lord Cauntelo, but before 1375 to William's son William (of age c. 1366, d. 1375). In 1364 it was held by Lady Isabel de Tours, presumably by a temporary tenure. In 1375 it passed from the younger William to the elder and apparently to William la Zouche, Lord Zouche, a coheir of the younger William.[53]

Zouche held the manor at his death in 1382. It passed to his son William, Lord Zouche (d. 1396),[54] and to that William's son William, Lord Zouche (d. 1415), who was named as owner in 1401–2, but it was acquired by that last William's brother Sir John, who held it in 1412[55] and 1434.[56] Sir John's daughter and heir Elizabeth, wife of Sir Nicholas Bowet, left as heirs her daughters Margaret, wife of John Chaworth, and Elizabeth, wife of William Chaworth and later of John Dunham.[57] The manor was apparently assigned to John and Margaret Chaworth in 1458,[58] passed on Margaret's death in 1482, when she was the relict of Humphrey Persall, to her son Thomas Chaworth,[59] and at Thomas's death without issue in 1486[60] reverted to Elizabeth. John Dunham held the manor from Elizabeth's death in 1502[61] to his own in 1524, it passed to their son Sir John Dunham[62] (d. 1533),[63] and descended to Sir John's daughter Anne, wife of Francis Meverell (d. 1564).[64] The Meverells were succeeded by their son Sampson (d. 1584), whose relict Elizabeth,[65] wife of Sir Edward Leighton (d. 1593),[66] held the manor until her death in 1620.[67] Before 1614 her eldest son Francis Meverell conveyed the reversion to

his brother Robert,[68] from whose death in 1627 Countess Court manor was held by his relict Elizabeth.[69] By 1632 the manor had passed to Robert's daughter and heir Elizabeth, wife of Thomas Cromwell, Lord Cromwell (cr. earl of Ardglass 1645),[70] who in 1646 sold it to Robert Gale[71] (d. 1656). In 1660 Gale's relict Elizabeth Gale sold a lease of the manor for 99 years from 1646 to John Wadman (d. 1688), and in 1674 Gale's son Robert sold the reversion to Wadman's son Robert (d. 1691). The manor descended to Robert Wadman's son John (d. 1745) and to that John's son John,[72] who in 1760 sold it to Charles, duke of Queensberry.[73]

In 1917 Sir Cosmo Antrobus sold Countess farm, 1,141 a., to Wort & Way,[74] the owner of Red House farm.[75] In 1929 Wort & Way sold the west part, 649 a., to the National Trust. In 1993 the trust owned that land,[76] members of the Wort family the remaining c. 500 a.[77]

In 1066 Earl Harold held 2 hides at *RATFYN*, Aluric 1 hide. Harvey of Wilton held land there in 1084, and in 1086 held the 2 hides in chief and the 1 hide of Edward of Salisbury.[78] Harvey gave the 1 hide, of which Edward's son Walter of Salisbury (d. 1147) was overlord at the time of the gift, and apparently the 2 hides, to Salisbury cathedral, and the cathedral endowed a prebend of Ratfyn with its land there; c. 1115 the king confirmed the arrangement,[79] and thenceforward the prebendary's was evidently the only estate at Ratfyn. The prebend was dissolved in 1545 by Act, and in an exchange the bishop of Salisbury gave the Ratfyn estate to Edward, earl of Hertford,[80] on whose attainder in 1552 it passed to the Crown.[81] In 1554 the reversion on the death of the last prebendary was granted to David Vincent.[82] In 1559 Vincent sold the estate to trustees of Ralph Lamb, and in 1562 the trustees conveyed it to St. John's hospital, Winchester.[83] The hospital owned Ratfyn farm, 502 a., until in 1841 it sold it to Sir Edmund Antrobus.[84] In 1916 Sir Cosmo Antrobus sold the land to A. C. Young, who in 1919 sold it to the Board of Agriculture and Fisheries. In 1960 the Ministry of Agriculture sold Ratfyn farm to Ratfyn Estates Ltd., a company controlled by H. J. Street;[85] in 1965 Street's executors

50 *Cal. Close, 1323–7*, 40.
51 *Cal. Pat. 1324–7*, 256; *Complete Peerage*, iv. 269–70; xii (1), 340–1.
52 *Cal. Pat. 1340–3*, 184–5; *Complete Peerage*, iii. 113–14; xii (1), 341.
53 *Cal. Inq. p.m.* xiv, p. 105; *Complete Peerage*, iii. 114–15; P.R.O., DL 43/9/25.
54 *Cal. Inq. p.m.* xv, p. 260; for the Zouches, *Complete Peerage*, xii (2), 941–4.
55 *Feud. Aids*, vi. 535, 630.
56 B.L. Add. Ch. 27332.
57 R. Thoroton, *Hist. Notts.* ed. J. Throsby, iii. 97.
58 *Feet of F. 1377–1509* (W.R.S. xl), pp. 137–8.
59 P.R.O., C 140/82, no. 12, rot. 4.
60 *Cal. Inq. p.m. Hen. VII*, i, pp. 1–2.
61 Ibid. ii, p. 381.
62 P.R.O., C 142/43, no. 69.
63 Ibid. C 142/56, no. 95.
64 Ibid. C 142/142, no. 114; ibid. CP 25/2/259/2 & 3 Eliz. I Mich.; *Visit. Staffs. 1614, 1663–4* (Wm. Salt Arch. Soc. pt. ii, vol. v), 212.   65 P.R.O., C 142/205, no. 174.
66 *Salop. Pedigrees* (Harl. Soc. xxix), 324.
67 P.R.O., C 2/Jas. I/A 7/5.

68 *Visit. Staffs. 1614, 1663–4* (Wm. Salt Arch. Soc. pt. ii, vol. v), 212.   69 P.R.O., C 142/432, no. 126.
70 *Complete Peerage*, i. 192–3, where Rob.'s d. is wrongly dated 1628; W.R.O. 192/24A, f. 4.
71 P.R.O., CP 25/2/512/22 Chas. I Mich.; B.L. Add. Ch. 59191.
72 Hoare, *Mod. Wilts.* Heytesbury, 165; W.R.O. 283/61; P.R.O., PROB 11/393, ff. 102–3; PROB 11/415, f. 96.
73 W.R.O. 1619, box 2, deed, Wadman to Queensberry, 1760.   74 G.P.L., Treas. Solicitor, 136/53.
75 Above, this section (Earldom).
76 Inf. from Nat. Trust, Wessex Regional Off.
77 Inf. from Mr. N. Morrison, Countess Farm.
78 *V.C.H. Wilts.* ii, pp. 75, 136, 166, 195.
79 *Reg. St. Osmund* (Rolls Ser.), i. 202; Le Neve, *Fasti, 1066–1300, Salisbury*, p. 92.
80 *L. & P. Hen. VIII*, xx (2), p. 411; W.R.O. 1883/59, copy of Act.   81 Above, this section (Earldom).
82 *Cal. Pat. 1553–4*, 477.
83 Hants R.O. 34M91W/199; 34M91W/205.
84 W.R.O. 1619, box 4, deed, Sumner to Antrobus, 1841.
85 G.P.L., Treas. Solicitor, 1136/75; above, this section (Earldom).

sold it, then 681 a., to Lincoln College, Oxford, the owner in 1992.[86]

Tithes from Amesbury parish may have been taken by Amesbury abbey, and in 1179 they were confirmed to Amesbury priory.[87] At the Dissolution the *RECTORY* estate consisted of the oblations given in the parish church, all tithes from the whole parish, and possibly a house.[88] Henry VIII gave it, with the priory's land in Amesbury, to Edward, earl of Hertford, in the exchange of 1541;[89] in 1547 Edward VI received it back from Edward, then duke of Somerset, in an exchange and gave it to St. George's chapel, Windsor.[90] It was confiscated by parliament in 1643,[91] assigned to the almshouses of Windsor castle in 1654,[92] and recovered by the chapel at the Restoration.[93] The tithes were valued at £955 in 1843 and commuted in 1847.[94]

In 1179 Henry II confirmed to Amesbury priory 5 a. of corn from Ratfyn, possibly representing an estate of tithes held until 1177 by Amesbury abbey.[95] In the early 15th century Amesbury priory apparently took corn from 6 a. in place of tithes from the demesne land of Ratfyn and tithes in kind from the other land there. Later the priory gave all the tithes to the prebendary of Ratfyn in exchange for a fee-farm rent of 26s. 8d., the sum at which the tithes were valued in 1341.[96] After the prebend was dissolved, the tithes remained part of the Ratfyn estate,[97] which was considered tithe free in 1843.[98] The rent, apparently not granted with the Rectory estate in 1541,[99] seems to have been kept by the Crown until 1553, when it was last mentioned, and to have been granted with the Ratfyn estate in 1554 and extinguished.[1]

From the Dissolution the demesne lands of Amesbury priory, reckoned 331 a. in 1843, were tithe free.[2] For the use of the curate serving the parish church, St. George's chapel reserved a parsonage house from leases of the Rectory estate from 1612,[3] and the oblations and some small tithes from 1630:[4] all three became part of the curate's living.[5]

AGRICULTURE. Amesbury, c. 3,100 a., and West Amesbury, c. 1,350 a., each had a set of open fields and common pastures until the 18th century. The lands of Countess Court manor, c. 800 a., and Ratfyn, c. 500 a.,[6] were separate from them, and in each of those two northern quadrants of the parish there was almost certainly a set of open fields and common pastures in the Middle Ages.[7]

AMESBURY. In 1086 the king's Amesbury estate had land for 40 ploughteams, and 39 were on it: there were 16 teams, 55 *servi*, and 2 coliberts on demesne land, 85 *villani* and 56 bordars had 23 teams, and there were 70 a. of meadow and 12 square leagues of pasture.[8] It is likely that much of the land of Durrington was reckoned as part of the estate, as land elsewhere may have been;[9] it is also likely that much, perhaps most, of the estate was at Amesbury, where later the demesne and customary lands of Amesbury manor seem to have been in a proportion roughly equal to that on the Amesbury estate in 1086.[10] Other land at Amesbury in 1086 was sufficient for 2 teams, and there were apparently 2 on it; there were 5 coscets and 3 *servi*, 6 a. of meadow, and 1 square furlong of pasture.[11]

In the later 12th century the demesne of Amesbury manor included several pasture for cattle,[12] and in the early 13th century extensive several pasture for sheep: nearly all Amesbury's other land, including some meadow and some pasture for cattle, was evidently used in common.[13] The demesne was in hand in 1295–6, when it was possibly cultivated largely by labour service: 309 a. of cereals and 11 a. of peas and vetch were sown, 36 a. were mown, 1,214 sheep and 46 draught beasts were kept, and there was a rabbit warren.[14] The demesne pastures were presumably on Slay down, as they were later.[15] In 1304–5 there were 1,229 sheep and 42 draught animals.[16] By 1364 half the demesne arable, 145 a., and some of the pastures in severalty, including two totalling 80 a. on which 300 sheep could be fed, had been leased. The leased arable was apparently in six open fields and consisted of 68 parcels, of which 11 were in hand in 1364 because no tenant could be found. The arable which had not been leased, 144 a. of which 83 a. were sown in 1364, was in only nine furlongs and apparently consisted of the whole of each furlong. That division of the demesne arable into larger parcels in hand and smaller parcels leased perhaps foreshadowed its separation from the open fields. There were 21½ a. of demesne meadow in 1364.[17]

The customary lands of Amesbury manor in 1364 were in yardlands (each of 24–50 a.), cotsetlands (each of 12 a.), and croftlings: 6½ yardlands were in 8 holdings shared among 7 tenants, 10 cotsetlands were shared among 9

86 Inf. from Mr. P. J. Rowland, Ratfyn Farm, and sale cat. in his possession; inf from the Land Agent, Lincoln Coll., Oxf.
87 *Cal. Chart. R.* 1257–1300, 157–8.
88 *Valor Eccl.* (Rec. Com.), ii. 93–4; for the ho. and for the tithes from Ratfyn, below, this section.
89 P.R.O., E 305/4/C 18; above, this section (Priory).
90 Ibid. E 305/15/F 42–3.
91 *V.C.H. Berks.* iii. 26.
92 *Acts & Ords. of Interr.* ed. Firth & Rait, ii. 1021.
93 D. & C. Windsor Mun. XV. 39. 24.
94 W.R.O., tithe award.
95 *Cal. Chart. R.* 1257–1300, 157–8.
96 *Inq. Non.* (Rec. Com.), 171; *Valor Eccl.* (Rec. Com.), ii. 92, 94; *Chandler's Reg.* (W.R.S. xxxix), p. 31.
97 P.R.O., E 318/37/2027; above, this section (Ratfyn).
98 W.R.O., tithe award.
99 P.R.O., E 318/13/572, rott. 17, 20; above, this section (Rectory).
1 P.R.O., E 318/37/2027; B.L. Harl. Roll I. 14, rot. 15.
2 *Antrobus D.* (W.R.S. iii), pp. 47–9; W.R.O., tithe award. 3 D. & C. Windsor Mun. XV. 39. 20.
4 Ibid. XV. 39. 22. 5 Below, churches.
6 W.R.O., tithe award; ibid. 490/1116.
7 Below, this section (Countess Ct.; Ratfyn).
8 *V.C.H. Wilts.* ii, p. 116.
9 Above, manors (preamble). 10 Below, this section.
11 *V.C.H. Wilts.* ii, p. 136.
12 *Bradenstoke Cart.* (W.R.S. xxxv), pp. 94–5.
13 *Rot. Chart.* (Rec. Com.), 155; P.R.O., DL 43/9/25.
14 P.R.O., DL 29/1/1, rot. 12 and d.
15 Cf. W.R.O., 490/1116; 944/2.
16 P.R.O., DL 29/1/2, rot. 21d.
17 Ibid. DL 43/9/25.

tenants, and there were 5 croftlings. The yard-landers, of whom 1 held freely and 6 in villeinage, 3 of the cotsetlanders, and those holding croftlings, did no labour service: all the cotsetlanders held in villeinage, and 6 of them had to make hay and serve as ploughmen, drovers, or shepherds. The yardlands were stinted at 8 pigs each free from pannage, and later evidence shows each to have included generous stints for sheep, horses, and cattle. Land in the open fields and rights to feed animals were also in other freeholds of Amesbury manor, the largest of which was presumably what became Coombes Court farm.[18] In 1437 Saucer's, 1 yardland, included 2 a. of meadow and feeding for 70 sheep, 4 horses, 8 fat beasts, and 8 pigs.[19]

The whole demesne of Amesbury manor had been leased by c. 1400.[20] In 1540 it had 320 a. of arable, apparently none of it in the open fields, 26 a. of meadow of which 20 a. in Wittenham were expressly said to be several, 60 a. of pasture called Northams, and feeding for 1,800 sheep (1,560 wethers and 240 ewes). Cattle other than the farmer's could be fed on Northams from 1 August to 11 November, the farmer could feed 16 cows and 1 bull in the open fields, and Sour mead, in which there were 6 a. of demesne, may have been a common meadow: otherwise the demesne, later called Earl's farm, was mainly in severalty, with feeding for 1,300 sheep on Earl's down (presumably Slay down) and for 500 on South down (presumably Blackcross Farm down).[21] On the other land of Amesbury husbandry in common was practised until the later 18th century.[22] In 1540 there may have been c. 10 open fields of which three, Barnard's (later Bartnett), Blackcross, and Cuckold's Hill, bore the names they had in the 18th century. Meadows in addition to Sour mead may have been used in common, and there were for cattle a downland pasture and a common pasture near the Avon and for sheep common downs including Woolston Hill and Kitcombe (later Kickdom). In 1540 the largest farms with open-field arable were apparently Coombes Court and Priory, but most of the fields was divided among c. 20 yardlands and c. 25 cotsetlands or 'corticels' held freely, by copy, or by other customary tenure of Amesbury manor. A yardland was typically of c. 30 a. with feeding for c. 75 sheep, 4 horses, and 4 cows, and a cotsetland of c. 13 a. with feeding for 1 cow or 1 horse. Some tenants had more than one holding, but only one tenant is known to have held, and only one other is likely to have held, more than 100 a., and in the mid 16th century much of Amesbury's open fields was apparently in farms of less than 50 a.[23]

At the Dissolution Amesbury priory's agricultural land in Amesbury parish was all in demesne. Of its 290 strips of arable in open fields, probably c. 175 were in Amesbury and the rest in West Amesbury; the priory could feed 74 sheep with the tenants' flocks in Amesbury and 300 on a several down in West Amesbury; its 22 a. of meadow were probably near the site of the priory.[24] Some of the arable was leased in parcels of 1–10 a. to tenants at will, later on lives, and was called Billet land: 86 a., mostly in Amesbury's fields, were Billet land in 1560.[25] The remainder was part of Priory farm, later called the Abbey lands,[26] which in the late 16th century was held by the tenant of Earl's farm.[27] In 1605 Coombes Court farm included c. 240 a. of arable and feeding for 420 sheep.[28]

From 1566 or earlier men of Boscombe claimed the right to feed sheep on all or part of Blackcross down, a claim denied by the men of Amesbury.[29] The dispute was lengthy: c. 1595, for example, the court of the Earldom manor ordered that the Boscombe sheep should be beaten back thrice a week or more.[30] It was apparently ended by assigning 36 a. of the down for use in common by Amesbury and Boscombe: that had been done by 1726.[31]

In 1586 it was agreed that every year the town flock, the hog flock of Earl's farm, and the Coombes Court farm flock should be folded as one on the open fields: three shepherds were to be employed, one to be provided by the owners or owner of the sheep in each flock, and those with open-field arable but no sheep were to pay 12d. an acre towards the keeping of the combined flock.[32] Whether the scheme was adopted and, if so, for how long are obscure.

In 1598 a plan was made to divide Earl's farm into 16 equal holdings of 1 yardland to be leased separately, but the plan came to naught: in 1608 the lessee of the whole farm agreed to build a new farmhouse.[33] In 1606–7 Priory farm was leased without the meadows and parkland around Lord Hertford's house; it too was to have a new farmhouse.[34] Lord Hertford's park contained 8 a. in 1605, when two burrows were made and 14 pairs of rabbits introduced,[35] and in 1635 c. 33 a. around the house.[36]

In 1635 Earl's farm had three several arable fields, 245 a., east of the village, 32 a. of several arable on Woolston Hill south of it, and a 12-a. parcel in an open field. Earl's down, c. 420 a., was several, and two other downs, Woolston Hill and part of Blackcross down, were for the exclusive use of a flock consisting of 400 sheep of Earl's farm and 74 of a copyholder: the farm included 8 a. of downland in two pennings and

18 Ibid.; below, this section.
19 *Antrobus D.* (W.R.S. iii), p. 21.
20 P.R.O., DL 29/728/11991.
21 Longleat Mun., Seymour papers, xii, f. 252v.
22 Below, this section.
23 Longleat Mun., Seymour papers, xii, ff. 247–55; W.R.O. 283/4, ct. bk. 1583–90, view 7 Oct. 27 Eliz. I; 944/1; for Priory farm, below, this section.
24 P.R.O., SC 6/Hen. VIII/3986, rott. 73–6; W.R.O. 283/6, bk. of surveys and leases, f. 42v.; 283/6, survey, c. 1741; Alnwick Castle Mun. X.II.11, box 6, survey, 1634, pp. 219–21.
25 *Antrobus D.* (W.R.S. iii), pp. 47–9; W.R.O. 283/83–5.

26 W.R.O. 283/6, survey, c. 1741.
27 Ibid. 283/6, bk. D, agreement, Hertford and Poore, 1595.   28 Ibid. 283/59, lease, Scot to Toppe, 1605.
29 Ibid. 283/6, bk. O, ct. 2 Apr. 1566.
30 Ibid. 283/4, ct. bk. 1581–96, memo. c. 1595.
31 Ibid. 944/1–2.
32 Ibid. 283/7, ct. 15 Mar. 28 Eliz. I.
33 Ibid. 283/6, bk. D, plan, 1598; *Antrobus D.* (W.R.S. iii), pp. 89–91.
34 *Antrobus D.* (W.R.S. iii), pp. 76–83.
35 W.R.O. 283/6, bk. D, note, 1605.
36 Alnwick Castle Mun. X.II.11, box 6, survey, 1634, p. 222.

the right to fold 1,200 sheep on the open fields. Apart from the first cut of 3 a., Wittenham mead was solely for the farm, as was most of the hay, but not the aftermath, of Sour mead, 8½ a.; the feeding of Northams was still shared in autumn. In 1635 Amesbury still had c. 10 open fields, on which a three-field rotation was evidently practised; each of the larger farms included meadow land, but apparently little meadow was cultivated in common. Sheep were fed in common on Blackcross down, c. 150 a., Kitcombe down, c. 50 a., and Southam down, c. 80 a. Cattle were fed in common on the lowland in Cow leaze, 7½ a., and on Rother down, c. 80 a.: Rother down was formerly part of Earl's down and was fed on by the town herd from 3 May to 11 November and by the wethers of Earl's farm from 11 November to 25 March. The largest holdings of open-field land were in Pavyhold, 190 a., and Coombes Court farm. Priory farm probably had c. 100 a., and four freeholds of the Earldom manor, including Saucer's, had a total of c. 110 a. Copyholds of the Earldom manor included c. 475 a.; Billet land measured c. 73 a. Only Pavyhold, Priory farm, and the yardlands, 3 freehold and 6½ copyhold, had feeding for sheep in common, and the flock numbered c. 1,350; Coombes Court farm may have had a several down for sheep, as it did later. The c. 15 cotsetlands of the Earldom manor included c. 170 a.: they and the larger holdings had feeding for cattle, but no feeding right was held with Billet land. There were three main copyholds, of 77 a., 108 a., and 115 a., with feeding for 192, 192, and 252 sheep respectively, and evidently more than two thirds of the open-field land was in holdings of more than 50 a.[37]

Between 1635 and 1725 the division of Amesbury's lands between several and commonable, the arrangement of open fields and common downs, and the division of the land among the farms seem to have changed little.[38] The watering of meadows may have begun c. 1658: in that year Moor hatches on the Amesbury–Normanton boundary were licensed by the Earldom manor court.[39] Some meadows remained in common use,[40] and c. 1724 Defoe praised the quality of Amesbury's meadow land.[41] By 1720 the lessee of Earl's farm, Windsor Sandys (d. 1729) of Brimpsfield (Glos.), had divided it by subletting 241 a. of its arable and meadows, and 180 a. of its downland, in six portions.[42] Over 200 a. of the farm's downland had been ploughed by 1726.[43] Pavyhold, 4 yardlands in 1646, Priory, held from 1725 or earlier without its land in West Amesbury, and Coombes Court remained among the largest farms with open-field land,[44] and in the early 18th century may all have been held by one tenant.[45] About 1702, as in 1635,

each of two copyholds included over 100 a. of arable, and one 77 a.[46] A proposal of 1725 to inclose Townend Little field and Cuckold's Hill field depended on the abandonment of the right to feed Earl's farm sheep on the two fields with the town herd after harvest and of the right to take the town herd across Earl's farm summer fields:[47] it was not implemented.[48]

In 1726 Amesbury had c. 1,300 a. of arable. There were c. 850 a. in nine open fields, Little field over the water (c. 15 a.) and Townend Little (22 a.), Cuckold's Hill (71 a.), Blackcross (175 a.), Bartnett (172 a.), Southmillhill (150 a.), Great Southam (167 a.), Little Southam (60 a.), and Woolston Hill (c. 30 a.): the fields contained c. 96 furlongs in which there were c. 730 parcels of land. In addition Earl's farm had c. 436 a. of several arable of which c. 191 a. were formerly downland pasture. There remained c. 1,540 a. of such pasture. The common downs for sheep were Blackcross Town (385 a. including 36 a. shared with men of Boscombe), Lower (139 a.), and Kickdom (78 a.). Earl's farm had Slay down (477 a.) in severalty and Blackcross Farm down (123 a.), Woolston Hill (53 a.), and Pigeon Hill (5 a.) shared with a copyholder; Coombes Court farm had a several down, Viner's (106 a.). Cow down, formerly Rother down and still shared by the town herd and Earl's farm sheep, was 172 a. Lowland pastures used in common totalled c. 19 a., and there were over 200 a. of meadow and other lowland pasture, some of which was in each of the larger farms. In addition there were c. 50 a. of grassland and parkland around Amesbury Abbey. Earl's farm contained 1,393 a., including Cow down, but was still sublet in portions. Coombes Court farm (otherwise Viner's or Southam) had 61 parcels in the open fields, Pavyhold 138: for reasons that are obscure the parcels belonging to Coombes Court farm were on average much larger than those of other farms, and the farm had its several down instead of feeding for sheep in common. Priory farm had a nominal 71 a. in the open fields, and the two largest copyholds nominally 138 a. and 83 a.; a nominal 160 a. was shared among c. 21 other holdings. The 602 a. of common sheep downs were for 1,301 sheep including 274 in respect of Pavyhold, 74 of Priory farm, and 636 of the two largest copyholds. Pavyhold, Coombes Court farm, and the two largest copyholds all had farmsteads in Salisbury Road.[49]

It appears that immediately on entering on the Earldom and Priory manors in 1725 Charles, duke of Queensberry,[50] adopted the policy of merging all the open-field land which he owned into a single farm. A farmhouse called the Red House had evidently been built by 1726 on the second largest copyhold,[51] and as other copy-

[37] Alnwick Castle Mun. X.II.11, box 6, survey, 1634, pp. 169–212; for Coombes Ct. down, below, this section. The acreage of open-field land recorded in 1635 was nominal.
[38] Cf. W.R.O. 944/1–2; Alnwick Castle Mun. X.II.11, box 6, survey, 1634, pp. 169–242.
[39] W.R.O. 283/4, ct. bk. 1658–60, ct. 14 Sept. 1658.
[40] Ibid. 283/6, ct. papers 1676–80, ct. 17 May 1677; 283/35, lease, Hayward to Bird, 1688.
[41] D. Defoe, Tour through Gt. Brit. ed. G. D. H. Cole, i. 211.   [42] V.C.H. Glos. vii. 143; W.R.O. 283/173.
[43] W.R.O. 944/2.

[44] Ibid. 283/61, deed, Clutterbuck to Gale, 1658; 283/87, deed, Hearst to Hayward, 1725; 944/1–2.
[45] Ibid. 334/22.   [46] Ibid. 283/16; above, this section.
[47] W.R.O. 283/174.   [48] e.g. ibid. 283/14, p. 131.
[49] Ibid. 283/6, survey, c. 1741; 283/178A; 944/1–2; for the subletting of Earl's farm, ibid. 283/48 and 283/198; for the acreage of the open fields, ibid. 283/168, description of fields.
[50] Above, manors (Earldom; Priory).
[51] W.R.O. 944/1–2; for a description of the ho., above, intro. (the town c. 1540 to c. 1900).

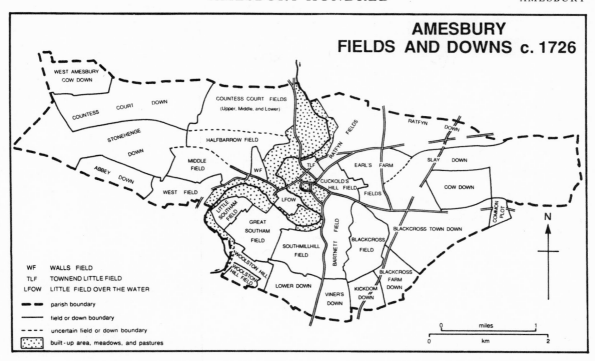

AMESBURY
FIELDS AND DOWNS c. 1726

WF   WALLS FIELD
TLF   TOWNEND LITTLE FIELD
LFOW   LITTLE FIELD OVER THE WATER

- - - -   parish boundary
_____   field or down boundary
- - - -   uncertain field or down boundary
[:::::]   built-up area, meadows, and pastures

holds and leaseholds fell in hand their lands were added to Red House farm.[52] To accelerate the process Queensberry leased land from some copyholders and leaseholders, bought out others, and became tenant of Saucer's.[53] In the mid 1750s nearly a third of the parcels in the open fields were in Red House farm.[54] From 1760, when Queensberry owned nearly all Amesbury's land,[55] the policy was refined. A dairy farm[56] and a farm apparently worked from Kent House were already in hand, and gradually all the other land was brought in hand: Red House farm was in hand at Michaelmas 1759, Viner's from 1760 or 1761,[57] part of Earl's by 1764, when 1,010 sheep were sheared on that part,[58] and Pavyhold and most of the other land by the later 1760s.[59] In 1770 the last tenant of a substantial copyhold gave up his open-field land in an exchange with Queensberry,[60] common husbandry was thus ended, and most of the former open fields and common downs were laid out as two several farms, Red House and Southam.[61] In 1771 there were between the town and the Avon c. 60 a. of the gardens and parkland of Amesbury Abbey, Earl's farm was 1,085 a., and Kent House farm was 80 a., including most of Townend Little field and most of Cuckold's Hill field. Red House farm was 853 a., including Blackcross and Bartnett fields, Blackcross Town and Blackcross

Farm downs, and part of Kickdom down: its 346 a. of arable had been arranged as four equally sized fields. Southam farm was 847 a., including Southmillhill, Great Southam, and Little Southam fields and Viner's, Lower, and Woolston Hill downs: 332 a. of its arable had been divided into four equally sized fields. Amesbury had a total of 102 a. of watered meadows, and the three main farms had 1,372 a. of 'maiden' down, 27 a. of downland pennings, and 223 a. of sown grass on downland formerly ploughed.[62] The farms remained in hand, and were evidently individually managed, until 1778, the year in which the duke of Queensberry died.[63]

From 1778 to c. 1900 the c. 5,800 a. of agricultural land of Amesbury parish was in few and very large farms.[64] Kent House or Park farm, to which the parkland around Amesbury Abbey was added as farmland, remained in hand until 1788.[65] Earl's, Red House, and Southam farms were leased from 1778: Red House and Southam were held together 1780–1915.[66] In 1809 Earl's was 1,106 a. including 635 a. of downland pasture and 439 a. of arable, of which 131 a. were downland; Red House was 872 a. including 462 a. of downland pasture and 366 a. of arable; Southam was 858 a. including 357 a. of downland pasture and 433 a. of arable. The watered meadows of Amesbury were admired by William

[52] Cf. W.R.O. 283/178A; 944/1–2.
[53] Ibid. 283/40, assignment, Compton to Queensberry, 1776; 283/81, copy, 1752; 283/133, lease, Osmond to Gatehouse, 1736; 283/186, rental; 377/1, memo. 1788; 944/3.
[54] Ibid. 283/178A.
[55] Above, manors (Coombes Ct.; Countess Ct.).
[56] W.R.O. 283/169.
[57] Ibid. 283/168, 1759–60, ff. 1–3, 17, 21, 30, 35, 39.
[58] Ibid. 283/168, 1764; 283/168, 1767–8, f. 46.
[59] Ibid. 283/168, e.g. 1767–8, f. 46.
[60] Ibid. 283/100, memo. 1770; 283/186, Harding's lands, 1770.

[61] Ibid. 283/186, Red House and Southam farms, 1770.
[62] Ibid.; ibid. 944/3; for the gardens and parkland, cf. 283/202.
[63] e.g. ibid. 283/168, 1777, f. 40; 283/168, 1778, f. 41; above, manors (Earldom).
[64] Below, this section; ibid. (W. Amesbury; Countess Ct.; Ratfyn).
[65] W.R.O. 377/1, memo. 1778; 377/2; 490/1116; 944/3; above, manors (Priory); for Kent Ho. farm 1778–1823, below, this section (W. Amesbury).
[66] W.R.O. 283/168, 1778, f. 44; 377/2; 776/6.

Marshall in 1794, and Earl's, Red House, Southam, and Kent House farms had a total of c. 117 a.[67] The need to repair Moor hatches led to a dispute with the owners of Normanton farm: in 1804 a new channel taking water away from Moor hatches was cut to the east, and 9 a. more of meadows, part of Southam farm, were watered.[68] In 1823 much of the land of Kent House farm east of the Avon was added to Earl's farm.[69] In 1825 Earl's was 1,173 a., the combined Red House and Southam 1,752 a.: the two farms were roughly divided by the Newton Tony road. Arable had been increased to c. 1,600 a. by 1825, when Earl's farm contained 315 a. of ploughed downland:[70] in riots against threshing machines two ricks were burnt at Amesbury in 1830,[71] and there had been a further small increase in arable by c. 1845.[72] On the combined Red House and Southam farm the lessee, William Long, employed 30 men, 16–18 women, and c. 17 boys in 1867.[73]

Earl's farm was divided in the early 20th century. In 1910 only the western part, then called Earls Court farm, 292 a., was worked from the principal buildings in Earls Court Road; the middle part was in Ratfyn farm; the eastern part of Slay down, 300 a. on which there were farm buildings, was, possibly as Beacon Hill farm, part of the Cholderton estate. From 1915 Earls Court farm's meadow and pasture near the Avon, 44 a., were detached from it.[74] From 1919 the Board of Agriculture and Fisheries used the remainder of Earls Court farm, 236 a. east of the town, bounded north by the railway and south by the Newton Tony road and extending east of the Marlborough road, as a farm colony: by 1923 c. 20 smallholdings, the smallest of 2 a., the largest of 30 a., had been leased, presumably to former soldiers.[75] Mainly after 1945 nearly all that land was built on.[76] The remainder of Earl's farm was in Ratfyn farm from 1915 to the 1930s, when Beacon Hill farm, c. 450 a., and Pennings farm, c. 260 a., were formed. Beacon Hill farm, 464 a., was mainly arable in 1993, when some cattle were kept for beef. Pennings, with buildings south of the London road and New Barn north of it, has since the 1930s been used in conjunction with land in West Amesbury: in 1993 its land was mainly arable and some of its buildings housed cattle.[77] Over 300 a. of the old Earl's farm, including Cow down, were still part of Ratfyn farm in 1993 and almost entirely arable.[78]

Red House farm, 964 a. between the main Salisbury road and the Newton Tony road, and Southam, thereafter Viney's, farm, 744 a. west of the Salisbury road, were separate again from 1915.[79] Both were entirely pasture in the 1930s.[80] Red House was greatly reduced from 1927 by the growth of Boscombe Down airfield.[81] In the later 20th century the reduced farm was worked from the farmstead called Stockport on the old Kickdom down and from large new buildings in the old Blackcross field. In 1993 Red House was an arable farm of 300 a. worked from the new buildings. Stockport farm, c. 150 a., but without Stockport farmstead, was separated from it in the later 1980s and, mainly arable in 1993, was worked in conjunction with Pennings farm and land in West Amesbury.[82] In 1993 Viney's, 705 a., was a mainly arable farm worked from later 20th-century buildings a little south of the town.[83]

WEST AMESBURY. There is evidence of open fields, common meadows, and common pasture for sheep and cattle in West Amesbury in the earlier 13th century. Holdings based in the village, like those based in Amesbury, included yardlands and cotsetlands,[84] and there was evidently no large demesne.[85] In the 14th century there were apparently three or more open fields.[86] Then and in the 15th sheep stints were generous: in 1328 a holding of 4 yardlands had feeding for 300 wethers,[87] in 1428 one of 1 yardland feeding for 200 sheep,[88] and in 1497 one of ½ yardland feeding for 50 sheep. Holdings also included rights to feed cattle and pigs.[89]

In the early 16th century most of West Amesbury's land was in West Amesbury manor, freeholds, and the demesne of Amesbury priory;[90] a few acres were in Coombes Court manor and customary holdings of Amesbury manor.[91] In 1502 the heirs of Thomas Hobbes shared c. 125 parcels, nominally c. 150 a., in the open fields;[92] in 1511 the demesne of West Amesbury manor, 4 yardlands, was said to include 80 a. of arable;[93] in 1535 Amesbury priory evidently had in the fields c. 115 parcels, of which after the Dissolution most were in Priory farm and some in smallholdings of Billet land.[94] In 1511 West Amesbury manor also included land held by tenants at will.[95]

In the early 16th century there were open fields called Halfbarrow, Middle West, and West;[96] in

67 W. Marshall, *Rural Econ. S. Cos.* ii. 337; W.R.O. 377/9.
68 W.R.O. 377/1, map, 1804; 377/8; 490/1116.
69 Cf. ibid. 283/202; 377/9. 70 Ibid. 283/202.
71 P.R.O., HO 52/11. 72 W.R.O., tithe award.
73 *Rep. Com. Children and Women in Agric.* [4202–I], p. 236, H.C. (1868–9), xiii.
74 *Kelly's Dir. Wilts.* (1907, 1911); W.R.O. 776/6; ibid. Inland Revenue, val. reg. 147; for Ratfyn farm, below, this section (Ratfyn); for the Cholderton estate and how it was managed, below, Cholderton, manors; econ. hist.
75 Wilts. Cuttings, xv. 216; W.R.O., G 1/500/1.
76 Above, intro. (the town from c. 1900).
77 W.R.O. 776/6; inf. from Mr. I. F. Sandell, Pikes Cottage, W. Amesbury; Mr. C. H. Crook, Mallards, Blackhorse Lane, Hurdcott.
78 Inf. from Mr. P. J. Rowland, Ratfyn Farm.
79 W.R.O. 776/6; ibid. G 1/500/1.
80 [1st] Land Util. Surv. Map, sheet 122.
81 Above, intro. (military activity).
82 Inf. from Mr. J. C. Salvidge, Home Farm, S. Tid-

worth; Mr. Sandell.
83 Inf. from Mr. R. C. Crook, 11 Salisbury Road.
84 *Rot. Chart.* (Rec. Com.), 155; P.R.O., CP 25/1/250/3, no. 34; CP 25/1/250/9, no. 26; above, this section (Amesbury).
85 Cf. above, manors (estates in W. Amesbury).
86 *Antrobus D.* (W.R.S. iii), pp. 15–16.
87 P.R.O., CP 40/273, rot. 30d.
88 *Antrobus D.* (W.R.S. iii), p. 19. 89 Ibid. pp. 21, 25–6, 32.
90 Above, manors (Priory; estates in W. Amesbury).
91 Alnwick Castle Mun. X.II.11, box 6, survey, 1634, pp. 187, 197; Longleat Mun., Seymour papers, xii, ff. 248v., 251v.–252; W.R.O. 944/2.
92 *Antrobus D.* (W.R.S. iii), pp. 33–6.
93 W.R.O. 283/8, rental, 1511; 283/136, deed, Littlebury to Gosnoll, 1635.
94 Ibid. 283/6, bk. of surveys and leases, ff. 51v.–55; 283/6, survey, c. 1741; P.R.O., SC 6/Hen. VIII/3986, rot. 73d.; Alnwick Castle Mun. X.II.11, box 6, survey, 1634, pp. 215–28.
95 W.R.O. 283/8, rental, 1511.
96 *Antrobus D.* (W.R.S. iii), pp. 40–1.

From the south-west in 1805

From the south-west in 1965

AMESBURY: AMESBURY ABBEY

Diana House

Gate piers of Amesbury Abbey

Kent House

AMESBURY

the early 17th there was a small fourth field called Walls covering Vespasian's camp.[97] In the early 17th century there was a common pasture for cattle near the Avon, and meadow land was used in common;[98] the watering of meadows in West Amesbury presumably began, as apparently in Amesbury, in the mid 17th century.[99] The downland pasture for sheep was extensive,[1] and stints remained generous.[2] At the Dissolution Amesbury priory had feeding for 300 sheep which were presumably then, as they were c. 1574 and later, kept on the open fields and in severalty on Abbey down:[3] in 1615 or 1616 it was claimed that for the Priory manor only 250 might be kept on the fields every fourth year.[4] There was also downland pasture for cattle in common.[5] In 1635 Abbey down was said to be c. 120 a., Cow down c. 90 a.[6]

In the 16th century several of the freeholds were brought into single ownership, and from the early 17th most land in West Amesbury belonged to the lord of West Amesbury manor.[7] The demesne farm of the manor was greatly increased, and in the earlier 17th century was one of apparently only four farms based in West Amesbury. In 1621 it had 246 a. of arable, including 235 a. in West Amesbury, 11 a. of apparently inclosed meadow, 3½ a. of common meadow, 13 a. of inclosed pasture, and feeding for 800 sheep; by then most of the arable had been accumulated into large pieces, including one of 52 a., one of 51 a., and one of 47 a. The manor also included farms of 93 a. and 60 a. with feeding for a total of 310 sheep.[8] Beckington's, said in 1635 to be 50 a., was 1½ yardland. Priory farm, with c. 87 a. and Abbey down in West Amesbury in 1635, was worked from Amesbury, and c. 20 a. of Billet land were in other holdings.[9]

In 1726 West Amesbury had 437 a. of arable in four open fields, Halfbarrow (176 a.), Middle (136 a.), West (101 a.), and Walls (24 a.); there were 814 a. of downland, Cow down (158 a.), Abbey down (152 a.), and Stonehenge down (504 a.), and West hill was a common pasture of 7 a. There were c. 20 a. of watered meadow, and c. 22 a. of other lowland pasture.[10] After 1678[11] none but the tenants of West Amesbury manor had a right to feed sheep on Stonehenge down or cattle on Cow down. The lord of the manor also owned c. 365 a. of the open fields; most of the remainder was in Priory farm.[12] With minor exceptions common husbandry ended either in 1725, when the West Amesbury lands of Priory

farm were sublet to the lord,[13] or in 1735, when the duke of Queensberry bought West Amesbury manor.[14] By 1735 c. 240 a. of downland, mostly the west part of Stonehenge down, had been ploughed, and it was intended then to plough a further 51 a.; immediately after the purchase 52 a. north-west of Amesbury Abbey were imparked, 19 a. of Walls field including Vespasian's camp, and 33 a. of Halfbarrow field; and in 1735 nearly all the other land was in two several farms, Homeward, 647 a., and Westward, 387 a. Homeward, probably worked from the new farmstead on the south side of the village street, included 7 a. of watered meadow, most, 121 a., of Halfbarrow field, and 491 a. of downland; Westward included a farmstead at the west end of the village, 13 a. of watered meadow, most, 192 a., of Middle and West fields, and 166 a. of downland.[15] About 1740 Abbey down was part of Westward farm.[16] The owner of Countess Court manor had the right to feed sheep on West Amesbury Cow down from 11 November to 2 February, and 160 sheep from West Amesbury could be fed for the whole year on Countess Court downs:[17] the arrangement probably ceased in 1760 when the duke of Queensberry bought Countess Court manor.[18]

By c. 1750 a further 36 a. had been imparked: sainfoin was grown on the 88 a. of former open field in the park.[19] At its maximum in the 1770s the park included c. 360 a., of which c. 250 a. were West Amesbury land, and was impaled.[20] Homeward farm and Westward farm were worked together from the mid 18th century, when they may have included no more than 400 a. of 'maiden' down.[21] Like farms in Amesbury the land was brought in hand c. 1760:[22] as West Amesbury farm it measured 935 a. including 30 a. of watered meadow, 86 a. of other meadow and lowland pasture, only 207 a. of arable, and 610 a. of downland pasture.[23] It was leased in 1778,[24] apparently without Cow down, which was added to Countess Court farm,[25] and 1,300 sheep were said to be kept on it in 1782.[26] In or soon after 1778 the parkland, including c. 50 a. of the former Countess Court manor, was added to Kent House farm, worked from Amesbury, and over 200 a. of it, including the former Halfbarrow field, were again ploughed. In 1809 West Amesbury, Kent House, and Countess Court farms were rearranged. From then to 1823 Abbey down, 223 a. of Stonehenge down, and part of Countess Court down, a total of 411 a.,

97   Ibid. p. 99; W.R.O. 944/1–2.
98   W.R.O. 283/8, ct. Mar. 13 Jas. I.
99   Above, this section (Amesbury).
1   Below, this section.
2   W.R.O. 283/8, ct. 25 Oct. 1645; 283/110, lease, South to Long, 1576.
3   Ibid. 283/6, bk. of surveys and leases, f. 42v.; P.R.O., SC 6/Hen. VIII/3986, rot. 73d.
4   W.R.O. 283/8, ct. Mar. 13 Jas. I.
5   *Antrobus D.* (W.R.S. iii), p. 110.
6   Alnwick Castle Mun. X.II.11, box 6, survey, 1634, p. 219.
7   Above, manors (W. Amesbury; South's).
8   *Antrobus D.* (W.R.S. iii), pp. 109–10.
9   Alnwick Castle Mun. X.II.11, box 6, survey, 1634, pp. 213, 219–21; W.R.O. 283/6, survey, c. 1741; above, this section (Amesbury).

10   W.R.O. 944/1–2.
11   Above, manors (Beckington's).
12   W.R.O. 944/2.
13   Ibid. 283/87, lease, Hearst to Hayward, 1725.
14   Above, manors (W. Amesbury).
15   W.R.O. 944/2; above, intro. (W. Amesbury).
16   W.R.O. 283/6, survey bk. [c. 1740].
17   Ibid.; ibid. 283/194.
18   Above, manors (Countess Ct.).
19   W.R.O. 283/194.
20   Ibid. 944/3.   21   Ibid. 283/194.
22   Ibid. 283/168, 1759–60, f. 20; 283/168, 1761, f. 17; above, this section (Amesbury).
23   W.R.O. 944/3.
24   Ibid. 283/168, 1778, f. 44.
25   Ibid. 377/9; 944/3.
26   D. & C. Windsor Mun., CC 120349; CC 120351.

were in Kent House farm; Cow down remained in Countess Court farm; and West Amesbury farm measured 700 a., including 33 a. of Countess Court down. In 1823 Kent House farm was divided between West Amesbury, Countess Court, and Earl's farms.[27]

West Amesbury farm was 1,071 a. in 1823, 1,010 a. in 1910. Cow down and *c.* 100 a. of West Amesbury land formerly in the park were in Countess Court farm. In 1823 West Amesbury farm had 33 a. of watered meadow, 32 a. of other meadow and lowland pasture, 503 a. of arable including 126 a. on Stonehenge down, and 501 a. of downland pasture. It was worked from West Amesbury House, and from the mid 19th century had an additional farmstead called Fargo.[28] From 1915 West Amesbury farm was 843 a. including 51 a. in Normanton but excluding West Amesbury House.[29] Stonehenge airfield was opened on the land in 1917, and Fargo farmstead was removed about then; in the 1920s 100 a. of the airfield and some of its buildings were used for a pig and poultry farm.[30] Also from 1915 Countess farm included *c.* 100 a. of Stonehenge down.[31] West Amesbury farm was divided after the National Trust bought it 1927–9.[32] In 1993 the east part was in a farm worked from 20th-century buildings north-west of the village and in conjunction with land formerly in Countess farm, with Pennings farm, and with Stockport farm, a total of 1,100 a.; the composite holding was an arable and beef farm. The west part of the old West Amesbury farm, *c.* 330 a., was worked from Winterbourne Stoke and was mainly arable.[33]

COUNTESS COURT. The lands called Countess field and Countess down in the 17th century[34] were almost certainly open fields and a common down in the Middle Ages. In 1726, and perhaps for long before, there were three fields, Lower, Middle, and Upper, *c.* 300 a., and 444 a. of downland.[35] In the early 14th century the demesne of Countess Court manor, with 200–300 a. of arable and feeding for many sheep, greatly outweighed other holdings:[36] it may have been in hand in 1332.[37] In 1311 there were on the manor three yardlanders, who presumably held land in the open fields and rights to feed sheep on the downs, and five cottars;[38] later evidence shows that a few, evidently no more than nine, parcels in the fields were parts of Amesbury manor and what became South's or Beckington's in West Amesbury,[39] and that 160 sheep from

West Amesbury could be fed on the downs. The land of Countess Court manor became a single farm, possibly in the later Middle Ages. The land not owned by the lord, 26 a., was concentrated in Lower field, 78 a. of down were assigned for the exclusive use of the West Amesbury sheep, but vestiges of common husbandry remained until 1760,[40] from when the duke of Queensberry owned all the land.[41]

In 1770 Countess Court farm was, like Queensberry's other farms in the parish, brought in hand;[42] *c.* 50 a. of its arable were imparked.[43] In 1771, when 880 sheep were sheared on it, the farm measured 965 a., including 30 a. of watered meadow, 86 a. of other meadow and lowland pasture, 257 a. of arable, 55 a. of downland formerly ploughed but then sown with grass, and 534 a. of 'maiden' down: the downland included West Amesbury Cow down.[44] The farm was leased in 1778, without the parkland but with Cow down. It was reduced to 778 a. in 1809, when its downland was reduced to 400 a. by the transfer of some to Kent House farm,[45] and increased to 1,102 a. in 1823, when Kent House farm was trisected. From 1823 to 1915 the farm included Cow down and *c.* 100 a. of West Amesbury land formerly imparked: in 1823 it had 49 a. of watered meadow, 44 a. of other meadow and lowland pasture, 592 a. of arable including 138 a. on the downs, and 418 a. of downland pasture.[46] From the mid 19th century to the later 20th it had an additional farmstead called Seven Barrows.[47] From 1915 the farm, then called Countess farm, was 1,169 a., to the west bounded on the south by the Exeter and Shrewton roads.[48] The west part of it was bought by the National Trust in 1929,[49] and in the later 20th century was entirely pasture: in 1993 *c.* 140 a. of that part were held with Countess farm, more with the composite farm based at West Amesbury, and more still with Manor farm, Winterbourne Stoke. In 1993 Countess, 640 a. including land north of Stonehenge and land in Durrington, was an arable and sheep farm.[50]

RATFYN. In 1086 Ratfyn had land for 1½ ploughteam: on demesne land there was 1 team, and on other land there were 8 bordars. There were 12 a. of meadow and 2¼ square furlongs of pasture.[51] Sheep-and-corn husbandry was practised in the Middle Ages: *c.* 1210 Ratfyn manor had demesne, stocked with 8 oxen and 450 sheep, and possibly customary tenants.[52] In 1405

27 W.R.O. 283/202; 377/1, memo. 1788; 377/9; 490/1116; for Kent Ho. farm, cf. above, this section (Amesbury); for the inclusion of Countess Ct. land, cf. W.R.O. 490/1116; 944/2.
28 O.S. Map 6", Wilts. LIV (1887 edn.); W.R.O., tithe award; ibid. Inland Revenue, val. reg. 147; ibid. 283/202.
29 W.R.O. 776/6.
30 Ashworth, *Action Stations*, v (1990), 254; O.S. Maps 6", Wilts. LIV. SW. (1901, 1925 edns.); W.R.O., G 1/500/1; above, intro. (military activity).
31 W.R.O. 776/6.   32 Above, manors (W. Amesbury).
33 Inf. from Mr. I. F. Sandell, Pikes Cottage, W. Amesbury.
34 Alnwick Castle Mun. X.II.11, box 6, survey, 1634, pp. 170, 201.   35 W.R.O. 944/2–3.
36 *Wilts. Inq. p.m.* 1242–1326 (Index Libr.), 385–6; 1327–77 (Index Libr.), 111.
37 *Tax List, 1332* (W.R.S. xlv), 109.

38 *Wilts. Inq. p.m.* 1242–1326 (Index Libr.), 385–6.
39 *Antrobus D.* (W.R.S. iii), pp. 33, 36; Alnwick Castle Mun. X.II.11, box 6, survey, 1634, p. 201; W.R.O. 944/2.
40 W.R.O. 283/194; 944/2.
41 Above, manors (Countess Ct.).
42 Ibid. this section (Amesbury; W. Amesbury); W.R.O. 283/168, 1772, f. 46.
43 Cf. W.R.O. 490/1116; 944/3; above, this section (W. Amesbury).   44 W.R.O. 283/168, 1771, f. 24; 944/3.
45 Ibid. 283/168, 1778, f. 44; 377/9; for the parkland, in Kent Ho. farm, above, this section (W. Amesbury).
46 W.R.O. 283/202; 776/6.
47 Above, intro. (Countess).   48 W.R.O. 776/6.
49 Above, manors (Countess Ct.).
50 Inf. from Mr. Sandell; Mr. N. Morrison, Countess Farm.   51 *V.C.H. Wilts.* ii, pp. 136, 166.
52 *Interdict Doc.* (P.R.S. N.S. xxxiv), 20.

the demesne included 1 carucate of arable and 5 a. of meadow, four tenants each held 10½ a., and three cottagers each held 2 a.: the arable is likely to have been in open fields, and a pasture for 500 sheep, presumably downland, was said to have been used in common.[53] In the 16th century Ratfyn's land was apparently all in Ratfyn farm, which in 1553 was said to have 12 a. of meadow, 12 a. of presumably lowland pasture, 240 a. of arable, and 140 a. of downland pasture for sheep, all in severalty.[54]

In 1846 Ratfyn farm was 502 a., including c. 28 a. of watered meadow, 7 a. of lowland pasture, c. 338 a. of arable, and c. 118 a. of downland pasture:[55] downland had presumably been converted to arable in the 18th century. In the early 20th century the middle part of Earl's farm was added to Ratfyn farm, which was 912 a. in 1910.[56] It was further enlarged in 1915 by the addition of the east part of Earl's farm, including Slay down, and 53 a. of Red House farm: from 1915 it measured 1,369 a. and, bounded on the south by the railway, comprised all the north-east part of the parish.[57] By 1923 it had been reduced to 1,223 a.;[58] Pennings farm and Beacon Hill farm were taken from it in the 1930s.[59] In 1965 Ratfyn farm was 681 a., including over 300 a. formerly in Earl's farm; in 1993 it was 600 a., mainly arable, and worked in conjunction with land in Bulford and Allington.[60]

MILLS. There were eight mills on the king's Amesbury estate in 1086;[61] it is unlikely that they were all in what became Amesbury parish.[62] Later, every mill in the parish was evidently driven by the Avon.

Geoffrey le Veel held a mill at Amesbury in the late 12th century and early 13th, possibly one of the two mills on Amesbury manor in 1269.[63] A mill was built or rebuilt on the manor in 1304–5,[64] but there was apparently none on it in the earlier 16th century.[65] The Earldom manor court frequently amerced a miller in the later 16th century;[66] a mill rebuilt c. 1560, after fire destroyed a predecessor,[67] was possibly on

the manor,[68] and may have been that near West bridge called Town Mill in 1593.[69] There was no mill on the Earldom manor in 1635[70] or later.

In the early 16th century Amesbury priory had two corn mills and a fulling mill immediately south-west of the parish church and probably under one roof.[71] Mills on the site, near that of Town Mill, were part of the Priory manor and later called West, Priory, or Abbey Mill.[72] In the mid 16th century the mills were used to grind wheat and malt, but the fulling mill was evidently taken down; in 1582 the mill buildings were seriously dilapidated and six floodgates were washed away.[73] The buildings had not been restored by 1590,[74] and in 1595, as a condition of a new lease, the mills were to be rebuilt.[75] West Mill was thereafter referred to as two grist mills and a fulling mill under one roof,[76] but in the 18th century it was used for tanning.[77] The mill was damaged by fire in 1761:[78] there is no evidence that it was used for milling after that, and it may have been the mill converted to stables 1778–81.[79] It had been demolished by 1812.[80]

In 1328 there were two mills, possibly under one roof, on what became West Amesbury manor,[81] and there was a mill at West Amesbury in 1428.[82] The site of one on the manor and near West Amesbury village was known in 1636, but it is very unlikely that a mill stood then[83] or later.

A mill at Amesbury descended with Countess Court manor from 1311 or earlier to c. 1760.[84] It was called Cleeve Mill in 1364 and 1602,[85] perhaps Townsend Mill in 1773,[86] but South Mill much more often. In the 14th century there were said to be two mills,[87] and in 1602 two mills under one roof.[88] In 1646 the buildings included a fulling mill said to be new, and in 1660 comprised that, the two corn mills, and a mill house.[89] A new house may have been built shortly before 1677.[90] It is not clear how long fulling continued. Between c. 1760 and 1838 there were several owners of the mill, including members of the Miles and Truckle families; it was bought by Sir Edmund Antrobus in 1838[91] and descended with his Amesbury estate until

53 *Chandler's Reg.* (W.R.S. xxxix), p. 31.
54 P.R.O., E 318/37/2027.
55 W.R.O., tithe award.
56 Ibid. Inland Revenue, val. reg. 147; *Kelly's Dir. Wilts.* (1907, 1911); above, this section (Amesbury).
57 W.R.O. 776/6.   58 Ibid. G 1/500/1.
59 Above, this section (Amesbury).
60 Inf. from Mr. P. J. Rowland, Ratfyn Farm, and sale cat. in his possession; inf. from the Land Agent, Lincoln Coll., Oxf.   61 *V.C.H. Wilts.* ii, p. 116.
62 Cf. above, manors (preamble).
63 *Bradenstoke Cart.* (W.R.S. xxxv), p. 94; *Rot. Chart.* (Rec. Com.), 155; *Close R. 1268–72*, 136.
64 P.R.O., DL 29/1/2, rot. 21.
65 Longleat Mun., Seymour papers, xii, ff. 247–58.
66 e.g. W.R.O. 283/4, ct. bks.; 283/5, ct. bk. 1586–96; 283/6, bk. O; 283/7.
67 *Antrobus D.* (W.R.S. iii), pp. 49–50.
68 W.R.O. 283/4, ct. bk. 1599–1612, notes of presentments 15 Oct. 3 Jas. I.
69 Ibid. 283/5, ct. bk. 1586–98, view 24 Apr. 1593.
70 Alnwick Castle Mun. X.II.11, box 6, survey, 1634, pp. 169–212.
71 P.R.O., C 1/421, no. 49; ibid. SC 6/Hen. VIII/3986, rot. 73d.
72 e.g. W.R.O. 283/5, ct. bk. 1581–2, view 3 Mar. 23 Eliz. I; 283/5, ct. bk. 1586–98, view 15 Apr. 38 Eliz. I; 283/6, bk.

O, ct. 16 Dec. 1566.
73 Ibid. 283/5, ct. bk. 1581–2, view 21 Mar. 24 Eliz. I; 283/7, view 8 Oct. 24 Eliz. I.
74 e.g. ibid. 283/5, ct. bk. 1586–98, view 24 Mar. 32 Eliz. I.
75 Ibid. 283/6, bk. B, lease, Hertford to Poore, 1595.
76 Alnwick Castle Mun. X.II.11, box 6, survey, 1634, p. 228.
77 W.R.O. 283/38, leases, Bruce to Andrews, 1714; Queensberry to Andrews, 1748; 944/1–2; below, trade and ind.
78 Wilts. Cuttings, xxvi. 33.
79 W.R.O. 377/2, payments, 1778–81.
80 Ibid. 490/1116.
81 P.R.O., CP 40/273, rot. 30d.
82 *Antrobus D.* (W.R.S. iii), p. 19.
83 Ibid. pp. 109–11; Alnwick Castle Mun. X.II.11, box 6, survey, 1634, p. 183.
84 *Wilts. Inq. p.m. 1242–1326* (Index Libr.), 385; W.R.O. 944/1–2; cf. above, manors (Countess Ct.).
85 P.R.O., DL 43/9/25; W.R.O. 130/49A, deed, Leighton to Smith, 1602.
86 *Andrews and Dury, Map* (W.R.S. viii), pl. 5.
87 *Wilts. Inq. p.m. 1327–77* (Index Libr.), 111.
88 W.R.O. 130/49A, deed, Leighton to Smith, 1602.
89 Ibid. 283/61, deeds, Clutterbuck to Gale, 1658; Gale to Wadman, 1660.
90 Ibid. 283/6, ct. papers 1676–80, ct. 17 May 1677.
91 Ibid. 1619, box 4, abstr. of title.

1915. The mill, separate from the house and apparently 18th-century, was raised to four storeys in the 19th century: it was for grinding corn, was driven by an undershot wheel, and housed three pairs of stones.[92] Between 1922 and 1948 it was used to generate electricity,[93] and was later converted for residence. A small mill house, apparently of the 18th century, survives.

MARKETS. A Thursday market was granted in 1219 and 1252 to the lord of Amesbury manor,[94] a Saturday market in 1317 to Amesbury priory,[95] and a Wednesday market in 1614 to the lord of the Earldom and Priory manors,[96] but it is unlikely that Amesbury ever had more than one weekly market. It was evidently a general market for food and agricultural produce: corn may have been marketed in 1301[97] and wine may have been in 1471,[98] and there were shambles in the 14th and 15th centuries.[99] Market sessions are known to have been held in 1607.[1] In 1635 there was a weekly market on Fridays;[2] the market house stood at the west end of the market place.[3]

Amesbury's market may never have been important, and in the late 17th century was described as inconsiderable and an occasion primarily for consuming the fish called loach.[4] It continued to be held on Fridays,[5] and in 1759 the market house was repaired and there were still shambles.[6] The market house was taken down in 1809.[7] By then the market may have been no more than nominal:[8] it was not revived.

FAIRS. A three-day fair at the feast of St. Melor, one of the patron saints of the church, was granted in 1252 to the lord of Amesbury manor, and a similar fair at the same feast, but not over the same three days, was granted in 1317 to Amesbury priory.[9] The second grant may indicate that the first grant had been ineffective or that the fair had lapsed, but it is more likely that the fair was in 1317 being held within, or was to be transferred to, the priory precinct, where it was evidently held later. St. Melor's day was 1 October, but the fair was probably held on and about the feast of St. John before the Latin Gate (6 May), when St. Melor was venerated again.[10] At the Dissolution a fair on St.

John's day was held by Amesbury priory,[11] almost certainly within its precinct. In the 1590s Edward, earl of Hertford, to whom the priory's right to hold the fair had passed, sought a new fairground away from the 'priory garden or abbey or priory green', and in 1607 leased the bailiwick of the fair on condition that the fair was held in the streets of the town: the old fairground was probably between the site of the priory, where Lord Hertford lived from c. 1600,[12] and High Street.

Two new fairs, to be held on 11 June and 23 December, were granted to Lord Hertford in 1614.[13] The three, the May fair, the Long fair, and the Short fair, continued until the 19th century; they were held in the streets, and seem to have been mainly for trade in livestock, especially horses and sheep.[14] After 1752 the May fair was held on 17 May, the Long fair on 22 or 23 June; the Short fair was held on 17 December from 1760, later on the first Wednesday after 12 December.[15] In 1830 the fairs were for trade in cattle and horses, in 1842 were said to be poorly attended,[16] and by 1888 had been discontinued.[17]

In 1680 a fair at Stonehenge on 25 and 26 September was granted to the lord of West Amesbury manor, despite an objection that it would harm the fair at Weyhill (Hants),[18] and in 1683 a fair on Countess Court downs and fields, also on 25 and 26 September, was granted to the lord of Countess Court manor:[19] it is unlikely that two fairs were held, and the second grant was presumably needed because the Stonehenge fairground was partly on Countess Court down. From 1752 the fair, on Countess Court down near Stonehenge, was held on 6 and 7 October.[20] It was presumably for sheep. It may have been held in the later 18th century[21] but apparently not thereafter.

TRADE AND INDUSTRY. It has been suggested that Amesbury priory had a tile factory at Amesbury in the 13th century.[22] In the mid and later 17th century clay pipes for smoking tobacco were made at Amesbury, and the Amesbury pipes were thought to be the best available. They were made by the Gauntlet family from clay dug on the downs of Chitterne St. Mary, were marked with the outline of a right-hand

92 W.R.O. 283/217; 776/6.
93 Above, intro. (public services).
94 Rot. Litt. Claus. (Rec. Com.), i. 392; Cal. Chart. R. 1226–57, 413.
95 Cal. Chart. R. 1300–26, 333.
96 Antrobus D. (W.R.S. iii), p. 119.
97 Cal. Inq. p.m. iv, p. 341.
98 Cal. Inq. p.m. Hen. VII, i, p. 394.
99 P.R.O., DL 43/9/25; ibid. SC 6/Hen. VII/975.
1 Early-Stuart Tradesmen (W.R.S. xv), pp. 6–7.
2 Alnwick Castle Mun. X.II.11, box 6, survey, 1634, p. 175.   3 Above, intro. (the town to c. 1540).
4 W.A.M. lii. 14.
5 T. Cox, Magna Brit. vi (1731), 56.
6 W.R.O. 283/168, 1759–60, ff. 11–12.
7 Ibid. 377/1, letter received 6 Mar. 1809; Wilts. Cuttings, vii. 225.
8 Pigot, Nat. Com. Dir. (1830), 790; Lewis, Topog. Dict. Eng. (1831), i. 36; H. Browne, Stonehenge and Abury (1823), 60.   9 Cal. Chart. R. 1226–57, 413; 1300–26, 333.

10 Antrobus D. (W.R.S. iii), p. xxx.
11 P.R.O., SC 6/Hen. VIII/3986, rot. 74d.
12 Hist. MSS. Com. 43, 15th Rep. VII, Ailesbury, p. 155; Antrobus D. (W.R.S. iii), pp. 80–3; above, manors (Priory).
13 Antrobus D. (W.R.S. iii), p. 119.
14 W.A.M. lii. 14; Poverty in Salisbury (W.R.S. xxxi), p. 121; Chandler and Goodhugh, Amesbury, 39; for the names, W.R.O. 283/168, 1759–60, ff. 10–11, 26.
15 Univ. Brit. Dir. ii (1793), 37; W.R.O. 283/168, 1759–60, ff. 10–11, 26, 28.
16 Pigot, Nat. Com. Dir. (1830), 790; (1842), 2.
17 Rep. Com. Mkt. Rights and Tolls [C. 5550], p. 213, H.C. (1888), liii.
18 Cal. S.P. Dom. 1679–80, 540, 573.
19 P.R.O., C 66/3234, no. 13.
20 Wilts. Cuttings, xxiv. 54.
21 Univ. Brit. Dir. ii (1793), 37.
22 W.A.M. xlvii. 367, 374; V.C.H. Wilts. iii. 245, 257. The suggestion depends on translating 'rogus' as 'kiln': cf. Close R. 1231–4, 46.

gauntlet, and had evidently become renowned nationally by 1651, when William Russell, earl of Bedford, bought a gross from Hugh Gauntlet at the Swan in High Street.[23] Gauntlet was succeeded as lessee of the Swan by William Gauntlet after 1675.[24] Gabriel Bailey, who may have acquired the Gauntlets' business, was a pipe maker at Amesbury in 1698;[25] no evidence that the industry flourished at Amesbury thereafter has been found.

Apart from its pipe making, Amesbury was not known for manufacturing, and until the 20th century its trade and industry was small-scale and mostly to satisfy local needs. As a small market town, on a main road and frequented by visitors to Stonehenge, innkeeping may for long have been its most prosperous trade.[26] A malthouse incorporating an oast house was to be built on Earl's farm in 1600,[27] there were two malthouses in High Street and one in Smithfield Street in the earlier 18th century,[28] there were still three malthouses in 1800,[29] and malting continued to the later 19th century.[30] A tanner was working in the town in 1426,[31] a currier in 1684.[32] Probably between 1698 and 1714 West Mill was converted to a tannery for Richard Andrews;[33] c. 1735 the tanyard incorporated a kiln for drying bark.[34] The tannery was evidently closed in 1761, when the mill was damaged by fire.[35] Tan pits, presumably elsewhere, were referred to in 1800.[36] A lime kiln at Southmill Hill was pulled down in 1761,[37] and lime pits were made in the former tanyard;[38] there was a lime kiln in Back Lane in 1845.[39] There was a tailor at Amesbury in 1364[40] and in the 16th century,[41] a clothworker in the 17th century,[42] shoemakers in the 17th and 18th,[43] a chandler in 1612[44] and c. 1735,[45] a soap boiler in 1755[46] and the 1790s. Members of the Hunt family made clocks and watches from the 1790s[47] or earlier to 1855 or later, James Abrahams in 1859.[48] A winnowing machine called the Amesbury heaver was invented by John Trowbridge (d. 1823) of Amesbury.[49] In the late 18th century and the 19th there were many tradesmen at Amesbury, 40–50 in the 1790s, c. 40 in 1865, c. 35 in 1898: most businesses were connected with food and drink, footwear and clothing, building, and equipment for agriculture. In the later 19th

century Thomas Sandell was a breeches maker, wholesale glover, tanner, and woolstapler.[50]

From c. 1900 many inhabitants of Amesbury were employed in the army camps at Bulford and Larkhill and at Boscombe Down,[51] and as the town grew many were engaged in the retail, motor, service, and building trades.[52] In the later 20th century c. 14 a. bounded by Porton Road, London Road, and the course of the railway were set aside for industry[53] and by 1993 had been built on. Chaplin & Co., goods agents of the London & South Western Railway, had premises in Amesbury, presumably from 1902, and had built a warehouse in Salisbury Road by 1923.[54] Chaplin & Co. was bought in the 1930s by the owners of Pickfords Ltd.:[55] the warehouse was used by Pickfords as a furniture depository until 1990, and was demolished in 1993. In 1990 Pickfords opened a warehouse on the new industrial land.[56] A warehouse for the NAAFI was built beside the London road east of the station in 1940; it was extended in 1970 and, to 211,000 square ft., in 1977. New offices were built in 1991–2, and in 1992 the NAAFI headquarters was moved to Amesbury. In 1992 at Amesbury the NAAFI had 170 employees in its warehouse, 330 in its offices.[57] Amesbury Transport Ltd. moved from Salisbury Street to London Road in the later 1950s, and soon after 1963 a new warehouse was built for it on the site of the station; other buildings nearby in London Road were built or converted for the company, which specialized in road haulage, warehousing, and distribution and in 1992 had 48 employees.[58] The Stonehenge Woollen Industry, a small company which was started at Lake House in Wilsford in an attempt to prevent rural depopulation, made cloth from local wool in Amesbury in the 1920s[59] and until 1932: its premises were behind houses on the south-east side of High Street.[60] Other companies to occupy premises on the new industrial land were Ross Group plc, makers of car alarms, and Haymills (Contractors) Ltd. The site of Stockport farmstead south of the town was used for industry in the late 20th century. In 1993 a meat-processing company, a company dealing in flooring materials wholesale, and a small engineering company had premises there.

[23] Aubrey, *Nat. Hist. Wilts.* ed. Britton, 35, 95; *V.C.H. Wilts.* iv. 242–3; *W.A.M.* lxv. 179–80, 185; W.R.O. 947/1456; for the Swan, cf. W.R.O. 283/6, survey, c. 1741.
[24] W.R.O. 283/24, f. 1.
[25] *V.C.H. Wilts.* iv. 243.
[26] Above, intro. (roads; Stonehenge; inns); mkts.
[27] *Antrobus D.* (W.R.S. iii), pp. 70–2.
[28] W.R.O. 283/6, survey, c. 1741.
[29] Ibid. 212B/89.
[30] *Early Trade Dirs.* (W.R.S. xlvii), 10–11, 102; *Kelly's Dir. Wilts.* (1848 and later edns.).
[31] *V.C.H. Wilts.* iv. 235.
[32] *W.N. & Q.* vii. 408.
[33] W.R.O. 283/24, ff. 2, 5.
[34] Ibid. 283/6, survey, c. 1741.
[35] Wilts. Cuttings, xxvi. 33; cf. W.R.O. 377/2, rent r. 1780–1.   [36] W.R.O. 212B/89.
[37] Ibid. 283/168, 1761, f. 18.
[38] Ibid. 283/168, 1771, f. 16.
[39] Ibid. tithe award.
[40] P.R.O., DL 43/9/25.
[41] *W.A.M.* xlv. 49.
[42] *Early-Stuart Tradesmen* (W.R.S. xv), p. 14.

[43] *Wilts. Apprentices* (W.R.S. xvii), pp. 10, 172; W.R.O. 283/132, lease, Hayward to Blake, 1686.
[44] *Antrobus D.* (W.R.S. iii), p. 92.
[45] W.R.O. 283/6, survey, c. 1741.
[46] *Wilts. Apprentices* (W.R.S. xvii), p. 147.
[47] *Early Trade Dirs.* (W.R.S. xlvii), 11.
[48] Ibid. 63, 102; *Kelly's Dir. Wilts.* (1848 and later edns.).
[49] *V.C.H. Wilts.* iv. 85.
[50] *Early Trade Dirs.* (W.R.S. xlvii), 10–11, 63, 102; *Kelly's Dir. Wilts.* (1848 and later edns.); *Harrod's Dir. Wilts.* (1865).
[51] e.g. W.R.O., G 1/132/105.
[52] e.g. *Kelly's Dir. Sar.* (1959).
[53] W.R.O., G 1/132/105.
[54] Ibid. G 1/500/1; *Kelly's Dir. Wilts.* (1903 and later edns.); O.S. Map 1/2,500, Wilts. LIV. 16 (1924 edn.); above, intro. (railways).
[55] G. L. Turnbull, *Traffic and Transport*, 171, 176.
[56] Inf. from Messrs. Pickfords, Porton Road.
[57] Inf. from Public Relations Off., NAAFI, Lond. Road.
[58] *Kelly's Dir. Sar.* (1953 and later edns.); ICC Inf. Group, *Regional Company Surv. Wilts.* (1993), 10.
[59] *V.C.H. Wilts.* vi. 219.   [60] W.R.O. 1821/37.

LOCAL GOVERNMENT. AMESBURY. In the Middle Ages Amesbury was sometimes called a borough[61] and had what was called a guildhall,[62] and in the mid 16th century the lord of the hundred, who was also lord of Amesbury manor, allowed an officer called the bailiff of the borough to attend some meetings of the hundred court,[63] but the town never had an institution for self government.

There is some evidence that there were two tithings in the 12th century.[64] Later in the Middle Ages the lord of Amesbury manor took view of frankpledge at Amesbury and held a manor court,[65] as did Amesbury priory.[66] In 1486–7, 1501–2, 1506–7, and 1511–12 on Amesbury manor the view was held twice a year, in October and April, and the manor court seven times a year. In 1503–4 and 1504–5 the manor court was said to have been held 17 times a year, either because it was or, as in legal principle it was a three-weekly court, it should have been. In 1535–6 the view was held twice, the manor court five times.[67] At the Dissolution Amesbury priory held its view and its manor court twice a year;[68] the Crown held the courts at the same frequency in 1539–40.[69]

From the mid 16th century such views and courts continued to be held separately for the Earldom and Priory manors, although the manors were in the same hands.[70] The boundaries of the manors, and presumably the jurisdiction of the courts, were defined in 1635–6: the Priory manor included the site of the priory, the north-west side of High Street, the south side of the market place, the west side of Frog Lane, and, it was claimed, West Amesbury; the Earldom manor included the rest of the town and parish except Ratfyn, the lord having claimed jurisdiction over Countess Court manor from 1580 or earlier. The guildhall or market house, in the middle of the entrance to the market place from High Street, stood on the boundary;[71] the courts of each manor were presumably held in its first-floor room from when it was built, as they were until it was taken down in 1809.[72] The records of the view (sometimes called the law court, sometimes the court leet) and the manor court (otherwise the court baron) of each manor survive from 1566 to 1771, with gaps. In the 16th and 17th centuries the views continued to be held twice a year, in spring and autumn; in

the 18th they were held yearly in autumn. They were held on the same day as each other, each in conjunction with a manor court; the records show that at each matters under leet jurisdiction were sometimes presented by an officer or officers and sometimes by a jury, but that more often a jury and the homage combined made a single body of presentments under the articles of both leet and manorial jurisdiction. Many of Amesbury's affairs were dealt with in the views and courts, and it is possible that twice a year a single assembly met to discuss them, and that only for the written record were its proceedings classified into those of two views and two manor courts.

To keep order the town had two constables, one each for the Earldom and the Priory manors, and four bailiffs, two to assist each constable. All were appointed by the courts, although from the later 17th century the constable nominated his bailiffs.[73] When officers made presentments at a view it was usually the bailiffs. By 1727 each constable had been armed with a watch bill,[74] one of which, of 1731 or earlier, was in Salisbury museum in 1936.[75] New stocks were made c. 1579,[76] and from 1660 orders were made for a pillory and a cuckingstool to be kept.[77]

Especially in the 16th and 17th centuries a wide range of offences was dealt with. Some offences were statutory, including playing unlawful games,[78] fishing with a net of a mesh smaller than 2½ in., not wearing a woollen cap on Sundays, not keeping a rook net,[79] not practising archery,[80] harbouring lodgers,[81] keeping greyhounds and beagles when holding land worth less than 40s., owning a fowling piece when holding land worth less than £100,[82] and failing to keep watch: for the last the statute of Winchester was invoked in 1581.[83] Some matters were the traditional business of the view, including assault, affray, reports that the hue had been raised or a felony committed, and the swearing of the oath of allegiance: one felony reported was the suicide of Sir George Rodney.[84] The assizes of bread and of ale were enforced, and in the 16th century and earlier 17th, when Amesbury had several inns and alehouses and held a market and fairs,[85] trade in food and drink was scrutinized generally. Bakers, brewers, wine sellers, innkeepers, alehouse keepers, butchers, and

61 P.R.O., SC 6/Hen. VII/975.
62 Ibid. SC 6/Hen. VIII/3986, rot. 73d.; for guildhall, mkt. ho., town hall, above, intro. (the town to c. 1540; the town c. 1540 to c. 1900).
63 W.R.O. 283/2, bk. M; above, Amesbury hund.
64 Pipe R. 1198 (P.R.S. N.S. ix), 73.
65 P.R.O., DL 43/9/25.
66 Valor Eccl. (Rec. Com.), ii. 93.
67 P.R.O., SC 6/Hen. VII/975; SC 6/Hen. VII/1364; SC 6/Hen. VII/1366–7; SC 6/Hen. VII/1369; SC 6/Hen. VIII/7022; SC 6/Hen. VIII/3841.
68 Valor Eccl. (Rec. Com.), ii. 93.
69 P.R.O., SC 6/Hen. VIII/3986, rot. 75.
70 This and the 5 following paras. based on W.R.O. 192/24A–B; 283/4, ct. bks. 1581–96; 1583–90; 1599–1611; 1599–1612; 1612–14; 1658–60; 283/5, ct. bks. 1581–2; 1586–96; 1586–98; 1599–1611; 1599–1614; 283/6, view 1576; ct. papers 1676–80; bk. O; 283/7; 283/14–15.
71 Ibid. 283/7; 944/1; Alnwick Castle Mun. X.II.11, box 6, survey, 1634, pp. 169–70, 183.

72 Wilts. Cuttings, vii. 225.
73 e.g. W.R.O. 283/4, ct. bk. 1658–60, ct. 16 Sept. 1659.
74 Ibid. 283/14, at p. 24.   75 W.A.M. xlvii. 526–7.
76 W.R.O. 283/7, views 20 Mar. 21 Eliz. I.
77 Ibid. 283/4, ct. bk. 1658–60, ct. 11 Apr. 1660; 283/6, ct. papers 1676–80, view 22 Apr. 1676; for the lock-up, above, intro. (public services).
78 W.R.O. 283/6, bk. O, ct. 2 Apr. 1566.
79 Ibid. 283/7, views 20 Mar. 21 Eliz. I; 20 Oct. 21 Eliz. I; 8 Oct. 24 Eliz. I.
80 Ibid. 283/5, ct. bk. 1586–98, view 20 Sept. 35 Eliz. I.
81 Ibid. 283/5, ct. bk. 1586–96, view 1 Mar. 1592.
82 Ibid. 283/4, ct. bk. 1583–90, views 12 Oct. 28 Eliz. I; 12 Mar. 31 Eliz. I.
83 Ibid. 283/4, ct. bk. 1581–96, view 18 Oct. 23 Eliz. I.
84 Ibid. 283/4, ct. bks. 1581–96, view 1 Mar. 24 Eliz. I; 1583–90, view 7 Sept. 32 Eliz. I; 283/5, ct. bks. 1586–96, view 18 Oct. 23 Eliz. I; 1586–98, view 28 Sept. 31 Eliz. I; 1599–1611, view 7 Oct. 1601; 283/7, view 20 Mar. 21 Eliz. I.
85 Above, intro. (inns); mkts.; fairs.

millers all came before the courts[86] either to pay a fine equivalent to a licence to trade or for misconduct. In 1580 an innkeeper allowed strangers to frequent his inn at prohibited times and the Earldom constable was authorized to weigh bread once a month or more often.[87] In 1588 the Priory constable was ordered to weigh bread once a week.[88] Overcharging and the use of unsealed measures were frequently punished. In 1603 innkeepers were required to show their sealed measures in court.[89] In 1614 an inspector of ale sold in the market was appointed.[90] From the mid 17th century, however, the assizes were enforced little in the courts, although the constables were still required to keep weights and pint and quart measures.[91] The measures were destroyed in the fire of 1751 and replaced c. 1759.[92]

Either under leet jurisdiction or as manorial business the courts dealt with many public nuisances. Orders to repair bridges, to make chimneys safe, and to maintain watercourses were frequent. In 1579 it was ordered that the inhabitants of West Amesbury should repair one arch of West bridge, those of the Priory manor the rest of it;[93] in 1582 the inhabitants of the Earldom manor were required to contribute.[94] In 1590 a rate was imposed for the repair of Grey bridge.[95] In 1580, presumably to lessen the risk of fire, baking bread after 8 p.m. was forbidden,[96] and in 1658 the churchwardens and overseers of the parish were ordered to repair two dangerous chimneys[97] presumably because the owner was too poor to do so. In 1596 it was ordered that the customary fall of the Avon, which had been altered by the construction of a bay, should be restored,[98] and unlawful fishing, in 1599 with angling rods,[99] was often reported. Orders were made to make safe or mend roads;[1] waymen were in office in 1592,[2] surveyors of highways in 1658.[3] In 1614 a committee of seven, including the two constables, was appointed to clear the streets of timber and other rubbish, to direct the cleaning of watercourses, and to check the safety of chimneys and fireplaces.[4] Firecrooks were kept in 1677.[5]

From the 16th century to the 18th normal tenurial business was transacted in the court of each manor, sometimes in courts not held in conjunction with the view: the death of tenants was presented, surrenders of and admissions to copyholds were performed or reported, and

unlicensed undertenants were presented. A few pleas of trespass or debt were heard.[6] Excluding West Amesbury, the Priory manor contained little agricultural land,[7] and the most frequent presentments of its homage were related to the dilapidation of buildings in the town: the condition of West Mill was of frequent concern.[8] Presentments that agrarian custom had been defined, refined, or infringed were normally recorded as those of the homage of the Earldom manor, and were sometimes made by the hayward.[9] Disputed or uncertain boundaries, use of common pastures, maintenance of common flocks and herds, and encroachment on common land or the land of neighbours were all presented, the dispute with the men of Boscombe over Blackcross down being the subject of several presentments. It was normal for the court to hear that stray animals had been caught, that the pound needed repair, that geese, ganders, and unringed pigs had been at large, and that hedges had not been made.[10] The court of each manor appointed an agrarian watchman ('agrophilax') in the later 17th century.[11]

In the 17th century the presentment of statutory offences, the old offences of the view, and offences under the assizes became less frequent, the presentment of public nuisances and agrarian matters more so. In the 18th the courts' business declined in amount and narrowed in range. Copyhold business continued to be done and officers appointed, orders were made to amend public nuisances, to maintain buildings and make chimneys safe, and agrarian custom was defended, but from c. 1750 most presentment was stereotyped and the courts were of little importance in local government. The last was held in 1854.[12]

WEST AMESBURY. In the 16th century and later West Amesbury was said to be a single tithing with Wilsford, although Wilsford was in Underditch hundred and was not a neighbour of West Amesbury;[13] West Amesbury's partner was not Wilsford but Normanton,[14] with which it had an administrative link in 1377, and which lies between West Amesbury and Wilsford and was in Durnford parish and Amesbury hundred.[15] The tithingman of the tithing called West Amesbury and Wilsford attended Amesbury hundred court.[16] The lord of the Priory manor evidently claimed jurisdiction over West Amesbury;[17] the

86 e.g. W.R.O. 283/6, bk. O, cts. 2 Apr. 1566.
87 Ibid. 283/7, views 13 Apr. 22 Eliz. I; 12 Oct. 1580.
88 Ibid. 283/5, ct. bk. 1586–98, view 3 Sept. 30 Eliz. I.
89 Ibid. 283/5, ct. bk. 1599–1611, view 3 May 1603.
90 Ibid. 283/5, ct. bk. 1599–1614, ct. 7 Oct. 1614.
91 e.g. ibid. 283/14, p. 101.
92 Ibid. 283/15, ct. 21 Oct. 1751; W.A.M. xlvii. 524; above, intro. (the town c. 1540 to c. 1900).
93 W.R.O. 283/7, view 20 Oct. 21 Eliz. I.
94 Ibid. 283/5, ct. bk. 1581–2, view 21 Mar. 24 Eliz. I.
95 Ibid. 283/4, ct. bk. 1583–90, view 7 Sept. 32 Eliz. I.
96 Ibid. 283/7, view 12 Oct. 22 Eliz. I.
97 Ibid. 283/4, ct. bk. 1658–60, ct. 14 Sept. 1658.
98 Ibid. 283/5, ct. bk. 1586–98, view 15 Apr. 38 Eliz. I.
99 Ibid. 283/4, ct. bk. 1599–1612, ct. 1 May 1599.
1 e.g. ibid. 283/5, ct. bk. 1586–96, view 5 Oct. 28 Eliz. I.
2 Ibid. 283/5, ct. bk. 1586–98, view 11 Sept. 1592.
3 Ibid. 283/4, ct. bk. 1658–60, ct. 14 Sept. 1658.
4 Ibid. 283/5, ct. bk. 1599–1614, ct. 7 Oct. 1614.
5 Ibid. 283/6, ct. papers 1676–80, view 10 Oct. 1677; for

the Amesbury fire engine, above, intro. (public services).
6 For pleas, W.R.O. 283/5, ct. bk. 1586–96, views 12 Sept. 1592; 4 Apr. 1593. 7 Above, agric. (Amesbury).
8 Ibid. mills; W.R.O. 283/5, ct. bk. 1581–2, view 21 Mar. 24 Eliz. I; 283/7, view 8 Oct. 24 Eliz. I.
9 For the hayward, e.g. W.R.O. 283/7, view 20 Mar. 21 Eliz. I.
10 e.g. ibid. 283/4, ct. bks. 1581–96, views 18 Oct. 23 Eliz. I; 2 Oct. 24 Eliz. I; 11 Sept. 1592; 24 Apr. 1593; 1583–90, view 7 Sept. 32 Eliz. I; 283/5, ct. bk. 1586–96, views 12 Sept. 1592; 2 Oct. 1595; 283/6, bk. O, view 16 Dec. 1566; 283/7, ct. 15 Mar. 28 Eliz. I.
11 Ibid. 283/6, ct. papers 1676–80, views 10 Oct. 1677.
12 Kemm, Amesbury Church and Abbey, 25.
13 V.C.H. Wilts. vi. 213–21; Longleat Mun., Seymour papers, xii, f. 256v.
14 W.R.O. 283/2, ct. bk. 1585–98, view 14 Mar. 28 Eliz. I.
15 V.C.H. Wilts. iv. 306; above, Amesbury hund.
16 W.R.O. 283/2, ct. bk. 1547–58, ct. 29 Oct. 3 & 4 Phil. and Mary. 17 Above, this section (Amesbury).

view of that manor ordered the inhabitants of West Amesbury to choose a tithingman for West Amesbury and Wilsford tithing in 1584,[18] itself presented a man to be the tithingman in 1587,[19] and chose a tithingman in 1599,[20] but the tithingman did not present at Amesbury courts and no West Amesbury business was done in them.[21]

Records of a court of West Amesbury manor exist for a few years in the period 1491–1645. The homage presented and the court transacted tenurial and agrarian business, dealing in the 1490s with the overstocking of common pasture with sheep, in the 1550s with the unsatisfactory condition of a hedge, and in 1645 with the arrangements for feeding cattle in common. The manor had few tenants, there was little copyhold business to be done,[22] and it is likely that few courts were held after 1645.

The parish spent £205 on poor relief in 1775–6, an average of £214 in the three years 1782–5. It had no workhouse and all relief was outdoor. The poor-rate was average for the hundred in 1802–3 when £845 was spent, only £7 of it on materials to be used in employment: 60 adults and 83 children were relieved regularly, 49 people occasionally; a further 52 who were relieved were not parishioners and were presumably travellers.[23] Expenditure is known to have exceeded £1,000 in only four years: in 1812–13, when it was £1,211, 118 adults were relieved regularly, 11 occasionally. It reached a peak of £1,310 in 1817–18, in the 1820s averaged £750,[24] and was £585 in 1834–5. The parish became part of Amesbury poor-law union in 1835,[25] of Salisbury district in 1974.[26]

CHURCHES. There was a church at Amesbury from when the abbey was founded c. 979,[27] and perhaps from before then. It is possible that St. Mary was invoked in the abbey church from its foundation and that St. Melor later became co-patron when some of his relics were brought to it.[28] The church is almost certain to have been the only one at Amesbury and to have been open to all inhabitants. When the abbey was dissolved in 1177 the church of St. Mary and St. Melor, evidently the abbey church, was granted to Amesbury priory.[29] A new priory church was

built between then and 1186,[30] and the old church apparently remained in use as the parish church.[31] Later the brethren of the priory had what is likely to have been a third church at Amesbury.[32] The parish church was served by chaplains, after the Reformation by curates: the right to appoint them belonged to the owners of the great tithes and was exercised by Amesbury priory until the Dissolution,[33] by the lessees of the Rectory estate from the mid 16th century to 1630, and by St. George's chapel, Windsor, from 1630.[34] From 1757, after the endowment of the curacy, the curates were presented to the bishop for institution.[35] Under the Incumbents Act of 1868 the living became a vicarage, which remains in the gift of St. George's chapel.[36]

Neither chaplains, curates, nor vicars were well remunerated. At the Dissolution the chaplain's stipend was £8:[37] from 1541 it was a charge on the Rectory estate,[38] and it had been increased to £15 by 1612, £20 by 1623, and £40 by 1660. From 1612 a house on the Rectory estate was reserved for use by the curate, and from 1630 St. George's chapel allowed him to take the oblations and some small tithes.[39] The tithes were later replaced by a modus of 6d. for each cow and each calf kept in the parish.[40] The living was augmented by the state in the Interregnum,[41] and six times in the period 1730–1829. Queen Anne's Bounty gave 8 a. in Hungerford (Berks.) in 1808 and met benefactions in 1730 and 1829, money was granted by parliament in 1814 by lot and in 1824 to meet benefactions,[42] and Susanna Bundy (d. 1828) gave by will the income from £500;[43] at £141, however, the curate's income remained low c. 1830.[44] The modus was commuted to a rent charge of £1 in 1847.[45] The Ecclesiastical Commissioners augmented the vicarage in 1880 and 1881,[46] and in 1881 the capital of Bundy's charity was spent on a new vicarage house.[47] The 8 a. given in 1808 were sold in 1919.[48] The curate had no glebe in Amesbury apart from his house, which stood very near the north-east corner of the church.[49] A house apparently of the mid or later 16th century[50] was enlarged in 1824 and 1859.[51] It was demolished when Wyndersham House on the south-east side of Church Street, formerly a school and later the Antrobus Arms, was bought as the vicarage house in 1881.[52] In 1916–17 that house was sold and a new one was built a little

[18] W.R.O. 283/7, view 9 Oct. 26 Eliz. I.
[19] Ibid. 283/5, ct. bk. 1586–98, view 28 Mar. 29 Eliz. I.
[20] Ibid. ct. bk. 1599–1611, view 1 May 1599.
[21] Inf. based on sources cited above, p. 48, n. 70.
[22] W.R.O. 283/8.   [23] Poor Law Abstract, 1804, 558–9.
[24] Ibid. 1818, 492–3; Poor Rate Returns, 1816–21; 185; 1822–4, 225; 1825–9, 215.
[25] Poor Law Com. 2nd Rep. App. D, 558; App. E, 398–9.
[26] O.S. Map 1/100,000, admin. areas, Wilts. (1974 edn.).
[27] Above, intro. (the town to c. 1540); for the hist. of Amesbury abbey and priory, V.C.H. Wilts. iii. 242–59.
[28] V.C.H. Wilts. iii. 242–3; for St. Melor, A. H. Diverres, 'St. Melor', Amesbury Millennium Lectures, ed. J. H. Chandler, 9–19.   [29] Cal. Chart. R. 1257–1300, 157–9.
[30] V.C.H. Wilts. iii. 244.
[31] The present church was standing in the earlier 12th cent.: below, this section [architecture].
[32] V.C.H. Wilts. iii. 246.   [33] P.R.O., E 305/4/C 18.
[34] D. & C. Windsor Mun. XV. 39. 18–28, 39–41; ibid. CC 120349.
[35] Phillipps, Wilts. Inst. ii. 77, 99, 106.

[36] 31 & 32 Vic. c. 117; Crockford (1896 and later edns.).
[37] P.R.O., E 326/12413.
[38] L. & P. Hen. VIII, xvi, pp. 380–1.
[39] D. & C. Windsor Mun. XV. 39. 20–4.
[40] W.A.M. xl. 268; W.R.O., tithe award.
[41] W. A. Shaw, Hist. Eng. Church, ii. 548; W.A.M. xl. 258.
[42] C. Hodgson, Queen Anne's Bounty (1864), p. cccxxxv; for the land, W.R.O. 2357, misc. papers.
[43] Endowed Char. Wilts. (S. Div.), 33; W.R.O., Ch. Com., bishop, 58.
[44] Rep. Com. Eccl. Revenues, 822–3.
[45] W.R.O., tithe award.
[46] Lond. Gaz. 21 Jan. 1881, p. 296; 5 May 1882, pp. 2081–2.
[47] Endowed Char. Wilts. (S. Div.), 33; below, this section.
[48] W.R.O. 2357, misc. papers.   [49] Ibid. tithe award.
[50] Chandler and Goodhugh, Amesbury, 91.
[51] W.R.O., D 1/11/43; D 1/11/140; cf. Chandler and Goodhugh, Amesbury, 115.
[52] Ch. Com. file 52126/2; above, intro. (the town c. 1540 to c. 1900); below, educ.

east of the church.[53] That in turn was sold in 1992, when a new vicarage house was built in its garden.[54]

Three lights and an obit in the church were endowed in the Middle Ages.[55] A Bible was bought in 1539–40.[56] In 1553, when Stephen Lyons was curate, no sermon had been preached for a year,[57] and in the 1580s quarterly sermons were not preached.[58] The curate, Uriah Banks, signed the *Concurrent Testimony* in 1648[59] and preached twice every Sunday in 1650.[60] In 1662, when Thomas Holland was curate, many parishioners were consistently absent from church, and the church had no Book of Homilies and no copy of Jewell's *Apology*.[61] Holland, said to be a good scholar and a painful preacher, was curate 1660–80, and his son Thomas, who in 1716 sought a patent for a water-raising device for use in agriculture and industry, was curate 1680–1730.[62] In 1783 the curate, Henry Richards, did not reside. His deputy, also curate of Allington, held two services every Sunday and services on Christmas day, Good Friday, and fast and thanksgiving days; he celebrated communion thrice a year with *c*. 25 communicants and catechized once or twice in Lent.[63] F. W. Fowle, curate 1817–68, vicar 1868–76, was also rector of Allington but lived at Amesbury. He too held services every Sunday, and on Census Sunday in 1851 had a congregation, excluding schoolchildren, of 194 in the morning and of 323 in the afternoon. Before the church was restored in 1852–3 he complained that it had too little accommodation for the poor. In 1864 he preached only at the afternoon services on Sundays. Morning services were also held on Wednesdays, Fridays, and saints' days but, except in Lent, were poorly attended; additional services were held on Christmas day and Good Friday. Communion, then with *c*. 70 communicants, was celebrated monthly and at Christmas, Easter, and Whitsun.[64]

A chapel, with an altar dedicated to All Saints, stood at Ratfyn in the early 15th century. Amesbury priory was responsible for providing a chaplain to hold services every Sunday, Wednesday, and Friday; the inhabitants of Ratfyn had all rights in their chapel except baptism and burial. A silver-gilt chalice was among the chapel's goods. In 1412 the priory was providing too few services and the inhabitants were neglecting the building.[65] A remark by William Cobbett in 1826 that its porch would accommodate all the inhabitants suggests that the chapel was standing then.[66] Cobbett's remark deserves little credence, and the chapel, the site of which may have been Church close a little south of

Ratfyn Farm,[67] is likely to have been demolished long before 1826.

The church of *ST. MARY AND ST. MELOR*, apparently the church of the abbey dissolved in 1177, is of rubble and ashlar, is cruciform, and has a chancel, a central tower, a north transept with east chapel, a south transept, and a clerestoried nave with south aisle.[68] The nave is of the earlier 12th century and is generally plain; east of it the crossing, transepts, and chancel were built in the early 13th century. At its north-west corner the nave is joined to the early 13th-century remains of what was evidently a gatehouse, probably a south-west gate of the priory, and a lean-to passage against the outside of the north wall of the nave apparently linked the north transept and the gatehouse. In the 13th century the north transept had two east chapels. The east part of the southern and smaller one had a door to the chancel and served as a chancel vestry: in the 14th century the chapel was demolished and the doorway replaced by a four-light window. At the same time a window of similar size was inserted at the centre of the south wall of the chancel. The south transept also had an east chapel in the 13th century. In the late 15th the chapel was rebuilt and, possibly slightly earlier, the nave aisle was built: the south wall of the chapel was aligned with that of the aisle. Also in the late 15th century much of the church was reroofed and a new east window and a new west window were inserted. In 1721, when a new doorway and two new windows were inserted in it,[69] the south wall of the south transept may have been completely rebuilt; the transept's chapel had been demolished by 1803.[70] In 1852–3 the church was restored to designs by William Butterfield, who evidently intended to remove all features later than *c*. 1400. The east window was replaced by one in 13th-century style, and a new more steeply pitched roof was made over the chancel; the tower staircase was removed from the north transept, the chapel of which was converted to a vestry, and in the angle of the chancel and the transept a new staircase and a boilerhouse were built; in the south transept the early 18th-century windows were replaced by lancets similar to the 13th-century ones in the north wall of the north transept, and the doorway was replaced by one in 13th-century style; the west wall of the nave was largely rebuilt, and the window in it was re-formed as three double lancets. Nearly all the furnishings, including a west gallery, a 15th-century rood screen, and an early 13th-century font, were removed from the church.[71] In 1905 the church was structurally restored

53 Ch. Com. file 52126/3; ibid. E 4542; W.R.O. 2357, misc. papers.　　54 Inf. from Ch. Com.; the vicar.
55 *W.N. & Q.* iii. 303 n.; *Cal. Pat.* 1580–2, p. 10.
56 P.R.O., SC 6/Hen. VIII/3986, rot. 76.
57 W.R.O., D 1/43/1, f. 108v.
58 Ibid. D 1/43/5, f. 36; D 1/43/6, f. 5B.
59 *Calamy Revised*, ed. Matthews, 557.
60 *W.A.M.* xl. 258.
61 W.R.O., D 1/54/1/3, nos. 41–2.
62 Ibid. D 1/21/5/2; Hist. MSS. Com. 58, *Bath*, iv, p. 269; *W.N. & Q.* ii. 247–8; P.R.O., SP 44/249, ff. 303–4.
63 *Vis. Queries, 1783* (W.R.S. xxvii), p. 24.
64 P.R.O., HO 129/262/2/4/5; W.R.O., D 1/21/5/2; D

1/56/7; below, this section [architecture].
65 *Chandler's Reg.* (W.R.S. xxxix), pp. 31, 63, 118–19.
66 W. Cobbett, *Rural Rides*, ed. E. W. Martin, 309.
67 W.R.O., tithe award.
68 Description based partly on J. Buckler, watercolours in W.A.S. Libr., vol. i. 3, for one of which, see below, plate facing p. 234; other illustrations and plans are in *Churches of SE. Wilts.* (R.C.H.M.), 103–7.
69 *Churches of SE. Wilts.* 103.
70 Buckler, watercolour in W.A.S. Libr., vol. i. 3.
71 *Churches of SE. Wilts.* 103–7; W.R.O. 1550/30; 1550/33; notes by W. C. Kemm (collated by P. Dyke; copy in Wilts. Libr. headquarters, Trowbridge).

under the direction of C. E. Ponting and Detmar Blow,[72] and in 1907 some of the furnishings removed in 1852–3, including the screen and the font, were replaced.[73]

In 1553 a 14-oz. chalice was left in the parish and 16 oz. of plate were taken for the king. A gilt plate was given by John Rose (d. 1677). In 1852–3 all the church plate was melted down and used in new plate consisting of two chalices of parcel gilt, a paten, a flagon, and an almsdish.[74] The parish retained all that plate in 1993.[75]

There were four bells in 1553.[76] The ring was increased to six, most likely in either 1619 or 1728, and later comprised two bells cast by John Wallis in 1619, one cast by Clement Tosier in 1713 and recast by John Warner & Sons in 1881, one cast by John Cor in 1728, one by a Cor between c. 1710 and 1740, and one by John Wells in 1801.[77] In 1905 the bells were rehung in a frame large enough for eight, and in 1946 the ring was increased to eight by two trebles cast by Taylor of Loughborough (Leics.).[78] Those eight bells hung in the church in 1993.[79]

There are registrations of baptisms 1624–40 and from 1660, of burials 1610–36 and from 1660, and of marriages 1610–39 and from 1661. In each case there are a few entries for earlier years; baptisms are lacking for 1809–10, burials for 1808–10.[80]

In 1931 a wooden church, dedicated to the *HOLY ANGELS*, was built beside Main Road to serve Boscombe Down.[81]

ROMAN CATHOLICISM.

From 1794 to 1800 an English convent of Augustinian canonesses driven from Louvain (Brabant) by the French Revolution lived in Amesbury Abbey.[82] A Roman Catholic church was opened in London Road in 1933;[83] chapels in several other parishes, including Ludgershall and Figheldean, were later served from it,[84] and a priest lived at Amesbury.[85] The church was replaced in 1985[86] by a new church of red brick.

PROTESTANT NONCONFORMITY.

Baptists lived at Amesbury in the 1650s, and a conventicle run by the Baptist chapel at Porton was held there.[87] In the 1660s and 1670s members of the Long family of West Amesbury were Baptists: in 1662 William Long and his wife Alice promised to attend church 'as soon as God

shall make them able', and in 1672 Thomas Long's house was licensed for meetings.[88] There were 10 protestant nonconformists in the parish in 1676,[89] and Thomas Long remained one in 1683.[90] A Quaker meeting house was licensed in 1719, and Independent ones in 1766, 1776, 1795, and 1815.[91]

John Wesley preached at Amesbury in 1779 and 1785,[92] and in 1806 a Methodist meeting house was licensed. A Methodist chapel had been built by 1816, and other Methodist meeting houses were licensed in 1816 and 1819. The chapel was relicensed in 1838,[93] possibly after alterations;[94] it stood behind buildings on the north-west side of High Street,[95] and on Census Sunday in 1851 congregations of 96 and 100, excluding schoolchildren, attended morning and evening service respectively.[96] In 1864 the curate of Amesbury described the Wesleyans as proselytizing and very active.[97] The chapel and its schoolroom were burnt down in 1899. A new chapel, of red brick and in middle Gothic style, was built to front the north-west side of High Street in 1900;[98] a new schoolroom was built behind it in 1931–2,[99] and a hall was built in 1961.[1] The chapel remained open in 1993.

A Primitive Methodist chapel, small and of corrugated iron, was built in Flower Lane between 1899 and 1910. It had been closed by 1922.[2]

EDUCATION.

A schoolmaster may have lived at Amesbury in the early 16th century.[3]

Rose's school was founded in 1677 by John Rose. It was to be kept 'on the south side of the parish church of Amesbury', where a school was formerly kept, presumably in the south transept. Rose gave land at Ditcheat (Som.), and provided for a master to be paid £30 a year to teach grammar, writing, and arithmetic: the pupils, up to 20 in number, were to be aged between 9 and 15, of the poorest inhabitants of Amesbury, and able to read and to recite the catechism. If income was sufficient a teacher was to be employed to prepare children for the grammar school.[4] One of the first masters, 1688–91, was the diarist Thomas Naish, subdean of Salisbury from 1694; the suggestion that one of his pupils was Joseph Addison, founder of the *Spectator*, may be invalid because Addison's father was neither poor nor resident in Amesbury.[5] Only six boys were taught in the grammar school in

72 *W.A.M.* xxxiv. 231; W.R.O., D 1/61/40/2.
73 *W.A.M.* xxxv. 502–3; Wilts. Cuttings, xvi. 28.
74 Nightingale, *Wilts. Plate*, 36–7.
75 Inf. from the vicar.   76 *W.A.M.* xii. 370.
77 Walters, *Wilts. Bells*, 13, 251, 297.
78 W.R.O. 2357, misc. papers.   79 Inf. from the vicar.
80 W.R.O. 1550/1–19; bishop's transcripts for 1622–3 and 1810 are ibid.
81 Inf. from Mr. P. S. Goodhugh, 34 Countess Road.
82 *V.C.H. Wilts.* iii. 94; *Gent. Mag.* lxvi (1), 6.
83 *Amesbury: Official Guide* (5th edn.), 14.
84 *V.C.H. Wilts.* iii. 97; xi. 150.
85 *Kelly's Dir. Wilts.* (1939).
86 *Clifton Dioc. Dir.* (1993).
87 *V.C.H. Wilts.* iii. 102–3, 112–13.
88 *Meeting Ho. Certs.* (W.R.S. xl), p. 172; W.R.O., D 1/54/1/3, nos. 41–2; D 1/54/3/2, no. 14.
89 *Compton Census*, ed. Whiteman, 124.

90 W.R.O., D 1/54/10/4, no. 47.
91 *Meeting Ho. Certs.* (W.R.S. xl), pp. 20, 28, 30–1, 43, 76.   92 Chandler and Goodhugh, *Amesbury*, 45.
93 *Meeting Ho. Certs.* (W.R.S. xl), pp. 61, 80–1, 89, 146.
94 Wilts. Cuttings, xiv. 222.
95 O.S. Map 1/2,500, Wilts. LIV. 16 (1887 edn.); cf. Chandler and Goodhugh, *Amesbury*, 126.
96 P.R.O., HO 129/262/2/4/6.
97 W.R.O., D 1/56/7.   98 Ibid. 1150/76.
99 Ibid. 1821/1; date on bldg.
1 Wilts. Cuttings, xxii. 46.
2 O.S. Maps 1/2,500, Wilts. LIV. 16 (1901, 1924 edns.); W.R.O., Inland Revenue, val. reg. 147; ibid. G 1/500/1; G 1/760/21.   3 *L. & P. Hen. VIII*, i (1), p. 213.
4 *Endowed Char. Wilts.* (S. Div.), 21–3.
5 *Naish's Diary* (W.R.S. xx), 8, 25; cf. below, Milston, intro.; church; Addison is not mentioned in a reg. of pupils 1677–90: W.R.O. 1550/38.

1818: none was of the poorest parents in the parish because, by the time they were 9 years old, most such children were already in paid employment, and children of mechanics, tradesmen, and artisans were admitted. About then Rose's trustees opened a preparatory school, at which 20 children were taught by a mistress paid £21 a year. Each school was held in the teacher's house. A house, formerly the Jockey inn, on the south-east side of High Street, was bought in 1807, and from 1831 was used as a school and schoolhouse for the grammar school. In 1833 that school had 6–13 pupils, of poor, but not the poorest, parents, and the master also taught six fee-paying pupils in the school; children aged 4 were admitted to the preparatory school, which boys left at 9 and girls at 11 or 12. The two schools were merged between 1833 and 1854.[6] In 1858 a master, who was paid £30, and a mistress, who was paid £20, taught a total of only 10 children.[7] By 1867 Rose's had become an elementary school for boys; in 1872 it was attended by 19, for 4 of whom fees were paid. Later it was again mixed, and most of the 36 pupils in 1891 were girls.[8] The school was closed in 1899. In 1900 its endowments were sold: an annuity was bought for the teacher, money was contributed to the building of a new National school, and Rose's Higher Education Fund was set up.[9] From 1906 the fund was managed with Harrison's charity to provide exhibitions at certain schools and bursaries for pupil-teachers and for those attending training college. By Schemes of 1953 and 1972 payments to help maintain the fabric of Amesbury Church of England school were permitted, and by the Scheme of 1972 and one of 1980 the educational purposes of the charities were widened.[10]

By will proved 1709 Henry Spratt of Southwark (Surr.) gave money for 15 boys and 15 girls to be taught English and the catechism: regular attendance was required although absence for harvest work was permitted. Spratt's school was opened in 1711, the master was paid £20 a year, a building was said to have been erected c. 1715, and in 1718 the endowment was used to buy land in Amesbury.[11] In 1818 the school had a mistress paid £44 a year and 45 pupils.[12] In 1832, when they were taught in the mistress's house, children were admitted aged 3–4 and left aged c. 9.[13] Spratt's continued as an elementary school kept in the teacher's house;

there were only 16 pupils in 1858, 27 in 1872.[14] The school was closed in 1896: from 1821 until then each of the three successive teachers was a Miss Zillwood. The endowment was sold in 1900: an annuity was bought for the teacher and a contribution given to the building of the National school.[15]

In addition to Rose's and Spratt's, two small schools in Amesbury had a total of 21 pupils in 1818.[16] They were apparently closed when a National school was started in 1825. The National school was attended by 17 boys and 47 girls in 1833:[17] it was probably the school in Amesbury run in the 1830s on the pupil-teacher system devised by Joseph Lancaster.[18] An infants' school was started in 1841.[19] In 1846–7 the National school, attended by 44, and the infants' school, attended by 64, each had a schoolroom and a teacher's house:[20] the buildings were those in Salisbury Street in use until 1900.[21] In 1858 an additional classroom was in use in each school,[22] and in 1867 average attendance was 70–80 at the National school, 50–60 at the infants' school. An evening school was held in winter from the 1850s to the 1870s; average attendance in 1866–7 was 47, of whom two thirds were over 12.[23] There was a school at the union workhouse in Salisbury Road in the 1850s, when 30–40 attended it,[24] but children from the workhouse later went to other schools in Amesbury.[25]

In 1901, after Rose's, Spratt's, and the workhouse schools had been closed, the National and infants' schools were replaced by a new National school, with five classrooms and five teachers, built in Back Lane: in 1902–3 the new school had 203 pupils, including 70 infants.[26] Average attendance was 182 in 1906,[27] 212 in 1927.[28] In 1928 a county infants' school was built behind the police station,[29] and the National school became Amesbury Church of England school; average attendance in 1937–8 was respectively 134 and 171.[30] Two new classrooms were added to the infants' school in 1933.[31] In the 1930s a fund was raised to provide a Church of England secondary school at Amesbury; a site was bought in 1938, but no school was built.[32] The Church of England school was enlarged in 1957; Amesbury secondary modern school, on the site off Antrobus Road bought in 1938, was opened in 1958 and enlarged in 1960–1; the infants' school was enlarged in 1962;[33] a Roman Catholic

[6] *Educ. of Poor Digest*, 1017; *Endowed Char. Wilts.* (S. Div.), 23–5, 28; O.S. Map 1/2,500, Wilts. LIV. 16 (1887 edn.); W.R.O. 814/15.
[7] *Acct. of Wilts. Schs.* 4.
[8] *Endowed Char. Wilts.* (S. Div.), 28; P.R.O., ED 21/18301.
[9] *Endowed Char. Wilts.* (S. Div.), 28–9; W.R.O., F 8/500, Amesbury, Rose's sch.
[10] W.R.O. 2357, misc. papers; for Harrison's charity, below, charities.
[11] *Endowed Char. Wilts.* (S. Div.), 25–6; Cox, *Magna Brit.* vi. 198; W.R.O. 1315/1; above, manors (Saucer's).
[12] *Educ. of Poor Digest*, 1017.
[13] *Endowed Char. Wilts.* (S. Div.), 26.
[14] *Acct. of Wilts. Schs.* 4; P.R.O., ED 7/18301.
[15] *Endowed Char. Wilts.* (S. Div.), 29–31; W.R.O. 1315/1.
[16] *Educ. of Poor Digest*, 1017.
[17] *Educ. Enq. Abstract*, 1027.
[18] Pigot, *Nat. Com. Dir.* (1830), 790; (1842), 2; *D.N.B.*
[19] P.R.O., ED 7/130, no. 7.
[20] Nat. Soc. *Inquiry, 1846–7*, Wilts. 2–3.
[21] O.S. Maps 1/2,500, Wilts. LIV. 16 (1887, 1901 edns.); W.R.O. 1550/48; below, this section.
[22] *Acct. of Wilts. Schs.* 4.
[23] *Rep. Com. Children and Women in Agric.* [4202–I], pp. 280–1, H.C. (1868–9), xiii; *Return of Public Elem. Schs. 1875–6* [C. 1882], pp. 280–1, H.C. (1877), lxvii.
[24] *Acct. of Wilts. Schs.* 4.
[25] W.R.O., F 8/500, Amesbury, Church of Eng. sch.
[26] Ibid.; ibid. F 8/220/1; *Endowed Char. Wilts.* (S. Div.), 33–5.   [27] *Return of Non-Provided Schs.* 18.
[28] *Bd. of Educ., List 21, 1927* (H.M.S.O.), 358.
[29] W.R.O., F 8/230/2/1.
[30] *Bd. of Educ., List 21, 1938* (H.M.S.O.), 421.
[31] W.R.O., F 8/230/2/1.
[32] Ibid. 1821/5; 2357/11.
[33] Ibid. F 8/230/2/2; ibid. 2357/11.

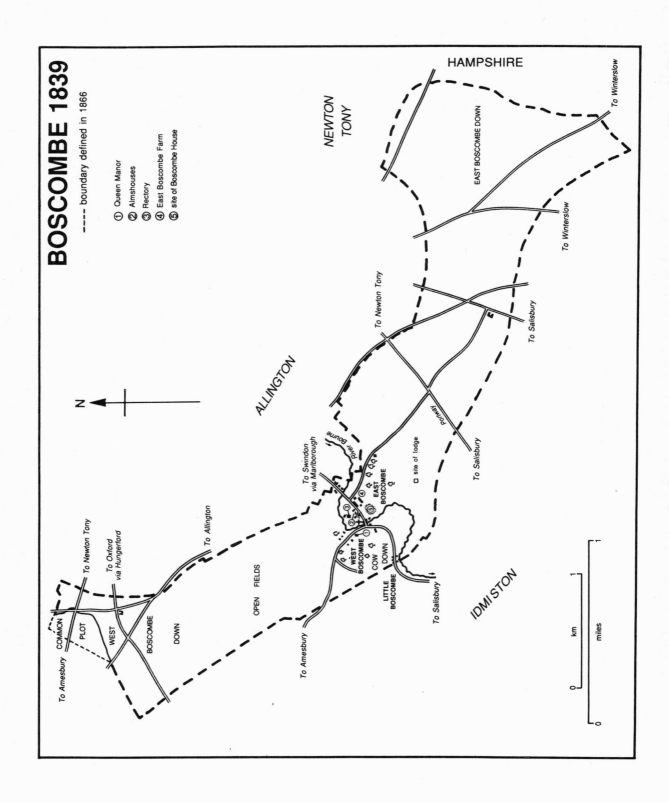

primary school, Christ the King school in Earls Court Road, was opened in 1964.[34] The secondary modern school, renamed Stonehenge school, became a comprehensive school in 1974.[35] In 1991, 141 pupils, aged 5–7, attended Amesbury Infants' school; 236, aged 5–11, attended Christ the King school; 250, aged 7–11, attended Amesbury Church of England school; 405, aged 11–16, attended Stonehenge school.[36]

From 1839 or earlier to 1867 or later Caroline Browne held a school for young ladies: it was a day school in 1842, a boarding school in 1855 and later.[37] Several small schools were held in the later 19th century. At one, a preparatory school held from c. 1867 to c. 1880 by the Revd. Arthur Meyrick in Wyndersham House,[38] later the Vicarage and the Antrobus Arms,[39] Walter Long (cr. Viscount Long 1921) was a pupil.[40] Avondale school, a preparatory school opened in 1923, was held in Countess Farm by F. A. Perks; it moved to Bulford in 1957.[41] Downlands school in Stonehenge Road was held in the 1950s by Eleanor F. B. Cowmeadow.[42]

CHARITIES FOR THE POOR. In 1601 Hugh Atwill gave 33s. 4d. as a stock to provide work for the poor of Amesbury, among whom the profits of the work were to be distributed. No more is known of the fund.[43]

Richard Harrison by will gave money for apprenticing boys of 12–16 who were sons of Amesbury's second poor and had attended Rose's or Spratt's school. Apprenticing evidently began c. 1727. Land in Allington was bought in 1780–1, and the charity's income was £11 in 1786. Between 1827 and 1832 nine boys were apprenticed, not all from the two schools. In 1881 £230 accumulated income was invested, in the 1890s three boys were apprenticed, and in 1904 the charity's income was £25.[44] From 1906 the charity was managed with Rose's Higher Education Fund.[45] The land, 21 a., was sold between 1910 and 1925.[46]

BOSCOMBE

BOSCOMBE[47] lies in the Bourne valley 11 km. north-east of Salisbury.[48] The parish, 1,688 a. (683 ha.), was added to Allington parish in 1934.[49] It was long and narrow, the river Bourne winds across the middle of it, and it contained two small villages, East Boscombe on the left bank and West Boscombe on the right: each village had a strip of land extending to the downs, East Boscombe's east of the river, West Boscombe's west.

The parish boundary crosses downland for most of its length; on the south-east the boundary with Hampshire follows a ridge, and near the north end of the parish a road and mounds marked the boundary with Allington. Near the river a zigzag in the boundary with Allington suggests a late division of common land, some of which may have been marshy. To the north-west the use of downland was disputed between Boscombe and Amesbury in the 16th and 17th centuries; by 1726 the dispute had been ended by allotting 36 a. for joint use by the two parishes, and in 1866 a line bisecting the common plot was adopted as the parish boundary.[50]

Chalk outcrops over the entire parish. There is gravel along the Bourne and in a tributary valley north-west of the church, and a small amount of alluvium has been deposited south of the church.[51] The downland, at over 160 m., is higher in the east than in the west. The Bourne, at c. 72 m., flows intermittently in winter and spring and is dry in summer and autumn. On each side of the river there was meadow land, and open fields lay between the meadows and the downs.[52] A few acres planted near the villages in the earlier 19th century[53] was the only woodland in the parish in the late 20th.[54] Both the east downs and the west downs have been used for military training in the 20th century.[55]

Portway, the Roman road from Silchester to Old Salisbury, crosses the east part of the parish:[56] it apparently remained in use locally until the 20th century.[57] The Oxford–Salisbury road via Hungerford (Berks.) crossed the west part, where it became a minor road after a new course was adopted for the Hungerford road between 1675 and 1773.[58] In 1835 the road linking the villages beside the Bourne to Salisbury was the last part of a Swindon–Salisbury road via Marlborough to be turnpiked; disturnpiked in

---

34 W.R.O., F 1/250/17.
35 Ibid. list of secondary schs. closed since 1945.
36 Wilts. co. council, *Sched. of Educ. Establishments* (1990), p. 1.
37 *Early Trade Dirs.* (W.R.S. xlvii), 102; *Kelly's Dir. Wilts.* (1848 and later edns.).
38 *Kelly's Dir. Wilts.* (1867 and later edns.); Chandler and Goodhugh, *Amesbury*, 46, 116–17.
39 Above, intro. (the town c. 1540 to c. 1900); church.
40 *W.A.M.* xlii. 518.
41 *Kelly's Dir. Sar.* (1927 and later edns.); notice on bldg. in High Street, Bulford; below, Bulford, educ.
42 *Kelly's Dir. Sar.* (1953 and later edns.).
43 W.R.O. 1550/1.
44 *Endowed Char. Wilts.* (S. Div.), 26–7, 31–2; *Char. Don.* H.C. 511 (1816), xvi (2), 1336–7; above, Allington, manors (Charity).   45 W.R.O. 2357, misc. papers; above, educ.
46 Above, Allington, manors (Charity).

47 This article was written in 1993.
48 Maps used include O.S. Maps 6", Wilts. LXI (1883 and later edns.); 1/25,000, 41/13, 41/23 (1948 and later edns.).
49 *Census*, 1931.
50 O.S. Map 6", Wilts. LXI (1883 edn.); W.R.O., EA/185; above, Amesbury, intro. [boundaries]; agric. (Amesbury).
51 Geol. Surv. Map 1/50,000, drift, sheet 298 (1976 edn.).
52 Below, econ. hist.
53 O.S. Map 1", sheet 14 (1817 edn.); P.R.O., IR 29/38/31; IR 30/38/31.
54 O.S. Map 1/50,000, sheet 184 (1988 edn.).
55 Below, this section.   56 *V.C.H. Wilts.* i (1), 25.
57 O.S. Maps 6", Wilts. LXI (1883 and later edns.).
58 Ibid. 1", sheet 14 (1817 edn.); J. Ogilby, *Brit.* (1675), pl. 83; *Andrews and Dury, Map* (W.R.S. viii), pl. 6; below, N. Tidworth, intro. [roads].

A HISTORY OF WILTSHIRE

1876, it remained the main Swindon–Salisbury road in 1993. A short new stretch was built in 1939 to take traffic eastwards away from the church.[59] At both ends of the parish roads or tracks were closed in the 20th century to allow for military training,[60] but in the 1950s one across the north corner was improved as a new route from Allington to Amesbury.[61] The London–Salisbury railway line was built for the L. & S.W.R. across the parish along the south-east side of Portway: it was opened in 1857 and remained a main line in 1993. A light railway between Amesbury and Grateley (Hants), diverging from the main line in Newton Tony parish, was opened across the north corner of Boscombe parish in 1902[62] and closed in 1963.[63]

Evidence of prehistoric activity is abundant in the parish. East of the village a prehistoric ditch crosses the parish and there are three bowl barrows.[64] On East Boscombe down a Bronze-Age enclosure of ¼ a. was possibly for cattle,[65] and iron may have been smelted on the site.[66] On West Boscombe down a hill fort was constructed in the mid 1st century A.D. and there is a cemetery of the late 3rd or early 4th century.[67] An Iron-Age enclosure c. 700 m. ESE. of Boscombe church was the site of a Romano-British villa.[68]

Boscombe's assessment for taxation in 1332 was high for a place in Amesbury hundred.[69] There were 46 poll-tax payers in 1377, but in 1428 fewer than 10 households. Between 1801 and 1851 the population of the parish rose steadily from 103 to 159, between 1851 and 1921 fell steadily to 81, and in 1931 was 117.[70] In 1991 no more than a third of the 469 inhabitants of Allington parish lived in Boscombe.[71]

East Boscombe and West Boscombe villages were on the gravel beside the Bourne, which divided them. In 1773 the river was forded by the Salisbury road, later called Tidworth Road, immediately south-west of the church and 350 m. north-east.[72] In each place a bridge had been built by 1817:[73] the south-western was rebuilt in brick as a single span in the later 19th century;[74] the north-eastern was rebuilt in 1930.[75] The two villages kept their separate identities until the mid 20th century but from then they and other settlement beside Tidworth Road have been collectively known as Boscombe village.[76]

East Boscombe had buildings on both sides of the main road, the church and the rectory house north-west and Boscombe House, a large manor house standing until the later 18th century,[77]

south-east. A lodge south-east of Boscombe House was demolished between 1773 and 1817.[78] Immediately north-east of the church a farmhouse called the Close in 1993 was built in the 18th century and enlarged in the 19th. In the early 19th century the principal farm buildings were on both sides of the main road north-east of the farmhouse. Two timber-framed granaries on staddle stones survive, one of the 18th-century north-west of the road, one of the 18th or early 19th century south-east of the road. A new farmhouse, East Farm, was erected south-east of the buildings on the south-east side between 1839 and 1877,[79] and the farmyard on that side remains in use. An 18th-century house survives between the Close and the rectory house; an almshouse and, near the church, two cottages are also 18th-century.[80]

In the early 19th century West Boscombe consisted of no more than Queen Manor, farm buildings, and a few cottages.[81] Queen Manor, lying east–west with a north entrance front, was built of brick in the 18th century. In 1832, to designs by John Peniston,[82] a north–south range, also of brick, was built at the east end. In the later 19th century an extension was built along the south side of the 18th-century range. In the later 20th the east side of the earlier 19th-century range was made into an entrance front and a large bay window was constructed on the south side. A large garden south of the house was enclosed with a high cob wall on brick and flint footings in the 18th century or earlier 19th. Farm buildings immediately west of the house in the early 19th century went out of use. Others further west included a long timber-framed and weatherboarded granary of the 18th century or early 19th on staddle stones, which survives: their site was a farmyard with mainly modern farm buildings in 1993. Near the old granary a thatched house was built in the late 19th century on the site of two cottages.[83] An early 17th-century cottage stands south-west of the church.

In the later 18th century small groups of buildings stood beside the main road near the parish boundary. That to the south-west, where buildings were on each side of the road, was called Little Boscombe in 1773,[84] Lower Boscombe in 1817.[85] On the north-west side of the road a 17th-century cottage of cob and thatch survives: buildings on the south-east side were demolished in the late 19th century.[86] The group to the north-east was on the south-east side of the road in 1773.[87] On the north-west side a

59 V.C.H. Wilts. iv. 257, 262, 266, 270.
60 Cf. O.S. Maps 6", Wilts. LXI. NW., SE., SW. (1901–10 edns.).   61 Above, Allington, intro. [roads].
62 V.C.H. Wilts. iv. 286, 291.
63 P. A. Harding, Bulford Branch Line, 28.
64 V.C.H. Wilts. i (1), 148, 250.
65 Ibid. i (2), 394, 396, 398, 402.
66 Ibid. 400, 408.
67 Ibid. i (1), 25–6; i (2), 431, 436.
68 W.A.M. lxv. 209; lxvi. 190–1.
69 Tax List, 1332 (W.R.S. xlv), 112.
70 V.C.H. Wilts. iv. 306, 314, 341.
71 Cf. above, Allington, intro.
72 Andrews and Dury, Map (W.R.S. viii), pl. 6.
73 O.S. Map 1", sheet 14 (1817 edn.).
74 W.R.O., A 1/531/2/1.
75 Date on bridge.

76 O.S. Maps 1/25,000, SU 13, SU 23 (1958 edns.); 1/10,000, SU 13 NE., SU 23 NW. (1977 edns.).
77 Below, manors (E. Boscombe).
78 Andrews and Dury, Map (W.R.S. viii), pl. 6; O.S. Map 1", sheet 14 (1817 edn.).
79 O.S. Map 6", Wilts. LXI (1883 edn.); P.R.O., IR 29/38/31; IR 30/38/31.
80 For the almshouse, below, charity.
81 P.R.O., IR 29/38/31; IR 30/38/31.
82 Early Trade Dirs. (W.R.S. xlvii), 85; W.R.O. 451/72, no. xvii.
83 For bldgs. standing in the early 19th cent., P.R.O., IR 29/38/31; IR 30/38/31.
84 Andrews and Dury, Map (W.R.S. viii), pl. 6.
85 O.S. Map 1", sheet 14 (1817 edn.).
86 Ibid. 6", Wilts. LXI (1883 edn.); LXI. NW. (1901 edn.).   87 Andrews and Dury, Map (W.R.S. viii), pl. 6.

cottage was built before 1817[88] and a school c. 1900:[89] those two buildings and a pair of late 19th-century cottages on the south-east side survived in 1993.

In the earlier 20th century Little Boscombe was linked to East and West Boscombe by a line of houses, including eight council houses, built on the north-west side of the main road.[90] To the north-east on what was the boundary with Allington until 1934 an estate of council houses was built in the late 1940s and the 1950s:[91] 12 are in the former Boscombe parish. A working men's club open by 1919[92] remained in Boscombe village in 1993. Between 1923 and 1939 a cemetery was opened beside the main road and south-west of the church.[93]

A barn was built on the downs of East Boscombe between 1773 and 1817,[94] and a farmstead with a house stood at its site in 1839.[95] The farmstead was removed between 1916 and 1923 when buildings associated with the Experimental Station based at Porton down in Idmiston were erected on the site. The downland east of them was used as firing ranges, and later more buildings were erected for what is now the Chemical and Biological Defence Establishment.[96] Boscombe gave its name to Boscombe Down airfield, the landing ground and buildings of which were in Amesbury parish, and from c. 1944 downland of West Boscombe has been used for some of the runways.[97]

MANORS AND OTHER ESTATES.

In 1086 William of Eu (d. c. 1095) held 7 hides in Boscombe, the later *EAST BOSCOMBE* manor, and Edward of Salisbury held them of him.[98] Like other estates of William, the overlordship of the manor descended to Walter Marshal, earl of Pembroke (d. 1245).[99] The overlordship has not been traced further.

Roger Bernard evidently held the manor in demesne c. 1175.[1] Eudes Bernard held it in 1242–3 and Mabel Bernard held it of him, possibly by a temporary tenure.[2] The manor may have been the estate held in 1288 by Walter of Durnford[3] and in 1298 settled by him and his wife Joan on Henry Thistleden and his wife

Thomasine: that estate was apparently held by trustees in 1322 when the remainder in it was settled on William Peverel and his wife Edith.[4] The manor was evidently that held at his death in 1362 by Sir Henry Peverel, who had a son Thomas.[5] It was probably the manor conveyed by Walter of Milcombe and his wife Margaret to Thomas Hungerford (d. 1397) in 1370,[6] and was the manor sold in 1382 by Sir Peter Courtenay and his wife Margaret to Sir John Thorp[7] (d. 1386). Sir John was succeeded by his son Edward.[8] Henry Thorp (d. 1416) held the manor in 1402 and from him it passed in the direct line to Ralph[9] (d. 1446), John[10] (d. 1464), and William[11] (d. 1509), an idiot by 1479. William was succeeded by his nephew William Clifford[12] (d. by 1536). The manor was held after Clifford's death by his relict Elizabeth (will proved 1544) and descended to her son Henry[13] (will proved 1578), to Henry's son Anthony[14] (d. 1580), and to Anthony's son Henry,[15] who conveyed it to his brother Simon in 1623.[16] In 1628 Simon sold it to William Kent[17] (d. 1632), who was succeeded by his son William[18] (d. 1666), a royalist in arms in the Civil War. The manor descended to the younger William's son William,[19] who sold it in 1675 or 1676 to his cousin John Kent[20] (d. s.p. 1710). John devised it to his nephew John Kent,[21] whose son John sold it to Robert Eyre in 1733.[22] Robert (d. 1752) devised the manor to his wife Mary (d. 1762), from whom it passed to her husband's cousin Samuel Eyre (d. 1794). Samuel's daughter and heir Susannah (d. 1833), whose husband William Purvis (d. 1810) assumed the surname Eyre in 1795, was succeeded by her daughter Harriet, wife of George Matcham (d. 1877). The manor passed to Harriet's son William Matcham (d. 1906), who assumed the surname Eyre-Matcham in 1889, and to William's son George Eyre-Matcham.[23] In 1919 the War Department occupied the downland of East Boscombe, c. 764 a., and in 1925 bought it; the Ministry of Defence owned it in 1993.[24] Between 1919 and 1922 George Eyre-Matcham sold East farm, c. 276 a., to W. C. Thomas.[25] In 1924 Thomas sold the farm, then c. 300 a., to John Bament (d. 1933), whose son Mr. A. G. Bament owned it in 1993.[26]

Members of the Clifford and Kent families

88 O.S. Map 1", sheet 14 (1817 edn.).
89 Below, educ.　　90 W.R.O., G 1/500/3.
91 Ibid. A 1/355/336; A 1/355/341; A 1/355/351; G 1/505/1; G 1/516/3; G 1/602/2–3.
92 Ibid. G 1/500/3.
93 O.S. Maps 1/2,500, Wilts. LXI. 6 (1925, 1939 edns.).
94 Ibid. 1", sheet 14 (1817 edn.); *Andrews and Dury, Map* (W.R.S. viii), pl. 6.
95 P.R.O., IR 29/38/31; IR 30/38/31.
96 G. B. Carter, *Porton Down*, 4, 15, 22; O.S. Maps 6", Wilts. LXI. NW. (1901, 1926 edns.).
97 Above, Amesbury, intro. (military activity).
98 *V.C.H. Wilts.* ii, p. 149; I. J. Sanders, *Eng. Baronies*, 119.
99 *V.C.H. Wilts.* ii, p. 111; *Bk. of Fees*, ii. 745; *Complete Peerage*, x. 374–6.
1 G. C. Gorham, *Hist. Eynesbury and St. Neots*, ii, p. cxxxv.　　2 *Bk. of Fees*, ii. 745.
3 *Abbrev. Plac.* (Rec. Com.), 215.
4 *Feet of F.* 1272–1327 (W.R.S. i), pp. 44, 110.
5 *Wilts. Inq. p.m.* 1327–77 (Index Libr.), 314–15.
6 *Feet of F.* 1327–77 (W.R.S. xxix), p. 138; *Complete Peerage*, vi. 613.
7 *Feet of F. 1377–1509* (W.R.S. xli), p. 11.
8 *Cal. Inq. p.m.* xvi, p. 175.
9 *Cal. Pat.* 1401–5, 95, 100–1; P.R.O., PROB 11/2B, f. 63 and v.　　10 P.R.O., C 139/126, no. 23, rot. 10.
11 Ibid. C 140/14, no. 28, rot. 6.
12 Ibid. C 140/69, no. 10, rot. 2; C 142/24, no. 24.
13 Ibid. PROB 11/26, f. 39; ibid. WARD 9/129, f. 211.
14 Ibid. PROB 11/60, ff. 44–5.
15 Ibid. PROB 11/62, ff. 407–9.
16 Ibid. CP 25/2/372/20 Jas. I Hil.; *Wilts. Pedigrees* (Harl. Soc. cv/cvi), 39.
17 W.R.O. 1369, deed, Clifford to Kent, 1628.
18 *Wilts. Inq. p.m.* 1625–49 (Index Libr.), 155–6.
19 P.R.O., PROB 11/322, f. 209 and v.
20 *W.N. & Q.* vii. 232.
21 P.R.O., PROB 11/515, ff. 264–265v.
22 *W.N. & Q.* vii. 233; W.R.O. 1369, deed, Kent to Eyre, 1733.
23 *V.C.H. Wilts.* xi. 30; Burke, *Land. Gent.* (1952), 1732; W.R.O. 1369, abstr. of title to E. Boscombe.
24 Carter, *Porton Down*, 4; inf. from Defence Land Agent, Durrington.　　25 W.R.O., G 1/500/3.
26 Inf. from Mr. A. G. Bament, East Farm.

lived at Boscombe,[27] presumably in Boscombe House, which stood on East Boscombe manor.[28] From c. 1733 Boscombe House was leased; one tenant was a doctor who in 1768 used it as an inoculation hospital. In 1768 it contained a large saloon and a hall, 4 parlours, and 18 bedrooms, and had gardens and a bowling green. It was demolished c. 1770:[29] the site of the house and the outline of the bowling green were visible in 1993.

In 1364 Thomas Peverel sold land, presumably in East Boscombe, to Sir Thomas Tyrell.[30] It passed in the Tyrell family[31] and was held of Sir Thomas Tyrell by John Clement (d. 1526). Clement was succeeded by his son Edward.[32] The estate has not been traced further.

In 1320 Richard Thistleden granted 1 yardland, presumably in East Boscombe, to the vicars choral of Salisbury cathedral in mortmain.[33] The later ownership of the land is obscure.

WEST BOSCOMBE was held in 1086 by Amesbury abbey.[34] In 1179 the manor was confirmed to Amesbury priory,[35] which was granted free warren in its demesnes in 1286,[36] and held the manor until the Dissolution.[37] The Crown sold it to Richard Reeves in 1599.[38] By 1609 it had been acquired by Sir Thomas Freke,[39] and in the earlier 17th century was evidently split into three portions.

In 1609 Freke sold the demesne and a copyhold of the manor to Simon Clifford[40] (d. 1640), the owner of East Boscombe manor. In 1628 Clifford sold 178 a. of the demesne to William Kent with East Boscombe manor.[41] They descended with that manor[42] and were reunited with the rest of West Boscombe manor between 1831 and 1866.[43]

The remainder of the demesne and the copyhold, called Queen's farm in the earlier 18th century,[44] descended to Clifford's son Simon, who sold it to Stephen Kent in 1641.[45] Kent sold the estate in 1656 to James Harris (will proved 1680), who sold an undivided moiety in 1667 to William Harris. James's moiety passed to Joan (d. 1734), relict of his son Thomas (d. 1679).[46] In 1734 it passed to Thomas's grandson James Harris (d. 1780), whose son Sir James Harris

(later earl of Malmesbury) sold it in 1785 to Thomas Waters.[47] The second moiety descended from William Harris (d. 1668) to his son James,[48] to James's son William[49] (d. 1746), and to William's daughter Sarah,[50] who married William Hayter (d. by 1780) and afterwards Henry Southby (d. 1797).[51] In 1799 Sarah's daughter Sarah Hayter sold it to Thomas Waters,[52] the owner of the first moiety. Waters (d. 1831) devised his estate to his nephew Robert Waters,[53] who sold it before 1866 to George Matcham,[54] the owner of the other two portions of the manor.

In 1646 Dorothy, relict of the younger Simon Clifford, sold 5 yardlands, formerly customary land of West Boscombe manor, to Bridget Thistlewaite.[55] In 1699 Francis Thistlewaite sold the land to Thomas Cooper, who immediately sold it to Robert Freemantle[56] (d. 1718). It passed to Freemantle's son Robert,[57] who sold it c. 1741 to Robert Eyre.[58] Thereafter it descended with East Boscombe manor along with the 178 a. of demesne.[59]

The whole of West Boscombe manor, called Queen Manor farm, descended with East Boscombe manor from the mid 19th century. George Eyre-Matcham sold the farm, 586 a., between 1919 and 1922 to R. E. Macan.[60] Queen Manor farm belonged to Macan's relict Dorothy Macan in 1945, was sold by her representatives to J. Read c. 1955, and belonged to Read's son, Mr. J. S. Read, in 1993.[61] The government bought c. 175 a. from Macan in 1925 and c. 75 a. from his relict in 1950, all for Boscombe Down airfield:[62] it owned the land in 1993.

Amesbury priory was evidently entitled to the tithes from the demesne of its manor of West Boscombe.[63] After the Dissolution the tithes belonged to the lord of the manor, and from the 17th century to the owners of that portion of the manor which passed in the Harris family.[64] In 1840, when they were due from 241 a. of land to which pasture rights were attached, they were valued at £95 and commuted.[65]

ECONOMIC HISTORY. EAST BOSCOMBE. In 1086 there were 3½ ploughteams although there

27 e.g. Wilts. Pedigrees (Harl. Soc. cv/cvi), 39; W.A.M. xxiv. 95–6.   28 Cf. above, intro.
29 Hoare, Mod. Wilts. Amesbury, 113; V.C.H. Wilts. v. 323; cf. Andrews and Dury, Map (W.R.S. viii), pl. 6.
30 Cal. Close, 1364–8, 44, 50.
31 Cf. V.C.H. Hants, v. 125.
32 P.R.O., C 142/58, no. 120.
33 Cal. Pat. 1317–21, p. 496.
34 V.C.H. Wilts. ii, p. 131.
35 Cal. Chart. R. 1257–1300, 157–9; for the hist. of the abbey and priory, V.C.H. Wilts. iii. 242–59.
36 Cal. Chart. R. 1257–1300, 336.
37 Valor Eccl. (Rec. Com.), ii. 94.
38 P.R.O., C 66/1530, m. 11.
39 W.R.O. 1369, deed, Freke to Clifford, 1609.
40 Ibid.
41 Ibid. 1369, deed, Clifford to Kent, 1628; P.R.O., PROB 11/182, f. 269.
42 e.g. P.R.O., IR 29/38/31; IR 30/38/31.
43 Below, this section.
44 W.R.O. 1369, survey, 1719.
45 Ibid. 1369, deed, Clifford to Kent, 1641.
46 Burke, Peerage (1963), 1588; P.R.O., C 11/2231/31; ibid. PROB 11/362, ff. 368v.–369; PROB 11/664, ff. 110–11.
47 Burke, Peerage (1963), 1588; W.R.O., A 1/345/43;

ibid. 1369, deed, Harris to Waters, 1785.
48 P.R.O., PROB 11/328, ff. 222–3.
49 Ibid. C 11/2231/31.
50 Ibid. PROB 11/750, ff. 117v.–119.
51 Burke, Land. Gent. (1855), 1121; W.R.O., A 1/345/43.
52 V.C.H. Wilts. vi. 185; W.R.O. 1369, deed, Hayter to Waters, 1799.
53 P.R.O., PROB 11/1789, ff. 370v.–372; W.R.O. 1068/29.   54 W.R.O., EA/185.
55 Hoare, Mod. Wilts. Amesbury, 112.
56 W.R.O. 1369, deeds, Thistlewaite to Cooper, 1699; Cooper to Freemantle, 1699.
57 Ibid. 1068/21; ibid. wills, archd. Sar., Rob. Freemantle, 1721.
58 Ibid. 1369, queries on Freemantle's title, c. 1741.
59 Above, this section.   60 W.R.O., G 1/500/3.
61 Ibid. G 1/516/1–3; inf. from Mr. J. S. Read, Queen Manor.
62 Boscombe Down: Record Site Plan (pub. After the Battle mag.: copy in Wilts. Libr. headquarters, Trowbridge); G.P.L., Treas. Solicitor, 2274/76.
63 P.R.O., SC 6/Hen. VIII/3986, rot. 86d.
64 Ibid. CP 25/2/371/13 Jas. I Mich.; W.A.M. xl. 259; W.R.O. 1369, deeds, Kent to Harris, 1653; Harris to Waters, 1785.   65 P.R.O., IR 29/38/31.

The Chinese pavilion

The bridge dated 1777 in the park

AMESBURY: AMESBURY ABBEY

West Amesbury street in the early 20th century

Antrobus House

AMESBURY

was land enough for 4; there were 2 teams and 2 *servi* on the 4½ demesne hides, and 3 *villani* and 4 coscets with 1½ team on land assessed at 2½ hides. There were 6 a. of meadow and there was pasture 12 furlongs square.[66]

In 1362 what was evidently the demesne of East Boscombe manor had 240 a. of arable, of which half was sown each year, 10 a. of meadow in severalty, a several cattle pasture worth 4s., and feeding in common for 4 working cattle, 18 oxen, and 500 sheep. None would hold land of the manor in bondage; free tenants held land but how many and how much are not known.[67] In 1446 the demesne was said to include 8 a. of meadow, 600 a. of downland pasture, but only 60 a. of arable; it also had a rabbit warren.[68]

Between 1577 and 1580 the lord, his tenants, and the rector exchanged lands, and from then all the land of East Boscombe was evidently in a single farm worked in severalty. In 1719 East Boscombe farm was said to have c. 300 a. of arable, 80 a. of 'ingrounds', and 700 a. of down. The c. 300 a. of arable were presumably former open fields; the 80 a. of 'ingrounds' included 20 a. of meadow, 40 a. of arable in inclosures formerly pasture, and a cattle pasture of 20 a. near the village; every part of the down had been burnbaked once or twice.[69] About 1840 the farm, 1,038 a., included 687 a. of arable, 35 a. of meadow and lowland pasture, and a downland field of 292 a. of which part was additional arable. It also included a downland farmstead,[70] and a flock of 1,130 sheep was kept.[71] For periods in the late 18th century and early 19th it was worked by the farmer who worked the land of West Boscombe.[72]

It is likely that in the later 19th century on East Boscombe farm arable was converted to pasture and that dairy and pig farming increased.[73] In the early 20th the two thirds of the farm east of the railway were taken for military training,[74] and in the 1930s East farm was about half arable and half pasture.[75] In 1993 East farm, c. 300 a., was mainly arable but had on it cattle reared for beef.[76] Of the c. 764 a. east of the railway, c. 75 a. were then cultivated for the Chemical and Biological Defence Establishment and the rest was rough grassland.[77]

WEST BOSCOMBE. There was land for 4 teams in 1086: there were 1 team and 1 *servus* on the demesne, 2½ hides; 2 *villani*, 5 coscets, and 2 cottars held 1 team on 1½ hide. There were 4 a. of meadow, and there was pasture 1 furlong by ½ furlong.[78]

In the Middle Ages and the 16th century West Boscombe is likely to have had as much arable as, and less pasture than, East Boscombe. In the 16th century the demesne was c. 147 a. and there were 4 copyholds, 2 of c. 70 a., 1 of c. 64 a., and 1 of c. 14 a. All five holdings had land in the three open fields, then called Church Hill, Brownberry, and West, and each holding except the smallest shared a common meadow of c. 8 a. There was a cow down and pasture for sheep on downs called Church Hill, Pike, and West.[79] The demesne included the right to feed 289 sheep in common.[80] In the 16th century and later downland on West Boscombe's boundary with Amesbury was disputed, and in the 18th and 19th centuries a sheep pasture of 36 a. was used in common by the farmers of both places.[81]

In the earlier 18th century there remained three open fields, Idmiston, Middle, and Church Hill or Allington, presumably south, middle, and north fields, nominally a total of 307 a. and shared among nine holdings. Between the earlier 18th century and the earlier 19th the amount of open field was increased, perhaps doubled. In 1839 there were 248 strips totalling 414 a.; the new arable to the west was divided into strips on a more regular pattern than the old arable to the east. Cow down, west of the church, was 31 a., and north of it a 26-a. pasture was used in common for sheep or pigs; together the two pastures were later called Little Boscombe down. Downland pasture for sheep, including half the common plot, was 113 a.[82] The arable was worked on a four-course rotation in which two fields were sown with corn, one was sown with grass, and one was left fallow.[83]

Common husbandry continued nominally until 1866, but between the earlier 18th century and the earlier 19th nearly all the land was absorbed into a single farm, Queen Manor farm,[84] and by c. 1840 linchets in the open fields had been ploughed. A flock of 1,210 sheep was kept c. 1840.[85] From 1780 or earlier to c. 1794 Thomas Waters worked nearly all the land in the parish, as did his nephew Robert Waters from c. 1832.[86]

In West as in East Boscombe arable may have been converted to pasture, and dairy and pig farming may have increased, in the later 19th century.[87] In 1910 Queen Manor farm was 586 a.[88] In the mid 20th century c. 250 a. were taken from the farm for Boscombe Down airfield.[89] In 1993 Queen Manor farm, c. 750 a., had all the other land in West Boscombe and much elsewhere: it was an arable and sheep farm with a flock of c. 1,000 breeding ewes.[90]

A windmill was built on Little Boscombe down

66 *V.C.H. Wilts.* ii, p. 149.
67 *Wilts. Inq. p.m.* 1327–77 (Index Libr.), 315.
68 P.R.O., C 139/126, no. 23, rot. 10.
69 Ibid. PROB 11/60, ff. 44–5; PROB 11/62, ff. 407–9; W.R.O. 1369, ct. bk. 1634–1796; ibid. 1369, survey, 1719.
70 P.R.O., IR 29/38/31; IR 30/38/31.
71 Ibid. IR 18/10914.
72 Below, this section.
73 P.R.O., MAF 68/151, sheet 8; MAF 68/493, sheet 10; MAF 68/1063, sheet 9; MAF 68/1633, sheet 16.
74 Above, intro.
75 [1st] Land Util. Surv. Map, sheet 122.
76 Inf. from Mr. A. G. Bament and Mr. D. Bament, East Farm.   77 Inf. from Defence Land Agent.
78 *V.C.H. Wilts.* ii, p. 131.

79 P.R.O., C 66/1530, m. 11; ibid. E 310/26/155, f. 47; E 310/26/156, ff. 35, 46; ibid. LR 2/191, ff. 130v.–131v.
80 *Valor Eccl.* (Rec. Com.), ii. 94.
81 P.R.O., IR 29/38/31; IR 30/38/31; above, Amesbury, agric. (Amesbury).
82 W.R.O. 1369, survey, 1719; P.R.O., IR 29/38/31; IR 30/38/31.   83 Hants R.O. 7M54/540/6.
84 W.R.O. 1369, survey, 1719; ibid. EA/185; P.R.O., IR 29/38/31; IR 30/38/31.   85 P.R.O., IR 18/10914.
86 W.R.O., A 1/345/43.
87 P.R.O., MAF 68/151, sheet 8; MAF 68/493, sheet 10; MAF 68/1063, sheet 9; MAF 68/1633, sheet 16.
88 W.R.O., Inland Revenue, val. reg. 149.
89 Above, intro.; manors (W. Boscombe).
90 Inf. from Mr. J. S. Read, Queen Manor.

between 1773 and 1793. It was a post mill,[91] which went out of use between c. 1876 and 1899 and was demolished before 1926.[92]

LOCAL GOVERNMENT. Amesbury priory held a court for West Boscombe manor 1315–18[93] and c. 1535.[94] No direct record of the court, or of the view held twice a year for the manor c. 1540,[95] survives. Records of a court for East Boscombe manor are extant 1634–1796. The court was convened very infrequently: it transacted copyhold business,[96] and was still held c. 1826.[97]

Annual expenditure on the poor in 1775–6 was high at £54, in the early 1780s low at an average of £25. In 1802–3 £79 was spent on relieving 23 paupers, a quarter of the inhabitants, 17 regularly and 6 occasionally.[98] A yearly average of £113 was spent 1812–15 on relieving c. 12 paupers.[99] Between 1816 and 1834 the few paupers may have been relieved comparatively generously: expenditure was highest, at £157, in 1832, lowest, at £49, in 1818.[1] The parish became part of Amesbury poor-law union in 1835.[2] It was included in Salisbury district in 1974.[3]

CHURCH. Boscombe church was mentioned in the 12th century.[4] In 1650 it was proposed to add Allington and part of Idmiston to the parish but the proposal was not implemented.[5] Boscombe rectory was united with Allington rectory in 1924,[6] the two parishes were united in 1970,[7] and the united benefice became part of Bourne Valley benefice in 1973.[8]

About 1175 Roger Bernard granted the advowson to St. Neots priory (Hunts.). In 1227 the priory gave it to the bishop of Salisbury in exchange for a pension of 13s. 4d.,[9] and the bishop afterwards collated rectors. John Barnaby presented in 1564, Thomas Painter in 1584, and Richard Hooker, the rector, in 1595, each time by grant of a turn.[10] From 1924 the bishop collated at alternate vacancies, and in 1973 became chairman of the Bourne Valley patronage board.[11]

The rectory was worth £4 6s. 8d. in 1291,[12] £14 in 1535,[13] £60 in 1650.[14] Valued at £330 c. 1830 it was one of the richer livings in Amesbury deanery.[15] The rector took all the tithes except

those from about half of West Boscombe. The rector's were valued at £250 10s. in 1840 and commuted.[16] From 1577 × 1580 all the rector's glebe was in West Boscombe.[17] It was nominally c. 24 a., presumably with pasture rights, in 1671,[18] c. 22 a. from inclosure in 1866.[19] It was sold in 1925.[20] The rectory house was built in the 15th century as a north–south hall, of which all but the north end survives; an upper floor was inserted in the 17th century. In the earlier 19th century a roofed cellar occupied the site of the north end. Near the north-west corner of the surviving part of the hall, and linked to it by a passage, an east–west range was built in 1836.[21] In the 20th century the ground floor of the medieval range was altered and an entrance hall was built in the angle between the two ranges.

The incumbents were in minor orders in 1309 and 1412.[22] William of Codford, curate in 1327,[23] rector in 1333, was a commissary of the court of Canterbury.[24] Augustine Church, rector 1498–9, was titular bishop of Lydda, and John Kite, 1499–1504, was archbishop of Armagh from 1513, bishop of Carlisle from 1521. Few later rectors were not pluralists. Nicholas Balgay, 1584–91, was also vicar of Idmiston and a canon, and from 1589 subdean, of Salisbury. Richard Hooker, 1591–5, also subdean of Salisbury, wrote part of his *Ecclesiastical Polity* while at Boscombe.[25] James White, 1632–61, was rector of Rollestone until 1644,[26] rector of Newton Tony 1660–1.[27] He preached once every Sunday in 1650, but did not observe fasts and thanksgiving days prescribed by parliament and used the Book of Common Prayer.[28] Charles Moss, 1738–50, was bishop of St. David's from 1766, of Bath and Wells from 1774.[29] John Jennings, 1750–68, was also vicar of Idmiston[30] and John Nairn, 1769–1815, was also rector of Pertwood. At Boscombe in 1783 a curate, who also served Bulford, held a service every Sunday, alternately morning and afternoon, and a service on some feast days. He administered the sacrament thrice a year to c. 5 communicants.[31] The rector held two services each Sunday in 1832.[32] On Census Sunday in 1851 a congregation of 73 attended morning and 79 afternoon service.[33] In 1864 the rector lived in the parish and held a service every Sunday, alternately morning and afternoon, for

91 *Andrews and Dury, Map* (W.R.S. viii), pl. 6; M. Watts, *Wilts. Windmills*, 4, 17.
92 O.S. Maps 6", Wilts. LXI (1883 and later edns.).
93 *V.C.H. Wilts.* iii. 250.
94 *Valor Eccl.* (Rec. Com.), ii. 94.
95 P.R.O., SC 6/Hen. VIII/3986, rot. 86d.
96 W.R.O. 1369, ct. bk. 1634–1796.
97 Hoare, *Mod. Wilts.* Amesbury, 113.
98 *Poor Law Abstract, 1804,* 558–9; *V.C.H. Wilts.* iv. 341.
99 *Poor Law Abstract, 1818,* 492–3.
1 *Poor Rate Returns, 1816–21,* 185; *1822–4,* 225; *1825–9,* 215; *1830–4,* 209.
2 *Poor Law Com. 2nd Rep.* App. D, 558.
3 O.S. Map 1/100,000, admin. areas, Wilts. (1974 edn.).
4 Gorham, *Hist. Eynesbury,* ii, p. cxxxv.
5 *W.A.M.* xl. 259–60.   6 Ch. Com. file 89944.
7 *Lond. Gaz.* 2 Oct. 1970, p. 10764.
8 Inf. from Ch. Com.
9 Gorham, *Hist. Eynesbury,* ii, pp. xlvi, cxxxv.
10 Phillipps, *Wilts. Inst.* (index in *W.A.M.* xxviii. 214).
11 Ch. Com. file 89944; inf. from Ch. Com.
12 *Tax. Eccl.* (Rec. Com.), 180.
13 *Valor Eccl.* (Rec. Com.), ii. 91.   14 *W.A.M.* xl. 259.

15 *Rep. Com. Eccl. Revenues,* 824–5.
16 P.R.O., IR 29/38/31; above, manors.
17 P.R.O., PROB 11/60, ff. 44–5; PROB 11/62, ff. 407–9; W.R.O. 1369, survey, 1719.
18 W.R.O., D 1/24/20/1.   19 Ibid. EA/185.
20 Ch. Com. file 89944.   21 W.R.O., D 1/11/71.
22 *Reg. Ghent* (Cant. & York Soc.), ii. 712; *Reg. Hallum* (Cant. & York Soc.), p. 177.
23 *Reg. Martival* (Cant. & York Soc.), ii. 551.
24 *Hemingby's Reg.* (W.R.S. xviii), p. 99.
25 *Alum. Oxon. 1500–1714,* i. 61; ii. 741, 867; Phillipps, *Wilts. Inst.* i. 179–80, 182, 234; *D.N.B.* (s.v. Ric. Hooker); for Hooker, see below, plate facing p. 75.
26 *Walker Revised,* ed. Matthews, 382; Phillipps, *Wilts. Inst.* ii. 16, 24.   27 Below, Newton Tony, church.
28 *W.A.M.* xl. 259.
29 *D.N.B.*; Phillipps, *Wilts. Inst.* ii. 69, 73.
30 Phillipps, *Wilts. Inst.* ii. 73; Hoare, *Mod. Wilts.* Amesbury, 117.
31 Phillipps, *Wilts. Inst.* ii. 84; *Vis. Queries, 1783* (W.R.S. xxvii), p. 38; W.R.O. 1807/2A.
32 Ch. Com. file, NB 34/32B/2.
33 P.R.O., HO 129/262/3/4/5.

a congregation of 50–60. He held services on Ash Wednesday, Good Friday, and Ascension day, and administered the sacrament six times a year to c. 20 communicants.[34] H. W. Barclay, rector from 1891, was also rector of Allington from 1895 and the first incumbent of the united benefice.[35]

ST. ANDREW'S church, so called in 1763,[36] is built of rubble with ashlar dressings and has a chancel and a nave with north transept and west bellcot. The thick walls of the chancel and of the nave may survive from the 12th-century church. The roofs were rebuilt, and the nave windows inserted, in the 15th century or early 16th. In the 17th the transept was built and new chancel windows were inserted. In 1709 the floors were repaved, box pews incorporating 17th-century panelling were fitted, the pulpit, dated 1623, was reset and given a sounding board, and above the pulpit a small casement window was inserted high in the south wall of the nave: the box pews and the pulpit remain in the church. In 1755 the east wall was rebuilt, in the 19th century the nave roof was reconstructed, and in the 20th century the transept was screened with re-used panelling to create a vestry. Weatherboarding on the sides of the bellcot was replaced by shingles after 1805.[37]

In 1553 a chalice of 6 oz. was left for the parish and 1 oz. of plate was taken for the king. A chalice, a paten, and a flagon, all hallmarked for 1708, were given in 1709,[38] and were held in 1993.[39] There were two bells in 1553. In 1993 a bell cast by Richard Florey in 1676 hung in the bellcot; a bell cast in the 18th century by William Tosier[40] fell in the 20th century and was stolen c. 1961.[41] Registrations of baptisms and marriages survive from 1696, of burials from 1698. Marriages are lacking for 1742–9 and burials for 1776–83.[42]

NONCONFORMITY. None known.

EDUCATION. There was a school with c. 14 pupils in 1833,[43] one with 27 in 1846–7,[44] and one with c. 10 in 1858. The older children went to school in Newton Tony or Idmiston in 1858.[45] Fewer children may later have gone to school in other parishes and c. 25 children were in Boscombe school, possibly held in a farm building, on attendance day in 1871.[46] That school lapsed and children again went to school in other parishes.[47] A new school opened in 1902. Anna Brunston, the teacher 1902–10, depicted Boscombe as 'Downlands' and gave an account of life at the school 1902–5 in *Letters of a School Ma'am* published in 1913.[48] Average attendance was 51 in 1906–7, 60 c. 1911, and 34 in 1938.[49] The school closed in 1972 and children from Boscombe afterwards attended school at Idmiston.[50]

CHARITY FOR THE POOR. John Kent (d. 1710) built at Boscombe a range of four one-roomed almshouses in 1708 and bequeathed £24 a year for the inmates, two widowers and two widows from either Boscombe or Winterbourne Dauntsey. Each inmate received 2s. 4d. a week. In 1833 three of the houses were held by the parish to house paupers and one was vacant. From the later 19th century those receiving the weekly payments were not required to live in the almshouses, which were often either empty or let.[51] In 1930 the almshouses were sold to the Bourne Valley Nursing Association and converted to a house for a nurse.[52] Weekly doles of 2s. 4d. or more were regularly paid to 3 or 4 recipients 1901–51.[53] The income of £22 a year was allowed to accumulate from 1973.[54]

BULFORD

BULFORD[55] village is 2.5 km. north-east of Amesbury; the rectangular parish is in the valley of the Christchurch Avon on the east side of the river and contains 1,474 ha. (3,642 a.).[56] Most parishes of Bulford's size in the Avon valley contained more than one settlement and tithing, and Bulford may have done so. Hindurrington was in the Middle Ages, but not later, the name of a settlement or a tithing or both: its name has led to the suggestion that it was in the neighbouring Durrington parish,[57] but the survival of the name for a farm and a field in Bulford in the 17th century,[58] and the size of Bulford parish, which contained only one settlement and one tithing without it, show that Hindurrington was in Bulford. In the 20th century a large army camp was built in the parish and from c. 1898 much land was used for military training.

34   W.R.O., D 1/56/7.
35   *Crockford* (1926); Ch. Com. file 89944.
36   J. Ecton, *Thesaurus* (1763), 391.
37   *Churches of SE. Wilts.* (R.C.H.M.), 54, 111; *Church Guide*; J. Buckler, watercolour in W.A.S. Libr., vol. i. 4.
38   Nightingale, *Wilts. Plate*, 37–8.
39   Inf. from the vicar, Allington.
40   Walters, *Wilts. Bells*, 31, 301, 303; inf. from the vicar.
41   Wilts. Cuttings, xxii. 48.
42   W.R.O. 1068/21–3; bishop's transcripts for some earlier years and for marriages 1742–9 are ibid.; marriages are printed in *Wilts. Par. Reg. (Mar)*, ed. W. P. W. Phillimore and J. Sadler, iii. 147–51.
43   *Educ. Enq. Abstract*, 1029.
44   Nat. Soc. *Inquiry, 1846–7*, Wilts. 2–3.
45   *Acct. of Wilts. Schs.* 7.
46   *Returns relating to Elem. Educ.* 426–7.

47   A. Brunston, *Letters of a Sch. Ma'am*, 58.
48   Ibid. 57; *Return of Non-Provided Schs.* 39; W.R.O. 1807/6; ibid. F 8/500, Boscombe sch. 1902–53.
49   *Bd. of Educ., List 21, 1908* (H.M.S.O.), 500; *1912*, 547; *1913*, 547; *1938*, 421.
50   W.R.O., F 8/500, Boscombe sch. 1953–72.
51   *Endowed Char. Wilts.* (S. Div.), 32–5; date on ho.
52   W.R.O. 992/7.   53   Ibid. L 2, Boscombe.
54   Inf. from the vicar.
55   This article was written in 1991–2.
56   Maps used include O.S. Maps 1", sheet 14 (1817 edn.); 1/50,000, sheet 184 (1988 edn.); 1/25,000, 41/14, 41/24 (1948 edns.); 6", Wilts. LIV–LV (1883–7 and later edns.).
57   *Tax List, 1332* (W.R.S. xlv), 110; *V.C.H. Wilts.* iv. 306.
58   P.R.O., LR 2/191, f. 126; W.R.O. 367/3, deed, Duke, 1744.

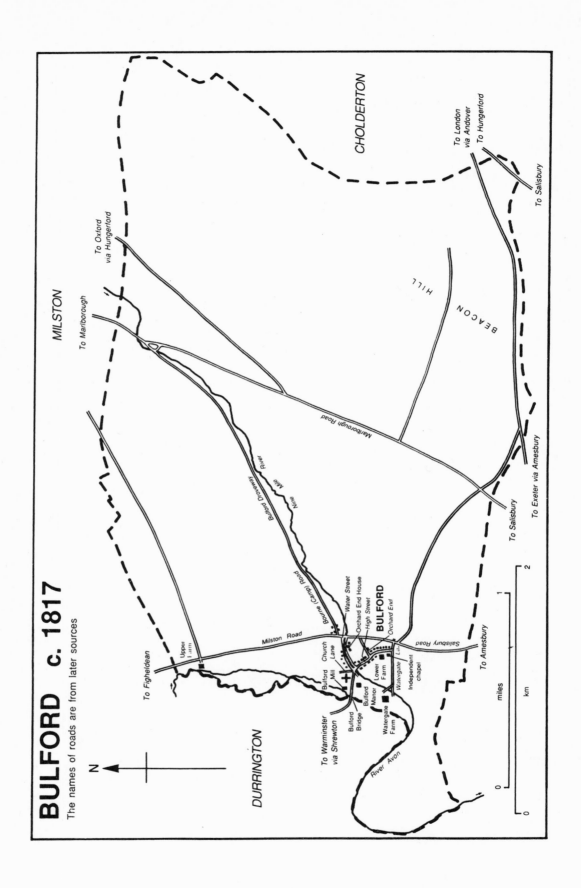

BULFORD c. 1817

The names of roads are from later sources

The parish boundaries may be those of Amesbury abbey's Domesday estate called Bulford,[59] and there is no evidence of a change in them. The western, with Durrington, is the Avon, part of the northern follows a dry valley, and the east part of the southern and the north part of the eastern, which separates Wiltshire from Hampshire, are marked by prehistoric ditches.

Chalk outcrops over nearly all the parish; a small area of Reading Beds is on the summit of Beacon Hill. Alluvium and gravel have been deposited by the Avon and its tributary, Nine Mile river, which flows south-west across the parish.[60] Apart from in the south-east corner, where Beacon Hill reaches 204 m., and along the eastern boundary, the relief in the parish is gentle. Land use was typical of the Wiltshire chalklands: there were meadows beside the Avon and Nine Mile river, open fields on the gravel and lower slopes of the downs, and rough pasture on the higher land furthest from the village.[61] In 1918–19, to commemorate the use of Bulford camp by New Zealand forces, the chalk on a north-west facing part of Beacon Hill was exposed to form the figure of a kiwi.[62]

Three main roads crossed the parish in the later 17th century. The road from Chipping Campden (Glos.) via Marlborough to Salisbury crossed the centre of the parish north–south, the road from Oxford via Hungerford (Berks.) to Salisbury crossed the south-east tip, and the road from London via Andover (Hants), Amesbury, Shrewton, and Warminster to Bridgwater (Som.) also crossed the south-east corner. By 1773 a new course, west of the old, had been adopted as the Hungerford road, which in the early 19th century ran north-east and south-west across the centre of the parish and merged with the Marlborough road east of the village.[63] A road on the north bank of Nine Mile river led south-west from the Marlborough road, crossed the Avon at Bulford village, ran through Durrington parish to Shrewton, and provided an alternative route between London and Warminster.[64] In 1761 the Andover–Amesbury road and a road across the south-west part of the parish through Bulford village to Durrington were turnpiked. A road linking the villages on the east bank of the Avon crossed the parish and through the village ran near the church. It was replaced by a road, leading from Figheldean through the east part of Bulford village to the London road at Folly bottom in Amesbury, also turnpiked in 1761. The roads were disturnpiked in 1871.[65] From 1958 the Andover–Amesbury road has been part of the London–Exeter trunk road.[66] The Hungerford road was still important in 1833 when the inhabitants of Bulford were summoned

to quarter sessions for failure to repair it.[67] That and the Marlborough road were used less after a more easterly road through the Bourne valley was turnpiked in 1835,[68] and north of the army camp were closed after the north-east part of the parish began to be used for military training.[69] The road linking the Marlborough road and Bulford village, called Bourne Road in 1838,[70] later Bulford Droveway and Camp Road, remained open and was joined across Sheep bridge to a new road, made in 1909–10 to replace the Hungerford road, running north-east and south-west below Beacon Hill between Tidworth camp and Bulford camp.[71]

The Amesbury and Military Camp Light Railway, a branch of the L. & S.W.R., was extended as a single track from Amesbury through Bulford village to a terminus 3 km. ENE. of the church in 1906. There was a station for the public south of the village, another station for passengers at Bulford camp, and a goods depot at the terminus. The line was closed to passengers in 1952 and entirely in 1963.[72]

A belief in the prehistoric significance of a large sarsen submerged in the Avon south of Bulford bridge and of another standing on high ground south-east of the village in the 19th century has been discredited.[73] The etymology of Haradon Hill, the name used for the summit of Beacon Hill in the 18th century, may refer to prehistoric religious rites.[74] Bulford is in an area of early settlement, and Neolithic, Bronze-Age, Pagan Saxon, and Romano-British artefacts have been found on Beacon Hill and other downland. A prehistoric ditch, distinct from the two on the boundaries, runs from Beacon Hill first north, then east, and again north into and across Milston parish. A small prehistoric field system lies south of Bulford village, and part of a large one extends into the south-east part of the parish from Amesbury.[75] There are numerous barrows of various types on the downs, and on Beacon Hill there is a cemetery of 70 or more bowl barrows with associated burials and cremations.[76]

Bulford and Hindurrington had a total of 125 poll-tax payers in 1377.[77] The population of the parish rose from 228 in 1801 to 408 in 1851, and declined to 343 in 1871: the decline from 383 in 1861 was caused by the death of more old people than usual, migration, and temporary absence of some families. The population remained almost constant 1871–91 but increased rapidly with the establishment of Bulford camp c. 1898. In 1901 it was 1,386 including 435 construction workers and 608 soldiers. The military population continued to grow and most of the 3,923 inhabitants in 1931, and of the 5,213 in 1951, lived in the

59 Below, manor (Bulford).
60 Geol. Surv. Map 1", drift, sheet 282 (1967 edn.).
61 Below, econ. hist.
62 N. D. G. James, *Plain Soldiering*, 111, 113.
63 J. Ogilby, *Brit.* (1675), pls. 32, 83, 85; *Andrews and Dury, Map* (W.R.S. viii), pl. 9; O.S. Map 1", sheet 14 (1817 edn.).
64 *Andrews and Dury, Map* (W.R.S. viii), pl. 9; *W.A.M.* xl. 258; Winch. Coll. Mun. 5908B.
65 *V.C.H. Wilts.* iv. 257, 261–2, 270; *L.J.* xxx. 138.
66 W.R.O., F 4/200/21.
67 Ibid. 814/31.

68 *V.C.H. Wilts.* iv. 257, 262, 270.
69 Below, this section.   70 P.R.O., IR 30/38/49.
71 James, *Plain Soldiering*, 99.
72 P. A. Harding, *Bulford Branch Line*, 3, 7–8, 27–8.
73 J. Britton, *Beauties of Wilts.* ii. 154; O.S. Map 1", sheet 14 (1817 edn.); cf. *W.A.M.* xxxvi. 636.
74 *Andrews and Dury, Map* (W.R.S. viii), pl. 9; *P.N. Wilts.* (E.P.N.S.), pp. xiv, 359, where it is wrongly identified with Earl's Farm down in Amesbury.
75 *V.C.H. Wilts.* i (1), 52, 251, 254, 272, 274; i (2), 380.
76 Ibid. i (1), 139, 162–4, 209, 217, 223, 235, 240.
77 Ibid. iv. 306.

camp.[78] The population declined to 4,125 in 1961, rose to 5,889 in 1971, and in 1991 was 5,255.[79]

Bulford village grew up on the gravel beside the Avon; Hindurrington, probably a settlement in the Middle Ages, is likely to have been on a similar site further north. The village had three main lines of settlement. The church, two 17th-century manor houses, a mill, and some principal farm buildings were all on or near the old road on the east bank of the Avon superseded in 1761. That road, part of which survives as Church Lane, was crossed at the church by the London–Warminster road, there wide enough for Nine Mile river to flow along the middle of it[80] and later called Water Street. A line of about eight houses, most perhaps the copyhold farmhouses of Bulford manor, survives in Water Street. The houses, characteristically of flint and red brick with thatched roofs, are apparently mostly 18th-century. One on the south side of the street, Orchard End House, was built of flint and chalk in the 17th century and altered in the early 19th, when new windows were inserted in the south entrance front and tall cob walls were built to enclose a garden. Water Street presumably went out of use as a thoroughfare after other roads through the village were turnpiked, and by the late 19th century was no more than a footpath beside the watercourse.[81] Thereafter local needs were served by the Old Coach Road north of it.

The ford which gave the village its name was replaced by a bridge, possibly c. 1761 when the road to Durrington was turnpiked. Through Bulford village that road is called High Street. Lower Farm on the west side of it is a 17th-century farmhouse, of flint with stone quoins, altered and extended in the 19th century. An inn, the site of a 19th-century school, and a house converted to a school are on the east side, and a nonconformist chapel stands at the junction with Watergate Lane.

Buildings in the village, possibly the north part, were destroyed by fire c. 1685,[82] and a farmstead called Hindurrington, apparently not far north of the church, had been demolished by 1758.[83] A new farmstead, Upper Farm, possibly replacing farm buildings at Bulford Manor,[84] had been built beside the turnpike road from Figheldean near the northern parish boundary by 1773.[85] The farmhouse, of flint with red-brick dressings, was altered and extended in the 19th century. Near the village a vicarage house was built in the late 19th century beside the Figheldean road, which was called Milston Road north of the village, Salisbury Road through and south of it, but otherwise there was little settlement beside the road before the 20th century.

There was one inn or more in the village from the earlier 16th century.[86] One was called the Lamb in 1604,[87] one the Maidenhead in 1764 and the 1820s.[88] The Rose and Crown in High Street was open in 1844,[89] rebuilt in 1896,[90] and open in 1992. A friendly society met at the Maidenhead in the late 18th century and early 19th: it had 70 members in 1803, c. 112 when the population of Bulford was only c. 230 between c. 1812 and 1815.[91] A friendly society which met at the Rose and Crown was dissolved in 1889.[92] There was a brass band and a choral society in the village in 1903.[93]

There were few buildings in the east part of the parish before c. 1898. Farm buildings erected on the east side of Beacon Hill in the earlier 19th century were demolished in the mid 20th;[94] the site of a cottage standing in the earlier 19th century near the boundary with Cholderton east of Beacon Hill was used c. 1900 for Scotland Lodge, a large house of flint and red brick on H. C. Stephens's Cholderton estate;[95] four cottages at Bulford Penning west of Beacon Hill in the mid 19th century were demolished in the early 20th.[96]

Bulford village grew north, south, and east in the 20th century. The new houses were presumably built for civilians working at Bulford camp, and in the late 1960s an eastwards extension of the village met a westwards extension of the camp.[97] The old part of the village, however, was little affected: on the site of the old school in High Street[98] an estate of private houses and a working men's club were built in the 1980s, in Orchard End two houses incorporating shops were built in 1927[99] and a large house in the grounds of Orchard End House was built in 1991,[1] and in Watergate Lane several houses were built after the Second World War. A reading room in High Street in the earlier 20th century was replaced by a village hall in Watergate Lane.[2] To the north the village was extended by the building of three large houses for army officers east of the Vicarage between 1901 and 1926,[3] of a police station and three terraces each of four council houses on the east side of Milston Road in the late 1920s,[4] and of three houses for soldiers between the Vicarage and the council houses in 1954.[5] After the rail-

78 V.C.H. Wilts. iv. 323, 325, 342; below, this section.
79 Census, 1961; 1971; 1991.
80 Andrews and Dury, Map (W.R.S. viii), pl. 9.
81 O.S. Map 6", Wilts. LV (1883 edn.).
82 W. A. Bewes, Church Briefs, 290.
83 P.R.O., PROB 11/837, ff. 72–9; below, econ. hist.
84 Below, econ. hist.
85 Andrews and Dury, Map (W.R.S. viii), pl. 9.
86 P.R.O., SC 6/Hen. VIII/3986, rot. 76d.
87 Ibid. LR 2/203, f. 369.
88 W.R.O. 367/3, deed, Southby to Southby, 1764; ibid. A 1/326/3.
89 Ibid. 1550/48; P.R.O., FS 4/55, Wilts. no. 231.
90 Date on bldg.
91 V.C.H. Wilts. iv. 342; Poor Law Abstract, 1804, 558–9; 1818, 492–3; P.R.O., FS 4/55, Wilts. no. 74.
92 P.R.O., FS 4/55, Wilts. no. 231.
93 W.R.O. 2770/2.
94 P.R.O., IR 29/38/49; IR 30/38/49; O.S. Maps 1", sheet 14 (1817 edn.); 1/25,000, 41/24 (1948 edn.); SU 24 (1958 edn.).
95 Below, Cholderton, intro.; P.R.O., IR 29/38/49; IR 30/38/49.
96 O.S. Maps 6", Wilts. LV (1883 and later edns.); W.R.O. 1550/48.   97 Below, this section.
98 Ibid. educ.
99 Date on bldgs.
1 Date on ho.
2 O.S. Maps 6", Wilts. LIV. SE. (1926 edn.); 1/10,000, SU 14 SE. (1976 edn.); W.R.O., Inland Revenue, val. reg. 142.
3 O.S. Maps 6", Wilts. LIV. SE. (1901, 1926 edns.).
4 Ibid. 6", Wilts. LIV. SE. (1926 edn.); W.R.O., A 1/355/266.   5 James, Plain Soldiering, 118.

way station was built at the south end of the village in 1906 the south-east extension of High Street, leading to the Andover–Amesbury road, was called Station Road. On the west side of Salisbury Road south of its junction with High Street private houses were built in the early 20th century;[6] on the east side of Station Road two terraces each of four council houses were built in 1927; Station Terrace, 16 council houses in pairs, was built on the west side of Station Road and the east side of Salisbury Road in 1931.[7] The station and a house and two cottages built nearby c. 1906 were demolished after c. 1965, and from 1969 the site has been occupied by extensive offices of the Property Services Agency.[8] The growth of the village eastwards took place after the Second World War when, to replace temporary housing north-east of the village, a large council estate was built east of Salisbury Road along the line and immediately south of Nine Mile river in the 1950s and 1960s. By 1955 c. 82 houses had been built near Salisbury Road in St. Leonard's Close, the Crescent (later Crescent Road), and Meadow Road.[9] In the 1960s building continued further east in John French Way and Churchill Avenue, parallel north-east and south-west roads, and in roads connecting them.[10] Also in the 1960s 11 old people's bungalows were built in the angle of High Street and Salisbury Road.[11]

Bulford camp,[12] mostly between Nine Mile river and the foot of Beacon Hill,[13] was a principal base of the Royal Artillery 1905–77, the base of the New Zealand expeditionary force 1914–18, and from 1977 the headquarters of South West District command. Rifle ranges were set up 1898–9, and by 1901 had been incorporated in a camp which was hutted to the south, tented to the north. The Marlborough–Salisbury road became the main road through the camp, there called Marlborough Road, but was closed a little north of it.[14] The south part of the camp was served by a new road, Bulford Road, leading south-east from Camp Road; east of the junction Bulford Droveway also served the camp. Permanent red-brick barracks were built on a grid pattern either side of Marlborough Road c. 1910. From 1914 Sling barracks to the north replaced the tents and housed the New Zealand forces. The barracks were all called after First World War battles 1922–38, but from 1938 were renamed; Beacon (now Picton) and Kiwi barracks are east of the road, Gordon, Ward, and Wing are west of it. Sling barracks had been partly demolished by 1923. Marlborough barracks were also west of the

road: they lost their identity after c. 1961 when part was merged with Ward, part with Gordon, and part with Wing barracks. Beacon barracks were rebuilt 1967–76, Gordon c. 1976. Carter barracks, a hutted camp north of Bulford Droveway, were built 1939–40 and demolished in 1978. At its most extensive, in the 1960s and 1970s, Bulford camp covered c. 640 a.

Mainly on the perimeter of the camp extensive housing estates, several with tree-lined roads, were built for soldiers and their families. To the north houses were built on the site of Sling barracks in 1937–8, 1952, and 1968; the Australian estate was built east of Kiwi barracks in 1963; in the north-west the Irish estate was built in 1968, and in the west the Canadian estate was built in the same year. Army housing built in 1969 in Dorset Close, Hampshire Close, and Wiltshire Close, all west of Bulford Road, linked the Canadian estate to the council housing in Churchill Avenue and John French Way.

Bulford camp has been provided with most of the facilities of a small town, including churches,[15] hospitals, schools,[16] sports grounds, a theatre, and cinemas. A new cinema opened in 1939 in Marlborough Road was standing in 1992 but not open. Before 1910 a dairy, shops, and branches of banks had opened.[17] On the site of a hospital west of Marlborough Road, a police station, opened in 1966,[18] a shopping centre, opened in the 1970s, and a NAAFI were built. The Saxon Warrior inn was opened in 1974. Two packs of Royal Artillery hounds have been based at the camp, harriers 1907–17 and 1919–39, for which kennels were built in 1934, and foxhounds from 1942.[19]

MANOR AND OTHER ESTATES. Amesbury abbey held *BULFORD* from before the Conquest: 3 hides held by Alward in 1086 were part of the abbey's estate in 1066 and probably again later.[20] When the manor was confirmed to Amesbury priory in 1179 it included land at Hindurrington,[21] and in 1286 the priory was granted free warren in its demesne at Bulford and Hindurrington.[22] From the Dissolution to 1614 the manor belonged to the Crown:[23] in 1610 James I settled it on Henry, prince of Wales (d. 1612).[24] In 1614 Leonard Welsted bought it and sold it to (Sir) John Daccombe, who sold it in moieties.[25]

The lordship and a moiety of the manor were bought in 1614 by George Duke[26] (d. 1618), who devised the estate, called Bulford manor and including Hindurrington farm, to his sons An-

6   O.S. Maps 6", Wilts. LIV. SE. (1901, 1926 edns.); above, this section [railway].
7   W.R.O., G 1/600/1.
8   Ibid. F 12/125/17; ibid. G 1/516/4; James, *Plain Soldiering*, 119; O.S. Maps 6", Wilts. SU 14 SE. (1961 edn.); 1/10,000, SU 14 SE. (1976 edn.).
9   O.S. Maps 1/25,000, 41/14 (1948 edn.); SU 14 (1958 edn.); W.R.O., G 1/501/1; G 1/505/1.
10   W.R.O., G 1/516/4; G 1/602/3–4.
11   O.S. Maps 6", Wilts. SU 14 SE. (1961 edn.); 1/10,000, SU 14 SE. (1976 edn.).
12   See plate facing p. 171.
13   This and the 2 following paras. are based on James, *Plain Soldiering*, 91–119, 247.
14   Above, this section [roads].

15   Below, churches; Rom. Cath.
16   Below, educ.
17   *Kelly's Dir. Wilts.* (1903 and later edns.).
18   Wilts. Cuttings, xxiii. 2.
19   N. D. G. James, *Gunners at Larkhill*, 208–10; James, *Plain Soldiering*, 110.
20   *V.C.H. Wilts.* ii, p. 131.
21   *Cal. Chart. R. 1257–1300*, 157–9; for the hist. of the abbey and priory, *V.C.H. Wilts.* iii. 242–59.
22   *Cal. Chart. R. 1257–1300*, 336.
23   P.R.O., C 66/2043, no. 10; ibid. SC 6/Hen. VIII/3986, rott. 76d.–77d.
24   Ibid. C 66/1879, no. 2.
25   *Cat. Anct. D.* vi, C 7911.
26   Ibid.

drew (d. 1633) and George, a lunatic from 1627, in moieties. Andrew devised his moiety to his brother John, to whom the younger George's son George sold his in 1647.[27] The estate passed from John (d. 1671) to his son Andrew (d. 1678) and to Andrew's relict Mary (fl. 1682) and son Andrew (d. 1730). In 1719 Andrew gave Hindurrington farm to his son Andrew (d. *s.p.* 1727) for life: he was succeeded in the whole estate by his son Richard[28] (d. 1757), who devised it in moieties to his sisters Anne (d. 1770), wife of Anthony Southby, and Mary. Anne's son Richard Southby inherited Mary's moiety and in 1764 Anne gave hers to him in an exchange. Richard (d. 1791) was succeeded in turn by his son Richard (d. 1791) and, as joint owners, by his daughters Charity (d. *s.p.* 1830), who married Sir John Pollen, Bt., and Mary[29] (will proved 1835).[30] In 1835 the estate passed to Mary Southby's kinsman Anthony Gapper (d. 1883),[31] who assumed the name Southby in 1835,[32] and from Anthony it passed to his son Edmund Southby (d. 1886). Edmund's trustees sold it in 1886 to J. L. Hill,[33] who in 1898 sold Bulford Manor and 1,899 a. to the War Department. The Ministry of Defence was the owner in 1992.[34]

Bulford Manor was built in the 17th century of stone and flint, and consisted of a long and narrow east–west range with a principal north front.[35] In the early 18th century, for Andrew Duke (d. 1730), a red-brick range incorporating a staircase was built on the south side to form a square house.[36] An embattled stone bay window was constructed on the west side of the 17th-century range in the mid 19th century, and in the 1890s a large service wing was built for J. L. Hill at the south-east corner of the 18th-century range. The service wing, of flint and stone to the north, red brick to the south, incorporates stables at its north-east corner.[37]

The second moiety of Bulford manor was bought in 1617 from Sir John Daccombe by Sir Laurence Washington[38] (d. 1643): it became known as Seymour's, afterwards as *WATERGATE* farm. It descended to Sir Laurence's son Laurence (d. 1661) and to Laurence's daughter Elizabeth, from 1671 the wife of Sir Robert Shirley, Bt. (Baron Ferrers from 1677, Earl Ferrers from 1711).[39] Elizabeth and Robert sold it in 1678 to Sir Edward Seymour[40] (Bt. from

1685, d. 1708), speaker of the House of Commons. It passed to Sir Edward's son Sir Edward[41] (d. 1740), who devised it to his son William (d. 1747).[42] It descended in the Seymour family, apparently belonged to Francis Seymour in 1780 and to William Seymour in 1808–9,[43] and in 1817 was Henry Seymour's. The farm, 1,633 a. in the south part of the parish, passed from Henry (d. 1849) to his sons Henry (d. 1877) and Alfred (d. 1888) successively. Alfred's heir, his daughter Jane (d. 1943), in 1897 sold 383 a. on Beacon Hill to H. C. Stephens:[44] that land passed with Stephens's Cholderton estate to P. M. L. Edmunds, who sold 101 a. in 1933, and Mr. H. A. Edmunds, who sold *c.* 200 a. in 1986. In 1992 the *c.* 300 a. belonged to the Ministry of Defence, the *c.* 80 a. to Mr. H. A. Edmunds.[45] Jane Seymour sold 751 a. in 1898, 11 a. in 1899, and 288 a. in 1901, all to the War Department: the Ministry of Defence owned that land in 1992.[46] About 200 a. passed in 1943 to Jane's cousin Sir Frederick Rawlinson, Bt.,[47] who sold them to H. J. Street in 1947. Street immediately sold Watergate House and 6 a. to Sir Noel Beresford-Peirse (d. 1953), whose relict Camilla sold them in 1985 to Dr. Charles Goodson-Wickes, M.P., the owner in 1992.[48] Of Street's other land some belonged in 1992 to Mr. M. Rowland, some to the Ministry of Defence.[49]

Watergate House was built in 1618,[50] evidently for Sir Laurence Washington, as a small stone house with an east entrance front and, on the ground floor, one room north and one room south of a central stack. About 1800 the addition of a block to the west, mostly of stone and flint, made the house square, and a south entrance front, of chequered flint and ashlar, was made across both the old and new parts. A verandah was built along the south front later in the 19th century. An L-shaped red-brick service wing was built on the north side of the house in the mid 19th century. Two large 17th- or early 18th-century aisled barns stand north-west of the house.

William Andrews (d. 1637) bought *c.* 50 a. in Bulford and Hindurrington from John Daccombe's feoffees, presumably *c.* 1614, and before 1633 *c.* 58 a. from Philip More.[51] The 108 a., with pasture rights, passed successively to his

27 *W.N. & Q.* viii. 196; P.R.O., C 142/510, no. 60; C 142/650, no. 126; W.R.O. 367/3, Duke's abstr. of title (deed, 1659); 492/45.
28 *W.N. & Q.* viii. 199, 295, pedigrees at pp. 300–1; Hoare, *Mod. Wilts.* Amesbury, 45; W.R.O. 367/3, Duke's abstr. of title (deed, Duke to Duke, 1719); ibid. wills, archd. Sar., Andrew Duke, 1678.
29 *W.N. & Q.* viii. 297–9; Burke, *Peerage* (1963), 1950; W.R.O., A 1/345/64; ibid. 367/3, deed, Southby to Southby, 1764. 30 P.R.O., PROB 11/1846, ff. 79v.–83v.
31 W.R.O. 2216/62; G.P.L., Treas. Solicitor, 432/51/4.
32 W. P. W. Phillimore and E. A. Fry, *Changes of Name*, 298.
33 *Endowed Char. Wilts.* (S. Div.), 82; Wilts. Cuttings, xvi. 23; G.P.L., Treas. Solicitor, 432/51/4.
34 Inf. from Defence Land Agent, Durrington.
35 See plate facing p. 267.
36 Inscription AD/1724 on rainwater head.
37 Date stone JLH/1890 on stables and inscription JLH/1893 in 17th-cent. range.
38 P.R.O., C 54/2336, no. 35.
39 *V.C.H. Wilts.* xiv. 90; W.R.O. 84/47/3; 367/3, Duke's

abstr. of title.
40 Leics. R.O. 26D53/1425.
41 *D.N.B.*; W.R.O. 1332, box 55, deed, Seymour to Reeves, 1735.
42 *Complete Peerage*, xii (1), 82; P.R.O., PROB 11/709, ff. 83v.–85. 43 W.R.O., A 1/345/64.
44 Ibid. 1340/1, deed, Seymour to Stephens, 1897; Burke, *Peerage* (1963), 2267; P.R.O., IR 29/38/49; IR 30/38/49; G.P.L., Treas. Solicitor, 2850/50, abstr. of title.
45 Below, Cholderton, manors; Wilts. Cuttings, xviii. 70; W.R.O. 1340/3; 1894/77; inf. from Mr. H. A. Edmunds, Cholderton Park; Defence Land Agent.
46 Inf. from Defence Land Agent.
47 Burke, *Peerage* (1963), 2033, 2267; W.R.O., Inland Revenue, val. reg. 142.
48 W.A.S. Libr., sale cat. xxxvii. 36; deeds in possession of, and inf. from, Dr. C. Goodson-Wickes, Watergate Ho.
49 Inf. from Mr. P. J. Rowland, Ratfyn Farm, Amesbury; Defence Land Agent.
50 A tablet bearing that date has been reset in the W. wall.
51 *Wilts. Inq. p.m.* 1625–49 (Index Libr.), 339–41.

relict Alice and grandson William Andrews, presumably the William Andrews who sold the estate to Lancelot Addison, rector of Milston, part in 1672 and part in 1674.[52] In 1692 Addison sold it to Andrew Duke, who added it to Bulford manor.[53]

A small estate, later *CHAFYN'S* farm, at Hindurrington was held *c.* 1550 by William Chafyn[54] (d. 1558), who devised it to James Foxhanger.[55] It was owned in 1604 by William Staples[56] and may have been the farm owned in 1804 by William Dyke, in 1825–6 by T. W. Dyke,[57] and in 1838–9, when it was 73 a. and included Orchard End House, by Richard and John Cooe.[58] The War Department owned the land in 1910,[59] the Ministry of Defence in 1992.[60]

The tithes from the parish may have been taken by Amesbury abbey, and in 1179 were confirmed to Amesbury priory.[61] The *RECTORY* estate, which included 1 yardland besides the tithes,[62] passed with Bulford manor to John Daccombe, and from 1614 with the reduced Bulford manor in the Duke and Southby families.[63] Watergate farm, owned by the Washington and Seymour families,[64] was free from great tithes, and the tithes from the reduced Bulford manor were merged with the land from which they arose. In 1838 the small tithes from Watergate farm, and the great and small tithes from remaining land in the parish, 76 a., were valued at £97 and commuted.[65]

ECONOMIC HISTORY. In 1086 Bulford had land for 9 ploughteams and 8 are known to have been there. On Amesbury abbey's 12-hide estate half was demesne, on which were 13 *servi* and 3 teams. Of the other half 3 hides may have been held by lease and have supported 1 team, and on 3 hides 3 *villani*, 20 coscets, and 3 cottars had 5 teams. There were 35 a. of meadow, and pasture 1 league by ½ league.[66]

Sheep-and-corn husbandry typical of Wiltshire chalk country prevailed in the parish in the Middle Ages and until the 20th century. Produce of the demesne was used to stock the larder of Amesbury priory in the early 14th century; in the mid 15th century and later the demesne was leased.[67] Apart from the demesne there were 25 copyholds, including 1 of 2½ yardlands, 1 of 2 yardlands, 2 of 1½ yardland, 5 of 1 yardland, and 14 of ½ yardland or less. A leasehold of 43 a. may formerly have been two copyholds, and,

since they shared Stewards mead with the lessee of the demesne, two copyholds, of 30 a. and 40 a., may formerly have been demesne.[68]

In the mid 16th century four open fields, North, Middle, South, and Hindurrington, contained 790 a., Michell mead was a common meadow of 25 a.,[69] and North and Hindurrington downs provided 500 a. of pasture in common.[70] The process of inclosure had begun in the early 16th century when William Chafyn, lessee of the demesne from 1502, inclosed *c.* 16 a. of arable, converted it to meadow land, and may have inclosed a further *c.* 72 a. of arable.[71] About 1550 the demesne included two several downs, Middle and South,[72] on which a flock of 1,200 sheep could be kept,[73] and 37 a. of mainly several meadows.[74] In 1584 the lessee inclosed his remaining open arable, 205 a. in North, South, and Hindurrington fields, and Michell mead. To compensate them for their loss of common rights at that inclosure the lessee gave to the customary tenants other open arable, later called High field and Low field, and New leaze, Middle leaze, both mainly inclosed, and Old leaze. In 1604 the demesne included pasture rights on the 200-a. Hindurrington down but was otherwise mainly several and was apparently a very large farm. The commonable lands of the parish remained extensive: there were still six open fields of which two, High and Low, contained 349 a., and the downland included North down, 300 a., but most of the tenants' 61 a. of meadow land had been inclosed.[75]

The large demesne farm was divided in the 17th century, presumably *c.* 1614 when Bulford manor was sold in portions.[76] The northern part had itself been divided by 1659 when it was in two farms, Manor and Hindurrington:[77] Manor may have been worked from buildings on the site of Bulford Manor, Hindurrington from buildings north of the church.[78] In 1678 Manor farm had on it *c.* 1,000 sheep and 16 cows.[79] The southern part of the demesne was later Watergate farm.[80] In the 18th century Upper Farm was built, apparently as a new farmstead for Manor, or Upper, farm, and new buildings were presumably erected for Hindurrington farm.[81] In 1604 there were 17 farms held on lives by copy or lease, much copyhold land having been converted to leasehold between 1584 and then;[82] in 1744 there were 16.[83] Richard Duke (d. 1757), lord of Bulford manor, directed that his successor should allow the tenancies of the leaseholds

52 W.R.O. 367/3, deeds, Andrews to Addison, 1672, 1674; below, Milston, church.
53 P.R.O., CP 25/2/888/4 Wm. and Mary Mich.
54 Ibid. LR 2/191, f. 126.
55 W.R.O., wills, archd. Sar., reg. 3, f. 141 and v.
56 P.R.O., LR 2/203, f. 368.
57 W.R.O., A 1/345/64.
58 P.R.O., IR 29/38/49; IR 30/38/49.
59 W.R.O., Inland Revenue, val. reg. 142.
60 Inf. from Defence Land Agent.
61 *Cal. Chart. R.* 1257–1300, 157–9.
62 *Valor Eccl.* (Rec. Com.), ii. 93.
63 P.R.O., C 142/650, no. 126; W.R.O. 367/3, deed, Southby to Southby, 1764; above, this section.
64 Above, this section.
65 P.R.O., IR 29/38/49; IR 30/38/49.
66 *V.C.H. Wilts.* ii, p. 131.
67 Ibid. iii. 249, 254; P.R.O., C 3/21/1.

68 P.R.O., LR 2/191, ff. 126–30; ibid. SC 6/Hen. VIII/3986, rott. 76d.–78.
69 Ibid. LR 2/191, ff. 126–30.
70 Ibid. E 310/26/155, f. 34; ibid. LR 2/203, ff. 372, 377v.; W.R.O. 367/3, deed, Daccombe to Castleman, 1614.
71 P.R.O., C 3/21/1; ibid. LR 2/191, f. 129; W.R.O. 865/182.　72 P.R.O., LR 2/191, f. 129.
73 *Cal. Pat.* 1563–6, p. 69.
74 P.R.O., LR 2/191, ff. 126–30.
75 Ibid. E 178/2424; ibid. LR 2/203, ff. 365–80.
76 Above, manor.
77 W.R.O. 367/3, deeds, Duke to Duke, 1719; Duke to Grist, 1728; Duke, 1744; 367/3, Duke's abstr. of title.
78 *W.N. & Q.* viii. 298.
79 W.R.O., wills, archd. Sar., Andrew Duke, 1678.
80 Above, manor.
81 Above, intro.　82 P.R.O., LR 2/203, ff. 365–80.
83 W.R.O. 367/3, deed, Duke, 1744.

and copyholds for lives to fall in and should add the land to Upper and Hindurrington farms. He also forbade his successor to plough or burnbake downland.[84] There was a private inclosure agreement in 1827,[85] and by 1838 the smaller farms had been absorbed by Upper and Hindurrington farms and open-field cultivation and common husbandry had been eliminated. In 1838 Upper farm was 810 a., Hindurrington farm 960 a., and Watergate farm 1,633 a. A fourth farm, 73 a., was worked from Orchard End House.[86]

Meadows beside the Avon and Nine Mile river were watered from the 17th century to the earlier 20th.[87] Although no downland in either Upper farm or Hindurrington farm was burnbaked, some in Watergate farm was, and in 1838 that farm had an additional farmstead on the downs at Bulford Penning. There was slightly more arable than pasture in the parish in 1838.[88] From c. 1860 about a third of the parish was arable and the chief grain crop was barley. Numbers of sheep pastured on the downs increased from c. 3,000 in 1867 to c. 4,500 in 1886. Arable was sown with temporary grasses, fewer sheep were kept, and herds of dairy cows increased 1886–96. Agriculture ceased on more than half the parish after 1898 as land was used for military training and for Bulford camp. On the other land arable continued to decline and cattle to replace sheep.[89] More land was ploughed after 1939. In 1992 of c. 350 a., mostly arable, in the south-west corner of the parish c. 150 a. were worked with Ratfyn farm, based in Amesbury;[90] the c. 250 a. of agricultural land in the north-west corner were used mainly for growing cereals; there was also arable on the c. 80 a. of farmland in the south-east corner.

There was no woodland in the parish until 38 a. in Sling plantation were planted between 1820 and 1838.[91] Plantations north-east of Nine Mile river and on Beacon Hill were made between c. 1877 and 1899.[92] More trees were planted around Bulford camp and on the downs from 1964, and in 1991 there were c. 360 a. of woodland in the parish.[93]

Amesbury abbey's Bulford estate had two mills in 1086,[94] and Amesbury priory is known to have had mills at Bulford in the 13th century[95] and the 14th.[96] In 1539–40 there were two mills on Bulford manor, possibly in one building.[97] All those mills were presumably on the Avon. A new mill was built between 1726 and 1735.[98] At Bulford mill, on the Avon near the church, paper was made from 1765 to the 1870s:[99] the mill house is a red-brick building of the 19th century.

In 1831 most men in Bulford were farm labourers, but a few followed retail trades, presumably outside the parish.[1] In the 20th century nearly all the trade and industry in the parish has been at Bulford camp.[2]

LOCAL GOVERNMENT. Presumably under a general confirmation of liberties to Amesbury priory in 1179, view of frankpledge, in addition to a manor court, was held for Bulford manor in the Middle Ages.[3] While the Crown owned the manor 1539–1614 tenants of neighbouring royal estates owed suit at Bulford,[4] and the lessee of the demesne was obliged to accommodate the steward who held the courts.[5] Views and courts for the smaller Bulford manor were held in 1675[6] but none is expressly mentioned afterwards.

In 1802–3 a quarter of the population of the parish received poor relief: £164 was spent on materials for employing some, on regular outrelief for 20 adults and 27 children, and on occasional relief for 8 adults.[7] An average of £193 a year was spent 1812–15, and on average 14 were relieved regularly and 8 occasionally.[8] Among the parishes of Amesbury hundred Bulford spent more than average on the poor 1816–21, less than average 1822–34.[9] Bulford became part of Amesbury poor-law union in 1835.[10] It was included in Salisbury district in 1974.[11]

CHURCHES. A church stood in Bulford in the early 12th century. It is likely to have belonged to Amesbury abbey and was confirmed to Amesbury priory in 1179.[12] Until the Dissolution the church was served by chaplains appointed by the priory,[13] and the right to nominate curates passed with the Rectory estate, the owners of which were lords of Bulford manor.[14] A proposal of 1650 to unite Bulford and Milston parishes

84 P.R.O., PROB 11/837, ff. 72–9.
85 G.P.L., Treas. Solicitor, 432/51/2.
86 P.R.O., IR 29/38/49; IR 30/38/49; W.R.O. 814/16.
87 W.A.M. xxxvii. 429; O.S. Maps 6", Wilts. LIV (1887 edn.); LIV. SE. (1926 edn.).
88 P.R.O., IR 29/38/49; IR 30/38/49.
89 Ibid. MAF 68/151, sheet 8; MAF 68/493, sheet 9; MAF 68/1063, sheet 9; MAF 68/1633, sheet 9; MAF 68/2203, sheet 8; MAF 68/2773, sheet 14; MAF 68/3319, sheet 14; MAF 68/3814, no. 191; [1st] Land Util. Surv. Map, sheet 122; above, intro.
90 Inf. from Mr. P. J. Rowland, Ratfyn Farm, Amesbury.
91 C. Greenwood, Map of Wilts. (1820); P.R.O., IR 18/10931; IR 29/38/49.
92 O.S. Maps 6", Wilts. LIV–LV (1883–7 edns.); LIV. SE. (1901 edn.); LV. SW. (1901 edn.).
93 [Property Services Agency], 25 Years of Landscape Design in Bulford and Tidworth, 2.
94 V.C.H. Wilts. ii, p. 131.
95 P.R.O., CP 25/1/250/7, no. 72.
96 Cal. Pat. 1381–5, 290.
97 P.R.O., SC 6/Hen. VIII/3986, rot. 77.
98 W.R.O. 367/3, deeds, Duke to Hickman, 1726, 1735.

99 V.C.H. Wilts. iv. 245–6; G.P.L., Treas. Solicitor, 432/51/1.
1 Census, 1831.
2 Above, intro.
3 V.C.H. Wilts. iii. 250; Cal. Chart. R. 1257–1300, 158–9; Valor Eccl. (Rec. Com.), ii. 93; P.R.O., C 142/650, no. 126; ibid. LR 2/191, ff. 126–30; LR 2/203, ff. 365–76; ibid. SC 6/Hen. VIII/3986, rot. 77d.; W.R.O. 865/333.
4 e.g. Cal. Pat. 1548–9, 290, 299.
5 Ibid. 1563–6, pp. 69, 338; 1566–9, p. 243; 1569–72, p. 289; 1572–5, p. 476.   6 W.R.O. 367/3, admittance, 1675.
7 Poor Law Abstract, 1804, 558–9; V.C.H. Wilts. iv. 342.
8 Poor Law Abstract, 1818, 492–3.
9 Poor Rate Returns, 1816–21, 185; 1822–4, 225; 1825–9, 215; 1830–4, 209.
10 Poor Law Com. 2nd Rep. App. D, 558.
11 O.S. Map 1/100,000, admin. areas, Wilts. (1974 edn.).
12 Cal. Chart. R. 1257–1300, 157–9; below, this section [architecture].
13 Valor Eccl. (Rec. Com.), ii. 93; P.R.O., SC 6/Hen. VIII/3986, rot. 79.
14 Rep. Com. Eccl. Revenues, 826–7; Vis. Queries, 1783 (W.R.S. xxvii), p. 49; P.R.O., E 178/1439; above, manor.

was not implemented.[15] From 1868 the living was a vicarage in the gift of the lord of the manor.[16] It was united with the benefice of Figheldean with Milston in 1982 and the Secretary of State for Defence, as lord of the manor, was allotted a share of the patronage.[17]

In 1535 the chaplain received a stipend of £5 6s. 8d. and a livery of 13s. 4d. By c. 1540 he had been allowed an extra 6s. 8d.[18] which he still received in 1567.[19] The stipend was £20 in 1650,[20] £51 c. 1830.[21] Between 1838 and 1864 the owner of the Rectory estate gave the rent charge at which the small tithes from Watergate farm were commuted, £75 in 1838, to the curate as a stipend.[22] The vicar received the same rent charge after 1868, and in 1883 the patron augmented it with £100 a year.[23] From the 16th century to the 19th a house for the curate was sometimes provided by the owner of the Rectory estate.[24] A vicarage house, built to C. E. Ponting's designs in 1893,[25] was sold in 1978.[26]

Before 1548 a small flock of sheep was given to pay for a candle in the church.[27] The curate lived in Amesbury in 1550. Liturgical practice was conservative in 1553, when the altar and crosses were still in the chancel and no sermon was preached.[28] The curate preached every Sunday in 1650.[29] The curates appointed in the 18th century were incumbents or curates of neighbouring or nearby parishes. George Lewis, curate from 1712 to c. 1724, was vicar of Figheldean.[30] In 1783 the curate was also curate of Boscombe and lived either there or in Amesbury. The service which he held at Bulford every Sunday morning was well attended, and at Christmas, Easter, and Whitsun he administered the sacrament to 6–10 communicants.[31] A service was held every Sunday in 1833,[32] and on Census Sunday in 1851 the service, held in the afternoon, was attended by 138.[33] T. D. Millner, curate from 1852 to c. 1868, was domestic chaplain to the Lord Lieutenant of Ireland and did not reside regularly. In 1859 the bishop enjoined him to do so: he apparently did not comply and employed a deputy. Each Sunday in 1864 two services were held: sermons were preached at both, except on the first Sunday in each month when, presumably after morning service, the sacrament was administered instead. Communion was also celebrated at Christmas, Easter, Ascension, and Whitsun, and there were 66 regular communicants. Weekday services

were held at minor festivals and on Wednesdays in Lent.[34]

The church of ST. LEONARD, so dedicated by c. 1900, was called St. John the Evangelist's in 1763 and c. 1875.[35] It is built of flint rubble with stone dressings and some brick patching, and most of it is rendered. It comprises a chancel and a nave with north transept and south porch above which is a tower.[36] The chancel arch and the east, south, and west walls of the nave survive from the early 12th century. The chancel and the north wall of the nave were rebuilt in the late 12th century, and in the 13th the south doorway of the nave was renewed and the porch and tower were built. Between c. 1300 and c. 1500 new tracery was inserted in most windows of the chancel and nave; in the 16th century the east window, possibly of three stepped lancets, was replaced by a traceried three-light window flanked inside by niches for statues. The chancel roof was reconstructed in the 16th century, the south doorway of the porch was renewed in the early 17th, and, also in the 17th, the nave roof was rebuilt and apparently designed for a flat ceiling. By 1826 an earlier north transept had been replaced by a narrower and longer one incorporating a north gallery above a vestry.[37] The church was restored to C. E. Ponting's designs 1902–11.[38] Traces of medieval wall paintings survive on the north and east nave walls.[39]

A 15½-oz. chalice was left for parish use and 15 oz. of plate were taken for the king in 1553. In 1891 and 1991 a chalice hallmarked for 1570 and a flagon hallmarked for 1636 belonged to the parish.[40] There were three bells in 1553. They were replaced by, or recast as, two bells made by John Wallis in 1614; those two were recast as one by Taylor of Loughborough (Leics.) in 1911.[41] Registrations of baptisms and marriages survive from 1654, of burials from 1655. Baptisms are lacking 1685–1761, marriages 1691–1790, and burials 1678–1766.[42]

To serve Bulford camp the church of ST. GEORGE was built 1920–7 to designs by Blount & Williamson.[43] It is a large church of stone consisting of a chancel with south vestry and transepts, an aisled nave, and a west baptistry, and is in 14th-century style.[44]

ROMAN CATHOLICISM. From 1910 there

15 W.A.M. xl. 258.
16 Incumbents Act, 31 & 32 Vic. c. 117; Clergy List (1866 and later edns.); Crockford (1896 and later edns.).
17 Inf. from Ch. Com.
18 Valor Eccl. (Rec. Com.), ii. 93; P.R.O., SC 6/Hen. VIII/3986, rot. 79.
19 P.R.O., E 310/26/153, f. 32.
20 W.A.M. xl. 258.
21 Rep. Com. Eccl. Revenues, 826–7.
22 P.R.O., IR 29/38/49; IR 30/38/49; W.R.O., D 1/56/7.
23 Ch. Com. file 912.
24 Ibid.; ibid. NB 34/58C; P.R.O., SC 6/Hen. VIII/3986, rot. 79; W.R.O., D 1/24/30/1.
25 Ch. Com. file, E 2688.   26 Ibid. deed 634692.
27 P.R.O., E 318/31/1729.
28 W.R.O., D 1/43/1, ff. 57v., 108v.
29 W.A.M. xl. 258.
30 W.R.O., bishop's transcripts, bdle. 2; ibid. D 26/3, f. 1.
31 Vis. Queries, 1783 (W.R.S. xxvii), pp. 48–9.
32 Ch. Com. file, NB 34/58C.
33 P.R.O., HO 129/262/2/5/7.
34 Clergy List (1866, 1881); W.R.O. 517/22; 814/32; ibid. D 1/56/7.
35 J. Ecton, Thesaurus (1763), 392; W.A.M. xv. 100; Lamb. Palace Libr., ICBS no. 10256.
36 Description partly based on watercolour by J. Buckler in W.A.S. Libr., vol. i. 7 (1805).
37 Hoare, Mod. Wilts. Amesbury, 44; W.R.O. 517/22; 517/25.   38 Kelly's Dir. Wilts. (1911); W.R.O. 517/25.
39 Church Guide (TS. in church).
40 Nightingale, Wilts. Plate, 38; inf. from the vicar, Figheldean.
41 Walters, Wilts. Bells, 43–4.
42 W.R.O. 517/2–9; 2014/1–3; bishop's transcripts for 1710–17, 1724–33, 1758–9, and 1786–9 are ibid.; marriages are printed in Wilts. Par. Reg. (Mar.), ed. W. P. W. Phillimore and J. Sadler, iii. 129–32.
43 Pevsner, Wilts. (2nd edn.), 152; James, Plain Soldiering, 102.
44 See plate facing p. 171.

were mass centres at Bulford camp in temporary accommodation on various sites. The Roman Catholic church of Our Lady of Victories was opened in 1925. It closed in 1968 when the church of Our Lady Queen of Peace, built to J. A. Douglas's designs, was opened.[45]

PROTESTANT NONCONFORMITY. Five or six Baptists were inhabitants of Bulford in 1669, a Baptist meeting house was licensed in 1672,[46] and there were two dissenters there in 1676.[47] A meeting house for Wesleyans at Bulford paper mill was certified by Thomas Mold in 1781,[48] but in 1783 there was said to be no nonconformist in Bulford.[49] Independents certified two houses in 1805, and in 1806 certified a new chapel partly paid for by Matthew Devenish of Watergate Farm.[50] The chapel was rebuilt in 1828; in 1851 on Census Sunday 119 attended the morning service, 128 the afternoon one.[51] From 1851 or earlier until 1955 the minister lived in a manse in High Street.[52] A register of births and baptisms survives for 1806–37.[53] From 1965 the chapel was an independent evangelical church in the Evangelical Fellowship of Congregational Churches.[54] Services were still held in 1991.

EDUCATION. By will proved 1758 Richard Duke gave money for a school to be built in Bulford churchyard and for land worth £8 a year to support a teacher and buy books. No land was bought, but a school was started. In 1833 £8 was paid to it by the tenant of Upper farm, afterwards, until 1892 or later, by the lords of Bulford manor, who gave an additional £12 until c. 1888, an additional £7 thereafter.[55] The school was attended by 12 in 1818,[56] 16 in 1833,[57] and 15–20 in 1858 when it was in a cottage near the churchyard.[58] On attendance day in 1871 there were 39 children present.[59] A new school was built in High Street in 1874.[60] Average attendance was 65 in 1906,[61] 46 in 1907–8, 79 in 1911–12. Figures fell slightly after schools were opened in Bulford camp, and in 1938 the average was 52.[62] The school was closed, and a new one in John French Way opened, in 1971. In 1991 a quarter of the 211 pupils were soldiers' children.[63]

In Bulford camp Haig county primary school in Haig Road opened in 1929, was enlarged in 1968 and 1974,[64] and had 108 children on roll in 1991.[65] A school in Wing barracks opened before 1915 was renamed Wing county junior school in 1955 and closed in 1964. Its pupils were transferred to Kiwi county primary school, opened in 1965 on the site of a former infants' school in Hubert Hamilton Road.[66] There were 231 children on roll in 1992.[67]

In 1858 a woman taught 20–30 children in a British school attached to the Independent chapel.[68] There is no later evidence of the school. A private school, Avondale, founded in Amesbury in 1923, moved in 1957 to the former manse in High Street.[69] It had 115 pupils in 1991.[70]

CHARITY FOR THE POOR. None known.

CHOLDERTON

CHOLDERTON,[71] 686 ha. (1,695 a.), is in the upper Bourne valley 15 km. north-east of Salisbury.[72] In 1086 there were eight estates called Cholderton, four in Wiltshire and four in Hampshire:[73] the Wiltshire four constitute Cholderton parish; the other four remained in Hampshire as part of the adjoining parish of Amport. In the 18th and 19th centuries the Wiltshire Cholderton was sometimes called West Cholderton,[74] the Hampshire one East Cholderton.[75]

On the north-east the parish boundary, with Hampshire, is marked by a prehistoric ditch, called Devil's ditch, and on the north-west crosses a summit of Beacon Hill. On the west another prehistoric ditch marks the east–west section of the boundary with Bulford, and roads mark the boundary on the south and east.

The parish is entirely on Upper Chalk. Where it crosses the east part, on a roughly north–south course, the Bourne has deposited gravel.[76] From c. 183 m. on Beacon Hill the land falls south-eastwards to the river, which leaves the parish at below 91 m., and in the south-east corner of the parish there is land at c. 100 m. The river

45 *V.C.H. Wilts*. iii. 97; James, *Plain Soldiering*, 103; Pevsner, *Wilts*. (2nd edn.), 152; *Cath. Dir.* (1991).
46 G. L. Turner, *Orig. Rec.* ii, p. 1074; *Meeting Ho. Certs.* (W.R.S. xl), p. 173.
47 *Compton Census*, ed. Whiteman, 124.
48 *Meeting Ho. Certs.* (W.R.S. xl), pp. 32–3.
49 *Vis. Queries, 1783* (W.R.S. xxvii), p. 49.
50 *Meeting Ho. Certs.* (W.R.S. xl), pp. 60–2; W.R.O. 1126/18.   51 P.R.O., HO 129/262/2/5/8.
52 *Kelly's Dir. Wilts.* (1855); W.R.O. 1550/48; 2770/2.
53 P.R.O., RG 4/2957.   54 W.R.O. 2770/2.
55 *Endowed Char. Wilts.* (S. Div.), 81–2; P.R.O., IR 29/38/49.   56 *Educ. of Poor Digest*, 1020.
57 *Educ. Enq. Abstract*, 1031.
58 *Acct. of Wilts. Schs.* 11.
59 *Returns relating to Elem. Educ.* 426–7.
60 W.R.O. 782/18; O.S. Map 6", Wilts. LIV (1887 edn.).
61 *Return of Non-Provided Schs.* 20.
62 *Bd. of Educ., List 21, 1909* (H.M.S.O.), 504; *1913*, 548; *1938*, 421; below, this section.
63 Inf. from the head teacher.
64 James, *Plain Soldiering*, 108.
65 Inf. from the head teacher.
66 James, *Plain Soldiering*, 108.
67 Inf. from Director of Educ., Co. Hall, Trowbridge.
68 *Acct. of Wilts. Schs.* 11.
69 Inf. outside ho.; W.R.O. 1550/48; above, Amesbury, educ.   70 Inf. from the head teacher.
71 This article was written in 1992.
72 Maps used include O.S. Maps 1", sheet 14 (1817 edn.); 1/50,000, sheet 184 (1988 edn.); 1/25,000, SU 24 (1958 edn.); 6", Wilts. LV (1883 and later edns.).
73 *V.C.H. Hants*, i. 484, 495, 498, 503; *V.C.H. Wilts.* ii, pp. 140, 149.
74 W.R.O. 1448/1; 1810/23; Ch. Com. file, NB 34/32B/1.
75 *V.C.H. Hants*, iv. 337.
76 Geol. Surv. Maps 1", drift, sheet 282 (1967 edn.); 1/50,000, drift, sheet 298 (1976 edn.).

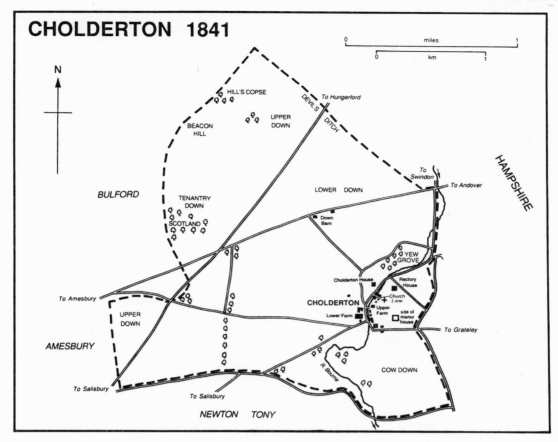

flows only in late winter; even then it is often intermittent, and its course is frequently dry all year. Sometimes, however, severe flooding has occurred.[77] There was downland pasture in the north and south parts of the parish, arable on lower land east, west, and north of Cholderton village, and meadow beside the Bourne.[78]

Two main roads crossed the parish in the later 17th century, the Oxford–Salisbury road via Hungerford (Berks.) across the west part, the London to Bridgwater (Som.) road via Andover (Hants) and Amesbury across the north part. A new course west of the parish had been adopted for the Hungerford road by 1773, and the old road through Cholderton parish decreased in importance.[79] The Andover–Amesbury road was turnpiked in 1761 and disturnpiked in 1871.[80] From 1958 it has been part of the London–Exeter trunk road,[81] and in 1988 a new dual-carriageway section was made across the parish a little north of the old course.[82] The road linking Cholderton village to Salisbury through the villages of the lower Bourne valley was blocked by imparking around Wilbury House in Newton Tony parish in the 18th century.[83] The old road south of the village fell into disuse, and Salisbury could be reached from Cholderton by

what was evidently a new stretch of road south-west of the village and either a road on the western edge of Wilbury park or the road on the boundary with Newton Tony and the old Hungerford road.[84] In 1835, however, a turnpike road from Swindon and Marlborough to Salisbury was completed, a new section of road was made in Newton Tony, and the road through and south-west of Cholderton village became part of a main Swindon–Salisbury road through the Bourne valley. That road was disturnpiked in 1876.[85] It was still a main road in 1992, when the road on the boundary with Newton Tony and the old Hungerford road were tracks. A road from Grateley (Hants) crosses the main road in the village and runs west to join the Andover–Amesbury road in Bulford parish.

The two ditches on the parish boundary and a ditch, now obliterated, which crossed the parish north-west and south-east, all formed part of a prehistoric network, possibly connected with cattle ranching, centred on Sidbury Hill in North Tidworth. Two field systems, one of 50 a. south-west of Devil's ditch, and another of 100 a. in the south-west corner of the parish and extending into Newton Tony, are associated with them. Near the Bulford boundary are three

77   E. P. Barrow, *Par. Notes* (1889), 18; *W.A.M.* lxxxiv. 137, 140; W.R.O. 1810/28, pp. 10, 110, 198, 205; 1810/31.
78   Below, econ. hist.
79   J. Ogilby, *Brit.* (1675), pls. 32, 83; *Andrews and Dury, Map* (W.R.S. viii), pl. 9; O.S. Map 1", sheet 14 (1817 edn.); below, N. Tidworth, intro. [roads].
80   *V.C.H. Wilts.* iv. 257, 270; *L.J.* xxx. 138.

81   Above, Amesbury, intro. (roads).
82   Inf. from Dept. of Planning and Highways, Co. Hall, Trowbridge.   83   Below, Newton Tony, intro.
84   *Andrews and Dury, Map* (W.R.S. viii), pl. 6; O.S. Map 1", sheet 14 (1817 edn.).
85   *V.C.H. Wilts.* iv. 257, 262, 270; below, Newton Tony, intro. [roads].

Bronze-Age bowl barrows, one of which contained a secondary Romano-British cremation. Romano-British coins have also been found in the parish.[86]

Cholderton's assessment for taxation 1332–4 showed it as relatively prosperous,[87] there were 46 poll-tax payers in 1377,[88] and taxation assessments of the 16th century and earlier 17th indicate moderate prosperity.[89] The population rose from 127 in 1801 to 191 in 1861. It fell to 161 in 1871, apparently because a large family was away from the parish, but rose to 238 in 1911. It was 188 in 1921, 204 in 1961, and 200 in 1991.[90]

Cholderton village stands on the gravel, with buildings on both sides of the Bourne along the Salisbury road where it follows the west bank. Buildings on the east bank are approached by bridges. Near the north end a new bridge for Church Lane was built in 1834; in the south a bridge was built of brick with iron railings in 1858 and rebuilt in 1908.[91] The chief building materials of houses in the village are chalk, brick, and flint, and some cottages have thatched roofs.

In 1773, and presumably earlier, the principal buildings of the village, the church, the Rectory, and Cholderton House, were at the north end. In Church Lane a range of single-storeyed cottages, partly thatched, was built on the north side, possibly c. 1800,[92] and a village school was later built on the south side.[93] South of the church stood a manor house which in 1773 and 1817 had a small park to the east: the house was demolished between 1817 and c. 1832.[94] On or near its site Upper Farm, later Drybrook Lodge, was built c. 1860 to designs by T. H. Wyatt[95] to replace a farmhouse which stood beside the road.[96]

In the south part of the village the buildings were in 1773 and 1992 more closely grouped.[97] On the west side Lower or Manor Farm had extensive farm buildings around it in the early 19th century.[98] The house, called Manor House in 1992, was built in the earlier 18th century on a square plan with a single-storeyed kitchen wing to the south. The principal east front, of five bays, has two storeys with attic dormers, and is built of red brick with decorations of black brick and a moulded brick cornice. A two-storeyed north service block was built from old materials in 1914 to designs by A. C. Bothams.[99] South of the house stand an earlier 18th-century

stable and a weatherboarded barn on staddle stones. In the 1980s a farm building was converted for residence and two private houses were built. At the road junction south-east of the house, a village hall with a clock tower was built in 1912 and, a little to the north, a fountain was built about the same time.[1] On the east side of the road most of the cottages were either rebuilt or altered in the 19th century. The Crown was an inn in 1855[2] and 1992. By 1773 settlement had extended south into what was later called Grateley Road,[3] and east along it there was later more. Holly Tree House on the north side was built of chalk in the late 18th century and extended in the early 19th; other houses were built in the early 19th.[4] North of Grateley Road in Edric's Close six council houses and six bungalows for old people were built 1952–4.[5]

North of the village a farmstead was built on downland beside a pond on the south side of the Andover–Amesbury road in the late 18th century or early 19th.[6] A coach house east of it[7] was later converted to a pair of cottages. The farmstead was burnt down in 1870[8] and was replaced by Down Barn.[9] A few other buildings, including a commercial garage and a large house of c. 1900,[10] were built beside the road. About 1900 H. C. Stephens, who owned most of the parish,[11] commissioned three houses and three pairs of cottages,[12] all of flint and red brick in vernacular style and built outside the village: Walnut Cottage, Ann's Farm (later Beacon House), and two pairs of cottages were built beside the road leading west from the village, later called Amesbury Road; Scotland Lodge was built beside the parish boundary in Bulford parish, and a pair of cottages was built beside the parish boundary north of the village. Also in Amesbury Road a pair of estate cottages was built in the 1920s or 1930s, and 12 council houses, 4 in 1927, 4 in 1932, 2 in 1939, and 2 in 1958,[13] and 4 private bungalows were built. A large private house, Cowden, was built of brick on the former Cow down south of the village in 1939.[14]

In 1904 waterworks, fed from springs in Hampshire and including reservoirs and a water tower in Cholderton, were constructed for the Cholderton Water Co. Ltd. to supply H. C. Stephens's Cholderton estate in Wiltshire and Hampshire. In 1992 the Cholderton & District Water Co. Ltd., so called from 1939, still supplied Cholderton and parts of other parishes.[15]

---

86 *V.C.H. Wilts.* i (1), 57, 166, 251, 254, 275; below, N. Tidworth, intro. [prehist. remains].
87 *Tax List, 1332* (W.R.S. xlv), 112; *V.C.H. Wilts.* iv. 297.   88 *V.C.H. Wilts.* iv. 306.
89 *Taxation Lists* (W.R.S. x), 2, 132; P.R.O., E 179/197/241; E 179/198/284; E 179/199/398.
90 *V.C.H. Wilts.* iv. 323, 344; *Census,* 1961; 1991.
91 P.R.O., IR 30/38/72; W.R.O. 1810/34 (annotated copy of Barrow, *Par. Notes*), n. on title p.; 1810/35.
92 *Andrews and Dury, Map* (W.R.S. viii), pl. 6; O.S. Map 1", sheet 14 (1817 edn.); P.R.O., IR 30/38/72.
93 Below, educ.
94 *Andrews and Dury, Map* (W.R.S. viii), pl. 6; Barrow, *Par. Notes*, 6–7; O.S. Map 1", sheet 14 (1817 edn.); P.R.O., IR 29/38/72; IR 30/38/72.
95 *Kelly's Dir. Wilts.* (1903); W.R.O. 776/39; 1810/34, n. on imprint p.
96 P.R.O., IR 29/38/72; IR 30/38/72.
97 *Andrews and Dury, Map* (W.R.S. viii), pl. 6.

98 P.R.O., IR 29/38/72; IR 30/38/72.
99 W.R.O. 1894/67.
1 Ibid. 1810/28, p. 31; 1810/35; date on bldg.
2 *Kelly's Dir. Wilts.* (1855).
3 *Andrews and Dury, Map* (W.R.S. viii), pl. 6.
4 O.S. Map 1", sheet 14 (1817 edn.); P.R.O., IR 30/38/72.   5 W.R.O., G 1/602/2.
6 *Andrews and Dury, Map* (W.R.S. viii), pl. 9; O.S. Map 1", sheet 14 (1817 edn.).
7 P.R.O., IR 29/38/72; IR 30/38/72.
8 W.R.O. 1810/35.
9 O.S. Map 6", Wilts. LV (1883 edn.).
10 Ibid. 6", Wilts. LV. SE. (1902, 1926 edns.).
11 Below, manors.
12 Inf. from Mr. H. A. Edmunds, Cholderton Park.
13 W.R.O., G 1/600/1; G 1/602/2.
14 Ibid. 1810/29, p. 71; W.A.S. Libr., sale cat. xxxvi, no. 55.
15 W.R.O. 776/39; 1340/90; 1340/93–4; 1340/96.

72

MANORS AND OTHER ESTATES. Alfsige (d. 959), archbishop of Canterbury, devised the reversion of either Cholderton or East or West Chittington (Suss.) to Alfwig.[16]

The estate of 3½ hides less 4 a. which became *CHOLDERTON* manor was held in 1086 by William of Eu (d. *c.* 1095).[17] Like other estates of William, the overlordship of the manor descended to Walter Marshal, earl of Pembroke (d. 1245).[18] The overlordship has not been traced further.

Bernard was William of Eu's tenant in 1086,[19] and the mesne lordship descended in his family to Roger Bernard (fl. *c.* 1175) and to Eudes Bernard who held it in 1242–3.[20] One of the family subinfeudated the manor to Reynold de Argentine,[21] and Richard de Argentine held it in 1242–3.[22] It passed to Reynold de Argentine (d. *c.* 1308) and his son John (d. *c.* 1323), who left a son John, a minor.[23] The family's interest has not been traced further.

The first Reynold de Argentine further subinfeudated the manor to a member of the Bassingbourn family.[24] Alan of Bassingbourn held it in 1242–3[25] and it passed like Bassingbourn manor in Wimpole (Cambs.) in the direct Bassingbourn line to Baldwin (d. 1275), Warin (d. 1323), Warin (d. 1348), who held in chief and was granted free warren in his demesne at Cholderton, and Warin.[26]

John Skilling and his wife Faith held Cholderton manor in 1382.[27] Another John Skilling held it in 1428,[28] and it descended in the Skilling family like Shoddesden manor in Kimpton (Hants) to Elizabeth, daughter of a John Skilling, who married John Wynnard (fl. 1465) and afterwards Thomas Wayte (d. 1482).[29] Sir Thomas Lovell held the manor in 1492–4: it is likely that it had been forfeited, perhaps in 1485, and granted to him by the king.[30] In a way that is obscure it passed to John Thornborough, who died seised of it in 1511. It passed to John's son Robert[31] (d. 1522) and to Robert's relict Anne, who later married Sir Anthony Windsor. It was held in 1562 by Robert's grandson John Thornborough,[32] and after John's death *c.* 1594 by his relict Margaret.[33] The manor was sold before 1603 to Sir George Kingsmill[34] (d. 1606), passed

to his relict Sarah[35] (d. 1629), afterwards wife of Edward la Zouche, Lord Zouche (d. 1625), and of Sir Thomas Edmundes,[36] and reverted to Bridget (will proved 1672), relict of Sir George's elder brother Sir Henry Kingsmill (d. 1624).[37] Bridget was succeeded by her son Daniel Kingsmill (will proved 1679) and Daniel by his relict Abigail (fl. 1681),[38] on whose death the manor reverted to Daniel's nephew Sir William Kingsmill (d. 1698). From Sir William's son and heir William (d. *s.p.* 1766) it descended to his niece Elizabeth (d. 1783), wife of Robert Brice, who took the name Kingsmill in 1766.[39] The manor was owned from 1781 or earlier by William Hayter (d. 1795) and afterwards by his nephew the Revd. Edward Foyle (d. 1832).[40] The manor house was that, south of the church, demolished in the earlier 19th century.[41]

Foyle, who already owned other land in the parish,[42] devised his Cholderton estate to his niece Frances Bolton (from 1835 Frances Nelson, Countess Nelson, d. 1878).[43] Her son and successor Sir Maurice Nelson sold the 1,016-a. estate in 1889 to the ink manufacturer H. C. Stephens[44] (d. 1918).[45] From 1893 Stephens owned nearly all the parish.[46] He devised it to his grandson P. M. L. Edmunds[47] (d. 1975), whose son Mr. H. A. Edmunds sold 380 a. in 1986[48] and owned over 1,000 a. in 1992.[49]

Other estates in Cholderton originated in small estates held in 1066 by Alwin and Ulvric (½ hide each), Sewi (1 hide), and Ulward (1 hide and 4 a.). Ernulf of Hesdin held them all in 1086 when Godric held the two ½ hides of him and Ulward held his 1 hide and 4 a. by lease.[50] The overlordship of the estates descended like Berwick St. James manor: it passed from Ernulf through the Chaworth family, in the 14th century was held by the earls and dukes of Lancaster, and as part of the duchy of Lancaster was attached to the Crown in 1399.[51]

Some estates held of Ernulf of Hesdin and his successors apparently merged to form *LOWER* farm. In 1203 Jordan Britton made good his claim against William Bacon to hold 3½ yardlands in Cholderton.[52] William Britton conveyed 1 hide in 1236 to Michael of Cholderton,[53] who held ½ knight's fee in 1242–3.[54] Land in

[16] Finberg, *Early Wessex Chart.* p. 47.
[17] *V.C.H. Wilts.* ii, p. 149; I. J. Sanders, *Eng. Baronies,* 119.
[18] *V.C.H. Wilts.* ii, p. 111; *Bk. of Fees,* ii. 745; *Complete Peerage,* x. 374–6.   [19] *V.C.H. Wilts.* ii, p. 149.
[20] *Bk. of Fees,* ii. 745; below, church.
[21] P.R.O., C 146/9292.   [22] *Bk. of Fees,* ii. 745.
[23] *Wilts. Inq. p.m.* 1242–1326 (Index Libr.), 346–7; *Cal. Inq. p.m.* vi, p. 105.
[24] P.R.O., C 146/9292.
[25] *Bk. of Fees,* ii. 745.
[26] *V.C.H. Cambs.* v. 265; *Wilts. Inq. p.m.* 1242–1326 (Index Libr.), 346–7; 1327–77 (Index Libr.), 191–2; *Cal. Chart. R. 1327–41,* 339.
[27] *Feet of F. 1377–1509* (W.R.S. xli), p. 9.
[28] *Feud. Aids,* v. 241.
[29] *V.C.H. Hants,* iv. 374; *Feet of F. 1377–1509* (W.R.S. xli), p. 144; *W.N. & Q.* ii. 16.
[30] Phillipps, *Wilts. Inst.* i. 175, 177; *D.N.B.*
[31] P.R.O., C 142/26, no. 82.
[32] Ibid. C 142/39, no. 109; C 142/58, no. 2; ibid. WARD 9/129, f. 259 and v.; Hants R.O. 19M61/1295, ff. 89v.–92.
[33] Hants R.O. 19M61/1295, ff. 96v.–100.
[34] Phillipps, *Wilts. Inst.* ii. 3.
[35] P.R.O., PROB 11/107, ff. 177v.–178v.; Hants R.O.

[36] *Complete Peerage,* xii (2), 949–54.
[37] P.R.O., PROB 11/339, ff. 357v.–359; ibid. WARD 7/72, no. 121; Hants R.O. 19M61/1130.
[38] Hants R.O. 19M61/1168; 19M61/1183; Oriel Coll., Oxf., Mun., DLL 8, notification, 1681; P.R.O., PROB 11/360, f. 168.
[39] G.E.C. *Baronetage,* v. 331–2; P.R.O., PROB 11/453, ff. 264–5; Hants R.O. 19M61/1209.
[40] *Musgrave's Obit.* iii (Harl. Soc. xlvi), 181; P.R.O., PROB 11/1119, ff. 143v.–145v.; W.R.O., A 1/345/108.
[41] *Andrews and Dury, Map* (W.R.S. viii), pl. 6; above, intro.   [42] Below, this section.
[43] *Complete Peerage,* ix. 465; P.R.O., PROB 11/1807, ff. 298–300v.
[44] Burke, *Peerage* (1963), 1781; W.R.O. 1340/1.
[45] W.R.O. 1821/145.
[46] Below, this section.
[47] Princ. Regy. Fam. Div., will of H. C. Stephens, 1919.
[48] Inf. from Mr. H. A. Edmunds.
[49] W.R.O. 1894/77.   [50] *V.C.H. Wilts.* ii, p. 140.
[51] Below, Berwick St. Jas., manors (Berwick St. Jas.); e.g. *Bk. of Fees,* ii. 716; *Cal. Inq. p.m.* i, pp. 113–15; xi, pp. 93, 110; *Cal. Close, 1360–4,* 208.   [52] *W.N. & Q.* i. 505.
[53] P.R.O., CP 25/1/250/10, no. 93.
[54] *Bk. of Fees,* ii. 716.

Cholderton, possibly the same, was confirmed to Peter of Cholderton and his wife Isabel in 1256.[55] In the later 13th century William Edmund conveyed land, again possibly the same, to John of Durnford, who conveyed it to Sir Henry Thistleden.[56] About 1330 Henry Thistleden held land in Cholderton later reputed a manor[57] and either he or a namesake held it in 1361.[58] It apparently passed to Walter Carbonell and by 1428 had been divided into five or more parts.[59] One part, held in 1428 by William Nail, was conveyed in 1440 by him or a namesake to Thomas Bailey.[60] Later it was said to comprise a house and c. 508 a. and was held by Robert Bailey. Robert's daughter and heir Elizabeth married Ralph Reeve and 1532 × 1544 their son John claimed it.[61] Called a manor, it was later owned by Cuthbert Reeve (d. 1594) and his relict Eleanor (fl. 1599).[62] Another part, also called a manor, was held in the later 16th century by William Pound and his wife Ellen;[63] others were held by Agnes Philpot (fl. 1540) and her son Edward Philpot,[64] by William Rutter,[65] and possibly by Henry Clifford (fl. 1599).[66] None of the five has been traced further, and some or all were apparently merged to form Lower farm, which Henry Hoare (d. 1785) owned in 1737 and William Blatch (d. 1820) in 1781.[67] Blatch's son William sold the farm in 1830 to Sir Alexander Malet, Bt. (d. 1886), whose son Sir Henry Malet, Bt., sold it, then 565 a., in 1893 to H. C. Stephens, the owner of most other land in the parish.[68]

Other estates held of Ernulf of Hesdin were possibly the origin of the *CHOLDERTON HOUSE* estate. One, perhaps the ½ knight's fee held in 1242–3 by John de Aure,[69] was conveyed by Robert Hungerford (d. 1352) to Ivychurch priory.[70] It passed to the Crown at the Dissolution,[71] and was sold through agents in 1582.[72] John Harding (d. 1609) owned it, and his son Thomas[73] sold it in 1613 to Sir Thomas White (will proved 1641), who owned it in 1638.[74] It passed, apparently like Claygate manor in Ash (Surr.), to Sir Thomas's cousin Robert Woodroffe (d. 1639). Robert was succeeded in turn by his sons Thomas (fl. 1658) and George.[75] In 1676 George sold it to Jonathan Hill (d. 1727), who already owned land in the parish.[76] Hill's estate descended to his grandson John Lee Hill (will

proved 1760), who owned it in 1737, and to John's son John Jonathan Hill.[77] J. J. Hill sold Cholderton House and 750 a. in 1771 to the Revd. Edward Foyle (d. 1784). The estate passed to Foyle's son the Revd. Edward Foyle and from 1795 descended with Cholderton manor.[78] In 1690 Cholderton House was built, of flint with red-brick dressings, as a two-storeyed house with attics above dentilled eaves and with a central doorway in a five-bayed east entrance front.[79] Features of 1690 to survive inside the house include panelling in rooms in the north-east corner, a staircase, doorcases, and doors. Other panelling was renewed or inserted in the 18th and 20th centuries. In the 19th the attics were made into a third storey. Before c. 1840 a west wing was built from the south end of the west elevation and a south wing from the west end of the south elevation.[80] The south wing was demolished in the mid 20th century.[81] West of the house the walls of a former kitchen garden incorporate a small, possibly early 19th-century, classical gazebo and a large doorway with a keystone dated 1780. North of the house, and perhaps of c. 1690, a grove of yew trees, c. 3 a., was aligned in four north–south rows c. 250 ft. long: the inner rows enclosed two circular clearings.[82] The grove was ruined by a gale in 1893.[83]

Mottisfont priory (Hants) held land at Cholderton at the Dissolution. It was possibly given by one of the Chaworths, overlords of land in Cholderton and descendants of the priory's founder. In 1536 the land was granted to William Sandys, Lord Sandys (d. 1540), and his wife Margery.[84] From their son Thomas, Lord Sandys (d. 1560), it descended to his grandson William, Lord Sandys (d. 1623), who owned it in 1600.[85] It was perhaps the estate owned in 1659 by Jonathan Hill (d. 1670). Hill devised his lands to his wife Elizabeth (d. 1675) and to his son Jonathan (d. 1727).[86] From 1676 they descended as part of the Cholderton House estate.[87]

Two yardlands at Cholderton were given to Monkton Farleigh priory by Roger son of Otes, possibly the Roger of Cholderton who leased them from the priory in 1210.[88] The priory held the estate in 1291.[89] No later evidence has been found.

Before 1737 Anthony Cracherode (d. 1752)

55 P.R.O., CP 25/1/251/18, no. 8.
56 Hist. MSS. Com. 78, *Hastings*, i, p. 242.
57 *Feud. Aids*, vi. 574.
58 *Cal. Close, 1360–4*, 208.
59 *Feud. Aids*, v. 241.
60 Ibid.; *Feet of F. 1377–1509* (W.R.S. xli), p. 114.
61 P.R.O., C 1/881, no. 10.
62 Ibid. C 142/240, no. 26; ibid. E 179/198/329.
63 Ibid. C 3/139/9.   64 Ibid. C 3/136/48.
65 Ibid. REQ 2/395/54.
66 Ibid. E 179/198/329.
67 Ibid. PROB 11/1637, ff. 11v.–12v.; Hoare, *Mod. Wilts.* Add. 14; Hants R.O. 19M61/2142; W.R.O., A 1/345/108.
68 Burke, *Peerage* (1963), 1585–6; W.R.O., A 1/345/108; ibid. 1340/1, deed, Malet to Stephens, 1893; above, this section.   69 *Bk. of Fees*, ii. 744.
70 *Cal. Inq. p.m.* x, p. 19; xi, p. 110; B.L. Add. Ch. 40047.
71 P.R.O., E 310/26/153, rot. 14.
72 *Cal. Pat. 1580–2*, pp. 251–2.
73 P.R.O., C 142/310, no. 7.
74 Ibid. C 5/27/48; ibid. PROB 11/185, ff. 78v.–80; W.R.O. 1553/19, deed, Harding to White, 1613.

75 *V.C.H. Surr.* ii. 618; iii. 342; B.L. Add. Ch. 63639.
76 W.R.O. 1553/19, deed, Woodroffe to Hill, 1676; P.R.O., PROB 11/618, ff. 89–91; below, this section.
77 Barrow, *Par. Notes*, 10; P.R.O., CP 43/726, rot. 367; ibid. PROB 11/854, ff. 69v.–71; Hants R.O. 19M61/2142.
78 Hoare, *Mod. Wilts.* Add. 45; Wilts. Cuttings, xxiv. 12; P.R.O., PROB 11/1119, ff. 143v.–145v.; W.R.O., A 1/345/108; above, this section.
79 Date on N., S., and W. elevations.
80 P.R.O., IR 30/38/72.
81 Inf. from Mr. J. V. Cornelius-Reid, Cholderton Ho.
82 *W.N. & Q.* ii. 87–8.   83 W.R.O. 1810/34, p. 7.
84 *V.C.H. Devon*, i. 567–8; *V.C.H. Hants*, ii. 172; *L. & P. Hen. VIII*, xi, p. 87; for the Sandys fam., *Complete Peerage*, xi. 441–6.
85 *Cal. Pat. 1558–60*, 329–30; *W.N. & Q.* iv. 556.
86 W.R.O., wills, archd. Sar., Jonathan Hill, 1672; ibid. 1293/1; P.R.O., PROB 11/618, ff. 89–91.
87 Above, this section.
88 *Interdict Doc.* (Pipe R. Soc. xxxiv), 17, 25; P.R.O., E 210/8815.
89 *Tax. Eccl.* (Rec. Com.), 185.

LUDGERSHALL
The south front of Biddesden House

NEWTON TONY
The south front of Wilbury House

LUDGERSHALL

Monument to Sir Richard Bridges (d. 1558) in the church

BOSCOMBE

Richard Hooker, rector 1591–5

acquired an estate in Cholderton. He devised it to his cousin Mordaunt Cracherode,[90] who in 1755 sold it, then 97 a., to Thomas Hayter.[91] From Thomas (d. 1779) it passed to his son William (d. 1795), and it was merged with Cholderton manor.[92]

ECONOMIC HISTORY. In 1086 the four estates at Cholderton had land for 5½ ploughteams which were there: apparently 3 teams were on demesne land and 2½ on land held by 5 bordars and 5 coscets. On the demesne of what became Cholderton manor there were 2 *servi*. There were 36 square furlongs of pasture but neither meadow nor woodland.[93]

Sheep-and-corn husbandry prevailed in the parish until the later 19th century. Until the later 18th there may have been roughly equal areas of open fields and common pasture. Nearly all the land north of the Andover–Amesbury road was apparently pasture for sheep: in the early 19th century, after inclosure, Tenantry down (*c.* 120 a.), Upper down (*c.* 200 a.), and Lower down (*c.* 200 a.) were mentioned, and a further 58 a. called Upper down lay west of the old Hungerford road in the south-west corner of the parish. In the south-east corner lay Cow down, *c.* 130 a. The open fields, mainly in the centre of the parish and perhaps *c.* 750 a., were called North, West or Middle, and South in the 16th, 17th, and 18th centuries. Meadows lay on either side of the Bourne.[94] A sheep down of 220 a., on which 560 sheep could be stinted, was inclosed in 1737,[95] other downland and some arable were inclosed in the period 1747–52,[96] and the remaining commonable land, *c.* 180 a. of arable and 73 a. of Cow down, was inclosed in 1806.[97] After it was inclosed most of the downland was ploughed. Some was burnbaked in the earlier 18th century,[98] and in the earlier 19th all the downland except 52 a. of Cow down was arable. About 40 a. more of Cow down were ploughed in the period 1840–7. In the later 18th century there were two small parks, West park, *c.* 40 a. in 1776, and that south-east of the church: both had been ploughed by *c.* 1840.[99]

In 1659 there were two large farms, Upper and Lower, and four others, 1 of 2½ yardlands, 2 of 1 yardland, and 1 of ½ yardland.[1] Sainfoin was grown on *c.* 30 a. of Lower farm in the earlier 18th century[2] and elsewhere in 1753.[3] From 1781 or earlier to *c.* 1797 nearly all the land in the parish was in Lower farm, worked by William Blatch. From *c.* 1798 Upper farm was again

separate.[4] In 1840 Upper farm was 953 a., of which *c.* 863 a. were arable, and Lower farm was 595 a., of which *c.* 550 a. were arable. The fields of both farms were of 20–30 a.[5]

There was less arable, but still about two thirds of the parish, in the period 1867–76, when grain, especially barley, was sown on about half the arable, root crops and vetches on the rest of it. More arable was laid to pasture 1876–86, and flocks totalling *c.* 2,000 sheep and herds averaging 60 pigs were kept.[6] Between 1889 and 1900 nearly the whole parish was brought in hand as part of H. C. Stephens's Cholderton estate based at Cholderton Lodge in Amport. It was divided into four farms, each with its arable divided into fields of 24 a. and its own manager. Michael's farm, 435 a. worked mainly from Down Barn, had 13 fields and *c.* 120 a. of woodland and downland; Ann's or Mount Pleasant farm, 389 a. worked from Beacon House, had 11 fields and *c.* 122 a. of woodland and downland; Pearl farm, 308 a. in the north corner of the parish, had 11 fields and *c.* 40 a. of woodland; Scotland farm, 330 a., had 11 fields and *c.* 62 a. of woodland. Cow down and other land east of the village was tenanted. The estate maintained a herd of Tamworth pigs, pedigree herds of Galloway and of Highland cattle, a stud of Cleveland Bays set up in 1885 from which carriage horses were supplied for the royal mews, and a flock of Hampshire Down sheep formed in 1890. Sainfoin was reintroduced as summer grazing for sheep. By the 1930s all the farms had been leased, the fields were again of different sizes, and all the downland north-east of the old Hungerford road was again pasture. In 1992 all except Ann's farm were again in hand as part of the Cholderton estate, which included about as much land in Hampshire as in Wiltshire: much of the Wiltshire land was arable and the Hampshire Down flock and Cleveland Bay stud were maintained.[7] Based at Beacon House, Cholderton Rare Breeds farm, *c.* 50 a., was open to the public.[8]

Hill's copse, 4 a. in 1817, was apparently the only woodland in the parish until *c.* 36 a., including the 14 a. of Scotland wood, were planted between 1817 and 1840.[9] Hill's copse was enlarged before *c.* 1878, and between 1889 and 1910 a total of 25 a. in four areas in the centre and west of the parish were planted. Between 1925 and 1948 trees were also planted along the parish boundary at its north corner.[10] All those woods were standing in 1992.

At a small factory opened at Down Barn *c.*

90 P.R.O., PROB 11/794, ff. 243v.–244v.; Hants R.O. 19M61/2142; W.R.O. 1293/1.   91 *W.N. & Q.* ii. 161–2.
92 *Musgrave's Obit.* iii (Harl. Soc. xlvi), 181; P.R.O., PROB 11/1055, ff. 136v.–140; W.R.O., A 1/345/108; above, this section.   93 *V.C.H. Wilts.* ii, pp. 140, 149.
94 P.R.O., E 310/26/153, rot. 14; ibid. IR 29/38/72; IR 30/38/72; W.R.O., D 1/24/49/1; ibid. wills, archd. Sar., John Bemon, 1676; Thomas Wheeler, 1679; Hants R.O. 19M61/2142.
95 Hants R.O. 19M61/1075; 19M61/2142; 19M61/2145–6.
96 Oriel Coll., Oxf., Mun., DLL 8, incl. proposal; Barrow, *Par. Notes*, 33; W.R.O. 1810/23.
97 W.R.O. 1448/1.   98 Hants R.O. 19M61/2145–6.
99 T. Mozley, *Reminiscences chiefly of Towns, Villages and Schs.* ii. 312–13; *Coroners' Bills, 1752–96* (W.R.S. xxxvi), p. 156; *Andrews and Dury, Map* (W.R.S. viii), pl. 6; O.S. Map

1", sheet 14 (1817 edn.); P.R.O., IR 29/38/72; IR 30/38/72.
1 W.R.O. 1293/1.   2 Hants R.O. 19M61/1075.
3 W.R.O. 1810/23, deed, Cracherode to Parry, 1753.
4 Ibid. A 1/345/108; Barrow, *Par. Notes*, 33; *Vis. Queries, 1783* (W.R.S. xxvii), p. 66.
5 P.R.O., IR 29/38/72; IR 30/38/72.
6 Ibid. MAF 68/151, sheet 29; MAF 68/493, sheet 15; MAF 68/1063, sheet 13.
7 *W.A.M.* xl. 277–8; W.R.O. 1340/3; 1340/22; 1340/40; 1340/44; 1894/77; [1st] Land Util. Surv. Map, sheet 122.
8 Inf. from Mr. D. W. Sydenham, Beacon Ho.
9 O.S. Map 1", sheet 14 (1817 edn.); P.R.O., IR 29/38/72; IR 30/38/72.
10 O.S. Maps 6", Wilts. LV (1883 and later edns.); 1/25,000, 41/24 (1948 edn.); W.R.O., Inland Revenue, val. reg. 148.

1990 Country Leisure Group Ltd. in 1992 employed 18 people in making equipment for swimming pools.[11] Extensive stabling and an indoor riding school were built c. 1980 west of Cholderton House for a commercial equestrian centre. In 1992 the buildings and the former kitchen garden of the house were used for dressage training.[12]

LOCAL GOVERNMENT. An average of £16 a year was spent on the poor 1783–5, and in 1802–3 c. £37 was spent on relieving 7 regularly and 6 occasionally. Between 1812 and 1815 c. £70 a year was spent on relieving c. 8 regularly and c. 6 occasionally: the total number relieved in Cholderton was a much smaller proportion of the population than was usual elsewhere.[13] Sums spent each year were low for Amesbury hundred: they averaged c. £44 in the early 1820s, c. £67 in the early 1830s.[14] There was no unemployed pauper in Cholderton in 1848.[15] The parish was included in Amesbury poor-law union in 1835,[16] in Salisbury district in 1974.[17]

CHURCH. A church stood in Cholderton c. 1175 when Roger Bernard, mesne lord of Cholderton manor, granted it to St. Neots priory (Hunts.).[18] The benefice remained a rectory and became part of Bourne Valley benefice in 1973.[19]

The advowson was held until 1337 by St. Neots priory, which presented rectors. Its right to present was challenged unsuccessfully in 1305 by Henry Spicer, who may have been undertenant of Warin of Bassingbourn's Cholderton manor. After 1337 the possessions of St. Neots, the cell of an alien house, were frequently in the king's hands, and the king presented rectors in 1337 and 1348. The lords of Cholderton manor presented from 1399, except in 1602 when Giles Hutchins presented by grant of a turn.[20] On the death of Sarah Edmundes in 1629 the advowson, unlike Cholderton manor, reverted to Sir George Kingsmill's nephew Sir William Kingsmill (d. 1661), whose wife Anne presented in 1651.[21] The advowson passed to Sir William's

and Anne's son Sir William Kingsmill (d. 1698), lord of Cholderton manor, who sold it in 1692 to the Revd. Thomas Cholwell[22] (will proved 1694). Cholwell devised it to Oriel College, Oxford.[23] John Potter (d. 1747), then regius professor of divinity, presented in 1709 by grant of a turn,[24] but thereafter the college presented and from 1973 was on the patronage board for Bourne Valley benefice.[25]

The rectory was valued at £4 6s. 8d. in 1291,[26] £11 10s. 6d. in 1535,[27] and £60 in 1650.[28] Its average income of £225 a year 1829–31 made it one of the poorer livings in Amesbury deanery.[29] Oriel College augmented the living in 1864.[30] The rector was entitled to all the tithes from the whole parish.[31] They were valued at £267 in 1840 and commuted.[32] The rector had 16 a. of glebe in 1341,[33] 12 a. in 1677,[34] 10 a. in 1840, and, after two exchanges, 8 a. from 1896:[35] 5 a. were sold in 1960, the remaining 3 a. c. 1967.[36] The rectory house was repaired in 1652–3, extended east in 1659,[37] and rebuilt c. 1722.[38] Most of the new house was demolished when another was built further east in 1828.[39] That was enlarged between 1836 and 1847.[40] It was sold c. 1967,[41] a new house having been built west of it c. 1965.[42]

Rectors, one of whom was licensed to study for a year in 1298, were often in minor orders in the late 13th century and early 14th.[43] In 1409 the rector was given a year's leave of absence.[44] A curate assisted the rector 1550–3[45] and one may have served the cure in 1565 when the rector, a pluralist, did not reside.[46] Nathaniel Noyes, rector 1622–51, signed the *Concurrent Testimony* and, although he did not live in Cholderton, preached twice on Sundays in 1650.[47] His successor, Samuel Heskins, was rector 1651–1709.[48] In 1662 the church lacked the Book of Homilies and Jewell's *Apology*.[49] The rectors were fellows of Oriel College 1709–1879.[50] George Carter, rector 1709–20, was provost of the college and employed a curate at Cholderton.[51] John Bradley, rector 1774–1801,[52] was also rector of Worting (Hants)[53] and employed Basil Cane, rector of Everleigh, as curate at Cholderton. Cane lived at Kimpton and was

11 *Wilts. Dir. of Employers* (Wilts. co. council, 1992); W.R.O. 1894/77.   12 Inf. from Mr. Cornelius-Reid.
13 *Poor Law Abstract, 1804,* 558–9; *1818,* 492–3; *V.C.H. Wilts.* iv. 344.
14 *Poor Rate Returns, 1816–21,* 185; *1822–4,* 225; *1825–9,* 215; *1830–4,* 209; *Poor Law Com. 2nd Rep.* App. D, 558.
15 T. Hughes, *Jas. Fraser,* 69.
16 *Poor Law Com. 2nd Rep.* App. D, 558.
17 O.S. Map 1/100,000, admin. areas, Wilts. (1974 edn.).
18 G. C. Gorham, *Hist. Eynesbury and St. Neots,* ii, p. cxxxv.   19 Inf. from Ch. Com.
20 Phillipps, *Wilts. Inst.* (index in *W.A.M.* xxviii. 216); *Feud. Aids,* v. 199.
21 Phillipps, *Wilts. Inst.* ii. 24, corrected by W.R.O. 1293/1; Hants R.O. 19M61/1154; P.R.O., PROB 11/305, ff. 236–7.
22 *V.C.H. Hants,* iv. 254; Oriel Coll., Oxf., Mun., DLL 8, notification, 1692; Hants R.O. 19M61/2149.
23 P.R.O., PROB 11/418, ff. 40–1.
24 Phillipps, *Wilts. Inst.* ii. 49; *D.N.B.*
25 Phillipps, *Wilts. Inst.* ii. 49, 56, 72, 84, 87, 102–3; *Crockford* (1896 and later edns.); *Clergy List* (1859 and later edns.); inf. from Ch. Com.
26 *Tax. Eccl.* (Rec. Com.), 180.
27 *Valor Eccl.* (Rec. Com.), ii. 91.
28 *W.A.M.* xl. 259.

29 *Rep. Com. Eccl. Revenues,* 830–1.
30 Ch. Com. file 28187.
31 W.R.O., D 1/24/49/1.   32 P.R.O., IR 29/38/72.
33 *Inq. Non.* (Rec. Com.), 172.
34 W.R.O., D 1/24/49/1.
35 Ibid. 1340/1; P.R.O., IR 29/38/72.
36 W.A.S. Libr., sale cat. xxxiii, no. 21; Wilts. Cuttings, xxiii. 90.   37 W.R.O. 1293/1.
38 Oriel Coll. Mun., DLL 8, agreement, 1721, letter, 1722, report, 1750.   39 W.R.O., D 1/61/5/38.
40 Mozley, *Reminiscences,* ii. 311.
41 Wilts. Cuttings, xxiii. 90.   42 W.R.O. 1810/15A.
43 *Reg. Ghent* (Cant. & York Soc.), ii. 674, 836; *Reg. Martival* (Cant. & York Soc.), i. 305–6; Phillipps, *Wilts. Inst.* i. 6.
44 *Reg. Hallum* (Cant. & York Soc.), p. 104.
45 W.R.O., D 1/43/1, ff. 58, 109v.
46 Ibid. D 1/43/4, f. 1v.
47 Ibid. 1293/1; *Subscription Bk. 1620–40* (W.R.S. xxxii), p. 18; *Calamy Revised,* ed. Matthews, 557; *W.A.M.* xl. 259.
48 W.R.O. 1293/1.   49 Ibid. D 1/54/1/3, no. 43.
50 Barrow, *Par. Notes,* 8.
51 *Alum. Oxon. 1500–1714,* i. 243; Phillipps, *Wilts. Inst.* ii. 49, 56; W.R.O. 1293/1.
52 Phillipps, *Wilts. Inst.* ii. 87, 102.
53 *W.N. & Q.* viii. 442.

also curate of Shipton Bellinger (Hants). He held two Sunday services at Cholderton and preached at the morning one; he administered the sacrament four times a year to 12–14 communicants.[54] James Pickford, rector 1802–36, was also perpetual curate of Little Eaton (Derb.). His curate at Cholderton preached at two services each Sunday in 1832, held some weekday services, and administered the sacrament four times a year.[55] Thomas Mozley, rector 1836–47,[56] was a pupil and brother-in-law of J. H. Newman. He was the first rector since 1709 to reside continuously and propagated the tenets of the Tractarians, locally by distributing *Tracts for the Times*, nationally through the *British Critic*, of which he became editor in 1841, and in articles in *The Times*.[57] James Fraser, rector 1847–59, continued Mozley's work and incurred the displeasure of leading parishioners by preaching in a surplice. He became bishop of Manchester in 1870.[58] In 1850–1 c. 80 people attended Sunday morning services, c. 100 those on Sunday afternoons.[59] The rector held two services on Sundays in 1864: he preached at all the services except the morning ones in alternate weeks. Weekday services were attended by c. 20. The sacrament was administered on Christmas day, Easter Sunday, either Whit Sunday or Trinity Sunday, and eight other Sundays. Of the c. 36 communicants, c. 20 received communion at the great festivals, c. 18 at other times.[60] The last fellow of Oriel College to be rector, 1875–9, was William Stubbs, who in those years lived at Cholderton each summer: Stubbs was regius professor of modern history at Oxford 1866–84 and later bishop of Chester and of Oxford.[61] The rectory was held in plurality with that of Newton Tony 1953–73.[62]

The church of *ST. NICHOLAS* was so called in 1763.[63] In the early 19th century the nave may have survived from the 12th-century church. The chancel may have been built in the early 13th century: it had a roof of lower pitch than the nave's but internally was undivided from the nave. Two windows were inserted in the south wall of the nave in the 15th century or early 16th. A west gallery was lit by a south dormer window. The church also had a west porch.[64] A new church was built 1841–50, mostly at the expense of Thomas Mozley, beside and north of the old, which was demolished in 1851. The new church, collegiate in plan and 15th- or early 16th-century

in style, comprises an undivided chancel and nave with west ante-chapel and north-west belfry. It was built of flint with dressings of Tisbury stone to designs by Mozley and T. H. Wyatt which allowed a late-medieval 10-bayed roof from Ipswich (Suff.) to be used. The pyramidal cap of the belfry was replaced by a wooden cage c. 1987.[65] A late 12th-century font and most of the mid 19th-century fittings survived in 1992.

In 1553 the king's commissioners took 2 oz. of plate and left a chalice of 8 oz. A paten and flagon given in 1848 and a chalice given in 1850 were held in 1992.[66] There were two bells in 1553, one presumably the medieval bell from the Salisbury foundry which alone hung in the belfry in 1992.[67] Registrations of baptisms and burials survive from 1652 and are complete. Marriage registrations survive from 1664 but are lacking 1753–1812.[68]

NONCONFORMITY. A house in Cholderton was certified for Independents in 1765, another for Methodists in 1813, and another in 1850.[69] There was only one dissenter in the parish in 1864.[70]

EDUCATION. A school for poor children was held in the earlier 18th century, evidently by the curate,[71] and Anthony Cracherode (d. 1752) gave by will £8 17s. a year to provide a teacher and books for 12 poor children.[72] Cracherode's school existed from 1753, and in 1818 a poorly qualified woman taught 6–8 children at it. Another school had c. 15 pupils in 1808 and was presumably the school with 16 pupils in 1818.[73] In 1833 the charity school had 28 pupils and was the only one in the parish;[74] in 1846–7 another ill qualified woman taught 14 children in it.[75] A new school in Church Lane was built from materials of the old church and opened in 1851,[76] when 17 attended. Numbers rose to 36, including children from other parishes, in 1853,[77] and in 1858 two teachers taught 40 children.[78] There were 30 pupils on attendance day in 1871.[79] The school was enlarged in the earlier 20th century;[80] the £8 17s. a year was added to its funds.[81] Average attendance was 53 in 1906–7, 34 in 1932, and 46 in 1938,[82] only 18 when the school was closed in 1978.[83]

An evening school was held twice weekly in

54 *V.C.H. Wilts.* xi. 141; *Vis. Queries, 1783* (W.R.S. xxvii), p. 66.   55 Ch. Com. file, NB 34/32B/1.
56 *Alum. Oxon. 1715–1886*, iii. 995.
57 *V.C.H. Wilts.* iii. 58–9, 64; *D.N.B.*
58 *Alum. Oxon. 1715–1886*, ii. 491; Hughes, *Fraser*, 80–1.
59 P.R.O., HO 129/262/3/1/1.   60 W.R.O., D 1/56/7.
61 *Alum. Oxon. 1715–1886*, iv. 1369; *D.N.B.*
62 *Crockford* (1955 and later edns.); Ch. Com. file, NB 34/32B/1.   63 J. Ecton, *Thesaurus* (1763), 391.
64 *W.A.M.* lxx/lxxi. 104; Hoare, *Mod. Wilts.* Amesbury, 101; J. Buckler, watercolour in W.A.S. Libr., vol. i. 5 (1805); see below, plate facing p. 235.
65 Barrow, *Par. Notes*, 24; *Churches of SE. Wilts.* (R.C.H.M.), 125; *V.C.H. Wilts.* iii. 62; *W.A.M.* lxx/lxxi. 107; W.R.O. 1810/19.
66 Nightingale, *Wilts. Plate*, 38; inf. from Brig. M. J. A. Clarke, the Brake, Cholderton.
67 Walters, *Wilts. Bells*, 52; inf. from Brig. Clarke.
68 W.R.O. 1293/1–3; 1810/3; bishop's transcripts for earlier periods and for marriages 1795–1812 are ibid.; mar-

riages 1664–1752 are printed in *Wilts. Par. Reg. (Mar.)*, ed. W. P. W. Phillimore and J. Sadler, vii. 95–8.
69 *Meeting Ho. Certs.* (W.R.S. xl), pp. 27–8, 74, 167.
70 W.R.O., D 1/56/7.
71 T. Cox, *Magna Brit.* vi (1731), 198.
72 *Endowed Char. Wilts.* (S. Div.), 93–5; cf. below, charities.
73 *Educ. of Poor Digest*, 1023; Lamb. Palace Libr., MS. 1732; W.R.O. 1810/23.
74 *Educ. Enq. Abstract*, 1033.
75 Nat. Soc. *Inquiry, 1846–7*, Wilts. 4–5.
76 Hughes, *Fraser*, 78–81.
77 P.R.O., ED 7/130, no. 75.   78 *Acct. of Wilts. Schs.* 15.
79 *Returns relating to Elem. Educ.* 426–7.
80 O.S. Maps 1/2,500, Wilts. LV. 15 (1910, 1924 edns.).
81 *Endowed Char. Wilts.* (S. Div.), 94.
82 *Bd. of Educ., List 21, 1908* (H.M.S.O.), 501; *1932*, 407; *1938*, 422.
83 W.R.O., F 8/600/70/1/3/2, pp. 122, 125; inf. from Director of Educ., Co. Hall, Trowbridge.

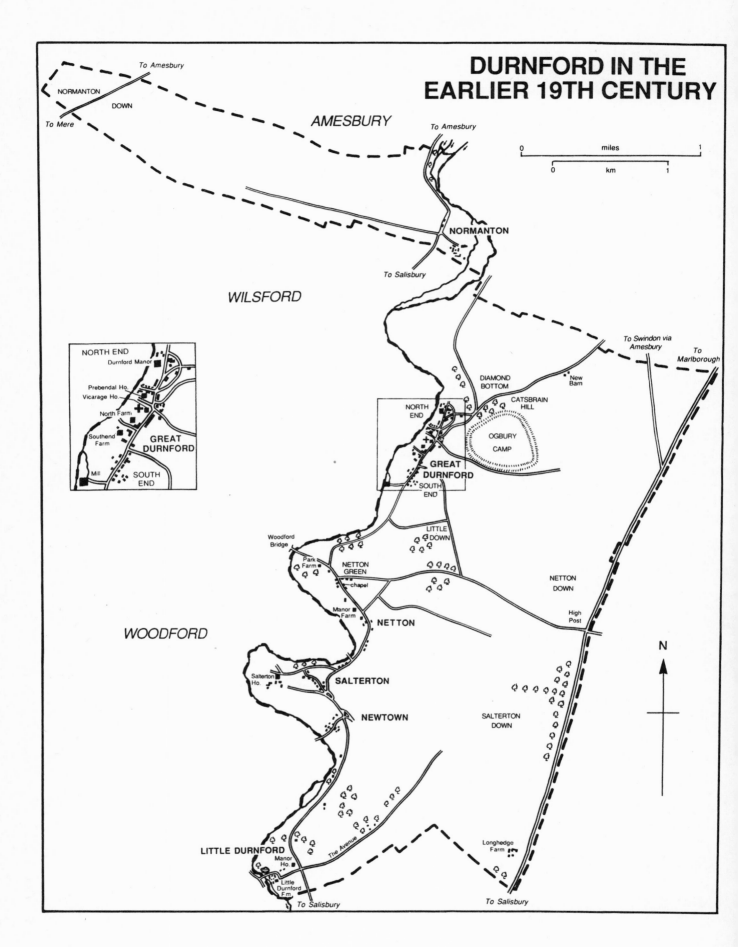

DURNFORD IN THE
EARLIER 19TH CENTURY

NORMANTON
DOWN

To Amesbury

To Mere

AMESBURY

To Amesbury

0   miles   1

0   km   1

NORMANTON

To Salisbury

WILSFORD

To Swindon via
Amesbury

To
Marlborough

DIAMOND
BOTTOM

New
Barn

NORTH
END

CATSBRAIN
HILL

OGBURY
CAMP

NORTH END

Durnford Manor

Prebendal Ho.
Vicarage Ho.

North Farm

Southend
Farm

GREAT
DURNFORD

Mill

SOUTH
END

GREAT
DURNFORD

SOUTH
END

LITTLE
DOWN

Woodford
Bridge

Park
Farm

NETTON
GREEN

chapel

NETTON
DOWN

High
Post

Manor
Farm

NETTON

WOODFORD

Salterton
Ho.

SALTERTON

SALTERTON
DOWN

N

NEWTOWN

LITTLE DURNFORD

The Avenue

Longhedge
Farm

Manor
Ho.

Little
Durnford
Fm.

To Salisbury

To Salisbury

winter 1851–3 by the rector and the schoolmistress.[84] The rector still held a night school in 1864.[85] At an evening continuation school held 1894–1900, attended by *c.* 9 pupils 1896–9 and *c.* 6 in 1900, arithmetic, geography, chemistry, botany, drawing, and music were taught.[86]

CHARITIES FOR THE POOR. Anthony Cracherode (d. 1752) gave £3 3*s.* a year for the poor at Christmas. The money was shared among 6–8 people in 1901,[87] among 3 in 1951.[88] The £12

yearly income from that and from Cracherode's educational charity was being allowed to accumulate *c.* 1992.[89]

Agnes, relict of the rector James Fraser, by deed of 1885 gave £250 for winter clothing for the poor. In 1901 £8 10*s.* was given to a clothing club and £1 10*s.* to old people.[90] Between 1933 and 1947 money was given to a nursing fund and to poor people. The £9 income was divided among 9 people in 1951.[91] The £25 yearly income was being allowed to accumulate *c.* 1992.[92]

DURNFORD

DURNFORD parish[93] lies between Salisbury and Amesbury.[94] Its main part, on the east bank of the Christchurch Avon, contains the villages or hamlets of Great Durnford, Little Durnford, Netton, Salterton, and Newtown; Normanton, nearby on the west bank, was a detached part. In 1885 Normanton, *c.* 656 a., was transferred to Wilsford parish, and Durnford parish was reduced to 3,102 a. (1,255 ha.).[95] In 1986 Durnford parish was increased to 1,325 ha. (3,274 a.) when a small part of it was transferred to Woodford and land of Laverstock was added.[96]

The parish has simple boundaries. The main part is bounded by the Avon on the west and a long and straight road across downland on the east: an estate in the south part of the parish was defined by those boundaries in the 10th century.[97] The short east and west boundaries of Normanton are marked by the Avon and a line of barrows respectively; the long boundaries between them cross downland and are roughly straight.

The main part of the parish lies on Upper Chalk, on which clay-with-flints on Netton and Salterton downs and alluvium and valley gravel beside the Avon have been deposited. Feeders of the Avon now dry have cut valleys across it, but in several places the land falls steeply to the river. The highest land is at *c.* 140 m. south-east of Great Durnford, and the Avon is at *c.* 55 m. where it leaves the parish. Normanton also lies on chalk. The highest land, at *c.* 110 m., is towards the east and covered by clay-with-flints; alluvium and valley gravel beside the river lie at *c.* 65 m. The downland to the west is almost flat.[98] In both parts of the parish, as normal on the Wiltshire chalklands, there were meadows on the alluvium, settlement sites on the gravel,

open fields on the chalk nearer to the settlements, and rough pasture on the downland further from them. The parish contains little woodland.[99] In the 20th century the high land south-east of Great Durnford was used for an airfield.[1]

The road on the parish's east boundary was the main road from Chipping Campden (Glos.) via Marlborough to Salisbury in the 17th century, and across the north-east corner of the parish a road from Amesbury converged on it.[2] The Amesbury road, which in Durnford parish was remade on a straight course, and the Marlborough road south of the junction were turnpiked in 1835 and from 1840 were part of a Swindon–Salisbury turnpike road via Amesbury: the road was disturnpiked in 1876[3] and remained important in 1993. The road on the east bank of the Avon linking the settlements of the parish with Salisbury may be of Saxon origin.[4] At the north end of Great Durnford it was diverted eastwards round Durnford Manor in the late 18th century:[5] the old course remains as a drive of the house. In the 19th century the road was superseded as the main route between Great Durnford and Amesbury by a road through Diamond bottom and the turnpike road.[6] There were evidently east–west roads between the Marlborough road and the Avon in the 10th century.[7] There were several in the later 18th, by when the Avon had been bridged in four places,[8] but evidently none was important. Apart from that through Diamond bottom only that between High Post on the Marlborough road[9] and Woodford bridge has been tarmacadamed. Normanton is crossed by a road linking the settlements on the west bank of the Avon with Salisbury. Normanton down is crossed by an

84   P.R.O., ED 7/130, no. 75.
85   W.R.O., D 1/56/7.
86   Ibid. F 8/500, Cholderton evening sch. 1894–1900.
87   *Endowed Char. Wilts.* (S. Div.), 93–5.
88   W.R.O., L 2, Cholderton.
89   Inf. from Brig. Clarke; cf. above, educ.
90   *Endowed Char. Wilts.* (S. Div.), 95.
91   W.R.O., L 2, Cholderton.
92   Inf. from Brig. Clarke.
93   This article was written in 1993.
94   Maps used include O.S. Maps 1", sheet 14 (1817 edn.); 1/50,000, sheet 184 (1974 edn.); 1/25,000, SU 13–14 (1958 edns.); 6", Wilts. LIV, LX, LXVI (1887 edns.).
95   *Census*, 1881; 1891; P.R.O., RG 11/2064, ff. 80v.–81.
96   Statutory Instruments, 1986, no. 72, Salisbury (Pars.) Order.

97   *W.A.M.* lxiv. 58–9.
98   Geol. Surv. Map 1/50,000, drift, sheet 298 (1976 edn.).
99   Below, agric.
1   Below, this section (Great Durnford).
2   J. Ogilby, *Brit.* (1675), pl. 85; cf. *Andrews and Dury, Map* (W.R.S. viii), pl. 5.
3   *V.C.H. Wilts.* iv. 257, 262, 270; above, Amesbury, intro. (roads); for the new course cf. O.S. Map 1", sheet 14 (1817 edn.).   4   *V.C.H. Wilts.* iv. 254.
5   Cf. *Andrews and Dury, Map* (W.R.S. viii), pl. 5; O.S. Map 1", sheet 14 (1817 edn.); below, manors (Great Durnford).
6   O.S. Maps 1", sheet 14 (1817 edn.); 6", Wilts. LIV, LX, LXVI (1887 edns.).
7   *Arch. Jnl.* lxxvii. 87–8.
8   *Andrews and Dury, Map* (W.R.S. viii), pl. 5.
9   For High Post, below, this section (Great Durnford).

Amesbury–Mere road turnpiked in 1761, disturnpiked in 1871,[10] and since 1958 part of the London–Exeter trunk road.[11] The down is also crossed by two roads leading from Netheravon towards Wilton; neither was of much importance in the 19th century[12] and neither has been tarmacadamed.

On the downs of both parts of the parish there was much prehistoric activity. In the main part a group of barrows on Little down is possibly Bronze-Age,[13] Ogbury camp is an early Iron-Age hill fort of c. 62 a.,[14] and there may have been a small settlement on the high ground south-east of Great Durnford from the early Iron Age to the 4th century A.D.[15] A prehistoric field system of 450 a. lies north of Ogbury camp, one of 400 a. and one of 160 a. lie south of it.[16] Normanton down is in the hinterland of Stonehenge. On it there is a Neolithic mortuary enclosure,[17] an extensive Bronze-Age cemetery with barrows of several types,[18] and a ritual shaft 100 ft. deep and 6 ft. wide which contained votive offerings.[19] A hoard of pewter, found c. 1635 and possibly Roman, may have been on the downland of Normanton.[20]

In 1377 the parish had 162 poll-tax payers, excluding Normanton which is likely to have had fewer than 20.[21] An outbreak of plague occurred in July 1627.[22] The population rose from 399 to 554 between 1801 and 1851; of 533 inhabitants in 1841 Great Durnford had 218, Little Durnford 67, Netton 107, Salterton 91, Newtown 28, and Normanton 22. The population fell from 553 to 380 between 1861 and 1891; a large part of the fall between 1881 and 1891 was caused by the transfer of Normanton. In the 20th century the population fluctuated between a high of 427 in 1951 and a low of 376 in 1931: it was 405 in 1991.[23]

The villages and hamlets of the parish all have Saxon names and all stand on gravel near the Avon. In the main part of the parish there were evidently only two estates in 1086, Durnford in the north and what was later called Little Durnford in the south.[24] There may already have been several settlements; later the larger estate was subdivided and there were five settlements in the main part of the parish each with an east–west strip of land on which there were open fields. The north end of Great Durnford, the south end of Great Durnford, Little Durnford, Netton, and Salterton were almost certainly such settlements in the 13th century;[25] Newtown had been planted as an offshoot of Salterton by the early 14th century[26] but did not have its own fields.

GREAT DURNFORD. The village has three elements, the north end, the south end, and a 20th-century part east of the south end. For the first two the riverside road from Amesbury formed a village street.

The north end includes the church, the site of a house which belonged to the prebendary of Durnford,[27] the vicarage house, and Durnford Manor. The prebendary's house stood north of the church,[28] and a farmhouse was built east of it in 1419–20.[29] The main house was lived in from c. 1743 by the author James Harris (d. 1780)[30] and was demolished c. 1860.[31] In 1773 there were buildings on each side of the street and a few near them beside the road through Diamond bottom.[32] Several on the east side of the street, thatched cottages typically of rendered cob and of one storey and attics, survived in 1993. Durnford Manor was built c. 1792[33] and a farmhouse was built south of the church about the same time. The farmhouse, North (later Church) Farm, of flint, stone, and brick, is of two storeys and attics; in the later 20th century the south front replaced the north as the entrance front and the north became the garden front. Land around Durnford Manor was imparked and by 1879 a lodge had been built beside the road at the east corner of the park.[34] In the earlier 19th century two pairs of cottages and a farmstead incorporating another pair were built beside the road through Diamond bottom. On high ground between the village and Ogbury camp Ogbury House, a large house of two storeys and attics, was built c. 1910 and extended c. 1946.[35]

The south end consisted mainly of farmsteads on each side of the street.[36] Southend Farm, on the west side and in 1993 called Church Farm Farmhouse, is the northernmost and may be medieval. It has a north–south hall range, partly timber-framed and partly of stone, and an east wing of two bays. A two-light trefoil-headed window possibly of the 14th century survives in the west wall of the hall range: it may have been reset. The existing hall roof, which retains smoke-blackened timbers, was constructed in the 16th century or later. The first floor of the wing is supported by an axial beam on a sampson post with heavy curved braces, and the existing roof is 16th-century. At the south end the hall was extended westwards in brick and flint in the 18th century, and brick additions were made to the wing in the 19th. Extensive alterations to the house were in progress in 1993. Piles Farm, later called the Old Hall, on the east side of the street was built in the 18th century and much enlarged in the early 20th, when 17th- and 18th-century panelling and fittings were introduced. In 1875

10 V.C.H. Wilts. iv. 270; L.J. xxx. 138.
11 Above, Amesbury, intro. (roads).
12 O.S. Maps 1", sheet 14 (1817 edn.); 6", Wilts. LIV, LX (1887 edns.).   13 V.C.H. Wilts. i (1), 170, 241, 243.
14 Ibid. 265.   15 W.A.M. lvii. 173–5.
16 V.C.H. Wilts. i (1), 272, 275.
17 Ibid. 122; i (2), 316–17.
18 Ibid. i (1), 145, 196–7, 219, 225.   19 Ibid. i (2), 395–6.
20 Ibid. i (1), 123.   21 Ibid. iv. 306.
22 T. Phillipps, Par. Reg. of Durnford (1823), 23–4.
23 V.C.H. Wilts. iv. 347; Census, 1961; 1971; 1981; 1991; P.R.O., HO 107/1165/6, f. 4v.
24 V.C.H. Wilts. ii, pp. 129, 148; W.A.M. lxiv. 56–7.
25 Cf. below, manors; agric.
26 Wilts. Inq. p.m. 1242–1326 (Index Libr.), 364–5.
27 For the prebend, below, manors (Rectory).
28 W.R.O., EA/36.
29 D. & C. Sar. Mun., press IV, Durnford prebend, 3.
30 D.N.B.; Andrews and Dury, Map (W.R.S. viii), pl. 5; Hants R.O. 7M54/210, lease, prebendary of Durnford to Harris, 1755.
31 W.A.S. Libr., annexe, box 3, MS. 15, W. H. Jones's MS. notes for Durnford, p. 59.
32 Andrews and Dury, Map (W.R.S. viii), pl. 5.
33 Below, manors (Great Durnford).
34 O.S. Map 6", Wilts. LX (1887 edn.).
35 Kelly's Dir. Wilts. (1911); W.R.O., G 1/760/484.
36 Andrews and Dury, Map (W.R.S. viii), pl. 5; W.R.O., EA/147.

a 19th-century farmhouse on the west side of the street was the Black Horse,[37] open in 1993. Near the south end of the street is a mill.

On the north side of Jubilee Hill, the road linking the south end to the High Post road, 4 council houses were built in 1922,[38] 2 in 1933.[39] On the south side 7 council houses were built in 1959,[40] 2 in 1965,[41] and 25 houses and bungalows since then.

The airfield south-east of the village was opened by the Wiltshire School of Flying Ltd. in 1931;[42] many buildings, mainly for manufacturing, have since been erected on the site.[43] Further east a guide post on the main road along the parish boundary gave a name to the High Post hotel built there in the 1930s; a petrol station was also built there in the 1930s.[44] The hotel was used as flats for factory workers in the Second World War[45] and until 1955[46] or later. It was rebuilt in the late 20th century.

LITTLE DURNFORD. In the Middle Ages Little Durnford was presumably, like the others in the parish, a small village beside the Avon. Most of its buildings were presumably near the ford, after which the village was named and by which an east–west road crossed the river. A new manor house, Little Durnford Manor, was built on higher ground to the east in the earlier 18th century, or perhaps earlier;[47] land around it was imparked, and in 1773 there was no more than a single farmstead, Little Durnford (later Home) Farm, near the river.[48] A bridge was built at the crossing in the 18th century, but the east–west road later went out of public use. The farmhouse, burned down c. 1973, was a 17th-century house of one storey and attics, of banded flint and chalk with stone quoins, and with a thatched roof; in 1993 a pair of cottages, faced in banded flint and chalk, and a bungalow built after c. 1973 stood west of the site.[49]

In the 19th and 20th centuries houses were built along the road between Little Durnford and Netton. On the east side, near Little Durnford Manor and possibly incorporating or on the site of an 18th-century hermitage,[50] a *cottage ornée* called Little Durnford Villa in 1851, the Hermitage in the 1870s,[51] was built in the early 19th century.[52] On the west side near Little Durnford Manor a lodge of flint with limestone dressings and with a timber-framed and jettied upper storey was built, possibly to designs by Detmar Blow, in the late 19th century.[53] A pair

of cottages near a chalk quarry had been built on the east side by c. 1840,[54] three pairs of stone estate cottages were built along the west side in the late 19th century and early 20th, and on high ground on the east side Roundabout is a house built between 1899 and 1915, when it was lived in by the architect A. C. Bothams.[55]

Between 1817 and c. 1840 a pair of cottages was built on the downs north-east of Little Durnford Manor, and a new farmstead, Longhedge Farm, was built beside the main Salisbury road at the parish boundary.[56] A pair of cottages was added to the farmstead between 1900 and 1923.[57]

NETTON. The road on the east bank of the Avon forms a street for Netton, which in the early 19th century consisted mainly of a few farmsteads west of the road:[58] all the farm buildings have since gone out of use. The house now called Manor Farm was built there in the 18th century: its three-bayed east entrance front is of red brick with stone dressings and has stone-mullioned windows and attic dormers. A long east–west service wing was built on the west in the early 19th century; later in the century a two-storeyed bay window was added on the south front and the staircase was rebuilt. The house was extended northwards in the later 20th century. The Round House, north of it, was built in the early 19th century: its principal north–south range has rounded ends. South of Manor Farm the Crown inn was open from 1851 or earlier[59] to c. 1962.[60] A thatched cottage of the 17th or 18th century also survives on the west side of the street. A little to the south a house was standing in the earlier 19th century on what later in the century was the site of an L-shaped house called Heale Cottage.[61] A new Heale Cottage was evidently built on the site in 1900 to designs by Detmar Blow.[62] It is a thatched house of two storeys; its west entrance front has two large half-hipped gables and a central porch.

In the later 18th century a group of buildings stood at Netton Green, the place a short distance north-west of Netton where the road from High Post to Woodford bridge joins the road on the east bank of the Avon. An elm tree at the junction in 1773[63] was still alive in 1993. Near it Corner Elm House was built in 1854 for William Hayter.[64] In the 19th century a nonconformist chapel and a school were built and rebuilt at Netton Green:[65] each was a private house in

37 *Kelly's Dir. Wilts.* (1875); W.R.O. 1550/48.
38 W.R.O., G 1/500/6.
39 Ibid. G 1/600/1.   40 Ibid. G 1/602/5.
41 Ibid. G 1/602/7.
42 N. C. Parker, *Aviation in Wilts.* (S. Wilts. Ind. Arch. Soc. v).   43 Cf. below, trade and ind.
44 *Kelly's Dir. Wilts.* (1939 and earlier edns.).
45 W.R.O. 1821/135; cf. below, trade and ind.
46 W.R.O., G 1/505/1.
47 Below, manors (Little Durnford).
48 *Andrews and Dury, Map* (W.R.S. viii), pl. 5.
49 Inf. from Mr. B. K. Allen, Home Farm, and photo. in his possession.
50 Cf. below, manors (Little Durnford).
51 O.S. Map 6", Wilts. LXVI (1887 edn.); W.R.O. 1550/48.
52 O.S. Map 1", sheet 14 (1817 edn.); P.R.O., IR 30/38/105.
53 O.S. Map 6", Wilts. LXVI (1887 edn.); LXVI. NW.

(1901 edn.); Dept. of Environment, list of bldgs. of hist. interest (1987).
54 P.R.O., IR 30/38/105.
55 O.S. Map 6", Wilts. LX. SE. (1901 edn.); *Kelly's Dir. Wilts.* (1915).
56 O.S. Map 1", sheet 14 (1817 edn.); P.R.O., IR 29/38/105; IR 30/38/105.
57 O.S. Maps 6", Wilts. LXVI. NE. (1901, 1926 edns.).
58 W.R.O., EA/147.
59 Ibid. 1550/48.
60 Ibid. G 1/505/2; O.S. Map 6", Wilts. SU 13 NW. (1961 edn.).
61 O.S. Map 6", Wilts. LX (1887 edn.); W.R.O., EA/147; P.R.O., IR 30/38/105.
62 O.S. Maps 6", Wilts. LX. SE. (1901, 1926 edns.); Dept. of Environment, list of bldgs. of hist. interest (1987).
63 *Andrews and Dury, Map* (W.R.S. viii), pl. 5.
64 Date and initials on ho.; P.R.O., HO 107/1845, f. 118v.
65 Below, nonconf.; educ.

1993. The Durnford friendly society, founded in 1815 and dissolved in 1892, was meeting in the school in 1859.[66] To the north-west a farmstead, Park Farm, was built beside the Woodford bridge road between 1824 and c. 1840.[67] The farmhouse was demolished in the late 19th century,[68] but a *cottage ornée* at Netton Green, which served as its lodge, a cob wall running c. 350 m. from the lodge to Woodford bridge, and a few farm buildings survive. On the High Post road as part of Netton Green a pair of cottages was built in the early 19th century[69] and a pair of council houses in 1933.[70] Several private houses were built at Netton Green in the mid and later 20th century.

On the downs east of Netton two farmsteads were built between c. 1840 and 1879,[71] Coffee Farm and, beside the High Post road, High Post Buildings. Beside the main road on the parish boundary a large farm building and a factory were built in the later 20th century.[72]

North-west of Netton, Woodford bridge was rebuilt in the early 19th century. Cricket was played at Netton c. 1793.[73]

SALTERTON. In the later 18th century Salterton lay east–west in a lane leading to the river off the road on the east bank of the Avon, and along the road itself.[74] In the early 19th century the only farmstead was that adjoining Salterton House at the west end of the lane; another house and about seven cottages stood along the lane. Five of the seven cottages strung out along the road c. 1840[75] had been demolished by 1879, another by 1899.[76] On the lane there were only two houses and a few cottages in 1993. Salterton House was built in the early 17th century on an east–west three-roomed plan. A short south wing was built at the west end before c. 1840.[77] In the later 20th century a similar wing was built at the east end, the east elevation was made into an entrance front, and the entire house was refitted. Possibly then 18th-century gate piers and gates were erected across a lane leading south of the hamlet to the house from the road. A small 18th-century farmhouse stands east of Salterton House. The cottages at Salterton in 1993 were mostly of cob and thatch. In the north part of the village a bridge of brick and stone was built across the Avon as an ornamental entrance to the grounds of Heale House in Woodford in the 18th century. A farmstead with a pair of cottages was built on the downland c. 1866.[78]

NEWTOWN was evidently colonized from Salterton, possibly in the 13th century. It was a small settlement in the early 14th when four or more tenants of Salterton manor are likely to have had farmsteads there.[79] The settlement was almost certainly then, as it was in the later 18th century, off the road on the east bank of the Avon along a lane leading to the river, a layout similar to Salterton's. The lane bridged the Avon and led to the nearby village of Lower Woodford in Woodford.[80] Newtown remained small and c. 1840 consisted of a farmstead and two cottages on the lane and a cottage on the east side of the road. Between c. 1840 and 1879, mostly c. 1867, all the buildings were demolished and replaced by a pair of cottages on the lane and farm buildings and a terrace of four cottages beside the road.[81] At its south end the lane was reduced to a footpath.[82] A new farmhouse was built beside the road in 1938.[83] A small mission hall stood at Newtown from the late 19th century to the late 20th.[84]

NORMANTON. There may have been several farmsteads at Normanton in the Middle Ages,[85] and there was a chapel.[86] In 1768 and later there was a single farmstead.[87] It stood between the road on the west bank of the Avon and the river. The present farmhouse, Normanton House, was built in the later 18th century and comprises two east–west ranges, of which the southern is longer than the northern; in the earlier 20th century the house was made taller and the roof reconstructed and a staircase and other fittings of c. 1700 were introduced.

West of the farmstead and beside the road two cottages stood on the waste c. 1840: they were demolished in the earlier 20th century. Between c. 1840 and 1879 three pairs of cottages were built on the west side of the road.[88] When Normanton was transferred to Wilsford in 1885 it had 9 houses and 39 inhabitants.[89]

MANORS AND OTHER ESTATES. In 1086 William of Eu (d. c. 1095) held a 16-hide estate called Durnford. Much of it evidently became Great Durnford manor, the remainder Southend manor and the manors and other estates of Netton and Salterton. In 1086 it included 4 houses in Wilton.[90]

GREAT DURNFORD manor, sometimes called Northend manor, was held by Richard FitzGilbert, earl of Pembroke[91] (d. 1176), possi-

66 *Acct. of Wilts. Schs.* 22; P.R.O., FS 4/55, Wilts. no. 63.
67 W.R.O., EA/147; P.R.O., IR 30/38/105.
68 O.S. Maps 6", Wilts. LX (1887 edn.); LX. SW. (1901 edn.).   69 W.R.O., EA/147; P.R.O., IR 30/38/105.
70 W.R.O., G 1/600/1.
71 O.S. Map 6", Wilts. LX (1887 edn.); P.R.O., IR 30/38/105.
72 O.S. Maps 1/25,000, SU 13 (1958 edn.); 1/10,000, SU 13 NW. (1983 edn.).
73 *V.C.H. Wilts.* iv. 378.
74 *Andrews and Dury, Map* (W.R.S. viii), pl. 5.
75 P.R.O., IR 30/38/105.
76 O.S. Maps 6", Wilts. LX (1887 edn.); LX. SW. (1901 edn.).
77 P.R.O., IR 30/38/105.
78 W.R.O., Ch. Com., bishop, 73, deed, Salisbury to Green, 1867.

79 *Wilts. Inq. p.m.* 1242–1326 (Index Libr.), 364–6; *P.N. Wilts.* (E.P.N.S.), 364; *Tax List, 1332* (W.R.S. xlv), 112.
80 *Andrews and Dury, Map* (W.R.S. viii), pl. 5.
81 O.S. Map 6", Wilts. LX (1887 edn.); P.R.O., IR 30/38/105; W.R.O., Ch. Com., bishop, 73.
82 W.R.O. 1550/48.
83 Inf. from Mrs. G. Langdon, Salterton Farm.
84 Below, church.
85 *Tax List, 1332* (W.R.S. xlv), 109.
86 *Reg. Chandler* (W.R.S. xxxix), p. 29.
87 W.R.O. 1619, map of Normanton, 1768.
88 O.S. Maps 6", Wilts. LX (1887 and later edns.); P.R.O., IR 30/38/105.
89 *Census,* 1891.
90 *V.C.H. Wilts.* ii, p. 148; I. J. Sanders, *Eng. Baronies,* 119.
91 Som. R.O., DD/SAS/H 348, f. 150.

bly a descendant of William. On Richard's death the overlordship may have been taken into the king's hands;[92] afterwards it was held by William, earl of Salisbury[93] (d. 1196), descended like Amesbury manor to William Longespée, styled earl of Salisbury (d. 1250), and was last mentioned in 1243.[94]

Richard, earl of Pembroke, subinfeudated the manor to John Bishop,[95] presumably the John Bishop who held it in 1191–2.[96] Jordan, son of John Bishop, held it in 1242–3,[97] and John Bishop (d. c. 1324), a Wiltshire coroner, held it in 1317. It passed to John's relict Alice and to their son Jordan,[98] who in 1344 conveyed it to his daughter Beatrice and her husband John Everard.[99] In 1361 Beatrice settled it on her daughter Edith and Edith's husband Richard Marwardine, who together sold it in 1416 to Sir John Blackett, perhaps a feoffee.[1] Blackett's feoffees sold it in 1426 to Walter Hungerford,[2] Lord Hungerford (d. 1449). The manor passed to Walter's son Sir Edmund, who in 1469–70 settled it on his son Edward (will proved 1507).[3] After Edward's death it passed in the direct line to Robert (d. 1517), Robert[4] (will proved 1558), Walter[5] (d. 1601), and John[6] (d. 1636). John's relict Elizabeth (will proved 1650) held the manor for life, after which it again passed in the direct line to Edward[7] (will proved 1667), Sir George[8] (d. 1712), and Walter (d. 1754). Walter devised it to his nephew John Keate[9] (d. 1755). It passed to John's son Lumley Hungerford Keate (d. s.p. 1766) and, as tenants in common, to Lumley's sisters Henrietta Maria, from 1769 the wife of George Walker, and Elizabeth Macie, a widow. At a partition of 1773 the manor was allotted to Elizabeth, who sold it in 1791 to James Harris, Lord Malmesbury[10] (cr. earl of Malmesbury 1800, d. 1820). The manor descended with the earldom to James's son James (d. 1841), that James's son James (d. 1889), that youngest James's nephew Edward Harris (d. 1899), and Edward's son James.[11] In 1868 Lord Malmesbury sold the manor house and park, c. 53 a., to John Pinckney (d. 1902),[12] whose relict sold them c. 1907 to George Tryon (cr. Baron Tryon 1940, d. 1940).[13] Between 1907 and 1910 James, Lord Malmesbury, sold the rest of the

manor, c. 760 a., to A. Robinson; c. 1912 Robinson sold that estate, on which he had built Ogbury House, to Tryon.[14] Lord Tryon was succeeded by his son Charles, Lord Tryon (d. 1976), whose son Anthony, Lord Tryon, in 1993 owned Great Durnford manor and other land in the parish, a total of c. 1,200 a.[15]

Durnford Manor, evidently built between 1791, when Lord Malmesbury bought the manor, and 1793,[16] is stylistically similar to contemporary houses in Bath. It is of red brick and of three storeys, and its main block is almost square. The west, garden, front is of five bays, has a central bow, and was extended north and south by low flanking pavilions. The east, entrance, front, also of five bays, is rusticated below the first floor, has tripartite central features, and, on the upper floors, shallow pilasters instead of quoins. In 1913, to designs by George Silley, a north service wing was built and the pavilions were raised to the height of the main block.[17]

In 1242–3 William Longespée, styled earl of Salisbury, was overlord of ¼ knight's fee in Durnford, later called SOUTHEND manor and presumably part of William of Eu's estate in 1086.[18] The overlordship apparently descended with the overlordship of Shrewton and the earldom of Salisbury until the 15th century[19] or later.

Walter son of Bernard was the mesne lord in 1242–3 and William of Durnford held the estate of him.[20] From then until 1410 the manor descended with Little Durnford manor.[21] From Nicholas Woodhill (d. 1410) it passed to his son Sir Thomas[22] (d. 1421), whose relict Elizabeth, wife of Thomas Ludsop, held it until her death in 1475. The manor descended to Sir Thomas's grandson John Woodhill[23] (d. 1490) and in the direct line to Fulk (d. 1511), Nicholas (d. 1531), and Anthony (d. 1542), whose daughter and heir Agnes (d. 1576), wife of Richard Chetwood and later of Sir George Calvely, was succeeded by her son Sir Richard Chetwood.[24] In 1612 Sir Richard sold the manor to Arthur Matravers,[25] who in 1618 sold it to Sir Laurence Hyde[26] (d. 1642). It passed in turn to Laurence's sons Robert (d. 1665) and Alexander (d. 1667),

92 Complete Peerage, x. 356; G. Ellis, Earldoms in Fee, 185; cf. V.C.H. Wilts. ii, p. 111.
93 Som. R.O., DD/SAS/H 348, f. 150v.
94 Complete Peerage, xi. 378, 382–3; Close R. 1242–7, 88; above, Amesbury, manors (Amesbury).
95 Som. R.O., DD/SAS/H 348, f. 150.
96 Pipe R. 1191–2 (P.R.S. N.S. ii), 98, 284, 290.
97 Bk. of Fees, ii. 744; Som. R.O., DD/SAS/H 348, ff. 150v.–151.
98 Feet of F. 1272–1327 (W.R.S. i), p. 96; Som. R.O., DD/SAS/H 348, f. 152.
99 Som. R.O., DD/SAS/H 348, ff. 152v.–153.
1 Feet of F. 1377–1509 (W.R.S. xli), p. 76; P.R.O., CP 40/583, rot. 646 and d.
2 Hants R.O. 7M54/207/1, Durnford, no. xxvii.
3 Complete Peerage, vi. 616; Feet of F. 1377–1509 (W.R.S. xli), pp. 150–1; W.A.M. xxxiv. 388–9.
4 P.R.O., C 142/32, no. 76.
5 Hist. Parl., Commons, 1509–58, ii. 412.
6 P.R.O., C 142/264, no. 161.
7 Wilts. Inq. p.m. 1625–49 (Index Libr.), 286–90; Wilts. Pedigrees (Harl. Soc. cv/cvi), 94; Hants R.O. 7M54/207/3.
8 P.R.O., C 5/248/34; ibid. PROB 11/325, ff. 93–94v.
9 Ibid. PROB 11/809, ff. 99–103; Hist. Parl., Commons, 1660–90, ii. 614–16; 1715–54, ii. 162.

10 Hants R.O. 7M54/209, abstr. of title.
11 For the earls, Burke, Peerage (1963), 1588–9.
12 W.A.M. xxxii. 233; Hants R.O. 7M54/215, agreement, 1868.
13 [F.] Antrobus, Sentimental and Practical Guide to Amesbury and Stonehenge (priv. print.); for the Tryon fam., Burke, Peerage (1963), 2441.
14 Inf. from Anthony, Lord Tryon, Durnford Manor; W.R.O., Inland Revenue, val. reg. 146; Hants R.O. 7M54/216, sale cat. 1874.
15 Who Was Who, 1971–80, 807; inf. from Lord Tryon.
16 W.R.O., EA/36.
17 Initials and date on S. front; Dept. of Environment, list of bldgs. of hist. interest (1987).
18 Bk. of Fees, ii. 744; above, this section.
19 Below, Shrewton, manors; e.g. P.R.O., C 140/55, no. 28.
20 Bk. of Fees, ii. 744.
21 Below, this section.
22 Cal. Inq. p.m. xix, p. 292.
23 P.R.O., C 138/57, no. 33; C 140/55, no. 28.
24 Ibid. C 142/65, no. 6; V.C.H. Beds. iii. 71–3; V.C.H. Bucks. iv. 165.
25 W.R.O. 492/61.
26 P.R.O., CP 25/2/371/16 Jas. I East.

bishop of Salisbury.[27] From 1665 to *c.* 1815 the manor descended with Milston and Brigmerston manor. It was held by Robert Hyde (d. 1722), Robert Hyde (d. 1723), Mary Levinz (d. 1730–1), and Mary (d. 1724) and Matthew Frampton (d. 1742). It passed to Matthew's nephews the Revd. Thomas Bull (d. 1743), Edward Polhill (d. 1759), and Simon Polhill (d. 1760). Simon was succeeded by the Revd. William Bowles (d. 1788),[28] assignees of whose son William sold the manor in 1815 to James, earl of Malmesbury.[29] Southend manor, 190 a. from inclosure in 1824, thereafter descended with Great Durnford manor.[30]

At the time of inclosure Lord Malmesbury sold 107 a. to Richard Webb.[31] That land, as Park farm, 121 a., in 1838 belonged to John Swayne, the owner of Netton manor,[32] and thereafter descended with that manor.[33]

King Edgar granted to his chamberlain Winstan 3 *cassati* in 963 and 4 *cassati*, including the 3, in 972.[34] Although said to be at Avon, Winstan's estate was that later called *LITTLE DURNFORD* manor.[35] It passed to Wilton abbey which held 4 hides at Durnford in 1066.[36] The manor was subinfeudated, but the abbey continued to receive a small rent from Little Durnford until the Dissolution.[37]

Three Englishmen held Little Durnford of Wilton abbey in 1066, Edward of Salisbury in 1086.[38] The manor may have passed to Edward's descendants, earls of Salisbury,[39] but by 1222 had been further subinfeudated.[40] William, styled earl of Salisbury, was recognized as overlord in 1242–3,[41] and the overlordship evidently descended like that of Shrewton to later earls of Salisbury.[42]

In 1222 John, son of Bernard, and his wife Sibyl conveyed the manor to William of Durnford,[43] who held it in 1242–3.[44] In 1286 William of Durnford, presumably another, conveyed it to (Sir) Henry de Préaux,[45] who conveyed it in 1322 to John Wahull or Woodhill[46] (d. 1336). It descended to John's son John Woodhill[47] (d. 1348) and from the younger John's relict Eleanor (fl. 1349) to his son John[48] (d. 1367). That John held jointly with his wife Isabel, who with her husband Sir Gerard Braybrooke conveyed the manor in 1376 to Nicholas Woodhill (d. 1410), her former husband's uncle and heir.[49] Nicholas's feoffees settled it in 1413 on his son Richard (d. 1470). Henry Etwall and his wife Mary bought the reversion from Richard's grandnephew and heir John Woodhill (d. 1490), but after Richard's death their title was disputed by Richard's nephew Richard Knesworth. As part of a compromise John Woodhill, Etwall, and Knesworth all joined in a sale of the manor to Thomas Tropenell in 1474.[50] Tropenell (d. 1488) was succeeded by his son Christopher[51] (d. 1503). The manor passed to Christopher's relict Anne,[52] by 1522 to his son Thomas (d. 1548),[53] to that Thomas's son Giles (d. 1553), and to Giles's sister Mary,[54] later the wife of John Young (d. 1588).[55] It descended in the direct line to Edward Young (d. 1608), John[56] (d. 1622), John (d. 1660), and John[57] (d. 1710), who devised it to his cousin Edward Young[58] (d. 1773). Edward's son Thomas (d. 1785) devised it to trustees, who may have held it for his illegitimate son William Young.[59] William or the trustees sold it in 1795 to Edward Hinxman. The manor, *c.* 420 a. in 1838, descended to Edward's son Edward (d. 1855)[60] and to that Edward's son Edward (d. 1896), whose relict Charlotte[61] sold it *c.* 1896 to M. H. W. Devenish (d. 1913). It descended to Devenish's son H. N. Devenish (d. 1934), who devised it in trust for sale.[62] J. Salmond, the owner in 1955,[63] sold it in 1966 to John Pelham, earl of Chichester,[64] the owner in 1993.

The manor house at Little Durnford in the Middle Ages was presumably beside the river on or near the site of Home Farm; in 1469 it included a hall and other rooms all described as new.[65] Little Durnford Manor, on higher ground to the north-east, was built for Edward Young and completed *c.* 1740;[66] although it is unlikely to be on the site of the medieval manor house, thick interior walls and several changes of floor level suggest that its north-east corner may have been part of a building standing before 1740. The new house was built of chequered limestone and flint and has two tall storeys, a south entrance front of five bays, and a west garden front of six.[67] The dining room in the north-west corner of the house retains richly decorated

[27] *Wilts. Pedigrees* (Harl. Soc. cv/cvi), 99; W.R.O. 492/40, deed, Hyde to trustees, 1653.
[28] Below, Milston, manors.
[29] Hants R.O. 7M54/212, abstr. of title; deed, Bowles's assignees to Vct. FitzHarris's trustees, 1815.
[30] W.R.O., EA/147.   [31] Ibid.
[32] P.R.O., IR 29/38/105; IR 30/38/105.
[33] Below, this section (Netton).
[34] Finberg, *Early Wessex Chart.* pp. 95, 98.
[35] *W.A.M.* lxiv. 56–7.   [36] *V.C.H. Wilts.* ii, p. 129.
[37] *Valor Eccl.* (Rec. Com.), ii. 111; P.R.O., CP 25/1/250/4, no. 13.   [38] *V.C.H. Wilts.* ii, pp. 70, 129.
[39] *Complete Peerage*, xi. 373–406.
[40] P.R.O., CP 25/1/250/4, no. 13.
[41] *Bk. of Fees*, ii. 744.
[42] *Cal. Inq. p.m.* viii, p. 16; xii, p. 154; xiv, p. 285; P.R.O., C 138/57, no. 33; C 142/686, no. 124; below, Shrewton, manors.   [43] P.R.O., CP 25/1/250/4, no. 13.
[44] *Bk. of Fees*, ii. 744.
[45] *Feet of F.* 1272–1327 (W.R.S. i), p. 28.
[46] *Tropenell Cart.* ed. J. S. Davies, ii. 271–2.
[47] *Cal. Inq. p.m.* viii, p. 16.
[48] Ibid. ix, pp. 108–9; *Cal. Close,* 1349–54, 60.
[49] *Cal. Inq. p.m.* xii, p. 154; xiv, p. 285; xix, p. 292; *Cal. Close,* 1374–7, 352–3.

[50] *Tropenell Cart.* ii. 286–90, 298–9, 305–7; Hoare, *Mod. Wilts.* Amesbury, 126–8.
[51] *Cal. Inq. p.m. Hen. VII*, i, pp. 146–7.
[52] Ibid. ii, pp. 437–9, 616.   [53] P.R.O., C 142/87, no. 93.
[54] Ibid. C 142/101, no. 116.
[55] Ibid. PROB 11/72, f. 224 and v.; Hoare, *Mod. Wilts.* Amesbury, 125.
[56] *Extents for Debts* (W.R.S. xxviii), p. 90; P.R.O., C 142/313, no. 87.
[57] *Cal. Cttee. for Compounding,* ii. 1039; Hoare, *Mod. Wilts.* Amesbury, 125; P.R.O., C 142/686, no. 124; ibid. PROB 11/298, f. 198 and v.
[58] P.R.O., PROB 11/513, ff. 10–15; W.R.O. 1985/2.
[59] P.R.O., PROB 11/986, ff. 305v.–307; PROB 11/1155, ff. 45–51v.; W.R.O. 1985/3; ibid. A 1/345/158.
[60] Hoare, *Mod. Wilts.* Amesbury, 128–9; P.R.O., IR 29/38/105; W.R.O. 1985/8.
[61] Princ. Regy. Fam. Div., will of Edw. Hinxman, 1896.
[62] Ibid. will of H. N. Devenish, 1934; *Kelly's Dir. Wilts.* (1898); R. J. Devenish and C. H. McLaughlin, *Hist. Devenish Fam.* 228, pedigree at pp. 228–9.
[63] W.R.O., G 1/505/1.   [64] Wilts. Cuttings, xxiii. 4.
[65] *Tropenell Cart.* ii. 317–31.
[66] Initials and date on rainwater head.
[67] See plate facing p. 186.

YOUNGE

BEHOLDE ALL YEE
Ẏ COME TO SEE

AS WE ARE NOWE
SO SHALL YEE BE

HIDE

HERE LYETH THE BODY OF EDWARD YOVNGE OF LITLE DORNEFORD Eꜱ^RQ̃ SONN & HEYRE OF IOHN YOVNG EꜱQ̃:& OF MARY HIS WIFE ONE OF Ẏ FOWER DAVGHTERS & COHEYRES OF THOM:TRAPNELL OF MOVNCKTON FARLEY E.ꜱQ̃: W^{ch} EDW:MARIED IOANE ẎELDEST DAVGHTER OF LAVRENCE HIDE OF WEST HATCHE EꜱQ̃:& HAD BY HER 6 SONES & 8 DAVGHTERS WHO DYED FEBR:18.1607.

BRASS IN THE CHURCH, COMMEMORATING EDWARD YOUNG AND HIS FAMILY

plasterwork of *c.* 1740. The entrance hall, a room east of it, and a room west of it were decorated for Edward Hinxman *c.* 1800. At the same time the first-floor rooms on the south side of the house were refitted, sash windows were inserted in most parts of the house, and three blind windows in the north-west corner were opened. An oak staircase and a landing screen, both in 17th-century style, were introduced by M. H. W. Devenish, who restored the house in 1896.[68] A long north-east service wing standing *c.* 1750 was replaced in 1937 by a smaller one.[69] Land around the house was imparked. By 1754 painted lead statues formerly at Wilton House and given to Edward Young by 1733 had been set up beside the Avon, and in woodland east of the house a hermitage decorated with grotesque figures had been erected.[70] The statues were later removed.[71] There were two fishponds beside the Avon in 1773;[72] a small lake was made between 1879 and 1900.[73] In 1993 20th-century sculptures were displayed on lawns south and west of the house.

Of what may have been a manor of *NETTON* Alice de Tony (fl. 1103) gave ½ hide, possibly the demesne land, to the Templars,[74] who held it at their suppression in 1308. It passed with their other lands to the Hospitallers, who held it from 1312 until the Dissolution.[75] In 1546 the estate was granted to (Sir) John Zouche[76] (d. 1585). It passed to Sir John's son Francis (d. 1600) and *c.* 1601, still 2 yardlands, it was sold to Thomas Mackerell (d. 1627), presumably by Francis's son Richard. From Mackerell's daughter and heir Anne (d. 1699), wife of John Swayne (d. 1676), the estate descended in the direct line to John Swayne, John (d. 1736), John (d. 1783), and John (d. *s.p.* 1804).[77] The last John devised it to his nephew John Swayne,[78] who by 1824 had acquired other land at Netton.[79] The estate, 200 a. in 1838[80] and later called Manor farm, descended from Swayne (d. 1865) to his son H. J. F. Swayne (d. 1892) and to his grandson J. M. Swayne.[81] It was acquired between 1910 and 1920, presumably by purchase, by Louis Greville (d. 1941),[82] and it descended to his

68   Initials and date on rainwater heads.
69   *Country Life*, 3 July 1975, pp. 19, 21.
70   *Travels through Eng. of Dr. Ric. Pococke*, ii (Camd. Soc. [2nd ser.], xliv), 135–6; *Complete Peerage*, x. 424–5.
71   For the hermitage, cf. above, intro. (Little Durnford).
72   *Andrews and Dury, Map* (W.R.S. viii), pl. 5.
73   O.S. Maps 6", Wilts. LXVI (1887 edn.); LXVI. NW. (1901 edn.).
74   *Rec. Templars in Eng.* ed. B. A. Lees, p. 52; *Complete Peerage*, xii (1), 761.
75   *V.C.H. Wilts.* iii. 328; *Rec. Templars in Eng.* p. xxv;

P.R.O., SC 6/Hen. VIII/7262, rot. 6.
76   *L. & P. Hen. VIII*, xxi (1), p. 687.
77   Hoare, *Mod. Wilts.* Amesbury, 124; ibid. Add. 49; *Wilts. Inq. p.m.* 1625–49 (Index Libr.), 140–1; *V.C.H. Wilts.* xiii. 95.   78   P.R.O., PROB 11/1424, ff. 261–3.
79   W.R.O., EA/147.
80   P.R.O., IR 29/38/105; IR 30/38/105.
81   *Kelly's Handbk.* (1924), 1466; Princ. Regy. Fam. Div., will of John Swayne, 1865.
82   *Kelly's Dir. Wilts.* (1920 and later edns.); Burke, *Peerage* (1963), 2510; W.R.O., Inland Revenue, val. reg. 146.

niece Phyllis, wife of Guy Rasch (d. 1955). She transferred it in 1955 to her son Major D. A. C. Rasch, who owned 355 a. at Netton in 1993.[83]

In 1242–3 William, styled earl of Salisbury, was overlord of two other estates in Netton, one of ¼ knight's fee held by Warin son of Gerald and of him by Robert Columbers, and one of ⅓ knight's fee held by Agace de Maizey.[84] The larger may have consisted of the customary lands of Netton manor and evidently descended with Salterton manor until 1309[85] or later, possibly until 1559, when 2 yardlands at Netton were part of that manor,[86] or later. In 1809 it seems to have been the estate, consisting of customary holdings totalling 83 a. with pasture rights, owned by Jacob Pleydell-Bouverie, earl of Radnor.[87] By 1824 that estate had been added to John Swayne's.[88] The smaller estate in 1242–3 may have been that owned by William Davis in 1635,[89] George Davis c. 1660,[90] another William Davis, and that William's sons William and George (fl. 1704); James Townsend, to whom the second William Davis was indebted, devised the estate to his son James (d. 1748).[91] It may have been the estate owned by William Bowles, lord of Southend manor, in 1809, when it was of 62 a. with pasture rights.[92] Bowles's estate belonged to John Newman in 1815[93] and 1838, when it was 90 a.[94] It has not been traced further.

What became *SALTERTON* manor was almost certainly part of William of Eu's estate in 1086.[95] Like other of his lands the overlordship of the manor descended to Walter Marshal, earl of Pembroke (d. *s.p.* 1245).[96] It was held in 1259 by Walter's nephew and coheir Richard de Clare, earl of Gloucester and of Hereford (d. 1262), passed with the earldom of Gloucester to Hugh de Audley (d. 1347),[97] and descended to Hugh's daughter Margaret, wife of Ralph de Stafford, Lord Stafford (cr. earl of Stafford 1351, d. 1372). It descended with the earldom of Stafford to Edmund de Stafford, earl of Stafford (d. 1403),[98] after whose death it was not mentioned.

Warin son of Gerald was the mesne lord in 1242–3 and Robert Columbers held the manor of him.[99] The lordship in demesne was held by Robert Waleran (d. 1273) who gave the manor to his brother William (d. by 1273) and to William's wife Isabel (d. 1284) in an exchange of 1259.[1] Before her death Isabel's lands were committed to her kinsman Alan Plucknet (d. *c.* 1299), a commission renewed in 1284 because her son Robert (d. by 1299) was an idiot.[2] Robert's brother and heir John Waleran (d. by 1309) was also an idiot.[3] In a partition of John's estate Salterton manor was allotted in 1310 to Isabel's grandnephew Ralph Butler (d. 1343).[4] It passed to Ralph's relict Hawise[5] (d. 1360) and to his grandson Sir Edward Butler[6] (d. 1412), whose heir was his cousin Sir Philip Butler.[7] In 1420 a moiety passed in turn to Sir Philip's sons Edward (d. 1420) and Philip, a minor. A moiety held in 1420 for life by John Judd and his wife Gillian, grantees of Sir Philip,[8] was held in reversion by Philip at his death in 1453. Philip Butler was succeeded by his son John[9] (d. 1504). Salterton manor descended in the direct line to John[10] (d. 1514), Sir Philip[11] (d. 1545), and Sir John,[12] who in 1569 sold it to Gerard Errington[13] (d. 1598). It descended in the direct line to Nicholas (d. 1604) and Gerard,[14] who in 1610 sold it to George Duke (d. 1618). It belonged, possibly from 1610 or soon after, to George's son John[15] (d. 1671), who by 1637 had divided it. John gave the lordship and all the land except the demesne to his son George[16] (d. 1655), from whom his estate passed in turn to his sons John (d. 1657) and George (d. 1690). From George it descended in the direct line to Robert (d. 1725), Robert (d. 1749), and Robert (d. 1793). The estate was held for life by the last Robert's relict Jane[17] (d. 1805) and passed to his cousin the Revd. Edward Duke, who sold it in 1809 to William Bowles, lord of Southend manor. Bowles's assignees sold the estate in 1813 to Edward Hinxman, lord of Little Durnford manor, who sold it in 1822 to John Davis[18] (d. 1860). The estate, 456 a. in 1838, passed to Davis's son John,[19] who sold it in 1866 to the Ecclesiastical Commissioners.[20] The commissioners, who also owned the demesne land from 1866, sold the whole manor in 1920 to G. D. Cole. Also in 1920 Cole sold the manor to Jeremiah Woodford,[21] in 1937–8 Woodford sold

83 Burke, *Peerage* (1963), 2027, 2510; inf. from Major D. A. C. Rasch, Heale Ho., Woodford.
84 *Bk. of Fees*, ii. 744.
85 *Wilts. Inq. p.m. 1242–1326* (Index Libr.), 364–5; below, this section (Salterton).
86 P.R.O., REQ 2/79/3.
87 W.R.O. 490/1126.
88 Ibid. EA/147.
89 Alnwick Castle Mun. X.II.11, box 6, survey, 1634, p. 186.
90 P.R.O., CP 25/2/744/13 Chas. II Mich.; W.R.O. 492/41, deed, Davis to Hyde, 1659.
91 *V.C.H. Wilts.* x. 45; *W.A.M.* lx. 116; P.R.O., C 5/634/34.
92 W.R.O. 490/1126.   93 Ibid. A 1/345/158.
94 P.R.O., IR 29/38/105.
95 Above, this section.
96 *Bk. of Fees*, ii. 745; *V.C.H. Wilts.* ii, p. 111; *Complete Peerage*, x. 374–6.
97 *Cal. Inq. p.m.* v, pp. 74–5; viii, p. 247; *Complete Peerage*, v. 694–719.
98 *Complete Peerage*, xii (1), 174–81; e.g. *Cal. Inq. p.m.* x, p. 463; xviii, p. 281.
99 *Bk. of Fees*, ii. 745.
1 Sanders, *Eng. Baronies*, 73–4; *Cal. Inq. p.m.* v, pp. 74–5.

2 *Cal. Pat.* 1281–92, 117; *Cal. Inq. p.m.* iii, pp. 416–17.
3 *Cal. Inq. p.m.* v, pp. 70, 74–9.
4 *Cal. Close*, 1307–13, 259; Sanders, *Eng. Baronies*, 146.
5 *Feet of F. 1272–1327* (W.R.S. i), p. 125.
6 *Cal. Inq. p.m.* x, pp. 462–3.   7 Ibid. xix, p. 374.
8 P.R.O., C 138/49, no. 78, rot. 6; C 139/33, no. 30, rot. 4.
9 Ibid. C 139/149, no. 27, rot. 8.
10 Ibid. PROB 11/14, f. 134 and v.
11 R. Clutterbuck, *Hist. Herts.* ii. 476. This acct. of the Butler fam. augments and corrects that given ibid. and in *V.C.H. Herts.* iii. 162.   12 P.R.O., C 142/73, no. 88.
13 W.R.O. 906/W/103.
14 P.R.O., C 60/464, no. 63; C 142/283, no. 84.
15 Ibid. CP 25/2/369/7 Jas. I Hil.; for the Duke fam., *W.N. & Q.* viii, pedigree at pp. 300–1.
16 P.R.O., CP 25/2/510/13 Chas. I East.
17 W.R.O. 906/W/104–7; 906/W/125; 906/W/127; 906/W/149–50.
18 Ibid. Ch. Com., bishop, 57/1, abstr. of title of John Davis; ibid. Ch. Com., bishop, 58; Hoare, *Mod. Wilts.* Underditch, 139; P.R.O., PROB 11/1231, ff. 38v.–41v.
19 P.R.O., IR 29/38/105; IR 30/38/105; Princ. Regy. Fam. Div., will of John Davis, 1860.
20 W.R.O., Ch. Com., bishop, 59/1.
21 Ch. Com. file 88585.

it to James Dugdale, and partly in 1968 and partly in 1981 Dugdale's trustees sold it to Geoffrey Langdon, the owner in 1993.[22]

The demesne of Salterton manor evidently passed, perhaps by gift, from John Duke (d. 1671) to his son John. It descended to the younger John's son George, to George's son John (d. 1743), and to that John's son John, who sold it in 1756 to Augustine Hayter (d. 1779).[23] It passed in turn to Hayter's sons William[24] (d. 1784) and Augustine (d. 1810),[25] who devised it to his daughters Anne Hayter (d. 1835), Susanna Bundy (d. 1828), and Mary Swayne (d. 1861) as tenants in common.[26] Mary owned c. 195 a. in 1838.[27] The land descended to her daughter Anne, whose husband John Davis owned the main part of the manor.[28] In 1866 Anne sold her land to the Ecclesiastical Commissioners.[29]

NORMANTON manor was ancient demesne of the Crown. It was granted to an ancestor of Roger la Zouche (d. 1285), and Roger claimed free warren in the demesne. In 1275 Roger held the manor by military service as overlord.[30] The overlordship was not afterwards mentioned.

The manor had been subinfeudated by 1268, when John son of Aucher held it.[31] In 1330 John Aucher settled it on himself for life and on Walter Norris and Walter's son Thomas.[32] In 1409 Thomas's daughter Joan and her husband Robert Craford held it,[33] and it descended to Joan's son John Mohun (fl. 1428), to John's son John, and to that John's daughter Christine, wife of Henry Trenchard.[34] Christine was succeeded by her son Sir John Trenchard (d. 1495). In 1483 the manor was taken from John because of his opposition to Richard III and in 1485 restored to him. It passed in the direct line to Sir Thomas (fl. 1543), Richard[35] (d. 1560), William[36] (will proved 1592), Francis (will proved 1622), and Francis (will proved 1636). The last Francis's daughter and heir Elizabeth died in infancy and was succeeded by Francis's brother Edward[37] (fl. 1668), whose nephew and heir William Trenchard[38] (d. 1710) devised the

manor in thirds to his daughters Anne (d. *s.p.*), wife of Richard Baxter, Frances (d. 1724), wife of John Hippisley, and Ellen (d. 1752), wife of Henry Long. Anne's sisters each inherited half her share. Frances's moiety descended to her son William Hippisley (d. 1755), whose trustees sold it *c.* 1767 to William Long (d. *s.p.* 1773), Ellen's son and heir.[39] A Mrs. Long, presumably William's relict, held the manor in 1780,[40] and in 1781 it belonged to his niece Elizabeth Long (d. *s.p.* 1807), wife of Robert Colebrooke (d. 1785) and later of John Crosdill.[41] In 1807 it passed to William Long's grandnephew the Revd. Bouchier Wrey,[42] who sold it in 1834 to Sir Edmund Antrobus, Bt.[43] The manor, 630 a. in 1838,[44] descended with his Amesbury estate from Sir Edmund (d. 1870) to Sir Edmund Antrobus, Bt. (d. 1899), Sir Edmund Antrobus, Bt. (d. 1915), and Sir Cosmo Antrobus, Bt.,[45] who sold it in 1915 to Edward Tennant, Lord Glenconner[46] (d. 1920). It passed to Glenconner's relict Pamela (d. 1928), wife of Edward Grey, Viscount Grey,[47] and, evidently between 1927 and 1933, was sold to F. G. G. Bailey.[48] In 1993 Mr. P. Bailey owned all the manor except Normanton House and *c.* 12 a., which belonged to Mr. and Mrs. L. Le Sueur.[49]

Salisbury cathedral owned Durnford church from *c.* 1150 or earlier.[50] Although no licence to appropriate is extant the cathedral is known from later evidence to have taken the great tithes from most of the parish.[51] By *c.* 1150 it had endowed a prebend with the *RECTORY* estate.[52] In addition to the tithes the estate included 3 houses and 1 yardland with pasture rights given to Durnford church by Isabel de Tony or her husband Walter son of Richard in the mid 12th century; Isabel and Walter also gave all tithes from their land in the parish.[53] In 1405 the prebendary was said to have 43 a.,[54] in 1622 *c.* 120 a.[55] In 1794 his tithes from Durnford Northend were exchanged for 246 a.,[56] and in 1838 his remaining tithes were valued at £490 and in 1842 commuted.[57] On the death of the prebendary in 1848 the manor passed to the Ecclesiastical Commissioners,[58] who sold the

22   Inf. from Mrs. G. Langdon, Salterton Farm.
23   Hoare, *Mod. Wilts.* Underditch, 135, 139; W.R.O., Ch. Com., bishop, 57/5, suppl. abstr. of title.
24   P.R.O., PROB 11/1060, ff. 168–70.
25   Hoare, *Mod. Wilts.* Underditch, 135.
26   P.R.O., PROB 11/1518, ff. 195–6; W.R.O., Ch. Com., bishop, 58; ibid. A 1/345/158.
27   P.R.O., IR 29/38/105; IR 30/38/105.
28   Hoare, *Mod. Wilts.* Add. 49, where Mary is erroneously called Anne: cf. W.R.O., Ch. Com., bishop, 58.
29   Ch. Com. file 32352.
30   *Rot. Hund.* (Rec. Com.), ii (1), 265; *Complete Peerage*, xii (2), 930–5.
31   P.R.O., JUST 1/998A, rot. 24d.
32   *Feet of F.* 1327–77 (W.R.S. xxix), p. 28.
33   Ibid. *1377–1509* (W.R.S. xli), pp. 63–4; J. Hutchins, *Dors.* i. 273.
34   Hutchins, *Dors.* i. 273; *Antrobus D.* (W.R.S. iii), p. 19.
35   Hutchins, *Dors.* iii. 326–7; *Cal. Inq. p.m. Hen. VII*, i, p. 537; *Rot. Parl.* vi. 246, 273; P.R.O., CP 25/2/52/378, no. 22.   36   P.R.O., E 150/1000, no. 2.
37   Ibid. C 142/530, no. 167; C 142/778, no. 151; *W.N. & Q.* iv. 177, 325–8; Burke, *Land. Gent.* (1846), ii. 1430–1.
38   W.R.O. 1953/66, deed, Trenchard, 1668.
39   Ibid. 1178/559/1, rep. on Hippisley's case, 1756–7; 1619, box 11, abstr. of Wrey's title; 1953/68, copy will of Wm. Trenchard; 1999/1; Burke, *Land. Gent.* (1846), i. 760;

ii. 1430–1; P.R.O., PROB 11/990, ff. 10v.–16.
40   W.R.O., A 1/345/158.
41   Ibid.; Burke, *Land. Gent.* (1846), i. 760; G.E.C. *Baronetage*, v. 116; P.R.O., PROB 11/990, ff. 10v.–16.
42   Burke, *Peerage* (1963), 2621–2; P.R.O., PROB 11/990, ff. 10v.–16.
43   W.R.O. 1619, box 11, deed, Wrey to Antrobus, 1834.
44   P.R.O., IR 29/38/105.
45   Above, Amesbury, manors (Earldom).
46   *W.A.M.* xxxix. 393.
47   *Who Was Who, 1929–1940*, 556; Burke, *Peerage* (1963), 1010; *Kelly's Dir. Wilts.* (1923, 1927); W.R.O., G 1/500/18.
48   W.R.O., G 1/501/1.
49   Inf. from Mr. P. Bailey, Springbottom Farm, Wilsford; Mrs. L. Le Sueur, Normanton Ho.
50   Le Neve, *Fasti, 1066–1300, Salisbury*, 65; *Reg. St. Osmund* (Rolls Ser.), i. 203.
51   P.R.O., IR 29/38/105.
52   Le Neve, *Fasti, 1066–1300, Salisbury*, 65.
53   *Reg. St. Osmund* (Rolls Ser.), i. 266; *Sar. Chart. and Doc.* (Rolls Ser.), 34–5.
54   *Chandler's Reg.* (W.R.S. xxxix), p. 29.
55   W.R.O., D 5/10/1/1.
56   Ibid. EA/36.
57   P.R.O., IR 29/38/105.
58   Ch. Com. file 2296.

land as Church farm, 371 a., in 1920.[59] The farm belonged to G. H. King in 1922,[60] and in 1993 was owned with Great Durnford manor by Anthony, Lord Tryon.[61]

AGRICULTURE. From the Middle Ages to the 20th century, when dairy farming increased, sheep-and-corn husbandry predominated throughout the parish. In 1086 William of Eu's estate evidently included the whole parish except Little Durnford and Normanton. It had land for 14 ploughteams: 2 were on the 4 demesne hides with 2 *servi*, 12 were shared by 26 *villani* and 37 bordars. There were 30 a. of meadow and 20 square leagues of pasture.[62] The numerous *villani* and bordars may already have lived in several separate settlements, each of which may have had its own open fields, common meadows, and common pastures, and later the north end of Durnford, the south end of Durnford, Netton, and Salterton were such settlements.

DURNFORD NORTHEND. The demesne of Great Durnford manor, which was leased in the 15th century,[63] seems in the 18th century to have been mainly in severalty and to have lain south and east of Ogbury camp.[64] It may have been separated from the customary land much earlier, and in the 15th and 16th centuries the three open fields may have been for the tenantry. In 1412 the fields were East (later Woodway), 100 a., Middle, 100 a., and North, 120 a. The tenantry had a cow down, possibly Ogbury camp and Catsbrain hill, and a sheep down in the north-east corner of the parish.[65] Part of the downland had been burnbaked by 1712.[66]

About 1412 the Rectory manor had four customary tenants who each held c. 2 a. and had to mow, make hay, and wash and shear sheep.[67] The demesne was of 4 yardlands in 1622, by when the customary holdings had evidently been merged with it; it had land in each of the three open fields, and a flock of 220 sheep could be fed with the flock on the demesne of Great Durnford manor.[68]

By the late 18th century nearly all the copyhold land of Great Durnford manor had been brought in hand and the owner of the manor had taken the Rectory manor on lease:[69] as a result 90 per cent of the land and pasture rights may have been in a single farm. In 1794 the c. 950 a. of arable and downland pasture of Durnford Northend were inclosed by Act, and some of the c. 50 a. of meadows and home closes were allotted in exchanges. The allotment to the prebendary of Durnford to replace the great

tithes, 246 a., was evidently so large because it was mainly of downland.[70] About 1840 there were 566 a. of arable, 65 a. of meadow and other land near the village, and 373 a. of downland pasture.[71] In 1910 the land was in two farms: one of 448 a. was worked from the farmstead in the south end at what was later called Church Farm Farmhouse and the 19th-century buildings north-east of the village; Church farm, 657 a., was worked from the farmstead at what was later called Church Farm.[72] In 1993 most of the land was in South farm, c. 800 a., and chiefly arable.[73]

Land north and east of Durnford Manor was imparked before 1820, probably in the 1790s,[74] and trees were planted on the steep north slopes of Ogbury camp. There were 40 a. of park and woodland in 1910[75] and 1993.

DURNFORD SOUTHEND. Open-field husbandry continued until 1824. There were three fields, Low, High to the east of it, and Ham to the south-west near Netton village. High field was subdivided into north, middle, and south fields. South of the village Little down may have been for cattle; east of the arable there was an extensive down presumably for sheep. South of the village c. 10 a. of meadow may formerly have been used in common. The c. 464 a. of open fields and common pastures were inclosed by Act in 1824.[76]

At the time of inclosure there were some seven farms, each with a farmstead in the street. The largest, Southend farm, was worked from the house on the west side of the street later called Church Farm Farmhouse. The other six farmsteads were further south on the east side. After inclosure the farms were of c. 192 a., c. 85 a., c. 47 a., c. 32 a., and 20 a. or less. Park farm, with buildings and 121 a. near Netton, was created in 1824.[77]

Nearly all the downland had been ploughed by c. 1840, when there were three principal farms. Southend farm, 280 a., had c. 246 a. of arable, a farm of 77 a. had c. 72 a. of arable, and Park farm had only 56 a. of arable: on Park farm a few acres of woodland had been planted on Little down.[78] Southend was a farm of c. 200 a. in 1874;[79] in 1910, when it had a down farmstead called South Farm, but not that at Church Farm Farmhouse, it was part of Church farm;[80] with land of Durnford Northend it was in 1993 in South farm.[81] By 1910 the smaller farms of Durnford Southend had been merged as a 206-a. farm:[82] in the 1930s much of its land was used as an airfield[83] and went out of cultivation. In 1910 Park farm was worked with land at Netton.[84]

59 W.A.S. Libr., sale cat. xvi, no. 10.
60 W.R.O., G 1/500/6.
61 Inf. from Lord Tryon, Durnford Manor.
62 *V.C.H. Wilts.* ii, p. 148.
63 P.R.O., SC 6/1119/11.   64 W.R.O., EA/36.
65 Ibid.; ibid. 2/3; D. & C. Sar. Mun., press III, Durnford prebend ct. rolls; Hants R.O. 7M54/207/7.
66 Hants R.O. 7M54/207/3.
67 D. & C. Sar. Mun., press III, Durnford prebend ct. rolls.   68 W.R.O., D 5/10/1/1–4.
69 Ibid. A 1/345/158; ibid. EA/36; Ch. Com. file 2296; Hants R.O. 7M54/210, lease, prebendary of Durnford to Harris, 1755.   70 W.R.O., EA/36.
71 P.R.O., IR 29/38/105; IR 30/38/105.

72 W.R.O., Inland Revenue, val. reg. 146 and map 60.
73 Inf. from Anthony, Lord Tryon, Durnford Manor.
74 C. Greenwood, *Map of Wilts.* (1820); cf. above, manors (Great Durnford).
75 W.R.O., Inland Revenue, val. reg. 146.
76 Ibid. EA/147.   77 Ibid.
78 P.R.O., IR 29/38/105; IR 30/38/105.
79 Hants R.O. 7M54/216.
80 W.R.O., Inland Revenue, val. reg. 146 and map 60; for Church farm, above, this section (Durnford Northend).
81 Inf. from Lord Tryon.
82 W.R.O., Inland Revenue, val. reg. 146 and map 60.
83 Above, intro. (Great Durnford).
84 W.R.O., Inland Revenue, val. reg. 146.

LITTLE DURNFORD. There were evidently open fields at Little Durnford in 963.[85] In 1086 there was enough land for 3 teams: there were 4 bordars and 1 team of 6 oxen on the demesne, and two Englishmen had 2 teams on the other arable land. There were 12 a. of meadow and 4 square furlongs of pasture.[86]

There were two open fields in 1348. The demesne of Little Durnford manor then had 60 a. in each, 4 a. of meadow, and pasture for 8 oxen.[87] It had been leased by 1409;[88] it perhaps included then, as it did later, all Little Durnford's farmland, making formal inclosure of the open fields unnecessary. Land around Little Durnford Manor was imparked in the 18th century,[89] and a new farmstead, later called Longhedge Farm, was built on the downs in the earlier 19th.[90] About 1840 Little Durnford, later Home, farm was 247 a., Longhedge farm was c. 95 a., and c. 30 a. were parkland and woodland. Of the farmland c. 267 a. were arable, of which 38 a. or more were burnbaked downland. Longhedge remained a farm of 95 a. in the later 19th century;[91] in 1910 its land, but not the farmstead, was part of Home farm, 401 a.[92] In 1993 there were c. 50 a. of woodland at Little Durnford; on Home farm, c. 370 a., cattle were reared for beef.[93]

NETTON. In 1309 there were at Netton probably eight customary tenants each holding 1 yardland, nominally 20 a.: five owed labour service on 32 occasions between 1 August and 29 September or 4s. additional rent. Three other yardlanders and two cottagers may also have held land at Netton.[94] There may also have been a small demesne farm.[95]

In the early 19th century there were 51 a. of inclosed meadow and pasture near the village, c. 183 a. of arable in four open fields, a common pasture of 6 a. near the village, and a common sheep down of 64 a. The open fields were North (35 a.), South (54 a.), East (35 a.), and Middle (59 a.): nearly all the strips were of less than 1 a. The men of Netton also had joint use of Salterton cow down in summer. In 1824 the open fields and common pastures were inclosed under the same Act and by the same award as Dunford Southend. All the land was then worked from farmsteads in the street; after inclosure there were apparently three farms, of 200 a., 91 a., and 51 a.[96] In 1840 the largest, later called Manor farm, may have been worked with the smallest.[97]

In the mid 19th century two downland farmsteads were erected, Coffee Farm and High Post Buildings.[98] In 1910 all the land was in a single

farm, 437 a. including the adjoining Park farm in Southend.[99] In 1993 Manor farm, 236 a., was worked with land in Woodford; the Netton land was mainly arable.[1]

SALTERTON AND NEWTOWN. The open fields of Salterton were worked from Salterton village and, by c. 1300, from Newtown. In 1299 the demesne of Salterton manor comprised 140 a. of arable, 18 a. of meadows, and a possibly several downland pasture worth 12s. The arable was estimated at 300 a. in 1309 and, if the figures for 1299 and 1309 are correct, there may have been a two-field system with an amount comparable to the 140 a. left fallow in 1299. On the manor 10½ yardlands, each nominally of 40 a., were in 20 holdings of 1 or ½ yardland in 1299. Labour service had been commuted: 15 ½-yardlanders each paid 2s. 8d., and 3 cottars each paid 8d., instead of autumn works. There was a common meadow. One or more of the holdings may have been based at Newtown.[2]

In 1309 the demesne comprised, besides the arable, a downland pasture for 250 sheep, and a pasture for 16 oxen. There was a freehold of 2 yardlands, and since 1299 the number of customary holdings had been reduced to eight, each of 1 yardland. Like tenants at Netton each yardlander owed labour service on 32 occasions between 1 August and 29 September or 4s. additional rent. The freehold and three or more of the customary holdings were evidently based at Newtown.[3] In 1421 the demesne was said to comprise c. 200 a. of arable, 40 a. of meadow, and 300 a. of pasture: some of the 300 a. were several.[4]

Open-field husbandry continued at Salterton until the earlier 19th century. There were three open fields in 1598.[5] In 1711 the common meadow was damaged when a ditch was dug to drain the demesne meadows.[6] By c. 1807 some arable had been inclosed. What then remained open was probably 300–350 a., and a 158-a. sheep down and a 96-a. cow down were used in common, the cow down also by the men of Netton in summer. In the earlier 19th century there were only two farms, the larger based in Newtown, the smaller in Salterton, and the same man was tenant of both. The land was inclosed between 1807 and 1838, presumably by private agreement. In 1838 the farms were of 457 a. and 195 a.: they had a total of 34 a. of meadow, 7 a. of orchard, 12 a. of lowland pasture, 374 a. of arable, and 219 a. of upland pasture.[7] All the land was in single ownership from 1866,[8] and in 1867 was leased as a single farm. About then most of the farm buildings along the lanes at

85 W.A.M. lxiv. 56, 59.
86 V.C.H. Wilts. ii, p. 129.
87 Wilts. Inq. p.m. 1327–77 (Index Libr.), 192.
88 Tropenell Cart. ii. 281–2.
89 Above, manors (Little Durnford).
90 O.S. Map 1", sheet 14 (1817 edn.); P.R.O., IR 29/38/105; IR 30/38/105.
91 P.R.O., IR 29/38/105; IR 30/38/105; W.R.O. 776/20.
92 W.R.O., Inland Revenue, val. reg. 146 and maps 60, 66.
93 Inf. from Mr. B. K. Allen, Home Farm.
94 Wilts. Inq. p.m. 1242–1326 (Index Libr.), 365.
95 Above, manors (Netton).
96 W.R.O. 490/1125–6; ibid. EA/147.

97 P.R.O., IR 29/38/105; IR 30/38/105.
98 O.S. Map 6", Wilts. LX (1887 edn.); P.R.O., IR 29/38/105; IR 30/38/105.
99 W.R.O., Inland Revenue, val. reg. 146; above, this section (Durnford Southend).
1 Inf. from Mrs. T. W. Baird, Manor Farm, Netton.
2 Wilts. Inq. p.m. 1242–1326 (Index Libr.), 229–30; for the demesne cf. ibid. 364.
3 Ibid. 364–5.
4 P.R.O., C 138/49, no. 78, rot. 6.
5 Ibid. C 60/464, no. 63, rot. 2.
6 W.R.O., Ch. Com., bishop, 60/1.
7 Ibid. 490/1125; P.R.O., IR 29/38/105; IR 30/38/105.
8 Above, manors (Salterton).

Salterton and Newtown were demolished and a farmstead beside the road at Newtown and a downland farmstead were built.[9] The new farmsteads remained in use in 1993, when Salterton farm, 625 a., was a mainly dairy farm.[10]

NORMANTON. In the earlier 14th century Normanton manor is likely to have had a demesne farm and a few customary holdings;[11] if it did there were almost certainly open fields and common pastures. By the 18th century, however, all Normanton's land was in a single farm and in severalty. In 1739 the farm included 35 a. of water meadow, 7 a. of pasture near the farmstead, and 211 a. of arable of which 39 a. were in small fields to the east.[12] About 1838 the farm, 631 a., included 28 a. of meadow, 9 a. of lowland pasture, 2 a. of orchard, 251 a. of arable, and 321 a. of downland; an additional 15 a. of down were furze[13] and in 1993 were woodland.

By 1915 little of the downland had been ploughed, and Normanton has evidently never had a farmstead on the downs. The 51 a. west of the Exeter road had been added to a farm based in Amesbury, and Normanton farm reduced to 604 a.[14] Much of the downland was afterwards ploughed, and in 1993 the farm, c. 590 a., was mainly arable; it was then worked from Springbottom Farm in Wilsford.[15] Some downland was used for training racehorses in 1992.[16]

MILLS. In 1086 there was a mill at Little Durnford and three others in the remainder of the parish excluding Normanton.[17] Great Durnford manor included a mill in the later 12th century and the earlier 14th.[18] There was a mill on Southend manor in 1389[19] and in 1612, when there were two or more under one roof.[20] Durnford Mill at the south end of Great Durnford is likely to stand on the site of the mills on Southend manor. It was reconstructed from the mid 18th century,[21] ceased to work after c. 1922,[22] was derelict in 1955,[23] and was restored as a house c. 1961.[24] In the 18th century there was a tradition, but no direct evidence, that a mill stood at Normanton.[25]

TRADE AND INDUSTRY. In the later 19th century members of the Dear family were woolstaplers and had a wool store on the south side of the Netton to High Post road.[26] Two other woolstaplers and a wool sorter had premises at Netton in 1881.[27]

An airfield north-west of High Post was used by the Wiltshire School of Flying Ltd. from 1931 and remained open until 1947.[28] The Wessex Aircraft Engineering Company Ltd., founded in 1933, had premises at High Post and later had buildings on the airfield. It made signalling equipment for aircraft and, during the Second World War, for ships. After the war the company, then called WAECO Ltd., made pyrotechnic devices for the armed forces and fireworks. The factory covered c. 27 a. in 1952.[29] In 1965 the company merged with James Pain & Sons, manufacturers of fireworks and civilian pyrotechnic devices, to form Pains-Wessex Ltd. In 1973 Schermuly, a firm which made marine pyrotechnics and specialized in rocket-powered line throwers, became part of the company to form Pains-Wessex Schermuly. Firework making ceased in 1976. In 1993 the company produced marine distress signals and military pyrotechnics: it had c. 450 employees and 150 or more buildings extending over c. 100 a.[30]

A factory built at High Post after the Second World War was used to process tobacco and manufacture cigarettes in the 1950s.[31] In 1990 a new factory was built at High Post and in 1993 was used by Air Cleaner Technical Services to make automatic components for air conditioners; c. 160 were employed by the company.[32]

LOCAL GOVERNMENT. Records of Great Durnford manor court survive for 1537–52, 1590–3, 1601, 1605, 1609, 1622–1713, and 1730–6. At the court common husbandry was regulated and copyhold tenants were admitted; among offences presented were fishing in the Avon from boats, encroaching on and building on the waste, and failing to repair buildings. John Duke, a freeholder, was often presented in the earlier 17th century for failing to keep his part of the river bank in good repair.[33]

Records of a court leet held twice yearly on the Rectory estate survive for 1412–14. The tithingman presented offences by brewers and at three courts the unlawful raising of the hue and cry.[34]

At Salterton manor court, records of which survive for 1674–1713, 1718–51, and 1766–1807, copyhold business was transacted, common husbandry was regulated, and encroachments on the waste were presented. From the later 18th century the court was held only when business required it.[35]

Records of courts held for Little Durnford

9 W.R.O., Ch. Com., bishop, 73; above, intro. (Salterton; Newtown).
10 Inf. from Mrs. G. Langdon, Salterton Farm.
11 Tax List, 1332 (W.R.S. xlv), 109.
12 W.R.O. 1619, map of Normanton, 1768; 1953/68, survey of Normanton, 1739.
13 P.R.O., IR 29/38/105; IR 30/38/105.
14 W.R.O. 776/6.
15 Inf. from Mr. P. Bailey, Springbottom Farm.
16 Wilts. Dir. of Employers (Wilts. co. council, 1992).
17 V.C.H. Wilts. ii, pp. 129, 148.
18 Som. R.O., DD/SAS/H 348, ff. 150, 152.
19 Extents for Debts (W.R.S. xxviii), p. 33.
20 W.R.O. 130/19B, deed, Steward to Poore, 1612; 492/61.
21 A. Tryon, Kingfisher Mill, 18.
22 W.R.O., G 1/500/6.

23 Ibid. G 1/505/1.
24 Tryon, Kingfisher Mill, 19, 22.
25 W.R.O. 1953/68, case, c. 1756.
26 Ibid. 1550/48; Kelly's Dir. Wilts. (1855, 1875); P.R.O., HO 107/1845, f. 118v.
27 P.R.O., RG 11/2064, f. 89 and v.
28 Parker, Aviation in Wilts.
29 V.C.H. Wilts. iv. 201–2.
30 Inf. from the Publicity Manager, Pains-Wessex Schermuly, High Post.   31 V.C.H. Wilts. iv. 242.
32 Inf. from the Financial Director, Air Cleaner Technical Services Ltd., High Post.
33 W.R.O. 2/3; Hants R.O. 7M54/207/2–12.
34 D. & C. Sar. Mun., press III, Durnford prebend ct. rolls.
35 W.R.O., Ch. Com., bishop, 60/1; 61/1; 62/1.

were extant c. 1407,[36] but none is known to have survived. In 1275 Roger la Zouche claimed to have gallows and hold the assize of bread and of ale in Normanton.[37] No record of a court of the manor is known.

In 1775–6 £58 was spent on the poor, in the earlier 1780s an average of £66. Durnford was a large parish with a small population, and in the early 19th century the poor-rate was low. In 1802–3 about a third of the inhabitants were paupers; 88 were relieved regularly, 24 occasionally.[38] Poverty had apparently been much reduced by 1812–15 when an average of £398 was spent on relieving c. 15 adults regularly and c. 5 occasionally.[39] Expenditure on the poor, average for a parish in Amesbury hundred, fluctuated 1816–34. At £524 it was highest in 1832, at £221 lowest in 1821.[40] The parish became part of Amesbury poor-law union in 1835,[41] and was included in Salisbury district in 1974.[42]

CHURCH. The present church at Great Durnford was built c. 1140,[43] evidently belonged to Salisbury cathedral c. 1150,[44] and was confirmed to the cathedral in 1158.[45] Its revenues were used to endow a prebend,[46] and a vicarage had been ordained by c. 1281.[47] A suggestion made in 1650 to transfer Little Durnford to Stratford-sub-Castle parish[48] was not carried out. In 1974 the benefice was united with the benefice of Wilsford and Woodford to form the Woodford Valley benefice and the three parishes were united.[49]

The prebendary of Durnford exercised archidiaconal jurisdiction in the parish and until 1848 presented vicars to the dean of Salisbury for institution. In 1848 the patronage was transferred to the bishop, who became patron of the Woodford Valley benefice in 1974.[50]

The vicarage was worth £9 a year in 1535,[51] £131 c. 1830.[52] The vicar received an annuity, which stood at £2 in 1535, £12 in 1650, and £30 in 1832, from the Rectory estate,[53] and the Ecclesiastical Commissioners augmented the vicarage with £14 a year in 1854, £8 in 1861, and £120 in 1864.[54] By 1405 the vicarage had been endowed with all the tithes from the Rectory estate, great tithes from 1 carucate at Little Durnford and 12 a. of Salterton's arable, some hay tithes from Netton, and the small tithes of

Little Durnford:[55] in 1622 and later the vicar was entitled to half the great tithes from Little Durnford.[56] The tithes of the Rectory estate and small tithes of Durnford Northend were exchanged for 31 a. at inclosure in 1794.[57] The vicar's remaining tithes were valued at £105 in 1838 and commuted in 1842.[58] Of the land, 29 a. were sold between 1910 and 1922.[59] The vicarage house was out of repair in the 1630s.[60] A new house was built in 1728,[61] and of the present house the west wing, of flint with brick dressings and with a five-bayed west front, survives from it. The principal east–west range and the east wing of the present house were both built in the 19th century; also in the 19th century a south drawing room was built between the wings. In 1905–6 additions were made on the north side of the house and the inside was rearranged, all to designs by C. E. Ponting.[62] The house was sold in 1974.[63]

A chapel at Normanton, dependent on Durnford, was served in 1405 by the rector of Landford to the detriment of his own parish;[64] no later evidence of it has been found. In 1864 the vicar of Durnford said that a chapel in the south part of it would make it easier to serve the whole parish.[65] A mission room at Newtown had been built by 1899;[66] it remained open until c. 1980[67] and was afterwards demolished.

Walter, the vicar, was murdered in the vicarage house c. 1281.[68] In the early 15th century the church was rich in service books and vestments, which included a chasuble of cloth of gold. It also possessed relics including a brooch containing bone fragments purported to be of St. Andrew and St. Blaise.[69] In 1459 Richard Woodhill, lord of Little Durnford manor, was excommunicated for not answering charges of heresy and failing to attend church, confess, or receive the sacrament at Easter.[70] He was afterwards reconciled and bequeathed to the church vestments and altar cloths, all of which were to bear his arms.[71] A chained copy of the 1571 edition of Jewell's *Apology*, presumably in the church from the later 16th century, was stolen in 1970.[72] In 1650, when the inhabitants of Normanton attended Wilsford church, the vicar of Durnford preached every Sunday.[73] After the Restoration several incumbencies were long, including those of Samuel Squire (d. 1723), vicar for nearly 50 years,[74] J. N. Hinxman, vicar 1849–

36 *Tropenell Cart.* ii. 277–9.
37 *Rot. Hund.* (Rec. Com.), ii (1), 265.
38 *Poor Law Abstract, 1804*, 558–9; *V.C.H. Wilts.* iv. 347.
39 *Poor Law Abstract, 1818*, 492–3.
40 *Poor Rate Returns, 1816–21*, 185; *1822–4*, 225; *1825–9*, 215; *1830–4*, 209.
41 *Poor Law Com. 2nd Rep.* App. D, 558.
42 O.S. Map 1/100,000, admin. areas, Wilts. (1974 edn.).
43 Below, this section [architecture].
44 Le Neve, *Fasti, 1066–1300, Salisbury*, 65.
45 *Reg. St. Osmund* (Rolls Ser.), i. 203–6.
46 Above, manors (Rectory).
47 P.R.O., JUST 1/1001, rot. 18d.
48 *W.A.M.* xl. 259.   49 Inf. from Ch. Com.
50 e.g. *Chandler's Reg.* (W.R.S. xxxix), p. 137; Cathedrals Act, 3 & 4 Vic. c. 113; inf. from Ch. Com.; above, manors (Rectory).   51 *Valor Eccl.* (Rec. Com.), ii. 91.
52 *Rep. Com. Eccl. Revenues*, 832–3.
53 *Valor Eccl.* (Rec. Com.), ii. 73; *W.A.M.* xl. 271; Ch. Com. file, NB 34/402B.
54 *Lond. Gaz.* 9 June 1854, pp. 1770–1; 15 Oct. 1861, pp.

4065–72; 2 Aug. 1864, pp. 3812–4.
55 *Chandler's Reg.* (W.R.S. xxxix), p. 29.
56 W.R.O., D 5/10/1/1; P.R.O., IR 29/38/105.
57 W.R.O., EA/36; above, econ. hist. (Durnford Northend).   58 P.R.O., IR 29/38/105.
59 W.R.O., Inland Revenue, val. reg. 146; ibid. G 1/500/6.
60 Ibid. D 5/10/1/2; D 9/3/1/2.
61 Ibid. D 1/21/5/1/4, f. 62.   62 Ch. Com. file 2300/1.
63 Wilts. Cuttings, xxvii. 224.
64 *Chandler's Reg.* (W.R.S. xxxix), p. 29.
65 W.R.O., D 1/56/7.
66 O.S. Maps 6", Wilts. LX (1887 edn.); LX. SE. (1901 edn.).
67 Inf. from Mrs. G. Langdon, Salterton Farm.
68 P.R.O., JUST 1/1001, rot. 18d.
69 *Chandler's Reg.* (W.R.S. xxxix), pp. 61–2.
70 *Cal. Papal Reg.* xi. 536–7.
71 *Tropenell Cart.* ii. 326.
72 *Church Guide*, 4–5.   73 *W.A.M.* xl. 258–9.
74 W.R.O., D 1/21/5/1/4, ff. 60v.–61.

97, and Leicester Selby, vicar 1898–1937.[75] The curate who served the church in 1832 held two services each Sunday and on festivals and lectured during Lent.[76] In 1851 on Census Sunday 204 attended morning service and 155 afternoon service.[77] In 1864 the vicar preached at the two services held each Sunday with an average congregation of *c.* 120; he also held weekday services on some fast and feast days. He celebrated communion at Christmas, Easter, and Whitsun for 30–40 communicants and on five other Sundays.[78]

the nave were reconstructed in the 14th, and new windows were inserted in the south wall of the chancel and in the nave in the 15th. Also in the 15th century timber-framed porches, and a rood stair in the north-east corner of the nave, were built: later the stair was removed and the north porch rebuilt mainly in brick. The top stage of the tower was rebuilt in the 17th century with a timber-framed and weatherboarded lantern.[82] In the 18th a gallery on two classical columns was erected along the north wall of the nave.[83] The chancel was partly rebuilt in 1890–1,[84] and in

THE NORTH DOORWAY OF THE CHURCH

THE SOUTH DOORWAY OF THE CHURCH

ST. ANDREW'S church was so called by *c.* 1150.[79] It is of rubble with ashlar dressings and comprises a chancel, a nave with north and south porches, and a west tower.[80] The chancel and the nave are both of *c.* 1140.[81] The chancel has thick walls and a pilaster buttress on the north side, and the chancel arch has a single order of chevrons. The north and south walls of the nave are divided into four bays by pilaster buttresses, and the doorways have semicircular patterned tympana surrounded by chevrons. The chancel was substantially altered in the 13th century and most of the architectural features to survive in it are of that date. The tower was built in the later 13th century, the roofs of the chancel and

1903–4 the nave and tower were restored by C. E. Ponting; the lantern was removed and the gallery reconstructed at the west end of the nave to form an organ loft.[85] There are two panels of medieval stained glass in a window in the nave, and the church contains a 12th-century font, benches and wall paintings of the 15th century or early 16th, a pulpit dated 1619, and a lectern and communion rails also of the 17th century.[86]

Among several items of plate the church had two chalices, each partly gilt and each with a paten, in the early 15th century.[87] In 1553 a chalice of 15 oz. was left and 3 oz. of plate were taken for the king.[88] The church had no chalice

75 *Clergy List* (1859); *Crockford* (1896, 1907); *Church Guide*, 12; Ch. Com. file 2300/2.
76 Ch. Com. file, NB 34/402B.
77 P.R.O., HO 129/262/2/2/2.
78 W.R.O., D 1/56/7.
79 *Reg. St. Osmund* (Rolls Ser.), i. 266.
80 Description based partly on J. Buckler, watercolour in W.A.S. Libr., vol. i. 6.

81 For the dating, *Churches of SE. Wilts.* (R.C.H.M.), 133.
82 *W.A.M.* xxxiii. 286.
83 Ibid. xlviii. 146.
84 *Churches of SE. Wilts.* 133.
85 *W.A.M.* xxxiii. 282, 422.
86 *Churches of SE. Wilts.* 133, 135.
87 *Chandler's Reg.* (W.R.S. xxxix), pp. 61–2.
88 Nightingale, *Wilts. Plate*, 38–9.

in 1674[89] but one, hallmarked for that year, was evidently acquired soon after. A flagon hall-marked for 1654 was given in 1707[90] and a salver hallmarked for 1689 was given c. 1710.[91] All three items of plate were held in 1993.[92] There were three bells in the church in 1553; one of them, cast at Salisbury c. 1400, was the fourth of a ring of five in 1993. The other four bells are 17th-century, the tenor cast in 1614 by John Wallis, the third cast in 1656, and the treble and the second cast in 1657 by Nathaniel Boulter.[93] Reg-istrations of baptisms, marriages, and burials survive from 1574 and are apparently complete.[94]

NONCONFORMITY. A house in the parish was certified in 1672 for Presbyterians,[95] one in 1818 probably for Methodists.[96] A Methodist chapel at Netton was certified in 1812, possibly for Wesleyans,[97] whose chapel stood on the east side of the road at Netton Green[98] until replaced by a new red-brick chapel built on the west side of the road in 1895.[99] It was open in 1974 but had been closed by 1988.[1]

EDUCATION. There was a school in the parish in 1808,[2] another was opened in 1824, and a third in 1827: the three had a total of 62 pupils in 1833.[3] A National school was opened in 1844 at Netton.[4] It had three teachers and 86 pupils c. 1846,[5] one teacher and 40–50 children in 1859. In 1859 there were two other schools, each of fewer than 10 children.[6] The National school was attended by c. 32 in 1871.[7] It was rebuilt in 1872;[8] it was attended by c. 58 child-ren in 1906–7 and 1910–11, by c. 43 in 1938.[9] There were 20 children on roll in 1972; the school closed in 1975, and its pupils were transferred to Woodford school.[10]

J. O. Parr, vicar 1824–40, kept a school for c. 5–6 boys in Durnford Manor, where he lived. Sir William Harcourt (d. 1904), leader of the Liberal party, was among his pupils.[11] A pre-paratory boarding school for girls was opened in Durnford Manor in 1942 by Etheldreda, Lady Tryon, and closed in 1992.[12]

CHARITY FOR THE POOR. None known.

DURRINGTON

DURRINGTON[13] is a long and narrow parish ad-joining Amesbury to the south and stretching westwards from the Christchurch Avon to the watershed of the Avon and the Till.[14] Beside the Avon to the north a detached 10 a. were from the mid 19th century considered part of Figheldean parish.[15] Thereafter Durrington par-ish measured 2,702 a. (1,094 ha.). Until the 20th century Durrington village was probably the only settlement, but it was in two parts appar-ently corresponding to the division of the parish into two manors, East End and West End.[16] A medieval settlement, tithing, or both called Hin-durrington has been thought, because of its name, to have been in Durrington parish,[17] but is more likely to have been in Bulford.[18] From 1898 much of Durrington parish was acquired by the army, and in the 20th century the building of barracks and houses has greatly altered it.

For much of its length the parish boundary runs straight across downland; the eastern part of the northern boundary follows a dry valley, and to the east the Avon is the boundary. The middle part of the south boundary is marked by the north bank of the prehistoric earthwork called the Cursus.

The whole parish is on Upper Chalk: to the east gravel deposited by the Avon forms a wide terrace, and there is a narrow strip of alluvium beside the river.[19] The highest point, at 134 m., is a little south-west of the village; land at c. 120 m. is in the centre of the parish, an area called Lark Hill in the mid 19th century.[20] From Lark Hill the downland falls gently westwards to c. 107 m. at the boundary; eastwards the fall to c. 75 m. beside the river is steeper. Near the river in the north-east corner of the parish high ground called Hackthorn Cliff reaches 87 m. As usual for a long and narrow downland parish there were meadows beside the river, open fields on the gravel and on the chalk nearer to the village, and rough pastures on the downs further from the village.[21] There was no woodland in 1773[22] and very little c. 1900.[23] In the 20th

89 W.R.O., D 9/3/1/9.
90 Nightingale, *Wilts. Plate*, 38–9.
91 P.R.O., PROB 11/513, ff. 10–15.
92 The flagon was displayed in Salisbury cath. in 1993: inf. from Mr. G. H. Hobbs, The Bungalow, Jubilee Hill.
93 Walters, *Wilts. Bells*, 79, 261–2; inf. from Mr. Hobbs.
94 W.R.O. 1985/1–6; registrations 1574–1650 are printed in Phillipps, *Par. Reg. Durnford*.
95 *Meeting Ho. Certs.* (W.R.S. xl), p. 173.
96 Ibid. p. 87.
97 Ibid. p. 71; *Kelly's Dir. Wilts.* (1848).
98 O.S. Map 6", Wilts. LX (1887 edn.); W.R.O. 1550/48.
99 O.S. Map 6", Wilts. LX. SE. (1901 edn.); G.R.O. Worship Reg. no. 34924; date on bldg.
1 O.S. Maps 1/50,000, sheet 184 (1974, 1988 edns.).
2 Lamb. Palace Libr., MS. 1732.
3 *Educ. Enq. Abstract*, 1036.
4 P.R.O., ED 7/130, no. 111.
5 Nat. Soc. *Inquiry, 1846–7*, Wilts. 6–7.
6 *Acct. of Wilts. Schs.* 22.
7 *Returns relating to Elem. Educ.* 426–7.

8 P.R.O., ED 7/130, no. 111.
9 *Bd. of Educ., List 21, 1908* (H.M.S.O.), 502; *1912*, 550; *1938*, 422.
10 W.R.O., F 8/500, Durnford sch. 1883–1975, 484, 488.
11 Ibid. D 1/21/5/1/4, f. 66; A. G. Gardiner, *Sir. Wm. Harcourt*, i. 22–4.
12 *Daily Telegraph*, 8 July 1992.
13 This article was written in 1992.
14 Maps used include O.S. Maps 1", sheet 14 (1817 edn.); 1/50,000, sheet 184 (1988 edn.); 1/25,000, 41/14 (1948 and later edns.); 6", Wilts. LIV (1887 and later edns.).
15 Ibid. 6", Wilts. LIV (1887 edn.); P.R.O., IR 29/38/106; IR 29/38/116; IR 30/38/106; IR 30/38/116.
16 Below, this section; manors.
17 *P.N. Wilts.* (E.P.N.S.), 364–5.
18 Above, Bulford, intro.
19 Geol. Surv. Map 1", drift, sheet 282 (1967 edn.).
20 Winch. Coll. Mun. 5667.
21 Below, econ. hist. (agric.).
22 *Andrews and Dury, Map* (W.R.S. viii), pls. 8–9.
23 O.S. Map 6", Wilts. LIV (1901 edn.).

DURRINGTON 1839

Some road names are of later date

Water meadows

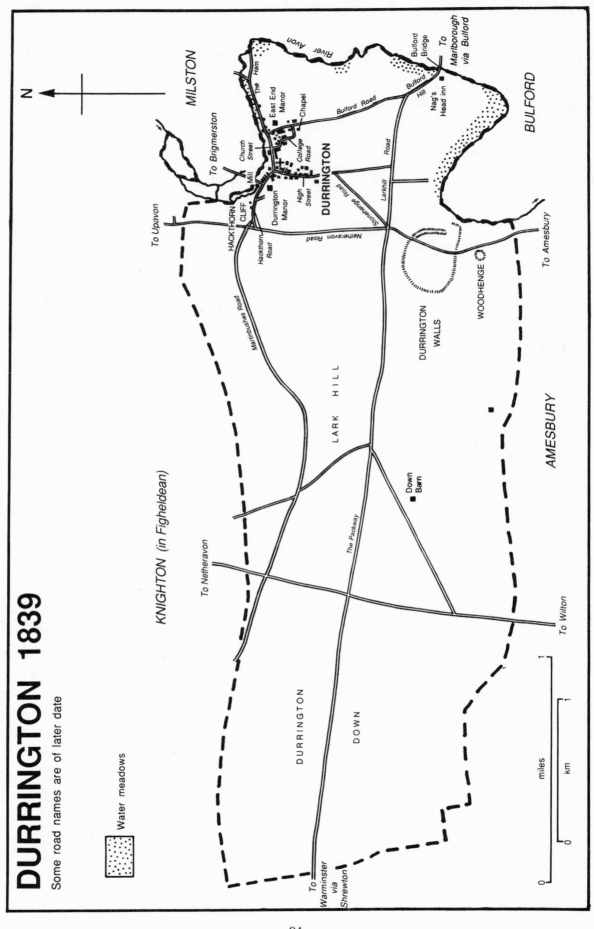

94

century *c.* 10 plantations, each of a few acres, have been made on the downs by the army.[24]

Two main roads cross the parish, one east–west and one north–south. The Bulford–Shrewton road, called Packway by *c.* 1555, was from the 17th century or earlier to the 19th part of a London–Warminster road via Marlborough;[25] between Bulford bridge and Lark Hill it was turnpiked in 1761, disturnpiked in 1871. The Upavon–Amesbury road, called Netheravon Road across Durrington parish, was turnpiked in 1840 and disturnpiked in 1877. It carries some traffic from Devizes and Marlborough to Salisbury. To avoid Woodhenge in the south part of the parish it was diverted to the east *c.* 1969, and a roundabout was made at its junction with the Bulford–Shrewton road.[26] Two other roads across the parish may have been well used in the 18th century: a north–south road led from Netheravon via Stonehenge towards Wilton, and an east–west road, called Martinbushes Road in the 20th century, linked Durrington village with the main Devizes–Salisbury road west of the parish.[27] By the early 19th century the Wilton road was apparently of little importance;[28] in the 20th both that and Martinbushes Road ceased to be through routes when part of each was closed to the public within a military training area. The Wiltway, east of and presumably parallel to the Wilton road, was evidently closed in Amesbury parish in the later 18th century[29] and had gone out of use in Durrington by the early 19th.[30]

What became Durrington parish was inhabited from Neolithic times, and the parish is rich in archaeological remains. It contains the sites of two large henge monuments, Durrington Walls and, south of it, Woodhenge. The monuments were built over what was apparently the site of a late Neolithic village, which included a long house.[31] South of Woodhenge a prehistoric ditch and an egg-shaped enclosure perhaps embracing the site of a circular house were possibly for agricultural use.[32] Cereals, mostly barley, were cultivated and pigs and other animals were reared;[33] north-east of Durrington Walls there were trial flint workings.[34] South-west of Durrington Walls a Romano-British village of the late 3rd century or early 4th, from which cereals were cultivated, stood on the site of a Neolithic settlement.[35] Elsewhere in the parish prehistoric artefacts have been discovered and there are barrows of various types, including four long barrows.[36] A prehistoric field system of *c.* 280 a. extends into the parish from Knighton in Figheldean parish.[37]

Durrington, with 139 poll-tax payers, was one of the most populous villages of the hundred in 1377.[38] The population rose from 339 in 1801 to 477 in 1851 and was 427 in 1901. Thereafter it increased rapidly as military camps on the downs and houses in the village were built. It was 897 in 1911, 3,005 in 1921, 5,784 in 1951.[39] The presence of fewer soldiers caused a decrease to 4,737 in 1961. The population was 6,734 in 1971, 6,926 in 1991.[40]

Durrington village stands on the gravel, off the main roads and within an eastwards meander of the Avon. It apparently contained two separate groups of buildings, each in a north–south street with, at the north end, the church between them on an elevated site.[41] Settlement also developed east and west along and beyond the street, now called Church Street, in which the church stands, and in the 20th century has grown extensively to the south.

In the eastern street, now called Bulford Road, few of the farmhouses, farm buildings, and cottages standing in 1839[42] survive. The principal one that does, on the east side, is East End Manor, the north–south hall range of which preserves the plan of a medieval house. The house was made **L**-shaped *c.* 1610, when, evidently for Anthony Trotman,[43] a timber-framed east–west range with a central chimney stack was built east from the south end. A large central stack was built in the hall, possibly at that time. The south and west walls of the house were reconstructed in flint rubble, possibly in the later 17th century, and the east and north walls of the hall range in brick in the earlier 19th. In the lane now called College Road, across the angle of Bulford Road and Church Street, Brown's Farmhouse was built in 1784, perhaps for Henry Dowling;[44] Red Cottage has early 19th-century cast-iron window frames with angular heads, as does a school built nearby in 1843.[45] A nonconformist chapel was built near the junction of College Road and Bulford Road evidently in the early 19th century.[46] The Plough inn was open in Bulford Road in 1851[47] and in 1992.

Most farmsteads in the village were in the western street, now called High Street, and perhaps seven of the farmhouses standing in 1839 survive, six on the west side. The northernmost on that side, Collins's Farm, was built in the early 19th century as a two-storeyed, three-bayed house with a slate roof. West End Manor Farm is a later 18th-century house, and the Red House is a mid 18th-century brick house heightened and refronted in the later 18th century. Further south, Parsonage Farm was almost

[24] O.S. Map, 1/50,000, sheet 184 (1988 edn.).
[25] Above, Bulford, intro. [roads]; Winch. Coll. Mun. 5663, f. 29.
[26] *V.C.H. Wilts.* iv. 257, 262, 264, 270–1; *L.J.* xxx. 138; inf. from Countryside Officer, Co. Hall, Trowbridge; for Woodhenge, below, this section [prehist. remains].
[27] *Andrews and Dury, Map* (W.R.S. viii), pls. 8–9.
[28] O.S. Map 1", sheet 14 (1817 edn.).
[29] *W.A.M.* xxxi. 7; above, Amesbury, intro. (roads).
[30] O.S. Map 1", sheet 14 (1817 edn.); W.R.O., EA/144. For a railway in the par., below, this section [Larkhill].
[31] *V.C.H. Wilts.* i (1), 65–6; i (2), 300–1, 318–19, 328–9.
[32] Ibid. i (1), 255; i (2), 398, 401.
[33] Ibid. i (2), 350.
[34] Ibid. 291, 302, 401.
[35] *W.A.M.* lxvii. 76, 83, 87.
[36] *V.C.H. Wilts.* i (1), 65–6, 140, 170–2, 217–18, 223, 225.
[37] Ibid. 275.
[38] Ibid. iv. 306.
[39] Ibid. 325–6, 347; below, this section.
[40] *Census*, 1961; 1971; 1991.
[41] *Andrews and Dury, Map* (W.R.S. viii), pls. 8–9; P.R.O., IR 30/38/106.
[42] P.R.O., IR 29/38/106; IR 30/38/106.
[43] Date and A/AT on ho.; cf. Winch. Coll. Mun. 5670, rot. C.
[44] Date and initials on ho.; cf. W.R.O., A 1/345/159.
[45] Below, educ.   [46] Below, nonconf.
[47] W.R.O. 1550/48.

entirely rebuilt as a red-brick house with stone quoins in the 19th century, when it was possibly extended southwards, but incorporates a north gable of *c.* 1700 built of flint rubble, banded stone, and red brick. Hollyhurst is a thatched early 18th-century farmhouse of four bays which may have been built of banded flint and stone. Pinckney's, the southernmost farmhouse on the west side, was built in brick for Philip and Jane Pinckney *c.* 1769.[48] On the east side, Church Farm is late 18th-century. South of it, and set back from the street, Durrington House was built as a gentleman's residence in the mid 19th century, evidently for G. P. Moore:[49] it was demolished after 1961.[50] A lodge for it survived in High Street in 1992.

By the early 19th century settlement had extended from the church along Church Street east to the Ham and west into Hackthorn Road.[51] In the late 18th century or early 19th a bridge over the Avon was made at the east end of the Ham[52] which then became the main route from Durrington to Milston: a footbridge survived in 1992. South of Hackthorn Road, Durrington Manor was built *c.* 1800, possibly on an old site:[53] it is a large red-brick house and has a five-bayed north entrance front in which is a central timber porch with columns; it was a hotel *c.* 1949[54] and was in flats in 1992. Durrington mill was on the north side of Hackthorn Road: a lane leading from it over Hatches bridge to Brigmerston in Milston in the early 17th century and the 19th[55] was a footpath in 1992. On the north side of Church Street a large early 17th-century farmhouse, with a two-storeyed porch and canted bay windows on the principal south front,[56] was lived in by the rector in the 19th century and early 20th: it was rebuilt *c.* 1920 after a fire.[57] In the 19th century cottages on the north side of Hackthorn Road were altered or rebuilt and cottages were built on the north side of Church Street. The junction of High Street, Church Street, and Hackthorn Road became a focal point of the village, and the base of a medieval cross was moved to the centre of the junction, perhaps from the churchyard and apparently in the 19th century.[58]

Houses and cottages of the 17th century, possibly of timber and cob and with thatched roofs, survive in College Road, High Street, and Church Street: most were altered in the 19th century and rendered. Between 1839 and *c.* 1900 the village grew little in extent. Outside it a farmhouse beside Bulford bridge was open as the Nag's Head in 1731. The house was rebuilt or extensively altered in the late 18th century or early 19th;[59] a friendly society met in it in 1836.[60] At the junction of the Upavon–Amesbury and Bulford–Shrewton roads west of the village the Stonehenge inn has been open since *c.* 1875. It may have taken trade from the Nag's Head which was closed between 1885 and 1898.[61] On the downs several groups of farm buildings had been erected by the 1880s, at one of which, Down Barn, there was a cottage in 1839.[62]

The growth of the village in the 20th century was stimulated by the presence of the army in the parish.[63] By 1923 houses and business premises had been built on both sides of Bulford Road from its junction with College Road south to the Bulford–Shrewton road; two new schools and buildings in east and west offshoots of Bulford Road had also been erected. Opposite College Road one of the eastern offshoots was later called School Road. The Bulford–Shrewton road was later called Bulford Hill east of Bulford Road, Larkhill Road west of it: by 1923 a few houses had been erected on the north side of Bulford Hill, a cinema on the south side of Larkhill Road. Also by 1923 a village hall had been built in High Street and eight cottages for the War Department on the west side of Netheravon Road.[64]

By the late 1930s there was a continuous line of settlement from Bulford bridge to the Stonehenge inn: 60 council houses were built on the north side of Larkhill Road 1927–32, and several private houses on the north side of Bulford Hill about the same time. Council houses were also built in the 1930s in Meads Road, as the south part of High Street came to be called, and by the late 1930s *c.* 12 more cottages had been built on the west side of Netheravon Road and private houses in and off Stonehenge Road, which links the junction of Larkhill Road and Netheravon Road with High Street.[65] In the 1950s a large council estate was built south of Coronation Road, a new east–west road linking Bulford Road and Meads Road, and the estate was extended northwards in the 1960s.[66] Private bungalows built over the grounds of Durrington House filled the space between the council estate and the old part of the village in the 1960s. Since then more private houses have been built in new roads east of Bulford Road and west of Stonehenge Road. In the old part of the village new building in the later 20th century, besides infilling, included a few new houses in the Ham and some old people's bungalows in College Road. At the north-west corner of the village *c.* 12 houses were built north of Hackthorn Road in the 1950s. As the village grew, various shops

48 W.R.O., A 1/345/159; Hoare, *Mod. Wilts.* Amesbury, 75; date and P/Pl on ho.; Min. of Housing and Local Govt., provisional list of bldgs. of hist. interest (1955); Winch. Coll. Mun. 21331; 21333.
49 P.R.O., IR 29/38/106; IR 30/38/106; W.R.O. 1550/48.
50 O.S. Map 6", Wilts. SU 14 SE. (1961 edn.); local inf.
51 P.R.O., IR 30/38/106.
52 *Andrews and Dury, Map* (W.R.S. viii), pls. 8–9; O.S. Map 1", sheet 14 (1817 edn.).
53 *Andrews and Dury, Map* (W.R.S. viii), pl. 8.
54 W.R.O. 776/71.
55 Ibid. 1550/48; O.S. Map 6", Wilts. LIV (1887 edn.); Winch. Coll. Mun. 5908B.
56 J. Buckler, watercolour in W.A.S. Libr., vol. x. 5.
57 Ch. Com. file 2301/2.

58 O.S. Map 6", Wilts. LIV (1887 edn.); Buckler, watercolour in W.A.S. Libr., vol. x. 5; see below, plate facing p. 251.
59 W.R.O. 402/90; P.R.O., E 134/4 Geo. II East./7; ibid. IR 29/38/106; IR 30/38/106.
60 P.R.O., FS 4/55, Wilts. no. 180.
61 *Kelly's Dir. Wilts.* (1875 and later edns.).
62 O.S. Map 6", Wilts. LIV (1887 edn.); P.R.O., IR 30/38/106.
63 Below, this section.
64 O.S. Map 6", Wilts. LIV. NE. (1901, 1926 edns.); W.R.O., G 1/500/7; below, econ. hist. (trade and ind.); educ.
65 O.S. Map 1", sheet 167 (*c.* 1952 edn.); W.R.O., G 1/600/1; G 1/602/2.
66 W.R.O., G 1/602/2.

and small businesses were opened,[67] a police station was built, a branch of the county library was opened in 1971,[68] and in 1974 a sports centre with a swimming bath was opened at the east end of School Road.[69]

The part of Salisbury Plain north-west of Durrington has been used by the army for artillery practice from 1899. A camp for those using the ranges was set up on Durrington down in 1899,[70] and in the 20th century the camps, barracks, houses, and other buildings on the down became known generally as Larkhill camp. From 1920 Larkhill camp has been the head-quarters of the School of Artillery, from 1970 the Royal School of Artillery,[71] and in the late 20th century was still used mainly for gunnery. It covered c. 800 a. in 1992.[72]

Before the First World War there were three tented camps, Durrington, Larkhill west of it, and Fargo near the western parish boundary.[73] The Larkhill light military railway was con-structed from Ratfyn in Amesbury to the Fargo camp in 1914, and served all three camps.[74] Between 1914 and 1918 the Fargo camp in-cluded a military hospital[75] and the tents were replaced by huts at Larkhill camp.[76] In the 1920s permanent brick buildings were erected throughout the camp and the Packway, which the camp stood astride, became the principal access route:[77] the railway had been closed by 1928 and its tracks removed by 1937,[78] and the Packway was tarmacadamed and in 1929 lined with trees. In 1928 Strangways, an estate of 23 houses for married officers, was built south-east of the camp, and in 1928–9 a row of 36 semi-detached houses for married soldiers was built in Fargo Road between Strangways and the camp. At the camp itself new barracks north of the Packway and 84 houses south of the Packway were built in the 1930s.[79] Two new messes for officers were built, one south of the Packway in 1938, one north of the Packway 1936–40: both are of red brick in neo-Georgian style.[80] By the late 1930s most of the buildings of the military hospital had been removed.[81]

Much of Larkhill camp was rebuilt in the 1960s, retaining the earlier grid system of roads;[82] most of the barracks and workshops are north of the Packway, most of the houses south. Alanbrooke barracks, begun c. 1960,[83] Stirling,

begun in 1966 and containing the headquarters of the Royal School of Artillery, Roberts, begun in 1964,[84] and Horne, the headquarters of two military bands, are all north of the Packway.[85] In the 1950s and 1960s more houses were built in the south and east parts of the camp and to the south-east between Strangways and Dur-rington Walls. In 1992 an ammunition store stood near the western parish boundary.

Larkhill camp has become like a small town. It has been provided with sports grounds, churches,[86] banks, shops, a school,[87] and a police station. A cinema built by 1915 was burned down in 1919; its replacement was closed c. 1971.[88] The Packhorse inn was opened on the south side of the Packway in 1962,[89] and a medical centre, a swimming pool, and a NAAFI were opened later. Between 1947 and 1952 a pack of beagles was kept.[90]

MANORS AND OTHER ESTATES. Until the 12th century Durrington was apparently part of the king's estate called Amesbury,[91] but by 1120 had become a separate manor.[92] About 1155 Henry II granted what became *WEST END* manor to Hugh Hussey.[93] The estate reverted to the king c. 1179[94] and was evidently granted to Stephen Chamber c. 1180.[95] On Stephen's death c. 1189 it passed to his relict Gillian, also relict of Alan de Neville. Gillian held it until c. 1195, as did Robert de Vipont from c. 1195 to 1199. Hugh de Neville acquired the manor in 1199:[96] his title was challenged unsuccessfully by Hugh Hussey's nephew Henry Hussey in 1201.[97] From Hugh de Neville (d. c. 1229) the manor descended to his son Ernis,[98] who successfully defended his title to it against Henry Hussey (d. 1290) in 1253.[99] From Ernis (d. 1257) it descended in the direct line to Gilbert[1] (d. 1294), John[2] (d. 1334), and Gilbert de Neville[3] (d. 1359). The younger Gilbert's heir was his daughter Elizabeth[4] (d. *s.p.* 1393), wife of Simon Simeon (d. 1387) and of John la Warre, Lord la Warre. John held the manor until his death in 1398,[5] and in 1399 his and Elizabeth's feoffees sold it to Winchester College.[6] The college owned it, c. 1,600 a. in 1838,[7] until the 20th century.[8]

From 1604 to 1718 the entire West End manor

[67] Below, econ. hist. (trade and ind.).
[68] Inf. from Local Studies Librarian, Co. Hall, Trow-bridge.
[69] Inf. from Manager, Swimming and Fitness Centre.
[70] N. D. G. James, *Gunners at Larkhill*, 8–9.
[71] Ibid. 55, 116.   [72] Ibid. 189.
[73] Ibid. 14.   [74] Ibid. 33–7.
[75] Ibid. 45.   [76] Ibid. 31, 42.
[77] Ibid. 54, 61–3.   [78] Ibid. 39.
[79] Ibid. 61–3.   [80] Ibid. 64–5.
[81] O.S. Map 1/2,500, Wilts. LIV. 10 (1939 edn.).
[82] James, *Gunners at Larkhill*, 189–90.
[83] Ibid. 102.
[84] Ibid. 107–8.
[85] Ibid. 189, 219.
[86] Below, churches; Rom. Cath.
[87] Below, educ.
[88] N. D. G. James, *Plain Soldiering*, 135–6.
[89] James, *Gunners at Larkhill*, 207.
[90] Ibid. 209–10.
[91] *W.A.M.* lii. 73–6; above, Amesbury, manors (pream-ble).

[92] *Reg. Regum Anglo-Norm.* ii, no. 1240A.
[93] *Plac. de Quo Warr.* (Rec. Com.), 808; *W.A.M.* lii. 73–5; *Pipe R.* 1156–8 (Rec. Com.), 57.
[94] *W.A.M.* lii. 75–6; *Pipe R.* 1179 (P.R.S. xxviii), 56; 1180 (P.R.S. xxix), 118, 122.
[95] *Pipe R.* 1181 (P.R.S. xxx), 94.
[96] Ibid. 1189 (Rec. Com.), 171; 1190 (P.R.S. N.S. i), 117, 121; 1194 (P.R.S. N.S. v), 195; 1195 (P.R.S. N.S. vi), 136; 1199 (P.R.S. N.S. x), 168; 1200 (P.R.S. N.S. xii), 155.
[97] *Rot. de Ob. et Fin.* (Rec. Com.), 177.
[98] *Ex. e Rot. Fin.* (Rec. Com.), i. 182.
[99] W. Farrer, *Honors and Knights' Fees*, iii. 86; P.R.O., KB 26/149, rot. 19.
[1] *Cal. Inq. p.m.* i, p. 101.
[2] Ibid. iii, p. 114.
[3] *Wilts. Inq. p.m.* 1327–77 (Index Libr.), 105–6.
[4] Ibid. 254–5.
[5] *Cal. Inq. p.m.* xvi, p. 241; xvii, pp. 504–6; *Cal. Inq. Misc.* vi, p. 44.
[6] *Cal. Pat.* 1388–92, 11; 1396–9, 332, 483.
[7] P.R.O., IR 29/38/106; IR 30/38/106.
[8] Below, this section.

was leased to members of the Poore family. Leases of East End manor descended in the same family.[9] Philip Poore (d. 1640) was followed as lessee of West End by his son Edward (d. 1656),[10] possibly by Edward's son Edward (d. 1672), by that Edward's nephew Philip Poore (d. 1693), and by that Philip's relict Elizabeth and son Philip (d. 1719).[11] From 1781 the lessees were Thomas Fowle (d. 1783),[12] his brother Henry (d. 1803),[13] Henry's son William (d. c. 1840), William's son T. E. Fowle (d. 1877),[14] and T. E. Fowle's son T. E. Fowle (d. 1932).[15]

The last lease of the entire manor apparently expired in the late 19th century. In 1899 Winchester College sold 292 a. and the reversion of 278 a. held by copy to the War Department, and in 1902 a further 400 a. and the reversion of a further 389 a. of copyhold. The Ministry of Defence owned nearly all that land in 1992.[16] The college kept c. 100 a.,[17] which it sold between 1921 and 1949.[18]

What became *EAST END* manor may have developed from one or both of two 11th-century estates. A thegn held 1 hide in 1066; that and 1½ hide were afterwards held and forfeited by Aubrey de Couci, and were held by the king in 1086.[19] What became the manor may have been held by Robert de Beaumont, count of Meulan (d. 1118), and in 1120 his sons Waleran, count of Meulan, and Robert, earl of Leicester, licensed their undertenant Ralph de Anquetil to grant it to the abbey of Bec-Hellouin (Eure).[20] In an exchange c. 1208 the abbey gave the manor to the bishop of Salisbury, who had assigned it by 1215 for the common fund.[21] The dean and chapter also held land at Knighton and treated it as part of East End manor. At inclosure in 1823 they were allotted c. 300 a. in Durrington but increased their holding there to 488 a. by giving land at Knighton in exchange.[22]

From the early 17th century to the 19th members of the Poore family, some of whom were lessees of West End manor,[23] held the entire manor by lease from the dean and chapter. Edward Poore (d. 1656) was lessee from 1606.[24] Leases were held by his son Edward (d. 1672), by that Edward's nephew Philip Poore (d. 1693), by Philip's relict Elizabeth (d. 1728), by Philip's and Elizabeth's daughter Venetia (d. 1741), and

by Venetia's cousin Edward Poore[25] (d. 1780). From 1780 Edward's nominees held the lease in trust for his daughters Eleanora Michel (d. s.p. 1812) and Charlotte Poore (will proved 1829); Charlotte devised her interest to Sir Edward Poore, Bt. (d. 1838), who was lessee from 1834. The lease presumably passed to Sir Edward's son Sir Edward Poore, Bt. (d. 1893), but was apparently not renewed after 1855. As lessees, members of the Poore family granted nearly all of the land of the manor to themselves by copy on lives.[26] In 1900 the Ecclesiastical Commissioners sold the freehold of 485 a. to the younger Sir Edward's son Sir Richard Poore, Bt. Of that land Sir Richard sold 213 a. to the War Department in 1902, his relict Ida sold some in 1955 and 1956,[27] and Ida's executors sold the remainder to the War Office in 1958. In 1992 the Ministry of Defence owned the land bought in 1902 and 1958.[28]

Hugh de Neville (d. c. 1229), lord of West End manor, granted 2 yardlands, which may have been the origin of *MARSH'S* farm, to Thomas Hiredman. The land was held in 1340 by Thomas's kinsman and heir Thomas Ward[29] (d. by 1361), whose relict Lettice in 1390 granted it to her son John Ward for life.[30] Like an estate in West Ashton in Steeple Ashton it passed to John Lyveden, who settled it in 1464 on his wife Amice (fl. 1497).[31] John Westley (d. 1521) held the estate in 1511; Anne (fl. 1562), wife of Henry Tichborne, held it for life c. 1527. The reversion passed to John Westley's son Thomas (d. 1561), to Thomas's son Leonard (d. 1562), and to Leonard's son Thomas,[32] who may have sold the estate after 1579.[33] It was perhaps the 2-yardland farm owned in 1608 by William Staples and sold by him c. 1613 to Thomas Staples.[34] The land was owned c. 1622 by Anthony Trotman[35] and in 1735 by John Batch (d. 1767). From Batch's sister Anne Marsh (d. 1770), Marsh's farm passed to her son Thomas Marsh, who in 1816 sold it to Charlotte Poore (will proved 1829).[36] At inclosure in 1823, when 74 a. were allotted in respect of it, the estate was given to the dean and chapter of Salisbury in exchange for land in Knighton and became part of East End manor.[37]

Hugh de Neville (d. c. 1229) granted lands to John de Bessin.[38] *BESSIN'S* was conveyed by

9 Below, this section.
10 *W.A.M.* xxxi. 341–2; Winch. Coll. Mun. 26390; P.R.O., PROB 11/257, f. 308 and v.
11 *W.A.M.* xxxi. 342; Winch. Coll. Mun. 26400–6; W.R.O. 84/23.
12 W.R.O., A 1/345/159; for the Fowle fam., *V.C.H. Wilts.* x. 36–7.
13 Winch. Coll. Mun. 21332; 26409; 26411.
14 Ibid. 21333–4; 26412A.
15 *Kelly's Dir. Wilts.* (1855 and later edns.); *V.C.H. Wilts.* x. 36.
16 *W.A.M.* xxxi. 342; inf. from Defence Land Agent, Durrington.
17 W.R.O., Inland Revenue, val. reg. 142.
18 Ibid. 776/70–1; ibid. G 1/500/7; G 1/760/11; *Kelly's Dir. Wilts.* (1923). 19 *V.C.H. Wilts.* ii, pp. 98–9, 134.
20 *Reg. Regum Anglo-Norm.* ii, no. 1240A; *Complete Peerage*, vii. 523, 526, 738.
21 *Reg. St. Osmund* (Rolls Ser.), i. 189–90; *Interdict Doc.* (Pipe R. Soc. N.S. xxxiv), 16; *Sar. Chart. and Doc.* (Rolls Ser.), pp. 78–9.
22 W.R.O., EA/144; P.R.O., IR 29/38/106; IR 30/38/106.   23 Above, this section.

24 *W.A.M.* xxxi. 342; xxxiii. 270.
25 Ibid. xxxiii. 272; W.R.O. 84/23; 1885/3; ibid. Ch. Com., chapter, 103/1; P.R.O., PROB 11/257, f. 308 and v.; PROB 11/340, f. 260 and v.
26 Below, Figheldean, manors (Knighton); W.R.O., A 1/345/159; ibid. EA/144; ibid. Ch. Com., chapter, 101; 103/2; ibid. 212B/2860; P.R.O., PROB 11/1754, ff. 297–304.
27 G.P.L., Treas. Solicitor, 1684/65; 2849/50.
28 Inf. from Defence Land Agent.
29 Above, this section (W. End); *Cal. Pat.* 1338–40, 532; Winch. Coll. Mun. 5601A, rot. E; 5601C, rot. A.
30 *W.A.M.* xxxvii. 10–11; Winch. Coll. Mun. 5644, rot. B.
31 *V.C.H. Wilts.* viii. 206; *W.A.M.* xxxvii. 14; Winch. Coll. Mun. 5657D.
32 *W.A.M.* xxxvii. 19–23, 30, 32–3; Winch. Coll. Mun. 5659, rot. E; 5663, f. 6.   33 W.R.O. 212B/2831.
34 Winch. Coll. Mun. 5669, rott. A, D.
35 Ibid. 5670, rot. C.
36 W.R.O. 402/93, deed, Marsh to Poore, 1816; 402/95, deed, Marsh to Coleman, 1813; 1885/4; P.R.O., PROB 11/1754, ff. 297–304.
37 W.R.O., EA/144; above, this section (E. End).
38 Winch. Coll. Mun. 5546.

the feoffees of Agnes, relict of Thomas Bessin, to Winchester College, lord of West End manor, in 1414,[39] but was afterwards held freely by John Greenleaf and his wife Maud, who together sold 2 yardlands in 1433 to Ralph Thorp[40] (d. 1446). The estate descended with East Boscombe manor[41] until Henry Clifford sold it to Philip Poore in 1595.[42] It descended in the Poore family, apparently like the lease of West End manor, to Philip Poore (d. 1719).[43] Its later descent is obscure.

Land held by Thomas Woodford 1435 × 1450[44] may have been the 2 yardlands, possibly the origin of LAWES farm, sold by Nicholas atte Mere to Sir Roger Tocotes in 1480.[45] Sir Roger (d. 1492) was deprived of the land in 1484–5.[46] Another Roger Tocotes owned it in 1494.[47] An estate which passed in the Wilkinson family from 1523 until Christopher Wilkinson sold it to Robert Wyryat c. 1537 was possibly the same land.[48] Wyryat sold the estate c. 1547 to John Flower, who sold it to William Stumpe (d. 1552). Stumpe's son Sir James apparently sold it in two portions: in 1553 he sold land to John Cowper, and c. 1555 other land to Richard Cowper[49] (d. 1558), who devised it to his daughter Maud and her husband Thomas Lovell.[50] John Cowper's 110-a. estate, which in 1561 passed to his relict Margaret (d. 1599), may have included both portions; it descended to his son Thomas (fl. 1618), a lunatic.[51] What is likely to have been the same estate belonged to Leonard Lawes (d. c. 1775),[52] and other land was added to it.[53] From Thomas Lawes (d. by 1809) Lawes farm passed to his sisters Jane Lawes (d. by 1812), Christian Lawes, Alice Lavington, and Susanna Amor. Alice sold her share in 1816 to Sir John Poore, Bt.[54] (d. 1820). At inclosure in 1823 Poore's grandnephew and heir Sir Edward Poore, Bt., gave that share, in respect of which 91 a. had been allotted, to the dean and chapter of Salisbury in exchange for land in Knighton, and it became part of East End manor.[55] The remainder of Lawes farm passed to Susanna Amor's son Thomas Amor, who sold it c. 1817 to George Moore (d. 1820). Moore devised it to his son Thomas (d. 1841), who held 275 a. in 1839. Thomas's successor was his brother G. P. Moore (d. 1884),[56] who sold the land in 1883 to A. T. Squarey, James Rawlence (d. 1894), and E. P. Squarey as tenants in common. In 1898 the Squareys sold all but c. 38 a. to the War Department. All was owned by the Ministry of Defence in 1992.[57]

An estate of 2–3 yardlands, later called IN-GRAM'S, was sold in 1409 by William Wake and his wife Amice to John Ingram.[58] It descended in the Ingram family, possibly until the earlier 18th century,[59] and in 1776 was part of Lawes farm.[60]

The tithes of Durrington may have belonged to Amesbury abbey, and in 1179 they were confirmed to Amesbury priory.[61] In the early 13th century the priory added to its estate in Durrington 3 yardlands granted by John Bonet and 1 yardland granted by Robert Goion;[62] free warren in its demesne was granted to it in 1286.[63] The RECTORY estate, the tithes and 6 yardlands in 1421,[64] passed to the Crown at the Dissolution and was granted in 1541 to the dean and chapter of Winchester.[65] They held 238 a. in 1838, when their tithes were valued at £590 and commuted.[66] From the later 17th century the whole estate was leased: the lessees were William Moore, c. 1679 to 1693, John Moore, 1693 to c. 1722, Thomas Moore (d. 1753), rector of Steepleton Iwerne (Dors.), Thomas Moore (d. 1783), Jonathan Moore (d. 1818), George Moore (d. 1820), and G. P. Moore (d. 1884).[67] In 1862 G. P. Moore surrendered the lease of £493 of rent charge to the Ecclesiastical Commissioners, and in 1865 he bought from them the freehold of Parsonage farm, 237 a., and of the £93 rent charge on it.[68] Moore sold the farm and the rent charge with Lawes farm to A. T. Squarey, James Rawlence, and E. P. Squarey in 1883, and the Squareys sold them to the War Department in 1898. The Ministry of Defence owned the land in 1992.[69]

ECONOMIC HISTORY. AGRICULTURE. The two Durrington estates described in 1086, totalling 2½ hides, had land for 2 ploughteams and included 10 a. of meadow; 1 hide was in demesne and there were 4 coscets and 1 bordar.[70]

The parish apparently contained two sets of open fields, one for West End manor in the south

39 Ibid. 5589–93.
40 Feet of F. 1377–1509 (W.R.S. xli), p. 102.
41 W.A.M. xxxi. 336; P.R.O., C 140/14, no. 28, rot. 6; above, Boscombe, manors (E. Boscombe).
42 W.R.O. 212B/2832.
43 Winch. Coll. Mun. 5669, rot. A; 5670, rot. A; 5887; 5889; 5892; 5894–5; above, this section (W. End).
44 Winch. Coll. Mun. 5655, rott. E, O.
45 Ibid. 5656, rot. E.
46 Cal. Pat. 1476–85, 501; Complete Peerage, xi. 302.
47 Winch. Coll. Mun. 5657.
48 Ibid. 5659, rott. C–F, H.
49 Ibid. 5663, ff. 9, 20v., 22v., 29; P.R.O., CP 25/2/65/533, no. 26.
50 P.R.O., C 142/124, no. 202.
51 Ibid. WARD 7/34, no. 190; below, Figheldean, manors (Abbot's).
52 W.R.O., wills, archd. Sar., Leonard Lawes, 1775.
53 Below, this section (Ingram's).
54 W.R.O. 212B/2860; 402/96, deed, Lavington to Poore, 1816; ibid. A 1/345/159; ibid. wills, archd. Sar., Thomas Lawes, 1809; wills, archd. Sar., Jane Lawes, 1812.
55 Burke, Peerage (1963), 1962; W.R.O., EA/144; above,

this section (E. End).
56 W.R.O., wills, archd. Sar., Jane Lawes, 1812; ibid. A 1/345/159; P.R.O., IR 29/38/106; IR 30/38/106; ibid. PROB 11/1637, ff. 245v.–246; mons. in church.
57 G.P.L., Treas. Solicitor, 442/51; inf. from Defence Land Agent.
58 Feet of F. 1377–1509 (W.R.S. xli), p. 64.
59 Winch. Coll. Mun. 5659; 5669–70; 5875; 5887; 5889; 5892–5; 5897.   60 Ibid. 21331.
61 Cal. Chart. R. 1257–1300, 157–9; for Amesbury abbey and priory, V.C.H. Wilts. iii. 242–59.
62 Winch. Coll. Mun. 5634.
63 Cal. Chart. R. 1257–1300, 336.
64 Winch. Coll. Mun. 5601.
65 L. & P. Hen. VIII, xvi, p. 417.
66 P.R.O., IR 29/38/106.
67 Ibid. E 126/14, f. 250; E 126/25, nos. 32, 35; E 134/36 Chas. II Trin./2; W.R.O. 1885/4; ibid. A 1/345/159; Winch. Coll. Mun. 21333; W.A.M. xxxiii. 274; mons. in church.
68 Ch. Com. files, NB 34/123; 2301/1.
69 G.P.L., Treas. Solicitor, 442/51; inf. from Defence Land Agent; above, this section (Lawes).
70 V.C.H. Wilts. ii, p. 134.

part of the parish and one, much smaller, for East End manor in the north. The extensive downland pasture, however, seems to have been used jointly by the men of each manor.[71] The location of the two sets of farmsteads, those of West End manor to the west in High Street, those of East End manor to the east in Bulford Road, apparently gave the manors their names.[72]

The fields of West End evidently included the arable of the demesne and customary holdings of West End manor and that of the Rectory estate and the holdings later called Marsh's, Bessin's, Lawes, and Ingram's. In 1229 the demesne of West End manor, on which there were 16 oxen and a flock of c. 200 sheep, was leased for three years to Amesbury priory, which could distrain upon the tenants for non-performance of customary services.[73] In the early 14th century six tenants at will held 15 a. of demesne by lease; two ploughmen, an oxherd, a doorkeeper, and a maid were employed on the remainder.[74] Sheep-and-corn husbandry was practised on West End manor, and there were apparently three West End open fields in 1334.[75] Demesne of the manor lay in North meadow, and there were other meadows called the Moor, East meadow, and South meadow.[76] Most demesne grain was sold in the earlier and mid 14th century, usually at Salisbury, and in 1331–2 some was bought for the king's household at Clarendon palace. In the 1320s demesne pasture was leased to the customary tenants for their flock, then c. 750 sheep. About 1340 the tenants, whose flock numbered 776 in 1353–4, were intercommoning in the south part of Durrington with men of Amesbury: such intercommoning had ceased by 1538. From c. 1334 to c. 1359 a small demesne flock was kept: at its largest, in 1350, it numbered 212. There were 17 yardlanders and 20 cottagers on West End manor in 1329, 16 and 20 in 1340. In 1340 the yardlanders, as part of their carting duties, had to carry grain off the manor for sale. The cottagers made hay and, when a demesne flock was kept, washed and sheared the sheep. There were only 12 yardlanders in the later 14th century, and from c. 1356 there were 4½-yardlanders who each had to do ploughing services.[77] The demesne of West End manor, on which a substantial farmstead was built in the earlier 15th century, was leased from 1389: there is evidence that John Langford, lessee 1458–78, managed it inefficiently.[78]

In the 16th century the West End arable was in four open fields, but in 1590 the number of fields was reduced to three and exchanges of land were made between tenants.[79] The fields were called Coombe, North, and South in 1622,[80] Coombe Bottom, Lark Hill, and Cuckoo Stone

in 1797.[81] They remained open until 1823.[82] Some land, however, was apparently used in severalty. In 1655 and later the demesne of West End manor included land in the open fields but also several arable in three farm fields and a several down of 150 a.; also in 1655 the 5-yardland demesne of the Rectory estate, then evidently worked from its own farmstead, had an apparently several down of 150 a.,[83] 11 a. of which had been burnbaked by 1684;[84] in 1776 the demesne of the manor included downs of 170 a. and 134 a. in severalty, part of the larger of which was occasionally burnbaked.[85] Those sharing the commonable downland, the freeholders and the tenants of West End manor, agreed in 1740 to burnbake 12 a. of down near the boundary with Shrewton, to elect a small committee to lease the land, and to use the rent to pay for a pond to be constructed on the land.[86] In 1776 there was a common sheep down of 824 a., a common cow down of 188 a.: in 1807 the downs were said to be of 837 a. and c. 200 a. Rights to use them also belonged to East End manor, and 1,796 sheep could be kept. In 1804 the demesne of West End manor included 505 a. of arable, the nine copyholds included 504 a., and Lawes farm was of 8 yardlands. The demesne was worked with some of the copyhold land; of its 239 a. of downland 104 a. were under the plough, and in the late 18th century a barn and penning was built on it. In 1807 the West End farms had c. 33 a. of apparently several water meadows.[87]

In addition to its open fields, East End manor had 4 a. of common pasture scattered about them, and c. 8 a. of water meadows. The fields contained c. 220 a. and those with land in them evidently had some rights to feed animals on the downs of the parish.[88] As lessees the Poores granted nearly all the land of the manor by copy to members of their family, and in the early 19th century it was worked as a single farm from East End Manor.[89]

The open fields and common pastures in the parish were inclosed in 1823 by Act. Apart from the home closes and closes between the village and the river, all the land of the parish was allotted, whether in common or several use before. As a result most of the farms were made compact. After inclosure the demesne of West End manor was 473 a., the East End manor farm 488 a., Parsonage farm 238 a., and Lawes farm 275 a.; copyholds of West End manor were of c. 280 a., 209 a., 195 a., 146 a., 104 a., 71 a., and 56 a. All 11 farms were worked from buildings in the village and some may have been worked together. About 1840 there were virtually equal amounts of arable and grassland in the parish,

71 Hants R.O., ECCLS. II, 59594, pp. 28–60.
72 Above, intro. [village].
73 *Archaeologia*, lix (1), 76.
74 Winch. Coll. Mun. 5934; 5936.
75 Ibid. 5631, rott. B, E; *Archaeologia*, lix (1), 78.
76 Winch. Coll. Mun. 5657; 5659, rott. A–B; 5932; 5934.
77 Ibid. 5659, rot. J; 5601A, rot. E; 5601C, rot. A; 5603, rot. C; 5607; 5932; 5934; 5936; 5944; *W.A.M.* lxxiv/lxxv. 137–47.
78 *W.A.M.* lxxiv/lxxv. 142, 145; *Archaeologia*, lix (1), 81; Winch. Coll. Mun. 5950d.; 5966–8; 5970; 6033–4; 6107.
79 Winch. Coll. Mun. 5659, rot. K.
80 Ibid. 5670, rot. C.

81 Ibid. 21332.
82 W.R.O., EA/144.
83 Winch. Coll. Mun. 5872.
84 P.R.O., E 134/36 Chas. II Trin./2.
85 Winch. Coll. Mun. 21331.
86 *W.N. & Q.* i. 415–16.
87 *Andrews and Dury, Map* (W.R.S. viii), pl. 8; W.R.O., EA/144; Hants R.O., ECCLS. II, 59594, *passim*; Winch. Coll. Mun. 21331–3.
88 W.R.O. 212B/2860; Hants R.O., ECCLS. II, 59594, pp. 57–61.
89 Hants R.O., ECCLS. II, 59594, p. 58; W.R.O., EA/144.

and the largest farms were composite ones of 683 a., 637 a., and 627 a., the second of which may have been worked with 421 a. in Knighton. There were two groups of farm buildings on the downs c. 1840,[90] five c. 1880.[91]

In the later 19th century the parish contained slightly more arable than pasture. The chief cereal crop was barley; on the grassland c. 3,000 sheep, c. 30 cattle, and c. 90 pigs were usually kept.[92] The amount of agriculture was reduced from 1899 by the building of Larkhill camp and the use of land for military training.[93] A. C. Young of Watergate Farm in Bulford occupied 1,830 a. of the parish in 1910, but much of it could not be used for agriculture; a farm of c. 290 a. was based at Durrington House, and three farms of less than 100 a. were apparently worked from farmsteads in the village.[94] Arable farming declined in the earlier 20th century, and in the early 1930s was restricted to c. 400 a. on both sides of the Upavon–Amesbury road. On the rest of the land not used by the army dairy and beef cattle and large flocks of sheep were kept.[95] Since then the agricultural land has been further reduced. In 1992 there was arable between the Upavon–Amesbury road and Larkhill camp and pasture in the south-west corner of the parish: those at Down Barn were apparently the only farm buildings in use in the parish.

MILL. A water mill north-west of the church was part of the demesne of West End manor from 1331–2 or earlier.[96] Its working was severely impeded by new mills built downstream in Milston in 1611.[97] Durrington mill evidently ceased to work between 1877 and 1899, and it was demolished between 1899 and 1923.[98]

TRADE AND INDUSTRY. Two weavers lived in Durrington in 1580,[99] one in 1754.[1] Malting was carried on in the 18th century[2] and early 19th, c. 1838 in a malthouse west of the church.[3] West of the village the Stonehenge inn incorporated the Crossroads brewery from c. 1875:[4] c. 1917 it was bought by Portsmouth (later Portsmouth & Brighton) United Breweries,[5] which had a depot there until c. 1981.[6] A bacon factor was based in the parish in the later 19th century. Then and in the earlier 20th racehorses were trained at stables at Durrington House.[7]

From c. 1911 various small businesses became established in the village, especially in Bulford

Road, to supply Larkhill camp.[8] A branch of Lloyds Bank was opened in Bulford Road in 1919 and closed in 1990.[9] A branch of the London Joint City & Midland Bank Ltd., later the Midland Bank, was open c. 1923 and in 1992.[10] From the 1920s the War Department's estate office has been at the Red House in High Street.[11] The number of shops and small businesses, still mostly in Bulford Road, increased as the village grew in the mid and later 20th century. Those in Bulford Road in 1992 included a motor repair works, a veterinary clinic, and a betting shop. In High Street there was a pets' undertaker and an animal crematorium. From 1971 protective packaging materials were made by Carton Industries Ltd. at a factory in Bulford Road where 11 people were employed in 1992.[12] In 1980 the firm of Hassett International was set up in Bulford Road by Mr. L. Hassett for the design and supply of infra-red heating equipment for industrial use; in 1989 the firm moved to a factory in Larkhill Road where 10 people were employed in 1992.[13] Also at premises in Larkhill Road the firm R.M.C. Ltd. has prepared ready mixed concrete from 1986 or earlier.[14]

LOCAL GOVERNMENT. Records of the court for West End manor survive with gaps from the early 14th century to the later 19th.[15] The court met four times a year 1319–24. From c. 1335 it met twice a year in spring and autumn, and its title reflected the lord's claim to leet jurisdiction and view of frankpledge. In the period 1426–36 the bailiff and the constable of Amesbury hundred were presented for having infringed the lord's franchises.[16] In the earlier 14th century the court heard and determined pleas of debt and of trespass, but otherwise there was little manorial business. The officers of the court included a tithingman, chosen at the autumn meeting, and an aletaster. From 1361 both leet and manorial business was energetically prosecuted. In 1400 the chaplain of Durrington was presented for assault. Five neifs, members of one family, were presented from 1511 for having left the manor; in 1514 a customary tenant was presented for taking his grain to a mill at Amesbury; and in 1511 and 1514 butchers and the miller of Durrington were presented for overcharging. Besides the usual

90 W.R.O., EA/144; P.R.O., IR 29/38/106; IR 29/38/116; IR 30/38/106; IR 30/38/116.
91 O.S. Map 6", Wilts. LIV (1887 edn.).
92 P.R.O., MAF 68/493, sheet 10; MAF 68/1063, sheet 10; MAF 68/1633, sheet 9.
93 Above, intro.
94 Kelly's Dir. Wilts. (1907); W.R.O., Inland Revenue, val. reg. 142.
95 [1st] Land Util. Surv. Map, sheet 122; P.R.O., MAF 68/2203, sheet 8; MAF 68/3814, no. 200.
96 Wilts. Inq. p.m. 1327–77 (Index Libr.), 105–6; Winch. Coll. Mun. 5878; 5934; 5954; 21333, pp. 6–9; 21334, pp. 1–2; P.R.O., IR 29/38/106.
97 Winch. Coll. Mun. 5908A; below, Milston, econ. hist. (mill).
98 O.S. Maps 6", Wilts. LIV (1887 and later edns.).
99 P.R.O., REQ 2/219/84.
1 Wilts. Apprentices (W.R.S. xvii), p. 99.
2 P.R.O., E 134/4 Geo. II East./7.
3 Ibid. IR 29/38/106; IR 30/38/106.

4 Kelly's Dir. Wilts. (1875, 1885); O.S. Map 6", Wilts. LIV (1887 edn.).
5 P.R.O., IR 29/38/106, altered apportionment.
6 Inf. from the Archivist, Whitbread plc, the Brewery, Chiswell Street, Lond. E.C. 1.
7 Kelly's Dir. Wilts. (1875 and later edns.).
8 Ibid. (1911 and later edns.).
9 W.R.O., G 1/760/10; inf. from the Archivist, Lloyds Bank plc, 71 Lombard Street, Lond. E.C. 3.
10 W.R.O., G 1/760/43.
11 Kelly's Dir. Wilts. (1923 and later edns.).
12 Inf. from Mr. J. Laing, Carton Industries Ltd., Bulford Road.
13 Inf. from Mr. L. Hassett, Hassett International, Larkhill Road.
14 Dir. of Firms (Wilts. co. council, 1986).
15 Para. based on Winch. Coll. Mun. 5629–31; 5634–6; 5639; 5644; 5649; 5651; 5653–7; 5659; 5663; 5667–70; 5672–4; 5679; 5719; 5743; 5748; 5780; 5804–10.
16 V.C.H. Wilts. v. 68.

manorial concerns, such as the regulating of common husbandry, copyhold transactions, and the repair of tenements, fishing in the Avon was closely regulated. In 1511 tenants of West End manor were forbidden to fish the common water more than twice a week, in 1515 a tenant of East End manor was presented for having removed a hatch and for catching trout and eels from his boat in the West End stretch of the river, and in 1518 two West End tenants were presented for netting trout in the lord's demesne waters. East End tenants were presented for trespassing with their animals on West End meadows in 1515. From 1604 the court was held by the lessees of the manor, and dealt mainly with manorial offences. In the 18th century, when the officers included a hayward and two hay weighers, it was usually held once a year in spring. From the mid 19th century, when it was held at Durrington Manor,[17] to 1884 it was held only when copyhold business required it.

Records of the court of East End manor survive with gaps for the period 1609–1854. In the 17th century and early 18th the court was called view of frankpledge and court, from the mid 18th court leet, view, and court baron. It was held both for that manor and for the manor of Knighton in the same ownership, but the business of the two was not distinguished in the records. It was held by the lessees of East End manor, usually twice a year in the 17th century, thereafter once a year or when copyhold business required it. The court appointed a hayward and a tithingman but dealt mainly with copyhold business. Exceptionally, pleas of debt and of trespass were heard in 1609.[18]

In 1802–3 a quarter of the population of the parish and 31 from outside it received poor relief at Durrington; £306 was spent on regular relief for 37 adults and 58 children, occasional relief for 20 adults, and instruction in spinning.[19] Poor relief was generous 1812–15 when an average of £364 a year was spent on regular relief for c. 27 adults and on occasional relief for c. 22.[20] Relief may have been less generous thereafter, especially as the population of the parish increased rapidly; in 1822–4 an average of £265 was spent, 1825–9 £361, and 1830–4 £419. Expenditure was highest at £471 in 1831.[21] The parish became part of Amesbury poor-law union in 1835[22] and of Salisbury district in 1974.[23]

A vestry, apparently select, governed the parish from c. 1810. In 1835 it paid for 11 labourers to be employed by local farmers, in 1838 collected a rate for paupers to emigrate, and c. 1839 owned two houses in Hackthorn Road and a cottage in the Ham.[24]

CHURCHES. Durrington church was standing in the early 12th century.[25] It is likely to have belonged to Amesbury abbey and was confirmed to Amesbury priory in 1179.[26] It was served by a chaplain or curate nominated by the owners of the Rectory estate: c. 1650 the lessees of the estate had the right to nominate; from c. 1763 nominations were by the dean and chapter of Winchester as owners.[27] Under the Incumbents Act of 1868 the benefice became a vicarage. From 1869, when as owners of the Rectory estate the Ecclesiastical Commissioners gave him some of the commuted great tithes and charged him with repairing the chancel, the vicar was usually styled rector.[28]

The curate's salary was £20 in 1641,[29] £40 in 1677, and £53 c. 1830; in addition he received a sack of wheat and a sack of malt from the Rectory estate each year.[30] Queen Anne's Bounty augmented the living by £200 in both 1813 and 1826.[31] By an endowment given in 1844 the Ecclesiastical Commissioners increased the stipend to £100,[32] and in 1869, as owners of the Rectory estate, they replaced the stipend, then £125, by £296 of tithe rent charge from the parish.[33] The lessee of the estate endowed the living with a house in the earlier 17th century,[34] probably the cottage in College Road which was unfit for use c. 1830.[35] In 1936 a new Rectory was built east of the church.[36]

Robert Maton gave a flock of 20 sheep for the church, and the profits from 8 more sheep and from 1 cow for three lights in the church, all by will proved 1510.[37] The income from the 8 sheep was used in 1548 for a candle which burned in the church in front of the corpses of parishioners.[38] John Marris, chaplain 1456–1509, was apparently summoned to testify during the canonization process of St. Osmund.[39] In 1553 no quarter sermon was preached and the church lacked the *Paraphrases* of Erasmus, and in 1564–5 the curate, a drunkard, was incapable of officiating.[40] Leonard Maton, appointed before 1623 when in minor orders,[41] served the cure until 1684.[42] He signed the *Concurrent Testimony* in 1648,[43] and preached every Sunday c. 1650.[44] The church still lacked the prescribed books in

17 W.R.O. 1885/11.
18 Ibid. 84/22–3; ibid. Ch. Com., chapter, 103/1–3; above, manors (E. End); below, Figheldean, manors (Knighton).
19 *V.C.H. Wilts.* iv. 347; *Poor Law Abstract, 1804,* 558–9.
20 *Poor Law Abstract, 1818,* 492–3.
21 *V.C.H. Wilts.* iv. 347; *Poor Rate Returns, 1816–21,* 185; *1822–4,* 225; *1825–9,* 215; *1830–4,* 209.
22 *Poor Law Com. 2nd Rep.* App. D, 558.
23 O.S. Map 1/100,000, admin. areas, Wilts. (1974 edn.).
24 *W.N. & Q.* iii. 190; W.R.O. 1885/11; 1885/15; P.R.O., IR 29/38/106; IR 30/38/106; Winch. Coll. Mun. 21333, pp. 92–3. 25 Below, this section [architecture].
26 *Cal. Chart. R. 1257–1300,* 157–9.
27 *W.A.M.* xl. 265; *Vis. Queries, 1783* (W.R.S. xxvii), p. 93; *Rep. Com. Eccl. Revenues,* 832–3; Phillipps, *Wilts. Inst.* ii. 81, 102, 104; Winch. Coll. Mun. 5553–4; P.R.O., SC 6/Hen. VIII/3986, rot. 84d.; above, manors (Rectory).
28 31 & 32 Vic. c. 117; Ch. Com. file 2301/2; above,

manors (Rectory); for the tithes, below, this section.
29 *W.A.M.* xl. 264.
30 *Rep. Com. Eccl. Revenues,* 832–3; W.R.O., D 1/24/81/2.
31 C. Hodgson, *Queen Anne's Bounty* (1864), p. cccxxxv.
32 *Lond. Gaz.* 3 May 1844, p. 1509.
33 Ibid. 17 Mar. 1871, p. 1454; W.R.O., D 1/56/7.
34 *W.A.M.* xl. 264.
35 *Rep. Com. Eccl. Revenues,* 832–3; Ch. Com. file, NB 34/123; P.R.O., IR 29/38/106; IR 30/38/106.
36 W.R.O., G 1/760/195; Ch. Com. file 2301/2.
37 *W.A.M.* xxxi. 339–40.
38 P.R.O., E 318/31/1729.
39 *W.A.M.* xxxiii. 276; Church Guide (TS.).
40 *V.C.H. Wilts.* iii. 33; W.R.O., D 1/43/1, f. 109.
41 *Subscription Bk. 1620–40* (W.R.S. xxxii), p. 26.
42 *W.A.M.* xxxiii. 275.
43 *Calamy Revised,* ed. Matthews, 557.
44 *W.A.M.* xl. 256.

1662.[45] Henry Head, curate from *c.* 1715 to *c.* 1748, was master of a free school in Amesbury and may not have resided.[46] Richard Head, appointed in 1763,[47] lived in Amesbury and was rector of Rollestone and vicar of Compton Chamberlayne. In 1783 he held a service at Durrington every Sunday alternately morning and afternoon, and administered the sacrament at Christmas, Easter, Whitsun, and Michaelmas to fewer than 20 communicants.[48] Nicholas Westcombe, appointed in 1804, was murdered in 1813 near Winchester, where he lived.[49] Henry Fowle, appointed in 1828, had an assistant curate who in 1832 held Sunday services alternately morning and evening.[50] Fowle's successor Richard Webb, curate 1833–62,[51] was possibly the first to reside since the 17th century. From 1838 or earlier to *c.* 1910 successive curates and rectors lived in a house in Church Street.[52] On Census Sunday in 1851 the morning service was attended by 270, the afternoon one by 290.[53] In 1864 Webb's successor C. S. Ruddle (d. 1910) held services with sermons on Sunday mornings attended by *c.* 150, and on Sunday afternoons or evenings attended by *c.* 270. He held some weekday services on holy days, others, at which he lectured, weekly between autumn and spring; he administered the sacrament to *c.* 40 communicants at Christmas and Easter, and on the first Sunday of each month.[54] He published articles on the history of Durrington.[55] He was succeeded as rector by his son A. G. Ruddle (d. 1935),[56] who lived in East End Manor.[57]

The church had no dedication in 1763[58] and was dedicated to *ALL SAINTS* in 1851.[59] It is built of knapped flint and freestone and has a chancel with south vestry, an aisled nave, and a west tower. Part of the north wall of an earlier 12th-century nave survived until the 19th century;[60] in the 13th the chancel was rebuilt, possibly on a larger scale, and the north wall of the nave and the south wall of the aisle were each given a pair of lancet windows.[61] About 1500 the double-lancet east window of the chancel was replaced by a triple lancet, and in the north wall of the nave a tall three-light window was inserted west of the doorway.[62] The tower was built in the earlier 16th century, partly into the nave, and has a west doorway and a north-east stair turret: its parapet and pinnacles, and the upper stage of the turret, were rebuilt from *c.* 1692, evidently after storm damage.[63] A west gallery erected in 1831[64] possibly replaced or extended an earlier one.[65] In 1851 the church was extensively re-stored to designs by J. W. Hugall. The walls of the chancel were restored, the chancel arch was rebuilt, the south aisle was widened, the north aisle was built, the gallery was removed, and all the roofs were renewed: a blocked earlier 12th-century doorway, which on the inside had been concealed by a wall on which there was a large painting of St. Christopher, was moved from the north wall of the nave to form a porch in the south aisle. The vestry was built in 1973.[66] The church contains numerous 17th-century fittings, including an altar table, the pulpit, and the tower screen. Box pews, which incorporated carved panels, were cut down and rearranged,[67] apparently in 1851.

A chalice weighing 13 oz. was left in the church and 16 oz. of plate were taken by the king's commissioners in 1553. In 1992 the parish held a later 16th-century chalice and a paten hallmarked for 1691.[68] There were three bells in 1553. They were replaced by, or recast as, three bells by John Wallis, one in 1602 and two in 1617. Two bells cast by John Lott, one in 1654 and one in 1660, were added to the ring. The bells were rehung in 1916,[69] and in 1953 a sixth bell was added.[70] Registrations of baptisms, burials, and marriages survive from 1591, and are apparently complete.[71]

The church of *ST. ALBAN THE MARTYR* at Larkhill camp was built in 1938 to replace a wooden church erected there in 1914. It is of brick to designs by W. Ross and consists of an apsidal chancel and a nave; the nave has narrow aisles, north and south porches at the east end, a short south-west tower, and a north-west baptistry.[72]

ROMAN CATHOLICISM. St. Anthony's church at Larkhill camp was open in the 1930s, and may have been in the 1920s or earlier. Later, a hut on a different site was used as a church, and in 1968 a new church of St. Barbara and St. Anthony was opened.[73] Our Lady Queen of Heaven church was opened in Durrington village in 1960.[74]

PROTESTANT NONCONFORMITY. In 1662 John West and his wife refused to have their child baptized, and they and another married couple would not attend church;[75] the group was described as anabaptist in 1669. West certified his house for Presbyterian worship in 1672,[76]

45 W.R.O., D 1/54/1/3, no. 40.
46 Ibid. bishop's transcripts, bdle. 2; *Alum. Oxon. 1500–1714*, ii. 684; *W.A.M.* xxxiii. 276.
47 Phillipps, *Wilts. Inst.* ii. 81.
48 *Vis. Queries, 1783* (W.R.S. xxvii), pp. 93–4.
49 Phillipps, *Wilts. Inst.* ii. 104; *W.N. & Q.* v. 8–9.
50 *Rep. Com. Eccl. Revenues*, 832–3; Ch. Com. file, NB 34/123.
51 *W.A.M.* xxxiii. 276; W.R.O. 1885/11.
52 O.S. Map 6", Wilts. LIV. NE. (1901 edn.); Ch. Com. file 2301/2; P.R.O., IR 29/38/106; IR 30/38/106.
53 P.R.O., HO 129/262/2/6/9.
54 Church Guide; W.R.O., D 1/56/7.
55 *W.A.M.* xxxi. 1–7, 331–42; xxxiii. 269–76.
56 Ch. Com. file 2301/2.
57 Ibid.; *Kelly's Dir. Wilts.* (1915, 1927, 1931).
58 J. Ecton, *Thesaurus* (1763), 392.
59 *W.A.M.* xxxiii. 279.
60 Below, this section.
61 *W.A.M.* xxxiii, pl. facing p. 277; Buckler, watercolour in W.A.S. Libr., vol. i. 17 (1805).
62 *W.A.M.* xxxi. 278–9.
63 *Churches of SE. Wilts.* (R.C.H.M.), 137; Aubrey, *Topog. Coll.* ed. Jackson, 357; W.R.O. 1885/10.
64 W.R.O. 1885/11.
65 Buckler, watercolour in W.A.S. Libr., vol. i. 17.
66 *Churches of SE. Wilts.* 136; W.R.O., D 1/61/7/18.
67 *Churches of SE. Wilts.* 137.
68 Nightingale, *Wilts. Plate*, 39; Church Guide.
69 Walters, *Wilts. Bells*, 79–80.
70 Church Guide.   71 W.R.O. 1885/1–9.
72 James, *Gunners at Larkhill*, 65, 202–3.
73 Ibid. 108, 111, 205.
74 *Cath. Dir.* (1992).
75 W.R.O., D 1/54/1/3, no. 40.
76 *Orig. Rec.* ed. G. L. Turner, ii, pp. 1066, 1074.

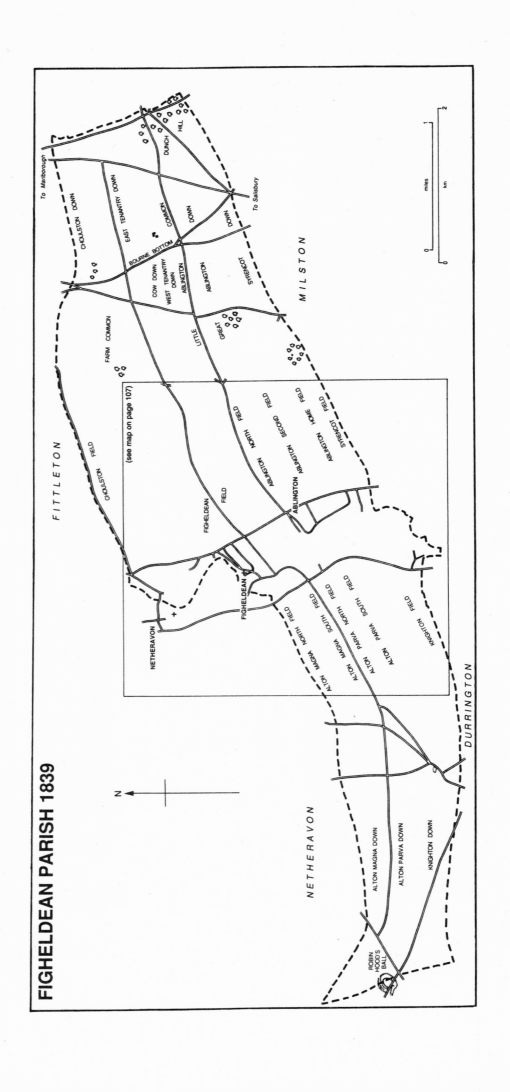

FIGHELDEAN PARISH 1839

N

To Marlborough

To Salisbury

CHOULSTON DOWN

EAST TENANTRY DOWN

DUNCH HILL

COMMON DOWN

BOURNE BOTTOM

COW DOWN

WEST TENANTRY DOWN

ABLINGTON DOWN

ABLINGTON DOWN

SYRENCOT

FARM COMMON

LITTLE

GREAT

CHOULSTON FIELD

(see map on page 107)

FIGHELDEAN FIELD

ABLINGTON NORTH FIELD

ABLINGTON SECOND FIELD

ABLINGTON HOME FIELD

SYRENCOT FIELD

ABLINGTON

FITTLETON

MILSTON

NETHERAVON

FIGHELDEAN

ALTON MAGNA NORTH FIELD

ALTON MAGNA SOUTH FIELD

ALTON PARVA NORTH FIELD

ALTON PARVA SOUTH FIELD

KNIGHTON FIELD

NETHERAVON

DURRINGTON

ALTON MAGNA DOWN

ALTON PARVA DOWN

KNIGHTON DOWN

ROBIN HOOD'S BALL

miles
km
0   1   2
0   1   2

and there were nine dissenters in 1676.[77] There was said to be no nonconformist in the parish in 1783.[78] A meeting house was certified in 1821, and in 1824 a chapel, almost certainly that standing near the junction of College Road and Bulford Road in 1839, was certified by Independents.[79] On Sunday afternoons in 1850–1 c. 40 attended the chapel,[80] and in 1864 four families.[81] The chapel, rebuilt or altered in 1860,[82] may have been used by Wesleyan Methodists c. 1880 but was for Congregationalists in 1899.[83] In 1905 it was replaced by a new Congregational chapel in Bulford Road, which in 1965 joined the Evangelical Fellowship of Congregational Churches.[84] Services were still held in 1992.

EDUCATION. The parish had one school in 1783,[85] three small schools in 1808,[86] and two schools with a total of c. 40 pupils in 1833.[87] A National school was built in College Road in 1843.[88] In it a woman taught c. 90 pupils in 1846–7,[89] 50–60 in 1858.[90] Average attendance was c. 52 in 1871, 74 in 1911–12.[91]

New schools were built in the village as the population of the parish increased in the 20th century. The school in College Road was reserved for infants when a new junior school was opened in School Road in 1912. In 1922 the school in College Road was closed, its pupils were transferred to that in School Road, and a new senior school was opened in Bulford Road.[92]

Average attendance in 1926–7 was 147 at School Road and 152 at Bulford Road. At School Road numbers had fallen to 124 by 1938; they had risen to 235 at Bulford Road[93] partly because pupils from outside the parish attended. The Bulford Road school became a secondary modern school in 1944.[94] In 1961 the School Road building was reserved for infants, the juniors were transferred to Bulford Road, and a new secondary school was built at the north-east corner of the village.[95] The new school became a comprehensive school, Upper Avon, in 1974. In 1992 it had 746 pupils on roll, the junior school had 223, and the infants' school had 139.[96]

A primary school was opened in Larkhill camp in 1962[97] and had 294 pupils on roll in 1992.[98]

CHARITIES FOR THE POOR. By will proved 1715 Thomas Allen gave £1 a year to the poor: the money was spent on bread c. 1833, was later given to a clothing club, and from the late 19th century was distributed in small sums to parishioners. Also in the 18th century 12s. a year was given to widows and 6s. a year to the poor: payments had ceased by 1833, and in 1901 the charities were deemed lost. About 1865 J. H. Alt, vicar of Enford, gave 12s. a year to be distributed on 1 January, 7s. to the oldest communicant, 5s. to the second oldest. Such payments were being made in the early 20th century but it is not clear how long they continued.[99]

FIGHELDEAN

FIGHELDEAN[1] is 18 km. north of Salisbury on Salisbury Plain.[2] The parish, 2,201 ha. (5,439 a.), includes 10 a. considered part of Durrington parish until the mid 19th century.[3] It lies east–west and is crossed from north to south by the Christchurch Avon. It contains six settlements beside the river: their names suggest that they are all of Saxon origin,[4] and each had a strip of land running from the river to the downs, Choulston, Figheldean, Ablington, and Syrencot to the east, Alton and Knighton to the west. Figheldean had a church, and Ablington, Knighton, and Syrencot, in the same ownership as Figheldean in the 12th and 13th centuries,[5] may have been in its parish early. Alton also had a church and may have been a parish in the

Middle Ages;[6] later both it and Choulston were in Figheldean parish.

The parish boundary, c. 30 km. in length, runs mostly in straight lines across downland. At the extremities a prehistoric ditch marks the boundary with South Tidworth (Hants until 1992) on Dunch Hill on the east, and a prehistoric earthwork, Robin Hood's Ball, straddles the boundary on the west. The Avon forms two stretches of the boundary, and in places both the northern and southern boundaries follow dry valleys.

The parish is entirely on Upper Chalk. Alluvium and gravel have been deposited by the Avon, and to the east there is gravel in Bourne bottom, a parallel valley cut by a tributary of the

77 *Compton Census*, ed. Whiteman, 124.
78 *Vis. Queries, 1783* (W.R.S. xxvii), p. 93.
79 *Meeting Ho. Certs.* (W.R.S. xl), pp. 95, 105; P.R.O., IR 29/38/106; IR 30/38/106.
80 P.R.O., HO 129/262/2/6/10.
81 W.R.O., D 1/56/7.
82 G.R.O. Worship Reg. no. 9750.
83 O.S. Maps 6", Wilts. LIV (1887 edn.); LIV. NE. (1901 edn.).
84 W.R.O. 2770/2.
85 *Vis. Queries, 1783* (W.R.S. xxvii), p. 93.
86 Lamb. Palace Libr., MS. 1732.
87 *Educ. Enq. Abstract*, 1036.
88 Church Guide; P.R.O., ED 7/130, no. 112.
89 Nat. Soc. *Inquiry, 1846–7*, Wilts. 6–7.
90 *Acct. of Wilts. Schs.* 22.
91 *Returns relating to Elem. Educ.* 426–7; *Bd. of Educ., List 21, 1913* (H.M.S.O.), 550.
92 W.R.O., F 8/500, Durrington junior sch. 1892–1941,

pp. 246, 355, 500.
93 *Bd. of Educ., List 21, 1927* (H.M.S.O.), 360; *1938*, 422.
94 *V.C.H. Wilts.* v. 355.
95 W.R.O., F 8/500, Durrington junior sch. 1941–72, p. 185; Durrington infant sch. 1961–72.
96 Inf. from Director of Educ., Co. Hall, Trowbridge.
97 W.R.O. 2036/89.
98 Inf. from Director of Educ.
99 *Endowed Char. Wilts.* (S. Div.), 157–9; W.R.O., L 2, Durrington.
1 This article was written in 1991.
2 Maps used include O.S. Maps 1", sheet 14 (1817 edn.); 1/50,000, sheet 184 (1988 edn.); 1/25,000, 41/14, 41/24 (1948 and later edns.); 6", Wilts. XLVII–XLVIII, LIV–LV (1883–9 and later edns.).
3 Above, Durrington, intro.
4 *P.N. Wilts.* (E.P.N.S.), 365–6.
5 Below, manors.
6 Below, churches.

Avon, Nine Mile river, now dry in Figheldean. There are ridges and dry valleys both east and west of the Avon, but much of the downland slopes gently. In the east the land exceeds 150 m. on Dunch Hill, and in the west reaches 147 m. on Knighton down and c. 140 m. at Robin Hood's Ball.[7] Each of the six settlements had meadow land beside the Avon, all their sites were on the gravel near the river, and to the east and west were large areas of open fields and downland pastures for sheep. Downland and some of the former open fields were included in military training areas after 1898.[8]

The eastern downs of the parish were crossed by a road from Chipping Campden (Glos.) to Salisbury via Marlborough prominent in the 17th century.[9] The road lost importance after a Marlborough–Salisbury road along the Bourne valley further east was turnpiked in 1835. North–south roads linked the villages on each bank of the Avon. That on the east was turnpiked from a little north of Figheldean parish to Amesbury in 1761 and disturnpiked in 1871. That on the west became more important. It was turnpiked in 1840, disturnpiked in 1877, and, via Upavon and Amesbury, took some Devizes–Salisbury and Marlborough–Salisbury traffic.[10] The two roads were linked by lanes through Figheldean village: to the north one crossed the river on a bridge, called Figheldean bridge in 1649,[11] near Figheldean mill, and to the south one forded the river. Between 1773 and 1817 a bridge was built near the ford:[12] it was an iron suspension bridge in 1851,[13] was later rebuilt, and was called Figheldean bridge by 1880.[14] The southern road, leading from the crossing northwards through Figheldean village, was turnpiked in 1840 and disturnpiked in 1877.[15] East–west roads across the parish fell out of civilian use after 1898.[16]

A Palaeolithic artefact was found in the parish, Robin Hood's Ball is a causewayed camp of the early Neolithic period, and Bronze-Age barrows of several types survive on the downs. East and west of Bourne bottom an Iron-Age field system of c. 1,500 a., divided by ditches and possibly associated with the contemporary fort on Sidbury Hill in North Tidworth, indicates settlement by agriculturalists and cattle farmers. The cultivated area now in Figheldean parish, c. 370 a., could have supported perhaps 22 families but no evidence of their dwellings has been found. There may have been other prehistoric field systems on the lower slopes of the downs west of Alton and on the boundary with Durrington further west, c. 220 a. and c. 280 a. respectively. Romano-British foundations and

pottery have been found west of the Upavon–Amesbury road at Alton Parva Farm.[17]

The six settlements had a total of c. 160 poll-tax payers in 1377, a high number for a parish in Amesbury hundred,[18] and the parish was apparently prosperous in the 16th century and early 17th.[19] The population was 367 in 1801. It rose from 342 in 1811 to 531 in 1831. Five people emigrated from the parish early in 1841 when there were 510 inhabitants. Increased mechanization of farming resulted in a declining population in the later 19th century and early 20th, and in 1911 the population was 429. Thereafter housing in the parish for military personnel caused the number of inhabitants to increase and fluctuate. The population was 893, including 500 civilians, in 1921, and 625 in 1931. New housing built at Figheldean and Ablington in the mid 20th century apparently caused the civilian population to increase. The parish had 977 inhabitants in 1951,[20] 675 in 1991.[21]

FIGHELDEAN. In the early 14th century Figheldean was apparently prosperous,[22] but in 1428 was said to have fewer than 10 households.[23] To judge from its surviving houses it was much the largest village in the parish in the 17th century and it was clearly so in the 19th and 20th: it had c. 288 inhabitants in 1841.[24]

The church stands on high ground at the north end of the village: the line of buildings south of it in Church Street and High Street has offshoots in Mill Lane and Pollens Lane. In the later 17th century there were houses on both sides of Church Street, the west side of Mill Lane, and the west side of High Street. The predominant building materials were timber, stone rubble, and brick, and many of the surviving houses retain thatched roofs. The earlier 17th-century houses are typically L-shaped with an internal chimney stack and a lobby entrance. Those of the later 17th century are typified by a house on the west side of Church Street built in 1676[25] and the Cottage on the west side of High Street. Melrose House, also on the west side of High Street, was built in 1666[26] and is L-shaped. Its principal timber-framed north–south range has an east entrance front with high symmetrical gables for second-floor attic windows and has end gables of flint and ashlar. That range contains the main rooms on either side of a central hall and at its north end a service wing projects eastwards. On the east side of High Street there was little more than two farmsteads in 1773:[27] Manor Farm was at the north end, Read's Farm at the south end. Both were demolished between

7 Geol. Surv. Map 1", drift, sheet 282 (1967 edn.).
8 Below, econ. hist.
9 J. Ogilby, *Brit.* (1675), pl. 85.
10 *V.C.H. Wilts.* iv. 257, 262, 264, 270–1; *L.J.* xxx. 138.
11 *W.A.M.* xl. 266.
12 *Andrews and Dury, Map* (W.R.S. viii), pl. 8; O.S. Map 1", sheet 14 (1817 edn.).
13 W.R.O. 1550/48.
14 O.S. Map 1/2,500, Wilts. LIV. 4 (1880 edn.).
15 *V.C.H. Wilts.* iv. 257, 264, 271.
16 Ibid. 266.
17 Ibid. i (1), 70–1, 140, 174–5, 218, 223, 225, 229, 233, 236, 239, 241, 243, 245, 254, 265, 275–6; i (2), 293–4, 296–7,

305; *W.A.M.* lxxvi. 19; *Proc. Prehist. Soc.* (N.S. xx), 103–14.
18 *V.C.H. Wilts.* iv. 306.
19 *Taxation Lists* (W.R.S. x), 2, 131, 135; P.R.O., E 179/197/152; E 179/197/241; E 179/198/284; E 179/198/329; E 179/199/370; E 179/199/398.
20 *V.C.H. Wilts.* iv. 319, 322, 326, 348.
21 *Census,* 1991.
22 *Tax List, 1332* (W.R.S. xlv), 111; *V.C.H. Wilts.* iv. 297.
23 *V.C.H. Wilts.* iv. 314.
24 P.R.O., HO 107/1165/8.
25 Date on ho.
26 Date on ho.
27 *Andrews and Dury, Map* (W.R.S. viii), pl. 8.

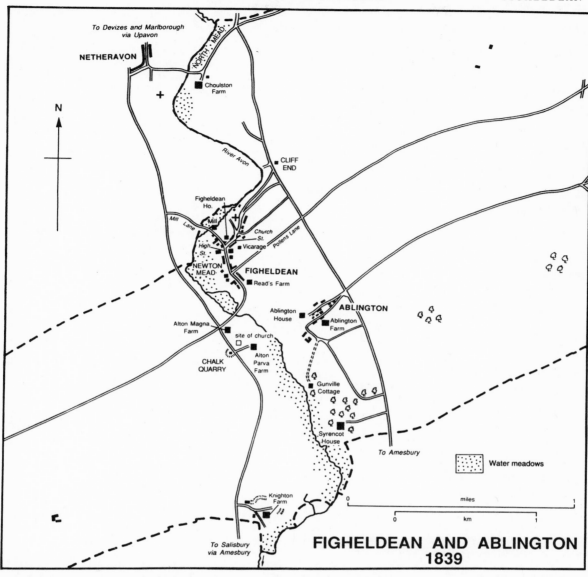

FIGHELDEAN AND ABLINGTON
1839

c. 1877 and *c.* 1957.[28] By 1817 other buildings, of which only a cottage south of the junction with Pollens Lane survives, had been erected to make a continuous line on the east side.[29] At the north end of High Street, Figheldean House, a large **L**-shaped house of pebble-dashed brick with label mouldings above the windows and a thatched roof, was built between 1820 and 1838 for Sir Edward Poore, Bt., whose relict lived there in 1848.[30] A range of five almshouses built in 1826 for Edward Dyke Poore (d. 1859) south-west of the church was demolished in the 1960s:[31] it is not known by whom or on what terms the houses were occupied. Also in the period 1820–38 two cottages were built beside the turnpike road north-east of the village at Cliff End; two more were built near the river north of the church, an area called Little London,

between 1838 and 1850. Of several farmsteads built on the open land east of the village in the mid 19th century only Figheldean New Buildings, 400 m. north-east of Cliff End, survives.[32]

The Wheatsheaf, on the west side of High Street, was open in 1855[33] and 1991. The Avon Valley lodge of the Order of Foresters met there 1866–1904.[34] A school and a nonconformist chapel were built on the east side of High Street in the later 19th century.[35] Houses in the later 19th century and the 20th, bungalows in the later 20th, have been built in High Street, those on the west side on old sites; at the south end of High Street on the west side offices and a working men's club were built in the 1980s. In the 20th century the village has also expanded eastwards, north and south of Pollens Lane. To the south, in Oak Lane, 4 council houses were

[28] O.S. Maps 6", Wilts. LIV (1887 and later edns.); 1/25,000, SU 14 (1958 edn.).
[29] Ibid. 1", sheet 14 (1817 edn.).
[30] *Kelly's Dir. Wilts.* (1848); C. Greenwood, *Map of Wilts.* (1820); P.R.O., IR 29/38/116; IR 30/38/116.
[31] Min. of Housing and Local Govt., provisional list of bldgs. of hist. interest (1955); inf. from the vicar; below,

manors (Ablington).
[32] Greenwood, *Map of Wilts.*; O.S. Maps 6", Wilts. XLVII (1889 and later edns.); P.R.O., IR 30/38/116; W.R.O., EA/162; ibid. 1550/48.
[33] *Kelly's Dir. Wilts.* (1855).
[34] P.R.O., FS 4/55, Wilts. no. 358.
[35] Below, nonconf.; educ.

built *c.* 1920,[36] several private houses were built, and 12 old people's bungalows were built in 1970[37] and later. To the north, 27 bungalows were built in Pollen Close in the 1960s and 10 in Hilltop Close in the 1980s. Council housing also extended the village south-eastwards towards Ablington: in Avon Banks 12 houses were built in 1949, 8 in 1957, and 6 in 1964–5.[38]

ABLINGTON. The small nucleated village lines both sides of an east–west lane: a new road was made to join it to Figheldean in the mid 19th century.[39] The village may have been as prosperous as Figheldean in the 14th century[40] but was later much smaller. It had 137 inhabitants in 1841.[41]

The village is notable for the survival of timber-framed and thatched houses and cottages of the 17th century, and in the 19th century two larger houses stood back from the lane, Ablington House to the north, Ablington Farm to the south. A house between them on the north side of the lane was built in 1631.[42] At the west end of the lane, also on the north side, a cottage of one storey and attics incorporates parts of three crucks. Further east, on the south side, a cottage was built in 1665.[43] A few other cottages were built or rebuilt in the 18th century or the 19th. In a back lane to the north the Terrace, a row of six houses, was built in the 1920s, north of that the Crescent, four pairs of houses, was built from the late 1930s, and nearby new farm buildings were also erected.

A farmstead was erected on the lower slopes of the downs east of Ablington in the later 20th century.[44] South of Ablington, Gunville Cottage, a rendered and thatched house of the 17th century, may be on the site of a mill.[45]

ALTON. In the early Middle Ages Alton was probably a small village and had a church.[46] The village was evidently small in 1377,[47] and in 1428 had fewer than 10 households.[48] The church was dilapidated in the late 16th century.[49] In 1773 there were only two farmsteads, each connected to the Upavon–Amesbury road by a short east–west lane,[50] and the site of the church was possibly between them.[51] The hamlet had 42 inhabitants in 1841.[52]

To the north Alton Magna Farm is an L-shaped house built of brick in the mid 18th century: in the early 19th it was enlarged on the south-east and its interior was altered. To the

south Alton Parva Farm was also an L-shaped 18th-century house but had flint walls and a thatched roof: it was burnt down during the First World War and a new house was built on the site *c.* 1920.[53]

A cottage on the west side of the Upavon–Amesbury road was built in 1828,[54] but two cottages built in 1854 apparently near Alton Magna Farm no longer stood *c.* 1877.[55] Barns were built on Alton down in the mid 19th century; a racecourse and a hunter trials course laid out there in 1930–1 and extended in the 1970s[56] were mainly for use by members of the armed services.

CHOULSTON. In the Middle Ages Choulston was apparently a small settlement.[57] In 1773 it consisted of no more than a single farmstead[58] and in 1841 had 23 inhabitants.[59] Choulston Farm, timber-framed and U-shaped, was built in the early 17th century and encased in red brick in the mid 18th. The house was made symmetrical with a central east entrance in the 19th century, and the inside was altered *c.* 1985.[60] Four mid 20th-century cottages are on the site of an older building nearby.[61]

In 1912–13 Netheravon airfield and its camp were constructed north-east of Choulston on either side of the Figheldean–Fittleton boundary. The officers' mess and quarters and a hospital were in Figheldean. The airfield was an operational base for the Royal Flying Corps during the First World War and was afterwards used for training pilots. Glider pilots were trained there during and after the Second World War. The R.A.F. police occupied the camp 1950–62. The airfield and camp were transferred to the army in 1963 and from 1966 were the headquarters of the Army Air Corps.[62]

The road from Netheravon via Choulston and the camp to Figheldean, with an offshoot to the south-east, was given the name Kerby Avenue. A Roman Catholic church on the west side and, *c.* 1952, a cemetery on the east side were opened there.[63] Married quarters were built in Choulston Close west of Kerby Avenue in the 1950s and in the south-east part of Kerby Avenue in the early 1960s, a total of *c.* 47 houses. Netheravon sewage disposal works were constructed west of the Figheldean road before 1948.[64]

KNIGHTON. There was a chapel and possibly a manor house at Knighton in the 13th century,[65]

36 W.R.O., G 1/500/8; G 1/603/1.
37 Ibid. G 1/602/8.
38 Ibid. G 1/600/1; G 1/602/3–5.
39 O.S. Map 6", Wilts. LIV (1887 edn.); P.R.O., IR 30/38/116.
40 *Tax List, 1332* (W.R.S. xlv), 111; *V.C.H. Wilts.* iv. 297.
41 *V.C.H. Wilts.* iv. 348.
42 Below, manors (Ablington estates).
43 Date on ho.
44 O.S. Maps 1/10,000, SU 14 NE. (1976 edn.); 1/25,000, SU 14 (1958 edn.).
45 Cf. below, econ. hist.
46 Below, churches.
47 *V.C.H. Wilts.* iv. 306.
48 Ibid. 314.   49 Below, churches.
50 *Andrews and Dury, Map* (W.R.S. viii), pl. 8.
51 *W.A.M.* xxx. 360–1.
52 P.R.O., HO 107/1165/8.

53 Inf. from Lt.-Col. and Mrs. G. J. Rudd, Alton Parva Farm, and photo. in their possession.
54 Date on ho.
55 Glos. R.O., D 2440, box 67, farm accts. 1858; O.S. Map 6", Wilts. LIV (1887 edn.).
56 N. D. G. James, *Gunners at Larkhill*, 160; O.S. Maps 6", Wilts. LIV (1887 edn.); SU 14 NW. (1961 edn.); 1/10,000, SU 14 NW. (1976 edn.); P.R.O., IR 30/38/116.
57 *Tax List, 1332* (W.R.S. xlv), 114; *V.C.H. Wilts.* iv. 297, 306.
58 *Andrews and Dury, Map* (W.R.S. viii), pl. 8.
59 P.R.O., HO 107/1165/8.
60 Inf. from Mr. C. L. Spencer, Choulston Farm.
61 P.R.O., IR 30/38/116.
62 C. Ashworth, *Action Stations* (1990), v. 134–8; *V.C.H. Wilts.* xi. 143.
63 *V.C.H. Wilts.* xi. 168; below, Rom. Cath.
64 O.S. Map 1/25,000, 41/24 (1948 edn.).
65 D. & C. Sar. Mun., press IV, E 2/Knighton/4.

and in the 14th century the settlement may have been more populous than it was later.[66] There was a single farmstead in 1773,[67] and in 1841 Knighton had 20 inhabitants.[68]

Knighton Farm was built in the early 18th century and was surrounded by an embankment as defence against floods. It has two east–west ranges. The tall south range is entirely of brick, has two storeys and attics, and contains the principal rooms. The lower north range, of mixed brick and chalk, contains service rooms. Two thatched cottages on the north side of the lane which linked Knighton Farm with the Upavon–Amesbury road were built in the late 18th century and altered in the 20th. On the west side of the main road a pair of cottages was built between c. 1840 and c. 1877. Farm buildings erected on Knighton down in the mid 19th century were demolished in the early 20th.[69]

Knighton down was used for military training in the early 20th century, and from the late 1920s the south part was used as an airfield by aircraft taking part in army exercises on Salisbury Plain. It was in R.A.F. Larkhill from 1936 to c. 1942 when it was returned to the army. In the later 20th century the Royal Aircraft Establishment had offices on Knighton down and there were several sports grounds.[70]

SYRENCOT. There was presumably a hamlet at Syrencot in the 14th century[71] but no building other than Syrencot House in 1773[72] and 1991.

MANORS AND OTHER ESTATES.

Harding held *FIGHELDEAN* in 1066 and 1086;[73] Henry Hussey held it in the later 12th century. The overlordship may have descended in the Hussey family until 1319 with Knighton manor but is not expressly said to have done so.[74]

Henry Hussey apparently granted Figheldean to his younger son Geoffrey, to whom the manor was confirmed in 1198. Geoffrey was succeeded by his son Geoffrey (d. c. 1218), who held the manor in 1210–12. The younger Geoffrey's estate passed to another Henry Hussey[75] (d. 1260 × 1263), who was succeeded by his son, Sir Hubert Hussey (d. before 1277).[76] The manor passed to Sir Hubert's daughters and coheirs Margaret, wife of Henry Sturmy, Maud (d. c.

1285, unmarried), and Isabel, in 1316 the wife of John of Thorney.[77] Margaret's moiety passed on her death c. 1320 to her son Henry Sturmy,[78] whose right was challenged successfully in 1321 by his brother John. In 1330, however, the moiety was returned to Henry[79] (d. c. 1338), and passed to his son Henry.[80] Isabel and John of Thorney held the other moiety in 1336[81] and on Isabel's death it reverted to the third Henry Sturmy, who in 1359 was granted free warren in the demesne of the reunited manor.[82] From Henry (d. 1381) Figheldean manor descended to his nephew Sir William Sturmy[83] (d. 1427), whose heirs were his daughter Agnes, wife of John Holcombe, and his grandson John Seymour.[84] It was allotted to Agnes and John Holcombe, who together held it in 1429.[85] The manor was afterwards owned by William Ringbourne (d. 1450), his relict Elizabeth, his son Robert[86] (d. 1485), Robert's relict Elizabeth (d. 1504), and Robert's brother William[87] (d. 1512). William was succeeded by his grandson Thomas Bruyn.[88] The manor was afterwards acquired, perhaps by inheritance, by John Seymour's great-great-grandson Edward Seymour, earl of Hertford, who in 1545 gave it to the bishop of Salisbury in an exchange.[89] The bishop owned the manor, c. 1,000 a., until it passed to the Ecclesiastical Commissioners in 1869.[90] Copyhold land was enfranchised in 1846 for the tenant Edward Dyke Poore (d. 1859) and descended to his son Edward Dyke Poore (d. 1874), whose daughters Frances, wife of the Revd. Henry Baker, and Alice Dyke Poore in 1879 sold 340 a. to Sir Michael Hicks Beach, Bt. Also in 1879 the Ecclesiastical Commissioners sold 394 a. to Hicks Beach,[91] who sold 489 a. to T. W. Hussey in 1897 and 247 a. to the War Department in 1898.[92] Hussey also owned 224 a., presumably former copyhold land, settled on his wife Mary (d. 1885) in 1871, and in 1898 sold c. 713 a. to the War Department.[93] The Ministry of Defence owned all the land in 1991.[94]

Part of the Figheldean estate held in 1066 by Harding was afterwards held by Aubrey de Couci and had been forfeited to the king by 1086.[95] It may have been the estate, later called *READ'S* farm, held in 1535 by Wilton abbey.[96] At the Dissolution the abbey's land in Figheldean passed to the Crown, and in 1544

[66] *Tax List, 1332* (W.R.S. xlv), 110; *V.C.H. Wilts.* iv. 297, 306.
[67] *Andrews and Dury, Map* (W.R.S. viii), pl. 8.
[68] P.R.O., HO 107/1165/8.
[69] Ibid. IR 30/38/116; O.S. Maps 6", Wilts. LIV (1887 and later edns.).
[70] Ashworth, *Action Stations*, v. 117–18; O.S. Map 1/10,000, SU 14 NW. (1976 edn.).
[71] *Tax List, 1332* (W.R.S. xlv), 110–11; *V.C.H. Wilts.* iv. 297, 306.
[72] *Andrews and Dury, Map* (W.R.S. viii), pl. 9; below, manors (Syrencot). [73] *V.C.H. Wilts.* ii, p. 163.
[74] W. Farrer, *Honors and Knights' Fees*, iii. 85; below, this section (Knighton).
[75] *Red Bk. Exch.* (Rolls Ser.), ii. 482; *Cal. Inq. p.m.* i, p. 287; *Pipe R. 1218* (P.R.S. N.S. xxxix), 10.
[76] *V.C.H. Wilts.* viii. 15; *Cal. Pat.* 1258–66, 290; *Suss. Arch. Colln.* viii. 47; B.L. Cott. MS. Vesp. E. xxiii, f. 75; D. & C. Sar. Mun., press IV, E 2/Knighton/5.
[77] *W.A.M.* xii. 7; li. 295; *Cal. Inq. p.m.* ii, pp. 339–40.
[78] *Cal. Inq. p.m.* vi, p. 167.
[79] *Feet of F.* 1272–1327 (W.R.S. i), p. 109; *Cal. Pat.*
1324–7, 161; *Cal. Close*, 1330–3, 92–3; *Wilts. Inq. p.m.* 1327–77 (Index Libr.), 16–17. [80] *Cal. Inq. p.m.* viii, p. 101.
[81] *Cal. Pat.* 1334–8, 310.
[82] *Cal. Chart. R.* 1341–1417, 164.
[83] *Cal. Inq. p.m.* xv, p. 202.
[84] P.R.O., C 139/28, no. 22, rot. 6.
[85] *Feet of F. 1377–1509* (W.R.S. xli), p. 95.
[86] P.R.O., C 139/138, no. 18.
[87] *Cal. Inq. p.m. Hen. VII*, ii, p. 508; iii, p. 359.
[88] P.R.O., C 142/27, no. 68.
[89] *L. & P. Hen. VIII*, xx (2), p. 411.
[90] P.R.O., IR 29/38/116; IR 30/38/116; G.P.L., Treas. Solicitor, 514/51, abstr. of title.
[91] Williamstrip Mun., MTC/37/13; G.P.L., Treas. Solicitor, 514/51, abstr. of title; mon. in church.
[92] Williamstrip Mun., MTD/23/6; G.P.L., Treas. Solicitor, 514/51, abstr. of title.
[93] *Salisbury Plain (Property Purchased)* [C. 9032], p. 3, H.C. (1898), liv; G.P.L., Treas. Solicitor, 514/51, abstr. of title.
[94] Inf. from Defence Land Agent, Durrington.
[95] *V.C.H. Wilts.* ii, pp. 46, 98–9, 163.
[96] *Valor Eccl.* (Rec. Com.), ii. 111.

was granted to Sir William Herbert (cr. earl of Pembroke 1551) and his wife Anne.[97] It descended with the Pembroke title to George, earl of Pembroke and of Montgomery, who in 1877 sold the 359-a. farm to T. E. Simpkins.[98] It passed with Simpkins's land in Ablington,[99] and the Ministry of Defence owned it in 1991.[1]

Ablington, held after 1066 by Aubrey de Couci, had been forfeited to the king by 1086.[2] Like Figheldean manor it was held in the later 12th century by Henry Hussey and by his son Geoffrey.[3] Geoffrey's son Geoffrey (d. c. 1218) apparently subinfeudated *ABLINGTON* manor to Geoffrey of Fundenhall. Henry Hussey, the younger Geoffrey's successor, subinfeudated it to Reynold of Whitchurch, to whom Geoffrey of Fundenhall ceded it in 1226[4] and it was confirmed in 1227.[5]

Ablington manor was later held in demesne by Bevis de Veel, whose son (Sir) Peter (d. c. 1343) held it in 1312. It was held by Sir Peter's relict Catherine[6] (d. 1386), who married Thomas Berkeley, Lord Berkeley, and passed to his grandson Sir John le Moyne[7] (d. 1429), whose daughter and heir Elizabeth married William Stourton (d. 1413).[8] From the Stourtons' son John, Lord Stourton (d. 1462), the manor passed with the barony to William Stourton[9] (d. 1478) and John Stourton[10] (d. 1485). It was held for life by John's relict Catherine (d. 1494), wife of Sir John Brereton, and passed to her brother-in-law William Stourton, Lord Stourton[11] (d. 1524). It descended to William's brother Edward, Lord Stourton (d. 1535), and to Edward's son William, Lord Stourton, who sold it to Thomas Long in 1544.[12] The manor passed from Long (d. 1562) and his relict Joan (d. 1583) to his nephew Edward Long[13] (d. 1622), and in the direct line to Gifford[14] (d. 1635), Edward[15] (d. 1644), and Henry Long (d. s.p. 1672).[16] Henry devised the manor to his nephew Richard Long (d. 1730), and it again descended in the direct line to Richard (d. 1760), Richard (d. 1787),[17] and Richard (d. 1835), who sold it in 1799 to William Dyke.[18] Dyke (d. 1818) was succeeded by his son Edward Dyke Poore (d. 1859), who in 1839 had c. 950 a. called Great Ablington.

The manor passed, with part of Figheldean manor, to Edward Dyke Poore (d. 1874)[19] and to Frances Baker and Alice Dyke Poore.[20] It was afterwards bought by George Knowles, who sold it to the War Department in 1898, and it belonged to the Ministry of Defence in 1991.[21]

Ablington Farm was built as a long east–west range with rendered walls and a thatched roof in the 17th or 18th century. A matching gabled extension was built on the west in the early 19th century and extended north in brick after c. 1890.

Geoffrey Hussey, probably he who died c. 1218, gave land in Ablington that became *ABBOT'S* farm to Durford abbey in Rogate (Suss.).[22] The abbey was granted free warren in its demesnes in 1252[23] and held the land until the Dissolution.[24] The estate was granted in 1537 to Sir William FitzWilliam (cr. earl of Southampton 1537, d. s.p. legit. 1542),[25] reverted to the Crown, and in 1546 was sold through agents to Richard Cowper (d. 1558).[26] It passed to John Cowper (d. 1561), his relict Margaret (d. 1599), and their son Thomas, a lunatic. John Cowper administered the estate for his cousin Thomas (fl. 1618) from c. 1603[27] and he was presumably the John Cowper who divided and sold it. Thomas Sheppard (d. 1665) bought part of it from Cowper in 1631. Another part was bought after 1623 by Geoffrey Bigge and in 1657 was sold to Sheppard by Joseph Bates, the husband of Bigge's daughter Anne. Sheppard's son Thomas was succeeded by his son William.[28] That William Sheppard or a namesake may have owned the farm in 1736.[29] By will dated 1771 it was given by, presumably another, William Sheppard to his four sisters, all of whom died unmarried. From the last sister, Anne, the farm passed to her brother Thomas, who by will proved 1806 gave it to his son Thomas Somerby *alias* Sheppard. In 1833 Thomas conveyed it to a trustee, who in 1837 sold it to Edwin Simpkins. The farm, 74 a. with c. 40 per cent of the rights to use a down of 279 a., was sold by Simpkins to T. E. Simpkins in 1842.[30] It became part of Simpkins's Ablington House estate.[31]

An **L**-shaped house, timber-framed with brick noggings, thatched, and jettied on all sides at first-floor level, was apparently built for Thomas

97 L. & P. Hen. VIII, xix (1), p. 38; for the Herbert fam., Complete Peerage, x. 405–29.
98 P.R.O., IR 29/38/116, and altered apportionment, 1856; IR 30/38/116; W.R.O., EA/162; ibid. 2057/A 1/97–8; W.A.S. Libr., sale cat. iii, no. 34.
99 Below, this section (Ablington).
1 Inf. from Defence Land Agent.
2 V.C.H. Wilts. ii, pp. 98–9, 134.
3 Cal. Chart. R. 1226–57, 394; Farrer, Honors and Knights' Fees, iii. 85.
4 Cur. Reg. R. xi, p. 537; P.R.O., CP 25/1/250/4, no. 33.   5 Cal. Chart. R. 1226–57, 58.
6 Year Bk. 6 Edw. II (Selden Soc. xxxiv), 32; Cal. Inq. p.m. viii, pp. 311–12; Cal. Close, 1343–6, 34.
7 Cal. Inq. p.m. xvi, pp. 81–2; Cal. Close, 1381–5, 442; 1385–9, 62.
8 P.R.O., C 139/43, no. 16; for the Stourton fam., Complete Peerage, xii (1), 300–6.
9 P.R.O., C 140/8, no. 18, rot. 17.
10 Ibid. C 140/63, no. 55, rot. 12.
11 Cal. Inq. p.m. Hen. VII, i, pp. 60–1, 478–9.
12 P.R.O., CP 25/2/46/323, no. 54.
13 V.C.H. Wilts. viii. 150; x. 48; Cal. Pat. 1560–3, 599–600.
14 P.R.O., C 142/393, no. 139; for the Long fam., Burke, Commoners, iv. 64–5, 67–9.

15 Wilts. Inq. p.m. 1625–49 (Index Libr.), 207–10, where Gifford is said to have d. 1634.
16 P.R.O., C 5/411/61, where Hen. is said to have d. 1645; ibid. CP 43/305, rot. 45.
17 Ibid. CP 43/513, Carte rott. 1–3d.; Glos. R.O., D 2440, box 36, abstr. of title to Alton Magna.
18 Long Estates Act, 39 Geo. III, c. 92 (Private and Personal, not printed).
19 P.R.O., IR 29/38/116; IR 30/38/116; Poore Estate Act, 11 Geo. IV, c. 29 (Private, not printed); mons. in church.
20 W.A.S. Libr., sale cat. iii, no. 34; above, this section (Figheldean).   21 Inf. from Defence Land Agent.
22 B.L. Cott. MS. Vesp. E. xxiii, f. 75; P.R.O., SC 6/Hen. VIII/3674, rott. 20d.–21.   23 Cal. Chart. R. 1226–57, 391.
24 Valor Eccl. (Rec. Com.), vi, p. xiii.
25 L. & P. Hen. VIII, xii (2), p. 352; Complete Peerage, xii (1), 118–21.
26 L. & P. Hen. VIII, xxi (1), pp. 243, 489; P.R.O., C 142/124, no. 202; ibid. E 318/19/938, rott. 3–5.
27 P.R.O., C 2/Jas. I/C 25/46; C 142/314, no. 155.
28 Ibid. C 3/395/109; W.R.O. 130/49A, settlements, 1638, 1668; ibid. bishop's transcripts, bdle. 1.
29 Q. Sess. 1736 (W.R.S. xi), p. 131.
30 P.R.O., IR 29/38/116; IR 30/38/116; G.P.L., Treas. Solicitor, 2374/50.   31 Below, this section.

Sheppard. The west lobby entrance with the date 1631 above it is set against the central chimney stack in the north–south range. The south ground-floor parlour retains some original panelling.

Other land in Ablington was granted before 1223, possibly also by Geoffrey Hussey (d. c. 1218), to St. Denis's priory, Southampton,[32] which held it until the Dissolution.[33] In 1539 the Crown granted the estate, possibly later *COW-PER'S*, to Charles Brandon, duke of Suffolk. He sold it to Edward Seymour, earl of Hertford (cr. duke of Somerset 1547, d. 1552), on whose execution and attainder it reverted to the Crown.[34] It was sold in 1560 to agents.[35] Margaret Cowper (d. 1599) may have owned the estate c. 1563, and Thomas Cowper (d. 1626), not her son, owned it in 1614. Cowper then settled a moiety on his son Edmund, who inherited the rest in 1626.[36] The farm descended to Thomas Cowper (d. 1728), who settled it for life on himself and his wife Sarah. His son Thomas (d. 1756) devised it for life to his wife Anne, who married John Neate, and in trust for sale after her death. The trustees sold it in 1783 to Edward Poore (d. 1787), evidently for his niece Mary Anne Poore, from 1789 wife of William Cox and from c. 1807 wife of the Revd. William Edwards.[37] She owned the farm, 95 a. with c. 50 per cent of the rights to use the 279-a. down, in 1839.[38] Her children, William Cox and Mary Anne, wife of F. J. Chapman, sold it in 1843 to T. E. Simpkins and it became part of the Ablington House estate.[39]

T. E. Simpkins (d. 1878) devised his estate, including Ablington House, c. 450 a. in Ablington, and Read's farm, in trust for sale. In 1883 the trustees transferred it to the beneficiaries, his sons T. H. Simpkins and Ernest Simpkins. Alfred Rawlins bought the estate c. 1890[40] and sold it to the War Department in 1897. The Ministry of Defence owned it in 1991.[41] Ablington House, built in the early 19th century, was a two-storeyed L-shaped house of brick with a hipped slated roof. Its north-west entrance front had five bays, the central one of which projected, was surmounted by a pediment, and had a stone porch.[42] The house was demolished in 1963.[43]

Godric and Bollo held a 5-hide estate at Alton in 1066. It was held in 1086 by John the doorkeeper, of whom Turstin and Frawin each held 1 hide.[44]

In 1179 *ALTON PARVA* manor was confirmed to Amesbury priory. The priory was granted free warren in its demesne in 1286[45] and held the manor until the Dissolution.[46] The manor was granted in 1541 to the dean and chapter of Winchester,[47] which in 1839 owned Alton Parva farm, 503 a.[48] In 1867 the dean and chapter sold the farm to the Ecclesiastical Commissioners,[49] who in 1875 allotted it to the dean and chapter of Salisbury, in 1896 received it back in exchange for other land, and in 1899 sold it to the War Department. The Ministry of Defence owned the land in 1991.[50]

The knight's fee that became *ALTON MAGNA* manor was held in 1242–3 by Simon de Montfort, earl of Leicester (d. 1265).[51] The overlordship of the manor descended with the honor of Leicester to Henry, earl of Lancaster (cr. duke of Lancaster 1351, d. 1361). It was allotted in 1362 to Henry's elder daughter Maud (d. *s.p.* 1362), wife of William, duke of Bavaria, and passed to her sister Blanche (d. 1369), wife of John of Gaunt (cr. duke of Lancaster 1362, d. 1399). When Blanche's son Henry, earl of Derby, became Henry IV in 1399 the honor of Leicester passed to the Crown.[52] The overlordship was still part of the honor in 1428,[53] but, apparently, was held in 1462 by Richard Nevill, earl of Warwick and of Salisbury,[54] and descended with the earldom of Salisbury; it was last mentioned in 1494.[55]

The lordship in demesne was held in 1242–3 by Robert of Layham,[56] in 1298 by John Barratt,[57] and in 1306 by Sir Richard Brompton. In 1307 Sir Richard's son Thomas sold it to Sir Robert Reydon,[58] who was granted free warren in the demesne in 1310.[59] Reydon sold the manor to John Goodhind in 1320.[60] Richard Woodford held it in 1330,[61] apparently William FitzWarin in 1332,[62] and Sir Adam Shareshill and his wife Alice in 1340. In 1342 the Shareshills settled Alton Magna on Sir Peter de Veel and his wife Catherine.[63] Thereafter the manor descended with Ablington manor until 1799,[64] when Richard Long sold it to Michael Hicks Beach[65] (d.

32 *Pat. R.* 1216–25, 480.
33 P.R.O., SC 6/Hen. VIII/3326, rot. 6.
34 *L. & P. Hen. VIII*, xiv (1), pp. 258, 468; *Complete Peerage*, xii (1), 59–64.
35 *Cal. Pat.* 1558–60, 315.
36 *Wilts. Inq. p.m.* 1625–49 (Index Libr.), 47–8; P.R.O., C 3/119/63; above, this section (Abbot's).
37 G.P.L., Treas. Solicitor, 2374/50; W.R.O. 1756/1–2; 1756/9.
38 P.R.O., IR 29/38/116; IR 30/38/116.
39 W.R.O., EA/162; G.P.L., Treas. Solicitor, 2374/50; below, this section.
40 *Kelly's Dir. Wilts.* (1889, 1895); W.A.S. Libr., sale cat. iii, no. 34; G.P.L., Treas. Solicitor, 2374/50; above, this section (Read's).
41 Inf. from Defence Land Agent.
42 Min. of Housing and Local Govt., provisional list of bldgs. of hist. interest (1955).
43 N. D. G. James, *Plain Soldiering*, 26.
44 *V.C.H. Wilts.* ii, p. 166.
45 *Cal. Chart. R.* 1257–1300, 157–9, 336.
46 *Valor Eccl.* (Rec. Com.), ii. 94.
47 *Cal. Pat.* 1575–8, p. 212.
48 P.R.O., IR 29/38/116, where the manor was said,

wrongly, to belong to Winchester Coll.; IR 30/38/116.
49 Ch. Com. file 29312.
50 Ibid. 27973; *Lond. Gaz.* 14 May 1875, pp. 2582–9; inf. from Defence Land Agent.
51 *Bk. of Fees*, ii. 746; *Complete Peerage*, vii. 546.
52 *Wilts. Inq. p.m.* 1242–1326 (Index Libr.), 218–19; *Feud. Aids*, vi. 574; *Complete Peerage*, vii. 378–410, 536–48.
53 *Feud. Aids*, v. 240.
54 P.R.O., C 140/8, no. 18, rot. 17.
55 *Cal. Inq. p.m. Hen. VII*, i, pp. 60–1, 478–9.
56 *Bk. of Fees*, ii. 746.
57 *Wilts. Inq. p.m.* 1242–1326 (Index Libr.), 218–19.
58 *Feet of F.* 1272–1327 (W.R.S. i), p. 57; P.R.O., C 146/8174.
59 *Cal. Chart. R.* 1300–26, 167.
60 *Feet of F.* 1272–1327 (W.R.S. i), pp. 104–5.
61 *Feud. Aids*, vi. 574.
62 Phillipps, *Wilts. Inst.* i. 28.
63 *Feet of F.* 1327–77 (W.R.S. xxix), pp. 61, 70.
64 Above, this section (Ablington); remainder of para. based on Glos. R.O., D 2440, box 36, abstr. of title to Alton Magna.
65 Hoare, *Mod. Wilts.* Amesbury, 75–6; for the Hicks Beach fam., Burke, *Peerage* (1963), 2134–5.

1830) as a trustee for his father-in-law William Beach (d. 1790).[66] On the death of Michael's relict Henrietta Maria in 1837 the manor, 627 a. in 1839,[67] descended to their son William (d. 1856), from 1838 called William Beach. William's son William Beach sold Alton Magna farm in 1861 to his cousin Sir Michael Hicks Beach, Bt.,[68] who sold it to the War Department in 1898.[69] The Ministry of Defence owned the land in 1991.[70]

Amesbury abbey held *CHOULSTON* manor in 1086 when Alward was tenant.[71] The manor was confirmed in 1179 to Amesbury priory, which in 1286 was granted free warren in the demesne.[72] The priory held Choulston until the Dissolution[73] when it passed to the Crown. The manor was apparently granted to Edward Seymour, duke of Somerset, and forfeited on his execution and attainder in 1552. The Crown sold it in 1557 to agents,[74] who immediately sold it to Ellis Fowler.[75] From Edmund Saunders *alias* Mills (d. 1596), possibly the owner in 1571, the manor descended in the direct line to Thomas Saunders *alias* Mills[76] (d. c. 1619), Edmund Saunders *alias* Mills, and Henry Saunders *alias* Mills, the owner in 1655. Edward Saunders *alias* Mills owned it in 1657. In 1659 the manor belonged to (Sir) Samuel Eyre[77] (d. 1698) and it descended in the direct line to Sir Robert (d. 1735) and Robert (d. 1752).[78] The younger Robert presumably sold it with Netheravon Lambert manor in Netheravon in 1750 to Charles Somerset, duke of Beaufort (d. 1756), and it passed with Cormayles manor in Netheravon to Charles's son Henry, duke of Beaufort, whose lands there were in 1773 settled upon trust for sale. William Beach (d. 1790) had bought Choulston manor by 1781, and it passed to his daughter Henrietta Maria, wife of Michael Hicks, from 1790 Michael Hicks Beach.[79] As Choulston farm, 378 a. in 1839, it passed in 1837 on Henrietta Maria's death to her grandson Sir Michael Hicks Beach, Bt.[80] (d. 1854), and in 1854 to Sir Michael's son Sir Michael Hicks Beach, Bt., who sold it with Alton Magna farm to the War Department in 1898.[81] The Ministry of Defence owned it in 1991.[82]

Harding held Knighton in 1066 and 1086;[83]

Henry Hussey held it in the later 12th century. The overlordship descended like the capital manor of Harting (Suss.), and possibly with the overlordship of Figheldean manor, from father to son from Henry Hussey (d. c. 1213) to Henry (d. by 1235), Sir Matthew (d. 1253), Sir Henry (d. 1290), and Henry, Lord Hussey (d. 1332). It was last mentioned in 1319.[84]

From Henry Hussey *KNIGHTON* manor passed with Figheldean manor to Geoffrey Hussey (fl. 1198), Geoffrey Hussey (d. c. 1218), and Henry Hussey (d. 1260 × 1263).[85] The second Henry apparently granted it to William Hussey whose title was challenged in 1239 by Maud Hussey, granddaughter of Henry Hussey (d. by 1235).[86] William held the manor in 1242–3[87] but Maud's claim was allowed in 1269 when Henry Hussey, the chief lord, conveyed to her and her husband William Paynel two thirds of it and the reversion of the third held in dower by William's relict Gillian.[88] In 1275 Maud and William conveyed the manor to another William Paynel[89] (d. 1317), who was succeeded by his brother John (d. 1319). John's daughter and heir Maud, wife of Nicholas of Upton,[90] afterwards married Edmund FitzAlan, earl of Arundel[91] (d. 1326), on whose execution and attainder Knighton was forfeited.[92] The manor was restored in 1343 to Edmund's son Richard, earl of Arundel (d. 1376),[93] on the execution and attainder of whose son Richard, earl of Arundel, in 1397 it was granted to Sir Henry Green.[94] In 1400 it was restored to Richard's son Thomas, earl of Arundel (d. s.p. 1415). From Thomas's heir, his cousin John d'Arundel, earl of Arundel[95] (d. 1421), it descended in the direct line with the Arundel title to John d'Arundel[96] (d. 1435) and to Humphrey FitzAlan (d. s.p. 1438). From Humphrey, Knighton manor passed to his uncle William FitzAlan, earl of Arundel[97] (d. 1487), and again descended in the direct line with the title to Thomas (d. 1524), William (d. 1544), and Henry, who in 1560 gave it to Elizabeth I in an exchange.[98]

Knighton farm, which may have represented the whole manor, was sold by Bartholomew Tookey to Samuel Linch in 1633.[99] In 1650 Linch sold it to Andrew Duke,[1] who sold it in 1659 to his brother John (d. 1671). John's relict Avice and son George sold the farm in 1675 to

66 *V.C.H. Wilts.* viii. 252.
67 P.R.O., IR 29/38/116; IR 30/38/116.
68 Glos. R.O., D 2440, box 36, agreement, 1861.
69 Williamstrip Mun., MTD/23/6.
70 Inf. from Defence Land Agent.
71 *V.C.H. Wilts.* ii, p. 131.
72 *Cal. Chart. R.* 1257–1300, 157–9, 336; for the hist. of the abbey and priory, *V.C.H. Wilts.* iii. 242–59.
73 *Valor Eccl.* (Rec. Com.), ii. 94.
74 *Cal. Pat.* 1557–8, 134–6; B.L. Harl. MS. 607, f. 43 and v.
75 Williamstrip Mun., MTD/84/1.
76 P.R.O., C 142/251, no. 136; ibid. E 179/198/284.
77 Williamstrip Mun., MTD/84/7–9; MTD/84/12; MTD/84/15A–B; MTD/84/17.
78 For the Eyre fam., Burke, *Commoners* (1833–8), iii. 291–2.
79 *V.C.H. Wilts.* xi. 169–71; W.R.O., A 1/345/177; Burke, *Peerage* (1963), 2134–5.
80 P.R.O., IR 29/38/116; IR 30/38/116.
81 Williamstrip Mun., MTD/23/6.
82 Inf. from Defence Land Agent.
83 *V.C.H. Wilts.* ii, p. 163.
84 *Cal. Chart. R.* 1226–57, 394; Farrer, *Honors and Knights' Fees*, iii. 83–6; *V.C.H. Suss.* iv. 14; *Bk. of Fees*, ii. 746; *Cal. Inq. p.m.* vi, pp. 110–12.
85 *Cal. Chart. R.* 1226–57, 394; P.R.O., CP 25/1/250/5, no. 31; above, this section (Figheldean).
86 *V.C.H. Suss.* iv. 14; *Sel. Cases in K.B.* ii (Selden Soc. lvii), pp. clvi–clvii.
87 *Bk. of Fees*, ii. 746.
88 P.R.O., CP 25/1/283/17, no. 448.
89 *Feet of F. 1272–1327* (W.R.S. i), p. 3.
90 *Cal. Inq. p.m.* vi, pp. 18, 110–12.
91 *Rot. Parl.* ii. 378–9; for the earls of Arundel, *Complete Peerage*, i. 241–52.   92 *Cal. Close*, 1343–6, 240.
93 *Cal. Pat.* 1343–5, 488; P.R.O., C 44/1, no. 14, f. 2.
94 *Cal. Pat.* 1396–9, 198, 221.
95 P.R.O., C 138/23, no. 54, rot. 31.
96 Ibid. C 138/59, no. 51, rot. 18.
97 Ibid. C 139/98, no. 28, rot. 10.
98 Hist. MSS. Com. 9, *Salisbury*, i, p. 256.
99 W.R.O. 212B/2834.
1 Ibid. 212B/2841.

Philip Poore[2] (d. 1693). Philip's relict Elizabeth in 1696 settled it on her son Philip Poore (d. 1719) and his wife Mary.[3] The farm later passed with Alton Rectory estate and a lease of the East End manor of Durrington, and was devised by Edward Poore (d. 1780) to his daughters Eleanora (d. s.p. 1812), wife of David Michel, and Charlotte (will proved 1829). Charlotte devised the farm, which was increased by exchange from c. 205 a. to c. 402 a. at inclosure in 1823, to Sir Edward Poore, Bt. (d. 1838).[4] It passed with the Poore baronetcy to Sir Edward's son Sir Edward (d. 1893) and that Sir Edward's son Sir Richard, who in 1898 sold it to the War Department.[5] The Ministry of Defence owned the land in 1991.[6]

Land at *KNIGHTON* was apparently subinfeudated in the 12th century by a member of the Hussey family. The mesne lordship descended with Figheldean manor to Sir Hubert Hussey and was last referred to in the later 13th century.[7]

Nicholas of Maund, probably in the 12th century, gave ½ knight's fee in Knighton to his daughter Eve and her husband William Percy.[8] The manor was later given to Bernard of Areines and his wife Isabel, possibly a Percy. Isabel's and Bernard's son Sir Guy of Areines, who held it in 1242–3, subinfeudated it to his son Jocelin.[9] It was afterwards acquired, apparently from Sir Guy, by John Burton, subdean of Salisbury cathedral, who conveyed it to the dean and chapter between c. 1260 and 1271.[10] It may have formed an endowment of a fund for the poor called Our Lady's Chamber.[11] Later it was treated as part of the East End manor of Durrington. The dean and chapter's estate in Knighton was reduced by exchange from c. 239 a. to 44 a. at inclosure in 1823.[12] The War Department bought it from the Ecclesiastical Commissioners in 1899 and the Ministry of Defence owned the land in 1991.[13]

SYRENCOT manor, like Figheldean manor, was held by Geoffrey Hussey (d. c. 1218) and Henry Hussey (d. 1260 × 1263).[14] Another Geoffrey Hussey held it of Henry in 1242–3.[15] It was held 1293 × c. 1306 by Reynold Hussey, who granted it for life to William of Kelsale. From Reynold the reversion may have passed with part of Teffont Evias manor, and Syrencot manor was held by Edmund Hussey (d. c. 1362),

by his relict Joan, and by their daughter Maud, who married Sir Philip de la Mere (fl. 1390).[16] Sir Ellis de la Mere (d. s.p. 1414 × 1428) held the manor in 1412. It passed with Fisherton de la Mere manor to his nephew Sir John Paulet (fl. 1460), to Sir John's son John (d. 1492), and to John's son Sir John (d. 1525).[17] It was possibly owned by William Skilling (d. 1608), whose nephew and heir Edward Skilling sold it in 1639 to Thomas Dyke (d. 1651).[18] The manor descended to Daniel Dyke (fl. 1700–31) and to William Dyke (will proved 1776), whose nephew and namesake was possibly the William Dyke (d. 1818) who owned it in 1781.[19] The manor, c. 300 a., passed like Ablington manor to Edward Dyke Poore[20] (d. 1859), Edward Dyke Poore (d. 1874), and Frances Baker and Alice Dyke Poore. In 1897 the 335-a. estate was sold to George Knowles, the tenant, and by him to the War Department in 1898. The Ministry of Defence owned it in 1991.[21]

The entrance hall and a room north of it, which in 1991 together formed the central portion of the east front of Syrencot House, are on the plan of a small 17th-century house. The house was enlarged to the south for William Dyke in 1738 when a three-storeyed brick block with stone quoins and a five-bayed east front was built.[22] In the early 19th century the east front of the 17th-century part of the house was altered and a wide Tuscan portico built. In the mid 19th century the 17th-century range was extended northwards and on its west side at the north end a three-storeyed service block was built. A single-storeyed billiards room was built c. 1898 west of the 18th-century block.[23] A park was created east of the house between 1773 and 1817.[24]

In the early 12th century and from 1157 Figheldean church belonged to the dean and chapter of Salisbury, and *FIGHELDEAN RECTORY* estate was appropriated to the treasurer of the cathedral, apparently before 1180–5.[25] The estate consisted of the great tithes of the whole parish except Alton, of other tithes, and of land. In 1839, when the treasurer held 49 a., the tithes were valued at £671 and commuted.[26] The estate passed to the Ecclesiastical Commissioners in 1841[27] and afterwards was merged with their other land in the parish.[28]

---

[2] Ibid. 212B/2844–5; *W.N. & Q.* viii. 197, 199–200; for the Poore fam., Burke, *Peerage* (1963), 1961–2.

[3] W.R.O. 212B/2850; 1885/4.

[4] Ibid. A 1/345/177; ibid. EA/144; Glos. R.O., D 2440, box 36, abstr. of title to Alton rectory; above, Durrington, manors (E. End); below, this section (Alton Rectory).

[5] *W.A.M.* xxxix. 297; *Salisbury Plain (Property Purchased)*, p. 3.   [6] Inf. from Defence Land Agent.

[7] *Bk. of Fees*, ii. 746; D. & C. Sar. Mun., press IV, E 2/Knighton/5.

[8] D. & C. Sar. Mun., press IV, E 2/Knighton/11.

[9] Ibid. press IV, E 2/Knighton/2; *Bk. of Fees*, ii. 746.

[10] *V.C.H. Wilts.* iii. 208; W. H. Jones, *Fasti Eccl. Sar.* ii. 439; D. & C. Sar. Mun., press IV, E 2/Knighton/4; press IV, E 2/Knighton/12.   [11] *V.C.H. Wilts.* iii. 168.

[12] W.R.O., EA/144.

[13] Inf. from Defence Land Agent.

[14] *Cur. Reg. R.* xii, p. 259; P.R.O., CP 25/1/250/5, no. 31; above, this section (Figheldean).

[15] *Bk. of Fees*, ii. 746.

[16] *V.C.H. Wilts.* xiii. 188; W.R.O. 490/1470, ff. 204,

209v.–211, 216.

[17] *Feud. Aids*, vi. 532; *Cal. Close*, 1454–61, 65; *V.C.H. Wilts.* viii. 38; P.R.O., SC 12/22/5.

[18] *V.C.H. Wilts.* x. 195; P.R.O., CP 25/2/511/15 Chas. I Mich.; ibid. PROB 11/218, f. 120.

[19] P.R.O., PROB 11/1018, ff. 229v.–231; W.R.O. 367/2, deeds, Naish to Dyke, 1730; Dyke to Naish, 1731; ibid. A 1/345/177; mon. in church.

[20] P.R.O., IR 29/38/116; IR 30/38/116; above, this section (Ablington).

[21] *Kelly's Dir. Wilts.* (1895); Wilts. Cuttings, xii. 206–7; inf. from Defence Land Agent.

[22] Date and initials on S. elevation.

[23] Wilts. Cuttings, xii. 206–7.

[24] *Andrews and Dury, Map* (W.R.S. viii), pl. 9; O.S. Map 1", sheet 14 (1817 edn.).   [25] Below, churches.

[26] *W.A.M.* xl. 266–8; *Inq. Non.* (Rec. Com.), 172; W.R.O. 413/450, no. 62; P.R.O., IR 29/38/116.

[27] Le Neve, *Fasti, 1541–1857, Salisbury*, 13; Cathedrals Act, 3 & 4 Vic. c. 113.

[28] Above, this section (Figheldean; Alton Parva).

The great tithes of Alton Parva and Alton Magna belonged at the Dissolution to Alton church which, as a free chapel, was appropriated by the Crown.[29] In 1607 the Crown conveyed those tithes, *ALTON RECTORY* estate, to agents,[30] who before 1616 sold them to the lessee Thomas Hanbury (d. 1618). Hanbury's son Thomas sold them in 1642 to John Rumball. John Duke, who bought them from Rumball in 1647,[31] settled them in 1662 on his son John Duke (d. 1671), whose son George sold them to Edward Poore in 1697.[32] Poore settled them on his son Edward (d. by 1726), and they passed to that Edward's wife Eleanor (d. by 1731) and son Edward (d. 1780). They passed with Knighton farm to Eleanora Michel and Charlotte Poore and to Sir Edward Poore, Bt. (d. 1838).[33] The tithes of Alton Magna were sold in 1831 to William Hicks Beach (William Beach from 1838), the owner in 1839 when they were valued at £88 and commuted. Those of Alton Parva descended to Sir Edward's son Sir Edward Poore, Bt. (d. 1893), and in 1839 were valued at £114 and commuted.[34]

In 1179 the Crown confirmed the tithes from the demesne and half the customary land of Alton Parva, which had presumably been part of the endowment of Alton church, and all the tithes of Choulston to Amesbury priory, lord of those two manors.[35] The priory held tithes valued at £4 6s. 8d. in 1291,[36] possibly all those confirmed in 1179, but by 1535 received only a pension of 6s. 8d. from the rector of Alton for the Alton Parva tithes.[37] That pension, payable to the owner of Alton Parva manor by the owner of Alton Parva tithes, was still recorded in the 19th century.[38] The tithes of Choulston were part of the Figheldean Rectory estate by 1839.[39]

ECONOMIC HISTORY. Each of the six settlements in the parish had its own long and narrow strip of land; the division in Saxon times possibly corresponded closely to that in the 19th century, when Figheldean had *c.* 1,400 a., Ablington *c.* 1,400 a., Alton *c.* 1,150 a., Choulston *c.* 380 a., Knighton *c.* 650 a., and Syrencot *c.* 300 a.[40] There was sheep-and-corn husbandry in all six areas, and generally it seems to have been on a three-field system.

FIGHELDEAN. In 1086 Figheldean had land for 5 ploughteams: on the demesne were 6 *servi* with 1 team, and 7 *villani* and 8 bordars had 4 teams. There were 24 a. of meadow, and the pasture measured 12 by 3 furlongs.[41]

Common husbandry continued until 1844.[42] In the 16th century there was a common meadow called North mead, open arable in North field, Foxlinch bottom, and the field next to Ablington, and extensive common pasture for sheep.[43] Later the fields were called Upper, Middle, and Lower, and there was a second common meadow called Newton. In 1839 the tenants of Figheldean manor had three areas of downland for use in common, East down and West down for sheep, and a cow down, a total of 505 a. The use of a further 206 a. of downland was shared between the demesne and the freehold later called Read's farm.[44]

One of the thirds of Figheldean manor in 1296 included 51 a. of demesne arable with common pasture for 4 oxen and 80 sheep; it had two customary tenants holding a total of 2 yardlands, and two cottars.[45] The reunited demesne had been leased by 1428.[46] Of the 12 customary tenants in 1504, 1 held 2½ yardlands, 2 held 2 yardlands each, 2 held ½ yardland each, 4 held 1 yardland each, and 3 cottagers held a few acres. Each yardland was of *c.* 30 a. and the tenants held 409 a. of arable and 16 a. of meadow.[47] The demesne, worked in the early 16th century by members of the Cowper family, included 89 a. of arable and 8 a. of inclosed meadows in the 1540s,[48] and in the 1560s what became Read's farm had 150 a. of arable, 7 a. of meadow, and pasture rights for 400 sheep, 7 cattle, and 7 horses.[49]

In 1769 the 17 copyholds of Figheldean manor had a total of 409 a., including meadow: none exceeded 50 a., each had a small amount of meadow beside the Avon, and each had a farmstead in the village. The demesne was then 236 a., and other farms, principally Read's, had a total of 262 a.[50] In the late 18th century and early 19th the number of farms decreased and in 1839 there was a composite farm of *c.* 680 a. with nearly all the rights to use the downland. The arable, *c.* 635 a. in *c.* 600 strips, *c.* 25 a. of meadow, and the 711 a. of commonable downland[51] were divided, allotted, and inclosed in 1844 by Act.[52]

ABLINGTON. In 1086 Ablington's land was mainly demesne, 2½ hides on which were 4 coscets and 1 team. The remaining ½ hide there was probably uncultivated. There were 35 a. of meadow, and 3 furlongs by 1 of pasture.[53]

For purposes of agriculture the lands of Ablington manor had been separated from those of the other Ablington estates by the 19th century.[54] In 1322 there were neifs who owed customary works on Ablington manor,[55] which in 1343 had 300 a. of demesne arable, a third

---

29 Below, churches.
30 P.R.O., C 66/1728, mm. 23–4.
31 Ibid. C 5/404/72; *Hist. Parl., Commons*, 1558–1603, ii. 246.
32 *W.N. & Q.* viii. 199–200. Remainder of para. based on Glos. R.O., D 2440, box 36, abstr. of title to Alton rectory.   33 Above, this section (Knighton).
34 P.R.O., IR 29/38/116.
35 *Cal. Chart. R.* 1257–1300, 157–9.
36 *Tax. Eccl.* (Rec. Com.), 180.
37 *Valor Eccl.* (Rec. Com.), ii. 94.
38 Glos. R.O., D 2440, box 36, abstr. of title to Alton rectory.
39 P.R.O., IR 29/38/116.

40 Ibid.; IR 30/38/116; W.R.O., EA/162.
41 *V.C.H. Wilts.* ii, p. 163.   42 Below, this section.
43 *First Pembroke Survey*, ed. Straton, i. 110–11.
44 P.R.O., IR 29/38/116; IR 30/38/116.
45 *Wilts. Inq. p.m.* 1242–1326 (Index Libr.), 160–1.
46 P.R.O., SC 6/1052/10.
47 Ibid. SC 12/22/5.   48 W.R.O. 192/52, f. 6.
49 *First Pembroke Survey*, i. 110–11.
50 W.R.O., Ch. Com., bishop, 92.
51 Ibid. A 1/345/177; P.R.O., IR 29/38/116; IR 30/38/116.   52 W.R.O., EA/162.
53 *V.C.H. Wilts.* ii, p. 134.
54 P.R.O., IR 29/38/116; IR 30/38/116.
55 Ibid. SC 12/1145/12.

worth 3*d.* an acre, a third 2*d.*, and a third 1*d.*[56] The manor had land in open fields called North, South, and Barrow in 1790,[57] later North, Second, and Third or Home,[58] and in the earlier 16th century had a copyholder with 12 a. and 3 leaseholders with a total of 52 a.[59] From 1790 or earlier, however, it consisted of a single long narrow farm, Great Ablington, *c.* 950 a., adjoining Syrencot's land on the south.[60]

On other Ablington land, a strip between Great Ablington's and Figheldean's, there was still common husbandry in the early 19th century, when there were three farms. There were *c.* 169 a. of arable in *c.* 120 strips and a down pasture of 279 a.[61] The land was in single ownership in 1844,[62] and had presumably been inclosed by then.

ALTON. In 1086 Alton had land for 4 teams: 3 teams were there, 2 with 3 *servi* on the demesne land, ½ held by 4 *villani* and 2 cottars, and ½ with 1 bordar and 1 cottar on subinfeudated land. There were 10 a. of meadow and 14 square furlongs of pasture.[63]

It is unlikely that much of the land of Alton was in severalty in the Middle Ages, and the 19th-century names of the two fields, North and South, in each of the Alton manors, may be evidence of earlier common husbandry.[64] In 1343 Alton Magna manor almost certainly had customary tenants, and the demesne had 280 a. of arable and 3 a. of meadow.[65]

The whole of Alton Parva manor was in a single farm in the later 16th century,[66] and the whole of Alton Magna manor was in a single farm in the 18th. In 1727 *c.* 800 lb. of wool were produced on Alton Magna farm. By 1731, when they were leased to the same tenant,[67] the two farms were presumably in severalty. In 1839 each was an east–west strip of land, to the north Alton Magna, 627 a., to the south Alton Parva, 503 a.[68]

CHOULSTON. In 1086 Choulston had 1½ team, which was all that there was land for. There were 2 *servi* and 3 coscets, 8 a. of meadow, and 5 square furlongs of pasture.[69]

There is no evidence of common husbandry at Choulston, nor of customary tenants. About 1557 the demesne farm was said to include 325 a. of arable, probably an exaggeration unless some lay elsewhere, 10 a. of meadow and pasture, and a 4-a. warren.[70] It was the only farm in Choulston in 1749,[71] and in 1839 was 378 a.[72]

KNIGHTON. In 1086 there was land for 6 teams,

and 5 were there: on the demesne there were 6 *servi* and 2 teams, and 7 *villani* and 6 coscets had 3 teams. There were 20 a. of meadow and the pasture was 12 by 4 furlongs.[73]

Open arable was in three fields, called North, Middle, and South in 1634;[74] in 1823 *c.* 275 a. were arable, Knighton down was *c.* 303 a., and there were probably *c.* 35 a. of common meadows.[75] In 1317 on William Paynel's manor there were said to be 216 a. of demesne arable of which 30 a. were sown with wheat, 40 a. with barley, 20 a. with oats, and 12 a. with vetches and peas; the demesne included common pasture for cattle and for 350 sheep.[76] There were 125 a. of arable and 8 a. of meadow on the demesne in a year between 1422 and 1461.[77] Knighton's land was worked in common in the 17th century,[78] and possibly until it was inclosed by Act in 1823.[79] In 1839 Knighton farm was 470 a., and most of the other land, a strip of 166 a. beside the southern parish boundary,[80] was apparently worked from Durrington.

SYRENCOT. The manor had only four tenants *c.* 1300,[81] and its land may have been in a single farm by the 15th century. In the 18th century Syrencot farm belonged to William Dyke, described by his contemporary Arthur Young as the greatest farmer in Wiltshire. There and on the adjoining Great Ablington farm in 1796 he had 1,000 a. of corn and *c.* 5,000 sheep, mostly Southdowns with which he was replacing the Wiltshire breed. After experimenting unsuccessfully on newly ploughed downland with temporary grasses and root crops he grew wheat on it in 1796.[82] Syrencot farm, 274 a. including *c.* 150 a. of arable, was worked from Great Ablington in 1839. There was then an 18-a. park, divided into Upper and Homeward, east of Syrencot House.[83]

In the whole parish in 1839 there were 2,299 a. of arable, 2,618 a. of downland pasture, and 194 a. of lowland pasture and meadow of which 80 a. were watered meadow. About 188 a., at Syrencot, Knighton, and Alton, had been burnbaked. The only woodland had apparently been planted by William Dyke after 1773, a total of *c.* 80 a. in plantations around Syrencot House and on Dunch Hill at the east end of Syrencot and Ablington downs.[84] Most of that woodland and several plantations made after 1898 were standing in 1991.[85]

Several farms in the parish were already large in the earlier 19th century, and some grew larger.

56 *Wilts. Inq. p.m.* 1327–77 (Index Libr.), 151.
57 Poore Estate Act, 11 Geo. IV, c. 29 (Private, not printed).
58 P.R.O., IR 29/38/116; IR 30/38/116.
59 W.R.O. 192/52, f. 10 and v.
60 Poore Estate Act, 11 Geo. IV, c. 29 (Private, not printed); P.R.O., IR 29/38/116; IR 30/38/116.
61 P.R.O., IR 29/38/116; IR 30/38/116.
62 W.R.O., EA/162. 63 *V.C.H. Wilts.* ii, p. 166.
64 P.R.O., IR 29/38/116; IR 30/38/116.
65 *Wilts. Inq. p.m.* 1327–77 (Index Libr.), 151.
66 D. & C. Winton. Mun., acct. rolls, 1545–72.
67 P.R.O., E 134/5 Geo. II Mich./3; E 134/8 Geo. II Hil./2.
68 Ibid. IR 29/38/116; IR 30/38/116.
69 *V.C.H. Wilts.* ii, p. 131.
70 B.L. Harl. MS. 607, f. 43 and v.

71 Williamstrip Mun., EMP/31/1.
72 P.R.O., IR 29/38/116; IR 30/38/116.
73 *V.C.H. Wilts.* ii, p. 163.
74 W.R.O., D 26/4.   75 Ibid. EA/144.
76 *Wilts. Inq. p.m.* 1242–1326 (Index Libr.), 413–14.
77 P.R.O., SC 11/33.
78 W.R.O., D 26/4; D. & C. Sar. Mun., press I, box 5, D–F/18.   79 W.R.O., EA/144.
80 P.R.O., IR 29/38/116; IR 30/38/116.
81 W.R.O. 490/1470, f. 204.
82 A. Young, *Annals of Agric.* xxviii. 361–4.
83 P.R.O., IR 29/38/116; IR 30/38/116.
84 *Andrews and Dury, Map* (W.R.S. viii), pl. 9; O.S. Map 1", sheet 14 (1817 edn.); Poore Estate Act, 11 Geo. IV, c. 29 (Private, not printed); P.R.O., IR 29/38/116; IR 30/38/116.
85 Inf. from Defence Land Agent.

In 1871 T. E. Simpkins farmed 1,600 a. from Ablington House, a farm of 1,700 a. was worked from Choulston, Alton Parva farm was 570 a., and Knighton farm was 468 a. In 1881 Great Ablington farm was 1,145 a., Little Ablington farm 850 a.[86] From 1867 to 1898 the parish was half arable and half pasture. Turnips and swedes were grown on an average of c. 600 a., barley on c. 500 a., wheat on c. 500 a., oats on c. 410 a., and vetches on c. 140 a. Temporary grasses, mostly for hay, made up a third of the grassland in 1867, nearly half in 1876, and less than a quarter in 1896. In the period 1867–98 there were usually c. 7,000 sheep, c. 70 cattle, and c. 95 pigs in the parish.[87]

About 1898 nearly all the parish was bought by the War Department,[88] and much of it was subsequently used for military training, from c. 1939 to c. 1956 about three quarters. Only three farms were based in the parish 1910–28: Choulston in 1920 was a grazing farm of 669 a., the farm based at Knighton, 1,147 a., included 519 a. of Alton's land and 74 a. of Figheldean's, and one based in Figheldean village had 739 a. In 1939 the farms were Ablington, Alton Magna, and Choulston. Sheep farming declined sharply in the earlier 20th century, and in the 1930s few sheep were kept. More land became available for farming from the late 1950s, most of it grazing land, and from then more cattle and sheep were kept.[89]

In 1990 there were still three farms based in the parish. East of the river Choulston farm had c. 2,000 a. and Ablington farm had c. 1,760 a.; west of it Knighton farm had only 106 a. and most of the agricultural land was worked from Wexland Farm in Netheravon. On both sides the downland was in military training areas and its agricultural use limited to grazing for cattle and sheep. Mixed farming, in which corn growing predominated, was practised on land nearer the river.[90]

Mills stood on the Avon at Figheldean and Knighton in 1086.[91] Figheldean mill stood south-west of the church[92] and ceased to work c. 1900.[93] Knighton mill was last mentioned in the 15th century.[94] A water mill stood on Ablington manor in 1422[95] and a similar mill for corn on Thomas Sheppard's Ablington estate in the 17th century.[96]

The manufacture of woollen cloth is suggested by the admission in 1653 of a Figheldean man as a freeman of the Weavers' company of London.[97] There was a disused fulling mill at Ablington in the 17th century[98] and new woollen mills at Figheldean in the 1790s.[99] In 1831, however, there was no clothmaker in the parish.[1]

There was a chalk quarry on the west side of the Upavon–Amesbury road near Alton Parva Farm in the 18th century:[2] in the early 19th chalk for building and for making lime and whiting was quarried at it.[3] A smith made hoes at Figheldean 1898–1903, horse trainers were based in the parish 1903–7 and 1928–38,[4] and in 1990 a small meat-processing factory and a travel company were based in Figheldean village.

LOCAL GOVERNMENT. Between 1189 and 1199 the lord of Figheldean manor was granted sac and soc, toll and team, infangthief, and quittance from county and hundred courts, liberties confirmed in 1252.[5] In the 13th century the lord held a three weekly court and twice yearly view of frankpledge at which cert money was paid: both were apparently attended by men of Figheldean and elsewhere.[6] The view was still held in 1504.[7] From the 17th century a court, called court leet, view, and manor court, was held, probably twice a year, by the lessee of the demesne farm. In the early 19th century a court was held only for the admission of copyholders.[8]

Amercements paid by his men attending the Figheldean view were granted to the lord of Ablington manor in 1227,[9] and between 1263 and 1277 the men of Durford abbey's Ablington estate were granted freedom from attending the three weekly court but not the view.[10] Men of Ablington, possibly tenants of Ablington manor, owed suit at the view for the honor of Wallingford (Berks., later Oxon.) held at Ogbourne St. George in the 15th century and earlier 16th; cert money was paid, a tithingman, a constable, and two affeerors were chosen, and business included nuisances such as blocked ditches, ruinous bridges, and overcharging by the miller.[11]

In 1539–40 tenants of Alton Parva and Choulston manors owed suit at courts for Bulford manor: all three manors formerly belonged to Amesbury priory.[12] The dean and chapter of Salisbury's Knighton manor was represented from the 17th century to the 19th at the dean and chapter's court for the East End manor of Durrington, but its business, if any, was not distinguished in the records.[13]

86 P.R.O., RG 10/1944, ff. 9v.–14; RG 11/2064, ff. 9, 11.
87 Ibid. MAF 68/151, sheet 18; MAF 68/493, sheet 11; MAF 68/1063, sheet 11; MAF 68/1633, sheet 9.
88 Above, manors.
89 Kelly's Dir. Wilts. (1939); P.R.O., MAF 68/2203, sheet 8; MAF 68/2773, sheet 8; MAF 68/3319, sheet 8; MAF 68/3814, no. 100; MAF 68/4145, no. 100; MAF 68/4552, no. 100; MAF 68/5004, no. 100; W.R.O., Inland Revenue, val. reg. 141; ibid. G 1/500/8.
90 Inf. from Mr. C. L. Spencer, Choulston Farm; Rawlins Bros., Ablington Farm; Lt.-Col. G. J. Rudd, Alton Parva Farm.   91 V.C.H. Wilts. ii, p. 163.
92 P.R.O., IR 29/38/116; IR 30/38/116.
93 Kelly's Dir. Wilts. (1903); O.S. Map 6", Wilts. LIV. NE. (1901 edn.).   94 P.R.O., SC 11/33.
95 Ibid. SC 2/212/3, rot. 2.
96 Ibid. C 3/463/12.   97 W.A.M. xxxviii. 573.
98 P.R.O., C 3/463/12.
99 W.R.O., Ch. Com., bishop, 94.

1 Census, 1831.
2 Andrews and Dury, Map (W.R.S. viii), pl. 8.
3 Lewis, Topog. Dict. Eng. (1848), ii. 233; P.R.O., IR 29/38/116; IR 30/38/116.
4 Kelly's Dir. Wilts. (1898 and later edns.); W.R.O., F 12/126/8.   5 Cal. Chart. R. 1226–57, 394.
6 Ibid. 58; Wilts. Inq. p.m. 1242–1326 (Index Libr.), 160–1; B.L. Cott. MS. Vesp. E. xxiii, f. 71.
7 P.R.O., SC 12/22/5.
8 Ibid. WARD 2/6/22C/43; W.R.O. 212B/3204; Williamstrip Mun., MTD/24/1–4.
9 Cal. Chart. R. 1226–57, 58.
10 B.L. Cott. MS. Vesp. E. xxiii, f. 71.
11 P.R.O., SC 2/212/3, rot. 2; SC 2/212/9, rot. 2d.; SC 2/212/14.
12 Ibid. SC 6/Hen. VIII/3986, rot. 84d.; Ch. Com. file 35487; above, manors; Bulford, manor; local govt.
13 W.R.O. 84/22–3; ibid. Ch. Com., chapter, 103/1–3; above, Durrington, local govt.

Paupers could be accommodated in a parish house c. 1769.[14] The amount raised for the poor in Figheldean parish rose from £91 in 1775–6 to £121 in 1783–5. In 1802–3 c. £3 each was spent on regular relief for 88 paupers, nearly a quarter of the inhabitants. In 1812–13, when £768 was spent on regular relief for 31 adults and on occasional relief for 25, in all about a sixth of the inhabitants, the poor were generously relieved. Lower expenditure 1814–15 represented a fall in the number relieved.[15] From 1816 to 1834 the average of c. £470 spent each year was among the highest in Amesbury hundred. The sums spent were highest at £629 in 1817 and £701 in 1818, lowest at £263 in 1834.[16] Figheldean became part of Amesbury poor-law union in 1835.[17] The parish was included in Salisbury district in 1974.[18]

CHURCHES. In 1115 Henry I granted Figheldean church to Salisbury cathedral and Bishop Roger. The bishop gave up his right in it to the dean and chapter, and Stephen confirmed the gift in 1139.[19] The church was taken from the cathedral, presumably in the 1140s, but, by a grant of 1157 and a confirmation of 1158, Henry II restored it.[20] The rectory was appropriated to the treasurer of the cathedral, apparently before 1180–5 when the church was granted for payments of £10 a year to him,[21] and by 1291 a vicarage had been ordained.[22] The treasurer fulfilled all the functions of the ordinary in the parish from c. 1190 until his peculiar jurisdiction was abolished in 1841; the church was also exempt from archidiaconal jurisdiction from c. 1190.[23] A proposal made in 1650 to unite Knighton to Durrington parish[24] was not implemented. The vicarage was united in 1940 with Milston rectory,[25] and in 1982 Bulford vicarage was added to the united benefice.[26]

Until 1821 the treasurer collated vicars.[27] His right of patronage passed in 1841 to the bishop of Salisbury,[28] who from 1940 was entitled to present alternately[29] and from 1982 at one turn in three.[30]

The vicarage was worth £4 6s. 8d. in 1291,[31] £14 in 1535.[32] The treasurer augmented it with £30 a year between 1634 and 1672,[33] and it was worth £50 c. 1654, £60 in 1705.[34] With an income of c. £106 in 1830 it remained poor.[35] A pension of £10 from the treasurer, possibly allotted to the vicar in the 18th century, was not received 1821–32 but was again paid from 1845.[36] The vicar took the small tithes, in 1535 some tithes of wool and lambs, and in 1705 some hay tithes and some great tithes from the land of the Figheldean Rectory estate.[37] The vicarial tithes were valued at £180 in 1839 and commuted.[38] Part of the rent charge was given to the treasurer for 1½ a. of glebe in 1840.[39] The Ecclesiastical Commissioners in 1859 gave the vicar an additional rent charge of £171 and c. 3 a. of glebe.[40] The vicarage house was out of repair in 1667.[41] A new house, with a brick plinth and mud walls, was built c. 1832; it was replaced by a new one in 1872,[42] and that was sold in 1976, when another was built in its grounds.[43]

A chapel at Knighton in the 13th century may have been manorial[44] and was not afterwards mentioned. A curate who either assisted the vicar or served the cure was in minor orders in 1634.[45] The vicar preached each Sunday in 1650.[46] The intruder who served the cure in 1660 was replaced by a vicar, collated in 1661,[47] who was reported in 1667 and 1673 for neglecting to catechize.[48] Vicars in the earlier 19th century were non-resident pluralists. J. H. Hume, vicar 1821–48, was also vicar of Calne and from 1835 of Hilmarton. David Owen, curate from 1814, was also curate of Durrington and of Milston, where he lived.[49] A curate held a service every Sunday, alternately morning and evening, in 1832.[50] Henry Carswell, Hume's last curate and his successor as vicar,[51] in 1850–1 held two services every Sunday: morning service was attended by an average of 175, afternoon service by one of 130.[52] He preached at morning and afternoon services on Sundays in 1864 and held weekday services on great festivals. He administered the sacrament on Christmas day, Easter day, Ascension day, Whit Sunday, and four other Sundays. The average number of communicants was 60, of whom 40 received at Easter and 30 at the other great festivals. Carswell thought that the counter-attraction of the Primitive Methodist meeting could be lessened by making church services more interesting for the

14 W.R.O., Ch. Com., bishop, 92.
15 *Poor Law Abstract, 1804*, 558–9; *1818*, 492–3; *V.C.H. Wilts.* iv. 348.
16 *Poor Rate Returns, 1816–21*, 185; *1822–4*, 225; *1825–9*, 215; *1830–4*, 209.
17 *Poor Law Com. 2nd Rep.* App. D, 558.
18 O.S. Map 1/100,000, admin. areas, Wilts. (1974 edn.).
19 *Reg. St. Osmund* (Rolls Ser.), i. 200–1; *Reg. Regum Anglo-Norm.* iii, no. 787.
20 *Sar. Chart. and Doc.* (Rolls Ser.), 29–30; *Reg. St. Osmund* (Rolls Ser.), i. 203–6; *V.C.H. Wilts.* iii. 159.
21 *Sar. Chart. and Doc.* (Rolls Ser.), 43–4.
22 *Tax. Eccl.* (Rec. Com.), 182.
23 *Reg. St. Osmund* (Rolls Ser.), i. 241–2; Cathedrals Act, 3 & 4 Vic. c. 113; Le Neve, *Fasti, 1541–1857, Salisbury*, 13.
24 *W.A.M.* xl. 256.
25 Ch. Com. file, NB 34/143; ibid. 100404.
26 Inf. from Ch. Com.
27 W.R.O., D 26/1, clergy appointments; D 26/3, subscription bk.   28 Cathedrals Act, 3 & 4 Vic. c. 113.
29 Ch. Com. file, NB 34/143; ibid. 100404.
30 Inf. from Ch. Com.
31 *Tax. Eccl.* (Rec. Com.), 182.
32 *Valor Eccl.* (Rec. Com.), ii. 91.
33 P.R.O., C 1/883, no. 69.
34 *W.A.M.* lxxvii. 105; D. & C. Sar. Mun., press I, box 5, D–F/18.
35 *Rep. Com. Eccl. Revenues*, 834–5.
36 Ibid.; Ch. Com. file, NB 34/58C; ibid. 9697.
37 *W.A.M.* lxxvii. 105; *Valor Eccl.* (Rec. Com.), ii. 91.
38 P.R.O., IR 29/38/116.
39 Ch. Com. files 5955; 9697.
40 *Lond. Gaz.* 12 July 1859, pp. 2677–8.
41 W.R.O., D 26/12, chwdns.' presentments, 1667.
42 Ch. Com. file, NB 34/58C; ibid. 2700/1–2.
43 W.R.O. 1756/25.
44 D. & C. Sar. Mun., press IV, E 2/Knighton/4.
45 *Subscription Bk. 1620–40* (W.R.S. xxxii), p. 65.
46 *W.A.M.* xl. 256.
47 W.R.O., bishop's transcripts, bdle. 1.
48 Ibid. D 26/12, chwdns.' presentments, 1667, 1673.
49 Ibid. D 26/1, clergy appointments; D 26/3, subscription bk.; *Alum. Oxon. 1715–1886*, ii. 713.
50 Ch. Com. file, NB 34/58C.
51 W.R.O., D 1/56/7.
52 P.R.O., HO 129/262/2/8/12.

poorer inhabitants. A parish library which he established had 70–80 subscribers in 1864.[53]

The church of *ST. MICHAEL AND ALL ANGELS*, so called in 1763,[54] is built of flint rubble and ashlar and is partly chequered. It comprises a chancel, an aisled and clerestoried nave with south porch, and a west tower with north vestry.[55] The church which stood in the early 12th century had a chancel and a nave, and the west tower was built later in that century. Chancel and nave were rebuilt, probably on their original plan, and the aisles were built, in the later 13th century. St. Edmund was invoked in a chapel in the church *c.* 1251.[56] In the 15th century or early 16th the clerestory was built and the chancel and rood stair were rebuilt. The chancel roof was renewed in the 17th century or the 18th, possibly in 1788 when other parts of the church were repaired.[57] During a restoration of the chancel by Ewan Christian in 1858–9 external parapets were removed, the east wall was rebuilt, and the arch was enlarged. The rest of the church was restored by J. W. Hugall in 1859–60: the tower and the south aisle roof were heightened, both aisles were refenestrated, the west gallery was removed, a new gallery was formed from the middle stage of the tower,[58] the vestry was built, and the porch was rebuilt.[59] In both 1858–9 and 1859–60 original materials were re-used. Two later 13th-century effigies of knights, in the church before 1671 and in the porch in 1991, may have been brought from elsewhere.[60]

The king's commissioners took 13 oz. of plate in 1553, and left a chalice of 14 oz. A paten hallmarked for 1787 was given in 1810, and a new chalice and flagon were added in 1858:[61] all were held for the parish in 1991.[62] There were three bells in 1553. Three new ones were cast in 1581 by John Wallis. The second, cracked and useless in the later 17th century, was recast in 1721 by William Tosier. All three were in the church in 1991.[63] Registrations of baptisms, marriages, and burials begin in 1653 and are complete.[64]

Alton church was recorded from the mid 12th century[65] to the 16th.[66] It appears to have been a parish church held in the later Middle Ages by sinecurists; in 1548 it was said that for long the vicars of Figheldean had received £2 a year for serving it, and *c.* 1547 the Crown appropriated it as a free chapel.[67] Jocelin, bishop of

Salisbury 1142–84, had granted the church to the dean and chapter of Salisbury,[68] but apparently they did not keep it. The advowson of the rectory descended from 1306 to the 16th century, apart from 1485–94, with the lordship in demesne of Alton Magna manor. Francis, Lord Stourton (d. 1487), held it 1485–7, William, Lord Stourton, to whom the manor reverted in 1494, from 1487. The bishop collated by lapse in 1364.[69] In a way that is not clear Edward Seymour, earl of Hertford, acquired the advowson, which was confirmed to him by Act in 1544.[70] The bishop collated under the Act in 1545.[71] In 1535 the rectory was worth £10 10s. and was endowed with all the tithes of Alton,[72] paying a pension for the share which Amesbury priory formerly held.[73] In 1548 the church had a chalice weighing 10 oz., a bell, a missal, and two vestments.[74] It was dilapidated *c.* 1590.[75] In 1831 the Alton Rectory estate was still paying the vicar of Figheldean £2 a year for serving the non-existent church.[76]

ROMAN CATHOLICISM. A church dedicated to St. Thomas More and St. John Fisher was opened in Kerby Avenue *c.* 1934, primarily for military personnel. In 1976 it was served by a priest from Amesbury, and in 1985–6 was closed.[77]

PROTESTANT NONCONFORMITY. Presbyterians, among whom were the vicar's son and members of the Sheppard, Smart, and Cowper families, certified a house at Figheldean in 1672; dissenters certified houses in 1700 and 1711, and Independents certified a house in 1797. A house on the east side of High Street at Figheldean, certified for Primitive Methodists in 1838,[78] was attended on Sundays in 1850–1 by average congregations of 30 in the morning, 63 in the afternoon, and 70 in the evening.[79] A small red-brick chapel, built near the site for the group in 1882,[80] was closed before 1971.[81]

EDUCATION. Small children were taught in a school approved of by the minister in 1667.[82] Two schools, one with 22 pupils, one with 20, were opened in 1831.[83] They were attended by a total of 60 children in 1846–7,[84] and apparently

53 W.R.O., D 1/56/7.
54 J. Ecton, *Thesaurus* (1763), 391–2.
55 For the church in the early 19th cent., J. Buckler, watercolour in W.A.S. Libr., vol. i. 7.
56 *Close R.* 1247–51, 455.   57 *Church Guide.*
58 Ch. Com. files 8471; 22379; W.R.O. 1756/36.
59 *Church Guide.*
60 Aubrey, *Topog. Coll.* ed. Jackson, 357–8; *W.A.M.* xxx. 360; xxxix. 398.
61 Nightingale, *Wilts. Plate*, 40.
62 Inf. from the vicar.
63 Ibid.; Walters, *Wilts. Bells*, 85; W.R.O., D 26/3, visitation bk. 1681–4, f. 14; D 26/12, chwdns.' presentments, 1681, 1683.
64 W.R.O. 1756/1–10.
65 B.L. Add. Ch. 37664.
66 e.g. *Valor Eccl.* (Rec. Com.), ii. 93.
67 P.R.O., E 301/58, no. 58.
68 B.L. Add. Ch. 37664.
69 *Feet of F.* 1272–1327 (W.R.S. i), p. 57; *Cal. Inq. p.m.*

Hen. VII, i, pp. 60–1, 123–4; Phillipps, *Wilts. Inst.* (index in *W.A.M.* xxviii. 212); above, manors (Alton Magna).
70 *L. & P. Hen. VIII*, xix (1), p. 14.
71 W.R.O., D 1/2/16, f. (2nd foliation) 27.
72 *Valor Eccl.* (Rec. Com.), ii. 93.
73 Above, manors.   74 P.R.O., E 301/58, no. 58.
75 Ibid. C 2/Eliz. I/H 24/29.
76 Glos. R.O., D 2440, box 36, abstr. of title to Alton rectory.
77 *V.C.H. Wilts.* iii. 97; xi. 150; *Cath. Dir.* (1985 and later edns.).
78 *Meeting Ho. Certs.* (W.R.S. xl), pp. 9, 17, 48, 145, 173; W.R.O., D 26/12, chwdns.' presentments, 1673; P.R.O., IR 29/38/116; IR 30/38/116.
79 P.R.O., HO 129/262/2/8/13.
80 Date on chapel.
81 G.R.O. Worship Reg. no. 26895.
82 W.R.O., D 26/12, chwdns.' presentments, 1667.
83 *Educ. Enq. Abstract*, 1037.
84 Nat. Soc. *Inquiry, 1846–7*, Wilts. 6–7.

merged before 1848. The single school stood west of Church Street in 1851 and was closed in 1858, when a new National school was built at the south end of High Street on the east side.[85] On return day in 1871 that school was attended by 57 pupils.[86] Average attendance, 100 in the years 1906–12, declined to 81 in 1914 and to 69 in 1938.[87] There were 60 children on roll in 1991.[88]

CHARITIES FOR THE POOR. A rent charge of £1 10s. was given in 1714 for paupers not

relieved by the parish.[89] It was received in 1826[90] but was deemed lost in 1833.[91]

In 1898 Alfred Rawlins gave the income from £100 for blankets, coal, or meat for the poor. In 1899 c. £3 was spent on coal and in 1900 £3 on meat.[92] Meat was bought for c. 24 people each year 1904–6, for 33 in 1912. Funds accumulated 1914–18, and meat was again given 1920–31. Fuel was bought for c. 12 people a year 1938–43, but from 1944 small money doles were given. From 1947 to 1954 eight people each received 7s. 6d. a year;[93] no distribution was made after 1982.[94]

LUDGERSHALL

LUDGERSHALL parish,[95] 724 ha. (1,789 a.), 774 ha. from 1992,[96] lies at the eastern edge of Salisbury Plain and borders Hampshire. The village, 11.5 km. WNW. of Andover (Hants), is the site of Ludgershall castle and of a medieval borough. Biddesden has been part of the parish from 1446 but most aspects of its history are dealt with separately under its own name.[97] Faberstown, a 20th-century settlement in Kimpton (Hants), adjoins Ludgershall on the east and was transferred to the parish in 1992.[98]

In the west the parish boundary is marked by a prehistoric ditch along a ridge, and the west half of the northern boundary is marked by the bank and ditch of the north park of the castle.[99] The north–south part of the boundary with Hampshire follows a dry valley, west of which the boundary with North Tidworth was on its present course in 901.[1] The north part of the eastern boundary is apparently the western boundary of Chute forest as defined in 1300:[2] it is not clear whether the line existed before, or was newly made in, 1300. It was considered indistinct in 1783,[3] but was on its present course across Long bottom in 1841.[4]

The whole parish is on Upper Chalk. Feeders of the river Anton, a tributary of the Test, deposited gravel in shallow valleys, now dry, in the centre of the parish but not in three deeper dry valleys in the north-east corner.[5] The highest land is in the west where Windmill Hill reaches 187 m.; the lowest is at c. 105 m. in the extreme south and at 102 m. in the south-east corner. Ludgershall's name may mean 'the nook of land

where traps are set' and suggests that its land was a hunting ground before the Conquest.[6] Much land in the west was in the castle parks in the Middle Ages; most of the parish's woodland was in the east. From the 16th century or 17th, after it was disparked, most of the land in the west was arable.[7] Windmill Hill has been in an army training area since c. 1898,[8] and other land in the west has been used by the army since 1939.[9]

Ludgershall is on an old Marlborough–Winchester road, an important route in the early 13th century.[10] The road, as part of an Andover–Devizes road, was turnpiked across the parish in 1762 and disturnpiked in 1873;[11] a turnpike house stood on the south side at the Hampshire boundary in 1841.[12] That no major road joins it in the west part of the parish may be attributed to the existence of the castle parks. In the east several mainly north–south lanes follow the valleys. The easternmost was diverted east of Biddesden House, presumably when the house was built in the early 18th century,[13] but Crawlboys Lane and the east–west road called Biddesden Lane are apparently on their original courses.[14] Crawlboys Road, leading north-east from an extension of Dewey's Lane, was made at inclosure in 1853, when roads leading north-east and south-west, and north-west and south-east, across Ludgershall common were closed.[15]

The Swindon, Marlborough & Andover Railway, from 1884 the Midland & South Western Junction Railway, in 1882 opened a line through Ludgershall parish, immediately south of the

[85] *Kelly's Dir. Wilts.* (1848, 1855, 1859); *Acct. of Wilts. Schs.* 23; W.R.O. 1550/48.
[86] *Returns relating to Elem. Educ.* 426–7.
[87] *Bd. of Educ., List 21, 1908–38* (H.M.S.O.).
[88] Inf. from the head teacher.
[89] *Char. Don.* H.C. 511 (1816), xvi (2), 1336–7.
[90] Hoare, *Mod. Wilts.* Amesbury, 36.
[91] *Endowed Char. Wilts.* (S. Div.), 171.
[92] Ibid. 171–2.
[93] W.R.O. 1756/42; ibid. L 2, Figheldean.
[94] Inf. from the vicar.
[95] This article was written in 1990, later additions being dated; maps used include O.S. Maps 1", sheet 14 (1817 edn.); 1/50,000, sheet 184 (1988 edn.); 1/25,000, SU 24–5 (1958 edns.); 6", Wilts. XLVIII–XLIX (1877–88 and later edns.).
[96] *Census*, 1991.   [97] Below, Biddesden.
[98] Statutory Instruments, 1991, no. 2247, Dors., Hants, W. Suss., and Wilts. (Co. Boundaries) Order; a brief acct. of Faberstown, which was built after the hist. of Kimpton was prepared for *V.C.H. Hants*, iv. 372–6, is given below,

this section.
[99] Cf. below, econ. hist. (parks).
[1] *Arch. Jnl.* lxxxiii. 98, 100.
[2] *V.C.H. Wilts.* iv. 425, 452–3.
[3] *Vis. Queries, 1783* (W.R.S. xxvii), p. 144.
[4] P.R.O., IR 30/38/178.
[5] Geol. Surv. Map 1/50,000, drift, sheet 283 (1975 edn.).
[6] *P.N. Wilts.* (E.P.N.S.), 367–8; *Eng. Place-Name Elements* (E.P.N.S.), i. 223; ii. 28–9.
[7] Below, econ. hist. (parks; agric.).
[8] O.S. Map 6", Wilts. XLVIII. NE. (1901 edn.); cf. below, manors (Ludgershall).
[9] Below, this section (Ludgershall).
[10] *Archaeologia*, xxii. 132, 138, 140–1.
[11] *V.C.H. Wilts.* iv. 257, 270; *L.J.* xxx. 232.
[12] P.R.O., IR 29/38/178; IR 30/38/178.
[13] Cf. below, Biddesden, manor.
[14] O.S. Map 1", sheet 14 (1817 edn.).
[15] C. Greenwood, *Map of Wilts.* (1820); W.R.O., EA/172.

LUDGERSHALL 1841

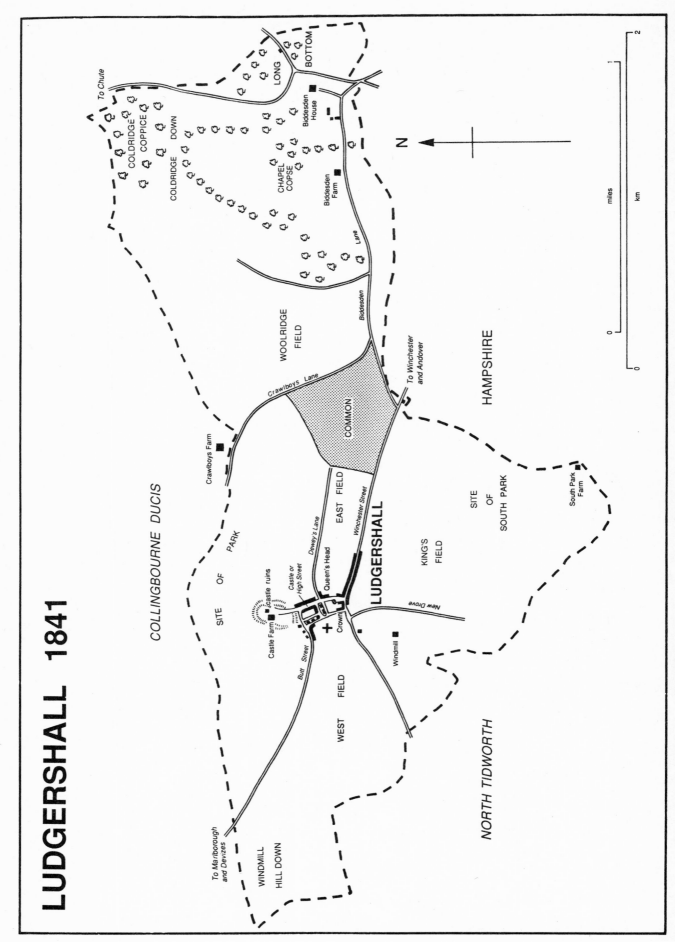

COLLINGBOURNE DUCIS

To Chute

COLDRIDGE
COPPICE

COLDRIDGE
DOWN

LONG
BOTTOM

Biddesden
House

CHAPEL
COPSE

Biddesden
Farm

Biddesden Lane

WOOLRIDGE
FIELD

Crawlboys Lane

To Winchester
and Andover

Crawlboys Farm

COMMON

EAST FIELD

HAMPSHIRE

SITE OF PARK

Dewey's Lane

Castle or
High Street

Queen's Head

Winchester Street

SITE
OF
SOUTH PARK

South Park
Farm

Castle ruins

Castle Farm

Crown

LUDGERSHALL

Butt Street

KING'S
FIELD

New Drove

WEST
FIELD

Windmill

To Marlborough
and Devizes

WINDMILL
HILL DOWN

NORTH TIDWORTH

N

miles

km

Andover–Devizes road east of the village and with a station south of the junction of Winchester Street and High Street. From west of the station a branch line to a station in South Tidworth (Hants) was opened for the army in 1901. The public used it from 1902 until it was closed in 1955.[16] In 1943 a line from an army depot south of Tidworth Road was built to join the Ludgershall–Tidworth line.[17] Ludgershall station was closed to passengers in 1961 and entirely in 1969.[18] The line from Andover to Ludgershall and the branch from south of Tidworth Road were used by the army in 1990: by 1974 the station had been demolished and the line across the north-west part of the parish dismantled.[19]

The ditch which marks the west boundary, and two Bronze-Age bowl barrows on Windmill Hill, attest prehistoric activity on what became Ludgershall parish. A late Bronze-Age axe has also been found. Three Romano-British skeletons, headless and perhaps of executed felons, were found in a pit in the west part of the parish.[20]

In 1377 Ludgershall and Biddesden had a total of c. 135 poll-tax payers.[21] The population of the parish rose from 471 in 1801 to 595 in 1861. It declined by a sixth between 1861 and 1871 and was 476 in 1891. It rose rapidly before the First World War as civilians working at the new army camps at North and South Tidworth were housed at Ludgershall and was 1,117 in 1911. It was 1,091 in 1921, 1,259 in 1931, and rose rapidly again from the 1930s, again stimulated by military activity in the parish and nearby. There were 1,906 inhabitants in 1951, 3,379 in 1991.[22]

LUDGERSHALL. To judge from its low assessment in Domesday Book, Ludgershall was no more than a very small village in the 11th century. Before 1103, and almost certainly after 1086, Ludgershall castle was built,[23] and later settlement was in a small grid of streets between the castle and the Marlborough–Winchester road, the natural line of which would sweep past the south end of High Street. Since the grid of streets is likely to have been built up before the church was built, west of the grid in the 12th century,[24] it is possible that the settlement is a planned borough of the early 12th century. The Marlborough–Winchester road was diverted through the main street: its old course to the east, Winchester Street, and its new course to the west, Butt Street, became boundaries of the

borough. A bank, part of which survives, was the east boundary, and a lane called Back Lane in 1511 and 1809,[25] possibly near the old course of the Marlborough–Winchester road, may have been the west boundary. The borough was one of the smallest in Wiltshire[26] and, although represented in parliament, did not grow as a town and developed no institution for self government.

All that survives of the medieval borough are its plan and the base and shaft of the high or market cross.[27] The main street was called High Street in 1598,[28] and part of it Castle Street in the 18th century:[29] in the early 20th century the north part was Castle Street, the south High Street.[30] It is wide, especially at its junction with Winchester Street; long and narrow burgage plots lay on both sides, and it was presumably the site of Ludgershall's markets and fairs, held from the 13th century. The cross was erected in the 15th century and around its base the Descent from the Cross, the Three Marys, the Incredulity of St. Thomas, and the Ascension are depicted in relief. In 1897, when it was railed,[31] it was halfway along the street on the east side. A lane parallel to and west of High Street was called Church Street in 1895,[32] St. James Street in 1903 and later.[33] The cross streets linking High Street and St. James Street were Church Lane, so called in 1631,[34] and to the north Cox's Lane, so called in the 19th century but later Chapel Lane.[35] There were burgage plots on the south side of Winchester Street and in Back Lane.[36] Butt Street was called Parsonage Lane in 1816 when the rector lived in it,[37] and by 1773 Dewey's Lane, so called in 1792, had breached the borough bank by leading east from High Street.[38]

The borough was seriously damaged by fire in 1679,[39] but before then had lost the importance it had in the earlier Middle Ages. Ludgershall was 'a poor thatch'd village' c. 1757,[40] its houses were 'mean' in 1764,[41] and in the later 18th century and earlier 19th gaol fever and smallpox were common causes of death among its inhabitants.[42] Its poverty occasioned a local rhyme:

'At Ludgershall the beer is small and very very thin,
At every door there stands a whore to call her cully in.'[43]

The chief building materials of the oldest surviving houses are brick and flint, and some houses retain thatched roofs. In 1775 the lord of the manor called Ludgershall beggarly,[44] an epithet echoed in 1826 by William Cobbett.[45] Part of the

16 V.C.H. Wilts. iv. 289–90; below, N. Tidworth, intro.
17 N. D. G. James, Plain Soldiering, 87.
18 Clinker's Reg. Closed Passenger Sta. 1830–1980 (1988 edn.), 90.
19 O.S. Map 1/50,000, sheet 184 (1974 edn.).
20 V.C.H. Wilts. i (1), 83, 181, 255.
21 Ibid. iv. 306.
22 Ibid. 325, 352; Census, 1991.
23 Below, castle.
24 Ibid. church [architecture].
25 Cat. Anct. D. i, C 349; W.R.O. 212B/3850.
26 V.C.H. Wilts. iv. 296; Tax List, 1332 (W.R.S. xlv), 7.
27 So called in the early 16th cent.: Cat. Anct. D. i, C 206, C 349; see below, plate facing p. 251.
28 W.R.O. 212B/3715.
29 Ibid. 212B/3835.
30 O.S. Map 1/2,500, Wilts. XLVIII. 12 (1924 edn.).
31 Tablet on base of cross.
32 Hants R.O. 46M84, box 37, abstr. of title, 1896.
33 W.R.O., G 10/760/5.
34 Ibid. 212B/3716.
35 Treas. Solicitor, regy. no. 293/50, copy lease, 1816; Hants R.O. 46M84, box 49, deed, 1891.
36 Cat. Anct. D. i, C 824; W.R.O. 212B/3852.
37 Treas. Solicitor, regy. no. 293/50, copy lease, 1816.
38 Andrews and Dury, Map (W.R.S. viii), pl. 9; overseers' and surveyors' acct. bk. 1792–1829 (in church).
39 W. A. Bewes, Church Briefs, 287.
40 Travels through Eng. of Dr. Ric. Pococke, ii (Camd. Soc. [2nd ser.], xliv), 246.
41 Eng. Illustrated (1764), ii. 330.
42 W.R.O., D 1/21/5/2.
43 W.A.M. l. 32.
44 Hist. MSS. Com. 42, 15th Rep. VI, Carlisle, p. 293.
45 W. Cobbett, Rural Rides, ed. G. D. H. Cole, i. 356.

village was designated a conservation area in 1981.[46]

By the mid 16th century Ludgershall castle had become ruinous and a lodge had been built on its site.[47] A banqueting house, possibly associated with it, still stood in 1703.[48] Castle Farm was built on part of the castle site in the late 18th century. In Castle Street, on the west side at its junction with Butt Street, a range of brick cottages, divided into bays by pilasters and retaining a thatched roof, was built in the later 17th century. On the east side a range of flint cottages with red-brick dressings was built in the 18th.[49] In High Street the Queen's Head, on the east side, survived the fire of 1679. Built in the 16th century, it was possibly the alehouse licensed in 1577;[50] it is timber-framed and contains a large 16th-century fireplace; its jettied west front was rebuilt in the 19th century. The Crown, on the west side near the junction with Winchester Street, retains timber-framing in its north part but was otherwise rebuilt in the 19th century. Also on the west side Erskine House was built of flint with red-brick dressings on an L-shaped plan as a two-storeyed house with attics in the late 18th century: it was altered and its west service wing heightened in the mid 19th century, and in 1968 it was again altered and was extended as an old people's home.[51] In the 19th century ranges of cottages were rebuilt on each side of High Street and a nonconformist chapel was built near the Crown,[52] but there are few 20th-century buildings in the street. Two ponds, one near the Crown[53] mentioned in 1655 and one near the Queen's Head mentioned in 1789, were drained between 1891 and 1899.[54]

On the north side of Butt Street the garden of a house had incorporated part of the castle earthworks as an ornamental mound by c. 1757:[55] the house was perhaps that owned or occupied by Sir Philip Meadows[56] (d. 1757)[57] and in 1816 lived in by the rector,[58] but no longer stood in 1841.[59] Cottages were built further west along Butt Street in the 17th century and early 18th, and a school was built on the south side in the 19th.[60] North of the church both sides of St. James Street had been built up by 1773.[61] A house built on the east side in 1737,[62] afterwards extended and altered, survives. St. James's well near the churchyard gate was arched over in 1759[63] and was still open in the 19th century,[64]

but it was covered, and the arch removed, before 1990. The chapel which gave its name to the lane formerly Cox's Lane was built in the earlier 19th century.[65]

Although both sides of Winchester Street had been built up by 1773,[66] the oldest building to survive in it is Perry's Cottage, built on the north side in 1791.[67] On the south side Highfield House was built at the west end and Laurel House at the east end between 1841 and c. 1878.[68] Also on the south side, near the junction with High Street, the Prince of Wales, a large red-brick inn, was built c. 1867:[69] it was closed between 1956 and 1965,[70] and in 1990 was being adapted for flats.

South of the village South Park Farm stood in 1720.[71] It was burned down in 1830, and in 1831, at Salisbury, Henry Wilkins was hanged for arson.[72] A barn stood on the site in 1841[73] and 1990.

Ludgershall was transformed into a small town in the 20th century. From c. 1900 the needs of nearby army camps encouraged the growth of commerce and the building of private and council houses in Ludgershall: shops and other business premises were built and public services were provided. To the west a few houses were built beside a bottling works in Simonds Road c. 1905 and c. 1911,[74] and more were built between 1930 and 1935 on the Astor estate south of Tidworth Road.[75] Army depots built in 1939 north and south of Tidworth Road restricted westward growth of housing,[76] but c. 1955 c. 60 council houses were built in New Crescent and Roberts Road[77] and in 1990 private houses were being built east of the Astor estate. Most development was to the east along a strip of former common pasture and on other land, but vacant sites were also built on in and around High Street. Early 20th-century speculative building to the east included Bell Street, two parallel terraces each of 16 red-brick cottages built by Walter Faber c. 1903,[78] and terraces of cottages in Andover Road dated 1900 and 1901. Building continued between 1918 and 1939: 6 council houses were built in Andover Road before 1924,[79] and 92 others were built in new roads on the former common, Short Street from the late 1920s, South View and Central Street from the early 1930s.[80] The council estate was enlarged eastwards in the 1950s when Coronation Road,

46 Inf. from Co. Planning Officer, Co. Hall, Trowbridge.
47 Leland, *Itin.* ed. Toulmin Smith, v. 6.
48 P.R.O., C 5/325/28.
49 The date 1680 on one of the cottages was introduced from elsewhere: inf. from Mr. P. Walker, C.B.E., 18 Castle Street.
50 *Sess. Mins.* (W.R.S. iv), 24.
51 Tablet on ho.
52 Cf. below, prot. nonconf.
53 See plate facing p. 218.
54 O.S. Map 6", Wilts. XLVIII. SE. (1901 edn.); Hants R.O. 46M84, box 49, deed, 1891; W.R.O. 212B/3718; ibid. D 1/21/5/2.
55 *Travels of Dr. Pococke*, ii. 246.
56 W. Stukeley, *Itin. Curiosum* (1724), 175.
57 *D.N.B.*
58 Treas. Solicitor, regy. no. 293/50, copy lease, 1816.
59 P.R.O., IR 30/38/178.   60 Below, educ.
61 *Andrews and Dury, Map* (W.R.S. viii), pl. 9.
62 Date on ho.
63 Capp's Diary, 1714–74, p. 28 (19th-cent. copy in church).
64 W.R.O., D 1/21/5/2.
65 Below, prot. nonconf.
66 *Andrews and Dury, Map* (W.R.S. viii), pl. 9.
67 Date on ho.
68 O.S. Map 6", Wilts. XLVIII (1883–8 edn.); P.R.O., IR 30/38/178.
69 *Kelly's Dir. Wilts.* (1867).
70 W.R.O., G 10/516/3–4; inf. from Mr. E. Levell, 18 Pretoria Road, Faberstown.
71 P.R.O., C 78/1814, no. 1.
72 Ibid. ASSI 21/57, Lent assizes, Wilts., 1831; ASSI 25/22/6.   73 Ibid. IR 29/38/178; IR 30/38/178.
74 W.R.O., G 10/760/20; G 10/760/53; cf. below, econ. hist. (trade and ind.).
75 W.R.O., A 1/355/265; A 1/355/290.
76 Below, this section.
77 W.R.O., A 1/355/370; ibid. G 10/132/38.
78 Ibid. A 1/355/136; A 1/355/141.
79 Ibid. G 10/500/14; G 10/516/1.
80 Ibid. A 1/355/265; A 1/355/290; A 1/355/345; ibid. G 10/516/1–2; O.S. Map 6", Wilts. XLVIII. SE. (1926 edn.).

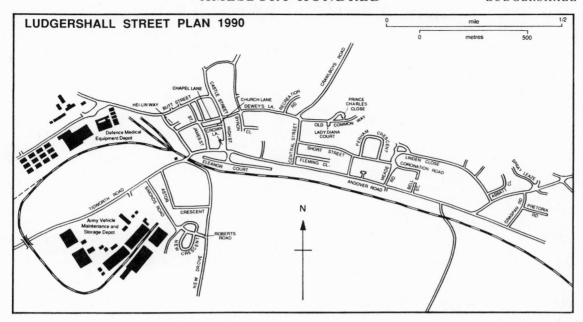

Linden Close, and Perham Crescent were built,[81] in the early 1960s council houses were built in Recreation Road and Byron Close, and in the late 1960s council houses were built in Hei-lin Way, Fleming Close, and, for old people, Crown Lane.[82] Private and council houses were built in Meade Road in the early 1960s,[83] in Wood Park, Spray Leaze, and St. Nicholas's Close in the early 1970s, in Abbatt Close in the late 1970s,[84] and in Lady Diana Court, Prince Charles Close, Old Common Way and on the site of the station in the 1980s.[85] After *c.* 1900 shops, including a co-operative stores, were opened in Andover Road.[86] In 1990 a garage and a supermarket were open in Andover Road and a total of *c.* 23 shops there and in High Street.

Three inns stood on the east side of High Street: the Falcon was closed before 1698,[87] the White Horse was closed before 1710,[88] and the George, next to the White Horse, was called the Queen's Head from between 1710 and 1721.[89] Three also stood on the west side, the Crown, open in 1695,[90] the Half Moon, open in 1728,[91] and the Star, open in 1756. Only the Queen's Head, the Crown, and the Star were open in 1756–7 when soldiers travelling to France were quartered in them.[92] The Star was closed before 1796;[93] the Queen's Head and the Crown remain open. The Prince of Wales was also called the Railway inn from 1882.[94]

Ludgershall had a police station, in Butt Street, by 1908, and an inspector and a constable were based there.[95] A new station was opened in Castle Street between 1947 and 1960.[96] Petty sessions were held at Ludgershall from *c.* 1907 to 1973.[97] From 1903 to 1959 or later Ludgershall was supplied by waterworks built by Walter Faber at Faberstown,[98] and a sewage disposal works and pumping station were built in the south corner of the parish in 1949.[99] Electricity was supplied from 1933,[1] a fire station was opened in High Street in 1939 and replaced by one built in Castle Street in 1968,[2] and a part-time branch of the county library was opened in the Memorial hall on the south side of Andover Road in 1968.[3] A health centre was opened in Central Street in 1980.[4] In 1966 many of the streets were renumbered.[5]

A friendly society in Ludgershall, presumably that which existed in 1819,[6] had *c.* 130 members, more than a quarter of the population, between 1813 and 1815.[7] The Prince of Wales gave its name to a lodge, which met in it, registered by the Modern Order of Foresters in 1869 and dissolved in 1912.[8] A craft lodge, 'Border', for freemasons, was formed in the Prince of Wales in 1905[9] and still met there in 1990. During the

81 W.R.O., A 1/355/370; ibid. G 10/132/38.
82 Ibid. A 1/355/395; A 1/355/420; A 1/355/440.
83 Ibid. A 1/355/420.
84 Ibid. A 1/355/440; A 1/355/465/1; A 1/355/490/2.
85 Ibid. A 1/355/515/3.
86 Ibid. Inland Revenue, val. reg. 139; ibid. G 10/500/14; G 10/516/1–4.
87 Ibid. 212B/3750–1; 212B/3760; 212B/3846.
88 Ibid. 212B/3779.
89 Ibid.; P.R.O., C 78/1814, no. 1.
90 W.R.O. 212B/3748.
91 Ibid. 212B/3796.
92 Capp's Diary, 1714–74, pp. 24–6.
93 Overseers' and surveyors' acct. bk. 1792–1829.
94 *Kelly's Dir. Wilts.* (1885).
95 W.R.O., F 5/250/7; ibid. Inland Revenue, val. reg. 139.
96 Ibid. A 1/355/395; ibid. F 5/510/1.

97 *Kelly's Dir. Wilts.* (1907 and later edns.); *V.C.H. Wilts.* xi. 136; inf. from the Clerk to the Justices, Everleigh and Pewsey Div., 10 Mkt. Place, Chippenham.
98 W.R.O., G 10/132/32.
99 Ibid. G 10/132/8.
1 Inf. from Mr. C. A. Williams, Southern Electric (Kennet Div.), Newbury, Berks.
2 P. Thorpe, *Moonraker Firemen*, 129; B. Humphrey, *Pictorial Hist. Ludgershall*, 12, 42; W.R.O., G 10/516/2.
3 Inf. from Local Studies Librarian, Co. Hall, Trowbridge.
4 Inf. from Mr. Levell.
5 W.R.O., G 10/132/9.
6 P.R.O., FS 4/55, Wilts. no. 50.
7 *Poor Law Abstract, 1818*, 492–3; *V.C.H. Wilts.* iv. 352.
8 P.R.O., FS 4/55, Wilts. no. 381.
9 *V.C.H. Wilts.* iv. 389.

First World War two cinemas were open at the west end of Winchester Street:[10] one on the north side was still open in 1920.[11] In 1853, when the common was inclosed, 2 a. south of Dewey's Lane were allotted to the parish as a recreation ground,[12] and in 1990 they were still used as such. A scout hall in Chapel Lane, given by G. J. Gribble in 1912,[13] was used in 1990. Other clubs in 1990 included a sports and working men's club, begun c. 1922, which had premises in Tidworth Road, the Old Castle club for Royal British Legion members, begun before 1945 in Castle Street, and a boys' club, begun c. 1949 in Andover Road.[14]

In 1939 the War Office transferred the Army Medical stores, from 1969 the Defence Medical Equipment Depot, to a 15-a. site west of Ludgershall station. The stores were rebuilt between 1971 and 1982. South of Tidworth Road, also in 1939, a mobilization depot and workshops for the manufacture and repair of vehicles were built for the army on a site of which c. 36 a. were in Ludgershall. In 1943–4 the United States army and navy prepared vehicles there for the invasion of Europe. The Armoured Vehicle Storage Depot was still used for maintenance and storage in 1990.[15]

FABERSTOWN is the name given to a group of houses in the east angle between Andover Road and Biddesden Lane, and alludes to Walter Faber (d. 1928), M.P. for Andover 1906–18,[16] who began the settlement as a speculative investment c. 1900. There are houses on the south side of Biddesden Lane, beside Andover Road, where bungalows on the south side occupy the site of the waterworks, in Pretoria Road where one is dated 1901 and another 1902, and in Graspan Road. Faberstown was, when begun, separate from Ludgershall, but by the 1970s Ludgershall's eastwards expansion had reached it, and since then it has generally been considered part of Ludgershall.

CASTLE, MANOR, AND OTHER ESTATES. King Ethelred (d. 1016) gave 3 hides at Ludgershall, likely to have been Ludgershall in Wiltshire, to his son Athelstan (d. 1014), who devised them to Godwine the driveller.[17] A hide at Ludgershall was held by Elward in 1066 and by Edward of Salisbury in 1086.[18] Before 1103 the king resumed the estate and Ludgershall castle was built on it.

LUDGERSHALL CASTLE had been built by 1103 when Henry I visited it.[19] Like Marlborough castle, it was fortified in 1138 by John FitzGilbert, the marshal,[20] for the Empress Maud who took refuge in it after the rout of Winchester in 1141 and was taken from it to Devizes castle disguised as a corpse on a bier.[21] After FitzGilbert's death in 1165,[22] Henry II committed the castle to William FitzPeter.[23] The king himself was at the castle in 1175–6 while on an extended visitation of forests.[24] On his brother John's marriage to Isabel of Gloucester in 1189 Richard I gave the castle to John,[25] presumably resumed it after John's rebellion in 1193–4, and in 1194 committed the keeping of it, with that of Marlborough castle, to Hugh de Neville.[26] The castles were linked administratively and both King John and Henry III favoured and improved them as residences and strengthened them as fortresses.

Ludgershall castle was garrisoned with knights, mounted serjeants, and foot soldiers in 1198–9,[27] the keep, a room within the keep, and the castle walls were strengthened in 1211,[28] and money was paid into the king's chamber in it in 1215–16,[29] but the castle may not have been one of John's provincial treasuries. The king visited it in 1200–1, 1204–5, 1207–8, and 1213–16,[30] and Queen Isabel was there in 1210.[31] Its assignment as jointure to Queen Eleanor (d. 1291) in 1236[32] indicates that the castle was not strategically important in the 13th century. The improvement of the living accommodation,[33] and the ordering of 119 casks of wine 1245–57,[34] show the castle to have been used mainly for recreation in the mid 13th century. Henry III was there in 1239, 1241,[35] and 1248.[36] In 1261, when the barons were opposing him, he entrusted the castle to Robert Waleran, as he did Marlborough castle. Probably at the insistence of Simon de Montfort, earl of Leicester, Waleran was replaced in 1262 by Roger de Clifford, an adherent of Montfort, but was reinstated in 1263 when Clifford returned to his allegiance.[37] Marauders who entered Ludgershall castle after the battle of Lewes in 1264 were ejected.[38] Henry III was again at the castle in 1267[39] and 1271,[40] and Queen Eleanor may have spent much of her widowhood there both before and after 1276, when she became a nun of Amesbury priory.[41] Edward I was at the castle in 1276,[42] 1278, 1281,

10 Inf. from Mr. Levell.
11 Ch. Com. file 53875/1.
12 W.R.O., EA/172.
13 Tablet on hall.
14 Ch. Com. file 89446; W.R.O., G 10/132/9; G 10/516/2; G 10/516/4; inf. from Mr. Levell.
15 James, *Plain Soldiering*, 87–8; inf. from Defence Land Agent, Durrington.
16 *Who Was Who, 1916–28*, 340.
17 D. Whitelock, *Anglo-Saxon Wills*, pp. 57–62, 173; *P.N. Wilts.* (E.P.N.S.), 368.
18 *V.C.H. Wilts.* ii, p. 136.
19 *Reg. Regum Anglo-Norm.* ii, nos. 630–1.
20 *Ann. Mon.* (Rolls Ser.), ii. 51.
21 John of Worcester in *Florentii Wigorn. Chron. ex Chronicis*, ed. B. Thorpe, ii. 134.
22 *Complete Peerage*, x, App. G, 95.
23 *Pipe R.* 1166–7 (P.R.S. xi), 130.
24 *V.C.H. Wilts.* iv. 393.

25 *Chron. Rog. de Houedene* (Rolls Ser.), iii. 6.
26 *V.C.H. Wilts.* xii. 166; *Pipe R.* 1198 (P.R.S. N.S. ix), 71.
27 *Pipe R.* 1199 (P.R.S. N.S. x), 174.
28 Ibid. 1211 (P.R.S. N.S. xxviii), 84.
29 Ibid. 17 John (P.R.S. N.S. xxxvii), 36.
30 *Archaeologia*, xxii. 131–2, 138–42, 145–9, 152, 156–7, 159.
31 *Rot. Lib.* (Rec. Com.), 152–3.
32 *Cal. Pat.* 1266–72, 736–7.
33 Below, this section.
34 *Cal. Lib.* 1245–51, *passim*; 1251–60, *passim*.
35 *Cur. Reg. R.* xvi, pp. xlvi–xlvii.
36 *Letters of Hen. III* (Rolls Ser.), ii. 50.
37 *V.C.H. Wilts.* xii. 166; *Close R.* 1261–4, 325–6.
38 *Cal. Lib.* 1260–7, 242.
39 Ibid. 291.
40 *Close R.* 1268–72, 537.
41 P.R.O., SC 1/16, nos. 152, 178, 187, 189; SC 1/23, nos. 30–2; SC 1/25, no. 91; SC 1/47, no. 109.
42 *Ann. Mon.* (Rolls Ser.), ii. 121.

and 1302,[43] and his brother Edmund was there in 1291.[44]

After *c.* 1300 the castle was used only as a house. Its residential quarters were called the king's houses and its lands a manor. In 1294 they were granted during pleasure to Almaric St. Amand, Lord St. Amand (d. 1310),[45] in 1317 for life to Edward II's sister Mary (d. 1332), a nun of Amesbury priory,[46] in 1334 to Queen Philippa,[47] and in 1356 for life to Edward III's daughter Isabel (d. 1379), wife of Ingram de Coucy (cr. earl of Bedford 1366), as her residence.[48] As part of the manor the castle was granted as dower in 1382 to Queen Anne (d. 1394)[49] and in 1403 to Queen Joan (d. 1437).[50] It was granted in 1440 for life, in 1449 in tail male, to William Ludlow (d. 1478), the parker of Ludgershall,[51] but both grants were revoked before 1453 when it was granted to Henry VI's half-brother Edmund Tudor, earl of Richmond (d. 1456).[52] It was granted to Edward IV's brother George, duke of Clarence, in 1464 but from his execution in 1478[53] it remained with the Crown until 1547.

The castle had around it a demesne farm and a park, and woodland was nearby:[54] resources from them may have been sufficient to support its daily administration and no serjeanty is recorded. The chief officer of the castle was the constable, first mentioned by that name in 1233[55] and also called the castellan or keeper, later keeper of the manor.[56] In the late 12th century and the 13th the constables were lessees of the lands around the castle[57] and were allowed wood from Chute forest for repairs.[58] Other officers included a bailiff, mentioned from 1226 and also responsible for Marlborough castle,[59] and, in 1255, a serjeant and a porter.[60] The castle was a common gaol in the 13th century but no reference to its delivery or to its use as such after 1289 has been found.[61]

The fortifications raised at Ludgershall before 1103 were within two embanked enclosures forming an irregular north–south figure eight.[62] The southern enclosure had timber revetting, later replaced in stone. Within it a timber building with a cellar was constructed in the 12th century and replaced in the 14th by a three-bayed building on stone foundations: the functions of both buildings are obscure. In the northern enclosure, on higher ground, timber buildings were erected in the late 11th century

and replaced in the early 12th by a stone keep with dressings of greensand ashlar. In the late 12th century the keep was replaced by a hall which possibly had aisles and an undercroft. Also in the late 12th century the inner edge of the northern half of the ditch was fortified at intervals with stone mural towers, the remains of one of which forms the main feature of the surviving ruins.[63] The buildings were often repaired 1198–1228, and in 1205 the construction of an oven large enough to roast two or three oxen was ordered. From 1234 rebuilding and alterations for Henry III converted the castle from a fortress to a country house. The royal chambers were redecorated, the king's in 1234–5 with wainscotting and a stained glass window, the queen's in 1241–2. The 12th-century hall was rebuilt from 1244. The new hall, measuring 40 ft. by 60 ft., was lit by gable dormers, and it had wooden pillars, painted to resemble marble, and opposite the king's dais a gable wall painted with the story of Dives and Lazarus. In 1247 the king's carpenter made a new dais. A covered passage between the hall and the queen's chamber was also built in 1247. The castle wall was repaired and crenellated in 1250. New service rooms, including a kitchen for the king and another for his household, were built from *c.* 1244. Other service rooms were rebuilt in 1250, and in 1251–2 a new chamber and two privy chambers were built for Henry III's son Edward. All those rooms of 1250–2 were possibly part of a range built east of the surviving mural tower and partly over the northern ditch, which was spanned by a latrine block. The castle was repaired in the period 1403–37 but was afterwards allowed to decay. About 1540 it was 'clean down'.[64]

A chapel in the castle in 1200[65] was repaired in 1205.[66] In the period 1234–44 there were two chapels, one invoking St. Catherine, the other St. Nicholas, and each was served by a chaplain; in 1244 two sets of vestments and a chalice were bought.[67] In 1250 a crucifix and a statue of St. Mary were ordered for the king's chapel, presumably a third. Another, for which a statue of St. Mary and Child was ordered in 1251, invoked St. Leonard.[68] The chaplain who served the king's chapel received a gown in 1267.[69] One of the chapels was rebuilt in 1285, and one in 1341–3 when glass, made by John the glazier of Calne and depicting the royal arms and the

43 H. Gough, *Itin. Edw. I*, i. 85–6, 118, 220.
44 *Sir Chris. Hatton's Bk. of Seals*, ed. L. C. Loyd and D. M. Stenton, no. 338.
45 *Cal. Close*, 1288–96, 391; *Complete Peerage*, xi. 297–8.
46 *Cal. Pat.* 1313–17, 625, 635.
47 *Cal. Fine R.* 1327–37, 414.
48 *Cal. Pat.* 1354–8, 190, 405; *Complete Peerage*, ii. 69–70.
49 *Cal. Pat.* 1381–5, 203.
50 Ibid. 1401–5, 235.
51 Ibid. 1436–41, 401; 1446–52, 247; *V.C.H. Wilts.* xi. 57.
52 *Cal. Pat.* 1452–61, 79; *Complete Peerage*, x. 825–6.
53 *Cal. Pat.* 1461–7, 331; *Complete Peerage*, iii. 260–1.
54 Below, econ. hist. (parks; agric.).
55 *Cal. Lib.* 1226–40, 205.
56 *Close R.* 1268–72, 222, 346–7.
57 *Pipe R.* 1198 (P.R.S. N.S. ix), 71; *Cal. Lib.* 1260–7,

128.
58 *Close R.* 1237–42, 85–6; 1247–51, 377–8.
59 *Cal. Lib.* 1240–5, 59; *Rot. Litt. Claus.* (Rec. Com.), ii. 139.
60 *Rot. Hund.* (Rec. Com.), ii (1), 233.
61 *V.C.H. Wilts.* v. 14; *Close R.* 1242–7, 326; 1264–8, 421; P.R.O., JUST 1/1006, rot. 66d.
62 Description based on accts. of P. V. Addyman's excavations 1964–71: *W.A.M.* lxi. 104–5; lxiii. 111–12; lxiv. 124–6; lxv. 205; lxvii. 176; *Hist. King's Works*, ed. R. A. Brown and others, i. 80, 121, 123–4, 128; ii. 729–31.
63 See plate facing p. 251.
64 Leland, *Itin.* ed. Toulmin Smith, v. 6.
65 *Pipe R.* 1200 (P.R.S. N.S. xii), 155.
66 *Rot. Litt. Claus.* (Rec. Com.), i. 40.
67 *Hist. King's Works*, ii. 731; *Cal. Lib.* 1226–40, 418; 1240–5, 59, 221; *Pipe R.* 1242 (ed. H. L. Cannon), 175.
68 *Cal. Lib.* 1245–51, 294–5, 363.
69 *Close R.* 1264–8, 406.

Passion, was inserted in its east window.[70] In St. Mary's chapel masses were said for the king, his heirs, and his ancestors in 1352.[71]

In 1547 *LUDGERSHALL* manor, including the remains of the castle, was granted to Edward Seymour, duke of Somerset, who was deprived of it in 1549. It was restored to him in 1550 but was forfeited on his execution and attainder in 1552.[72] The manor was granted in 1553 to John Russell, earl of Bedford, and Edmund Downing. In that year they sold it to William Allen,[73] in 1556 Allen sold it to Richard Taverner,[74] and in 1558 Taverner sold it to Sir Richard Bridges (d. 1558), the lessee from 1539, and Richard's wife Jane, later wife of Sir Simon Harcourt (d. 1577). On Jane's death in 1593 the manor passed to her son Anthony Bridges,[75] who apparently sold it then to his son-in-law Sir George Browne (d. 1614). Two thirds of it were forfeited by Sir George for recusancy in 1610. He was succeeded as owner by his son George (d. 1664), by George's son Sir George (d. 1678), and by Sir George's son John (cr. baronet 1665, d. c. 1680). The manor passed with the baronetcy to Sir John's son Sir Anthony (d. 1688), and to Sir Anthony's brothers Sir John (d. 1692) and Sir George.[76] In 1703 Sir George sold it to Sir Walter Clarges, Bt.[77] (d. 1706), and it passed to Clarges's relict Elizabeth (d. 1728), who devised it to her sons Christopher and Gould Clarges as tenants in common.[78] They sold it in 1741 to John Selwyn[79] (d. 1751). It descended to John's son George (d. 1791) and to his grandson Thomas Townshend, Viscount Sydney (d. 1800). Thomas's son John, Lord Sydney, sold it c. 1817 to Sir James Graham, Bt.[80] Sir James (d. 1825) was succeeded by his son Sir Sandford Graham, Bt.,[81] who c. 1833 sold his burgage tenements[82] and in 1845 sold the rest of the manor to the trustees of the will (proved 1837) of W. H. Maund. In 1876 Maund's trustee sold the estate to Nathaniel Young, after whose death his mortgagee sold it in 1898 to the War Department.[83] In 1990 the Ministry of Defence owned 225 ha. in Ludgershall.[84]

SOUTH PARK farm, formerly part of Ludgershall manor, was owned by John Richmond Webb (d. 1724) in 1720.[85] As part of Shoddesden

manor in Kimpton it descended to his daughter Frances and her husband Thomas Humphreys, who sold it in 1756 to John Peachy.[86] John's son William (d. 1790) owned it in 1780, and it passed to William's son William (d. 1839), whose relict Susannah[87] sold it to James Henry in 1839. Henry sold the land, 145 a., to Richard Pollen and his wife Charlotte in 1849. In 1854 the Pollens sold it to Richard's uncle Sir John Pollen, Bt. (d. s.p. 1863) and his wife Charlotte (d. 1877).[88] From Charlotte it passed back to Richard, who had succeeded to his uncle's baronetcy. From Sir Richard (d. 1881) it descended to his son Sir Richard Pollen, Bt., who sold it in 1907 to A. J. Kemble.[89] In 1910 and 1924, when the land was still part of an estate based in Shoddesden, the owner was R. Young.[90] From c. 1943 South Park farm was owned by the firm of W. E. & D. T. Cave. It was bought in 1983 by Mr. R. D. Hendry, the owner in 1990.[91]

St. Mary's chantry in Ludgershall church[92] had in the parish two burgage tenements in Winchester Street given before 1405,[93] two houses in the same street, one given before 1518 and one before 1525, and, all given in 1528, two messuages in Ludgershall, one in Biddesden, and a total of 6 a. in the fields of Ludgershall and Biddesden.[94] The estate passed to the Crown in 1548.[95]

The great tithes from Ludgershall were apparently due to Amesbury priory between 1228 and 1446. From 1446 to the Dissolution the rector of Ludgershall paid the priory £4 a year instead.[96]

ECONOMIC HISTORY. PARKS AND WOODLAND. Land near Ludgershall castle had been imparked by 1203.[97] There was a South park in the late 13th century:[98] its name, and the existence of a bank and ditch north of the castle,[99] show that there was also a north park. In the early 13th century the parkland to the south apparently extended into Hampshire.[1] A park was inclosed by a ditch and a hedge in 1244,[2] and in 1271 was impaled.[3] Deer from it were sent to William de Valence's park at Collingbourne Kingston in 1254,[4] and in 1265 three

70 *Hist. King's Works*, ii. 731.
71 *Cal. Pat.* 1350–4, 212; cf. below, church.
72 *Cal. Pat.* 1547–8, 121; 1549–51, 430; *Complete Peerage*, xii (1), 63–4.
73 *Cal. Pat.* 1547–53, 266, 281–3.
74 P.R.O., CP 25/2/81/694, no. 10.
75 Ibid. C 142/124, no. 191; ibid. CP 25/2/81/695, no. 16; ibid. E 368/347 Recorda Mich. rot. 89; *Hist. Parl., Commons*, 1509–58, i. 534–5; *V.C.H. Oxon.* xii. 275.
76 P.R.O., C 66/1874, no. 24; C 142/341, no. 87; W.R.O. 212B/3739; for the Browne fam., *V.C.H. Berks.* iv. 239–40.
77 W.R.O. 212B/3766.
78 Hist. MSS. Com. 43, *15th Rep. VII, Ailesbury*, p. 199; *Musgrave's Obit.* ii (Harl. Soc. xlv), 4; *Hist. Parl., Commons*, 1660–90, ii. 81; P.R.O., PROB 11/677, f. 268 and v.
79 W.R.O. 212B/3814.
80 Ibid. A 1/345/266; *Hist. Parl., Commons*, 1715–54, ii. 416; 1754–90, iii. 420–1; *Complete Peerage*, xii (2), 590–2.
81 *Hist. Parl., Commons*, 1790–1820, iv. 55.
82 Hants R.O. 46M84, box 37, sale cat. 1833.
83 Treas. Solicitor, regy. no. 293/50, Ludgershall deeds.
84 Inf. from Defence Land Agent, Durrington.
85 P.R.O., C 78/1814, no. 1.
86 *V.C.H. Hants*, iv. 374, which this descent corrects and

amplifies.
87 W.R.O., A 1/345/266; ibid. 2216/16, deed, Peachy to Henry, 1839; P.R.O., PROB 11/1196, ff. 128–9.
88 W.R.O. 2216/16, deeds, Peachy to Henry, 1839; Henry to Pollen's trustees, 1849; Pollen to Pollen, 1854; 2216/29, Barnes's declaration, 1865; for the Pollens, Burke, *Peerage* (1963), 1949–50.
89 W.R.O. 2216/30/1, abstr. of title, 1907.
90 Ibid. Inland Revenue, val. reg. 139; ibid. G 10/500/14.
91 Inf. from Mr. R. D. Hendry, Lower Ho. Farm, Everleigh.
92 Below, church.
93 Soc. Antiq. MS. 817, Ludgershall.
94 *Cat. Anct. D.* i, C 59, C 674, C 824; ii, C 2044; iii, C 3318.
95 P.R.O., E 301/58, no. 19.
96 W.R.O., D 1/2/10, ff. 74–5; below, church.
97 *Pipe R.* 1203 (P.R.S. N.S. xvi), 161; *Rot. Hund.* (Rec. Com.), ii (1), 233.
98 *P.N. Wilts.* (E.P.N.S.), 369.
99 Above, intro. [boundaries].
1 *Rot. Litt. Claus.* (Rec. Com.), ii. 52.
2 *Cal. Lib.* 1240–5, 234.
3 *Close R.* 1268–72, 346–7.
4 Ibid. 1254–6, 17.

deer leaps were built in Ludgershall park for the Lord Edward.[5] In 1305 royal officials spent three weeks trapping beasts in Chute forest and carting them to Ludgershall to stock the park.[6] The parkland was increased in 1348 when arable was imparked,[7] and was possibly enlarged to the north in 1464 when George, duke of Clarence, was licensed to impark 200 a. of Collingbourne woods, to construct a deer leap, and to have free warren there.[8] The office of parker, mentioned in 1332,[9] was from 1400 or earlier usually held by the farmer of Ludgershall manor.[10] The south park was still stocked with deer in 1549[11] and was presumably later the land of South Park farm. There is no further evidence of parkland north of the castle.

Ludgershall had woodland ½ league by 2 furlongs in 1086.[12] By 1203 some near the castle had been taken into the parkland,[13] and there is likely to have been little other woodland in the west part of the parish. Ludgershall forest, so called in 1189,[14] may have been the name for all or part of Chute forest, and Ludgershall woods, including North grove, were part of Chute forest: they are likely to have lain to the east, were disafforested in 1300 but as ancient demesne remained subject to the forest law, and in 1332 were administered by the keepers of the castle park.[15] In the 16th century Ludgershall manor included Coldridge coppice, which was inclosed between 1510 and 1539. It was partly coppiced in the late 16th century,[16] amounted to 37 a. in 1838,[17] and was still woodland in 1990.

AGRICULTURE. In 1086 Ludgershall had land for 3 ploughteams: there were 2 on the demesne with 3 *servi*, and 8 coscets had a third. Pasture measured 2 furlongs by ½ furlong.[18]

The demesne or barton of Ludgershall castle may have included land south, east, and west of the castle: later evidence shows arable to have been in King's field, south of the Marlborough–Winchester road, and Woolridge field, north of Biddesden Lane. Sheep-and-corn husbandry was practised. In 1222 the tenants were enjoined to plough on the demesne, money was sent from the Exchequer to buy grain, and an officer was sent to oversee cultivation.[19] Corn for seed was sent from Ludgershall to Marlborough in 1223, and in 1225 surplus grain was sold to pay for repairs at Ludgershall castle.[20] In 1291 c. 180 a. of demesne were sown, mostly with barley and oats, and a hayward, a shepherd, and a ploughman were employed; a further 48 a., possibly Woolridge field, were leased to the tenants.[21]

Before the castle and the borough were built arable at Ludgershall was almost certainly in open fields, and Windmill Hill down may have been a common pasture for sheep. Afterwards, East and West may have survived as open fields, but customary tenure was apparently ended. The inhabitants of the borough may have taken over the open arable: they were required to cultivate the barton, but commuted the service before 1233.[22] From 1291 they held, in addition to the 48 a. of arable, 84 a. of Woolridge,[23] the later Ludgershall common.[24] Rights claimed in the 17th century may have been long held: the tenant of each burgage had the right to keep a beast in the open fields after harvest and on Coldridge down and Spray leaze, to take wood from Coldridge coppice and dig chalk for repairs, and to use dirt from the street for compost.[25] Feeding was lost when demesne arable was imparked in 1348 and Coldridge coppice was inclosed in the earlier 16th century. In the 16th and 17th centuries the tenants held, for 6d. an acre, land in the three, possibly open, fields, Woolridge, East, and West: an attempt by the lord of the manor to raise the rent to 8d. in the late 16th century provoked a riot in which a tenant was killed.[26] Between 1614 and 1647 part of Coldridge down was lost to the tenants and added to Biddesden, possibly c. 1636 when a ditch was dug to distinguish Coldridge and Biddesden downs.[27] In 1682, by agreement, land, most of it almost certainly open arable, was inclosed, divided, and allotted to 16 tenants in portions, apparently one each, which all adjoined a track called the Drove:[28] if the Drove was the road called New Drove in 1838 and 1990 the allotments were of c. 90 a. south of High Street.[29] There is no later evidence of open arable or, apart from Ludgershall common, of common pasture, and the allotments of 1682 may have been to compensate the tenants for their exclusion from such lands.

In 1786 most of Ludgershall's land was in three farms, Manor or Castle based near the castle ruins, South Park based in the south corner of the parish, and Crawlboys based in Collingbourne Ducis and including c. 145 a. in Ludgershall. Ludgershall common remained open for the cattle of tenants in the borough, and the rector was accustomed to provide a bull from Whit Sunday to 21 December each year.[30] In 1838 Castle farm was 563 a., South Park was 147 a., and Crawlboys still included 145 a. A farm of 56 a. was worked from buildings north of Butt Street, and one of 52 a. from the Queen's Head.

5 Ibid. 1264–8, 77.
6 P.R.O., SC 6/1276/8, nos. 1–2, 9.
7 *Cal. Pat.* 1348–50, 148–9.
8 Ibid. 1461–7, 331.
9 Ibid. 1330–4, 375.
10 Ibid. 1391–6, 422; *Cal. Fine R.* 1399–1405, 142–3.
11 *W.A.M.* viii. 299.
12 *V.C.H. Wilts.* ii, p. 136.
13 *Pipe R.* 1203 (P.R.S. N.S. xvi), 161; *Rot. Hund.* (Rec. Com.), ii (1), 233.
14 *Chron. Rog. de Houedene* (Rolls Ser.), iii. 6.
15 *V.C.H. Wilts.* iv. 424–5; *Cal. Pat.* 1330–4, 375; P.R.O., E 159/48, rot. 2d.; ibid. SC 6/1054/22.
16 P.R.O., E 134/27 Eliz. I East./4.
17 Ibid. IR 29/38/178; IR 30/38/178.
18 *V.C.H. Wilts.* ii, p. 136.

19 *Rot. Litt. Claus.* (Rec. Com.), i. 491; *Cal. Lib.* 1226–40, 205; *Pat. R.* 1216–25, 323–4; *Tax List, 1332* (W.R.S. xlv), 7; P.R.O., E 134/27 Eliz. I East./4; ibid. IR 29/38/178; IR 30/38/178.
20 *Rot. Litt. Claus.* (Rec. Com.), i. 530; ii. 53.
21 P.R.O., SC 6/1054/22.
22 *Cal. Lib.* 1226–40, 205.
23 P.R.O., E 134/27 Eliz. I East./4; ibid. SC 6/1054/22.
24 Ibid. IR 29/38/178; IR 30/38/178.
25 Ibid. E 134/23 Chas. I Mich./6.
26 Ibid. C 3/213/3; ibid. E 134/27 Eliz. I East./4; E 134/23 Chas. I Mich./6.
27 Ibid. E 134/23 Chas. I Mich./6.
28 W.R.O. 212B/3732.
29 P.R.O., IR 29/38/178; IR 30/38/178.
30 W.R.O., D 1/24/137/1.

Apart from Windmill Hill down, 105 a. in Castle farm, nearly all the land was arable. In the earlier 19th century sheep-and-corn husbandry was practised on a four-field system in which wheat, barley, and temporary grasses including sainfoin, were grown in rotation. By 1838 that arrangement had been modified to include the cultivation of turnips.[31] The 87 a. of Ludgershall common were inclosed and allotted by Act in 1853: 36 a. were added to Castle farm and 5 a. to South Park farm.[32] In the later 19th century racehorses, including two winners of the Grand National, were trained on gallops on Windmill Hill down.[33]

Possibly in the later 19th century, certainly in the earlier 20th, arable was laid to grass: sheep rearing was largely replaced by dairying and pig keeping.[34] In the mid and late 20th century agricultural land was appreciably reduced by new housing and building for military purposes.[35] In 1990 the 371 a. of Castle farm were worked mainly from Court Farm in Collingbourne Ducis, and South Park farm, with 500 a. in Ludgershall, was part of Lower House farm based in Everleigh:[36] the Ludgershall lands of the two farms were largely arable. A commercial horticultural nursery was open in Astor Crescent in 1966[37] and 1990, and a poultry farm in Crawlboys Lane in 1978[38] and 1990.

MILLS. A horse mill was built on the castle barton in 1250.[39] The windmill standing on the barton in 1274[40] was perhaps the mill held on lease from the king 1291–3.[41] In 1585 there was a windmill in West field,[42] and in 1773 one stood east of Dewey's Lane.[43] The only windmill at Ludgershall in 1838 was one owned by James Hunt south of Tidworth Road.[44] It was still working in 1865[45] but no longer stood in 1878.[46]

MARKETS AND FAIRS. A market was presumably held in 1255 when inhabitants of Ludgershall committed market offences,[47] and Ludgershall market attracted people from elsewhere in 1268.[48] The tolls were held by lease from the Crown in 1291.[49] In 1348 it was claimed that the closure of roads on land taken to enlarge the

king's park discouraged trade, and quittance from toll was granted to those attending the market.[50] A small market was still held in 1756,[51] possibly on a Wednesday[52] and around the market cross in High Street, but c. 1757 Ludgershall was of no importance as a market town.[53] No market was held in 1792.[54]

In 1248 the king proclaimed a three-day fair at the Nativity of St. Mary (7–9 September).[55] In 1291, however, the fair was on the eve and day of St. James (24–5 July).[56] Freedom from toll was granted in 1348.[57] In the later 16th century the lord of the manor was reported to have taken away the weights used at the fair.[58] A small pleasure fair, held on 25 July in the later 19th century,[59] was last mentioned in 1903.[60]

TRADE AND INDUSTRY. Ludgershall may have prospered as a trading centre in the late 14th century, when an apparently prosperous merchant represented it in parliament,[61] and in the 15th. Oil, herrings, and wool were brought from Southampton in 1443–4, fish in 1528,[62] and Henry Bridges, keeper of Ludgershall manor 1510–38, may have dealt in cloth.[63] The request of four Germans from Westphalia to live in Ludgershall, granted in 1436, suggests commercial opportunities.[64] Later, an itinerant tobacco seller was licensed to trade in Ludgershall in 1637,[65] and in 1665 a Ludgershall tradesman issued a token.[66]

Cloth was worked in Ludgershall in the 17th and 18th centuries: there was a weaver in 1647,[67] a serge weaver in 1671–2,[68] and in 1706 a Mr. Cook employed 150–200 of the poorer inhabitants in spinning,[69] but c. 1757 no trace of the cloth industry remained.[70] A roper worked in Ludgershall in 1426.[71] Tiles from Ludgershall used to repair Devizes castle in 1411–12 may have been second-hand and not made there.[72] A butchers' shambles was near the market cross in 1515,[73] and several butchers, seven in 1620, traded at Ludgershall in the later 16th century and earlier 17th.[74] There was a malthouse in 1671–2, presumably the large one which stood in Winchester Street in 1692,[75] and another at the Crown in 1735.[76] In the later 19th century

31 P.R.O., IR 18/11074; IR 29/38/178; IR 30/38/178.
32 W.R.O., EA/172.
33 W.A.S. Libr., sale cat. vii, no. 67.
34 [1st] Land Util. Surv. Map, sheet 122; P.R.O., MAF 68/151, sheet 21; MAF 68/493, sheet 12; MAF 68/1063, sheet 11; MAF 68/1663, sheet 12; MAF 68/2203, sheet 6; MAF 68/2773, sheet 8; MAF 68/3319, sheet 8; MAF 68/3814, no. 103.
35 Above, intro. (Ludgershall).
36 Inf. from Mrs. P. J. Gordon, Court Farm; Mr. R. D. Hendry, Lower Ho. Farm.
37 W.R.O., G 10/516/4.
38 O.S. Map 1/10,000, SU 25 SW. (1978 edn.).
39 Cal. Lib. 1245–51, 276.
40 Cal. Close, 1272–9, 96.
41 P.R.O., SC 6/1054/22.
42 Ibid. E 134/27 Eliz. I East./4.
43 Andrews and Dury, Map (W.R.S. viii), pl. 9.
44 P.R.O., IR 29/38/178; IR 30/38/178.
45 Harrod's Dir. Wilts. (1865).
46 O.S. Map 6", Wilts. XLVIII (1883–8 edn.).
47 Close R. 1254–6, 91.
48 P.R.O., JUST 1/998A, rot. 27.
49 Ibid. SC 6/1054/22.
50 Ibid. C 81/333, no. 19709; Cal. Pat. 1348–50, 148–9.
51 Capp's Diary, 1714–74, pp. 24–5.
52 Lewis, Topog. Dict. Eng. (1831), iii. 175–6.

53 Travels of Dr. Pococke, ii. 246.
54 Rep. Com. Mkt. Rights and Tolls [C. 5550], p. 214, H.C. (1888), liii.   55 Close R. 1247–51, 22.
56 P.R.O., SC 6/1054/22.
57 Cal. Pat. 1348–50, 148–9.
58 W.R.O., D 1/43/6, f. 6.
59 Rep. Com. Mkt. Rights and Tolls (1888), 214.
60 Kelly's Dir. Wilts. (1903).
61 Hist. Parl., Commons, 1386–1421, i. 702.
62 Brokage Bk. of Southampton, 1443–4 (Southampton Rec. Ser. iv), i. 30, 131; 1477–8, 1527–8 (Southampton Rec. Ser. xxviii), 200.
63 Hist. Parl., Commons, 1509–58, i. 531–2.
64 Cal. Pat. 1429–36, 571, 574.
65 Early-Stuart Tradesmen (W.R.S. xv), pp. 100–1.
66 G. C. Williamson, Trade Tokens, ii, p. 1238.
67 P.R.O., E 134/23 Chas. I Mich./6.
68 W.R.O. 212B/3724–5.
69 T. Carew, Rights of Elections (1754), 357.
70 Travels of Dr. Pococke, ii. 247.
71 Cal. Pat. 1422–9, 309.
72 V.C.H. Wilts. x. 244.
73 Cat. Anct. D. i, C 206.
74 Sess. Mins. (W.R.S. iv), 119; Early-Stuart Tradesmen (W.R.S. xv), p. 15; P.R.O., C 2/Eliz. I/B 29/16.
75 W.R.O. 212B/3724–5; 212B/3743.
76 Ibid. 212A/37/3.

and early 20th malting was carried on by the Berry family at Laurel House in Winchester Street,[77] and there were other 20th-century businesses concerned with drink.[78] A brick kiln in Ludgershall in 1796 was apparently near Crawlboys Farm.[79]

Economic activity in Ludgershall was stimulated by the opening of the station in 1882 and the construction of an army camp in North Tidworth from 1897.[80] Three banks had opened by 1907, and that opened by the Wilts. and Dorset Banking Co. in Winchester Street in 1901, a branch of Lloyds Bank from 1914, remained open in 1990.[81] A branch of the Midland Bank was open in High Street from 1938 to 1983.[82] H. & G. Simonds, brewers and wine and spirit merchants, opened offices and bottling works on the south side of Tidworth Road in 1903.[83] From 1960 the works belonged to Courage, Barclay, & Simonds Ltd., based in Reading, after 1970 Courage (Central) Ltd., and were closed in 1988.[84] Waugh Bros. made mineral water in Ludgershall in 1903,[85] in 1907 the Crown Mineral Water Works Ltd. did so,[86] and in 1910 the Aqua Pura Mineral Water Co. had a factory in St. James Street.[87] George Younger & Sons Ltd., brewers, apparently had a depot in Ludgershall in 1939.[88] Other new businesses were White & Co. Ltd., camp furnishers, open in 1903, the South Wilts. Grocery Stores, also open in 1903,[89] the Crown Sanitary Laundry, open in St. James Street in 1907,[90] and the Adjutants Press, opened in Butt Street in 1914[91] and closed in 1989. There was much unemployment in Ludgershall in 1921, presumably caused by reduced military activity after the First World War; the army camp at North Tidworth remained the chief source of employment.[92] New businesses opened after 1918 included a gravel merchant's at Faberstown before 1923,[93] E. Roy's furniture showroom in High Street c. 1931[94] (open in 1990), Seawell Electronics in St. James Street after 1978,[95] and B.M.G. Concrete Products in Tidworth Road in 1984.[96]

LOCAL GOVERNMENT.
Although its inhabitants farmed the borough in 1233 and later,[97] and

claimed their own coroner in 1289,[98] Ludgershall developed no civic institution and there was no justification for the inhabitants' claims, made in the later 16th century and earlier 17th, to be incorporated and to have a common seal.[99] The borough was governed by the castle bailiff, the sheriff was excluded, royal writs were returned direct to Westminster, the bailiff, assisted by catchpoles, took view of frankpledge twice a year, and the king had a gallows.[1] View of frankpledge was granted with Ludgershall manor in 1449,[2] and the view may have been held by the lessees of the manor in the earlier 16th century and by the lords of the manor thereafter, but no direct record of it survives.[3] At quarter sessions in 1648 the lord was ordered to repair the cage, blindhouse, stocks, and pillory.[4] The borough officers, a bailiff and two constables, the successors of the castle bailiff and catchpoles, and two aldermen were appointed at the court leet in the earlier 17th century.[5] Earlier the bailiffs may have been elected yearly, but some evidently served for several years: the same man was bailiff in 1518 and 1525, and another, appointed c. 1597, served for 14 years.[6] An impression of a bailiff's seal of the 15th century, on which the castle is depicted, survives.[7] A manor court was held by the castle bailiff several times in 1291–2,[8] and was held near the castle ruins c. 1757,[9] but its records do not survive.

References in the later 18th century and earlier 19th to Ludgershall being beggarly may have implied a lack of gentility rather than extreme poverty.[10] In 1802–3 only 18 people received regular poor relief, but between 1813 and 1815 the number averaged 79,[11] a sixth of the inhabitants.[12] The average of c. £400 a year spent on relief 1813–35 was not exceptional for a parish with c. 500 inhabitants. Ludgershall became part of Andover poor-law union in 1835[13] and was transferred to Pewsey union in 1879.[14] It became part of Kennet district in 1974.[15]

The accounts of the two surveyors of highways exist for 1792–1829.[16]

PARLIAMENTARY REPRESENTATION.
Ludgershall returned two burgesses to parliament in 1295, and was represented nine times in the period 1300–30. Although summoned in 1360–1 the borough was not represented again

77 Hants R.O. 46M84, box 56, sched. of deeds; box 56, deed, Berry to Berry, 1907; box 56, fire policy, 1927.
78 Below, this section.
79 Overseers' and surveyors' acct. bk. 1792–1829 (in church); P.R.O., IR 29/38/178; IR 30/38/178.
80 Above, intro. [railway]; below, N. Tidworth, intro.
81 Kelly's Dir. Wilts. (1903 and later edns.); W.R.O., G 10/760/5; inf. from the Archivist, Lloyds Bank plc, 71 Lombard Street, Lond. E.C. 3.
82 Inf. from the Archivist, Midland Group, Mariner Ho., Pepys Street, Lond. E.C. 3.
83 W.R.O., G 10/760/2; G 10/760/10.
84 Ibid. G 10/516/3–4; inf. from the Archivist, Courage Ltd., Countership, Bristol.
85 Kelly's Dir. Wilts. (1903).   86 Ibid. (1907).
87 W.R.O., Inland Revenue, val. reg. 139.
88 Kelly's Dir. Wilts. (1939).   89 Ibid. (1903).
90 Ibid. (1907).   91 W.A.M. xlvi. 140.
92 Humphrey, Pictorial Hist. Ludgershall, 7; Ch. Com. file 53875/1.   93 Kelly's Dir. Wilts. (1923).
94 W.R.O., G 10/760/111.
95 Inf. from the rector.
96 Inf. from Mr. B. M. Gloyne, B.M.G. Concrete Products.

97 Cal. Lib. 1226–40, 205.
98 P.R.O., JUST 1/1006, rot. 66d.
99 Ibid. C 3/213/3; ibid. E 134/23 Chas. I Mich./6.
1 Ibid. JUST 1/1006, rot. 66d.; ibid. SC 6/1054/22; Cal. Close, 1272–9, 31.   2 Cal. Pat. 1446–52, 247.
3 e.g. L. & P. Hen. VIII, xiv (2), pp. 220–1; Hist. MSS. Com. 42, 15th Rep. VI, Carlisle, pp. 286, 293; P.R.O., E 134/23 Chas. I Mich./6.
4 Hist. MSS. Com. 55, Var. Colln. i, p. 117.
5 P.R.O., E 134/23 Chas. I Mich./6.
6 Ibid.; Cat. Anct. D. i, C 59; ii, C 2044.
7 B.L., Seals, cv. 38; see below, plate facing p. 219.
8 P.R.O., SC 6/1054/22.
9 Travels of Dr. Pococke, ii. 246.
10 Above, intro. (Ludgershall).
11 Poor Law Abstract, 1804, 558–9; 1818, 492–3.
12 V.C.H. Wilts. iv. 352.
13 Poor Rate Returns, 1816–21, 185; 1822–4, 225; 1825–9, 251; Poor Law Com. 1st Rep. App. D, 248.
14 V.C.H. Wilts. iv. 336.
15 O.S. Map 1/100,000, admin. areas, Wilts. (1974 edn.).
16 Overseers' and surveyors' acct. bk. 1792–1829 (in church).

until 1378: Robert Monk, a resident merchant, sat for it 1378–80 and in 1382–3, and Roger Sotwell, parker of Ludgershall, 1380–5. Ludgershall was represented in nearly all parliaments from 1421 to 1832.[17]

Ludgershall was a royal borough in the 15th century and earlier 16th. The son and grandson of Sir William Sturmy (d. 1427), joint keeper of Ludgershall manor from c. 1412, sat in 1422.[18] In 1432–3, 1435, 1437, 1453–4, and 1455–6 one of the borough's members was William Ludlow, who kept Ludgershall park from 1433 and held the manor from 1440.[19] In the earlier 16th century Henry Bridges and his son Sir Richard were successive lessees of the manor,[20] possibly resident, and together represented the borough in 1523, 1529, and 1536. As lessee and as bailiff and ex officio returning officer, Sir Richard secured his own election in 1553 and 1558.[21] The members returned in 1562–3 may have had the patronage of Sir Richard's relict Jane, but for the rest of the 16th century the borough was apparently open.[22]

In the 17th century most elections may have been influenced by members of the Browne family, the owners of Ludgershall manor, but from 1660 to 1689 the Brownes shared the influence with the owners of the Savernake estate, the Seymours and Bruces.[23] Among the members returned was John Selden, the jurist, in 1628.[24] The franchise may originally have been limited to those holding burgage tenements but before 1660 was extended to other inhabitants. In 1699 the right to vote was restricted to those with a freehold or leasehold estate of inheritance in Ludgershall.[25] In the early 18th century elections took place at the market cross and the interest was split between John Richmond Webb, the owner of Biddesden manor, and members of the Clarges family, owners of Ludgershall manor. Webb, a Tory and the only resident member since Sir Richard Bridges or earlier, was returned 11 times in the period 1695–1722, and his son was elected in 1724 and 1727. John and George Selwyn owned Ludgershall manor 1741–91 and Ludgershall became their pocket borough. Charles Selwyn was returned in 1741, George four times in the period 1754–90, but at other times the seats were sold to the government, in 1768 for £9,000. Lord George Gordon was one of the members returned in 1774.[26]

Between 1790 and 1793 Thomas Everett, the owner of Biddesden manor, unsuccessfully challenged the Selwyn interest, held from 1791 by John Townshend, Viscount Sydney. He petitioned against the returns made in 1790 and at a byelection of 1791 on the grounds that the Selwyns had increased the number of voters by dividing estates to which the franchise was attached, and between c. 1716 and 1792 the number of voters had increased from 70 to 149. Everett was returned in 1796 and 1806–7, and his son J. H. Everett in 1810 and 1812. Sydney sold his interest c. 1812 to Sir James Graham, Bt., whose son Sandford, returned in 1812, 1818, 1830, and 1831, voted successfully in 1832 for the borough's disfranchisement.[27]

CHURCH. A church stood at Ludgershall in the 12th century.[28] It was granted to Amesbury priory in 1228[29] and appropriated,[30] but no vicarage was ordained: in 1446 the church was united with Biddesden church and the benefice was again called Ludgershall rectory.[31] Faberstown was added to the ecclesiastical parish in 1945.[32] From 1979 the benefice was called Ludgershall and Faberstown rectory and in 1986 was united with Tidworth rectory.[33]

The king presented rectors until 1228.[34] Amesbury priory, appropriator of Ludgershall and patron of Biddesden, was from 1446[35] to the Dissolution[36] entitled to present rectors of Ludgershall. In 1547 the advowson was granted to Edward, duke of Somerset,[37] and it descended with Ludgershall manor until the 19th century.[38] In 1553 William Nottingham presented by grant of a turn from the prioress of Amesbury.[39] Because members of the Browne family who owned it were recusants,[40] the advowson may have been leased in the 17th century and early 18th. As either lessees or grantees Gregory Geering presented in 1670 and Morgan Randall and Peter Birch together in 1707.[41] The lord of Ludgershall manor still held the advowson in 1824.[42] By 1859 the advowson had been bought by Jason Smith, and it may have been from his devisees that West Awdry bought it in 1867. Awdry's trustees, to whom he conveyed it in 1868, sold it in 1899 to Charles Awdry (d. 1912). The advowson passed to Charles's son C. S. Awdry (d. 1918). In 1941 C. E. Awdry owned it and in 1964 he conveyed it to the Salisbury diocesan board of finance, which shared the patronage of the united benefice from 1986.[43]

17 Hist. Parl., Commons, 1386–1421, i. 701–2; returns are listed in W.A.M. xxxiv. 151–6.
18 Hist. Parl., Commons, 1386–1421, i. 701–2; iv. 520–3.
19 Ibid. 1439–1509, 561.
20 L. & P. Hen. VIII, xiv (2), pp. 220–1.
21 Hist. Parl., Commons, 1509–58, i. 226, 531–2, 534–5.
22 Ibid. 1558–1603, i. 274; V.C.H. Wilts. v. 120–1.
23 Hist. Parl., Commons, 1660–90, i. 450–1; V.C.H. Wilts. v. 159.
24 V.C.H. Wilts. v. 132.
25 Carew, Rights of Elections, 354, 356.
26 W.A.M. xxxiv. 154–5; Hist. Parl., Commons, 1715–54, i. 347–8; 1754–90, i. 416–17; Hist. MSS. Com. 43, 15th Rep. VII, Ailesbury, pp. 211–12; Letters of the Earl of Chesterfield to his Son, ed. C. Strachey, ii. 479.
27 Hist. Parl., Commons, 1790–1820, ii. 421–2; W.A.M. xxxiv. 156; V.C.H. Wilts. v. 301; T. H. B. Oldfield, Hist. Boroughs, iii (1792), 191–3.
28 Below, this section [architecture].
29 Cal. Chart. R. 1226–57, 80.
30 Tax. Eccl. (Rec. Com.), 180.
31 W.R.O., D 1/2/10, ff. 74–5; below, Biddesden, church.
32 Ch. Com. file 53875/2.
33 Ibid. NB 34/340C.
34 Rot. Litt. Pat. (Rec. Com.), 27, 88; Rot. Chart. (Rec. Com.), 197; Pat. R. 1216–25, 350.
35 W.R.O., D 1/2/10, ff. 74–5.
36 Phillipps, Wilts. Inst. (index in W.A.M. xxviii. 224).
37 Cal. Pat. 1547–8, 121.
38 Phillipps, Wilts. Inst. (index in W.A.M. xxviii. 224).
39 Phillipps, Wilts. Inst. i. 215.
40 e.g. P.R.O., C 66/1874, no. 24; W.R.O., A 1/310, rot. 15.
41 Phillipps, Wilts. Inst. ii. 30, 48.
42 Clerical Guide (1829).
43 Kelly's Dir. Wilts. (1859, 1867); W.R.O. 374/130/61; Ch. Com. files, CB 13057; NB 34/340C; 53875/2; Soc. Antiq. MS. 817, vi, Ludgershall.

All the tithes of Ludgershall were presumably taken by the rector until 1228, and the tithes of both Ludgershall and Biddesden were assigned to the rector in 1446, subject to a payment to Amesbury priory.[44] The rectory was worth £16 in 1535,[45] £100 in 1650,[46] and an average of £296 a year 1829–31.[47] The tithes were valued at £427 in 1838 and commuted.[48] There was no glebe house until 1920 when one on the west side of High Street, lived in by the curate in the late 19th century, was bought.[49] That house was sold in 1966,[50] and a new Rectory fronting St. James Street was built in its garden.[51]

St. Mary's chantry was founded apparently between 1352 and 1395 in the north chapel of the church, the chapel being called St. Mary's in 1395. That the chaplain serving it was paid £2 a year to say masses for the king, his heirs, and his ancestors, and that a chaplain had been similarly paid for such services in a chapel in the castle in 1352, suggests that the chantry chapel replaced the castle chapel.[52] It was dissolved in 1548.[53]

Ralph de Neville (d. 1244), rector from 1215 to c. 1222, and from 1224 bishop of Chichester, was a pluralist who presumably owed his presentation to Hugh de Neville, constable of Ludgershall castle.[54] It is not clear how Ludgershall church was served between 1228 and 1352, but in 1352 the inhabitants of Ludgershall appointed and paid a chaplain to serve it. The chaplain also served St. Mary's chapel in Ludgershall castle, and later served St. Mary's chantry in the church.[55] A curate assisted the rector in 1550.[56] In 1565 no sermon had been preached during the past year and the church lacked Erasmus's *Paraphrases*.[57] Bartholomew Parsons, rector 1620–42, was a royalist preacher and author of sermons.[58] Curates either assisted him or served the cure in his absence.[59] Andrew Reade, rector 1642–70, was described as an idle and simple man who neglected to preach. He was ejected, and Henry Cusse, intruded c. 1646,[60] preached twice on Sundays in 1650.[61] Only three rectors served Ludgershall 1670–1823.[62] In 1783, when the church was a confirmation centre,[63] the third, John Selwyn, held two services each Sunday and preached every Sunday morning, but had recently discontinued weekday services because few attended them. Selwyn administered the sacrament four times a year, but only 15 received it on Easter day in 1783.[64] He was the borough bailiff in 1791 and succentor of Salisbury cathedral from that year.[65] He was resident 1777–83 and seems to have resided frequently even after 1791.[66] John Pannell, rector 1824–72,[67] was assisted 1829–31 by a curate.[68] Morning and evening services with sermons were held in 1832.[69] Curates may have served alone in 1844 and 1859.[70] In 1851 on Census Sunday 79 people attended morning, and 70 afternoon, service.[71] In 1864 W. H. Awdry, curate from 1862, held two services each Sunday and preached, to a congregation averaging 150, at both. He also held services on Friday evenings and administered the sacrament monthly and at the great festivals. Of c. 120 communicants an average of 31 attended at the great festivals and 24 each month.[72] Awdry became rector in 1872 and rectors have since resided.[73] In the 1920s inhabitants of Faberstown were already being treated as parishioners and attending Ludgershall church.[74]

The church of *ST. JAMES*, so called in 1763[75] and probably in the Middle Ages,[76] is built of stone rubble with ashlar dressings and comprises a chancel, a nave with north and south chapels and south porch, and a west tower.[77] The nave, which has thick walls, is of the 12th century: surviving features of that date are a window in the north wall, a blocked doorway in the north wall, and the inner arch of the south doorway. The chancel, with plain lancet windows, was rebuilt in the earlier 13th century. In the 14th two windows were inserted in the north wall of the nave, and the north chantry chapel was built. The outer lancets of the chancel's triple-lancet east window were blocked, and the central one was replaced by a traceried three-light window, in the 15th century. The south chapel was apparently built in the earlier 16th century. All or part of the tower fell before 1662[78] and it was rebuilt or extensively repaired in 1675.[79] In 1727 a west nave gallery was built.[80] It was removed in the early 1870s, when the church was restored under the direction of J. L. Pearson.[81] The porch and the top stage of the tower were then rebuilt, two new windows were inserted in the nave,[82]

44 W.R.O., D 1/2/10, ff. 74–5; above, manor [tithes].
45 *Valor Eccl.* (Rec. Com.), ii. 91.
46 *W.A.M.* xl. 257.
47 *Rep. Com. Eccl. Revenues*, 840–1.
48 P.R.O., IR 29/38/178.
49 Ch. Com. file, CB 13057.
50 Ibid. deed 593098.
51 Inf. from the rector.
52 *Cal. Pat.* 1350–4, 212, 214; *Cal. Close*, 1392–6, 346; above, castle; cf. below, this section [architecture].
53 P.R.O., E 301/58, no. 19.
54 *Rot. Chart.* (Rec. Com.), 197; *D.N.B.*; above, castle.
55 *Cal. Pat.* 1350–4, 212, 214; *Cal. Close*, 1392–6, 346.
56 W.R.O., D 1/43/1, f. 58.
57 Ibid. D 1/43/4, f. 2.
58 *Alum. Oxon. 1500–1714*, iii. 1122; *D.N.B.*
59 *Subscription Bk. 1620–40* (W.R.S. xxxii), pp. 20, 26, 38, 73; W.R.O., bishop's transcripts, bdle. 1.
60 *Walker Revised*, ed. Matthews, 379.
61 *W.A.M.* xl. 257.
62 *Alum. Oxon. 1500–1714*, iv. 1497 (s.v. Torbock), 1698 (s.v. Yalden); *1715–1886*, iv. 1273 (s.v. Selwyn).
63 *V.C.H. Wilts.* iii. 52.

64 *Vis. Queries, 1783* (W.R.S. xxvii), pp. 143–5.
65 W. H. Jones, *Fasti Eccl. Sar.* ii. 444; *Hist. Parl., Commons, 1790–1820*, ii. 422.
66 *Vis. Queries, 1783* (W.R.S. xxvii), pp. 143–4; Hist. MSS. Com. 42, *15th Rep. VI, Carlisle*, p. 460; par. reg. in church.
67 *Alum. Oxon. 1715–1886*, iii. 1063; *Clergy List* (1859).
68 *Rep. Com. Eccl. Revenues*, 840–1.
69 Ch. Com. file, NB 34/340C.
70 *W.A.M.* xlviii. 174 n.; *Clergy List* (1859).
71 P.R.O., HO 129/118/2/10/13.
72 Ch. Com. file 53875/1; W.R.O., D 1/56/7.
73 *Clergy List* (1881 and later edns.); *Crockford* (1896 and later edns.).
74 Ch. Com. file, NB 34/340C.
75 J. Ecton, *Thesaurus* (1763), 391.
76 P.R.O., SC 6/1054/22.
77 For the church in the early 19th cent., J. Buckler, watercolour in W.A.S. Libr., vol. i. 13.
78 W.R.O., D 1/54/1/3, no. 44.
79 *Church Guide*.
80 W.R.O., D 1/21/5/1, f. 125.   81 *Church Guide*.
82 Vestry min. bk. 1860–1920 (in church).

and the 13th-century appearance of the east window was restored by replacing the 15th-century window with a lancet and unblocking the flanking lancets. All the roofs were renewed, and that of the south chapel, formerly flat and surrounded by an embattled parapet, was rebuilt with a transeptal ridge ending in a gable. The south chapel may have been built for the Bridges family and was used by Jane (d. 1593), wife of Sir Richard Bridges and of Sir Simon Harcourt.[83] She and Sir Richard (d. 1558) are commemorated on a canopied tomb placed between the chapel and the nave. The tomb is open on both sides and, although of traditional late-medieval form, incorporates Corinthian columns and has Renaissance decoration on the panelling.[84]

The parish holds a paten hallmarked for 1707. A chalice hallmarked for 1708 was replaced when a new set of plate, also held in 1990, was given in 1867.[85] There were three bells in 1553. They were replaced by a treble cast by John Danton in 1631, a second cast by Richard Purdue in 1638, and a tenor cast by Clement Tosier in 1686. A new treble and second, cast in 1749 by J. Burrough, were added to make a ring of five. Of that ring the treble was replaced in 1818 by a bell cast by James Wells of Aldbourne, the second and the tenor were replaced in 1859 by bells cast by John Warner & Sons. The ring was increased to six and rehung in 1908 when a new treble by Taylor of Loughborough (Leics.) was added.[86] The registers survive from 1609.[87]

ROMAN CATHOLICISM. From the time of Sir George Browne (d. 1614) to 1703 the lords of Ludgershall manor were Roman Catholics, but they did not live at Ludgershall and are unlikely to have encouraged recusancy there.[88] There was one recusant in 1663, five 1675–80,[89] none in 1783.[90] A chapel of ease, served from Amesbury, was opened west of the church in 1943.[91] It remained open in 1990.[92]

PROTESTANT NONCONFORMITY. There was no protestant nonconformity in Ludgershall in 1676[93] or 1783.[94] A house was certified in 1806 for a group described as Baptists and

Independents: the same group certified a new building nearby in Cox's (later Chapel) Lane in 1810 and another house in 1818, and may have been the group which certified a house in 1822. The group's minister was John Walcot in 1818[95] and 1832.[96] By 1851, when its minister was John Smith, it had become Strict Baptist. On Census Sunday in 1851 morning and evening services were attended by 60, afternoon services by 50: the chapel, possibly the building erected in 1810 but said to have been built in 1818, was in Chapel Lane and was rebuilt in 1903.[97] The chapel was open in 1910,[98] closed before 1915, ruinous c. 1920,[99] and later demolished. Registrations of births and baptisms survive for 1817–36,[1] of births only for 1835–7.[2] Stock given for the graveyard, which survived on the north side of Chapel Lane in 1990, in 1924 produced £1, which was given to the Gospel Standard Aid Society, £3 in 1990.[3]

Methodists were active in Ludgershall in 1818.[4] They may have been the Primitive Methodists who in 1844 certified the chapel[5] which on Census Sunday in 1851 was attended by 100 people in the afternoon and 180 in the evening.[6] The chapel was presumably that near the Crown:[7] it was closed between 1885 and 1889.[8] A mission hall built on the north side of Winchester Street in 1904 for Wesleyan Methodists was open in 1907.[9] Services were held in 1990 in a hall on the south side, registered in 1921 for the Ludgershall Evangelical Mission.[10]

EDUCATION. Interest on £1,000 stock was used by a daughter of the rector, John Selwyn, for a school for 15 girls, some of whom were provided with clothing, in 1818 and possibly still in 1831. Another school, begun c. 1828, was attended in 1831 by 40 children.[11] In 1833 a total of 46 children, and in 1846–7 a total of 85, were taught in three schools.[12] An existing school was reserved for younger children when a new National school was built in Butt Street in 1856. In the old schoolroom 50–60 children, in the new 60, were taught in 1858.[13] An evening school was held in 1864,[14] and 74 children were present at the National school on attendance day in 1871.[15] The Butt Street school was enlarged in 1894 and was reserved for the younger children when a new primary school was built in St. James Street

83 W.A.M. xxx. 139–40; above, manor (Ludgershall).
84 See plate facing p. 75.
85 Nightingale, Wilts. Plate, 40–1; inf. from the rector.
86 Walters, Wilts. Bells, 124–5, 289, 298; W.R.O., D 1/24/137/1; inf. from the rector.
87 In church. There are transcripts for 1602: W.R.O., bishop's transcripts, bdle. 1.
88 Cal. S.P. Dom. 1603–10, 356; Cal. Cttee. for Money, ii. 740; W.N. & Q. viii. 343; W.A.M. xviii. 363; V.C.H. Wilts. iii. 89 and n.; G.E.C. Baronetage, iv. 14; P.R.O., E 126/5, f. 208 and v.
89 Williams, Cath. Recusancy (Cath. Rec. Soc.), 86, 230.
90 Vis. Queries, 1783 (W.R.S. xxvii), p. 143.
91 V.C.H. Wilts. iii. 97; W.R.O., G 10/516/3–4.
92 Cath. Dir. (1990).
93 Compton Census, ed. Whiteman, 124.
94 Vis. Queries, 1783 (W.R.S. xxvii), p. 143.
95 Meeting Ho. Certs. (W.R.S. xl), pp. 62, 65–6, 85, 97.
96 R. W. Oliver, Strict Bapt. Chapels Eng. (Strict Bapt. Hist. Soc.), v. 24–5.
97 Ibid.; P.R.O., HO 129/118/2/10/15; ibid. IR 29/38/178; IR 30/38/178; W.R.O. 1458/54.

98 W.R.O., Inland Revenue, val. reg. 139.
99 Kelly's Dir. Wilts. (1915); Ch. Com. file 53875/1.
1 P.R.O., RG 4/2131.
2 Ibid. RG 4/2235.
3 W.R.O., L 2, Ludgershall; inf. from Mr. E. Levell, 18 Pretoria Road, Faberstown.
4 Educ. of Poor Digest, 1031.
5 Meeting Ho. Certs. (W.R.S. xl), p. 159.
6 P.R.O., HO 129/118/2/10/14.
7 W.R.O. 776/119.
8 Kelly's Dir. Wilts. (1885, 1889).
9 W.R.O., G 10/760/8; Hants R.O. 46M84, box 56, map attached to deed, Berry to Berry, 1907.
10 G.R.O. Worship Reg. no. 48235.
11 Endowed Char. Wilts. (S. Div.), 1292; Educ. of Poor Digest, 1031; Lewis, Topog. Dict. Eng. (1831), iii. 175–6; P.R.O., PROB 11/1550, ff. 278v.–280.
12 Educ. Enq. Abstract, 1041; Nat. Soc. Inquiry, 1846–7, Wilts. 8–9.
13 Acct. of Wilts. Schs. 31; Kelly's Dir. Wilts. (1903).
14 W.R.O., D 1/56/7.
15 Returns relating to Elem. Educ. 418–19.

in 1906.[16] Average attendance at the two schools rose from 148 in 1906–7 to 251 in 1938,[17] and the St. James Street school was enlarged in 1914.[18] The Butt Street school was closed in 1941, and between then and 1954, when new classrooms were opened in Central Street, the scout hall in Chapel Lane and other buildings provided additional school accommodation.[19] When Tidworth Down secondary school in North Tidworth was reserved for boys in 1965, a new secondary school for girls, Ludgershall Castle school, was opened in Short Street.[20] In 1978 the St. James Street school and the Central Street classrooms were closed, Ludgershall Castle school became a primary school, and the boys' school in North Tidworth became a mixed comprehensive school.[21] In 1990 there were 340 children on roll at Ludgershall Castle school.[22]

CHARITIES FOR THE POOR. By will dated 1624 Peter Blake gave to the poor of Ludgershall £1 5s. a year; in 1833 the money was spent on clothes or shoes for three or four ploughboys. By deed of 1627 Henry Smith ('Dog' Smith), alderman of London, gave income from lands to parishes including Ludgershall, which received £7 a year from 1641 and c. £21 a year 1823–30. Before c. 1823 the money was spent on bread and clothes, but 1823–33 was distributed among 12–18 old or single people in sums of between 5s. and £5. The income averaged £28 a year 1867–9, £13 10s. 1900–5. By a Scheme of 1905 Blake's and Smith's charities were administered together to relieve poverty generally:[23] in 1905 and 1912 money, coal, and groceries were distributed, in 1906 and 1912 donations to Savernake hospital were made, and in 1912 a contribution was made to Ludgershall coal club.[24]

Before c. 1682 c. 2 a. were bought with money given to the poor of Ludgershall by a Mr. Mundy. The income of £1 4s. was distributed on 21 December in 1786. Distribution of the £1 income, to 40 widows who received 6d. each in the early 19th century, ceased in 1828.[25]

Anna Maria Everett by will proved 1851 gave £200, Martha Everett by will proved 1867 gave £200 stock, and Ellen Everett by will proved 1884 gave £300, all for the poor. Until 1898 the total yearly income of c. £18 was distributed to a clothing club and in gifts to the sick and poor. That only small sums were given 1898–1905 was attributed to the parish's increased prosperity arising from military activity nearby.[26] In 1908 £19 from the Everett charities was spent on coal for 70 people, meat for 33 sick people, and groceries for 80 people.[27]

From 1921 Blake's, Smith's, and Everetts' charities were administered jointly. The £35 total income was given in small money doles to 34 people in 1935, and in 1950 spent on groceries for 48.[28] In 1989 £5 was given to each of 20 old people.[29]

BIDDESDEN

IN THE Middle Ages Biddesden had a church and was apparently a parish until 1446.[30] It had little land, possibly less than 400 a., and the village, although separately assessed for taxation in the 14th century[31] and with poll-tax payers in 1377,[32] was clearly very small. There has been a manor house there from the 16th century.[33] In 1841, when its population was 12,[34] the hamlet consisted of a farmstead and of the manor house and its farm buildings. There has since been little new building. North-west of the manor house, Chapel copse may mark the site of the church.

Biddesden Farm, west of Biddesden House, was built in the early 18th century, possibly about the same time as Biddesden House, and was standing in 1732.[35] It is of flint with red-brick dressings, and above the windows of the south entrance front has decorative cut heads and moulded plaitboards. It was originally one room deep with a stair turret which projected to the north. The staircase was embraced when the house was extended northwards between 1841 and c. 1870, perhaps in 1864 when the north garden was walled.[36] Internal decorations of the 1930s by Roland Pym survived in 1990. An aisled barn stands south-east of, and is possibly contemporary with, the house. Further south-east, on the south side of Biddesden Lane, a pair of estate cottages was built in the early 20th century. North-east of Biddesden House an 18th-century aisled barn stands in Long bottom. A pair of brick and flint cottages was built there in the later 19th century and a bungalow in the 20th.

MANOR. A yardland that became BIDDESDEN manor was held in 1066 by Coolle and in 1086 by Robert son of Gerald.[37] Amesbury priory held the estate in 1272,[38] was granted free warren in its demesne in 1286,[39] and kept it until the Dissolution.[40]

In 1543 Biddesden manor was granted to (Sir) Richard Bridges[41] (d. 1558). It passed to his son

[16] Kelly's Dir. Wilts. (1903, 1911); P.R.O., ED 7/131, no. 178.
[17] Bd. of Educ., List 21, 1908 (H.M.S.O.), 504; 1938, 423.
[18] Kelly's Dir. Wilts. (1923). [19] W.R.O., F 8/230/2/3.
[20] Ibid. F 8/700, list of secondary schs.; ibid. G 10/516/3–4.
[21] Ibid. F 8/700, list of schs.; inf. from the head teacher, Ludgershall Castle sch.
[22] Inf. from Director of Educ., Co. Hall, Trowbridge.
[23] Endowed Char. Wilts. (S. Div.), 291–4.
[24] W.R.O., L 2, Ludgershall.
[25] Endowed Char. Wilts. (S. Div.), 290–2.
[26] Ibid. 296–8. [27] W.R.O., L 2, Ludgershall.
[28] Ibid. [29] Inf. from the rector.
[30] Below, church.
[31] V.C.H. Wilts. iv. 297; Tax List, 1332 (W.R.S. xlv), 113.
[32] V.C.H. Wilts. iv. 306. [33] Below, manor.
[34] P.R.O., HO 107/1165/10.
[35] Ibid. C 78/1814, no. 1.
[36] Ibid. IR 30/38/178; O.S. Map 6", Wilts. XLVIII (1883–8 edn.); date on wall. [37] V.C.H. Wilts. ii, p. 153.
[38] P.R.O., CP 25/1/252/22, no. 30.
[39] Cal. Chart. R. 1257–1300, 337.
[40] Valor Eccl. (Rec. Com.), ii. 94.
[41] L. & P. Hen. VIII, xviii, p. 281.

Anthony[42] (d. 1613), and to Anthony's son-in-law Sir George Browne.[43] From Sir George (d. 1614)[44] the manor descended like Ludgershall manor to Sir Anthony Browne, Bt. (d. *s.p.* 1688), who devised it to his mother Elizabeth Browne. She sold it in 1693 to John Webb,[45] later John Richmond Webb. Webb (d. 1724) bought other land in the parish and devised the enlarged estate to his son Borlace Richmond Webb (d. *s.p.* 1738), on the death of whose relict Hester (fl. 1749)[46] it reverted to his half-brother John Richmond Webb (d. *s.p.* 1766). In 1766 it passed to John's sister Frances (d. 1777), the wife of Thomas Humphreys, whose children[47] sold the Biddesden estate in 1786 to Thomas Everett.[48]

From Thomas (d. 1810) the estate, 802 a. in 1838, passed to his son J. H. Everett (d. 1853),[49] who was succeeded by his sons the Revd. Thomas Everett (d. 1860) and Henry Everett (d. 1892) in turn. From Henry it passed to his nephew C. E. Everett,[50] who in 1908 sold it to Sir John Denison-Pender. Sir John sold it to G. J. Gribble, from whom Guy Baring bought it in 1913. In 1925 Baring's relict Olive sold all except Biddesden House and *c.* 200 a. to her brother O. H. Smith. In 1926 Smith conveyed his land to trustees, in 1930 the trustees sold it to C. E. Stern and Stern sold it to Nellie L. Bates, and in 1931 she sold Biddesden farm, 313 a., to Charles Hatt, the owner in 1966. In 1928–9 Biddesden House and the *c.* 200 a. were sold, presumably by Olive Baring, to E. R. Fothergill, who sold them in 1931 to Bryan Guinness (from 1944 Lord Moyne). In 1990 Lord Moyne and members of his family owned *c.* 600 a. in Ludgershall including Biddesden farm.[51]

Biddesden House, of chequered brick with stone dressings, was built for John Richmond Webb (d. 1724)[52] and replaced a manor house mentioned in the 16th and 17th centuries.[53] Irregularities in its internal plan show that, despite its external symmetry, the new house was built in stages, west, south, and east ranges in that order. The staircase, which has corkscrew balusters and an enriched handrail, was built in the angle of the west and south ranges. Each main elevation is of three storeys and seven bays. The principal south entrance front has ground- and first-floor windows with semicircular heads and prominent keystones, attic windows, above a carved and moulded cornice, with segmental heads and keystones, and, in the three central projecting bays which are surmounted by a semicircular pediment, circular mezzanine windows.[54] Three bays in each of the east and west

elevations are blind. At the north end of the east range a castellated circular tower was built to house a bell from Lille (Nord) given to Webb *c.* 1708.[55] Soon after the east range was built the court between the three ranges was built over, and a two-storeyed north service range and, north of that, an outhouse court were built. Inside the house the entrance hall, which is lit by the mezzanine windows, is cubic, west of it the drawing room has been extended north by the inclusion of a smaller room, and east of it the dining room may also have been enlarged.

In the early 19th century a wide pillared porch was built across the projecting bays of the south front and, among other alterations, a new service staircase was made. The porch was later re-used as the front of an ornamental temple in gardens north-west of the house. In the 1930s the west part of the service range was altered to form a first-floor library, and trompe d'oeil scenes were painted by Dora Carrington and Roland Pym in blank windows in both the east and west ground-floor elevations.

Rising ground west of the house was terraced, possibly in the early 18th century, and west of the terraces lay a walled garden.[56] Outside the garden's north-west corner a swimming pool was built, with a changing pavilion designed in 1932 by George Kennedy and decorated with mosaics in 1937 by Boris Anrep.[57]

ECONOMIC HISTORY. There was land for 1 ploughteam at Biddesden in 1086: 1 *villanus*, 4 *servi*, and 2 bordars had 1 team on 1 yardland, and there were 2 square furlongs of pasture.[58] Much nearby land may have been wooded, and the cultivated land was perhaps a recent assart. Biddesden was summoned to Chute forest eyres in the 13th century and from 1300 was bisected by the west boundary of the forest. Westcroft wood at Biddesden was disafforested in 1330,[59] and later only a small proportion of Biddesden's land was woodland.[60] In 1838 and 1990 there were, apart from Coldridge copse to the north, *c.* 40 a. of woodland at Biddesden.[61]

Common husbandry was practised at Biddesden in 1528,[62] but there is no evidence of it later, and by *c.* 1636, when inclosed downland separated from Ludgershall's land was added to Biddesden farm,[63] all the cultivated land may have been in one farm. Biddesden farm was the only one in 1786.[64] In 1838, when copses and long lines of trees gave nearly all Biddesden's land the appearance of a park, Biddesden farm

42 P.R.O., C 142/124, no. 191.
43 Ibid. CP 25/2/261/32 Eliz. I Hil.; *V.C.H. Berks.* iv. 239.
44 P.R.O., C 142/341, no. 87.
45 Ibid. CP 25/2/888/4 & 5 Wm. and Mary Hil.; W.R.O. 212B/3737; 212B/3739; above, Ludgershall, manor.
46 P.R.O., C 78/1814, no. 1; W.R.O. 130/48B, deed, Webb to Chandos, 1749.
47 *Misc. Herald. et Geneal.* (5th ser.), vii. 45–6; P.R.O., C 78/1814, no. 1.
48 W.R.O., A 1/345/266; P.R.O., CP 25/2/1477/27 Geo. III East. no. 8; CP 25/2/1477/27 Geo. III Mich. no. 21.
49 *Hist. Parl., Commons,* 1790–1820, iii. 718–19; P.R.O., IR 29/38/178.
50 P.R.O., PROB 11/2173, ff. 394v.–397v.; Hants R.O. 46M84, box 49, abstr. of title, 1892.
51 Inf. from Lord Moyne, Biddesden Ho., and abstr. of

title in his possession.
52 No evidence has been found to confirm the building date of 1711 given in *Country Life,* 28 June 1919, p. 787 and 2 Apr. 1938, p. 352.
53 e.g. P.R.O., C 142/124, no. 191; W.R.O. 212B/3737.
54 See plate facing p. 74.
55 *Country Life,* 28 June 1919, pp. 786, 789.
56 *Andrews and Dury, Map* (W.R.S. viii), pl. 9.
57 Pevsner, *Wilts.* (2nd edn.), 110; *Country Life,* 9 Apr. 1938, p. 380.
58 *V.C.H. Wilts.* ii, p. 153.
59 Ibid. iv. 425, 452–3.
60 *Andrews and Dury, Map* (W.R.S. viii), pl. 9.
61 P.R.O., IR 29/38/178; IR 30/38/178.
62 *Cat. Anct. D.* i, C 674.
63 P.R.O., E 134/23 Chas. I Mich./6.
64 W.R.O., D 1/24/137/1.

was 370 a., of which *c.* 297 a. were arable; 169 a., including 19 a. of woodland, a park of 6 a. near the house, *c.* 58 a. of pasture, *c.* 85 a. of arable, and farm buildings south of the house, were held with Biddesden House.[65] The buildings included a dairy in 1990, when mixed farming was practised on the *c.* 600-a. Biddesden estate.[66]

LOCAL GOVERNMENT. A court for Biddesden manor may have been held in the Middle Ages,[67] but no record of one held then or later survives.

CHURCH. A church had been built at Biddesden by 1297.[68] Between then and 1446, when it was united with Ludgershall church, it was served by rectors presented by Amesbury priory, and in 1446 it was called a parish church.[69]

The rectors presumably took the tithes of Biddesden, which were part of the endowment of Ludgershall rectory after 1446.[70]

Two early 14th-century rectors of Biddesden were in minor orders. Roger of Purbrook, the second of them, was licensed in 1312 to study at Oxford or Cambridge for a year.[71] Roger Tonge, rector *c.* 1438, was also rector of Broughton Gifford *c.* 1438 and rector of Steeple Ashton 1429–38.[72] By 1446 no rector of Biddesden had resided for many years.[73]

As a chapel of Ludgershall church from 1446 Biddesden church was to be served by the rector of Ludgershall, who was to maintain the chancel and churchyard. Mass was to be said on All Saints' day, on the anniversary of the church's dedication, and on All Souls' day or in the following week for those buried there.[74] The church evidently fell into disuse, and its exact site is not now known.

BIDDESDEN HOUSE

[65] P.R.O., IR 29/38/178; IR 30/38/178.
[66] Inf. from Lord Moyne.
[67] *Cal. Inq. p.m. Hen. VII*, i, p. 154.
[68] *Cal. Pat.* 1292–1301, 263.
[69] Phillipps, *Wilts. Inst.* (index in *W.A.M.* xxviii. 215); W.R.O., D 1/2/10, ff. 74–5.
[70] Above, Ludgershall, church.
[71] *Reg. Ghent* (Cant. & York Soc.), ii. 883, 911.
[72] Phillipps, *Wilts. Inst.* i. 129; A. B. Emden, *Biog. Reg. Univ. Oxf. to 1500*, iii. 1884.
[73] W.R.O., D 1/2/10, ff. 74–5.
[74] Ibid.

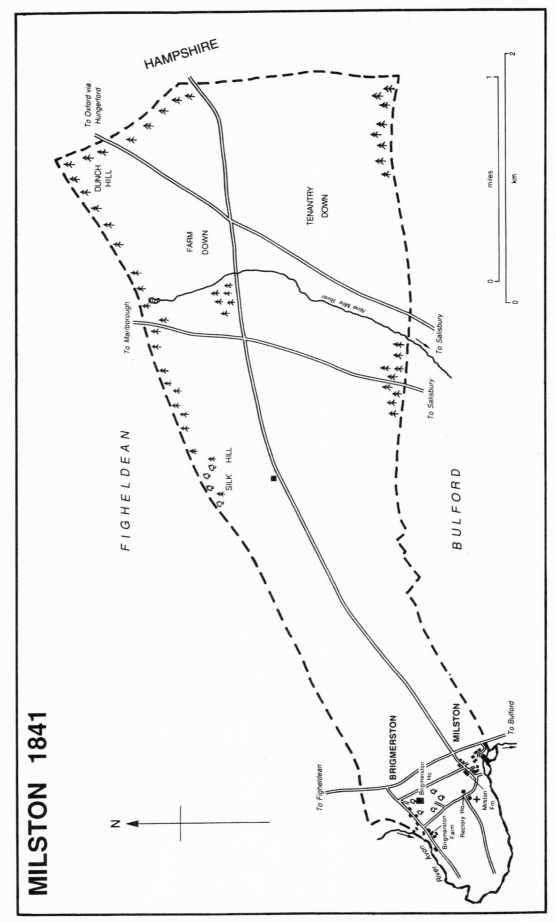

MILSTON 1841

N

HAMPSHIRE

To Oxford via Hungerford

DUNCH HILL

FARM DOWN

TENANTRY DOWN

To Marlborough

Nine Mile River

To Salisbury

To Salisbury

FIGHELDEAN

SILK HILL

BULFORD

BRIGMERSTON

MILSTON

To Figheldean

River Avon

Brigmerston Farm

Rectory Ho.

Brigmerston Ho.

Milston Fm.

To Bulford

miles
km

MILSTON

MILSTON parish, 917 ha. (2,265 a.), is 15 km. north of Salisbury.[75] Long and narrow, it reaches 6.5 km. across Salisbury Plain from the Christchurch Avon in the west to Hampshire in the east, and it contains two small villages, Milston to the south, Brigmerston to the north.[76] Their etymology suggests that both villages are of Saxon origin, and both stand near the river, Brigmerston on slightly higher ground than Milston; Brigmerston took its name from its lord in 1066,[77] and later 18th- and earlier 19th-century references to it as Brigmilston were misconceived.[78]

The parish boundary is very simple, long straight lines across the downs, the Avon in the west. Parts of both the northern and southern boundary follow dry valleys; the eastern follows a ridge and for much of its length is marked by a prehistoric ditch.

The whole parish is on Upper Chalk. The Avon has deposited gravel, on which the two villages stand, and, west of Milston, alluvium. To the east the downland is crossed from north to south by a tributary of the Avon, Nine Mile river, which rises on Brigmerston down and has also deposited gravel. The land is at c. 70 m. beside the Avon and c. 85 m. beside Nine Mile river; the highest land is over 165 m. on Dunch Hill at the north-east corner of the parish. West of Nine Mile river the chalkland slopes gently, east of it more steeply. The alluvium was meadow land, on the gently sloping chalk there were open fields, and to the east there was rough pasture. After 1899 some arable in the west was converted to pasture when the eastern part of the parish became part of a military training area.[79]

Two main roads crossed the parish's downland. That from Chipping Campden (Glos.) via Marlborough to Salisbury was prominent in the later 17th century,[80] that from Oxford via Hungerford (Berks.) to Salisbury in the later 18th. The Oxford–Salisbury road did not cross the parish until a new more westerly route was brought into use for it after 1675. Both roads were superseded in the earlier 19th century by a turnpiked road in the Bourne valley further east,[81] and both were closed by the army in the earlier 20th. The old Marlborough road has retained its name. Across the west part of the parish the road linking the villages on the east bank of the Avon was turnpiked between Figheldean and Bulford in 1761 and disturnpiked in 1871.[82]

Much evidence of prehistoric activity has been found in Milston parish, the oldest being Bronze-Age artefacts found on Brigmerston down. There are barrow cemeteries on Silk Hill and Milston down. There are Iron-Age enclosures on Milston and Brigmerston downs, Iron-Age or Romano-British pottery has been found near the site of Milston mill, and a field system based on an Iron-Age hill fort on Sidbury Hill in North Tidworth extends into the parish. A north–south ditch crossing the parish, east of Nine Mile river, and the parallel Devil's ditch, which marks the eastern parish boundary, may be associated with the field system.[83]

There were 55 poll-tax payers in 1377.[84] The population, 139 in 1801, had declined to 98 by 1821, its lowest known point. Numbers had increased to 155 by 1881, declined to 121 by 1901, and risen to 162 by 1921. The population was 154 in 1951 and, after new houses were built,[85] 251 in 1961. Thereafter numbers fell rapidly and there were only 126 inhabitants in 1991.[86]

The villages of Milston and Brigmerston apparently originated within a westwards meander of the Avon, Milston on the north bank, Brigmerston on the south, and grew round a rectangle of lanes.[87] The east side of the rectangle was a track in 1841[88] and did not survive in 1851.[89] The name Church Road was applied to both the south and the west sides in the 20th century. Both villages were bypassed by the Figheldean–Bulford turnpike road. Brigmerston may have been the wealthier of the two settlements in the 14th century;[90] Milston was more populous in the mid 19th century,[91] Brigmerston in the later 20th.

MILSTON. The parish church stands at Milston at the south-west corner of the rectangle of lanes. East of it the rectory house may have been the birthplace, and was the childhood home, of Joseph Addison (1672–1719), a founder of *The Spectator*.[92] On the north side of the churchyard a house, of flint with ashlar dressings, was built for Roger Pinckney in 1613 and may have incorporated an older building.[93] The new house may have been **U**-shaped with a principal east–west range, containing a central hall, and short north wings. The north-west wing may have contained a parlour and a staircase, the north-east wing a kitchen. If there was a north-west wing, it was presumably demolished in the 18th century when a staircase was inserted in the

75 This article was written in 1991.
76 Maps used include O.S. Maps 1", sheet 14 (1817 edn.); 1/50,000, sheet 184 (1988 edn.); 1/25,000, 41/14, 41/24 (1948 edns.); 6", Wilts. XLVIII, LIV–LV (1883–7 and later edns.).
77 P.N. Wilts. (E.P.N.S.), 369; below, manors (Brigmerston).
78 Andrews and Dury, Map (W.R.S. viii), pl. 9; O.S. Map 1", sheet 14 (1817 edn.).
79 Geol. Surv. Map 1", drift, sheet 282 (1967 edn.); below, econ. hist.   80 J. Ogilby, Brit. (1675), pl. 85.
81 Ibid. pl. 83; Andrews and Dury, Map (W.R.S. viii), pl. 9; below, N. Tidworth, intro. [roads].
82 V.C.H. Wilts. iv. 257, 262, 266, 270; L.J. xxx. 138.
83 V.C.H. Wilts. i (1), 89, 142, 183–4, 210, 218–19, 225–6,

229, 236, 239, 241, 244, 254, 267, 273, 276; W.A.M. xlv. 197.   84 V.C.H. Wilts. iv. 306.
85 Ibid. 354; for the housing, below, this section (Brigmerston).   86 Census, 1961; 1991.
87 Andrews and Dury, Map (W.R.S. viii), pl. 9.
88 P.R.O., IR 30/38/197.   89 W.R.O. 1550/48.
90 Tax List, 1332 (W.R.S. xlv), 110.
91 V.C.H. Wilts. iv. 354.
92 D.N.B.; W.N. & Q. i. 527; vii. 380. Baptisms in par. reg. are missing for 1672 and his baptism is not recorded in the bishop's transcript for 1672: W.R.O. 1469/1–2; ibid. bishop's transcripts, bdle. 1.
93 Date and initials on N. gable; W.R.O. 367/2, deed, Pinckney to Pinckney, 1612.

north-east wing, which survives. In the 19th century several stone-mullioned windows, and two canted bay windows on the ground floor in the north and west elevations, were inserted. A farmhouse on the north side of Church Road was built in the 17th century as a four-bayed timber-framed and thatched house with banded brick and flint infilling. The ground floor was reconstructed in brick in the 18th century, and in the early 20th a lower two-storeyed fifth bay was built on the west end. The house became cottages when a new Milston Farm was built north-west of it c. 1850,[94] and was two houses in 1991. A pair of cottages east of it is also timber-framed, thatched, and 17th-century. The farm buildings on the south side of Church Road were apparently built in the late 18th century or early 19th.[95] Further south on the Avon stood two mills.[96] In 1991 an early 19th-century mill house, of flint rubble with red-brick dressings, thatched, and with a later north-west extension, and south-east of it an early 19th-century cottage built of the same materials, stood on the north side of the lane which linked the mills to the Figheldean–Bulford road. A farmstead was built c. 1 km. north-east of the village in the mid 19th century.[97] Milston's population was 77 in 1841[98] and, there having been very few houses built since then, evidently much less in 1991. A burial ground was opened west of Church Road midway between Milston and Brigmerston in 1918.[99]

BRIGMERSTON. The north side of the rectangle of lanes, extending west beyond Church Road, formed a village street for Brigmerston.[1] A 'very meanly built' manor house and a dovecot stood in the village in 1274,[2] and the lord of Milston and Brigmerston manor apparently had a house there in the earlier 14th century and the later 16th.[3] The site of the early manor house is unknown but the dovecot survives on the south side of the street. It retains a medieval buttress at the north-east corner and possibly traces of others at the south-east and north-west corners. It was lined with stone nesting boxes. Much of the walling has been renewed and its present pyramidal roof was constructed in the 18th century. The dovecot was made into a cottage in the early 20th century and replanned internally in 1969.[4] A fire destroyed 11 houses in

Brigmerston in 1768.[5] The principal farmstead in the village, Brigmerston Farm, was at the west end of the street on the south side, the farm buildings west of the house.[6] A new farmhouse was built south-west of the buildings between 1851 and c. 1877.[7] Brigmerston House, a large square stone building with a long south-east and north-west range at its north corner, was built in a 3-a. park between 1820 and 1841, probably for C. E. Rendall in the 1830s.[8] It was converted to seven flats c. 1950.[9] At the junction of Brigmerston street and the Figheldean–Bulford road a pair of cottages was built in the mid 19th century, and west of that, all on the north side of the street, three pairs were built in the early 20th.[10] West of them on the north side eight council houses and four old people's bungalows were built in 1956,[11] taking settlement back to the old part of the village, where a few cottages of the 18th century or the 19th survive. At Brigmerston Corner, east of the junction of Brigmerston street and the Figheldean–Bulford road, temporary housing was erected after the Second World War and apparently removed in the 1960s.[12] Brigmerston's population was 33 in 1841,[13] evidently much more in 1991.

MANORS AND OTHER ESTATES. Osmund held Milston in 1066; Turold held it in 1084 and in 1086 as tenant of Roger de Montgomery[14] (d. 1094). MILSTON manor passed successively to Roger's sons Hugh de Montgomery (d. 1098) and Robert de Bellême, who forfeited it in 1102.[15] It was granted to Gilbert de Villiers who held it 1201–4.[16] In 1204 King John granted it to Walter de Cauntelo,[17] who held it 1210–12.[18] Henry III confirmed the manor in 1227 to Walter's son William[19] (d. 1239),[20] and it passed in the direct male line to William[21] (d. 1251), William (d. 1254), and George (d. s.p. 1273). George also held Brigmerston manor,[22] and in 1274 the united manor of MILSTON AND BRIGMERSTON was allotted to his sister Millicent[23] (d. 1299), who in 1285 settled it on Eve[24] (d. 1314), her daughter by Eudes la Zouche. Eve's widower Maurice de Berkeley, Lord Berkeley (d. 1326),[25] forfeited the manor in 1322.[26] Maurice's son Maurice, the reversioner, held the manor in 1329,[27] and on his death in 1347 it passed to his son Thomas[28] (d.

94 W.R.O. 1550/48.
95 *Andrews and Dury, Map* (W.R.S. viii), pl. 9; O.S. Map 1", sheet 14 (1817 edn.).   96 Below, econ. hist. (mills).
97 W.R.O. 1550/48.
98 *V.C.H. Wilts.* iv. 354.   99 Ch. Com. file 86813.
1 *Andrews and Dury, Map* (W.R.S. viii), pl. 9; O.S. Map 1", sheet 14 (1817 edn.); P.R.O., IR 30/38/197.
2 *Wilts. Inq. p.m.* 1242–1326 (Index Libr.), 75.
3 Ibid. 1327–77 (Index Libr.), 179; *Taxation Lists* (W.R.S. x), 132–3; *Tax List, 1332* (W.R.S. xlv), 110; below, manors.   4 Inf. from Miss A. D. Hooper, the Dovecote.
5 B.L. Church Briefs, B. ix. 4.
6 P.R.O., IR 29/38/197; IR 30/38/197.
7 O.S. Map 6", Wilts. LIV (1887 edn.); W.R.O. 1550/48.
8 C. Greenwood, *Map of Wilts.* (1820); P.R.O., IR 29/38/197; IR 30/38/197; below, manors (Milston and Brigmerston); inf. from Miss Hooper.
9 W.R.O., A 1/355/346.
10 O.S. Maps 6", Wilts. LIV (1887 and later edns.); P.R.O., IR 29/38/197; IR 30/38/197.

11 W.R.O., G 1/602/2.
12 Ibid. A 1/355/331; *Census*, 1961; 1971.
13 *V.C.H. Wilts.* iv. 354.   14 Ibid. ii, pp. 133, 194.
15 *Complete Peerage*, i. 230–3.
16 *Rot. Normanniae* (Rec. Com.), i. 6; *Pipe R.* 1202 (P.R.S. N.S. xv), 283; 1203 (P.R.S. N.S. xvi), 43; 1204 (P.R.S. N.S. xviii), 231.   17 *Rot. Litt. Claus.* (Rec. Com.), i. 8.
18 *Red Bk. Exch.* (Rolls Ser.), ii. 482.
19 *Pat. R.* 1225–32, 138; *D.N.B.* (s.v. Wm. de Cantelupe)
20 For the Cauntelo fam., I. J. Sanders, *Eng. Baronies*, 39–40.   21 *Bk. of Fees*, ii. 747.
22 *Wilts. Inq. p.m.* 1242–1326 (Index Libr.), 74–6; below, this section (Brigmerston).   23 *Cal. Fine R.* i. 18.
24 *Feet of F.* 1272–1327 (W.R.S. i), p. 25.
25 *Complete Peerage*, ii. 128–9.
26 J. Smyth, *Berkeley Manuscripts: Lives of the Berkeleys*, ed. J. Maclean (Glouc. 1883), 246.
27 I. H. Jeayes, *Descriptive Cat. of Chart. and Mun. at Berkeley Castle*, p. 157.
28 *Wilts. Inq. p.m.* 1327–77 (Index Libr.), 178–9.

1361).[29] Thomas's relict Catherine (d. 1388), wife of Sir John Thorp (d. 1386), successfully defended her right to it against Thomas, Lord Berkeley, the great-grandson of Maurice, Lord Berkeley. The manor passed to her son Maurice Berkeley[30] (d. 1400), to Maurice's son Sir Maurice[31] (d. 1464), and to Sir Maurice's son Sir William,[32] who forfeited it in 1485. It was granted in 1486 to Jasper Tudor, earl of Bedford (d. 1495),[33] and on his death, in accordance with a royal grant of 1489, reverted to Sir William (d. c. 1500) and his wife Anne (fl. 1515).[34] William's grandson and heir John Berkeley sold the manor in 1544 to Richard Buckland.[35]

Richard Buckland (d. 1558) was succeeded in turn by his sons Matthew[36] (d. 1559) and Walter,[37] who in 1572 sold Milston and Brigmerston manor to Francis Green.[38] In 1606 Green sold it to (Sir) Laurence Hyde[39] (d. 1642).[40] In 1643 moieties were allotted to Hyde's sons Alexander (d. 1667), bishop of Salisbury from 1665, and Henry (d. 1651),[41] but Henry's was not afterwards mentioned and the two were merged. Alexander was succeeded by his son Robert[42] (d. 1722) and Robert by his cousin Robert Hyde (d. s.p. 1723). The manor passed with Heale manor in Woodford to the second Robert's sister Mary Levinz (d. 1730–1). It was apparently settled on the marriage of Mary's daughter Mary Levinz (d. 1724) with Matthew Frampton (d. 1742), to whom the elder Mary devised the reversion.[43] From 1742 it passed with part of Linley manor in Tisbury to Matthew's nephews the Revd. Thomas Bull (d. 1743), Edward Polhill (d. 1759), and Edward's brother Simon (d. 1760) in turn, and to Simon's cousin twice removed the Revd. William Bowles (d. 1788). Bowles's son and successor William became bankrupt in 1810[44] and by 1815 the manor had been sold to Thomas Rendall (will proved 1831). Rendall was succeeded by his son C. E. Rendall[45] (d. 1872) and he by his grandniece Rachel Pinckney (d. 1926), from 1877 wife of F. S. Holden (F. S. Rendall from 1877).[46] The War Department bought the 2,205-a. estate, without Brigmerston House and 3 a., in 1899 and the Ministry of Defence owned it in 1991.[47]

In 1066 Brismar and in 1086 Robert son of Gerald held 1½ hide that became MILSTON GUDGEON manor.[48] The overlordship was part of the honor of Camel (Som.) in the 14th century and was held by Edmund of Woodstock, earl of Kent (d. 1330),[49] his sons Edmund, earl of Kent (d. 1331),[50] and John, earl of Kent (d. 1352), and his daughter Joan,[51] countess of Kent (d. 1385), wife of Thomas de Holand, Lord Holand. The overlordship passed with the earldom to Joan's son Thomas de Holand (d. 1397) and to that Thomas's sons Thomas (d. 1400) and Edmund (d. 1408); from Edmund it passed to his sister Margaret (d. 1439), wife of John Beaufort, earl of Somerset.[52]

Robert held the 1½ hide of Robert son of Gerald in 1086.[53] The estate was afterwards held by Geoffrey le Dun and in 1203 by his relict Aubrey (fl. 1226), wife of Ellis the huntsman.[54] Geoffrey's heir was his grandson Simon le Dun and the estate passed to William le Dun (d. 1286) and his son John[55] (d. s.p. c. 1331).[56] In 1331 Stephen of Brigmerston claimed it under a settlement of 1309,[57] and in 1339 Nicholas of Wylye and his wife Isabel conveyed it to John Gudgeon.[58] In 1350 Joan, wife of Sir John Winchester, established her right as heir of John le Dun,[59] and in 1351 Gudgeon's relict Joan released the manor to her.[60] Sir John Winchester and Joan conveyed it to Walter of Coombe in 1357.[61] It was held in 1365 by Catherine Thorp and became part of Milston and Brigmerston manor.[62]

The 4 hides that became BRIGMERSTON manor were Brismar's in 1066 and held by Robert of Robert son of Gerald in 1086.[63] George de Cauntelo (d. 1273) held the manor,[64] which afterwards descended with Milston.[65]

Francis Court held land worth £17 in Milston and Brigmerston in 1412.[66] Possibly the same estate was conveyed in 1468 by Elizabeth Mountain and her husband Richard to Nicholas Forthey,[67] and was perhaps the one forfeited by Sir Roger Tocotes in 1483. In 1484 Tocotes's estate was granted to Edward Redmayne,[68] after 1485 it was restored to Tocotes (d. 1492),[69] and in 1535 another Roger Tocotes sold it to William

29 Ibid. 272.
30 Cal. Inq. p.m. xvi, pp. 175, 244–5; Cal. Fine R. x. 223; P.R.O., CP 40/487, rot. 386.
31 Cal. Inq. p.m. xviii, p. 128; Feud. Aids, v. 240.
32 P.R.O., C 140/14, no. 29, rot. 5.
33 Cal. Pat. 1485–94, 64; Complete Peerage, ii. 73.
34 Cal. Pat. 1485–94, 266; Smyth, Lives of the Berkeleys, ed. Maclean, 262; P.R.O., C 142/29, no. 97.
35 P.R.O., C 54/434, no. 76; C 142/29, no. 97.
36 Ibid. C 142/124, no. 172.
37 Ibid. C 142/124, no. 174.
38 Ibid. CP 25/2/239/14 & 15 Eliz. I Mich.
39 Ibid. CP 25/2/369/4 Jas. I Mich.
40 For the Hyde fam., Wilts. Pedigrees (Harl. Soc. cv/cvi), 98–100.
41 W.R.O. 130/49A, deed, Hyde to Hyde, 1643.
42 Ibid. 130/49A, lease, Hyde to Lawes, 1683; 367/2, deed, Hyde to Pinckney, 1707.
43 V.C.H. Wilts. vi. 224, which this acct. expands; Alum. Oxon. 1500–1714, ii. 528, 783; D.N.B. (s.v. Baptist Levinz); P.R.O., PROB 11/586, ff. 196v.–200; PROB 11/643, ff. 355v.–357v.
44 V.C.H. Wilts. xiii. 216; Milston and Brigmerston Incl. Act, 19 Geo. III, c. 8 (Priv. Act); W.R.O., A 1/345/298.
45 P.R.O., PROB 11/1782, ff. 75–76v.; W.R.O., A 1/345/298.

46 Kelly's Handbook (1924), 1280; Burke, Land. Gent. (1937), 1907; G.P.L., Treas. Solicitor, 440/50.
47 Inf. from Defence Land Agent, Durrington.
48 V.C.H. Wilts. ii, p. 153.
49 Cal. Inq. Misc. ii, p. 278; Complete Peerage, vii. 143–7.
50 Wilts. Inq. p.m. 1327–77 (Index Libr.), 59–60.
51 Cal. Inq. p.m. x, pp. 41, 54.
52 Complete Peerage, vii. 148–162; xii (1), 39–45; Cal. Close, 1409–13, 248.
53 V.C.H. Wilts. ii, p. 153.
54 Cur. Reg. R. ii. 229; iii. 76; xii, p. 362.
55 Ibid. xii, p. 362; Cal. Fine R. i. 230.
56 Wilts. Inq. p.m. 1327–77 (Index Libr.), 59–60.
57 Cal. Pat. 1307–13, 157; P.R.O., C 260/143, no. 16.
58 Feet of F. 1327–77 (W.R.S. xxix), p. 56.
59 P.R.O., CP 40/363, rot. 72.
60 Feet of F. 1327–77 (W.R.S. xxix), pp. 97–8.
61 Ibid. p. 111.
62 Extents for Debts (W.R.S. xxviii), p. 26.
63 V.C.H. Wilts. ii, p. 153.
64 Wilts. Inq. p.m. 1242–1326 (Index Libr.), 74–6.
65 Above, this section (Milston).
66 Feud. Aids, vi. 535.
67 Feet of F. 1377–1509 (W.R.S. xli), p. 148.
68 Cal. Pat. 1476–85, 501.
69 Complete Peerage, xi. 303.

Stumpe[70] (d. 1552). William's son Sir James[71] sold it in 1553 to John Cowper[72] (d. 1561), who owned a house and 100 a. in Milston. John's son Thomas[73] held the estate in 1572,[74] but it has not been traced further.

Some tithes from the demesne of Milston and Brigmerston manor were held with 24 a. by Wherwell abbey (Hants) at the Dissolution.[75] The estate, called *HORRELL*, had been acquired by a lord of the manor by 1650 and became part of the manor. In respect of it 776 a. were deemed tithe free at inclosure in 1778.[76]

In 1179 Henry II confirmed to Amesbury priory 1 a. of wheat in Milston and 2 a. of wheat in Brigmerston, possibly representing an estate of tithes held until 1177 by Amesbury abbey.[77] Tithes worth 3s. 4d. from Milston parish belonged to the priory at the Dissolution. It was customary to lease them to the rector.[78] Tithes granted to Bermondsey priory (Surr.) had been exchanged before 1317 for 6d. yearly, but the pension was no longer paid in 1319.[79]

ECONOMIC HISTORY. In 1086 Milston had 3½ ploughteams on land for 3: 1 was on demesne land of 2 hides, and 3 *villani*, 2 *servi*, and 9 coscets had 2½ teams. There were 12 a. of meadow, and there was pasture 1 league by 3 furlongs and 12 furlongs by 1. At Brigmerston there was land for 2 teams which, with 11 bordars, were there on the demesne. There were 10 a. of meadow, and there was pasture 12 by 4 furlongs.[80]

In 1274 the demesne of Milston manor may have been worked with that of Brigmerston, and at Milston the united manor had only five customary tenants each holding ½ yardland for 4s. rent, autumn boonworks, and other labour services. There were also three cottagers. Milston Gudgeon manor in 1331 included tenants, but its 160 a. of arable, 3 a. of meadow, and sheep pasture worth 14s. were apparently demesne. In 1274 the demesne land worked from Brigmerston was extensive: there were 432 a. of arable, 14 a. of meadow, and two several pastures, one for 1,000 sheep and one for 18 draught animals. At Brigmerston four customary tenants each held ½ yardland for 4s. 4½d. and labour service between 1 August and 29 September, four customary tenants each held ¼ yardland for 2s. 8d., autumn boonworks, and shearing and weeding services, and there was a cottager. Hay

was made in the lord's meadows apparently by the customary tenants of both Milston and Brigmerston. The united manor also had five free tenants holding a total of 6 yardlands. In 1347 there were 300 a. of demesne arable worked from Brigmerston.[81]

The three manors in the parish were in single ownership from c. 1365[82] and if, as is likely, Milston and Brigmerston each had a separate set of open fields and common pastures in the earlier Middle Ages the two had apparently been merged by c. 1600. Although some demesne was inclosed c. 1595 and in 1616,[83] and c. 64 a. of common down were inclosed in 1611,[84] sheep-and-corn husbandry continued mostly in common. In the later 17th century the four open fields were named after the points of the compass.[85] Under an Act of 1778 the fields, c. 700 a. of arable all east of the Figheldean–Bulford road, and the north part of the downland, c. 525 a., were inclosed.[86] The inclosed downland became part of the demesne farm, apparently still worked from Brigmerston. That remaining, c. 754 a., was for use in common by the rector and the tenantry and was for 1,360 sheep.[87]

The number of tenants of Milston and Brigmerston manor was reduced from c. 25 in 1618[88] to c. 14 in 1778[89] and 6 in 1813.[90] The owner of the manor from c. 1815 was apparently himself a farmer, and by 1840 nearly all the land of the parish was in the lord's hand. Between 1778 and 1840 c. 70 a. of the demesne down and c. 60 a. of the open down were burnbaked, and c. 54 a. of plantations were made between 1817 and 1840 on Silk Hill and along downland stretches of the parish boundary. In 1840 the parish had 884 a. of arable, 1,130 a. of downland, and c. 32 a. of meadow, of which c. 10 a. were watered. There were farm buildings at both Brigmerston and Milston and near Silk Hill.[91] From c. 1850 Milston farm and Brigmerston farm were separate, each of over 1,000 a., and Milston farm included the glebe and the rector's right to feed sheep on the downland.[92] On both, new farmhouses were built in the mid 19th century[93] and sheep-and-corn husbandry continued: barley was the chief crop and c. 2,000 sheep were kept.[94] In 1856 it was intended to plough a further 60 a. of downland and plant more trees.[95]

From 1899 the east part of the parish was used for military training, and by the 1920s much more woodland had been planted on it.[96]

70 W.R.O. 88/1/22.
71 P.R.O., WARD 7/6, no. 121.
72 Ibid. CP 25/2/65/533, no. 26.
73 Ibid. WARD 7/34, no. 190.
74 Ibid. CP 25/2/239/14 & 15 Eliz. I Mich.
75 Ibid. SC 6/Hen. VIII/3342, rot. 89.
76 Ibid. IR 18/11093; IR 29/38/197; Milston and Brigmerston Incl. Act, 19 Geo. III, c. 8 (Priv. Act); W.A.M. xl. 256.
77 Cal. Chart. R. 1257–1300, 157–9; for the hist. of the abbey and priory, V.C.H. Wilts. iii. 242–59.
78 P.R.O., SC 6/Hen. VIII/3986, rot. 86.
79 Reg. Martival (Cant. & York Soc.), iii, pp. 35, 54.
80 V.C.H. Wilts. ii, pp. 133, 153.
81 Wilts. Inq. p.m. 1242–1326 (Index Libr.), 75–6; 1327–77 (Index Libr.), 59–60, 179.
82 Above, manors.
83 P.R.O., E 134/13 Jas. I Hil./17.
84 W.R.O. 2/1, rot. 3.
85 Ibid. 130/49A/13.
86 Milston and Brigmerston Incl. Act, 19 Geo. III, c. 8 (Priv. Act).
87 W.A.M. xxxi. 2; P.R.O., IR 29/38/197; IR 30/38/197.
88 W.R.O. 2/1, rot. 11.
89 Ibid. A 1/345/298.
90 W.A.M. xxxi. 2.
91 O.S. Map 1", sheet 14 (1817 edn.); P.R.O., IR 29/38/197; IR 30/38/197.
92 Kelly's Dir. Wilts. (1848 and later edns.); W.R.O. 906/W/202, lease, Rendall to Hussey, 1856.
93 Above, intro.
94 P.R.O., MAF 68/151, sheet 22; MAF 68/493, sheet 12; MAF 68/1063, sheet 12.
95 W.R.O. 906/W/202, lease, Rendall to Hussey, 1856.
96 Above, manors; O.S. Maps 6", Wilts. XLVIII. SW., LV. NW. (1901, 1925 edns.).

The land was still used for military training in 1991. In the west part in the earlier 20th century dairy farming increased at the expense of arable and sheep farming.[97] In 1991 a farm of *c.* 2,000 a., including land in other parishes, was worked from the farmstead built north-east of Milston in the mid 19th century: on it corn and potatoes were grown and cattle for beef were raised.[98]

MILLS. A mill on Robert son of Gerald's Milston estate in 1086[99] was on Milston Gudgeon manor in 1331.[1] It presumably stood on the Avon where two new grist mills were built in 1611.[2] There were still two mills in 1761,[3] one in 1840:[4] it ceased working in the 1920s.[5]

A mill at Brigmerston was mentioned in 1086[6] but not later.

LOCAL GOVERNMENT. Courts for Milston and Brigmerston manors were held, either separately or together, in the later 13th century,[7] and a court was held for Milston Gudgeon manor in the earlier 14th.[8] Later a single court was held for the composite manor of Milston and Brigmerston.[9] Some of its records survive for 1606–41. The court baron was generally held twice a year in spring and autumn. Presentments included the deaths of tenants, ruinous tenements, illegal undertenancies, encroachments on the common pastures, and in 1610, unusually, an assault. The court regulated common husbandry, in 1611 appointed surveyors to oversee an inclosure, and in 1626 sanctioned a subscription to induce an undesirable parishioner and his wife to move away. Manorial officers appointed at the court included a hayward and, occasionally, a water bailiff, who in 1631 was also ordered to act for the lord of a manor in Durrington.[10]

In 1775–6 £16, in the years 1783–5 an average of £33, and in 1802–3 £47 was spent on the poor: in 1802–3 the parish relieved a quarter of its inhabitants, 15 adults and 18 children.[11] Afterwards fewer were relieved regularly, 9 in 1812–13 when £176 was spent and relief was generous, 8 in 1813–14 when £113 was spent, and 8 in 1814–15 when £50 was spent and relief was less generous.[12] As might be expected of a small parish the sums spent on poor relief remained low, between 1816 and 1836 exceeding £100

only in 1817–18 and 1827–8. The parish became part of Amesbury poor-law union in 1835.[13] It was included in Salisbury district in 1974.[14]

CHURCH. The chapel recorded at Milston in 1274 had by 1299 become a parish church served by a rector.[15] It was consecrated in 1413.[16] A proposal made in 1650 that the parishes of Milston and Bulford should be united[17] was not implemented. Milston rectory was united in 1940 with Figheldean vicarage, and Bulford vicarage was added to the united benefice in 1982.[18]

The advowson of Milston church descended with Milston and Brigmerston manor until the early 19th century and the lords or their representatives usually presented. In 1361 the king presented for Thomas Berkeley who died in that year, and in 1392–3 the right of Maurice Berkeley (d. 1400) was challenged by Thomas, Lord Berkeley. In 1392 Lord Berkeley presented a rector and the ordinary collated one; in 1393 the king and Lord Berkeley each presented and Lord Berkeley's nominee may not have been instituted. Lord Berkeley may have surrendered his claim to the advowson *c.* 1394. The king presented in 1411 because (Sir) Maurice Berkeley was a minor, and the bishop collated for an unknown reason in 1458.[19] From 1572 to 1606 the lord of the manor, Francis Green, was a recusant,[20] and Henry Poole and his brother George, to whom Henry gave the advowson by will proved 1604,[21] may have been his trustees. The advowson passed with Alexander Hyde's moiety of the manor and his brother Sir Frederick Hyde presented, in each case presumably by grant of a turn, in 1663 and 1670. In 1703 the ordinary collated through lapse.[22] The advowson was sold, possibly *c.* 1810,[23] to Peter Templeman (d. 1824), who devised it to the Revd. Christopher Erle.[24] Before 1832 Erle sold it to the Revd. Peter Hall (d. 1849), whose trustees in 1834 presented him as rector.[25] It was bought by C. E. Rendall and again passed with the manor.[26] In 1940 the War Office became entitled to present alternately for the united benefice and in 1982 the Ministry of Defence at two of every three turns.[27]

The rectory was worth £13 6s. 8d. a year in 1535,[28] £100 in 1650,[29] and £275 c. 1830.[30] The

97 P.R.O., MAF 68/2203, sheet 8; MAF 68/2773, sheet 8; MAF 68/3319, sheet 8; MAF 68/3814, sheet 106; MAF 68/4182, no. 106; MAF 68/4552, no. 106.
98 Inf. from Mrs. S. Parsons, Addison Ho.
99 *V.C.H. Wilts.* ii, p. 153.
1 *Wilts. Inq. p.m.* 1327–77 (Index Libr.), 59–60.
2 P.R.O., E 134/13 Jas. I Hil./17; Winch. Coll. Mun. 5908A.
3 W.R.O. 367/2, lease, Bowles to Southby, 1761.
4 P.R.O., IR 29/38/197; IR 30/38/197.
5 *Kelly's Dir. Wilts.* (1923 and later edns.); W.R.O., G 1/500/11.   6 *V.C.H. Wilts.* ii, p. 153.
7 *Wilts. Inq. p.m.* 1242–1326 (Index Libr.), 74–6.
8 Ibid. 1327–77 (Index Libr.), 59–60.
9 Cf. above, manors.
10 W.R.O. 2/1; 549/42; B.L. Add. Ch. 58418.
11 *Poor Law Abstract, 1804,* 558–9; *V.C.H. Wilts.* iv. 354.
12 *Poor Law Abstract, 1818,* 492–3.
13 *Poor Rate Returns, 1816–21,* 185; *1822–4,* 225; *1825–9,* 215; *1830–4,* 209; *Poor Law Com. 2nd Rep.* App. D, 558.
14 O.S. Map 1/100,000, admin. areas, Wilts. (1974 edn.).

15 *Wilts. Inq. p.m.* 1242–1326 (Index Libr.), 76; *Reg. Ghent* (Cant. & York Soc.), ii. 600.
16 *Reg. Hallum* (Cant. & York Soc.), pp. 122, 140.
17 *W.A.M.* xl. 258.
18 Ch. Com. file, NB 34/143; inf. from Ch. Com.
19 Phillipps, *Wilts. Inst.* (index in *W.A.M.* xxviii. 225); Smyth, *Lives of the Berkeleys,* ed. Maclean, 247; above, manors.   20 *V.C.H. Wilts.* iii. 89.
21 P.R.O., PROB 11/104, f. 141 and v.
22 Phillipps, *Wilts. Inst.* ii. 26, 30, 47; *Wilts. Pedigrees* (Harl. Soc. cv/cvi), 99.
23 Cf. above, manors (Milston and Brigmerston).
24 Hoare, *Mod. Wilts.* Amesbury, 38; P.R.O., PROB 11/1688, ff. 365v.–367v.
25 *D.N.B.*; *Alum. Oxon. 1715–1886,* ii. 588; Ch. Com. file, NB 34/58C; P.R.O., IR 18/11093.
26 *Kelly's Dir. Wilts.* (1855 and later edns.).
27 Ch. Com. file, NB 34/143; inf. from Ch. Com.
28 *Valor Eccl.* (Rec. Com.), ii. 93.
29 *W.A.M.* xl. 256.
30 *Rep. Com. Eccl. Revenues,* 842–3.

rector was entitled to all the tithes of the parish except some from the demesne of Milston and Brigmerston manor.[31] From inclosure in 1778 the rector took all the tithes except those from 776 a. and those other than wool and lambs from 31 a. They were valued at £204 in 1840 and commuted.[32] In the 17th century and early 18th the rector had a house, a nominal 8 a. of arable with pasture rights, and 1 a. of meadow.[33] At inclosure in 1778, when some tithes were given up and land was exchanged, the glebe was increased to 101 a. with rights to feed 286 sheep on the tenantry down.[34] The land and grazing rights were sold to the War Department in 1907.[35] The thatched house in which the rector lived in 1671 was of recent construction. A new taller wing, also thatched, was built on the west in the 18th century.[36] The large stone house in 17th-century style which replaced it c. 1870 was sold c. 1940.[37]

Before the Reformation a small flock of sheep was given to pay for a light in the church.[38] The rector was licensed in 1299 to study for two years provided that he supplied a chaplain to serve the cure. His successor, apparently in minor orders when instituted in 1299, received licences to study in 1299, 1301, and 1306[39] and may rarely have resided. In 1565 the rector was said to be a drunken pluralist.[40] Curates served the cure 1622–31 and 1640–2.[41] Edward Hyde, rector 1641–59,[42] was sequestered. John Smith, who was intruded, preached twice on Sundays in 1650.[43] Thomas Rutty, who served the cure c. 1654, was ejected in 1660.[44] William Gulston, rector 1663–70,[45] either delegated the cure to, or was assisted by, curates,[46] and in 1669 received a royal dispensation to hold in plurality a rectory in Sussex.[47] His successor Lancelot Addison, rector 1670–1703[48] and author of theological and devotional works, did not reside after he became dean of Lichfield (Staffs.) in 1683, and a curate served Milston.[49] William Bowles, rector 1757–61, resigned after inheriting Milston and Brigmerston manor and presented a kinsman Edward Polhill, rector 1761–1800.[50] In 1783 Polhill, who lived in Milston but not in the glebe house, held two Sunday services at one of which he preached, held weekday services on principal feast days, and administered the sacrament four

times a year to c. 10 communicants.[51] His successor J. J. Toogood, rector 1801–34 and from 1815 also vicar of Broad Hinton, lived at Milston in 1832 and held a service there every other Sunday.[52] Peter Hall, rector 1834–49, published topographical and theological works and an edition of the *Preces Privatae* of Lancelot Andrews.[53] Toogood, Hall, and Richard Webb, rector 1850–62 and perpetual curate of Durrington, were all assisted by curates.[54] On Census Sunday in 1851 the curate held morning and afternoon services attended by 58 and 72 people respectively.[55] From 1863 the rector had no curate and in 1864 held and preached at two services every Sunday, held poorly attended weekday services in Lent, and administered the sacrament to c. 25 communicants six times a year.[56]

The church of *ST. MARY*, so called in 1763,[57] consists of a chancel and a nave with north vestry, south porch, and west bellcot,[58] and is built of flint and of stone rubble with dressings of limestone and greensand. A lancet window of the late 13th century survives in the south wall of the chancel. The chancel arch and the nave were rebuilt, and a piscina was placed in the chancel, in the 14th century. New windows were inserted in both nave and chancel in the 15th and 16th centuries, and traces of early 16th-century wall paintings survive in the nave. The church was out of repair in the later 16th century,[59] and then or in the 17th the nave and chancel roofs were reconstructed. The chancel arch was restored in 1786.[60] The entire church was restored in 1860, and again in 1906 when the vestry, designed by C. E. Ponting, was built.[61] Probably also in 1906 a new bellcot supported on buttresses replaced a timber one, and the timber-framed porch was rebuilt to incorporate a 17th-century door and frame.

In 1553 the king's commissioners took 2 oz. of plate and left a chalice of 10 oz. In 1891 and 1991 the parish held a chalice hallmarked for 1576 and a paten hallmarked for 1694 and given in 1718.[62] A 13th-century bell hangs in the bellcot.[63] Registrations of marriages and burials survive from 1540, of baptisms from 1541: those of baptisms are lacking 1654–1702, of marriages 1653–1703.[64]

31 W.R.O., D 1/24/149/1–3.
32 P.R.O., IR 29/38/197.
33 W.R.O., D 1/24/149/1–3.
34 P.R.O., IR 29/38/197; IR 30/38/197.
35 Inf. from Defence Land Agent.
36 W.R.O., D 1/24/149/2–3; Ch. Com. file, NB 34/58C; J. Buckler, watercolour in W.A.S. Libr., vol. i. 14; see below, plate facing p. 251.
37 *Church Guide.*
38 P.R.O., E 318/31/1729.
39 *Reg. Ghent* (Cant. & York Soc.), ii. 838–9, 845, 877.
40 W.R.O., D 1/43/4, f. 1v.
41 Ibid. bishop's transcripts, bdle. 1; *W.N. & Q.* vii. 498; *Cal. S.P. Dom.* 1640–1, 384.
42 Phillipps, *Wilts. Inst.* ii. 20; *Wilts. Pedigrees* (Harl. Soc. cv/cvi), 99.
43 *W.A.M.* xl. 256.
44 *Calamy Revised*, ed. Matthews, 421.
45 Phillipps, *Wilts. Inst.* ii. 26, 30.
46 W.R.O., bishop's transcripts, bdle. 1; ibid. D 1/54/3/2, no. 13.
47 *Cal. S.P. Dom.* 1668–9, 407, 412.
48 Phillipps, *Wilts. Inst.* ii. 30, 47.
49 *D.N.B.*; *W.A.M.* xxxiii. 276; W.R.O., bishop's transcripts, bdle. 1.

50 Phillipps, *Wilts. Inst.* ii. 77, 80, 101; above, manors.
51 *Vis. Queries, 1783* (W.R.S. xxvii), pp. 158–9.
52 *Alum. Oxon. 1715–1886*, iv. 1426; Ch. Com. file, NB 34/58C.
53 *D.N.B.*; *Alum. Oxon. 1715–1886*, ii. 588.
54 *Alum. Oxon. 1715–1886*, iv. 1516; W.R.O., bishop's transcripts, bdle. 5.
55 P.R.O., HO 129/262/2/7/11.
56 W.R.O., D 1/56/7.
57 J. Ecton, *Thesaurus* (1763), 391.
58 For the church in the early 19th cent., Buckler, watercolour in W.A.S. Libr., vol. viii. 5.
59 W.R.O., D 1/43/1, f. 109; D 1/43/4, f. 1v.; D 1/43/5, f. 36; D 1/43/6, f. 4.
60 Date on chancel arch.
61 Pevsner, *Wilts.* (2nd edn.), 351; *W.A.M.* xxxiv. 335; W.R.O. 1469/10.
62 Nightingale, *Wilts. Plate*, 41; inf. from the vicar, Figheldean.
63 Walters, *Wilts. Bells*, 140; inf. from the vicar.
64 W.R.O. 1469/1–4; bishop's transcripts of some of the missing reg. are ibid.; marriages are printed in *Wilts. Par. Reg. (Mar.)*, ed. W. P. W. Phillimore and J. Sadler, iii. 123–8.

NONCONFORMITY. After his ejection from Milston in 1660, Thomas Rutty was a nonconformist preacher in Trowbridge and elsewhere.[65] Parishioners may have attended Baptist conventicles in the later 17th century,[66] but in 1676 there was said to be no nonconformist in Milston.[67]

EDUCATION. In 1858 an old woman taught 15–20 younger children, and older ones attended school at Durrington.[68] The school at Milston, apparently affiliated to the National Society, was attended by 13 children on return day in 1871.[69] It was open in 1875 but closed c. 1880.[70] Milston children attended schools at Bulford, Durrington, and Figheldean in 1923,[71] at Bulford and Durrington in 1991.[72]

CHARITY FOR THE POOR. None known.

NEWTON TONY

NEWTON TONY[73] lies in the Bourne valley 13 km. north-east of Salisbury.[74] The parish, 965 ha. (2,386 a.), is on Wiltshire's border with Hampshire, and the river Bourne winds from north-east to south-west across the middle of it. The suffix Tony is the surname of the lords of the capital manor in the 13th century and early 14th, and was in use in 1332.[75]

The parish boundary consists mostly of straight lines across downland. A barrow lies on the northern boundary, and roads mark the west part of the northern and the north part of the eastern. Between c. 1817 and c. 1826 a belt of trees was planted along the entire boundary, a distance of c. 7 miles.[76]

The parish is entirely on Upper Chalk. The Bourne, which is dry for much of the year, meanders across it in a wide valley and has deposited gravel but no alluvium; east and west of it tributaries have deposited gravel in valleys now dry.[77] The highest land is in the south-east corner at over 170 m. on Tower Hill, which took its name from a folly built on it and was so called in 1817.[78] West of the river the land reaches 109 m. on the western parish boundary, 110 m. on the northern. The lowest point is at c. 80 m. and, except in the south-east corner, the relief is gentle. The village stands on the gravel, which has also been used for meadow land. There were open fields, evidently on both sides of the river, and rough pastures in the north-west and south-east corners of the parish.[79] Much land was imparked for Wilbury House in the 18th century and between 1773 and 1817,[80] and much was planted with trees in the 19th century.[81] A racecourse laid out in the south-east corner before 1839 had become disused by 1874.[82] Also in the south-east corner land was used for military training in the 20th century.[83]

Portway, the Roman road from Silchester to Old Salisbury, runs through the south-east part of the parish, where it is flanked by V-shaped ditches:[84] it seems to have remained in use as a local route until the 20th century,[85] and was a track in 1992. A main road from Oxford to Salisbury via Hungerford (Berks.), important in the 17th century, touched the north-west corner of the parish until, between 1675 and 1773, a new course further west was adopted for it.[86] A road linking Newton Tony to Cholderton, Allington, and other villages of the Bourne valley was blocked by imparking at Newton Tony in the 18th century and diverted to the western edge of the park. An alternative route was by a road on the east edge of the park and Portway.[87] In 1835 the Bourne valley road was turnpiked as part of a Swindon–Salisbury road via Marlborough, and a new section across the west part of Newton Tony parish was made; disturnpiked in 1876,[88] it was still a main road in 1992. In 1871 the Cholderton road on the north-west edge of the park was closed and the north-west and south-east section of the road was extended to join the turnpike road.[89] A road to Amesbury, from which the road on the western edge of the park diverged, remained on its old course in Newton Tony in 1992 but was closed in Amesbury parish in the mid 20th century.[90] The eastern route round the park was in places a rough track in 1992, as was the road along the west part of the northern parish boundary which from the early 18th century to the early 19th was important as a link between Cholderton and the old Hungerford road.[91]

The London–Salisbury railway line, opened by the L. & S.W.R. in 1857, was constructed across the parish along the south-east side of Portway. In 1902 the Amesbury and Military

65 V.C.H. Wilts. iii. 105.   66 Ibid. 112.
67 Compton Census, ed. Whiteman, 124.
68 Acct. of Wilts. Schs. 34.
69 Returns relating to Elem. Educ. 426–7.
70 Kelly's Dir. Wilts. (1875, 1880).
71 Ch. Com. file 100404.   72 Inf. from the vicar.
73 This article was written in 1992.
74 Maps used include O.S. Maps 1", sheet 14 (1817 edn.); 1/50,000, sheet 184 (1988 edn.); 6", Wilts. LV, LXI (1883 and later edns.).
75 P.N. Wilts. (E.P.N.S.), 370; below, manors (Newton Tony).
76 Hoare, Mod. Wilts. Amesbury, 103; O.S. Map 1", sheet 14 (1817 edn.).
77 Geol. Surv. Maps 1/50,000, drift, sheet 298 (1976 edn.); sheet 299 (1975 edn.).
78 O.S. Map 1", sheet 14 (1817 edn.); below, manors

(Newton Tony).   79 Below, econ. hist.
80 Ibid. manors (Newton Tony).
81 Ibid. econ. hist. [woodland].
82 O.S. Map 6", Wilts. LXI (1883 edn.); P.R.O., IR 29/38/208; IR 30/38/208.
83 O.S. Map 1/50,000, sheet 184 (1974 edn.); cf. below, manors (Newton Tony).   84 V.C.H. Wilts. i (1), 91.
85 O.S. Maps 6", Wilts. LXI (1883 and later edns.).
86 Ibid. 1", sheet 14 (1817 edn.); J. Ogilby, Brit. (1675), pl. 83; Andrews and Dury, Map (W.R.S. viii), pl. 6; below, N. Tidworth, intro. [roads].
87 O.S. Map 1", sheet 14 (1817 edn.); for the park, below, manors (Newton Tony).
88 V.C.H. Wilts. iv. 257, 262, 270; P.R.O., IR 30/38/208.
89 W.R.O., A 1/110/1871 Mich.
90 Above, Amesbury, intro. (roads).
91 Ibid. Cholderton, intro. [roads].

Camp Light Railway was opened between Grateley (Hants) and Amesbury, diverging from the main L. & S.W.R. line in Newton Tony. A station on the Amesbury line was built at the west edge of Newton Tony village. At the junction a short curve to enable trains to run between Amesbury and Salisbury was added in 1904. The branch line was closed to passengers and Newton Tony station completely in 1952; the curve was taken out of use in 1954; the line was closed entirely in 1963 and its track removed in 1965.[92] The main line remained open in 1992.

Eighteen bowl barrows, most in the south part of the parish, have been recorded,[93] and east of the village a pit used in the Iron Age has been found.[94] On high ground north-west of the village a prehistoric field system of 100 a. extends into Cholderton, and on similar ground east of the village another, of 180 a., is near the Hampshire boundary. There is a prehistoric ditch on Tower Hill.[95]

Although Newton Tony's assessment for taxation in 1332, when it may have had a resident lord, seems high,[96] it was described as a hamlet in 1401 and had fewer than 10 households in 1428.[97] Taxation assessments of the 16th century and early 17th suggest that the village was then of average size.[98] The population was 286 in 1801, 268 in 1831. It had risen to 351 by 1861, fallen to 292 by 1891, and was 407 in 1901 and 306 in 1911: inhabitants in 1901 may have included workmen constructing the branch railway. Between 1951 and 1971 the population increased from 304 to 395 as new houses were built in the village. In 1991 it was 373.[99]

Until the 20th century much the greater part of Newton Tony village was beside a single street,[1] in 1992 called High Street, the north part of which was the course of the Bourne valley road blocked in the earlier 18th century. By 1773 the village had also extended north-west along the south side of the road, in 1992 called Beechfield, leading both to Amesbury and, round the west edge of the park, to Cholderton. The river flowed down the middle of the street.[2] Between 1773 and 1839 two bridges were built at the north end, where a small green was formed, and the river was diverted west of the street at that end.[3] Further south two footbridges were built between c. 1875 and 1899. Between 1899 and 1923 an iron girder road bridge was built at the junction with the Allington road;[4] thereafter traffic through the village has used a road on the east bank of the river, but the road on the west bank has also been tarmacadamed to serve buildings there.

The church stands towards the south end of

the street and when first built may have been at the southernmost end. The rectory house was presumably near it and was replaced in the later 18th century[5] by one set back from the street almost behind the church. South of the church, possibly on a new site at what was then the southern end of the village,[6] Manor Farm was built in the early 19th century, the farmhouse, like the rectory house, set back from the street on the east side, and extensive farm buildings on the west side. The house is of red brick, and a contemporary three-arched brick bridge over the Bourne links it to the farm buildings. Also at the south end of the village on the east side of the street a nonconformist chapel, a school,[7] and a reading room were built in the 19th century, a village hall in 1920. The reading room was converted for residence c. 1915.[8]

Three substantial houses were built in the north part of the street. What was Newton Tony manor house until the earlier 18th century stood on the west side.[9] On the east side the main north–south range of West Farm, which has thick stone walls and possibly had a cross passage, was built in the 16th century or earlier. An east–west cross wing, with a three-bayed roof incorporating arch-braced collars, was built at the south end of that range in the 16th century. The main range was greatly altered in the later 17th century, and in 1985 the house was restored throughout and extended to the east.[10] On the west side of the street a house of 17th-century origin retains timber framing and a central chimney stack. It was altered and extended in the early or mid 18th century, possibly for Thomas Hayter:[11] it was an inn, the Malet Arms, from the late 19th century.[12]

Several small houses of the 17th or 18th century survive in the street. On the west side at the south end a range of houses has walls of moulded cob, some timber framing, and a thatched roof; two cottages with cob walls stand on the south side of the Amesbury and Cholderton road. Other houses on the west side of the street, including one dated 1726 and one 1741, are of flint. South of West Farm on the east side a house of cob, flint, and brick, of two storeys and attics, has labels above the ground-floor windows of the west front and is dated 1690: it was altered and extended in the 20th century. Between the church and Manor Farm a range of cottages, of flint with red-brick dressings, was built in 1857,[13] but not many other houses were built in the village in the 19th century. In the late 19th century a few cottages in the middle part of the street on the east side were demol-

92   *V.C.H. Wilts.* iv. 286, 291; P. A. Harding, *Bulford Branch Line*, 27–8; Wilts. Tracts, 220, no. 11, p. 46.
93   *V.C.H. Wilts.* i (1), 184–5.
94   *W.A.M.* lxv. 209.
95   *V.C.H. Wilts.* i (1), 250, 275, 277.
96   *Tax List, 1332* (W.R.S. xlv), 112; cf. below, manors (Newton Tony).
97   *V.C.H. Wilts.* iv. 314; *Cal. Pat.* 1399–1401, 435.
98   *Taxation Lists* (W.R.S. x), 130; P.R.O., E 179/197/152; E 179/197/241; E 179/198/284; E 179/198/329; E 179/199/370; E 179/199/398.
99   *V.C.H. Wilts.* iv. 354; *Census,* 1971; 1991; above and below, this section.
1   O.S. Map 6", Wilts. LXI. NW. (1901 edn.).

2   *Andrews and Dury, Map* (W.R.S. viii), pl. 6.
3   Ibid.; P.R.O., IR 30/38/208.
4   O.S. Maps 6", Wilts. LXI (1883 and later edns.).
5   Below, church.
6   O.S. Map 1", sheet 14 (1817 edn.).
7   Below, nonconf.; educ.
8   Ch. Com. file 53780; inf. from Capt. N. I. C. Kettlewell, Old Rectory; Wilts. Tracts, 220, no. 11, p. 42.
9   Below, manors (Newton Tony).
10   Inf. from Capt. Kettlewell.
11   Cf. *Andrews and Dury, Map* (W.R.S. viii), pl. 6; below, manors (Norris's).
12   O.S. Map 6", Wilts. LXI. NW. (1901 edn.).
13   Date on bldg.

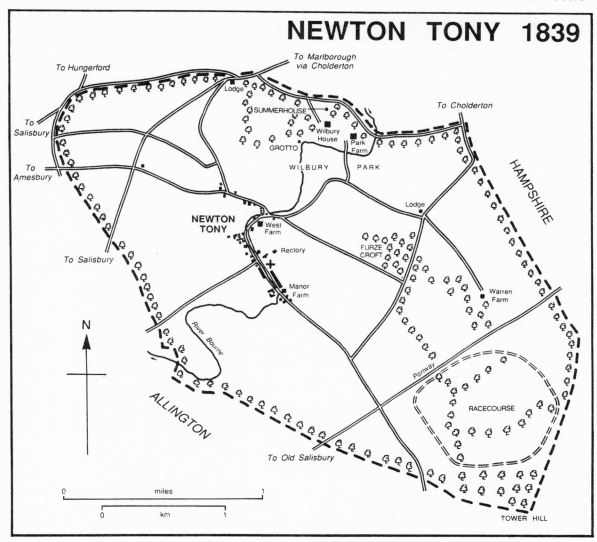

NEWTON TONY 1839

ished,[14] and an open space there was a recreation ground in 1992.

Newton Tony village grew in the 20th century. On the Allington road near High Street a stationmaster's house and a pair of cottages, each of red brick, were built *c.* 1900,[15] and St. Just Close, an estate of *c.* 15 private bungalows, was built between them and High Street *c.* 1966.[16] The Croft, a council estate of 8 houses and 10 old people's bungalows, was built west of High Street on the site of the old manor house from *c.* 1948:[17] it is approached by a new bridge over the Bourne. There has also been some infilling in High Street, but most 20th-century building has been in Beechfield. On the north side 18 council houses were built between *c.* 1924 and 1957 and a block of 4 council flats in 1965; on the north side of the Amesbury road 4 old people's

bungalows were built in 1958.[18] On the south side of Beechfield *c.* 10 private bungalows were built in the 1960s.[19] On part of the park near the north side a terrace of four red-brick estate cottages was built in 1947.[20] A cemetery was opened beside the Cholderton road in 1927.[21]

Outside the village the mansion called Wilbury House was built in the early 18th century.[22] Four lodges were built on the perimeter of its park, those on the north-west (Salisbury Lodge) and the east between 1817 and 1839,[23] those on the north-east (Grateley Lodge) and the south (Newton Tony Lodge) between 1900 and 1923.[24] Newton Tony Lodge, at the entrance to the park from the village, is in classical style. A farmhouse, Park (later Home) Farm, was built, evidently in the earlier 19th century,[25] a little east of Wilbury House on the site of buildings

14   O.S. Maps 6", Wilts. LXI (1883 edn.); LXI. NW. (1901 edn.).
15   Ibid. LXI. NW. (1901 edn.); cf. above, this section.
16   W.R.O., G 1/132/117; ibid. 1293/12.
17   Ibid. G 1/600/1.
18   Ibid.; ibid. G 1/132/117; G 1/500/12; G 1/602/2–4.
19   O.S. Map 1", sheet 167 (1960 edn.); 1/50,000, sheet 184 (1974 edn.).

20   Date on bldg.
21   Ch. Com. file 90999.
22   Below, manors (Newton Tony).
23   O.S. Map 1", sheet 14 (1817 edn.); P.R.O., IR 30/38/208.
24   O.S. Maps 6", Wilts. LV. SW., LXI. NW. (1901, 1926 edns.).
25   W.R.O. 776/124.

standing in the later 18th century,[26] and Warren Farm, near the east edge of the park, was built between 1817 and 1839.[27] New (later Red) Cottage, a house of red brick and flint, was built in the mid 19th century where, from 1871, a new section of the Cholderton road diverged from an older section;[28] above, this section.[28] a similar house, an animal sanctuary in 1992, was built in the early 20th century at the junction of the Amesbury road and the Marlborough–Salisbury road.[29] A pair of cottages built beside the main railway line and Portway c. 1857 was demolished in the later 20th century.[30]

An inn called the Swan was open in Newton Tony in 1773[31] and was perhaps the meeting place of a friendly society registered in 1817.[32] There was apparently no inn c. 1822.[33] In the mid 19th century the Three Horse Shoes was an alehouse in the village, and the Malet Arms was an inn on the south side of what is now Beechfield.[34] The Malet Arms was perhaps the meeting place of a friendly society formed in 1857.[35] Between c. 1875 and 1896 the Malet Arms was closed and its name transferred to the Three Horse Shoes, and between 1896 and 1899 that Malet Arms was closed and the name transferred to the inn opened in the house which may have been built for Thomas Hayter.[36] The Malet Arms remained open in 1992.

MANORS AND OTHER ESTATES. In 1086 Alfred of Marlborough held what became *NEWTON TONY* manor.[37] A dispute over the manor in the early 13th century suggests that the estate was acquired soon after 1086 by Edward of Salisbury. It may have passed from Edward to his daughter Maud, wife of Humphrey de Bohun, and to Maud's son Humphrey de Bohun, whose son Humphrey held it in 1179; the right to it of that Humphrey's son Henry (cr. earl of Hereford 1200, d. 1220) was challenged in 1212 by Edward's great-great-granddaughter Ela Longespée, countess of Salisbury (d. 1261).[38] Henry's son Humphrey, earl of Hereford and of Essex (d. 1275), had defeated Ela's claim by 1229.[39] The manor had been subinfeudated by 1257.[40] The overlordship passed with the Hereford and Essex titles to

Humphrey's grandson Humphrey de Bohun (d. 1298), to that Humphrey's son Humphrey (d. 1322),[41] and to that Humphrey's sons John (d. s.p. 1336) and Humphrey (d. 1361).[42] The last Humphrey's heir was his nephew Humphrey de Bohun, earl of Hereford, of Essex, and of Northampton (d. 1373),[43] to whose daughter Mary, wife of Henry of Lancaster, earl of Derby (from 1399 Henry IV), the overlordship was allotted in 1384.[44] Thereafter it was part of the duchy of Lancaster.[45]

In 1257 Roger de Tony (d. 1263 or 1264) held the manor. It descended in the direct line to Ralph de Tony (d. 1295) and Robert de Tony, Lord Tony (d. s.p. 1309). Robert was succeeded by his sister Alice (d. c. 1325), relict of Thomas Leyburn and later wife of Guy de Beauchamp, earl of Warwick (d. 1315), and of William la Zouche, Lord Zouche.[46] On Zouche's death in 1337 the manor passed to Alice's son Thomas Beauchamp, earl of Warwick[47] (d. 1369). Thomas granted it for life to his brother John, Lord Beauchamp (d. 1360),[48] and settled it on his younger son Sir William, who gave it by exchange to Sir Thomas West (d. 1386). Sir Thomas granted it for life to John or Roger New.[49]

By c. 1401 Newton Tony manor had reverted to Sir Thomas West's son Sir Thomas (Lord West from 1402, d. 1405), who was succeeded in turn by his sons Thomas, Lord West (d. 1416), and Reynold,[50] Lord la Warre (d. 1450). From Reynold it passed in the direct line to Richard,[51] Lord la Warre (d. 1476), and Thomas,[52] Lord la Warre, who sold it in 1489 to a London goldsmith, (Sir) Bartholomew Reed[53] (d. 1505). Sir Bartholomew's relict Elizabeth held the manor until her death in 1532, and from then the profits were apparently taken for 10 years by the Goldsmiths' company. The profits reverted to Reed's grandnephew John Reed[54] (d. by 1545).[55] From John the manor passed to his relict Elizabeth (d. by 1568), who married Henry Reynolds.[56] John's son John sold it in 1581 to Thomas Crane[57] (d. 1596). Crane's coheirs were his daughters Elizabeth, wife of David Waterhouse, Sarah, wife of William Brockett, Frances, wife of (Sir) James Bouchier, and Eluzai, wife of John Jones.[58] In 1599 Eliza-

[26] *Andrews and Dury, Map* (W.R.S. viii), pl. 6.
[27] O.S. Map 1″, sheet 14 (1817 edn.); P.R.O., IR 30/38/208.
[28] O.S. Map 6″, Wilts. LV (1883 edn.); P.R.O., IR 30/38/208; above, this section [roads].
[29] O.S. Maps 6″, Wilts. LXI. NW. (1901, 1926 edns.).
[30] W.R.O. 1294/11; cf. above, this section.
[31] W.R.O. 1408, PCC/3/1.
[32] P.R.O., FS 4/55, Wilts. no. 28.
[33] W.R.O., A 1/326/3.
[34] *Kelly's Dir. Wilts.* (1848 and later edns.); O.S. Map 6″, Wilts. LXI (1883 edn.).
[35] Wilts. Tracts, 220, no. 11, p. 29.
[36] O.S. Maps 6″, Wilts. LXI (1883 edn.); LXI. NW. (1901 edn.); W.R.O. 1810/34 (annotated copy of E. P. Barrow, *Par. Notes*), n. at end; above, this section.
[37] *V.C.H. Wilts.* ii, p. 141.
[38] Ibid. x. 207; *Cal. Chart. R.* 1257–1300, 158; *Complete Peerage*, vi. 457–77; xi. 373–82; *Cur. Reg. R.* vi. 320.
[39] *Bk. of Fees*, ii. 744; P.R.O., CP 25/1/580/8, no. 11.
[40] *Wilts. Inq. p.m.* 1242–1326 (Index Libr.), 22.
[41] Ibid. 373–4, 409–10.
[42] Ibid. 1327–77 (Index Libr.), 265–6.

[43] Ibid. 371–2; *Cal. Close*, 1360–4, 471.
[44] *Cal. Close*, 1381–5, 514–15.   [45] *Feud. Aids*, vi. 632.
[46] *Wilts. Inq. p.m.* 1242–1326 (Index Libr.), 22, 373–4, 409–10; for the Tony fam., *Complete Peerage*, xii (1), 771–4; for the Beauchamp fam., ibid. xii (2), 370–4.
[47] *Cal. Inq. p.m.* viii, pp. 65–6.
[48] *Cal. Chart. R.* 1341–1417, 64–5; *Wilts. Inq. p.m.* 1327–77 (Index Libr.), 265–6; *Complete Peerage*, ii. 50–1.
[49] *Cal. Inq. p.m.* xvi, pp. 185–7; *Complete Peerage*, i. 24–6; P.R.O., C 88/55, no. 110.
[50] *Feud. Aids*, vi. 632; P.R.O., C 138/19, no. 28, rot. 13; for the West fam., *Complete Peerage*, iv. 152–6; xii (2), 519–21.   [51] P.R.O., C 139/142, no. 21, rot. 15.
[52] Ibid. C 140/57, no. 62, rot. 12.
[53] *Feet of F.* 1377–1509 (W.R.S. xli), p. 164; *Cal. Close*, 1485–1500, p. 165.
[54] *Cal. Inq. p.m. Hen. VII*, iii, pp. 123–4; *V.C.H. Surr.* iii. 477–8; P.R.O., C 142/55, no. 55; ibid. PROB 11/14, ff. 321–4; the descent 1505–96 corrects and amplifies that in *V.C.H. Wilts.* xi. 242.   [55] P.R.O., C 142/72, no. 81.
[56] Phillipps, *Wilts. Inst.* i. 213–14, 216, 219, 223.
[57] *W.A.M.* xxxvi. 112–14.
[58] P.R.O., C 60/449, no. 14; C 142/251, no. 154.

beth and Sarah conveyed their shares of the manor to John's father William (d. 1610). Those shares descended to John[59] (d. 1611), who devised them to Eluzai,[60] later the wife of Henry Cromwell. From Eluzai (d. 1620) three quarters of the manor descended to her son Francis Jones:[61] Francis had apparently acquired Frances Bouchier's quarter by 1656, when he sold the manor to Nathaniel Fiennes[62] (d. 1669). Nathaniel devised it to his wife Frances (d. 1691) for life, and afterwards in trust for sale.[63] It was bought, possibly soon after 1691, by Sir William Benson, whose title Nathaniel's grandson Nathaniel Fiennes, Viscount Saye and Sele, confirmed in 1709.[64]

Sir William Benson settled the manor in 1710 on his son William (d. 1754), M.P. for Shaftesbury, an amateur architect and a patron of literature,[65] who built Wilbury House on it.[66] William sold it after 1729 to his nephew Henry Hoare (d. 1785), who sold it c. 1739 to Fulk Greville, M.P. for Monmouth.[67] Greville sold it c. 1783 to Thomas Bradshaw (will proved 1800), whose brother John sold it c. 1803 to Sir Charles Malet, Bt.[68] The manor, which comprised nearly all the parish in 1839, descended in the direct line from Sir Charles (d. 1815), to Sir Alexander (d. 1886), and to Sir Henry (d. 1904).[69] It passed to Sir Henry's brother Sir Edward (d. s.p. 1908), to Sir Edward's cousin Sir Edward Malet, Bt. (d. 1909), to that Sir Edward's son Sir Charles (d. 1918), and to Sir Charles's uncle Sir Harry Malet, Bt.[70] In 1918 the War Department occupied 198 a. south-east of the main railway line, and in 1925 bought that land from Sir Harry; the Ministry of Defence owned the land in 1992.[71] In 1925 Sir Harry also sold Manor farm, West farm, and Village farm, a total of c. 1,000 a. He sold Wilbury House, Home farm, and Warren farm, a total of c. 764 a., c. 1925 to J. A. St. G. F. Despencer-Robertson,[72] who sold that land in 1939 to Edward Grenfell, Lord St. Just (d. 1941). Grenfell was succeeded by his son Peter, Lord St. Just (d. 1984), whose relict Maria was the owner in 1992.[73]

Newton Tony manor house on the west side of High Street[74] was in the later 17th century the home of the Fiennes family. The traveller and author Celia Fiennes spent much of her girlhood at Newton Tony and was buried there in 1741.[75] The house presumably became a farmhouse when Wilbury House was built in the early 18th

century[76] and was largely demolished in the early 19th, presumably when Manor Farm was built.[77] Its kitchen was later the Three Horse Shoes and may have been the malthouse adjoining the west side of the street in 1839;[78] a cob wall north of that site was associated with the house.

Wilbury House,[79] so called c. 1739,[80] was designed c. 1710 as a small classical villa by William Benson, who was inspired by the architecture of Inigo Jones. Although parts of a timber-framed building may have been re-used in it, it is likely that no building preceded it on its site. Aspects of the design echo that of Amesbury Abbey, of which Benson took a 21-year lease in 1708.[81] Wilbury House, however, was smaller, lacked Amesbury Abbey's tall ground floor, and had its two staircases in different positions from the staircases in Amesbury Abbey. The house, of rendered brick with stone dressings on a rusticated stone basement, comprised a single-storeyed east–west range with attics surmounted by a central cupola, and had long flanking walls extending east and west from the south front. From under a pedimented portico on that front the main entrance to the house was into a principal central room. In the later 18th century, apparently after 1773,[82] and presumably for Thomas Bradshaw, the north elevation was converted to an entrance front, the attics were heightened to form a second storey, and the cupola was removed. The flanking walls were replaced by short single-storeyed wings with canted south bays. The eastern was used as a Roman Catholic chapel from 1797 to c. 1800.[83] Alterations made for Sir Charles Malet by 1813 included the extension of the south portico and pediment to the length of the principal room. Later the pediment was removed and three second-storey windows were inserted above the portico.[84] Fittings and decorations of the earlier 18th century survive inside the house, particularly in the central south room. The original east staircase was replaced in the later 18th century.

A park of c. 175 a. was laid out round the house from c. 1710. It had avenues, vistas, and woodland mainly north and north-west of the house. There were in the park in 1773 an octagonal summerhouse above a grotto north of the house, a grotto beside the Bourne south-west, a temple on a hill south-east, and a formal garden northeast of the house. Outside the park on Tower Hill the ornamental tower called Benson's Folly

59   Ibid. C 142/680, no. 30; ibid. CP 25/2/242/41 & 42 Eliz. I Mich.   60   Ibid. C 142/325, no. 187.
61   Ibid. C 142/379, no. 91.
62   Ibid. CP 25/2/609/1656 East.; CP 43/293, rot. 38.
63   Ibid. PROB 11/334, ff. 318–319v.; for the Fiennes fam., Complete Peerage, xi. 489–90; Hoare, Mod. Wilts. Amesbury, 105.
64   P.R.O., CP 25/2/980/8 Anne Trin.
65   Ibid. C 113/205, deed, Benson to Austen, 1710; Hist. Parl., Commons, 1715–54, i. 455.
66   Below, this section.
67   Hist. Parl., Commons, 1715–54, ii. 85–6; Hoare, Mod. Wilts. Amesbury, 104; P.R.O., CP 43/586, rot. 196 and d.; W.R.O. 383/226.
68   W.R.O., A 1/345/308; P.R.O., PROB 11/1343, ff. 454v.–456v.
69   P.R.O., IR 29/38/208; IR 30/38/208; for the Malet fam., Burke, Peerage (1963), 1585–7.
70   W.R.O., Inland Revenue, val. reg. 148; ibid. 776/124.
71   G. B. Carter, Porton Down, 4; inf. from Defence Land

Agent, Durrington.
72   Kelly's Dir. Wilts. (1927); W.A.S. Libr., sale cat. xlviii, no. 32; W.R.O., G 1/500/12.
73   Burke, Peerage (1963), 2148–9; Who Was Who, 1981–9, 664.
74   The foundations were exposed c. 1948 during the construction of the Croft: inf. from Capt. N. I. C. Kettlewell, Old Rectory.
75   C. Fiennes, Journeys of Celia Fiennes, ed. C. Morris (1949 edn.); W.R.O., bishop's transcripts, bdle. 2.
76   Below, this section.   77   Above, intro.
78   P.R.O., IR 29/38/208; IR 30/38/208; W.R.O. 1810/34 (annotated copy of Barrow, Par. Notes), n. at end.
79   Description of ho. and park based on J. Bold, Wilton Ho. and Eng. Palladianism (R.C.H.M.), 124–35.
80   W.R.O. 383/226.
81   Ibid. 283/44, lease, Bruce to Benson, 1708; above, Amesbury, manors (Priory).
82   cf. Andrews and Dury, Map (W.R.S. viii), pl. 6.
83   Below, nonconf.   84   See plate facing p. 74.

in 1773 was the focal point of a southern vista;[85] it may have borne an inscription which, if it did, would have suggested that it incorporated all or part of an ornamental tower built in the park of Edward Seymour, earl of Hertford, at Amesbury in 1600.[86] The temple and the tower had been demolished by 1817.[87] Between 1773 and 1817 the park was enlarged to c. 490 a.,[88] and on its

Peverel[96] to Henry Peverel (d. 1302) and to Henry's son William.[97] They were afterwards held by Robert Noble (d. 1361), who held the 2 yardlands of Robert of Wolverton. His heirs were his daughters Joan and Alice;[98] in 1386 Alice and her husband Roger Champion conveyed the estate to Walter Chippenham and his wife Alice.[99] John Chippenham held it in 1412.[1]

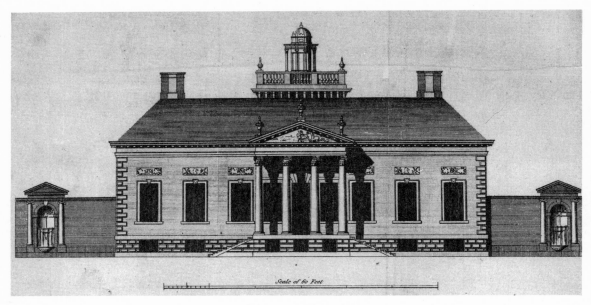

WILBURY HOUSE

perimeter, c. 3¾ miles, a fence of oak palings was erected.[89] Trees planted in the south and east parts of the park were obscuring the vistas in 1817, and soon afterwards much of the park was again used for agriculture.[90] New formal gardens were made south of the house in the period 1941–59.[91]

Of Alfred of Marlborough's estate 3 hides held of him in 1086 by Girard[92] may have included the land which later became the manor called NORRIS'S. From 1242–3 to 1489 the overlords of an estate likely to have been Girard's were those of Newton Tony manor.[93]

The estate likely to have been Girard's was held in demesne by John de Neville in 1179[94] and by another John de Neville in 1242–3.[95] Agnes Peverel (d. 1257) held 1 yardland of it and held as tenant of Christine of Harsfield 2 further yardlands which may have been part of it. Agnes's lands descended from her son Thomas

The estate was held of Thomas Norris by John Hall (d. c. 1479),[2] possibly by a temporary tenure; shortly before his death in 1489 Norris sold it to John Mompesson.[3] On John's death in 1500 Norris's passed to his son William, and on William's c. 1504 it passed to John's grandson John Mompesson (d. 1511). It descended to the younger John's son Edmund (d. 1553), whose heirs, his nephew Gilbert Wells and his sisters Anne wife of William Wayte, Elizabeth wife of Richard Perkins, and Susan Mompesson, sold the manor in 1554 to Richard Mompesson.[4] From Richard the manor passed to his grandson Thomas Mompesson,[5] who in 1586 sold it to William Gore[6] (d. 1587). It descended to Gore's son William[7] (d. 1598) and grandson William Gore, a minor,[8] whose trustees sold it in 1605 to (Sir) Laurence Hyde (d. 1642).[9] In 1609 Hyde sold it to William Jones (d. 1610) and his grandson Gabriel Jones.[10] Gabriel's son Wil-

85 Andrews and Dury, Map (W.R.S. viii), pl. 6.
86 Bold, Eng. Palladianism, 133; above, Amesbury, manors (Priory).
87 O.S. Map 1", sheet 14 (1817 edn.).
88 Ibid.; Andrews and Dury, Map (W.R.S. viii), pl. 6; P.R.O., IR 29/38/208; IR 30/38/208.
89 Hoare, Mod. Wilts. Amesbury, 103.
90 O.S. Map 1", sheet 14 (1817 edn.); below, econ. hist.
91 Country Life, 10 Dec. 1959.
92 V.C.H. Wilts. ii, p. 141.
93 Bk. of Fees, ii. 744; Cal. Inq. p.m. Hen. VII, i, pp. 203–4.   94 Cal. Chart. R. 1257–1300, 158–9.
95 Bk. of Fees, ii. 744.
96 Wilts. Inq. p.m. 1242–1326 (Index Libr.), 22.
97 Cal. Fine R. i. 518.

98 Wilts. Inq. p.m. 1327–77 (Index Libr.), 312.
99 Feet of F. 1377–1509 (W.R.S. xli), pp. 19–20.
1 Feud. Aids, vi. 539.
2 P.R.O., C 140/70, no. 33, rot. 3.
3 Cal. Inq. p.m. Hen. VII, i, pp. 203–4.
4 Ibid. ii, pp. 317–18; V.C.H. Wilts. xiv. 189; P.R.O., C 142/104, no. 123; ibid. CP 25/2/83/709, no. 25; ibid. PROB 11/14, f. 13.   5 P.R.O., REQ 2/62/21.
6 Ibid. CP 25/2/241/28 Eliz. I Hil.
7 Ibid. C 142/224, no. 26.
8 Ibid. C 142/258, no. 140.
9 Ibid. CP 25/2/369/3 Jas. I Trin.; for Hyde, above, Milston, manors.
10 P.R.O., PROB 11/116, ff. 386v.–387v.; W.R.O. 1408, MTD/M 3.

liam, in possession *c.* 1650,[11] sold the manor in portions.

Parts were sold in 1658 and 1662 to Jonathan Hill[12] (d. 1670). Hill devised them to his son Augustine, whose brother Alexander was party to a sale of the estate to William Salt in 1679.[13] Also in 1679 Salt sold the reversion after the death of him and his wife Catherine to William Braxton[14] (will proved 1688), who devised the estate to his son James.[15] James's devisee, his mother Elizabeth Braxton, sold it in 1709 to John Judd,[16] whose daughter Catherine sold it in 1740 to Thomas Hayter[17] (d. 1779). Hayter added other land in Newton Tony to the estate, which passed to his son William (d. 1795) and grandson F. T. Hayter.[18] In 1792 F. T. Hayter changed his surname to Egerton, and in 1807 sold his 578 a. in the parish to Sir Charles Malet, Bt.: the land afterwards passed with Newton Tony manor.[19]

Part of Norris's, 1 yardland, was sold in 1660 by William Jones to Robert Bevis[20] (d. 1720). Robert's son Thomas[21] sold it in 1744 to Henry Quaite[22] (will proved 1751), a London pastry cook, who devised it to his brother William and William's wife Anne for life and afterwards to William's sons William and Henry as tenants in common.[23] William and Henry each sold the reversion of his moiety, in 1769 and 1770 respectively,[24] to Thomas Hayter, and on the death of the elder William in 1773[25] the estate was merged with Hayter's other estate in the parish.

Thomas Hayter (d. 1779) acquired two other small estates in the parish. Land sold in 1567 by John Day to Philip Poore[26] descended to Philip Poore (d. 1719).[27] In 1725 Philip's daughters Mary Poore and Anne Poore sold 1 yardland to William Swanton,[28] whose mortgagee Thomas Hayter foreclosed him in 1736.[29] John Smart owned 2 yardlands in 1598 and 1608.[30] William Smart sold them, possibly in the early 18th century, to Henry Gilbert, who sold them to Hayter in 1740.[31]

Amesbury abbey may have owned tithes in the parish. The yearly render from the parish of 12 a. of corn and 12 lambs confirmed to Amesbury priory in 1179[32] may represent an estate of tithes, and tithes from the parish passed from the priory to the Crown at the Dissolution.[33] In 1563 they were granted to William Revett and Thomas Bright,[34] and soon afterwards may have been acquired by the lord of Newton Tony manor. From 1605 or earlier those tithes were repre-

sented by the exemption of the manorial demesne from tithes of 20 ridges of wheat, 20 ridges of barley, all oats, and 102 lambs.[35] Later the demesne was reckoned as 665 a., and 20 ridges were deemed 21 a.[36]

ECONOMIC HISTORY. In 1086 Newton Tony had land for 7 ploughteams and was fully cultivated. There were 2 teams and 6 *servi* on the demesne, and 10 *villani* and 9 bordars had 5 teams. There were 3 a. of meadow and 9 square furlongs of pasture.[37]

Sheep-and-corn husbandry prevailed in the parish. In 1315 the demesne of Newton Tony manor included 220 a. of arable, probably all in the open fields; that 100 a. could be sown each year, and 120 a. were evidently fallow, suggests a two-field system. The demesne had 8 a. of meadow and a several pasture worth 4*s.* a year. There were on the manor 14 yardlanders and 6½-yardlanders. Their labour service was light: each had to do haymaking and harvest work on the demesne only between 1 August and 29 September on Saturdays which were not feast days.[38] In 1360 there was clearly a two-field system. The demesne of Newton Tony manor then included 160 a. of arable, 8 a. of meadow, and two several pastures, one for 16 oxen and one for 400 sheep. The meadows were common after haymaking. There were still 6½-yardlanders, but then only 9 yardlanders:[39] the decrease in the number of yardlanders from 1315 is likely to have been caused by land going out of cultivation and by consolidation of holdings. What became Norris's manor included 59 a. of arable and 6 a. of meadow in 1361.[40] In 1591 the demesne flock comprised 1,086 sheep and 286 lambs. The shepherd was allowed to pasture with it 30 sheep of his own, including no more than 10 ewes.[41]

In the 17th century the demesne arable of Newton Tony manor may not have been in the open fields. It may have been mainly east of the village, and its several down for sheep was presumably in the south-east corner of the parish. The open fields, of which there were *c.* 10, contained much land west of the village, and the downland in the north-west corner of the parish was presumably common for sheep. There were two common pastures for cattle, evidently one north of the village and one south. The commonable land seems to have been shared mainly

11 P.R.O., CP 25/2/608/1650 East.; W.R.O. 1408, MTD/M 6.
12 W.R.O. 1408, MTD/M 7; 1408, MTD/M 9.
13 Ibid. 1293/1; 1408, MTD/M 11–12B; ibid. wills, archd. Sar., Jonathan Hill, 1672.
14 Ibid. 1408, MTD/D 2–3.
15 Ibid. 1408, MTD/D 7.
16 Ibid. 1408, MTD/D 10.
17 Ibid. 1408, MTD/D 23–4.
18 *Musgrave's Obit.* iii (Harl. Soc. xlvi), 181; P.R.O., PROB 11/1055, ff. 136v.–140; below, this section.
19 W. P. W. Phillimore and E. A. Fry, *Changes of Name,* 105; W.R.O. 1408, MTD/E 13–14.
20 W.R.O. 1408, MTD/E 1.
21 Ibid. wills, cons. Sar., Rob. Bevis, 1720.
22 Ibid. 1408, MTD/E 5B.
23 Ibid. 1408, MTD/E 7.
24 Ibid. 1408, MTD/E 8A–B; 1408, MTD/E 9A–B.

25 Ibid. wills, cons. Sar., Wm. Quaite, 1773.
26 *Antrobus D.* (W.R.S. iii), p. 52.
27 W.R.O. 1408, MTD/J 1.
28 Ibid. 1408, MTD/J 3–4.
29 Ibid. 1408, MTD/J 9.
30 Ibid. 1408, MTD/L 1; 1408, MTD/L 3A.
31 Ibid. 1408, MTD/L 13–14.
32 *Cal. Chart. R.* 1257–1300, 157–9; for the hist. of the abbey and priory, *V.C.H. Wilts.* iii. 242–59.
33 P.R.O., SC 6/Hen. VIII/3986, rot. 86d.
34 *Cal. Pat.* 1560–3, 519–20.
35 W.R.O., D 1/24/156/1.
36 P.R.O., IR 29/38/208.
37 *V.C.H. Wilts.* ii, p. 141.
38 P.R.O., C 134/50, no. 34.
39 *Wilts. Inq. p.m.* 1327–77 (Index Libr.), 265–6.
40 Ibid. 312.
41 P.R.O., REQ 2/79/25.

by the customary tenants of Newton Tony manor, the rector, and the freeholders of a few small estates. Downland of Norris's manor was fenced with thick crab-tree hedges in the mid 17th century and was presumably several.[42]

The open fields and common pastures were inclosed c. 1710 by private agreement. Demesne downland was burnbaked c. 1712, other downland was ploughed then or later, and the lack of sheep in the parish c. 1712 impoverished the arable.[43] The amount of agricultural land was reduced by imparking from c. 1710;[44] the farms may have been reduced in number,[45] but until the early 19th century all were evidently worked from farmsteads in the village.

Two new farmsteads were built in the early 19th century, Manor in the village street and Warren east of the village.[46] Park Farm was evidently built about then;[47] from 1821 or earlier the park was again used for agriculture[48] and most of it was ploughed. In 1839 there were 1,798 a. of arable in the parish, only 354 a. of grassland. Manor farm was then 696 a., Park 398 a., and Warren 467 a.; West farm, with buildings in the street, was 317 a. In all the farms the average size of the arable fields was c. 20 a., and the land was farmed partly on a four-year and partly on a five-year rotation. Meadow land lay beside the Bourne, and the only extensive areas of pasture were in the park and on the west slopes of Tower Hill. Wheat and barley were the chief cereal crops, and temporary grasses were sown on 500 a., of which c. 220 a. were for hay. There were again large flocks: c. 1,700 sheep, most of them ewes, were kept.[49] Barley was the main cereal grown in the later 19th century, when the arable acreage declined and more land was sown with temporary grasses mostly for hay. Between c. 1886 and c. 1916 more land became permanent pasture and dairy farming increased, although flocks totalling more than 1,000 sheep were still kept.[50] There were still four large farms in 1924: Home was 408 a., including 283 a. of arable, Warren 345 a. including 184 a. of arable, Manor 603 a., and West 288 a. A dairy herd was kept on each. On Manor cattle were reared for beef, and on West sheep were kept. Village farm was 107 a., and there was also a farm of 63 a.[51] The parish was about half arable in the 1930s.[52] More land was ploughed after 1939.[53] In the 1960s Manor farm was 670 a. including 36 a. in Allington: it had c. 526 a. of arable, and a flock of breeding ewes, a herd of pigs, and a herd of

c. 100 Friesian cows were kept.[54] In 1992 farming in the parish was predominantly arable. Of the 198 a. in the south-east corner of the parish taken in 1918 for military training, in 1992 c. 75 a. were cultivated for the Chemical and Biological Defence Establishment, based at Porton down in Idmiston, and the rest was woodland.[55]

There may have been woodland at Furze Croft, 19 a., east of the village, but otherwise there was apparently little in the parish until some was planted between c. 1710 and 1773 in the park of Wilbury House.[56] The planting along the parish boundary c. 1820 greatly increased the woodland,[57] and between c. 1817 and 1839 plantations were made in the south-east part of the parish, especially on Tower Hill. There were c. 255 a. of woodland in 1839.[58] A new 48-a. plantation was made north of that on Tower Hill between 1839 and 1877,[59] and in 1925 there were 289 a. of woodland.[60] The acreage and disposition were similar in 1992.

In 1086 there was a mill on the estate which became Newton Tony manor,[61] but its site is unknown.

LOCAL GOVERNMENT. In 1347 view of frankpledge was granted to the lord of Newton Tony manor, a grant confirmed in 1401.[62] No record of a view survives. A manor court was held in the early 14th century; in the 18th it was evidently held infrequently and only when copyhold business required it.[63]

The parish spent £98 on the poor in 1775–6, an average of £156 from 1782–3 to 1784–5. In 1790 it acquired a building as a workhouse, but there is no evidence of indoor relief. In 1802–3 all relief was outdoor: about a fifth of the inhabitants of Newton Tony and 15 who were not parishioners received it, 39 adults and children regularly and 30 occasionally. Materials bought for £2 were used by the poor, who earned £12.[64] Between 1812 and 1815 an average of £390 was spent on occasional relief for a few paupers and on regular relief for c. 20.[65] The poor of Newton Tony seem to have been generously relieved, and in 1816–21 an average of £296 was spent. Expenditure declined in the 1820s and averaged £148 in the early 1830s, but it remained high for a parish of Newton Tony's size.[66] The parish became part of Amesbury poor-law union in 1835.[67] It was included in Salisbury district in 1974.[68]

42 P.R.O., IR 29/38/208; IR 30/38/208; Aubrey, Nat. Hist. Wilts. ed Britton, 105; W.R.O., D 1/24/156/1–2.
43 W.R.O., D 1/24/156/3; Camb. Univ. Libr., Queens' Coll. Mun. 80/NT 12.
44 Above, manors (Newton Tony).
45 W.R.O. 1408, PPC/3/1.
46 O.S. Map 1", sheet 14 (1817 edn.); P.R.O., IR 29/38/208; IR 30/38/208.   47 W.R.O. 776/124.
48 Ibid. 1408, MTD/G 4.
49 P.R.O., IR 18/11104; IR 29/38/208; IR 30/38/208.
50 Ibid. MAF 68/151, sheet 13; MAF 68/493, sheet 12; MAF 68/1063, sheet 12; MAF 68/1633, sheet 16; MAF 68/2203, sheet 9; MAF 68/2773, sheet 16.
51 W.R.O. 776/124.
52 [1st] Land Util. Surv. Map, sheet 122.
53 e.g. P.R.O., MAF 68/4552, no. 214; MAF 68/5004, no. 214.   54 W.R.O. 1268/13.
55 Inf. from Defence Land Agent, Durrington; cf. above, Allington, econ. hist.

56 Andrews and Dury, Map (W.R.S. viii), pl. 6; above, manors (Newton Tony).
57 Above, intro. [boundary].
58 O.S. Map 1", sheet 14 (1817 edn.); P.R.O., IR 29/38/208; IR 30/38/208.
59 O.S. Map 6", Wilts. LXI (1883 edn.); P.R.O., IR 30/38/208.   60 W.R.O., G 1/500/12.
61 V.C.H. Wilts. ii, p. 141.
62 Cal. Chart. R. 1341–1417, 64–5; Cal. Pat. 1399–1401, 435.
63 Wilts. Inq. p.m. 1242–1326 (Index Libr.), 409–10; W.R.O. 1408, PPC/3/1, ff. 1, 3.
64 Poor Law Abstract, 1804, 558–9; V.C.H. Wilts. iv. 354; W.R.O. 1408, PPC/3/1, f. 3.
65 Poor Law Abstract, 1818, 492–3.
66 Poor Rate Returns, 1816–21, 185; 1822–4, 225; 1825–9, 215; 1830–4, 209.
67 Poor Law Com. 2nd Rep. App. D, 558.
68 O.S. Map 1/100,000, admin. areas, Wilts. (1974 edn.).

CHURCH. Newton Tony church was standing in the 12th century. In 1179 Amesbury priory held an estate in the parish, evidently of tithes, and received 5s. a year in respect of the graveyard, suggesting that earlier the church had been served by Amesbury abbey and had not had burial rights. There was a graveyard at Newton Tony in 1179,[69] and a rector was serving the church in 1296.[70] The rector paid the 5s. a year to the priory's successors in title to the tithes until 1677 or later.[71] The rectory was included in Bourne Valley benefice in 1973.[72]

Until the 17th century the advowson descended with Newton Tony manor and most presentations were by the lord or his representative. The king presented in 1296 and 1545, in each case when the lord was his ward; Sir George Paulett presented in 1556, William Blacker and Christopher Harrison jointly in 1568, in each case by grant of a turn.[73] In 1636 Francis Jones sold the advowson to John Davenant, bishop of Salisbury,[74] who in 1637 gave it to Queens' College, Cambridge.[75] Thomas Clarke, a canon of Salisbury, presented in 1660 by grant of a turn from Davenant. Queens' College presented thereafter,[76] and from 1973 was represented on the patronage board of Bourne Valley benefice.[77]

The rectory was worth £6 in 1291,[78] £20 in 1535,[79] and £130 in 1650.[80] It was leased for £100 a year in 1699 and for £150 a year in 1701 and 1706.[81] About 1830 the rector's income, c. £440, was high for a living in Amesbury deanery.[82] In the Middle Ages all tithes from the parish except Amesbury priory's were due to the rector;[83] in 1839 the rector's were valued at £433 and commuted.[84] There was 1 yardland of glebe in 1341,[85] c. 31 a. with pasture rights in the 17th century and early 18th,[86] and 42 a. after inclosure c. 1710.[87] About 18 a. were sold in 1955 and 32 a. remained in 1992.[88] The parsonage house, mentioned in 1605,[89] was uninhabitable in 1662.[90] It was replaced in 1778.[91] The new house, of two storeys and attics and of red brick on foundations incorporating re-used ashlar and several pieces of medieval carved stonework, has a west entrance front of five bays and a longer south garden front with a canted central bay. An internal 17th-century door was re-used in the service quarters. The house was sold in 1955.[92]

Elizabeth Reed (d. 1532) by will endowed obits for herself and her husband Sir Bartholomew Reed (d. 1505), lord of Newton Tony manor, and before the Reformation 4d. a year was given for a candle in the church.[93] In 1301–2 the rector William Cliff, in minor orders, was licensed to study away from the parish.[94] Roger Bellham, rector from c. 1346, was pardoned in 1350 for disturbing the peace and for inciting others to do likewise.[95] John Chitterne, rector 1415–19, was a local landowner.[96] In 1553 a curate assisted the rector.[97] By 1565 no sermon had been preached for five years, and the parish then lacked the Bible, the *Paraphrases* of Erasmus, and the Book of Homilies.[98] The rector in 1584–5 did not wear a surplice, failed to observe holy days, and declined to baptize with the sign of the cross.[99] In the early 17th century cockfighting was allowed in the church.[1] Christopher Riley, rector from 1633, observed the Friday fast, denied that Sunday observance was a moral law of God, and considered it more profitable to read the Bible than to listen to sermons.[2] He was deprived c. 1648. The intruder, John Watts, was a prominent nonconformist: he signed the *Concurrent Testimony* in 1648 and preached twice on Sundays in 1650.[3] Riley died in 1660 before he could be restored. His successor, James White, also rector of Boscombe, committed suicide in 1661.[4] From 1661 until 1955 most rectors were fellows or graduates of Queens' College and several incumbencies, particularly in the 18th and 19th centuries, were long. Joseph Kelsey, rector 1669–1710, was also rector of Fugglestone from 1681, vicar of Highworth from 1705, and archdeacon of Salisbury from 1695.[5] John Ekins, rector 1776–1808, was also rector of Trowbridge and from 1786 dean of Salisbury.[6] He resided in 1783, when he held two services each Sunday and preached at the morning one. The sacrament was administered on Christmas day, Easter day, and Whit Sunday to c. 20 communicants.[7] In the 1790s and the early 19th century curates, including Ekins's son Charles in 1802 and son Robert in 1810, often served the cure.[8] Hugh Price,

69 *Cal. Chart. R.* 1257–1300, 157–9; above, manors.
70 *Cal. Pat.* 1292–1301, 223.
71 W.R.O., D 1/24/156/2.   72 Inf. from Ch. Com.
73 Phillipps, *Wilts. Inst.* (index in *W.A.M.* xxviii. 226); *Cal. Pat.* 1292–1301, 223.
74 P.R.O., CP 25/2/510/11 Chas. I Hil.
75 Camb. Univ. Libr., Queens' Coll. Mun. 80/NT 4.
76 Phillipps, *Wilts. Inst.* (index in *W.A.M.* xxviii. 226).
77 Inf. from Ch. Com.   78 *Tax. Eccl.* (Rec. Com.), 180.
79 *Valor Eccl.* (Rec. Com.), ii. 92.
80 *W.A.M.* xl. 259.   81 P.R.O., C 5/337/12.
82 *Rep. Com. Eccl. Revenues*, 842–3.
83 *Inq. Non.* (Rec. Com.), 172.
84 P.R.O., IR 29/38/208.
85 *Inq. Non.* (Rec. Com.), 172.
86 W.R.O., D 1/24/156/1–3.
87 P.R.O., IR 29/38/208; IR 30/38/208; above, econ. hist.
88 Inf. from Capt. N. I. C. Kettlewell, Old Rectory.
89 W.R.O., D 1/24/156/1.   90 Ibid. D 1/54/1/3, no. 48.
91 Ibid. D 1/11/1A; ibid. 1294/3.
92 Inf. from Capt. Kettlewell.
93 *Cal. Pat.* 1569–72, pp. 341, 347; 1572–5, p. 408; P.R.O., PROB 11/14, ff. 168v.–172v.

94 *Reg. Ghent* (Cant. & York Soc.), ii. 845, 853.
95 Phillipps, *Wilts. Inst.* i. 40; *Cal. Pat.* 1348–50, 582.
96 Phillipps, *Wilts. Inst.* i. 104, 108; e.g. *V.C.H. Wilts.* xi. 87; xiii. 110; below, N. Tidworth, manors (Hussey); Bathampton, manors (Great Bathampton).
97 W.R.O., D 1/43/1, f. 109v.   98 Ibid. D 1/43/4, f. 2.
99 Ibid. D 1/43/5, f. 37v.; D 1/43/6, f. 5v.
1 *V.C.H. Wilts.* iii. 38.
2 Phillipps, *Wilts. Inst.* ii. 17; *Walker Revised*, ed. Matthews, 379–80, where his date of d. is wrongly given: cf. W.R.O. 1294/2, list of rectors.
3 *Cal. Cttee. for Compounding*, i. 79; *Calamy Revised*, ed. Matthews, 514; W. A. Shaw, *Hist. Eng. Church*, ii. 454; *W.A.M.* xl. 259.
4 *W.N. & Q.* v. 5; viii. 366; above, Boscombe, church.
5 Phillipps, *Wilts. Inst.* (index in *W.A.M.* xxviii. 226); e.g. *Alum. Cantab. to 1751*, i. 57 (s.v. Austen), 244 (s.v. Bryan); iii. 4 (s.v. Kelsey), 397 (s.v. Price); iv. 451 (s.v. Wood); *1752–1900*, v. 193 (s.v. Ekins); *Crockford* (1896 and later edns.).   6 *W.N. & Q.* viii. 431, 503.
7 *Vis. Queries, 1783* (W.R.S. xxvii), p. 166.
8 *Alum. Cantab. 1752–1900*, ii. 398; *W.A.M.* lxi. 72; W.R.O., bishop's transcripts, bdle. 3.

rector 1809–53, held two services, at both of which he preached, on each Sunday in 1832.[9] In 1851, when he was assisted by a curate, morning service on Census Sunday was attended by 89, afternoon service by 114.[10] Each Sunday in 1864 the rector held two services, each with a sermon; he did likewise on Christmas day and Good Friday, and held services on Ash Wednesday,

century. New windows were inserted in the south wall of the nave in the later Middle Ages. The simple porch was possibly 18th century. The chapel was built c. 1803[16] and the church was repaired in 1804.[17] The new church, to designs by T. H. Wyatt and D. Brandon,[18] is of flint rubble with stone dressings, is in a 14th-century style, and has a chancel with north

ST. ANDREW'S CHURCH, REBUILT 1844

Ascension day, and, with sermons, on Wednesday evenings in Lent. When communion was celebrated at Christmas, Easter, and Whitsun c. 37 received it; on the first Sunday in alternate months c. 26 did so.[11] The rectory was held in plurality with that of Cholderton 1953–73.[12]

The church was wholly rebuilt in 1844 and dedicated to ST. ANDREW.[13] The old church, which may have been undedicated,[14] had a chancel and a nave with south porch and north chapel; the tower which was part of the church in 1662[15] may have been the large wooden belfry above the west end of the nave in 1805. The small size of the chancel and the nave suggests that they were built no later than the 12th

vestry and a nave with south-west porch above which is a tower with a spire: the chancel and the nave are undivided.

In 1553 a 9-oz. chalice was left and 2 oz. of plate were taken for the king. There was no silver chalice in 1662. In 1891 and 1992 the parish had a chalice hallmarked for 1659, its paten cover, a paten hallmarked for 1686, and a flagon hallmarked for 1692.[19] There were four bells in 1553 and 1992. The tenor is a medieval bell cast in Salisbury. The present treble was cast by Robert Wells of Aldbourne in 1792, and the present second and third were cast by C. & G. Mears in 1851.[20] Registrations of baptisms and burials begin in 1586, those of marriages in 1591: those

9 *Alum. Cantab. 1752–1900*, v. 193; Ch. Com. file, NB 34/32B/2.
10 P.R.O., HO 107/1845, ff. 244–5; HO 129/262/3/2/2.
11 W.R.O., D 1/56/7.
12 *Crockford* (1955 and later edns.); Ch. Com. file, NB 34/32B/1.
13 *Churches of SE. Wilts.* (R.C.H.M.), 163–4; W.R.O. 1294/10; ibid. D 1/61/6/6.
14 J. Ecton, *Thesaurus* (1763), 391.

15 W.R.O., D 1/54/1/3, no. 48.
16 Hoare, *Mod. Wilts.* Amesbury, 104; J. Buckler, watercolour in W.A.S. Libr., vol. i. 5; see below, plate facing p. 235.
17 W.R.O. 1294/7. 18 *Churches of SE. Wilts.* 163.
19 Nightingale, *Wilts. Plate*, 42; W.R.O., D 1/54/1/3, no. 48; inf. from Capt. Kettlewell.
20 Walters, *Wilts. Bells*, 147; W.R.O. 1294/7; inf. from Capt. Kettlewell.

of baptisms are lacking 1640–5, those of marriages 1641–58.[21]

NONCONFORMITY

NONCONFORMITY. Thomas Bradshaw, who was lord of Newton Tony manor until c. 1800, in 1797 certified a room in Wilbury House as a Roman Catholic chapel and employed a resident chaplain.[22]

Presbyterians were encouraged by Nathaniel Fiennes, lord of Newton Tony manor, and his wife Frances, and in 1669 a conventicle met at their house in the village. Several ministers ejected for nonconformity preached to the group: they included Thomas Taylor, ejected from Burbage, George Whitmarsh from Rowner (Hants), and John Crouch from Alderbury. Frances Fiennes employed John Crofts, ejected rector of Mottisfont (Hants), as her chaplain, and in 1672 the house was certified for Presbyterian meetings.[23] A second group of nonconformists was led c. 1668 by John Girle,[24] whose house was certified for Congregationalists in 1672.[25] There were 26 nonconformists at Newton Tony in 1676.[26] Members of the Girle family remained dissenters in the 1680s.[27]

In 1816 Primitive Methodists certified a house,[28] and in 1851 dissenters certified a house at Warren Farm.[29] A small red-brick chapel was built in High Street for Wesleyan Methodists in 1877.[30] It was closed in 1981.[31]

EDUCATION

EDUCATION. There was a school in the parish in 1808,[32] and in 1818 one attended by 22 children.[33] In 1833 there were three schools with a total of 27 pupils,[34] in 1846–7 two with 38.[35] A National school was built in High Street in 1857; 40–50 children, including some from Allington and Boscombe, were taught at it in 1858.[36] A separate room for lectures and for an evening school was built in 1858.[37] On return day in 1871 the school was attended by 70 pupils.[38] It was enlarged in 1894.[39] Average attendance was 42 in 1906–7, 69 in 1926–7, 34 in 1938.[40] At a new school, which replaced the old in 1959, there were 32 children on roll in 1992, including some from other parishes.[41]

CHARITY FOR THE POOR

CHARITY FOR THE POOR. J. N. Peill (d. 1879), rector from 1853,[42] bequeathed the interest on £50 to be distributed among poor widows on 30 November each year. In 1894–5 four widows shared £1 5s.; there were three beneficiaries in 1901 and 1904, nine in 1911; £2 10s. a year was distributed 1918–31.[43] About 1988 the income contributed to an old people's Christmas tea.[44] In 1992 it was £7.50.[45]

NORTH TIDWORTH

NORTH TIDWORTH village[46] is 13.5 km. WNW. of Andover (Hants) on the eastern edge of Salisbury Plain.[47] It seems that a large estate called Tidworth had been fragmented by 1066 when seven estates were so called: three were in Wiltshire and became North Tidworth parish, four were in Hampshire and became the adjoining South Tidworth parish.[48] After 1897 both parishes were greatly affected by the army, which built a garrison town across their boundary.[49] North Tidworth parish, 1,253 ha. (3,096 a.), is rectangular and lies east and west across the valley of the river Bourne. Few prominent features mark its boundaries, which mostly run over downland, but part of the northern is marked by an ancient ditch and crosses the summit of Windmill Hill. The parish was in Chute forest until 1300.[50]

The whole parish is on chalk, overlain by clay-with-flints and clay of the Reading Beds on Sidbury Hill and by a small area of clay-with-flints east of the village. The Bourne, which for a century or more has usually been dry, has deposited gravel and, to the north, a small amount of alluvium in its north–south valley across the middle of the parish, and there is also gravel in three east–west dry valleys to the west. The relief is sharper in the west where Sidbury Hill at 224 m. is the highest point in the parish and Clarendon Hill reaches 178 m. To the east Windmill Hill, over 183 m., and Pickpit Hill, 173 m., are on the watershed of the Bourne and

21 W.R.O. 1294/1–6; marriages are printed in *Wilts. Par. Reg. (Mar.)*, ed. W. P. W. Phillimore and J. Sadler, iii. 133–42.
22 *V.C.H. Wilts.* iii. 91; P.R.O., PROB 11/1343, ff. 454v.–456v.; above, manors (Newton Tony).
23 *V.C.H. Wilts.* iii. 106; *Orig. Rec.* ed. G. L. Turner, ii. 1071; *Calamy Revised*, 145, 151, 479, 527.
24 W.R.O., D 1/54/3/2, no. 23.
25 *Meeting Ho. Certs.* (W.R.S. xl), p. 172.
26 *Compton Census*, ed. Whiteman, 124.
27 W.R.O., D 1/54/10/4; D 1/54/11/4, no. 10; D 1/54/12/3.   28 *Meeting Ho. Certs.* (W.R.S. xl), p. 78.
29 Ibid. p. 169.
30 Date on bldg.; *Kelly's Dir. Wilts.* (1885).
31 Inf. from Capt. Kettlewell.
32 Lamb. Palace Libr., MS. 1732.
33 *Educ. of Poor Digest*, 1034.
34 *Educ. Enq. Abstract*, 1044.
35 Nat. Soc. *Inquiry, 1846–7*, Wilts. 8–9.
36 *Acct. of Wilts. Schs.* 35; W.R.O. 782/79.
37 *Kelly's Dir. Wilts.* (1875); W.R.O., D 1/56/7.

38 *Returns relating to Elem. Educ.* 426–7.
39 *Kelly's Dir. Wilts.* (1898).
40 *Bd. of Educ., List 21, 1908* (H.M.S.O.), 505; *1927*, 361; *1938*, 424.
41 W.R.O. 1810/31; date on bldg.; inf. from the head teacher.
42 Wilts. Tracts, 220, no. 11, p. 47.
43 *Endowed Char. Wilts.* (S. Div.), 354; W.R.O., L 2, Newton Tony.   44 Wilts. Tracts, 220, no. 11, p. 1.
45 Inf. from Capt. Kettlewell.
46 This article was written in 1990; any later addition is dated.
47 Maps used include O.S. Maps 1", sheet 14 (1817 edn.); 1/50,000, sheet 184 (1988 edn.); 1/25,000, SU 24–5 (1958 edns.); 6", Wilts. XLVIII (1883–8 and later edns.).
48 *V.C.H. Hants*, iv. 391; below, manors. In 1992 S. Tidworth was transferred to Wilts.: Statutory Instruments, 1991, no. 2247, Dors., Hants, W. Suss., and Wilts. (Co. Boundaries) Order.
49 Below, this section.
50 *V.C.H. Wilts.* iv. 425, 453.

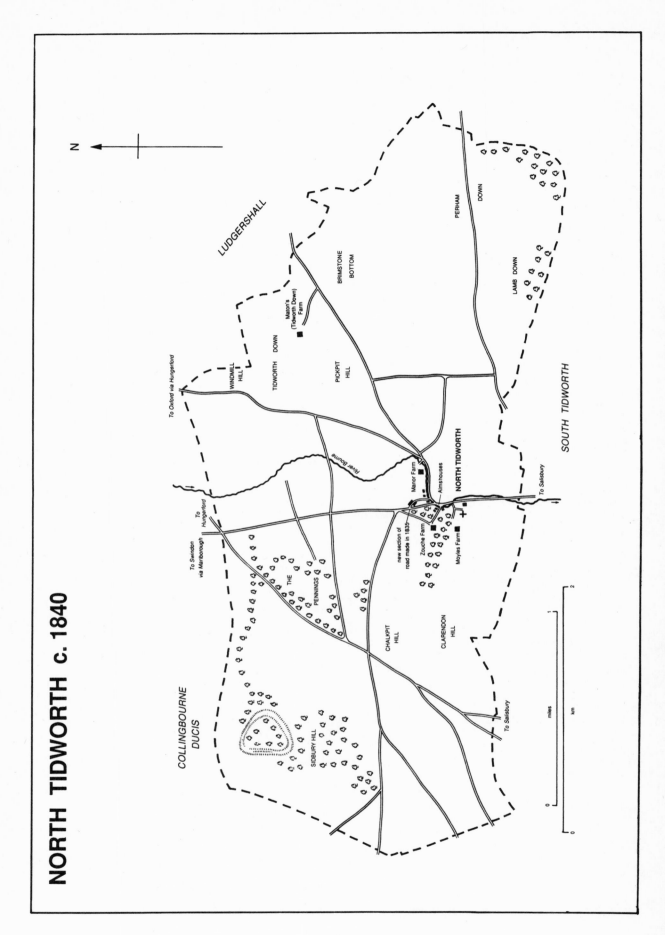

NORTH TIDWORTH c. 1840

N

LUDGERSHALL

PERHAM DOWN

BRIMSTONE BOTTOM

LAMB DOWN

Maton's (Tidworth Down) Farm

TIDWORTH DOWN

PICKPIT HILL

WINDMILL HILL

To Oxford via Hungerford

River Bourne

SOUTH TIDWORTH

Manor Farm

Almshouses

NORTH TIDWORTH

new section of road made in 1835

Zouche Farm

Moyles Farm

To Salisbury

To Hungerford

To Swindon via Marlborough

THE PENNINGS

CHALKPIT HILL

CLARENDON HILL

To Salisbury

COLLINGBOURNE DUCIS

SIDBURY HILL

miles

km

the river Anton, and south-east of them on Perham down and Lamb down the relief is gentler. The lowest land is at *c.* 100 m. in the south-east corner of the parish.[51] Like many other Wiltshire villages North Tidworth had meadow land beside the river, arable on the lower slopes of the downs nearest the village, and extensive pastures for sheep on the higher and further downs. In the 19th century wood-land for coverts was planted on the downs, and in the 20th agriculture was greatly reduced after the army acquired the land for training, bar-racks, workshops, and housing.[52]

In the 17th century the main Oxford–Salisbury road via Hungerford (Berks.) ran southwards over Windmill Hill and passed through North Tidworth village, where it turned sharply south.[53] By the late 18th century a new course had been adopted for the road: it left the old Oxford road north of the parish, crossed the western part of the parish between Sidbury Hill and Clarendon Hill, and bypassed the village.[54] It was turnpiked between the northern parish boundary and Hungerford in 1772,[55] and was disturnpiked in 1866. From 1835, however, the north–south road through the village, then the last part of a Swindon–Salisbury road via Marlborough and the villages of the Bourne valley to be turnpiked, was again a main road.[56] North of the church a new straight section was made.[57] The road was disturnpiked in 1876,[58] and in 1990 remained an important north–south route. The road to Salisbury between Sidbury Hill and Clarendon Hill presumably decreased in importance from 1835 and it was among several roads in the west part of the parish closed by the army *c.* 1900.[59] In the east part of the parish a road to Ludgershall is apparently on its original course,[60] but the old Hungerford road, from which it branched, went out of use in the mid 20th century.[61] The army built a new road between North Tidworth, where it is called Meerut Road, and Bulford in 1909–10,[62] and military activity has increased the importance of a road leading from Andover to South Tidworth across Perham down and of Somme Road be-tween Brimstone bottom and Perham down.

A railway for the army was built from the Midland & South Western Junction Railway in Ludgershall to a terminus in South Tidworth and opened in 1901. The public used it from 1902[63] until it was closed in 1955.[64]

Prehistoric artefacts have been found in the parish and there are bowl barrows on Sidbury Hill and Pickpit Hill. A prehistoric field system extends into North Tidworth from the west. It was later crossed by parts of the seven ditches which converge on the Iron-Age hill fort cover-ing 17 a. on Sidbury Hill; the ditches may be associated with cattle ranching. A smaller field system is further east. Romano-British remains have been found near Sidbury Hill and on Perham down, and a Pagan-Saxon burial on Perham down.[65]

North Tidworth was seriously affected by the plague of 1349,[66] and there is no evidence that any inhabitant paid poll tax in 1377.[67] There were 140 inhabitants in 1527.[68] The population rose from 240 in 1801 to 417 in 1841, but had fallen to 241 by 1891 and was 259 in 1901. Thereafter barracks and new housing, mainly for the army, were built and the population was greatly increased, although numbers varied with the amount of military activity. The population was 1,541 in 1911, 1,253 in 1921, 2,771 in 1931, 4,916 in 1951,[69] and 2,824 in 1961. After more housing was built the population was 7,280 in 1971, 5,813 in 1991 when it was still mainly soldiers and their families.[70]

North Tidworth was a small village on the gravel beside the Bourne, strung out along the old Oxford–Salisbury road which, with its sharp southward bend, closely followed the river. North of the bend an offshoot of the village lay along the part of the Collingbourne Ducis road which from 1835 has been a back lane.[71] A bridge over the river was called Church bridge in 1701.[72] At the south end of the village the church is west of the main road; the rectory house was immediately south-east of the church, a farm-stead, demolished in the mid 19th century, immediately west of it. Two other large farm-steads were in the village in the 19th century. Zouche Farm, of which the farmhouse survives as Zouch Manor, was on higher ground north-west of the church and away from the main road; a manor house stood on the site in the 18th century. Manor Farm, on the north side of the road east of the bend,[73] was rebuilt in the early 20th century and was ruinous in 1990. Few of the cottages in the village before 1900 survive: two stand near the church, several estate cot-tages, including a trio of brick and flint bearing a plausible date stone for 1890, stand at the old bend of the main road, an 18th-century cottage stands in the back lane, and a 19th-century flint and brick house stands at the junction of the back lane and the new section of road which replaced it in 1835. The village was often flooded in the early 19th century.[74]

There was a church house in 1566,[75] new cottages were licensed in 1591,[76] and almshouses

51 Geol. Surv. Map 1", drift, sheet 282 (1967 edn.); 1/50,000, drift, sheet 283 (1975 edn.).
52 Below, this section; econ. hist.
53 J. Ogilby, *Brit.* (1675), pl. 83.
54 *Andrews and Dury, Map* (W.R.S. viii), pl. 9.
55 *L.J.* xiii. 299.
56 *V.C.H. Wilts.* iv. 257, 262, 270.
57 P.R.O., IR 30/38/259.   58 *V.C.H. Wilts.* iv. 270.
59 Cf. ibid. 266.
60 Ogilby, *Brit.* (1675), pl. 83; *Andrews and Dury, Map* (W.R.S. viii), pl. 9.
61 O.S. Maps 6", Wilts. XLVIII. SE. (1926 edn.); 1/25,000, SU 24 (1958 edn.); 1", sheet 122 (1940 edn.).
62 N. D. G. James, *Plain Soldiering*, 99.
63 *V.C.H. Wilts.* iv. 290.

64 *Clinker's Reg. Closed Passenger Sta. 1830–1980*, 135.
65 *V.C.H. Wilts.* i (1), 92, 185, 254–7, 268, 276–7; i (2), 403, 412.
66 *Wilts. Inq. p.m.* 1327–77 (Index Libr.), 204.
67 *V.C.H. Wilts.* iv. 306.
68 *L. & P. Hen. VIII*, iv (2), p. 1645.
69 *V.C.H. Wilts.* iv. 325–6, 359.
70 *Census*, 1961; 1971; 1991.
71 Cf. above, this section [roads].
72 W.R.O. 2159/25.
73 O.S. Map 6", Wilts. XLVIII (1883–8 edn.); P.R.O., IR 29/38/259; IR 30/38/259; below, manors (Zouche).
74 W.R.O. 2159/2.
75 P.R.O., REQ 2/240/75.
76 *Sess. Mins.* (W.R.S. iv), 140.

were built in the late 17th century.[77] A friendly society in the parish in 1805 had an average of 83 members 1813–15.[78] There was an alehouse in 1587,[79] the Old Bull was open in the 1820s[80] but had been replaced by the Ram by 1848, and the Ram was rebuilt c. 1935.[81] The house of John Mompesson in the village attained national notoriety in the early 1660s for allegedly being haunted by a poltergeist.[82]

On downland called the Pennings, north-west of the village, there was a barn in 1773, and by 1820 Tidworth Cottage had been built amid woodland on roughly the same site.[83] Neither building was standing c. 1839.[84] Tidworth Down Farm was built on the downs between Brimstone bottom and Windmill Hill c. 1800:[85] it incorporates a red-brick house, extended in the later 19th century, and was called Sweetapple Farm in 1990. A new farmstead at the Pennings, incorporating barns and two cottages, was built in the mid 19th century.[86]

North Tidworth was transformed after 1897, the year in which nearly all the parish, together with nearly all of South Tidworth parish, was bought by the War Department for military training.[87] Much land was built on for the garrison attached to the headquarters of the Southern Military Command based at Tidworth House in South Tidworth; most of the barracks were in South Tidworth, most of the houses, for both soldiers and civilians, in North Tidworth. Tented camps were on Windmill Hill and Perham down and at the Pennings in 1899.[88] In the village Lucknow and Mooltan barracks were built south-west of the church and completed in 1905; they had been extended westwards by 1926.[89] Zouch Manor and Manor Farm were used as officers' quarters.[90] Also in the village, east of the church, a Royal Army Ordnance depot was erected, probably during the First World War.[91] On Perham down a hutted camp[92] had been built by 1915, new buildings were erected north and south of the Andover road in the 1920s, and brick barracks were built 1933–6. Perham Down barracks were rebuilt 1972–4 and renamed Swinton barracks. South of the Ludgershall road in Brimstone bottom Fowler barracks were built on the west side, and Busigny barracks on the east side, of Somme Road in 1938.[93] In the village, east of the Ordnance depot, Mathew barracks were built c. 1939,[94] and north-east of the village, adjoining

Fowler barracks, Busigny barracks, and Ludgershall, extensive military workshops were built in 1939.[95] Mathew barracks and Fowler barracks were demolished in the 1960s and Busigny barracks c. 1976,[96] but Lucknow, Mooltan, and Swinton barracks remained in use in 1990.

An isolation hospital was built in Brimstone bottom in 1900[97] and a military cemetery was opened north of the village in 1904.[98] As the garrison grew other buildings were erected for sport and recreation: they included a British Legion club and a cinema before 1923.[99] Later, when there was much new housing, a police station, schools, shops, and health and community centres were built.

In the 20th century the main north–south road through the village has been renamed Pennings Road, and its old southward bend and the road leading east from it have together been called Ludgershall Road. The many houses built in the 20th century are in roughly equal numbers east and west of Pennings Road. The first to be built by the army were those north-west of the church in Nepaul Road dated 1922 and those south-east of the church on the north side of Ordnance Road standing in 1923.[1] The earliest council houses are apparently 18 in Ludgershall Road built c. 1930 and 8 on the west side of Pennings Road.[2] Many more houses were built north-west of Nepaul Road, an area called the Zouch estate, especially in the 1960s; in the angle between the Zouch estate and Pennings Road the Gason Hill council estate was built, mainly in the early 1950s.[3] East of Pennings Road much new housing, blocks of flats and small houses, was built for the army in the mid and later 1960s to designs by the Austin Smith, Salmon, and Lord Partnership: c. 90 houses on the Mathew estate, on the site of the Mathew barracks, were sold by the Ministry of Defence to Kennet district council in 1990.[4] South of Ludgershall Road and adjoining that housing an estate of council houses, including bungalows for old people, was built in the later 1960s.[5] East of the village, labourers employed on the construction of the garrison soon after 1900 were accommodated in a hutted encampment in Brimstone bottom called Tin Town. It included a hospital, mission hall, school, recreation rooms, and baths.[6] There are houses of the 1920s or 1930s in Lambdown Terrace off the Andover road,[7] and a large estate of houses was built by the army south of the road

77 Below, charities.
78 *Poor Law Abstract, 1818*, 492–3; P.R.O., FS 4/55, Wilts. no. 60.
79 *Sess. Mins.* (W.R.S. iv), 118.
80 W.R.O., A 1/326/3.
81 Ibid. G 10/760/227; *Kelly's Dir. Wilts.* (1848).
82 *Cal. S.P. Dom.* 1667–8, 149–50; Hoare, *Mod. Wilts.* Amesbury, 93–9; Aubrey, *Nat. Hist. Wilts.* ed. Britton, 121.
83 *Andrews and Dury, Map* (W.R.S. viii), pl. 9; O.S. Map 1", sheet 14 (1817 edn.); C. Greenwood, *Map of Wilts.* (1820).
84 P.R.O., IR 30/38/259.
85 *Andrews and Dury, Map* (W.R.S. viii), pl. 9; O.S. Map 1", sheet 14 (1817 edn.).
86 O.S. Map 6", Wilts. XLVIII (1883–8 edn.); P.R.O., IR 29/38/259; IR 30/38/259.
87 Below, manors (Moels).
88 James, *Plain Soldiering*, 59, 79, 242; for the Perham down camp, see below, plate facing p. 170.
89 *Kelly's Dir. Wilts.* (1903, 1907); O.S. Map 6", Wilts.

XLVIII. SE. (1926 edn.); W.R.O. 9, newspaper cutting, 27 Dec. 1900; date on bldg.
90 *Kelly's Dir. Wilts.* (1911 and later edns.).
91 James, *Plain Soldiering*, 49; see below, plate facing p. 170.   92 See plate facing p. 170.
93 James, *Plain Soldiering*, 82–5.
94 Ibid. 72.   95 Ibid. 87.
96 Ibid. 76, 84–5.   97 Ibid. 47.
98 W.R.O., D 1/60/17/11.
99 Ibid. G 10/760/343; ibid. 1612/15; *Kelly's Dir. Wilts.* (1923).
1 O.S. Map 6", Wilts. XLVIII. SE. (1926 edn.).
2 *Kelly's Dir. Wilts.* (1927, 1931 edns.); W.R.O., G 10/516/2.   3 James, *Plain Soldiering*, 76.
4 Pevsner, *Wilts.* (2nd edn.), 359; O.S. Map 1/10,000, SU 24 NW. (1976 edn.); W.R.O. 1612/15; *Daily Telegraph*, 4 Jan. 1991.
5 James, *Plain Soldiering*, 76.
6 *Kelly's Dir. Wilts.* (1903, 1907).
7 O.S. Map 1", sheet 167 (1940 edn.).

on Perham down from the late 1920s. North of the road smaller estates were built in 1968 and 1977.[8]

From the 11th century, when Croc the huntsman held estates at North Tidworth and South Tidworth, North Tidworth may have been a centre for sport.[9] Game, particularly hares and partridges, were abundant in the 17th century,[10] and in the 19th North Tidworth was part of a large sporting estate. In 1895 coursing meetings were held there.[11] Cricket was played on Perham down in the 18th century, and from c. 1787 to c. 1797 players from Hambledon (Surr.) and the rest of England met there.[12] Between c. 1926 and c. 1984 there was a polo ground on Perham down; it was a general sports ground in 1987.[13] In 1935 Salisbury Plain Race club had a course and stands on Windmill Hill.[14]

MANORS AND OTHER ESTATES. A 4-hide estate that became *MOELS* or Moyles manor was held in 1066 by Alward and in 1086 by Edward of Salisbury.[15] It descended in the direct line to Walter of Salisbury (d. 1147), Patrick, earl of Salisbury (d. 1168), and William, earl of Salisbury (d. 1196),[16] and to William's daughter Ela (d. 1261), wife of William Longespée, earl of Salisbury (d. 1226). From Ela, who took the veil in 1238, the overlordship descended like the overlordship of Shrewton;[17] it was last mentioned in 1428, when Thomas Montagu, earl of Salisbury, held it.[18]

Either William, earl of Salisbury (d. 1196), or, more likely, William, earl of Salisbury (d. 1226), granted the manor to William de Moels.[19] Philip de Moels held it in 1242–3,[20] and before 1250 granted it to William of Widworthy. Hugh of Widworthy held it in 1263–4,[21] but later it belonged to Richard of Coombe (d. c. 1293) and his son Richard.[22] Moels manor was settled in 1313 by the younger Richard on himself and his wife Anstice and passed to his nephew Richard of Coombe (d. c. 1329) and to that Richard's son Sir Richard (d. 1361).[23] Walter of Coombe held the manor in 1379, his son or nephew Robert of Coombe (d. by 1416) held it in 1409 and c. 1411, and Robert's son John, M.P. for Ludgershall 1436–7, held it in 1428. John was succeeded by

his sons Richard (d. by 1460) and John in turn.[24] The younger John's heir, his daughter Joan, wife of Ralph Bannister (d. 1492), was succeeded by her daughter Joan (fl. 1534), wife of Thomas Dauntsey and later of William Walwyn. On the younger Joan's death the manor passed to Edmund Walwyn, who sold it in 1538 to William Dauntsey[25] (d. 1543). It passed to William's brother Ambrose (d. 1555) and to Ambrose's son John (d. 1559), who was succeeded in turn by his sons Ambrose (d. 1562) and Sir John.[26] In 1627 Sir John Dauntsey sold the manor to James Ley, earl of Marlborough[27] (d. 1629), the owner of an adjacent estate in South Tidworth.[28] The earl's relict Jane and her husband William Ashburnham sold Moels manor in 1650 to Thomas Smith.[29] It descended in the direct line to John Smith (d. 1690), John Smith (d. 1723), speaker of the House of Commons and Chancellor of the Exchequer,[30] and William Smith (d. 1773). William devised it to his nephew Thomas Assheton (d. 1774), who assumed the name Smith. Thomas's son Thomas Assheton Smith[31] (d. 1828) was succeeded by his son Thomas Assheton Smith (d. 1858), a noted sportsman,[32] who in 1844 owned nearly all the parish. As part of the Tidworth estate, which also included nearly all of South Tidworth parish, he devised it to his relict Matilda (d. 1859). She devised the estate to her nephew F. S. Stanley who sold it in 1877 to Sir John Kelk, Bt.[33] (d. 1886). Kelk's son Sir John sold it in 1897 to the War Department.[34] The Ministry of Defence owned most of the parish in 1990.[35]

The 5-hide estate that came to be called *HUSSEY* manor after its 13th-century lords was held in 1066 by Eddulf and in 1086 by Odo, bishop of Bayeux.[36] It was among the bishop's estates which may have been held by John the marshal (d. 1165) and passed to William Marshal, earl of Pembroke (d. 1219), who held it by serjeanty of marshalcy. The overlordship passed with the marshalcy to William's son William, earl of Pembroke (d. 1231), whose relict Eleanor (d. 1275) and her husband Simon de Montfort, earl of Leicester, held it in 1248.[37] The overlord in 1290 was the marshal, Roger le Bigod, earl of Norfolk (d. s.p. 1306),[38] and the marshal was overlord in the 14th century.[39]

8 James, *Plain Soldiering*, 85.
9 *V.C.H. Wilts.* iv. 425.
10 Aubrey, *Nat. Hist. Wilts.* ed. Britton, 108.
11 *V.C.H. Wilts.* iv. 383; W. Cobbett, *Rural Rides*, ed. G. D. H. Cole, i. 110; *D.N.B.* (s.v. Thomas Assheton Smith); below, manors (Moels).
12 *V.C.H. Wilts.* iv. 378.
13 O.S. Map 6", Wilts. XLVIII. SE. (1926 edn.); James, *Plain Soldiering*, 83.   14 W.R.O., G 10/516/1.
15 *V.C.H. Wilts.* ii, p. 136.
16 Ibid. p. 107; for the earldom of Salisbury, *Complete Peerage*, xi. 373–95.   17 Below, Shrewton, manors.
18 P.R.O., C 139/41, no. 57.
19 Hoare, *Mod. Wilts.* Amesbury, 90.
20 *Bk. of Fees*, ii. 744.
21 Hoare, *Mod. Wilts.* Amesbury, 90–1.
22 *Cal. Inq. p.m.* iii, pp. 66–7.
23 *V.C.H. Wilts.* xi. 120; *Feet of F.* 1272–1307 (W.R.S. i), p. 84; *Feud. Aids*, v. 241.
24 *W.N. & Q.* vii. 502–5; P.R.O., C 139/41, no. 57; above, Amesbury, manors (Coombes Ct.).
25 *Cal. Inq. p.m. Hen. VII*, i, pp. 349–50; P.R.O., C 1/686, no. 10; C 1/917, no. 7; C 1/922, no. 5; ibid. CP

25/2/46/322, no. 5B.
26 *V.C.H. Wilts.* xi. 120.
27 P.R.O., E 159/468, Recorda East. rot. 13.
28 *Wilts. Inq. p.m.* 1625–49 (Index Libr.), 232–6; *V.C.H. Hants*, iv. 393.
29 *Complete Peerage*, viii. 488–90; P.R.O., CP 25/2/616/1650 East.
30 *Hist. Parl., Commons*, 1660–90, iii. 442–3; *D.N.B.* (s.v. John Smith 1655–1723).
31 Burke, *Peerage* (1963), 771; W. P. W. Phillimore and E. A. Fry, *Changes of Name*, 291; Smith Estate Act, 17 Geo. III, c. 53 (Priv. Act); W.R.O. 2159/24, pp. 18–19.
32 *D.N.B.*
33 *V.C.H. Hants*, iv. 393; P.R.O., IR 29/38/259; IR 30/38/259.
34 Burke, *Peerage* (1890), 768; W.R.O., D 1/21/5/2.
35 Inf. from Defence Land Agent, Durrington.
36 *V.C.H. Wilts.* ii, p. 122.
37 *Cal. Chart. R.* 1257–1300, 157–9; *Red Bk. Exch.* (Rolls Ser.), ii. 487; *Complete Peerage*, vii. 543–7; x. 358–68; x, App. G, 93–5; *Wilts. Inq. p.m.* 1327–77 (Index Libr.), 340–1.
38 *Cal. Inq. p.m.* ii, pp. 473–4; *Complete Peerage*, ii. 611.
39 *Cal. Inq. p.m.* vii, pp. 332–3; xi, p. 66.

In 1086 another Odo held the estate of Odo, bishop of Bayeux.[40] It was held in 1218 by Henry Hussey[41] (d. by 1235) and descended in the direct line to Sir Matthew (d. 1253) and Sir Henry (d. 1290),[42] who was granted free warren in his demesnes in 1271.[43] The manor was assigned to Sir Henry's relict Agnes (fl. 1326), and she and her husband Peter de Breuse held it in 1307.[44] It passed to her son Henry Hussey, Lord Hussey (d. 1332), who was succeeded by his son Henry,[45] Lord Hussey (d. 1349). That Lord Hussey settled it on his son Richard[46] (d. s.p. 1361), from whom it passed to his brother Sir Henry (d. 1383).[47] By 1401 it had apparently been acquired by John Chitterne, a clerk.[48] In 1239 Maud, granddaughter of Henry Hussey (d. by 1235), successfully claimed 1 carucate against her uncle Sir Matthew Hussey,[49] and she and her husband William Paynel held the estate in 1269.[50] Their land in North Tidworth may also have been acquired by John Chitterne in the early 15th century as their manor of Littleton Pannell in West Lavington was.[51] In 1409 and 1412 feoffees held what was probably the whole Hussey manor,[52] which evidently passed, like Upton Knoyle manor in East Knoyle and Great Bathampton manor in Steeple Langford, to John Chitterne's sister Agnes, wife of William Milbourne. Hussey manor was held by Agnes's son Richard Milbourne[53] (d. 1451) and passed in the direct line to Simon[54] (d. 1464), Sir Thomas[55] (d. 1492), Henry[56] (d. 1519), and Richard Milbourne,[57] who was succeeded by his cousin William Fauconer[58] (d. 1558). Fauconer's son William[59] (d. c. 1610) was a recusant and two thirds of his estate were held by the Crown in 1592–3 and 1600. The manor passed to his niece Jane (d. 1615), wife of Francis Eyton, and afterwards to his daughter Anne, wife of Benet Winchcomb.[60] Anne Winchcomb sold it in 1624 to Sir James Ley, Bt.[61] (cr. earl of Marlborough 1626),[62] and from 1627 it descended with Moels manor.

Three hides, from which ZOUCHE manor may have originated, were held by three thegns in 1066. In 1086 Croc held 2 hides and 3 yardlands and Edward of Salisbury held 1 yard-land. Croc's 2 hides were held of him by a knight.[63] Some or all of those lands may have been held by Hugh de Lacy (d. 1186)[64] and were possibly the estate in North Tidworth held by the king 1187–91.[65] Later John Bisset (d. 1241) was overlord of Zouche manor. It was held of him by Roger la Zouche who was succeeded by his son Sir Alan (d. 1270). The Zouches subinfeudated the manor in portions: their successors Roger la Zouche (d. 1285), Alan la Zouche, Lord Zouche (d. 1314), and that Alan's daughters Ellen, wife of Sir Nicholas Seymour, and Maud, wife of Sir Robert de Holand, were mesne lords.[66]

Between 1199 and 1227 Roger la Zouche gave ½ yardland to Maiden Bradley priory.[67] Sir Alan la Zouche gave the priory rent from a carucate of the manor,[68] and in 1273 the lessee Sir Nicholas Vaux surrendered the land to the priory,[69] which held it until the Dissolution.[70] It was granted in 1536 to Sir Edward Seymour, Viscount Beauchamp (cr. earl of Hertford 1537, duke of Somerset 1547),[71] was presumably forfeited on his execution and attainder in 1552, and was granted in 1559 to John Cutt and Richard Roberts.[72] What was probably the same land was sold in 1567 by John Stockman and his wife Dorothy to John Knight,[73] who sold it in 1579 to John Thornborough.[74] In 1592 Thornborough sold it to John Pitman,[75] who owned Zouche manor in 1600.[76] William Pitman, more likely the elder, owned it in 1621 and, apparently before 1649, sold it to John Bulkeley. In 1662 Bulkeley sold it to Thomas Pierce[77] (d. 1691), president of Magdalen College, Oxford, and later dean of Salisbury. The manor descended to Thomas's son Robert (d. 1707), rector of North Tidworth, and to Robert's son Thomas,[78] who sold it in 1724 to Smart Poore[79] (d. 1747).[80] Poore's son Edward (d. 1787) devised the manor successively to his nephew Edward Poore (d. s.p. 1803) and Edward Dyke, who assumed the name Poore in 1803. Edward Dyke Poore sold the manor, 930 a.,[81] to Thomas Assheton Smith in 1832, and it became part of Smith's Tidworth estate.[82]

A house on Zouche manor was built on Tidworth Hill of local stone for Edward, duke of

40 V.C.H. Wilts. ii, p. 122.
41 Pipe R. 1218 (P.R.S. N.S. xxxix), 10.
42 Bk. of Fees, ii. 744; Cal. Inq. p.m. ii, pp. 473–4; for the Hussey fam., Complete Peerage, vii. 1–11.
43 Cal. Chart. R. 1257–1300, 176.
44 Cal. Inq. p.m. ii, pp. 474–5; iv, p. 299.
45 Ibid. vii, pp. 332–3.
46 Ibid. ix, pp. 212, 214.
47 Ibid. xi, p. 66; Feet of F. 1327–77 (W.R.S. xxix), p. 147.
48 Cal. Close, 1399–1402, 325.
49 Sel. Cases in K.B. ii (Selden Soc. lvii), pp. clvi–clvii.
50 P.R.O., CP 25/1/283/16, no. 448.
51 V.C.H. Wilts. vii. 201.
52 Feet of F. 1377–1509 (W.R.S. xli), p. 63; Feud. Aids, vi. 530.
53 V.C.H. Wilts. xi. 87; Feud. Aids, v. 241; below, Bathampton, manors.
54 P.R.O., C 139/142, no. 19.
55 Ibid. C 140/12, no. 12, rot. 6.
56 Cal. Inq. p.m. Hen. VII, i, pp. 351, 356–7.
57 P.R.O., C 142/34, no. 58.
58 Ibid. C 142/57, no. 6.
59 Ibid. C 142/124, no. 195.
60 Ibid. C 2/Jas. I/W 12/23; C 142/662, no. 133; Recusant R. 1592–3 (Cath. Rec. Soc. xviii), p. 352; 1593–4 (Cath. Rec. Soc. lvii), pp. 184–5.
61 P.R.O., CP 25/2/372/22 Jas. I East.
62 Complete Peerage, viii. 488.
63 V.C.H. Wilts. ii, p. 166.
64 Cal. Chart. R. 1257–1300, 157–9; I. J. Sanders, Eng. Baronies, 95.
65 Pipe R. 1186–7 (P.R.S. xxxvii), 180; 1191–2 (P.R.S. N.S. ii), 120.
66 Cal. Inq. p.m. ii, pp. 173–4; v, pp. 255, 257; for the Zouche fam., Complete Peerage, xii (2), 930–6.
67 Sir Chris. Hatton's Bk. of Seals, ed. L. C. Loyd and D. M. Stenton, pp. 128–9.
68 Cat. Anct. D. iii, D 1021.
69 Feet of F. 1272–1307 (W.R.S. i), p. 2.
70 Valor Eccl. (Rec. Com.), ii. 98.
71 L. & P. Hen. VIII, x, p. 526; Complete Peerage, xii (1), 59–64.
72 Cal. Pat. 1558–60, 464–5.
73 P.R.O., CP 25/2/239/9 Eliz. I Trin. no. 374.
74 Ibid. CP 25/2/240/21 Eliz. I Hil.
75 Ibid. CP 25/2/242/34 & 35 Eliz. I Mich.
76 Ibid. C 78/110, no. 7.
77 Ibid. CP 25/2/372/18 Jas. I Hil.; W.A.M. xl. 265–6; W.R.O. 212B/6557; for Pitman, below, this section (N. Tidworth).
78 Alum. Oxon. 1500–1714, iii. 1137; below, church.
79 P.R.O., CP 25/2/1079/11 Geo. I Mich.
80 Mon. in Figheldean church.
81 Poore Estate Act, 11 Geo. IV, c. 29 (Private, not printed).
82 Endowed Char. Wilts. (S. Div.), 701; above, this section (Moels).

Somerset, 1547-9.[83] In 1773 Edward Poore had a house, on rising ground north of the church,[84] which c. 1800 was described as small and secluded.[85] It was replaced in the early 19th century by Zouch Manor,[86] a square house with a principal east front, rendered and of three bays with a central door, and with a west service wing of red brick.

Between 1220 and 1238 Roger la Zouche subinfeudated part of the manor to his daughter Laura and her husband Gilbert of Sandford. Laura settled the land on Arabel, wife of Henry of Pembridge, and on Arabel's son Fulk of Pembridge (d. 1296),[87] who held it in 1282.[88] Fulk's heirs held it in 1314, and in 1339 another Fulk of Pembridge granted the reversion after the death of the life tenant, Henry of Birmingham, to Robert of Pembridge.[89]

What may have been the same estate was held in 1412 by Alice Sotwell,[90] and in 1579, when it was called *NORTH TIDWORTH* manor, by William Sotwell.[91] That manor descended to William Sotwell (d. 1639), passed to his daughter Elizabeth, wife of Francis Trenchard and, after 1646, of John Bulkeley, and apparently reverted to his nephew John Sotwell, who sold it to William Pitman and William's son William. The Pitmans sold it in 1654 to John Bulkeley and it was reunited with Zouche manor.[92]

In the later 13th century Sir Nicholas de Vaux granted 1 yardland, the nucleus of an estate later called *TIDWORTH* manor and perhaps formerly part of Zouche manor, to John Irish.[93] The estate was later held by Simon Irish.[94] In 1423 Richard Etton and his wife Joan, whose inheritance it was, settled it on themselves and on William Ludlow (d. 1478) and his wife Margaret.[95] From William's son John (d. 1487)[96] the estate descended, apparently in the direct line, to George Ludlow (d. 1580), Sir Edmund Ludlow (d. 1624), Henry Ludlow (d. 1639), and Edmund Ludlow,[97] who sold it to William Maton (will proved 1687). It was presumably merged with Maton's other estate in North Tidworth.[98]

In the mid 12th century one Roland gave to Bradenstoke priory a messuage and 5 a. in North Tidworth which he had acquired from Benet of Angreville, and in the early 13th Gerard of Coombe gave the priory 5½ yardlands formerly his brother Baldwin's.[99] The estate passed to the

Crown at the Dissolution[1] and was granted in 1540 to John Goddard.[2] It was possibly the later *MATON'S* or Tidworth Down farm devised by John Maton (d. 1590) to his son Leonard.[3] Maton's apparently passed to Leonard's brother Francis (will proved 1663), to Francis's son William[4] (will proved 1687), and to William's grandson John Maton[5] (d. 1737), who devised it to his nephew Edmund Brickenden.[6] Brickenden's daughter and heir Ann (will proved 1788), wife of John Hughes, devised the estate to her cousin John Yaldwin, who sold it in 1793 to Thomas Assheton Smith: it was added to the Tidworth estate.[7]

Amesbury abbey may have received tithes from lands in North Tidworth held by John the marshal (d. 1165) and Hugh de Lacy (d. 1186), and in 1179 such tithes were confirmed to Amesbury priory.[8] The priory kept the tithes until the Dissolution.[9] In 1541 they were granted to Winchester cathedral,[10] the owner in 1843 when they were valued at £80 and commuted.[11]

ECONOMIC HISTORY. In 1086 North Tidworth had land for 6½ ploughteams and 6½ were there with 3 *villani*, 8 bordars, 5 *servi*, and 2 coscets: 6¾ hides were in demesne. The estates had pastures measuring 12, 6, and 2 square furlongs.[12]

In the Middle Ages the usual sheep-and-corn husbandry of the Wiltshire chalklands apparently prevailed at North Tidworth. It is likely that there were separate groups of open fields on each side of the river, and later evidence suggests that each of the main manors, Moels, Hussey, and Zouche, had its own open fields,[13] but where the lands of each lay is obscure. There were bondmen on Zouche manor in the period 1199–1227.[14]

On the minor part of Zouche manor in 1279 there were 4 yardlands of demesne and 9 yardlands held by customary tenants. In 1296 that estate included 89 a. of arable, 1 a. of meadow, and pasture worth £1 a year. The major part of Hussey manor in 1290 included 210 a. of demesne arable and a several pasture worth 3s. a year; there were eight customary tenants.[15] In 1332 it included 90 a. of arable and the pasture. The tenants, who paid £5 yearly, may have been more numerous than in 1290. They were all dead

83 Hist. MSS. Com. 58, *Bath*, iv, p. 335.
84 *Andrews and Dury, Map* (W.R.S. viii), pl. 9.
85 J. Britton, *Beauties of Wilts.* ii. 154–5.
86 Cf. P.R.O., IR 30/38/259.
87 *Cal. Inq. p.m.* ii, pp. 173–4; iii, pp. 208–9.
88 *Abbrev. Plac.* (Rec. Com.), 204.
89 *Cal. Inq. p.m.* v, p. 257; *Feet of F. 1327–77* (W.R.S. xxix), p. 56.   90 *Feud. Aids*, vi. 539.
91 P.R.O., REQ 2/187/19.
92 Ibid. CP 25/2/528/22 Chas. I Trin.; CP 25/2/608/1654 Hil.; *Visit. Yorks.* (Surtees Soc. xxxvi), 304–5; W.R.O. 212B/6557.   93 P.R.O., E 210/2976.
94 *Feud. Aids*, v. 241.
95 *Feet of F. 1377–1509* (W.R.S. xli), p. 83; for the Ludlow fam., *V.C.H. Wilts.* xi. 57.
96 *Cal. Inq. p.m. Hen. VII*, i, p. 154.
97 *Wilts. Inq. p.m. 1625–49* (Index Libr.), 94–7, 306–7; P.R.O., C 142/191, no. 122.
98 W.R.O., wills, archd. Sar., Wm. Maton, 1687; below, this section (Maton's).
99 *Bradenstoke Cart.* (W.R.S. xxxv), pp. 93–4.

1 P.R.O., SC 6/Hen. VIII/3985, rot. 56.
2 *L. & P. Hen. VIII*, xv, p. 296.
3 P.R.O., PROB 11/76, f. 139 and v.
4 *Wilts. Pedigrees* (Harl. Soc. cv/cvi), 127; W.R.O., wills, archd. Sar., Francis Maton, 1663.
5 W.R.O., wills, archd. Sar., Francis and Wm. Maton, 1687.   6 Ibid. wills, archd. Sar., John Maton, 1737.
7 Hants R.O. 2M53/8, deeds, 1777, 1793; copy will of Ann Hughes; above, this section (Moels).
8 *Cal. Chart. R. 1257–1300*, 157–9; above, this section (Hussey; Zouche); for the hist. of the abbey and priory, *V.C.H. Wilts.* iii. 242–59.
9 P.R.O., SC 6/Hen. VIII/3986, rot. 83d.
10 *L. & P. Hen. VIII*, xvi, p. 417.
11 P.R.O., IR 29/38/259; IR 30/38/259.
12 *V.C.H. Wilts.* ii, pp. 122, 136, 166.
13 W.R.O., D 1/24/203/1–2.
14 *Sir Chris. Hatton's Bk. of Seals*, ed. Loyd and Stenton, pp. 128–9.
15 *Wilts. Inq. p.m. 1242–1326* (Index Libr.), 124, 182, 209–10.

in 1349 and their arable, 40 a., was held by the lord. The demesne, 120 a. in 1349, was worked in a three-field system. In 1361 the demesne arable, 160 a., was worth only 1d. an acre, and there were then 2 bond and 3 free tenants. A demesne flock of 300 sheep could be kept on the common pastures in 1349 and 1361.[16]

By the late 18th century both common husbandry and customary tenure had been eliminated in North Tidworth, and nearly all the land was in four several farms. Zouche, or Great House, farm, 956 a., had 539 a. of arable of which 15 a. were sown with French grass, 33 a. of meadow, and 383 a. of pasture including downland and 50 a. of former lanes; Moyles, 666 a., had 367 a. of pasture, 283 a. of arable, and 16 a. of meadow; Manor, 718 a., had 449 a. of arable, 256 a. of pasture, and 9 a. of meadow, of which c. 5 a. were watered; Maton's, 655 a., had 477 a. of arable, 165 a. of pasture, and 9 a. of meadow, mostly watered. Manor and Maton's included newly ploughed downland,[17] but all four farms were apparently worked from buildings in the village. About 1800 new buildings were erected outside the village for Maton's, thereafter Tidworth Down farm, and in the mid 19th century buildings were erected at the Pennings for Zouche farm.[18] On Zouche farm between 1790 and 1839 c. 200 a. were planted with trees, mostly after 1832 when the farm was bought by the sportsman Thomas Assheton Smith, and more land was ploughed. Land on the other farms in 1839 remained much as in 1790.[19]

Between c. 1839 and 1896 about half the arable was laid to grass:[20] in 1896 grain was grown on only half the arable, and temporary grasses were sown on much of the former arable. Sheep farming predominated until the late 19th century when dairying began to increase. Farming ceased on about a third of the parish when the War Department bought the land in 1897, and more agricultural land was later taken for housing. In the earlier 20th century there were three large farms: between 1900 and 1906 Manor and Zouche, a total of 1,367 a., were worked together and Tidworth Down, 636 a., separately;[21] between 1910 and 1939 Manor and Tidworth Down were worked together as a dairy farm and Zouche was worked separately.[22] After the Second World War the agricultural land was worked from Collingbourne Ducis and was used for mixed farming.[23] In 1990 nearly all the parish was in use for military training or had been built on.[24]

North Tidworth had no woodland in 1086, but there was some on Hussey manor in the mid 13th century.[25] In 1790 Manor farm and Maton farm each had 4 a. of woodland on its downs.[26] Between 1790 and 1830 c. 50 a., mainly ash, elm, beech, and fir, were planted on Zouche manor.[27] Other woodland was also planted, probably in the 1830s, and in 1839 there were 207 a. of woods, mainly on Perham down, at the Pennings, and on Sidbury Hill.[28] About 1900 a total of 175 a. of new woodland was planted, on the south-east slope of Sidbury Hill and on Chalkpit Hill, Clarendon Hill, and Windmill Hill.[29] All those woodlands, c. 380 a., were standing in 1990.

There was a windmill on the major part of Hussey manor in 1290,[30] one on Tidworth manor in 1487,[31] and one on Maton's estate in 1590.[32] A windmill stood on Windmill Hill in 1773[33] but not in the early 19th century.[34]

A brick kiln on the northern slopes of Sidbury Hill in 1773 was probably in the parish.[35] Chalk from the downs was quarried c. 1796 and carried by way of Bristol to Birmingham and other manufacturing centres.[36] In 1831 three quarters of the men in North Tidworth were agricultural labourers and the remaining quarter worked at rural trades and handicrafts.[37] The increase in population from c. 1900 encouraged some commercial enterprises, such as a creamery depot c. 1912, a photographic studio c. 1911, and a depot for McEwan-Younger Ltd., brewers, c. 1939,[38] but most business development was centred on Ludgershall.[39] The Royal Army Ordnance depot in Ordnance Road employed 150 civilians in 1928. A tank workshop was built in 1929; the works were extended in 1938–9 and employed 90 civilians in 1952.[40] About 1980 c. 80 civilians were employed and the works still maintained armoured vehicles and provided support for the Armoured Vehicle Storage depot at Ludgershall,[41] part of which was in North Tidworth parish.

LOCAL GOVERNMENT. A court was held for Hussey manor in the late 13th century and the 14th,[42] and for part of Zouche manor in 1296, the mid 16th century, and 1781.[43]

From £60 in 1776 and c. £86 a year 1783–5 sums spent on the poor increased greatly, and in the earlier 19th century a twelfth of the inhabitants was relieved generously. In 1802–3 £208

16 *Wilts. Inq. p.m.* 1327–77 (Index Libr.), 84, 204, 284–5.
17 W.R.O. 2159/24, pp. 14–25.
18 Above, intro.
19 Poore Estate Act, 11 Geo. IV, c. 29 (Private, not printed); above, manors (Zouche); P.R.O., IR 29/38/259; IR 30/38/259.
20 Para. based on P.R.O., IR 18/11169; ibid. MAF 68/151, sheet 23; MAF 68/493, sheet 13; MAF 68/1063, sheet 12; MAF 68/1633, sheet 12; MAF 68/2203, sheet 6; MAF 68/2773, sheet 8; MAF 68/3319, sheet 8; MAF 68/3814, no. 111; MAF 68/4145, no. 111; MAF 68/4552, no. 111.
21 W.R.O., G 10/510/12.
22 Ibid. Inland Revenue, val. reg. 139; *Kelly's Dir. Wilts.* (1935, 1939).
23 W.R.O., G 10/516/3.
24 Inf. from Defence Land Agent, Durrington.
25 *Close R.* 1254–6, 102.
26 W.R.O. 2159/24, pp. 20–5.
27 Poore Estate Act, 11 Geo. IV, c. 29 (Private, not printed).
28 P.R.O., IR 29/38/259; IR 30/38/259.
29 O.S. Maps 6", Wilts. XLVIII (1883–8 and later edns.); W.R.O., Inland Revenue, val. reg. 139.
30 *Wilts. Inq. p.m.* 1242–1326 (Index Libr.), 182.
31 *Cal. Inq. p.m. Hen. VII*, i, p. 154.
32 P.R.O., PROB 11/76, f. 139 and v.
33 *Andrews and Dury, Map* (W.R.S. viii), pl. 9.
34 O.S. Map 1", sheet 14 (1817 edn.).
35 *Andrews and Dury, Map* (W.R.S. viii), pl. 9.
36 A. Young, *Annals of Agric.* xxviii. 363.
37 *Census*, 1831.
38 Above, intro.; *V.C.H. Wilts.* iv. 226; *Kelly's Dir. Wilts.* (1911, 1939).
39 Above, Ludgershall, econ. hist. (trade and ind.).
40 *V.C.H. Wilts.* iv. 206; above, intro.
41 *Tidworth Guide*, 1980, 19.
42 *Wilts. Inq. p.m.* 1242–1326 (Index Libr.), 182; 1327–77 (Index Libr.), 84, 204, 284–5.
43 Ibid. 1242–1326 (Index Libr.), 209–10; P.R.O., C 3/137/11; ibid. REQ 2/187/19; W.R.O. 130/49B/40.

was spent on regular out-relief for 17 people and on occasional relief for 20, and in 1813–15 £338 was thus spent for 28 and 10 respectively.[44] In 1790 the parish had a cottage for housing paupers, and others could be admitted to Pierce's almshouses.[45] Although the poor-rates raised 1816–34 were average for Amesbury hundred, it is likely that in North Tidworth a smaller number of paupers was still generously relieved.[46] The parish became part of Andover union in 1835,[47] was transferred to Pewsey union in 1879,[48] and became part of Kennet district in 1974.[49]

CHURCH. The church may have been standing in the 12th century,[50] but the earliest reference to it is of 1291.[51] In 1972 the rectory and parish were united with those of South Tidworth; North Tidworth church became the parish church, and the new parish is in Salisbury diocese. The united benefice, Tidworth, was united with the rectory of Ludgershall and Faberstown in 1986.[52]

The advowson apparently passed with the overlordships of Moels manor and Shrewton as part of the earldom of Salisbury, which was forfeited to the king in 1326. From 1327 it may have been held with the honor of Shrewton; the king presented in 1348 and 1354 and Edward, prince of Wales, in 1350 and 1351. Evidently from 1361 and until the death in 1484 of Edward Plantagenet, earl of Salisbury, the advowson again passed with the earldom. The king presented in 1481, because the earl was a minor, and at all vacancies after 1484.[53] The Crown became patron of Tidworth rectory in 1972, and in 1986 became entitled to present alternately for Tidworth, Ludgershall, and Faberstown.[54]

The rectory was worth £8 in 1291,[55] £12 in 1535,[56] and £115 in 1650.[57] The living was accounted good in 1707,[58] and the income of £266 was above average for the benefices in Amesbury deanery c. 1830.[59] The rector took all tithes from the parish except those from 595 a. In 1843 his tithes were valued at £327 and commuted.[60] The glebe was 1 yardland in 1341,[61] 15 a. from the 17th century to the early 20th,

and was sold in portions 1901–22.[62] The rector had a house in 1341.[63] In 1783 the glebe house had two wainscotted rooms and five bedrooms.[64] It was sold in 1962 and was later demolished.[65] A new Rectory was built in St. George's Road.[66]

There was a chapel on Hussey manor in the early 14th century.[67] In 1299 the rector, Simon of Walcot, was licensed to study at Oxford for a year provided that he resided on his return: his leave was extended in 1300 on condition that he employed a curate at North Tidworth and gave alms and in 1301 on condition that he resided from mid Lent to Easter.[68] Thomas Shifford, who resigned the benefice in 1371, was also a canon of Hereford.[69] In the years 1348–54 and after 1481 some rectors were royal protégés. Andrew Tracy, rector 1531–44, was a minister of a royal chapel,[70] and John Panke, rector c. 1600, published anti-Catholic works.[71] John Mompesson, rector 1617–37, seldom preached,[72] and he employed a curate who was apparently not ordained.[73] John Graile, rector 1646–54, preached twice on Sundays in 1650, signed the *Concurrent Testimony*, and defended himself in print against charges of Arminianism.[74] Prescribed books were lacking in 1668 and 1674, and in the 1660s the parish clerk could neither read, write, nor sing.[75] Robert Pierce, rector 1680–1707, owned Zouche manor and was described by the bishop as 'a very ill man of a turbulent spirit and loose behaviour that had given him much trouble and uneasiness in the county'.[76] From the later 17th century to the earlier 19th many rectors were pluralists and either were assisted by, or delegated the cure to, curates.[77] Thomas Fountaine, 1780–8, who succeeded his father as rector, was vicar of Old Windsor (Berks.) and a royal chaplain.[78] In 1783 the curate held two Sunday services and preached at one of them. Weekday services were held on Christmas day, fast days, and feast days.[79] Francis Dyson, rector 1829–58, was also rector of South Tidworth, a canon of Salisbury, and a royal chaplain.[80] In 1832 and 1850–1 only one service was held on Sundays at North Tidworth, in the morning or evening by alternation with South Tidworth; an average of 250 attended morning services 1850–1.[81] In 1864 the

44 *Poor Law Abstract, 1804*, 558–9; *1818*, 492–3; *V.C.H. Wilts.* iv. 359.
45 W.R.O. 2159/24, p. 28; below, charities.
46 *Poor Rate Returns, 1816–21*, 185; *1822–4*, 225; *1825–9*, 215; *1830–4*, 209.
47 *Poor Law Com. 1st Rep.* App. D, 248.
48 *V.C.H. Wilts.* v. 258, 260.
49 O.S. Map 1/100,000, admin. areas, Wilts. (1974 edn.).
50 Below, this section [architecture].
51 *Tax. Eccl.* (Rec. Com.), 180.
52 Ch. Com. files, NB 34/340B–C.
53 Phillipps, *Wilts. Inst.* (index in *W.A.M.* xxviii. 231–2); *Complete Peerage*, xi. 385–99; above, manors (Moels); below, Shrewton, manors.   54 Ch. Com. files, NB 34/340B–C.
55 *Tax. Eccl.* (Rec. Com.), 180.
56 *Valor Eccl.* (Rec. Com.), ii. 92.   57 *W.A.M.* xl. 256.
58 *Naish's Diary* (W.R.S. xx), 61–2.
59 *Rep. Com. Eccl. Revenues*, 850–1.
60 W.R.O., D 1/24/203/1–2; P.R.O., IR 29/38/259; above, manors.   61 *Inq. Non.* (Rec. Com.), 172.
62 *Kelly's Dir. Wilts.* (1907 and later edns.); W.R.O., D 1/24/203/1–2; ibid. 2159/24, pp. 10–11; G.P.L., Treas. Solicitor, 528/51; Ch. Com. file, NB 34/340C.
63 *Inq. Non.* (Rec. Com.), 172.
64 W.R.O., D 1/24/203/2.

65 Ibid. 1612/12; Ch. Com. deed 584028.
66 Inf. from the rector, Ludgershall.
67 Phillipps, *Wilts. Inst.* i. 14.
68 *Reg. Ghent* (Cant. & York Soc.), ii. 839, 843, 850.
69 *Cal. Pat. 1370–4*, 54.
70 *L. & P. Hen. VIII*, v, p. 150; Phillipps, *Wilts. Inst.* i. 210.   71 *D.N.B.*; *Alum. Oxon. 1500–1714*, iii. 1112.
72 Phillipps, *Wilts. Inst.* ii. 9; *Cal. S.P. Dom. 1636–7*, 369; *V.C.H. Wilts.* iii. 41.
73 *Subscription Bk. 1620–40* (W.R.S. xxxii), p. 73; W.R.O., bishop's transcripts, bdle. 1.
74 *D.N.B.*; W. A. Shaw, *Hist. Eng. Church*, ii. 328; *W.A.M.* xl. 256; *Calamy Revised*, ed. Matthews, 557.
75 W.R.O., D 1/54/1/3, no. 45; D 1/54/3/2, no. 11; D 1/54/6/4, no. 39.
76 Phillipps, *Wilts. Inst.* ii. 37, 49; *Naish's Diary* (W.R.S. xx), 61–2; above, manors (Zouche).
77 W.R.O., bishop's transcripts, bdles. 1–3; ibid. 2159/25; ibid. D 1/21/5/1, f. 184; D 1/21/5/2.
78 *Alum. Cantab. to 1751*, ii. 166; *1752–1900*, ii. 550; Phillipps, *Wilts. Inst.* ii. 81, 90.
79 *Vis. Queries, 1783* (W.R.S. xxvii), pp. 212–13.
80 *Alum. Oxon. 1715–1886*, i. 401.
81 Ch. Com. file, NB 34/340C; P.R.O., HO 129/118/2/9/12.

resident rector held two services every Sunday, in winter and spring in the morning, when he preached, and afternoon, and in summer and autumn in the afternoon, when he preached, and evening, when he lectured. The sacrament was administered at the four great festivals, when *c.* 30 received it, and on Ascension day and every six weeks, when *c.* 24 received it.[82] In 1990 the parish was served by a deacon who assisted the rector and lived in the Rectory.[83]

The church of *HOLY TRINITY*, so called in 1763,[84] is of stone rubble with ashlar dressings and extensive red-brick patching, and consists of a chancel with north organ chamber, a nave with south porch, and a west tower with north vestry. It contains a 12th-century font, but the oldest dateable part of its structure is a 14th-century niche which was reset when the church was rebuilt in the 15th century. The tower had been patched by 1805[85] and was repaired again in 1859.[86] In a restoration of the church in 1882, to plans by J. L. Pearson, a gallery was removed, the chancel and the nave were reroofed, the porch was rebuilt, and the organ chamber was built. The vestry was built in 1912.[87]

In 1553 the king took 4 oz. of plate and left a chalice of 15 oz. for the parish. A chalice hallmarked for 1576 and a chalice and paten of 1838 belonged to the parish in 1891 and 1990.[88] There were three bells in 1553. They were replaced by three cast by John Wallis in 1619, to which were added a treble cast by Clement Tosier in 1700 and a tenor cast by James Wells of Aldbourne in 1809:[89] those five bells hung in the church in 1990.[90] The registers date from 1700; an older one was burnt in the earlier 18th century.[91]

NONCONFORMITY. William Fauconer (d. *c.* 1610), a recusant who owned Hussey manor,[92] is unlikely to have lived in North Tidworth. There was no papist or dissenter in 1662 or 1676.[93] Primitive Methodists certified houses in 1816 and 1818 and Baptists from Ludgershall did so in 1831.[94] Each group still had a few adherents in the parish in 1864.[95]

EDUCATION. Children were taught in several small schools in the parish in 1783.[96] In 1818 a total of 46, of whom 22 were from a neighbouring parish, presumably South Tidworth, was taught in three schools,[97] but there was only one

school in 1833 when 12 were taught in it.[98] In 1846–7 there were two schools, one with 71 pupils and one with 9,[99] and in 1859 the 40 older children attended a school opened in South Tidworth in 1856 and 5–10 others were taught in a cottage.[1] North Tidworth children attended South Tidworth school until Clarendon junior and infants' schools were opened east of the church and of Pennings Road in, respectively, 1962 and 1964.[2] Zouch junior and infants' schools were opened in 1969 west of the Gason Hill estate and merged in 1985 as Zouch primary school.[3] In 1990 there were on roll 228 children at Clarendon junior school, 184 at Clarendon infants' school, and 309 at Zouch primary school.[4]

A mixed secondary school was opened on Tidworth down in 1940 for children from North Tidworth, South Tidworth, and Ludgershall, and became a secondary modern school in 1944. It was reserved for boys when a secondary modern school for girls was opened in Ludgershall in 1965. In 1978 the Ludgershall school became a primary school, and thereafter all the older children attended Castledown comprehensive school housed in the buildings on Tidworth down.[5] There were 450 children on roll in 1990.[6]

A school at Tin Town for an average of 83 children was open from 1903 to 1906.[7] There were classrooms at the barracks on Perham down from 1926 and at Fowler barracks in Brimstone bottom in 1965–6. There was also a school in the parish for the children of Gurkha soldiers in 1965–6.[8] A private preparatory school was open between 1934 and 1966.[9]

CHARITIES FOR THE POOR. Elizabeth Willis (d. 1637) bequeathed the income from £5 for distribution to the poor each Good Friday. The charity was lost before 1833.[10]

In 1656 John Bulkeley gave a rent charge of £1 to the poor.[11] Firewood was given on St. Andrew's day (30 November) in the early 19th century, but the charity had been discontinued by the late 1860s. It was revived and in 1905 the £1 was distributed by the rector with other money collected for the sick and poor.[12] In 1933 £4 was distributed among five people.[13] The £1 was given each year to the same old woman 1965–72.[14]

In 1689 Thomas Pierce (d. 1691) built four almshouses on the west side of the main road

82 W.R.O., D 1/56/7.
83 Inf. from the rector.
84 J. Ecton, *Thesaurus* (1763), 391.
85 For the church in the early 19th cent., J. Buckler, watercolour in W.A.S. Libr., vol. i. 13.
86 W.R.O. 2159/25.
87 Ibid. D 1/21/5/1, ff. 161–2.
88 Nightingale, *Wilts. Plate*, 42; inf. from the rector.
89 Walters, *Wilts. Bells*, 217.
90 Inf. from the rector.
91 *Vis. Queries, 1783* (W.R.S. xxvii), pp. 212–13; W.R.O. 2159/1–10; bishop's transcripts for 1620–36, 1668, 1671–4, 1695–7 are ibid.   92 Above, manors (Hussey).
93 *Compton Census*, ed. Whiteman, 119; W.R.O., D 1/54/1/3, no. 45.
94 *Meeting Ho. Certs.* (W.R.S. xl), pp. 81, 86, 127.
95 W.R.O., D 1/56/7.
96 *Vis. Queries, 1783* (W.R.S. xxvii), pp. 212–13.

97 *Educ. of Poor Digest*, 1039.
98 *Educ. Enq. Abstract*, 1049.
99 Nat. Soc. *Inquiry, 1846–7*, Wilts. 10–11.
1 *Acct. of Wilts. Schs.* 44.
2 Inf. from Director of Educ., Co. Hall, Trowbridge.
3 W.R.O., F 8/500, Zouch infants'.
4 Inf. from Director of Educ.
5 *V.C.H. Wilts.* v. 355; W.R.O., F 8/500, Tidworth Down; above, Ludgershall, educ.
6 Inf. from Director of Educ.
7 *Return of Non-Provided Schs.* 26, 40.
8 James, *Plain Soldiering*, 82, 84; W.R.O., G 10/516/4.
9 W.R.O., G 10/516/4; G 10/760/182.
10 *Endowed Char. Wilts.* (S. Div.), 701.
11 W.R.O. 212B/6557.
12 *Endowed Char. Wilts.* (S. Div.), 702, 705.
13 W.R.O., L 2, N. Tidworth.
14 Char. Com. file.

near the church. The almspeople, preferably tenants of Zouche manor, were endowed with £21 a year, 2s. a week each, and could also work. Pierce also bequeathed the income from £20 for repairs. The repair fund was lost before 1833. The almshouses were a range of two-roomed red-brick cottages. By a Scheme of 1901 no new almsperson was to be appointed and each cottage, as it became vacant, was to be sold. The proceeds and the £21 yearly were to be invested and weekly pensions

of 3s. to be paid to needy parishioners, preferably employees of the former Zouche manor who received no poor relief. In 1905 only one almsperson remained and three of the cottages were let. From the rents and the £21 the almsperson and two more old people received weekly pensions of 4s. 6d.[15] The almshouses were sold in 1913: in 1914 and in 1928 £52 was distributed in monthly pensions.[16] From 1966 to 1976 the yearly income of £35 7s. was given in small pensions to 5–7 widows.[17]

15 *Endowed Char. Wilts.* (S. Div.), 699–705; above, manors (Zouche).

16 W.R.O., L 2, N. Tidworth.
17 Char. Com. file.

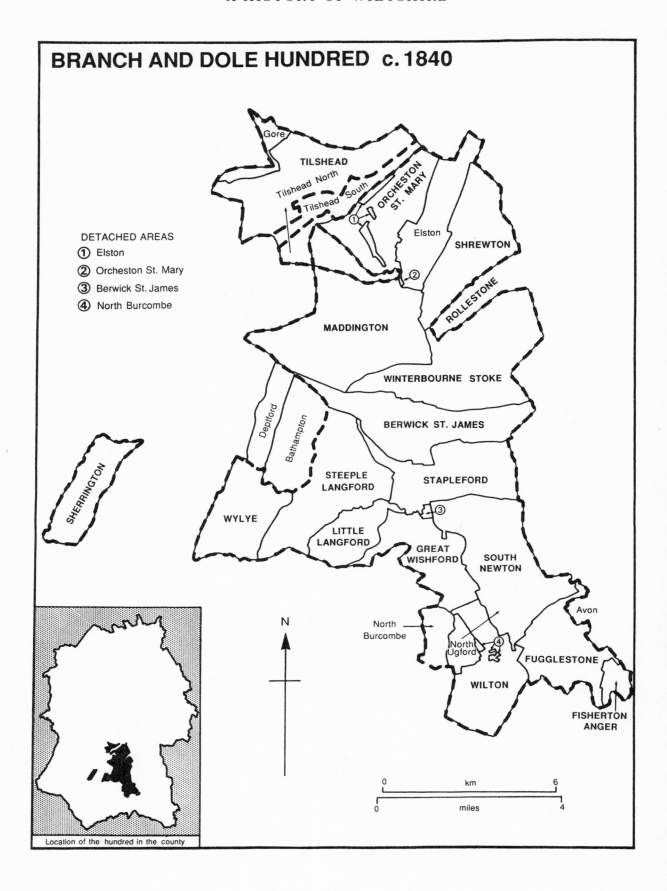

BRANCH AND DOLE HUNDRED c.1840

Gore

TILSHEAD

Tilshead North

Tilshead South

ORCHESTON ST. MARY

Elston

SHREWTON

ROLLESTONE

DETACHED AREAS
① Elston
② Orcheston St. Mary
③ Berwick St. James
④ North Burcombe

MADDINGTON

WINTERBOURNE STOKE

BERWICK ST. JAMES

Deptford

Bathampton

STEEPLE LANGFORD

STAPLEFORD

SHERRINGTON

WYLYE

LITTLE LANGFORD

GREAT WISHFORD

SOUTH NEWTON

Avon

N

North Burcombe

North Ugford

④

FUGGLESTONE

WILTON

FISHERTON ANGER

| 0 | km | 6 |
| 0 | miles | 4 |

Location of the hundred in the county

BRANCH AND DOLE HUNDRED

Branch hundred was called Brencesberga hundred in 1084[1] and may have taken its name from a barrow at which it met.[2] In 1084 it included all the lands in Sherrington, Stapleford, and Stockton parishes, some of those in Steeple Langford parish, and possibly all those in Fisherton Anger and Great Wishford parishes; it also included extensive estates of Wilton abbey, probably all the lands in the parishes of Fugglestone, Little Langford, and South Newton, and some of those in Burcombe, Stratford-sub-Castle, Wilton, and Wylye.[3] Stockton, a possession of St. Swithun's priory, Winchester, was transferred to Elstub hundred, which was also the priory's, before 1249.[4] Otherwise the composition of Branch hundred in 1332 was what it seems to have been in 1084. It included in Burcombe parish North Burcombe and part of Ditchampton but not South Burcombe and South Ugford which were in Cadworth hundred, in Fugglestone parish Fugglestone, Bemerton, and Quidhampton, in Steeple Langford parish Steeple Langford and Hanging Langford but not Bathampton which was in Heytesbury hundred, in South Newton parish South Newton, Little Wishford, Stoford, Chilhampton, North Ugford, and possibly Burden's Ball, in Wilton parish most of Ditchampton, and in Wylye parish Wylye but not Deptford which was in Heytesbury hundred. Avon in Stratford-sub-Castle was in the hundred in 1332[5] but later is more likely to have been considered part of Underditch hundred.[6] The lands of Branch hundred are north-west of Salisbury in the Nadder and Wylye valleys. At the confluence of the two rivers Wilton borough was not part of the hundred,[7] but after the Middle Ages was often linked administratively with it.[8] In 1255 and presumably until, between 1604 and 1839, it ceased to be considered part of Great Wishford parish, the northern half of Grovely forest was part of the hundred.[9]

By an early grant or by prescription some of Wilton abbey's estates, including all those in the hundred in Burcombe, South Newton, and Wylye parishes, were evidently exempt from the jurisdiction of the hundred,[10] and in the 12th century exemption was granted to other lords for Stapleford and Great Wishford. Great Wishford's was disputed 1226–7 but established. Exemption for Hanging Langford was claimed in the 13th century and had been established by the 15th.[11]

Dole hundred was called Dolesfeld hundred in 1084[12] and may have taken its name from a field in which it met.[13] In 1084 it included all the lands in Shrewton and Rollestone parishes and probably all those in Berwick St. James, Maddington, Orcheston St. Mary, and Winterbourne Stoke parishes; it also included Gore, a

1 *V.C.H. Wilts.* ii, p. 209.
2 *P.N. Wilts.* (E.P.N.S.), 225.
3 *V.C.H. Wilts.* ii, pp. 129–30, 209; vi. 9, 41, 207; below, S. Newton, manors; Wylye, manors (Wylye).
4 *V.C.H. Wilts.* xi. 105.
5 *Tax List, 1332* (W.R.S. xlv), 22–3, 70, 81–4; for Burden's Ball, below, S. Newton, intro.
6 *V.C.H. Wilts.* vi. 196, 199.   7 Ibid. ii, p. 115.
8 Ibid. iv. 327; *Taxation Lists* (W.R.S. x), 109–14.

9 *Rot. Hund.* (Rec. Com.), ii (1), 244; below, Great Wishford, intro.
10 *First Pembroke Survey*, ed. Straton, i. 104–5; Finberg, *Early Wessex Chart.* 84, 86, 96; cf. below, Wylye, manors (Wylye).
11 Below, Hanging Langford, local govt.; Stapleford, local govt.; Great Wishford, local govt.
12 *V.C.H. Wilts.* ii, p. 179.
13 *P.N. Wilts.* (E.P.N.S.), 232.

detached part of Market Lavington parish, and Elston in Orcheston St. George.[14] Tilshead was a royal borough in 1086:[15] by the early 12th century most of it, Tilshead North manor, had evidently been added to Dole hundred, of which it was later part;[16] by the mid 13th the remainder, Tilshead South manor, had been added to Whorwellsdown hundred, which was held by the lord of that manor.[17] In 1332 Dole hundred comprised the parishes of Berwick St. James (including Asserton), Maddington (including Addestone, Bourton, and Homanton), Orcheston St. Mary, Shrewton (including Netton), Winterbourne Stoke, and probably Rollestone, and Elston, Gore, and Tilshead North.[18] Rollestone was transferred to Elstub hundred between 1428 and 1524 although it had no known connexion with St. Swithun's priory.[19] Nearly all the lands of the hundred are in the valley of the river Till, and most of the Till valley was in the hundred.

Maddington manor and Tilshead North manor, held by respectively Amesbury priory and Holy Trinity abbey, Caen (Calvados), was each free from suit of the hundred by grant,[20] and Shrewton and Winterbourne Stoke may also have been freed from the jurisdiction of the hundred by 1255, when each manor was held with view of frankpledge.[21] Attempts to reimpose hundredal jurisdiction over Tilshead North in the later 13th century were unsuccessful.[22] Orcheston St. Mary manor was held with view of frankpledge in the 15th century,[23] as was Berwick St. James manor in the 16th, when it was in the duchy of Lancaster.[24]

Branch and Dole hundreds were combined for some purposes from 1236;[25] the two shared a bailiff with Cawdon hundred in 1249[26] and with Dunworth hundred in 1255.[27] Branch and Dole evidently remained two hundreds in the earlier 14th century,[28] but were named as one in 1383[29] and 1428[30] and had been combined by 1439.[31] The last known reference to Branch or Dole as a separate hundred is of 1487.[32]

The Crown's ownership of Branch and Dole hundreds and of the combined hundred was largely uninterrupted. Caen abbey may have had rights over the whole of Dole hundred in the early 12th century,[33] but in the 13th that hundred was the king's.[34] A tourn for Branch and Dole hundred was held at 'Wirdescliff' in 1439. It was attended by tithings called Tilshead, Orcheston, Elston, Maddington, Addestone, Asserton, Sherrington, Wylye, Steeple Langford, Wishford, Newton, Bemerton, and Burcombe. It is not clear why it was attended by so many tithings for which exemption had been granted or claimed and not by several for which no exemption had been granted or claimed; Gore was the only tithing against which action was taken for not attending.[35] Later Hanging Langford and Little Langford formed a single tithing.[36] In 1651 a hundred court, at which actions under 45s. could be tried, was said to meet every three weeks, and a leet court on Lady day

14 *V.C.H. Wilts.* ii, pp. 179–80.
15 Ibid. pp. 116–17.
16 *Caen Chart.* ed. M. Chibnall, 47; *Rot. Hund.* (Rec. Com.), ii (1), 254; below, Tilshead, manors (Tilshead N.); local govt.
17 *V.C.H. Wilts.* viii. 194; below, Tilshead, manors (Tils-head S.); local govt.
18 *Tax List, 1332* (W.R.S. xlv), 76–9; for Rollestone, cf. *Rot. Hund.* (Rec. Com.), ii (1), 254; *Feud. Aids,* v. 243.
19 *V.C.H. Wilts.* xi. 106.
20 *Cal. Chart. R.* 1257–1300, 157–9; *Plac. de Quo Warr.* 806; below, Maddington, manors (Maddington); Tilshead, manors (Tilshead N.).
21 *Rot. Hund.* (Rec. Com.), ii (1), 237.
22 *Plac. de Quo Warr.* 806.
23 Below, Orcheston St. Mary, local govt.
24 Ibid. Berwick St. Jas., manors (Berwick St. Jas.); local govt.
25 *V.C.H. Wilts.* v. 3.
26 *Crown Pleas, 1249* (W.R.S. xvi), pp. 44, 241, 251–3.
27 *Rot. Hund.* (Rec. Com.), ii (1), 238.
28 *V.C.H. Wilts.* iv. 297, 299.
29 *Proc. before the Justices* (Ames Foundation), 385.
30 *Feud. Aids,* v. 242.
31 *W.A.M.* xiii. 114.
32 *V.C.H. Wilts.* iv. 429.
33 *Caen Chart.* 47.
34 *V.C.H. Wilts.* v. 51.
35 *W.A.M.* xiii. 114–15.
36 Below, Little Langford, local govt.; Hanging Langford, local govt.

and at Michaelmas. The meeting place was said to be in Stapleford at a corner made by a hedge,[37] possibly 'Wirdescliff'. No detailed record of the courts survives.

In 1255 Branch hundred was valued at £4 6s. 4d. and from Dole hundred the sheriff received £4 as tithing penny and aid.[38] In 1651 cert money totalling £7 16s. 2d. was paid and fines were said to be worth £20; the duties of steward and bailiff of Branch and Dole hundred were performed by the sheriff and his officers.[39] The hundred had two constables;[40] until 1844 a high constable was appointed to collect the county rate in it.[41]

The histories of most of the parishes in Branch and Dole hundred are given below, but not those of Fisherton Anger parish, given with that of Salisbury,[42] Fugglestone parish and Ditchampton, given with Wilton borough,[43] Gore, given with Market Lavington,[44] and Avon, given with Stratford-sub-Castle,[45] while those of North Burcombe and Elston are reserved for future volumes relating to Cawdon and Cadworth hundred and Heytesbury hundred. Bathampton and Deptford in Heytesbury hundred and Tilshead South in Whorwellsdown hundred are included below in the histories of their respective parishes.

[37] P.R.O., E 317/Wilts. no. 4.
[38] *Rot. Hund.* (Rec. Com.), ii (1), 233, 237.
[39] P.R.O., E 317/Wilts. no. 4.
[40] *Sess. Mins.* (W.R.S. iv), 35, 121.

[41] *V.C.H. Wilts.* v. 234.
[43] Ibid. 1–50.
[44] Ibid. x. 82–106.
[45] Ibid. vi. 199–213.

[42] Ibid. vi. 180–94.

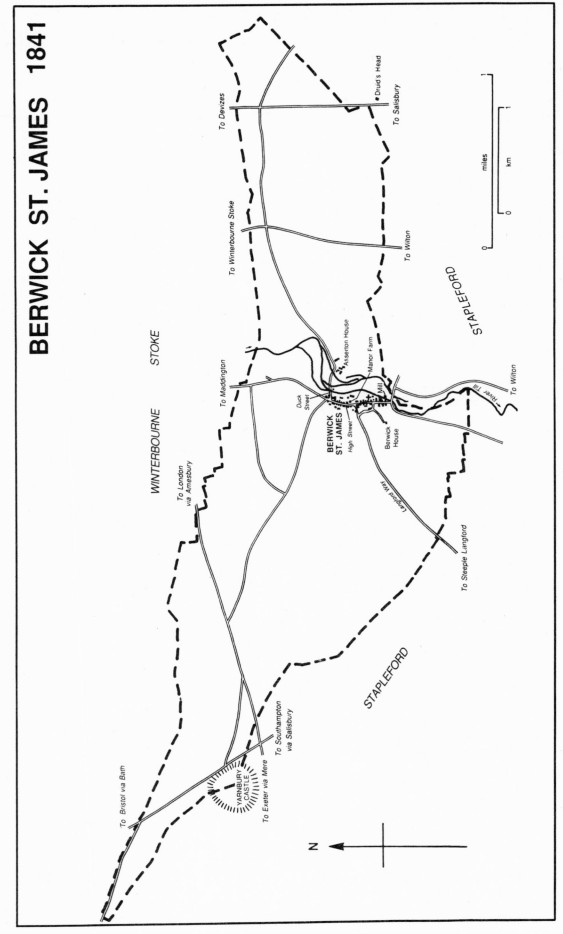

BERWICK ST. JAMES 1841

WINTERBOURNE STOKE

STAPLEFORD

STAPLEFORD

To Devizes

To Salisbury

• Druid's Head

To Winterbourne Stoke

To Wilton

To Maddington

Asserton House

Manor Farm

Mill

Duck Street

BERWICK
ST. JAMES

High Street

Berwick
House

To Wilton

River Till

Langford Way

To London
via Amesbury

To Steeple Langford

To Bristol via Bath

YARNBURY
CASTLE

To Southampton
via Salisbury

To Exeter via Mere

N

miles

km

BERWICK ST. JAMES

BERWICK ST. JAMES village is 8 km. WSW. of Amesbury.[1] It is in an elongated parish, 8.5 km. from east to west, crossed from north to south by the river Till. In the 11th century, when the Till was called the Winterbourne, the estate on the west bank at what was later called Berwick St. James was, like many other estates in the valley, called Winterbourne, but by the late 12th century the village bore its present name and probably had then, as it had later, a parish church.[2] One of two estates said to be in Winterbourne Stoke in 1086[3] was probably that on the east bank said to be Little Winterbourne in the early and mid 13th century,[4] Asserton in 1279.[5] Asserton became part of Berwick St. James parish, and was said to be so in 1609,[6] but it had its own church in the Middle Ages and a recommendation of 1650 that it be wholly united with Berwick St. James suggests that there was then uncertainty about its affiliation.[7] The parish also had a detached part, 33½ a., c. 2.5 km. south of Berwick St. James church:[8] it was transferred to Stapleford in 1884, from when the parish measured 2,497 a. (1,011 ha.).[9]

Boundary mounds divide the parish from Winterbourne Stoke east of the Till; the parish boundary is marked by two short lengths of a prehistoric ditch in the extreme east and crosses a prehistoric settlement site in the west. Elsewhere few natural or man-made features mark the boundary.

Chalk outcrops over the whole parish. Alluvium and gravel have been deposited beside the Till, and gravel lines two valleys running east towards the Till and now dry.[10] The lowest point in the parish is where the Till leaves it at c. 64 m. Westwards the downs rise gradually to reach 166 m. at the westernmost corner; eastwards the land rises more steeply, reaches 144 m. on the watershed of the Till and the Christchurch Avon, and declines gently to 112 m. at the parish boundary. From the Middle Ages land use in the parish followed the pattern usual for Wiltshire chalklands: there were meadows beside the Till and in the detached part of the parish, and open fields lay on the downs between the meadow land and the rough pasture at the east and west ends. The parish had little woodland until the 19th century,[11] in the 13th century the lord of Berwick St. James manor took housebote and haybote from a coppice probably in Grovely forest,[12] and in 1603 the men of Berwick St. James were accustomed to take wood and ferns

from the forest, although their right to do so was denied.[13] Trees were planted in the parish from the mid 19th century, especially in the east part,[14] and in 1979 there were c. 200 a. of woodland.[15]

Langford Way, a road across the downs from Berwick St. James village to Steeple Langford, may have been part of the ancient Harrow way, thought to link Kent and Somerset,[16] but no part of such a road survives in the east half of the parish. The Southampton–Bristol road via Salisbury and Bath crossed the parish's western tip, became less important in the 18th century,[17] and was a track in the late 20th. The Devizes–Salisbury road across the east corner of the parish and a downland road between Amesbury and Mere across the west part were turnpiked in 1761, disturnpiked in 1870 and 1871 respectively.[18] Both remained important in the late 20th century, the Amesbury–Mere road as part of the London–Exeter road, a trunk road from 1958.[19] The road from Maddington and Shrewton to Wilton followed the Till and passed through Berwick St. James village, where it was on its present course in 1773. Where it crossed the river south of the church a new bridge was built after its predecessor was destroyed in a flood in 1841. Near the northern boundary the road forked: the eastern branch, from Winterbourne Stoke village, was a footpath in the late 20th century. A road on higher ground east of the Till also led between Winterbourne Stoke and Wilton in the 18th century, and it remained open across the parish in 1992. In the 18th century a road diverging from Langford Way linked Berwick St. James village with the Mere and Bath roads, but in the late 20th century only parts of it survived as tracks.[20] A military railway was built north–south across the east end of the parish in 1914–15; it had been dismantled by 1923.[21]

Yarnbury castle, on the parish boundary at the west corner, is an Iron-Age hill fort occupied until Romano-British times; north of it lies a barrow and south of it there is a site where Romano-British remains were found. Apart from those features, evidence of early ploughing of both the east and west downland, and the boundary ditch, the parish is not rich in prehistoric remains.[22]

In 1377 Berwick St. James had 80 poll-tax payers, Asserton 27.[23] The population of the parish was 226 in 1801. It had risen to 294 by

[1] This article was written in 1992. Maps used include O.S. Maps 6", Wilts. LIII, LIX–LX (1887–9 and later edns.); 1/25,000, SU 03–04, SU 13–14 (1958 edns.); 1/50,000, sheet 184 (1979 edn.).
[2] P.N. Wilts. (E.P.N.S.), 10, 232–8; below, churches.
[3] V.C.H. Wilts. ii, p. 136.
[4] Cur. Reg. R. ii. 214; Bk. of Fees, ii. 721; below, manors (Asserton).
[5] P.N. Wilts. (E.P.N.S.), 233.
[6] W.R.O., D 1/24/13.
[7] W.A.M. xl. 395; below, churches (St. Mary Magdalene).   [8] W.R.O., tithe award.
[9] Census, 1891.
[10] Geol. Surv. Map 1/50,000, drift, sheet 298 (1976 edn.).
[11] Below, econ. hist.; W.R.O., tithe award.

[12] V.C.H. Wilts. iv. 423, 432.
[13] W.A.M. xxxv. 305.
[14] Below, econ. hist. (Asserton).
[15] O.S. Map 1/50,000, sheet 184 (1979 edn.).
[16] H. W. Timperley and E. Brill, Anct. Trackways of Wessex, 64.
[17] Below, Steeple Langford, intro. [roads].
[18] V.C.H. Wilts. iv. 270; L.J. xxx. 77, 138.
[19] W.R.O., F 4/200/21.
[20] Ibid. A 1/533/39; Andrews and Dury, Map (W.R.S. viii), pl. 5.
[21] N. D. G. James, Plain Soldiering, 198, 203, 206; O.S. Map 6", Wilts. LX. NW. (1926 edn.).
[22] V.C.H. Wilts. i (1), 37–8, 155, 252, 262, 273; i (2), 417.
[23] Ibid. iv. 308.

1851 but fell thereafter, to 191 in 1891 and 133 in 1931. It rose again in the mid and later 20th century and was 153 in 1991.[24]

A benefit society for the parish was founded in 1817. It was to meet weekly and provide relief for any member in need who had contributed for a year. Although it was intended to dissolve the society and to divide its stock between the members after 10 years,[25] it may have continued until the early 20th century.[26]

BERWICK ST. JAMES. The principal buildings of Berwick St. James stand on alluvium rather than the valley gravel, exceptionally for a south Wiltshire village[27] and for no evident reason. The Maddington–Wilton road passes through the village and its earliest line is likely to have been east of the church and through the main farmsteads. In 1773, however, it was on its present course west of the church, on the line between the alluvium and gravel, and formed a village street: east of it and near the river were the church, the mill, and, at right angles to the street, the principal farmhouses; on the west side of it and fronting it a line of buildings was on the gravel.[28] The village street has been given the name High Street; the lane leading to Asserton from the crossroads at the north end has been called Duck Street.

East of High Street two farmyards, a mill, and several houses of 17th-century or earlier origin survived in 1992. North of the church Manor Farm has a back wing of c. 1600, in which a ground-floor room has a six-part ceiling of moulded beams, and a south range built in the early 18th century. South of the church the Dairy House was built in the 17th century as a cottage of two rooms and later much enlarged. Two houses north of Manor Farm, Goodwin House and the Boot inn, are also 17th-century. The Boot, in the angle of High Street and Duck Street, was open in 1848[29] and 1992, and much altered in the 1890s.[30] Also on the east side of High Street a school was built near the church in the mid 19th century.[31]

In 1992 only one cottage west of High Street was older than c. 1800. Near the street's south end Berwick House, a square house of two storeys and tall attics, was built in the early 19th century. Most buildings fronting the street are cottages of the 19th or 20th century. Three pairs, two rendered and one of banded stone and flint, are estate cottages built in 1874.[32] North of them a row of estate cottages and a reading room are of c. 1900.

There was little building in the village be-

tween c. 1900 and 1945. Thereafter most was near the crossroads at the north end. In North Rise, to the west, four council houses were built in 1949 and two in 1962.[33] A pair of cottages north of them was built in 1954,[34] and a few houses and bungalows were built on the east side of the road north of Duck Street. Several houses were also built at the south end of High Street on the west side. West of the village few buildings have been erected on the downs.[35] Farm buildings near the village beside Langford Way, and others west and north-west of them, are mainly of the mid and later 20th century.

ASSERTON. In the Middle Ages Asserton was a hamlet or village[36] presumably on or near the site of Asserton House, but in 1655 was apparently no more than a single farmstead.[37] Asserton House was built in the late 17th century: c. 1830 it was altered, a new west block with a principal west front was built, and a single-storeyed east service court was added. Extensive farm buildings stood nearby c. 1841: most were removed and one was replaced by a pair of cottages when a new Asserton Farm was built on downland 750 m. further east between then and 1886. White Lodge, a thatched house in picturesque style, was built 500 m. north-east of Asserton House in the same period.[38] Beside the parish's northern boundary at the east corner there was a building from 1923 or earlier,[39] two bungalows had been built by 1958,[40] and extensive farm buildings and two more bungalows were built c. 1990.

MANORS AND OTHER ESTATES. In 1066 Edric held what became *BERWICK ST. JAMES* manor, and in 1086 Nubold held it of Ernulf of Hesdin.[41] The manor was later part of the barony of Kempsford (Glos.) and presumably passed with Kempsford before 1096 to Patrick de Chaworth, probably Ernulf's son-in-law, and after 1133 to Patrick's son Patrick (d. by 1155).[42] It was held in 1169 by the younger Patrick's son Pain, also called Pain de Mundubleil,[43] in 1194 by Pain's son Patrick de Chaworth,[44] in 1219 by that Patrick's son Pain[45] (fl. 1236), and in 1242–3 by that Pain's son Patrick,[46] who in 1243 was granted free warren in his demesne at Berwick St. James.[47] In 1258 the manor was assigned as dower to Patrick's relict Hawise[48] and by 1275 had passed to his son Pain,[49] who was succeeded c. 1279 by his brother Patrick (d. by 1283). Patrick's relict Isabel was granted it as dower: the reversion

24 *V.C.H. Wilts.* iv. 340; *Census*, 1991.
25 W.R.O. 130/10, rules of benefit soc. 1818.
26 D. Last et al. *Berwick St. Jas.* (priv. print. 1987), 15.
27 Geol. Surv. Map 1/50,000, drift, sheet 298 (1976 edn.).
28 *Andrews and Dury, Map* (W.R.S. viii), pl. 5; W.R.O., tithe award.
29 *Kelly's Dir. Wilts.* (1848).
30 W.R.O. 130/78, sale cat. 1898.
31 Below, educ.
32 Date on bldgs.
33 W.R.O., G 11/602/2; G 11/603/1.
34 Date on bldg.
35 e.g. O.S. Maps 6", Wilts. LIX (1889 and later edns.); 1/25,000, SU 03–04 (1958 edns.); W.R.O., tithe award.
36 e.g. *Tax List, 1332* (W.R.S. xlv), 78.

37 W.R.O. 1553/72.
38 Ibid. tithe award; O.S. Maps 6", Wilts. LIX–LX (1887–9 edns.).
39 O.S. Map 6", Wilts. LX. NW. (1926 edn.).
40 Ibid. 1/25,000, SU 03 (1958 edn.).
41 *V.C.H. Wilts.* ii, p. 140.
42 *V.C.H. Glos.* vii. 98, on which the following acct. of the Chaworth fam. is based; the descent amplifies and corrects that given in *V.C.H. Wilts.* xiv. 55–6.
43 *Pipe R. 1169* (P.R.S. xiii), 21.
44 Ibid. 1194 (P.R.S. N.S. v), 18.
45 *Cur. Reg. R.* viii. 153.   46 *Bk. of Fees*, ii. 742.
47 *Cal. Pat. 1232–47*, 372.
48 *Close R. 1256–9*, 348.
49 *Rot. Hund.* (Rec. Com.), ii (1), 254.

Perham Down camp in 1910

Perham Down camp 1910 × 1915

Royal Army Ordnance depot in the mid 20th century

NORTH TIDWORTH

Part of the camp in the earlier 20th century

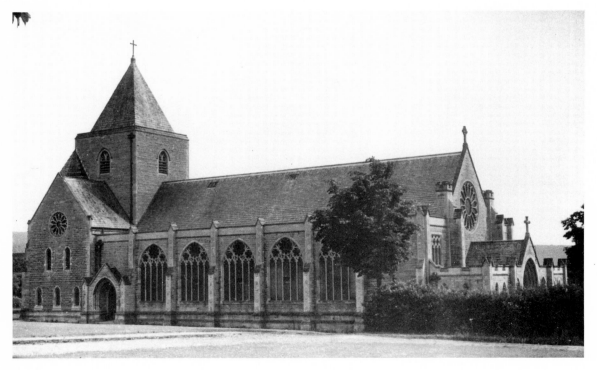

St. George's church

BULFORD: BULFORD CAMP

passed to his daughter Maud[50] (d. *c.* 1322), who married Henry of Lancaster, earl of Leicester from 1324 and of Lancaster from 1326.[51] Henry held the manor in 1307;[52] it passed on his death in 1345 to his and Maud's son Henry, earl of Lancaster (cr. duke of Lancaster 1351),[53] who granted it for life to Sir Robert de la Mare (fl. 1376).[54] On Henry's death in 1361 the reversion was assigned to his daughter Maud, wife of William, duke of Bavaria; on her death in 1362 it passed to her sister Blanche, wife of John of Gaunt, earl of Lancaster (cr. duke of Lancaster 1362, d. 1399).[55] John granted the manor in 1382 to Sir Nicholas Sharnesfield for life.[56] As part of the duchy of Lancaster it passed with the Crown from the accession of John's son as Henry IV in 1399 to 1591 or later.[57]

The manor was acquired by Adam Snow, who died in 1618 leaving an elder son William[58] and a younger son Nicholas. In performance of Adam's nuncupative will William in 1632 conveyed the manor to Nicholas[59] (d. 1639), whose heir was his son Nicholas.[60] By 1680 it had passed to William's daughter Catherine and her husband the Revd. James Crawford.[61] Catherine may have been the Catherine who in 1692 held the manor with her husband the Revd. John Stevens.[62] It passed to Catherine's and James's daughter Mary (d. 1740), wife of the Revd. Edward Wake and later of William Swainton,[63] and to Mary's son William Wake, who sold it to James Harris in 1742.[64] Harris (d. 1780) was succeeded by his son Sir James (cr. Baron Malmesbury 1788, earl of Malmesbury 1800),[65] who sold the manor in 1815 to Alexander Baring[66] (cr. Baron Ashburton 1835, d. 1848). In 1841 Lord Ashburton owned 1,603 a. in the parish. With the barony the manor passed to his sons William (d. 1864) and Francis (d. 1868), to Francis's son Alexander (d. 1889), and to Alexander's son Francis,[67] who sold it in 1896 to E. T. Hooley. In 1898, following Hooley's bankruptcy, Manor farm, *c.* 1,500 a., was bought by Sir Christopher Furness (cr. Baron Furness 1910, d. 1912);[68] in 1915 Furness's son Marmaduke, Lord Furness, sold it to Mary, wife of Cecil Chubb (cr. baronet 1919), and in 1919 Mary sold it to the Board of Agriculture and Fisheries.[69] E. K. Collins bought it in 1921 and sold it in 1945 to Frank Bucknell, whose son Mr. Michael Bucknell owned Manor farm, 612 a., in

1992.[70] In 1954 Mr. George Street bought 820 a., which he owned as Berwick Hill farm in 1992.[71]

Before 1127 Patrick de Chaworth may have granted part of Berwick St. James manor, as he did Great Wishford manor, to his son-in-law Henry Daubeney. In 1258 Henry's great-grandson Henry Daubeney held 1 hide and ½ yardland freely of Berwick St. James manor.[72] That estate, later *BONHAM'S*, passed to the younger Henry's sons Walter (d. by 1273) and Henry (d. *c.* 1278) and thereafter usually with a moiety of Great Wishford manor. From Maurice Bonham (d. 1302), a grandnephew of Henry (d. *c.* 1278), it passed in turn to his sons William (d. by 1316) and Sir John,[73] and in turn to Sir John's sons Robert[74] (fl. 1356) and Nicholas (d. 1386). Nicholas devised it to his son John (d. 1411),[75] and in 1435 it was held by John's nephew Thomas Bonham (d. 1473). It presumably passed to Thomas's son Walter (d. 1476), to Walter's son William (fl. 1514), in turn to William's sons Walter (d. 1527) and Nicholas (d. 1559), and to Nicholas's son John (d. a minor in 1559). John's brother Walter[76] in 1598 conveyed Bonham's to Sir Richard Grobham[77] (d. 1629). Thereafter it descended with Great Wishford manor in the Grobham and Howe families to John Howe, Lord Chedworth (d. 1804),[78] who held 294 a. in Berwick St. James in 1790.[79] The lands were sold by Chedworth's executors in 1806 or 1807 to James, earl of Malmesbury, and reunited with Berwick St. James manor.[80]

Until the Dissolution a chantry at Marnhull (Dors.) owned a messuage and 1½ yardland at Berwick St. James.[81]

ASSERTON manor derived from one of two estates, of 1½ hide and 1 hide, said in 1086 to be in Winterbourne Stoke and then held of Edward of Salisbury by Walter: the smaller estate was held in 1066 by Alwi, possibly as part of an estate of 1½ hide.[82] Overlordship of the manor passed with Shrewton to Edward's descendants, earls of Salisbury, and from the earlier 13th century to the earlier 15th with the overlordship of Shrewton.[83] It was held by Thomas Montagu, earl of Salisbury (d. 1428),[84] but has not been traced further.

Asserton manor was presumably the estate, then said to be in Little Winterbourne, held by Geoffrey of Poulton in 1203 and apparently held

[50] *Cal. Inq. p.m.* ii, p. 288; *Cal. Close, 1279–88*, 217.
[51] *Complete Peerage*, vii. 396–402.
[52] *Wilts. Inq. p.m. 1242–1326* (Index Libr.), 343–4.
[53] *Complete Peerage*, vii. 400–2.
[54] *V.C.H. Wilts.* v. 76.
[55] *Cal. Pat. 1361–4*, 50; *Complete Peerage*, vii. 401–11.
[56] *John of Gaunt's Reg.* ii (Camd. 3rd ser. lvii), p. 320.
[57] R. Somerville, *Duchy of Lanc.* i. 199, 338; P.R.O., DL 42/115, ff. 48–62.
[58] P.R.O., C 142/370, no. 56.   [59] W.R.O. 492/1.
[60] *Wilts. Inq. p.m. 1625–49* (Index Libr.), 276.
[61] Hoare, *Mod. Wilts.* Branch and Dole, 28; W.R.O. 130/10, deed, Crawford to Crawford, 1680.
[62] P.R.O., CP 25/2/888/4 Wm. and Mary Trin.
[63] Hoare, *Mod. Wilts.* Branch and Dole, 28.
[64] *Par. Reg. Wylye*, ed. G. R. Hadow, 77; W.R.O. 212B/188; 212B/190.   [65] *Complete Peerage*, viii. 358–60.
[66] W.R.O. 212B/212.
[67] Ibid. tithe award; *Complete Peerage*, i. 277–8.
[68] Burke, *Peerage* (1931), 1011; W.R.O. 130/78, sale cat. 1898; Ch. Com. file, F 382.

[69] Burke, *Peerage* (1931), 542, 1011; *W.A.M.* xxxix. 394; Ch. Com. file 40354/2.
[70] Inf. from Mr. M. Bucknell, Manor Farm.
[71] Inf. from Mr. G. Street, Dairy Ho.
[72] *Wilts. Inq. p.m. 1242–1326* (Index Libr.), 25; below, Great Wishford, manor.
[73] G. J. Kidston, *Bonhams of Wilts. and Essex*, 7, facing p. 9; *Cal. Inq. p.m.* ii, p. 156; below, Great Wishford, manor.
[74] *Feet of F. 1327–77* (W.R.S. xxix), p. 87.
[75] Kidston, *Bonhams*, facing p. 9, 25.
[76] Ibid. facing p. 9, 44, 46–7; *Cal. Close, 1435–41*, 36; for the date 1476, P.R.O., C 140/58, no. 69.
[77] B.L. Add. Ch. 15114.
[78] Below, Great Wishford, manor.
[79] W.R.O., EA/50.
[80] Ibid. 317/12; *W.A.M.* xxv. 311.
[81] *Cal. Pat. 1548–9*, 305, 308.
[82] *V.C.H. Wilts.* ii, p. 136; below, Winterbourne Stoke, intro.; manors (Winterbourne Mautravers).
[83] Below, Shrewton, manors.
[84] *Cal. Fine R. 1413–22*, 97.

previously by his brother William.[85] In 1242–3 the manor was held by William son of Walter,[86] probably William Waleran whose son Robert died seised of it in 1273. It was assigned to Robert's relict Maud as dower, may have passed to his nephew Robert Waleran (d. by 1299), an idiot, and in 1299 was held by the Crown for the younger Robert's brother John, also an idiot.[87] John's mother Isabel was also said to have held the manor at her death in 1284, by what right is not known. John was dead by 1309, and in 1310, when it was called Asserton, the manor was assigned to Joan, wife of (Sir) Alexander de Freville (d. by 1328), her grandniece and a coheir of her and John.[88] Joan (d. by 1339) conveyed it to Henry Willington (d. 1349) and his wife Isabel (d. after 1349). It passed to the Willingtons' son Sir John[89] (d. 1384)[90] and in turn to Sir John's sons Ralph, who died a minor, and John, who died a minor and insane in 1397.[91] After John's death Asserton manor was assigned to his sister Isabel, wife of William Beaumont.[92] From Isabel (d. 1424) it descended to her son Sir Thomas Beaumont[93] (d. 1450) and to Sir Thomas's son William[94] (d. 1453). It probably passed with Brompton Ralph manor (Som.) to William's brother Philip (d. 1473) and to Philip's half-brother Thomas Beaumont.[95] Thomas (d. 1488) was succeeded by his brother Hugh,[96] who held Asserton manor in 1501. John Basset (later knighted), nephew of Philip Beaumont, also had an interest in the manor in 1501:[97] he was acknowledged as Hugh's heir and in 1504 the manor was settled on Giles Daubeney, Lord Daubeney (d. 1508), whose son Henry was betrothed to Basset's daughter.[98] Although no marriage took place Henry, Lord Daubeney (cr. earl of Bridgwater 1538, d. 1548), acquired the manor and in 1547 conveyed it to Edward Seymour, duke of Somerset.[99] On Somerset's attainder in 1552[1] it passed to the Crown. It was granted in 1565 to (Sir) Arthur Basset (d. 1586), grandson of Sir John Basset, and passed to his son Sir Robert (fl. 1626)[2] and to Sir Robert's son Arthur (d. 1672), whose estates were sequestered in 1646, restored in 1650, and sequestered again and restored in 1654. Arthur was succeeded by his grandson John Basset (d. 1686) and he by his

son John (d. 1721).[3] Another John Basset held the manor in 1736,[4] and it was sold in 1773, perhaps by trustees of the Basset family, to Henry Biggs[5] (d. 1800). As Asserton farm, 824 a. in 1841, it passed to Henry's son Harry (d. 1856).[6] It was offered for sale under Harry's will in 1861,[7] and in 1864 was bought by E. C. Pinckney[8] (d. 1899).[9] It was acquired by Sir Christopher Furness, presumably from Pinckney's executors, was offered for sale by him in 1909, and may have been bought by F. B. Beauchamp.[10] In 1910 it was part of A. P. Cunliffe's Druid's Lodge estate based in Stapleford.[11] Cunliffe sold Asserton farm, 518 a., in 1912[12] to D. H. S. Awdry (fl. 1915).[13] It was later reunited with the Druid's Lodge estate, was held by J. V. Rank at his death in 1952, and thereafter passed as part of the estate to the Fenston Trust and in 1989 to Mr. R. A. Hurst, the owner in 1992.[14]

A manor house of Asserton was standing in the 14th century.[15]

Berwick St. James church was appropriated in 1406 or 1407 by Mottisfont priory (Hants).[16] At the Dissolution the *RECTORY* estate, of land and tithes, passed to the Crown, and in 1536 it was granted to William Sandys, Lord Sandys[17] (d. 1540). It passed with the title to William's son Thomas (d. 1560), Thomas's grandson William Sandys (d. 1623), and that William's son William (d. *s.p.* 1629), whose nephew Henry Sandys held it in 1631. Henry was killed in 1644 while fighting in the Royalist cause, and his estates were apparently confiscated.[18] In 1650 the Rectory belonged to Simon Spatchurst[19] who sold it to John Duke in 1659.[20] Duke (d. 1671) settled it in 1662 on his son John, whose son George sold it in 1699 to Thomas Kellow[21] (d. by 1736).[22] In 1737 it was bought by Edward Hearst[23] (d. 1767). Edward was succeeded by his daughter Caroline, who in 1768 married H. P. Wyndham,[24] and in 1790 the Wyndhams sold the estate. The Berwick St. James part of it, great tithes from, and 48 a. with pasture rights in, that part of the parish, was bought by James, Lord Malmesbury: it passed with Berwick St. James manor to Alexander, Lord Ashburton, who in 1841 merged the tithes on 1,327 a. and

85 *Cur. Reg. R.* ii. 214.
86 *Bk. of Fees,* ii. 721.
87 *Cal. Close,* 1272–9, 67; *Cal. Inq. p.m.* v, pp. 70–8; *Cal. Pat.* 1292–1301, 397; above, Durnford, manors (Salterton).
88 *Wilts. Inq. p.m.* 1242–1326 (Index Libr.), 355–7, 368–71; *Cal. Inq. p.m.* v, pp. 70–8, 125; vii, p. 110; *Reg. Martival* (Cant. & York Soc.), i. 238.
89 *Cal. Inq. p.m.* viii, pp. 158–9; ix, pp. 195–6.
90 Ibid. xv, p. 61.
91 Ibid. xvii, p. 344.
92 *Cal. Close,* 1396–9, 170–1.
93 P.R.O., C 139/11, no. 28.
94 Ibid. C 139/143, no. 30.
95 *V.C.H. Som.* v. 20.
96 *Cal. Inq. p.m. Hen. VII,* i, p. 179.
97 *Feet of F. 1377–1509* (W.R.S. xli), pp. 171–2.
98 *V.C.H. Som.* v. 20; P.R.O., C 142/25, no. 5.
99 *Complete Peerage,* iv. 105; P.R.O., CP 25/2/66/545, no. 26.
1 *Complete Peerage,* xii (1), 63–4.
2 *Cal. Pat.* 1563–6, pp. 202–3; *V.C.H. Som.* v. 20; P.R.O., C 142/209, no. 21; ibid. E 126/3, f. 107v.
3 Burke, *Land. Gent.* (1846), i. 65; *Cal. Cttee. for Compounding,* ii. 1878–9.
4 P.R.O., CP 25/2/1233/10 Geo. II Hil. no. 697.

5 Ibid. CP 25/2/1446/13 Geo. III Mich. no. 720; Hoare, *Mod. Wilts.* Branch and Dole, 31.
6 Burke, *Land. Gent.* (1937), 157; W.R.O., tithe award.
7 W.R.O. 384/4, partic. of estates, 1861.
8 Last, *Berwick St. Jas.* 9.
9 Burke, *Land. Gent.* (1937), 1813.
10 W.A.S. Libr., sale cat. ix, no. 15.
11 W.R.O., Inland Revenue, val. reg. 145; below, Stapleford, manor (Druid's Lodge).
12 W.R.O. 776/368.
13 *Kelly's Dir. Wilts.* (1915).
14 Inf. from the manager, Druid's Lodge, Woodford; below, Stapleford, manor (Druid's Lodge).
15 *Cal. Inq. p.m.* xvii, p. 48.
16 *Cal. Papal Reg.* vi. 200; *Cal. Pat.* 1405–8, 176.
17 *L. & P. Hen. VIII,* xi, p. 87.
18 *Complete Peerage,* xi. 441–7; P.R.O., CP 25/2/509/7 Chas. I Mich.
19 *W.A.M.* xl. 395.
20 W.R.O. 212B/163.
21 Ibid. 212B/164; 212B/172–3; Burke, *Commoners* (1833–8), i. 285–6.
22 *L.J.* xxv. 15, 90.
23 W.R.O. 212B/185.
24 Ibid. 212B/195; *V.C.H. Wilts.* vi. 145.

was allotted a rent charge of £10 for those on *c.* 45 a. The Asserton part of the estate, *c.* 18 a. with pasture rights, the great tithes from 226 a., and half of the great tithes from 407 a., was bought by Henry Biggs in 1790: it passed with Asserton manor to Harry Biggs who in 1841 merged the tithes.[25]

The abbess of Wilton *c.* 1191 claimed 15 a. of corn each year from the demesne of Berwick St. James manor for South Newton prebend in the conventual church,[26] possibly representing an estate of tithes. In 1291 a pension of 10s. was due to the prebendary from the rector,[27] who may have held the tithes. Later, after the rectory was appropriated, the prebendary may again have taken great tithes from the Berwick St. James part of the parish. Such tithes were owned by Wilton abbey, which appropriated the prebend in 1450,[28] and with the abbey's other estates were granted in 1544 to Sir William Herbert[29] (cr. earl of Pembroke 1551) and passed with the earldom.[30] In 1841 they arose from 203 a., were valued at £50, and were commuted.[31]

The endowment in Asserton of Asserton chapel, *c.* 14 a. and tithes from the demesne of Asserton manor, was held by the Crown from *c.* 1547[32] to 1607, when it was granted to Sir Roger Aston and John Grimsditch.[33] In 1614 Grimsditch sold it to Thomas Atkins, who conveyed it in 1615 to Sir Richard Grobham (d. 1629).[34] With Bonham's and Great Wishford manor it passed to Sir Richard Howe, Bt. (d. 1730),[35] who devised the tithes to a school at Great Wishford.[36] In the early 18th century the tithes were said to be from five twelfths of Asserton manor.[37] In 1805 the estate consisted of great tithes from Asserton, all those from 200 a. and half those from 407 a.[38] The school was allotted a rent charge of £72 10s. when the tithes were commuted in 1841.[39]

ECONOMIC HISTORY. BERWICK ST. JAMES.

In 1086 the estate, of 1 hide and 2½ yardlands, which became Berwick St. James manor had on it only 1 ploughteam and 2 *servi*; it had 8 a. of pasture.[40] Berwick's lands were later extensive, *c.* 1,650 a. in 1841,[41] and it is not clear why no more demesne and no customary land was mentioned in 1086.

In 1258 the manor had 96 a. of demesne in a north field, 99 a. in a south field: the two fields were probably open, also containing land of freeholders and customary tenants, and were possibly the only two of Berwick St. James. The downland, on which 300 demesne sheep could be kept, was almost certainly used in common, and there was a common pasture for 80 beasts of which 32 belonged to the demesne. There were also cattle pastures called Kyggersmers and Sterce, used in common for 16 beasts of the demesne and 24 of the freeholds. A total of 1 hide and 1½ yardland was in three freeholds; there were only five customary tenants, each of whom held ½ yardland; four servants on the manor held ¼ yardland each. The demesne was then or formerly cultivated partly by customary works.[42] Later evidence shows the rector to have held 3 yardlands.[43]

By 1283 the amount of demesne arable had been increased to 300 a., and the number of customary tenants to 22 and their holdings to 8½ yardlands. The customary tenants also held 'acreland'. It is likely that the increases were the result of new land being brought into cultivation. There were only 124 a. of demesne arable in 1307, when 18 ½-yardlanders held customarily.[44] In the 15th century the demesne included a several sheep pasture called Worham: the demesne flock numbered 301 in 1435, 418 in 1441, and 260 in 1449. Approximately a third of the flock was sold yearly in the mid 15th century.[45]

By the early 17th century each of the two open fields had apparently been divided into an in- and an out-field, and a separate demesne field may have been created. The demesne had its own downland sheep pasture in the late 16th century, when the common Cow down was on the south part of the downland.[46] The 8½ customary yardlands were held by 15 tenants in 1591.[47] Sheep stints were generous, to judge from the Rectory estate, which in the Berwick St. James part of the parish had 48 a. of arable and feeding for 200 sheep in 1609.[48] In 1591 the lands of the manor were said to be not very fertile but reasonably apt for corn and with reasonably good sheep pasture. There was said to be a shortage of meadow even though the detached part of the parish was meadow and in Berwick St. James manor. There were *c.* 850 a. of upland pasture.[49]

In 1735 an agreement was made for watering meadows south of the village.[50] Other water meadows lay north of the village in 1790.[51] In 1841 Berwick St. James had *c.* 30 a. of water meadows,[52] in 1898 *c.* 40 a.[53] Watering of the meadows ceased in the mid 20th century.[54]

25 W.R.O. 212B/199–202; ibid. tithe award; ibid. D 1/24/13.   26 *Sar. Chart. and Doc.* (Rolls Ser.), 52.
27 *Tax. Eccl.* (Rec. Com.), 181.
28 P.R.O., SC 6/Hen. VIII/3985, rot. 15; W.R.O., D 1/2/10, ff. (2nd foliation) 65–6.
29 *L. & P. Hen. VIII*, xix (1), p. 38.
30 *Complete Peerage*, x. 405–28.
31 W.R.O., tithe award.
32 P.R.O., E 301/58, no. 75; below, church (St. Mary Magdalene).
33 W.R.O. 753/1, f. 168v.
34 P.R.O., E 126/3, f. 107v.
35 Above, this section; below, Great Wishford, manor.
36 *Endowed Char. Wilts.* (S. Div.), 909–10; below, Great Wishford, educ.
37 P.R.O., E 134/13 Wm. III East./2.
38 *Endowed Char. Wilts.* (S. Div.), 909–10.

39 W.R.O., tithe award.
40 *V.C.H. Wilts.* ii, p. 140.
41 W.R.O., tithe award.
42 *Wilts. Inq. p.m. 1242–1326* (Index Libr.), 24–5.
43 *Inq. Non.* (Rec. Com.), 179.
44 *Wilts. Inq. p.m. 1242–1326* (Index Libr.), 146–7, 344.
45 P.R.O., DL 29/683/11068; DL 29/684/11078; DL 29/685/11098.
46 *W.A.M.* vi. 196; W.R.O., D 1/24/13.
47 P.R.O., DL 42/115, ff. 59v.–61v.
48 W.R.O., D 1/24/13.
49 Ibid. tithe award; *W.A.M.* vi. 196.
50 W.R.O. 317/3.
51 Ibid. EA/50.
52 Ibid. tithe award.
53 Ibid. 130/78, sale cat. 1898.
54 Wilts. Cuttings, xxi. 209.

The open fields and much of the downland, a total of *c.* 1,300 a., were inclosed in 1790 under an Act of 1789. On the 169 a. of downland which remained open eight holdings included rights to graze sheep in a flock for which a single shepherd was appointed; six allottees continued to feed cattle in common on 6 a. of meadow between 12 May and 12 December.[55] Common grazing of the meadow but not of the downs was apparently still practised in 1841.[56]

In 1806 Berwick farm, derived from the demesne, comprised 539 a. The farm derived from Bonham's was then of over 300 a. and included 166 a. of arable, 98 a. of pasture, and 8 a. of water meadow; 29 a. of the arable were burnbaked. There were also farms of 230 a. and 220 a., and two totalling *c.* 70 a.[57] In 1815 Berwick farm included 106 a. of newly broken arable.[58] In 1841 all the land was in a single farm, with its principal buildings in the street. More of the downland pasture had been ploughed, and some of the former open fields was pasture. There were 216 a. of old arable, 166 a. of lowland pasture, and *c.* 100 a. of meadow including the detached part of the parish.[59] The lands remained in one farm, still worked from the village, in the earlier 20th century.[60] In 1954 they were divided into Manor farm and Berwick Hill farm,[61] for both of which farmyards in the street were still used in 1992. Between 1954 and 1992 on Berwick Hill farm, *c.* 820 a., cereals and peas were grown and a herd of 150 suckler cattle was kept.[62] In 1992 Manor, 612 a., was a mixed farm on which cereals, peas, and rape were grown and sheep and pigs were kept.[63] From 1898 or earlier 225 a., the westernmost part of the downland, were in farms based in Steeple Langford.[64] In the 1950s poultry houses were built west of the village by Geoffrey Sykes, an early exponent of intensive poultry farming.[65] Much of the business was later transferred to Winterbourne Stoke.[66]

The mill held freely of Berwick St. James manor in 1258 was possibly the windmill so held in 1307.[67] There was a water mill at Berwick St. James in 1591 when a complaint was made against the lord of Winterbourne Stoke whose newly built mill, presumably that rebuilt between 1546 and 1574, was said to reduce both the flow of water to Berwick mill and its trade.[68] In 1773 the mill was on the Till near the bridge at the south end of the street;[69] the mill house may have been repaired or rebuilt in 1785.[70] The mill was replaced in the mid 19th century by Bean Mill 100 m. upstream.[71] Bean Mill is of flint and clunch with red-brick dressings; after

1921, when grinding presumably ceased, its machinery, including a cast-iron undershot wheel, was used to provide electricity for Berwick House and to pump water from a bore hole.[72]

ASSERTON. There was 1 ploughteam at Asserton in 1086.[73] Asserton later had *c.* 850 a.,[74] and, as in the case of Berwick St. James, it is not clear why no more cultivated land was mentioned in 1086.

In 1309 Asserton had north and south open fields: they were said to comprise *c.* 530 a., but later there was less arable and that figure may have been an exaggeration. There was downland used in common for *c.* 1,000 sheep. Those lands included the demesne of Asserton manor, the holdings of the free and customary tenants of the manor, and glebe of the rector of Berwick St. James. The demesne was said to have 321 a. or 351 a. of arable, pasture rights for 250 sheep, a pasture close of 3 a., and 3 a. of pasture in severalty for part of the year. Customary tenants included 7 yardlanders, each said to hold 24 a. with grazing rights for 65 sheep, 3 ½-yardlanders, each said to hold 12 a. with rights for 32 sheep, and 5 cottagers. The yardlanders had to carry dung, harrow, carry corn to Salisbury, Wilton, and Amesbury, wash and shear sheep, and mow, cut, and carry hay. They were to do five works weekly between 29 August and 29 September and for four weeks in autumn. The ½-yardlanders and cottagers had proportionately smaller obligations. For each beast which the yardlanders and ½-yardlanders fed on the demesne after harvest they were to plough 1 a. The rector had rights for 65 sheep, as did each of two free tenants. The only meadow land of the manor was apparently 9½ a. in Great Wishford.[75]

In the mid 17th century North field was 107 a., South field 111 a., and a third field was 127 a. on higher ground to the east. South field was in two parts, divided by Little down, 75 a. To the east Great down was 313 a. There were then 9 a. of meadow beside the Till west of North field,[76] and the first cut of hay from Asserton meadow, 12 a., in Great Wishford belonged to men of Asserton then[77] and in the early 20th century.[78] There were also 20 a. of closes of pasture in the mid 17th century. By then the demesne of Asserton had absorbed three or more former copyholds or freeholds. The Rectory estate included *c.* 18 a. of arable and feeding for 60 sheep, but in 1655 nearly all Asserton's lands were in a single farm and the only farmstead was

55 W.R.O., EA/50.
56 Ibid. tithe award.
57 Ibid. 212B/207; 317/12.
58 Ibid. 212B/212.
59 Ibid. tithe award.
60 Ibid. 130/78, sale cat. 1898; ibid. Inland Revenue, val. reg. 145.
61 Above, manors (Berwick St. Jas.).
62 Inf. from Mr. G. Street, Dairy Ho.
63 Inf. from Mr. M. Bucknell, Manor Farm.
64 Below, Steeple Langford, econ. hist.; Bathampton, econ. hist.
65 Wilts. Cuttings, xxi. 209–10.
66 Below, Winterbourne Stoke, econ. hist.
67 *Wilts. Inq. p.m. 1242–1326* (Index Libr.), 25, 344.

68 P.R.O., DL 42/115, f. 61v.; below, Winterbourne Stoke, econ. hist. (mills).
69 *Andrews and Dury, Map* (W.R.S. viii), pl. 5.
70 Date on ho.
71 W.R.O., tithe award; O.S. Map 6", Wilts. LIX (1889 edn.).
72 Last, *Berwick St. Jas.* 12.
73 *V.C.H. Wilts.* ii, p. 136.
74 W.R.O., tithe award.
75 *Wilts. Inq. p.m. 1242–1326* (Index Libr.), 362–3, 368–71. 76 W.R.O. 1553/72.
77 Ibid. 753/1, f. 1v.; *Wilts. Inq. p.m. 1625–49* (Index Libr.), 243; for the area of the meadow, *Endowed Char. Wilts.* (S. Div.), 909.
78 W.R.O. 776/368.

that on the demesne: two smaller holdings were possibly worked from Berwick St. James village in 1655.[79] In the 1690s one of the smaller holdings and the lands of the Rectory estate were added to the principal farm, later called Asserton farm. About 1690 the farmer had c. 1,200 sheep. After 1695, however, part of the down was ploughed, and 75 a. of it were sown with corn in 1699.[80]

In 1805 Asserton farm was 846 a.,[81] and in 1841 it included c. 450 a. of arable, c. 350 a. of pasture, and c. 20 a. of water meadow. Asserton Farm was built on the downs in the mid 19th century,[82] probably soon after 1864 when E. C. Pinckney bought the land. Pinckney planted much woodland, including 1,000 beech trees a year, principally between Asserton House and Asserton Farm; in the east corner of the parish 63 a. largely bounded by plantations were laid out as a park between 1880 and 1909, presumably before Pinckney's death in 1899. In 1909 the farm included 265 a. of arable, 320 a. of pasture, and 21 a. of water meadow.[83] In 1912 the farm was only 518 a.,[84] and what was formerly the east part of it was presumably managed with lands in adjacent parishes. In the later 20th century Asserton's land was part of a large farm, extending into several parishes, based at Druid's Head Farm in Stapleford. In 1992 it was used for mixed farming, partly from the extensive new buildings in the parish.[85]

A water mill was part of Asserton manor in 1309.[86]

LOCAL GOVERNMENT. Berwick St. James and Asserton were distinct tithings in the 14th and 15th centuries,[87] but there is no evidence that they were later.

In 1591 Berwick St. James manor was said to be held with waifs, strays, felons' goods, and other liberties.[88] Records survive of a court and view of frankpledge for the manor held together thrice in 1542 and once in 1543. The tithingman paid cert money and presented strays and breaches of assize. A jury was sworn, found on the tithingman's presentments, and presented breaches of the peace and games played illegally. The homage presented defaulters from the court and misuse of common pastures, and orders were published for common grazing and against unlicensed subletting of tenements. There was

little tenurial business.[89] A court of survey was held in 1591.[90]

The parish spent £59 on poor relief in 1776, c. £58 in 1785; £260 was spent in 1803, when the poor-rate was about the average for the hundred, and 30 adults and 46 children received relief regularly and 12 people occasionally.[91] Expenditure rose from £179 in 1816 to a peak of £330 in 1818. In the 1820s it fluctuated: in 1823 it was £116, in 1826 £312. It fell from 1829, and was only £86 in 1834.[92] The parish became part of Wilton poor-law union in 1836,[93] and of Salisbury district in 1974.[94]

CHURCHES. Berwick St. James church was standing in the mid 12th century.[95] It was served by a rector until it was appropriated by Mottisfont priory in 1406 or 1407. The appropriation was conditional upon the ordination of a vicarage,[96] and there was a vicar in 1422.[97] In 1924 the vicarage was united with that of Stapleford;[98] in 1992 the united benefice became part of Lower Wylye and Till Valley benefice, served by a rector.[99]

The advowson of the rectory was held for life by Maud de Cauntelo (fl. 1258), apparently by grant from a lord of Berwick St. James manor.[1] It was held with the manor by Patrick de Chaworth (d. by 1283),[2] and as dower by his relict Isabel.[3] By 1299 it had been acquired by Mottisfont priory,[4] and the prior presented rectors. In 1311 a presentation by an excommunicate prior was set aside and the bishop of Salisbury collated.[6] In 1291 the rectory was valued at £10, about the average for a living in Wylye deanery.[7] The rector was apparently entitled to all tithes from most of the parish[8] In 1341 the glebe included pasture worth 40s. and 3 yardlands.[9]

The advowson of the vicarage belonged to Mottisfont priory, and priors presented at all but two vacancies before the Dissolution: in 1468 the abbess of Shaftesbury (Dors.) presented, by what right is not known, and in 1516 John Claymond, executor of James Zouche, presented by grant of a turn.[10] The advowson passed with the Rectory estate, the Crown granting it in 1536 to William, Lord Sandys.[11] The bishop presented by lapse in 1566, the king did so in 1612,[12] and there may have been doubt about who was patron 1644–59.[13] Between 1671 and 1730 no

79 Ibid. 1553/72; ibid. D 1/24/13; P.R.O., C 2/Eliz. I/G 5/56.
80 P.R.O., E 126/17, f. 218v.; E 134/13 Wm. III East./2.
81 Endowed Char. Wilts. (S. Div.), 909.
82 O.S. Map 6", Wilts. LX (1887 edn.); W.R.O., tithe award.
83 Last, Berwick St. Jas. 9; O.S. Map 6", Wilts. LX (1887 edn.); W.A.S. Libr., sale cat. ix, no. 15; above, manors (Asserton). 84 W.R.O. 776/368.
85 Inf. from the manager, Druid's Lodge, Woodford.
86 Wilts. Inq. p.m. 1242–1326 (Index Libr.), 369.
87 Tax List, 1332 (W.R.S. xlv), 78; V.C.H. Wilts. iv. 299, 308; W.A.M. xiii. 115. 88 W.A.M. vi. 196.
89 P.R.O., DL 30/127/1902.
90 Ibid. DL 42/115, f. 58.
91 Poor Law Abstract, 1804, 558–9.
92 Poor Rate Returns, 1816–21, 186; 1822–4, 225; 1825–9, 215; 1830–4, 209.
93 Poor Law Com. 2nd Rep. App. D, 560.
94 O.S. Map 1/100,000, admin. areas, Wilts. (1974 edn.).

95 Below, this section [architecture].
96 Cal. Pat. 1405–8, 176.
97 Phillipps, Wilts. Inst. i. 112.
98 Lond. Gaz. 9 Dec. 1924, pp. 8972–3.
99 Inf. from the rector, Great Wishford.
1 Cal. Inq. p.m. i, p. 114.
2 Ibid. ii, p. 288.
3 Cal. Close, 1279–88, 252.
4 Reg. Ghent (Cant. & York Soc.), ii. 587.
5 Phillipps, Wilts. Inst. i. 6–7, 28, 30, 49.
6 Reg. Ghent (Cant. & York Soc.), ii. 772–3.
7 Tax. Eccl. (Rec. Com.), 181.
8 Above, manors (Rectory); for the exceptions, above, manors; below, this section (St. Mary Magdalene).
9 Inq. Non. (Rec. Com.), 179.
10 Phillipps, Wilts. Inst. i. 112, 131, 134, 140, 145, 157, 192, 194–6.
11 Above, manors (Rectory).
12 Phillipps, Wilts. Inst. i. 222; ii. 7.
13 W.A.M. xl. 395; cf. above, manors (Rectory).

owner of the advowson presented. Avice Duke presented in 1671, Edward Hearst in 1682 and 1683 probably by grant, the king in 1728 by lapse, and Anthony Kellow in 1730 probably by grant.[14] With the Rectory estate and Berwick St. James manor the advowson passed to Mary, Lady Chubb.[15] In 1919 she conveyed it to St. George's chapel, Windsor, patron of the united benefice from 1924[16] and entitled to present at every third vacancy from 1992.[17]

In 1535 the vicar's income, £8 5s. 8d., was well below the average for the deanery.[18] Although augmentations of £200 from the patron and £300 from Queen Anne's Bounty were received in 1810,[19] the living remained poor, valued at only £54 c. 1830.[20] The vicar received a stipend from the owner of the Rectory estate and some small tithes:[21] in 1841 the tithes were valued at £30 11s. and commuted. The glebe may have comprised only the churchyard and the site of a house until c. 1813 when 14 a. in the parish were bought:[22] that land was sold in 1922.[23] The vicarage house, described as unfit for residence c. 1830,[24] stood on the east side of the village street near the church.[25] It was let as a labourer's cottage in 1865[26] and was demolished in 1900.[27]

A rent of 20s. was paid for a lamp in the church until the Dissolution.[28] Roger Powell signed the *Concurrent Testimony* as minister of Berwick St. James in 1648,[29] and in 1650 was said to preach twice every Sunday.[30] In 1680 two parishioners were presented for not receiving communion at Easter: one claimed that he was prevented from doing so by a suit brought against him by the vicar, Anthony Sadler, who was also said to have failed to give due notice of a meeting to elect churchwardens.[31] From the late 18th century no incumbent is known to have lived in the parish, and it was usual to have only one service there each Sunday. In 1783 the curate who served both Berwick St. James and Stapleford lived in Salisbury;[32] in 1805 the vicar lived at Fisherton Anger,[33] between 1817 and 1879 the vicars were also incumbents of and lived at Winterbourne Stoke, and between 1879 and 1924 they were also vicars of and lived at Stapleford.[34] A morning or afternoon service was held every Sunday in 1783. Communion was celebrated at Christmas, Easter, and Whitsun: there were usually 16 Easter communicants. The curate's custom of catechizing and of preparing children and servants for confirmation[35] apparently bore fruit in 1787 when there were 51 candidates for confirmation, a very high figure for such a parish.[36] In 1851 a service on the afternoon of Census Sunday was attended by 164 people.[37] Services were held each Sunday afternoon in

1864 and there were additional services in Lent and on Christmas day; communion was celebrated at the principal festivals and on one other Sunday with c. 20 communicants.[38]

The church of *ST. JAMES*, apparently so called c. 1191,[39] is built of flint rubble, chequered flint and freestone, and ashlar. It has a chancel, a clerestoried nave with north and south chapels and north porch, and a west tower. The nave is of the mid 12th century: on the inside the north doorway has an order of chevrons on the arch

THE NORTH DOORWAY OF THE CHURCH

and a lintel decorated with diaper carving. In the early 13th century a north chapel was built; in the later 13th century the chancel was rebuilt, probably longer than before, and a tower was built; in the 14th a new window was made in the west part of the nave's south wall. The north chapel was rebuilt, apparently in the 15th century and probably to incorporate a rood stair at its southeast corner; the porch, clerestory, and south chapel were built probably in the early 16th century. The tower was rebuilt in 1651.[40] A stone pulpit of the 15th century against the north wall of the nave was entered by a stair from the north chapel: it was moved to the south side of the chancel arch after 1825.[41]

14 Phillipps, *Wilts. Inst.* ii. 31, 38–9, 61–2.
15 Above, manors (Berwick St. Jas.).
16 Ch. Com. file 40354/2.
17 Inf. from the rector.
18 *Valor Eccl.* (Rec. Com.), ii. 104.
19 C. Hodgson, *Queen Anne's Bounty* (1864), p. cccxxxv.
20 *Rep. Com. Eccl. Revenues*, 824–5.
21 *W.A.M.* xl. 395; Ch. Com. file, F 382.
22 W.R.O., tithe award; ibid. 212B/211.
23 Ch. Com. deed, D 2582.
24 *Rep. Com. Eccl. Revenues*, 824–5.
25 W.R.O., tithe award.   26 Ch. Com. file 40354/1.
27 J. P. Adams, *Berwick St. Jas. and its Associations* (priv. print. 1981), 8.   28 *W.A.M.* xii. 382.

29 *Calamy Revised*, ed. Matthews, 557.
30 *W.A.M.* xl. 395.
31 W.R.O., D 1/39/2/13, f. 130v.
32 *Vis. Queries, 1783* (W.R.S. xxvii), p. 32.
33 Ch. Com. file, F 382.
34 Ibid. 40354/1–2.
35 *Vis. Queries, 1783* (W.R.S. xxvii), p. 32.
36 *V.C.H. Wilts.* iii. 52.
37 P.R.O., HO 129/265/1/7/16.
38 W.R.O., D 1/56/7.
39 *Sar. Chart. and Doc.* (Rolls Ser.), 52.
40 Date on bldg.
41 Adams, *Berwick St. Jas.* 5; Hoare, *Mod. Wilts.* Branch and Dole, 27.

A chalice of c. 1200[42] and a paten of c. 1500 remained in use in the parish until given in 1879 to the British Museum. In 1553 plate weighing 4 oz. was confiscated. A flagon, given in 1739, and a chalice and paten, given in 1879, belonged to the parish in 1992.[43]

In 1553 there were three bells. One of 1683 and one of 1687, both cast by Clement Tosier, one of 1727 by William Tosier, and one of 1748 by William Cockey hung in the church in 1992: only that of 1748 was usable. A bell of the late 17th century or the early 18th was sold in 1835.[44]

Registers of burials survive from 1731, of baptisms and of marriages from 1746.[45]

The church of Little Winterbourne recorded in 1291[46] was evidently the chapel of *ST. MARY MAGDALENE* at Asserton mentioned in 1349 and 1599.[47] The chapel had a rector in the 13th century,[48] but from 1299 or earlier it was served by chaplains, who were presented to the bishop for institution.[49] As a free chapel its endowment was confiscated c. 1547,[50] and in 1650 it was said to have been long unused. Whether in the Middle Ages it had all the attributes of a parish church is obscure: the recommendation of 1650 that Asserton be united with Berwick St. James suggests that it had some of them.[51]

The advowson was held with Asserton manor in 1299[52] and passed with it to John Willington (d. 1397). Rights of presentation at alternate vacancies were allotted to Willington's coheirs, his sister Isabel Beaumont and nephew John Wroth. Isabel's right was inherited with the manor by her son Sir Thomas Beaumont.[53] Wroth's was presumably that conveyed to Sir William Poulton and his wife Elizabeth in 1412.[54] Sir Thomas acquired it, probably by purchase, and held the undivided advowson at his death in 1450.[55] With Asserton manor it descended to Hugh Beaumont (fl. 1501): it may have continued to pass with the manor but was not mentioned after 1505.[56] Few owners of the advowson presented chaplains. In 1299 and 1305 the king presented because of the idiocy of John Waleran,[57] and in 1349 the bishop presented, presumably by lapse. The king again presented in 1399 and 1403; in 1427 the patrons were feoffees of Sir Thomas Beaumont; in 1493 Robert Willoughby, Lord Willoughby de Broke, presented by grant of a turn.[58]

In 1309 the endowment, valued at £1 6s. 8d., comprised great tithes from the demesne of Asserton manor and from 13 a. of customary land, and small tithes from the whole manor.[59] Later a lord of Great Wishford manor gave the first cut of 8 a. of Asserton meadow in Great Wishford, and evidently tithes from the meadow, to the chaplains in return for prayers for his ancestors.[60]

In 1399 and 1403 the chaplain was instituted on an exchange: John Wotton, chaplain from 1399, was also rector of Iwerne Courtney (Dors.)[61] and in 1402 was licensed to hold another benefice with cure of souls.[62]

The church was said in 1391 to be a chapel in the manor house of Asserton.[63] In the mid 16th century it was apparently a separate building[64] and in 1650 was in ruins.[65] A silver chalice and a pair of vestments belonging to it were sold c. 1548; it then had a bell.[66]

NONCONFORMITY. Three houses in the parish were certified for meetings of nonconformists, two for Baptists, one in 1796 and one in 1816, and one in 1815 for Independents.[67] In 1864 there were 13 Baptists, but there was no nonconformist place of worship then[68] or later.

EDUCATION. A dame school in the parish had 25 pupils in 1818.[69] A school, perhaps the same one, had 50 pupils in 1833[70] and was a National school in 1846.[71] A new schoolroom was built north-west of the church in 1856, and in the 1870s a teacher's house was provided.[72] In 1871 there were 47 pupils:[73] average attendance was 24 in 1910, 32 in 1936[74] when the school was replaced by a new one in Stapleford parish but near Berwick St. James village and for children of both.[75] The school, called Berwick St. James school, had six pupils on roll in 1992, when it was closed.[76]

CHARITY FOR THE POOR. In 1784 a clergyman named Birch gave £2 2s. for the poor of the parish. The charity gave nothing to the poor from 1817: its income in 1833 was £1. In 1904 the endowment was considered lost.[77]

42 See plate facing p. 187.
43 Nightingale, *Wilts. Plate*, 66–7; inf. from the rector.
44 Walters, *Wilts. Bells*, 23; inf. from the rector.
45 W.R.O. 2090/2–5; bishop's transcripts for earlier years are ibid.   46 *Tax. Eccl.* (Rec. Com.), 181.
47 *Cal. Inq. p.m.* ix, p. 196; W.R.O. 753/1, f. 1v.
48 *Tax. Eccl.* (Rec. Com.), 181; *Cal. Inq. p.m.* iv, p. 341.
49 *Cal. Pat.* 1292–1301, 397; Phillipps, *Wilts. Inst.* i. 2, 6, 18, 48, 86, 90, 117, 152, 176.
50 P.R.O., E 301/58, no. 75; E 310/26/153, f. 17.
51 *W.A.M.* xl. 395.
52 *Cal. Pat.* 1292–1301, 397; *Cal. Inq. p.m.* iv, p. 341.
53 *Cal. Inq. p.m.* xvii, p. 344; *Cal. Close*, 1396–9, 170–1; above, manors (Asserton).
54 *Feet of F. 1377–1509* (W.R.S. xli), p. 68.
55 P.R.O., C 139/143, no. 30.
56 *Feet of F. 1377–1509* (W.R.S. xli), p. 178; above, manors (Asserton).
57 *Cal. Pat.* 1292–1301, 397; 1301–7, 316.
58 Phillipps, *Wilts. Inst.* i. 48, 86, 90, 117, 176.

59 *Wilts. Inq. p.m. 1242–1326* (Index Libr.), 371.
60 P.R.O., C 2/Eliz. I/G 5/56; below, Great Wishford, manor.
61 *Cal. Pat.* 1399–1401, 111, 127; 1401–5, 301.
62 *Cal. Papal Reg.* vi. 21–2.
63 *Cal. Inq. p.m.* xvii, p. 48.
64 P.R.O., E 301/58, no. 75.
65 *W.A.M.* xl. 395.
66 P.R.O., E 301/58, no. 75.
67 *Meeting Ho. Certs.* (W.R.S. xl), pp. 44, 76, 80.
68 W.R.O., D 1/56/7.
69 *Educ. of Poor Digest*, 1018.
70 *Educ. Enq. Abstract*, 1028.
71 *Nat. Soc. Inquiry, 1846–7*, Wilts. 2–3.
72 Last, *Berwick St. Jas.* 14; P.R.O., ED 7/130, no. 16.
73 *Returns relating to Elem. Educ.* 428–9.
74 *Bd. of Educ., List 21, 1911* (H.M.S.O.), 545; *1936*, 422.
75 Last, *Berwick St. Jas.* 14.
76 *The Independent*, 10 July 1992.
77 *Endowed Char. Wilts.* (S. Div.), 40.

LITTLE LANGFORD

LITTLE LANGFORD[78] is in the Wylye valley 12 km. north-west of Salisbury.[79] The river Wylye to the north, the Grovely Grim's ditch to the south, and a coomb to the east marked part of its boundary in the 10th or 11th century and became parish boundaries. The Powten stone on the south boundary before 1066 may still have marked Little Langford's boundary in the 14th century.[80] A minor course of the Wylye called the Back river, which is forded east of the village, later marked part of the northern boundary.[81] Taking in a north-east and south-west coomb and half another the parish, 1,020 a. (413 ha.), took its shape in response to relief: it reached from the river south-west to the watershed and was roughly rectangular. At its north-east corner it projected eastwards: the projection, from which the men of Wylye took some of the hay, may have been the shared meadow assigned to Little Langford in the early recital of its boundaries.[82] The epithet Little was in use to distinguish the village from its neighbours Steeple Langford and Hanging Langford in 1210–12.[83] In 1934 the whole of Little Langford parish was added to Steeple Langford.[84]

The land falls from c. 185 m. on Grim's ditch to c. 70 m. by the Wylye. There is alluvium near the river, and valley gravel south of it around the village and in the coombs; chalk outcrops further south, covered by clay-with-flints near the southern boundary. Most of the parish is downland and it had roughly equal amounts of open fields, of down pasture, both on the chalk, and of woodland, on the clay. The woodland was extensively cleared in the 19th century, and in the later 20th the downs were used much more for tillage than pasture.[85] The parish was in Grovely forest at all perambulations in the Middle Ages: most of its woodland was part of the forest in 1589 but not 1603.[86]

The Wilton–Warminster road linking the villages on the right bank of the Wylye between Great Wishford and Bishopstrow crosses the parish. It was turnpiked between Little Langford and Stockton in 1761, disturnpiked in 1871.[87] A road across the downs between the Wylye and the Nadder marked the west boundary of Little Langford in the early Middle Ages,[88] and later other north–south tracks linked Little Langford and the Grovely ridge way, which in the later 16th century may have crossed

the southern extremity of the parish.[89] The Salisbury–Warminster section of the G.W.R. was made across the parish very near the turnpike road in 1856: the nearest station was at Hanging Langford in Steeple Langford until 1857, afterwards at Great Wishford until 1955.[90]

There were 32 poll-tax payers in 1377, a total which suggests that Little Langford was more populous than at any time except perhaps the later 19th century,[91] and probably 20 adult inhabitants in 1676.[92] The population was 25 in 1801 and had risen to 39 by 1861. After new building in the 1860s it stood at 67 in 1871 and reached a peak of 82 in 1881. There were 64 inhabitants in 1931,[93] almost certainly fewer in 1981.

The Iron-Age hill fort now called Grovely castle is in the parish, a barrow lies on the boundary with Steeple Langford, and other archaeological remains may have come from downland in the parish. There was a prehistoric field system east of Grovely castle.[94]

Little Langford village stood on the gravel terrace near the river and was the smallest of the three markedly different villages called Langford.[95] For most of its history, certainly from the later 16th century to the 1860s, it consisted of little more than the church and two farmsteads: the village had fewer houses than its neighbours because neither of its manors had customary tenants living on it.[96] In the 18th century the three main houses in the parish, each with three principal ground-floor rooms, may have been of similar size: east of the church Little Langford (later Lower) Farm was a stone house with five first-floor rooms, west of the church Stourton (later Upper) Farm, as rebuilt in 1737, was also a stone house but had only three first-floor rooms,[97] and in 1783 the rectory house north of the church was a stone and thatch house with two first-floor rooms.[98] Before 1761 the village was possibly on the Great Wishford to Bishopstrow road, and parts of an old road are visible east and west of the church. From when that road was turnpiked, however, if not earlier, it ran across higher ground to the south. In 1773 the parish contained no building other than those on the line of the old road, presumably including a few cottages.[99] The whole village, including the church, was rebuilt in the later 19th century. In 1864 a new farmhouse, of stone and in Gothic style, and model farm buildings

78 A map of the par. is below, s.vv. Steeple Langford.
79 This article was written in 1990. Maps used include O.S. Maps 1", sheet 167 (1960 edn.); 1/50,000, sheet 184 (1974 edn.); 1/25,000, SU 03 (1958 edn.); 6", Wilts. LIX, LXV (1889–90 edns.).
80 Arch. Jnl. lxxvi. 278–83; V.C.H. Wilts. iv. 431, 456.
81 W.R.O., tithe award.
82 Ibid.; Arch. Jnl. lxxvi. 281; below, econ. hist.
83 Red Bk. Exch. (Rolls Ser.), ii. 483.
84 V.C.H. Wilts. iv. 351.
85 Geol. Surv. Map 1/50,000, drift, sheet 298 (1976 edn.); W.R.O., tithe award; below, econ. hist.
86 V.C.H. Wilts. iv. 431–2, 456–7; W.R.O. 212B/7190H.
87 V.C.H. Wilts. iv. 257, 262, 270; L.J. xxx. 138.
88 Arch. Jnl. lxxv. 105.

89 H. W. Timperley and E. Brill, Anct. Trackways of Wessex, 134 and map 6; O.S. Map 1", sheet 14 (1817 edn.); W.R.O. 212B/7190H.
90 V.C.H. Wilts. iv. 281, 283–4, 293; below, Great Wishford, intro. 91 V.C.H. Wilts. iv. 307.
92 Compton Census, ed. Whiteman, 125.
93 V.C.H. Wilts. iv. 351; for the new building, below, this section. 94 V.C.H. Wilts. i (1), 107, 191, 269, 276.
95 Cf. below, Steeple Langford, intro.; Hanging Langford, intro.
96 W.R.O. 212B/7190H; ibid. tithe award; below, manors; econ. hist.
97 W.R.O. 2057/S 30, pp. 51, 55; ibid. tithe award.
98 Ibid. D 1/24/125/2.
99 Andrews and Dury, Map (W.R.S. viii), pl. 5.

incorporating four cottages were built south of the railway and beside the turnpike road, and a group of eight cottages, of red brick and slate, was built in 1863 near the site of Lower Farm.[1] Upper Farm, Lower Farm, and cottages were demolished[2] and a new rectory house was built.[3] The eight cottages, forming three sides of a rectangle, were sometimes called the Barracks,[4] later Stourton Cottages. Six more houses were built in the 20th century, four east of the church on or near the old line of the village and two near the road west of the new farmstead.

MANORS AND OTHER ESTATE. Land at Little Langford was the subject of three grants in the mid 10th century: in 943 King Edmund granted 3 hides, the west half of what became the parish; c. 950 King Eadred granted to Wulfheah 1 *mansa*; and in 956 King Eadwig granted to Byrnric 6 *mansae*, comprising what became the whole parish. The first and third grants are recorded in Wilton abbey's cartulary, the second in that of Glastonbury abbey (Som.).[5]

In 1066 Wilton abbey held 3 hides at Little Langford, an estate mainly in the west half of the parish and later called *LANGFORD DANGERS* manor. Its tenant was an Englishman whose two sons had by 1086 acquired the abbey's right to hold the land in demesne.[6] The abbey remained overlord until the Dissolution.[7]

In 1242–3 the manor was held of the abbey as ½ knight's fee by William Tracy,[8] who with his wife Margery conveyed it to Ralph Dangers in 1252.[9] In 1428 John Tracy was said to be the mesne lord.[10] The manor descended in the Dangers family with Lambert's estate in West Amesbury.[11] John Dangers held it in 1294[12] and 1309,[13] his son Ralph in 1317, and Ralph's son John[14] apparently 1323–54. One or more William Dangers (d. by 1443) held it in 1379–1435, and William Dangers's feoffees, including John Stourton, held it in 1443.[15] In 1448 it was conveyed to Stourton (cr. Baron Stourton 1448, d. 1462),[16] already the owner of a second manor in the parish.[17]

In 1086 Glastonbury abbey held 2 hides at Little Langford and claimed as thegnland 1 hide

held of the king by Edward of Salisbury, who also held the 2 hides of the abbey.[18] Edward's successors were overlords of both estates, together called *LITTLE LANGFORD* manor and comprising land in the east half of the parish.[19] The overlordship descended to Edward's son Walter (d. 1147), Walter's son Patrick, earl of Salisbury (d. 1168), and with the earldom to Patrick's son William (d. 1196) and William's daughter Ela (d. 1261) and her husband William Longespée, earl of Salisbury (d. 1226). It passed with the overlordship of Shrewton,[20] and was held by Thomas Montagu, earl of Salisbury (d. 1428).[21]

The 1 hide held by Edward of Salisbury in 1086 had been held by Azor in 1066 and was held of Edward by Letard.[22] The tenant in demesne of Little Langford manor in the later 12th century was Stephen of Langford, whose heir was his brother William of Langford.[23] The manor passed in the Langford family, apparently to Turbert Langford (fl. 1203),[24] to John Langford who held it as ½ and ¹⁄₁₀ knight's fee in 1242–3,[25] to Alan Langford (fl. 1300),[26] to Alan's son John (fl. 1329),[27] and to Thomas Langford (fl. 1348).[28] In 1388 it belonged to William Dun,[29] who by 1397 had conveyed it to William Stourton[30] (d. 1413). Stourton was succeeded by his son John, Lord Stourton (d. 1462),[31] who also acquired Langford Dangers.[32]

Langford Dangers and Little Langford manors descended with the barony from Lord Stourton in the direct line to William (d. 1478), John (d. 1485), and Francis (d. 1487), with the barony to Francis's uncles William Stourton (d. 1524) and Edward Stourton (d. 1535), and again in the direct line to William, Lord Stourton (d. 1548), and Charles, Lord Stourton, whose lands were forfeited in 1557 on his execution and attainder for felony.[33]

About 1573 Edward Seymour, earl of Hertford (d. 1621), claimed Little Langford manor as an escheat on the grounds that he was a successor of the earls of Salisbury as lord of Amesbury manor, to which the overlordship of Little Langford manor had been attached. Hertford's claim was evidently made good,[34] and apparently matched by a successful claim for Langford Dangers manor by Henry Herbert, earl of

1 W.R.O. 2057/A 1/83, p. 90; 2057/E 2/4, pp. 50, 117.
2 Cf. O.S. Map 6", Wilts. LIX (1889 edn.).
3 Below, church.   4 W.R.O., G 11/505/3.
5 Finberg, *Early Wessex Chart.* pp. 87–8, 90–2; *Arch. Jnl.* lxxvi. 278–83; *V.C.H. Wilts.* ii, p. 93; *Chart. Glaston.* (Som. Rec. Soc. lix), p. 201.
6 *V.C.H. Wilts.* ii, p. 130; for the location cf. P.R.O., E 134/34 Eliz. I Hil./28; E 178/2427; W.R.O. 212B/7190H; 2057, deeds, Little Langford, Pembroke to Biggs, 1732; ibid. tithe award.
7 P.R.O., SC 6/Hen. VIII/3985, rot. 11; W.R.O. 2057/D 3, reg. of deeds, 1642, f. 51.
8 *Bk. of Fees*, ii. 715.
9 P.R.O., CP 25/1/251/17, no. 23.
10 *Feud. Aids*, v. 243.
11 Above, Amesbury, manors (Lambert's).
12 Hist. MSS. Com. 43, *15th Rep. VII, Somerset*, p. 148.
13 *Feet of F. 1272–1327* (W.R.S. i), p. 123.
14 Hist. MSS. Com. 43, *15th Rep. VII, Somerset*, p. 148; *Year Bk. 12 Edw. II* (Selden Soc. lxx), 118.
15 Phillipps, *Wilts. Inst.* (index in *W.A.M.* xxviii. 223); *Feud. Aids*, v. 243; vi. 534; W.R.O. 2057/D 3, reg. of deeds, 1642, f. 50v.
16 *Complete Peerage*, xii (1), 301–2; P.R.O., C 140/8, no. 18.   17 Below, this section.

18 *V.C.H. Wilts.* ii, pp. 46, 80, 124, 205.
19 e.g. *Red Bk. Exch.* (Rolls Ser.), ii. 483; *Bk. of Fees*, ii. 721; *V.C.H. Wilts.* iv. 456.
20 *Complete Peerage*, xi. 373–95; below, Shrewton, manors; cf. *Feet of F. 1272–1327* (W.R.S. i), p. 132; *Cal. Inq. p.m.* xvii, p. 321.
21 *Cal. Inq. p.m.* xix, p. 233; *Feud. Aids*, v. 243.
22 *V.C.H. Wilts.* ii, pp. 138–9.
23 *Bradenstoke Cart.* (W.R.S. xxxv), p. 95.
24 P.R.O., CP 25/1/250/2, no. 13.
25 *Bk. of Fees*, ii. 721.
26 *V.C.H. Wilts.* iv. 456.
27 *Cal. Pat. 1321–4*, 390; W.R.O. 2057/D 3, reg. of deeds, 1642, f. 50v.
28 *Feet of F. 1327–77* (W.R.S. xxix), p. 87.
29 *Feet of F. 1377–1509* (W.R.S. xli), p. 22.
30 P.R.O., C 1/68, no. 84.
31 *Complete Peerage*, xii (1), 300–2.
32 Above, this section.
33 *Complete Peerage*, xii (1), 302–8; P.R.O., C 140/8, no. 18; C 140/63, no. 55; ibid. E 178/2427.
34 *Antrobus D.* (W.R.S. iii), pp. 54–5; W.R.O. 2057/D 3, reg. of deeds, 1642, f. 49; Longleat Mun., Seymour papers, xii, f. 253v.; above, Amesbury, manors (Amesbury; Earldom).

Pembroke, the successor to Wilton abbey as overlord.[35] In 1585 the Crown claimed both manors on the grounds that Lord Stourton held them without intermediary at his death,[36] and in the same year granted both to agents. Langford Dangers was acquired by Lord Pembroke, probably by 1590, certainly by 1595,[37] and descended with the Pembroke title as part of the Wilton estate: it was sometimes called Stourton farm, presumably after the Stourtons who were lessees in the 16th and 17th centuries, and later Upper farm.[38] Little Langford manor was conveyed to Lord Hertford in 1586.[39] In 1621 it passed to his grandson and heir William, earl of Hertford, who in 1626 sold the reversion after the death of his sister-in-law Lady (Anne) Beauchamp, to William, earl of Pembroke.[40] Lady Beauchamp sold her interest to Lord Pembroke in 1636,[41] and Little Langford manor thereafter descended with Langford Dangers: it was called Lower farm in the 19th century.[42] In 1921 the Wilton estate sold both manors as Little Langford farm to Frederick Andrews, from whom they were bought back in 1939.[43] In 1990 the Wilton estate owned nearly the whole parish.[44]

In the later 12th century Stephen of Langford granted 1 yardland in Little Langford to Bradenstoke priory. The priory apparently conveyed it to Ralph Dangers in an exchange c. 1243 × 1260[45] and it was presumably added to Langford Dangers manor.

ECONOMIC HISTORY. In 1086 Little Langford had land for 4 ploughteams, on which were 3 or more teams, and there were 51 a. of meadow, much for so small a place, and 50 a. of pasture. The land was nearly all demesne, on which were 4 *servi* and 9 bordars, and was in 2–4 holdings. No *villanus* was mentioned in Domesday Book[46] and there is no later evidence of customary tenure. The land was presumably worked in demesne by Wilton abbey and Glastonbury abbey from when they acquired it; it was possibly in only two holdings before they acquired it; and almost certainly from the 13th century, certainly from the 16th to the mid 19th, there were two farms corresponding to the two manors in the parish.[47]

Sheep-and-corn husbandry predominated in the parish.[48] Between the village and the downs

there were three open fields, c. 280 a., which were never formally inclosed. Common husbandry ceased when the two farms were worked as one: that may have been before 1796, when the open fields were still so called,[49] and was certainly before 1838.[50] Vestiges of open-field cultivation were removed c. 1860 when glebe in the former open fields was exchanged for other land.[51] Sheep were pastured in common on the downs, also c. 280 a.,[52] until a separate down was allotted to each farm, evidently in the late 18th century.[53] The extensive meadow land was shared with men of other parishes, Duttenham mead (16 a.) with Wylye, Chitterne or Jordan mead (10 a.) with Chitterne, and 1 a. of Broad mead apparently with Dinton: after the hay was taken Little Langford had the pasture of all 27 a.[54] Rights to the hay were acquired for Little Langford in respect of Duttenham mead c. 1860, Chitterne mead in 1906, and Broad mead between c. 1860 and 1920.[55]

Presumably from the mid 15th century, certainly from the mid 16th, the two manors were leased.[56] In the later 16th century Little Langford farm to the east, occupied by members of the Hayter family and in the early 17th century called Hayter's farm, was slightly larger than Stourton farm to the west, occupied by Christopher Stourton from 1528, Leonard Stourton in the later 16th century, and Hercules Stourton in the earlier 17th century. Both farms were said to include only c. 90 a. of arable: Little Langford farm had 80 a. of several down.[57] Both were leased for years on lives by the earls of Pembroke, and from 1753 to 1857 members of the Biggs family held both leases. In 1701 Little Langford farm included c. 33 a. of meadows, c. 9 a. of several pasture, 106 a. in the open fields, c. 36 a. of inclosed arable, and 101 a. of woodland. Stourton farm, held by Tristram Biggs from 1681, included c. 25 a. of meadows, c. 12 a. of several pasture, 153 a. in the open fields, and 23 a. of woodland. Cows were kept on Little Langford farm but both were mainly sheep and arable farms: the downs were common for 1,100 sheep. Some meadows were watered, although in the early 18th century a dispute between the lessees prevented the watering of Broad mead, c. 13 a.[58] By c. 1750 a coppice at the extreme south end of the parish had been grubbed up for

35 *L. & P. Hen. VIII*, xix (1), p. 38; P.R.O., SC 6/Hen. VIII/3985, rot. 11; below, church; for the earls of Pembroke, *Complete Peerage*, x. 405–30; *Debrett's Peerage* (1976), 898.
36 P.R.O., E 178/2427.
37 W.R.O. 2057/D 3, reg. of deeds, 1642, ff. 49 and v., 50v.
38 e.g. ibid. ff. 50v.–51; 2057/S 60, p. 101; ibid. tithe award; below, econ. hist.
39 P.R.O., CP 43/10, Carte rott. 5–6; CP 43/15, Carte rott. 24d.–25d.
40 *Complete Peerage*, vi. 507; *Wilts. Inq. p.m.* 1625–49 (Index Libr.), 100; W.R.O. 1332, box 53, deed, Pembroke to Hertford, 1626.
41 W.R.O. 2057/D 3, reg. of deeds, 1642, f. 49.
42 Ibid. tithe award.
43 Ibid. 2057/R 106, f. 110; 2057/R 107, f. 154.
44 Inf. from Mr. D. Jenkins, Wilton Estate Off., Wilton.
45 *Bradenstoke Cart.* (W.R.S. xxxv), pp. 95, 103.
46 *V.C.H. Wilts.* ii, pp. 124, 130, 138–9.
47 Above, manors; below, this section.

48 e.g. W.R.O. 2057/S 30, pp. 51, 55.
49 Ibid. 2057, deeds, Little Langford, Pembroke to Biggs, 1796; below, this section.
50 W.R.O., tithe award.
51 Ibid. 2057/S 205; below, church.
52 W.R.O., tithe award.
53 Ibid. 2057, deeds, Little Langford, Pembroke to Biggs, 1777, 1796.
54 *First Pembroke Survey*, ed. Straton, i. 278; *Tithe Apportionments* (W.R.S. xxx), pp. 35–6, 47, 110; W.R.O., tithe award; ibid. 2057/S 30, p. 51; 2057/S 63, f. 20; 2057, deeds, Little Langford, Pembroke to Biggs, 1796.
55 W.R.O. 776/93; 2057/S 176; 2057/S 205.
56 *Antrobus D.* (W.R.S. iii), pp. 54–5; P.R.O., E 178/2427; above, manors.
57 *Wilts. Inq. p.m.* 1625–49 (Index Libr.), 100; *Cal. S.P. Dom.* 1639, pp. 103, 252; 1639–40, pp. 341–2; P.R.O., C 2/Jas. I/E 7/19; ibid. E 134/34 Eliz. I Hil./28; E 178/2427; W.R.O. 2057/D 3, reg. of deeds, 1642, f. 51.
58 W.R.O. 2057/S 30, pp. 51–2, 55–6; 2057, deeds, Little Langford.

arable.[59] In 1796 Little Langford (Lower) farm, 507 a., included 12 a. of pasture, 24 a. of water meadows, 46 a. of inclosed arable, 120 a. of open arable, 96 a. of woodland, and 200 a. of downland; Stourton (Upper) farm, 394 a., included 15 a. of dry meadow and pasture, 20 a. of water meadows, 6 a. of inclosed arable, 162 a. of open arable, 55 a. of woodland, and 120 a. of downland.[60] In 1838 the parish had 355 a. of arable, 69 a. of meadows of which 52 a. were watered, 35 a. of lowland pasture, 281 a. of downland pasture, and 249 a. of woodland: Lower farm to the east, 504 a., and Upper farm to the west, 465 a., were worked together.[61]

Lower farm and Upper farm fell in hand in 1857 and 1860 respectively,[62] and by 1865 Little Langford had become one of the places most affected by improvements on the Wilton estate. The model farm buildings of Little Langford farm replaced both Lower Farm and Upper Farm, new buildings were erected on the downs, all the cottages in the village were replaced, 156 a. of woodland were grubbed up for arable, and downland pasture was ploughed. Land in Great Wishford was added to Little Langford farm, 1,432 a. c. 1864,[63] and has remained part of it. In 1920 the farm, 1,562 a., was for corn, sheep, and dairying.[64] Arable was laid to grass between 1920 and 1941[65] but ploughed again later. In 1990 Little Langford farm, 1,422 a., was an arable and dairy farm, had buildings at Little Langford and in Great Wishford parish, specialized in cereal production, and maintained a herd of pedigree Holstein Friesian cattle. Most of c. 90 a. of woodland remaining in the parish was managed by the Forestry Commission.[66]

A mill on the Englishmen's Little Langford estate was mentioned in 1086[67] but no mill is known later.

LOCAL GOVERNMENT.
Little Langford was part of a single tithing with Hanging Langford from the 16th century or earlier.[68] There is no evidence of a manor court held for Little Langford and, since there was apparently no customary tenure,[69] none may have been held.

Few paupers lived in the parish. Expenditure on them 1783–5 averaged £9; the poor-rate was low and only £18 was spent in 1802–3, when two adults were relieved regularly. In the period 1813–15 no poor rate was levied because there was only one farmer in the parish.[70] Yearly expenditure was over £34 from 1815 to 1819, later fell, and was nil in 1831–2.[71] In 1836 the parish joined Wilton poor-law union;[72] in 1974, as part of Steeple Langford parish, it became part of Salisbury district.[73]

CHURCH.
Little Langford church was standing in the later 12th century.[74] The benefice remained a rectory. A plan of 1650 to add Hanging Langford to the parish was not implemented.[75] In 1973 Little Langford was united with Steeple Langford as the parish and benefice of the Langfords, that benefice was then united with the benefice of Wylye and Fisherton de la Mere, and in 1979 Stockton was added to create the new benefice of Yarnbury.[76]

From 1309 or earlier the advowson passed with Langford Dangers manor.[77] Sir Walter Sutton, who presented ineffectually in 1323, may have been a relative of John Dangers who presented successfully in the same year,[78] and in 1349 John Dangers successfully resisted Robert More's claim to the advowson.[79] William Dangers's feoffees presented in 1443 and John Barrow in 1527 by grant of Sir William Stourton (probably Lord Stourton d. 1548).[80] Henry, earl of Pembroke, presented in 1573, and the advowson descended with the manor and the Pembroke title until 1972, when it was transferred to the bishop of Salisbury. John Gauntlet presented in 1694 by grant of a turn. The bishop shared the right to present for the new benefices created in 1973 and 1979.[81]

The church was valued at £20 in 1349,[82] at only £7 7s. in 1535,[83] and at £65 in 1650[84] and 1705. The rector was entitled to all tithes from the whole parish:[85] in 1838 they were valued at £147 and commuted.[86] The rector had a house and c. 5 a. of arable in 1592 when, perhaps unsuccessfully, he claimed rights to feed animals on Stourton farm.[87] In 1705 he had a house and 10 a., in 1783 a small house and 10 a. including 2 a. in place of some hay tithes.[88] The house was demolished and a new one built north of the church in 1798.[89] It was repaired, altered, and enlarged in 1827.[90] After 1856, probably in the early 1860s, the glebe was concentrated near the church and rectory house by exchange with the earl of Pembroke;[91] in 1872 a new house was

59 Ibid. 1553/25, p. 174; ibid. tithe award.
60 Ibid. 2057, deeds, Little Langford, Pembroke to Biggs, 1796.   61 Ibid. tithe award.
62 Ibid. 2057/S 30, p. 52; 2057/S 60, p. 101.
63 Ibid. 2057/A 1/83, pp. 82–5, 90; 2057/I 28; 2057/S 176; 2057/S 205; ibid. tithe award; V.C.H. Wilts. iv. 95.
64 W.R.O. 776/93.
65 Ibid. 2057, deeds, Little Langford, agreement to let, 1941.   66 Inf. from Mr. Jenkins.
67 V.C.H. Wilts. ii, p. 130.
68 Taxation Lists (W.R.S. x), 112; Eton Coll. Mun., Ric. Rowden's bk.; W.R.O., A 1/345/253.
69 Above, econ. hist.
70 Poor Law Abstract, 1804, 558–9; 1818, 492–3.
71 Poor Rate Returns, 1816–21, 186; 1822–4, 225; 1825–9, 216; 1830–4, 209.
72 Poor Law Com. 2nd Rep. App. D, 560.
73 O.S. Map 1/100,000, admin. areas, Wilts. (1974 edn.).
74 Below, this section [architecture].
75 W.A.M. xl. 393.   76 Ch. Com. file, NB 34/412C.

77 Feet of F. 1272–1327 (W.R.S. i), p. 123; Phillipps, Wilts. Inst. (index in W.A.M. xxviii. 223).
78 Feet of F. 1272–1327 (W.R.S. i), p. 123; Reg. Martival (Cant. & York Soc.), i. 289–90; Hist. MSS. Com. 43, 15th Rep. VII, Somerset, p. 149.
79 P.R.O., CP 40/359, rot. 39d.
80 Phillipps, Wilts. Inst. i. 134, 199.
81 Ibid. (index in W.A.M. xxviii. 223); Ch. Com. file, NB 34/412C; above, manors.
82 P.R.O., CP 40/359, rot. 39d.
83 Valor Eccl. (Rec. Com.), ii. 104.
84 W.A.M. xl. 393.
85 W.R.O., D 1/24/125/1.
86 Ibid. tithe award.
87 P.R.O., E 134/34 Eliz. I Hil./28.
88 W.R.O., D 1/24/125/1–2.
89 Ibid. D 1/61/4/29.
90 Ibid. D 1/11/58.
91 Ibid. 2057/S 176; 2057/S 205; ibid. tithe award; above, intro.

built north-west of the church, and the old house was demolished.[92] The house and glebe were sold in 1926.[93]

In 1324 John Langford, lord of Little Langford manor, gave land in Little Langford and elsewhere to St. John's hospital, Wilton, to endow a chantry of which the chaplain should celebrate daily in Little Langford church. Each year the hospital was to present a chaplain to the archdeacon of Salisbury for admission and to provide him with food, clothes, and a house at Little Langford.[94] The chaplain accused of stealing a chalice, a breviary, a surplice, and a towel from the church in 1389 was possibly the chantry chaplain.[95] The hospital may have failed to present chaplains, and from 1397 or earlier the advowson of the chantry was claimed by Langford's successors as lord of the manor.[96] Sir Reynold Stourton, a relative of the lord, and the lord, William, Lord Stourton, presented in 1457 and 1502 respectively. That chaplains were presented to the bishop for institution suggests that chaplaincies were for longer than a year, and the chaplain who died c. 1502 may have been the prior of St. John's.[97] No reference to the chantry has been found after 1502. The hospital may have kept the endowment, and the patron, also patron of the parish church, have presented no other chaplain.

Thomas Green was apparently the rector deprived for Roman Catholicism before 1570.[98] In 1630 John Lee, rector of Wylye and treasurer of Salisbury cathedral, and in 1634 Alexander Hyde, rector of Wylye and 1665–7 bishop of Salisbury, were instituted as rectors, and in the 1630s curates served the church.[99] Hyde was sequestrated in 1645[1] and resigned in 1660.[2] In 1650 the minister John Wilson preached every Sunday.[3] In 1662 the parish lacked Jewell's *Apology* and a chalice.[4] Curates often served the church in the 18th century and earlier 19th.[5] In 1783 the rector Henry Hawes lived at Box: the curate, rector of Steeple Langford, held a service every Sunday and communion four times a year. There had been no wedding, christening, or burial for three years.[6] From 1798 to 1827 the rector was William Moody, the lord of Great Bathampton manor and of a manor in Hanging Langford.[7] Morning and evening services were held every Sunday in 1851 with average congregations of, respectively, 20 and 46: half those attending evening service were from outside the parish.[8] When a new rector was instituted in 1863 he found no communicant and parishioners who he said knew little of Christian worship: in 1864, in his own drawing room while the church

was being rebuilt, he held two services every Sunday, morning prayers every day, and communion at festivals and monthly for six communicants.[9] A retreat attended by Walter Hamilton, bishop of Salisbury, was conducted in the church in 1865,[10] and from 1867 the rector also served St. Martin's chapel at Grovely Wood[11] (later in Barford St. Martin). The rectory was held with Great Wishford rectory 1926–73.[12]

THE SOUTH DOORWAY OF THE CHURCH

The church of *ST. NICHOLAS*, so called in 1324,[13] is built of chequered flint and ashlar, and consists of a chancel with north vestry and a nave with south transeptal chapel and east bell turret. The reset south doorway is of the later 12th century and has a decorated tympanum above a lintel carved with a hunting scene.[14] Most features of the church were apparently reproduced when it was rebuilt in 1864 to T. H. Wyatt's designs. They suggest that the small nave and chancel were 12th-

92 Inf. from Miss S. Rooke, the Old Rectory.
93 Ch. Com. file, NB 34/203.
94 *Reg. Martival* (Cant. & York Soc.), ii. 493–8.
95 P.R.O., JUST 3/179, rot. 14.
96 W.R.O. 2057/D 3, reg. of deeds, 1642, f. 51.
97 Phillipps, *Wilts. Inst.* i. 148, 181; Hoare, *Mod. Wilts.* Mere, 48; *V.C.H. Wilts.* iii. 366–7.
98 *V.C.H. Wilts.* iii. 87; Phillipps, *Wilts. Inst.* i. 227.
99 *Subscription Bk. 1620–40* (W.R.S. xxxii), pp. 22, 26, 48, 52, 63; below, Wylye, church.
1 *Walker Revised*, ed. Matthews, 374.
2 Phillipps, *Wilts. Inst.* ii. 23.
3 *W.A.M.* xl. 393.
4 W.R.O., D 1/54/1/4, no. 38B.

5 Ibid. D 1/51/1, ff. 101, 182; ibid. bishop's transcripts, bdles. 1–2.
6 *Vis. Queries, 1783* (W.R.S. xxvii), p. 136.
7 W.R.O. 475/33, letter, Maitland to Moody, 1827; 475/50; below, Bathampton, manors; Hanging Langford, manors.
8 P.R.O., HO 129/265/1/9/19.
9 W.R.O., D 1/4/2/101; D 1/56/7.
10 *V.C.H. Wilts.* iii. 70.
11 W.R.O., D 1/4/2/143.
12 *Crockford* (1930 and later edns.); Ch. Com. files, NB 34/412C; 53753.
13 *Feet of F.* 1272–1327 (W.R.S. i), p. 115.
14 Hoare, *Mod. Wilts.* Branch and Dole, pl. facing p. 19.

century and that the chapel was added in the earlier 14th. Most of the windows were enlarged in the 15th century or the 16th. A north porch was rebuilt as the vestry, and the bell turret built, in 1864.[15] The bell turret was renewed in 1965.[16]

The chalice stolen in 1389 was apparently not replaced until soon after 1662: the church had no plate in 1553. In 1990 the parish held a chalice hallmarked for 1660 or 1662 and a new set of plate given in 1864.[17] There were two bells in 1553,[18] one in 1783.[19] A sanctus bell was hung in the turret in 1864.[20] The registers begin in 1699: baptisms and burials are lacking for 1767–85 and 1764–85 respectively.[21]

NONCONFORMITY. A rector was deprived for Roman Catholicism before 1570[22] and a papist lived in the parish in 1676.[23] There is no evidence of protestant dissent.

EDUCATION. A day school in the parish was attended by eight children in 1846–7.[24] No other day school is recorded, and an evening school started by the rector in 1863 or 1864 was attended by few and may have been short lived.[25]

CHARITY FOR THE POOR. Between 1899 and 1913 Sidney, earl of Pembroke and of Montgomery, gave land for almshouses and shared with the tenant of Little Langford farm, Frederick Andrews, the cost of building two cottages for poor and aged residents of Little Langford. The Little Langford almshouse charity was created by Scheme of 1923 and endowed with the cottages and £200 collected in Little Langford as a war memorial.[26] The cottages remained in use as almshouses in 1990.[27]

STEEPLE LANGFORD

STEEPLE LANGFORD parish is in the Wylye valley 13 km. north-west of Salisbury and 19 km. ESE. of Warminster.[28] It contains Steeple Langford, Bathampton, and Hanging Langford, a total of 4,018 a. (1,626 ha.), with villages at Steeple Langford and Hanging Langford. In 1934 Little Langford was added to Steeple Langford parish,[29] thereafter 2,039 ha. (5,038 a.). In this article most aspects of the histories of Bathampton and Hanging Langford are dealt with separately under their own names.

Much of the parish is downland across which its boundaries are generally straight and in most places ignore relief. The south part of the eastern boundary, with Little Langford, the south part of the western, with Wylye, and, apparently, the north part of the western, with Deptford in Wylye, were described in the 10th century.[30] To the south-west part of the boundary follows a dry valley, and for short distances courses of the Wylye are the boundaries with Wylye and Little Langford. The northern boundary is on the watershed of the Wylye and Till, the southern on that of the Wylye and Nadder. The boundaries were drawn across two prehistoric settlement sites and the southern is marked by an ancient ditch.

Chalk outcrops over the whole parish. It is covered by clay-with-flints along the southern boundary where, at c. 185 m., the flat land

between the Wylye and Nadder valleys is the highest in the parish. The northern downs reach 167 m. There are ridges and dry valleys in both north and south parts of the parish, but also a flat area of 300–350 a. at c. 125 m. in the north. The Wylye falls little as it crosses the middle of the parish from west to east; it has deposited a wide band of alluvium and, on each side, a strip of gravel on which stand the main settlements. The flat land near the river is at c. 75 m.[31]

From the Middle Ages the parish conformed to the pattern of sheep-and-corn husbandry normal on the Wiltshire chalklands: there were meadows on the alluvium beside the river, pastures on the gravel between the alluvium and the chalk, open fields on the lower slopes of the downs, and extensive pastures mainly for sheep on the upland beyond. Steeple Langford and Hanging Langford each had a system of arable fields and common meadows and pastures which was not inclosed until the mid 19th century.[32] The clay-with-flints of the Wylye–Nadder watershed supports woodland, but nearly all that now in Steeple Langford parish had apparently been cleared by 1086 when none of the estates of Steeple Langford, Bathampton, and Hanging Langford had recorded woodland.[33] Hanging Langford had a wood called Ridgely,[34] later Stourton Hat,[35] c. 10 a. in the south-east corner of the parish; a few acres were planted at

15 J. Buckler, watercolours in W.A.S. Libr., vol. iii. 10; W.R.O. 1421/17; 1421/19; ibid. D 1/61/15/10; Wilts. Cuttings, xvi. 271; for the turret cf. Walters, Wilts. Bells, 116.
16 W.R.O. 1421/15.
17 Nightingale, Wilts. Plate, 70; inf. from Major-Gen. J. M. Brockbank, Manor Ho., Steeple Langford.
18 Walters, Wilts. Bells, 116.
19 W.R.O., D 1/24/125/2.
20 Wilts. Cuttings, xvi. 271.
21 W.R.O. 1421/1–3.
22 V.C.H. Wilts. iii. 87.
23 Compton Census, ed. Whiteman, 125.
24 Nat. Soc. Inquiry, 1846–7, Wilts. 6–7.
25 W.R.O., D 1/56/7.
26 Ibid. 2057, deeds, Little Langford, Pembroke to

Turnbull, 1922; O.S. Map 6", Wilts. LIX. SE. (1901 edn.).
27 Inf. from Miss Rooke.
28 This article was written in 1991. The following maps have been used: O.S. Maps 6", Wilts. LIII, LIX (1889 and later edns.); 1/25,000, SU 03–04 (1958 edns.); 1/50,000, sheet 184 (1974 edn.).
29 V.C.H. Wilts. iv. 351 n.
30 Arch. Jnl. lxxvi. 261–6, 278–83.
31 Geol. Surv. Map 1/50,000, drift, sheet 298 (1976 edn.).
32 Below, econ. hist.; Bathampton, econ. hist.; Hanging Langford, econ. hist.
33 V.C.H. Wilts. ii, pp. 133, 144–5, 151.
34 First Pembroke Survey, ed. Straton, i. 217; Som. R.O., DD/WY, box 156, ct. bk. 1609–57; Eton Coll. Mun. 43/77.
35 W.R.O. 212B/7190H; ibid. EA/153.

Bathampton between 1773 and 1838, and several coverts were planted on the downs of Steeple Langford in the 19th and 20th centuries.[36] No trade unconnected with agriculture has ever been prominent in the parish.

From the 11th century or earlier the Wylye was used to drive mills in the parish and from the 17th century or earlier to drown meadows:[37] partly because of its low fall the river was diverted into leets and minor courses. The main public bridge may for long have been that immediately west of the church, called Maskell's from 1592 or earlier.[38] Further east the river was forded, presumably the long ford from which three villages take their name, until a three-arched concrete road bridge was built c. 1880.[39] East of that bridge lakes were formed north and south of the river by mid 20th-century gravel extraction.[40]

The Roman road thought to link Winchester and Old Salisbury to the Mendips,[41] and a ridge way, sometimes called the Grovely ridge way, leading from Wilton along the Wylye–Nadder watershed, may have crossed the southern tip of the parish. Berwick Lane may have been part of the Harrow way, an ancient road thought to link Kent and Somerset, which may have crossed the Wylye at the ford.[42] A road crossing the northern downs was the main road from Southampton and Salisbury to Bath and Bristol, via Tinhead in Edington, and a road branched from it leading to Chitterne.[43] It was superseded by two other roads to Bath turnpiked in 1761, one through Steeple Langford village linking the villages on the left bank of the Wylye between Wilton and Warminster, the other via Market Lavington over the downs further east. Both were disturnpiked in 1870.[44] In the 20th century the road through Steeple Langford became the main Southampton–Bristol road, and it was designated a trunk road in 1946.[45] A new section to bypass the village was built in 1989.[46] A downland road across the north part of the parish, crossing the old Bath road near the north-east boundary, was turnpiked between Amesbury and Mere in 1761 and disturnpiked in 1871. As part of the main London–Exeter road it was designated a trunk road in 1958. A Wilton–Warminster road through Hanging Langford, linking the villages between Great Wishford and Bishopstrow on the right bank of the Wylye, was turnpiked between Little Langford and Stockton, also in 1761, and disturnpiked in 1871.[47]

The Salisbury–Warminster section of the G.W.R. was opened across the parish in 1856. A halt at Hanging Langford was closed in 1857,[48] after which the nearest station was at Wylye.

Artefacts of the Neolithic period and later have been found in the parish, nine bowl barrows have been identified, and four prehistoric settlement sites and the Grovely Grim's ditch are on or near the parish boundary.[49] To the north Yarnbury castle is a large circular hill fort constructed c. 650 × c. 400 B.C. and extended all around 400–100 B.C. and by a west enclosure in Roman times.[50] To the south-east East castle is a much smaller hill fort or enclosure possibly of the Iron Age,[51] and to the south-west Church End ring and Hanging Langford camp were late Iron-Age settlements, with enclosures for livestock, and were still occupied in the Roman period.[52] There were prehistoric field systems on both the north and south downs.[53]

Later settlement was beside the Wylye and, even in the 19th and 20th centuries, there has been virtually no settlement on the downs. With 230 poll-tax payers the parish was very populous in 1377.[54] The population was 523 in 1801. It rose steadily to reach a peak of 634 in 1851 but was again 523 in 1881. The decline continued, with fluctuations, and the population was 410 in 1931.[55] The addition of Little Langford and new housing after the Second World War increased it, and it was 517 in 1991.[56]

Steeple Langford, with c. 1,640 a., had more land than either Hanging Langford or Little Langford:[57] it had 83 poll-tax payers in 1377, slightly fewer than Hanging Langford,[58] and had 354 inhabitants in 1841, when it was more populous than Hanging Langford.[59] It was sometimes called Great Langford:[60] the epithet Steeple, in use in 1285,[61] is probably derived from a spire on the church.[62] Like others in the Wylye valley Steeple Langford church stands near the river: the rectory house, the demesne farm buildings of Steeple Langford manor, and a mill are nearby, respectively east, north, and west.[63] The old Salisbury–Bath trunk road crosses the village east–west: most of the village is beside that and Duck Street, which leads south to the former ford and the bridge. The demesne farmhouse, Manor House, was built in the later 17th century with a seven-bayed south front of chequered limestone and flint and a small twin-gabled stair and service projection at the rear: a

36 *Andrews and Dury, Map* (W.R.S. viii), pl. 5; O.S. Maps 6", Wilts. LIX (1889 and later edns.); W.R.O., tithe award.
37 Below, econ. hist.; Bathampton, econ. hist.; Hanging Langford, econ. hist.   38 Eton Coll. Mun. 43/73.
39 K. D. D. Henderson, *Short Acct. of the Par. of Steeple Langford* (priv. print. 1973), 3; *P.N. Wilts.* (E.P.N.S.), 227; W.R.O. 502/23.
40 Inf. from Mr. D. H. Andrews, East Clyffe.
41 I. D. Margary, *Rom. Roads in Brit.* (1973), pp. 101–2; O.S. Map 1/625,000, Rom. Brit., S. (1978 edn.).
42 H. W. Timperley and E. Brill, *Anct. Trackways of Wessex*, 59, 64, 134, and map 6; W.R.O. 212B/7190H.
43 Timperley and Brill, op. cit. 39; *Andrews and Dury, Map* (W.R.S. viii), pls. 5, 7–8; *V.C.H. Wilts.* viii. 239–40; O.S. Map 1", sheet 14 (1817 edn.).
44 *V.C.H. Wilts.* iv. 257, 270; *L.J.* xxx. 77.
45 W.R.O., F 4/200/3.

46 *Wilts. Co. Council News* (Wilts. co. council), Feb. 1989.
47 *V.C.H. Wilts.* iv. 257, 270; *L.J.* xxx. 138; W.R.O., F 4/200/21.
48 *V.C.H. Wilts.* iv. 281, 283–4, 293.
49 Ibid. i (1), 107–8, 191, 251, 262, 269.
50 Ibid. i (2), 410 and pl. facing that p., 417–18, 430.
51 Ibid. i (1), 269.
52 Ibid. i (2), 421, 429, 432, 445–6.
53 Ibid. i (1), 273, 278.   54 Ibid. iv. 306–7.
55 Ibid. 351.   56 *Census*, 1991; below, this section.
57 W.R.O., tithe award.   58 *V.C.H. Wilts.* iv. 307.
59 P.R.O., HO 107/1167.
60 *Tax. Eccl.* (Rec. Com.), 181.
61 P.R.O., CP 40/60, rot. 3.
62 *P.N. Wilts.* (E.P.N.S.), 227; cf. below, church [architecture].
63 For the demesne farm, W.R.O., tithe award.

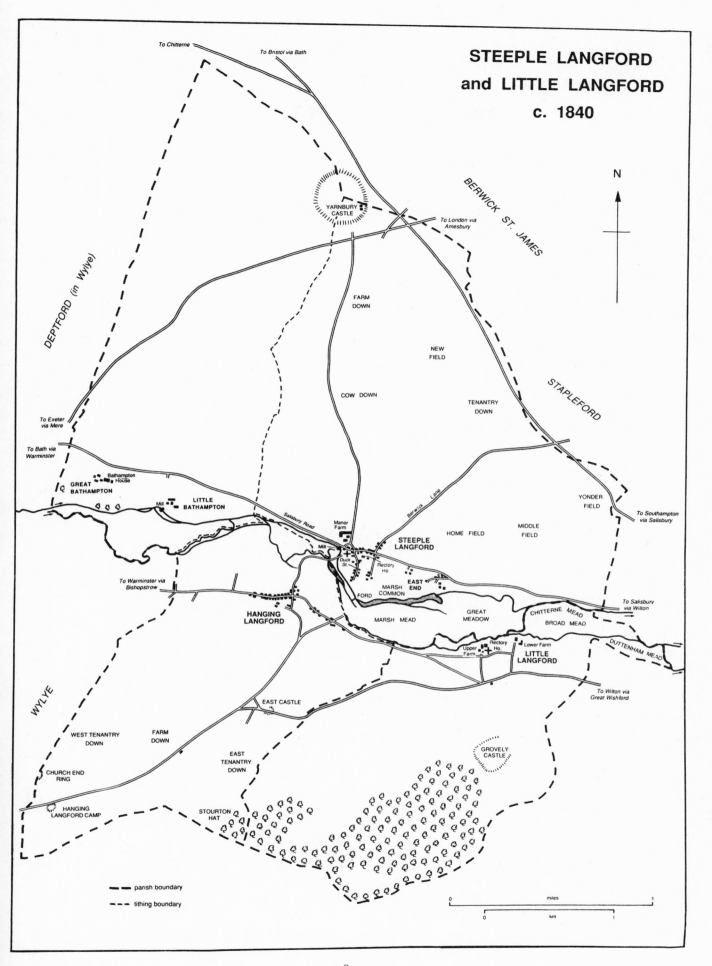

STEEPLE LANGFORD
and LITTLE LANGFORD
c. 1840

N

To Chitterne

To Bristol via Bath

BERWICK ST. JAMES

YARNBURY
CASTLE

To London via
Amesbury

DEPTFORD (in Wylye)

FARM
DOWN

NEW
FIELD

COW DOWN

TENANTRY
DOWN

STAPLEFORD

To Exeter
via Mere

To Bath via
Warminster

GREAT
BATHAMPTON

Bathampton
House

Mill

LITTLE
BATHAMPTON

Salisbury Road

Manor
Farm

Berwick Lane

HOME FIELD

MIDDLE
FIELD

YONDER
FIELD

To Southampton
via Salisbury

STEEPLE
LANGFORD

Mill

Duck
St.

Rectory
Ho.

EAST
END

To Warminster via
Bishopstrow

MARSH
COMMON

HANGING
LANGFORD

FORD

MARSH MEAD

GREAT
MEADOW

CHITTERNE MEAD

To Salisbury
via Wilton

BROAD MEAD

Upper
Farm

Rectory
Ho.

Lower Farm

LITTLE
LANGFORD

DUTTENHAM MEAD

WYLYE

EAST CASTLE

To Wilton via
Great Wishford

WEST TENANTRY
DOWN

FARM
DOWN

EAST
TENANTRY
DOWN

GROVELY
CASTLE

CHURCH END
RING

HANGING
LANGFORD CAMP

STOURTON
HAT

parish boundary
tithing boundary

0   miles   1

0   km   1

mullion bears the date 1679. The ground floor and its windows were apparently altered in the earlier 19th century, the first floor and staircase in the later 19th when a red-brick north-east kitchen wing was built to incorporate an earlier single-storeyed limestone and flint extension. The drawing room contains reset 17th-century panelling. North of the house are extensive 19th- and 20th-century farm buildings. Until *c.* 1800 most of Steeple Langford's land was worked from the village, thereafter as much from buildings further east.[64] Several farmhouses but very few farm buildings except for those of Manor farm survive in the village.

In Duck Street, south of the church and the rectory house, stand a timber-framed and weatherboarded barn, a stone and thatch house dated 1635, and a pair of cottages and a farmhouse both of the 18th century and much altered in the 20th. On the north side of Salisbury Road at the junction with Duck Street is a late 17th-century farmhouse of chequered limestone and flint. A line of buildings east of it includes two red-brick houses of the 18th century, one dated 1788, and an early 19th-century farmhouse with a red-brick façade. On the south side of the road three pairs of rendered estate cottages are dated 1870 and a fourth pair 1871. Several other 18th- and 19th-century cottages and the school stand beside the road; in 1936 a large house was built on the north side of the road at the west end of the village,[65] and about then another south of the road at the east end. A church house built in the churchyard, possibly in the 16th century, was in use as cottages in 1838[66] and 1991; the cottages were renovated in 1947.[67] North of Salisbury Road there were in 1773 a few buildings at the south end of Berwick Lane,[68] of which only a chequered and thatched cottage at the junction with Salisbury Road survives. Several cottages, one dated 1802, were built in the lane in the 19th century. In Duck Street 12 council houses were built in 1956–7, and between then and 1991 a total of *c.* 13 private houses in all parts of the village. In the earlier 19th century a terrace of four cottages was built south of Salisbury Road and east of Duck Street, and in the mid 20th century a road to them from Salisbury Road was remade and called the Wirr. In the Wirr four council houses were built in 1947 and five old people's bungalows in 1969;[69] *c.* 20 homes for old people were built in the 1970s in Edgar's Close off the Wirr.

Steeple Langford had innholders in the 17th century,[70] a public house called the Bell in 1751,[71] and beer retailers in the 19th century.[72] A public house in Salisbury Road at the junction with Berwick Lane was rebuilt and named the Bell between 1880 and 1903:[73] it was closed soon after the village was bypassed in 1989.[74] A private room in the village was used as a parish reading room until 1909.[75]

Tucking Langford, which took its name from a fulling mill,[76] was referred to as a settlement in 1435[77] and had at least 4 households and 23 inhabitants in 1528.[78] It was almost certainly the hamlet east of the village called East End in 1773.[79] Between *c.* 1800 and 1869 the eastern lands of Steeple Langford were worked mainly from the three farmsteads there.[80] The southernmost of the three farmhouses, an 18th-century house of chequered stone and flint, survives. The other buildings were demolished, presumably when, in 1869,[81] East Clyffe Farm was built north of them and the Salisbury–Bath road. The new farmstead consisted of a large farmhouse, of white brick with dressings of red brick and ashlar, model farm buildings, and a pair of cottages. Another pair of cottages was built in the early 20th century[82] and a large bungalow in 1990. On the south side of the road between the village and East Clyffe Farm the East End inn was opened in 1898.[83] It was later called the Rainbow's End.

MANOR AND OTHER ESTATE. Osulf held Steeple Langford in 1066; Waleran the huntsman held it as 10 hides in 1086.[84] The manor of *STEEPLE LANGFORD* descended to Waleran's heirs, possibly in the direct male line and presumably to William son of Waleran, Waleran (fl. 1131) son of William, Walter Waleran (fl. 1166), and Walter Waleran (d. 1200–1).[85] The second Walter's heirs were his daughters Cecily, Aubrey, and Isabel; Cecily married John of Monmouth, Aubrey Sir John de Ingham (d. *c.* 1203) and William de Botreaux (d. *c.* 1209), and Isabel William de Neville. The husbands held the manor jointly in the early 13th century,[86] and John of Monmouth, Aubrey de Botreaux, and Isabel's daughter Joan de Neville (d. *c.* 1263), who married Jordan de St. Martin (d. *c.* 1223), held it jointly and in chief in 1242–3.[87] John of Monmouth (d. *c.* 1248) and Cecily were succeeded by their son John (d. 1257) who settled the manor or his right in it on his brother, evidently half-brother, John of Monmouth.[88] The brother was hanged for mur-

64 Below, econ. hist.
65 W.R.O., G 11/760/249.
66 Ibid. tithe award.
67 Ibid. G 11/760/615.
68 *Andrews and Dury, Map* (W.R.S. viii), pl. 5.
69 W.R.O., G 11/615/1A.
70 Ibid. 492/178; *Early-Stuart Tradesmen* (W.R.S. xv), p. 12.   71 *W.N. & Q.* i. 129.
72 *Kelly's Dir. Wilts.* (1859 and later edns.).
73 O.S. Map 6", Wilts. LIX. SE. (1901 edn.); W.R.O. 1075/001/70.   74 Local inf.
75 W.R.O. 776/106; Eton Coll. Mun., bursary estate files, sundry corresp., letter from Holden, 1913.
76 Below, econ. hist. (mills).
77 *Feet of F. 1377–1509* (W.R.S. xli), p. 106.
78 *L. & P. Hen. VIII,* iv (2), p. 1700.

79 *Andrews and Dury, Map* (W.R.S. viii), pl. 5.
80 W.R.O., tithe award; below, econ. hist.
81 Date on farmho., farm bldgs., and cottages.
82 O.S. Maps 6", Wilts. LIX. SE. (1901, 1926 edns.).
83 Date on bldg.   84 *V.C.H. Wilts.* ii, p. 151.
85 *V.C.H. Hants,* iv. 351, 521; I. J. Sanders, *Eng. Baronies,* 96, where Walter (d. 1200–1) is said to be the son of Waleran (fl. 1131); Hoare, *Mod. Wilts.* Cawden, 73; *Red Bk. Exch.* (Rolls Ser.), i. 241.
86 *Red Bk. Exch.* (Rolls Ser.), i. 153–4; ii. 483; *V.C.H. Hants,* iv. 521; Sanders, *Eng. Baronies,* 96–7, which this acct. of Walter Waleran's successors corrects at several points.
87 *Cal. Inq. p.m.* i, p. 166; *Ex. e Rot. Fin.* i. 100; *Bk. of Fees,* ii. 716; P.R.O., CP 40/355, rot. 89 and d.
88 Sanders, *Eng. Baronies,* 96; *Cal. Inq. p.m.* i, p. 101; *Close R. 1256–9,* 63; P.R.O., CP 40/355, rot. 89 and d.

DURNFORD
Little Durnford Manor from the south-west

STEEPLE LANGFORD
Bathampton House from the north-east

WYLYE

The chalice of 1525

BERWICK ST. JAMES

The chalice of c. 1200

der in 1281.[89] Aubrey (d. *c.* 1270) had a son Walter de Ingham (d. *c.* 1253) and a grandson and heir Oliver de Ingham (d. 1282),[90] and Joan had a son William de St. Martin (d. *c.* 1291).[91] Oliver and William claimed the manor but Edward I took it as an escheat, asserting that John of Monmouth (d. 1281) held it in chief,[92] and in 1299 settled it as dower on Queen Margaret.[93] In 1304 Oliver's son Sir John de Ingham and William's son Reynold de St. Martin petitioned parliament for the manor, acknowledging the king's right to have held it for a year and a day but claiming it as their escheat on the grounds that John of Monmouth (d. 1281) held it not in chief but of the heirs of his brother John as coparceners.[94] In 1306 they recovered seisin,[95] and by 1310 had partitioned the manor,[96] which thereafter descended in moieties until 1588.

Sir John de Ingham's moiety passed at his death *c.* 1310 to his son Sir Oliver, from 1328 Lord Ingham (d. 1343 or 1344). Lord Ingham's relict Elizabeth held it[97] until her death in 1350, when it passed to his daughter Joan, Baroness Ingham (d. between 1360 and 1365), wife of Sir Roger Lestrange, Lord Strange (d. 1349), and later of Sir Miles de Stapleton (d. 1364). It descended with the Ingham title to Joan's son Sir Miles de Stapleton[98] (d. 1419), to that Sir Miles's son Sir Brian[99] (d. 1438), and to Sir Brian's son Sir Miles[1] (d. 1466), after whose death it was assigned to his daughter Joan (d. 1519), wife of Christopher Harcourt and later of Sir John Huddelstone (d. 1512).[2] Joan was succeeded by her son Sir Simon Harcourt (d. 1547), from whom the moiety descended in the direct line with the manor of Stanton Harcourt (Oxon.) to Sir John (d. 1565), Sir Simon (d. 1577), and Sir Walter. In 1581 Richard Knapton bought it from Sir Walter[3] and in 1585 sold it to Thomas Mompesson (d. 1587) of Little Bathampton.[4] In 1588 Mompesson's executors sold it to Nicholas Mussell, who already owned the second moiety.[5]

Reynold de St. Martin (d. *c.* 1315)[6] settled his moiety on the marriage of his son Laurence (d. 1318), whose relict Sibyl,[7] wife of John Scures, held it until her death in 1349. It passed to Laurence's son Laurence[8] (d. 1385) who settled it on his nephew Henry Popham[9] (d. 1418).[10] Popham's relict Margaret (fl. 1428) held the

moiety as dower[11] and it passed to his son Sir Stephen (d. 1444), whose heirs were his four daughters, all minors.[12] The moiety passed to his daughter Alice (d. 1477), was held by her husband Humphrey Forster (d. 1500), and passed in the direct line to Sir George Forster[13] (will proved 1533) of Aldermaston (Berks.), Sir Humphrey (d. 1556), and William (d. 1574),[14] who in 1557 sold it to John Mussell for a rent charge of £34.[15] The rent charge descended to William's son Sir Humphrey (d. 1602) and to Sir Humphrey's son Sir William,[16] who in 1605 sold it to trustees under the settlement on the marriage of Tristram Mussell and Bridget Whitaker.[17] The moiety of the manor descended from John Mussell (d. 1576) to his son Nicholas, who united the two moieties in 1588.[18]

From Nicholas Mussell (d. 1619) Steeple Langford manor passed to his son Tristram[19] (d. 1624) and to Tristram's son Nicholas,[20] who in 1628 sold it to Sir Richard Grobham (d. 1629) of Great Wishford.[21] Grobham devised it to his wife Margaret (d. 1637) for life, to his brother John (will proved 1646) for life, to a relative George Grobham, who evidently predeceased John, and to his own heirs.[22] By 1647 it had passed to Sir Richard's nephew and heir John Howe (cr. baronet 1660).[23] From then until *c.* 1807 the manor descended with Great Wishford manor and was held after Sir John by Sir Richard Grobham Howe, Bt. (d. 1703), Sir Richard Howe, Bt. (d. 1730), Mary Howe (d. 1735), John Howe, Lord Chedworth (d. 1742), John, Lord Chedworth (d. 1762), Henry, Lord Chedworth (d. 1781), and John, Lord Chedworth (d. 1804).[24] About 1807 Chedworth's executors sold the manor, *c.* 1,660 a., to Alexander Baring[25] (cr. Baron Ashburton 1835, d. 1848). It passed with the barony to Alexander's sons William (d. 1864) and Francis (d. 1868), to Francis's son Alexander (d. 1889), and to Alexander's son Francis,[26] who in 1896 sold it to E. T. Hooley, a fraudulent financier declared bankrupt in 1898. Sir Christopher Furness bought the manor in 1898 and, through the Cavendish Land Company, offered it for sale in lots in 1909.[27]

In 1910 Manor farm, 878 a., including land in Berwick St. James, was bought by W. N. D.

[89] *Rot. Parl.* i. 185.

[90] *Cal. Inq. p.m.* i, p. 232; *Complete Peerage*, vii. 65 n.

[91] *Cal. Inq. p.m.* i, p. 166; *Cal. Fine R.* 1272–1307, 295; P.R.O., CP 40/355, rot. 89 and d.

[92] *Cal. Fine R.* 1272–1307, 185; P.R.O., CP 40/60, rot. 3; CP 40/355, rot. 89 and d.

[93] *Cal. Pat.* 1292–1301, 452.

[94] *Rot. Parl.* i. 168, 184–7.

[95] *Cal. Pat.* 1301–7, 505.

[96] *Cal. Inq. p.m.* v, p. 124; P.R.O., CP 40/355, rot. 89 and d.

[97] *Cal. Inq. p.m.* v, p. 124; viii, pp. 374, 377, 381; for the Ingham title, *Complete Peerage*, vii. 58–66.

[98] *Cal. Inq. p.m.* ix, p. 395; xv, p. 20.

[99] P.R.O., C 138/39, no. 47, rot. 10.

[1] Ibid. C 139/92, no. 34, rot. 10.

[2] Ibid. C 140/19, no. 19; *Complete Peerage*, vii. 65.

[3] Burke, *Land. Gent.* (1898), i. 679–80; *V.C.H. Oxon.* xii. 275; P.R.O., C 1/414, no. 1; ibid. CP 40/1394, Carte rott. 23–4.

[4] W.R.O. 492/161; P.R.O., C 142/215, no. 266.

[5] W.R.O. 492/156, deed, South to Mussell, 1588; below, this section.   [6] *Cal. Inq. p.m.* v, pp. 295–6.

[7] Ibid. vi, p. 110; P.R.O., C 143/190, no. 4.

[8] *Cal. Inq. p.m.* ix, p. 184.

[9] Ibid. xvi, pp. 108–9; P.R.O., C 143/402, no. 4.

[10] P.R.O., C 138/33, no. 36.   [11] *Feud. Aids*, v. 244.

[12] P.R.O., C 139/121, no. 18.

[13] Ibid. C 140/56, no. 41; *Cal. Inq. p.m. Hen. VII*, ii, p. 235.

[14] *V.C.H. Berks.* iii. 389; *Hist. Parl., Commons*, 1558–1603, ii. 146; P.R.O., PROB 11/25, f. 4; ibid. STAC 2/25/34.

[15] P.R.O., CP 25/2/81/694, no. 44.

[16] *V.C.H. Berks.* iii. 389–90; *Hist. Parl., Commons*, 1558–1603, ii. 146.

[17] W.R.O. 492/156, deed, Foyle to Whitaker, 1607.

[18] P.R.O., C 142/175, no. 109; above, this section.

[19] P.R.O., C 142/379, no. 45.

[20] Ibid. C 142/403, no. 12.

[21] *Wilts. Inq. p.m.* 1625–49 (Index Libr.), 106–7; W.R.O. 492/156, deed, Mussell to Grobham, 1628.

[22] *W.N. & Q.* v. 37; Hoare, *Mod. Wilts.* Branch and Dole, facing p. 46; *V.C.H. Wilts.* xiii. 101.

[23] W.R.O. 492/170.

[24] Below, Great Wishford, manor.

[25] *W.A.M.* xxxv. 311; W.R.O. 374/128/45.

[26] *Complete Peerage*, i. 276–8.

[27] *V.C.H. Wilts.* x. 23; W.A.S. Libr., sale cat. ii, no. 18; W.R.O. 776/106.

Burrows,[28] whose executors sold it to his son-in-law E. F. Andrews. Apart from its water meadows and c. 220 a. north of the Amesbury–Mere road, including the land in Berwick St. James, Andrews sold it in 1948 to Mr. D. F. H. McCormick, who in 1989 sold it with the greater part of Little Bathampton manor to Mr. R. P. Merrick, the owner in 1991. The land north of the Amesbury–Mere road was bought c. 1948 by B. G. Ivory, the owner of Little Bathampton manor, was sold by him to Lord Hugh Russell in 1962, and passed with Great Bathampton manor to Mr. and Mrs. A. J. Maitland-Robinson, the owners in 1991.[29] East Clyffe farm, 826 a. including land in other parishes, was bought by Henry Andrews in 1909, was given by him to his four unmarried daughters, and in 1948 was bought from them by his son E. F. Andrews. In 1948 Andrews conveyed it to his son Mr. D. H. Andrews who, with members of his family, owned the farm in 1991.[30]

A small estate in Steeple Langford later called *KINGSTON'S* was possibly that in 1242–3 assessed as ⅒ knight's fee and held by John de Campeny.[31] John of Kingston held it in 1291.[32] It passed to Nicholas Kingston (d. c. 1323), who left a wife Anstice and as heir a brother John. John forfeited his lands as a contrariant but on the return to England of Queen Isabella in 1326 he re-entered by force.[33] The estate passed with Little Corsley manor in Corsley to his son Thomas and to Thomas's son Sir John (fl. 1383), and perhaps with that manor in the Kingston family until the death of Mary Kingston, wife of Thomas Lisle, in 1539.[34] It belonged to John Brimsden in 1560[35] and probably to Thomas Brimsden of Steeple Langford in 1587. Thomas Brimsden of East Stowell in Wilcot held it in 1599[36] and 1632,[37] and in 1652 his son Thomas (d. 1685) settled it on himself and his wife Anne (d. 1711).[38] Thomas's son Thomas married Eleanor Blagden[39] and Kingston's passed to a spinster Eleanor Brimsden, presumably the youngest Thomas's daughter and heir. In 1713 and 1717 Eleanor held it jointly with Edward Blagden[40] (d. 1730) of Keevil,[41] who was evidently her heir or assign. By 1733 it had passed to Edward's relict Anne Blagden (d. 1769)[42] and in 1770 was sold by her daughters Anne and Eleanor Blagden to Thomas Blake[43] (d. 1808). Blake devised Kingston's, 62 a. and pasture rights, to his niece Mary Dredge (d. 1816), wife of George Smith, for life, and to his grand-nephew John Dredge (d. 1812), whose son Solomon Dredge held it from 1816[44] to his death in 1856. Dredge's heirs were his sister Anne (d.

1858), wife of William Blake, and nephew J. J. Marshall.[45] Francis, Lord Ashburton, bought the estate, a moiety from Marshall in 1867 and a moiety from Anne Blake's trustees in 1868,[46] and added it to Steeple Langford manor.

ECONOMIC HISTORY. In some aspects of agriculture Steeple Langford showed remarkable continuity: the proportions, two fifths and three fifths respectively, in which the land was divided between demesne and tenantry, the largely several cultivation of the demesne, and the arrangement of the tenantry's common meadows, common pastures, and three open fields are all likely to have changed little between the late 11th century and the mid 19th.[47] In 1086 there was land for 5 ploughteams: 2 were on the 5 demesne hides with 5 *servi*, and 8 *villani* and 4 bordars had 3 teams. There were 30 a. of meadow, and pasture ½ league by 2 furlongs.[48] In the 1290s the demesne was in hand and c. 260 a. were sown each year: in 1295–6, for example, 81 a. of wheat, 83 a. of barley, 11 a. of dredge, 70 a. of oats, 10 a. of peas, and 9 a. of vetch were sown. Livestock included a flock of 200–250 sheep and a small herd of cows. Stock was brought to Steeple Langford from Adam de Stratton's lands in north-east Wiltshire while both were in the king's hands c. 1290. In Steeple Langford c. 21 yardlands were held by freeholders (3), the rector (c. 2), customary tenants (15), and the tenant of the corn mill (1). The customary holdings were small, 11 of 1 yardland, 6 of ½ yardland, 3 of ⅓ yardland, and 13 of little more than a cottage. Instead of rent and other service one yardlander had to represent the manor at hundred and county courts and to carry the king's writs.[49]

The working of the land was unaffected by the partition of the manor which took place between 1306 and 1310.[50] The demesne was possibly leased in the early 14th century, and was so in the later 15th. In the early 16th century it was held by a member of the Mussell family,[51] which later owned the manor, and presumably remained a sheep-and-corn farm, but in the 1560s feeding on it for 500 sheep was leased to the owner of Great Bathampton manor.[52] In 1628 the large and mainly several farm was reckoned 12 yardlands; 26 tenants, who had open fields called East, Middle, and West, and of whom 9 were lessees, then held a total of 19 yardlands, and some holdings, one of 3 yardlands, one of 2½, and two of 1½, were larger than before. The rector held a few acres in the farm

28 W.R.O., Inland Revenue, val. reg. 143; ibid. 776/107.
29 Inf. from Mr. D. H. Andrews, East Clyffe; Mr. D. F. H. McCormick, Mawarden Ct., Stratford-sub-Castle; Mr. A. J. Maitland-Robinson, Bathampton Ho.; map of Yarnbury Grange estate, 1958, and sale cat., 1989, in possession of Mr. Maitland-Robinson; below, Bathampton, manors.
30 Inf. from Mr. Andrews.
31 *Bk. of Fees*, ii. 716.
32 *Feet of F.* 1272–1327 (W.R.S. i), p. 37.
33 *Cal. Inq. p.m.* vi, p. 252; P.R.O., SC 6/1148/19A.
34 *V.C.H. Wilts.* viii. 16; P.R.O., C 260/94, no. 59.
35 P.R.O., CP 25/2/239/2 Eliz. I Hil.
36 Hist. MSS. Com. 55, *Var. Colln.* i, p. 69; W.R.O. 212B/6211.
37 W.R.O. 212B/6217.

38 Ibid. 212B/6221; 212B/6224–5; 502/1.
39 Ibid. 212B/6227.
40 Ibid. 212B/6228–9.   41 Ibid. 653/1.
42 Ibid. 212B/6231; 653/5.
43 Ibid. 212B/6235.
44 Ibid. 212B/6240; 212B/6244.   45 Ibid. 212B/6246.
46 Ibid. 212B/6258; 212B/6260.
47 Below, this section.
48 *V.C.H. Wilts.* ii, p. 151.
49 *Stratton Accts.* (W.R.S. xiv), p. xxv; P.R.O., SC 6/1058/7; for the glebe, W.R.O., D 1/24/126/1.
50 Above, manor (Steeple Langford).
51 P.R.O., STAC 2/25/34.
52 Ibid. REQ 2/238/37; above, manor (Steeple Langford).

fields although he kept his sheep in the tenants' flock;[53] on the other hand, by the later 17th century some customary land had been added to the farm.[54] By 1662 a new meadow had been made, presumably by controlling the flow of the Wylye over marshy ground and evidently that south-east of the village later called Marsh mead, 27 a.,[55] and by 1685 downland north-east of the village had been ploughed to form New field, 48 a.: the new meadow was divided and allotted in small closes but the new arable, divided into 36 strips, was open field. In 1685 a yardland consisted of c. 20 a. in the old open fields, c. 2 a. in New field, 1½ a. in the common meadows, 1 a. in the new meadow, and feeding for 6 beasts and 42 sheep: 5½ yardlands were then in a single holding.[56]

Common husbandry on the tenantry lands continued throughout the 18th century. To supervise the watering of meadows the manor court sometimes appointed surveyors of waterworks, who were paid 5s. for each acre watered;[57] the court also appointed overseers of fences and overseers of furrows.[58] The demesne, Manor farm, 567 a. in 1807 and 1838, occupied the west part of Steeple Langford tithing with buildings at the north-west corner of the village: it included Farm down, 196 a., 21 a. of meadow of which 19 a. were watered in 1807, c. 34 a. of lowland pasture, c. 310 a. of arable, and the exclusive right to feed sheep on Cow down in winter. To the east Yonder, 164 a., Middle, c. 134 a., Home, c. 131 a., and New were open fields with a total of c. 814 strips. Tenantry down, 281 a., and 25 a. of slopes too steep to plough were for c. 1,175 sheep throughout the year; Marsh common, 27 a. immediately south-east of the village, was for cattle, Cow down, 95 a., was for cattle in summer, and Great meadow, 51 a., was fed on by cattle after haymaking. The farmer of the demesne took the hay from two fifths of Great meadow and could keep 40 beasts in the herd of c. 100. In 1807 the open arable was held by the rector (c. 38 a.), the owner of Kingston's (c. 56 a.), and c. 9 tenants of Steeple Langford manor (between 6 a. and 115 a.).[59]

The commonable lands were inclosed by Act in 1866,[60] but before then, especially between 1807 and 1838, the number of those sharing them was reduced by accumulation of holdings. In 1838 a single tenant held 509 a. including 734 strips, c. 376 a., in the open fields. His farm was apparently worked mainly from buildings at East End. The only other farm on the commonable

lands was Kingston's, 60 a., also worked from East End.[61] After inclosure and the absorption of Kingston's into Steeple Langford manor 1867–8[62] nearly all the land of the manor was in two long and narrow farms, and in 1869 new buildings, East Clyffe Farm, were erected for the eastern one. In 1898 Manor farm was 874 a., including Cow down and 184 a. of downland in Berwick St. James, and East Clyffe farm was 824 a., including the old open fields, Tenantry down, and 41 a. of downland in Berwick St. James.[63] The tenant of East Clyffe from 1894, Henry Andrews, invented the Andrews sacklifter.[64] There was no major change of land use before 1939,[65] but afterwards more of the downland was ploughed. In 1989 Manor farm, 905 a. including Little Bathampton land, was mainly arable: coverts had been planted earlier and game birds were shot for sport.[66] East Clyffe farm had a dairy herd until the early 1960s. In 1991, then c. 800 a., it was an arable and sheep farm on which land was leased for pig and poultry rearing.[67]

Clothmaking at Steeple Langford is suggested by references to a weaver there in 1575,[68] to a clothier in 1632,[69] and to women who carded and spun wool in the late 18th century.[70] In the later 17th century Thomas Sadler of Steeple Langford prepared flints for use in guns.[71] Gravel was extracted from beside the Wylye in the 1940s and 1950s.[72]

MILLS. There was a mill at Steeple Langford in 1086,[73] and a corn mill was part of Steeple Langford manor until the 20th century.[74] It was in hand in 1294, when it needed repair: new stones were installed and the mill was leased in 1297–8.[75] From the early 14th century to 1588 there was a moiety of the mill in each part of the manor.[76] In the early 16th century the mill was rebuilt to house a grist and a malt mill, and in the 1530s and 1540s there were disputes over how the Wylye was divided into streams to serve Steeple Langford mill to the north and Hanging Langford mill to the south.[77] Steeple Langford mill was described as a grist and malt mill in 1796:[78] it is not clear for how long it was used for malt. The corn mill, which was bought by G. H. Chilcott in 1909,[79] was used until the First World War.[80] The mill was refronted with red brick in the late 18th or early 19th century.

A fulling mill stood in Steeple Langford in the 13th century but in the 1290s was said to have fallen to the ground.[81] It was rebuilt, or a new fulling mill was built, and by 1435 had given a name to Tucking Langford.[82] The mill and its

53 W.R.O., D 1/24/126/1; ibid. 492/156, deed, Mussell to Grobham, 1628.   54 Ibid. 492/186.
55 Ibid. 130/11, lease, Chedworth to Thring, 1760; 374/128/45; 492/178.
56 Ibid. 374/128/45; 492/196; ibid. tithe award.
57 Ibid. 130/11, ct. papers.
58 Ibid. 2057/M 75.
59 Ibid. 212B/6240; 374/128/45; ibid. D 1/24/126/3; ibid. tithe award.
60 Ibid. EA/186.
61 Ibid. 374/128/45; ibid. tithe award.
62 Above, manor.
63 W.A.S. Libr., sale cat. ii, no. 18; W.R.O. 776/106; date on bldgs.
64 Inf. from Mr. Andrews.
65 [1st] Land Util. Surv. Map, sheet 122.
66 Sale cat., 1989, in possession of Mr. Maitland-Robinson.
67 Inf. from Mr. Andrews.

68 Cal. Pat. 1572–5, p. 515.
69 W.R.O. 212B/6220.
70 W. Cobbett, Rural Rides, ed. E. W. Martin, 324.
71 Aubrey, Nat. Hist. Wilts. ed. Britton, 43.
72 W.A.M. liii. 251; inf. from Mr. Andrews.
73 V.C.H. Wilts. ii, p. 151.
74 W.R.O. 776/106.
75 P.R.O., SC 6/1058/7; SC 12/16/66.
76 e.g. ibid. STAC 3/3/13; Wilts. Inq. p.m. 1327–77 (Index Libr.), 159; above, manor (Steeple Langford).
77 P.R.O., C 60/393, no. 24; ibid. STAC 2/20/333; STAC 2/33/5; STAC 3/3/13.
78 W.R.O. 531.
79 W.A.S. Libr., sale cat. ix, no. 15.
80 Kelly's Dir. Wilts. (1915 and later edns.).
81 P.R.O., SC 6/1058/7.
82 Feet of F. 1377–1509 (W.R.S. xli), pp. 105–6; above, intro.

A HISTORY OF WILTSHIRE

pond were mentioned as late as 1698[83] but fulling may have ceased before then.

FAIR. A fair at Yarnbury castle on 23 and 24 September for cattle and general merchandise was granted to Sir Richard Howe in 1718.[84] No evidence supports the tradition that the fair was ancient.[85] It apparently flourished in the 18th century, and by the late 18th century, when it was held within the hill fort on 5 October, buildings had been erected for it. It was later for sheep on 4 October[86] and for hiring or amusements on a second day. It declined in the late 19th and early 20th century, and was moved to Wylye in 1917.[87] In the 1920s it was for sheep and a few cattle and horses,[88] and it has not been held since c. 1929.[89]

LOCAL GOVERNMENT. Neither Bathampton nor Hanging Langford was in Steeple Langford tithing.[90] A court of Steeple Langford manor was held in the late 13th century,[91] but no formal record of it before 1716 survives. The court baron, at which the homage presented rules for common husbandry, met six times in the period 1716–24, each time in autumn; most of the presentments were repeated at each meeting, but the rules were sometimes varied or added to. From 1722 orders to repair the stocks were made.[92] The court was held yearly 1782–1800, and at each meeting the homage presented the same list of orders governing aspects of common husbandry; the death of tenants was reported and a hayward was appointed.[93]

Steeple Langford parish's spending on poor relief was above average in the later 18th century: £139 was spent in 1775–6, an average of £149 1783–5. In the early 19th century the two overseers gave most relief as regular doles: 20 adults were relieved regularly in 1802–3, c. 15 in 1809–10, c. 25 in 1819–20, and c. 40 in 1829–30. Other relief included payments for clothing, medical services, and fuel. Total expenditure on the poor fluctuated between £734, in 1812–13,[94] and £305, in 1829–30.[95] The parish became part of Wilton poor-law union in 1836,[96] and of Salisbury district in 1974.[97]

CHURCH. Steeple Langford church was ap-

parently standing in the 12th century.[98] Recommendations of 1650 that Hanging Langford should be transferred to Little Langford parish and half of Bathampton to Fisherton de la Mere parish were not adopted.[99] In 1973 Steeple Langford was united with Little Langford to form the parish and benefice of the Langfords, and that benefice was united then with the benefice of Wylye and Fisherton de la Mere. In 1979 Stockton was added to create the new benefice of Yarnbury.[1]

John of Monmouth, who held Steeple Langford manor 1257–81, presented a rector,[2] the king, who held the manor 1281–99, presented in 1295, 1298, and 1299,[3] and Queen Margaret, who held the manor 1299–1306, presented in 1304.[4] When, between 1306 and 1310, the manor was partitioned Sir John de Ingham and Reynold de St. Martin was each allotted the right to present alternate rectors. Sir John was to have the first turn[5] and his son Sir Oliver (later Lord Ingham) presented in 1321.[6] In 1348 Reynold's grandson Laurence de St. Martin and the king disputed the patronage and made rival presentations. On the grounds that it had not been partitioned with the manor the king claimed that the advowson was the inheritance of Lord Ingham's granddaughter Mary Curzon who was then a minor. Although a nominee of the king may have been instituted in 1348,[7] Laurence established his right, and subsequently the advowson descended in moieties with the moieties of Steeple Langford manor, each lord to present alternately. In 1507 Henry Mervyn and William Tomson, possibly trustees of the Mompesson family, presented Henry Mompesson by grant of a turn from Sir George Forster, and Michael Scot, the grantee of Sir Humphrey Forster, presented in 1548.[8] John Mussell bought William Forster's moiety in 1557:[9] in 1572 he granted a turn to John Bailey, who became lessee of the rectory after his own grantee James Parham alias Wiseman presented John Parham, rector 1572–1607.[10] In 1586 Sir Walter Harcourt sold his moiety of the advowson to, apparently, trustees for Bailey, and Bailey also bought Mussell's moiety. Bailey (d. 1600), a mayor of Salisbury, devised the advowson to his son Samuel,[11] but in 1607–8 his elder son and executor John sold it to Joseph Collier, by whose grant his father Giles Collier presented him as

83 P.R.O., C 60/393, no. 24; W.R.O. 502/24.
84 P.R.O., C 66/3530, no. 21.
85 Henderson, *Steeple Langford*, 8.
86 *Rep. Com. Mkt. Rights and Tolls* [C. 5550], p. 215, H.C. (1888), liii; W.R.O. 130/11, lease, Chedworth to Swayne, 1771; 776/106; ibid. tithe award.
87 Henderson, *Steeple Langford*, 8; W. H. Hudson, *Shepherd's Life*, 160–1; *W.A.M.* xlvi. 198; D. Howell, *Remember the Wylye Valley*, 24.
88 *Mkts. and Fairs* (H.M.S.O. 1929), iv (E. and S. Mkts.), 209, 220.
89 *Kelly's Dir. Wilts.* (1920 and later edns.); inf. from Major-Gen. J. M. Brockbank, Manor Ho.
90 Below, Bathampton, local govt.; Hanging Langford, local govt.   91 P.R.O., SC 6/1058/7.
92 W.R.O. 130/11, ct. papers.   93 Ibid. 2057/M 75.
94 Ibid. 502/18; *Poor Law Abstract, 1804*, 558–9; *1818*, 492–3.
95 *Poor Rate Returns, 1816–21*, 186; *1822–4*, 225; *1825–9*, 216; *1830–4*, 209.

96 *Poor Law Com. 2nd Rep.* App. D, 560.
97 O.S. Map 1/100,000, admin. areas, Wilts. (1974 edn.).
98 Below, this section [architecture].
99 *W.A.M.* xl. 299, 393.
1 Ch. Com. file, NB 34/412C.
2 P.R.O., CP 40/355, rot. 89 and d.
3 *Cal. Pat.* 1292–1301, 130, 385, 397.
4 *Reg. Ghent* (Cant. & York Soc.), ii. 629.
5 P.R.O., CP 40/355, rot. 89 and d.
6 Phillipps, *Wilts. Inst.* i. 18.
7 Ibid. 43; *Cal. Pat.* 1348–50, 38, 132, 192, 216; 1354–8, 153; *Wilts. Inq. p.m.* 1327–77 (Index Libr.), 159–62; P.R.O., CP 40/355, rot. 89 and d.
8 Phillipps, *Wilts. Inst.* i. 107, 126–7, 134, 141, 143, 165, 184, 187, 189, 191, 213.
9 *Cal. Pat.* 1555–7, 332–3; P.R.O., CP 25/2/81/694, no. 44.
10 Phillipps, *Wilts. Inst.* i. 226; ii. 5; *Hatcher Review*, ii. 87; P.R.O., C 78/94, no. 9.
11 *Hatcher Review*, ii. 86–8; P.R.O., CP 25/2/241/28 & 29 Eliz. I Mich.

rector in 1607.[12] The advowson descended in the Collier family, of which three more were rectors: trustees presented in 1635 and 1670 and Anne Collier, relict of Arthur Collier, rector 1670–98, presented in 1698, 1703, and 1704. Arthur Collier, rector 1704–32,[13] sold the advowson to Corpus Christi College, Oxford, in 1725.[14] The college was assigned a share of the patronage in 1973 and 1979.[15]

The living was highly valued: in 1291 it was worth £20,[16] in the early 15th century £50 a year from it was paid to a rector who had resigned it,[17] it was worth £300 in 1650,[18] the glebe and tithes were leased for a total of £610 c. 1795,[19] and it yielded £594 net c. 1830.[20] The rector was entitled to all the tithes except those from the Hanging Langford manor of which Wilton abbey was overlord,[21] but by 1600 had lost most of the hay tithes.[22] The tithes were valued at £680 in 1838 and commuted.[23] From c. 1600 to the mid 19th century the glebe was c. 50 a. with pasture rights,[24] 60 a. after inclosure in 1866:[25] 37 a. were sold in 1947,[26] 11 a. were sold in 1989, and 7 a. were retained in 1991.[27] A new glebe house was built, apparently in the later 17th century and possibly soon after the Restoration,[28] of chequered flint and limestone with a main south front of seven irregularly disposed bays, a rear stair turret, and possibly a short rear service wing at the west end. In the mid 19th century, possibly soon after 1853 when Michael Harrison was instituted as rector,[29] the windows were renewed, the interior, apart from the staircase, was refitted, a porch on the south and other extensions on the north were built, and a coach house, other outbuildings, and garden walls were all built in chequerwork to match the house. A new house was built c. 1960 and the old one was sold in 1961.[30]

Bathampton and Hanging Langford each had its own chapel in the Middle Ages.[31] At the Reformation there was a light in the parish church endowed with c. 4 a.[32]

John of Winchester, rector 1299–1304, in 1300 was licensed as a subdeacon to be absent for three years to study: he proceeded to the orders of deacon and priest in 1301.[33] Nicholas of Winchester (alias Nicholas Fulflood), rector 1304–21, was an acolyte when instituted: in

1304, when a curate was appointed, Nicholas too was licensed to study for three years and he was ordained priest in 1307.[34] Many later rectors were resident but not, apparently, Cuthbert Tunstall, rector 1509–11 and later bishop of London and of Durham,[35] and R. T. Coates, rector 1802–53 and rector of Sopworth.[36] Joseph Collier, 1607–35, his son Henry, 1636–70, Henry's son Arthur, 1670–97, and Arthur's son Arthur, 1704–32, was each rector.[37] Henry was a royalist in arms and allegedly his wife and 11 children were left homeless in deep snow when he was ejected after the Civil War. The intruders included John Jessop 1646–8 and Nathaniel Giles, 1648–60, who is said to have preached twice on Sundays wearing a pistol at his neck[38] and was later a nonconformist.[39] In 1662 the church lacked a Book of Homilies and Jewell's Apology.[40] Arthur Collier (d. 1732) was the author of the metaphysical treatise Clavis Universalis.[41] In 1783 the rector, Samuel Weller, who was also curate of Little Langford, held two services at Steeple Langford each Sunday, services on other days, and communion with 30–40 communicants five times a year.[42] He died in the pulpit on Easter Sunday in 1795.[43] In 1864 two services were still held each Sunday, with an average congregation of 200, and communion was celebrated at the great festivals, with c. 30 communicants, and on six other Sundays.[44]

By will proved 1853 R. T. Coates gave the income from £100 to Sunday school children or, if no such school was held, to regular churchgoers. In 1904 and 1923 it was used to give treats and prizes to children.[45] Emily Straton (d. 1905) gave the income from £50 for the upkeep of the churchyard,[46] and Mrs. E. M. Brockbank (d. 1964) gave money for a similar purpose. In 1990 the income from all three charities was used as the donors intended.[47]

The church of ALL SAINTS, so called in 1763,[48] is of flint and ashlar, some of it coursed, and has a chancel with north vestry, a nave with north aisle and south porch, and a west tower with a short lead spire. The Purbeck marble font is of the 12th century and the east wall of the nave, which bears the scars of responds for a narrow, aisled, nave, may also be of that date. The chancel arch and the tower arch are 13th-

12 Phillipps, Wilts. Inst. ii. 5; P.R.O., CP 25/2/369/5 Jas. I Hil.
13 Phillipps, Wilts. Inst. ii. 18, 31, 44, 47, 64.
14 Inf. from Mr. C. Butler, Corpus Christi Coll., Oxf.
15 Ch. Com. file, NB 34/412C.
16 Tax. Eccl. (Rec. Com.), 181.
17 W.R.O., D 1/2/8, f. (2nd foliation) 18v.
18 W.A.M. xl. 393.
19 W.R.O. 529/218, Barnard's draft agreement.
20 Rep. Com. Eccl. Revenues, 838–9.
21 Inq. Non. (Rec. Com.), 177; below, Hanging Langford, manors.
22 W.R.O., D 1/24/126/1.
23 Ibid. tithe award.
24 Ibid.; ibid. D 1/24/126/1–3; ibid. 502/24; 592/218, glebe terrier, 1770.   25 Ibid. 451/44.
26 Ch. Com. file 92863.
27 Inf. from Deputy Dioc. Sec. (Property), Church Ho., Crane Street, Salisbury.
28 Below, this section.
29 W.R.O., D 1/48/5, f. 101.
30 Ch. Com. file 574617.
31 Below, Bathampton, church; Hanging Langford,

church.
32 P.R.O., E 309/5/18 Eliz. I/19, no. 5.
33 Reg. Ghent (Cant. & York Soc.), ii. 589, 629, 841, 846.
34 Ibid. 629, 868, 883; Reg. Martival (Cant. & York Soc.), i. 228; P.R.O., CP 40/355, rot. 89 and d.
35 Phillipps, Wilts. Inst. i. 187, 189; D.N.B.
36 Rep. Com. Eccl. Revenues, 838–9; Kelly's Dir. Wilts. (1848); Wilts. & Glos. Standard, 25 June 1853; Ch. Com. file, NB 34/412C.
37 Phillipps, Wilts. Inst. ii. 5, 18, 31, 44, 47, 64; mon. in church.
38 Walker Revised, ed. Matthews, 371–2, 375; W.A.M. xiv. 47–9; Hist. MSS. Com. 55, Var. Colln. i, p. 125.
39 W.N. & Q. viii. 153.
40 W.R.O., D 1/54/1/4, no. 37B.
41 R. Benson, Memoirs of Arthur Collier (1837).
42 Vis. Queries, 1783 (W.R.S. xxvii), pp. 136, 203–4.
43 Sar. Jnl. 13 Apr. 1795.
44 W.R.O., D 1/56/7.
45 Ibid. L 2, Steeple Langford; Endowed Char. Wilts. (S. Div.), 663.   46 Char. Com. file.
47 Inf. from Major-Gen. J. M. Brockbank, Manor Ho.
48 J. Ecton, Thesaurus, 397.

century. The church was largely rebuilt in the 14th century, and was rededicated in 1326:[49] the arcade, the north windows of the aisle, and the windows of the nave are early 14th-century, the tower is largely 14th-century, and the chancel may also have been. In the 15th century a rood stair was built against the south-east corner of the nave, windows were placed in the east and west walls of the aisle, and the upper stage of the tower was built. The porch was 15th- or early 16th-century,[50] and the spire was on the tower in 1589.[51] The chancel was rebuilt on its

1553, when 18 oz. of plate were taken for the king. In 1991 the parish had a chalice of 1609, an almsdish of 1694 given in 1732, a paten of 1695, and a flagon hallmarked for and given in 1768.[58] There were three bells in 1553. Three new bells cast at Salisbury by William Purdue were hung in 1656. A tenor cast in 1737 by William Cockey and a treble cast at Salisbury in 1903 were added later, and one of the bells of 1656 was recast in 1903. Those five bells remained in the church in 1991.[59] The registers begin in 1674 and are complete.[60]

MOMPESSON MONUMENT IN THE CHURCH

old foundations c. 1857 to designs of William Slater.[52] The vestry was built, the porch rebuilt, and the rest of the church reroofed and extensively restored in 1875 to designs by R. H. Carpenter. In 1782–3 two large pews were erected for the Moody family of Great Bathampton at the east end of the aisle, and other seats in the church were re-allotted: the church was reseated in 1875 when the west gallery, which had been erected by 1783, was removed.[53] Parts of a three-decker pulpit dated 1613, which was against the south wall in the mid 19th century, were re-used in 1875 in the reading desk and the pulpit.[54] The church contains monuments to the Mompesson family, an altar tomb commemorating John Mussell (d. 1576), and a stone slab incised, possibly c. 1300, to represent a man carrying a horn.[55] A Saxon cross shaft found at Hanging Langford c. 1937 was placed in the church.[56] A lych gate based on a design by Sir Gilbert Scott was erected in 1902.[57]

A chalice of 12 oz. was kept by the parish in

NONCONFORMITY. Several parishioners failed to attend Steeple Langford church in the later 16th century,[61] and Thomas Brimsden, who probably held the estate called Kingston's, was suspected of recusancy in 1587.[62] There was a protestant nonconformist in the parish in 1676,[63] and one or more papist until 1706 or later.[64] Nonconformists at Hanging Langford and possibly at Great Bathampton are mentioned below.[65]

EDUCATION. There were in the parish in 1818 four small schools at which a total of 67 children too young for agricultural labour were taught to read,[66] but there was no more than a Sunday school in 1833.[67] In 1846–7 there were two Sunday schools united to the National society, and two dame schools.[68] The rector's proposal to extend the aisle of the church eastwards to provide a schoolroom was resisted by the parish in 1856,[69] and in 1858 the only schooling was

49 *Reg. Martival* (Cant. & York Soc.), ii. 501–2.
50 Description based partly on J. Buckler, watercolours in W.A.S. Libr., vol. iii. 9.   51 W.R.O. 212B/7190H.
52 Ibid. D 1/61/10/2.
53 Ibid. D 1/61/1C; D 1/61/26/6; ibid. 502/12.
54 *Church Guide*; watercolour in church.
55 *W.A.M.* xxxv. 383–6; *W.N. & Q.* vii. 145–7.
56 W.R.O., D 1/61/86/14; below, Hanging Langford, intro.   57 Wilts. Cuttings, xvi. 283.
58 Nightingale, *Wilts. Plate*, 70–1; inf. from Major-Gen. Brockbank; *W.A.M.* xxvi. 334 lists a paten of 1717.
59 Walters, *Wilts. Bells*, 116, 291, 319; inf. from Major-

Gen. Brockbank.
60 W.R.O. 502/1–8A; bishop's transcripts for 1608–38 and 1672–4 are ibid.
61 Ibid. D 1/43/2, f. 8; D 1/43/5, f. 28; D 1/43/6, ff. 13v.–14.
62 Hist. MSS. Com. 55, *Var. Colln.* i, p. 69; above, manors (Kingston's).   63 *Compton Census*, ed. Whiteman, 125.
64 Williams, *Cath. Recusancy* (Cath. Rec. Soc.), 228, 259.
65 Below, Bathampton, nonconf.; Hanging Langford, nonconf.   66 *Educ. of Poor Digest*, 1030.
67 *Educ. Enq. Abstract*, 1040.
68 Nat. Soc. *Inquiry, 1846–7*, Wilts. 6–7.
69 W.R.O., D 1/61/10/2.

in two cottages where 15–20 children were 'kept out of mischief'. A National school incorporating a schoolhouse was built at Steeple Langford in 1861.[70] In 1864 boys left school at 9, girls at 12, and an evening school for boys was held.[71] In 1875–6 average attendance was 56 in the day, 17 in the evening.[72] The building was enlarged in 1895.[73] Average attendance, 108 in 1906–7, declined from 100 in 1913–14 to 38 in 1937–8,[74] and from 1938 older pupils attended school at Wilton.[75] Steeple Langford school was enlarged by new buildings in 1973.[76] In 1991 it had c. 27 on roll.[77]

CHARITIES FOR THE POOR.

By deed of 1575 Susan Mompesson gave £1 6s. 8d. a year charged on her manor of Little Bathampton for distribution in Lent to the poor: in the early 19th century the curate distributed the money to elderly widows, sometimes biennially. Payment of the rent charge later lapsed but was revived c. 1905. Money was given to 13 widows in 1910–11 and 1923.[78] In 1991 the income was being allowed to accumulate.[79]

Susan Mompesson's sister Elizabeth (d. 1581), relict of Richard Perkins and Sir John Mervyn,[80] gave by will for the poor of Steeple Langford and Wylye parishes yearly 4 qr. of wheat to be distributed as bread in Lent, and, to be distributed on Good Friday, 25 ells of canvas for making shirts and smocks and 25 yd. of blue cloth for making coats and cassocks. The gifts

were a charge on her Great Bathampton estate, and the parishes claimed them from the sequestrators of Francis Perkins's estate in 1651. In the early 19th century the tenant of Great Bathampton farm gave on Good Friday 3-lb. loaves of bread, possibly c. 750, to the old and needy, and, to 16 of the most needy, different recipients each year, a total of £3 6s. 8d. in place of cloth. The numbers of beneficiaries from Steeple Langford and from Wylye are likely to have been about equal. By a Scheme of 1875 Steeple Langford's share of the charity was commuted to yearly payments of £8 5s. In the early 20th century the income was used to pay for clothing and groceries for the poor:[81] there were 71 recipients in 1923, 2 in 1952,[82] 10 in 1960.[83] The rent charge was redeemed c. 1988 and the income was being allowed to accumulate in 1991.[84]

From 1628 or earlier £1 6s. 8d. a year for the poor was charged on Steeple Langford manor,[85] from 1675 or earlier by lease on the demesne lands:[86] no payment was made after c. 1811, and later it could not be shown that a perpetual charity had been endowed.[87] Thomas Mompesson (d. 1640) gave the interest from £20 to the poor: by 1655 only one year's interest had been paid, and the charity was apparently lost.[88] By the inclosure award of 1866 the poor were allotted 3 a., subject to a rent charge of £2. By Act of 1894 the land was transferred to the parish council, and it was used as garden allotments.[89]

BATHAMPTON

THE TWO Bathampton estates were called by the name Wylye in 1086,[90] and for long afterwards the name Batham Wylye was applied to each;[91] only from the 15th century did the name Bathampton become more usual.[92] Two groups of buildings c. 500 m. apart, Great Bathampton and Little Bathampton, each including a manor house and a farmstead, correspond to the two estates,[93] and it is unlikely that there was ever a single village or hamlet of Bathampton. Each group may be on the site of what in the early Middle Ages may have been a small settlement consisting of a demesne farmstead and a few

tenants' farmsteads.[94] The estates had a total of c. 1,290 a.,[95] and Bathampton had 60 poll-tax payers in 1377[96] and 49 inhabitants in 1841.[97]

John Mompesson (d. 1500) had a house at Bathampton, almost certainly Little Bathampton,[98] and the present manor house, Ballington Manor, may be on its site. There was a mill nearby.[99] From, probably, the later 18th century to the early 20th the manor house was occupied by tenant farmers,[1] and in 1910 that house, extensive farm buildings, and five cottages were at Little Bathampton.[2] In 1939 a pair of stone and thatch cottages in vernacular style was built,

[70] Ibid. 782/60; *Acct. of Wilts. Schs.* 30; P.R.O., ED 7/131, no. 259.   [71] W.R.O., D 1/56/7.
[72] *Return of Public Elem. Schs. 1875–6* [C. 1882], pp. 284–5, H.C. (1877), lxvii.
[73] W.R.O., F 500, Steeple Langford sch. 1907–36.
[74] *Bd. of Educ., List 21, 1908* (H.M.S.O.), 506; *1914*, 554; *1938*, 425.
[75] W.R.O., F 8, corresp. files, primary schs., special ser., Steeple Langford.
[76] Ibid. 2499/220/3.
[77] Wilts. co. council, *Sched. of Educ. Establishments* (1990), p. 17.
[78] *Endowed Char. Wilts.* (S. Div.), 660–1; W.R.O., L 2, Steeple Langford.
[79] Inf. from Major-Gen. Brockbank.
[80] Below, Bathampton, manors.
[81] *Endowed Char. Wilts.* (S. Div.), 662, 924–5; *Cal. Cttee. for Compounding*, iii. 2390; *Char. Don.* H.C. 511 (1816), xvi (2), 1338–9; for the number of loaves, cf. *V.C.H. Wilts.* xiii. 247–8.   [82] W.R.O., L 2, Steeple Langford.
[83] Char. Com. file.

[84] Inf. from Major-Gen. Brockbank.
[85] W.R.O. 492/156, deed, Mussell to Grobham, 1628.
[86] Ibid. 492/186.
[87] *Endowed Char. Wilts.* (S. Div.), 660, 662.
[88] Hist. MSS. Com. 55, *Var. Colln.* i, p. 131; P.R.O., PROB 11/183, ff. 232–4; below, Bathampton, manors (Little Bathampton).
[89] *Endowed Char. Wilts.* (S. Div.), 663.
[90] *V.C.H. Wilts.* ii, pp. 144–5; for the estates, below, manors.
[91] e.g. *Feet of F. 1377–1509* (W.R.S. xli), p. 15; *Bk. of Fees*, ii. 726.   [92] *P.N. Wilts.* (E.P.N.S.), 227.
[93] Below, manors.   [94] Ibid. econ. hist.
[95] W.R.O., tithe award.
[96] *V.C.H. Wilts.* iv. 306.
[97] P.R.O., HO 107/1167.
[98] Ibid. PROB 11/13, f. 135; *W.A.M.* ii. 266–7; below, manors.   [99] Below, econ. hist.
[1] Ibid. manors.
[2] O.S. Map 6", Wilts. LIX. NW. (1901 edn.); W.R.O., Inland Revenue, val. reg. 143.

the manor house was altered and extended, the mill house and farm buildings were altered, the latter to incorporate garages and a squash court, and stables were converted to a cottage.[3]

The survival near it of a medieval cruck barn of four bays, extended by three bays in the 17th century, suggests that Bathampton House is on the site of the medieval farmstead at Great Bathampton. Bathampton House was built in the late 17th century, and in the later 18th, presumably soon after 1764,[4] a farmhouse was built nearby. Great Bathampton farm had 11 cottages in 1910, most of them near the manor house.[5] In 1991 the farmhouse, a later 20th-century house, and extensive farm buildings, some of the later 20th century, were near Bathampton House, and two bungalows, a cottage, and farm buildings were elsewhere.

In the 1960s and until the late 1980s the Wylye horse trials were held yearly at Great Bathampton.[6]

MANORS. The grant by King Edward to his thegn Aelfric of 10 *mansae* at Wylye in 977 was possibly of Bathampton land. Of the two estates at Bathampton in 1066 Aluric held the larger, Edwin the smaller, and in 1086 Humphrey Lisle held both.[7] They passed through Adelize Lisle, wife of Reynold de Dunstanville and almost certainly Humphrey's daughter and heir, to Reynold de Dunstanville (cr. earl of Cornwall c. 1141, d. *s.p.m.* 1176), the son of Henry I and possibly of Adelize. From Reynold, earl of Cornwall, they passed to his son-in-law Walter de Dunstanville (d. 1194),[8] whose relict Sibyl and her husband Ingram de Pratell held them in 1204 and 1222. The larger estate had been subinfeudated by 1222, part of the smaller was subinfeudated by Earl Reynold.[9] The overlordship of the subinfeudated land, and a fee farm rent of £8 paid for the rest from the mid 12th century,[10] presumably passed to Walter's son Walter de Dunstanville (d. 1241); that Walter's son Walter (d. 1270) was overlord in 1242–3.[11] The overlordship passed to the youngest Walter's daughter Parnel, whose husband John de la Mare held it until his death in 1313. From John it passed to Bartholomew de Badlesmere, Lord Badlesmere (d. 1322), who bought the reversion from Parnel's son William de Montfort in 1309.

Bartholomew's son Giles, Lord Badlesmere (d. 1338),[12] was succeeded as overlord by his sister Maud[13] (d. 1366) and her husband John de Vere, earl of Oxford (d. 1360), and Maud by her son Thomas de Vere, earl of Oxford (d. 1371). Thomas's son Robert, earl of Oxford (d. *s.p.* 1392), forfeited his estates in 1388.[14] In 1390 the overlord was said to be the lord of Castle Combe, then Giles de Badlesmere's grandniece Millicent (d. 1446), wife of Stephen Scrope.[15] Millicent's later husband Sir John Fastolf was overlord from 1409 to 1459, and thereafter the overlordship descended in the Scrope family with Castle Combe.[16] The £8 was still being paid to the overlord in 1476.[17] Richard Scrope was named as overlord in 1555.[18]

The more highly assessed estate at Bathampton, presumably GREAT BATHAMPTON manor, was held by Gilbert of Milford in 1222 and, as ½ knight's fee, in 1242–3.[19] It descended with Upper Woodfalls manor in Downton: Sir Stephen of Milford (*alias* Stephen of Woodfalls, d. c. 1260) presumably held it, and it passed to his son William of Milford (later Sir William of Woodfalls, d. by 1323), who in 1307 settled it on himself and his wife Margaret (or Margery, fl. 1342) and their issue. Margaret held it in 1316.[20] In 1338 it was held, possibly by a temporary tenure, by John Buckland, presumably the Sir John Buckland (d. 1362) who held a manor adjoining Woodfalls.[21] By 1369 the estate had passed with Upper Woodfalls to Joan, daughter of Joan of Woodfalls,[22] and it was held by her husband Sir Hugh Cheyne (d. 1390),[23] apparently by John Dauntsey (fl. 1391), who may have been her husband,[24] and by her husbands Sir Thomas Blount (d. 1400)[25] and Thomas Linford[26] (d. 1423).[27] It was apparently bought by John Chitterne, a clerk, c. 1409:[28] it evidently passed, like Upton Knoyle manor in East Knoyle and Hussey manor in North Tidworth, to his sister Agnes and her husband William Milbourne, and it descended in the direct line[29] to Richard Milbourne (d. 1451), Simon Milbourne[30] (d. 1464), and Sir Thomas Milbourne,[31] who in 1483 sold it to John Mompesson[32] (d. 1500), the owner of the second Bathampton estate. Both estates descended to John's grandson John Mompesson[33] (d. 1511) and to that John's son Edmund[34] (d. *s.p.* 1553).[35] At the partition of Edmund Mompesson's estates

3 W.R.O., G 11/760/443; G 11/760/445; G 11/760/452; G 11/760/474–5. 4 Below, manors.
5 O.S. Map 6", Wilts. LIX. NW. (1901 edn.); W.R.O., Inland Revenue, val. reg. 143.
6 Inf. from Mr. A. J. Maitland-Robinson, Bathampton Ho. 7 V.C.H. Wilts. ii, pp. 86, 144–5.
8 Ibid. pp. 110–11; G. Poulett Scrope, Castle Combe (priv. print. 1852), 19; I. J. Sanders, Eng. Baronies, 28; W.A.M. ii. 137–8; Cal. Chart. R. 1257–1300, 152; Pipe R. 1190 (P.R.S. N.S. i), 22.
9 W. Farrer, Honors and Knights' Fees, iii. 38–9; Cal. Chart. R. 1257–1300, 152; Rot. Litt. Claus. (Rec. Com.), i. 1; P.R.O., CP 25/1/282/8, no. 23.
10 Below, this section (Little Bathampton).
11 Sanders, op. cit. 28; Bk. of Fees, ii. 726.
12 Poulett Scrope, Castle Combe, 19, 41–2; Cal. Inq. p.m. vii, p. 96; for the Badlesmeres, Complete Peerage, i. 371–3.
13 Cal. Inq. p.m. viii, pp. 137–8, 143; Cal. Close, 1339–41, 282.
14 Cal. Inq. p.m. xiii, p. 98; Complete Peerage, x. 222–32.
15 Cal. Inq. p.m. xvi, p. 316; Poulett Scrope, Castle Combe, 141–5.

16 Poulett Scrope, Castle Combe, 171, 185, 350.
17 W.A.M. ii. 268.
18 P.R.O., C 142/104, no. 123.
19 Bk. of Fees, ii. 726; P.R.O., CP 25/1/282/8, no. 23.
20 V.C.H. Wilts. xi. 32–3; Feet of F. 1272–1327 (W.R.S. i), p. 58; Feud. Aids, v. 211.
21 V.C.H. Wilts. xi. 31–2; Cal. Inq. p.m. viii, p. 137.
22 Feet of F. 1327–77 (W.R.S. xxix), p. 134.
23 Cal. Inq. p.m. xvi, p. 316; Cal. Fine R. 1383–91, 325–6.
24 P.R.O., C 260/147, no. 18; cf. V.C.H. Wilts. xi. 33.
25 Cal. Inq. p.m. xviii, p. 66.
26 Cal. Close, 1399–1402, 440.
27 V.C.H. Wilts. xi. 33.
28 Cal. Close, 1405–9, 494; Feet of F. 1377–1509 (W.R.S. xli), p. 63; cf. V.C.H. Wilts. vii. 201; V.C.H. Hants, iv. 327.
29 V.C.H. Wilts. xi. 87; above, N. Tidworth, manors (Hussey). 30 P.R.O., C 139/142, no. 19.
31 Ibid. C 140/12, no. 12. 32 B.L. Eg. Ch. 1805.
33 Cal. Inq. p.m. Hen. VII, ii, pp. 317–18; below, this section. 34 P.R.O., C 142/26, no. 117.
35 Ibid. C 142/104, no. 123; ibid. PROB 11/36, f. 31.

in 1556 Great Bathampton manor was allotted to his sister Elizabeth, wife of Richard Perkins[36] (d. 1560)[37] and later of Sir John Mervyn (d. 1566).[38] Although claimed by her heirs, under a settlement of 1573 it passed at Elizabeth's death in 1581 to her grandnephew Francis Perkins (d. 1616) who was also Richard Perkins's nephew and heir.[39] Two thirds of the manor were held by the Crown, apparently from 1590 to 1600, because Perkins failed to pay fines for recusancy.[40] He was succeeded by his son Francis (d. 1661), from whom two thirds were confiscated for the same reason in 1628 and 1650.[41] Francis was succeeded by his grandson Francis Perkins (d. 1694) and he by his son Francis (d. 1736),[42] whose sons Francis (d. 1749 or 1750),[43] James (d. 1755), Charles (d. 1762), and John (d. 1769) held the manor in turn. In 1764 it was sold to William Moody[44] (d. 1774),[45] and it descended in the direct line to William Moody (d. 1798), the Revd. William Moody (d. 1827), and Henry Moody (d. 1827). The manor, 713 a. in 1838, was held by Henry's relict Felicia Moody (d. 1888)[46] and passed to his daughter Henrietta Moody (d. 1911), who was succeeded in turn by her cousin J. H. S. Seagram[47] (d. 1920) and by Seagram's son T. O. Seagram (d. 1958).[48] Great Bathampton manor was sold in 1959 to Lord Hugh Russell, who sold it in 1986 to Mr. and Mrs. A. J. Maitland-Robinson, the owners in 1990.[49]

Bathampton House[50] was built in the late 17th century and bears a date stone for 1694 with initials FP for Francis Perkins. Its seven-bayed north entrance front is of ashlar with rusticated quoins and had mullioned and transomed windows. On the south side two short wings projected slightly east and west of the main range, and the fall of the ground allowed for a third, basement, storey. The chimneys, which have rusticated bases and tall fielded panelled sides, are set at the four corners of the house. In the 18th century, presumably soon after 1764, the mullions and transoms were removed from the windows of the north front, and the space between the wings was filled to make an unbroken south elevation.[51] Early in the 19th century a three-storeyed canted bay window was added towards the east end of the south front, and the wooden semicircular north porch is possibly of

similar date. Inside the house the east wing has a late 17th-century staircase with turned newels and twisted balusters, there is some bolection-moulded panelling, and a first-floor room has reset early 17th-century panelling, but most of the decoration is of the later 18th century or early 19th. The fireplace surround in the north-east room on the ground floor, of carved white marble with half-quatrefoil shafts of variegated brown marble, is reputedly from Fonthill Abbey in Fonthill Gifford.[52] East of the house is a late 17th-century stable block, and south-east later 18th-century walled gardens.

In the mid 12th century Reynold, earl of Cornwall, granted an estate at Bathampton, apparently what was later *LITTLE BATHAMPTON* manor, in two parts to John of Wylye and his wife Agace, 1 hide as ⅕ knight's fee, possibly the demesne, and land at fee farm, possibly the customary land.[53] The two parts were held by Agace and her husband Nicholas of Merriott in 1203.[54] John had a son Thomas[55] (d. by 1204)[56] whose heir was Nicholas of Wylye;[57] in 1242–3 Nicholas held the hide of Alfred of Lincoln who held of the overlord, and Philip of Deptford held it of Nicholas; Nicholas held the other land as ¼ knight's fee.[58] John of Wylye held the two parts in 1270[59] and, apparently as one estate, in 1276. Maud of Wylye, possibly his relict, held the estate in 1316[60] and Nicholas Lambert held it in 1338,[61] possibly by a temporary tenure. Presumably after the death of a husband, Elizabeth, in 1385 wife of John Knottingley, held the estate for life with reversion to Catherine, wife of Thomas Bonham, probably the earlier husband's daughter, and in 1386 it was also settled on John for life subject to rent of £5 if he survived Elizabeth.[62] The Knottingleys died after 1391,[63] Catherine Bonham died apparently before 1405,[64] and in 1409 Thomas Bonham held the estate.[65] At his death in 1420 it passed to his granddaughter Alice Godwin, wife of Robert Mompesson,[66] and at Robert's death c. 1433[67] to her son John Mompesson, a minor until 1442 or later.[68] John held the estate until his death in 1500,[69] and the two Bathampton estates descended together until 1556 when Little Bathampton manor was allotted to Edmund Mompesson's sister Susan Mompesson[70] (d. 1583).[71] In 1582 Susan settled

36 *W.A.M.* xliii. 291–2.
37 *V.C.H. Berks.* iii. 441.
38 *Wilts. Pedigrees* (Harl. Soc. cv/cvi), 132; P.R.O., C 142/154, no. 116.
39 P.R.O., C 2/Eliz. I/P 5/54; C 142/197, no. 91; C 142/366, no. 181.
40 *Recusant R.* 1593–4 (Cath. Rec. Soc. lvii), pp. lxxxiv, 3.
41 *V.C.H. Berks.* iii. 441; *Cal. Cttee. for Compounding,* iii. 2390; P.R.O., C 66/2420, no. 12.
42 *V.C.H. Berks.* iii. 441.
43 W.R.O. 475/3, copy will.
44 Ibid. 475/1, deed, Myddleton to Cooper, 1764; *V.C.H. Berks.* iii. 441.
45 Hoare, *Mod. Wilts.* Branch and Dole, 122.
46 Mon. in church; W.R.O., tithe award.
47 W.R.O. 475/17; 475/46.
48 *Who Was Who, 1951–60,* 980; W.A.S. Libr., sale cat. xxix (C), no. 11.
49 Inf. from Mr. A. J. Maitland-Robinson, Bathampton Ho.
50 See plate facing p. 186.

51 Cf. W.R.O. 475/22.   52 Ibid. 475/37.
53 *Cal. Chart. R.* 1257–1300, 152.
54 *Pipe R.* 1203 (P.R.S. N.S. xvi), 21.
55 *Cal. Chart. R.* 1257–1300, 153.
56 *Rot. Litt. Claus.* (Rec. Com.), i. 1.
57 *Cal. Chart. R.* 1257–1300, 153.
58 *Bk. of Fees,* ii. 713, 726, 739.
59 *Cal. Chart. R.* 1257–1300, 152–3.
60 *Feet of F. 1272–1327* (W.R.S. i), p. 7; *Feud. Aids,* v. 211.   61 *Cal. Inq. p.m.* viii, p. 138.
62 *Feet of F. 1377–1509* (W.R.S. xli), pp. 15, 20; cf. below, Hanging Langford, manors.
63 P.R.O., C 260/147, no. 18.
64 *Feet of F. 1377–1509* (W.R.S. xli), p. 55.
65 *Cal. Close,* 1405–9, 530.
66 P.R.O., C 138/48, no. 67; the Mompesson geneal. to 1556 is from ibid. C 142/104, no. 123.
67 *W.A.M.* ii. 267; B.L. Add. Ch. 18555.
68 B.L. Add. Ch. 18556.
69 *Cal. Inq. p.m. Hen. VII,* ii, pp. 317–18.
70 *W.A.M.* xliii. 291–2; P.R.O., C 142/104, no. 123.
71 P.R.O., PROB 11/66, ff. 52–4.

the manor on the marriage of her cousin once removed Thomas Mompesson, who died holding it in 1587. Thomas's heir was his son, the politician and extortioner Sir Giles Mompesson,[72] the profits of whose lands were taken by the Crown and leased to trustees of his wife Catherine in 1621.[73] In 1624 Little Bathampton manor was sold to Sir Giles's brother Thomas[74] (d. 1640). In 1638 Thomas settled it in tail on Sir Giles (d. 1651 or later), on his brother John, rector of North Tidworth 1617–37, and on John's son John (fl. 1669),[75] but by 1659 it had passed to his son Thomas[76] (knighted 1662, d. 1701), who was M.P. for Wilton from 1661.[77] Sir Thomas was succeeded by his son Charles (d. 1714), who built a house in the Close in Salisbury,[78] and by Charles's son Henry (d. 1733). Henry devised the manor to his mother Elizabeth Mompesson (d. 1751), who devised it to Charles's grandnephew Thomas Walker (d. 1782). In 1783 Walker's relict Elizabeth sold it to John Drummond, who sold it in the same year to Edward Seymour, duke of Somerset[79] (d. 1792). The manor, 564 a. in 1838, descended with the title to Webb Seymour (d. 1793), Edward Seymour (d. 1855), Edward Seymour (d. 1885), Archibald St. Maur (d. 1891), Algernon St. Maur (d. 1894), and Algernon St. Maur (d. 1923), from the last of whom it was bought after 1910[80] by E. J. Ashford. In 1929 Ashford sold it to Mrs. E. M. Brockbank, in 1939 she sold it to Philip Lyle, and in 1946 or 1947 Lyle sold it to B. G. Ivory.[81] In 1962 Ivory sold c. 200 a. north of the Amesbury–Mere road with other land there to Lord Hugh Russell, who sold it all with Great Bathampton manor to Mr. and Mrs. A. J. Maitland-Robinson, the owners in 1991. In 1962 Ivory sold the manor house and c. 350 a. to D. F. H. McCormick, the owner of Manor farm in Steeple Langford, who in 1989 sold his estate to Mr. R. P. Merrick, the owner in 1991.[82]

The house on Little Bathampton manor, called Ballington Manor in 1990, is of coursed stone rubble and bears a reset date stone for 1580 with initials SM for Susan Mompesson. The oldest part of the house is apparently an east–west range at the south-west corner, which has an early 18th-century staircase, possibly original, and a short south wing. North of that main range is an extension, with two north gables, in which an early 17th-century fireplace and 17th-century beams are probably reset. In 1939 a small single-storeyed west extension of the gabled range was built and, in a style to match its older parts, the house was more than doubled in size

by an extension eastwards which, at its east end, incorporated outbuildings.[83] A north porch was built, and much of the house refitted, in 1990. Near the house are 18th-century brick-walled gardens and a square dovecot of stone.

ECONOMIC HISTORY. In 1086 there were 6½ ploughteams on land for 6 at Bathampton. On the larger estate, presumably Great Bathampton, there were 1 hide and 1 yardland of demesne with 3 teams and 12 servi, 2 villani and 6 coscets with 1½ team, 10 a. of meadow, and pasture ½ league square. On the smaller, presumably Little Bathampton, there were 2 hides of demesne with 1 team, 2 villani and 1 coscet with 1 team, 5 a. of meadow, and 8 a. of pasture.[84] There is evidence of sheep-and-corn husbandry in the Middle Ages,[85] but it is not clear whether the two Bathampton estates, like the two at Hanging Langford, shared a single set of open fields and common meadows and pastures,[86] or whether Bathampton was divided in a way similar to nearby Stockton with a separate set for each estate.[87] About 1440 Little Bathampton manor had a demesne farm, which was leased, and several customary tenants: a dispute between the farmer and the tenants over a pasture, in which the tenants claimed feeding in common, may be evidence that Little Bathampton had its own fields and pastures.[88]

There is no later evidence of common husbandry or customary tenants at either Great or Little Bathampton, which were in the same ownership 1483–1566.[89] Probably in that period common rights over Great Bathampton farm and Little Bathampton farm were eliminated and the farms became, as they were later, the only ones at Bathampton. Each was mentioned in the 17th century,[90] and then and until the 20th century each normally seems to have been leased. Each was a long strip between the Wylye and the northern parish boundary and in each case the farm buildings were near the river west of the manor house.[91]

In 1763 Great Bathampton farm was 712 a. including 54 a. of meadow, 29 a. of lowland pasture, c. 430 a. of arable, and 178 a. of downland pasture: 156 a. of downland had earlier been converted to arable,[92] and the weirs and sluices for watering meadows mentioned in 1779 had presumably been built much earlier.[93] The proportions of arable, lowland and downland pasture, and meadow were almost the same in 1838.[94] In the later 19th century and earlier 20th the farm was reduced by c. 50 a. of grassland

72 Wilts. Pedigrees (Harl. Soc. cv/cvi), 132–3; D.N.B.; P.R.O., C 142/215, no. 266.   73 B.L. Eg. Ch. 1813.
74 Ibid. Eg. Ch. 1811.
75 Wilts. Inq. p.m. 1625–49 (Index Libr.), 295–6; D.N.B.; above, N. Tidworth, church; W.R.O. 1332, box 2, deed, Mompesson to Ash, 1669.
76 Cal. Cttee. for Compounding, i. 753.
77 Hist. Parl., Commons, 1660–90, iii. 71–2.
78 Hoare, Mod. Wilts. Heytesbury, 216; Nat. Trust, Mompesson Ho. (1984).
79 Gent. Mag. ii. 586; W.R.O. 1332, box 22, deed, Drummond to Som., 1783; P.R.O., PROB 11/790, ff. 295–6.
80 Complete Peerage, xii (1), 83–8; W.R.O., tithe award; ibid. Inland Revenue, val. reg. 143.
81 Inf. from Major-Gen. J. M. Brockbank, Manor Ho.,

Steeple Langford.
82 Henderson, Steeple Langford, 15; Wilts. Cuttings, xxii. 129; inf. from Mr. Maitland-Robinson, and sale cat., 1989, and map of Yarnbury Grange estate, 1958, in his possession.
83 W.R.O., G 11/760/475.
84 V.C.H. Wilts. ii, pp. 144–5.
85 Feet of F. 1272–1327 (W.R.S. i), p. 50.
86 Cf. below, Hanging Langford, econ. hist.
87 Cf. V.C.H. Wilts. xi. 217.
88 Poulett Scrope, Castle Combe, 258–9; B.L. Add. Ch. 18555–6.   89 Above, manors.
90 W.A.M. xl. 299; B.L. Eg. Ch. 1808.
91 W.R.O., tithe award.   92 Ibid. 475/22.
93 Ibid. 475/3, particulars, 1782.
94 Ibid. tithe award.

and woodland which formed a small park for Bathampton House.[95] In 1962 c. 420 a. of downland, including some of Little Bathampton's, were added to the farm and from 1987 much land in Hanging Langford was worked with it. In 1991 Great Bathampton farm was 1,900 a., of which 1,500 a. were for growing cereals and in large fields; sheep and cattle for beef were kept on the remainder.[96] Little Bathampton farm was 564 a. in 1838, when there were 30 a. of meadow, 24 a. of lowland pasture, 374 a. of arable, and 131 a. of downland pasture. North of the Amesbury–Mere road 81 a. of downland had been converted to arable, presumably in the 18th century. The lessee in 1838 was also tenant of 541 a. in Hanging Langford.[97] The farm buildings at Little Bathampton were converted for dairying in 1939.[98] From c. 1948 to 1962 the farm included c. 220 a. of Steeple Langford's and Berwick St. James's downland: after 1962 the reduced farm was worked with the adjoining Manor farm, Steeple Langford.[99]

MILLS. There was a mill on each Bathampton estate in 1086.[1] From the mid 15th century to the 20th there was a mill at Little, but apparently not at Great, Bathampton,[2] and in the early 17th century there were said to be two.[3] A water mill stood south-west of the farm buildings and from the later 18th century to the earlier 20th was leased with the farm.[4] There is no evidence that it was used to grind corn after the First World War. An 18th-century stone mill house and a

19th-century weatherboarded mill north of it survived in 1991.

LOCAL GOVERNMENT. Bathampton and Deptford were linked as a single tithing, usually called Bathampton, in Heytesbury hundred, and the tithingman attended the view of frankpledge for the hundred in the 15th century and early 16th. Among matters presented were the tithingman's failure to bring statutory measures, the taking of excess toll by millers, payment for licences by brewers and tapsters, and failure to keep watch.[5]

CHURCH. In the late Middle Ages there was a chapel at Bathampton, almost certainly at Little Bathampton, at which the Mompesson family heard divine service and received the sacrament.[6] It was called St. Nicholas's and was apparently rebuilt shortly before 1500.[7] Edmund Mompesson made the expenses of the priest serving it a charge on his lands for 20 years after his death in 1553.[8] No later reference to the chapel has been found.

NONCONFORMITY. Robert Hall of Great Bathampton in the 1580s absented himself from church 'upon a special inward zeal of his own conscience'.[9] Members of the Perkins family, owners of Great Bathampton manor on which they may sometimes have lived, were recusants.[10]

HANGING LANGFORD

HANGING LANGFORD, so called in 1242–3,[11] is a street village with c. 1,010 a. south of the Wylye.[12] The plan of the village, in which farmhouses face each other across the straight street of c. 500 m. with rectangular plots of roughly equal size behind them,[13] and its site along the gravel strip, with arable south of it and meadows and pastures north of it, suggest planned colonization. In 1556 a lessee of land in Hanging Langford destroyed a cross,[14] and part of a cross shaft was found c. 1937 built into a cottage in Hanging Langford: if the cross stood in Hanging Langford its carving, possibly of the mid 9th century,[15] may indicate the village's foundation date. By 1066 the land had been divided between two estates:[16] later evidence shows that it was shared in a complex and

carefully organized way, that the two manors were of equal size and with the same amounts of demesne and customary land as each other, and that along both sides of the street the copyhold farmhouses belonged alternately to one manor and the other. The street is part of the Great Wishford to Bishopstrow road, called Wylye Road in 1991; the demesne farmsteads of each manor were beside the road east of the buildings in the street, and further east was the village mill. Away from the street and the road there was no other building in 1763.[17]

Hanging Langford was in Grovely forest, of which the northern boundary was the Wylye, and attended swanimotes. The west lodge of the forest was possibly on Hanging Langford's downs.[18] At the west end of the street a non-

95 Ibid. Inland Revenue, val. reg. 143; ibid. 475/37; O.S. Map 6", Wilts. LIX (1889 edn.).
96 Above, manors; Steeple Langford, manors; inf. from Mr. Maitland-Robinson.
97 W.R.O., tithe award.
98 Ibid. G 11/760/474.
99 Above, manors; Steeple Langford, manors; sale cat., 1989, in possession of Mr. Maitland-Robinson.
1 V.C.H. Wilts. ii, pp. 144–5.
2 B.L. Add. Ch. 18556; W.R.O., Inland Revenue, val. reg. 143.
3 B.L. Eg. Ch. 1822.
4 W.R.O., tithe award; ibid. Inland Revenue, val. reg. 143; ibid. 1332, box 3, lease, Som. to Rowden, 1789.
5 Ibid. A 1/345/252; W.A.M. xiii. 115; xxxvii. 375; P.R.O., SC 2/208/62, rott. 9 and d., 11; SC 2/208/64–8; SC 2/208/71; SC 2/208/74; SC 2/208/77; SC 2/208/79.

6 P.R.O., STAC 2/28/95.
7 Ibid. PROB 11/8, f. 134; PROB 11/13, f. 135.
8 Ibid. C 142/104, no. 123.
9 V.C.H. Wilts. iii. 36; Sess. Mins. (W.R.S. iv), 113.
10 Cf. V.C.H. Berks. iii. 441; W.N. & Q. vii. 203; above, manors.
11 Bk. of Fees, ii. 742.
12 W.R.O., tithe award.
13 Ibid. 475/22; Eton Coll. Mun. 51/313.
14 W.R.O., D 1/43/2, f. 8.
15 Ibid. D 1/61/86/14; W.A.M. xlviii. 183; V.C.H. Wilts. ii, p. 36.
16 V.C.H. Wilts. ii, pp. 133, 151.
17 W.R.O. 475/22; ibid. EA/153; Eton Coll. Mun. 51/313; below, econ. hist.
18 V.C.H. Wilts. iv. 431, 457; First Pembroke Survey, ed. Straton, i. 194; W.R.O. 212B/7190H.

conformist chapel was built[19] and by 1859, perhaps by 1857 when Hanging Langford halt was closed, the Railway tavern was opened.[20] The inn was closed in 1966.[21] To the east, at the junction of Wylye Road and the Steeple Langford road, a parish reading room was built c. 1913:[22] it remained open as a parish hall in 1991. With 87 poll-tax payers the village may have been more populous than Steeple Langford in 1377,[23] but with 272 inhabitants was less so in 1841:[24] the two villages were of roughly equal size in 1991. Few farm buildings in the village were used in the late 20th century.

In 1763 Hanging Langford street was faced by c. 17 farmhouses, perhaps in origin one for each copyhold of the two manors and for a freehold.[25] About 12 survive, all small and apparently built in the 17th century or early 18th. Most incorporate chequered or banded walling of stone and flint, some incorporate timber framing, and a few are mainly of stone: several have been much altered. A malthouse was rebuilt on the south side of the street c. 1799.[26] None of the eight cottages on the waste in 1763, seven at the west end of the street,[27] survives, but there are several 19th-century cottages in the street. A new farmstead was built at the west end on the north side in 1937,[28] and after the Second World War c. 30 houses and bungalows were built to fill most of the spaces along the street.

Immediately east of the buildings in the street, on the north side of the road, the demesne farmhouse of one of the manors is probably of c. 1700: a cob and thatch wall encloses what was its farmyard,[29] in which a thatched building has been converted for residence. Further east, also on the north side of the road, the demesne farmhouse of the second manor was replaced in or soon after 1770 by a smaller house west of it: the new house, Peartree House, of stone and in early 18th-century style, was apparently built to match the demesne farmhouse of the first manor. Nearby, a small thatched house of chequered stone and flint, apparently built in the 17th century, and an earlier 18th-century thatched house were copyhold farmhouses which presumably replaced buildings in the street.[30] Near the site of the mill a thatched 17th-century house adjoins a pair of 19th-century cottages. Wylye Road east of Hanging Langford street has itself acquired the appearance of a village street: two council houses were built in 1937, four in 1948,[31] and 12 private houses thereafter.

MANORS AND OTHER ESTATE. There were two 5-hide estates at Hanging Langford in 1066, and topographical evidence suggests that they were the halves of a former single estate. Chetel held one in 1066, and Robert, count of Mortain (d. 1090), held it in 1086. It apparently passed with the countship to Robert's son William (attainted 1106), Henry I's nephew Stephen (count of Mortain from 1115 or earlier, king from 1135, d. 1154), and Stephen's son William (d. s.p. 1159). The countship was resumed by the Crown in 1159[32] and Richard I (1189–99) granted his manor of *HANGING LANG-FORD*, one of two so called, to the collegiate church of St. Evroul, Mortain (Manche).[33] The dean and canons of Mortain held it in 1207, when the king gave possession of it to Henry Lovel, who was waiting to recover a prebend in the church,[34] and the church kept it. For several periods in the 14th century and early 15th it was held by the king in time of war with France,[35] and was apparently resumed when the alien priories were suppressed. In 1414 it was assigned in dower to Queen Joan[36] (d. 1437), relict of Henry IV, and in 1438 was granted for life to Humphrey, duke of Gloucester.[37] The Crown granted the reversion to Eton College (Bucks.) in 1441,[38] and in 1443 Humphrey surrendered his life interest to the college.[39] In 1914 the college sold its land, 373 a. later called College farm, to Albert Whatley.[40] In the 1930s the farm apparently belonged to V. W. Perrett.[41] In 1987 it was bought by Mr. and Mrs. A. J. Maitland-Robinson, the owners in 1991.[42]

The second estate in Hanging Langford was held by Norman in 1066 and by Waleran the huntsman in 1086. Erenburgis held it of Waleran.[43] There is no evidence that Waleran's heirs held the estate and from 1243 or earlier until the 16th century Wilton abbey was overlord.[44] Nicholas of Wylye may have held the estate in 1231,[45] and he held the second *HANGING LANGFORD* manor in 1242–3.[46] The manor may have descended, like Little Bathampton manor, in the Wylye family and was apparently held by another Nicholas of Wylye in 1300[47] and by Joan of Wylye c. 1316.[48] Thomas Bonham and his wife Catherine (d. apparently by 1405) owned it in 1382,[49] and from his death in 1420 it was held by Thomas's relict Alice.[50] From Alice's death before 1428[51] to the death of Edmund Mompesson in 1553 the

[19] Below, nonconf.
[20] *Kelly's Dir. Wilts.* (1859); above, Steeple Langford, intro. [21] Henderson, *Steeple Langford*, 3.
[22] Eton Coll. Mun., bursary estate files, sundry corresp., letter from Holden, 1913. [23] *V.C.H. Wilts.* iv. 307.
[24] P.R.O., HO 107/1167.
[25] W.R.O. 475/22; 475/24; Eton Coll. Mun. 51/313; cf. below, econ. hist.
[26] W.R.O. 475/24; ibid. tithe award.
[27] Ibid. 475/22.
[28] Ibid. G 11/760/346. [29] Ibid. 475/22.
[30] Ibid.; ibid. 475/24; Eton Coll. Mun. 43/143, letter from Moody, 1770; 51/313.
[31] W.R.O., G 11/615/1A.
[32] *V.C.H. Wilts.* ii, pp. 133, 151; *Complete Peerage*, iii. 427–9; ix. 243; for the topographical evidence, above, intro.; below, econ. hist.
[33] *Bk. of Fees*, ii. 742.

[34] *Rot. Litt. Claus.* (Rec. Com.), i. 77; *Pipe R.* (P.R.S. N.S. xxiii), 198. [35] e.g. *Cal. Pat.* 1385–9, 42.
[36] Ibid. 1413–16, 165.
[37] Ibid. 1436–41, 189. [38] *Rot. Parl.* v. 47.
[39] Eton Coll. Mun. 39/16–17; 39/20.
[40] Ibid. ALHC 3/4, draft conveyance to Smith and Whatley, 1914; for the extent of the coll.'s land, below, econ. hist. [41] W.R.O., G 11/760/346.
[42] Inf. from Mr. A. J. Maitland-Robinson, Bathampton Ho. [43] *V.C.H. Wilts.* ii, p. 151.
[44] *Bk. of Fees*, ii. 742; *Cal. Inq. p.m. Hen. VII*, ii, pp. 317–18. [45] *Close R.* 1227–31, 479.
[46] *Bk. of Fees*, ii. 742.
[47] *Feet of F. 1272–1327* (W.R.S. i), p. 46.
[48] *First Pembroke Survey*, i. 6.
[49] *Feet of F. 1377–1509* (W.R.S. xli), pp. 11, 55.
[50] P.R.O., C 138/48, no. 67.
[51] *Feud. Aids*, v. 244.

manor descended in the Mompesson family with Little Bathampton manor, and from 1483 with Great Bathampton manor.[52] In 1556 Hanging Langford was allotted to Richard and Elizabeth Perkins,[53] and from then it descended in the Perkins and Moody families with Great Bathampton[54] until c. 1831 when, after a contract of 1826, the trustee of the Revd. William Moody (d. 1827) sold it to William Wyndham[55] (d. 1841) of Dinton. From inclosure in 1836 the manor measured c. 630 a.[56] It descended in the direct line to William (d. 1862), William (d. 1914),[57] and William Wyndham, who sold most of it in 1916 and the rest in 1918.[58] Thereafter the land descended in various farms[59] two of which, a total of c. 370 a., were bought in 1987 by Mr. and Mrs. A. J. Maitland-Robinson, who owned c. 750 a. of Hanging Langford in 1991.[60] Mr. W. Helyar then owned 214 a. of downland.[61]

The rector of North Newnton had been endowed with 1/20 of the revenues of Steeple Langford church by 1291:[62] later evidence shows it to have been tithes from the land in Hanging Langford of which Wilton abbey was overlord.[63] The prebendary of North Newnton, whose church was a prebend in Wilton abbey apparently from 1299,[64] owned the tithes until the Dissolution. They were among the abbey's possessions granted in 1544 to Sir William Herbert (cr. earl of Pembroke 1551).[65] Until the later 19th century earls of Pembroke appointed sinecure prebendaries: a condition of appointment was that the endowments of the prebend, including the tithes from Hanging Langford, were leased to the patron,[66] and successive earls held them until in 1838 they were valued at £42 and commuted.[67]

ECONOMIC HISTORY. In 1086 there were 4 ploughteams on land for 4½ at Hanging Langford, 3 on the 8 hides and 1 yardland of demesne and 1 on the land of 3 *villani* and 9 bordars. There were 40 a. of meadow, and 30 a. and 4 square furlongs of pasture. The two estates there, each of 5 hides in 1086,[68] remained of equal size until the 19th century. The lands of the two were intermingled in the open fields, and the meadows, lowland pasture, and downland pasture were common to each.[69] Before the late 16th century, however, the demesne lands were separated from the tenantry lands so that the two demesnes shared a central north–south strip, in which lay all four kinds of land, running from the Wylye to the downs, and the two sets of customary tenants shared similar north–south strips to the east and west.[70]

The lands of the two demesnes consisted mainly of 28 a. of meadows, 19 a. of lowland pasture, c. 142 a. of arable, and 224 a. of downland pasture: the two farms were of equal size and used that land in common, taking equal amounts of hay from the meadows and keeping a joint demesne flock.[71] There were three open fields, East, Middle, and West, in the later 16th century, when they lay divided into ridges estimated at ¾ a. each.[72] In 1617 each field was in furlongs averaging c. 4½ a. but by then was apparently not divided into strips, and each farm had an equal number of furlongs in each field.[73] In the later 16th century, but apparently not from the later 17th, tenantry cattle could be fed in the fields by night in autumn.[74] The three fields were of roughly equal size in 1763.[75] The boundaries between the furlongs were obliterated in the 18th century, when the two farms may have been in single occupation.[76] In the later 18th century the two demesnes made up a farm of c. 427 a., several except that each tenantry had the right to feed animals for part of the year on the meadows and lowland pasture, a few tenants had a few acres in the arable, 36 tenantry sheep might be in the flock, a few acres of demesne arable were in the tenantry fields, and a few acres of demesne meadow were in Towning mead.[77] In the later 17th century part of Farm down was covered by bushes and it was the practice to plough 15 a. of it each year,[78] in the later 18th century c. 22 a. were sometimes ploughed,[79] and by 1836 the southernmost 100 a. of the down had been converted to arable.[80] The demesne meadows were drowned from the later 17th century or earlier.[81]

Eton College's demesne was held on lease by two bondmen in 1443: when they took it 300 sheep could be kept, 30 a. were sown with wheat, 35 a. with barley, 8 a. with dredge, and 8 a. with peas and vetch.[82] It was leased to another bondman in 1455.[83] The Mompessons' demesne was leased in the earlier 16th century[84] and perhaps earlier. From 1756 or earlier to the late 19th century the college leased its demesne to the lord of the second manor,[85] and from 1754 or earlier members of the Thring family occupied both demesnes.[86] On the north side of the road and east of the village the college demesne included

52   Above, Bathampton, manors.
53   *W.A.M.* xliii. 291–2.
54   Above, Bathampton, manors.
55   W.R.O. 475/1, copy will of Wm. Moody; Som. R.O., DD/WY, box 156, copy letters, 1829; case for Brodie's opinion, 1830.
56   W.R.O., EA/153.
57   Burke, *Land. Gent.* (1937), 2511.
58   *V.C.H. Wilts.* viii. 28; W.R.O. 475/39.
59   W.R.O., G 11/505/2.
60   Inf. from Mr. Maitland-Robinson.
61   Sale cat. 1991; local inf.
62   *Tax. Eccl.* (Rec. Com.), 181.
63   W.R.O. 475/24.
64   *V.C.H. Wilts.* x. 133–4.
65   *First Pembroke Survey*, i. 298; *L. & P. Hen. VIII*, xix (1), p. 38; *Complete Peerage*, x. 406–7.
66   *V.C.H. Wilts.* x. 134.
67   W.R.O., tithe award.
68   *V.C.H. Wilts.* ii, pp. 133, 151.
69   Below, this section.
70   Eton Coll. Mun. 43/69; 43/128; cf. W.R.O. 475/22.
71   Eton Coll. Mun. 43/138; W.R.O. 475/22.
72   Eton Coll. Mun. 4/424.
73   Som. R.O., DD/WY, box 156, ct. bk. 1609–57, ct. 5 May 15 Jas I.   74   Eton Coll. Mun. 43/69; 43/99.
75   W.R.O. 475/22; 475/24.
76   Ibid. 475/22; Eton Coll. Mun. 43/158.
77   W.R.O. 475/22; 475/24; for Towning mead, below, this section.   78   Eton Coll. Mun. 43/156.
79   W.R.O. 475/24.   80   Ibid. EA/153.
81   Eton Coll. Mun. 43/99.   82   Ibid. 43/44.
83   Ibid. 43/49.
84   P.R.O., C 3/176/9.
85   Eton Coll. Mun. 43/18–42.
86   W.R.O. 475/3, partic. of estates.

a farmstead and *c.* 4 a. of several pasture, and on the same side at the east edge of the village the other demesne included a farmstead and *c.* 6 a.[87]

The customary tenants of each manor had small home closes but all their other lands remained commonable until 1836. West of the demesne meadow land they had a meadow called Towning, 16 a., east of it *c.* 34 a. of lowland pasture for *c.* 50 cattle called the Marsh and the Moor. The arable south of the Great Wishford to Bishopstrow road was in four hill fields, called Upper and Lower East and Upper and Lower West in the late 17th century, but may earlier have been in two. North of the road and west of the village other arable was in smaller 'hitch' fields. All the arable was in strips of *c.* ½ a. and all the tenants of each manor had strips scattered throughout the fields, *c.* 245 a. in all. Some or all of the arable north of the road may have been converted from pasture. South of the arable and on each side of Farm down was a tenantry down, each of *c.* 120 a., on which *c.* 500 sheep could be fed. A communal shepherd and a communal cowherd were employed in the 16th and 17th centuries. In 1659 *c.* 20 a. of the Marsh were converted to water meadow: 14 equal portions were designated and the hay from each taken by yearly lot. From 1723 a further 4 a. of the Marsh were watered and mown, and the hay from it was made into a rick from which the tenantry flock was fed. From, possibly, the early 18th century there were three hill fields and three 'hitch' fields after Upper and Lower West field were merged and one of the 'hitch' fields was divided.[88] From 1797, when it was agreed to convert the south end of each of East Tenantry down and West Tenantry down to arable, there were two new areas of open field: on each down 14 plots of 1 a. were assigned to the tenants by lot.[89] On the west down more land may have been ploughed before 1836.[90]

On both manors customary holdings were small. In 1443 Eton College's 9 tenants held a total of 5½ yardlands and there were 4 cottagers.[91] In the 17th century each manor had *c.* 7 copyholds. On each a yardland included *c.* 25 a. of arable, 1 a. of meadow, and feeding for *c.* 40 sheep. There was a freehold of ½ yardland, and ½ yardland was held with the mill.[92] In 1763 Eton College had 7 copyholders holding *c.* 106 a. of arable, the other manor 9 holding *c.* 120 a. The largest copyhold was of 2 yardlands.[93] By 1788 holdings of 76 a. and 72 a. had been accumulated,[94] and the concentration of the tenantry lands into fewer farms continued in the early 19th century.[95]

All the demesne and tenantry lands were in-closed by Act in 1836. Although their manors were nearly equal, Eton College was allotted only 357 a., William Wyndham 611 a.: the discrepancy is only partly explained by Wyndham's acquisition of a sale allotment and the inclusion of a higher proportion of down in his allotment. The college's land was a strip, beside the western parish boundary, of which the eastern part, 163 a., was held on lease by Wyndham.[96] In 1838 there was a farm of 541 a., held by the lessee of Little Bathampton farm, one of 248 a., and one of 196 a., the college's western strip then worked from buildings on the north side of the street.[97] The two larger farms were merged as Manor farm in 1842. The farm remained *c.* 785 a. until the 163 a. leased to Wyndham were reunited with College farm in the late 19th century.[98] In the early 20th century Manor farm and College farm had the same tenant.[99] About 1918 Manor farm was split into several farms, some of which may have been for dairying,[1] and new buildings, incorporating a dairy, were erected for College farm in 1937.[2] Dairying ceased in the later 20th century: in 1991 *c.* 750 a., including College farm and mainly arable, were part of Great Bathampton farm,[3] and 162 a. of downland in addition were arable.[4]

A linen weaver was mentioned in 1716.[5]

MILL. A mill stood at Hanging Langford from 1086[6] or earlier to the mid 17th century, apparently east of the village near the junction of Wylye Road and the Steeple Langford road.[7] For its whole life the lords of the two manors owned equal shares in it.[8] In the Middle Ages the Wylye was divided north of Hanging Langford village by a great stone, presumably a cutwater, from which a stream led south to Hanging Langford mill, and in 1455 a causeway between the stone and the Hanging Langford bank needed repair.[9] The mill itself was in great decay in 1459.[10] It was presumably rebuilt, and a new wheel was fitted in the early 16th century.[11] In the 1530s and 1540s, however, the men of Hanging Langford claimed that alterations to the Steeple Langford bank to benefit the Steeple Langford mills obstructed the flow of water to Hanging Langford mill,[12] which was again ruinous in 1564.[13] By 1575 it had again been rebuilt,[14] and in the earlier 17th century Eton College's copyholders were obliged to have their corn ground at it.[15] The division of the water continued to be disputed with Steeple Langford,[16] and the mill was once more in decay in 1636.[17] There is no later evidence of milling at it, and by 1689 mill and mill house had fallen down.[18]

[87] W.R.O. 475/22.
[88] Ibid.; ibid. 475/24; ibid. EA/153; Eton Coll. Mun., Ric. Rowden's bk.; for the shepherd and cowherd, Eton Coll. Mun. 43/69; Som. R.O., DD/WY, box 156, ct. bk. 1609–57, list of orders. [89] W.R.O. 475/3, agreement, 1797.
[90] Ibid. EA/153. [91] Eton Coll. Mun. 43/44.
[92] Ibid. 43/136; W.R.O. 475/22; Som. R.O., DD/WY, box 156, ct. bk. 1609–57, ct. 5 May 15 Jas. I.
[93] W.R.O. 475/22; 475/24.
[94] Ibid. 529/218, survey of Hanging Langford, 1788.
[95] Below, this section. [96] W.R.O., EA/153.
[97] Ibid. tithe award.
[98] Som. R.O., DD/WY, box 155, survey, 1892; DD/WY, box 156, partic. of estates, 1875; DD/WY, box 232, rental, 1840–6. [99] W.R.O., Inland Revenue, val. reg. 143.
[1] Ibid. 475/39; ibid. G 11/132/28; G 11/505/2.
[2] Ibid. G 11/760/346.
[3] Inf. from Mr. Maitland-Robinson.
[4] Local inf.
[5] *Wilts. Apprentices* (W.R.S. xvii), p. 116.
[6] *V.C.H. Wilts.* ii, pp. 133, 151.
[7] W.R.O. 475/22; 475/24; ibid. EA/153.
[8] e.g. *V.C.H. Wilts.* ii, pp. 133, 151; Eton Coll. Mun. 43/51 (1459); 43/64 (1564); 43/126 (1492).
[9] Ibid. 43/47, rot. 10. [10] Ibid. 43/51.
[11] Ibid. 43/127.
[12] P.R.O., STAC 2/20/333; STAC 2/33/5; STAC 3/3/13.
[13] Eton Coll. Mun. 43/64.
[14] Ibid. 43/128. [15] Ibid. 43/83, nos. 1, 20.
[16] Ibid. 43/230, cts. 17 June 9 Jas. I; 30 July 16 Jas. I.
[17] Ibid. 43/83, no. 39.
[18] Ibid. 43/138.

LOCAL GOVERNMENT. From the 16th century or earlier Hanging Langford and Little Langford were united as a single tithing.[19]

The dean and canons of Mortain claimed the assize of bread and of ale, view of frankpledge, and freedom from suit of shire and hundred for their manor of Hanging Langford[20] and from 1443 Eton College held a view of frankpledge and court at Hanging Langford, apparently attended by the men of only their own manor. In the 15th century the view and court was usually held twice a year. The assize of ale was enforced, and matters dealt with under leet jurisdiction included assault and the taking by the miller of excess toll. The tithingman presented and a jury affirmed his presentments. The homage presented manorial matters such as the death of tenants and disrepair of tenements. The lord often claimed incidents of bondage: those living away from the manor paid chevage, licences to marry were paid for,[21] and in 1455 a bondman was amerced for attending school at Winchester, at the expense of the rector of Steeple Langford, without licence.[22] In 1442 a Deptford man assaulted, and broke the right leg of, a bondman; negotiations over what damages were due to the college were referred to the provost in 1447.[23]

The court may have been held less frequently in the 16th century.[24] Leet business, including assault, petty larceny, and the miller's offences, was still transacted; the usual manorial matters were dealt with, and in 1566 letters of manumission granted to a bondman and eight of his family in 1537 were shown in court.[25] The jury and the homage coalesced and increasingly the court tried to enforce agreed practice in common husbandry. That was apparently the main function of the court in the 17th century, although a few matters under leet jurisdiction were still presented. In 1611, for example, jurors presented an assault and that three had sworn allegiance to the king, but there were c. 17 presentments dealing with rights of way, watercourses, tree felling, and the use of commonable land.[26] The taking of a trout under 8 in. long contrary to statute was punished in 1617;[27] in 1636 it was said that the tithing had no butt and none proficient in the use of bows and arrows and that men frequented alehouses;[28] and in 1664 the constable was ordered to make stocks.[29] In 1640 two surveyors of highways were presented for not mending a road, a failure which they attributed to being too busy pressing soldiers:[30] it is not clear whether they acted for Hanging Langford alone or for all Steeple Langford parish.

In the 17th century the court of the second manor of Hanging Langford dealt only with tenurial matters and the rules for common husbandry.[31] In agrarian matters consultation between the lords or stewards of the two manors was sometimes reported,[32] sometimes the same offence was presented at each court,[33] and sometimes a court for each manor was held on the same day.[34] From the late 17th century Eton College's court seems to have dealt only with tenurial business and to have been held infrequently.[35]

CHURCH. A chapel on Eton College's manor, presumably built by the dean and canons of Mortain, was ruinous in 1463,[36] and is not recorded later.

NONCONFORMITY. A house in Hanging Langford was certified for Baptist meetings in 1829, and in 1849 a small red-brick chapel was built for Primitive Methodists.[37] The chapel was attended by congregations totalling 125 at the three services on Census Sunday in 1851.[38] It was closed in 1960.[39]

MADDINGTON

MADDINGTON, a downland parish WNW. of Amesbury,[40] contained the settlements called Maddington, Homanton, Bourton, and Addestone, each of which had a strip of land running from the river Till in the east to the downs in the west.[41] It may also have included a hamlet called Newport.[42] A total of 12 a. in three detached parcels to the east[43] was transferred to Winterbourne Stoke in 1885, leaving Maddington parish with 3,968 a. (1,606 ha.).[44] In 1934 the whole parish was added to Shrewton parish.[45]

An earlier name for the Till was the Winterbourne: in the 11th century many estates in its

19 *Taxation Lists* (W.R.S. x), 112; Eton Coll. Mun., Ric. Rowden's bk.; W.R.O., A 1/345/253.
20 P.R.O., JUST 1/1004, rot. 104d.
21 Eton Coll. Mun. 43/44–52.
22 Ibid. 43/47, rot. 10; A. B. Emden, *Biog. Reg. Univ. Oxf. to 1500*, i. 521.
23 Eton Coll. Mun. 43/46.
24 Para. based on ibid. 1/242; 2/230–2; 2/235; 4/424; 43/53–103.
25 Ibid. 43/65.
26 Ibid. 43/77.
27 Ibid. 43/78; 1 Eliz. I, c. 17, s. 2.
28 Ibid. 43/83, no. 39.
29 Ibid. 43/95.
30 Ibid. 43/83, no. 48.
31 Som. R.O., DD/WY, box 156, ct. bks. 1609–57; 1663–1769.
32 Eton Coll. Mun. 43/87.
33 Ibid. 43/77; Som. R.O., DD/WY, box 156, ct. bk. 1609–57.
34 Eton Coll. Mun., Ric. Rowden's bk.
35 Ibid. 43/100–2.
36 Ibid. 43/44.
37 *Meeting Ho. Certs.* (W.R.S. xl), pp. 122, 166.
38 P.R.O., HO 129/265/1/8/18.
39 W.R.O. 1150/338A–B.
40 This article was written in 1990–1. Maps used include O.S. Maps 1/50,000, sheet 184 (1979 edn.); 1/25,000, SU 04 (1958 edn.); 6", Wilts. LIII (1889 and later edns.).
41 W.R.O., tithe award.
42 Bristol Univ. Libr., Wansbrough MS. 4.
43 W.R.O., tithe award.
44 *Census*, 1891; O.S. Map 6", Wilts. LIII (1889 edn.).
45 *V.C.H. Wilts.* iv. 357.

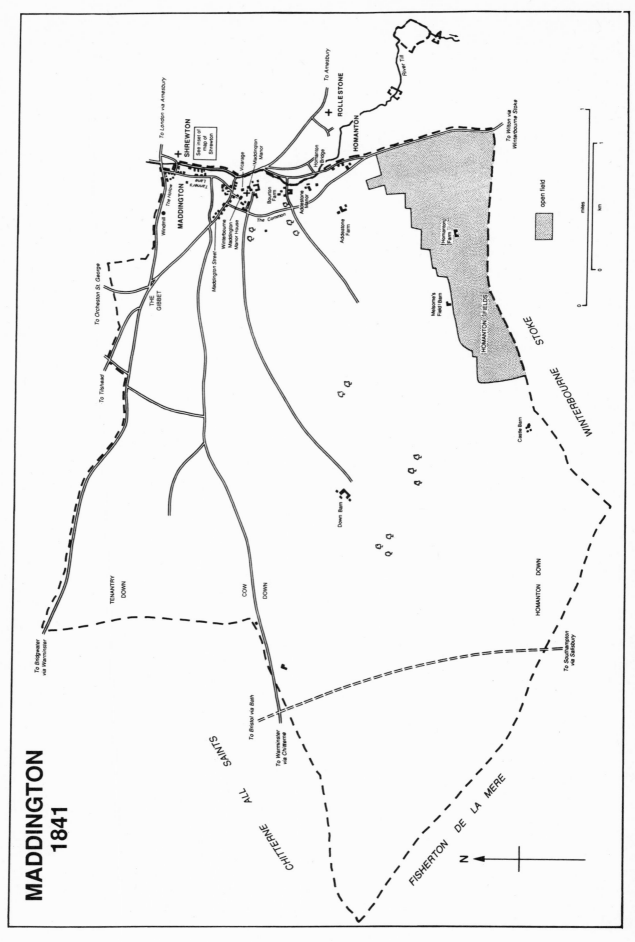

MADDINGTON
1841

SHREWTON

ROLLESTONE

To Amesbury

To London via Amesbury

See inset of
map of
Shrewton

HOMANTON

River Till

To Wilton via
Winterbourne Stoke

Vicarage

Maddington
Manor

Homanton
Bridge

Windmill

The Hollow

MADDINGTON

Tanner's Lane

Bourton
Farm

Adastone
Manor

The Common

Addestone
Farm

Homanton
Farm

open field

miles

km

Winterbourne
Maddington
Manor House

Maddington Street

To Orcheston St. George

THE
GIBBET

Melsome's
Field Barn

HOMANTON FIELDS

STOKE

WINTERBOURNE

To Tilshead

Castle Barn

TENANTRY
DOWN

COW

DOWN

Down Barn

HOMANTON DOWN

To Bridgwater
via Warminster

ALL

SAINTS

To Bristol via Bath

To Southampton
via Salisbury

To Warminster
via Chitterne

CHITTERNE

FISHERTON   DE   LA   MERE

N

valley were called Winterbourne, and several became part of Maddington parish. Maiden Winterbourne, so called because it belonged to the nuns of Amesbury, became Maddington and gave its name to the parish. Addestone, called Winterbourne in 1086, Abboteston in the 13th century, took its new name because it belonged to Hyde abbey, Winchester.[46]

On the north-east the parish's boundary with Shrewton was marked by the Till, and the east part of the southern boundary and part of the boundary in the extreme west follow dry valleys. A road marks the south part of the eastern boundary, and elsewhere the boundary is followed by roads and tracks.

Chalk outcrops over the whole parish, overlain by gravel near the Till and in several northerly dry valleys. The downland relief is gentle: the highest land is over 160 m. on the west part of the southern boundary, the lowest is below 91 m. in the Till valley and its tributaries.[47] The Till sometimes floods in winter and, as its old name indicates, sometimes dries out in summer.[48] From the Middle Ages land use was typical of Wiltshire's downland parishes. There were open fields between meadow land beside the river and rough grazing on the downs. Some of the meadows were watered and in the 17th century were said to produce extraordinarily long grass. Downland was ploughed from the 18th century.[49] Woodland was sparse: some was planted in the 18th century and early 19th, and in 1841 and 1990 there were c. 30 a. of scattered woods.[50] From c. 1940 the west half of the parish has been used for military training.[51] Since 1980 c. 70 a. near the southern boundary have been part of Parsonage Down national nature reserve.[52]

Two early main roads crossed the parish away from the village. The Southampton–Bristol road via Salisbury and Bath across the west part of the parish declined in importance in the 18th century,[53] and the east–west road from Amesbury to Warminster across the northern tip of the parish and along its boundary,[54] part of the road from London to Bridgwater (Som.) in the later 17th century,[55] was surpassed in importance by a new Amesbury–Warminster turnpike road made soon after 1761. The turnpike road crossed the Till near Maddington church, bisected Maddington village, and followed a dry valley westwards over the downs towards Chitterne: it was disturnpiked in 1871.[56] In 1773 roads running south from Orcheston St. George and south-east from Tilshead met the old east–west road at a junction, now called the Gibbet,

where a gibbet was standing in 1666 and 1773, and a road linked that junction with the turnpike road and Maddington village.[57] A north–south route led from the old Amesbury–Warminster road towards Winterbourne Stoke and Wilton: north of the church it survives as Tanner's Lane, south of it as the Common. A parallel road on the east bank of the Till in Shrewton has become more important. From the north–south route in Maddington other roads led west and south-west across the downs.[58] The Tilshead road and the eastern part of the turnpike road became part of a Devizes–Salisbury road which replaced another further east across Salisbury Plain c. 1900[59] and was the main road through the parish in 1990.

Evidence of prehistoric activity includes a barrow at the western tip of the parish known from the early 19th century as Oram's Grave, and the sites of others at the Gibbet and in the parish's south-east corner. Near the south-west boundary is a circular enclosure of c. 1 ha. In the south-east corner Romano-British pottery and coins have been found, and near the church other artefacts of similar date, perhaps associated with a burial;[60] the site of a Pagan-Saxon burial ground is on the northern boundary near the village.[61] There is evidence of prehistoric ploughing on the downs.[62]

There were 115 poll-tax payers in the parish in 1377. In 1801 the population was 327: it had risen to 445 by 1841 but fell in the next decade as people sought work elsewhere. It remained c. 400 from 1851 until 1881, had fallen to 343 by 1891, rose again in the early 20th century, but had declined to 329 by 1931, the last date for which a figure is available.[63]

MADDINGTON was the principal settlement in the parish and had almost half the poll-tax payers in 1377.[64] It apparently originated as a village closely grouped around its church. A large farmstead stood south of the church, three large farmsteads and the vicarage house north of it.[65] To the south were the three subsidiary settlements of the parish, to the north there may have been early settlement in Tanner's Lane, and to the north-west there was settlement, presumably later, along the turnpike road now called Maddington Street. On the east bank of the Till buildings of the less closely grouped Shrewton village were strung out south of Shrewton church along the Winterbourne Stoke road, now called High Street, parallel to the line of settlement in Maddington:[66] the turnpiking of the south part of that road as part of the

46 *P.N. Wilts.* (E.P.N.S.), 10, 232–7; below, manors. Shrewton, in which the church belonged to Lacock abbey, was also called Maiden Winterbourne: below, Shrewton, intro.
47 Geol. Surv. Maps 1", drift, sheet 282 (1967 edn.); 1/50,000, drift, sheet 298 (1976 edn.).
48 Below, Shrewton, intro.
49 *W.A.M.* xvii. 301; below, econ. hist.
50 Dors. R.O., D 124, box 177, Maddington accts. 1756–9; W.R.O., tithe award.
51 Inf. from Defence Land Agent, Durrington; below, manors.
52 Below, manors (Homanton); econ. hist. (Homanton).
53 Above, Steeple Langford, intro. [roads].
54 Dors. R.O., D 124, box 19, plan of Chitterne–Ames-

bury roads, 18th-cent.
55 J. Ogilby, *Brit.* (1675), pl. 32.
56 *V.C.H. Wilts.* iv. 270; *L.J.* xxx. 138; above, Amesbury, intro. (roads).
57 *Andrews and Dury, Map* (W.R.S. viii), pls. 5, 8; *W.N. & Q.* iii. 333–4.
58 *Andrews and Dury, Map* (W.R.S. viii), pls. 5, 8.
59 *V.C.H. Wilts.* iv. 266.
60 Ibid. i (1), 191, 269; J. M. J. Fletcher and A. S. Robins, *Guide to Shrewton, Maddington and Rollestone* (priv. print. 1938), 10–11; Wilts. Cuttings, xvi. 227.
61 *W.A.M.* lxiv. 128.   62 *V.C.H. Wilts.* i (1), 278.
63 Ibid. iv. 308, 321, 352.   64 Ibid. 308.
65 W.R.O., tithe award.
66 Below, Shrewton, intro.

Amesbury–Warminster road in 1761 and the increased importance of the road after 1900[67] apparently drew Shrewton's centre of gravity south from its own church towards Maddington's. As a result the two villages coalesced,[68] and later building has embraced the hamlet of Netton in Shrewton and the village of Rollestone. The unified and enlarged village is called Shrewton, and since 1934 use of the name Maddington has greatly decreased.

South of Maddington church stand Maddington Manor and large farm buildings, some of which have been converted for residence. North of the church were the manor houses of Winterbourne Maddington manor, one of which may survive as the Priory,[69] and its principal farmstead. South of the Priory in 1990 stood the remains of a nine-bayed barn of 17th-century origin. North of the church the Grange, built of stone and flint, has a central east–west range of the 17th century, a parallel 18th-century range to the north, and an early 19th-century wing to the south. Maddington House is **L**-shaped and was built of banded flint and stone in the late 17th century: it was extended northwards in red brick in the 18th century and given a new south front, also of brick, c. 1800. Nearby stand Pear Tree Cottage, of flint and stone and possibly of 17th-century origin, and an earlier 19th-century lodge of Maddington Manor[70] built of cob.

Houses had been built in Tanner's Lane by the 17th century. Plots extended from the east side of the lane to the river, and surviving houses of the 17th and 18th centuries, some thatched and built of cob, lie at right angles to the lane. By 1773 a row of houses of which two survive had been built at the east end of several plots: the houses were approached by bridges over the Till and formed a west side to Shrewton village street. By that date also a group of cottages had been built in the angle between the west side of Tanner's Lane and the old Amesbury–Warminster road: the road there was later called the Hollow, and the cottages were replaced by three pairs of estate cottages in the later 19th century. There were buildings on both sides of Maddington Street in 1773.[71] At the north-west end a pair of cottages built c. 1842 was one of several pairs in villages of the Till valley paid for by public subscription after a flood of 1841.[72] Other cottages were built beside Maddington Street in the 19th century.

Maddington village expanded little between the late 18th century and the mid 20th. On the west side of Tanner's Lane three pairs of council houses were built c. 1950 and the Butts, an estate of 12 private houses, c. 1985. In the Hollow 15 bungalows were built, mainly in the 1950s, and in the 1980s and 1990 houses were built near the

church on the farmyard of which the Priory was part. Elsewhere there was infilling.

HOMANTON had 25 poll-tax payers in 1377,[73] and in the 18th century was a hamlet of c. 10 houses on the east side of the Common; several houses in Shrewton and Winterbourne Stoke parishes were part of the hamlet.[74] Homanton House was built in the 17th century of banded stone and flint to a two-roomed plan with a gable stack at the east end. An 18th-century western extension was itself extended northwards in the 19th century. In the late 19th century a northern service block was added and a large central staircase, comprising re-used parts of various dates, some of high quality, was inserted. Between 1817 and 1841 a new farmstead was built of flint in Gothic style 750 m. south-west of the hamlet; it was called Homanton Farm in the later 19th century and Cherry Lodge Farm in the 20th. By 1841 some buildings in the hamlet had been demolished, and in 1886 as in 1990 only two or three within the Maddington part of it remained.[75]

BOURTON had only 20 poll-tax payers in 1377, although in 1334 its assessment for taxation had been considerably higher than that for Homanton.[76] In the early 19th century its buildings were on the west bank of the Till, linked by a ford to buildings in Shrewton on the east bank.[77] In 1841 only Bourton House and its farmstead stood west of the ford.[78] The house was rebuilt in the mid 19th century, and in the 20th another farmhouse was built east of it.

ADDESTONE, with only nine poll-tax payers in 1377,[79] may have been no more than a hamlet in the Middle Ages, and in 1773 consisted only of Addestone Manor and its farm buildings.[80] A second farmstead, Addestone Farm, was built 250 m. south-west of Addestone Manor between 1817 and 1841,[81] and a new farmhouse was built between the two in the 1980s.

OTHER SETTLEMENT. A house was said to be in Newport in 1538[82] but no other reference to a settlement of that name in the parish has been found. There was no building on the downs in 1773.[83] Down barn, later the site of cottages, was built c. 3 km. WSW. of the church probably in 1806 and certainly before 1817. Melsome's field barn and Castle barn, both west of Homanton Farm, and farm buildings near the turnpike road in the west part of the parish were all erected between 1817 and 1841.[84] Those near the road had been demolished by 1886. New downland barns and farmsteads of the mid or later 19th century included Maddington Farm, built be-

67 Above, this section.
68 Cf. below, Shrewton, intro. (map).
69 Ibid. manors (Maddington; Winterbourne Maddington). 70 W.R.O., tithe award.
71 *Andrews and Dury, Map* (W.R.S. viii), pl. 8.
72 *Endowed Char. Wilts.* (S. Div.), 302; below, charities.
73 *V.C.H. Wilts.* iv. 308.
74 *Andrews and Dury, Map* (W.R.S. viii), pl. 8.
75 O.S. Maps 1", sheet 14 (1817 edn.); 6", Wilts. LIII (1889 edn.); W.R.O., tithe award.
76 *V.C.H. Wilts.* iv. 299, 308.

77 O.S. Map 1", sheet 14 (1817 edn.).
78 W.R.O., tithe award.
79 *V.C.H. Wilts.* iv. 308.
80 *Andrews and Dury, Map* (W.R.S. viii), pl. 8.
81 O.S. Map 1", sheet 14 (1817 edn.); W.R.O., tithe award.
82 Bristol Univ. Libr., Wansbrough MS. 4.
83 *Andrews and Dury, Map* (W.R.S. viii), pl. 8.
84 O.S. Map 1", sheet 14 (1817 edn.); Dors. R.O., D 124, box 177, Maddington bills and receipts, 1806; W.R.O., tithe award.

side the turnpike road 2 km. west of the church between 1841 and 1853, and Bushes Farm near the parish's western corner, Tile barn north-east of Down barn, and Bourton field barn south-east of Down barn, all built between 1841 and 1886.[85] The three most westerly, Down barn, Bushes Farm, and Castle barn, were demolished, presumably when military training began c. 1940.[86] In the mid 20th century Middlecroft Farm was built between Maddington Farm and the village.

MANORS AND OTHER ESTATES. In 1066 Amesbury abbey held 4½ hides,[87] later *MADDINGTON* manor. In 1179 the estate was confirmed to Amesbury priory,[88] which in 1286 was probably granted free warren in Maddington as in other manors.[89] Maddington manor passed to the Crown at the Dissolution, and in 1564 was granted to Sir Walter Hungerford and Thomas Hungerford.[90] Thomas apparently had no later interest in it. Sir Walter (d. 1596) was succeeded by his half-brother Sir Edward Hungerford (d. 1607), who devised his estates to his grandnephew Sir Edward Hungerford (d. 1648).[91] The younger Sir Edward's relict Margaret (d. 1673) claimed a life interest in Maddington[92] but his half-brother and heir Anthony Hungerford evidently held the manor in 1650. Anthony (d. 1657) was succeeded by his son Sir Edward.[93] In 1673 Sir Edward conveyed the manor to Sir Richard Mason and Richard Kent,[94] probably trustees of Sir Stephen Fox who held it in 1678.[95] Sir Stephen (d. 1716) was succeeded by his son Stephen (cr. Baron Ilchester 1741, earl of Ilchester 1756), who took the name Fox-Strangways in 1758 and died in 1776. The manor passed in turn to Stephen's son Henry, earl of Ilchester (d. 1802), and Henry's son Henry, earl of Ilchester,[96] who sold it in 1809 as an estate of 1,500 a. to John Maton (d. 1827) and his brother James (d. 1856).[97] In 1850 James conveyed it to L. P. Maton[98] (d. 1865), who was succeeded by his son L. J. Maton. The manor was apparently sold c. 1896 by Maton to E. T. Hooley,[99] after whose bankruptcy it was sold in 1898 to Sir Christopher

Furness.[1] In 1909–10 Furness sold the estate in parcels through the Cavendish Land Company. J. C. Hayward bought Manor farm, 1,164 a., and A. Wallis bought land called Ingram's, 207 a.[2] In 1938 Hayward sold most of Manor farm to the War Department: the Ministry of Defence owned the land in 1990.[3] Tanner's Lane farm, 128 a., later called Middlecroft farm, was bought in 1910 by Wiltshire county council, the owner in 1990.[4]

A house on or near the site of Maddington Manor was lived in by Stephen Fox, later earl of Ilchester, from 1727. It burned down in 1741 and a larger house, built in 1742,[5] was used by Ilchester for some months of most years until his death.[6] It was replaced in 1833[7] by Maddington Manor, a red-brick house of three bays.

An estate of 4 hides held by Ulward in 1066 and by Matthew de Mortain in 1086[8] was later called *WINTERBOURNE MADDINGTON* manor.[9] It was probably among lands formerly Matthew's granted by Henry I to a member of the le Moyne family to be held by the serjeanty of serving as the king's larderer.[10] The estate was held by serjeanty c. 1200;[11] a claim to serve as larderer at the coronation of George IV in 1821 was made in respect of it, not by its owner but by the Maton brothers who presumably believed theirs to be the estate in question.[12]

Geoffrey le Moyne held Winterbourne Maddington in 1162[13] and 1198.[14] By 1212 it had passed to Ralph le Moyne,[15] probably Geoffrey's grandnephew Ralph who held it in 1230.[16] Ralph (d. by 1238) left a son and heir.[17] William le Moyne (fl. 1252, d. by 1295)[18] had by 1278 conveyed all or part of the manor to his son Henry,[19] who at his death c. 1315 held the whole jointly with his wife Joan[20] (d. by 1340). She was succeeded in turn by her son John le Moyne[21] (d. by 1349), John's son Sir Henry[22] (d. 1374), and Sir Henry's son John[23] (d. by 1381), whose heir was a minor.[24] Sir John le Moyne (fl. 1398) held the manor at his death in 1429 and was succeeded in turn by his grandson John Stourton[25] (cr. Baron Stourton 1448, d. 1462) and Stourton's son William, Lord Stourton (d. 1478), whose relict Margaret, later wife of John Cheyne, Lord Cheyne,[26] had a life interest in it.

85 O.S. Map 6", Wilts. LIII (1889 edn.); W.R.O., tithe award; ibid. EA/173.   86 Above, this section.
87 *V.C.H. Wilts.* ii, p. 132.
88 *Cal. Chart. R.* 1257–1300, 157–9; for the hist. of the abbey and priory, *V.C.H. Wilts.* iii. 242–59.
89 *Cal. Chart. R.* 1257–1300, 336.
90 *Cal. Pat.* 1563–6, p. 154.
91 *Complete Peerage,* vi. 626.
92 *V.C.H. Wilts.* x. 163; P.R.O., C 78/1924, no. 26.
93 P.R.O., CP 25/2/616/1650 Mich.; below, Winterbourne Stoke, manors (Winterbourne Stoke).
94 P.R.O., C 54/4397, no. 3.
95 Dors. R.O., D 124, box 129, deed, Fox to Sopp, 1678.
96 *Complete Peerage,* vii. 46–7.
97 Hoare, *Mod. Wilts.* Branch and Dole, 37; W.A.S. Libr., sale cat. xi, no. 11; mons. in church.
98 TS. abstr. of title of Maddington manor, in possession of Mrs. E. Broadbent, Maddington Manor.
99 Burke, *Land. Gent.* (1937), 1558; *Kelly's Dir. Wilts.* (1895, 1898).
1 Hants R.O. 11M65/28.
2 W.A.S. Libr., sale cat. ix, no. 15.
3 Inf. from Major R. D. Hayward, Bourton Farm.
4 Inf. from the Property Manager, Co. Hall, Trowbridge.

5 G. S. H. F. Strangways, *Hen. Fox, First Lord Holland,* 47, 54.
6 Dors. R.O., D 124, box 177, Maddington farm accts. 1752–77.   7 Date on bldg.
8 *V.C.H. Wilts.* ii, p. 159.
9 *Cal. Inq. p.m.* iii, p. 159; *Cal. Close,* 1461–8, 122; *Cal. Inq. p.m. Hen. VII,* i, p. 60.
10 J. H. Round, *King's Serjeants and Off. of State,* 235.
11 *Bk. of Fees,* i. 341.
12 Round, op. cit. 233–4, 241; Hoare, *Mod. Wilts.* Branch and Dole, 37.
13 Round, op. cit. 236.
14 *Bk. of Fees,* i. 12.
15 *Red Bk. Exch.* (Rolls Ser.), ii. 485.
16 *Bracton's Note Bk.* ed. Maitland, ii, pp. 330–1.
17 *Close R.* 1237–42, 52.
18 *Cal. Inq. p.m.* iii, p. 159; *Cal. Chart. R.* 1226–57, 407.
19 *Abbrev. Rot. Orig.* (Rec. Com.), i. 200.
20 *Wilts. Inq. p.m.* 1242–1327 (Index Libr.), 398.
21 *Cal. Inq. p.m.* viii, p. 199.
22 *V.C.H. Glos.* xi. 249.
23 *Cal. Inq. p.m.* xiv, p. 76.
24 *Cal. Pat.* 1377–81, 626.
25 Ibid. 1396–9, 356; P.R.O., C 139/43, no. 16.
26 *Complete Peerage,* xii (1), 301–3.

After her death in 1503 the manor passed in turn to her sons William Stourton, Lord Stourton[27] (d. 1524), and Edward Stourton, Lord Stourton (d. 1535), and to Edward's son William, Lord Stourton.[28] William sold it in 1544 to Thomas Long,[29] and Long in 1546 to William Bailey.[30]

In 1552 Bailey's relict Mary conveyed the manor to John Tooker[31] (d. 1558), who was succeeded in turn by his son George[32] (d. 1561) and George's son Henry[33] (d. 1570). From Henry two thirds of the manor passed to his uncle Charles Tooker and a third to his sister Agnes.[34] No later record of Agnes's share has been found. Charles (d. 1571) was succeeded by his son Giles[35] (d. 1623), who devised Winterbourne Maddington manor to his wife Elizabeth for life.[36] The manor passed to their son Edward (d. c. 1671)[37] and to Edward's son Sir Giles Tooker, Bt. (d. 1675), whose heirs were his sisters Philippa, wife of Sir Thomas Gore, and Martha, wife of Sir Walter Ernle, Bt.[38] (d. 1682).[39] It apparently passed from Martha (d. 1688)[40] to her grandson Sir Walter Ernle, Bt. (d. 1690). Thereafter, until 1917, it descended with Etchilhampton manor. Sir Walter was succeeded by his brother Sir Edward (d. 1729), whose heir was his daughter Elizabeth (d. 1759), wife of Henry Drax (d. 1755). Elizabeth and Henry were succeeded in turn by their sons Thomas (d. 1789) and Edward (d. 1791), whose daughter and heir Sarah married Richard Grosvenor, later Erle-Drax-Grosvenor (d. 1819). From Sarah (d. 1822), Winterbourne Maddington manor passed successively to her son Richard Erle-Drax-Grosvenor (d. 1828) and daughter Jane, wife of John Sawbridge, later Sawbridge-Erle-Drax. Jane (d. 1853) was succeeded in turn by her daughters Maria (d. 1885) and Sarah (d. 1905), wife of F. A. P. Burton (d. 1865) and later of J. L. Egginton, who took the name Ernle-Erle-Drax in 1887. Sarah's heir was her daughter Ernle Plunkett, Baroness Dunsany (d. 1916), who took the surname Plunkett-Ernle-Erle-Drax.[41] Ernle devised the manor to her son Reginald Plunkett-Ernle-Erle-Drax, who offered it for sale in 1917 as an estate of 1,039 a. In 1918 Maddington farm, 961 a.,[42] later called Grange farm, was bought by G. H. Barnes,[43] who sold it, part in 1938 and part in 1943,

to the War Department. The Ministry of Defence owned the land in 1990.[44]

The building now called the Priory stood on the manor. It is a single range built of flint with stone-mullioned windows c. 1600. It may originally have been a house, was apparently used later as a barn,[45] and was restored as a house c. 1990.[46] It is likely to have been built for Giles Tooker, who had a manor house at Maddington in 1618,[47] and was possibly the house lived in by Sir Walter Ernle (d. 1690), who was of Maddington.[48] A much larger house was built east of it and in 1773 was lived in by Thomas Drax.[49] Later owners of the manor may have occupied that house occasionally until it was demolished in the later 19th century.[50]

An estate of 1½ hide, later HOMANTON manor, was part of the honor of Wallingford (Berks., later Oxon.) in 1242–3[51] and 1300.[52] Thomas of Appleton held it as mesne tenant in 1242–3[53] and his right in it passed, presumably with Appleton manor (Berks.), to Giles de la Mote (d. c. 1334).[54]

The estate was probably that granted to Richard Rous and in 1203 confirmed to his nephew Richard the chamberlain.[55] John Rous held it in 1242–3,[56] Thomas Rous in 1275,[57] and John Rous at his death c. 1330.[58] From John the manor passed to his son Sir John (d. c. 1339) and afterwards to Sir John's son Richard (d. by 1374),[59] whose relict Elizabeth held it in 1375.[60] In 1438 Richard's grandson William Rous conveyed the manor to Walter Hungerford, Lord Hungerford, for an annuity for life.[61] Hungerford (d. 1449) was succeeded by his son Robert, Lord Hungerford (d. 1459), whose relict Margaret, Baroness Botreaux and Hungerford,[62] in 1472 gave the manor to the dean and chapter of Salisbury to found a chantry in the cathedral for her husband and his parents.[63] A Crown grant of Homanton manor as concealed land in 1582 to Theophilus Adams and James Woodshaw[64] was ineffective. The dean and chapter retained it,[65] and in 1869 the Ecclesiastical Commissioners sold it as an estate of 422 a. to Charles Wansborough[66] (d. 1890). Wansborough's executors conveyed Homanton farm to the mortgagee J. G. Simpkins, who owned it in 1894.[67] It was acquired, probably by purchase in 1896, by John Fallon, who owned it in 1914.[68]

27 Cal. Inq. p.m. Hen. VII, ii, p. 505.
28 Complete Peerage, xii (1), 304–6.
29 P.R.O., CP 25/2/46/323, no. 54.
30 L. & P. Hen. VIII, xxi (1), p. 151.
31 Cal. Pat. 1550–3, 428.
32 P.R.O., C 142/124, no. 201.
33 Ibid. C 142/131, no. 202.
34 Ibid. C 142/154, no. 115.
35 Ibid. C 142/159, no. 85.
36 Wilts. Inq. p.m. 1625–49 (Index Libr.), 38–41.
37 Ibid. 296; W.R.O., Ch. Com., chapter, 133/5.
38 Burke, Ext. & Dorm. Baronetcies (1844), 529, where Edw.'s death is wrongly dated 1688.
39 Burke, Land. Gent. (1952), 690.
40 Hoare, Mod. Wilts. Branch and Dole, 39.
41 Burke, Land. Gent. (1952), 690–1; V.C.H. Wilts. x. 73; Complete Peerage, iv. 556.
42 W.A.S. Libr., sale cat. xii, no. 23.
43 Inf. from Mrs. E. H. Woods, the Grange.
44 Inf. from Major Hayward; Defence Land Agent, Durrington.
45 See plate facing p. 267.   46 W.A.M. lxxxi. 80–3.

47 Wilts. Inq. p.m. 1625–49 (Index Libr.), 40.
48 Burke, Land. Gent. (1952), 690.
49 Andrews and Dury, Map (W.R.S. viii), pl. 8.
50 W.A.M. lxxxi. 82–3.   51 Bk. of Fees, ii. 742.
52 Cal. Inq. p.m. iii, p. 446.   53 Bk. of Fees, ii. 742.
54 V.C.H. Berks. iv. 336–7; Cal. Inq. p.m. vii, p. 222.
55 Rot. Chart. (Rec. Com.), 109.
56 Bk. of Fees, ii. 742.
57 Rot. Hund. (Rec. Com.), ii (1), 254.
58 Cal. Inq. p.m. vii, p. 222.
59 Ibid. xiv, pp. 83–4; for the Rous fam., Hoare, Mod. Wilts. Heytesbury, 160–1.   60 Cal. Close, 1374–7, 120.
61 Feet of F. 1377–1509 (W.R.S. xli), p. 110.
62 Complete Peerage, vi. 613–18.
63 Cal. Pat. 1467–77, 311; W.A.M. xlvii. 458–9.
64 Cal. Pat. 1580–2, p. 258.
65 D. & C. Sar. Mun., press D, I, box 31/26, ct. bk. 1538–1606.   66 Ch. Com., copy deeds, vol. xcvii, no. 8785.
67 W.A.S. Libr., sale cat. xxi, no. 22; Wilts. Cuttings, v. 107; vii. 30.
68 W.R.O. 1232/1, mortgage, Fallon to Leslie, 1914; 2132/187.

R. C. Dawson owned the land in 1920–1,[69] and in 1927 it was sold as part of his Scotland Lodge estate, based in Winterbourne Stoke parish, to Robert Wales (d. 1979). On Wales's instructions the estate was sold in 1980 for less than the market price to the Nature Conservancy Council, whose successor English Nature owned 283 a. in Maddington in 1991.[70]

In 1242–3 William Longespée, styled earl of Salisbury, was overlord of ½ knight's fee said to be in Maddington.[71] The overlordship passed with the overlordship of Shrewton and the earldom of Salisbury until 1462[72] or later. Sir Ellis Giffard (d. 1248) held the land in 1242–3, Hugh Giffard held of Ellis, and Gilbert Giffard, Hugh Francis, and William Franklin held of Hugh.[73] William Botreaux, Lord Botreaux, held it at his death in 1462.[74] In 1464 his relict Margaret and her husband Sir Thomas Burgh conveyed the estate, nominally 110 a. and pasture rights, to feoffees, possibly of Botreaux's daughter Margaret, Baroness Botreaux and Hungerford.[75] It was apparently conveyed with Homanton manor to the dean and chapter of Salisbury in 1472.[76] It was not afterwards a separate estate and, since the dean and chapter held no land in the parish except Homanton's,[77] it was apparently absorbed by Homanton manor.

Lands at *BOURTON* may have formed the estate near Shrewton called Winterbourne held by Sir Ellis Giffard in 1242–3.[78] Gilbert Giffard was overlord of land in Maddington, perhaps the same, in 1278,[79] as was John Giffard in 1327[80] and Hugh Giffard in 1428.[81] Henry Daubeney died seised of the estate held of Gilbert Giffard c. 1278.[82]

In 1435 lands in Bourton were part of Winterbourne Stoke manor, held by Walter, Lord Hungerford (d. 1449).[83] They seem to have passed with that manor in the Hungerford and Hastings families and to have been sold with it by Sir Edward Hungerford in 1674 to Sir John Nicholas (d. 1704) and by Nicholas's son Edward in 1715 to John Howe (d. 1721) or Howe's son John (cr. Baron Chedworth 1741, d. 1742):[84] Sir Walter Hungerford owned 2 yardlands in Bourton in 1582[85] and Howe owned them in

1730.[86] With his title the land passed to Howe's sons John (d. 1762) and Henry (d. 1781) and to their nephew John Howe (d. 1804),[87] whose executors sold it in 1807 to Harry Biggs.[88]

Biggs inherited two other estates in Bourton. In 1428 Sir John le Moyne, lord of Winterbourne Maddington manor, held lands in Maddington of Hugh Giffard,[89] from which was perhaps derived an estate in Bourton held in 1617 by Giles Tooker, lord of the same manor.[90] The estate, of 3 yardlands in 1634,[91] passed with the manor to Thomas Drax (d. 1789)[92] and before 1780 was acquired by Henry Biggs.[93] Another 3-yardland estate in Bourton belonged in 1582 to John Eyre of Bromham[94] and in 1617 to his son Thomas,[95] who sold it in 1633 to Henry Miles.[96] In or before 1635 Miles settled it on his son Richard.[97] A Henry Miles died in or before 1685;[98] another died in 1726 and was succeeded in turn by his son Henry (d. 1765) and daughter Jane, wife of Tristram Biggs.[99] By 1780 the estate had passed to Jane's son Henry Biggs.[1] Henry (d. 1800) was succeeded by his son Harry,[2] the purchaser of Lord Chedworth's lands, who in 1841 held the whole of Bourton, 495 a.[3] From Harry (d. 1856) Bourton farm may have passed to his son H. G. Biggs (d. 1877), whose heir was A. G. Yeatman, later Yeatman-Biggs.[4] It was held in 1903 and 1910 by J. H. Barrington,[5] and in 1921 by J. C. Hayward:[6] with Manor farm it passed to the Ministry of Defence, the owner in 1990.[7]

Lands at *ADDESTONE* were given to the New Minster at Winchester c. 950 probably by King Eadred:[8] the estate was 2 hides in 1086.[9] The monastery, called Hyde abbey from the early 12th century,[10] retained Addestone manor until the Dissolution. The Crown may have granted the manor to William Gilbert, who held it at his death in 1548 leaving as heir a son John.[11] In 1572 and 1585 John or a namesake held it.[12] In 1604 John Gilbert died holding the manor and was succeeded by his son John,[13] perhaps the John Gilbert who died in 1661.[14] Another John Gilbert held Addestone manor in 1662.[15] Later members of the Gilbert family who may have held it include William (fl. 1688–

69   Ibid. G 1/500/10; Wilts. Cuttings, xiv. 125.
70   Inf. from Chief Site Manager, Eng. Nature, S. Region, Foxhold Ho., Crookham Common, Newbury, Berks.
71   *Bk. of Fees*, ii. 721.
72   *Cal. Inq. p.m.* xvii, pp. 314, 321; P.R.O., C 140/7, no. 15; below, Shrewton, manors.
73   *Bk. of Fees*, ii. 721; below, Sherrington, manor.
74   P.R.O., C 140/7, no. 15.
75   *Feet of F. 1377–1509* (W.R.S. xli), pp. 143–4; *Complete Peerage*, iii. 242–3.
76   *Cal. Pat.* 1467–77, 311; above, this section (Homanton).
77   W.R.O., tithe award.
78   *Bk. of Fees*, ii. 721.
79   *Cal. Inq. p.m.* ii, p. 156.
80   Ibid. vii, pp. 42–5.
81   *Feud. Aids*, v. 243.
82   *Cal. Inq. p.m.* ii, p. 156.
83   P.R.O., SC 6/1062/6.
84   Below, Winterbourne Stoke, manors (Winterbourne Stoke).   85   W.R.O. 442/1, f. 10v.
86   Ibid. 906/W/192.
87   *Complete Peerage*, iii. 156–7.
88   Hoare, *Mod. Wilts.* Branch and Dole, 37–8; W.R.O. 374/128/49.   89   *Feud. Aids*, v. 243.
90   W.R.O. 906/W/176.
91   Ibid. 906/W/179.

92   Ibid. 906/W/187; above, this section (Winterbourne Maddington).
93   W.R.O., A 1/345/270.
94   Ibid. 442/1, f. 10.
95   Ibid. 906/W/176; *Wilts. Pedigrees* (Harl. Soc. cv/cvi), 58.   96   Ibid. 906/W/177.
97   Ibid. 906/W/179.
98   Ibid. wills, archd. Sar., Hen. Miles, 1685.
99   Ibid. 1336/38; Burke, *Land. Gent.* (1937), 157.
1   Burke, *Land. Gent.* (1937), 157; W.R.O., A 1/345/270.
2   *V.C.H. Wilts.* xi. 214.
3   W.R.O., tithe award.
4   *V.C.H. Wilts.* xi. 214.
5   *Kelly's Dir. Wilts.* (1903); W.R.O., Inland Revenue, val. reg. 140.
6   W.R.O., G 1/500/10.
7   Inf. from Major Hayward; above, this section (Maddington).   8   Finberg, *Early Wessex Chart.* p. 90.
9   *V.C.H. Wilts.* ii, p. 127.
10   *V.C.H. Hants.* ii. 117.
11   P.R.O., C 142/92, no. 128.
12   Ibid. CP 25/2/241/27 Eliz. I Hil.; *Cal. Pat.* 1569–72, p. 425.
13   P.R.O., C 142/282, no. 32.
14   *W.N. & Q.* iii. 374.
15   Wilts. Cuttings, xvi. 363.

1700),[16] William (fl. 1736),[17] Joseph (d. 1759), and Joseph's son William (d. 1777).[18] By 1780 it had been acquired by William Roles (d. 1781), who was succeeded by James Roles (fl. 1831).[19] The manor, 385 a., was held by William Davis as trustee for J. Festing in 1841[20] and was sold by Davis in 1877. It may have been bought by W. K. Melsome[21] and was offered for sale in 1894 by George Melsome.[22] C. M. Lesley owned the land in 1907 and 1931.[23] It was offered for sale several times in the later 20th century, and in 1987, as a farm of 505 a.,[24] was bought by Mr. G. Etherington, who sold it soon afterwards to the Ministry of Defence.[25]

Addestone Manor has a west range of flint and limestone apparently built in the early 18th century. Later in the century a north-east service wing of rubble was added and the west front was altered and given two Venetian windows. In the early 19th century the house was extended to the south in brick, a new staircase was made, and parts of the house were refitted.

Maddington church, with tithes and ½ hide, may have been held by Amesbury abbey and was confirmed to Amesbury priory in 1179.[26] The priory held the *RECTORY* estate until the Dissolution, and the land was presumably absorbed by Maddington manor. The tithes were granted with the manor to Sir Walter Hungerford and Thomas Hungerford in 1564[27] and descended with it to James Maton who in 1841 received all tithes from c. 2,700 a. in the parish, tithes of hay from 581 a. of Winterbourne Maddington manor, tithes from a further 10 a. of wheat and a further 10 a. of barley, and some further small tithes. Those tithes were then valued at £528 and commuted.[28]

Tithes from Addestone manor were held by Hyde abbey in 1223 and probably in 1341. Amesbury priory held the tithes by lease in 1223[29] and, after the Dissolution, they were apparently part of the rectory estate: tithes from Addestone were due to James Maton in 1841.[30]

In 1291 Salisbury cathedral and Bradenstoke priory each received a pension of 13s. 4d. out of the rectory:[31] nothing further is known of Bradenstoke's. In 1341 the dean and chapter of Salisbury were entitled to tithes from Maddington,[32] and in the 16th and 17th centuries they received those from Winterbourne Maddington manor not due to the owner of the rectory estate.[33] In 1841 those tithes were valued at £107 and commuted.[34]

Tithes from Bourton belonged in 1730 to John Howe, later Lord Chedworth (d. 1742), and

passed with his lands there to Harry Biggs (d. 1856):[35] they were valued at £80 at commutation in 1841. Other tithes from Bourton belonged to the vicar of Winterbourne Stoke. They were valued at £21 5s. in 1841 and commuted.[36]

Among endowments of Dartford priory (Kent) in 1372 were the services of tenants in Maddington.[37] The priory had 2 yardlands or less in Maddington at the Dissolution.[38]

In 1689 Sir Stephen Fox endowed a hospital at Farley in Alderbury with a rent charge of £188 from Maddington manor. The payment, from 1909 made by the owners of Manor farm,[39] ceased in 1959.[40]

ECONOMIC HISTORY. Maddington, Homanton, Bourton, and Addestone each had its own system of fields and pastures. In the early 19th century Maddington had c. 2,500 a., Homanton 550 a., Bourton c. 500 a., and Addestone 385 a.; Winterbourne Maddington manor included land in both Maddington and Homanton.[41]

MADDINGTON. In 1086 the two Maddington estates had a total of 4½ demesne hides, with 2 teams and 1 *servus*, and, also with 2 teams, of 6 *villani*, 8 bordars, and 2 cottars. They had 8 a. of meadow, 10 a. of pasture, and pasture 4 furlongs square.[42]

In the later 16th century Maddington's land was apparently about half arable, and there were apparently three sets of open fields. Of one set 440 a. of c. 505 a. were demesne of Maddington manor; the c. 65 a. were in copyholds of the manor. Another set, which later evidence suggests was of c. 200 a., may have been primarily demesne of Winterbourne Maddington manor, and the customary tenants of both manors may have shared a third set, of c. 500 a. Each demesne farm had downland largely for the use of its own sheep; other downland was used in common, and the sheep of the tenants of both manors may have fed together. Each manor, however, had a separate Cow down: in winter that of Maddington manor, 50 a., was for sheep of the lessee of the demesne, in summer for the cattle of all tenants; that of Winterbourne Maddington manor was called the Heath. There were a few acres of common meadow, and the demesne of Maddington manor included 5 a. of meadow and 22 a. of several pasture.[43]

The demesne lands of Maddington and Winterbourne Maddington manors had been

16 V.C.H. Wilts. viii. 211.
17 Q. Sess. 1736 (W.R.S. xi), p. 2.
18 Hoare, Mod. Wilts. Branch and Dole, 38.
19 W.R.O., A 1/345/270; ibid. 502/2.
20 Ibid. tithe award.
21 W.N. & Q. iii. 374; W.A.S. Libr., sale cat. iii, no. 25.
22 Wilts. Cuttings, v. 107.
23 Kelly's Dir. Wilts. (1907, 1931); W.R.O., G 1/500/10.
24 W.A.S. Libr., sale cat. xxx, no. 4; xxxv, no. 7; xliv, no. 52.
25 Inf. from Major Hayward.
26 Cal. Chart. R. 1257–1300, 157–9.
27 Cal. Pat. 1563–6, p. 154.
28 W.R.O., tithe award.
29 Dugdale, Mon. ii. 337; Inq. Non. (Rec. Com.), 178.
30 W.R.O., tithe award.
31 Tax. Eccl. (Rec. Com.), 181.
32 Inq. Non. (Rec. Com.), 178.
33 W.A.M. xli. 124–5; W.R.O., Ch. Com., chapter, 133/1.
34 W.R.O., tithe award.
35 Ibid. 906/W/192.
36 Ibid. tithe award.
37 Cal. Close, 1389–92, 241.
38 P.R.O., SC 6/Hen. VIII/1757, rot. 28.
39 Endowed Char. Wilts. (S. Div.), 5, 10–11, 14; W.R.O., L 2, Pitton and Farley.
40 Inf. from Defence Land Agent.
41 W.R.O., tithe award.
42 V.C.H. Wilts. ii, pp. 132, 159.
43 W.R.O. 442/1, ff. 10v.–15v.; for the later evidence, ibid. 148, terrier, 1815, ff. 113–14.

inclosed by the early 19th century, a total of *c.* 1,675 a.[44] Both Cow downs had possibly been inclosed by the late 17th century, when the demesne of Maddington manor included 100 a. of several pasture on the downs;[45] the demesne of Winterbourne Maddington manor later included 58 a. of former Cow down. The other land of the two manors remained open. In the early 19th century 509 a. of open arable were north and north-west of the village, and Tenantry down, 211 a., was presumably for sheep. Of the arable *c.* 275 a. were part of Maddington manor, *c.* 235 a. part of Winterbourne Maddington manor.[46] Parts of both Tenantry down and the demesne pastures may have been ploughed in 1726 when the lord of Winterbourne Maddington manor and others agreed to burnbake 203 a. of down. From the late 17th century the lord of Maddington manor had pasture rights on 12 a. in Fisherton de la Mere adjoining Maddington's western boundary.[47] The detached 12 a. of the parish were watered meadows, some of which apparently remained in common use in the early 19th century.[48]

From the early 16th century, as presumably earlier, the demesne of Maddington manor was held with the lands of the rectory estate, said in 1341 to be 2 yardlands and 4 a. of meadow. The demesne was apparently stocked with 371 sheep when first leased,[49] and the farmer had a flock of 500 *c.* 1560.[50] Including *c.* 200 a. of downland the demesne was *c.* 670 a. in 1582.[51] By 1797, when much of the farm's downland had been ploughed, a flock of sheep, 30–40 young cattle, 30–40 pigs, and two or three Alderney cows, all of poor quality, were kept. Suggested improvements to the farm then included building a barn and stable on the downs and doubling the acreage of turnips to feed more and better stock.[52] Down barn was built soon afterwards,[53] and in 1809 the demesne, Manor farm, was 1,094 a.[54]

The demesne of Winterbourne Maddington manor in 1295 comprised 100 a. of arable and pasture for 100 sheep;[55] the flock remained 100 in the early 16th century.[56] In 1815 the demesne, later Maddington farm, was 581 a., including 346 a. of arable of which 150 a. were on the downs, 8 a. of meadow, and 224 a. of pasture. There was apparently also a hopyard.[57]

In 1582 nine tenants of Maddington manor shared 16 yardlands, which included *c.* 397 a. of arable, and could pasture 650 sheep, 17 horses, and 40 cattle. The largest holding had 56 a., the smallest 30 a., of arable.[58] By 1715 five holdings had been accumulated by one tenant, who was also lessee of the demesne. There were 11 copyholders and 5 leaseholders *c.* 1730, 8 and 6 *c.* 1755,[59] and 4 and 7 in 1783.[60] In 1809 three copyholds totalled 40 a. and there were leaseholds of 120 a., 77 a., and 74 a.[61] There were customary tenants of Winterbourne Maddington manor in the late 13th century,[62] and in 1624 two tenants held 4 yardlands each in Maddington and a third held 52 a., some in Maddington and some in Shrewton.[63] In 1815 a total of *c.* 264 a. was held by 11 tenants: the largest holding was of 83 a. and three were of 30–50 a.[64]

By 1841 the number of farms in Maddington had been reduced to five. Manor, 998 a., worked from buildings south of the church, and Maddington, 608 a. worked from the buildings of which the Priory was one, were the largest farms. Both also had buildings on the downs. A farm of 200 a. was worked from the Grange, one of 184 a. from Maddington House, and one of 93 a. from other buildings near the church. Also by 1841 the land in the open fields had apparently been redistributed into much larger parcels for the three smaller farms, which presumably had feeding in common on those fields after harvest and on Tenantry down. There were *c.* 1,400 a. of arable and *c.* 1,000 a. of pasture.[65] All common husbandry was eliminated by an award of 1853 under an Act of 1845. Some divisions of the open fields made before 1841 were confirmed, others were altered, and Tenantry down was inclosed: *c.* 1,000 a. were thus allotted.[66]

From the 1860s until *c.* 1900 Manor farm measured *c.* 1,300 a. and was worked from buildings near Maddington Manor, in Tanner's Lane, and on the downs.[67] Some arable was converted to pasture in the late 1870s, but *c.* 1880 there were still 942 a. of arable and only 315 a. of downland pasture, 19 a. of meadow, and 22 a. of wood and plantation. A rotation of wheat, barley, clover, and turnips was practised on the better land, and a five-crop rotation on the poorer. A flock of 900–1,000 breeding ewes was kept. The farmer employed 5 shepherds, 14 'horsemen', and a varying number of labourers.[68] In or before 1909 the farm was reduced to *c.* 1,150 a., and 128 a. of it were taken for smallholdings. Then and in the 1920s an arable holding of 207 a., Ingram's land, was worked either separately or with Maddington farm.[69] Both Manor and Maddington, later Grange, were sheep and corn farms in the early 20th

44 Ibid. 148, terrier, 1815, ff. 113–14; W.A.S. Libr., sale cat. xi, no. 11.
45 Dors. R.O., D 124, box 19, case papers, Woodruffe v. Saywell, 1696–7.
46 W.R.O. 148, terrier, 1815, ff. 114–15.
47 Ibid. tithe award; Dors. R.O., D 124, box 19, case papers, Woodruffe v. Saywell, 1696–7; Bristol Univ. Libr., Wansbrough MS. 9, lease, Ernle to Holloway, 1726.
48 W.R.O., EA/104; ibid. tithe award.
49 *Valor Eccl.* (Rec. Com.), ii. 194; *Inq. Non.* (Rec. Com.), 178.   50 P.R.O., C 3/79/25.
51 W.R.O., 442/1, ff. 14, 15v.
52 Dors. R.O., D 124, box 177, letter, Stone to Ilchester, 1797.   53 Above, intro. (Maddington).
54 W.A.S. Libr., sale cat. xi, no. 11.
55 *Cal. Inq. p.m.* iii, p. 159.

56 P.R.O., C 1/1072, no. 42.
57 W.R.O. 148, terrier, 1815, ff. 112–14.
58 Ibid. 442/1, ff. 10v.–13v.
59 Dors. R.O., D 124, box 19, surveys, 1715, 1727–34, 1752–60.   60 Ibid. D 124, box 338, rental, 1783.
61 W.A.S. Libr., sale cat. xi, no. 11.
62 *Cal. Inq. p.m.* iii, p. 159.
63 *Wilts. Inq. p.m.* 1625–49 (Index Libr.), 38–9.
64 W.R.O. 148, terrier, 1815, ff. 115–38.
65 Ibid. tithe award.   66 Ibid. EA/173.
67 O.S. Map 6", Wilts. LIII (1889 edn.); W.A.S. Libr., sale cat. ii, no. 18; xxviii (F), no. 45.
68 *Minutes of Evidence to Agric. Com.* [C. 3096], pp. 696–704, H.C. (1881), xvii.
69 W.A.S. Libr., sale cat. ix, no. 15; Wilts. Cuttings, xvii. 19; W.R.O., Inland Revenue, val. reg. 140; ibid. G 1/500/10.

century.[70] In the late 20th century their farm-steads in Maddington village were disused and the lands were worked from the more easterly downland farmsteads. On Grange farm sheep had been replaced by pigs and dairy cattle by the 1940s. Pig rearing and dairying ceased in the 1970s. In 1990 the farm, 2,000 a. including land outside the former parish, was worked from Maddington Farm: there were over 350 a. of arable and 1,600 a. of rough grazing on which 200 suckler cows and their offspring were kept.[71] Manor farm, including the land of Bourton, was a stock farm of 1,300 a. in the 1950s. It was worked as two farms 1967–88, afterwards as Barleycroft farm. In 1990 it had 500 a. of rough grazing on which 80–100 beef cattle and 1,200 sheep were kept, 350 a. of leys, and 450 a. of arable, chiefly used for winter wheat.[72] Middle-croft farm was then a small dairy farm with, north-west of the village, buildings which re-placed those of Tanner's Lane farm in the village.[73]

A windmill standing at Maddington in the 1580s and 1662 may have been built between 1576 and 1578.[74] It was presumably that stand-ing west of the village south of the old Amesbury–Warminster road in 1675.[75] The mill was still wind-powered in 1841[76] but was steam-powered in the late 19th century.[77] It went out of use between 1899 and 1923,[78] and had been demolished by 1958.[79]

HOMANTON. In 1472 Homanton manor was said to include 200 a. of arable, 300 a. of pasture, and 8 a. of meadow.[80] Attempts at inclosure by the farmer of the demesne in the mid 16th century were unsuccessful, although some copy-hold land was then untenanted and uncultivated.[81] In the early 19th century Homanton remained little affected by inclosure: there were open fields called Upper, Middle, Home, and Stoke, totalling c. 300 a., in the parish's south-east corner, and a common down of 238 a. further west.[82] In 1815 five tenants of Winterbourne Maddington manor held 93 a. in the open fields with pasture rights.[83] In 1841 the fields and downs were shared by only two farms: most of the five holdings of Winterbourne Mad-dington were in one, and the two holdings of Homanton manor, with 160 a. and 69 a., were worked together.[84] The fields and downs were inclosed in 1855 under an Act of 1845.[85] The proportion of arable to pasture, two thirds to a third, changed little between the 1860s and the 1890s. In 1894 Homanton (Cherry Lodge) farm, c. 400 a., was well stocked with sheep.[86] From the earlier 20th century the farm was worked with lands in Winterbourne Stoke. Cattle were introduced in the early 20th century and from the 1940s rare breeds of both cattle and sheep were kept. Arable farming ceased c. 1985. In 1991 English Nature managed 283 a. in the former parish of Maddington, of which 70 a. were part of a national nature reserve and stocked with sheep and cattle, including some rare breeds.[87]

BOURTON. In the later 16th century Bourton had four open fields, Home, Down, North, and South, and common pasture on downs south of Maddington's. A yardland included 25–30 a. of arable and, at 60 sheep, 4 beasts, and 2 horses, was generously stinted. Each yardland may have had land in only three of the fields.[88] In the 17th century there was a common meadow of 8 a.[89] Open fields were called North, Middle, and House in the later 17th century and early 18th.[90] In 1674, for each of c. 10 yardlands, there were pasture rights for 60 sheep and 10 lambs, 4 beast leazes on Cow down in Winterbourne Stoke, and 2 horse leazes in Bourton mead.[91] From 1730 or earlier the land was worked as a single farm.[92] In 1809 and 1841 it measured c. 500 a., of which a little over half was arable and the remainder downland pasture. Pasture rights in Winter-bourne Stoke, part of the farm in 1809,[93] were replaced by an allotment of 21 a. in 1812.[94] From the 1920s the land was worked with that of Manor farm, Maddington.[95]

There may have been a mill at Bourton in 1674.[96]

ADDESTONE. There were 2 ploughteams at Addestone in 1086, 1 on the demesne of 1 hide with 3 servi, and 1 held by 1 villanus and 4 bordars; there were 4 a. of meadow and 60 a. of pasture.[97] No later record has been found of cultivation in common, and in the 16th century the lands formed one farm, said in 1551 to comprise 300 a. of arable, 200 a. of downland pasture, and a pasture close of 10 a.[98] In 1576 there was a flock of 300 sheep.[99] In 1841 and 1894 the farm, c. 390 a., included 310 a. of arable, 40–50 a. of pasture, and 5–10 a. of wood.[1] Between 1910 and 1921 c. 70 a. were added to the farm,[2] and in the later 20th century it was

70 W.A.S. Libr., sale cat. ix, no. 15; xii, no. 23.
71 Inf. from Mrs. E. H. Woods, the Grange.
72 Inf. from Mr. John Young, Barleycroft Farmhouse.
73 W.A.S. Libr., sale cat. ix, no. 15; local inf.
74 Sess. Mins. (W.R.S. iv), 88; M. Watts, Wilts. Wind-mills, 22; W.R.O. 442/1, ff. 13v.–14.
75 Ogilby, Brit. pl. 32.   76 W.R.O., tithe award.
77 Wilts. Cuttings, xxi. 146.
78 O.S. Maps 6", Wilts. LIII. NE. (1901, 1926 edns.).
79 Wilts. Cuttings, xxi. 146.
80 Cal. Pat. 1467–77, 311.
81 D. & C. Sar. Mun., press D, I, box 31/26, ct. bk. 1538–1606.   82 W.R.O., tithe award.
83 Ibid. 148, terrier, 1815, ff. 115–38.
84 Ibid. tithe award.   85 Ibid. EA/176.
86 Ch. Com., copy deeds, vol. xcvii, no. 8785; W.A.S. Libr., sale cat. xxi, no. 22; for the farmstead, above, intro. (Homanton).

87 Inf. from Chief Site Manager, Eng. Nature, S. Region, Foxhold Ho., Crookham Common, Newbury, Berks.; cf. below, Winterbourne Stoke, econ. hist.
88 W.A.M. xxxiv. 214–15; W.R.O. 442/1, f. 10 and v.
89 W.R.O. 906/W/179.
90 Ibid. 906/W/192; W.A.M. xxxiv. 215.
91 W.A.M. xxxiv. 214–15; W.R.O. 906/W/188.
92 W.R.O. 906/W/188; 906/W/192.
93 Ibid. 374/128/49; ibid. tithe award.
94 Ibid. EA/104.
95 Ibid. G 1/500/10; inf. from Major R. D. Hayward, Bourton Farm.   96 W.A.M. xxxiv. 215.
97 V.C.H. Wilts. ii, p. 127.
98 Cal. Pat. 1553, 369; P.R.O., SC 6/Hen. VIII/3341, rot. 47.   99 P.R.O., C 3/173/48.
1 W.R.O., tithe award; Wilts. Cuttings, v. 107; vii. 30.
2 W.R.O., Inland Revenue, val. reg. 140; ibid. G 1/500/10.

an arable and stock farm of *c.* 500 a. In 1987 there were 420 a. of arable, a flock of 240 ewes, and 20 cows.[3]

LOCAL GOVERNMENT. A tithing called Maddington is recorded in the 13th, 15th, and 16th centuries;[4] how much of the parish it included is not clear. A tithingman, said to be from Maiden Winterbourne, who attended Wallingford honor courts in the 15th and 16th centuries, may have represented a tithing which included Homanton,[5] and in the 15th century Addestone was considered a tithing.[6]

From 1179 Amesbury priory held its lands, including Maddington manor, with extensive liberties.[7] In 1255 the prioress had view of frankpledge and return of writs in Maddington,[8] rights which were confirmed in 1286. The court at Maddington evidently claimed jurisdiction over Bourton in the early 14th century.[9] In the earlier 16th century a tourn and a manor court were both held twice a year.[10] A court for Maddington manor was held in most years between 1716 and 1783. Although in 1716 it was said to be held twice a year by custom, it usually met only once, in May or June until 1750, thereafter in October or November; none is recorded between 1743 and 1749 or between 1770 and 1782. It was called a court leet in 1716 and 1718, at other times a court baron: the business transacted did not vary. The homage presented rights of common pasture and other customs of the manor, death of copyholders, and repairs needed to field boundaries and the pound. Offences for which fines were imposed included felling the lord's trees in 1743, making a path across a field in 1749, and encroaching on the waste in 1751. In 1716 the bay mare of a thief caught within the manor was claimed by the lord, and in 1758 a fine was set for pasturing diseased horses on the common. A tithingman was appointed by the court in 1716 and later, and a hayward from 1719. From 1760 those appointments and the admission of copyholders were the chief business of the court.[11]

Men from Bourton attended the court of Winterbourne Stoke manor in the early 16th century.[12] Between 1542 and 1606 a court baron for Homanton manor was held, usually every three or four years. Although the homage presented minor inclosures, repairs needed to roads and buildings, and subletting of customary hold-

ings, most business concerned surrenders and admittances, especially at the later courts.[13] Occasional meetings of the court are recorded between 1661 and 1751, and from 1751 until 1841 the court met every two or three years: the only business was tenurial.[14]

In 1671 Maddington parish spent *c.* £6 on the poor, relieving *c.* 3 parishioners each month. Annual expenditure had increased to £10 by 1700, and in 1707 it was agreed that all secular costs laid upon the parish, including payments for bridges and vagrants, should be borne from the poor rate; £35 spent by the overseers of the poor in 1712 presumably included such costs. Of £61 spent in 1761 over half was regular relief to 13 parishioners. Other payments were for nursing, midwifery, clothing, and rents. The number receiving regular relief rose from 16 in 1771[15] to 49 adults and 65 children in 1803, when occasional relief was given to a further 22, a total of £424 was spent, and the parish rate was above the average for Branch and Dole hundred.[16] In 1814–15 regular relief was given to 27 adults and occasional to 12; £350 was spent.[17] Spending reached a peak of £701 in 1818, was much lower in the 1820s and 1830s,[18] and was on average £242 a year between 1833 and 1835. Maddington became part of Amesbury poor-law union in 1835,[19] and with the remainder of Shrewton parish part of Salisbury district in 1974.[20]

CHURCH. Maddington church may have been held by Amesbury abbey and was confirmed to Amesbury priory in 1179.[21] Until the Dissolution it was presumably served by chaplains provided by the priory; thereafter curates were appointed by lords of Maddington manor, owners of the rectory estate.[22] A proposal of 1650 that Maddington should be the parish church of a combined parish of Maddington, Shrewton, and Rollestone[23] was not then implemented. From 1868 the incumbent of Maddington was called vicar.[24] In 1869 the benefice was united with Shrewton vicarage,[25] and in 1923 Rollestone rectory was added.[26] The three ecclesiastical parishes were united in 1970,[27] and the benefice was called Shrewton from 1972.[28] Maddington church was declared redundant in 1975[29] and vested in the Redundant Churches Fund in 1979.[30]

In 1865 the executors of L. P. Maton conveyed

3   W.A.S. Libr., sale cat. xxx, no. 4; xliv, no. 52.
4   *Crown Pleas, 1249* (W.R.S. xvi), pp. 241–2; *W.A.M.* xiii. 115; *Sess. Mins.* (W.R.S. iv), 139.
5   P.R.O., SC 2/212/2; SC 2/212/9; SC 2/212/14; SC 2/212/18; SC 2/212/20; SC 2/212/24; above, manors (Homanton).   6   *W.A.M.* xiii. 115.
7   *Cal. Chart. R. 1257–1300,* 157–9.
8   *Rot. Hund.* (Rec. Com.), ii (1), 237.
9   *V.C.H. Wilts.* iii. 247, 250; cf. above, manors (Bourton).
10   P.R.O., SC 6/Hen. VIII/3986, rot. 82d.
11   Dors. R.O., D 124, box 19, Maddington ct. papers, 1716–43, 1749–70, 1783.
12   P.R.O., SC 2/208/67.
13   D. & C. Sar. Mun., press D, I, box 31/26, ct. bk. 1538–1606.
14   Ibid. press D, I, box 7, M–N/23, ct. papers, 1661–1751; W.R.O., Ch. Com., chapter, 135/1.

15   W.R.O. 1336/69–70.
16   *Poor Law Abstract, 1804,* 558–9.
17   Ibid. *1818,* 492–3.
18   *Poor Rate Returns, 1816–21,* 186; *1822–4,* 225; *1825–9,* 216; *1830–4,* 209.
19   *Poor Law Com. 2nd Rep.* App. D, 558.
20   O.S. Map 1/100,000, admin. areas, Wilts. (1974 edn.).
21   Above, manors (Rectory).
22   Ibid.; e.g. *Vis. Queries, 1783* (W.R.S. xxvii), pp. 147–8; *Clerical Guide* (1822); W.R.O., D 1/48/4, p. 14.
23   *W.A.M.* xl. 394.
24   Incumbents Act, 31 & 32 Vic. c. 117.
25   Ch. Com. file, F 3124.
26   *Lond. Gaz.* 2 Feb. 1923, pp. 782–3.
27   Ibid. 4 June 1970, p. 6218.
28   Ibid. 10 Feb. 1972, p. 1695.
29   Ibid. 30 Dec. 1975, p. 16384.
30   *Church Guide* (1985).

to the Ecclesiastical Commissioners the right to appoint vicars of Maddington:[31] they evidently transferred it to the bishop of Salisbury, patron of the united benefice between 1869 and 1923. The bishop held two of three turns of the presentation from 1923[32] until 1958 when the Crown became the sole patron by an exchange.[33]

In 1650 the curate received £60, of which £40 derived from an endowment given by Sir Edward Hungerford (d. 1648), the owner of the rectory estate.[34] In 1688 Sir Stephen Fox gave £40 yearly to the curate from Maddington manor and the rectory estate;[35] in 1783 it was the curate's sole income from Maddington and was from small tithes.[36] By the late 19th century the payment had ceased.[37] A grant of £200 was made from Queen Anne's Bounty in 1827,[38] raising the curate's income to c. £50 in 1830.[39] A house of chequered flint and limestone built for the curate in 1704 was enlarged in the early 19th century; a larger extension, in banded red brick and flint, was completed in 1877.[40] It was the vicarage house for the united benefice from 1869[41] until 1974, when it was sold and a new house was built in Shrewton.[42]

In 1553 the church had the income from a flock of 28 sheep, presumably for its maintenance, but money was owed to it by two men who may have bought ornaments made superfluous by the 1552 prayer book.[43] In 1584 the churchwardens reported that no sermon had been preached for nine months,[44] and in 1585 the curate served both Maddington and Rollestone churches.[45] William Arnold, who served Maddington in 1650, conformed to the *Directory of Public Worship* and preached twice on Sundays, but was nevertheless said to be unfit for the ministry.[46] In 1662 the churchwardens promised to replace a missing copy of Jewell's *Apology* and presented that they had no poor box: they had warned parishioners who claimed poverty as an excuse for absence to attend the church.[47]

From the late 17th century incumbents of neighbouring benefices were often curates of Maddington. Thomas Harward, curate 1681–1722, was rector of Rollestone and vicar of Winterbourne Stoke.[48] Charles Digby, curate in 1783 and 1787, did not serve the church, and in 1783 the curate of Orcheston St. Mary and of Shrewton held a service at Maddington each Sunday alternately in the morning and the afternoon. He celebrated communion at Christmas, Easter, and Whitsun with c. 30 communicants, but did not have time to catechize.[49] Frederick Bennett, curate from 1851, also served

Shrewton and became incumbent of the united benefice in 1869.[50] On Census Sunday in 1851 the congregation at morning service was c. 185, at evening service c. 260.[51] In 1864 the morning congregation usually numbered c. 140 and the evening congregation c. 190. Additional services were held on holy days, in Advent and Lent, and daily in Holy Week. Communion was celebrated at Christmas, Easter, and Whitsun, and monthly: there were c. 30 communicants.[52]

Land in Winterbourne Stoke was said in 1904 to have belonged to the churchwardens of Maddington for many years. The income from it, 10s. yearly, was used for church expenses in 1904 and the 1920s.[53] Payments from the land had ceased by 1990.[54]

ST. MARY'S church, so called in 1763,[55] is built of flint and ashlar, partly chequered, and has a chancel, a nave with north porch and south chapel and aisle, and a west tower. The nave is narrow and may be contemporary with fragments of 12th-century stonework which survive in the church. The chancel and tower are 13th-century. The aisle, also narrow and with a partly reconstructed west lancet window, may be of early 13th-century origin, but its two-part arcade is later: the two eastern bays may be late 13th-century, the three western early 14th. The nave roof was renewed in 1603.[56] The upper part and south side of the tower and the south wall of the aisle were rebuilt, the north wall of the nave was apparently moved c. 0.5 m. further north, and the porch was added, all possibly c. 1603. Medieval windows were reset in the nave and aisle. A decorated plaster panel of 1637 on the inside west wall of the nave may date the insertion of a west gallery, and the transeptal south chapel is also of the mid 17th century. The chancel's east window was blocked and the interior was elaborately decorated with plasterwork c. 1700. A new east window and chancel arch were made, the plasterwork was removed, and the gallery was taken down during a restoration by T. H. Wyatt and D. Brandon between 1843 and 1853. Further restoration was undertaken 1896–1900[57] and pinnacles on the tower, added or replaced in 1755,[58] were removed c. 1970.[59]

In 1553 a chalice weighing 8 oz. was left in the parish and 2½ oz. of plate were confiscated. A chalice with paten cover, a paten, and a flagon, all given c. 1700, and a chalice and paten, given in the late 19th century,[60] belonged to the combined parish in 1990.[61]

Of three bells in the church in 1553 one was

31 Ch. Com. file 30980/1–2.
32 Fletcher and Robins, *Guide to Shrewton*, 10; *Lond. Gaz.* 2 Feb. 1923, pp. 782–3.
33 *Lond. Gaz.* 31 Jan. 1958, p. 687.
34 *W.A.M.* xl. 393–4.
35 *Endowed Char. Wilts.* (S. Div.), 302.
36 *Vis. Queries, 1783* (W.R.S. xxvii), p. 148.
37 *Endowed Char. Wilts.* (S. Div.), 303.
38 C. Hodgson, *Queen Anne's Bounty* (1864), p. cccxxxvi.
39 *Rep. Com. Eccl. Revenues*, 840–1.
40 Dates on bldg.   41 Ch. Com. file 30980/1–2.
42 Inf. from Mrs. E. Broadbent, Maddington Manor.
43 W.R.O., D 1/43/1, f. 119v.
44 Ibid. D 1/43/5, f. 29.
45 Ibid. D 1/43/6, f. 16A.
46 *W.A.M.* xxxiv. 175; xl. 393–4.
47 W.R.O., D 1/54/1/4, no. 126.
48 *W.N. & Q.* ii. 482.
49 *Vis. Queries, 1783* (W.R.S. xxvii), pp. 147–8; Dors. R.O., D 124, box 177, receipt, 1787.
50 *W.A.M.* xxxiii. 174.
51 P.R.O., HO 129/262/1/5/6–7.
52 W.R.O., D 1/56/7.
53 *Endowed Char. Wilts.* (S. Div.), 301; W.R.O., L 2, Maddington.   54 Inf. from Mrs. Broadbent.
55 J. Ecton, *Thesaurus* (1763), 348.
56 Date on bldg.
57 *Churches of SE. Wilts.* (R.C.H.M.), 158–60.
58 Dors. R.O., D 124, box 177, Maddington accts. 1755.
59 W.R.O. 1336/65.
60 Nightingale, *Wilts. Plate*, 73–4.
61 Inf. from Mrs. Broadbent.

replaced in 1587 and one in 1699: the new bells were cast by John Wallis and William Cor respectively.[62] Those two bells and the medieval bell hung in the church in 1990.[63]

There are registers of baptisms, marriages, and burials from 1652.[64]

NONCONFORMITY. There was one dissenter in Maddington in 1676,[65] none in 1783.[66] A house was certified in 1815 for Independent meetings,[67] and before 1858 there was a chapel.[68] In 1864 a fifth of the inhabitants were Baptists or Wesleyan Methodists and apparently attended chapels in Shrewton.[69]

EDUCATION. A school in Maddington attended by 30 children in 1818[70] had closed by 1833.[71] A schoolroom standing north of the vicarage house in 1841[72] was used as a National school in 1847, when it was attended by children from Shrewton.[73] It was for girls and infants in 1856, when boys attended a school in Shrewton.[74] The Maddington school, attended by 50–60 children from Maddington, Shrewton, and Rollestone, received a very favourable report in 1858.[75] It and the Shrewton school were replaced in 1868 by a new building in Shrewton.[76] Additional buildings were erected between Tanner's Lane and High Street, in the former Maddington parish, c. 1968.[77] A dissenters'

school with 30 pupils was recorded in Maddington in 1858[78] but not thereafter.

CHARITIES FOR THE POOR. Those living on Maddington manor were eligible for admission to Farley hospital, endowed by Sir Stephen Fox in 1689 with an income from the manor. No inmate of the hospital from Maddington was known in the late 19th century,[79] but those living on the lands of the manor remained eligible in the 20th.[80]

A rent charge of £3 11s. 6d. from Winterbourne Maddington manor, given by either Edward Tooker (d. c. 1671) or Sir Giles Tooker, Bt. (d. 1675), and another of £4 from Shrewton, which apparently replaced the income from £100 given by William Woodroffe by will proved 1753, were distributed to the poor of Maddington under the name Candlemas money in the early 19th century. The £4 was replaced by rent from 1 a. in Shrewton in 1899.[81] In the 1970s the total income, £28, was distributed annually to about six recipients.[82]

Rents from the cottages built after the flood of 1841, including those in Maddington, were used to buy clothing and fuel for the poor from the mid 19th century. A seventh of the total was due to Maddington, and with that income 27 sheets were bought for poor householders in 1904.[83] The cottages were later used as almshouses.[84]

SOUTH NEWTON

SOUTH NEWTON parish, 3,502 a. (1,417 ha.) in 1879, consisted of a main part immediately north of Wilton and a detached part, North Ugford, immediately west of Wilton.[85] The main part is essentially the land of a 10th-century estate bounded on the west by the river Wylye and on the east by a way along the ridge dividing the valleys of the Wylye and the Christchurch Avon; to the south-east the estate extended east of the watershed to the Avon.[86] Four settlements grew up by the Wylye, South Newton, Little Wishford, Stoford, and Chilhampton: each stands on gravel,[87] bears a Saxon name,[88] and had a strip of land extending from the river to the downland of the watershed.[89] In the south-east extension

there may have been, or it may have been intended to plant, a settlement beside the Avon with land extending west to the ridge way and comparable to those of Wilsford, Woodford, and Durnford parishes,[90] but there is no direct evidence of one; later the land nearest the river was in Fugglestone parish.[91] To the south Burden's Ball, a fifth settlement standing on gravel beside the Wylye and evidently having a strip of land extending east to the ridge way,[92] had been added to South Newton parish by the 16th century:[93] c. 40 a. of its meadows, however, had been added to Wilton parish by the earlier 19th.[94] North Ugford, a small village on the north bank of the river Nadder with a triangle

[62] Walters, *Wilts. Bells*, 128, 296.
[63] Inf. from Mrs. Broadbent.
[64] W.R.O. 1336/38–48; bishop's transcripts for some earlier years are ibid.
[65] *Compton Census*, ed. Whiteman, 128.
[66] *Vis. Queries, 1783* (W.R.S. xxvii), p. 148.
[67] *Meeting Ho. Certs.* (W.R.S. xl), p. 76.
[68] *Acct. of Wilts. Schs.* 32.
[69] W.R.O., D 1/56/7; below, Shrewton, nonconf.
[70] *Educ. of Poor Digest*, 1032.
[71] *Educ. Enq. Abstract*, 1042.
[72] W.R.O., tithe award.
[73] *Nat. Soc. Inquiry, 1846–7*, Wilts. 8–9.
[74] P.R.O., ED 7/131, no. 245.
[75] *Acct. of Wilts. Schs.* 32; *V.C.H. Wilts.* xi. 212.
[76] Ch. Com. file 38678.
[77] Below, Shrewton, educ.
[78] *Acct. of Wilts. Schs.* 32.
[79] *Endowed Char. Wilts.* (S. Div.), 302–3; above, manors.
[80] Char. Com. file.
[81] *Endowed Char. Wilts.* (S. Div.), 298–301.
[82] Char. Com. file.
[83] *Endowed Char. Wilts.* (S. Div.), 302.
[84] Below, Shrewton, charities.
[85] This article was written in 1993. Maps used include O.S. Maps 6", Wilts. LIX–LX, LXV–LXVI (1887–90 and later edns.); 1/25,000, SU 03/13 (1988 edn.); 1/50,000, sheet 184 (1979 edn.); 1", sheets 14–15 (1811–17 edns.).
[86] *Arch. Jnl.* lxxvi. 271–4.
[87] Geol. Surv. Map 1/50,000, drift, sheet 298 (1976 edn.).
[88] *P.N. Wilts.* (E.P.N.S.), 228, 231.
[89] Below, agric.
[90] Cf. *V.C.H. Wilts.* vi. 213, 222, 225; above, Durnford, intro.   [91] W.R.O., Fugglestone tithe award.
[92] Ibid. tithe award; *First Pembroke Survey*, ed. Straton, i. 242–3; Geol. Surv. Map 1/50,000, drift, sheet 298 (1976 edn.).
[93] *Valor Eccl.* (Rec. Com.), ii. 100; below, church.
[94] *First Pembroke Survey*, i. 243; W.R.O., Wilton tithe award.

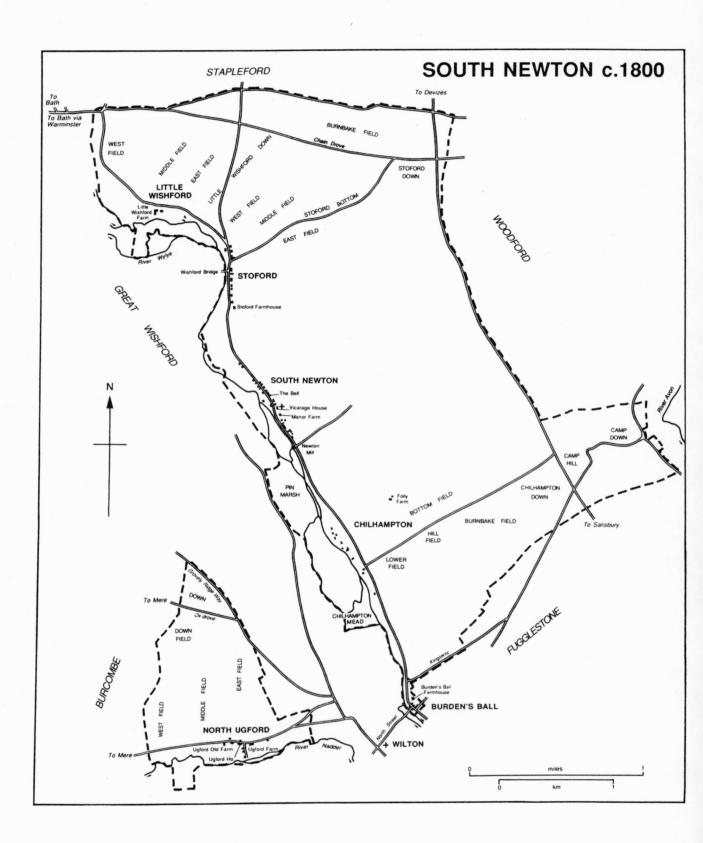

SOUTH NEWTON c.1800

of land extending northwards to downland, was presumably added to South Newton parish in the late 12th century, when tithes from it were part of the endowment of South Newton prebend.[95]

At the south-east corner of North Ugford c. 7 a. were deemed to be part of South Newton parish in 1844, part of Wilton parish in 1879. The remainder of North Ugford, 372 a., was transferred to Burcombe parish in 1884;[96] in 1934 the east part was transferred to Wilton.[97] When Wilton was incorporated in 1885 the borough included 7 a. of Burden's Ball, on which stood buildings which were part of the town. The 7 a. were designated South Newton Within parish in 1894, and transferred to Wilton parish in the same year. The remainder of South Newton parish became South Newton Without in 1894 but was evidently not so called for long.[98] In 1934 a further 195 a. of South Newton parish were transferred to Wilton,[99] and in 1986 the c. 183 a. east of the ridge way in the south-eastern corner were transferred to Woodford.[1] As a result of all those changes South Newton parish was reduced to 1,111 ha. (2,745 a.).[2]

Much of the long western boundary of the parish follows the main course of the Wylye, but in places deviates from it or follows a minor course. To the north and east the roads which mark the boundary are ancient,[3] and another road marks the boundary on the south-west. In the Avon valley the boundary follows a coomb on the north and a ridge on the south. The Nadder is North Ugford's boundary on the south, and a probably ancient road[4] and a prehistoric ditch mark parts of it on the east and west respectively; elsewhere the boundary is marked by no natural or man-made feature.

Chalk outcrops over the whole parish. All three rivers, the Wylye, Avon, and Nadder, have deposited alluvium and gravel, although only a little of the Avon's alluvium is in the parish; dry valleys lined with gravel, of which Stoford bottom is the longest and deepest, lead from downland to all three. To the south-east on the watershed of the Wylye and the Avon there are deposits of clay-with-flints and plateau gravel. The downs reach 157 m. in the north-east; North Ugford's highest point is its northern tip at 144 m. The Wylye leaves the parish at c. 55 m., the Nadder at c. 60 m.; near the Avon the land is at c. 60 m.[5] In the Wylye and Nadder valleys land use has been typical of Wiltshire's chalk downland, with meadows beside the river, most extensive at Little Wishford and Chilhampton, open fields on the lower slopes of the chalkland, and pasture on the downs. In the

Avon valley the land descends steeply to the river: there was some meadow land but evidently no open field. From the 18th century or earlier much of the downland in all parts of the parish was brought under the plough.[6] At the highest point, east of Stoford, a police wireless station was erected in the mid 20th century.[7]

In 1086 the estate on which the parish was based included 200 a. of woodland, the right to take from Melchet forest in the south-east corner of the county 80 cartloads of wood and the wood needed to repair houses and fences, and the right to feed 80 pigs in the forest.[8] There is no later evidence that men of the parish had rights in Melchet forest. The main part of the parish was within Grovely forest in 1184–5, but not in 1219 or later. North Ugford was within the forest in the Middle Ages,[9] and in 1567 men of the village were eligible to serve on the jury at swanimotes.[10] There was very little woodland in the parish in 1773.[11] Between c. 1805 and 1844 scattered plantations totalling c. 8 a. were made on the downs;[12] there were c. 30 a. of woodland in the parish c. 1863[13] and in the later 20th century.

A Roman road from Winchester and Old Salisbury to the Mendips is thought to have passed through the parish, crossing the Wylye c. 300 m. south of the church, but no trace of it has been found.[14] The ancient road along the eastern boundary became the main Devizes–Salisbury road. A downland road from Bath converged on it across the north part of the parish. The Devizes road, on which a turnpike road from Bath via Market Lavington converged further north, was turnpiked in 1761, and in the same year the Wilton–Warminster road linking settlements on the left bank of the Wylye, including those in South Newton parish, was turnpiked as part of a Salisbury–Bath road. Both roads were disturnpiked in 1870 and remained important in 1993. The Salisbury–Bath road was designated a trunk road in 1946 as part of the main Southampton–Bristol road:[15] between 1958 and 1972 improvements to it caused the main course of the Wylye to be moved westwards south of the church.[16] The old Bath road across the parish decreased in importance; in 1993 it was a track called Chain Drove. East–west roads across the main part of the parish included one through Stoford bottom, one to Chilhampton, and one, later called Kingsway, to Burden's Ball.[17] Kingsway, which linked the villages of the Avon valley to Wilton, and the road through Stoford bottom were metalled public roads in the late 20th century. The ancient road on the northern boundary[18] remained a track in 1993.

95 *Sar. Chart. and Doc.* (Rolls Ser.), p. 52; for the prebend, below, church.
96 O.S. Map 6", Wilts. LXVI (1887 edn.); W.R.O., tithe award.   97 *V.C.H. Wilts.* iv. 342.
98 Ibid. 354, 360; *Census*, 1891; 1901; O.S. Maps 6", Wilts. LXVI. NW., SW. (1901 edn.).   99 *Census*, 1931.
1 Statutory Instruments, 1986, no. 72, Salisbury (Pars.) Order.   2 *Census*, 1991.
3 *Arch. Jnl.* lxxvi. 271–4.   4 Ibid. 290–1.
5 Geol. Surv. Map 1/50,000, drift, sheet 298 (1976 edn.).
6 Below, agric. (s.v. Chilhampton for the Avon valley land).
7 O.S. Maps 6", Wilts. LX. SW. (1926 edn.); 1/25,000,

SU 03 (1958 edn.); SU 03/13 (1988 edn.).
8 *V.C.H. Wilts.* ii, pp. 129–30.   9 Ibid. iv. 432, 457.
10 *First Pembroke Survey*, i. 194.
11 *Andrews and Dury, Map* (W.R.S. viii), pl. 5.
12 W.R.O. 861/15; 861/17; ibid. tithe award.
13 Ibid. 2057/S 179, p. 21.
14 I. D. Margary, *Rom. Roads in Brit.* (1973), pp. 101–2.
15 *Arch. Jnl.* lxxv. 93–4; *L.J.* xxx. 77; *V.C.H. Wilts.* iv. 270; above, Steeple Langford, intro. [roads].
16 O.S. Maps 1/25,000, SU 03 (1958 edn.); 1/50,000, sheet 184 (1979 edn.); local inf.
17 *Andrews and Dury, Map* (W.R.S. viii), pl. 5.
18 *Arch. Jnl.* lxxv. 94.

North Ugford's three roads are all ancient. That along the north bank of the Nadder was called Portway between Wilton and North Ugford in the 11th century;[19] diverging from Portway the Grovely ridge way is the road on the east boundary;[20] and diverging from that Ox drove crossed the north corner. The south part of the ridge way and Ox drove were part of a main Wilton–Mere road, along which milestones were erected in 1750,[21] but declined in importance from 1761, when the riverside road was turnpiked as a Wilton–Mere road. The Mere road was disturnpiked in 1870.[22] As part of the London–Penzance road the North Ugford part of it was designated a trunk road in 1936; it was distrunked in 1958,[23] but in 1993 remained the main road between Salisbury and Shaftesbury (Dors.).

Two railways diverging at Wilton crossed the parish, each carried by a bridge over the Warminster road at Burden's Ball. The Salisbury–Warminster section of the G.W.R. along the Wylye valley was opened in 1856 with Wilton station north-west of Kingsway at Burden's Ball. The line crosses only the south-west corner of the main part of the parish. The Salisbury & Yeovil Railway opened a line along the Nadder valley through North Ugford in 1859; it was extended to Exeter in 1860. Wilton G.W.R. station was closed in 1955 but both lines remained open in 1993.[24]

The parish is not rich in known prehistoric remains. In the south-east on the watershed of the Avon and Wylye there was a small Romano-British settlement, and there was an associated field system of over 100 a. on Camp Down in the Avon valley. Another prehistoric field system lay west of it on the downs of Chilhampton, and part of one of 450 a. lay in the north-east corner of the parish. North-east of South Newton village three barrows stand beside the Devizes road. Little, if any, trace remains of a prehistoric ditch said to have run south-west from Camp Down or of another along the parish's northern boundary.[25]

The parish, including North Ugford but possibly not Burden's Ball, had 176 poll-tax payers in 1377: South Newton had 69, Little Wishford 18, Stoford 38, Chilhampton 14, and North Ugford 37. The population of the whole parish was 541 in 1801, 516 in 1811 when South Newton had 223 inhabitants, Little Wishford 8, Stoford 64, Chilhampton 64, Burden's Ball 112, and North Ugford 45. The increase from 565 in 1831 to 692 in 1841 was caused by the opening of Wilton union workhouse at Burden's Ball. A peak of 768 was reached in 1871 but the population had fallen to 675 by 1881 and was further reduced by the transfer of North Ugford and Burden's Ball. The parish had 454 inhabitants in 1901, 478 in 1911; in 1931 and 1951 it had 436 despite a further reduction in its size between those dates.[26] The population had increased to 763 by 1961, presumably because of new housing in South Newton village; in 1991 it was 696.[27]

SOUTH NEWTON. With c. 40 per cent of the poll-tax payers in 1377 and of the population in 1811 South Newton has long been the largest settlement in the parish.[28] In the Middle Ages its land belonged to Wilton abbey, and by 1243 the village had attracted its prefix,[29] evidently to distinguish it from North Newnton, where the abbey also owned the land.[30]

The village stands on a wide band of gravel beside the Wilton–Warminster road. The church, vicarage house, and demesne farmstead formed a group on the east side of the road. The demesne farmhouse, Manor Farm, was rebuilt in 1799[31] as a square house with a five-bayed west entrance front of chequered flint and stone. The vicarage house immediately west of church was demolished in the mid 19th century.[32]

North of the church there were farmsteads and other buildings on both sides of the road in the late 18th century and earlier 19th, more on the east than the west.[33] Those to survive include, on the east side, Newton Cottage, of brick and flint rubble, thatched, and dated 1679, and, on the west side, a brick and flint house of the 18th century. The Bell inn, on the east side, occupies an 18th-century house and was open in 1759[34] and 1993. The Plough was an inn in the early 18th century[35] but where it stood is obscure. In 1752 a fire destroyed seven houses and three barns in the village.[36]

About 400 m. south of the church South Newton mill has long stood on the Wylye,[37] and between it and Manor Farm its main leat was along the west side of the road: the leat was stopped in the mid 20th century.[38] By 1773 a line of buildings stood along the east side of the road north of the mill,[39] evidently including some of the 11 cottages which stood on the waste there c. 1844.[40] A school was built there in the 1830s.[41] A few of the cottages survived in 1993 but not the school.

Several large new houses were built in the 19th century, all east of the road. Newton House, a white-brick house of c. 1840 incorporating a reset doorcase of earlier date, and a new vicarage house were built north of the church;[42] each was

[19] *Arch. Jnl.* lxxvi. 290.
[20] H. W. Timperley and E. Brill, *Anct. Trackways of Wessex*, 134.
[21] *V.C.H. Wilts.* viii. 26; *Wilts. Ind. Arch.* (S. Wilts. Ind. Arch. Soc.), v. 30–1.
[22] *V.C.H. Wilts.* iv. 270; *L.J.* xxx. 77.
[23] *V.C.H. Wilts.* v. 291; W.R.O., F 4/200/21.
[24] *V.C.H. Wilts.* iv. 284, 286, 293.
[25] Ibid. i (1), 106, 191, 258, 278; O.S. Map 1/10,000, SU 13 SW. (1982 edn.).
[26] *V.C.H. Wilts.* iv. 306–7, 354; for the workhouse, below, this section (Burden's Ball).
[27] *Census*, 1961; 1991; below, this section (S. Newton).

[28] Above, this section.
[29] *P.N. Wilts.* (E.P.N.S.), 228; below, manors (S. Newton).   [30] *V.C.H. Wilts.* x. 128.
[31] Date on bldg.   [32] Below, church.
[33] *Andrews and Dury, Map* (W.R.S. viii), pl. 5; W.R.O., tithe award.   [34] *W.A.M.* xxxi. 256.
[35] W.R.O. 2057/M 31; 2057/M 50.
[36] Wilts. Cuttings, i. 16.   [37] Below, mills.
[38] Above, this section [roads].
[39] *Andrews and Dury, Map* (W.R.S. viii), pl. 5.
[40] W.R.O., tithe award.
[41] Below, educ.
[42] For the vicarage ho., below, church.

used as a nursing home in 1993, the vicarage house having been much extended in the 1980s and renamed Glenside Manor. South of the church Spex Hall, also of white brick, was built c. 1860, and east of the mill a large farmstead was built between 1844 and 1860.[43] Some cottages were also built or rebuilt, chiefly in red brick, in the mid or later 19th century. Pembroke Cottages, a terrace of four flint and brick estate cottages north of the church, bear the date 1859.

In the 20th century most new building was north of the church. At the north end of the village 4 council houses, West View, were built on the east side of the road in 1927,[44] c. 12 private houses from c. 1920, and a large garage and other industrial buildings in the mid 20th century. On the west side of the road c. 10 private houses were built in the 1980s. There has been building on land behind the houses east of the road since the 1930s: the local authority built 6 houses and 2 bungalows in Jubilee Terrace 1935–7,[45] 2 bungalows were built as a peace memorial in 1946,[46] a total of 73 council houses and bungalows were built in several streets 1947–56, and 6 council bungalows were built in 1966.[47]

Outside the village barns on the site of Folly Farm were standing in 1773,[48] and the farmstead incorporated a house in 1844.[49] The number of buildings there was reduced after c. 1940.[50] A pair of cottages beside the Wilton–Warminster road south of the village was built between 1844 and 1860[51] and rebuilt in 1927.[52] Keeper's Lodge, a red-brick house 500 m. east of the church, and Field Barn 1.5 km. north-east, were probably built soon after 1860.[53]

LITTLE WISHFORD was a small settlement in the 14th century[54] and had a church in the 15th.[55] In the later 18th century and the early 19th it consisted of no more than two groups of farm buildings, both of which stood south of the Warminster road; only the western group included a farmhouse in 1844.[56] The house, Little Wishford Farmhouse, was rebuilt apparently in the early 19th century, using the long narrow plan of an earlier house and re-using 18th-century bricks in a gable wall; in the later 19th century bay windows were added on the south front. Between 1844 and 1860 the eastern group of buildings was demolished and a pair of estate cottages in banded brick and flint built north of the road.[57] A large farm building called Crough's Barn was built 400 m. north of Little Wishford Farmhouse between 1957 and 1969.[58]

STOFORD village comprised a line of farm-steads, on small freeholds or copyholds of South Newton manor, on the east side of the Warminster road.[59] The ford between it and Great Wishford on the west bank of the Wylye had been replaced by a bridge evidently by the early 18th century;[60] the bridge was largely rebuilt in 1841,[61] and was called Wishford bridge in the earlier 19th century,[62] Stoford bridge in the 1870s and later.[63] In 1844 there were about five farmsteads in the line; only a cottage, which survives, stood west of the road.[64] Two farmhouses of 18th-century origin survive. Stoford House opposite the bridge was altered or rebuilt in 1822;[65] Stoford Farmhouse at the south end of the line was also much altered in the 19th century. Several 18th-century cottages were also standing in 1993.

An inn in the village was called the Swan in 1740,[66] the White Swan in 1789.[67] The Swan was open in 1844 and 1993, north of the junction of the Warminster road and the road through Stoford bottom:[68] it was rebuilt in the 19th century, was again called the White Swan c. 1863,[69] and was called the Black Swan in 1919.[70]

Between 1844 and 1879 three pairs of cottages, later called Verandah Cottages, and in 1912 a nonconformist chapel were built between Stoford House and Stoford Farmhouse.[71] Off the main road and north-east of the Swan c. 40 houses and bungalows were built in the mid 20th century, mainly in Mount Pleasant. Two halls for the joint use of South Newton and Great Wishford parishes were built at the south end of Stoford in 1949–50 and 1980.[72] There was some infilling in the 1980s, including the building of two bungalows and a house in Riverside, north of the Swan.

There was no building on the downs east of Stoford in 1817:[73] by 1844 a barn, later part of a farmstead called Stoford Hill Buildings, had been built near the parish's north-east corner.[74] Additional buildings and a bungalow were erected in the 20th century.

CHILHAMPTON. In the Middle Ages and until the mid 19th century Chilhampton seems to have been a small settlement, like Stoford consisting of a line of farmsteads on small freeholds or copyholds of South Newton manor and mainly on the east side of the Warminster road.[75] The road is likely to have been remade on a new course east of the village when it was turnpiked in 1761, and the street along which the farm-

43 W.R.O., tithe award; ibid. 2057/P 1/42.
44 Ibid. G 11/132/39.   45 Ibid. G 11/602/1.
46 Below, charities.   47 W.R.O., G 11/602/1–2.
48 *Andrews and Dury, Map* (W.R.S. viii), pl. 5.
49 W.R.O., tithe award.
50 Cf. O.S. Map 1/2,500, Wilts. LXVI. 1 (1940 edn.).
51 W.R.O., tithe award; ibid. 2057/P 1/42.
52 Date on bldg.
53 O.S. Map 6", Wilts. LX (1887 edn.); W.R.O. 2057/P 2/22.
54 *Tax List, 1332* (W.R.S. xlv), 82; *V.C.H. Wilts.* iv. 367.
55 Below, church.
56 *Andrews and Dury, Map* (W.R.S. viii), pl. 5; W.R.O., tithe award.   57 W.R.O., tithe award; ibid. 2057/P 1/42.
58 O.S. Maps 1/25,000, SU 03 (1958 edn.); 1/50,000, sheet 184 (1974 edn.).
59 Cf. *First Pembroke Survey*, i. 18–19, 24–6; W.R.O.,

tithe award.
60 Dept. of Environment, list of bldgs. of hist. interest (1986).   61 Date on bridge.
62 W.R.O., tithe award.
63 O.S. Maps 6", Wilts. LX (1887 and later edns.).
64 W.R.O., tithe award.
65 Date on bldg.   66 W.R.O. 2057/M 50.
67 Ibid. 2057, deeds, S. Newton, Pembroke to Swayne, 1789.   68 Ibid. tithe award.
69 Ibid. 2057/S 179, p. 153.   70 Ibid. 776/357.
71 Ibid. tithe award; O.S. Map 6", Wilts. LX (1887 edn.); below, nonconf.
72 Inf. from Mr. H. Smith, Bramscote, S. Newton.
73 O.S. Map 1", sheet 14 (1817 edn.).
74 W.R.O., tithe award.
75 Ibid. 2057/P 1/10; *Tax List, 1332* (W.R.S. xlv), 83; *V.C.H. Wilts.* iv. 306, 354; *First Pembroke Survey*, i. 19, 26–7.

steads stood in 1773 was presumably the old course.[76] In 1800 there were about four farmsteads, one of which was on the west side of the street, and several other houses or cottages.[77] Most of the buildings were standing in 1844,[78] none in 1993. Most were probably demolished in 1856 when new red-brick farm buildings were erected to adjoin the west side of the main road;[79] Chilhampton Farmhouse, a red-brick house on higher ground east of the road, was built then or soon afterwards.

East of Chilhampton near the Avon a substantial house called the Bays was built c. 1900.

BURDEN'S BALL. There was probably little more than a single farmstead at Burden's Ball in the 16th century.[80] A chapel which stood there early in that century, and possibly from the 13th or earlier,[81] had probably been demolished by 1650 when only Burden's Ball Farm and two other houses stood there.[82] The farmstead stands, as did most of the others in the main part of the parish, on the east side of the Warminster road. Burden's Ball Farmhouse is a small mid 18th-century house of brick and rubble with a north-eastern kitchen wing; a new south-west front of brick was added in the mid or later 19th century, and a second north-eastern service wing was built c. 1900.

In 1773 there were several other buildings beside the main road,[83] and in the 19th century Wilton expanded along North Street into Burden's Ball. North-west of its junction with North Street the Warminster road was called Queen Street, south-east of it King Street. Primrose Hill led north-east from King Street. Several of the c. 10 houses in those streets in 1844 survive:[84] the oldest, at the junction of King Street and Primrose Hill, bears the date 1725. Burden's Ball House, at the junction of North Street and Queen Street, is a two-storeyed house of three bays built c. 1830; in 1844 it was the Shepherd inn, possibly having replaced the Tap open in 1822, and was open as the Shepherd, the Shepherd's Tap, or the Shepherd's Crook until the 1850s.[85] At the junction of North Street and King Street a house also of the earlier 19th century was open as the Wheatsheaf in 1844–5[86] and 1993. Several cottages were rebuilt in the 19th century.

In 1837 the Wilton union workhouse was built north-west of Kingsway, and a chapel in 14th-century style was built for it in 1864.[87] North-east of the workhouse a railway station was opened in 1856 and closed in 1955;[88] a

gasworks had been built by 1859 and was closed in 1934.[89] In the 1990s the former workhouse and the sites of the station and the gasworks were used for industry. Some 19th-century buildings remained in use and there were some 20th-century buildings.

NORTH UGFORD. Ugford was a village on the south side of the riverside road from Wilton to Mere. It had a church in the Middle Ages and its land belonged to Wilton abbey:[90] it was called Ugford St. John in the 12th and 13th centuries,[91] Ugford Abbess in the 16th,[92] and Ugford St. Giles in the 17th,[93] but much more often North Ugford. The epithets distinguished it from a village called Ugford, otherwise South Ugford, on the south side of the Nadder.[94] South Ugford had apparently lost its identity by the late 18th century, since when North Ugford has usually been called simply Ugford.[95]

In 1773 North Ugford had buildings beside the road and in a short lane leading to the river; most were on the south side of the road.[96] There were c. 10 houses in 1798, 1844,[97] and 1993. At the east end of the village Ugford Farm is a timber-framed house of the 16th century with a 17th-century cross wing of chequered flint and stone. At the west end Ugford Old Farm is also timber-framed and has a four-bayed **A**-framed roof of the late 16th century or early 17th. In the middle Ugford House is apparently 18th-century, is of chequered flint and stone, and was altered and extended southwards in the early 19th century; in the mid or later 19th century large red-brick buildings were erected west of it. North of the road a brick cottage was built in the early 20th century[98] and two council houses, Nadder Vale Cottages, replaced other buildings in 1944.[99]

Between 1844 and 1879 a barn was built beside Ox drove. It was replaced by Ugford Red Buildings, built at the junction of Ox drove and the Grovely ridge way between 1879 and 1900;[1] the buildings are of red brick and incorporate a pair of cottages. East of the village a cemetery for Wilton was opened in 1901 on land regarded as part of South Newton parish in 1844;[2] later in the 20th century houses were built as part of Wilton town on land which was in the parish until 1884.

MANORS AND OTHER ESTATES. In 943 King Edmund granted to his thegn Wulfgar 10 *mansae*, evidently all the main part of South

76 *Andrews and Dury, Map* (W.R.S. viii), pl. 5.
77 W.R.O. 2057/P 1/10.
78 Ibid. tithe award.
79 Ibid. 2057/P 2/30.
80 *First Pembroke Survey*, i. 242.
81 Below, church.
82 *W.A.M.* xl. 394.
83 *Andrews and Dury, Map* (W.R.S. viii), pl. 5.
84 W.R.O., tithe award.
85 Ibid.; ibid. A 1/326/3; *Kelly's Dir. Wilts.* (1848, 1855, 1859).
86 W.R.O., tithe award; ibid. 2057, deeds, S. Newton, Pembroke to Taylor, 1845.
87 *V.C.H. Wilts.* vi. 24; below, church.
88 Above, this section [railways].
89 *V.C.H. Wilts.* vi. 23; *Kelly's Dir. Wilts.* (1859); O.S.

Map 6", Wilts. LXVI (1887 edn.).
90 Below, manors (N. Ugford); church.
91 *Sar. Chart. and Doc.* (Rolls Ser.), p. 52; P.R.O., JUST 1/1001, rot. 29.
92 *L. & P. Hen. VIII*, xix (1), p. 38.
93 W.R.O., D 1/24/255/1.
94 For the site of S. Ugford, O.S. Map 1/25,000, SU 03/13 (1988 edn.).
95 *Andrews and Dury, Map* (W.R.S. viii), pl. 5.
96 Ibid.
97 W.R.O. 2057/P 1/19; ibid. tithe award.
98 O.S. Maps 6", Wilts. LXVI. SW. (1901, 1926 edns.).
99 W.R.O., G 11/600/1.
1 Ibid. tithe award; O.S. Maps 6", Wilts. LXVI (1887 and later edns.).
2 *Kelly's Dir. Wilts.* (1901); W.R.O., tithe award.

LUDGERSHALL
The pond near the Crown inn in the earlier 20th century

STAPLEFORD
Cottages near the church

LUDGERSHALL

The seal of the borough bailiff

GREAT WISHFORD

The fire engine bought in 1728

Newton parish except Burden's Ball. The estate, except Little Wishford, was later held by Wulfthryth and became *SOUTH NEWTON* manor. It was granted by King Edgar to Wilton abbey in 968.[3] The manor, which comprised South Newton, Stoford, and Chilhampton, belonged to the abbey until the Dissolution. It was granted by the Crown in 1544 to Sir William Herbert[4] (cr. earl of Pembroke 1551) and descended with the Pembroke title.[5] In 1993 Henry, earl of Pembroke and of Montgomery, owned most of the land in South Newton, Stoford, and Chilhampton.[6]

Henry de Bohun, earl of Hereford (d. 1220), held 2 carucates in South Newton in 1212. The estate passed to his son Humphrey, earl of Hereford and of Essex, who resisted a claim to it by his kinswoman Ela Longespée, countess of Salisbury.[7] Humphrey held it in 1242–3, when it was part of the honor of Trowbridge.[8] By the 16th century it had presumably been added to South Newton manor.[9]

In 1335 Richard of Chiseldon was licensed to grant 1 yardland in South Newton to the hospital of St. John the Baptist, Wilton.[10] The grant may not have been made, as in 1361 Richard or a namesake was licensed to grant what may have been the same estate to Wilton abbey.[11]

Two estates in Stoford were held freely of South Newton manor. Henry Quintin (d. 1284) held 61¼ a., presumably with pasture rights.[12] Like land in Great Wishford the estate descended to William Quintin (d. by 1290), William Quintin (d. by 1341), and William Quintin (d. 1351). It was inherited by the last William's daughters Edith and Isabel.[13] With the land in Great Wishford it was held by another pair of sisters, Edith, wife of John Stone, and Agnes, wife of John Dykeman. Edith and Agnes died in 1433. Edith's heir was her grandnephew Hugh Moleyns, Agnes's her granddaughter Maud, wife of John Cooper.[14] In 1466 the Coopers conveyed the Stoford estate to Maurice Berkeley[15] (d. 1474). It probably passed with East Hayes House farm in Sedgehill in turn to Maurice's son William (d. *s.p.* 1485) and daughter Catherine (d. 1494), wife of John Stourton, Lord Stourton (d. 1485), and later of Sir John Brereton, and to Catherine's daughter Werburgh Brereton (d. 1525), wife of Sir William Compton (d. 1528). It passed to Werburgh's son

Peter Compton (d. 1544), whose relict Anne, wife of William, earl of Pembroke, held it until her death in 1588,[16] and in turn to Peter's son Henry, Lord Compton (d. 1589), and Henry's son William, Lord Compton, who sold it to William Gray *c.* 1598.[17] Gray sold it in 1602 to Barnaby Lewis,[18] who in 1609 sold it to Sir Richard Grobham.[19] By will Grobham (d. 1629) gave it to endow an almshouse at Great Wishford:[20] in 1948 the trustees sold the estate, 69 a.[21]

The second freehold in Stoford, 1¼ yardland, which was held with 1 yardland in South Newton, belonged in 1462 to William Stourton, Lord Stourton (d. 1478).[22] In 1468 William gave it to his son John (Lord Stourton from 1478, d. 1485) and John's wife Catherine (d. 1494), later wife of Sir John Brereton.[23] It passed in turn to John Stourton's brothers William, Lord Stourton (d. 1524), and Edward, Lord Stourton (d. 1535), and with the Stourton title to Edward's son William (d. 1548), that William's son Charles (d. 1557), Charles's sons John (d. 1588) and Edward (d. 1633), Edward's son William (d. 1672), William's grandson William Stourton (d. 1685), and that William's son Edward,[24] who sold it to Henry Blake between 1693 and 1704. In 1704 Henry conveyed it to John Blake, who sold it in 1720 to John Powell[25] (d. 1737). It passed in turn to Powell's son (Sir) Alexander (d. 1784), Alexander's son Francis (d. 1786), and Francis's son Alexander.[26] Between 1815 and 1820 Alexander sold the estate, 112 a., to George, earl of Pembroke and of Montgomery, who added it to South Newton manor.[27]

An estate in Chilhampton, sometimes reputed a manor,[28] was held of the lord of South Newton manor by knight service. Walter of Calstone's heirs held it in 1242–3.[29] Roger of Calstone (d. by 1292) held at Chilhampton 1 hide which passed to his son Roger.[30] The estate was granted by Sir Thomas Kingston to Margery and Walter Barrow and, after Margery's death, was held by Walter in 1358.[31] From Walter's relict Isabel (d. 1369), wife of Sir Hugh Tyrell, it passed to his son John,[32] whose relict Christine held it at her death in 1396. It passed to John's son John (born *c.* 1378),[33] who in 1431 settled it on Drew Barrow and Drew's wife Anne in tail with reversion to himself.[34] In 1455 John Barrow (d. 1456), presumably he born *c.* 1378, settled it on his son Walter and Walter's wife Anne.[35] On Walter's

3 Finberg, *Early Wessex Chart.* pp. 87, 96; *Arch. Jnl.* lxxvi. 271–6.
4 *L. & P. Hen. VIII*, xix (1), p. 38.
5 *Complete Peerage*, x. 405–30.
6 Inf. from the agent, Wilton Estate Off., Wilton.
7 *Abbrev. Plac.* (Rec. Com.), 86; *Cur. Reg. R.* xii, pp. 528–9; *Pat. R. 1225–32*, 300; *Complete Peerage*, vi. 475–9.
8 *Bk. of Fees*, ii. 742.
9 *First Pembroke Survey*, ed. Straton, i. 18–20.
10 *Cal. Pat. 1334–8*, 61.
11 Ibid. *1361–4*, 22.
12 *Cal. Inq. p.m.* ii, p. 307.
13 Ibid. ix, p. 445; below, Great Wishford, manor (Quintin's).
14 *Cal. Fine R. 1445–52*, 26–7; P.R.O., C 139/57, no. 7; C 139/118, no. 16.
15 *Feet of F. 1377–1509* (W.R.S. xli), p. 145.
16 *V.C.H. Wilts.* xiii. 172; *Complete Peerage*, x. 409; *First Pembroke Survey*, i. 19.
17 *Complete Peerage*, iii. 390–1; P.R.O., REQ 2/210/94.
18 P.R.O., CP 25/2/242/44 & 45 Eliz. I Mich.

19 W.R.O. 753/1, f. 40.
20 *Endowed Char. Wilts.* (S. Div.), 921; below, Great Wishford, charities [almshouse].
21 W.R.O. 2007/48.
22 Ibid. 2057/S 1, pp. 83, 85; *Cal. Close, 1461–8*, 122; *Complete Peerage*, xii (1), 302–3.
23 *Cal. Fine R. 1485–1509*, pp. 217–18; *Complete Peerage*, xii (1), 303; *Cal. Close, 1485–1500*, pp. 229–30; *Cal. Inq. p.m. Hen. VII*, i, pp. 478–9.
24 *Complete Peerage*, xii (1), 303–12.
25 W.R.O. 212B/6120–1.
26 Burke, *Commoners* (1833–8), i. 375.
27 W.R.O., EA/94; ibid. 2057/S 133.
28 e.g. *Feet of F. 1377–1509* (W.R.S. xli), p. 134.
29 *Bk. of Fees*, ii. 723.
30 *Cal. Inq. p.m.* iii, pp. 6–7.
31 *Cal. Close, 1354–60*, 533.
32 *Cal. Inq. p.m.* xii, pp. 404–5.
33 Ibid. xvii, pp. 283–4.
34 *Feet of F. 1377–1509* (W.R.S. xli), p. 98.
35 Ibid. p. 134; P.R.O., C 139/161, no. 8.

death after 1469 the estate was held by his relict Eleanor, later wife of Charles Bulkeley. On Eleanor's death in 1476 it passed to Walter's son Maurice.[36] John Barrow (d. by 1550) held the estate in 1538 and was succeeded by his grandson Edward Barrow,[37] who in 1585 sold it to Giles Estcourt[38] (d. 1587). It passed in turn to Giles's son Sir Edward (d. 1608) and grandson Sir Giles Estcourt (cr. baronet 1627), who in 1646 sold it to (Sir) Samuel Eyre[39] (d. 1698). Sir Samuel was succeeded in turn by his son Sir Robert (d. 1735) and Sir Robert's son Robert (d. 1752), whose relict Mary held the estate until her death in 1762. It was inherited by the younger Robert's cousin Samuel Eyre (d. 1794), who was succeeded by his daughter Susannah, wife of William Purvis. In 1795 William took the surname Eyre.[40] In or soon after 1806 Susannah and William sold the estate, c. 300 a. with pasture rights, to George, earl of Pembroke and of Montgomery,[41] who added it to South Newton manor.

In 1407, under a licence of 1403, William Chitterne granted a total of 12½ a. in places including Chilhampton and South Newton to the hospital of St. Giles and St. Anthony, Wilton:[42] 2 a. in Chilhampton belonged to the hospital in 1801.[43] In 1567 Eton College (Bucks.) owned 6 a. and feeding for 30 sheep, probably in Chilhampton:[44] it owned 15 a. in Chilhampton in 1844.[45]

In 1086 Wilton abbey held *LITTLE WISHFORD*.[46] The manor belonged to the abbey until the Dissolution, was presumably granted with South Newton manor to Sir William Herbert in 1544, belonged to him c. 1553,[47] and, like South Newton, descended with the Pembroke title. Lord Pembroke owned most of the land in 1993.[48]

BURDEN'S BALL manor, in the Middle Ages sometimes called Fugglestone manor, was held by Robert Burden (d. c. 1280). After Robert's death it was held for life by William of Chardstock though claimed as dower by Robert's relict Mary.[49] The manor passed to Robert's son Nicholas (d. by 1304)[50] and descended to John Burden (d. 1395). It passed to John's daughter Cecily[51] (fl. 1419), wife of Henry Thorp (d. 1416),[52] and to Cecily's son Thomas Thorp, whose relict Agnes held it in 1423.[53] In 1424 it was held by Thomas's brother Ralph[54] (d. 1446), from whom it passed with East Bos-

combe manor in turn to John Thorp (d. 1464) and William Thorp (d. 1509). William was succeeded by his nephew William Clifford (d. by 1536), whose son Henry held Burden's Ball manor in 1536[55] and sold it in 1547 to Sir William Herbert.[56] Thereafter it descended with South Newton manor.

In 956 King Edwy granted 4 *mansae* at *NORTH UGFORD* to Wistan.[57] Wilton abbey held the manor in 1086[58] and until the Dissolution. In 1544 the manor was granted to Sir William Herbert,[59] and thereafter, like South Newton manor, it descended with the Pembroke title. Lord Pembroke owned most of the land in 1993.[60]

Small areas of land in North or South Ugford were granted in 1195 by Gervase son of Sprackling to St. James's hospital at Wilton, presumably the hospital later called St. John the Baptist's,[61] and in or after 1333 by Robert Hungerford (d. 1352) to Ivychurch priory.[62]

From the earlier Middle Ages the prebendary of South Newton[63] evidently held all the tithes from the main part of the parish, including Burden's Ball;[64] he held North Ugford's from c. 1191 or earlier.[65] The *PREBENDAL* estate was worth £20 in 1291, when the prebendary also received £5 16s. 8d. from other parishes,[66] and is later known to have included 1 yardland in South Newton.[67] Wilton abbey appropriated the prebend in 1450[68] and held it until the Dissolution. Like South Newton manor the estate was granted to Sir William Herbert in 1544[69] and descended with the Pembroke title. The land was absorbed by South Newton manor. The tithes from all but 400 a. of the parish had been merged with the land from which they arose by 1844, when the remaining tithes were valued at £115 and commuted.[70]

AGRICULTURE. SOUTH NEWTON.
In 1086 the estate of 19 hides and 3 yardlands called Newton almost certainly included Stoford and Chilhampton besides South Newton. It had land for 14 ploughteams. The demesne, assessed at 2 hides and with 6 coliberts and only 2 teams, was small and, to judge from later evidence, may have been restricted to South Newton itself. There were 20 *villani* and 16 bordars with 12 teams. There were 20 a. of meadow and 150 a. of pasture.[71]

36 P.R.O., C 140/56, no. 49.
37 Ibid. C 142/125, no. 12; ibid. SC 6/Hen. VIII/3985, rot. 21.   38 Ibid. CP 25/2/241/27 & 28 Eliz. I Mich.
39 *V.C.H. Wilts.* xi. 210; Hoare, *Mod. Wilts.* Add. 40.
40 Burke, *Commoners* (1833–8), iii. 291–2.
41 Hoare, *Mod. Wilts.* Add. 40; W.R.O. 861/15.
42 *Cal. Pat.* 1401–5, 189; *V.C.H. Wilts.* iii. 463.
43 W.R.O. 2057/S 134.
44 *First Pembroke Survey*, i. 20.
45 W.R.O., tithe award.
46 *V.C.H. Wilts.* ii, p. 130.
47 *L. & P. Hen. VIII*, xix (1), p. 38; W.R.O. 2057/S 1, p. 83.   48 Inf. from the agent, Wilton Estate Off.
49 *V.C.H. Wilts.* vi. 41; *Cal. Close*, 1279–88, 72.
50 *Cal. Close*, 1302–7, 186.
51 *Cal. Inq. p.m.* xvii, p. 184.
52 *Cal. Close*, 1419–22, 9; above, Boscombe, manors (E. Boscombe).   53 *Cal. Close*, 1422–9, 27.
54 *Feet of F.* 1377–1509 (W.R.S. xli), p. 85; P.R.O., C 139/8, no. 76.

55 P.R.O., CP 25/2/321, no. 22; above, Boscombe, manors (E. Boscombe).
56 W.R.O. 2057/D 3, reg. of deeds, 1642, f. 18.
57 Finberg, *Early Wessex Chart.* p. 93; *Arch. Jnl.* lxxvi. 236–8.   58 *V.C.H. Wilts.* ii, p. 130.
59 *L. & P. Hen. VIII*, xix (1), p. 38.
60 Inf. from the agent, Wilton Estate Off.
61 *Feet of F.* 1182–96 (Pipe R. Soc. xvii), 33; *V.C.H. Wilts.* iii. 364.
62 *Wilts. Inq. p.m.* 1327–77 (Index Libr.), 98–9, 226.
63 Cf. below, church.
64 Cf. *First Pembroke Survey*, i. 31–2.
65 *Sar. Chart. and Doc.* (Rolls Ser.), p. 52.
66 *Tax. Eccl.* (Rec. Com.), 180–1.
67 *First Pembroke Survey*, i. 23; *Inq. Non.* (Rec. Com.), 177.   68 W.R.O., D 1/2/10, ff. (2nd foliation) 65–6.
69 *L. & P. Hen. VIII*, xix (1), p. 38.
70 W.R.O., tithe award.
71 *V.C.H. Wilts.* ii, pp. 129–30; below, this section (Stoford; Chilhampton).

South Newton had c. 1,300 a., about half of which was arable in open fields. In the 16th century some of the arable was demesne of South Newton manor and most was in freeholds and copyholds of the manor; in the Middle Ages some belonged to the prebendary of South Newton. In 1567 all c. 650 a. of arable was in three fields, North, Middle, and South. On the higher ground mainly east of the arable there were then three pastures for sheep; one of 300 a. to the north and one of 200 a. to the south were used in common, and between them one of 100 a. was shared only by the farmer of the demesne and a freeholder. Pin marsh, 30 a. west of the Wylye, was demesne pasture for cattle and horses in winter; at other times customary tenants of both South Newton and Stoford had rights to feed animals there, as they did throughout the year in Long marsh, 10 a., and Little marsh, 4 a. The first cut of Duttenham mead, 22 a., was shared by the demesne, freeholds, and copyholds of South Newton, and the men of Great Wishford had the aftermath.[72] Some arable had been inclosed by 1750.[73] Although some rights to common pasture on the downs for sheep were said to survive c. 1805, the open fields and most, if not all, of the common pastures had by then been inclosed, presumably by private agreement, and much of the downland had been ploughed.[74] Any remaining common pasture had been inclosed by 1844.[75]

In 1341 the prebendary's estate included 30 a. of arable and the right to feed 200 sheep.[76] By 1561 the land and rights had been added to the demesne farm, which was leased then. The combined farm included 195 a. of arable with pasture for 620 sheep and c. 60 cattle, 15½ a. of meadows in severalty, and the first cut of 10½ a. of Duttenham mead.[77] About 1805 it was worked from Manor Farm and comprised 336 a. of arable, 24 a. of lowland pasture and dry meadows, 18 a. of watered meadows, and 49 a. of downland pasture.[78]

In 1315 the customary tenants of South Newton held 400 a. There were 7 yardlanders, 18 ½-yardlanders, and 1 ⅓-yardlander. All except a single ½-yardlander owed labour services, each yardlander more than each ½-yardlander. Each yardlander owed four boon works, two of ploughing and two of harrowing, had to work daily between 1 August and 29 September, and had to provide a man for an additional two days' work at harvest; he had to wash and shear sheep, to mow, carry, and stack hay from Duttenham mead, Long mead, and Reeve's mead, and once a year to carry grain or malt anywhere within the county and to carry dung for one day.[79] In the mid 16th century tenants had to mow and carry hay and to carry fuel and timber to Wilton, and each yardlander had to find a man for one day's work in autumn, but other services had apparently been commuted. By 1567 holdings had been merged: 10 copyholders, one of whom held 4½ yardlands, then had c. 420 a. of arable with pasture for c. 1,000 sheep.[80] Some copyholds were converted to leaseholds in the 18th century. About 1805 the seven copyholds and leaseholds included 717 a. of arable, and the largest leasehold included the barns on the site of Folly Farm; the copyholders were then said to share pasture rights for 233 sheep.[81]

Freeholds in South Newton were neither numerous nor large. In 1315 there were four totalling 4½ yardlands; two included rights to feed 24 beasts, 13 pigs, and 175 sheep in the demesne pastures. In 1567 the four freeholders had 68½ a. of arable with pasture for 160 sheep and 22 cattle and draught animals.[82] There was a freehold of 73 a. c. 1805.[83]

In 1844 over 1,000 a. were arable, only c. 100 a. of the downland were pasture, and there were 73 a. of water meadows. The land was worked in six farms, some including land in Stoford or Chilhampton. Manor farm was a compact farm of 560 a., extending north-east from the farmstead and including 462 a. of arable, 49 a. of water meadows, and 34 a. of downland pasture. South-east of it was a single farm of 319 a., including 60 a. in Chilhampton, a farmstead in South Newton village, and Folly Farm: of its South Newton land 222 a. were arable, 28 a. down, and 8 a. meadow and lowland pasture. North-west of Manor farm three other farms had farmsteads in the village. The largest, 217 a. including 10 a. in Stoford, had 151 a. of arable, 69 a. of down, and 6 a. of water meadows: the two others were of 82 a., including c. 30 a. in Stoford, and of 73 a.[84] In 1863 only two farms were based in South Newton village, Manor farm, 485 a., and Mill farm, 328 a., for which a new farmstead had been built at the south end of the village. The south-east lands and Folly Farm were part of Chilhampton farm. The land remained principally arable.[85] The pattern of farms and land use had changed little by 1920;[86] there was a dairy herd on Manor farm in the mid 20th century. In 1993 Manor farm, 545 a., and Mill farm, 351 a., were worked in partnership and were mainly arable; a small herd of beef cattle was kept.[87]

LITTLE WISHFORD. In 1086 Little Wishford, with land for 3 teams, may have had twice as much demesne as other land. There were 2 teams on the demesne, 1 villanus and 16 bordars had 1 team, and there were 8 a. of meadow and 9 a. of pasture.[88] In 1315 there were 10 customary tenants holding ½ yardland each and 3 holding ⅓ yardland each; a freehold was of 1½ yardland. Seven of the ½-yardlanders had to

72 *First Pembroke Survey*, ed. Straton, i. 18–21, 23–4, 28–9; W.R.O. 2057/S 1, pp. 83, 85–93.
73 W.R.O. 2057, deeds, S. Newton, Herbert to Sage, 1750.
74 Ibid. 861/15; 2057/P 1/7.
75 Ibid. tithe award.
76 *Inq. Non.* (Rec. Com.), 177.
77 *First Pembroke Survey*, i. 23.
78 W.R.O. 861/15; 2057/P 1/7.
79 *First Pembroke Survey*, ii. 538–41.

80 Ibid. i. 20–2, 29–30; W.R.O. 2057/S 1, pp. 87–90.
81 Ibid. 861/15; 2057/P 1/7; 2057/S 23, ff. 12–17.
82 *First Pembroke Survey*, i. 18–20; ii. 537–8.
83 W.R.O. 861/15.
84 Ibid. tithe award.
85 Ibid. 2057/S 179, pp. 1–2, 7–9; above, intro. (S. Newton); below, this section (Chilhampton).
86 W.R.O. 2057/S 294.
87 Inf. from Mrs. J. H. Swanton, Manor Farm.
88 *V.C.H. Wilts.* ii, p. 130.

carry dung, wash and shear sheep, harrow and weed, mow, stack, and carry hay, and work daily between 1 August and 29 September; each had to provide a man for an additional day's work at harvest. Three others, who held no meadow, owed slightly lighter services. A reeve, a ploughman, a shepherd, and an ox herd were appointed from among the customary tenants.[89]

Common husbandry continued on the c. 420 a. of Little Wishford until the early 19th century.[90] In the mid 16th century there were three open fields, East, Middle, and West, and, north-east of the settlement, a common down for sheep.[91] By 1567 all the customary land except a holding of 6½ a. with feeding for 25 sheep had been added to the demesne, which then comprised 180 a. of arable, 25 a. of meadow and pasture in severalty, and feeding for 420 sheep. The freehold was then of 50 a. with feeding for 130 sheep.[92] Those holdings remained distinct in the early 19th century,[93] but by c. 1820 had been merged into a single farm. About 1820 the farm comprised 79 a. of downland pasture, 14 a. of dry meadow, 19 a. of water meadow, and 279 a. of arable; of the arable 60 a. were former downland pasture, including 15 a. which had been burnbaked.[94] The remaining downland had been ploughed and the area of water meadow increased to 35 a. by c. 1863: the farm was then 537 a.[95] The lands remained principally arable and were worked from Little Wishford Farm in the late 20th century.[96]

STOFORD. All Stoford's land, c. 500 a., was in copyholds and small freeholds of South Newton manor.[97] Of 13 customary holdings in 1315 there were 4 of 1 yardland, 8 of ½ yardland, and 1 of ¼ yardland. Labour services due from the tenants were similar to those due from the tenants of South Newton but in addition each yardlander of Stoford had to find a man for 24 days every year to prepare land to be ploughed, and all Stoford yardlanders and ½-yardlanders were required to carry salt.[98]

In the mid 16th century there were three open fields, East, Middle, and West, a total of c. 360 a., and a common pasture in the north-east corner of the parish for 615 sheep said in 1567 to be of 100 a.; cattle were grazed on the common pasture of South Newton. Detached from its other land Stoford had a 12-a. common meadow between two courses of the Wylye north-west of the village. Six copyholders and a tenant at will held between them 8¼ yardlands, sharing 262 a. of arable and pasture for 405 sheep. Some labour services at haymaking and harvest were still owed. Three free tenants held 98½ a. of arable with rights for 210 sheep.[99]

Probably in the 18th century, certainly by the early 19th, a new open field of c. 90 a. was made

by burnbaking the northern part of the downland; strips in it were larger than in the older open fields.[1] Common cultivation was ended by an award of 1815 under an Act of 1809.[2] There were apparently about seven farms in Stoford c. 1805,[3] but between 1815 and c. 1820 the number was reduced to four. The remaining downland was ploughed after inclosure,[4] and in 1844 there were 439 a. of arable.[5]

About 1863 all Stoford's land was in a 530-a. farm, which included buildings in the village and on the downs.[6] In the 1920s the lands, still principally arable, lay in farms of 325 a., 114 a., and 131 a.[7] There was no farmstead in the village in the late 20th century, when the lands were worked as parts of farms based nearby; 180 a., including Stoford Hill Buildings, were part of Manor farm, Great Wishford, and provided sheep pasture.[8]

CHILHAMPTON. The 600 a. of Chilhampton included the land of South Newton parish east of the Devizes–Salisbury road and in the Avon valley, c. 183 a.[9] It was all shared by free and customary tenants of South Newton manor, the freeholders having the greater share.[10] In 1315 two customary tenants held ½ yardland each, three held ¼ yardland each, and there were two cottagers: all owed labour services similar to those required of South Newton and Stoford tenants with similar holdings.[11]

In the mid 16th century there were three open fields, North, South, and East, later called Bottom, Hill, and Lower respectively. The downland east of the fields evidently included all the land east of the Devizes road. Chilhampton mead, 33 a. west of the main course of the Wylye, was then used in common. In three copyholds there were 84½ a. of arable, 5½ a. in Chilhampton mead, 8 a. of inclosed pastures, and pasture rights for 190 sheep; in two freeholds there were 203 a. of arable, 26 a. of meadow, 16 a. in pasture closes, and pasture for 420 sheep.[12]

By 1788 some arable had evidently been laid to grass, and in that year a new open field was created by burnbaking 82 a. of downland adjoining Hill and Bottom fields: strips in it were assigned in proportion to the pasture rights given up. Another 21 a. were added to the field in 1790.[13] About 1805 there were c. 332 a. of arable, 90 a. of meadow and lowland pasture, and 170 a. of downland pasture. One farm included 239 a. of arable, 60 a. of meadow and lowland pasture, and rights to feed sheep on the downland; three others included a total of 93 a. of arable and feeding for 190 sheep.[14]

The fields and downs were inclosed before c.

89 *First Pembroke Survey*, ii. 548–50.
90 For the area cf. W.R.O., tithe award.
91 Ibid. 2057/S 1, p. 98; 2057/P 1/11.
92 *First Pembroke Survey*, i. 33–5.
93 W.R.O. 861/15; 2057/P 1/11.
94 Ibid. 2057/S 133. 95 Ibid. 2057/S 179, pp. 3–4.
96 Inf. from the agent, Wilton Estate Off., Wilton.
97 *First Pembroke Survey*, i. 18–20, 24–6; W.R.O., tithe award.
98 *First Pembroke Survey*, ii. 542–4; *V.C.H. Wilts.* iv. 14; above, this section (S. Newton).
99 *First Pembroke Survey*, i. 18–20, 24–6, 29.

1 W.R.O. 861/15; 2057/P 1/7.
2 Ibid. EA/94. 3 Ibid. 861/15.
4 Ibid. EA/94; ibid. 2057/S 133.
5 Ibid. tithe award. 6 Ibid. 2057/S 179, pp. 5–6.
7 Ibid. 2057/S 294.
8 Inf. from Mr. R. Huntley, Manor Farm, Great Wishford. 9 W.R.O. 2057/P 1/7.
10 *First Pembroke Survey*, i. 19, 26–7.
11 Ibid. ii. 541–2; above, this section (S. Newton).
12 *First Pembroke Survey*, i. 19, 26–7; W.R.O. 2057/P 1/7.
13 W.R.O. 861/21.
14 Ibid. 861/15; 2057/P 1/7.

1820, presumably soon after the lord of South Newton manor bought the main freehold c. 1806. By c. 1820 another 90 a. of downland had been ploughed and the largest farm, 373 a., was two-thirds arable. There were then c. 70 a. of meadow of which c. 55 a. were watered;[15] in 1820 a common drowner was appointed to oversee the watering.[16] From the mid 19th century most of the land was in Chilhampton farm, for which a new farmstead was erected beside the Wilton–Warminster road in 1856; presumably about then the old farm buildings were demolished.[17] In 1863 Chilhampton farm, 616 a., included Folly Farm and land around it, both previously parts of a farm based in South Newton; the land east of the Devizes road was part of Avon farm based in Stratford-sub-Castle.[18] Chilhampton farm c. 1920 comprised 474 a. of arable, 105 a. of meadow, 85 a. of which were watered, and 39 a. of downland pasture.[19] In 1993 land west of the Devizes road was worked with that of Burden's Ball and land outside the parish. Much of it was arable, on which early wheat and break crops were grown in rotation; sheep and suckler cattle were also kept. Most of the land east of the Devizes road was pasture and used from outside the parish.[20]

BURDEN'S BALL. Although Burden's Ball had only c. 215 a.,[21] it is possible that in the Middle Ages it had its own open fields, that its downland pasture was commonable, and that the manor included both demesne and a few customary tenants. In 1550 and probably earlier all the land was in Burden's Ball farm, which in 1567 comprised 126 a. of arable in fields called North, East, and West, and 60 a. of downland on which 400 sheep could be fed. The farmer was entitled to the first cut of 3 a. of meadow, 2 a. of which were in Chilhampton.[22] By 1735 the number of sheep which could be kept had been reduced to 120 in summer and 160 in winter, suggesting that some downland had been ploughed,[23] and c. 1805 the farm was entirely arable except for 10 a. of inclosed meadows and pasture.[24] It remained mainly arable throughout the 19th century and early 20th; it was worked with lands outside South Newton parish from c. 1863 or earlier,[25] in 1993 also with Chilhampton farm.[26]

NORTH UGFORD. In 1086 there were 2 teams on land enough for 3: one was on the 3-hide demesne, and 2 *villani* and 4 bordars held the other. There were 6 a. of meadow.[27]

In the mid 16th century c. 250 a. lay in open fields called East, Middle, and West. There was

a tenantry sheep down of 80 a., there were c. 10 a. of common meadows, and 18 a., including 9 a. taken from the open fields, provided common grazing for cattle.[28] The demesne, including c. 60 a. of arable, may have been leased as one farm in the early 16th century, but by c. 1553 most of its lands had been distributed among customary tenants.[29] In 1567 seven copyholders shared 193 a. of arable with pasture rights for 400 sheep; four of them also each held 10 a. of court land, formerly demesne arable, in ½-a. parcels. Another 20 a. of court land with pasture rights for 40 sheep were held by lease. Grain rents were due for all court land. A meadow of 3½ a. remained in the lord's hand and the tenants were obliged to cut and carry the hay from it.[30]

By 1632 c. 15 a. of arable had been inclosed,[31] by 1705 another 5 a.[32] By 1798 a total of c. 50 a. of the open fields had been inclosed and about half the downland converted to a fourth open field. Pasture rights for 380 sheep were said to remain on 37 a. of down, and there were 23 a. of meadow, some of which had been watered since the 1730s or earlier. The fields and downland were inclosed between 1798 and 1844, presumably by private agreement; there may have been about five farms in 1798, and by 1844 most of the land had been absorbed into two, of 182 a. and 150 a., worked from buildings respectively north and south of the Wilton–Mere road. In 1844 there were c. 270 a. of arable, 29 a. of meadow of which 24 a. were watered, 8 a. of orchards, and 38 a. of downland used to grow sainfoin.[33] All the downland was under the plough c. 1863.[34] New farm buildings were erected in the village and on the downs in the mid and later 19th century,[35] and in the early 20th Ugford farm was based at those in the village. About 1920 the farm comprised 284 a. of arable, 27 a. of dry meadows, 18 a. of watered meadows, and 5 a. of orchards.[36] In 1993 cereals were grown on most of the land and a small flock of sheep was kept.[37]

MILLS. In 1086 there were two mills on South Newton manor, two at Little Wishford, and one at North Ugford.[38] In 1305 and 1315 a mill perhaps in or near South Newton village belonged to members of the Imbert family, owners of corn mills at Wilton;[39] a different mill at South Newton was mentioned in 1335 and 1361,[40] a mill at Little Wishford in 1303 and 1315,[41] and one at North Ugford in 1338.[42] They were presumably the four mills in the parish in 1341.[43]

From the 16th century there is evidence of only

[15] Ibid. 2057/S 133; above, manors.
[16] W.R.O. 2057/M 68.
[17] Above, intro. (Chilhampton).
[18] W.R.O. 2057/S 179, pp. 1–2; above, this section (S. Newton).   [19] W.R.O. 2057/S 294.
[20] Inf. from Mr. T. Goodman, Burden's Ball Farm.
[21] W.R.O., tithe award.
[22] Ibid. 2057/S 1, p. 229; *First Pembroke Survey*, i. 262–3.   [23] W.R.O. 2057/S 30.
[24] Ibid. 861/15.
[25] Ibid. tithe award; ibid. 2057/S 179, p. 111; 2057/S 294.
[26] Inf. from Mr. Goodman; the agent, Wilton Estate Off.
[27] *V.C.H. Wilts.* ii, p. 130.
[28] *First Pembroke Survey*, i. 35–9.
[29] P.R.O., SC 6/Hen. VIII/3985, rot. 8; W.R.O. 2057/S

[30] *First Pembroke Survey*, i. 35–9.
1, pp. 69–74.
[31] *Pembroke Manors, 1631–2* (W.R.S. ix), pp. 136–7.
[32] W.R.O. 2057/S 15, ff. 7, 27–8, 30–1.
[33] Ibid. f. 31; 2057/S 104; ibid. tithe award.
[34] Ibid. 2057/S 179, pp. 70–80.
[35] Above, intro. (N. Ugford).
[36] W.R.O. 2057/S 294.
[37] Inf. from Mr. D. Hankey, Priory Farm, Burcombe.
[38] *V.C.H. Wilts.* ii, pp. 129–30.
[39] Ibid. vi. 18; *Feet of F.* 1272–1327 (W.R.S. i), p. 53; *First Pembroke Survey*, ed. Straton, ii. 537.
[40] *Cal. Pat.* 1334–8, 61; 1361–4, 22.
[41] *Feet of F.* 1272–1327 (W.R.S. i), p. 48; *First Pembroke Survey*, ii. 548.   [42] *Cal. Close*, 1337–9, 308.
[43] *Inq. Non.* (Rec. Com.), 177.

one mill, at South Newton. In 1567 the customary tenants of South Newton manor were required to use the mill,[44] and in 1679 the level of the fine for failure to do so and of the miller's charges were published at the manor court.[45] The mill was used for both grinding and fulling from c. 1680:[46] fulling may have ceased c. 1820, when the mill was rebuilt.[47] It remained in use as a corn mill until 1960. The miller's house was later demolished,[48] the mill building was converted for residence, and in 1993 an iron undershot wheel survived.

TRADE AND INDUSTRY. The fulling mill at South Newton[49] was probably used to produce medleys in the earlier 18th century.[50] A starch maker lived in the parish in 1752.[51]

In South Newton village there was a machinist, presumably an engineer, in the 1880s, a cycle or motor cycle dealer in the 1920s. A garage built in the mid 20th century and adjacent land were used in 1993 by Real Motors for coach hire and car sales. Between 1907 and 1939 or longer W. M. Chalke & Sons traded as road contractors, from 1931 until the 1950s as timber merchants. Their former sawmills and associated buildings were occupied in 1993 by businesses including the Wessex Peat Co. Ltd. and a handle manufacturer. From 1911 members of the Moulding family worked from South Newton as builders: the firm R. Moulding & Co. Ltd. was a building contractor in 1993.[52]

There was a malthouse at the north end of Stoford village c. 1805.[53] There were brewers at Stoford in 1848 and 1855, and a corn dealer and haulier worked there between 1867 and 1885.[54]

Traders at Burden's Ball included a coal dealer in 1859, presumably working from the station, a wine and spirit merchant 1859–75, and a brewer 1867–75. There was a coal depot at the station until 1895 or later. In 1863 E. H. Cooke opened a whiting works: later, hearthstone and putty were also made at the works, which was still open in 1939[55] and later moved to Quidhampton.[56] In 1993 the Wilton workhouse buildings were used in part as a furniture depository; north of them were a garage and small engineering works, and the sites of the gasworks and former railway buildings were occupied by small industrial units.

LOCAL GOVERNMENT. South Newton, Little Wishford, Stoford, Chilhampton, and North Ugford may each have been a tithing in the Middle Ages, being separately assessed for taxation in the 14th century.[57] By grants of 943 and 968 South Newton was held free of all but the three common dues,[58] and later all five places were evidently represented at the tourn of Chalke hundred, a private hundred of Wilton abbey.[59]

There are records of the court of South Newton manor, including Stoford and Chilhampton, held in 1559, 1567, and 1584. Tenants of North Ugford manor attended in 1567 but not at other times. The court was held in spring and autumn, and presentments were made by the homage of each place. Most business concerned transfers of copyholds, and presentments were made of buildings needing repair.[60] A court held for South Newton, Stoford, Chilhampton, and Little Wishford is recorded in the mid and later 17th century and for the period 1690–1844. Until 1800 a court met every year and often several times a year. After 1800 a court was held every two or three years, less frequently after 1820. From the 17th century to the 19th century a single homage presented. Transfers of copyholds formed the sole business on many occasions and predominated on most. Orders were made to repair buildings, often specifying that timber be provided by the lord; the pound was presented for repair in 1635, 1691, 1713, when it was rebuilt, and 1740. A perambulation, apparently of the whole of South Newton manor, was ordered in 1635; occasionally separate inspections of the bounds of South Newton, Stoford, and Chilhampton were ordered until the later 18th century. Between 1688 and 1820 there were occasional elections of a hayward. The drowner of Chilhampton meadows was appointed at the court in 1820.[61]

There are records of a joint court held for North Ugford and South Burcombe manors in 1559, 1584, 1632, and 1651, and from 1675 to 1796. In the late 17th century and the 18th North Ugford business did not always come before it, and from the 1740s was transacted only every three or four years. Sometimes a combined homage of South Burcombe and North Ugford presented, but usually North Ugford's business was presented by its own homage. Most business concerned the transfer of copyholds. From the late 17th century orders were frequently made for marking or repairing field boundaries, in the early 18th tenants subletting without licence were presented, and from 1715 inheritance customs and regulations for common grazing were published.[62]

Of £223 raised by the poor rate in 1776, only £118 was spent on the poor. The rate was a little below the average for the hundred in 1803, when 30 adults and 45 children received regular relief and 21 people occasional relief, but by then

44 *First Pembroke Survey*, i. 24.
45 W.R.O. 2057/M 15.   46 Ibid. 1195/20.
47 Ibid. 2057, deeds, S. Newton, Pembroke to Maslen, 1822.
48 TS. hist. of S. Newton mill, in possession of Mr. C. B. J. Miller, Old Mill Ho.   49 Above, mills.
50 *V.C.H. Wilts.* iv. 158.
51 Wilts. Cuttings, i. 16.
52 *Kelly's Dir. Wilts.* (1880 and later edns.); D. Howell, *Remember the Wylye Valley*, 84; inf. from Mr. H. Smith, Bramscote, S. Newton.
53 W.R.O. 861/15; 2057/P 1/7.

54 *Kelly's Dir. Wilts.* (1848 and later edns.).
55 Ibid. (1859 and later edns.).
56 *Kelly's Dir. Sar.* (1953).
57 *Tax List, 1332* (W.R.S. xlv), 82–3.
58 Finberg, *Early Wessex Chart.* pp. 87, 96–7.
59 *First Pembroke Survey*, ed. Straton, i. 104–5.
60 B.L. Add. Ch. 24440–1; 24718.
61 W.R.O. 2057/M 5; 2057/M 8; 2057/M 11; 2057/M 13–16; 2057/M 31; 2057/M 50; 2057/M 68.
62 Ibid. 2057/M 4; 2057/M 8; 2057/M 11–13; 2057/M 15; 2057/M 41; 2057/M 58; 2057/S 12; B.L. Add. Ch. 24440; 24718.

expenditure had almost quadrupled.[63] In 1813 regular relief was given to 76 adults and occasional relief to 10 at a total cost of £1,145; by 1815 the cost had fallen to £645 and the number receiving regular relief to 60.[64] Expenditure was £793 in 1822, was lower until 1831, when it rose to £861, and was between £640 and £750 until 1836. The parish became part of Wilton poor-law union in 1836,[65] of Salisbury district in 1974.[66]

CHURCH. From its foundation South Newton church probably belonged to Wilton abbey and may have been served by a rector. Before c. 1191 a prebend of South Newton in the conventual church had been endowed,[67] and the prebendary evidently held the entire rectory estate.[68] For South Newton church to be served a vicarage had been ordained by 1325.[69] In 1650 it was recommended that Burden's Ball should be transferred to Fugglestone and that Ugford, presumably North Ugford, should form part of Burcombe parish:[70] neither recommendation was implemented. In 1992 South Newton vicarage became part of the benefice of Lower Wylye and Till Valley.[71]

From 1325 to 1450 each vicar was presented by the incumbent prebendary.[72] From 1450, when Wilton abbey appropriated the prebend, until the Dissolution the abbey was patron.[73] The advowson was granted in 1544 to Sir William Herbert,[74] and descended with South Newton manor and the Pembroke title. From 1992 Lord Pembroke shared the patronage of the new benefice.[75]

In 1535 the vicarage was worth £12 19s. 4d., a little below the average for a living in Wilton deanery,[76] and in 1830 c. £222.[77] The vicar took tithes of wool and lambs, tithes of hay from some meadows, and other small tithes.[78] In 1844 his tithes were valued at £280 and commuted.[79] There was a vicarage house in 1598:[80] in 1609 and 1705 it was described as a small thatched house with three rooms on each of its two storeys.[81] In the later 18th century a new house with a five-bayed west front was built, probably on the site of its predecessor, west of the church.[82] Although the house was described as unfit for residence c. 1830,[83] in 1832 the vicar lived in it.[84] In 1865 it was demolished, and a

new house built north of the church.[85] That house was sold in 1981.[86]

A church at Little Wishford was mentioned in 1428[87] but at no other time. All Saints' church in a suburb of Wilton in 1281[88] may have stood at Burden's Ball, and in 1464 the lord of Burden's Ball manor claimed the right to appoint a chaplain to serve a church there.[89] Services in Burden's Ball chapel were provided by the vicar of South Newton in 1535;[90] no later reference to the chapel has been found. A church of St. John was standing at North Ugford in 1281[91] and almost certainly c. 1191.[92] A chapel there in 1535, in which the vicar of South Newton provided services, was probably dedicated to St. Giles;[93] no later record of it has been found.

In 1550 no service was held because of the incapacity of the vicar, presumably through illness; the church also lacked a covering for the communion table.[94] Leonard Dickenson, vicar 1631–63, signed the *Concurrent Testimony* in 1648 and preached regularly in 1650.[95] In 1783 one service was held each Sunday, and there were also services on Good Friday and Christmas day. Communion was celebrated at Christmas, Easter, and Whitsun, and on the Sunday after Michaelmas: no more than 10 people received the sacrament, and some parishioners attended churches in other parishes which were nearer to their homes than South Newton church. The vicar, Henry Hetley, formerly tutor to George, Lord Herbert (from 1794 earl of Pembroke and of Montgomery), lived in Salisbury and from 1782 was also vicar of Aldworth (Berks.).[96] Two services were held each Sunday in 1832;[97] in 1851 on Census Sunday 105 people attended morning service and 112 evening service, congregations smaller than usual because of an outbreak of measles.[98] In 1864 there were additional services on Good Friday, Ash Wednesday, Ascension day, and Wednesdays and Fridays in Lent. The average congregation was 80 on Sunday mornings, between 150 and 200 on Sunday evenings: there were 49 communicants. The vicar was also chaplain of Wilton union workhouse and held a Sunday and a Friday service there each week;[99] the chapel, built at the workhouse in 1864, was served by vicars of South Newton until 1940.[1]

By will proved 1844 J. H. Flooks gave £50, the

---

[63] *Poor Law Abstract, 1804*, 558–9.
[64] Ibid. *1818*, 492–3.
[65] *Poor Rate Returns, 1822–4*, 225; *1825–9*, 216; *1830–4*, 209; *Poor Law Com. 2nd Rep.* App. D, 560.
[66] O.S. Map 1/100,000, admin. areas, Wilts. (1974 edn.).
[67] *Sar. Chart. and Doc.* (Rolls Ser.), p. 52.
[68] Above, manors (Prebendal).
[69] *Reg. Martival* (Cant. & York Soc.), i. 344.
[70] *W.A.M.* xl. 392, 394.
[71] Ch. Com file, NB 34/209B/2.
[72] Phillipps, *Wilts. Inst.* i. 22, 33, 43, 58, 60, 63, 76, 84, 86, 89, 121, 128, 131.
[73] Ibid. 154, 175, 205; above, manors (Prebendal).
[74] *L. & P. Hen. VIII*, xix (1), p. 38.
[75] Phillipps, *Wilts. Inst.* ii. 2–3, 16, 26, 37–8, 64, 66, 71–2, 75, 86, 94; Ch. Com. file 53779; ibid. NB 34/209B/2.
[76] *Valor Eccl.* (Rec. Com.), ii. 100.
[77] *Rep. Com. Eccl. Revenues*, 842–3.
[78] W.R.O., D 1/24/155/1.   [79] Ibid. tithe award.
[80] P.R.O., C 2/Eliz. I/G 14/45.
[81] W.R.O., D 1/24/155/1–2.

[82] Ibid. tithe award; drawing in possession of Mr. J. H. Swanton, Manor Farm.
[83] *Rep. Com. Eccl. Revenues*, 842–3.
[84] Ch. Com. file, NB 34/209B.
[85] W.R.O. 2077/13.   [86] Ch. Com. deed 644257.
[87] *Feud. Aids*, v. 297.   [88] *V.C.H. Wilts.* vi. 32.
[89] P.R.O., C 140/14, no. 28.
[90] *Valor Eccl.* (Rec. Com.), ii. 100.
[91] P.R.O., JUST 1/1001, rot. 29.
[92] *Sar. Chart. and Doc.* (Rolls Ser.), p. 52.
[93] *Valor Eccl.* (Rec. Com.), ii. 100; cf. W.R.O., D 1/24/155/1.   [94] W.R.O., D 1/43/1, f. 61.
[95] *Subscription Bk.* (W.R.S. xxxiii), p. 51; *Calamy Revised*, ed. Matthews, 557; *W.A.M.* xl. 394; Phillipps, *Wilts. Inst.* ii. 26.
[96] *Vis. Queries, 1783* (W.R.S. xxvii), pp. 165–6; *Clerical Guide* (1829).   [97] Ch. Com. file, NB 34/209B.
[98] P.R.O., HO 129/265/1/4/9.
[99] W.R.O., D 1/56/7.
[1] *Clergy List* (1866); *Crockford* (1907 and later edns.); above, intro. (Burden's Ball).

income from which was to be spent each year on a coat; every other year a new coat was to be given to the clerk, every other year one to the sexton. In the late 19th century and until 1950 or later a coat was bought every second year for the holder of the joint office of sexton and clerk.[2]

The church of *ST. ANDREW*, so called in 1763,[3] is mainly of rubble with ashlar dressings, and has some flint and stone chequerwork. It consists of a chancel with north chapel and south vestry, a nave with north aisle and south porch, and a west tower. Nearly all the external walling was rebuilt on the old foundations in 1861–2 to designs by T. H. Wyatt,[4] the south doorway to incorporate reset masonry of the 12th century. Features of the church as it was before 1861 survive inside. The chancel and the aisle were built in the early 13th century: of that date are the chancel arch, which in 1861–2 was moved to become the tower arch, and the east bay of the arcade. The generous width of the aisle suggests that it was rebuilt in the 14th century, the date of the two other bays of the arcade. The tower, perhaps of 12th-century origin,[5] was also altered or rebuilt in the 14th century. In the early 19th the nave had a low-pitched roof, to the north continuous with that of the aisle and covered with lead.[6]

In 1553 plate weighing 3½ oz. was confiscated and a chalice of 8½ oz. was left in the parish. The chalice was replaced by one hallmarked for 1576, which, with a chalice, a paten, and a flagon all given in 1862, belonged to the parish in 1993.[7]

Of four bells in 1553, two cast in Salisbury still hung in the church in 1993. Bells cast by John Wallis in 1603 and 1610 replaced the others. A fifth bell was added in 1862, a sixth in 1887, when that of 1603 was replaced: the bells of 1862 and 1887 were all cast by John Warner & Sons. There were still six bells in 1993.[8]

Registers of baptisms, marriages, and burials are complete from 1695.[9]

NONCONFORMITY.

NONCONFORMITY. A Baptist chapel at Porton in Idmiston had members from Stoford in 1655.[10] In 1662 three Baptists of South Newton parish were presented for not bringing children for baptism; they were also among 10 parishioners, of whom eight were Baptists, who were presented for not attending church.[11] Baptist meetings were appar-

ently held in the parish in 1669,[12] perhaps at Stoford, where a house was licensed for them in 1672.[13] In 1676 there were 20 Protestant dissenters in the parish,[14] in 1678 a house was licensed for Presbyterian meetings,[15] and Quakers from South Newton were apparently part of a group centred on Fovant in the late 17th century.[16] Although a house was licensed for Independent meetings in 1777,[17] in 1783 the only dissenters were said to be a few Presbyterians who had no meeting place.[18] A dissenters' meeting house was licensed in 1798.[19]

In 1807 a licence was granted for Methodist meetings, and a Methodist chapel was built in South Newton village in 1812.[20] In 1851 on Census Sunday 15 Wesleyans attended an afternoon service there.[21] The chapel was apparently used by Primitive Methodists c. 1879 and had been demolished by 1900.[22] A small red-brick chapel was built at Stoford for United Methodists in 1912:[23] it was closed in 1986.[24] In 1843 a house at North Ugford and in 1845 one at Chilhampton were licensed for meetings,[25] and in 1864 dissenters from Burden's Ball attended a chapel at Wilton.[26]

The former workhouse chapel at Burden's Ball was Wilton Spiritualist church in 1993.

EDUCATION.

EDUCATION. There was no school in the parish in 1783.[27] In 1818 three dame schools had a total of 75 pupils: 35 were the children of paupers but the poor still had inadequate means of education.[28] Two small schools, attended by 7 boys and 17 girls, were open in 1833.[29] In 1838 a National school, with a teacher's house, was built in South Newton village. It had 58 pupils in 1846, when there was also a dame school with 10 pupils in the parish.[30] The National school was described as tidy and well conducted in 1858, when there were 30–40 pupils.[31] The number of pupils had risen to 75 by 1873,[32] and in 1909 average attendance was 58. Attendance had fallen to 22 by 1927, and the school was closed in 1935.[33]

In 1883 Stoford House was certified for use as a residential industrial school for a maximum of 15 girls.[34]

CHARITIES FOR THE POOR.

CHARITIES FOR THE POOR. Some of the money given by a Mr. Daniel for poor widows

[2] *Endowed Char. Wilts.* (S. Div.), 352–3; W.R.O., L 2, S. Newton.
[3] J. Ecton, *Thesaurus* (1763), 396.
[4] For the work of 1861–2 and for illustrations of the church at var. dates, *Churches of SE. Wilts.* (R.C.H.M.), 187–9.
[5] Hoare, *Mod. Wilts.* Branch and Dole, 53.
[6] J. Buckler, watercolour in W.A.S. Libr., vol. i. 28.
[7] Nightingale, *Wilts. Plate*, 146–7; inf. from Mr. H. Smith, Bramscote, S. Newton.
[8] Walters, *Wilts. Bells*, 146–7; inf. from Mr. Smith.
[9] W.R.O. 2077/1–9; bishop's transcripts for some earlier years are ibid.
[10] *V.C.H. Wilts.* iii. 102–3.
[11] W.R.O., D 1/54/1/4, no. 1B.
[12] *Orig. Rec.* ed. G. L. Turner, ii, p. 1075.
[13] *Meeting Ho. Certs.* (W.R.S. xl), p. 172.
[14] *Compton Census*, ed. Whiteman, 126.
[15] *Meeting Ho. Certs.* (W.R.S. xl), p. 6.
[16] *V.C.H. Wilts.* iii. 117.
[17] *Meeting Ho. Certs.* (W.R.S. xl), p. 31.

[18] *Vis. Queries, 1783* (W.R.S. xxvii), p. 165.
[19] *Meeting Ho. Certs.* (W.R.S. xl), p. 52.
[20] Ibid. pp. 62, 71; O.S. Map 6", Wilts. LXVII (1887 edn.).
[21] P.R.O., HO 129/265/1/4/11.
[22] O.S. Maps 6", Wilts. LXVI (1887 edn.); LXVI. NW. (1901 edn.).
[23] Foundation stone on bldg.
[24] Inf. from Mr. Smith.
[25] *Meeting Ho. Certs.* (W.R.S. xl), pp. 156, 162.
[26] W.R.O., D 1/56/7.
[27] *Vis. Queries, 1783* (W.R.S. xxvii), p. 165.
[28] *Educ. of Poor Digest*, 1033.
[29] *Educ. Enq. Abstract*, 1044.
[30] Nat. Soc. *Inquiry, 1846–7*, Wilts. 8–9; P.R.O., ED 7/131, no. 247.
[31] *Acct. of Wilts. Schs.* 35.
[32] P.R.O., ED 21/18544.
[33] Bd. of Educ., List 21, 1910 (H.M.S.O.), 510; 1927, 362; 1936, 426.
[34] *Lond. Gaz.* 9 Mar. 1883, p. 1328.

of the parish had been lost by 1786; thereafter Daniel's charity comprised the income from £10 and was distributed annually. In the early 1830s J. H. Flooks yearly increased the amount distributed to 10s., and by will proved 1844 he gave £50 to augment the charity. In 1901 each of 10 widows received 3s. 4d.;[35] in 1930 £2 0s. 5d. was distributed and in 1950 £1 10s. 4d.[36] In the later 20th century the income was allowed to accumulate; £34 was distributed in 1981.[37]

By his will Flooks also gave the income from £500 for bread for the poor of South Newton and Wilton. South Newton was to receive the bread in alternate years, but in the late 19th century received c. £7, half the income, annually: 210 gallons of bread were distributed in 1901,[38] 102 gallons were shared by 227 recipients in 1930, and in 1950 £6 7s. was spent on bread for 21 parishioners.[39] There was no distribution of bread recent to 1993.[40]

Two bungalows, built in South Newton village in 1946 as a peace memorial and later designated almshouses, were let at low rents to parishioners.[41]

ORCHESTON ST. MARY

ORCHESTON ST. MARY lies in the upper Till valley 11 km. WNW. of Amesbury.[42] Before the late 11th century there may have been a single large estate called Orcheston, but in 1086 four estates, probably divisions of it, bore the name,[43] and Orcheston St. Mary parish was formed from two of them. In the late 13th century the parish was called Orcheston Bovill: the suffix, the surname of lords of the principal manor, was replaced from the 14th century by the suffix St. Mary, the dedication of the church.[44] The other two Domesday estates made up Orcheston St. George parish: a detached part of a southern tail of Orcheston St. Mary parish lay between the two main parts of Orcheston St. George, and the parish embraced several islands of Orcheston St. George. Further south down the Till valley, surrounded mainly by Winterbourne Stoke, a field of less than 1 a. may have formed a detached part of Orcheston St. Mary in 1812 but not in 1841.[45] In 1885 the detached part of the tail, c. 3 a., was transferred to Orcheston St. George, and the detached parts of Orcheston St. George, c. 139 a., were transferred to Orcheston St. Mary. Thereafter Orcheston St. Mary comprised 1,895 a. (766 ha.).[46] The parishes were united as Orcheston in 1934.[47]

Most of the parish boundary, nearly all of which was with Orcheston St. George, crossed gently sloping downland on Salisbury Plain and largely ignored relief. To the north-west the boundary with Tilshead was marked by the prehistoric Old Ditch, other ditches marked short stretches of boundary with Orcheston St. George, and to the south the Till marked the eastern boundary of the tail.[48] Chalk outcrops over the whole parish and gravel has been deposited in the valleys.[49] The Till, which flows mainly in winter,[50] follows a curving course across the southern part of the parish. Only in its valley and in a dry valley in the south-east corner of the parish is the land below 100 m.: it rises to 130 m. on Orcheston down and to 158 m. at the northern corner. In the 19th century and presumably earlier the arable was in the south and centre of the parish, and the western and northern downs provided pasture. The tail brought within the parish part of a strip of unusually valuable meadow, and the detached land in Winterbourne Stoke was also meadow. There was little woodland, c. 25 a. in 1841,[51] 31 a. in scattered plantations on the downs in 1899, probably c. 35 a. in 1991. Nearly all the parish was bought by the War Department between 1897 and 1934, and the northern downs became part of artillery ranges extending north-west from Larkhill in Durrington.[52]

The Devizes–Salisbury road, turnpiked in 1761, disturnpiked in 1870, and closed c. 1900 to allow for military training,[53] crossed the parish's northern tip; the road which superseded it, linking West Lavington and Tilshead in the north to Shrewton and Maddington in the south, was thereafter the principal route through the parish, crossing its western corner in the Till valley. A road leading from Tilshead to the Bustard inn in Shrewton across the parish's northern downland may have been prominent in the earlier 19th century, when it was wide and called London Road,[54] but was apparently never a major route. In the mid 20th century it was diverted to a more northerly and indirect course[55] but was a tarmacadamed road in public use on roughly its old course in 1991. In the late 18th century other roads radiated from Orcheston St. Mary village south to Maddington and Shrewton, south-east to Elston in Orcheston St. George, south-west towards Warminster, north to the Devizes–Salisbury road, and north-east towards Netheravon.[56] Only that leading

35 *Endowed Char. Wilts.* (S. Div.), 351, 353.
36 W.R.O., L 2, S. Newton.
37 Inf. from Mr. Smith.
38 *Endowed Char. Wilts.* (S. Div.), 352–3.
39 W.R.O., L 2, S. Newton.
40 Inf. from Mr. Smith.
41 Char. Com. file; date on bldgs.
42 This article was written in 1991. Maps used include O.S. Maps 1/50,000, sheet 184 (1979 edn.); 1/25,000, SU 04 (1958 edn.); 6", Wilts. XLVI, LIII (1889 and later edns.).
43 *V.C.H. Wilts.* ii, pp. 136, 155.
44 *P.N. Wilts.* (E.P.N.S.), 234; Phillipps, *Wilts. Inst.* i. 37, 58; below, manors (Orcheston St. Mary); church.
45 W.R.O., tithe award; Orcheston St. Geo. tithe award;

Winterbourne Stoke tithe award; ibid. EA/104.
46 *Census,* 1891.   47 *V.C.H. Wilts.* iv. 355.
48 W.R.O., tithe award.
49 Geol. Surv. Map 1", drift, sheet 282 (1967 edn.).
50 Cf. below, Shrewton, intro.
51 W.R.O., tithe award; ibid. EA/104; below, econ. hist.
52 O.S. Maps 6", Wilts. XLVI, LIII (1889 and later edns.); below, manors; inf. from Defence Land Agent, Durrington.   53 *V.C.H. Wilts.* iv. 266, 270; *L.J.* xxx. 77.
54 W.R.O., tithe award; for the Bustard, below, Shrewton, intro. [inns].
55 O.S. Maps 1/25,000, SU 04 (1958 edn.); 6", Wilts. LIII. NE. (1926 edn.).
56 *Andrews and Dury, Map* (W.R.S. viii), pl. 8.

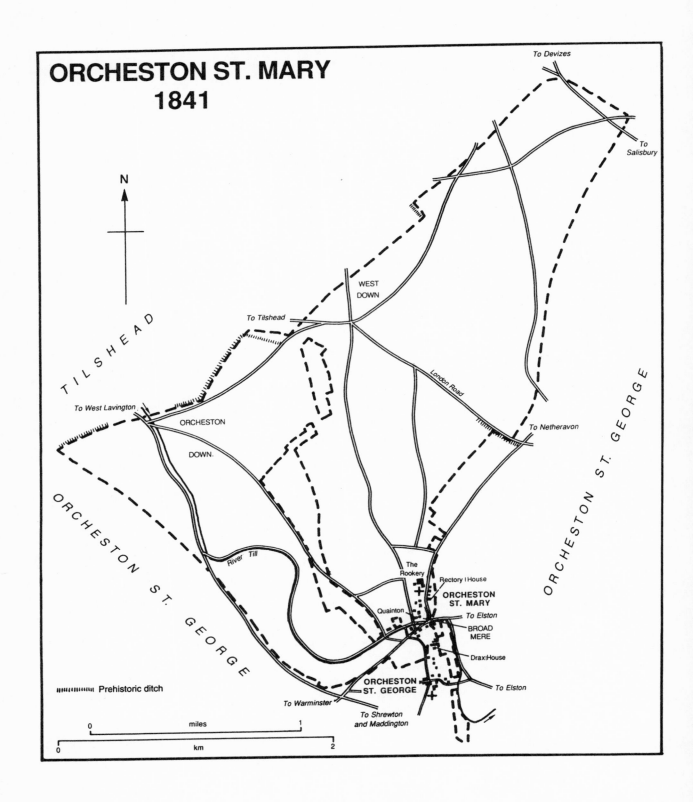

ORCHESTON ST. MARY
1841

N

To Devizes

To Salisbury

TILSHEAD

WEST DOWN

To Tilshead

London Road

To West Lavington

ORCHESTON

To Netheravon

DOWN.

ORCHESTON ST. GEORGE

ORCHESTON ST. GEORGE

River Till

The Rookery

Rectory House

ORCHESTON ST. MARY

Quainton

To Elston

BROAD MERE

Draxl House

To Elston

ORCHESTON ST. GEORGE

|||||||||||||| Prehistoric ditch

To Warminster

To Shrewton and Maddington

0   miles   1
0   km   2

south to the modern Devizes–Salisbury road and Shrewton was in regular public use in 1991.

The north part of the parish is the site of an extensive prehistoric field system, c. 900 a., crossed north-west and south-east by a long and possibly contemporary ditch. The ditch was prominent across the parish in the earlier 19th century but was later visible only from the air. Other nearby ditches are on the parish boundary and another field system, c. 80 a., is on Orcheston down. Two barrows have been identified on West down and two on Orcheston down: one of those on Orcheston down may have been the site of intrusive Saxon burials.[57]

Orcheston St. Mary had 26 poll-tax payers in 1377. In the earlier 19th century the population fluctuated: it was 133 in 1801 and 134 in 1831, but only 106 in 1811 and 113 in 1841. For reasons which are not clear the population rose by 55 per cent between 1841 and 1851, when it was 175. It declined steadily from 177 in 1861 to 117 in 1921. In 1931, the last date for which a figure for Orcheston St. Mary is available, there were 134 inhabitants.[58]

Orcheston St. Mary village lies on the gravel where the Till valley and a northern tributary valley meet. Its church is 750 m. north of Orcheston St. George's. The two villages which grew up between the churches coalesced only in the 20th century but some older buildings on the southern and eastern edges of Orcheston St. Mary village lay within Orcheston St. George parish. In 1773 and 1991 most houses in the village were beside a lane, straight at its north and south ends but winding in the middle where it crossed the Till. Beside the river in the late 18th century there was an open space,[59] in 1841 called Broad Mere.[60] Between 1773 and 1817 a second lane parallel with the first was made leading north from the western edge of Broad Mere.[61]

The principal farmhouse in the village was the Rookery, north of the church. In 1753 it was extensively repaired,[62] sashes were made for windows on the east front, a new staircase was built, and new roof tiles replaced what may have been thatch. A kitchen block was added in the later 18th century, and in the mid 19th a new main entrance, with a porch, was made in the south front. Quainton, 250 m. south of the church, is a brick house of the late 17th or early 18th century with stone dressings: it has a nearly symmetrical south front, with a central main doorway, and end chimneys. Also of 17th-century origin is a timber-framed and thatched cottage east of the church. Further south the farm buildings of Drax House, a building of

17th-century origin in Orcheston St. George, were in the parish: a large weatherboarded barn of the mid 18th century survives. A house south of the church was the rectory house until c. 1827, thereafter one south-east of the church;[63] in the late 18th century there were cottages south and west of Broad Mere.[64] A flood of 1841 destroyed several cottages, presumably those west of Broad Mere and closest to the river, and in 1842 two pairs of cottages, paid for by a public subscription to aid victims of the flood, were built on higher ground further south.[65] Later in the 19th century a house and a small school were built near the church.[66] Thereafter there was little new building until a line of council houses was erected in Whatcombe Brow to link Orcheston St. Mary and Orcheston St. George villages, in one parish from 1934:[67] 6 houses were built soon after 1919,[68] 10 in 1948,[69] and 10 in 1957.[70] There was little other 20th-century building in Orcheston St. Mary.

In 1841 there was no building in the parish outside the village.[71] By 1886 three new farmsteads had been built, New Buildings 500 m. south of the Tilshead boundary beside what became the main Devizes–Salisbury road, Prospect Farm at the parish's northern corner, and Keeper's Farm 1.5 km. north of the church. Presumably because of military training Prospect Farm had passed out of use by 1899 and Keeper's Farm was demolished between 1899 and 1923.[72] New Buildings remained in use in 1991. By 1903 two army camps had been built, West Down North straddling the northern part of the boundary with Tilshead, and West Down South on the north side of the road from Tilshead to the Bustard inn. Both were demolished c. 1925,[73] and in the mid 20th century Greenland camp 1.75 km. NNE. of the church and another camp west of New Buildings were built.[74] Most of Greenland camp had been demolished by 1979,[75] and in 1991 a crescent of huts used by the Wiltshire Army Cadet Force was all that remained of the camp near New Buildings.

MANORS AND OTHER ESTATE. In 1066 Godric held lands in Orcheston St. Mary, from which geld was paid for 4½ hides, and Alwin held 2 hides. Both estates were held of Edward of Salisbury in 1086, Godric's by Hugh and Alwin's by William.[76] Overlordship of both apparently descended with Shrewton to Edward's descendants and with the overlordship of Shrewton and the earldom of Salisbury.[77] Thomas Montagu, earl of Salisbury, was apparently overlord in 1409.[78]

57 V.C.H. Wilts. i (1), 187, 244, 258, 274, 277; W.R.O., tithe award.   58 V.C.H. Wilts. iv. 308, 355.
59 Andrews and Dury, Map (W.R.S. viii), pl. 8.
60 W.R.O., tithe award.
61 Andrews and Dury, Map (W.R.S. viii), pl. 8; O.S. Map 1", sheet 14 (1817 edn.).
62 Plaque in ho.   63 Below, church.
64 Andrews and Dury, Map (W.R.S. viii), pl. 8.
65 W.A.M. xlix. 262; below, Shrewton, intro.; plaque on bldg.   66 Below, educ.
67 Above, this section.
68 O.S. Map 6", Wilts. LIII. NE. (1926 edn.); W.R.O., G 1/603/1.
69 W.R.O., G 1/600/1.
70 Ibid. G 1/602/3; G 1/602/5.
71 Ibid. tithe award.
72 O.S. Maps 6", Wilts. XLVI, LIII (1889 and later edns.).
73 N. D. G. James, Plain Soldiering, 129, 243; Wilts. Cuttings, xi. 25.
74 O.S. Maps 1/25,000, SU 04 (1958 edn.); 6", Wilts. XLVI. SE. (1926 edn.); LIII. NE. (1926 edn.).
75 Ibid. 1/50,000, sheet 184 (1979 edn.).
76 V.C.H. Wilts. ii, p. 136.
77 Below, Shrewton, manors.
78 Cal. Close, 1405–9, 457–8.

In 1242–3 Sir Ellis Giffard (d. 1248) was mesne lord of what became *ORCHESTON ST. MARY* manor.[79] His interest may have passed to John Giffard who held ½ knight's fee in Orcheston St. Mary at his death *c.* 1327.[80]

What became the manor was held by Matthew de Bovill in 1168 and 1169.[81] Henry de Bovill held it in 1242–3,[82] and in 1297 it was settled on Parnel de Bovill (fl. 1308) with reversion to William of Rollestone and his wife Margaret.[83] William held it in 1316[84] and it may have passed by 1332 to Nicholas of Rollestone.[85] The manor was apparently conveyed to Hugh de Audley, earl of Gloucester, and his wife Margaret: in 1337 Nicholas held it from them for a term of years.[86] From Hugh (d. 1347) it passed to his daughter Margaret, Baroness Audley, wife of Ralph de Stafford, Lord Stafford (cr. earl of Stafford 1351, d. 1372), and from her to her son Hugh, earl of Stafford (d. 1386). Hugh was succeeded by his sons Thomas, earl of Stafford (d. 1392), William, earl of Stafford (d. 1395), and Edmund, earl of Stafford (d. 1403), and by Edmund's son Humphrey, earl of Stafford (cr. duke of Buckingham 1444, d. 1460). From Humphrey the manor passed to his grandson Henry, duke of Buckingham, executed in 1483,[87] and in 1484 it was granted for seven years to trustees for payment of Henry's debts. Although the reversion was granted in 1485 to John Howard, duke of Norfolk,[88] the manor was probably restored later that year with Henry's other lands to his son Edward, duke of Buckingham. It was again forfeited on Edward's execution in 1521,[89] and in 1522 was granted in tail male to Sir Edward Darell[90] (d. 1530), whose heir was his grandson Sir Edward Darell.[91] In 1544 the king granted the reversion to Edward Seymour, earl of Hertford,[92] but in 1545 the manor was assured to Darell and his heirs by an exchange with Hertford. Darell (d. 1549) devised the manor to his daughter Eleanor,[93] who with her brother William conveyed it in 1575 to Robert Downe.[94] It apparently passed to Nicholas Downe (fl. 1585), who had a son Edward.[95] By conveyances of 1609–16 it was settled on Nicholas's son-in-law John Low[96] (d. 1632), and it passed to John's son John[97] (fl. 1657)[98] and to that John's son Laurence. With Semington manor in Steeple Ashton it apparently passed to

Laurence's relict Lucy (d. 1697) who married George Pitt (d. 1734). From 1697 it was apparently held for life by Lucy's sister Elizabeth Freke and after her death in 1714 or 1715 probably passed to Lucy's son George Pitt (d. 1745).[99] That George's son George (cr. Baron Rivers 1776, d. 1803)[1] held Orcheston St. Mary manor in 1753.[2] By 1780 it had been acquired, presumably by purchase, by Gifford Warriner who from *c.* 1785 held all but *c.* 600 a. of the parish.[3] Warriner (d. 1787) was succeeded by his son Gifford (d. 1820), who devised the estate to his son Ernle.[4] From Ernle it passed, probably by sale in 1841 with an estate of tithes in Chirton, to Stephen Mills, who in that year held 1,117 a. in Orcheston St. Mary.[5] Mills (d. 1857) was succeeded by his sister Martha Mills[6] (d. 1903), who sold 676 a. to the War Department in 1897 and devised the remainder to her cousin Frederick Mills[7] (d. 1914). In 1911 Mills sold a further 487 a. to the War Department. He devised Rookery farm, 112 a., to his brother Stephen, who in 1916 sold it to George Williams (d. 1926). Williams's daughter Alice, wife of E. W. Grant, bought the farm from his executors in 1927[8] and sold most of it to the War Department in 1934.[9] Nearly all of what had been Orcheston St. Mary manor belonged to the Ministry of Defence in 1991.[10]

The second estate held of Edward of Salisbury became a manor sometimes called *LITTLE-COTT'S*.[11] William son of Everard of Littlecott held lands in the parish in the late 12th century,[12] and in 1242–3 Adam of Littlecott held lands as ⅓ knight's fee there.[13] In 1423 Thomas Quinton and his wife Alice granted lands, evidently those formerly William of Littlecott's, to John Pocock and his wife Joan for life.[14] In 1428 Joan held them with reversion to John Quinton, and Richard Littlecott held other land, formerly Nicholas of Rollestone's.[15] One or both of those estates was presumably the manor held after 1428 by John Littlecott and by 1466 by Ralph Littlecott. Ralph settled the manor for life on his son Edward (fl. 1497), from whom it passed to Alice Littlecott, daughter of Edward's brother Simon and later wife of Robert Thornborough (d. 1522).[16] Simon's relict Joan Gorge held it, perhaps as lessee, at her death in 1524.[17] Thereafter it passed in turn to Alice's son William Thorn-

79 *Bk. of Fees*, ii. 721; below, Sherrington, manor.
80 *Cal. Inq. p.m.* vii, p. 44.
81 *Pipe R.* 1168 (P.R.S. xii), 164; 1169 (P.R.S. xiii), 21.
82 *Bk. of Fees*, ii. 721.
83 *Feet of F. 1272–1327* (W.R.S. i), p. 44; Phillipps, *Wilts. Inst.* i. 9.   84 *Feud. Aids*, v. 203.
85 *Tax List, 1332* (W.R.S. xlv), 76.
86 *Cal. Close, 1337–9*, 201–2.
87 *Complete Peerage*, ii. 388–90; xii (1), 201–2.
88 *Cal. Pat. 1476–85*, 497–8.
89 *Complete Peerage*, ii. 390–1.
90 *L. & P. Hen. VIII*, iii (2), p. 915.
91 *V.C.H. Wilts.* xii. 28.
92 *L. & P. Hen. VIII*, xix (2), pp. 313–14.
93 H. Hall, *Soc. in Elizabethan Age*, 192, 236–7.
94 *Cal. Pat. 1572–5*, p. 403.
95 P.R.O., CP 25/2/369/7 Jas. I Trin.; W.R.O., D 1/43/6, f. 17v.
96 *Wilts. Pedigrees* (Harl. Soc. cv/cvi), 120; P.R.O., CP 25/2/369/7 Jas. I Trin.; CP 25/2/370/11 Jas. I East.; ibid. index of fines, xiv, 14 Jas. I East. Wilts.
97 *Wilts. Inq. p.m. 1625–49* (Index Libr.), 326–9.
98 P.R.O., index of fines, xxiv, 1657 Trin. Wilts.
99 Ibid. CP 25/2/897/1 Wm. and Mary Trin.; *V.C.H. Hants*, iv. 22; *V.C.H. Wilts.* viii. 205; xiii. 11, 20; J. Hutchins, *Hist. Dors.* iv. 91.   1 *Complete Peerage*, xi. 30–1.
2 Plaque in the Rookery.
3 W.R.O., A 1/345/318; below, this section.
4 Act for sale of lands of Gifford Warriner, 11 Geo. IV, c. 41 (Private).
5 *V.C.H. Wilts.* x. 65; W.R.O., tithe award.
6 Princ. Regy. Fam. Div., will of Steph. Mills, 1857.
7 Ibid. will of Martha Mills, 1903; James, *Plain Soldiering*, 18; inf. from Defence Land Agent, Durrington.
8 G.P.L., Treas. Solicitor, 274/50; 739/59.
9 Inf. from Mrs. E. G. N. Grant, Quainton; Defence Land Agent.   10 Inf. from Defence Land Agent.
11 P.R.O., C 1/1111, no. 27.
12 *Bradenstoke Cart.* (W.R.S. xxxv), p. 28.
13 *Bk. of Fees*, ii. 721.
14 *Feet of F. 1377–1509* (W.R.S. xli), p. 83.
15 *Feud. Aids*, v. 243–4.
16 Phillipps, *Wilts. Inst.* i. 156, 185; *V.C.H. Wilts.* xi. 122; P.R.O., DL 7/1/83.   17 P.R.O., C 142/56, no. 83.

borough (d. 1535)[18] and William's son John. In 1590 John sold it to John Eyre[19] (d. 1599), who left a wife Anne and daughter Eleanor, later wife of John Boys. Anne held the manor for life, and c. 1616 she and Eleanor disputed the inheritance with Giles Tooker, Eyre's executor and formerly Eleanor's guardian.[20] Tooker owned the manor at his death in 1623 and it passed to his son Edward[21] (d. c. 1671) and to Edward's son Sir Giles Tooker, Bt. (d. 1675), whose heirs were his sisters Philippa, wife of Sir Thomas Gore, and Martha, wife of Sir Walter Ernle.[22] In a way that is not clear the lordship and perhaps half the lands had passed to John Gibbs by 1779.[23] From Gibbs they passed c. 1785 to Gifford Warriner, presumably by sale:[24] thereafter they descended with Orcheston St. Mary manor.

Land of Littlecott's manor was apparently inherited by Martha Ernle (d. 1688) and presumably passed with Winterbourne Maddington manor in Maddington in turn to her grandsons Sir Walter Ernle, Bt. (d. 1690), and Sir Edward Ernle, Bt. (d. 1729), to Sir Edward's daughter Elizabeth Drax (d. 1759) and her sons Thomas (d. 1789) and Edward (d. 1791), and to Edward's daughter Sarah, whose husband Richard Erle-Drax-Grosvenor held c. 580 a. in 1815. From Richard (d. 1819) the land passed successively to his son Richard (d. 1828) and daughter Jane (d. 1853), wife of John Sawbridge-Erle-Drax, to Jane's daughters Maria (d. 1885) and Sarah (d. 1905), and to Sarah's daughter Ernle, Baroness Dunsany (d. 1916).[25] In 1911 Lady Dunsany sold 281 a. to the War Department. In 1917 her son Reginald Plunkett-Ernle-Erle-Drax sold 207 a. to E. W. Grant and 113 a. to Archibald Wallis. Grant's lands were conveyed to his wife Alice in 1931,[26] and sold with Rookery farm to the War Department in 1934. Wallis also sold his lands to the War Department in 1934.[27]

In the late 12th century William son of Everard of Littlecott gave two thirds of the tithes from his demesne to Bradenstoke priory.[28] By 1291 the tithes had apparently been replaced by a pension of 16s.[29] which was still payable at the Dissolution.[30]

ECONOMIC HISTORY. In 1086 Orcheston St. Mary had land for 3 ploughteams: 5 bordars and 7 *servi* had 2 teams, and the larger of the two estates had demesne on which was 1 team. That estate had pasture 4 furlongs by 2, the smaller had 80 a. of pasture.[31]

There were apparently two sets of open fields

and common pasture in the 17th century corresponding with the manors of Orcheston St. Mary and Littlecott's and presumably of long standing.[32] The demesne of Orcheston St. Mary manor, held at farm in 1394,[33] comprised 168 a. of arable, 3 a. of meadow, and pasture for 200 sheep in 1397. On it were a hall house and a barn, both thatched and old. The 10 tenants held between them 13 yardlands, each nominally of 24 a.[34] Littlecott's manor may have comprised both demesne and customary land in the 16th century. A copyholder held 57 a. of arable in East, West, and Middle fields and pasture for 100 sheep c. 1590.[35] The fields of Littlecott's were still open in 1677,[36] and common husbandry in that part of the parish may not have ceased until the early 19th century.[37]

Land in the parish was not inclosed by formal agreement or award, and common husbandry in each part apparently ended when the lands were merged in a single holding. In 1780 the lands of Orcheston St. Mary manor were apparently a single farm, those of Littlecott's manor were apparently in two farms, one of which was probably worked from Drax House, and there was a much smaller glebe farm.[38] In 1841 all but the glebe formed a single farm. There were c. 870 a. of pasture on the downs in the west and north and c. 900 a. of arable, including c. 25 a. which had been burnbaked, in the south and centre. There were c. 50 a. of meadow beside the Till, and there was a hopyard north of the church. Most of the land was worked with neighbouring estates of Stephen Mills, owner of the principal farm probably from 1841 and a prominent sheep farmer.[39]

Although in the mid or later 19th century new farmsteads were built on the downs,[40] and some new land was presumably ploughed, the proportion of arable to pasture changed little before 1900. In 1896 farms based in the parish had flocks totalling 3,750 sheep and grew c. 550 a. of cereals and c. 400 a. of fodder crops.[41] Thereafter lands owned by the War Department were presumably less intensively used and some passed out of cultivation. In 1910 there were two farms, the Rookery, c. 1,250 a. including War Department lands, and Drax farm, c. 500 a.[42] By 1917 Drax had become a farm of c. 313 a.: it was worked from Drax House and New Buildings and more than two thirds of its land was arable.[43] Much of the parish was pasture in the 1930s.[44] In 1991 Rookery was a dairy and beef farm of c. 250 a.,[45] and nearly all the rest of the parish was rough grassland used for military training.[46]

18 Ibid. C 142/58, no. 2.
19 Ibid. CP 25/2/241/32 & 33 Eliz. I Mich.
20 Ibid. C 2/Jas. I/M 11/14; C 142/260, no. 127.
21 *Wilts. Inq. p.m.* 1625–49 (Index Libr.), 38–9.
22 Above, Maddington, manors (Winterbourne Maddington).   23 P.R.O., CP 25/2/1446/19 Geo. III Mich.
24 W.R.O., A 1/345/318.
25 Ibid. 148, terrier, 1815, ff. 104–7; above, Maddington, manors (Winterbourne Maddington).
26 W.A.S. Libr., sale cat. xii, no. 23; G.P.L., Treas. Solicitor, 739/59.
27 Inf. from Mrs. Grant; Defence Land Agent.
28 *Bradenstoke Cart.* (W.R.S. xxxv), p. 28.
29 *Tax. Eccl.* (Rec. Com.), 181.
30 *Valor Eccl.* (Rec. Com.), ii. 101.
31 *V.C.H. Wilts.* ii, p. 136.

32 W.R.O., D 1/24/162/1.   33 P.R.O., SC 2/209/8.
34 *Cal. Inq. Misc.* vi, pp. 146–7.
35 P.R.O., REQ 2/57/86.
36 W.R.O., D 1/24/162/2.
37 Clare Coll., Camb., Mun., BF08/3/1 (Safe B: 75/11), letter, Cantley to Clare, 1827.
38 W.R.O., A 1/345/316; A 1/345/318; cf. above, manors (Littlecott's).
39 *V.C.H. Wilts.* iv. 86; W.R.O., tithe award.
40 Above, intro.
41 P.R.O., MAF 68/1633, sheet 9.
42 W.R.O., Inland Revenue, val. reg. 140.
43 W.A.S. Libr., sale cat. xii, no. 23.
44 [1st] Land Util. Surv. Map, sheet 122.
45 Inf. from Mrs. Grant.
46 Inf. from Defence Land Agent.

In the 17th century John Aubrey reported that grass in a meadow in Orcheston St. Mary grew as much as 17 ft. in a season.[47] The prolific grass was grown in the 1790s on 2–3 a. beside the Till in the parish's tail and was mown once or twice a year: the meadows were watered naturally when the river flooded.[48] The grass was still famous for its prolificacy in 1939.[49]

There was a windmill on Orcheston St. Mary manor in 1623.[50]

LOCAL GOVERNMENT. A manor court and a view of frankpledge were held for Orcheston St. Mary manor in the Middle Ages. At a court held in 1394 the homage presented the disrepair of buildings on the demesne and the death of cottagers.[51] A leet court was apparently held annually in the 15th century.[52] The view of frankpledge and the court recorded for 1452–3 and 1458–60 were held together once or twice a year: cert money was paid, a tithingman presented defaulters, the homage presented boundaries and buildings in need of repair, and customary tenants were admitted.[53]

In the 1770s and 1780s the annual cost of poor relief in the parish was c. £45.[54] In 1797–8 regular relief was given to 8 or 9 people and occasional payments were made for clothes, midwifery, and rents.[55] The cost had risen to £81 by 1803, when 13 adults and 17 children received regular relief and 20 people occasional relief: the poor rate was slightly lower than the average for Branch and Dole hundred.[56] Expenditure reached a peak of £169 in 1813, although only 12 adults then received regular relief.[57] By 1820 it had fallen to £118 and thereafter was always less than £100 and often less than £70.[58] An average of £94 was spent yearly 1833–5. In 1835 the parish became part of Amesbury poor-law union;[59] in 1974 Orcheston parish was included in Salisbury district.[60]

CHURCH. There was a church at Orcheston St. Mary probably in the 12th century and certainly in the 13th.[61] Recommendations of 1650 that the parish be united with Orcheston St. George and that Orcheston St. George's be the parish church[62] were not carried out. The two rectories were united in 1933 as the Orcheston benefice,[63] which in 1991 became part of the united benefice of Tilshead, Orcheston and Chitterne.[64]

In 1297 Parnel de Bovill claimed the advowson.[65] It may have passed with Orcheston St. Mary manor to Nicholas of Rollestone, patron in 1342. A rector was presented in 1364 by Henry Fleming and his wife Joan and another by Joan in 1380, by what right is unknown. Four presentations were made between 1405 and 1416 by Richard Littlecott and another four between 1434 and 1468 by Ralph Littlecott, who by 1466 had become lord of Littlecott's manor. Lords of that manor owned the advowson until the early 17th century but did not always present. The bishop of Salisbury presented by lapse in 1480 and the king presented in 1526, perhaps by lapse, and in 1534, when William Thornborough was a minor. By grants of a turn John Wroe presented in 1538, Laurence Clifton in 1637.[66] In the earlier 17th century the advowson was acquired, presumably by purchase, by a lord of Orcheston St. Mary manor, and in 1632 John Low, lord of the manor from that year, sold it to Giles Thornborough[67] (d. 1637), the rector.[68] It descended in the direct line to Giles (fl. 1661), Giles (fl. 1691), and Giles (fl. 1718), each of whom was rector.[69] In 1680 Richard Hayter and Robert Wansborough presented by grant of a turn.[70] Clare Hall, later Clare College, Cambridge, bought the advowson from Thornborough in 1718.[71] From 1933 the college was patron of the united benefice at alternate turns:[72] its rights were transferred to the Salisbury diocesan patronage board in 1961.[73]

The rectory's value was below average for a living in Wylye deanery in 1291 when it was £6 13s. 4d.,[74] about average in 1535 when it was £13 13s. 4d.[75] In 1830 the rector's income, c. £360, was above the diocesan average.[76] Some tithes from the parish were not the rector's in the late 12th century[77] but later the rector received all tithes. They were valued at £350 and commuted in 1841.[78] In 1341 the rector had 2 yardlands and received 4s. rent from other land.[79] The glebe comprised c. 40 a. of arable with pasture rights for 80 sheep in the 17th century.[80] In 1827 the arable was only 25 a.,[81] and in 1841 the glebe was a compact holding of 21 a.[82] All but 3 a. was

47 Aubrey, *Nat. Hist. Wilts.* ed. Britton, 51.
48 W. Marshall, *Rural Econ. S. Cos.* ii. 331, 339–40; W.R.O., tithe award.   49 *Kelly's Dir. Wilts.* (1939).
50 *Wilts. Inq. p.m.* 1625–49 (Index Libr.), 38–9.
51 P.R.O., SC 2/209/8.
52 Ibid. SC 6/1051/16.
53 Ibid. SC 2/209/46.
54 *Poor Law Abstract, 1804,* 558–9.
55 W.R.O. 1360/13.
56 *Poor Law Abstract, 1804,* 558–9.
57 Ibid. *1818,* 492–3.
58 *Poor Rate Returns, 1816–21,* 186; *1822–4,* 225; *1825–9,* 216; *1830–4,* 209.
59 *Poor Law Com. 2nd Rep.* App. D, 558.
60 O.S. Map 1/100,000, admin. areas, Wilts. (1974 edn.).
61 *Bradenstoke Cart.* (W.R.S. xxv), p. 28; below, this section [architecture].   62 *W.A.M.* xl. 299.
63 *Lond. Gaz.* 16 Oct. 1925, pp. 6682–4; Ch. Com. file, NB 34/341.
64 Inf. from Dioc. Registrar, Castle Street, Salisbury.
65 *Feet of F.* 1272–1327 (W.R.S. i), p. 44.
66 Phillipps, *Wilts. Inst.* i. 37, 58, 65, 93–4, 105, 125, 137,

156, 158, 167, 185, 198, 202, 207, 227; ii. 18; *L. & P. Hen. VIII,* vii, p. 55; above, manors.
67 Clare Coll., Camb., Mun., BF08/1/1 (Safe B: 75/9), 1; above, manors.   68 *W.A.M.* xxxiv. 187.
69 *Alum. Oxon. 1500–1714,* iv. 1479; Clare Coll. Mun., BF08/1/1 (Safe B: 75/9), 3, 6, 18; below, this section.
70 Phillipps, *Wilts. Inst.* ii. 36; Clare Coll. Mun., BF08/1/1 (Safe B: 75/9), 3.
71 Clare Coll. Mun., BF08/1/1 (Safe B: 75/9), 18; *V.C.H. Cambs.* iii. 345.
72 *Lond. Gaz.* 16 Oct. 1925, pp. 6683–4; Ch. Com. file, NB 34/341.
73 Inf. from the archivist, Clare Coll., Camb.
74 *Tax. Eccl.* (Rec. Com.), 181.
75 *Valor Eccl.* (Rec. Com.), ii. 101.
76 *Rep. Com. Eccl. Revenues,* 844–5.
77 *Bradenstoke Cart.* (W.R.S. xxxv), p. 28.
78 W.R.O., tithe award.
79 *Inq. Non.* (Rec. Com.), 179.
80 W.R.O., D 1/24/162/1–2.
81 Clare Coll. Mun., BF08/3/1 (Safe B: 75/11), letter, Cantley to Clare, 1827.   82 W.R.O., tithe award.

sold to the War Department in 1912.[83] A rectory house standing in the 1530s[84] may have been that which was rebuilt or extensively altered in the early 18th century, perhaps soon after the advowson was bought by Clare Hall. The brick and flint house was said in 1783 to be too small for a family[85] and ceased to be the rectory house c. 1827.[86] Thereafter the northern half was re-roofed and used as a barn, the southern end was a cottage: the whole was restored as a house in the later 20th century.[87] A new house was built

there had never been a pulpit in the church: a carpet for the communion table was also lacking.[91] Three parishioners failed to receive Easter communion in 1584: two of them had been refused the sacrament by the minister then and at Whitsun.[92] Members of the Thornborough family owned the advowson from the earlier 16th century to 1590 and from 1632 to 1718, and, except 1680–90, were rectors from 1575 to 1735. John Thornborough, presented by a namesake in 1575,[93] held other livings in Wiltshire and

ST. MARY'S CHURCH IN 1836

c. 1827. It consists of a three-storeyed square block built of white brick with a red-brick northern service wing of slightly later date: extensive gardens to the east were walled in red brick and cob. The house was sold when the Orcheston benefice was formed in 1933.[88]

Dispensations to hold additional livings were granted in 1451 and 1463 to the rector Thomas Chippenham, from 1459 a canon of Exeter.[89] In the earlier 16th century the churchwardens held 2 a. and stock including 2 cows and 35 sheep for obits and lights in the church, including a light on the high altar.[90] In 1553 it was reported that

Dorset and was later bishop of Limerick, Bristol, and Worcester.[94] His successor at Orcheston St. Mary was his brother Giles, rector 1588–1637 and subdean of Salisbury. Giles's son Giles, rector 1637–60, was said in 1650 to preach every Sunday but may later have been sequestrated. He presented his son Giles, rector 1660–80,[95] who received a dispensation to hold an additional living in 1679[96] and presented his son Giles as rector in 1690.[97] Giles was still rector in 1718:[98] James Thornborough was replaced as rector in 1735.[99]

In 1783 the rector did not reside and the curate

83 Ch. Com. file 85127.
84 P.R.O., C 1/1111, no. 28.
85 *Vis. Queries, 1783* (W.R.S. xxvii), p. 173.
86 W.R.O., D 1/61/5/35.
87 Inf. from Major H. Dumas, the Old Rectory.
88 W.R.O. 776/128.
89 *Cal. Papal Reg.* x. 100–1; xi. 652–3; Le Neve, *Fasti, 1300–1541, Exeter*, 54.
90 P.R.O., E 301/58, no. 19; E 318/31/1729.
91 W.R.O., D 1/43/1, f. 119.
92 Ibid. D 1/43/5, f. 27.
93 Phillipps, *Wilts. Inst.* i. 227; above, this section;

manors (Littlecott's).
94 *D.N.B.*
95 *Alum. Oxon. 1500–1714*, iv. 1479; Phillipps, *Wilts. Inst.* ii. 23, 36; *Walker Revised*, ed. Matthews, 380; *Subscription Bk. 1620–40* (W.R.S. xxxii), p. 72, where 1636 is given for 1637.
96 *Cal. S.P. Dom. 1679–80*, 162.
97 *Alum. Oxon. 1500–1714*, iv. 1479.
98 Clare Coll. Mun., BF08/1/1 (Safe B: 75/9), 18; BF08/3/1 (Safe B: 75/11), deed, Thornborough to Clare, c. 1718.
99 Phillipps, *Wilts. Inst.* ii. 66.

also served Shrewton and Maddington churches. At Orcheston St. Mary one service was held each Sunday, none on weekdays. There were usually 12 communicants at the celebrations at Christmas, Easter, and Whitsun.[1] On Census Sunday in 1851 the congregation at the only service, held in the afternoon, was 51.[2] In 1864 the average congregation was between 50 and 60; additional services were held on Christmas day, Good Friday, Ascension day, and Wednesdays and Fridays in Lent. Communion was celebrated at Christmas and Easter, on Whit Sunday or Trinity Sunday, and on four other Sundays: there were 41 regular communicants.[3]

ST. MARY'S church, so called in 1297,[4] is built of limestone rubble and flint and has a chancel, a nave with south aisle and south porch, and a south-west tower. The nave has thick east and west walls, possibly surviving from a small 12th-century church; the aisle and tower were built in the 13th century. A staircase was made in the south-east corner of the tower, and the aisle was refenestrated, in the 14th century, and the chancel was apparently rebuilt or extensively altered in the 16th century. In 1832-3 the chancel, the north wall of the nave, and the aisle walls were rebuilt, the nave was reroofed, and the porch, until then of timber, was rebuilt in stone.[5]

In 1553 a chalice weighing 9½ oz. was retained and 2½ oz. of plate were confiscated. An early 16th-century paten and a late 16th-century chalice belonged to the parish in 1991, as did a flagon given in 1730.[6] Of three bells hanging in the church in 1553 two, cast at Salisbury, survived until 1914: a third bell was replaced in 1715 by one cast by Clement Tosier. The three bells were destroyed by fire in 1914; three cast by Taylor of Loughborough (Leics.)[7] hung in the church in 1991.[8]

Incomplete series of registers survive, of baptisms from 1688 and of marriages and of burials from 1691.[9]

NONCONFORMITY. Although in 1765 a house was certified for dissenters' meetings and in 1801 another for Baptist meetings,[10] there was said to be no nonconformist in the parish in 1783.[11] In 1864 there was no meeting house and the 32 Baptists and 4 Wesleyan Methodists who lived in the parish presumably attended chapels elsewhere.[12]

EDUCATION. A small red-brick school built in 1854[13] was attended by 15-20 pupils in 1859, when it was said to be very good of its kind.[14] By 1871 it had become a National school.[15] Apparently from 1894, when the school was enlarged, it was attended by children from Orcheston St. George: average attendance was 50 in 1900, 40 in 1910.[16] There were 16 pupils on roll in 1931 and the school was closed in 1932.[17]

CHARITIES FOR THE POOR. With other Till valley parishes Orcheston St. Mary benefited from the Shrewton Flood charity established in 1843. Four cottages were built in 1842 and the parish was entitled to a seventh of the charity's income, to be spent on clothing or fuel for the poor: 27 sheets were distributed in 1904.[18] In the later 20th century the income was spent on repairing the cottages, and in 1991 their transfer to a housing association was being negotiated.[19]

By will proved 1904 Martha Mills (d. 1903) gave the income from £250 to buy coal for the poor of Orcheston St. Mary. About £6 a year was spent until 1949; thereafter the income was allowed to accumulate.[20]

SHERRINGTON

SHERRINGTON is in the Wylye valley 10 km. south-east of Warminster; the long and narrow parish is south of the river, and the village is on the south bank.[21] The boundaries of an estate defined in 968 became those of the parish, the Wylye on the north, the Grovely Grim's ditch on the south, a road along a coomb on the east, and a barrow on part of the west.[22] To the north changes to the main course of the Wylye, presumably to drive Sherrington mill and to water meadows,[23] left some Sherrington land north of it. The southernmost part of the eastern boundary, with Stockton, had been obscured by 1794 and was redefined between then and 1839.[24] A

[1]   *Vis. Queries, 1783* (W.R.S. xxvii), pp. 172-3.
[2]   P.R.O., HO 129/262/1/2/1.
[3]   W.R.O., D 1/56/7.
[4]   *Cal. Close, 1296-1302*, 92.
[5]   *Churches of SE. Wilts.* (R.C.H.M.), 173-4.
[6]   *W.A.M.* xii. 367; Nightingale, *Wilts. Plate*, 71-2; inf. from the priest-in-charge, the Vicarage, Tilshead.
[7]   Walters, *Wilts. Bells*, 153-4, 262, 303, 322; Wilts. Cuttings, iii. 126.
[8]   Inf. from the priest-in-charge.
[9]   W.R.O. 1360/3; 1360/5-6; bishop's transcripts for some earlier and missing years are ibid.
[10]   *Meeting Ho. Certs.* (W.R.S. xl), pp. 56, 169.
[11]   *Vis. Queries, 1783* (W.R.S. xxvii), p. 172.
[12]   W.R.O., D 1/56/7.
[13]   *Kelly's Dir. Wilts.* (1903).
[14]   *Acct. of Wilts. Schs.* 36.

[15]   *Returns relating to Elem. Educ.* 426-7.
[16]   *Kelly's Dir. Wilts.* (1885 and later edns.); P.R.O., ED 21/18513.
[17]   W.R.O., F 8/500, Orcheston St. Mary sch.
[18]   *Endowed Char. Wilts.* (S. Div.), 359; above, intro.; below, Shrewton, charities.
[19]   Inf. from the secretary, Shrewton Flood charity, Maddington Place, Shrewton.
[20]   W.R.O., L 2, Orcheston; inf. from the priest-in-charge.
[21]   This article was written in 1992. Maps used include O.S. Maps 6", Wilts. LVIII (1889 and later edns.); 1/25,000, ST 93 (1958 edn.); 1/50,000, sheet 184 (1974 edn.).
[22]   *Arch. Jnl.* lxxvii. 110-11.
[23]   Below, econ. hist.; cf. maps listed above, n. 21; W.R.O., EA/41.
[24]   W.R.O., EA/41; ibid. tithe award.

TILSHEAD
St. Thomas à Becket's church in 1805

AMESBURY
The church of St. Mary and St. Melor in 1803

GREAT WISHFORD: ST. GILES'S, MOSTLY REBUILT 1863–4

CHOLDERTON: ST. NICHOLAS'S, DEMOLISHED *c.* 1841

WYLYE: ST. MARY'S, MOSTLY REBUILT 1844–6

NEWTON TONY: DEMOLISHED 1844

CHURCHES IN 1804–5

detached 8 a. of meadow north of the Wylye, from which tithes were paid to the rector of Sherrington from *c.* 1783 or earlier,[25] were transferred to Codford St. Peter in 1884.[26] Since then Sherrington parish has been 1,315 a. (532 ha.). Sometimes in the 15th century it was called Sherrington Mautravers, after the lords of the manor.[27]

Chalk outcrops over the whole parish. To the south on Great Ridge, the Wylye–Nadder watershed, it is covered by clay-with-flints. Flat land on the ridge near the boundary is at 213 m. The downland north of it, where Stony Hill reaches 201 m., is broken by deep dry valleys, but north of Park bottom the relief is gentler except where the Cliff, 100 m. to 140 m., forms a barrier south of the village. North and east of the Cliff the chalk is covered by a large area of gravel, which also extends along the eastern boundary in the coomb southwards as far as the foot of Stony Hill. A narrow strip of alluvium lies beside the Wylye, which leaves the parish at *c.* 80 m.[28] Sheep-and-corn husbandry typical of the Wylye valley was long practised in Sherrington, with meadows on the alluvium, open fields on the gravel and lower lying part of the chalk, and rough pasture and woodland beyond that.[29] At the south end of the parish Sherrington's extensive woodland, Snailcreep hanging and Sherrington wood, is part of the Great Ridge woodland.

A Roman road thought to link Winchester and Old Salisbury to the Mendips crossed the southernmost part of the parish east and west,[30] and the Grovely ridge way, leading from Wilton along the watershed, was on or near the same course.[31] The old road on Sherrington's eastern border[32] was never of much importance: it was a local route to Hindon in the 18th and 19th centuries[33] but across the ridge went out of general use in the 20th. The minor Wilton–Warminster road linking the villages on the right bank of the Wylye between Great Wishford and Bishopstrow crosses the parish: if it ever ran through the village it had been diverted away from it by 1773 when it had one course above the Cliff and one, via Boyton village, below it.[34] East of Sherrington the road was turnpiked between Little Langford and Stockton in 1761 and linked by a new or improved crossing of the Wylye to the main road on the left bank at Codford St. Mary,[35] and from then the road through Sherrington may have been of even less importance. The upper road was never tarmacadamed and in the 20th century access to

Sherrington village was from the lower road. Also of decreasing importance was the downland Wilton–Warminster road which crossed Sherrington parish a little north of Park bottom:[36] it may have been little used in the 19th century[37] but has survived as a track. In 1856 the Salisbury–Warminster section of the G.W.R. was opened across the north-east corner of the parish: the nearest station was Codford, closed in 1955.[38]

A bowl barrow and a long barrow lie on Sherrington's western boundary and either may be the Maiden barrow mentioned in 968. There are two bowl barrows on the Cliff and a third on downland south of Park bottom. A Pagan-Saxon long barrow east of the village is unusual because it is on a lowland site near a river. To the south Grim's ditch may be later than the Roman road which it intersects, and on the downs between Park bottom and Stony Hill there are prehistoric field systems on the eastern and western boundaries, respectively 120 a. and 80 a.[39]

The parish has never been populous. It had only 37 poll-tax payers in 1377[40] and fewer than 10 households in 1428.[41] With 36 adult males it was more populous in 1641–2[42] and may have had 72 inhabitants in 1676.[43] The population was 134 in 1801. It rose from 133 in 1811 to a peak of 194 in 1841, remained steady until 1871, but between then and 1911 fell from 186 to 97. It remained below 100 except in 1921, when it was 122,[44] and 1961, when it was 104. In 1991 the parish had 70 inhabitants.[45]

Typical of the Wylye valley, Sherrington village was founded on the gravel terrace near the river. It was designated a conservation area in 1973.[46] Grouped in the north part were the church, the rectory house, a Norman castle or fortified house, the demesne farm buildings, and the mill. In the south part most of the copyhold farmsteads formed a street running north-east and south-west.[47] A motte was raised, presumably in the late 11th century or the 12th by a Giffard,[48] and in 1796 the circular moat around it, connected to the Wylye, was still clearly defined.[49] Evidence of a west bailey was found *c.* 1972[50] but no masonry of a keep or a house on the motte is *in situ*, and how long a building on it may have been used is obscure. An expanse of water much wider than the moat still lay around the motte on the east in 1992 but on the west the moat was dry. The demesne farmstead stood south-west of it in the 18th century[51] or earlier. The farmhouse has a long main south front, of ashlar and in 18th-century style, and may have

25 Ibid. D 1/24/180/5; cf. ibid. tithe award.
26 *Census*, 1891.
27 Phillipps, *Wilts. Inst.* i. 157; below, manor.
28 Geol. Surv. Maps 1/50,000, solid and drift, sheet 297 (1972 edn.); drift, sheet 298 (1976 edn.).
29 W.R.O., EA/41; below, econ. hist.
30 *V.C.H. Wilts.* i (1), 105; I. D. Margary, *Rom. Roads in Brit.* (1973), pp. 100–3.
31 H. W. Timperley and E. Brill, *Anct. Trackways of Wessex*, 133–4 and map 6.   32 *Arch. Jnl.* lxxvii. 110.
33 W.R.O., EA/41; ibid. tithe award.
34 Ibid. EA/41; *Andrews and Dury, Map* (W.R.S. viii), pl. 5.
35 *V.C.H. Wilts.* iv. 270; *L.J.* xxx. 138. The map in *V.C.H. Wilts.* iv. 257 shows the turnpike road extending too far W.: cf. W.R.O., A 1/371/36.

36 *Andrews and Dury, Map* (W.R.S. viii), pls. 4–5; O.S. Map 1", sheet 14 (1817 edn.).
37 W.R.O., tithe award.
38 *V.C.H. Wilts.* iv. 281, 284; xi. 213.
39 Ibid. i (1), 105, 143, 161, 190, 251–2, 278; i (2), 303; *Arch. Jnl.* lxxvii. 111.   40 *V.C.H. Wilts.* iv. 307.
41 Ibid. 314.
42 *W.N. & Q.* vii. 166.
43 *Compton Census*, ed. Whiteman, 125.
44 *V.C.H. Wilts.* iv. 357.
45 *Census*, 1961; 1971; 1981; 1991.
46 Inf. from Co. Planning Officer, Co. Hall, Trowbridge.
47 W.R.O., EA/41; ibid. tithe award.
48 Below, manor.   49 W.R.O., EA/41.
50 *W.A.M.* lxviii. 137–8.
51 W.R.O., EA/41.

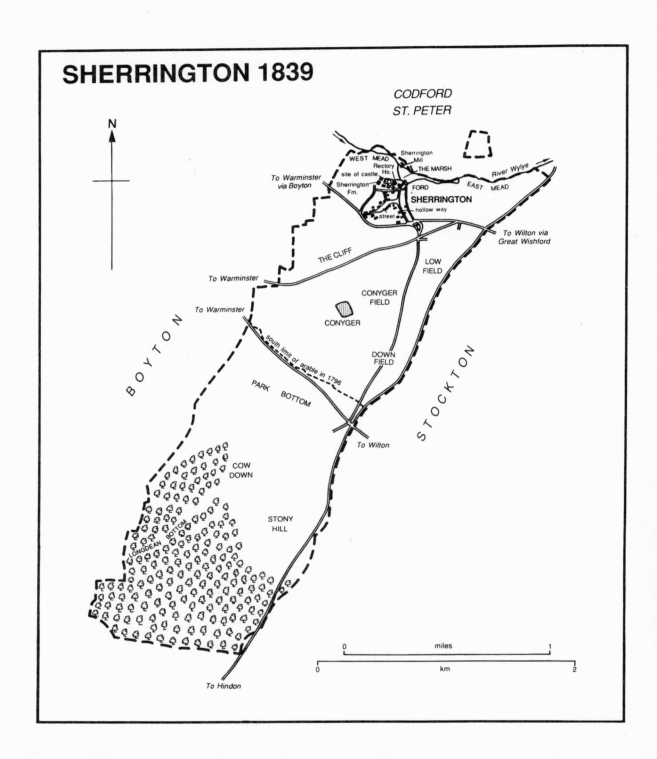

SHERRINGTON 1839

N

CODFORD
ST. PETER

WEST MEAD
Sherrington Mill
Rectory Ho.
THE MARSH
site of castle
River Wylye
To Warminster via Boyton
Sherrington Fm.
EAST MEAD
FORD
SHERRINGTON
hollow way
street
To Wilton via Great Wishford

THE CLIFF
LOW FIELD
To Warminster
CONYGER FIELD
To Warminster
CONYGER
DOWN FIELD
south limit of arable in 1796
B O Y T O N
S T O C K T O N
PARK   BOTTOM
To Wilton
COW DOWN
LONGDEAN BOTTOM
STONY HILL

	miles		1
0			

0	km	2

To Hindon

been largely rebuilt in the 19th century.[52] A freehold farmstead stood east of the church:[53] its farmhouse was replaced by a house in the mid 20th century. Where the road from the village to the mill fords what is now the main course of the Wylye a footbridge on circular stone piers had been erected by 1796.[54]

A stream rising near the Boyton road may have flowed along Sherrington street, which was very wide at its north-east end. From that end a deeply cut hollow way led south-eastwards round the east end of the Cliff to Sherrington's open fields and downs. In the later 19th century the north-east end of the street and the north-west end of the hollow way were intentionally flooded for growing watercress, and the hollow way apparently went out of use. Several former copyhold farmhouses and several cottages, a total of eight buildings, survive in the street, all from before 1839. One copyhold farmstead on the south-east side and two beside the hollow way were demolished between 1884 and 1899. Most of the surviving buildings are thatched and apparently 17th- or early 18th-century, and most of the walling of the larger ones is of stone. A house with chequered walling is dated 1724, a pair of red-brick and thatch cottages 1756. In the later 19th century a red-brick cottage was built, almost surrounded by water,[55] presumably when the street was flooded, and at the south-west end of the street a house was built in the later 20th century.

Between the street and the church stand two cottages, apparently one 17th-century and one 18th-, and a later 20th-century house. In the east and south parts of the village two cottages were built before 1796, possibly in the 18th century, and one between 1796 and 1839, all perhaps on the waste and all later enlarged; a cottage was built in the mid 19th century[56] and a pair of estate cottages in 1958.[57] East of the village on the boundary with Stockton a small house and a pair of cottages were built in the mid 19th century,[58] and between them and the village a pair of villas in a style of c. 1900 was built c. 1934.[59]

There may have been a lodge in the woods at the south end of the parish in 1773,[60] perhaps near where a forester's shelter stood in 1992. Otherwise there has been no settlement in the parish south of the village.

MANOR. Between 959 and 968 King Edgar granted Sherrington, 10 hides, to Wulfthryth. Wilton abbey acquired it, Edgar confirming the abbey's title in 968,[61] but did not keep it. In 1066 it comprised two 5-hide estates, one held by Algar, one by Smalo, and by 1084 Osbern Giffard had acquired both. A burgess of Wilton held his burgage of the estate in 1086.[62] SHER-RINGTON manor was held in chief[63] for 1 knight's fee[64] and descended in the Giffard family.[65] It probably had a fortified house,[66] and it became the head of a small honor.[67]

From Osbern Giffard (d. by 1096) the manor descended in the direct line to Ellis (d. by 1130), Ellis (d. by 1162), Ellis (d. by 1190),[68] Sir Ellis (d. 1248),[69] Sir John, from 1295 Lord Giffard (d. 1299),[70] who in 1281 was granted free warren in the demesne,[71] and John, Lord Giffard, who was hanged as a contrariant in 1322. The manor was granted in 1322 to Hugh le Despenser,[72] earl of Winchester (executed 1326),[73] and resumed in 1327.[74] Although others put in their claims to his lands, the heir of Lord Giffard, who died without issue, was John Callaway, the great-great-grandson of Ellis Giffard (d. by 1190):[75] Sherrington manor was among lands formerly Giffard's which Edward III, to reward John Mautravers, licensed Callaway to convey to Mautravers,[76] and for £1,000 Callaway conveyed them in May 1330.[77] In November 1330 Mautravers (Lord Mautravers from 1330) forfeited his lands and went into exile.[78] In 1337 the king granted Sherrington manor to Maurice Berkeley, Mautravers's brother-in-law, who in 1339 settled it on himself for life with remainder to Mautravers's son John.[79] On Berkeley's death in 1347 the king disregarded the settlement and took the land because Berkeley's heir was a minor: the younger John Mautravers claimed it[80] but it is not clear whether he, who died in 1349, or his infant son Henry, who died in 1350,[81] recovered it. In 1351 the forfeiture of Lord Mautravers was reversed and Sherrington manor was restored to him.[82] At his death in 1364 it passed to his wife Agnes,[83] and at her death in 1375 to his granddaughter Eleanor Mautravers, *suo jure* Baroness Mautravers (d. 1405), wife of John FitzAlan (from 1377 John d'Arundel, Lord Arundel, d. 1379) and of Reynold Cobham, Lord Cobham (d. 1403).[84] Eleanor was succeeded by her grandson John

---

52 For the mill, below, econ. hist.; for the church and rectory ho., ibid. church.
53 W.R.O., EA/41; ibid. tithe award.
54 Ibid. EA/41.
55 Ibid.; ibid. tithe award; O.S. Maps 1/2,500, Wilts. LVIII. 8 (1889 and later edns.); for the watercress growing, below, econ. hist.
56 O.S. Map 6", Wilts. LVIII (1889 edn.); W.R.O., EA/41; ibid. tithe award.
57 W.R.O. 2499/305/2.
58 Ibid. tithe award; O.S. Map 6", Wilts. LVIII (1889 edn.).   59 W.R.O., G 12/760/107.
60 *Andrews and Dury, Map* (W.R.S. viii), pl. 4; cf. W.R.O., tithe award.
61 Finberg, *Early Wessex Chart.* p. 96; *Arch. Jnl.* lxxvi. 110.
62 *V.C.H. Wilts.* ii, pp. 155, 209.
63 *Bk. of Fees*, ii. 742.
64 *Cal. Inq. p.m.* vii, p. 43.
65 Below, this section.
66 Above, intro.   67 e.g. *Cal. Inq. p.m.* vii, p. 44.

68 For the Giffards, *Complete Peerage*, v. 639–49; for the date 1162, *V.C.H. Glos.* vii. 143.
69 *Cal. Inq. p.m.* i, p. 30.
70 Ibid. iii, p. 419.
71 *Cal. Chart. R.* 1257–1300, 252.
72 Ibid. 1300–26, 444.
73 *Complete Peerage*, iv. 262–6.   74 Ibid. v. 646.
75 *Cal. Inq. p.m.* vii, pp. 43, 48–9; x, p. 162; G. Wrottesley, *Pedigrees from the Plea R.* 60–1; *Feet of F.* 1327–77 (W.R.S. xxix), pp. 26–7.
76 *Complete Peerage*, v. 648–9; viii. 581–3; *Cal. Pat.* 1327–30, 527.
77 *Feet of F.* 1327–77 (W.R.S. xxix), pp. 26–7.
78 *Complete Peerage*, viii. 583.
79 Ibid. 584–5; ii. 129; *Cal. Pat.* 1334–8, 563; 1338–40, 239.
80 *Cal. Inq. p.m.* ix, p. 29; *Cal. Pat.* 1348–50, 239–40.
81 *Complete Peerage*, viii. 585.
82 *Cal. Close*, 1349–54, 312.
83 *Cal. Inq. p.m.* xi, p. 452.
84 Ibid. xiv, p. 191; *Complete Peerage*, i. 259–60; viii. 586.

d'Arundel,[85] Lord Mautravers, from 1415 earl of Arundel (d. 1421), whose relict Eleanor (d. 1455) married Sir Richard Poynings (d. *c.* 1430) and Walter Hungerford, Lord Hungerford (d. 1449).[86] From that Eleanor the manor passed to her son William FitzAlan or Mautravers, earl of Arundel[87] (d. 1487), and it descended from father to son with the Arundel title to Thomas FitzAlan (d. 1524), William FitzAlan (d. 1544), and Henry FitzAlan (d. 1580).[88]

In 1560–1 Lord Arundel sold Sherrington manor to Richard Lambert,[89] and with the neighbouring Boyton manor it descended in the Lambert family.[90] Richard (d. 1567) was succeeded by his son Edmund[91] (d. 1608), whose relict Anne held Sherrington manor until her death in 1619.[92] The manor passed to her son Thomas Lambert (d. 1638), whose relict Anne held it[93] until her death in 1649,[94] to Thomas's grandson Thomas Lambert (d. 1692), and to that Thomas's son Edmund (d. *s.p.* 1734).[95] Edmund was succeeded by his nephew Edmund Lambert[96] (d. 1751), he by his son Edmund (d. 1802), and he by his son Aylmer Bourke Lambert (d. *s.p.* 1842),[97] who in 1839 owned the whole parish except the glebe and *c.* 70 a.[98] From A. B. Lambert the manor passed to Lucy Benett (d. 1845), the daughter of his half-sister, and her husband the Revd. Arthur Fane (d. 1872). The Fanes were succeeded by their son E. D. V. Fane (d. 1900) and he by his son H. N. Fane.[99]

In 1874 E. D. V. Fane sold the south half of the parish, 680 a., to Alfred Morrison[1] (d. 1897), who added it to his Fonthill House estate then based in Fonthill Gifford. As part of that estate the land descended in the direct line to Hugh Morrison (d. 1931) and John, Baron Margadale, whose son the Hon. James Morrison owned *c.* 670 a. in 1992.[2] In 1935 H. N. Fane sold the north half of the parish as part of the Boyton estate to Sidney Herbert[3] (cr. baronet 1935, d. 1939). As part of that estate Sir Sidney devised it to his cousin Sir George Herbert, Bt. (d. 1942), for life and to his second cousin the Hon. David Herbert,[4] who in 1946 sold it to the land company of Henry Pelham-Clinton-Hope, duke of Newcastle.[5] The Newcastle estate sold it to trustees of C. J. H. Wheatley in 1962, since when the beneficiaries of the trust have been Mrs. E. R. Wheatley-Hubbard and her son Mr. T. H. Wheatley-Hubbard.[6]

ECONOMIC HISTORY. Of Sherrington's 10 hides 9 were in demesne in 1086. There was land for 5 ploughteams: in demesne were 4 teams and 10 *servi*, and 4 *villani* had 1 team. There were 12 a. of meadow, 120 a. of pasture, and 80 a. of wood.[7]

In the mid 13th century the demesne of Sherrington manor was still apparently much more extensive than the customary lands and apparently was, or could be, cultivated largely by customary labour.[8] Compared to those of 1086 figures for the holdings of the manor in 1299, when a yardland was nominally 20 a. of arable, suggest that by then the demesne had been reduced by granting parts of it freely. The demesne then included 380 a. of arable, 6 a. of meadow, and woodland; 7 free tenants held 10½ yardlands (210 a.), possibly former demesne; 12 customary tenants held 6 yardlands (120 a.); and there were 6 cottars. Of the customary tenants 6 were ½-yardlanders, each of whom was required to work on the demesne on Mondays, Wednesdays, and Fridays from Michaelmas to 1 August and six days a week from 1 August to Michaelmas: no work was done in Christmas week or on feast days. The other 6 customary tenants also held ½ yardland each; 1 was described as a ½-yardlander, the other 5 as keepers of houses or farms; each had to weed, wash and shear sheep, and mow and carry hay, but their autumn services had been commuted. The cottars also had to weed and to wash and shear sheep. Of the free tenants' holdings one, 2½ yardlands in 1299,[9] remained a freehold but the others became copyholds of the manor.[10] The demesne apparently remained in hand until 1347 or later,[11] but by 1328 the ½-yardlanders' labour services had apparently been commuted.[12] In 1327 the demesne included 350 a. of arable, 12 a. of meadow, 100 a. of woodland, pasture worth 12*d.*, pasture for sheep in common, a dovecot, a fishpond, and fishing in the mill pond; in 1347 it included 360 a. of arable.[13] It had been leased by the 16th century.[14]

Customary and demesne arable was almost certainly intermingled in the open fields, which covered *c.* 440 a. There may have been a three-field system in the 14th century, with two fields on the lower land to the north and one large field on the higher ground to the south, but in the 17th and 18th centuries there were four fields: to judge from the rector's, the strips in them

85 *Cal. Inq. p.m.* xviii, p. 381.
86 *Complete Peerage*, i. 247.
87 P.R.O., C 139/159, no. 35, rot. 18.
88 *Complete Peerage*, i. 248–52.
89 P.R.O., CP 25/2/239/3 Eliz. I East.
90 Hoare, *Mod. Wilts.* Heytesbury, 202.
91 P.R.O., C 142/145, no. 2; ibid. PROB 11/49, ff. 191v.–194.
92 Ibid. C 142/311, no. 124; Hoare, *Mod. Wilts.* Heytesbury, 206.
93 *Wilts. Inq. p.m.* 1625–49 (Index Libr.), 331–5.
94 W.R.O. 1507/2.
95 For the Lamberts after 1649, Hoare, *Mod. Wilts.* Heytesbury, 203; for the date 1734, W.R.O. 1507/4.
96 W.R.O. 857/15, office copy of decree, 1814.
97 *D.N.B.*
98 W.R.O., tithe award; cf. ibid. EA/41.
99 Hoare, *Mod. Wilts.* Heytesbury, 203; Burke, *Land. Gent.* (1937), 2117; Boyton Manor Archive, statement of Revd. Arthur Fane's title; ibid. survey, 1873.

1 Fonthill Estate Off., Fonthill Bishop, deed, Fane to Morrison, 1874–6.
2 *V.C.H. Wilts.* xiii. 161; inf. from Fonthill Estate Off.
3 Wilts. Cuttings, xviii. 168; Ch. Com. file 45476/1.
4 Burke, *Peerage* (1959), 1765; Princ. Regy. Fam. Div., will of Sir Sidney Herbert, 1939.
5 Ch. Com. file 45476/1.
6 Wilts. Cuttings, xxii. 58; inf. from Mr. E. R. Wheatley-Hubbard, the Dower Ho., Boyton.
7 *V.C.H. Wilts.* ii, p. 155.
8 *Wilts. Inq. p.m.* 1242–1326 (Index Libr.), 5.
9 Ibid. 230–2; P.R.O., SC 6/1119/1.
10 *Feet of F.* 1272–1327 (W.R.S. i), p. 73; P.R.O., SC 1/35/184; cf. W.R.O., EA/41.
11 *Wilts. Inq. p.m.* 1327–77 (Index Libr.), 178–9.
12 P.R.O., SC 6/1119/1.
13 *Wilts. Inq. p.m.* 1327–77 (Index Libr.), 11, 179.
14 P.R.O., SC 6/Hen. VIII/5722–4; Boyton Manor Archive, B 320B.

averaged a little less than 1 a. Beside the Wylye there were in East mead, West mead, and Mill mead 20 a. of meadow, some, if not all, commonable:[15] meadows were watered by the later 17th century.[16] On the downs there were c. 415 a. of rough pasture. A reference to a tenantry flock in 1609 suggests that there were separate demesne and tenants' downs, and the rector's stint of 60 sheep to a yardland, presumably the same for the freeholder and copyholders, was generous. Part of the downland, 41 a., was set aside as a cow down, presumably between 1609 and 1671 when a sixth of the rector's sheep stint was replaced by the right to feed cattle in common, and cattle may also have been fed in common in the Marsh, c. 5 a. near the Wylye. A rabbit warren of 2 a. amid the open arable above the Cliff, c. 15 a. of demesne pasture, and c. 25 a. of home closes in the village were inclosed lands. The warren may have replaced an earlier one in Longdean bottom on the west boundary. In the 18th century the demesne was reckoned to be 9½ yardlands, the freehold 3, the glebe 2, and 11 other holdings c. 11, but by 1794 the farms were probably fewer and larger than those figures suggest.[17]

More than half the parish was inclosed in 1796 under an agreement of 1794. The lord of the manor was allotted a strip of arable and pasture adjoining Boyton on the west in respect of four copyholds which were in hand, and east of that a similar strip for the demesne, Sherrington farm. Those two strips were separate farms in 1839, respectively 195 a. and 318 a., each with buildings in the village. In 1796 the freeholder was allotted 60 a. immediately east of the village, including 4 a. of East mead. The rector and six copyholders were also allotted arable in severalty, 100 a. near the village, but three fields, Low, Conyger, and Down, a total of c. 108 a., were left open. The inclosure award laid down the rules for husbandry; in most cases the rector and each copyholder had one parcel in each field, and there were only 25 parcels in all. Those with land in the open fields also shared a downland sheep pasture, 145 a. including Stony Hill, for a common flock of 380. Also not inclosed were part of East mead, in which three copyholders shared the hay and the aftermath, and the Marsh, Cow down, and the c. 330 a. of woodland, in all of which a common herd of 46 cattle, including 25 in respect of Sherrington farm and the copyholds in the lord's hand, could feed.[18]

In 1839 the parish had 32 a. of meadow, 10 a. of lowland pasture, 450 a. of arable, 356 a. of upland pasture, and c. 330 a. of woodland. By

then all rights to feed cattle in the woodland had been replaced by an allotment of 50 a. of woodland, and 25 a. of the inclosed downland had been burnbaked; 277 a. of several woodland were in the lord's hand in 1839 and leased in 1841. Common husbandry was still practised but in 1839 four of the six copyholds were occupied by the lessee of Sherrington farm and one by the owner of the freehold farm.[19] Vestiges of it continued until 1874–6 when the lord of the manor bought out a copyholder, made exchanges with the rector, and conveyed the feeding rights over the south half of the parish to the new owner of the land.[20]

From 1874 the 680 a. of woodland and downland south of Park bottom were part of the Fonthill House estate, managed directly for the owners and worked from outside the parish.[21] By 1910 the woodland had been increased to 372 a., its approximate area in 1992 when some was used for commercial forestry. The c. 300 a. of downland remained pasture in the 1930s, but were ploughed during or soon after the Second World War. In 1991 cereals were grown on most of it.[22]

In the north part of the parish in 1878 there were three farms, Sherrington, later Manor, 234 a., Mill, 163 a., and the former freehold farm, 62 a.: in addition 117 a. were worked from Boyton.[23] From the 1880s to the mid 20th century sometimes there was one farm, sometimes there were two, and more land, 186 a. in 1910, was worked from Boyton.[24] By the 1930s c. 100 a. had been converted from arable to pasture.[25] After 1946 more land was worked from Boyton parish but until the early 1970s there remained a small farm based at Sherrington. Since then 508 a. of Sherrington have been part of a large arable and dairy farm based at Corton in Boyton: a new dairy was built near Conyger in 1972,[26] and that was the only significant farm building in the parish in 1992.

In the later 19th century 3 a. of watercress beds were made by controlling the water from springs feeding the Wylye. The larger part of the beds covers what was the wide village street. In 1895 the cress was said to have great pungency.[27] It was grown at Sherrington until 1974–5.[28]

MILL. There was a mill at Sherrington in 1086,[29] and from the mid 13th century[30] to the 20th a corn mill, north of the village on the Wylye, was part of Sherrington manor.[31] In the later 15th century or early 16th new leats or weirs were made.[32] Milling continued until the early 20th century.[33] The mill and mill house,

15 *Wilts. Inq. p.m. 1327–77* (Index Libr.), 179; W.R.O., D 1/24/180/2; D 1/24/180/5; ibid. EA/41; Boyton Manor Archive, B 357; B 371A.
16 *Bayntun Commonplace Bk.* (W.R.S. xliii), p. 19.
17 W.R.O., D 1/24/180/2–3; D 1/24/180/5; ibid. EA/41; for the earlier warren, Boyton Manor Archive, B 138.
18 W.R.O., EA/41; ibid. tithe award.
19 Ibid. tithe award; Boyton Manor Archive, lease of Sherrington woods, 1841.
20 W.R.O. 857/13; 1508/19; Boyton Manor Archive, survey, 1873; Fonthill Estate Off., deed, Fane to Morrison, 1874–6; above, manor.
21 Estate map in Fonthill Estate Off.
22 [1st] Land Util. Surv. Map, sheet 122; W.R.O., Inland Revenue, val. reg. 135; inf. from the Hon. Mrs. J. I.

Morrison, Hawking Down, Hindon.
23 W.R.O. 1508/15; cf. *Kelly's Dir. Wilts.* (1880).
24 *Kelly's Dir. Wilts.* (1885 and later edns.); W.R.O. 1508/16–17; ibid. G 12/501/1; ibid. Inland Revenue, val. reg. 135.
25 [1st] Land Util. Surv. Map, sheet 122; W.R.O., tithe award.   26 Inf. from Mr. Wheatley-Hubbard.
27 *W.N. & Q.* i. 513; above, intro.
28 Inf. from Mr. Wheatley-Hubbard.
29 *V.C.H. Wilts.* ii, p. 155.
30 *Wilts. Inq. p.m. 1242–1326* (Index Libr.), 5.
31 W.R.O., Inland Revenue, val. reg. 135; Boyton Manor Archive, B 334–5; B 339; B 341.
32 P.R.O., SC 6/Hen. VIII/5722.
33 *Kelly's Dir. Wilts.* (1903).

partly of stone rubble and partly of brick, were rebuilt in the early 19th century when existing walling was re-used. They became derelict and in the later 20th century were restored for residence.[34]

LOCAL GOVERNMENT. In the Middle Ages the lord of Sherrington manor had the right to hold an honor court at Sherrington every three weeks.[35] There is evidence of a manor court being held from the 13th century to the 19th: two courts were held in 1328–9.[36] The enrolled records of the court do not survive.

There are overseers' accounts for 1678–1796. The earliest payments recorded were of the income from Gregory's charity, but from 1688 parish rates were also levied to relieve the poor. In 1694 a total of £9 7s. was spent. In 1697–8 £22 was spent, more on rent, fuel, clothing, shoes, and coffins than on doles. In the 18th century the overseers also paid for the heads of polecats, hedgehogs, moles, jackdaws, and sparrows, for apprenticing, and for repairs to roads and bridges. The parish apparently appointed no surveyor of highways. Most of what the overseers spent, however, was on poor relief, increasingly as regular doles. Of £12 spent in 1722–3 monthly doles cost £3 15s., rents £3 18s. Expenditure increased from the 1760s. It was £16 in 1762–3, £48 in 1772–3 when £36 was given in doles and payments were made for rent, clothing, and medical services, £76 in 1782–3, and £163 in 1795–6 when £91 was spent on weekly pay, £49 on extraordinary items, and £14 on doctoring.[37] In 1802–3 more than a third of the inhabitants received relief.[38] From £314 in 1812–13, when 19 adults were relieved regularly and 6 occasionally,[39] expenditure declined to averages of £140 a year 1816–20, £108 a year 1825–9, and £147 a year 1830–4.[40] The parish joined Warminster poor-law union in 1835,[41] and became part of West Wiltshire district in 1974.[42]

CHURCH. A priest of Sherrington mentioned 1130 × 1135[43] may have served a church there, and there was a chaplain at Sherrington in 1249;[44] the church was first referred to directly in 1252 when it was served by a rector.[45] The rectory was united with Boyton rectory in 1909.[46] With the benefices of Codford St. Peter with St. Mary and of Upton Lovell the united benefice became part of Ashton Gifford benefice in 1979.[47]

The advowson of Sherrington descended with the manor, and from 1874 with the north half of the parish.[48] The king presented in 1252 when John Giffard was a minor,[49] in 1300 when John's son John was a minor,[50] and in 1329 after the resumption of 1327.[51] From 1909 the lord of the manor was entitled to present alternately,[52] and in 1950 the advowson of the united benefice was transferred to the Salisbury diocesan patronage board.[53]

The church, valued at £6 13s. 4d. in 1291,[54] £11 in 1535,[55] £100 in 1650,[56] and £238 c. 1830,[57] was well endowed. The rector was entitled to all tithes from the whole parish.[58] In 1839 they were valued at £259 and commuted.[59] The glebe consisted of the rectory house, another house, ½ a. of pasture, 27½ a. of arable in the open fields, and feeding for 120 sheep. The second house was later two cottages, feeding for cattle replaced some of that for sheep,[60] and in 1796 the arable was replaced by allotments totalling 20 a.[61] In 1874 the rector exchanged his right to feed cattle and sheep on the downland for 7 a. of lowland arable.[62] The two cottages were demolished between 1884 and 1899,[63] the rectory house was sold in 1931,[64] 29 a. of glebe were sold in 1947,[65] and the remaining glebe, ½ a., was sold in 1971.[66] The rectory house was built of ashlar with a principal south-west front of six bays in the early 17th century, probably for Henry Gregory.[67] Each end room of the main range, which had a symmetrical ground-floor plan, has ceilings divided into nine compartments by beams with plain chamfers. In 1827 the service rooms to the rear of the south-east part of the house were replaced by a red-brick range containing a principal room on each floor and an entrance hall and staircase.[68] In 1935 a single-storeyed service building in the angle between the 17th- and the 19th-century ranges was replaced by a two-storeyed kitchen wing.[69]

In the Middle Ages 1½ a. in Sherrington was given for a lamp in the church.[70] Hugh de la Penne, rector from 1252, was a clerk of the queen's chapel;[71] Geoffrey de Beuseval, an acolyte when presented in 1311 and a priest from 1312, was French.[72] Lionel Hollyman, rector

34 Inf. from Mr. S. G. Davenport, Sherrington Mill.
35 e.g. *Cal. Inq. p.m.* iii, p. 419; iv, p. 192; vii, p. 44.
36 e.g. *Wilts. Inq. p.m. 1242–1326* (Index Libr.), 231–2; P.R.O., SC 6/1119/1; W.R.O. 857/13; Boyton Manor Archive, B 385–98.
37 W.R.O. 1508/7; for Gregory's charity, below, charities.
38 *Poor Law Abstract, 1804*, 558–9; *V.C.H. Wilts.* iv. 357.
39 *Poor Law Abstract, 1818*, 492–3.
40 *Poor Rate Returns, 1816–21*, 186; *1825–9*, 216; *1830–4*, 209.
41 *Poor Law Com. 2nd Rep.* App. D, 560.
42 O.S. Map 1/100,000, admin. areas, Wilts. (1974 edn.).
43 *Reg. St. Osmund* (Rolls Ser.), i. 349.
44 *Crown Pleas, 1249* (W.R.S. xvi), p. 252.
45 *Cal. Pat. 1247–58*, 127.
46 Ch. Com. file 45476/1.   47 Ibid. NB 34/412C.
48 Ibid. 45476/1; Phillipps, *Wilts. Inst.* i. 10, 25, 51, 53, 110, 112, 157, 201, 217, 221; ii. 5, 31, 35, 43, 54, 60, 85, 89, 95; *Clergy List* (1870, 1894).
49 *Cal. Pat. 1247–58*, 127; *Cal. Inq. p.m.* i, p. 30.
50 *Cal. Pat. 1292–1301*, 490; *Cal. Inq. p.m.* iii, p. 419.
51 *Cal. Pat. 1327–30*, 344; above, manor.
52 Ch. Com. file 45476/1.   53 W.R.O. 1507/1.
54 *Tax. Eccl.* (Rec. Com.), 181.
55 *Valor Eccl.* (Rec. Com.), ii. 102.
56 *W.A.M.* xl. 392.
57 *Rep. Com. Eccl. Revenues*, 846–7.
58 *Inq. Non.* (Rec. Com.), 178; W.R.O., D 1/24/180/2.
59 W.R.O., tithe award.   60 Ibid. D 1/24/180/2–5.
61 Ibid. EA/41.   62 Ibid. 1508/19.
63 Ibid. 1508/10; O.S. Maps 6", Wilts. LVIII (1889 edn.); LVIII. NE. (1901 edn.).
64 Ch. Com. file 45476/1.
65 Ibid. 95016.   66 Ibid. deed 611418.
67 For Gregory, below, this section.
68 W.R.O., D 1/11/50.   69 Ibid. G 12/760/123.
70 P.R.O., E 301/58, no. 120.
71 *Cal. Pat. 1247–58*, 127.
72 *Reg. Ghent* (Cant. & York Soc.), ii. 766–7, 902, 906; *Reg. Martival* (Cant. & York Soc.), iii, p. 142.

until 1609, was rector of Boyton 1600–9. His successor at Sherrington, and husband of his relict, was Henry Gregory, his curate in 1608.[73] Gregory's successor Robert Dyer, rector from 1634,[74] signed the *Concurrent Testimony* in 1648:[75] in 1650 he preached twice every Sunday.[76] His successor William Hobbes, rector 1657–70, was also rector of Boyton,[77] and Edmund Sly, 1670–7, was also rector of Upton Lovell and employed a curate to serve Sherrington.[78] Thomas Lambert, rector 1677–94, was also rector of Boyton and archdeacon of Salisbury and formerly a domestic chaplain of Charles II; Thomas Lambert, 1695–1717, and Robert Sawyer, 1717–26, were also rectors of Boyton.[79] Curates often served Sherrington in the period 1677–1726, but later rectors were apparently resident and only occasionally assisted by a curate.[80] An exception was Richard Scrope, rector 1772–8, who was also rector of Aston Tirrold (Berks., later Oxon.).[81] In 1783 the rector held two services every Sunday and some weekday services, administered the sacrament at the great festivals to some seven communicants, and catechized in Lent: some parishioners explained that they did not attend services because they had children and insufficient clothes.[82] On Census Sunday in 1851 morning service was attended by 68, afternoon or evening service by 109.[83] In 1864 the rector still held two services on Sundays, then with congregations which he said averaged 100 in the morning and 150 in the evening; he held services on saints' days, on Wednesdays and Fridays in Lent, and on Monday and Tuesday after Lent, all with congregations of 30–40; and he celebrated communion eight times with *c.* 35 communicants.[84] From 1909 the rector of Boyton with Sherrington lived at Boyton.[85]

The church of *ST. COSMAS AND ST. DAMIAN*, saints invoked in it long before 1341,[86] was so called in 1352.[87] From the 18th century to the 20th it was sometimes called St. Michael's.[88] It is built of ashlar, has a chancel and a nave with south porch and west bellcot, and was rebuilt, apparently completely, in 1624.[89] Until then the church, which had three bells in 1553,[90] may have had a tower, but the plan of the new church may match that of part of the old one, and the early 14th-century style

of the tracery of many of the windows in the new church may reflect the appearance of the old. The present bellcot is of the later 19th century. The church has a 13th-century font, and fragments of 14th-century stained glass reset in the chancel windows. Most fittings, including the pulpit, the communion table and rail, and the benches are contemporary with the rebuilding. Painted wall texts dated 1630 were restored in 1939.[91]

In 1553 the church kept a chalice of 9 oz., and 2 oz. of plate were taken for the king. The chalice may be that, fitted with a new bowl in 1844, belonging to the church in 1992, when the church also had a paten of the later 17th century, a flagon given in 1694, an almsdish given in 1873, a chalice and a paten given in 1928, and other items of 20th-century plate.[92] From 1624 the church has had a single bell. That in the bellcot in 1992 is probably 14th-century and was presumably one of the three in 1553.[93] It was repaired in 1793.[94] Registers of baptisms begin in 1677, of burials in 1678, and of marriages in 1705. Those of burials are lacking for 1703–7, of marriages 1713–34.[95]

NONCONFORMITY. In 1836 a cottage near the church was certified for meetings,[96] but there is no other evidence of dissent in the parish.

EDUCATION. A Sunday school was started at the rectory house in 1832,[97] and in 1833 was united to the National society.[98] Later the rector converted a barn near the rectory house for a day school, at which 7 boys and 11 girls were taught in 1846–7 and 20–30 children in 1858.[99] In 1864 boys left at 8, girls at 11.[1] The school was a National school,[2] had an average attendance of 17 in 1882, and was closed in 1883.[3]

CHARITIES FOR THE POOR. Henry Gregory, rector 1609–34, gave the interest from £30 to the poor: in the 1680s and 1690s small sums of money were given biennially, in 1686 £3 5s. among 13. In the later 17th century Thomas Lambert (rector 1677–94) gave a further £20 and in the early 18th Edmund Lambert (presumably

73 Phillipps, *Wilts. Inst.* ii. 1, 5; W.R.O., bishop's transcripts, bdle. 1; ibid. 1508/18.
74 *Subscription Bk. 1620–40* (W.R.S. xxxii), p. 50; W.R.O., bishop's transcripts, bdle. 1.
75 *Calamy Revised*, ed. Matthews, 558.
76 *W.A.M.* xl. 392–3.
77 *Walker Revised*, ed. Matthews, 374.
78 Phillipps, *Wilts. Inst.* ii. 25, 31, 35; W.R.O., D 1/54/5, f. 23.
79 Phillipps, *Wilts. Inst.* ii. 35, 43, 54, 60–1; Le Neve, *Fasti, 1541–1857, Salisbury*, 17; *W.A.M.* xxxix. 50.
80 W.R.O., bishop's transcripts, bdles. 1–3; ibid. D 1/48/1, f. 10; D 1/48/2, f. 38; D 1/48/3, f. 7; ibid. 1508/7.
81 Ibid. bishop's transcripts, bdle. 3; Phillipps, *Wilts. Inst.* ii. 85, 89; B.L. Add. Ch. 18463.
82 *Vis. Queries, 1783* (W.R.S. xxvii), pp. 190–1.
83 P.R.O., HO 129/260/3/6/8.
84 W.R.O., D 1/56/7.
85 *Kelly's Dir. Wilts.* (1911 and later edns.).
86 *Inq. Non.* (Rec. Com.), 178.
87 Phillipps, *Wilts. Inst.* i. 51.
88 e.g. J. Ecton, *Thesaurus* (1763), 397; Walters, *Wilts.*

Bells, 197; P.R.O., HO 129/260/3/6/8.
89 Date stones on chancel and porch. C. E. Ponting thought that parts of the old church were incorporated in the new: *W.A.M.* xxvii. 258–9.
90 Walters, *Wilts. Bells*, 197.
91 *W.A.M.* l. 63–5; Wilts. Cuttings, xxi. 142; plaque in church.
92 Nightingale, *Wilts. Plate*, 72–3; W.R.O. 1508/11; inf. from Major N. J. Lewis, Rectory Cottage.
93 Walters, *Wilts. Bells*, 197, 251; inf. from Major Lewis.
94 W.R.O. 1508/7.
95 Ibid. 1508/1–6; bishop's transcripts for some earlier years are ibid.; marriages are printed in W. P. W. Phillimore and J. Sadler, *Wilts. Par. Reg. (Mar.)*, xii. 109–13.
96 *Meeting Ho. Certs.* (W.R.S. xl), p. 142; W.R.O., tithe award.   97 *Educ. Enq. Abstract*, 1047.
98 W.R.O. 1688/1.
99 *Acct. of Wilts. Schs.* 41; Nat. Soc. *Inquiry, 1846–7*, Wilts. 10–11.
1 W.R.O., D 1/56/7.
2 *Returns relating to Elem. Educ.* 424–5.
3 P.R.O., ED 2/464, no. 10976.

he who d. 1734 or he who d. 1751) and Anne Lambert each a further £10;[4] in 1760 the parish had an endowment of £67 for the poor. In the earlier 19th century and earlier 20th the income from the charity, called the Poor's money, was used to buy bread which was given away at Christmas: 35 families shared 117 loaves, tea, and money in 1901.[5] In the 1930s bread, sugar, and tea were given each year to c. 25 recipients; in 1946 loaves were delivered to all the cottages in Sherrington.[6] In 1992 the assets of the charity were transferred to Edmund Lambert's charity.[7]

By will proved 1878 Edmund Lambert gave £100 for food and fuel for the poor, aged, and sick at Christmas. In the 20th century coal was given, in 1901–2 to the value of £5. In 1946 a free delivery of 1 cwt. was made to all the cottages in Sherrington.[8] The income was being allowed to accumulate in the 1990s.[9]

Sir Sidney Herbert, Bt. (d. 1939), gave by will £500 for the poor of Boyton and Sherrington.[10] From the income, each year two old people in Sherrington were each given £1 in the 1940s.[11] No inhabitant of Sherrington received a gift in the early 1990s.[12]

SHREWTON

SHREWTON[13] lies on Salisbury Plain 9 km. WNW. of Amesbury. The parish, which also contained the village or hamlet of Netton, in 1800 had 22 a. in three detached parcels surrounded mainly by Winterbourne Stoke parish.[14] In 1885 the detached lands were transferred to Winterbourne Stoke and a further 2 a. to Rollestone. Thereafter Shrewton parish measured 2,203 a. (892 ha.); it was increased to 7,041 a. (2,849 ha.) by the addition of Maddington and Rollestone parishes in 1934.[15]

The three estates which together made up the old Shrewton parish, taking their name from the river later called the Till, were among many called Winterbourne in 1086.[16] In the late 12th century the village was apparently called Winterbourne on the Hills (super montes),[17] although its lands were no higher than those of its neighbours and namesakes, and from the mid 13th century, when the nuns of Lacock acquired its church, it was sometimes called Maiden Winterbourne.[18] The name Shrewton (sheriff's 'tun'), in use from 1236, commemorates the shrievalties of Edward of Salisbury, who held the three estates in 1086, and his successors as owner and sheriff, and it replaced the name Winterbourne.[19] The village was sometimes called Shrewton Virgo.[20]

Shrewton's south-west boundary follows the Till. Its other boundaries, across downland, are mainly straight: that to the west was straightened at inclosure in 1801.[21] To the east the boundary crosses a low summit on which is a Neolithic camp,[22] and elsewhere there are minor diversions where it crosses roads.

Chalk outcrops over the whole parish; gravel has been deposited beside the Till and in a dry valley north-east of the church. Near the river the land is below 91 m., on the downs mainly between 107 m. and 131 m.: the highest points, c. 140 m., are in the north and east corners.[23] As its old name suggests, the Till sometimes fails in summer, and from the 18th century severe winter floods are recorded.[24] From the Middle Ages the more northerly downs provided pasture, chiefly for sheep, and the lower slopes were ploughed.[25] The detached portions of the parish were meadow land.[26] In the 11th century one of the three estates was well wooded,[27] but in the late 18th there was little woodland in the parish.[28] On scattered sites 25 a. of wood had been planted by c. 1840;[29] and in the late 20th century there were c. 70 a., mainly firs on the downland. From c. 1900 the northern half of the parish was used for military training and not cultivated.[30]

An east–west road across the parish, crossing the Till near the church, was the main road between London and Bridgwater (Som.), via Amesbury and Warminster, in 1675.[31] It was closed in Amesbury parish probably c. 1761, and soon after then a new Amesbury–Warminster turnpike road was made further south, crossing the Till near Maddington church. West of Shrewton church the earlier road has become a rough track; east of the church it has been tarmacadamed and, as London Road, remains in

[4] Char. Don. H.C. 511 (1816), xvi (2), 1338–9; W.R.O. 1508/7; for the Lamberts, above, manor; church.
[5] Endowed Char. Wilts. (S. Div.), 626–7.
[6] W.R.O., L 2, Sherrington.
[7] Inf. from Major Lewis; below, this section.
[8] Endowed Char. Wilts. (S. Div.), 627; W.R.O., L 2, Sherrington.
[9] Inf. from Major Lewis.
[10] Princ. Regy. Fam. Div., will of Sir Sidney Herbert, 1939.
[11] W.R.O., L 2, Sherrington.
[12] Inf. from Major Lewis.
[13] This article was written in 1990, later additions being dated. Maps used include O.S. Maps 6", Wilts. XLVII, LIII–LIV (1887–9 and later edns.); 1/25,000, SU 04, SU 14 (1958 edns.); 1/50,000, sheet 184 (1979 edn.); 1", sheet 14 (1817 edn.).
[14] W.R.O., EA/59.
[15] Census, 1881; 1891; 1931.
[16] V.C.H. Wilts. ii, pp. 136, 138, 179–80; P.N. Wilts. (E.P.N.S.), 10; below, manors.

[17] Bradenstoke Cart. (W.R.S. xxxv), pp. 94–5, 104, 187.
[18] Lacock Chart. (W.R.S. xxxiv), p. 12; Cal. Close, 1413–19, 436; Cal. Inq. p.m. Hen. VII, ii, pp. 458–9; below, church. Maddington, in which a manor belonged to Amesbury priory, was also called Maiden Winterbourne: above, Maddington, intro.
[19] P.N. Wilts. (E.P.N.S.), 236; Cal. Chart. R. 1226–57, 221; Complete Peerage, xi. 373–9; below, manors.
[20] J. Speed, Map of Wilts. (1611); J. Ogilby, Brit. (1675), pl. 32.
[21] W.R.O., EA/59.
[22] Below, this section.
[23] Geol. Surv. Map 1", drift, sheet 282 (1967 edn.).
[24] Bristol Univ. Libr., Wansbrough MS. 10/25; ibid. 68; W.R.O. 1336/88; inf. from Sir Rohan Delacombe, Shrewton Manor.
[25] Below, econ. hist.
[26] W.R.O., EA/59.
[27] V.C.H. Wilts. ii, p. 136.
[28] Andrews and Dury, Map (W.R.S. viii), pl. 8.
[29] W.R.O., tithe award.
[30] Below, this section.
[31] Ogilby, Brit. pl. 32.

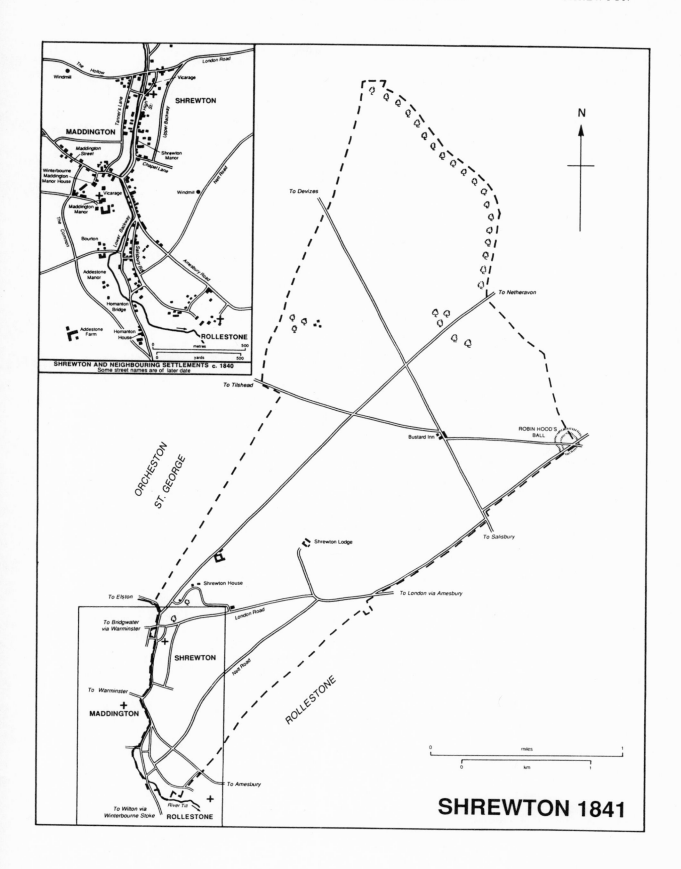

SHREWTON AND NEIGHBOURING SETTLEMENTS c. 1840
Some street names are of later date

SHREWTON 1841

use. The second Amesbury–Warminster road was disturnpiked in 1871. Where it left the south end of the village it was called Amesbury Road in 1990. A Devizes–Salisbury road across the north part of the parish was turnpiked in 1761 and disturnpiked in 1870.[32] Two roads, each on the course it followed in 1773, link the old London–Bridgwater road and the turnpike road which superseded it. Across high ground to the east Nett Road was so called in the 1880s. Near the river the other leads from the church to Winterbourne Stoke and Wilton: it crosses the river over Homanton bridge, rebuilt in 1956, and in 1990 was called High Street north of the turnpike road, Lower Backway south of it. From the junction of Lower Backway and Amesbury Road, Salisbury Road leads between them to Rollestone. The north part of Salisbury Road and the south part of Lower Backway were tarmacadamed and in the later 20th century took the Winterbourne Stoke and Wilton traffic. The north part of Lower Backway was then a footpath. In the late 18th century there were various tracks across the plain,[33] and new roads were made to farmsteads on the downs in the early 19th.[34] When artillery ranges were opened on the plain c. 1900 the Devizes–Salisbury road was closed north of the Bustard inn and the Amesbury–Warminster road became part of a new Devizes–Salisbury road.[35] In 1990 a road leading west from the Bustard to Tilshead was also a public road. In 1898 the London & South Western Railway was empowered to build a spur from its line at Grateley (Hants) to Amesbury and Shrewton; it did not build the Shrewton portion.[36]

Evidence of prehistoric activity within the parish has been found chiefly in the northern half. A Neolithic causewayed camp, Robin Hood's Ball, on the boundary at the east corner may have been the site of earlier occupation. Nearby there are five barrows or their sites, and others lie further west and north-west. In the north a field system extended over 40 a. Pagan Saxon artefacts associated with a burial were found west of Nett Road.[37]

In 1377 Shrewton had 49 poll-tax payers, Netton 40.[38] The population of the parish was 269 in 1801: an increase to 399 in 1811 prompted contemporary comment but no explanation. The population continued to increase until 1871 and there was another exceptionally steep rise from 571 to 682 between 1851 and 1861. Between 1871 and 1891 it fell from 757 to 548 but it rose again thereafter, reaching 631 in 1931. The population of the enlarged parish was 1,259 in 1951,[39] 1,780 in 1991.[40]

Before 1800 Shrewton village[41] consisted of buildings around the church and on the east side of High Street. Buildings on the other side of the Till in Maddington made a west side to High Street, at the north end of which some west of the Till were in Shrewton. In 1800 the eastern limit of the plots in High Street was marked by a parallel lane, called Backway or Upper Backway from the 1880s. A large farmstead was north of the church and London Road, the vicarage house was north-west of the church, and Shrewton Manor and two or more farmyards were south of the church in High Street.[42] After the Amesbury–Warminster road was turnpiked more buildings were erected at and south of its junction with High Street. As a result of that and of later growth,[43] Shrewton and Maddington villages coalesced. The enlarged settlement, now known only as Shrewton, also embraced Netton and Rollestone.[44] Apart from the church, the vicarage house, and Shrewton Manor, the original Shrewton part of the settlement contains few buildings of earlier than the 19th century. A lock-up or blindhouse of c. 1700 standing between the turnpike road and the river at the south end of High Street was moved a few metres south in 1974.[45]

Netton village or hamlet may have stood on the gravel beside lanes east of the Winterbourne Stoke road in the south corner of the parish: c. 15 buildings stood there in 1773[46] and the names Nett and Netton survived for fields, downs, and a road in the south and east parts of the parish.[47] In 1800 there were buildings beside Lower Backway and Salisbury Road.[48] Two thatched cottages, possibly 17th-century, survive.

The growth of Shrewton as a minor centre of trade and commerce in the 19th century,[49] and the rapid increase in its population,[50] were accompanied by the rebuilding of many houses, usually in brick or rendered, and the building of many cottages, some in pairs or short terraces. A terrace of cottages, some with entrances above street level, replaced earlier buildings on the south side of London Road. Between 1800 and 1840 there was building on the north-east side of Amesbury Road, north-west of its junction with Nett Road, and beside Salisbury Road, where a nonconformist chapel was built. Another chapel was built at right angles to High Street in what became Chapel Lane.[51] A severe flood in January 1841 affected all the villages of the Till valley and apparently caused greatest destruction in Shrewton, although reports of 28 houses destroyed and 300 people left homeless may have included the Maddington part of the village. In 1842 four cottages, paid for by a relief fund subscribed to nationally, were built in Salisbury Road.[52] A nonconformist chapel and a

32 L.J. xxx. 77, 138; V.C.H. Wilts. iv. 270; above, Amesbury, intro. (roads).
33 Andrews and Dury, Map (W.R.S. viii), pl. 8; O.S. Map 6", Wilts. LIII (1889 edn.); date on bridge.
34 O.S. Map 1", sheet 14 (1817 edn.); W.R.O., tithe award.
35 V.C.H. Wilts. iv. 266; for the Bustard, below, this section.   36 V.C.H. Wilts. iv. 291.
37 Ibid. i (1), 105, 178, 190, 233, 278, 293; W.A.M. xlvi. 169–70.   38 V.C.H. Wilts. iv. 308.
39 Ibid. 357; Hoare, Mod. Wilts. Branch and Dole, 34.
40 Census, 1991.   41 See plate facing p. 250.

42 Andrews and Dury, Map (W.R.S. viii), pl. 8; O.S. Map 6", Wilts. LIII (1889 edn.); W.R.O., EA/59; above, Maddington, intro. (Maddington).   43 Above and below, this section.
44 For Rollestone, V.C.H. Wilts. xi. 208–12.
45 Wilts. Gaz. and Herald, 16 Feb. 1978.
46 Andrews and Dury, Map (W.R.S. viii), pl. 8.
47 P.N. Wilts. (E.P.N.S.), 236; W.R.O., tithe award.
48 W.R.O., EA/59.   49 Below, econ. hist.
50 Above, this section.
51 W.R.O., EA/59; ibid. tithe award; below, nonconf.
52 W.A.M. xlix. 262, where the flood's date is wrongly given as 1871; W.R.O. 1336/98; below, charities.

school were built in High Street in the 1860s, and other new buildings between 1840 and 1886 included a large house called Highfield House, near the south end of High Street, and a group of houses called Chalk Hill around the junction of Nett Road and Amesbury Road.[53] A road running south from the junction was later called Chalk Hill.

In the 20th century the village doubled in size, and most new building was in the old Shrewton parish. Between 1900 and 1950 cottages, including two trios dated 1911 and 1914, houses, bungalows, and farmsteads were built in Nett Road, and houses, including two pairs with thatched roofs, and bungalows were built on new sites in Salisbury Road and Chalk Hill. Sundial Cottages, a pair of cottages on the north side of London Road, were rebuilt in vernacular style in 1934.[54] Council houses were built in Chalk Hill, 12 in 1936,[55] and east of the village in London Road, 12 in 1927 and 6 in 1933. Mainly in the 1950s the local authority built c. 75 houses on rising ground at the north end of the village east of Upper Backway.[56] Old people's bungalows were built in Parson's Green, c. 30 in the 1960s west of Upper Backway further south, and Hindes Meadow, 16 in the 1980s on the site of the large farmstead north of the church. In addition to infilling, private building in the 1960s, 1970s, and 1980s included Meadway, c. 50 houses south-west of Amesbury Road, Copper Beech Close, 6 houses south-east of Chalk Hill, Highfield Rise, 45 bungalows east of Upper Backway, and 6 houses in Chapel Lane. More bungalows were being built between Highfield Rise and Nett Road in 1990.

In 1800 there was no building within the parish on the downs. The Bustard inn was built beside the Devizes–Salisbury road between 1800 and 1811,[57] and between 1800 and 1817 Shrewton Lodge, a thatched *cottage ornée*, was built 1.5 km. north-east of the church.[58] Shrewton House, set in ornamental grounds north of the village, was built between 1820 and 1840 to replace the farmstead north of the church. The new house, a plain classical villa, has a Doric loggia along the main south front. A lodge was built south-west of it and a farmstead north-east of it. Barns of similar date near the parish's north-western boundary[59] were demolished in the earlier 20th century, when scattered military buildings were erected north of the Bustard.[60]

Inns stood beside the three main roads across the parish. The George, in 1840 and 1990 on the south side of London Road near its junction with

High Street, was presumably on that site when mentioned in 1607 and 1780.[61] That and the Sun, mentioned in 1746[62] but not by name thereafter, were presumably among the four alehouses in the parish in the 1750s and 1760s.[63] The Catherine Wheel, mentioned in 1780,[64] was presumably built soon after 1761 to serve the Amesbury–Warminster turnpike road[65] and stands at its junction with High Street: friendly societies may have met there and at the George in 1803.[66] The Royal Oak on the north side of Amesbury Road was open in 1867;[67] the Wheatsheaf in Salisbury Road, open c. 1886, was apparently closed soon afterwards;[68] the Plume of Feathers north-west of the church was opened c. 1910.[69] The Bustard was open c. 1840[70] and from the 1860s,[71] may have been a private house in the 1850s,[72] and was a temperance hotel in 1900.[73] It, the George, the Catherine Wheel, the Royal Oak, and the Plume of Feathers were open in 1990.

From 1863 rook hawking on Salisbury Plain was organized from the Bustard; the Old Hawking club, founded in 1864, had its headquarters there until c. 1875 and again from 1903 until 1924.[74] There was a croquet ground south of Shrewton House c. 1886[75] and a polo ground near Shrewton Lodge in 1900.[76]

The northern half of the parish, c. 1,100 a., was acquired for the army between 1897 and 1902[77] and was thereafter the site of artillery ranges used by the (Royal) School of Artillery based at Larkhill in Durrington. A narrow-gauge railway in the north corner of the parish was built between 1923 and 1958 to serve the ranges and was dismantled before 1984.[78] Between 1940 and 1944 land west of the Bustard was used as a military airfield.[79]

Sir Cecil Chubb, Bt. (1876–1934), who bought Stonehenge in 1915 and gave it to the nation in 1918, was born in Shrewton.[80]

MANORS AND OTHER ESTATES. Estates in Shrewton were held in 1066 by Alric, 13 hides and 3 yardlands, Alward, 3 hides, 1 yardland, and 4 a., and Ulueva, 3 hides. All 20 hides were held in 1086 by Edward of Salisbury, from whom Godfrey held Ulueva's estate and Tetbald held Alward's.[81] Edward's estates passed in turn to his son Walter (d. 1147), Walter's son Patrick, earl of Salisbury (d. 1168), and with the earldom to Patrick's son William (d. 1196) and William's daughter Ela (d. 1261) and her husband William Longespée, earl of Salisbury (d. 1226). Ela took

53 O.S. Map 6", Wilts. LIII (1889 edn.); W.R.O., tithe award; below, nonconf.; educ.
54 Date on bldg.   55 W.R.O., G 1/602/2.
56 Ibid.; ibid. G 1/501/1; G 1/603/1.
57 Ibid. EA/59; Bristol Univ. Libr., Wansbrough MS. 122.
58 O.S. Map 1", sheet 14 (1817 edn.); W.R.O., EA/59.
59 C. Greenwood, *Map of Wilts.* (1820); W.R.O., tithe award.
60 O.S. Maps 6", Wilts. LIV. NW. (1901, 1926 edns.).
61 P.R.O., C 142/375, no. 43; W.R.O., A 1/345/367; ibid. tithe award.   62 Wilts. Cuttings, xxiv. 43.
63 W.R.O., A 1/326/1–2.
64 Ibid. A 1/345/367.   65 Above, this section.
66 *Poor Law Abstract, 1804*, 558–9.
67 *Kelly's Dir. Wilts.* (1867).

68 O.S. Maps 6", Wilts. LIII (1889 edn.); LIII. SE. (1901 edn.).
69 W.R.O., Inland Revenue, val. reg. 140.
70 Ibid. tithe award.
71 *Kelly's Dir. Wilts.* (1867 and later edns.).
72 Wilts. Cuttings, xviii. 58.   73 Ibid. xvi. 365.
74 R. Upton, *O for a Falconer's Voice*, 32, 36, 45, 130, 149, 167, 171.
75 O.S. Map 6", Wilts. LIII (1889 edn.).
76 Wilts. Cuttings, xvi. 365.
77 Below, manors.
78 O.S. Maps, 1/25,000, SU 04 (1958 edn.); 6", Wilts. LIV. NW. (1901, 1926 edns.); 1/10,000, SU 04 NE. (1984 edn.).
79 N. D. G. James, *Plain Soldiering*, 175–6.
80 *W.A.M.* xlvii. 130.
81 *V.C.H. Wilts.* ii, pp. 136, 138.

the veil in 1238,[82] and in 1242–3 her son William Longespée (d. 1250), styled earl of Salisbury, was overlord of 3 knights' fees in Shrewton. William was succeeded by his son Sir William Longespée (d. 1257), and he by his daughter Margaret, from 1261 countess of Salisbury,[83] wife of Henry de Lacy, earl of Lincoln (d. 1311). Henry held the overlordship with a small honor of Shrewton. The overlordship and honor passed from him to his daughter Alice, countess of Lincoln and of Salisbury, wife of Thomas, earl of Lancaster (d. 1322).[84]

The honor may have been granted in 1319 to John de Warenne, earl of Surrey, for life and, under duress, in 1322 may have been granted by John to the elder Hugh le Despenser, earl of Winchester (d. 1326). A life interest was restored in 1327 to John (d. 1347) and his wife Joan (d. 1361),[85] who in 1348 granted her interest to Edward, prince of Wales.[86] In 1361 the honor reverted to William de Montagu, earl of Salisbury[87] (d. 1397), possibly under a grant of 1337 to his father,[88] and it apparently passed to his son John, earl of Salisbury, who died and was attainted in 1400. In 1409 it was restored to John's son Thomas, earl of Salisbury.[89] No later reference to the honor has been found.

The overlordship was in 1325 granted by Alice, countess of Lincoln, and her husband Ebles Lestrange to the younger Hugh le Despenser, Lord le Despenser, who forfeited it on his execution in 1326.[90] It may have been granted in 1337 with the earldom of Salisbury to William de Montagu (d. 1344) and was held with the honor by his son William, earl of Salisbury (d. 1397).[91] It passed to the younger William's relict Elizabeth,[92] reverted on her death in 1415 to Thomas, earl of Salisbury,[93] and thereafter evidently descended with the earldom.[94]

Alexander Cheverell held 2 knights' fees in Shrewton in 1242–3[95] and was succeeded in 1260 by his son Sir John (d. 1281). The estate passed to Sir John's son Sir Alexander (d. by 1310),[96] to Sir Alexander's daughter Joan, wife of John St. Lo (d. 1313 or 1314), and presumably with Little Cheverell manor in turn to her son Sir John St. Lo (d. after 1372) and Sir John's son Sir John (d. 1375). The younger Sir John's relict Margaret (d. 1412) held the estate with her husband Sir Peter Courtenay (d. 1405) and was succeeded by her grandson William Botreaux, Lord Botreaux (d. 1462),[97] who held it in 1417.[98]

John of Kingston held land in Shrewton in 1291,[99] possibly the 4 yardlands and 14 a. later held by Nicholas Kingston (d. c. 1323) and forfeited by Nicholas's brother John, a rebel.[1] John may have re-entered the estate in 1326, as he did an estate in Steeple Langford.[2] It descended to his son Thomas and in 1380 was held by Thomas's son Sir John (fl. 1383).[3]

SHREWTON manor, perhaps derived from the Cheverells' estate, the Kingstons', or both, was held in 1493 by Thomas Hussey (d. 1503), who was succeeded by his son Henry.[4] It later belonged to Sir William Brounker (d. 1596), may have belonged to his father Sir Henry Brounker, and in 1596 was sold by his relict Martha and his son Henry in portions. The lordship and demesne lands were bought by Robert Wansborough (d. 1630)[5] and passed from father to son to Robert (d. 1639), Robert (d. 1675), Robert (d. 1697), Robert (d. 1700), Robert (d. 1704), Robert (d. 1706), Robert (will proved 1715), Robert (fl. 1725), and Robert (d. 1783).[6] The last Robert's estate was divided between his sons John (d. 1833) and Charles. John's portion was acquired after 1831[7] by the Revd. Samuel Heathcote who, having bought other land in Shrewton, owned 860 a. in the parish c. 1840.[8] Most of Heathcote's estate was sold after his death in 1846.[9] The lands formerly John Wansborough's were bought as Shrewton Lodge estate, 425 a., by C. R. M. Smith, husband of Heathcote's granddaughter Katherine Heathcote.[10] Charles Wansborough (d. 1834) devised his estate, including the lordship of Shrewton manor, jointly to his children Charles, Robert, Martha, and Jane.[11] About 1840 Charles and Robert held 240 a. in Shrewton,[12] and by will dated 1848 Charles devised the estate for sale.[13] The lordship, however, passed to his son Charles and grandson Charles Wansborough[14] (d. 1890).[15] The land was probably bought c. 1848 by C. R. M. Smith (d. 1882) whose Shrewton Lodge estate, 680 a., was sold in 1883 to H. N. B. Good.[16] In 1891 the estate was bought by George Kirby. In 1898 Kirby sold 330 a. to the War Department, and the Ministry of Defence owned that land in 1990.[17] The rest of the estate

82 *Complete Peerage*, xi. 373–81.
83 Ibid. 382–4; *Bk. of Fees*, ii. 721.
84 *Rot. Hund.* (Rec. Com.), ii (1), 254; *Complete Peerage*, vii. 686–7.
85 *Cal. Pat.* 1327–30, 21; *Complete Peerage*, iv. 262–6; xii (1), 508–11; cf. *V.C.H. Wilts.* vii. 128; above, Amesbury, manors (Amesbury).   86 *Cal. Pat.* 1348–50, 93.
87 Ibid. 1361–4, 131.
88 *W.A.M.* lii. 84; *Cal. Inq. p.m.* xvii, p. 322; for the earls of Salisbury, *Complete Peerage*, xi. 385–93.
89 *Cal. Close*, 1405–9, 443.
90 *Feet of F.* 1272–1327 (W.R.S. i), pp. 132–3; *Complete Peerage*, iv. 267–70.   91 *Cal. Inq. p.m.* xvii, p. 321.
92 *Cal. Close*, 1396–9, 188–9.
93 *Cal. Fine R.* 1413–22, 97.
94 e.g. *Cal. Inq. p.m. Hen. VII*, ii, pp. 458–9.
95 *Bk. of Fees*, ii. 721.
96 *V.C.H. Wilts.* x. 55; *Cal. Inq. p.m.* v, p. 145.
97 *Cal. Close*, 1402–5, 440; *V.C.H. Wilts.* x. 55.
98 *Cal. Close*, 1413–19, 436.
99 *Feet of F.* 1272–1327 (W.R.S. i), p. 37.
1 *Cal. Inq. p.m.* vi, p. 252; *Cal. Fine R.* 1319–27, 330.

2 Above, Steeple Langford, manor (Kingston's).
3 *Cal. Pat.* 1377–81, 490; P.R.O., C 260/94, no. 59.
4 *Cal. Inq. p.m. Hen. VII*, ii, pp. 458–9.
5 *W.A.M.* liv. 416–17; Bristol Univ. Libr., Wansbrough MS. 11; ibid. 14; below, local govt.
6 Bristol Univ. Libr., Wansbrough MS. 42/3.
7 Ibid.; W.R.O., A 1/345/367; mon. in church.
8 W.R.O., tithe award; below, this section.
9 E. D. Heathcote, *Fam. of Heathcote* (Winchester, 1899), 134; Hants R.O. 27M54/12.
10 Heathcote, op. cit. 133; W.A.S. Libr., sale cat. xxviii (H), no. 3.
11 Bristol Univ. Libr., Wansbrough MS. 34; ibid. 42/3.
12 W.R.O., tithe award.
13 Bristol Univ. Libr., Wansbrough MS. 107.
14 Ibid. 42/11; *Kelly's Dir. Wilts.* (1859 and later edns.).
15 *Endowed Char. Wilts.* (S. Div.), 299–300; Wilts. Cuttings, xvi. 365.
16 Wilts. Cuttings, i. 198; G.P.L., Treas. Solicitor, 511/51.
17 Wilts. Cuttings, vii. 30; inf. from Defence Land Agent, Durrington.

was sold in 1900,[18] perhaps to Robert Coombes, the owner in 1910.[19] By 1921 Coombes's estate had been bought by John Wort, George Way, and J. H. Wort, in business together as Wort & Way, builders. After the firm was dissolved in 1967,[20] the land belonged to members of the Wort family, from whom the southern portion was bought by Mr. J. C. J. Tarrant, the northern by Mr. E. G. N. Grant, the owners in 1990.[21]

Shrewton Manor, apparently built for Robert Wansborough (d. 1630) and occupied by Wansboroughs until 1890,[22] has a long north–south range of flint and stone with a short northern cross wing dated 1602. The wing was extended eastwards in the 18th century and the extension was refitted in the early 19th. Service rooms at the south end of the main range were replaced c. 1900. East of the house was a walled farmyard,[23] now a garden, in which a timber-framed granary and a flint and stone pigeon house, both possibly 18th-century, survive.

In 1596 Martha and Henry Brounker sold part of Shrewton manor to Thomas Tooker,[24] who was succeeded in 1607 by his son Charles.[25] The land was held in 1638 by Thomas Tooker (d. by 1650), in 1656 by John Sainsbury, and in 1662 by John Gilbert[26] (fl. 1690).[27] In 1712 a moiety was settled on Charles Gilbert.[28] Lands bought by Robert Gennings from William Gilbert and from William Maundrell and Thomas Franklin probably comprised both moieties of the estate; Gennings bought other land in Shrewton and at his death in 1739 held 3⅛ yardlands, which he devised to his wife Mary and son Robert.[29] In 1751 the estate was held by John Gennings[30] (d. 1762), who devised it to Robert Gennings.[31] One or more of that name held the estate, c. 250 a., until 1829,[32] when a Robert Gennings was succeeded by his kinsman John Ingram[33] and Ingram sold it to the Revd. Samuel Heathcote.[34] Some lands were apparently sold between 1846 and 1850,[35] probably including 150 a. bought in 1898 by the War Department and owned in 1990 by the Ministry of Defence.[36] The remainder passed with Rollestone manor.[37]

Other lands perhaps derived from Shrewton manor were held in 1780 by Elizabeth Colebrooke and in 1785 by Jane Folliott, who in 1800 held c. 290 a. in Shrewton.[38] As Jane Fussell she sold the lands c. 1818 to Joseph Gilbert. With Gil-

bert's other Shrewton estate they were sold to Thomas Sheppard.[39]

By the mid 13th century Bradenstoke priory had acquired piecemeal an estate in Shrewton, later *WINTERBOURNE SHREWTON* manor. In the later 12th century 1 yardland was granted by Boemund to John son of Stephen and by John to the priory. William, earl of Salisbury (d. 1196), confirmed that grant and between 1168 and 1179 gave 100s. a year from Shrewton to the priory. Also between 1168 and 1179 Nicholas d'Epaignes gave 3 yardlands which he had been granted by the earl, and in the early 13th century Roger Young sold to the priory ½ yardland which he held of Sir Alexander Cheverell. The priory also held in Shrewton 3 yardlands given in 1246 by John Cheney and his wife Margery, 10s. rent received in an exchange with Stanley abbey in 1247, 3 yardlands given in 1256 by Robert le Veel,[40] 3 yardlands given before 1275 by Richard Langford, who in 1242 held ½ knight's fee there of the earldom of Salisbury,[41] and 2 yardlands given in 1303 by Nicholas Ingram.[42] The estate passed to the Crown at the Dissolution and was bought in 1560 by Robert Davye and Henry Dynne,[43] possibly feoffees for Sir Henry Brounker who held it in 1564 or 1565.[44] Brounker (d. 1569) was succeeded in turn by his son (Sir) William[45] (d. 1596), and by Sir William's son Henry.[46] The manor was sold before Henry's death in 1598, probably in 1596: the lordship may have been bought then with that of Shrewton manor by Robert Wansborough,[47] and the lands by William Goldisborough who held them at his death in 1608. From Goldisborough the lands descended in the direct line to Robert (d. 1632), Nicholas (d. 1642), Robert (d. 1702), and Robert (d. 1739), whose relict Elizabeth held them until her death in 1765. They apparently passed to her nephew R. G. Cripps (d. 1782),[48] whose relict Sarah (d. c. 1810) held c. 450 a. in Shrewton in 1800, when she was the wife of William Goddard.[49] The estate passed to Sarah's nephew Joseph Gilbert,[50] who with William Gilbert sold it and other lands in Shrewton in 1832 to Thomas Sheppard.[51] By will proved 1858 Sheppard gave his estate there, c. 800 a., to his son Walter (fl. 1871). In 1876, however, it was sold to perform trusts under the will[52] and was bought by T. L. Mills (d. 1909).[53] Mills sold 570

18 W.R.O. 776/315.
19 Ibid. Inland Revenue, val. reg. 140.
20 Ibid. G 1/500/16; above, Amesbury, manors (Earldom).
21 Inf. from Mr. J. C. J. Tarrant, Rollestone Manor Farm.   22 Wilts. Cuttings, xvi. 365.
23 W.R.O., EA/59.
24 *Antrobus D.* (W.R.S. iii), p. 66.
25 P.R.O., C 142/375, no. 43.
26 Bristol Univ. Libr., Wansbrough MS. 36/1; 36/6–7.
27 P.R.O., CP 25/2/887/2 Wm. and Mary Trin.
28 Ibid. CP 25/2/980/11 Anne Mich.
29 W.R.O. 451/492, copy will of Rob. Gennings, 1739.
30 Ibid. 451/492, deed, Gennings to Keevil, 1751.
31 Ibid. 451/492, copy will of John Gennings, 1762.
32 Ibid. 451/493, lease, Estcourt to Gennings, 1776; ibid. A 1/345/367; ibid. EA/59.
33 Ibid. 451/492, copy will of Rob. Gennings, 1829.
34 Ibid. 451/492, deed, Ingram to Heathcote, 1829.
35 Hants R.O. 27M54/12.
36 Inf. from Defence Land Agent.
37 Below, this section.

38 W.R.O., A 1/345/367; ibid. EA/59.
39 Ibid. A 1/345/367; Hoare, *Mod. Wilts.* Branch and Dole, 35; below, this section.
40 *Bradenstoke Cart.* (W.R.S. xxxv), pp. 103–4, 159–60, 187.
41 *Rot. Hund.* (Rec. Com.), ii (1), 254; *Bk. of Fees*, ii. 721.
42 *Bradenstoke Cart.* (W.R.S. xxxv), p. 162.
43 *Cal. Pat.* 1558–60, 276.
44 *W.N. & Q.* v. 179–80.
45 P.R.O., C 142/152, no. 166.
46 Ibid. C 142/247, no. 98.
47 Ibid. C 142/257, no. 80; above, this section.
48 A. Goldsborough, *Memorials of Goldesborough Fam.* (priv. print. 1930), 276, 287, pedigree facing p. 274; W.R.O., A 1/345/367.   49 W.R.O., A 1/345/367; ibid. EA/59.
50 Hoare, *Mod. Wilts.* Branch and Dole, 35.
51 W.R.O. 2210/2, acct. of Alfred Whitaker, 1832; above, this section.
52 Burke, *Land. Gent.* (1871), 1254; W.R.O., tithe award; ibid. 2210/2, draft order, Harvey v. Harvey, 1876.
53 Wilts. Cuttings, xvi. 365.

a. to the War Department in 1897, and the Ministry of Defence owned that land in 1990.[54] In 1919 Mills's executors sold the remaining 230 a. to George Williams (d. 1926),[55] whose great-grandchildren J. and E. Grant held c. 270 a. in the old parish of Shrewton in 1990.[56]

In the later 16th century Rollestone manor included land and pasture rights in Shrewton,[57] and at inclosure in 1801 an allotment of 143 a. was made to the lord of that manor, Sir Nathaniel Holland, Bt.[58] (d. 1811). It passed with the manor to his relict Harriett (will proved 1825), to her nephew Robert Brudenell, earl of Cardigan, and by sale in 1827 to the Revd. Samuel Heathcote (d. 1846). With Rollestone c. 210 a. in Shrewton passed to Heathcote's son William in trust for William's children, were divided in 1882 among the children, and, as the subject of a Chancery suit, were sold in 1902.[59] The War Department bought 54 a., which the Ministry of Defence owned in 1990,[60] and T. W. Pratt the rest. Pratt's land passed in 1932 to G. R. Smith (d. 1972).[61] In 1990 part was owned by his relict, Mrs. Janetta Smith, part by Mr. J. C. J. Tarrant, and part by Mr. D. W. Johnson.[62]

Lacock abbey appropriated Shrewton church under a grant of 1241. In 1242 Ives the merchant and his wife Sibyl gave to the abbey a tenement and rents in Shrewton, and Hugh Burgoyne and his wife Maud gave 20s. rent from Ives's tenement.[63] The *RECTORY* estate consisted of tithes and two small closes at the Dissolution,[64] probably only of tithes in the 17th century.[65] In 1545 it was granted to John Pope,[66] perhaps a trustee for John Lambert, to whom he conveyed it in 1546.[67] Lambert (d. 1553) was succeeded by his son William,[68] who sold the estate in 1570 to William Partridge[69] (d. 1578). Partridge was succeeded by his son Robert[70] (d. 1600), who devised it to his daughters Elizabeth, wife of William Cartwright, and Anne, wife of Edward Masters.[71] Cartwright and Masters held it in 1650.[72] In 1655 William Cartwright, Thomas Cartwright, and Thomas's wife Susan held a moiety and between 1663 and 1674 Thomas and Susan sold portions of tithes.[73] Thomas retained some tithes in 1681,[74] but they were apparently sold thereafter. By 1657 the Masterses' moiety had passed to their daughter Elizabeth[75] and it too was later sold in portions. In 1801, when

they were exchanged for land, the rectorial tithes of Shrewton were held by 17 owners.[76]

St. Denis's priory, Southampton, had lands in Shrewton in 1249.[77] In 1275 St. Denis's held 3 yardlands there, Ivychurch priory held 2 yardlands, and Breamore priory (Hants) 1 yardland.[78] Breamore had lands in Netton in 1432:[79] nothing further is known of the holding. After the Dissolution the holdings of Ivychurch, 5 yardlands, and St. Denis's, c. 45 a. and 8s. rent, were granted, in 1562, to Richard Middlecot:[80] the later history of the land has not been traced. Before 1275 Richard Syfrewast granted to Durford abbey (Suss.) ½ knight's fee in Shrewton,[81] which he had held of the earldom of Salisbury in 1242–3.[82] At the Dissolution the abbey held only rents from free tenants in Shrewton.[83] Edington priory had rights of pasture for 50 sheep in Shrewton held with land in Orcheston St. George at the Dissolution.[84]

ECONOMIC HISTORY. In 1086 Shrewton had land for 12 ploughteams. The three estates had 7 teams and 11 *servi* on the demesne lands, and there were 17 *villani* and 15 bordars with 4 or more teams. There were 16 a. of meadow, pasture measuring 13 a., 6 furlongs by 4, and 1 league by ½, and 30 a. of woodland. Of two of the estates the demesne was the greater part.[85]

Evidence from the 16th century shows Shrewton and Netton to have each had open fields and common downland pasture, but then, as later, each was shared by the lord and tenants of both manors in the parish.[86] Shrewton's lands probably formed a strip between the Till and the northern corner of the parish, Netton's presumably a similar strip between the Till and the east corner. Each had three open fields: in the 16th and 17th centuries Netton's were called Middle, Middlehurst, and South or the field next to Rollestone,[87] in the 18th Shrewton's were called Middle, Down, and the field next to Elston.[88] Shrewton had a cow down[89] but otherwise the downs were for sheep. There were c. 650 a. of open fields, c. 1,250 a. of downland pasture.[90] In the earlier 17th century Netton's arable was assessed as 26 yardlands, each of 24 a. with pasture for 40 sheep.[91] Landholders of Shrewton parish had common rights in the meadows which

54 Inf. from Defence Land Agent.
55 Wilts. Cuttings, xiv. 108; above, Orcheston St. Mary, manors (Orcheston St. Mary).
56 Inf. from Mrs. E. G. N. Grant, Quainton, Orcheston St. Mary.
57 P.R.O., C 3/61/9.
58 W.R.O., EA/59.
59 *V.C.H. Wilts.* xi. 210; G.E.C. *Baronetage*, v. 334; Heathcote, *Fam. of Heathcote*, 134.
60 Inf. from Defence Land Agent.
61 W.R.O. 776/142; ibid. Inland Revenue, val. reg. 140.
62 Inf. from Mr. Tarrant.
63 *Lacock Chart.* (W.R.S. xxiv), pp. 66–7; below, church.
64 P.R.O., SC 6/Hen. VIII/3985, rot. 30d.
65 Ibid. CP 25/2/372/22 Jas. I Mich.
66 *L. & P. Hen. VIII*, xx (2), p. 323.
67 Ibid. xxi (1), p. 693.
68 P.R.O., C 142/108, no. 126.
69 *Cal. Pat.* 1569–72, p. 144.
70 P.R.O., C 142/185, no. 85.
71 Ibid. C 142/268, no. 146.
72 *W.A.M.* xl. 395.

73 P.R.O., CP 25/2/609/1655 East.; CP 25/2/744/14 & 15 Chas. II Hil.; CP 25/2/746/26 Chas. II Trin.; W.R.O. 451/491, abstr. of title.
74 P.R.O., E 134/33 Chas. II Trin./1.
75 Bristol Univ. Libr., Wansbrough MS. 15/4.
76 W.R.O., EA/59.
77 P.R.O., CP 25/1/251/15, no. 32.
78 *Rot. Hund.* (Rec. Com.), ii (1), 254.
79 *Cat. Anct. D.* ii, B 3262.
80 *Cal. Pat.* 1560–3, 234; P.R.O., E 318/46/2436; ibid. SC 6/Hen. VIII/3969, rot. 28d.
81 *Rot. Hund.* (Rec. Com.), ii (1), 254.
82 *Bk. of Fees*, ii. 271.
83 P.R.O., SC 6/Hen. VIII/3674, rot. 17.
84 Ibid. SC 6/Hen. VIII/3985, rot. 36d.
85 *V.C.H. Wilts.* ii, pp. 136, 138.
86 *W.A.M.* xxiii. 33–9.
87 W.R.O., D 1/24/183/1; ibid. 906/W/223.
88 Bristol Univ. Libr., Wansbrough MS. 94.
89 P.R.O., C 3/61/9.
90 W.R.O., EA/59.
91 Ibid. D 1/24/183/1; *W.N. & Q.* vii. 573.

formed its detached parts[92] and were entitled to the hay, but not the aftermath, of a meadow in Winterbourne Stoke.[93]

In 1599 orders were made for the fields and pastures of Shrewton and Netton, which had apparently been mismanaged since the suspension of Shrewton manor court in 1596; how far they reflected earlier practice is not clear. Because sheep had died in recent winters for want of fodder, provisions were made for a common flock of weaker animals and for money to be collected at midsummer to buy hay. Shrewton and Netton each had a common flock: no more than 12 lambs were to be bred for each yardland in Shrewton and no more than 10 for each in Netton. Other rules governed the grazing of cattle and horses and the appointment of a hogherd each for Shrewton and Netton and of a hayward.[94] In the 1650s there were still separate flocks for Shrewton and Netton.[95]

There was little inclosure in the parish before 1800. Inclosures in Netton fields were ordered to be removed in 1615 and 1616[96] and apparently were not reinstated. In the 1670s part of Netton down, perhaps c. 70 a., was brought into cultivation by burnbaking and divided among those with pasture rights at the rate of 2 a. to the yardland.[97]

After the two manors in the parish were broken up in the later 16th century, mostly by sale to the tenants, there was little copyhold. No copyholder was mentioned in the orders of 1599 and tenurial business rarely came before the manor court. The orders were subscribed by 23 people, presumably all those occupying lands in the parish.[98] The largest farms may have been those derived from the demesnes of the two manors. The demesne of Shrewton manor comprised 160 a. and pasture rights in 1596,[99] and in 1654 the farmer had 190 a. sown and 302 sheep with 105 lambs. In the 1630s, although he sold wool, a larger part of his income was derived from corn. On some fields a three-course rotation of wheat, barley, and fallow was practised, on others there may have been a fourth course of oats.[1] In the 1660s the principal farm derived from Winterbourne Shrewton manor comprised 224 a. of arable, 10 a. of meadow, and rights of pasture.[2]

Common husbandry was ended by an award of 1801 under an Act of 1798. Allotments were made of the whole parish, except the village, replacing rights to arable, pasture, meadow, and rectorial tithes. On the arable, to the south-west, fields of 156 a., 99 a., and 75 a. were allotted; otherwise the average size of the new fields was c. 8 a. To the north-east 1,060 a. of downland were allotted in six parcels. About 1840 the parish was still about half arable and half pasture. There were 55 a. of meadow, including the detached 22 a., and 25 a. of wood, chiefly plantation on the downs. Most of the land lay in four farms. A scattered holding of 191 a. was worked from Shrewton Manor, and a farm of 410 a. was worked from buildings immediately north of it. The two others were worked from buildings outside the village, all built after 1800. The larger, 790 a., was worked from the farmstead near Shrewton House and from barns near the north-west boundary of the parish, and a compact farm of 445 a. was worked from Shrewton Lodge.[3]

The proportion of pasture apparently increased in the later 19th century. In 1886 lands worked from farmsteads in the parish included c. 650 a. of arable; from the 1870s permanent rough pasture apparently replaced sown grasses and clover. In 1876 there were c. 2,500 sheep and lambs and only 20 cattle. Less land was available for agriculture after military training began in the north part of the parish c. 1900: in 1916 only c. 400 a. were arable and only c. 700 sheep were kept. Cattle rearing, however, increased and c. 100 cattle, mainly for beef, were kept in 1916.[4] Most of the parish was pasture in the 1930s;[5] in 1990 there was arable and mixed farming in the south-western part, which was worked from farmsteads outside the old parish.[6]

A glover lived at Shrewton in 1755.[7] Shrewton's rapid growth in the 19th century was apparently achieved by becoming a minor centre for trade in an area where there were few towns. In 1841 c. 60 people in Shrewton were engaged in c. 30 trades, of which none was unusual for a rural village and none became prominent, but the proportion of tradesmen in the population was much larger than for surrounding villages. Shrewton Laundry at the north end of High Street was open in 1931.[8] It employed 25 people in 1986.[9]

MILLS. There was a mill on Godfrey's estate in 1086,[10] and a mill stood in Shrewton in 1341[11] and perhaps 1630. Between 1773 and 1793 a thatched, timber windmill was built north-west of Nett Road. From 1848 it was worked by members of the Maslen family.[12] It passed out of use between 1867 and 1886,[13] perhaps in 1877 when James Maslen was declared bankrupt,[14] and had been demolished by 1899.[15]

LOCAL GOVERNMENT. Shortly before 1275 honor courts for the earldom of Salisbury, previously held twice yearly at Chitterne, were

92 P.R.O., C 3/61/9.
93 *W.A.M.* xxxiv. 214.
94 Ibid. xxiii. 33–9; for the manor ct., below, local govt.
95 *W.A.M.* liv. 417.
96 Bristol Univ. Libr., Wansbrough MS. 36/1.
97 P.R.O., E 134/33 Chas. II Trin./1.
98 *W.A.M.* xxiii. 36–7; above, manors; below, local govt.
99 Bristol Univ. Libr., Wansbrough MS. 14.
1 *W.A.M.* liv. 417–19.
2 Goldsborough, *Goldesborough Fam.* 282.
3 W.R.O., EA/59; ibid. tithe award.
4 P.R.O., MAF 68/74, sheet 21; MAF 68/493, sheet 13; MAF 68/1063, sheet 12; MAF 68/1633, sheet 9; MAF 68/2203, sheet 8; MAF 68/2773, sheet 14.

5 [1st] Land Util. Surv. Map, sheet 122.
6 Inf. from Mr. J. C. J. Tarrant, Rollestone Manor Farm.   7 *Wilts. Apprentices* (W.R.S. xvii), p. 110.
8 *Kelly's Dir. Wilts.* (1848 and later edns.); P.R.O., HO 107/1167/12.
9 Wilts. Cuttings, xxx. 250.
10 *V.C.H. Wilts.* ii, p. 136.
11 *Inq. Non.* (Rec. Com.), 179.
12 M. Watts, *Wilts. Windmills*, 21–2; *Andrews and Dury, Map* (W.R.S. viii), pl. 8; W.R.O., EA/59.
13 *Kelly's Dir. Wilts.* (1867); O.S. Map 6", Wilts. LIII (1889 edn.).
14 Watts, *Wilts. Windmills*, 22.
15 O.S. Map 6", Wilts. LIII. SE. (1901 edn.).

moved to Shrewton and became three-weekly.[16] They were apparently held at Shrewton until 1361[17] or later. The overlord also had franchisal jurisdiction in Shrewton: in 1255 Sir William Longespée had return of writs and view of frankpledge, and in 1275 Henry, earl of Lincoln, also had pleas of vee de naam and the assize of bread and of ale.[18] Exemption from such jurisdiction was successfully claimed by Bradenstoke priory under a grant by William Longespée (d. 1250) of quittance from hundred courts and other services.[19] There is no evidence that the priory held its own court for what became Winterbourne Shrewton manor, but Nicholas Kingston may have done so for his estate before 1323.[20]

View of frankpledge and a manor court were held for Shrewton manor, Winterbourne Shrewton manor, or both by Sir Henry Brounker in 1567 and (Sir) William Brounker in 1580.[21] The lordship of both manors may have been bought by Robert Wansborough in 1596,[22] and he and his heirs held a court and claimed jurisdiction over Winterbourne Shrewton manor.[23] The claim was disputed by Nicholas Goldisborough, who held the lands of that manor, but in 1639 he accepted it, renounced a claim to hold his own court, agreed to attend the law days of Shrewton manor, and was given the right to keep a third of strays taken in Netton.[24] No court was held between 1596 and 1599.[25] Between 1615 and 1691 the view of frankpledge and court baron was recorded for 20 years. It usually met in October and was held yearly between 1630 and 1635, but there was also a spring meeting in 1630. Free tenants were summoned, orders for the use of common pastures were published, and a tithingman was elected. Matters presented by the jury included absence from the court, repairs needed to roads, buildings, and in 1638 the stocks, encroachments on and inclosures of the open fields, and selling ale without licence.[26]

Spending on poor relief in Shrewton rose from c. £66 in 1775 to £114 in 1785, when regular relief was given to 19 people and occasional payments were made for clothing, to the sick, and to the unemployed. In 1804, when poor rates in the parish were about the average for the hundred, 46 adults and 57 children were regularly relieved at a cost of £273; none, apparently, received occasional relief.[27] Expenditure rose to

a peak of £652 in 1818, fell to £294 in 1823, and was usually between £300 and £400 in the following 12 years. Shrewton became part of Amesbury poor-law union in 1835,[28] and of Salisbury district in 1974.[29]

CHURCH. There was a church at Shrewton in 1236.[30] In 1241 Lacock abbey was licensed to appropriate it when it became vacant: a vicarage was to be ordained[31] but no vicar was recorded until 1323.[32] A proposal of 1650 that Shrewton, Rollestone, and Maddington should form a single parish[33] was not then implemented, but in 1869 Shrewton and Maddington vicarages were united,[34] and in 1923 Rollestone rectory was added.[35] The three ecclesiastical parishes were united in 1970,[36] and from 1972 the benefice was called Shrewton.[37]

In 1236 Ela, countess of Salisbury, with the agreement of her son William Longespée gave the advowson of Shrewton rectory to Lacock abbey.[38] In 1241 the advowson of the vicarage was reserved to the bishop of Salisbury;[39] the bishop presented at most if not all vacancies of the vicarage and of the united benefice of Shrewton with Maddington.[40] The bishop could present at two of every three vacancies from 1923[41] until the Crown became sole patron by an exchange in 1958.[42]

A valuation of the church at £8 in 1291[43] may have been of the rectory estate; the figure was about the average for a living in Wylye deanery but in 1535 and c. 1830, when he received £7 and c. £200 respectively,[44] the vicar's income was below the average. In the late 16th century the vicar claimed a pension of 20s. from the rectory estate: it had not then been paid for 20 years[45] and was apparently not paid thereafter. At its ordination the vicarage was implicitly endowed with all tithes except those from grain,[46] and vicarial tithes were due from the whole parish in the 16th century,[47] as in the early 19th. In 1838 they were valued at £219 and commuted.[48] The vicar had 1 yardland of glebe in 1341,[49] for which 28 a. were allotted at inclosure in 1801.[50] In the 1870s Frederick Bennett, then vicar, augmented the glebe;[51] 27 a., including 3 a. given by Bennett, were sold in 1918.[52] The rector's principal house was assigned to the vicar in 1241 until another could

16 *Rot. Hund.* (Rec. Com.), ii (1), 254.
17 *Cal. Pat.* 1361–4, 131.
18 *Rot. Hund.* (Rec. Com.), ii (1), 237, 254.
19 *Bradenstoke Cart.* (W.R.S. xxxv), p. 180.
20 *Cal. Inq. p.m.* vi, p. 252.
21 Bristol Univ. Libr., Wansbrough MSS. 11–12.
22 *W.A.M.* xxiii. 36; above, manors.
23 Bristol Univ. Libr., Wansbrough MSS. 36/1–7.
24 *W.N. & Q.* vii. 573–4.
25 *W.A.M.* xxiii. 36.
26 Bristol Univ. Libr., Wansbrough MSS. 36/1–7; 40/1–23; 146/1–9; W.R.O. 121/1.
27 *Poor Law Abstract, 1804,* 558–9; W.R.O. 1336/36.
28 *Poor Rate Returns, 1816–21,* 186; *1822–4,* 225; *1825–9,* 216; *1830–4,* 209; *Poor Law Com. 2nd Rep.* App. D, 558.
29 O.S. Map 1/100,000, admin. areas, Wilts. (1974 edn.).
30 *Cal. Chart. R.* 1226–57, 221.
31 *Lacock Chart.* (W.R.S. xxxiv), p. 66.
32 Phillipps, *Wilts. Inst.* i. 20.
33 *W.A.M.* xl. 394.
34 Ch. Com. file, F 3124.

35 *Lond. Gaz.* 2 Feb. 1923, pp. 782–3.
36 Ibid. 4 June 1970, p. 6218.
37 Ibid. 10 Feb. 1972, p. 1695.
38 *Cal. Chart. R.* 1226–57, 221; *Lacock Chart.* (W.R.S. xxxiv), p. 12.
39 *Lacock Chart.* (W.R.S. xxxiv), p. 66.
40 Phillipps, *Wilts. Inst.* i. 20, 36, 47, 61, 126, 131, 160, 216, and pp. listed in *W.A.M.* xxviii. 230; *Rep. Com. Eccl. Revenues,* 846–7; Ch. Com. file, F 3124.
41 *Lond. Gaz.* 2 Feb. 1923, pp. 782–3.
42 Ibid. 31 Jan. 1958, p. 687.
43 *Tax. Eccl.* (Rec. Com.), 181.
44 *Valor Eccl.* (Rec. Com.), ii. 104; *Rep. Com. Eccl. Revenues,* 846–7.   45 W.R.O., D 1/24/183/1.
46 *Lacock Chart.* (W.R.S. xxxiv), p. 66.
47 W.R.O., D 1/24/183/1.
48 Ibid. tithe award.
49 *Inq. Non.* (Rec. Com.), 179.
50 W.R.O., EA/59.
51 Ch. Com. file, K 6963; ibid. NB 34/304.
52 W.A.S. Libr., sale cat. xxvii, no. 13.

ALLINGTON
The village in the earlier 20th century

SHREWTON
High Street in the later 19th century

LUDGERSHALL: THE MARKET CROSS IN 1805

LUDGERSHALL: THE CASTLE RUINS IN 1805

DURRINGTON: THE CHURCH CROSS IN 1805

MILSTON: THE RECTORY HOUSE c. 1805

be provided.[53] A vicarage house recorded in 1609[54] was probably on the site of that built in the 17th century[55] and sold in 1870.[56] The house, of three bays, may originally have been timber-framed but its walls were later of flint rubble and ashlar. New fittings of the 18th century included some panelling and the house was extended westwards in the 19th century. The vicarage house of the united benefice was at Maddington from 1869 until 1974, when a new house was built in Chapel Lane.[57]

In 1488 the vicar received a dispensation to hold another living.[58] Parishioners who owed money to the church in 1553[59] may have bought ornaments and furniture made superfluous by the 1552 prayer book; some ornaments had not been recovered by 1556.[60] In 1585 the vicar did not reside and the curate, who served two churches, did not preach or read a homily every Sunday, or catechize.[61] Thomas Grange, vicar 1613–61, was expelled and the vicarage seques-trated during the Interregnum: in 1650 the intruder Thomas Worthen was said to preach twice every Sunday.[62] The church lacked Jew-ell's *Apology* and an almschest in 1662.[63] One service every Sunday, alternately in the morning and afternoon, was held in 1783: there was no weekday service. John Skinner, vicar 1782–1801, was master of Salisbury cathedral choristers' school and did not reside in Shrewton. His curate there in 1783 also served two neighbour-ing churches, lived at Orcheston St. Mary, and did not have time to catechize. Communion was celebrated at Christmas, Easter, when there were 36 communicants, and Whitsun.[64] There was still only one service on Sundays in 1832,[65] but in 1851 on Census Sunday 70 people attended a morning and 200 an afternoon service.[66] In 1864 there were three services on Sundays, each with a sermon, and services on Wednesdays, Fridays, and holy days. Communion was celebrated monthly and at Christmas, Easter, and Whit-sun.[67] Shrewton and Maddington vicarages were held in plurality from 1854 until 1869,[68] and from 1938 the incumbent of the united benefice also served Winterbourne Stoke.[69]

ST. MARY'S church, so called in 1488,[70] is built of flint and ashlar and has a chancel with north organ chamber and south chapel, an aisled and clerestoried nave with north porch, and a west tower. In the early 13th century the church had a chancel and an aisled nave of two bays. The tower was added in the late 15th century;

by then the aisles had been widened. In 1854 the church was restored and enlarged in a generally 16th-century style to designs by T. H. Wyatt. The nave was extended eastwards by one bay, the arcades were restored, the aisles were rebuilt, and the clerestory was added. In a new chancel with organ chamber and chapel the respond of the old chancel arch, the piscina, and a small window, all of the 13th century, were reset.[71]

Lands or pasture rights given for the upkeep of the church, perhaps by William Goldisbor-ough in 1608,[72] were replaced at inclosure in 1801 by an allotment of 10 a., which yielded £10–£16 yearly in the 19th century and the early 20th.[73] The church still held land in 1990.[74]

In 1553 plate weighing 20 oz., an unusually large amount, was confiscated and a chalice of 12½ oz. was left in the parish. The church has a 17th-century chalice, the cover of which was exchanged for a dish in 1851. An early 19th-century salver was altered to form a paten in 1854, and a new chalice and a new flagon were given in 1855.[75]

The three bells in the church in 1553 were replaced by three cast by John Wallis in 1619. A fourth, by Clement Tosier, was added in 1717, a fifth, by Abel Rudhall, in 1757, and a sixth, by Mears & Stainbank, in 1928.[76] Those six bells hung in the church in 1990.[77]

Registers of baptisms, marriages, and burials survive from 1557.[78]

NONCONFORMITY. Two parishioners who refused to pay Easter dues, one in 1662 and one in 1674,[79] and another, presented for absence from church in 1665, may have been protestant dissenters.[80] A dissenter was recorded in the parish in 1676,[81] and a meeting house was certi-fied in 1694 and, for Baptists, in 1697.[82] By 1783 nonconformity had apparently died out,[83] but in the 1790s Baptists from Imber began to preach in Shrewton.[84] Seven Shrewton residents marked or signed a certificate for a meeting house in 1795,[85] and in 1796–7 a Baptist chapel, described as a mud-walled house in a cottage garden, was built.[86] It was replaced in 1816 by the Zion chapel,[87] a plain brick building at the junction of Lower Backway and Salisbury Road. By 1831 a second chapel had been built:[88] it stood on the north side of what was later Chapel Lane and was evidently called Bethesda.[89] It had probably been closed by 1851, when it was said

53 *Lacock Chart.* (W.R.S. xxxiv), p. 66.
54 W.R.O., D 1/24/183/2.
55 Ibid. D 1/24/183/4.   56 Ibid. 1336/80.
57 Above, Maddington, church; Ch. Com. deed 618766.
58 *Cal. Papal Reg.* xv, p. 115.
59 W.R.O., D 1/43/1, f. 119.
60 Ibid. D 1/43/2, f. 6.   61 Ibid. D 1/43/6, f. 17A.
62 *W.A.M.* xxxiv. 188; xl. 395.
63 W.R.O., D 1/54/1/4, no. 8B.
64 *Vis. Queries, 1783* (W.R.S. xxvii), pp. 193–4; Phillipps, *Wilts. Inst.* ii. 91, 102.
65 Ch. Com. file, NB 34/304.
66 P.R.O., HO 129/262/1/4/4.
67 W.R.O., D 1/56/7.   68 *W.A.M.* xxxiii. 174.
69 *Crockford* (1940 and later edns.).
70 *Cal. Papal Reg.* xv, p. 115.
71 J. Buckler, watercolour in W.A.S. Libr., vol. iii. 32; W.R.O., D 1/61/8/13.   72 *W.A.M.* xxiii. 35.
73 *Endowed Char. Wilts.* (S. Div.), 630, 634–5; W.R.O.

1336/28.
74 Inf. from Mrs. E. Broadbent, Maddington Manor.
75 Ibid.; Nightingale, *Wilts. Plate*, 73–4.
76 Walters, *Wilts. Bells*, 198, 297; J. M. J. Fletcher and A. S. Robins, *Guide to Shrewton, Maddington and Rollestone* (priv. print. 1938), 6.   77 Inf. from Mrs. Broadbent.
78 W.R.O. 1336/1–12.
79 Ibid. D 1/54/1/4, no. 8B; D 1/54/6/5, no. 37.
80 Williams, *Cath. Recusancy* (Cath. Rec. Soc.), 340.
81 *Compton Census*, ed. Whiteman, 125.
82 *Meeting Ho. Certs.* (W.R.S. xl), pp. 5–6.
83 *Vis. Queries, 1783* (W.R.S. xxvii), p. 194.
84 *V.C.H. Wilts.* iii. 137–8.
85 *Meeting Ho. Certs.* (W.R.S. xl), p. 43.
86 *Bapt. Mag.* 1812, pp. 269–70; W.R.O. 1112/141.
87 Date on bldg.
88 Lewis, *Topog. Dict. Eng.* (1831), iv. 75.
89 O.S. Map 6", Wilts. LIII (1889 edn.); W.R.O., tithe award.

that on Census Sunday 300 people attended morning, 250 afternoon, and 350 evening service at the Zion chapel.[90] A manse was built in Salisbury Road in 1909.[91] A schismatic group from the Baptist congregation became Wesleyan Methodists[92] and in 1861 built a brick chapel in High Street.[93] Both chapels were open in 1990.

EDUCATION. A schoolmaster lived in Shrewton in 1811,[94] and 25 children attended a school there in 1818.[95] Another school, opened in 1823, had 18 pupils in 1833.[96] In 1847 children from Shrewton attended the National school in Maddington.[97] A building in Shrewton was adapted for use as a National school in 1855;[98] it was attended by 20–30 boys from Shrewton, Tilshead, and Maddington in 1858, when girls and infants from Shrewton attended Maddington school.[99] In 1868 a new school and a teacher's house near the south end of High Street, with help from Anne Estcourt's charity, replaced the old Shrewton and Maddington schools. Until 1904 or later the school received £10 yearly from the charity and more for repairs.[1] It had 95 pupils in 1871,[2] and average attendance rose from 156 in 1910 to 178 in 1936.[3] About 1968 additional buildings were erected west of High Street in what had been Maddington parish, and in 1990 there were 140 children on roll.[4]

A British school, open in 1859,[5] had c. 80 pupils in 1871,[6] and was closed in or after 1879.[7]

CHARITIES FOR THE POOR. By will dated 1704 Anne Estcourt gave a rent charge of £30 from an estate in Long Newnton (now Glos.) and Rollestone to apprentice six boys yearly from those parishes and from the part of Rollestone manor in Shrewton. No payment was made before 1711 when the income, including the arrears which were used to buy land, was divided equally between the three parishes, from each of which two boys were to be apprenticed annually. In 1742 trustees for the Shrewton part of the charity bought 6½ a. there which, with

some rectorial tithes, were replaced by an allotment of 5 a. at inclosure in 1801. Shrewton's £10 of the rent charge was unpaid from 1779 to 1806, when the arrears for those years were paid with interest. That money was later invested, and the investment, rent charge, and land yielded £34 10s. in 1833. The income was never absorbed by premiums, there were fewer apprenticeships than intended, and not all beneficiaries were from Rollestone manor: 12 boys were apprenticed between 1748 and 1771, only 1 between 1786 and 1806, and 16 between 1821 and 1833. From 1862 £10 a year was paid to Shrewton school. Under a Scheme of 1867 the trustees continued to provide apprenticeships, helped to pay for the new school, and gave money to maintain the school.[8] By a Scheme of 1910 the Shrewton and Rollestone charities were merged. Money not used for apprenticeships could thereafter be used to help boys attending Dauntsey's agricultural school or, under a Scheme of 1919, for any training of poor children from the two parishes.[9] Money was occasionally given to apprentices in the later 20th century, and in 1991 a new Scheme, to allow the income to be used for wider educational purposes, was under consideration.[10]

The sites of the four cottages built in 1842, after the flood of 1841, were transferred to trustees in 1843, the rents from those and similar cottages in neighbouring parishes to be used for clothing and fuel for the poor. The conveyance was enrolled and rules for distribution of the income of the Shrewton Flood charity were issued in 1863. Shrewton received two sevenths of the income but no distribution there is recorded before 1883 when 98 people each received a pair of sheets. Between 1889 and 1904 sheets were distributed every year;[11] in the 1920s tickets, each worth 2s. 6d., were distributed.[12] The cottages, occupied by needy parishioners at very low rents in the mid 20th century, were converted to almshouses by a Scheme of 1984, when the charity's income from rents and investments was £4,500.[13]

STAPLEFORD

STAPLEFORD village is 11 km. north-west of Salisbury.[14] The parish is crossed north–south by the river Till, and consists of a rectangle on each side of it; from the smaller, western rectangle a tapering tail of downland extends c. 2 km. north-westwards. On the Till's east bank stand

Stapleford village, part of which may have been called Church Street, and Uppington hamlet; on the west bank stand the small villages called Over Street and Serrington. In 1884, 33½ a. south of Stapleford village, until then a detached part of Berwick St. James parish, were transferred

90 P.R.O., HO 129/262/1/4/5.   91 Date on bldg.
92 W.R.O., D 1/56/7.
93 Wilts. Cuttings, xxi. 391.
94 W.R.O. 451/492, copy will of Rob. Gennnings, 1811.
95 Educ. of Poor Digest, 1037.
96 Educ. Enq. Abstract, 1047.
97 Nat. Soc. Inquiry, 1846–7, Wilts. pp. 10–11.
98 P.R.O., ED 7/131, no. 245.
99 Acct. of Wilts. Schs. 42; above, Maddington, educ.
1 Endowed Char. Wilts. (S. Div.), 631, 633; W.R.O. 782/94; below, charities.
2 Returns relating to Elem. Educ. 426–7.
3 Bd. of Educ., List 21, 1910 (H.M.S.O.), 510; 1936, 426.
4 Inf. from the head teacher.

5 Kelly's Dir. Wilts. (1859).
6 Returns relating to Elem. Educ. 426–7.
7 P.R.O., ED 21/18541.
8 Endowed Char. Wilts. (S. Div.), 628–34; V.C.H. Wilts. xi. 212; W.R.O. 1336/27; above, educ.   9 Char. Com. file.
10 Inf. from the secretary, Anne Estcourt's charity, High Down, Salisbury Road, Shrewton.
11 Endowed Char. Wilts. (S. Div.), 635–7; W.R.O. 1336/89.   12 W.R.O., L 2, Shrewton.
13 Char. Com. file; inf. from the secretary, Shrewton Flood charity, Maddington Place, Shrewton.
14 This article was written in 1992. Maps used include O.S. Maps 1/50,000, sheet 184 (1979 edn.); 1/25,000, SU 03 (1958 edn.); 6", Wilts. LIX–LX (1887–9 and later edns.).

to Stapleford parish, thereafter 2,118 a. (857 ha.).[15]

Most of the parish boundary ignores relief. To the south-west it follows a side stream of the river Wylye. At their confluence and for short distances east and south of it the Till and the main course of the Wylye marked, until 1884, the boundary between Stapleford and the detached part of Berwick St. James. Boundary mounds define the north-western tail of the parish. On the east and on the south at the east end the roads which mark the boundary are ancient.[16]

Chalk outcrops over the whole parish. Beside the Wylye in the south-west and beside the Till alluvium and valley gravel have been deposited. On the eastern downs gravel has also been deposited at the head of a tributary valley of the Christchurch Avon, and a small area of clay-with-flints is in the south-east corner of the parish.[17] The highest land, 155 m., is at the end of the tail. There are steep slopes on either side of the Till, but to the east there is flat land at c. 140 m. on the watershed of the Till and the Avon. The land is at c. 65 m. beside the Wylye. The parish had extensive meadow land, much of it watered from the 18th century. The open fields were on the chalk nearer to the settlements on either side of the Till, and the eastern and western ends of the parish were pasture.[18]

The Devizes–Salisbury road along the eastern boundary was turnpiked in 1761, disturnpiked in 1870;[19] it remained a major road in the late 20th century. Until the 18th century traffic between Southampton and Bristol via Salisbury and Bath used the Devizes road northwards from Salisbury; the Bath road branched from the Devizes road, entered the parish c. 750 m. south-east of the church, crossed the Till at Serrington, ran north-westwards across the west part of the parish, and followed the west boundary of the tail. It became less important from 1761, when other roads to Bath were turnpiked, and on both sides of the Till in Stapleford parish was no more than a rough track in 1992. A road linking the villages of the Till valley and leading south from Maddington and Shrewton to Wilton crossed the Bath road south of the church, and a road leading to Warminster through villages on the north bank of the Wylye diverged from the Bath road at Serrington. In 1761 the Wilton and Warminster roads were turnpiked as part of a main Salisbury–Bath road: that road, disturnpiked in 1870,[20] became more important in the 20th century and was designated a trunk road in 1946.[21] The Till valley road, on the east bank of the river and called Uppington Lane north of Stapleford village in 1886 and later,[22] continued to carry local traffic in 1992. A parallel road west

of the Till, part of which was made after 1773, has never been tarmacadamed north of Over Street. Other roads that crossed the parish in 1773[23] survived as tracks in 1992: the north part of that parallel to and west of the Devizes road was tarmacadamed; Berwick Lane, linking Berwick St. James and Steeple Langford, crosses the north-western tail and is thought to have been part of the ancient Harrow way running from Kent to Somerset.[24]

Most evidence of prehistoric activity in the parish has been found on downland in the eastern part. A large saddle quern of the early Iron Age was found in the north-east corner. The South Kite is a quadrilateral earthwork enclosing 22 a., possibly the site of a Romano-British settlement, and within it, north-west of it, and in the parish's south-eastern corner, lie barrows. To the west, in the tail, there may be another Romano-British settlement site. A field system covering 450 a. lies across the east part of the boundary with South Newton, and another field system extends across the tail.[25]

Stapleford may have been more populous in 1377, when it had 89 poll-tax payers, than in 1801, when it had 233 inhabitants. The population had risen to 337 by 1831; it fell from 309 to 260 between 1851 and 1861, a decrease attributed to a reduction of road traffic following the opening of the Salisbury–Warminster section of the G.W.R. in 1856. Numbers continued to fall, with some fluctuations, in the later 19th century and the early 20th. They rose from 215 in 1931 to 267 in 1951[26] but had fallen to 212 by 1961. The parish had 252 inhabitants in 1981, 249 in 1991.[27]

Each of the settlements beside the Till stands on a narrow strip of gravel, and the names of three of them, Stapleford, Uppington (called Uphampton in 1249 and the 17th century), and Serrington (called Southampton in the early 14th century), suggest a Saxon origin:[28] the names of Uppington and Serrington evidently refer to their relationship to Stapleford. In the 18th century the largest settlements were Stapleford and Over Street, and each was stretched out along a road.[29] Over Street was so called c. 1537. Then and until the 19th century Church Street may have been a hamlet;[30] it was possibly the group of buildings at the south end of the continuous line of settlement called Stapleford village in 1773 and later, and if so was evidently losing its separate identity in the later 18th century and early 19th.[31] Notwithstanding the names Church Street and Over Street settlement seems to have grown gradually along the gravel strips; neither road is built up with houses on both sides and there is no evidence of early planning.

[15] Census, 1891; W.R.O., tithe award; ibid. Berwick St. Jas. tithe award.   [16] Arch. Jnl. lxxvi. 273.
[17] Geol. Surv. Map 1/50,000, drift, sheet 298 (1976 edn.).
[18] Below, econ. hist.
[19] V.C.H. Wilts. iv. 270; L.J. xxx. 77.
[20] Andrews and Dury, Map (W.R.S. viii), pl. 5; V.C.H. Wilts. iv. 257, 270; L.J. xxx. 77.
[21] Below, Wylye, intro. [roads].
[22] O.S. Maps 6", Wilts. LIX (1889 and later edns.).
[23] Andrews and Dury, Map (W.R.S. viii), pl. 5.
[24] Above, Steeple Langford, intro. [roads].

[25] V.C.H. Wilts. i (1), 107, 191, 269, 273, 278; inf. from Arch. section, Co. Hall, Trowbridge.
[26] V.C.H. Wilts. iv. 284, 322, 358.
[27] Census, 1961; 1981; 1991.
[28] P.N. Wilts. (E.P.N.S.), 229–30; Cal. Pat. 1313–17, 206; Civil Pleas, 1249 (W.R.S. xxvi), p. 70.
[29] Andrews and Dury, Map (W.R.S. viii), pl. 5.
[30] Longleat Mun., Seymour papers, xii, f. 237v.; W.R.O. 212B/6157.
[31] Andrews and Dury, Map (W.R.S. viii), pl. 5; O.S. Map 1", sheet 14 (1817 edn.).

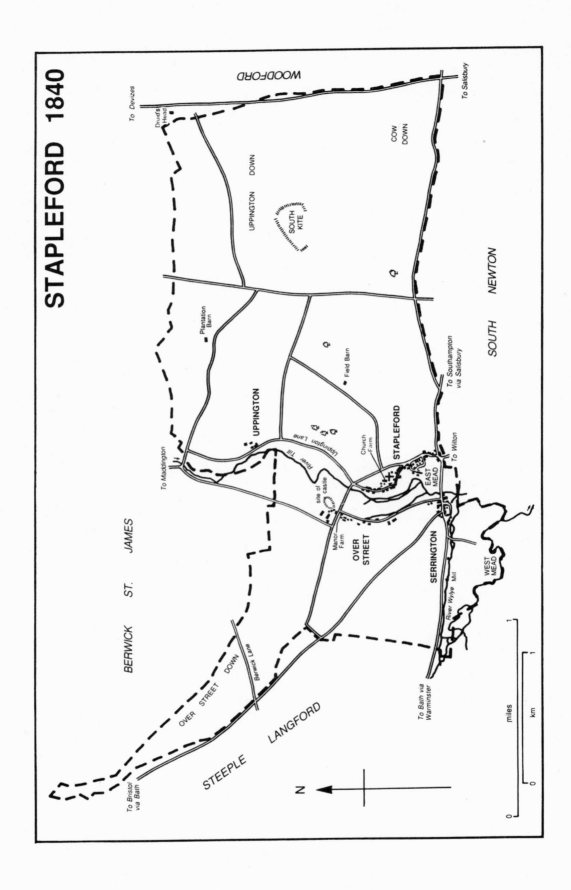

STAPLEFORD. In the late 18th century Stapleford village extended along the Maddington road from a little north of the church to the Bath road. In the south part of the village a lane, a footpath in 1992, formed a loop to the west.[32] The site of a demesne farmstead is immediately north of the church: a substantial house there was apparently built in the mid 19th century. South of the church and west of the road four 17th-century farmhouses of chequered flint and limestone survive: two of them, Parsonage House, which was extended in the early 19th century, and Seymour Cottage, which stands in the loop, are mid 17th-century. On the east side of the road and a little south of the church stand two early 18th-century cottages, one timber-framed and rendered, one of brick, and the Malthouse, a thatched 17th-century house of four bays, with a former malthouse as a long single-storeyed extension.[33] All those older buildings were included in a conservation area designated in 1988.[34]

Between 1773 and 1817 cottages built on the waste on the east side of the road took settlement north towards the lane which linked Stapleford and Over Street over Bury bridge,[35] so called in the late 19th century,[36] and by 1812 a back lane east of the north part of the village had been defined.[37] In the later 19th century some houses and cottages were rebuilt, and a school beside the western lane and a new vicarage house beside the eastern were built.[38]

There was little new building in the earlier 20th century. At the north end of the village six council houses were built in Riverside Terrace in 1950, and the local authority also built four houses and six bungalows in Hillside beside the eastern lane in 1961.[39] Private building after c. 1960 included small groups of houses and bungalows north of Riverside Terrace, in the eastern lane, in Church Pasture north of the church, and at the south end of the village.

OVER STREET. West of the Till a small castle or a fortified house was apparently built in the 12th century or early 13th for a lord of Stapleford manor, held from the mid 12th century by members of the Hussey family.[40] The mound and ditch survive, but no masonry or other direct evidence of a building has been found. Over Street village is mainly on the west side of the road south of the castle site, and has changed little in extent since the late 18th century.[41] A demesne farmstead stood immediately south of the castle site.[42] The farmhouse, Manor Farm, was built in the 17th century as a small house of two storeys with attics, and, on the ground floor,

had one room on each side of the main chimney stack: a large extension to the east was built c. 1860. Two cottages, of flint and limestone rubble, between Manor Farm and the castle mound are also of 17th-century origin. Manor Cottage, south of Manor Farm, and two cottages east of the road are early 18th-century, and a house of slightly later date stands at a right angle to the road on the west side further south. In the later 19th century farm buildings west of the castle mound were renewed and several cottages were built or rebuilt beside the road. Brooklet Farm, comprising a house west of the road and a farmyard east of it, was built c. 1930, and several private houses have been built west of the road in the later 20th century.

SERRINGTON. In the later 18th century Serrington was a hamlet of some eight houses beside the Warminster road;[43] its modern name was in use in the early 19th.[44] Several of the houses standing in 1773 survive. Bridge House, on the north side of the road at the junction with the road to Over Street, was built c. 1700; a north-west range was added in 1777.[45] On the south side of the road the Pelican, a building of late 17th- or early 18th-century origin, was an inn in 1751[46] and 1992. West of the Pelican, Southington is a three-bayed house built of chequered flint and limestone c. 1700, and Pembroke Cottage is of similar date. A mill stood west of the village until the mid or later 19th century.[47] By 1840 more houses had been built near Bridge House.[48] Among them was the New Inn, which was open in 1848 and demolished c. 1908.[49] In the later 20th century four houses were built north of Bridge House, two police houses and two bungalows at the west end of the hamlet, and a house and a commercial garage near the Pelican. The bridge over the Till, called Southington bridge in 1705[50] and Pelican bridge in 1899,[51] was rebuilt in 1937.[52]

UPPINGTON. Only three buildings stood at Uppington in 1773,[53] although earlier there may have been three small farmsteads there.[54] In 1992 a small farmhouse apparently of c. 1800 and a house of the earlier 20th century stood there.

OTHER SETTLEMENT. There was no building on the downs in 1817.[55] By 1840 Plantation Barn north-east of Uppington and Field Barn north-east of the church had been built.[56] Between 1840 and 1879 Plantation Barn was demolished and two new farmsteads, Druid's Head Farm and York Yard, were built respectively 500 m.

32 *Andrews and Dury, Map* (W.R.S. viii), pl. 5.
33 See plate facing p. 218; for the malthouse, W.R.O., tithe award.
34 Inf. from Dept. of Planning and Highways, Co. Hall, Trowbridge.
35 *Andrews and Dury, Map* (W.R.S. viii), pl. 5; O.S. Map 1", sheet 14 (1817 edn.).
36 O.S. Map 6", Wilts. LIX. SE. (1901 edn.).
37 W.R.O., EA/103.
38 Below, church; educ.
39 W.R.O., G 11/602/1–2.
40 Below, manor (Stapleford).
41 *Andrews and Dury, Map* (W.R.S. viii), pl. 5.
42 W.R.O., tithe award.
43 *Andrews and Dury, Map* (W.R.S. viii), pl. 5.
44 O.S. Map 1", sheet 14 (1817 edn.).
45 Date on bldg.
46 W.R.O. 1126/19, deed, Seymour to Stanes, 1751.
47 Below, econ. hist. [mills].
48 W.R.O., tithe award.
49 Ibid. 776/106; *Kelly's Dir. Wilts.* (1848, 1907).
50 W.R.O., D 1/24/191/3.
51 O.S. Map 6", Wilts. LIX. NE. (1901 edn.).
52 Date on bridge.
53 *Andrews and Dury, Map* (W.R.S. viii), pl. 5.
54 Below, econ. hist.
55 O.S. Map 1", sheet 14 (1817 edn.).
56 W.R.O., tithe award.

south-east and 1.5 km. east of its site. The new farmsteads were linked by a road which in the later 20th century was called York Road. Druid's Head Farm was enlarged c. 1900 and again in the later 20th century; it incorporates a pair of bungalows. York Yard was also enlarged c. 1900 and, perhaps then, was converted to a stable yard; a house and two cottages west of it were built in the mid 20th century.[57] In Woodford parish near the north-east corner of Stapleford parish a small settlement called Druid's Head developed c. 1800[58] and survived in 1992. In Stapleford parish, a house called Druid's Lodge[59] and a large stable block are part of the settlement. In the south-east part of the parish a farmstead called Chain Hill Farm was built near the southern boundary between 1840 and 1879 and another, called Cowdown Farm, in the south-east corner between 1879 and 1899.[60] Most of Chain Hill Farm has been demolished; Cowdown Farm is the site of Camp Cottages, a group of seven early 20th-century cottages. In the mid 20th century a few houses were built beside the Warminster road in the south-west corner of the parish, and a school beside the Maddington road near Berwick St. James village.[61]

MANOR AND OTHER ESTATES. In 1084 and 1086 Suain held 10½ hides which his father had held in 1066 and which became *STAPLE-FORD* manor.[62] Geoffrey Hussey held the manor in 1166–7.[63] It passed to Henry Hussey and, probably after 1189, to Henry's son Geoffrey, to whom it was confirmed in 1198.[64] With Figheldean manor it passed to Geoffrey's son Geoffrey (d. c. 1218), who was succeeded by another Henry Hussey.[65] By 1226 Henry (d. 1260 × 1263) had subinfeudated Stapleford manor to his son Sir Hubert:[66] the overlordship apparently passed to Henry's relict Maud (fl. 1263)[67] and presumably reverted to Sir Hubert, successors of whom held in chief.[68] The heirs of Sir Hubert (d. before 1277) were his daughters Margaret, who married Henry Sturmy (d. 1305), Maud (d. c. 1285, unmarried), and Isabel, who married John of Thorney:[69] the manor descended in moieties, presumably from c. 1285.

Before her death c. 1320 Margaret Sturmy may have granted her moiety to her son John Sturmy, who by 1325 had granted it to Hugh le Despen-ser, earl of Winchester[70] (executed 1326).[71] John recovered the moiety and by 1327 had granted it to John Mautravers (from 1330 Lord Mau-travers).[72] By 1330, however, the moiety had been successfully claimed by John Sturmy's brother Henry[73] (d. c. 1338), whose son Henry[74] (d. 1381) was in 1359 granted free warren in his demesne lands at Stapleford. The moiety passed to Henry's nephew Sir William Sturmy[75] (d. 1427), whose heirs were his daughter Agnes, wife of John Holcombe, and grandson (Sir) John Seymour.[76] It was allotted to Seymour[77] (d. 1464), who in 1447 settled it on his son John (d. 1463) and that John's wife Elizabeth,[78] later wife of Richard Whiteley. On Elizabeth's death in 1472 the moiety passed to her son John Sey-mour[79] (d. 1491), who was succeeded in turn by his son (Sir) John[80] (d. 1536) and Sir John's son Sir Edward (cr. Viscount Beauchamp 1536, earl of Hertford 1537, duke of Somerset 1547). Like the Earldom manor in Amesbury it was forfeited on Somerset's death and attainder in 1552, and was restored in the same year to his son Edward (cr. earl of Hertford 1559, d. 1621), a minor until 1558.[81] It was held for life by Hertford's relict Frances (d. 1639), wife of Ludovic Stuart, duke of Richmond, and passed to the earl's grandson William Seymour, earl of Hertford (cr. mar-quess of Hertford 1641, duke of Somerset 1660, d. 1660).[82] William devised the moiety to trus-tees,[83] but its descent 1660–1743 is obscure. William's successors as duke were his grandson William Seymour (d. 1671), that William's uncle John Seymour (d. 1675), John's cousin Francis Seymour (d. 1678), and Francis's brother Char-les (d. 1748),[84] but in 1743 the moiety belonged to William Seymour of East Knoyle[85] (d. 1747). It passed to William's brother Francis (d. 1761), in turn to Francis's son Henry (d. 1805) and grandson Henry Seymour (d. 1849), in turn to the younger Henry's sons Henry (d. 1877) and Alfred (d. 1888), and to Alfred's daughter Jane (d. 1943),[86] who held c. 890 a. in Stapleford parish in 1923.[87] The lands were bought after Jane's death by J. V. Rank and have since been part of the Druid's Lodge estate.[88]

The second moiety of Stapleford manor was conveyed by Isabel and John of Thorney to John Giffard, Lord Giffard, probably in 1316.[89] From then until 1560–1 the moiety descended almost like Sherrington manor.[90] In 1322 Giffard was

57 O.S. Maps 6", Wilts. LX (1887 and later edns.); W.R.O., tithe award.
58 *Andrews and Dury, Map* (W.R.S. viii), pl. 5; O.S. Map 1", sheet 14 (1817 edn.).
59 Below, manor (Druid's Lodge).
60 O.S. Maps 6", Wilts. LX (1887 and later edns.); W.R.O., tithe award.   61 Below, educ.
62 *V.C.H. Wilts.* ii, pp. 165, 209.
63 *Pipe R.* 1167 (P.R.S. xi), 131.
64 *V.C.H. Wilts.* iii. 269; *Cal. Chart. R.* 1226–57, 394.
65 *Cal. Inq. p.m.* i, p. 287; *Ex. e Rot. Fin.* (Rec. Com.), i. 35; above, Figheldean, manors (Figheldean).
66 *Cur. Reg. R.* xii, p. 340; *Bk. of Fees*, ii. 728; above, Figheldean, manors (Figheldean).
67 *Cal. Pat.* 1258–66, 290.
68 e.g. *Cal. Inq. p.m.* vi, p. 167.
69 Ibid. ii, pp. 330, 339–40; *W.A.M.* li. 295, 301.
70 *Cal. Inq. p.m.* vi, p. 167; *Cal. Pat.* 1324–7, 161.
71 *Complete Peerage*, xii (2), 754.
72 Ibid. viii. 583; *Cal. Pat.* 1327–30, 130.
73 *Cal. Close*, 1330–3, 92–3.

74 *Cal. Inq. p.m.* viii, p. 101.
75 Ibid. xv, p. 202; *Cal. Chart. R.* 1341–1417, 164.
76 *Cal. Pat.* 1446–52, 121; P.R.O., C 139/28, no. 22.
77 *Cal. Pat.* 1422–9, 449.
78 Ibid. 1446–52, 121; Hoare, *Mod. Wilts.* Mere, 117.
79 P.R.O., C 140/40, no. 16.
80 *Cal. Inq. p.m. Hen. VII*, ii, pp. 328–9.
81 *Complete Peerage*, vi. 505–6; xii (1), 59–64; P.R.O., E 328/117; above, Amesbury, manors (Earldom).
82 *Wilts. Inq. p.m. 1625–49* (Index Libr.), 20–2; *Complete Peerage*, vi. 505–7; W.R.O. 192/24B, f. 25v.
83 W.R.O. 1300/200.
84 *Complete Peerage*, xii (1), 74–9.
85 W.R.O. 1126/19, deed, Seymour to Saph, 1743.
86 Burke, *Peerage* (1963), 2267.
87 W.R.O., G 11/505/2.
88 Inf. from the manager, Druid's Lodge, Woodford; below, this section (Druid's Lodge).
89 *Feud. Aids*, v. 202; *Feet of F.* 1272–1327 (W.R.S. i), p. 94.
90 Above, Sherrington, manor, where more details are given.

executed and the moiety was granted to Hugh le Despenser, earl of Winchester (executed 1326);[91] unlike Sherrington it was granted as dower in 1327 to Giffard's relict Aveline (d. 1327).[92] Like Sherrington the moiety was conveyed in 1330 by John Callaway to John Mautravers (from 1330 Lord Mautravers, d. 1364);[93] between 1337 and 1347, while Mautravers was in exile, it was held by Maurice Berkeley.[94] It was restored to Mautravers in 1351,[95] passed to his relict Agnes (d. 1375) and granddaughter Eleanor, Baroness Mautravers (d. 1405),[96] and descended to Eleanor's grandson John d'Arundel, earl of Arundel (d. 1421).[97] Two further life interests were granted, between 1375 and 1379 to Thomas Adderbury (d. 1415),[98] and in 1416 to Joan Beauchamp (d. 1435), relict of William Beauchamp, Lord Bergavenny. Lord Arundel's grandson Humphrey FitzAlan, earl of Arundel (d. 1438), held the moiety from 1435, and Humphrey's uncle William, earl of Arundel (d. 1487), from 1438.[99] Like Sherrington it passed in the direct line, and in 1561 Henry, earl of Arundel, conveyed it by exchange to the Crown.[1] In 1580 the moiety was granted to John Castillion[2] (d. 1597), whose son Sir Francis sold it in 1611 to George Tattershall[3] (fl. 1624).[4] In 1642 it belonged to Tattershall's son George,[5] who conveyed it in 1667 to John Woolfe, perhaps a trustee.[6] Woolfe conveyed it in 1673 to Bernard Howard,[7] and Howard in 1693 to Sir Richard Grobham Howe, Bt.[8] (d. 1703). From then until 1808 the moiety descended with Great Wishford manor and was held by Sir Richard Howe, Bt. (d. 1730), John Howe, Lord Chedworth (d. 1742), John, Lord Chedworth (d. 1762), Henry, Lord Chedworth (d. 1781), and John, Lord Chedworth (d. 1804).[9] In 1808 that last Chedworth's executors sold it to Alexander Baring[10] (cr. Baron Ashburton 1835, d. 1848),[11] who in 1840 owned c. 1,030 a. in Stapleford.[12] The land passed with the barony to Alexander's sons William (d. 1864) and Francis (d. 1868), to Francis's son Alexander (d. 1889), and to Alexander's son Francis,[13] who sold it to E. T. Hooley probably in 1896. In 1898, following Hooley's bankruptcy,[14] the land was bought by Sir Christopher Furness, who in 1909 offered it for sale

through the Cavendish Land Company. Manor farm, 407 a. west of the Till, was bought by Frank Moore:[15] in 1992 it belonged to his grandsons Mr. Roger Moore and Mr. Geoffrey Moore.[16]

Druid's Head farm, 478 a. east of the Till, may have been bought by F. B. Beauchamp in 1909.[17] In 1910 it belonged to A. P. Cunliffe as part of the *DRUID'S LODGE* estate.[18] The estate, the principal buildings of which stood on the boundary between Stapleford and Woodford, included land in Berwick St. James and Winterbourne Stoke parishes.[19] Cunliffe sold it in 1934 to J. V. Rank, after whose death in 1952 it was bought by the Fenston Trust. In 1989 the trust sold it to Mr. R. A. Hurst, the owner in 1992 when the estate included c. 1,400 a. in Stapleford.[20] Druid's Lodge, a plain red-brick house of two storeys with attics, was built in the north-east corner of the parish c. 1895.[21]

In 1406 John Bonham (d. 1411) and his son John held land in Uppington.[22] *BONHAM'S* was held in 1435 by the elder John's nephew Thomas Bonham[23] (d. 1473) and passed with an estate in Berwick St. James to Walter Bonham, who held it in 1559.[24] It was perhaps the estate held in 1780 by Sir James Harris (cr. Baron Malmesbury 1788, earl of Malmesbury 1800),[25] which comprised 193 a. in 1812.[26] Harris sold that estate c. 1815 to Alexander Baring, who added it to his moiety of Stapleford manor.[27]

Three estates held by religious houses were combined after the Dissolution, probably as *SAPH'S*. St. Denis's priory, Southampton, held land valued at 12s. in 1291,[28] 12 a. at the Dissolution;[29] Bath abbey held 1 yardland, probably given by Sir Hubert Hussey (d. before 1277);[30] in 1314 Andrew of Aldbourne was licensed to grant 4 yardlands to Keynsham abbey (Som.),[31] which held 86 a. at the Dissolution. The Crown granted the combined estate twice in 1557, first to Anselm Lane,[32] possibly a trustee, and secondly to William Northcote and his son John.[33] It was probably that held in 1631 by John Saph,[34] which passed in the direct line from John to John (d. 1683), John (d. 1699), Charles (d. 1726), and Charles (d. 1736).[35] By 1753 Saph's had apparently passed to another John Saph,[36] who was succeeded c. 1782 by his

91   *Cal. Chart. R. 1300–26*, 443–4.
92   *Cal. Close, 1327–30*, 36; *Complete Peerage*, v. 647.
93   *Feet of F. 1327–77* (W.R.S. xxix), pp. 26–7.
94   *Cal. Pat. 1334–8*, 363.
95   *Cal. Close, 1349–54*, 312.
96   Ibid. 1374–7, 184; *Cal. Inq. p.m.* xi, pp. 452–3; xiv, pp. 189–91.   97   *Complete Peerage*, i. 247; viii. 586.
98   *Cal. Fine R. 1413–22*, 125.
99   *Complete Peerage*, i. 24–6, 247–9; P.R.O., C 139/71, no. 37.   1   *Cal. Pat. 1560–3*, 43–4.
2   Ibid. 1578–80, p. 184.
3   *V.C.H. Berks.* iv. 105; W.R.O. 130/44, deed, Castillion to Tattershall, 1611.
4   W.R.O. 130/44, deed, Tattershall to Awstell, 1624.
5   Ibid. 212B/6135.
6   P.R.O., CP 25/2/745/18 & 19 Chas. II Hil.
7   Ibid. CP 25/2/762/24 & 25 Chas. II Hil.
8   Ibid. CP 25/2/888/5 Wm. and Mary Hil.
9   Below, Great Wishford, manors.
10   W.R.O. 212B/6157.
11   *Complete Peerage*, i. 276–7.
12   W.R.O., tithe award.
13   *Complete Peerage*, i. 277–8.
14   W.R.O. 130/78; above, Berwick St. Jas., manors (Berwick St. Jas.).   15   W.A.S. Libr., sale cat. ix, no. 15.

16   Inf. from Mr. R. Moore, Manor Farm.
17   W.A.S. Libr., sale cat. ix, no. 15.
18   W.R.O., Inland Revenue, val. reg. 145.
19   Above, intro. (other settlement); Berwick St. Jas., manors (Asserton); below, Winterbourne Stoke, manors (Winterbourne Stoke).
20   P. Mathieu, *Druid's Lodge Confederacy*, 161–2; inf. from the manager, Druid's Lodge; cf. above, this section.
21   Mathieu, *Druid's Lodge Confederacy*, 14.
22   *Cal. Close, 1405–9*, 221–2; B.L. Add. Ch. 15301.
23   *Cal. Close, 1435–41*, 36.
24   B.L. Add. Ch. 15106; above, Berwick St. Jas., manors (Bonham's).
25   *Complete Peerage*, viii. 358–9; W.R.O., A 1/345/379.
26   W.R.O., EA/103.   27   Ibid. A 1/345/379.
28   *Tax. Eccl.* (Rec. Com.), 181.
29   P.R.O., SC 6/Hen. VIII/3326, rot. 6.
30   *Tax. Eccl.* (Rec. Com.), 181; *V.C.H. Som.* ii. 79; above, this section (Stapleford).
31   *Cal. Pat. 1313–17*, 206.
32   P.R.O., E 318/41/2188.
33   *Cal. Pat. 1557–8*, 271–2.
34   W.R.O. 212B/6135.
35   Ibid. 317/25.
36   Ibid. 212B/6154.

son John. The son sold the estate, 125 a. in 1812, to Alexander Baring *c.* 1822.[37]

Lands in Stapleford granted by Henry Hussey and his son Geoffrey were confirmed to Stanley abbey in 1189;[38] at the Dissolution the abbey received 8s. rent from land in the parish.[39] In 1291 Hyde abbey, Winchester, had lands in Stapleford valued at 10s.,[40] at the Dissolution 2 a.[41] St. Thomas's church, Salisbury, was entitled to 13s. 4d. a year from Stapleford in the earlier 16th century; the rent was given by Easton priory, probably in the 16th century, for an obit, and was a charge on the Rectory estate;[42] it was apparently not paid after the Dissolution. In 1535 Salisbury cathedral received pensions of 1s. and 3s. 4d. respectively from the Rectory estate and Stapleford vicarage:[43] no later reference to the pensions has been found. From 1712 to 1981 Great Wishford church owned a rent charge of £10 from Stapleford.[44]

In 1446 Stapleford church was appropriated by Easton priory,[45] which held it until the Dissolution. In 1536 the *RECTORY* estate, consisting of tithes and land, was granted to Sir Edward Seymour, Viscount Beauchamp (later duke of Somerset),[46] who in 1547 gave it to the king in an exchange. Also in 1547 the king gave it to St. George's chapel, Windsor.[47] In 1840 the rectorial tithes were valued at £420 and commuted: St. George's chapel then held 122 a. in Stapleford.[48] The land passed to the Ecclesiastical Commissioners and was sold in 1871 to Thomas Powell.[49] Between then and 1910 it passed, presumably by purchase, to Alfred or Jane Seymour and was added to their moiety of Stapleford manor.[50]

ECONOMIC HISTORY. In 1086 Stapleford had land for 10 ploughteams. On the demesne were 2 teams with 1 *servus*; 17 *villani* and 10 bordars shared 8 teams. There were 40 a. of meadow, and pasture ½ league square.[51]

When Stapleford manor was divided in the late 13th century[52] demesne and customary land was allotted to each moiety. In the 1320s John Giffard's moiety included 214 a. of arable, 20 a. of meadow, and pasture for 400 sheep: the arable, assessed at three different values, is likely to have been in three open fields. Seven customary tenants of the moiety held 1 yardland each, and one held ½ yardland; there were 10 cottagers.[53] The demesne was leased to members of the Harris family in the mid 15th century and the late 16th.[54] The demesne of the other moiety

was leased in two portions in 1432 and in three in 1453, when one was described as in the west and one was of pasture only. In 1432 the moiety had 16 customary tenants, of whom 13 shared 17 yardlands and 3 were cottagers.[55] With the right to feed 212 sheep in 1341 the rector's 2 yardlands were probably more generously stinted than other holdings; the rector also had 3 a. of meadow.[56]

There were farmsteads in all four or five settlements in the parish, throughout which there was sheep-and-corn husbandry in common. Holdings of the Seymours' moiety were based in each of the settlements, holdings of the Howes' moiety in Stapleford or Church Street, Over Street, and Serrington, but apparently not Uppington; the Howes, however, may have had Bonham's, based at Uppington. The lands of the two moieties remained intermingled until inclosure in 1812.[57] In the early 16th century the Seymours' moiety and the Rectory estate, about half the parish, included *c.* 535 a. of arable, *c.* 20 a. of meadow, and pasture rights for 1,076 sheep and 121 cattle and horses. The arable was in seven fields: the names of five, Church Street, Stapleford, Over Street, Uppington, and Serrington, presumably indicate where they lay; two larger fields, Marnham and Berry, are likely to have been east of the Till. Over Street down was in the parish's tail, Cow down was in the southeast corner, and Marnham down and Berry down were probably east of the fields bearing those names.[58]

About 1537 the demesne in the Seymours' moiety, 182 a. with rights to feed 420 sheep and 24 beasts, was held by lease with the lands of the Rectory estate, 45 a.; the demesne apparently became Church farm, which had its principal buildings immediately north of the church. Also *c.* 1537 that moiety had 7 other holdings based in Stapleford village and Church Street, 4 in Over Street, 2 in Uppington, and 1 in Serrington.[59] The demesne of the Howes' moiety became Manor farm, based in Over Street with principal buildings near the site of the castle; in the early 19th century the moiety had 11 other holdings of over 10 a., 5 based in Stapleford village, including Church Street, 2 in Over Street, and 4 in Serrington.[60] The main part of the Saphs' estate, assessed at 3 yardlands, was based at Uppington.[61] Nearly all the arable of each holding was almost certainly in the field or fields adjacent to the settlement in which the holding was based;[62] sheep of holdings based in Stapleford, Church Street, and Uppington were

37 W.R.O., A 1/345/379; ibid. EA/103.
38 *V.C.H. Wilts.* iii. 269.
39 P.R.O., SC 6/Hen. VIII/3969, rot. 23.
40 *Tax. Eccl.* (Rec. Com.), 181.
41 *Cal. Pat.* 1553, 369.
42 P.R.O., E 301/58, no. 90; E 318/39/2087; below, this section (Rectory).
43 *Valor Eccl.* (Rec. Com.), ii. 80, 103.
44 *Endowed Char. Wilts.* (S. Div.), 912, 920–1; below, Great Wishford, church.
45 W.R.O., D 1/2/10, ff. (2nd foliation) 68–9.
46 *Cat. MSS. D. & C. Windsor,* ed. J. N. Dalton, p. 421; below, church. 47 *Antrobus D.* (W.R.S. iii), p. 67.
48 W.R.O., tithe award. 49 Ch. Com. file 39899.
50 W.R.O., Inland Revenue, val. reg. 145.
51 *V.C.H. Wilts.* ii, p. 165.

52 Above, manor (Stapleford).
53 *Wilts. Inq. p.m.* 1327–77 (Index Libr.), 11–12.
54 P.R.O., C 3/94/18; C 3/145/94; ibid. SC 6/1119/12.
55 W.R.O. 192/35A; 192/35C.
56 *Inq. Non.* (Rec. Com.), 178.
57 Hoare, *Mod. Wilts.* Branch and Dole, 20; W.R.O., EA/103; Longleat Mun., Seymour papers, xii, ff. 234–42; for Bonham's, cf. above, manor; Berwick St. Jas., manors (Bonham's).
58 Longleat Mun., Seymour papers, xii, ff. 234–42; W.R.O., EA/103.
59 Longleat Mun., Seymour papers, xii, ff. 234–240v.; O.S. Map 6", Wilts. LIX (1889 edn.).
60 W.R.O. 212B/6157.
61 Ibid. 212B/6137; 212B/6145.
62 Ibid. 906/W/232; Longleat Mun., Seymour papers, xii, ff. 234–240v.; P.R.O., E 318/41/2188.

apparently fed on downs east of the Till, those of Over Street and Serrington on downs west of the Till, although there were some exceptions.[63] Rights to use West mead, beside the Wylye, East mead, beside the Till, and Cow down were, however, included in holdings based in all four or five settlements.[64]

Uppington field, in the north-east part of the parish, was apparently subdivided after c. 1537; in 1743 there were North, Middle, and South fields at Uppington.[65] An agreement of 1735 to water meadows adjacent to each other in Stapleford and Berwick St. James may have related to Uppington meadows.[66] In the later 18th century Uppington down was grazed for six months of every year by the demesne flock of the Howes' moiety of the manor:[67] part of it had been burnbaked by 1812.[68] In the south-east part of the parish, Cow down was 254 a. in 1808, Church Street down was 106 a.; an additional 250 a. of downland, which could support 1,000 sheep, were grazed only by the demesne flock of each moiety and by the flock on the Rectory estate. In the south-west part Serrington had a sheep down of 30 a. in 1808;[69] in the later 18th century part of it, or other land, beside the Steeple Langford boundary, was apparently used for cattle.[70] West mead, c. 70 a., was being watered in the early 19th century[71] and almost certainly much earlier. In the north-west Over Street down was 121 a. in 1808. Between Stapleford village and Over Street, East mead and other meadows totalled c. 25 a.[72]

Manor farm was apparently in hand in the 1690s, when a flock of 300 of Sir Richard Grobham Howe's sheep was moved between pastures in Stapleford and Great Wishford parishes.[73] In 1808 the farm included 133 a. of arable, 8 a. of water meadow, and pasture rights for 400 sheep. Other holdings in the Howes' moiety, seven held by lease, three by copy, and one at rack rent, then included 308 a. of arable and rights of pasture for 748 sheep, and nine more holdings were of less than 5 a. each.[74] In the late 18th century the Seymours' moiety apparently included Church farm and 12 smaller holdings,[75] and in 1715 the Rectory estate included 35 a. of arable, 7½ a. of meadow and inclosed pasture, and grazing for 200 sheep.[76] Although many of the holdings based in each of the four or five settlements remained small c. 1800, it is likely that by subletting they had by then been absorbed into substantial farms.

Common husbandry ceased in 1812, when the whole parish was inclosed under an Act of 1810. Between 1810 and 1840 more downland

in the north-east corner of the parish and some in the south-east corner was ploughed, and in 1840 the parish had c. 1,040 a. of arable, c. 640 a. of downland pasture, c. 70 a. of lowland pasture, and c. 130 a. of meadow, mainly water meadow. In 1840 Manor farm was 750 a., Church farm 580 a.: the lands of each were scattered throughout the parish, and, in addition to its main farmstead, each had a barn and yard on high ground east of the Till. In addition to Church farm, there were apparently farms of 122 a., 38 a., and 34 a. based in Stapleford village, and, in addition to Manor farm, farms of 83 a. and 58 a. based in Over Street: those of 122 a. and 58 a. may have been worked together. Holdings of 52 a. and 26 a., each with a house at Serrington, may have been small farms, and a holding of 22 a. may have been worked from Uppington.[77]

New farmsteads were built on the downs in the east part of the parish in the 19th century,[78] and arable was converted to pasture; probably less than half the parish was ploughed in the 1890s, about a quarter in the 1920s. All of the parish west of the Till was grassland c. 1930: most of the arable then lay immediately east of Stapleford village. The increased areas of pasture were mainly for sheep.[79] In the later 19th century and the early 20th there were four principal farms. By 1898 Manor farm, then 475 a. including 51 a. in Steeple Langford, had been limited to land west of the Till: it was still predominantly arable,[80] but in 1929, when it was 371 a., was entirely pasture.[81] In 1992 it was a specialist arable farm of 528 a., including land in Winterbourne Stoke parish.[82] In 1898 Druid's Head Farm was the base for a farm of 516 a. in the north-east part of the parish. The farm was half downland pasture, much of it recently converted from arable, and half arable.[83] Presumably then, as in 1912, it was principally a sheep farm.[84] In 1910 Church farm comprised 755 a., Parsonage farm 122 a.[85] By 1934 they had been combined as Parsonage farm, 879 a., including 477 a. of arable, 234 a. of downland, and 42 a. of water meadow: the principal buildings were then on the west side of the Maddington road west of the church and at Field Barn.[86] In the late 20th century Druid's Head Farm became the main farm buildings of the Druid's Lodge estate, which included Druid's Head farm, Parsonage farm, and lands in Winterbourne Stoke and Berwick St. James, a total of c. 2,500 a. In 1992 the agricultural land of the estate was in hand and worked mainly from Druid's Head Farm and buildings in Berwick St. James as a mixed farm, on which sheep and

63 For an exception, W.R.O. 2057/M 75.
64 Ibid. 212B/6157; Longleat Mun., Seymour papers, xii, ff. 234–240v.
65 W.R.O. 1126/19, deed, Seymour to Saph, 1743.
66 Ibid. 317/3.   67 Ibid. 2057/M 75.
68 Ibid. EA/103.
69 Ibid. 212B/6157.
70 Ibid. 2057/M 75.
71 Ibid. 212B/6164; ibid. EA/103; ibid. tithe award.
72 Ibid. 212B/6157; ibid. EA/103.
73 P.R.O., E 126/17, f. 128v.; ibid. E 134/11 Wm. III Mich./5.
74 W.R.O. 212B/6157.
75 Ibid. A 1/345/379.
76 Cat. MSS. D. & C. Windsor, pp. 429–30.
77 W.R.O., EA/103; ibid. tithe award.
78 Above, intro. (other settlement).
79 [1st] Land Util. Surv. Map, sheet 122; P.R.O., MAF 68/1633, sheet 17; MAF 68/2203, sheet 7; MAF 68/3319, sheet 15.
80 W.R.O. 130/78.
81 Ibid. G 11/505/2; above, this section.
82 Inf. from Mr. R. Moore, Manor Farm.
83 W.R.O. 130/78.
84 Ibid. 776/368.
85 Ibid. Inland Revenue, val. reg. 145.
86 Ibid. 1265/80; O.S. Map 1/2,500, Wilts. LIX. 12 (1939 edn.).

cattle were kept and cereal and fodder crops were grown.[87]

From 1855 until c. 1923 members of the Williams family were nurserymen and seedsmen.[88] In 1898 and the 1920s the nursery was at Serrington south of the Warminster road.[89]

A racing stable built for A. P. Cunliffe about the same time as Druid's Lodge was opened in 1895. The gallops lay mainly outside the parish. The stable was very successful until the First World War, when it was requisitioned. It was used again for some years in the 1920s by Cunliffe and from 1934 by J. V. Rank, for whom more stables were built. Training ceased c. 1954.[90]

In 1086 Stapleford had woodland 1 league long and ½ league broad,[91] but later the parish was sparsely wooded. In 1603 parishioners were accustomed to take wood and ferns from Grovely forest c. 3 km. to the south. They were then said to do so without authority,[92] but in the early 19th century apparently still claimed the right.[93] In 1840 there were a few acres of withy bed and, on the eastern downs, c. 10 a. of plantation.[94] Further planting took place from the later 19th century, and in the 1970s there were c. 150 a. of woodland in the parish.[95]

In 1239 the lord of Stapleford manor was granted a yearly fair on 7 September and the three days following.[96] No fair is known to have been held at Stapleford.

There were two mills at Stapleford in 1086.[97] A moiety of a water mill was apparently assigned as part of each moiety of Stapleford manor in the late 13th century,[98] and the mill continued in joint ownership until 1840[99] or later. In 1773, as presumably earlier, it stood west of Serrington on the Wylye.[1] It was demolished between 1840 and 1886.[2]

Charles Rowden, a maker of clocks and watches, lived in the parish between 1859 and 1875.[3]

LOCAL GOVERNMENT. In 1198 Geoffrey Hussey was granted freedom from shire and hundred courts for Stapleford manor.[4]

The right to hold view of frankpledge for the whole parish descended with the moiety of the manor held by the Sturmy and Seymour families.[5] The records of courts held 1331–4 and in 1343 and 1364 survive. In the period 1331–4 and in 1343 a court met between three and five times

each year. The court leet and the manor court were usually held separately; the number of each in a year varied, as did the dates at which they were held. Pleas between tenants provided much of the business. Presentments by the tithingman at the court leet included defaulters from the court, breaches of the assize of ale, many instances of the raising of the hue, and, in 1333, the killing of six ewes and theft of their skins. An aletaster was sometimes appointed at the court leet. Matters before the manor court included infringement of grazing rights and of the lord's rights to timber and certain hay crops, besides tenurial business. The court held in 1364 was apparently a court of survey.[6] A court was held 1453–4[7] but no record of its business survives. The only business at the manor court 1559–60 was a few presentments by the homage and the admission of tenants.[8] At a view of frankpledge held in April 1651 a tithingman was sworn, the jury presented a road in need of repair, the homage presented the death of a copyholder, and other tenurial business was transacted.[9]

For the moiety of the manor held by the earls of Arundel and members of the Howe family[10] a court was mentioned for the years 1327–9, 1579, and 1712,[11] but little is known of its business. An annual court baron was held between 1782 and 1800: the homage presented defaulters from the court, regulations for the use of common pastures and other customs of the manor, encroachments by tenants of other manors, and the need to repair the stocks. In 1796 and 1797 the lessee of the Rectory estate was presented for not keeping a boar or a bull for parish use. Tenants were admitted to copyholds and a hayward was appointed.[12]

The parish spent £106 on poor relief in 1776, c. £135 in 1785. Expenditure had risen to £149 by 1803, when 10 adults and 23 children were relieved regularly, 4 people occasionally. The poor rate was then about the average for the hundred, its level presumably reduced by the £24 earned by the poor: Stapleford was one of the few parishes in which there was no workhouse but some earnings by the poor were recorded.[13] Expenditure on poor relief reached a peak in 1813, when 24 adults received permanent and 9 occasional relief at a cost of £394.[14] The amount raised by the poor rate varied considerably between then and 1829: in 1816 it was £129, in 1818 £397, in 1822 £269.[15] Average annual expenditure 1833–5 was £253. Stapleford

87 Inf. from the manager, Druid's Lodge, Woodford.
88 Kelly's Dir. Wilts. (1855 and later edns.).
89 O.S. Map 6", Wilts. LIX. SE. (1926 edn.); W.R.O. 130/78.
90 Mathieu, Druid's Lodge Confederacy, 14, 49, 68, 115, 161–2.
91 V.C.H. Wilts. ii, p. 165.
92 W.A.M. xxxv. 305.
93 Hoare, Mod. Wilts. Branch and Dole, 22.
94 W.R.O., tithe award.
95 O.S. Maps 6", Wilts. LIX–LX (1887–9 and later edns.); 1/50,000, sheet 184 (1979 edn.).
96 Cal. Chart. R. 1226–57, 243.
97 V.C.H. Wilts. ii, p. 165.
98 Cal. Inq. p.m. vii, p. 44; W.R.O. 192/35A; above, manor (Stapleford).
99 W.R.O., tithe award.

1 Andrews and Dury, Map (W.R.S. viii), pl. 5.
2 O.S. Map 6", Wilts. LIX (1889 edn.); W.R.O., tithe award.   3 Kelly's Dir. Wilts. (1859 and later edns.).
4 Cal. Chart. R. 1226–57, 394.
5 Above, manor; cf. W.R.O. 2057/M 75.
6 W.R.O. 192/15A–D.
7 Ibid. 192/35C.
8 Ibid. 192/15E.
9 Ibid. 192/24B, ff. 25v.–26v.
10 Above, manor.
11 Wilts. Inq. p.m. 1327–77 (Index Libr.), 11–12; P.R.O., E 318/43/2299; ibid. SC 6/1119/1; W.R.O. 317/7.
12 W.R.O. 2057/M 75.
13 Poor Law Abstract, 1804, 558–9.
14 Ibid. 1818, 492–3.
15 Poor Rate Returns, 1816–21, 186; 1822–4, 225; 1825–9, 216.

became part of Wilton poor-law union in 1836,[16] and of Salisbury district in 1974.[17]

CHURCH. Stapleford church, which belonged to Salisbury cathedral in the earlier 12th century,[18] was served by a rector in 1220[19] and until the church was appropriated in 1446 by Easton priory. A vicarage was evidently ordained in 1446.[20] In 1924 it was united with that of Berwick St. James,[21] and in 1992 the united benefice became part of Lower Wylye and Till Valley benefice, served by a rector.[22]

In 1220 Gundreda de Warenne, relict of Geoffrey Hussey (fl. 1198), acknowledged Salisbury cathedral's right to present a rector,[23] but later the advowson was disputed by the Hussey family and the dean and chapter. In 1236 Sir Hubert Hussey challenged a recent presentation by the dean and chapter,[24] and at the institution in 1305 of a rector presented by Maud Hussey an equal right of patronage was said to belong to the cathedral.[25] The cathedral's claim was not mentioned thereafter, and, like Stapleford manor, the advowson of the rectory descended in moieties to Sir Hubert's heirs, Margaret Sturmy and Isabel of Thorney.[26] Between 1337 and 1443 the successors to Margaret's title presented eight or nine times, the successors to Isabel's twice or thrice. In 1337 Henry Sturmy (d. 1381) presented, in 1338 the king presented as keeper of the estate of Henry Sturmy (d. c. 1338), between 1393 and 1423 Sir William Sturmy presented four times, once by grant of a turn, and in 1429 Agnes Sturmy and her husband John Holcombe presented. In 1361 John, Lord Mautravers, and in 1400 Reynold Cobham, Lord Cobham, husband of Eleanor, Baroness Mautravers, presented:[27] no successor of Isabel presented after 1400. Feoffees of Sir William Sturmy presented in 1434: one of them, John Benger, presented in 1442 by grant of a turn[28] and in 1443 granted the advowson to Easton priory.[29] Vicars were presented by the priors of Easton from 1446 to the Dissolution, except in 1473 when four *confratres* of Easton presented, probably because there was no prior, and in 1487, when Laurence Cox presented by grant of a turn.[30] In 1536 the

advowson passed with the Rectory estate to Sir Edward Seymour, Viscount Beauchamp, and in 1547 to St. George's chapel, Windsor.[31] John Biggs, lessee of the Rectory estate, presented in 1551, 1554, and 1571, but thereafter St. George's chapel presented a vicar at every vacancy but one:[32] in 1854 the bishop presented by lapse.[33] The chapel was patron of the united benefice formed in 1924,[34] and from 1992 shared the patronage of Lower Wylye and Till Valley benefice.[35]

The rectory was valued at £8 in 1291, a little below the average for a living in Wylye deanery.[36] The rector apparently received most, if not all, tithes from the parish and had 2 yardlands with pasture for 212 sheep.[37] In 1446 Easton priory endowed the vicarage with £8 a year, personal tithes, 3 a. and a house, and mortuaries and oblations.[38] In 1535 the vicar's income, £9 7s. 2d., was well below the average for the deanery;[39] despite augmentations by Queen Anne's Bounty in 1816 and 1819, and of £15 a year by St. George's chapel in 1818,[40] at c. £106 it remained so in 1831.[41] A further augmentation of £400, of which Queen Anne's Bounty gave £200, was made in 1856.[42] The £8 a year was paid from the Rectory estate in the mid and later 16th century:[43] the amount had been increased to £12 by 1610 and to £34 by 1671.[44] The vicar was entitled to some small tithes,[45] which in 1840 were valued at £30 and commuted. His glebe never exceeded c. 3 a.[46] In 1650 his house was of two storeys, each of two rooms.[47] In 1705 it was said to be old and thatched,[48] c. 1825 mean and inhabited by paupers.[49] The old house, which stood immediately west of the church,[50] was replaced c. 1860 by a red-brick one north-east of the church; the new house, much enlarged in 1884,[51] was sold in 1991.[52]

In 1249 James, rector of Stapleford, was committed to gaol for wrongful disseisin.[53] John Bath, rector 1400–2, was licensed in 1402 to hold with Stapleford another living with cure of souls.[54] Other 15th-century rectors were more eminent and probably all absentees: John Perch, 1402–15, whose successor as rector claimed against his executors for dilapidation of the church and rectory house, was registrar of a

[16] *Poor Law Com. 2nd Rep.* App. D, 560.
[17] O.S. Map 1/100,000, admin. areas, Wilts. (1974 edn.).
[18] *Reg. St. Osmund* (Rolls Ser.), i. 200–1, 203–4.
[19] *Sar. Chart. & Doc.* (Rolls Ser.), 100.
[20] *Cal. Papal Reg.* xiii (2), 832–3; Phillipps, *Wilts. Inst.* i. 138; W.R.O., D 1/2/10, ff. (2nd foliation) 68–9.
[21] *Lond. Gaz.* 9 Dec. 1924, pp. 8972–3.
[22] Inf. from the rector, Great Wishford.
[23] *Sar. Chart. & Doc.* (Rolls Ser.), 100; W. Farrer, *Honors and Knights' Fees*, iii. 34.
[24] *Close R. 1234–7*, 392.
[25] *Reg. Ghent* (Cant. & York Soc.), ii. 662.
[26] *Feet of F. 1272–1327* (W.R.S. i), pp. 94, 109; above, manor (Stapleford).
[27] Phillipps, *Wilts. Inst.* i. 33, 53, 80, 86, 89, 104, 113, 119; *Cal. Pat. 1338–40*, 23.
[28] Phillipps, *Wilts. Inst.* i. 125, 134; *W.A.M.* xxxix. 173.
[29] *Cal. Pat. 1441–6*, 228.
[30] Phillipps, *Wilts. Inst.* i. 138, 146, 151, 153, 163, 169–70, 174.
[31] *Cat. MSS. D. & C. Windsor*, ed. Dalton, p. 421; *Antrobus D.* (W.R.S. iii), p. 67; above, manors (Rectory).
[32] Phillipps, *Wilts. Inst.* i. 215–16, 225; ii. 11, 25, 39, 51,

75, 78, 91, 106.
[33] W.R.O., D 1/2/34, f. 226v.
[34] *Lond. Gaz.* 9 Dec. 1924, pp. 8972–3.
[35] Inf. from the rector.
[36] *Tax. Eccl.* (Rec. Com.), 181.
[37] *Inq. Non.* (Rec. Com.), 178.
[38] Phillipps, *Wilts. Inst.* i. 138; Longleat Mun., Seymour papers, xii, f. 241v.
[39] *Valor Eccl.* (Rec. Com.), ii. 103.
[40] C. Hodgson, *Queen Anne's Bounty*, pp. cxcvi, cccxxxvi.
[41] *Rep. Com. Eccl. Revenues*, 848–9.
[42] Hodgson, *Queen Anne's Bounty, Supplt.* p. lxxiv.
[43] *Cal. Pat. 1547–8*, 148–50; W.R.O., D 1/24/191/1.
[44] *Cat. MSS. D. & C. Windsor*, p. 429.
[45] *W.A.M.* xl. 395–6; W.R.O., D 1/24/191/2.
[46] W.R.O., tithe award; ibid. D 1/24/191/1.
[47] *W.A.M.* xl. 396.
[48] W.R.O., D 1/24/191/3.
[49] Hoare, *Mod. Wilts.* Branch and Dole, 22.
[50] W.R.O., tithe award. [51] Ch. Com. file 40354.
[52] Inf. from the rector.
[53] *Civil Pleas, 1249* (W.R.S. xxvi), p. 70.
[54] *Cal. Papal Reg.* v. 418; Phillipps, *Wilts. Inst.* i. 86, 89.

court of Canterbury;[55] Nicholas Upton, 1434–42, an author of treatises on war and heraldry, became precentor of Salisbury in 1446;[56] Adam Moleyns, 1442–5, was dean of Salisbury 1441–5 and later bishop of Chichester.[57] The prior of Easton, William Marshall, was himself vicar 1487–91.[58] In 1553 the churchwardens complained that the services were not held at the proper times because the vicar also served Winterbourne Stoke; it was also said that, having celebrated communion in that parish, he would return to administer but not receive the sacrament in Stapleford. In the same year the churchwardens reported that crosses had not been removed from the chancel.[59] Some or all of the quarterly sermons were omitted in 1585, probably because the vicar was not qualified to preach.[60] Humphrey Wall, vicar from 1622, signed the *Concurrent Testimony* in 1648, and in 1650 preached twice each Sunday at Stapleford.[61] Few 18th-century incumbents resided in the parish:[62] in 1783 the church was served with Berwick St. James by a curate who held one service at Stapleford each Sunday, alternately in the morning and the afternoon. Communion was celebrated at Christmas, Easter, and Whitsun: there were *c.* 20 communicants.[63] John Matthews, vicar 1808–53, was also vicar of Shrewton, where he lived. He was assisted in 1851 by a curate who lived at Little Langford: on Census Sunday in that year 85 people attended morning service in Stapleford church and 136 afternoon service. George Carpenter, vicar 1854–64, was probably the first resident incumbent for over a century.[64] In 1864 he held a service with a sermon each Sunday morning and Sunday evening. Services were also held on Wednesdays in Lent, on Good Friday, and on Ascension day. Communion was celebrated at Christmas and Easter, on Whit and Trinity Sundays, and on eight other Sundays: there were *c.* 17 communicants at festivals, *c.* 13 at other times.[65] From 1879 until the benefices were united in 1924 Stapleford was held in plurality with Berwick St. James: vicars usually lived at Stapleford.[66]

From 1793, and probably long before, the rent from *c.* 1 a. in Stapleford was used to maintain the church. The rent was 2s. in 1793, £3 3s. in 1873. In 1898 the land was sold and the proceeds invested.[67] The income of *c.* £8 a year from the investment was spent on repairs in the early 20th century,[68] but the charity had apparently been lost by 1992.[69]

The church of *ST. MARY* was so called in 1446 and probably in 1239 or earlier.[70] It is of chalk ashlar and flint and has a chancel and a clerestoried nave with north chapel, south chapel, north tower, south aisle, and two-storeyed south porch.[71] The oldest parts of the church, the north and west walls of the nave, the south arcade, and the west wall of the aisle, are late 12th-century, but the nave is narrow and its shape may be that of the nave of an earlier church. The chancel, wider than the nave, was

THE SOUTH ARCADE OF THE CHURCH

rebuilt in the later 13th century, and the north chapel was built about the same time. The tower was built, after and west of the chapel, in the late 13th century or early 14th, and in the mid 14th the south chapel was built and the south wall of the aisle was rebuilt on its old foundations. New windows and a piscina with triple sedilia were made in the chancel in the 14th century. In the 15th the nave was raised to accommodate the clerestory, and the porch was built. The upper stage of the tower was rebuilt in 1674.[72] The church was extensively restored in 1861: some walls and most of the roofs were rebuilt and windows were altered.[73]

In 1553 plate weighing 1½ oz. was confiscated and a chalice of 6 oz. was left in the parish. Plate belonging to the church in 1992 included a cup and a paten of 1678 but not a plated flagon bought in 1876.[74]

Three bells hung in the church in 1553. The ring was increased to five, apparently by two bells cast by John Wallis, one in 1611 and one in 1615. Three bells cast by Nathaniel Boulter in 1655 presumably replaced the old bells. The bell of 1615 was replaced by one of 1887 cast by Mears & Stainbank, who recast that of 1611 in 1907.[75] The bells of 1655, 1887, and 1907 hung in the church in 1992.[76]

Registers of burials survive from 1633, of

55 *Reg. Chichele* (Cant. & York Soc.), iv. 29, 59–60; Phillipps, *Wilts. Inst.* i. 89, 104.
56 *D.N.B.*; Phillipps, *Wilts. Inst.* i. 125, 134.
57 *D.N.B.* (s.v. Molyneux); Le Neve, *Fasti, 1300–1541, Salisbury,* 4; Phillipps, *Wilts. Inst.* i. 134, 138.
58 *W.A.M.* li. 374.   59 W.R.O., D 1/43/1, f. 117v.
60 Ibid. D 1/43/6, f. 16A.
61 *W.A.M.* xl. 395; *Subscription Bk.* (W.R.S. xxxii), p. 23. There is no evidence that John Saph, described in *W.A.M.* xxxiv. 171 as vicar *c.* 1646, served the church.
62 *Stapleford* (priv. print. 1990 under initials J.P.A., copy in church), 9.
63 *Vis. Queries, 1783* (W.R.S. xxvii), pp. 201–2.
64 *Stapleford* (priv. print. 1990), 9; P.R.O., HO 129/265/1/6/14.
65 W.R.O., D 1/56/7.
66 *Kelly's Dir. Wilts.* (1885 and later edns.); Ch. Com. file 40354/1; above, this section.
67 *Endowed Char. Wilts.* (S. Div.), 638–9.
68 W.R.O., L 2, Stapleford.   69 Inf. from the rector.
70 *Cal. Chart. R.* 1226–57, 243; Longleat Mun., Seymour papers, xii, f. 241v.
71 Illustrations and plans of the church are in *Churches of SE. Wilts.* (R.C.H.M.), pp. 192–4.   72 Date on bldg.
73 J. Buckler, watercolour in W.A.S. Libr., vol. iii. 33; W.R.O., D 1/61/13/17.
74 Nightingale, *Wilts. Plate,* 74–5; inf. from the rector.
75 Walters, *Wilts. Bells,* 204, 297.
76 Inf. from the rector.

baptisms and marriages from 1637; they are incomplete for the 17th century and early 18th.[77]

NONCONFORMITY. In 1605 George Tattershall, then resident in Stapleford and from 1611 owner of a moiety of the manor, was indicted as a recusant.[78] His father-in-law Christopher Biggs, also of Stapleford, was convicted of recusancy in 1609 and c. 1629,[79] and his son George forfeited a lease of the Rectory estate as a papist and a royalist in 1645.[80] Biggs's wife Alice was an excommunicate recusant at her death c. 1619. It was said that her corpse was buried secretly in Stapleford church by an unknown priest: the bishop later ordered its removal.[81] John Saph (probably he who d. 1683) owned an estate in the parish and was a papist in 1657,[82] three papists who lived in the parish in 1676[83] may have been members of the Saph family, and Charles Saph (d. 1726), successor of John Saph as owner of the estate, was a Roman Catholic.[84] In 1783 there was said to be no papist in the parish.[85]

There were three protestant nonconformists in Stapleford in 1676.[86] There was a Quaker meeting house in 1690 and 1703,[87] and Quakers lived in the parish 1682–1715.[88] There was said to be no protestant dissenter in 1783.[89] In 1816 several Baptists lived in Stapleford and in 1820 a house was certified for their meetings. A Methodist chapel beside the western lane at the south end of Stapleford village was built c. 1820 and certified in 1824. On Census Sunday in 1851 Wesleyan Methodists held a morning and an evening service there, attended by 48 and 92 people respectively.[90] No service was held in the chapel after 1946 and it was demolished c. 1970.[91]

EDUCATION. A school attached to the Methodist meeting house in 1824 was probably a Sunday school.[92] In 1833 there was a school in the parish for c. 10 infants but most children attended Great Wishford school.[93] A National school which had 20 pupils in 1847[94] may have been that in Over Street which had 30–40 pupils in 1859.[95] It was presumably closed when a new school incorporating a teacher's house was built at the south end of Stapleford village in 1874.[96] Average attendance at the new school fell from 31 in 1906[97] to 9 in 1914, when some children living in the parish attended Berwick St. James and Great Wishford schools. In 1914 the county council withdrew approval and funding from the school but it continued privately for several years and was re-adopted by the county in 1919 or 1920. In 1925, when there were 10 pupils, it was closed.[98] It was used as a school for 24 boys who were evacuated to neighbouring parishes in 1939 and 1940,[99] but was later a village hall.

In the north part of the parish Berwick St. James school was built in 1936 and closed in 1992.[1]

CHARITY FOR THE POOR. None known.

TILSHEAD

TILSHEAD lies on Salisbury Plain 13 km. WNW. of Amesbury at the head of the valley of the river Till.[2] Its name is first recorded as a form of 'Theodwulf's hide' in the 11th century; the modern form of the name was in use in the 16th century, and the name of the river is derived from it.[3] In 1086 Tilshead was a borough and a large royal estate. The borough may have been planted as a collection centre for wool when sheep farming increased in the late Saxon period,[4] and the estate was evidently far more extensive than the modern parish.[5] Where the additional lands lay is not clear: lands of most neighbouring parishes can be otherwise identified in Domesday Book and it is perhaps most likely that much land worked from Tilshead in 1086 later went out of cultivation and was absorbed as rough pasture by other settlements around the plain.[6] There was extensive early arable on the downs around Tilshead.[7] The

77 W.R.O. 2089/1–6; bishop's transcripts for earlier and some missing years are ibid.
78 Hist. MSS. Com. 9, *Salisbury*, xvii, p. 231; above, manors (Stapleford).
79 *Cal. S.P. Dom.* 1603–10, 557; *W.N. & Q.* viii. 343; P.R.O., STAC 8/271/8.
80 *Cal. Cttee. for Compounding*, i. 78, 699–700.
81 P.R.O., STAC 8/271/8.
82 Williams, *Cath. Recusancy* (Cath. Rec. Soc.), 228; above, manors (Saph's).
83 *Compton Census*, ed. Whiteman, 125; W.R.O., D 1/54/6/5.
84 Williams, *Cath. Recusancy* (Cath. Rec. Soc.), 80, 228; above, manor (Saph's).
85 *Vis. Queries, 1783* (W.R.S. xxvii), p. 202.
86 *Compton Census*, 125.
87 *Meeting Ho. Certs.* (W.R.S. xl), pp. 3, 12.
88 *W.N. & Q.* v. 405, 453, 514; vii. 512; 'Wilts. Quarterly Meeting Min. Bk.' (TS. in W.R.O.), *passim*.
89 *Vis. Queries, 1783* (W.R.S. xxvii), p. 202.
90 *Meeting Ho. Certs.* (W.R.S. xl), pp. 80, 91, 106; O.S. Map 6", Wilts. LIX (1889 edn.); P.R.O., HO 129/265/1/6/15.

91 Inf. from the rector.
92 *Meeting Ho. Certs.* (W.R.S. xl), p. 106.
93 *Educ. Enq. Abstract*, 1084.
94 Nat. Soc. *Inquiry, 1846–7*, Wilts. 10–11.
95 *Acct. of Wilts. Schs.* 42.
96 Ch. Com. file 43910.
97 *Return of Non-Provided Schs.* 28.
98 P.R.O., ED 21/18553; W.R.O., F 8/600/251/1/26/1.
99 W.R.O., F 8/600/251/8/1.
1 Above, Berwick St. Jas., educ.
2 This article was written in 1991. Maps used include O.S. Maps 1", sheet 14 (1817 edn.); 1/50,000, sheet 184 (1979 edn.); 1/25,000, SU 04–05 (1958 edns.); 6", Wilts. XLVI, LIII (1889 and later edns.).
3 *P.N. Wilts.* (E.P.N.S.), 10, 236–7; for the river, below, this section.
4 *V.C.H. Wilts.* ii, pp. 116–17; iv. 1.
5 Ibid. ii, pp. 116–17; below, econ. hist.
6 Pars. N. and E. of Tilshead are described in *V.C.H. Wilts.* x and xi; for Orcheston St. Geo., Imber, and Chitterne All Saints, ibid. ii, pp. 137, 152, 155; for Orcheston St. Mary, above.
7 *V.C.H. Wilts.* i (1), 274–8.

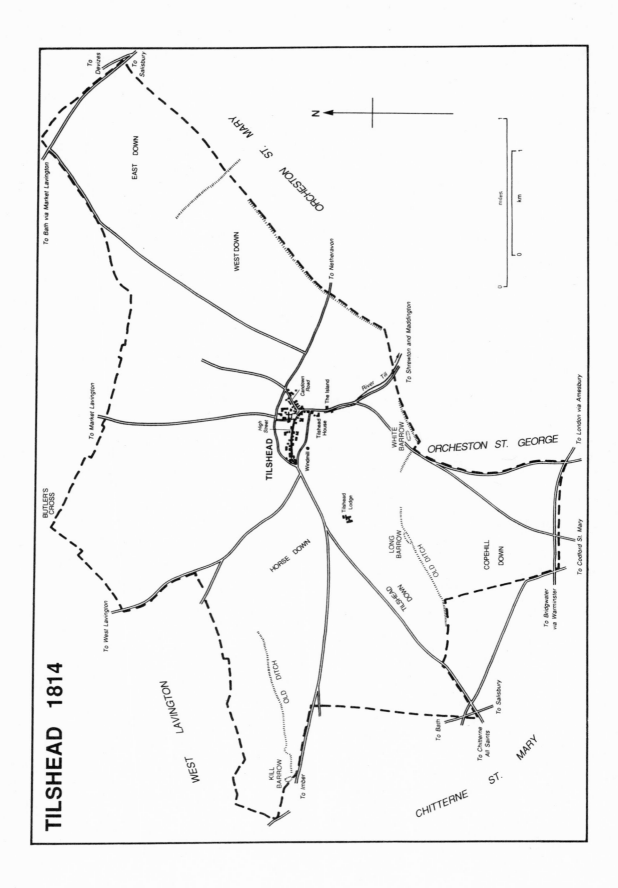

TILSHEAD 1814

parish had two tithings, Tilshead North and Tilshead South, and measured 1,572 ha. (3,883 a.). Tilshead South tithing was in Whorwellsdown hundred,[8] but there is no evidence to support a suggestion that other Tilshead land was in Rowborough hundred.[9] Vestiges of a borough may perhaps be seen[10] but there was no reference to a burgess after 1086.

The parish boundary, unchanged since 1814,[11] is marked chiefly by man-made features, some of which are ancient. The southern of the two lines of the prehistoric Old ditch marks parts of the south-eastern and south-western boundaries. Three crosses stood on the boundaries: one was to the south-west in 1623, Cole's cross had by then been removed from the northern boundary, and the name of Butler's cross, which had marked an angle in the boundary north of Tilshead village,[12] was still in use in the late 20th century. Mounds marked other parts of the northern boundary in the late 19th century and the 20th, and in several other places the boundary is along roads.[13]

Chalk outcrops over the whole parish. The Till is no more than an occasional stream or winter bourne, and it was called the Winterbourne in the 16th century and earlier:[14] the name Till was not apparently used until c. 1900.[15] The large number of mills and the great area of meadow on the 11th-century royal estate called Tilshead suggest that the flow of the river was then more regular.[16] The Till has sometimes flowed with considerable force through Tilshead village, most notably in a destructive flood of 1841.[17] Its valley, mainly below 107 m. and broadening towards the southern parish boundary, and dry valleys which lead north-east and south-west towards it south of the village are lined with gravel; another tongue of gravel lies in a dry valley north-east of the village. The downland is highest, over 152 m., at the west corner of the parish and on East down and near Butler's cross in the northern corners; it reaches c. 140 m. on Copehill down to the south-west.[18]

From the Middle Ages arable seems to have been on the lower slopes of the downs nearer the village, with the higher slopes and land further from the village having been used principally for pasture.[19] From the early 20th century much of the parish has been rough grassland used for military training.[20] The estate called Tilshead included woodland 2 leagues long and 1 league broad in 1086[21] but later the parish was sparsely wooded. In 1886 there was scattered woodland on the downs, some in the north-east and some near Tilshead Lodge, all probably planted after 1814.[22] Most of the plantations survive and some

additional woodland was planted in the later 20th century.[23]

The parish was crossed by many roads over the plain, some of more than local importance. The road from London to Bridgwater (Som.) via Amesbury and Warminster, a major route in the later 17th century, crossed the southern tip of the parish,[24] the main Salisbury–Bath road, important until the mid 18th century,[25] crossed the south-west corner, and another downland Salisbury–Bath road, turnpiked in 1758 and disturnpiked in 1873,[26] crossed the north-eastern tip. On the last of those roads the main Devizes–Salisbury road converged at the parish's easternmost corner. In 1773 an apparently minor road linked Tilshead village to West Lavington to the north and Shrewton and Maddington to the south-east, other minor roads led from the village east across the downs to Netheravon, south-west to Codford St. Mary, and west to Imber, and there were various other downland routes. From the Imber road a road leading south-west to Chitterne All Saints was made between 1773 and 1814;[27] it was improved in the early 19th century.[28] Military use of the downs from the early 20th century led to the diversion or closure of roads, including those from Bath and Devizes to Salisbury. The route from West Lavington via Tilshead to Shrewton became part of a new Devizes–Salisbury road c. 1900.[29] The only other roads in the parish in public use in the late 20th century were one leading east from the village to join the old Salisbury road at the Bustard inn in Shrewton and the road to Chitterne.

Archaeological evidence of much prehistoric activity survives within the parish. The southern line of Old ditch, although broken, extends for c. 3.5 km. within Tilshead and along its boundaries, the northern line for 1.4 km. To the east, a third ancient ditch runs north-west and south-east, crossing the southern line of Old ditch and dividing East and West downs. A long barrow on Old ditch south-west of Tilshead village is 274 m. long and perhaps the largest in England. Beside the ditch south of the village lies White barrow, 233 m. long; its site, c. 2 a., was acquired by the National Trust in 1909. In the extreme west lies Kill barrow, 52 m. long, and there are other long and bowl barrows on the southern and eastern downs. A few artefacts, some associated with the barrows and ditches, have been found and date from periods from the Neolithic to the Pagan Saxon. There is evidence of prehistoric field systems on the western downs.[30]

In 1086, with 66 burgesses among its inhabitants, Tilshead was unusually populous but

8   Below, local govt.
9   *V.C.H. Wilts.* ii, p. 197.
10   Below, this section.
11   W.R.O., EA/127.   12   Ibid. 412/1.
13   O.S. Maps 6", Wilts. XLVI, LIII (1889 and later edns.).
14   Hoare, *Mod. Wilts.* Branch and Dole, 44; *P.N. Wilts.* (E.P.N.S.), 10.
15   O.S. Map 6", Wilts. LIII. SE. (1901 edn.).
16   *V.C.H. Wilts.* ii, pp. 56 n., 116–17.
17   *W.A.M.* xlix. 262, where 1871 is given for 1841.
18   Para. based on Geol. Surv. Map 1", drift, sheet 282 (1967 edn.).
19   Below, econ. hist.

20   Ibid.; below, this section.
21   *V.C.H. Wilts.* ii, p. 117.
22   O.S. Maps 6", Wilts. XLVI, LIII (1889 edns.); W.R.O., EA/127; for Tilshead Lodge, below, this section.
23   Inf. from Defence Land Agent, Durrington.
24   J. Ogilby, *Brit.* (1675), pl. 78.
25   Above, Steeple Langford, intro. [roads].
26   *V.C.H. Wilts.* iv. 257, 270; *L.J.* xxix. 367.
27   *Andrews and Dury, Map* (W.R.S. viii), pl. 8; W.R.O., EA/127.
28   W.R.O. 823/16, MS. acct. of Tilshead by J. H. Johnson.   29   *V.C.H. Wilts.* iv. 266.
30   Ibid. i (1), 114, 144–5, 192–3, 253, 258, 275, 278; *W.A.M.* xxxvi. 188; lxxvii. 139–42.

taxation assessments suggest that by the 14th century that was no longer so. In 1377 there were 125 poll-tax payers in the parish.[31] The population was 327 in 1801, for reasons that are not clear had risen sharply to 397 by 1811, and had reached 523 by 1851. Between 1861 and 1871 emigration reduced the number from 500 to 467, and the population was under 400 between 1891 and 1921. It rose from 395 in 1921 to 610 in 1931, evidently because army camps in the parish were more fully occupied at the later date. The total had risen to 989 by 1951[32] but, probably because no camp was in residential use, had fallen to 314 by 1961 and 287 by 1981. There were 343 inhabitants in 1991.[33]

Tilshead village lies on the gravel near the parish's centre. The church stands north of a triangular open space at a road junction. The space and the width of the village street west of it may be evidence of the plan of the borough.[34] North and south of the junction stand houses called North Manor and South Manor: their sites may be those of the demesne farmsteads of the two manors in the parish.[35] In the late 18th century building extended west from the junction c. 500 m. along the street, later High Street, and south c. 250 m. along the Shrewton road to a farmstead east of the road and later called the Island. East of the church in the Netheravon road, later Candown Road, there are houses possibly of the 17th century, and in 1760 there was a line of settlement along the road. From the west end of High Street back lanes lead on the north to the Netheravon road and on the south to the Shrewton road.[36] Between 1760 and 1814 a few cottages were built in the centre of the triangle at the road junction south of the church.[37]

Some buildings of 17th-century or earlier origin survive in High Street. West of the church on the north side the Rose and Crown is a late-medieval timber-framed house of four bays: the roof of what was its central hall was smoke-blackened and may have a central cruck truss. In the early 17th century a chimney stack and an upper floor were built in the hall and the south front was rebuilt in banded flint and ashlar: a north wing was added at the west end in the later 17th century. Further west on the south side Bell Cottage and the Black Horse may both be of 16th-century origin. Near the middle of the street on the north side Dean and Chapter House, timber-framed, was built in the earlier 17th century and refronted in brick in the early 19th. South Manor, a small house with a north

front of banded flint, and, immediately west of the Rose and Crown, Hooper's Farm, timber-framed and fronted in bands and chequerwork of flint and ashlar, may also be 17th-century. The houses possibly of 17th-century origin in Candown Road are Slades Farm, north-west of the road, and Lower Farm, south-east of the road.

North Manor was built c. 1800 and extended in the early 19th century. Between 1773 and 1814 there was new building in Candown Road, including a farmstead on the south-east side at the village's eastern edge.[38] In 1820 Tilshead House, a red-brick house of three storeys and three bays, was built for Richard Norris on the west side of the Shrewton road:[39] it was used as a home for the elderly in 1991. Many cottages in the village in the early 19th century were mud-walled[40] and thus vulnerable to damage by floods such as that of 1841 in which nine were destroyed. In 1842 two cottages, paid for by a national subscription to aid victims of the flood in Tilshead and neighbouring villages, were built on the south side of High Street.[41] New building of the later 19th century and the early 20th included a nonconformist chapel and, on the site of a house north of the church, a school.[42] Drax House, at the junction of High Street and Candown Road, and May Villa, near the Island, bear the dates 1900 and 1901 respectively. At the village's western end, called Townsend in 1886 and 1957 but later West End,[43] six council houses were built north of the Devizes road and six south of it in 1938–9.[44] A commercial garage was later built north of the road and two bungalows south of it. In Imber Place, north-west of Candown Road, 10 council houses were built in 1949[45] and another 8 and 2 bungalows in the early 1960s. South-east of Candown Road four old people's bungalows were built in the late 1970s. Between 1957 and 1982 the buildings in the centre of the triangle south of the church were demolished,[46] and in 1991 there was a camping and caravan site south of Tilshead House.

In 1814 the only building in the parish outside the village was Tilshead Lodge,[47] built in the early 18th century, presumably as a sporting lodge. It was leased to Francis Godolphin (from 1712 earl of Godolphin, d. 1766) in 1704, 1730, and 1736,[48] and later to William, duke of Cumberland (d. 1765).[49] Another tenant may have been either William Graham, duke of Montrose (d. 1790), or his son James, duke of Montrose (d. 1836).[50] Formal gardens had been made

[31] V.C.H. Wilts. ii, pp. 116–17; iv. 299, 308, 311; Tax List, 1332 (W.R.S. xlv), 76.
[32] V.C.H. Wilts. iv. 324, 326, 359; for the camps, below, this section.   [33] Census, 1961; 1981; 1991.
[34] See plate facing this p.
[35] Below, manors; econ. hist.
[36] Andrews and Dury, Map (W.R.S. viii), pl. 8; W.R.O. 1252/1.
[37] W.R.O. 1252/1; ibid. EA/127.
[38] Ibid. EA/127; Andrews and Dury, Map (W.R.S. viii), pl. 8.
[39] Date on bldg.; below, manors (Tilshead S.).
[40] Hoare, Mod. Wilts. Branch and Dole, 44.
[41] Endowed Char. Wilts. (S. Div.), 706; W.A.M. xlix. 262.
[42] Below, nonconf.; educ.; W.A.S. Libr., MS. acct. of

Tilshead by J. H. Johnson, photo. of church and Old Parsonage.
[43] O.S. Maps 1/25,000, SU 04 (1958 edn.); 6", Wilts. XLVI (1889 and later edns.); 1/10,000, SU 04 NW. (1983 edn.).
[44] W.R.O., G 1/501/1; G 1/602/2.
[45] Ibid. G 1/600/1.
[46] O.S. Maps 1/25,000, SU 04 (1958 edn.); 1/10,000, SU 04 NW. (1983 edn.).
[47] W.R.O., EA/127.
[48] Ibid. 130/7, lease, Scawen to Godolphin, 1736; Hoare, Mod. Wilts. Branch and Dole, 44; Complete Peerage, v. 748–9.
[49] Complete Peerage, iii. 573; Wilts. Cuttings, xvi. 373.
[50] Hoare, Mod. Wilts. Branch and Dole, 44; Complete Peerage, ix. 156–7.

The east end of the village street in the mid 19th century

Tilshead Lodge, demolished in the later 20th century

TILSHEAD

MADDINGTON: THE BUILDING CALLED THE PRIORY

GREAT WISHFORD: THE 18TH-CENTURY SCHOOL

GREAT WISHFORD: THE 17TH-CENTURY ALMSHOUSE

BULFORD: THE NORTH FRONT OF BULFORD MANOR

south of the house by 1760.[51] The house was apparently rebuilt *c.* 1800[52] and was demolished between 1957 and 1982.[53] Between 1814 and 1841 two downland farmsteads were built, one of them on Copehill down.[54] In 1886 there were farm buildings in the parish's north-eastern and north-western corners, and cottages in the south-west corner. All were demolished in the 20th century.[55]

There were two inns in the parish in the 1750s,[56] probably the Crown, from 1822 or earlier the Rose and Crown, and the Bell, which stood south-east of Candown Road in 1814.[57] Friendly societies recorded in the parish 1813–15[58] may have met at the two inns. The Rose and Crown was open in 1991, the Bell was closed after 1939,[59] and the Black Horse was open in 1848[60] and 1991.

In the early 19th century and the early 20th racehorses were trained at Tilshead Lodge.[61] Hares were coursed in the parish, and a hare warren straddled the eastern boundary with Orcheston St. Mary *c.* 1820.[62] In 1924 and 1925 the Old Hawking club had its headquarters in Tilshead,[63] and in the 1950s the Royal Artillery (Salisbury Plain) and Wylye Valley hunts met at the Black Horse.[64]

Lands in the east part of the parish bought by the War Department in 1897[65] had by 1910 become part of artillery ranges extending north-west from Larkhill in Durrington: later the west part of the parish was included in the Imber ranges. The parish was used for training in the use of tanks for much of the 20th century. In the First World War there was a kite balloon school at Tilshead, in the Second a landing ground was made west of the village,[66] and there was a landing strip north of the village *c.* 1980.[67] West Down North camp had been set up in the parish's north-eastern corner by 1903. It was replaced *c.* 1925 by West Down camp immediately east of the village, and temporary camps, some tented, were set up elsewhere in the parish between 1918 and 1945.[68] West Down camp remained in summer use in the 1990s.[69] Groups of military buildings which stood *c.* 400 m. north of the village and south and west of Tilshead Lodge in 1957 had mostly been demolished by

1982:[70] a brick water tower stood south of the Chitterne road in 1991.

MANORS AND OTHER ESTATES.

In 1066 and 1086 the large estate called Tilshead belonged to the king. It had to render to him yearly the cost of a night's food and lodging for him and his household.[71]

What became *TILSHEAD NORTH* manor was granted, perhaps before 1113, by Henry I to Holy Trinity abbey, Caen (Calvados).[72] The grant was confirmed in 1131.[73] The manor was in royal keeping during wars with France in the 14th century and the early 15th.[74] It was apparently among Caen's Wiltshire possessions which in 1416 were granted to Syon abbey (Mdx.), founded the previous year:[75] a confirmation of Syon's endowments in 1424 expressly included it.[76] In 1442, however, Henry VI granted the manor to King's College, Cambridge; in 1444 Syon abbey was pardoned for illegal entry on that and other manors formerly Caen's,[77] and the college's right to it was confirmed.[78] The abbey still claimed the manor in 1459, when the college held it,[79] and in 1461 Edward IV restored it to Syon. In 1462 the college conceded the abbey's right,[80] which was confirmed by Edward IV in 1465[81] and by Henry VI in 1470.[82] After the Dissolution the Crown retained the manor until 1583[83] or later. By 1593 it had passed, presumably by sale, to Sir Robert Cecil[84] (cr. earl of Salisbury 1605, d. 1612). Cecil or his son William, earl of Salisbury,[85] apparently sold the manor in portions.[86]

Giles Tooker (d. 1623) bought the lordship and demesne and held them in 1616. He was succeeded in turn by his son Edward[87] (d. *c.* 1671) and grandson Sir Giles Tooker, Bt. (d. 1675). Sir Giles's estate was divided between his heirs, his sisters Philippa, wife of Sir Thomas Gore, and Martha, wife of Sir Walter Ernle, Bt.[88] The lordship and most of the lands passed to Philippa's son William Gore and in turn to William's sons Thomas (d. 1728) and William (d. 1769). The younger William's heir may have been his cousin John Gore,[89] named as owner of the estate 1780–95.[90] John's heir was probably

51 W.R.O. 1252/1.
52 W.A.S. Libr., sale cat. xi, no. 12; see above, plate facing p. 266.
53 O.S. Maps 1/25,000, SU 04 (1958 edn.); 1/10,000, SU 04 NW. (1983 edn.).
54 W.R.O., EA/127; P.R.O., HO 107/1167.
55 O.S. Maps 6", Wilts. XLVI, LIII (1889 and later edns.); 1/10,000, SU 04 NW. (1983 edn.).
56 W.R.O., A 1/326/1–2.
57 Ibid. A 1/326/3; ibid. EA/127.
58 *Poor Law Abstract, 1818,* 492–3.
59 *Kelly's Dir. Wilts.* (1939).
60 Ibid. (1848).
61 Hoare, *Mod. Wilts.* Branch and Dole, 44; W.R.O. 776/327.
62 *V.C.H. Wilts.* iv. 382; C. Greenwood, *Map of Wilts.* (1820).
63 R. Upton, *O for a Falconer's Voice,* 167; above, Shrewton, intro.
64 *V.C.H. Wilts.* iv. 377.
65 Below, manors (Tilshead S.).
66 N. D. G. James, *Plain Soldiering,* 82, 122–3, 128, 176.
67 O.S. Map 1/10,000, SU 04 NW. (1983 edn.).
68 James, *Plain Soldiering,* 123, 137; Wilts. Cuttings, xi. 25.

69 Inf. from Mrs. A. M. Dixon, Rose and Crown.
70 O.S. Maps 6", SU 04 NW. (1961 edn.); 1/10,000, SU 04 NW. (1983 edn.).   71 *V.C.H. Wilts.* ii, pp. 116–17.
72 *Caen Chart.* ed. M. Chibnall, p. xxxi; Hoare, *Mod. Wilts.* Branch and Dole, 43.
73 *Reg. Regum Anglo-Norm.* ii, no. 1692.
74 e.g. *Cal. Pat.* 1343–5, 224; 1401–5, 46; 1413–16, 108–9.
75 *Cal. Pat.* 1416–22, 34–5; *V.C.H. Mdx.* i. 182.
76 *Cal. Pat.* 1422–9, 205–7.
77 Ibid. 1441–6, 111–12, 256.
78 *Rot. Parl.* v. 89.
79 *V.C.H. Cambs.* iii. 379–80.
80 *Cal. Pat.* 1461–7, 56–7, 177.
81 *V.C.H. Mdx.* i. 185.
82 *Rot. Parl.* v. 456.
83 P.R.O., E 310/26/154, f. 33.
84 Ibid. REQ 2/229/2.
85 *Complete Peerage,* xi. 403–4.
86 Below, this section.
87 *Wilts. Inq. p.m.* 1625–49 (Index Libr.), 38–41; W.R.O. 412/1.
88 Above, Maddington, manors (Winterbourne Maddington).
89 Hoare, *Mod. Wilts.* Heytesbury, 183; W.R.O. 101/119/1.   90 W.R.O., A 1/345/394.

his nephew Montague Gore, whose father the Revd. Charles Gore apparently held the estate, c. 800 a., as trustee in 1814 and c. 1825.[91] Some of the land had been sold by 1844.[92] After Montague's death in 1864[93] other land was sold to W. D. Hulbert (d. 1890). Hulbert's executors sold Tilshead Manor farm, 344 a., in 1890 to Joseph Jackson. In 1908 the farm was bought by John Chamings,[94] who later bought other land in the parish.[95] Chamings sold c. 130 a. to the War Department in 1911; in 1920, after his death, his estate of 450 a. was sold,[96] perhaps to R. J. Evans who owned 440 a. in 1924.[97] Those lands too were later bought by the War Department: the Ministry of Defence owned them and nearly all the other land in the parish in 1991.[98]

In 1844 Walter Long (d. 1867) held c. 200 a. in Tilshead, formerly part of Charles Gore's estate. The land descended to Walter's son Richard (d. 1875) and to Richard's son W. H. Long, who in 1905 sold it to the Cavendish Land Company. The company sold it in 1906 to R. J. Farquharson, and it was part of an estate sold by Farquharson to the War Department in 1933.[99]

The lands inherited by Martha (d. 1688) and Sir Walter Ernle (d. 1682) passed with Winterbourne Maddington manor in Maddington in turn to their grandsons Sir Walter Ernle, Bt. (d. 1690), and Sir Edward Ernle, Bt. (d. 1729), to Sir Edward's daughter Elizabeth Drax (d. 1759), and to her son Thomas Drax. Thomas (d. 1789) was succeeded in turn by his brother Edward (d. 1791) and by Edward's daughter Sarah (d. 1822), wife of Richard Erle-Drax-Grosvenor, who held c. 160 a. in Tilshead in 1815. Those lands passed from Richard's and Sarah's son Richard (d. 1828) to their daughter Jane (d. 1853), wife of John Sawbridge-Erle-Drax, and in turn to Jane's daughters Maria Sawbridge-Erle-Drax (d. 1885) and Sarah, wife of F. A. P. Burton. Sarah (d. 1905) was succeeded by her daughter Ernle Plunkett, Baroness Dunsany (d. 1916), who sold 78 a. to the War Department in 1911. Ernle's son Reginald Plunkett-Ernle-Erle-Drax[1] sold the remaining 83 a. in 1917[2] to John Chamings: they were part of the estate sold in 1920 after Chamings's death.[3]

Several estates in the parish traceable from the late 16th century or the early 17th may have been derived from copyholds sold by Robert, earl of Salisbury.[4] One such estate, comprising 83 a.

and pasture for 220 sheep, was sold in 1603 by John Eaton to John Long.[5] It passed from father to son to a second, third, and fourth John Long,[6] the last of whom held it in 1697.[7] In 1706 Catherine Stockdale sold the estate to Sir William Scawen[8] (d. 1722). Sir William was succeeded by his nephew Thomas Scawen (d. 1774), whose estate included *TILSHEAD LODGE*. Thomas or his son James[9] sold the estate, which may have been dispersed. In 1802 the house and a few acres were sold by Elizabeth Pratt to Gorges Lowther,[10] who bought several estates in the parish c. 1805, including the Rectory estate.[11] His combined estate, the Tilshead Lodge estate, 1,026 a. from inclosure in 1814,[12] was held in 1816 and 1817 by H. P. Isherwood[13] and sold in 1819[14] presumably to John Long, who held it in 1820 and 1829. It was acquired c. 1830 by George Watson-Taylor[15] (d. 1841) and his wife Anne (d. 1852) and passed as part of their Erlestoke estate to their son Simon (d. 1902) and to his son G. S. A. Watson-Taylor.[16] In 1907 H. W. Hooper bought 292 a., which he sold in 1911 to the War Department. The remainder was bought in 1908 by R. J. Farquharson and sold by him in 1933 to the War Department.[17]

The estate which John Elliott *alias* Hill inherited from his father and in 1594 devised to his son John[18] may have been another former copyhold. It was conveyed with other holdings to Thomas Naishe in 1654,[19] and in 1694 was conveyed by Jonathan Hill and his wife to Laurence Cooper.[20] By will proved 1705 Cooper devised the estate to John Wansborough.[21] It was later bought by Joan Harris and passed to her kinsman James Harris, who held it in 1745.[22] James (d. 1780) was succeeded by his son Sir James (cr. Baron Malmesbury 1788, earl of Malmesbury 1800, d. 1820),[23] from whom the estate was acquired, presumably by purchase, by W. N. Maton c. 1787. A Mrs. Hayden held it in 1796 and 1804, as did Gorges Lowther from 1805.[24] It became part of the Tilshead Lodge estate.[25]

Peter Crook (d. 1633) sold to John Randall (fl. 1666) c. 100 a. of arable and pasture rights for 80 sheep, perhaps formerly part of Tilshead North manor. In 1692 Randall's son John sold that and other estates to Robert Goldisborough,[26] who in 1699 held c. 170 a. and pasture rights for 180 sheep in Tilshead.[27] In 1724 the

91 Hoare, *Mod. Wilts.* Branch and Dole, 43; ibid. Heytesbury, 183; W.R.O., EA/127. 92 Below, this section.
93 Burke, *Land. Gent.* (1871), 522.
94 G.P.L., Treas. Solicitor, 1755/67.
95 Below, this section.
96 W.A.S. Libr., sale cat. xiii, no. 13; inf. from Defence Land Agent. 97 W.R.O., G 1/500/17.
98 Inf. from Defence Land Agent.
99 Burke, *Land. Gent.* (1906), 1039–40; G.P.L., Treas. Solicitor, 1638/67; below, this section (Tilshead Lodge).
1 Above, Maddington, manors (Winterbourne Maddington); W.R.O. 148, terrier, 1815, f. 102; G.P.L., Treas. Solicitor, 739/59.
2 W.A.S. Libr., sale cat. xxiv, no. 25.
3 Ibid. sale cat. xiii, no. 13; above, this section.
4 P.R.O., REQ 2/229/2.
5 W.R.O. 412/1; ibid. A 1/200/1, m. 2.
6 Ibid. 130/7, deed, Cole to Roberts, 1672.
7 Ibid. 649/8/8, deed, Eyre to Cooper, 1688; 649/8/10, deed, Eyre to Petty, 1697.

8 Ibid. 130/7, deed, Stockdale to Scawen, 1706.
9 Ibid. 130/7, lease, Scawen to Godolphin, 1736; O. Manning and W. Bray, *Hist. Surr.* ii. 510.
10 W.R.O. 323/4. 11 Below, this section.
12 W.R.O., EA/127.
13 Ibid. A 1/345/128A; A 1/345/394.
14 W.A.S. Libr., sale cat. xi, no. 12.
15 W.R.O., A 1/345/128A; A 1/345/394.
16 *V.C.H. Wilts.* vii. 84; Burke, *Land. Gent.* (1871), 1361.
17 G.P.L., Treas. Solicitor, 275/50; 1216/76.
18 W.R.O. 323/1, will of John Elliott *alias* Hill, 1594.
19 Ibid. 323/1, deed, Foote to Naishe, 1654.
20 Ibid. 323/2, deed, Hill to Cooper, 1694.
21 Ibid. 323/2, will of Laurence Cooper, 1705.
22 Ibid. 212B/5950. 23 *Complete Peerage*, viii. 358–9.
24 W.R.O., A 1/345/394.
25 Above, this section (Tilshead Lodge).
26 *W.N. & Q.* vii. 37; W.R.O. 323/2, deeds, Randall to Goldisborough, 1692.
27 W.R.O. 323/2, deed, Goldisborough to Gilbert, 1699.

Revd. William Aishton sold an estate which may have included lands formerly Goldisborough's to the dean and chapter of Salisbury.[28] The cathedral owned 94 a. in Tilshead from inclosure in 1814.[29] The Ecclesiastical Commissioners sold the land to the War Department in 1928–9.[30]

In 1206 Romsey abbey (Hants) held 1 hide or more in Tilshead:[31] the estate became *TILSHEAD SOUTH* manor.[32] The manor was presumably part of Steeple Ashton manor granted in 1539 by the abbey to Thomas Seymour[33] (cr. Baron Seymour 1547), and on his attainder in 1549 apparently passed to the Crown.[34] As part of Steeple Ashton manor it was sold by the Crown in 1629 and descended in the Long family from *c.* 1630.[35] It was held by Sir Walter Long, Bt. (d. 1672), Sir Walter Long, Bt. (d. 1710), Calthorpe Long (d. 1729), Sir Philip Long, Bt. (d. 1741), the Revd. John Long (d. 1748), and Walter Long (d. 1807).[36] Between 1760 and 1780 most of the land was sold[37] but Catherine Long was lord of the manor in 1814.[38] Of the farms derived from the manor the largest, South, was held in 1780 by a Mr. Miles and from 1791 by the Revd. Dr. Kent, perhaps Ambrose Kent (d. 1793), who also had several smaller holdings in the parish.[39] What had been Kent's estate belonged *c.* 1800 to a Mrs. Norris and *c.* 1810 to Richard Norris (d. 1826). Norris's estate, *c.* 850 a. from inclosure in 1814, was retained by his relict until *c.* 1838 and was acquired *c.* 1840 by Stephen Mills[40] (d. 1857),[41] who was succeeded by his sister Martha Mills. Martha (d. 1903) sold 500 a. in 1897 to the War Department and devised the remainder to her cousin T. L. Mills[42] (d. 1909). Most of T. L. Mills's lands were sold by his executors to the War Department in 1911.[43]

Lands which had been part of Tilshead South manor were apparently divided between William Wallis and Thomas Stevens. Wallis's share was bought by Joseph Houlton (d. 1720) and Stevens's by Joseph's son Joseph. The elder Joseph devised his portion to the young Joseph's son Nathaniel and in 1723 the younger Joseph (d. 1731) settled his on Nathaniel[44] (d. 1754). In 1768 Nathaniel's relict Mary (d. 1770) apparently held the lands.[45] The estate may have been that in the southern part of the parish held by William Cooper in 1781, acquired by Gorges Lowther *c.* 1804, and thereafter part of Tilshead Lodge estate.[46]

In 1086 four thegns held land at Tilshead. Alward held 1 hide, Alestan ½ hide, and Alvric Parvus and Almar 2½ yardlands each.[47] The holdings were apparently represented by four Tilshead estates recorded in 1242–3. Alvric's was probably the hide held by serjeanty in 1198 by William Spileman[48] (fl. *c.* 1212).[49] In 1242–3 Laurence le Gras was said to hold it of Spileman; no later reference to the estate has been found. Hyde abbey (Hants) held ⅕ knight's fee in 1242–3. Herbert of Stoke held the estate of the abbey and Robert Omedieu of Herbert.[50] Both Herbert and Robert were alive in 1249,[51] and in 1428 an estate was still said to be held by Robert's heirs.[52] It may have been that settled in 1444 on Isabel, relict of John Romsey, for life: the settlement was acknowledged before the abbot of Hyde in 1462[53] but the estate has not been traced thereafter. The other estates in 1242–3 were of ⅕ knight's fee, held by Eustace of Hull of Ellis of Hull who held of Sir Ellis Giffard, and of 1/10 knight's fee, held by Walter de Baynton of the honor of Trowbridge.[54] Either Hull's or Baynton's estate may have been that including 62 a. in Tilshead held by Peter of Middleton in 1315[55] and by his son Robert in 1350.[56] The Middletons' estate was settled in 1414 on Henry Pyres and his wife Christine[57] and may have been that claimed *c.* 1510 by Elizabeth, wife of John Tremayle, and Joan, wife of Thomas Brooke, as daughters and heirs of John Speke.[58] Thomas and Joan apparently held a moiety of an estate in Tilshead in 1527.[59] That or the other moiety was held in 1544 by Thomas Horton[60] (d. 1549) and passed to his son Edward (d. 1603), who devised his estates to his grand-nephew Edward Horton (d. 1605). The Tilshead lands, however, passed to William Horton, nephew of Edward (d. 1603). In 1610 they were settled by William on his son Toby, who in 1618 conveyed them to Sir John Horton (d. 1667), brother and heir of Edward (d. 1605).[61] In 1654 they were among lands conveyed to Thomas Naishe,[62] and with Naishe's other holdings later became part of the Tilshead Lodge estate.[63]

An estate including what became *COPEHILL* farm belonged to William Slade from *c.* 1780 until *c.* 1787, James Slade from *c.* 1788 until 1793, and another William Slade from *c.* 1794.[64] It comprised 221 a. in 1814[65] and was sold after William's death in 1838.[66] It was conveyed in 1897 to John Coleman. Copehill farm, 143 a.,

28 *V.C.H. Wilts.* iii. 199.   29 W.R.O., EA/127.
30 Inf. from the Librarian, Salisbury cath.
31 *Rot. Chart.* (Rec. Com.), 162.
32 Hoare, *Mod. Wilts.* Branch and Dole, 44.
33 *L. & P. Hen. VIII,* xiv (1), p. 75.
34 *Complete Peerage,* xi. 637–9.
35 *V.C.H. Wilts.* viii. 202.
36 Ibid. vii. 173.
37 W.R.O. 1252/1; ibid. A 1/345/128A.
38 Ibid. EA/127.
39 Ibid. A 1/345/128A; *Alum. Oxon. 1715–1886,* ii. 788.
40 W.R.O., A 1/345/128A–B; ibid. EA/127; for Ric. Norris's d., mon. in church.
41 Princ. Regy. Fam. Div., will of Steph. Mills, 1857.
42 Ibid. will of Martha Mills, 1903; inf. from Defence Land Agent.   43 G.P.L., Treas. Solicitor, 2105/64.
44 *W.A.M.* xliii. 298, 306–7; *W.N. & Q.* vi. 212; for the Houltons, ibid. pedigree at pp. 272–3.
45 *W.A.M.* xliii. 298.
46 W.R.O., A 1/345/128A; above, this section.

47 *V.C.H. Wilts.* ii, pp. 160–1.
48 Ibid. p. 78; *Bk. of Fees,* i. 12; ii. 722, 728, 734, 742.
49 *Red Bk. Exch.* (Rolls Ser.), ii. 485.
50 *Bk. of Fees,* ii. 734, 742.
51 P.R.O., CP 25/1/251/16, no. 55.
52 *Feud. Aids,* v. 244.
53 *Cal. Close, 1461–8,* 93–4.
54 *Bk. of Fees,* ii. 722, 728; for the honor, *V.C.H. Wilts.* vii. 128.
55 *Feet of F. 1272–1327* (W.R.S. i), p. 92.
56 Ibid. *1327–77* (W.R.S. xxix), p. 94.
57 *Feet of F. 1377–1509* (W.R.S. xli), p. 73.
58 P.R.O., C 1/367, no. 49.
59 Ibid. CP 25/2/46/319, no. 32.
60 Ibid. CP 25/2/46/323, no. 55.
61 *W.A.M.* v, pedigree at pp. 316–17; xli. 245–6, 249, 252.   62 W.R.O. 323/1, deed, Foot to Naishe, 1654.
63 Above, this section.
64 W.R.O., A 1/345/394.   65 Ibid. EA/127.
66 W.A.S. Libr., sale cat. xi, no. 18.

was offered for sale in 1909 after Coleman's death;[67] it was sold, apparently by Coleman's trustees, in 1920 to J. C. Henley. In 1934 Henley sold it to the War Department.[68]

Tilshead church was appropriated by Ivychurch priory in 1317.[69] The *RECTORY* estate, comprising tithes and 2 yardlands,[70] passed from the priory to the Crown at the Dissolution[71] and was granted in 1602 to Robert Hopton.[72] Robert was succeeded by his son Sir Ralph (cr. Baron Hopton 1643, d. 1652),[73] whose estates were sequestrated in or before 1650.[74] By 1662 they had been restored to his coheirs, his sisters Catherine, wife of John Wyndham, and Mary, relict of Sir Thomas Hartop, his niece Elizabeth, wife of Sir Trevor Williams, Bt., and his brother-in-law Sir Baynham Throckmorton, who in that year jointly sold the Rectory estate to Edward Tripp.[75] In 1678 Tripp sold it to Edward Halliday[76] (d. 1701 or 1702), who was succeeded in turn by his son John (d. 1737) and by John's son John (d. 1754). The younger John's relict Mary (will proved 1792) held the estate for life[77] and John Hayter acquired it *c.* 1801, Gorges Lowther *c.* 1804.[78] In respect of the estate 493 a. were allotted at inclosure in 1814:[79] that land was added to Lowther's Tilshead Lodge estate.[80]

Tithes worth 4*s.* from Romsey abbey's demesne in Tilshead were granted in 1252 to the vicar of Ashton,[81] presumably Steeple Ashton: no later reference to them has been found. Tithes from Tilshead were also due to the abbey in 1341.[82]

Before 1317 tithes from the demesne of Tilshead North manor were held by the prebendary of South Newton.[83] As an endowment of the prebend in the conventual church, they were appropriated by Wilton abbey in 1450, passed to the Crown at the Dissolution, and were granted in 1551 to William Herbert, earl of Pembroke.[84] They descended with the earldom and in 1814 were exchanged for 87 a. in Tilshead.[85] In 1911 that land was sold by Sidney, earl of Pembroke and of Montgomery, to the War Department.[86]

ECONOMIC HISTORY. The royal estate called Tilshead comprised in 1086 land for 40 ploughteams: there were 9 teams with 22 *servi* and 10 coliberts on the demesne, and 34 *villani* and 32 coscets shared 18 teams. It was said to

include meadow 1 league by ½ league and there was pasture 1½ league by 1 league. Of the four smaller estates Alward's was worked by the single team which the land could sustain and included 1 furlong of pasture, and Alvric's had land for ½ team.[87]

It is probable that each of the two tithings in the parish had its own open fields and common pastures: Tilshead North was *c.* 3,000 a., Tilshead South *c.* 900 a.[88] In the 16th century there were apparently two open fields in each tithing, in both cases called East and West,[89] and in the 18th century the lands of the two main manors were not intermixed. The fields of Tilshead South tithing in 1760, then called East and South, lay east and south-west of the village and beyond them were East and South downs.[90] In the 17th century some downland pasture, perhaps on Copehill down, was several.[91] The two fields of Tilshead North presumably abutted those of Tilshead South east and west of the village. In the late 14th century Tilshead North manor included downland cattle pasture called Oxen leaze,[92] and Horse down west of the village was so called in 1814.[93] In the early 18th century some of the western downland was burnbaked.[94]

The demesne of Tilshead North manor may rarely have been in hand in the Middle Ages. About 1170, when it was worked as a farm by a group of nine tenants, it had 130 a. of sown arable, 8 oxen, and 252 sheep and lambs. By 1299 the area sown had increased to 362 a. and the stock to 18 oxen and 558 sheep.[95] Later it was further expanded or better exploited. In 1397 the farmhouse and outbuildings had recently been rebuilt or enlarged and there were then and in 1562 *c.* 400 a. of sown arable: the pasture was sufficient for 1,000 sheep in 1397[96] and 1,300 in 1623.[97] In the earlier 16th century the demesne was leased to a single tenant.[98]

Customary tenants of Tilshead North manor *c.* 1170 included 16 who held between them 2 hides and 12 yardlands, 3 who held ½ yardland each, and 13 cottagers: the 16 each owed autumn works of carrying corn, the rest owed reaping services. Other men held 'gafol land', claimed common pasture in Tilshead, owed rents totalling 10*s.*, and were required to plough 2 a. for each animal grazed.[99] The number of customary tenants had fallen by 1397 to 10, all yardlanders who still owed autumn works; there were then 12 cottagers and another 2 cottages were in hand because no tenant could be found.[1] A freehold,

[67] W.A.S. Libr., sale cat. xxvi, no. 29.
[68] G.P.L., Treas. Solicitor, 2829/67; inf. from Defence Land Agent.
[69] *Reg. Martival* (Cant. & York Soc.), ii. 201–3.
[70] Below, church.
[71] P.R.O., SC 6/Hen. VIII/3969, rot. 28.
[72] W.R.O. 216/1. [73] *Complete Peerage*, vi. 576–7.
[74] *W.A.M.* xl. 395.
[75] *Complete Peerage*, vi. 577; G.E.C. *Baronetage*, ii. 178; W.R.O. 323/2, deeds, Williams to Cowch, 1662; Wyndham to Cowch, 1662.
[76] W.R.O. 323/3, deed, Sainsbury to Halliday, 1678.
[77] Burke, *Land. Gent.* (1858), i. 504; P.R.O., PROB 11/1226, f. 90. [78] W.R.O., A 1/345/128A.
[79] Ibid. EA/127. [80] Above, this section.
[81] *Edington Cart.* (W.R.S. xlii), p. 23.
[82] *Inq. Non.* (Rec. Com.), 178.
[83] *Reg. Martival* (Cant. & York Soc.), ii. 201–3; for the

prebend, cf. above, S. Newton, manors (Rectory); church.
[84] *Cal. Pat.* 1550–3, 196.
[85] W.R.O., EA/127.
[86] Ibid. 2057/R 108, f. 303.
[87] *V.C.H. Wilts.* ii, pp. 116–17, 160–1.
[88] W.R.O., EA/127; below, local govt.
[89] P.R.O., E 310/26/154, f. 27; ibid. LR 2/191, f. 81.
[90] W.R.O. 1252/1.
[91] Ibid. 323/1, deed, Foote to Naishe, 1654.
[92] *Cal. Inq. Misc.* vi, p. 148.
[93] W.R.O., EA/127.
[94] Ibid. 101/119/1.
[95] *Caen Chart.* ed. M. Chibnall, pp. xlv, 28–9, 47–9.
[96] *Cal. Inq. Misc.* vi, p. 148; P.R.O., E 310/26/153.
[97] W.R.O. 412/1.
[98] P.R.O., LR 2/191, f. 81.
[99] *Caen Chart.* 47–8.
[1] *Cal. Inq. Misc.* vi, p. 148.

described as ½ carucate in 1198 and as 5 yard-lands *c.* 1210,[2] and 2 yardlands, with pasture for *c.* 200 sheep, which belonged to the vicarage in the 14th century but earlier and later to the rectory,[3] may also have been in the north part of the parish. In the mid 16th century the 2 yardlands were leased to the tenant of the de-mesne.[4] The 11 customary tenants then shared *c.* 700 a. of arable,[5] and in 1623 tenants, presum-ably including free tenants, had pasture rights for *c.* 1,000 sheep.[6] In the later 17th century holdings derived from the customary lands in-cluded one of 63 a. with pasture for 125 sheep, one of 83 a. with rights for 220 sheep, and one of 107 a. with pasture for 80 sheep.[7] Between 1706 and 1710 Sir William Scawen complained of the management of his estate, that of 83 a.: the land had been inadequately ploughed, some intended for sowing had been left unbroken, and unfit seed had been used. Pasture rights on that and other estates in Tilshead North tithing had recently been reduced by a fifth.[8]

An estate of 1 hide, with pasture for 16 oxen and 200 ewes, held of Romsey abbey in 1206, may have been the demesne of Tilshead South manor.[9] In 1586 the lands of the manor were leased in two portions: one included 208 a. of arable, the other 57 a.[10] The manor may have had customary tenants earlier but none is re-corded. In the late 18th century the largest farm in Tilshead South was apparently derived from the demesne: a smaller holding belonged to the lord of the manor and there were two or more other holdings.[11]

Open-field cultivation continued in both tith-ings until 1814, when the whole parish was inclosed under an Act of 1811. Allotments were made for land, pasture rights, and tithes, but no holding became unified.[12] For the rest of the 19th century and in the early 20th the largest farm was part of the Tilshead Lodge estate. In 1819 and 1907 it measured over 700 a. and was a sheep and corn farm. A new house and buildings in the village and a barn on the downs, perhaps Field barn in the parish's north-western corner, were built for the farm before 1819.[13] Although most farms continued to be worked from the village, additional farmsteads were built in the parish's north-eastern corner and on Copehill down between 1814 and 1886,[14] presumably to work downland arable created by burnbaking. In 1890 Tilshead Manor farm, *c.* 350 a. worked from buildings north of the church, was almost

all arable and included 107 a. of burnbaked downland, and in 1911 Glebe farm, *c.* 240 a. worked from buildings on the north side of High Street, included 132 a. of poor arable and down-land called the Bake land.[15]

Lands north-east and south-west of the new Devizes–Salisbury road were withdrawn from cultivation by the War Department before and after 1925 respectively.[16] Thereafter much of the parish was used as rough grazing only when military activities allowed. There was arable immediately north and south of the village in the 1930s,[17] and *c.* 550 a. remained arable in the 1990s. Approximately half of the remaining lands was used as pasture, principally for sheep, in 1991.[18]

There were 9 mills on the royal estate called Tilshead in 1086:[19] if any stood in or near the village there was more water in the upper reaches of the Till in the 11th century than in the 19th or the 20th. In 1341 the vicar was entitled to tithes of mills,[20] perhaps indicating that there was one or more in the parish, and a miller was a tenant of Tilshead North manor in 1517 and 1518.[21] Between 1773 and 1785 a windmill was built on the south-western edge of the village. When demolished *c.* 1904 it was a post mill with a thatched roof: the timbers were then used to repair Tilshead church.[22]

The Tilshead pipe company, founded in 1981, produced hand-made briar pipes in a small factory in Candown Road in 1991.[23]

LOCAL GOVERNMENT. In the early 12th century, when the lord of what became Tilshead North manor, Caen abbey, may have had rights over the whole of Dole hundred, Tilshead may have been the head of the hundred,[24] and Tils-head North became a tithing of the hundred.[25] In the early 13th century the lord of what became Tilshead South manor also held Whor-wellsdown hundred,[26] which included Tilshead South tithing from the earlier 14th century until the 19th.[27] The boundary between the tithings ran roughly north-east and south-west; Copehill down was a detached part of Tilshead North tithing, and the division of the village between the two tithings was complex.[28] In 1377 Tilshead North had 99 poll-tax payers and Tilshead South 26;[29] in 1814 they had respectively *c.* 45 and *c.* 10 houses.[30]

Caen abbey had extensive privileges,[31] in 1131

[2] *Bk. of Fees*, i. 12; *Red Bk. Exch.* (Rolls Ser.), ii. 485.
[3] W.R.O. 412/1; below, church.
[4] P.R.O., E 310/26/153; ibid. SC 6/Hen. VIII/3969, rot. 28.   [5] Ibid. LR 2/191, f. 81.
[6] W.R.O. 412/1.
[7] Ibid. 323/1, deed, Foote to Naishe, 1654; 323/2, deeds, Randall to Goldisborough, 1692; 649/817, deed, Roberts to Eyre, 1679.   [8] P.R.O., E 134/8 Anne Mich./28.
[9] *Rot. Chart.* (Rec. Com.), 162.
[10] P.R.O., E 310/26/154, f. 27.
[11] Hoare, *Mod. Wilts.* Branch and Dole, 44; W.R.O., A 1/345/128A.   [12] W.R.O., EA/127.
[13] Ibid. 776/327; W.A.S. Libr., sale cat. xi, no. 12; O.S. Map 6", Wilts. XLVI (1889 edn.).
[14] O.S. Maps 6", Wilts. XLVI, LIII (1889 edns.); W.R.O., EA/127.
[15] W.A.S. Libr., sale cat. ii, no. 12; Ch. Com. file 83636.
[16] Wilts. Cuttings, xii. 25.

[17] [1st] Land Util. Surv. Map, sheet 122.
[18] Inf. from Mr. T. N. Blake, Glebe Farm.
[19] *V.C.H. Wilts.* ii, pp. 116–17.
[20] *Inq. Non.* (Rec. Com.), 178.
[21] W.R.O. 192/18.
[22] Ibid. EA/127; *Andrews and Dury, Map* (W.R.S. viii), pl. 8; M. Watts, *Wilts. Windmills*, 23; Wilts. Cuttings, xvi. 373.   [23] Wilts. Cuttings, xxix. 185.
[24] *Caen Chart.* 47; above, Branch and Dole hund.; ibid. manors.
[25] e.g. *Tax List, 1332* (W.R.S. xlv), 76; W.R.O., A 1/345/394.
[26] *V.C.H. Wilts.* viii. 194; above, manors.
[27] e.g. *Tax List, 1332* (W.R.S. xlv), 51; W.R.O., A 1/345/128A.
[28] W.R.O., EA/127; above, Branch and Dole hund., map.
[29] *V.C.H. Wilts.* iv. 308, 311.   [30] W.R.O., EA/127.
[31] *Caen Chart.* 47.

including sac and soke, toll and team, and infangthief.[32] Although the exemption of all the abbey's English estates from suit of shire and of hundred was confirmed in 1189 and 1190, the exemption of Tilshead North was challenged, unsuccessfully, in 1267 and 1281.[33]

View of frankpledge and a manor court for Tilshead North were recorded for 1517–18, 1612–16, and 1623. Both a view and a court were usually held in spring and autumn. A tithingman presented strays, buildings needing repair, and in 1612 and 1616 the disrepair of the butts. Orders were made to enforce or vary the rules of common husbandry, and in 1612 tellers for sheep and for cattle were appointed. In that year the right to glean was restricted to those of the poor unable to work. Then and in 1615 the jury was ordered to view the bounds and a survey of the boundaries, apparently of the whole parish, was recorded in 1623.[34]

In 1261 and 1262 a tithingman from Tilshead South presented at Whorwellsdown hundred court, and a suit between parties from Tilshead concerning a broken contract to build houses was heard in the court in 1261.[35] Romsey abbey was entitled to hold a Tilshead South manor court, but from 1457 or earlier Tilshead business may have come before the court of Steeple Ashton manor, also held by the abbey,[36] and no separate court for Tilshead South is recorded.

Two overseers of the poor were appointed annually in the 18th century. Between 1711 and 1732 their yearly expenditure fluctuated between £13 and £28.[37] The overseers were summoned at least once in both 1744 and 1745 and twice in 1746 for failing to relieve members of the Whitley family: only once did they show good cause for the omission.[38] The annual cost of poor relief had risen to £139 by 1776 and to £262 by 1803, when 39 adults and 68 children received regular relief and 20 people occasional relief. The level of the poor rate in 1802–3 was about the average for parishes of Branch and Dole hundred.[39] A poor house was recorded in the parish in 1807[40] but not thereafter. Although the number of recipients had apparently fallen since 1803, expenditure on poor relief was at its peak, £450, in 1813. From 1815 until 1834 it was between £200 and £300 a year.[41] Tilshead became part of Amesbury poor-law union in 1835,[42] and of Salisbury district in 1974.[43]

CHURCH. There was a church at Tilshead in the early 12th century.[44] A rector was recorded c. 1170.[45] The patron was the king[46] and the living, valued at £16 13s. 4d. in 1291,[47] was rich although some tithes had already been granted away.[48] In the early 13th century the rectors were evidently absentees, since the church was served by vicars presented by the rectors.[49] A vicarage was apparently ordained, and by 1291 had been consolidated with the rectory.[50] In 1317 Edward II gave the advowson to Ivychurch priory with licence to appropriate the church.[51] A vicarage was again ordained[52] and in 1991 became part of the united benefice of Tilshead, Orcheston and Chitterne.[53]

Ivychurch priory held the advowson of the vicarage, the Crown presenting in 1361 when there was no prior, until the Dissolution. Thereafter the Crown retained the advowson[54] until it was bought in 1902 by the bishop of Salisbury,[55] who shared the patronage of the united benefice from 1991.[56]

The endowment of the vicarage, assigned in 1319, included lands formerly the rector's, pasture for 200 sheep, and small tithes apparently excluding those of wool and hay. The vicar was to be responsible for repairing the chancel.[57] In 1341 the vicar had 2 yardlands as part of his estate[58] but by the early 15th century, when he unsuccessfully sought augmentation of his living,[59] the lands may have been exchanged with Ivychurch priory for wool and hay tithes. In the 16th and 17th centuries the vicar had all tithes except those of corn and only c. 1 a. of glebe;[60] responsibility for the chancel had by then passed to the owner of the Rectory estate.[61] In 1535 the vicarage was valued at £7 15s. 8d.,[62] well below the average for livings in Wylye deanery. In 1806 it was augmented by £200 from Queen Anne's Bounty and £200 from private donations.[63] The money was used in 1814 to buy 8 a. in Beckington (Som.),[64] and at inclosure in the same year most of the vicar's tithes were replaced by 241 a. in Tilshead.[65] In 1830 his income, c. £200,[66] was still below average. The remaining tithes, from the windmill, were replaced in 1853 by a rent charge of £1 1s.[67] In 1911 the War Department bought 78 a. of the glebe, and in 1912 a further 157 a. were sold.[68] The vicar had a house from 1319,[69] in the late 16th century a thatched house of perhaps three rooms.[70] A vicarage house

32 Reg. Regum Anglo-Norm. ii, no. 1692.
33 Plac. de Quo War. (Rec. Com.), 806.
34 W.R.O. 192/18; 412/1.
35 V.C.H. Wilts. viii. 195; Sel. Pleas in Manorial Cts. (Selden Soc. ii), 179; P.R.O., SC 2/208/1.
36 V.C.H. Wilts. viii. 202, 216; P.R.O., E 326/9089.
37 W.R.O. 823/9.
38 Hunt's Notebook (W.R.S. xxxvii), pp. 35, 38, 51, 53.
39 Poor Law Abstract, 1804, 558–9.
40 W.R.O. 823/9.
41 Poor Law Abstract, 1818, 492–3; Poor Rate Returns, 1816–21, 186; 1822–4, 225; 1825–9, 216; 1830–4, 209.
42 Poor Law Com. 2nd Rep. App. D, 558.
43 O.S. Map 1/100,000, admin. areas, Wilts. (1974 edn.).
44 Below, this section [architecture].
45 Caen Chart. 47.
46 Pat. R. 1216–25, 541.
47 Tax. Eccl. (Rec. Com.), 181.
48 Edington Cart. (W.R.S. xlii), p. 23.
49 Pat. R. 1216–25, 541; Cal. Pat. 1232–47, 234.
50 Tax. Eccl. (Rec. Com.), 181.

51 Cal. Pat. 1313–17, 631.
52 Reg. Martival (Cant. & York Soc.), i. 101.
53 Inf. from Dioc. Registrar, Castle Street, Salisbury.
54 Reg. Martival (Cant. & York Soc.), i. 101; Phillipps, Wilts. Inst. (index in W.A.M. xxviii. 232); Clerical Guide (1822 and later edns.); Clergy List (1859 and later edns.); Crockford (1896).   55 Ch. Com. file 53830.
56 Inf. from Dioc. Registrar.
57 Reg. Martival (Cant. & York Soc.), ii. 251–3.
58 Inq. Non. (Rec. Com.), 178.
59 W.R.O., D 1/2/9, f. 114v.
60 Ibid. D 1/24/204/1; D 1/24/204/3; W.A.M. xl. 395.
61 P.R.O., SC 6/Hen. VIII/3969, rot. 28.
62 Valor Eccl. (Rec. Com.), ii. 104.
63 C. Hodgson, Queen Anne's Bounty, pp. clxxxi, cccxxxvi.   64 Ch. Com. deed 511296.
65 W.R.O., EA/127.
66 Rep. Com. Eccl. Revenues, 850–1.
67 W.R.O., tithe award.   68 Ch. Com. file 83636.
69 Reg. Martival (Cant. & York Soc.), ii. 251–2.
70 W.R.O., D 1/24/204/1.

of red brick was built in the early 1820s south-west of the church:[71] it was sold and a new house was built in High Street *c.* 1972.[72]

John Hobbes, vicar 1529–75,[73] was presented for not preaching all the quarter sermons in 1553; the communion table then lacked a covering.[74] In 1646 the vicar Richard Foote was said to have deserted his cure and was replaced by Robert Sharpe, whose constancy in preaching was commended in 1650.[75] In the later 18th century and the early 19th successive vicars were evidently non-resident pluralists, and curates served the church. In 1783 the curate, Thomas Davies, lived at Chitterne All Saints and served three cures. At Tilshead he held one service on Sundays and celebrated communion at Christmas, Easter, Whitsun, and Michaelmas, but held no other weekday service.[76] Henry Gauntlett, a prominent supporter of the Anglican evangelical revival, was curate from 1786 until *c.* 1800.[77] J. H. Johnson became curate *c.* 1824 and was vicar from 1837 until 1884. He oversaw, as curate, the building of a new vicarage house and, as incumbent, the building of a new glebe farmhouse and the restoration of the church, for which he made some stone carvings and coloured and fired most of the stained glass windows. He also prepared and produced in the vicarage house engravings to illustrate leaflets appealing for church funds and was an early photographer.[78] Each Sunday in 1864 he held either a morning or afternoon service and an evening service with a sermon. Services were held on all red-letter days, with an average attendance of 30; additional services held on winter Wednesday evenings, at which Johnson preached, had congregations of *c.* 60. Communion was celebrated at Christmas and Easter, on Ascension day, and on Whit and Trinity Sundays.[79] From 1966 until 1971 Tilshead was held in plurality with the benefices of Orcheston St. Mary and Orcheston St. George.[80] A chapel had been opened at West Down camp by 1982[81] and remained in use in 1991.[82] In 1687 Hugh Cox gave by will the income from £10 for a sermon on Ascension day. The endowment had been lost by the early 20th century.[83]

A tradition that the early invocation of Tilshead church was of St. James is unsupported by evidence beyond the holding in the early 20th century of a feast or fair on or about St. James's day, 25 July.[84] A suggestion that the invocation was altered to *ST. THOMAS À BECKET* when the church was given to Ivychurch priory receives some support from the tradition that the

saint was connected with the priory.[85] The dedication is first recorded in 1763.[86] The church is built of flint rubble and ashlar: some of the walls are chequered. It has a chancel, a central tower with north vestry, and an aisled and clerestoried nave with south porch.[87] The foundations of a south transept which were seen in 1846[88] suggest that the church was cruciform. The nave arcades and the responds of the tower arches are early 12th-century. The nave was then built or rebuilt with narrow aisles and no clerestory. In the 13th century the chancel was rebuilt or, more likely, lengthened, the upper part of the tower was built, and the south aisle was altered. The porch may have been built in the 14th century, and the clerestory was probably made in the early 16th when hood moulds were constructed over the windows in the north aisle. Extensive repairs took place in the 17th and 18th centuries. In 1845–6, to designs by T. H. Wyatt and D. Brandon, west and south galleries were removed from the nave, the narrow north aisle was replaced by one as wide as the nave, the vestry was built, and buttresses and a parapet were added to the south aisle and buttresses to the chancel.[89] The triple lancet east window in the chancel[90] was then replaced by one in 15th-century style. The roof was repaired in 1904, with timbers from the windmill, and in 1965.[91]

In 1553 plate weighing 15 oz. was confiscated from the church, and a chalice of 9½ oz. was left. A cup and cover of 1787, perhaps incorporating part of an earlier cup, and a flagon of 1885 belonged to the church in 1991.[92] Three bells cast in 1764 by Thomas Bilbie, presumably to replace the three at Tilshead in 1553, hung in the church in 1991.[93] Registers of baptisms, marriages, and burials survive from 1664.[94]

NONCONFORMITY. There was one dissenter in Tilshead in 1676,[95] none in 1783.[96] In 1801 a house was certified for Independent meetings: houses certified in 1816 and 1818 were probably also used by Independents.[97] In 1851 a Baptist church or meeting was begun[98] but in 1864 there was no regular meeting in the village and only two professed dissenters: they, and presumably others, attended occasional sermons given in a cottage.[99] A small plain brick Baptist chapel, built in 1882,[1] was open in 1991.

EDUCATION. A boarding school opened at Tilshead in the mid 18th century had 63 pupils

71 Ibid. 823/16, MS. acct. of Tilshead by J. H. Johnson.
72 Wilts. Cuttings, xxvi. 86.
73 Phillipps, *Wilts. Inst.* i. 200, 227.
74 W.R.O., D 1/43/1, f. 117.
75 *Walker Revised*, ed. Matthews, 372; *W.A.M.* xl. 395.
76 *Vis. Queries, 1783* (W.R.S. xxvii), p. 212; *Rep. Com. Eccl. Revenues*, 850–1.   77 *D.N.B.*
78 W.R.O. 823/16, MS. acct. of Tilshead by J. H. Johnson, ch. appeal, and letter, Johnson to Amery; W.A.S. Libr., MS. acct. of Tilshead by J. H. Johnson; for one of his photos., see above, plate facing p. 266.
79 W.R.O., D 1/56/7.
80 Inf. from Dioc. Registrar.
81 O.S. Map 1/10,000, SU 04 NW. (1983 edn.).
82 Inf. from Defence Land Agent.
83 W.R.O. 823/16, extract from Wylye deanery mag. 1907.   84 *Church Guide.*
85 *V.C.H. Wilts.* iii. 290 n.

86 J. Ecton, *Thesaurus*, 398.
87 See plate facing p. 234.   88 Plan in church.
89 *Churches of SE. Wilts.* (R.C.H.M.), 197–8.
90 J. Buckler, watercolour in W.A.S. Libr., vol. iii. 34.
91 Wilts. Cuttings, xvi. 373; xxii. 293; above, econ. hist. [mills].
92 Nightingale, *Wilts. Plate*, 77, which gives the date 1855 for the flagon; inf. from the priest-in-charge, the Vicarage.
93 Walters, *Wilts. Bells*, 217; inf. from the priest-in-charge.
94 W.R.O. 823/1–7; bishop's transcripts for some earlier years are ibid.
95 *Compton Census*, ed. Whiteman, 125.
96 *Vis. Queries, 1783* (W.R.S. xxvii), p. 212.
97 *Meeting Ho. Certs.* (W.R.S. xl), pp. 56, 80, 86.
98 *V.C.H. Wilts.* iii. 138.
99 W.R.O., D 1/56/7.   1 Date on bldg.

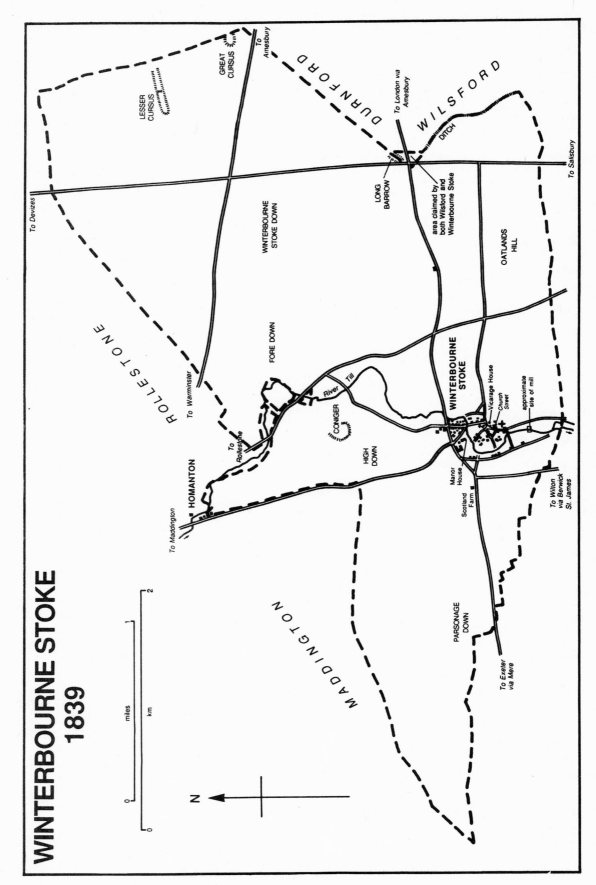

WINTERBOURNE STOKE
1839

miles

km

N

LESSER CURSUS

GREAT CURSUS

To Amesbury

DURNFORD

To London via Amesbury

WILSFORD

DITCH

To Salisbury

To Devizes

WINTERBOURNE STOKE DOWN

LONG BARROW

area claimed by both Wilsford and Winterbourne Stoke

OATLANDS HILL

ROLLESTONE

FORE DOWN

To Warminster

River Till

CONIGER

WINTERBOURNE STOKE

Vicarage House

Church Street

approximate site of mill

To Rollestone

HIGH DOWN

Manor House

Scotland Farm

To Wilton via Berwick St. James

HOMANTON

To Maddington

MADDINGTON

PARSONAGE DOWN

To Exeter via Mere

274

in 1779; they included Henry Hunt, the radical politician of the early 19th century.[2] The school was called Tilshead academy in 1819,[3] apparently flourished c. 1825,[4] may have had only 6 pupils in 1833,[5] and was probably closed soon afterwards.

In 1833 there were two day schools in the parish, with a total of 37 pupils.[6] A National school, on a site south of the church given in 1841,[7] had between 30 and 40 pupils in 1859. Three or four boys from Tilshead then attended Shrewton school.[8] A new school built north of the church c. 1905[9] was attended by c. 80 children in 1908–9, 50 in 1935–6,[10] and c. 28 in 1991.[11]

CHARITIES FOR THE POOR. Rents from two cottages built in Tilshead after the flood of 1841 formed part of an endowment to provide fuel and clothing for the poor of parishes affected by the flood. Tilshead was entitled to a seventh of the income, c. £7 in 1901 when it was used to provide sheets for 45 people.[12] In the mid 20th century most of the income was used to maintain the cottages:[13] in 1991 it was proposed to convert them to almshouses.[14]

By will proved 1876 John Parham gave the income from £200 to buy blankets for the poor of Tilshead. Little of the income was spent before 1899: from then c. £6 a year was spent on blankets until 1939. Thereafter no distribution was made until 1960 when money was given. In 1990 four beneficiaries received £5 each.[15]

WINTERBOURNE STOKE

WINTERBOURNE STOKE village is 8 km. west of Amesbury.[16] North of the village the parish had on its boundary or as islands within it five pieces of meadow land, c. 36 a. in all, detached parts of the parishes of Maddington, Shrewton, and either Orcheston St. George or Orcheston St. Mary.[17] The Orcheston land had been absorbed into Winterbourne Stoke by the 1880s,[18] and in 1885 that of Maddington and Shrewton was transferred to the parish.[19] A few acres on their common boundary were claimed by both Winterbourne Stoke and Wilsford parishes in the early 19th century: they were in Wilsford in the 1880s, since when Winterbourne Stoke has measured 3,572 a. (1,445 ha.).[20]

Winterbourne Stoke parish is crossed by the river Till, which was for long called the Winterbourne; many estates in the valley were called Winterbourne in the 11th century. Three were called Winterbourne Stoke: one of those became part of Berwick St. James parish, and Winterbourne Stoke parish was made up of the other two, on one of which was a church, and possibly included a third estate called Winterbourne. No other estate in the Till valley called Winterbourne was distinguished by suffix or prefix in 1086, and only Winterbourne Stoke has kept the name.[21]

On the west the boundary with Maddington in part follows a dry valley and in part is marked by a road. The parish is divided from Berwick St. James east of the Till by boundary mounds and from Wilsford by a prehistoric ditch. Barrows mark other parts of the eastern boundary.

Most of Winterbourne Stoke parish is downland, and chalk outcrops over all of it. The Till flows north–south across the centre and, as its earlier name implies, is sometimes dry in summer. It has deposited gravel and small amounts of alluvium, and there is also gravel in dry valleys leading from the north-east and north-west towards the river.[22] The relief is mostly gentle: from c. 70 m. by the river the land rises to 126 m. on Parsonage down in the south-west, to 135 m. west of that, and to 129 m. on Oatlands Hill, formerly Short, Slourt, or Stourt Hill,[23] in the south-east. From the Middle Ages the slopes of the downland nearest to the village were arable, and the downs further east and west were chiefly pasture. There were extensive meadows beside the river, some watered, but woodland was scarce.[24] In or soon after 1967 c. 400 a. in the west were declared a Site of Special Scientific Interest: 394 a. of them were, with adjacent land in what had been Maddington parish, part of Parsonage Down national nature reserve from 1980.[25] Between 1941 and 1946 Oatlands Hill was the site of a military airfield.[26]

The Amesbury–Mere road runs east–west across the south side of the parish: it was

2   Whitaker's Diaries (W.R.S. xliv), p. xliv n.
3   W.A.S. Libr., sale cat. xi, no. 12.
4   Hoare, Mod. Wilts. Branch and Dole, 44.
5   Educ. Enq. Abstract, 1049.   6   Ibid.
7   P.R.O., ED 7/131, no. 274; inscription on bldg.
8   Acct. of Wilts. Schs. 44; above, Shrewton, educ.
9   P.R.O., ED 21/18570.
10   Bd. of Educ., List 21, 1910 (H.M.S.O.), 510; 1936, 427.
11   Wilts. co. council, Sched. of Educ. Establishments (1990), p. 22.
12   Endowed Char. Wilts. (S. Div.), 637, 706; above, intro.
13   W.R.O. 823/16, notice concerning flood charity, 1952–3.   14   Char. Com. file; above, Shrewton, charities.
15   Endowed Char. Wilts. (S. Div.), 706–7; W.R.O., L 2, Tilshead; inf. from Mrs. E. Druce, Elmhurst, High Street.
16   This article was written in 1992. Maps used include O.S. Maps 6", Wilts. LIII–LIV, LIX–LX (1887–9 and later edns.); 1/25,000, SU 04, SU 14 (1958 edns.); 1/50,000, sheet 184 (1974 edn.); 1", sheet 14 (1817 edn.).

17   Above, Maddington, intro.; Orcheston St. Mary, intro.; Shrewton, intro.; W.R.O., Winterbourne Stoke tithe award, which wrongly identifies Shrewton's lands as Rollestone's.
18   O.S. Maps 6", Wilts. LIII (1889 edn.); LIV (1887 edn.).   19   Census, 1891.
20   O.S. Map 6", Wilts. LIV (1887 edn.); W.R.O., tithe awards.
21   P.N. Wilts. (E.P.N.S.), 10, 232–7; V.C.H. Wilts. ii, pp. 136, 179; below, manors.
22   Geol. Surv. Maps 1", drift, sheet 282 (1967 edn.); 1/50,000, drift, sheet 298 (1976 edn.).
23   Andrews and Dury, Map (W.R.S. viii), pl. 5; O.S. Map 1", sheet 14 (1817 edn.); W.R.O. 442/1, f. 21.
24   Below, econ. hist.
25   Inf. from Chief Site Manager, Eng. Nature, S. Region, Foxhold Ho., Crookham Common, Newbury, Berks.; above, Maddington, intro.
26   C. Ashworth, Action Stations, v. 140.

turnpiked on its present course in 1761, was disturnpiked in 1871,[27] and has been part of the London–Exeter trunk road since 1958.[28] The bridge carrying it over the Till was rebuilt in 1939.[29] The main Devizes–Salisbury road, also turnpiked in 1761, disturnpiked in 1870,[30] ran north–south across the east part of the parish. The two roads cross at the Longbarrow Cross Roads. Across the north-east corner of the parish a turnpike road linking Amesbury and Warminster was evidently made soon after 1761 and was disturnpiked in 1871: west of its junction with the Devizes–Salisbury road, which was closed north of the Bustard inn in Shrewton parish to allow for military training, it has been since c. 1900 part of the main Devizes–Salisbury road.[31] Minor roads in 1773 included one joining Maddington and Shrewton with Berwick St. James and Wilton, and one leading south-east from Rollestone across the downs. Other roads linked those two with Winterbourne Stoke village and the major routes.[32] Of the minor roads only that from Maddington to Berwick St. James, and the south part of that from Rollestone, were in public use in 1992. Near Winterbourne Stoke village an eastwards diversion of the Maddington road made between 1817 and 1839 created a widely staggered junction with the main road.[33] A military railway was built north–south across the east end of the parish in 1914–15; it had been dismantled by 1923.[34]

The parish is rich in archaeological remains, particularly in the east part, in the hinterland of Stonehenge. The Lesser Cursus, a possibly Neolithic earthwork over 400 m. long with a transverse ditch, lies in the north-east corner: south of it the rounded western end of the Great Cursus extends into the parish from Amesbury. The barrow c. 73 m. long on the boundary with Wilsford, which gave its name to Longbarrow Cross Roads, is one of a group of 19, some of which are outside the parish. Smaller groups are at the parish's north-east corner, south and west of the Lesser Cursus, on Fore down, and at the Coniger. High down and Winterbourne Stoke down are sites of Romano-British settlement, and medieval earthworks have been identified on Winterbourne Stoke down, on Fore down, north of Longbarrow Cross Roads, and at the Coniger.[35] Prehistoric field systems have been traced on Winterbourne Stoke down, north of Parsonage down, and straddling the eastern boundary with Berwick St. James.[36]

Winterbourne Stoke had 93 poll-tax payers in 1377, the second highest figure for a place in Dole hundred. In 1801 the population was 256.

It had fallen to 215 by 1811, was 281 in 1821, and had risen to 383 by 1861. A sharp fall, to 293 in 1871, was attributed to a decline in demand for agricultural labour and the departure of young women for domestic service in towns. The population was 205 in 1921, remained c. 200, and was 193 in 1991.[37]

In the later 18th century Winterbourne Stoke village, standing on gravel beside the Till, consisted mainly of buildings along a winding street between the church and the Amesbury–Mere road and carried across the river by a bridge. The street was later called Church Street. West of the main line of settlement were the 17th-century Manor House, and, south of it, a farmstead which may have included a house described in 1588 as new.[38] The farmstead was demolished in the mid 19th century.[39] The oldest surviving buildings in Church Street are on the east side. Church Cottage, at the south end, and Old Glebe Farmhouse, 250 m. further north, are both of flint and limestone and of 17th-century origin. Riverside Cottage, by the Till south of the bridge, is also of 17th-century origin and is ornamented with flint and limestone chequerwork. In the early 19th century both sides of Church Street were lined with buildings at the north end. An alehouse, open in 1756, was probably the Bell inn which in 1812 and 1839 stood on the east side of the street near the main road.[40] In 1841 the Till flooded and 16 houses in Winterbourne Stoke were destroyed.[41] Most probably stood between the street and the river south of the bridge: between 1839 and 1886 several houses or cottages there, in addition to the farmstead, were demolished. At the south end of the street about five buildings on the east side were also demolished, probably c. 1850 when a new vicarage house was built.[42] At the north end, two bungalows and a village hall were built in the 1920s: the hall was converted to a house c. 1962.[43] West of the street near the south end seven houses and two bungalows in New Street in the early 1960s, and four houses and two bungalows in St. Peter's Close in 1970, were all built for the local authority.[44] Apart from four houses at the north end, there was little private building in Church Street in the later 20th century.

Between 1773 and 1812 about six cottages were built beside a back lane west of the Till and parallel to Church Street.[45] Two survive, one a stone and thatch farmhouse, probably of the late 18th century. The others had been demolished by 1923.[46]

North of the Amesbury–Mere road there were

27 *Andrews and Dury, Map* (W.R.S. viii), pl. 5; *V.C.H. Wilts.* iv. 270; *L.J.* xxx. 138.
28 Above, Amesbury, intro. (roads).
29 Date stone on bridge.
30 *V.C.H. Wilts.* iv. 270; *L.J.* xxx. 77.
31 *V.C.H. Wilts.* iv. 266, 270; *L.J.* xxx. 138; above, Amesbury, intro. (roads); Shrewton, intro. [roads].
32 *Andrews and Dury, Map* (W.R.S. viii), pls. 5, 8.
33 O.S. Map 1", sheet 14 (1817 edn.); W.R.O., tithe award.
34 N. D. G. James, *Plain Soldiering*, 198, 203, 206; O.S. Maps 6", Wilts. LIV. SW. (1925 edn.); LX. NW. (1926 edn.).
35 *V.C.H. Wilts.* i (1), 146, 201–3, 206, 212–13, 221, 224–5, 271; i (2), 305, 332; *W.A.M.* xlv. 209.

36 *V.C.H. Wilts.* i (1), 273, 279; O.S. Map 1/10,000, SU 04 SE. (1974 edn.).
37 *V.C.H. Wilts.* iv. 308, 325, 361; *Census,* 1961; 1971; 1981; 1991.
38 *Andrews and Dury, Map* (W.R.S. viii), pl. 5; P.R.O., PROB 11/73, f. 239; below, manors (Winterbourne Stoke).
39 O.S. Map 6", Wilts. LIX (1889 edn.); W.R.O., tithe award.
40 W.R.O., A 1/326/1; ibid. EA/104; ibid. tithe award.
41 *W.A.M.* xlix. 262; above, Shrewton, intro.
42 O.S. Map 6", Wilts. LIX (1889 edn.); W.R.O., tithe award; above, this section; below, church.
43 Wilts. Cuttings, xxii. 138.   44 W.R.O., G 1/602/8.
45 Ibid. EA/104; *Andrews and Dury, Map* (W.R.S. viii), pl. 5.   46 O.S. Map 6", Wilts. LIX. NE. (1926 edn.).

a few buildings opposite Church Street in 1773,[47] three houses, farm buildings, and a smithy in 1839.[48] Settlement later spread east and west beside the road. A house built on the north side of the road in the mid 19th century was open in 1886 and 1992 as the Bell inn, having replaced the inn of that name in Church Street. Two cottages in a style to match the house were also built on the north side of the road in the mid 19th century, and a new farmstead was built north of the Bell. In 1886 settlement extended west to the Maddington road, and there was more building on the north side between 1886 and 1899.[49] Five pairs of council houses, three on the north side west of Church Street, two on the south side east of Church Street, were built in the mid 1950s.[50]

Cottages on the northern edge of the parish were part of Homanton hamlet, mainly in Maddington parish. One stood there in 1812,[51] and a pair was built in 1842 with money raised to aid victims of the 1841 flood. The pair was demolished in 1987 and new houses were built on the site.[52] A farmstead called Scotland stood beside the Amesbury–Mere road west of the village in 1773.[53] The farmhouse, later called Scotland Lodge, comprises a single range with an east front of chequered flint and stone of the late 18th century: bay windows and a central porch, all in brick and of two storeys, were added in the 19th century. Other buildings erected in the parish away from the village in the 19th century included, between 1817 and 1839, a barn beside the Amesbury–Mere road east of the village[54] on or near the site of Grant's Barn, a group of farm buildings standing in 1866 and demolished c. 1990. Farmsteads called Foredown Barn and Greenland Farm were built respectively 1 km. and 3.5 km. north-east of the village between 1839 and 1866.[55] Hill Farm, 750 m. east of the village, was built between 1839 and 1879:[56] the farmhouse was demolished c. 1990, but several cottages and extensive farm buildings remained there in 1992. Wisma Poultry Farm was built south of the village in the late 1940s: later it was extended and two houses were built there.[57]

A cross stood on or near the parish boundary close to the Longbarrow Cross Roads in 1773:[58] its remains there in the later 20th century were in Wilsford parish.[59] A cross said to have stood east of the Devizes road in Winterbourne Stoke parish was moved in the mid 19th century. The base was reportedly placed beside the road, the shaft at a crossroads in Shrewton parish:[60] neither could be seen in those places in 1992, and the cross may in fact have been that at the Longbarrow Cross Roads in 1773 and the later 20th century. A stone monument was erected in 1912 at the junction of the Devizes–Salisbury and Amesbury–Warminster roads to commemorate a fatal aircraft accident.[61]

MANORS AND OTHER ESTATES. What became *WINTERBOURNE STOKE* manor, 2 hides and 1 yardland, was held by the king in 1086, and earlier by Queen Edith. An estate of 1 hide called Winterbourne, held of Alfred of Marlborough by Edward in 1086, may have become part of the manor.[62] Robert, earl of Leicester, held the manor in 1170.[63] It was apparently confiscated on his rebellion in 1173 but may have been restored with his other estates in 1177.[64] Robert (d. 1190) probably gave the manor to his daughter Amice on her marriage to Simon de Montfort, who held it in 1185, and in 1188 and 1189 it was held by William des Barres, then her husband.[65] It was confirmed in 1205 to Amice[66] (styled countess of Leicester from 1204, d. 1215), but in 1207, when the estates of her brother Robert, earl of Leicester (d. 1204), were partitioned, moieties of the manor were allotted to her son Simon de Montfort, earl of Leicester (d. 1218), and Saier de Quency, earl of Winchester, her sister Margaret's husband.[67] Simon's moiety presumably passed to his son Simon, from 1239 earl of Leicester, whose estates were confiscated on his death in 1265 and granted in the same year to Edmund, earl of Leicester and later of Lancaster.[68] Edmund was overlord of 1 carucate in Winterbourne Stoke in 1275,[69] but there is no evidence that the overlordship descended to his successors. Saier's moiety may have been held after his death in 1219 by Margaret (d. 1235) and passed to their son Roger, earl of Winchester (d. 1264).[70] On the partition of Roger's estates in 1277 the overlordship of land in Winterbourne Stoke was allotted to his daughter Helen or Ellen[71] (d. 1296), relict of Sir Alan la Zouche. It passed to her grandson Alan la Zouche, from 1313 Lord Zouche (d. 1314), and to that Alan's daughter Maud, wife of Robert de Holand, from 1314 Lord Holand[72] (d. 1328): it was presumably confiscated with Robert's other estates in 1322 and restored in 1327. Maud (d. 1349)[73] was overlord of Winter-

47 *Andrews and Dury, Map* (W.R.S. viii), pl. 5.
48 W.R.O., tithe award.
49 O.S. Maps 6", Wilts. LIX (1889 edn.); LIX. NE. (1901 edn.). 50 W.R.O., G 1/602/2.
51 Ibid. EA/104.
52 *Endowed Char. Wilts.* (S. Div.), 899; inf. from the Secretary, Shrewton Flood charity, Maddington Place, Shrewton.
53 *Andrews and Dury, Map* (W.R.S. viii), pl. 5.
54 O.S. Map 1", sheet 14 (1817 edn.); W.R.O., tithe award.
55 W.R.O., tithe award; ibid. 776, lease, Ashburton to Brown, 1866.
56 Ibid. tithe award; O.S. Map 6", Wilts. LX (1887 edn.).
57 Inf. from Mr. J. K. Woodford, Goodwin Ho., Berwick St. Jas. 58 *Andrews and Dury, Map* (W.R.S. viii), pl. 5.
59 O.S. Map 1/10,000, SU 14 SW. (1974 edn.).
60 *W.A.M.* xxxvi. 142–3.

61 James, *Plain Soldiering*, 166; Wilts. Cuttings, xxii. 297.
62 *V.C.H. Wilts.* ii, pp. 118, 141, 179.
63 *Pipe R.* 1170 (P.R.S. xv), 62.
64 Ibid. 1173 (P.R.S. xix), 103; *Complete Peerage*, vii. 531.
65 *Complete Peerage*, vii. 532–3, 536–7; *Pipe R.* 1185 (P.R.S. xxxiv), 194; 1188 (P.R.S. xxxviii), 142; 1189 (Rec. Com.), 178.
66 *Rot. Litt. Claus.* (Rec. Com.), i. 30, where Amice is wrongly described as wife of Saier de Quency.
67 Ibid. 77; *Complete Peerage*, vii. 535–8; Hist. MSS. Com. 78, *Hastings*, i, p. 340.
68 *Complete Peerage*, vii. 379, 540–7.
69 *Rot. Hund.* (Rec. Com.), ii (1), 254.
70 *Complete Peerage*, xii (2), 750–3.
71 Hist. MSS. Com. 78, *Hastings*, i, p. 237.
72 *Complete Peerage*, xii (2), 934–7; *Cal. Inq. p.m.* v, p. 257; *Cal. Close, 1330–3*, 186.
73 *Complete Peerage*, vi. 529–31.

bourne Stoke manor in 1331:[74] thereafter the overlordship has not been traced.

In 1242–3 Winterbourne Stoke manor was held in demesne by Sir Robert de Quency[75] (d. by 1266), whose coheirs were his sisters Joan, wife of Humphrey de Bohun (d. 1265), and Hawise, wife of Sir Baldwin Wake. It was allotted to Joan and on her death in 1284 passed to Hawise.[76] In 1292 one of Wake's sons, John, conveyed it to another, Hugh[77] (d. by 1312). Hugh's relict Joan, wife of Nicholas of Braybrook, held the manor until her death c. 1329.[78] It passed to her grandson (Sir) Thomas Wake (fl. 1390),[79] who, probably by 1399, was succeeded by his son Thomas[80] (will proved 1413).[81] The younger Thomas's relict Elizabeth, in 1416 wife of Thomas Trewin and later wife of Sir John Hamlin (d. by 1428), held the manor in 1430,[82] presumably for life. Thomas Wake's kinsman Thomas Poynings, Lord St. John, in 1416 conveyed the reversion to his son Sir Hugh Poynings *alias* St. John.[83] In 1427 Sir Hugh conveyed it to Walter Hungerford, Lord Hungerford,[84] who held the manor in 1435.[85] Hungerford (d. 1449) was succeeded in turn by his son Robert, Lord Hungerford (d. 1459), and Robert's son Robert, Lord Hungerford and Moleyns (d. 1464). The younger Robert's estates were forfeited on his attainder in 1461[86] and Winterbourne Stoke may have been granted to Richard, duke of Gloucester: by an agreement of 1469 with Gloucester it was assigned for life to Margaret Hungerford, *suo jure* Baroness Botreaux[87] (d. 1478), relict of Robert, Lord Hungerford (d. 1459).[88] In 1474, however, the king granted it to Gloucester, who, as Richard III, granted it to John Howard, duke of Norfolk, in 1483.[89] It reverted to the Crown on Norfolk's attainder in 1485 and was probably among estates restored in that year to Sir Walter Hungerford, son of Robert, Lord Hungerford (d. 1464). Sir Walter (d. 1516)[90] held the manor in 1487 and 1505,[91] and it probably passed to his son Sir Edward (d. 1521) and to Sir Edward's son Sir Walter. It was, however, claimed by George Hastings, Lord Hastings (cr. earl of Huntingdon 1529), great-grandson of Robert, Lord Hungerford (d. 1464),[92] and was listed among lands settled on his marriage in 1532. Disputes over the Hungerford inheritance were

settled by arbitration in 1535;[93] Winterbourne Stoke was presumably confirmed to Sir Walter (cr. Lord Hungerford 1536), who held it in 1536. It was forfeited on his attainder in 1540[94] and became part of the jointure of Queen Catherine (d. 1548). In 1552 it was restored to Hungerford's son (Sir) Walter,[95] who was succeeded in 1596 by his half-brother Sir Edward Hungerford (d. 1607). Sir Edward devised his estates to his grandnephew Sir Edward Hungerford (d. 1648), who was succeeded by his half-brother Anthony Hungerford (d. 1657). Anthony's son Sir Edward[96] sold Winterbourne Stoke manor in 1674 to Sir John Nicholas[97] (d. 1704), whose son Edward sold it in 1715 to John Howe[98] (d. 1721) or his son John (cr. Baron Chedworth 1741, d. 1742). It descended with Great Wishford manor to John, Lord Chedworth (d. 1762), Henry, Lord Chedworth (d. 1781), and John, Lord Chedworth (d. 1804).[99] In 1807 the manor was sold by Lord Chedworth's executors to Alexander Baring[1] (cr. Baron Ashburton 1835, d. 1848). It passed with the barony to Alexander's sons William (d. 1864) and Francis (d. 1868), to Francis's son Alexander (d. 1889), and to Alexander's son Francis,[2] who sold it probably in 1896 to E. T. Hooley. Following Hooley's bankruptcy the manor, comprising c. 2,500 a., was sold to Sir Christopher Furness, probably in 1899.[3] It was offered for sale by Furness through the Cavendish Land Company in 1909: then or in 1910 Cary Coles (fl. 1915) bought Manor farm, c. 1,600 a., and probably Greenland farm, c. 400 a.[4] In 1923 G. C. Alexander owned the farms[5] and in 1945 sold them to L. E. Turner. In 1958 Turner sold the farms to his son Mr. J. L. Turner, owner in 1992 of c. 1,900 a. in the parish.[6]

Hill farm, 644 a., part of Winterbourne Stoke manor until 1909, was part of the Druid's Lodge estate, based in Stapleford and Woodford, between 1909 and 1912 and from the 1930s. F. B. Beauchamp may have bought the farm in 1909;[7] A. P. Cunliffe owned it in 1910,[8] and, probably in 1912, sold it to T. N. Coles, who owned it in 1923[9] and sold it in 1936 to J. V. Rank (d. 1952). As part of the Druid's Lodge estate it was bought by the Fenston Trust and in 1989 sold to Mr. R. A. Hurst, the owner in 1992.[10]

Manor House is a long gabled house of flint

---

[74] *Cal. Close, 1330–3*, 186.   [75] *Bk. of Fees*, ii. 731.

[76] *Cal. Inq. p.m.* ii, p. 323; *Complete Peerage*, vi. 463; W.R.O. 490/1470, f. 34.   [77] W.R.O. 490/1470, f. 34.

[78] Ibid. f. 36; *Cal. Inq. p.m.* vii, p. 165.

[79] *Wilts. Inq. p.m. 1327–77* (Index Libr.), 68–9; *Cal. Close, 1389–92*, 301; W.R.O. 490/1470, f. 37.

[80] W.R.O. 490/1470, f. 43v.

[81] *W.N. & Q.* v. 187.

[82] *Cal. Close, 1429–35*, 55; *Feud. Aids*, v. 245; W.R.O. 490/1470, ff. 44v.–45.

[83] *Complete Peerage*, xi. 328–30; W.R.O. 490/1470, f. 44.

[84] *Feet of F. 1377–1509* (W.R.S. xli), p. 90.

[85] P.R.O., SC 6/1062/6.

[86] *Complete Peerage*, vi. 616–20.

[87] Hist. MSS. Com. 78, *Hastings*, i, p. 290.

[88] *Complete Peerage*, vi. 617–18.

[89] *Cal. Pat. 1467–77*, 466–7; *1476–85*, 359.

[90] *Complete Peerage*, vi. 622–5; ix. 610–12.

[91] P.R.O., SC 6/Hen. VII/960; SC 6/Hen. VII/964.

[92] *Complete Peerage*, vi. 622–4; E. M. Oliver, *Memoirs of Hungerford Fam.* (priv. print. 1930), 13.

[93] Hist. MSS. Com. 78, *Hastings*, i, pp. 292–3, 309–10.

[94] *Complete Peerage*, vi. 626; P.R.O., SC 2/208/80; SC 6/Hen. VIII/3918.

[95] *D.N.B.*; *Cal. Pat. 1550–3*, 438–9; P.R.O., E 318/30/1720.

[96] *Complete Peerage*, vi. 626; *V.C.H. Wilts.* xii. 129; W.R.O. 490/1537.

[97] Folger Shakespeare Libr., MS. V. a. 420.

[98] Hoare, *Mod. Wilts.* Alderbury, 96; W.R.O. 530, abstr. of title.

[99] *Complete Peerage*, iii. 156–7; below, Great Wishford, manor.   [1] *W.A.M.* xxxv. 311; W.R.O. 317/2.

[2] *Complete Peerage*, i. 276–8.

[3] W.R.O. 131/78, sale cat. of Hooley's estate; 1232, sched. of exchange, 1896; W.A.S. Libr., sale cat. ii, no. 18.

[4] *Kelly's Dir. Wilts.* (1915); W.A.S. Libr., sale cat. ix, no. 15; W.R.O., Inland Revenue, val. reg. 144.

[5] W.R.O., G 1/500/22.

[6] Inf. from Mr. J. L. Turner, Manor Ho.

[7] W.A.S. Libr., sale cat. ix, no. 15; above, Stapleford, manor.   [8] W.R.O., Inland Revenue, val. reg. 144.

[9] Ibid. 776/368; ibid. G 1/500/22.

[10] Inf. from the manager, Druid's Lodge, Woodford.

and chalk. The central range and northern wing of the older part of the present house are early 17th-century: a southern service wing was added in the later 17th century, forming a **U**-shaped house with its open court to the west. The house was substantially extended northwards *c.* 1920 when new kitchens and servants' rooms were added.

In 1066 Alwi held an estate in Winterbourne Stoke possibly of 1½ hide: the ½ hide held by his wife in 1086 may have been her dower, was then held of the king, and may have become part of Winterbourne Stoke manor; 1 hide, formerly Alwi's, was held in 1086 by Edward of Salisbury and of him by Walter. Another estate, of 1½ hide, was also held of Edward by Walter in 1086. One of Edward's estates became Asserton in Berwick St. James,[11] the other became *WIN-TERBOURNE MAUTRAVERS* manor, overlordship of which evidently passed to Edward's descendants with the manor and overlordship of Shrewton and the earldom of Salisbury.[12] Thomas Montagu, earl of Salisbury, was overlord in 1409,[13] after which the overlordship has not been traced.

The manor was held in demesne by Nicholas Hall (de Aula) in 1275,[14] by Ralph Hall (de la Sale) and his wife Parnel in 1320,[15] and perhaps by Richard Hall in 1332.[16] In 1356 it was held by John Mautravers, Lord Mautravers (d. 1364).[17] From 1375 to 1560–1 it descended with Sherrington manor.[18] It was held by Mautravers's granddaughter Eleanor, Baroness Mautravers (d. 1405), her grandson John, earl of Arundel (d. 1421), and his relict Eleanor (d. 1455),[19] and from 1455 by successive earls of Arundel.[20] Henry, earl of Arundel, sold it to Nicholas Snow in 1562.[21] Snow (will proved 1588) was succeeded in turn by his son Adam[22] (d. 1618) and Adam's son William.[23] In 1664 William settled the manor on himself and his son William.[24] It was held by Edward Duke (d. 1705) and passed to his granddaughter Rebecca Duke, wife of George or Gorges Hely[25] (d. 1760). It passed to the Helys' son John (fl. 1791), whose son Gorges[26] sold the manor in 1805 to Hampden Hely[27] (will proved 1814). Hampden's son Hampden held Scotland (or Arundell) farm, 501 a., in 1839, and in 1859 was succeeded by

his sister Anne, wife of Henry Bowen. From Anne (d. 1859) the farm passed to her son Henry Bowen.[28] In 1880 Henry sold it to William Salway,[29] who conveyed it to his son William in 1889.[30] The younger William sold it in 1895 or 1896 to George Saunders.[31] In 1910 and 1914 John Fallon owned Scotland farm[32] which, with adjoining land in Maddington parish,[33] was called the Scotland Lodge estate from the earlier 20th century. It was offered for sale, probably by Fallon, in 1920[34] and was bought about then by R. C. Dawson, the owner in 1923.[35] In 1927 Robert Wales (d. 1979) bought the estate, which to fulfil his will was sold in 1980 for less than the market price to the Nature Conservancy Council. The council sold Scotland Lodge and *c.* 330 a. in 1980: its successor English Nature owned 394 a. in Winterbourne Stoke parish in 1991.[36]

Between 1227 and 1241 the abbey of Jumièges (Seine Maritime) was licensed to appropriate Winterbourne Stoke church when it next became vacant. The vacancy apparently occurred *c.* 1248 when Hayling priory (Hants), a dependent house of the abbey, disputed the church with a cleric claiming it by papal provision.[37] The appropriation by the abbey was confirmed in 1249.[38] The *RECTORY* estate was among the priory's possessions confiscated during wars with France in the 14th century,[39] passed to the Crown at the priory's dissolution in 1413, and was among the endowments of Sheen priory (Surr.), founded in 1414.[40] Before 1248 the rector's estate evidently comprised 1 carucate and all tithes from the whole parish.[41] Some tithes were taken from it to endow the vicarage in 1248, and more may have been alienated at other times.[42] The estate passed to the Crown on Sheen priory's dissolution in 1539,[43] was granted in 1541 to Arundel college (Suss.), and reverted to the Crown on the college's dissolution in 1544.[44] In 1562 it was sold to Basil Johnson.[45] It had been acquired by Sir Walter Hungerford by 1587,[46] possibly by 1580,[47] and afterwards passed with Winterbourne Stoke manor. By 1839 the lands had been absorbed into the manor, and tithes from 2,115 a. had been merged. The remaining rectorial tithes were valued at £131 in 1839 and merged.[48]

11 *V.C.H. Wilts.* ii, p. 136.
12 Above, Shrewton, manors; cf. *Rot. Hund.* (Rec. Com.), ii (1), 254; *Feet of F. 1272–1327* (W.R.S. i), pp. 132–3; *Cal. Inq. p.m.* xv, p. 80; xviii, p. 381.
13 *Cal. Close, 1405–9,* 458.
14 *Rot. Hund.* (Rec. Com.), ii (1), 254.
15 *Feet of F. 1272–1327* (W.R.S. i), p. 106.
16 *Tax List, 1332* (W.R.S. xlv), 77.
17 *Feet of F. 1327–77* (W.R.S. xxix), p. 109; *Complete Peerage,* viii. 584.   18 Above, Sherrington, manor.
19 *Cal. Close, 1419–22,* 190.
20 Ibid. *1454–61,* 87–8.
21 P.R.O., CP 25/2/239/3 Eliz. I Hil.
22 Ibid. PROB 11/73, f. 239.
23 Ibid. C 142/370, no. 56.
24 Ibid. CP 25/2/744/16 Chas. II East.
25 Ibid. CP 25/2/980/9 Anne Mich.; Burke, *Commoners* (1833–8), i. 286.
26 Burke, *Land. Gent. of Ireland* (1904), 255; W.R.O., A 1/345/446.
27 W.R.O. 1232/1, notification of sale, 1805.
28 Ibid. 1232/1, abstr. of Salway's title; ibid. tithe award.
29 Ibid. 1232/1, deed, Bowen to Salway, 1880.
30 Ibid. 1232/1, abstr. of Salway's title.
31 W.A.S. Libr., sale cat. xiii, no. 16; Wilts. Cuttings, v. 281, 380.
32 W.R.O., Inland Revenue, val. reg. 144; ibid. 1232/1, mortgage, Fallon to Leslie, 1914.
33 Above, Maddington, manors (Homanton).
34 W.A.S. Libr., sale cat. xiii, no. 16.
35 W.R.O., G 1/500/22.
36 Inf. from Chief Site Manager, Eng. Nature, S. Region.
37 *Cal. Papal Reg.* i. 257.
38 *Hist. de l'Abbaye de Jumièges* (Soc. de l'Hist. de Normandie, xiii), ii. 6–7.
39 e.g. *Cal. Pat. 1338–40,* 127; *1367–70,* 305; *1388–92,* 497.   40 *V.C.H. Hants,* ii. 219; *V.C.H. Surr.* ii. 89.
41 *Chartes de l'Abbaye de Jumièges* (Soc. de l'Hist. de Normandie, xlv), ii, p. 24.
42 Below, this section; church [tithes].
43 *V.C.H. Surr.* ii. 93.
44 L. & P. Hen. VIII, xvi, p. 504; *V.C.H. Suss.* ii. 109.
45 *Cal. Pat. 1560–3,* 220.
46 W.R.O. 442/1, f. 27v.
47 Phillipps, *Wilts. Inst.* i. 230.
48 W.R.O., tithe award.

By 1291 Salisbury cathedral had acquired tithes of Winterbourne Stoke valued at £2,[49] and in 1650 had the rectorial and some other tithes from Winterbourne Mautravers manor.[50] The tithes, from 501 a., were valued at £95 in 1839 and commuted.[51]

Rents from Winterbourne Stoke belonged to Amesbury priory in 1435[52] and at the Dissolution, when they totalled 30s.[53] The suggestion that Bradenstoke priory's manor of Winterbourne Shrewton in Shrewton parish included lands in Winterbourne Stoke probably arose from the use of the name Winterbourne[54] and cannot be verified.

ECONOMIC HISTORY. By far the largest estate at Winterbourne Stoke in 1086 was the king's, which had 11 ploughteams on land for 12, 8 a. of meadow, and pasture 2 leagues square: the demesne, with 3 teams, 11 *servi*, and 5 coliberts on land assessed at only ½ yardland, was small, and most of the land was held by 15 *villani* and 15 bordars who between them had 8 teams. The other three estates of which two may have been in Winterbourne Stoke had on them 3 teams, 1 *servus*, 1 bordar, and 2 cottars, and included 1 a. of meadow and 6 a. of pasture.[55]

The arable in the demesne of Winterbourne Stoke manor apparently remained much less than in its customary holdings. The demesne included 300 a. of arable in 1284 and 1331: in 1331 *c.* 25 yardlands, each shown by later evidence to contain *c.* 27 a. of arable with feeding for *c.* 60 sheep, were held customarily. There were 19 customary tenants in 1284, 34 in 1331; customary works owed in summer may have been commuted in part by 1331. The demesne had 6½ a. of meadow in 1284, 20 a. of meadow and a flock of *c.* 500 sheep in 1331.[56] Although it had less arable than the customary tenants it may have had as much downland pasture, and in the 15th century management of the demesne flock was integrated with sheep farming on other estates of the Hungerford family, lords of the manor. New stock, in 1443–4 including 200 wethers, was sent from Heytesbury, and fleeces, wool, and animals for breeding were sent from Winterbourne Stoke to Farleigh Hungerford (Som.). The flock at Winterbourne Stoke numbered 1,330 in 1435–6, 940 in 1454–5. The arable had been leased by 1435, and part of it was leased in the 1440s in parcels of between 29 a. and 50 a. On what was in hand barley and wheat were the chief crops in the mid 15th century: from 164 a. sown in 1450 half the crops of wheat and of barley were sold and 40 qr. of grain were sent to the Hungerfords' household. In 1486 and

1504 demesne land was leased in two portions, one of pasture only.[57]

A warren, recorded in the late 14th century, was part of Winterbourne Stoke manor[58] and presumably at the site called the Coniger. In 1435–6 and 1440–1 it was leased: 42 couple of rabbits were caught in 1435–6.[59] The warren was leased as pasture in 1486 and 1545,[60] and was not recorded thereafter.

In the 1170s the rector's land was assessed at 1 carucate and had five tenants on it.[61] It was proposed in 1352 to repair buildings on the estate and to erect a new barn,[62] but in 1393 the farmhouse was dilapidated.[63]

Open-field husbandry, with common meadows and pasture, continued until the 19th century. In 1331 the demesne included arable assessed at three different values and perhaps therefore in three fields, but evidence that half the demesne arable was sown in the 15th century suggests a two-field system.[64] There may then have been distinct fields for the demesne, as there were later. In the 16th century the parish was probably half arable, including some recently broken land, and half pasture. The arable was mainly in two groups of fields: the demesne arable was in North and Breach fields, north of the village, and in Hide field, East Cranham field, and West Cranham field; a freeholder, 14 copyholders, and *c.* 6 leaseholders had *c.* 935 a. in Longbarrow or East field, Shorthill or South field, and Burden or West field, respectively east, south-east, and west of the village. The 180 ridges of arable on the Rectory estate may have been in the demesne fields. Of the three tenantry fields two were sown and one left fallow: other arable was sown on a three-year rotation of wheat, barley, and 'lenten' grain. Demesne pastures included Fore down and Chissels down: Summer down, 400 a., and Little down, 6 a., were tenantry sheep pastures near the eastern parish boundary. Cow down, 350 a. in the north-east, and sheep downs called Middle down, south of Cow down, and Gore down, in the south-east corner of the parish, each of 100 a., were shared by men holding either demesne or tenantry arable, and some men of Bourton in Maddington had rights to use Cow down. Fore mead, Midsummer mead, Stopples, Lammas mead, and Lot mead may all have been common meadows. The two groups of fields and those downs and meadows may also have included the lands of Winterbourne Mautravers manor, which were possibly in a single farm in the late 16th century.[65]

The demesne sheep pastures of Winterbourne Stoke manor remained in the lord's hand in the late 16th century, and the lord excluded the right to feed sheep from a lease of the land of the

49 *Tax. Eccl.* (Rec. Com.), 181.
50 *W.A.M.* xli. 124.
51 W.R.O., tithe award.
52 P.R.O., SC 6/1062/6.
53 Ibid. SC 6/Hen. VIII/3986, rot. 82.
54 *V.C.H. Wilts.* iii. 282–3; *Bradenstoke Cart.* (W.R.S. xxxv), pp. 103–4; above, Shrewton, manors (Winterbourne Shrewton).
55 *V.C.H. Wilts.* ii, pp. 118, 136, 141.
56 *Wilts. Inq. p.m. 1242–1326* (Index Libr.), 157–8; 1327–77 (Index Libr.), 69.
57 R. C. Payne, 'Agrarian conditions on Wilts. estates of

Duchy of Lanc., Lords Hungerford, etc.' (Lond. Univ. Ph.D. thesis, 1940), 123, 131, 177–216, 302, and App. III, p. xi; P.R.O., SC 6/1062/6–9; SC 6/1062/11–13.
58 *Proc. before the Justices* (Ames Foundation), 385.
59 P.R.O., SC 6/1062/6; SC 6/1062/8.
60 Ibid. SC 6/Hen. VII/390; SC 6/Hen. VIII/3918.
61 *Chartes de Jumièges*, ii, p. 24.
62 *Cal. Pat. 1350–4*, 359.
63 *V.C.H. Wilts.* iii. 25.
64 *Wilts. Inq. p.m. 1327–77* (Index Libr.), 69; Payne, 'Agrarian conditions', 123–4.
65 *W.A.M.* xxxiv. 208–15; W.R.O. 442/1, ff. 18–34.

Rectory. Some arable may also have remained in hand but much was leased, mainly in five parcels of *c*. 80 ridges and two of 40. Although the tenants of the demesne arable had no right of pasture for sheep, the lord's flock was folded on their land: grain rents were paid and the tenants had to carry hay from the demesne farmhouse to the lord's wether fold. The freeholder, the 14 copyholders, and the *c*. 6 lessees of customary land had rights to feed *c*. 2,140 sheep in common.[66]

By *c*. 1610 the demesne sheep pastures, *c*. 400 a. of several downland for *c*. 1,200 sheep, had been leased with 200 ridges of demesne arable, 20 a. of meadow, 8 a. in pasture closes, and the 180 ridges of the Rectory arable: the farm was apparently that later called Manor farm. The largest copyhold 1545–1610 was one of 5 yardlands, including 135 a. of arable and feeding for 305 sheep, and in the late 16th century there were, excluding demesne arable, 8–9 holdings each exceeding 50 a. with feeding for more than 100 sheep.[67]

Between *c*. 1600 and *c*. 1800 the amount of arable in the parish may have declined slightly, although small areas of downland were brought into cultivation by burnbaking.[68] In the late 18th century and early 19th Mill mead and Lammas mead were being watered.[69] In 1806 Manor farm was 1,027 a., worked from buildings near Manor House, and mainly several: it included *c*. 400 a. of pasture, *c*. 600 a. of arable, and 20 a. of watered meadow. Scotland farm, the land of Winterbourne Mautravers manor, was 496 a. in 1805 and half arable and half pasture.[70] In 1806 the 20 tenants of Winterbourne Stoke manor, including six copyholders, held *c*. 750 a. of arable and pasture for 1,260 sheep.[71]

Common husbandry in the parish was ended by an award of 1812 under an Act of 1810: open fields, tenantry downs, and common meadows were inclosed and allotments were made of 2,659 a.[72] In 1839 there were approximately equal areas of arable and pasture, and *c*. 60 a. of meadow. All four principal farms were worked from farmsteads in the village: Manor farm was then 1,875 a., two other farms were of 678 a. and 287 a., and Scotland farm had 501 a. in two blocks west of the village.[73]

Between 1839 and 1880 new farmsteads were built on the downs in the east,[74] and in the late 19th century and the earlier 20th the lands which they served were in either Manor farm, *c*. 1,500 a., or Hill farm, *c*. 600 a.; Scotland farm remained *c*. 500 a. and was worked from the earlier 20th century with adjacent lands in Maddington parish.[75] In the 1860s and 1880s almost half the land worked from farmsteads in the parish was arable, and on half of that cereals were produced. Farms based in the parish had *c*. 3,000 sheep in 1866, over 5,000 in 1886.[76] On Manor farm there was a prize-winning flock of Hampshire Down sheep numbering *c*. 1,000 in 1899.[77] The area of arable declined sharply in the 1920s and less than a third of the parish was ploughed in the 1930s. Fewer sheep were kept but more cattle.[78] On Scotland farm, principally a sheep farm in the 1920s, cattle were kept in increasing numbers from the 1930s, and from the 1940s included rare breeds such as Gloucesters, Highlands, and Longhorns; Jacob sheep were also kept. Most of the land was never worked intensively and from 1980 the 394 a. of it in the Parsonage Down nature reserve have been grazed by cattle and sheep.[79] Manor and Greenland farms have been worked together from the 1940s, as a dairy and cereal farm in the 1940s and 1950s, since 1960 as a beef and cereal farm of *c*. 1,900 a.[80] In the 1990s the lands of Hill farm were worked with others in Berwick St. James and Stapleford as part of a large mixed farm.[81]

Horses were trained at Scotland Lodge from 1895;[82] in 1920 there was extensive stabling, *c*. 70 a. of pasture set aside for horses, and gallops on 260 a. of downland.[83] Horses were again trained there in the 1980s.[84]

Poultry houses for a business based in Berwick St. James were built at Wisma Poultry Farm in Winterbourne Stoke in the late 1940s and later.[85]

MILLS. There was a mill on the king's Winterbourne Stoke estate in 1086,[86] and one on Winterbourne Stoke manor from the 13th century to the 17th. The mill mentioned in 1284[87] may have been the water mill repaired in 1435 and given a new wheel in 1436.[88] The water mill was untenanted and in disrepair in 1486 and 1546.[89] It had been rebuilt by 1574,[90] was in use *c*. 1610,[91] but had been demolished by 1773.[92] Its site was presumably south of the village where a pasture was called Mill Pond in 1839.[93]

LOCAL GOVERNMENT. In 1255 Winterbourne Stoke manor was held with return of writs and view of frankpledge.[94] A court for the manor was held from the 13th century.[95] In 1436 and 1437 a view of frankpledge was held in April,

66 W.R.O. 442/1, ff. 18–34.
67 Ibid. ff. 19–21; 442/2, pp. 77–92; P.R.O., SC 6/Hen. VIII/3918. 68 W.R.O. 317/12.
69 Ibid. EA/50; EA/104.
70 Ibid. 1232/1, abstr. of Salway's title.
71 Ibid. 317/12. 72 Ibid. EA/104.
73 Ibid. tithe award.
74 Ibid.; O.S. Maps 6", Wilts. LIV (1887 edn.); LIX (1889 edn.).
75 W.A.S. Libr., sale cat. ix, no. 15; W.R.O. 130/78, sale cat. 1898; ibid. G 1/500/22; above, Maddington, econ. hist. (Homanton).
76 P.R.O., MAF 68/74, sheet 73; MAF 68/1063, sheet 14. 77 Wilts. Cuttings, viii. 76.
78 P.R.O., MAF 68/3319, sheet 16; MAF 68/3814, sheet 239; [1st] Land Util. Surv. Map, sheet 122.
79 Inf. from Chief Site Manager, Eng. Nature, S. Region.

80 Inf. from Mr. J. L. Turner, Manor Ho.
81 Inf. from the manager, Druid's Lodge, Woodford; above, Stapleford, econ. hist. 82 Wilts. Cuttings, v. 281.
83 W.A.S. Libr., sale cat. xiii, no. 16.
84 Inf. from Mr. J. Singleton, Scotland Lodge.
85 Inf. from Mr. J. K. Woodford, Goodwin Ho., Berwick St. Jas. 86 V.C.H. Wilts. ii, p. 118.
87 Wilts. Inq. p.m. 1242–1326 (Index Libr.), 158.
88 P.R.O., SC 6/1062/6–7.
89 Ibid. SC 6/1062/12; SC 6/Hen. VIII/3918.
90 Ibid. DL 42/115, f. 61v.; W.A.M. xxxiv. 211–12.
91 W.R.O. 442/2, p. 85.
92 Andrews and Dury, Map (W.R.S. viii), pl. 5.
93 W.R.O., tithe award.
94 Rot. Hund. (Rec. Com.), ii (1), 237.
95 Wilts. Inq. p.m. 1242–1326 (Index Libr.), 158; 1327–77 (Index Libr.), 43–4, 69.

and in 1436 the manor court was held four times.[96] The lord was said to keep both a court leet and a court baron twice each year in the late 16th century.[97] There are records of the manor court and the view of frankpledge, held together and usually in spring and autumn, for the periods 1512–46 and 1592–7,[98] and a court of survey, at which the customs of the manor were presented, is known to have been held in 1574[99] and c. 1610.[1]

By 1574 the obligation to serve as tithingman had been attached to 15 holdings, presumably the copyholds of Winterbourne Stoke manor: the tithingman was chosen, and a hayward sworn, presumably at the combined view and manor court.[2] At earlier 16th-century meetings of the court the tithingman paid cert money and presented free tenants owing suit: also on his presentment the court dealt with stray animals, breaches of the assize of bread and of ale, and infringements of rules for the use of common pastures. At most meetings the homage also presented: their presentments included encroachment on the waste, pigs at large in places or at times forbidden by the court, obstruction of the highway, and removal of boundary stones. Both tithingman and homage presented the death of customary tenants. A jury found on both sets of presentments, and itself presented breaches of the peace, defaulters from the court, a burglary in 1533, and in 1517 failure to give doles due to the poor from the Rectory estate. In the 1590s the only formal presentments of the tithingman and the homage related respectively to free tenants and to strays and the death of tenants; none was made by the jury. Other business of the court included agreements for the use of common pastures and for keeping the river clear, orders to repair tenements and boundaries and to perform customary works, and admission to holdings.[3]

At the court and view of frankpledge held together yearly in October between 1782 and 1800 a joint jury and homage was sworn. Defaulters were presented, a hayward and a tithingman were appointed, and customs chiefly concerned with the common pastures were published. Copyholds were surrendered and new tenants admitted at the court and at an additional court baron held in 1788.[4]

In 1767–8 the parish spent £65 on poor relief; five parishioners received regular relief, and occasional payments were made for rents, clothing, and nursing. Expenditure was c. £70 a year

in the 1770s and 1780s. In 1802–3 £303 was spent. The high cost may have resulted from payments to paupers travelling through the parish: 20 non-parishioners were relieved, among 28 adults and 38 children who received regular relief and 22 people relieved occasionally, and Winterbourne Stoke was then the only rural parish of the hundred to relieve more than two from outside the parish.[5] Expenditure reached a peak of £376 in 1813–14, although only 16 people then received regular relief and 8 occasional relief.[6] In the 1820s it was usually between £150 and £200 a year, and in 1833–4 was £134.[7] Winterbourne Stoke became part of Amesbury poor-law union in 1835,[8] of Salisbury district in 1974.[9]

CHURCH. A church stood on the king's Winterbourne Stoke estate in 1066, when it was served by a chaplain.[10] It was given to Jumièges abbey in the period 1078–83,[11] and later the abbey evidently presented rectors. The abbey appropriated the church, apparently c. 1248:[12] a vicarage had been ordained by 1246.[13]

The advowson of the vicarage apparently belonged to Jumièges abbey, and vicars may have been presented by its dependant, Hayling priory. During wars with France the king presented 12 vicars between 1338 and 1406.[14] In 1412 Queen Joan, wife of Henry IV, was patron for a turn.[15] The advowson was granted to Sheen priory, presumably with the Rectory estate in 1414, and passed to the Crown at the Dissolution.[16] It was apparently not granted with the estate in 1541 or 1562,[17] and the king presented in 1542. By 1580, however, the advowson had been acquired by Sir Walter Hungerford, lord of Winterbourne Stoke manor and owner of the Rectory estate from 1587 or earlier. Thereafter until the 20th century lords of the manor presented at most vacancies:[18] an exception was in 1615 when Francis Manners, earl of Rutland, presented,[19] presumably in the right of his wife Cecily, relict of Sir Edward Hungerford (d. 1607).[20] In 1909 or 1910 Cary Coles bought the advowson with Manor farm. His executors were patrons in 1935, 1943, and 1962, and the bishop of Salisbury presented by lapse in 1937.[21] The executors conveyed the advowson to the bishop in 1973.[22]

With land and apparently all tithes from the whole parish the rectory was valuable.[23] Jumièges abbey gave the vicar 15s. a year until 1248, when it augmented the living.[24] The vicarage, valued at £4 6s. 8d. in 1291,[25] £10 12s. 8d.

96 P.R.O., SC 6/1062/6–7.
97 *W.A.M.* xxxiv. 209; W.R.O. 442/1, f. 34.
98 P.R.O., SC 2/208/64–70; SC 2/208/72–3; SC 2/208/75–6; SC 2/208/78–80; SC 6/Hen. VIII/3918; W.R.O. 490/1536–9.   99 *W.A.M.* xxxiv. 208–9.
1 W.R.O. 442/2, p. 77.   2 *W.A.M.* xxxiv. 209–10.
3 P.R.O., SC 2/208/64–70; SC 2/208/72–3; SC 2/208/75–6; SC 2/208/78–80; SC 6/Hen. VIII/3918; W.R.O. 490/1536–9; for the doles, below, charities.
4 W.R.O. 2057/M 75.
5 Ibid. 1968/11; *Poor Law Abstract, 1804*, 558–9.
6 *Poor Law Abstract, 1818*, 492–3.
7 *Poor Rate Returns, 1822–4*, 225; *1825–9*, 216; *1830–4*, 209.   8 *Poor Law Com. 2nd Rep.* App. D, 558.
9 O.S. Map 1/100,000, admin. areas, Wilts. (1974 edn.).
10 *V.C.H. Wilts.* ii, p. 118.
11 *Reg. Regum Anglo-Norm.* i, no. 194.
12 *Cal. Papal Reg.* i. 257; above, manors (Rectory).

13 *Sar. Chart. and Doc.* (Rolls Ser.), 314–15.
14 Phillipps, *Wilts. Inst.* i. 33, 46, 65, 68, 76, 82, 84, 94; *Cal. Pat.* 1367–70, 305; 1377–81, 334; 1381–5, 152; 1391–6, 123.   15 *Reg. Hallum* (Cant. & York Soc.), p. 42.
16 Phillipps, *Wilts. Inst.* i. 110, 114, 118, 134, 149, 151, 172, 184, 191; above, manors (Rectory).
17 *L. & P. Hen. VIII*, xvi, p. 504; *Cal. Pat.* 1560–3, 220.
18 Phillipps, *Wilts. Inst.* i. 210, 230; ii. 26–7, 29, 32, 36, 49, 51–2, 76–7, 80, 102; W.R.O., D 1/2/30, pp. 135, 143, 148; Ch. Com. file 7372; above, manors (Rectory).
19 Phillipps, *Wilts. Inst.* ii. 8.
20 *Complete Peerage*, xi. 261–2.
21 Ch. Com. file 7372; above, manors (Winterbourne Stoke).
22 Inf. from Dioc. Registrar, Castle Street, Salisbury.
23 *Chartes de Jumièges*, ii, p. 24.
24 *Sar. Chart. and Doc.* (Rolls Ser.), 314–15.
25 *Tax. Eccl.* (Rec. Com.), 181.

in 1535,[26] and £172 c. 1830,[27] was among the poorer livings of Wylye deanery. From 1248 it was endowed with half the hay tithes and all the tithes of lambs, wool, and mills from the whole parish except the demesne of the Rectory estate.[28] By 1609 the vicar's tithes from Winterbourne Mautravers manor had been compounded to renders of only 3 fleeces, 3 lambs, and half the tithe hay from 4 a. The vicar was, however, entitled then to tithes of grain from the whole Rectory estate.[29] In 1839 the tithes and the renders of 3 fleeces and 3 lambs were valued at £220 and commuted.[30] From 1609 or earlier the vicar also received tithes of wool, of lambs, and of hay from 7 yardlands in Bourton:[31] they were valued in 1841 at £21 5s. and commuted.[32] The glebe was 3 a. in 1609 and later. A vicarage house was built or renewed in 1586. In 1783 it had three rooms on the ground floor and two above, walls partly of flint and partly of lath and plaster, and a thatched roof.[33] The house, fit for residence c. 1830,[34] was replaced c. 1850 by a larger building of cob with a tiled roof.[35] That house was sold in 1938.[36]

The vicarage changed hands 11 times between 1379 and 1416, 10 by exchange.[37] In 1393 the font had no cover and the church windows and the churchyard fence were in need of repair.[38] In 1553 the vicar did not reside and had not provided a curate: Sunday services were held by the vicar of Stapleford but not at the proper times, no service had been held on Wednesdays or Fridays for three years, and there was no cover for the communion table.[39] In 1556 a parishioner was presented for refusing to contribute to the purchase of ornaments, presumably those required by the restoration of Roman Catholicism: 33s. owed to the church by another parishioner may have been for furnishings removed from the church under Edward VI.[40] The vicar preached regularly in 1584,[41] and in 1650 the vicar, Roger Maton, who in 1648 signed the *Concurrent Testimony*, was commended as a preacher.[42] Mark King, vicar from 1658, was ejected for nonconformity in 1662.[43] Thomas Harward, vicar 1684–1708, was curate of Maddington, where he lived, and rector of Rollestone.[44] John Tomkinson, vicar 1713–55, and Neville Wells, vicar 1762–1801, were also pluralists: Wells lived at West Grimstead. In 1783 the curate, who was also curate of Orcheston St. George, where he lived, held one service at Winterbourne Stoke each Sunday alternately in the morning and the afternoon. He celebrated communion at Christmas and Michaelmas and on Easter and Whit Sundays: there were usually 20 communicants.[45] In 1851 two services were usually held each Sunday in summer, one each

Sunday for the rest of the year: in summer the morning congregation comprised c. 110 adults, the afternoon one c. 150, and c. 70 children attended Sunday school.[46] Additional services were held in 1864 on Wednesdays in Lent and on Good Friday, Ascension day, and Christmas day: communion was celebrated at the four principal festivals and on the first Sunday in October, and the average number of communicants was 25.[47] The living was held with Berwick St. James vicarage from 1817 until 1879,[48] and

THE NORTH DOORWAY OF THE CHURCH

from 1938 until c. 1980 with the united benefice of Shrewton, Maddington, and Rollestone: from 1981 the incumbent of the united benefice was also priest-in-charge of Winterbourne Stoke.[49]

At inclosure in 1812 land and pasture rights given earlier for the upkeep of the church were replaced by an allotment of c. 1 a. The land, which was let for between £2 and £3 in the 19th century and for only 3s. in 1932,[50] was sold in 1954.[51]

ST. PETER'S church presumably took its dedication, recorded in 1163, from St. Peter's abbey, Jumièges. The church is of flint rubble with ashlar dressings, except for the chancel which is of yellow brick, and has a chancel with south organ chamber, a central tower with transepts, and a nave with north porch.[52] The nave

26 *Valor Eccl.* (Rec. Com.), ii. 104.
27 *Rep. Com. Eccl. Revenues*, 854–5.
28 *Sar. Chart. and Doc.* (Rolls Ser.), 314–15.
29 W.R.O., D 1/24/226/1.
30 Ibid. tithe award.   31 Ibid. D 1/24/226/1.
32 Ibid. Maddington tithe award.
33 Ibid. D 1/24/226/1; D 1/24/226/3; Hoare, *Mod. Wilts.* Branch and Dole, 31.
34 *Rep. Com. Eccl. Revenues*, 854–5.
35 Ch. Com. file 7372.   36 Ibid. 34/398.
37 Phillipps, *Wilts. Inst.* i. 65–6, 68, 82, 84, 105; *Cal. Pat.* 1377–81, 334; 1388–92, 497; 1391–6, 123; *Reg. Hallum* (Cant. & York Soc.), p. 42.   38 *V.C.H. Wilts.* iii. 25.
39 W.R.O., D 1/43/1, f. 117 and v.
40 Ibid. D 1/43/2, f. 5v.   41 Ibid. D 1/43/5, f. 30.
42 *W.A.M.* xl. 393; *Calamy Revised*, ed. Matthews, 557.
43 *Calamy Revised*, 309; *W.N. & Q.* viii. 358.
44 Phillipps, *Wilts. Inst.* ii. 36, 49; *W.N. & Q.* ii. 481–2.
45 Phillipps, *Wilts. Inst.* ii. 52, 76, 80, 102; *W.N. & Q.* i. 366; *Vis. Queries, 1783* (W.R.S. xxvii), pp. 111, 239–40.
46 P.R.O., HO 129/262/1/7/9.
47 W.R.O., D 1/56/7.   48 Ch. Com. file 40354/1.
49 *Crockford* (1940 and later edns.).
50 *Endowed Char. Wilts.* (S. Div.), 897–8; W.R.O., L 2, Winterbourne Stoke.
51 Inf. from Lt.-Col. J. H. Price, Old Glebe Farmhouse.
52 For plans and illustrations of the church, *Churches of SE. Wilts.* (R.C.H.M.), 226–8.

is 12th-century with a north doorway of two orders and a blocked south doorway with a square-headed opening beneath a moulded arch of one order. The crossing is 13th-century and may be on the site of an earlier chancel. The transepts and the new chancel, with lancets in the north wall, were added at various dates in the 13th and 14th centuries, and the present tower was built in the later 14th. The north and south walls of the nave were each given a large new window at the east end in the 15th century, and the west wall was rebuilt with a doorway and a large window in the early 16th.[53] The church was extensively restored 1838–40. The main alterations to the nave were that the tracery of the windows at the east end was replaced in a 14th-century style, the north and south walls were each given a similar window at the west end, the porch was added, the floor was raised, and the roof replaced. The chancel was rebuilt: its north window has tracery in a 15th-century style, perhaps that removed from the windows at the east end of the nave.[54] The north transept, which had been demolished by the early 19th century,[55] was rebuilt in 1880, and the organ chamber was added in 1881.[56] The church contains a 12th-century font, with a 17th-century cover, and a 17th-century pulpit. In the north and south windows at the west end of the nave there are stained glass panels with figures of saints and dated 1835.

In 1553 plate weighing 16 oz. was confiscated and a chalice weighing 8 oz. left in the parish. A cup, apparently larger than that chalice, a flagon or mug, and a plate, all of silver, were replaced in 1848 by a chalice and a paten, both of silver, and a flagon of plated metal.[57] The vessels of 1848 belonged to the parish in 1992.[58]

There were four bells in the church in 1553. Two of them, cast at Salisbury, a bell of 1712 by Robert and William Cor, and a bell of the late 18th century by James and Robert Wells[59] hung in the church in 1992.[60]

Registers of burials, baptisms, and marriages survive from 1726.[61]

NONCONFORMITY. In 1662 the vicar was

ejected as a nonconformist and three women of the parish, one the mother of a child who had not been baptized, were presented for not attending church.[62] Two of the women were presented again c. 1670, one for absence from church, the other, with her husband, for remaining excommunicate.[63] Those may have been the three dissenters, probably Anabaptists, in the parish in 1676.[64] The curate claimed that there was no dissenter in the parish in 1783:[65] a house was certified in 1795 for Independent meetings, as others were in 1798 and 1811 for Baptist meetings.[66] In 1864 there were c. 12 Baptists and c. 12 Wesleyan Methodists:[67] they and later nonconformists presumably attended chapels outside the parish.

EDUCATION. In 1684 the vicar, Thomas Harward, proposed to open a school in a building newly erected or converted.[68] A dame school in Winterbourne Stoke had c. 23 pupils in 1818,[69] when a schoolroom was built.[70] The school, affiliated to the National society, had 34 pupils in 1833,[71] 40–50 in 1858 and 1871.[72] The schoolroom was replaced in 1875 by a gabled red-brick school on the west side of Church Street near the Vicarage.[73] Average attendance was 35 in 1895,[74] 47 in 1909–10, and 17 in 1935–6.[75] The school was closed in 1949.[76]

CHARITIES FOR THE POOR. Seven strikes of wheat and 7d., due yearly from the Rectory estate to the poor of the parish, had not been given for four years in 1517.[77] The tenant of the estate was required to make the gift in 1562,[78] but no later reference to the charity has been found.

Winterbourne Stoke was entitled to a seventh of the income of the Shrewton Flood charity, derived from the rents of cottages including the two on the north edge of the parish. Its share was to provide clothing or fuel for the poor: in 1904 c. £5 was spent on 27 sheets. From the mid 20th century the charity's income was spent chiefly on its cottages; in 1987 those in the parish were sold and the proceeds used to repair others.[79]

GREAT WISHFORD

GREAT WISHFORD village is 8.5 km. north-west of Salisbury.[80] The parish measures 680 ha. (1,679 a.).

The parish's boundary with Little Langford follows a dry valley and had been fixed by the 10th or 11th century.[81] On the north and east

53 For the church in the early 19th cent., J. Buckler, watercolour in W.A.S. Libr., vol. viii. 73.
54 Churches of SE. Wilts. 227–8; W.R.O. 1968/12.
55 Buckler, watercolour in W.A.S. Libr., vol. viii. 73.
56 Churches of SE. Wilts. 227; Ch. Com. file 57260.
57 Nightingale, Wilts. Plate, 77; W.R.O., D 1/24/226/3.
58 Inf. from Lt.-Col. Price.
59 Walters, Wilts. Bells, 238–9.
60 Inf. from Lt.-Col. Price.
61 W.R.O. 1968/1–8; bishop's transcripts for some years between 1608 and 1726 are ibid.
62 Ibid. D 1/54/1/4, no. 7B; above, church.
63 W.R.O., D 1/54/5, no. 29.
64 Compton Census, ed. Whiteman, 125; V.C.H. Wilts. iii. 113. 65 Vis. Queries, 1783 (W.R.S. xxvii), p. 240.
66 Meeting Ho. Certs. (W.R.S. xl), pp. 43, 52, 68.
67 W.R.O., D 1/56/7. 68 W.N. & Q. ii. 481–2.

69 Educ. of Poor Digest, 1041.
70 P.R.O., ED 7/131, no. 324.
71 Educ. Enq. Abstract, 1052.
72 Acct. of Wilts. Schs. 51; Returns relating to Elem. Educ. 426–7. 73 Kelly's Dir. Wilts. (1885); W.R.O., F 8/320.
74 Kelly's Dir. Wilts. (1895).
75 Bd. of Educ., List 21, 1910 (H.M.S.O.), 554; 1936, 428.
76 W.R.O. 1821/155. 77 P.R.O., SC 2/208/67.
78 Cal. Pat. 1560–3, 220.
79 Endowed Char. Wilts. (S. Div.), 638, 899; above, intro.; Shrewton, charities; inf. from the Secretary, Shrewton Flood charity, Maddington Place, Shrewton.
80 This article was written in 1993. Maps used include O.S. Maps 6", Wilts. LIX–LX, LXV–LXVI (1887–90 and later edns.); 1/25,000, SU 03/13 (1988 edn.); 1/50,000, sheet 184 (1979 edn.).
81 Arch. Jnl. lxxvi. 282–3.

the boundary follows the river Wylye and may also have been fixed early: the boundary is marked by the main course of the river in some places, by side-streams in others. To the south, where the woodland of Grovely forest lay between Great Wishford and Barford St. Martin, the boundary may have been defined equally early, but, if so, was later changed. In 1604 the jurors of a forest court gave the prehistoric Grim's ditch as the boundary of the two parishes: that boundary left seven coppices of the forest in Great Wishford,[82] but in 1609 the rector claimed tithes from only the easternmost, Bonham's copse, later called Heath wood.[83] In 1839 Heath wood, bounded to the south by Grim's ditch, was in the parish, but the other six coppices were not: by then the rest of the southern boundary of the parish had been moved north from Grim's ditch to what was until c. 1800 the north edge of the woodland.[84]

Chalk outcrops over the whole parish, and the relief is sharp. The downs reach 170 m. on Ebsbury Hill and 155 m. on Hadden Hill and are crossed by deep valleys, now dry, cut by tributaries of the Wylye. Heath wood is on clay-with-flints at c. 150 m., and there is also a small area of clay-with-flints on the west side of the village. Near the Wylye, at c. 60 m., there is alluvium, and gravel has been deposited along the Wylye and in the tributary valleys.[85] There were open fields on the lower slopes of the chalk and, mostly further from the river, the steeper slopes and higher downland provided pasture. There is extensive meadow land beside the river, especially in the north part of the parish. Apart from Heath wood, there was until c. 1800 little woodland in the parish as defined in 1839.[86]

The Roman road from Winchester and Old Salisbury to the Mendips is thought to have crossed the south-east end of the parish, running west from the Wylye and north of Heath wood.[87] Also to the south-east the Grovely ridge way was apparently on the same course as Grim's ditch along the south boundary of Heath wood in 1589:[88] a track remained there in the late 20th century. Unusually for a Wiltshire parish no road in Great Wishford was turnpiked. The principal road through it is that, apparently of Saxon origin,[89] between Wilton and Warminster linking the villages on the right bank of the Wylye. From it a road led across Stoford bridge[90] to the road on the left bank, which became a trunk road in the 20th century. In 1773 and 1993 minor roads led south-west from Great Wishford village.[91] The Salisbury–Warminster section of the G.W.R., opened in 1856, runs beside the principal road. A station built in the village in 1856 or soon after was closed in 1955.[92]

Earthworks covering c. 100 a. on Ebsbury Hill provide evidence of Iron-Age and Romano-British settlement, and coin hoards probably deposited in the 5th century A.D. have been found. A Romano-British field system extends over part of the site, and other prehistoric field systems have been identified west of Ebsbury Hill and on Hadden Hill. Grim's ditch may be of slightly later date than the Roman road to the Mendips.[93]

The parish had 138 poll-tax payers in 1377. The population was 346 in 1801, 291 in 1811, 372 in 1821: the reason for such large changes is obscure. From 1821 to 1871, when there were 381 inhabitants, numbers were roughly constant. Thereafter they fell, reaching a low point of 234 in 1951.[94] From the 1950s new housing was accompanied by a sharp increase: 328 people lived in the parish in 1971, 360 in 1991.[95]

Great Wishford village is close to the Wylye. The church stands at the centre of an arc of gravel, and the village grew west and south along the arc to form two streets, West Street and South Street.[96] Great Wishford manor house stood 200 m. north-west of the church: part was evidently demolished in 1785, the rest in the mid 19th century[97] when a new farmhouse was built among farm buildings near its site. Near the church at the junction of West Street and South Street stand the old rectory house, a mid 17th-century almshouse, and an early 18th-century school.[98] In West Street the principal surviving house is Wishford House, on the north side. It consists of a main 18th-century range, on which a new south front of brick was built in the early 19th century; a north extension was built in the early 19th century apparently to replace a kitchen wing, a north service wing of flint and brick was built in the late 19th century, and the interior of the main range was much altered in the mid 20th century. In South Street, on the east side, Shatfords is a farmhouse of chequered flint and limestone and of 17th-century origin. South of it on the same side Wishford Farmhouse may also be of 17th-century origin. It was altered in the mid 18th century, probably for Sir Edward Knatchbull, Bt. (d. 1789), the tenant in 1773:[99] a new west front of brick was built, and a high-quality oak staircase was inserted. West Street and South Street are each built up on both sides, and in each several cottages and small houses of 17th- or 18th-century origin survive: some are timber-framed, some are of flint and stone, and some are of brick with stone dressings. Both streets were in a conservation area designated in 1974.[1]

A little east of the village a mill stood on the Wylye at Stoford bridge.[2] A little south of the village one of two houses standing close to a

---

[82] *W.A.M.* xxxv. 304.   [83] W.R.O., D 1/24/228/1.
[84] Ibid. tithe award; *Andrews and Dury, Map* (W.R.S. viii), pl. 5; below, econ. hist. [woodland].
[85] Geol. Surv. Map 1/50,000, drift, sheet 298 (1976 edn.).
[86] Below, econ. hist.
[87] I. D. Margary, *Rom. Roads in Brit.* (1973), pp. 101–2; O.S. Map 6", Wilts. LXV (1890 edn.).
[88] H. W. Timperley and E. Brill, *Anct. Trackways of Wessex,* 133–6; W.R.O. 212B/7190H.   [89] *Arch. Jnl.* lxxv. 105.
[90] For the bridge, above, S. Newton, intro. (Stoford).
[91] *Andrews and Dury, Map* (W.R.S. viii), pl. 5.
[92] *V.C.H. Wilts.* iv. 284; *Kelly's Dir. Wilts.* (1859);

Clinker's Reg. Closed Passenger Sta. 1830–1977, 150.
[93] *V.C.H. Wilts.* i (1), 74, 251, 266, 276; i (2), 429, 465; O.S. Map 1/10,000, SU 03 NE. (1980 edn.).
[94] *V.C.H. Wilts.* iv. 307, 361.   [95] *Census,* 1971; 1991.
[96] Geol. Surv. Map 1/50,000, drift, sheet 298 (1976 edn.).
[97] Below, manor (Great Wishford).
[98] Ibid. church; educ.; char.; for the almshouse and the sch., above, plates facing p. 267.
[99] *Andrews and Dury, Map* (W.R.S. viii), pl. 5; G.E.C. *Baronetage,* ii. 118; W.R.O., A 1/345/449.
[1] Inf. from Co. Planning Officer, Co. Hall, Trowbridge.
[2] Below, econ. hist. [mills].

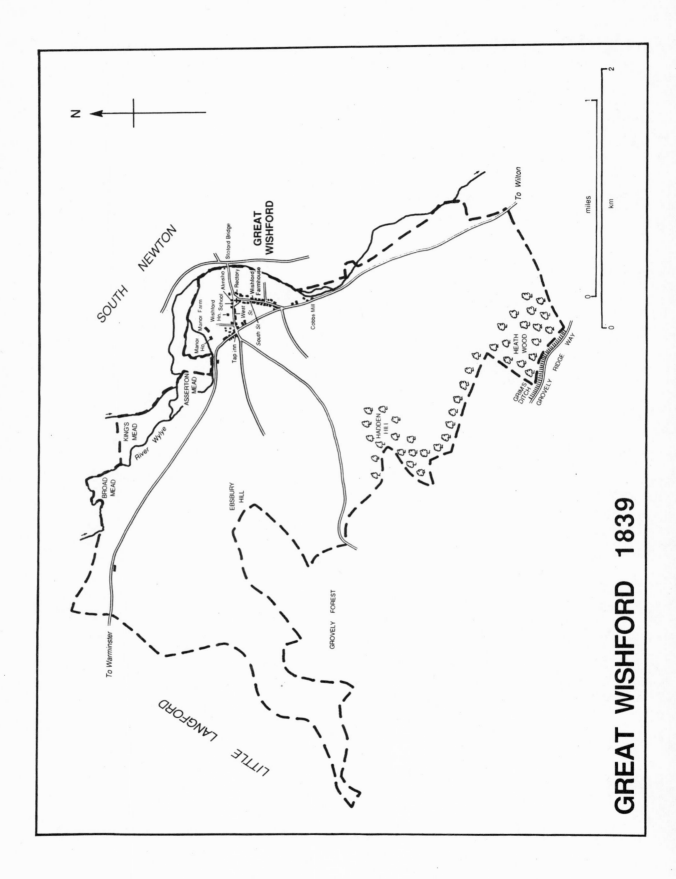

GREAT WISHFORD 1839

branch of the Wylye in 1773 was later called Cobbs Mill:[3] between 1773 and 1802 a third house was added to form a group. By 1773 both West Street and South Street had been built up between the church and the Wilton–Warminster road, and there were then several buildings beside the road near the junction with West Street. Several more had been erected there by 1802,[4] and, also beside the road, two more between the south end of South Street and Cobbs Mill by 1839.[5] An alehouse at Great Wishford was recorded in 1618.[6] On the west side of the Warminster road at its junction with West Street an inn called the Tap was open in 1822 and 1839.[7] By 1848 it had been renamed the Royal Oak,[8] under which name it remained open in 1993.

In the mid 19th century new farm buildings, south of Wishford Farmhouse, and a terrace of four estate cottages of banded brick and flint north of it, were erected in South Street, and Wishford station was built beside the Wilton–Warminster road. There was evidently little new domestic building in the late 19th century. In the 20th the principal road came to be called Station Road between its junctions with West Street and South Street, Langford Road to the north-west. About 1900 a pair of brick villas and in 1929 four council houses were built at the south end of South Street.[9] The southern end of the village was further developed 1949–54 when Grovely Cottages, 22 council houses and bungalows,[10] and c. 1987 when Kingsmead, an estate of 12 private houses, were built. At the north end in Langford Road 4 estate cottages were built in 1953[11] and Bonhams Close, 6 flats and 11 bungalows, in 1969.[12] In Station Road the stationmaster's house survives: a later 19th-century goods shed was demolished after 1980.[13] In the later 20th century c. 10 private houses were built beside the road. In 1993 there were few buildings within the triangle formed by Station Road and the houses in West Street and South Street: one there, among farm buildings west of South Street, was a weatherboarded granary of the 18th century.

Outside the village beside the Warminster road a thatched cottage was built between 1773 and 1802[14] and a barn between 1817 and 1839.[15] In the north-west corner of the parish Hungerford Lodge Farm was built near the site of the barn from the mid or later 19th century; a pair of cottages was added in the early 20th.[16] Dairy Cottages and farm buildings were erected 1 km. south of the church between 1839 and 1886;[17]

the farmstead was enlarged in the 20th century. A sewage works was built in the parish's south-east corner between 1958 and 1969.[18]

Great Wishford was within the bounds of Grovely forest.[19] In the mid 13th century it was represented at forest inquests,[20] the jurors at the forest court of 1604 were drawn from Great Wishford and Barford St. Martin,[21] and inhabitants of Great Wishford owed suit at a similar court in 1618.[22] A small estate in Great Wishford was attached to the office of keeper of the north bailiwick of the forest,[23] and it included housebote, haybote, and firebote from the underwood of Grovely.[24] Men of Great Wishford had rights to pasture in the forest by the mid 13th century and rights to wood by the 16th century. In 1597 the lord of the manor was entitled to certain loads of wood each year, and his tenants had the right to fetch boughs from Grovely on Saturdays and holidays from 1 May to Whitsun, to fell a load of wood annually, and at all times to take dead wood and wood from Grim's ditch.[25] In 1604 it was customary for the men of the manor to claim their rights by going in procession to Salisbury cathedral on the Tuesday after Whitsun and there reciting the words 'Grovely! Grovely! And all Grovely!'. After 1660 the date of the procession was changed to 29 May. The right to take boughs in May was compounded for in 1681, and pasture rights were extinguished in 1809, but the ceremonial claim continued to be made. In the early 19th century the procession was replaced by a deputation of two women who placed boughs from Grovely forest on the cathedral altar. By 1885 the ceremonial claim in Salisbury cathedral had been replaced by a yearly procession in Great Wishford village.[26] From c. 1890 processions and other events were organized by the Oak Apple club, and from 1951 a claim to rights in Grovely forest was again made in Salisbury cathedral.[27]

In 1728 a fire engine made by Richard Newsham was bought for the parish.[28] It remained in use until the 1920s or later, and from 1972 was preserved in the church.[29]

The price of bread at various dates between 1800 and 1984 is recorded on stones inserted in the north-east wall of the churchyard.

MANOR AND OTHER ESTATES. In 1066 Avitius and in 1086 William Corniole, one of the king's servants, held what became *GREAT*

3 *Andrews and Dury, Map* (W.R.S. viii), pl. 5; O.S. Map 6", Wilts. LX (1887 edn.).
4 *Andrews and Dury, Map* (W.R.S. viii), pl. 5; W.R.O. 2057/P 1/11.   5 W.R.O., tithe award.
6 Ibid. 212A/36/9B.
7 Ibid. A 1/326/3; ibid. tithe award.
8 *Kelly's Dir. Wilts.* (1848).
9 W.R.O., G 11/603/1.
10 Ibid. G 11/602/1–2.   11 Date on bldgs.
12 Inf. from the housing manager, Salisbury district council, 26 Endless Street, Salisbury.
13 Cf. *W.A.M.* lxxiv/lxxv. 174.
14 *Andrews and Dury, Map* (W.R.S. viii), pl. 5; W.R.O. 2057/P 1/11.
15 O.S. Map 1", sheet 14 (1817 edn.); W.R.O., tithe award.
16 O.S. Maps 6", Wilts. LIX (1889 and later edns.); W.R.O., tithe award.

17 O.S. Map 6", Wilts. LXV (1890 edn.); W.R.O., tithe award.
18 O.S. Maps 1/25,000, SU 03 (1958 edn.); 1", sheet 167 (1971 edn.).
19 *V.C.H. Wilts.* iv. 457.
20 Ibid. 431.
21 *W.A.M.* xxxv. 304.
22 W.R.O. 212B/36/9B.
23 Below, manor (Quintin's).
24 *V.C.H. Wilts.* iv. 433.
25 *W.A.M.* xxxv. 295–6, 313; for the pasture rights, below, econ. hist.
26 *W.A.M.* xxxv. 300–1; W.R.O. 2057, deeds, Wishford, box 1, Howe to Pembroke, 1681; ibid. EA/81; below, church.
27 G. Frampton, *Grovely! Grovely! And all Grovely!* 15, 30.   28 W.R.O. 1160/11.
29 M. Paskin, *Church of Wishford Magna* (1983), 55; see above, plate facing p. 219.

WISHFORD manor.[30] Henry I gave the estate to Patrick de Chaworth, who before 1127 subinfeudated the manor to his son-in-law Henry Daubeney.[31] From Patrick the overlordship descended with Berwick St. James manor, until the 14th century in the Chaworth family: Patrick de Chaworth was overlord of 1½ knight's fee in 1242–3,[32] and Maud de Chaworth, wife of Henry of Lancaster, earl of Leicester from 1324 and of Lancaster from 1326, was overlord at her death *c.* 1322.[33] The overlordship thereafter descended with the earldom and dukedom of Lancaster.[34]

Henry Daubeney was succeeded by his son Robert, who gave Great Wishford manor to his brother Niel (fl. 1166).[35] The manor passed to Niel's son William and before 1207 to William's son Henry, who held it in 1242–3. Ralph de St. Amand held a third of the manor in 1242–3, possibly as tenant by the courtesy, and of that third stood as mesne lord between Henry and Patrick de Chaworth. Henry (fl. 1258) was succeeded in or before 1268 by his son Walter[36] (d. by 1273). Walter was succeeded by his brother Henry[37] (d. *c.* 1278), whose heirs were his sister Clarice Daubeney and grandnephew Maurice Bonham.[38] From *c.* 1278 to 1576 the manor descended in moieties.

Maurice Bonham (d. 1302) was succeeded in turn by his sons William (d. by 1316) and Sir John[39] (fl. 1348).[40] His moiety passed to Sir John's son Robert, who in 1356 granted it to his brother Nicholas (d. 1386).[41] Nicholas's relict Edith (fl. 1387) may have held the moiety for life[42] and in 1391 his son Thomas held it.[43] From Thomas (d. 1420) it passed in turn to his sons William and Thomas (d. 1473). Thomas, who held the moiety in 1429, was succeeded by his son Walter[44] (d. 1476). It passed to Walter's son William[45] (fl. 1514), and in turn to William's sons Walter (d. 1527) and Nicholas[46] (d. 1559), who devised it for life to his relict Alice. In 1574 Alice and her husband Anthony Styleman surrendered their interest to Nicholas's son Walter,[47] who acquired the second moiety and in 1597 sold the whole manor to Sir Richard Grobham.[48]

Grobham (d. 1629) settled the manor for life

on his wife Margaret (d. 1637), with reversion to a kinsman George Grobham. George presumably died without issue, and the manor passed, probably before 1650, to Sir Richard's nephew John Howe (cr. baronet 1660).[49] In 1661 Sir John (d. by 1672) settled it on his son (Sir) Richard[50] (d. 1703), who was succeeded by his son Sir Richard (d. 1730). The manor was held for life by the younger Sir Richard's relict Mary (d. 1735)[51] and passed to his second cousin John Howe[52] (cr. Baron Chedworth 1741, d. 1742). With the barony it passed to John's sons John (d. 1762) and Henry (d. 1781) and their nephew John Howe (d. 1804).[53] In 1808 the last Lord Chedworth's executors sold the manor to George Herbert, earl of Pembroke and of Montgomery.[54] Thereafter it passed with the Pembroke title,[55] and in 1993 Henry Herbert, earl of Pembroke and of Montgomery, owned most of the land in the parish.[56]

A chapel belonging to Walter Daubeney (d. by 1273) may have been at a manor house at Great Wishford;[57] John Bonham was taxed at Great Wishford in 1332;[58] and in 1408 and 1410 Thomas Bonham was licensed to hear mass there in an oratory in his manor house,[59] where his descendants evidently lived in the 16th century.[60] A manor house was lived in by Sir Richard Grobham (d. 1629), and probably by Sir Richard Howe (d. 1703) and Sir Richard Howe (d. 1730).[61] In 1773 Lady Chedworth, presumably Dorothy (d. 1777), relict of John, Lord Chedworth (d. 1742), lived in it.[62] Nothing is known of the architecture of the house; it was said to have been demolished in 1785,[63] but part of it remained a house until demolished between 1839 and 1886.[64]

The second moiety of Great Wishford manor was held in 1281 by Clarice Daubeney's husband Sir Edmund Spigurnel (d. by 1296)[65] and in 1298 by her son Adam de la Ford[66] (d. by 1326). It passed to Adam's son Sir Adam (d. by 1349) and was evidently held by Sir Adam's relict Elizabeth, wife of Sir Robert of London, until 1390 or later.[67] Sir Adam's heir may have been Robert Brent, probably his nephew, and in 1402 the

30 *V.C.H. Wilts.* ii, p. 168.
31 *Reg. Regum Anglo-Norm.* ii, no. 1517.
32 *Bk. of Fees,* ii. 716, 728; above, Berwick St. Jas., manors.
33 *Cal. Inq. p.m.* vi, p. 414; *Complete Peerage,* vii. 396–400.   34 e.g. P.R.O., C 142/44, no. 140.
35 *W.N. & Q.* v. 48.
36 *Cur. Reg. R.* v. 44; *Cal. Inq. Misc.* i, pp. 120–1; *Bk. of Fees,* ii. 716, 728; *Wilts. Inq. p.m.* 1242–1326 (Index Libr.), 25.   37 *Cal. Inq. p.m.* ii, p. 24.
38 Ibid. p. 156.
39 G. J. Kidston, *Bonhams of Wilts. and Essex,* facing p. 9; *Feud. Aids,* v. 202; B.L. Add. Ch. 15084.
40 *Feet of F.* 1327–77 (W.R.S. xxix), p. 87.
41 Kidston, *Bonhams,* facing p. 9; W.R.O. 383/560.
42 Kidston, *Bonhams,* 20; *Cal. Close,* 1385–9, 292.
43 Kidston, *Bonhams,* facing p. 9; B.L. Add. Ch. 15085.
44 B.L. Add. Ch. 15088–9; P.R.O., C 138/48, no. 67; C 140/45, no. 41.   45 P.R.O., C 140/58, no. 69.
46 Kidston, *Bonhams,* facing p. 9.
47 P.R.O., C 142/119, no. 201; C 142/124, no. 199; ibid. CP 25/2/242/16 Eliz. I East.
48 Ibid. CP 25/2/242/39 Eliz. I Trin.; below, this section.
49 *Wilts. Inq. p.m.* 1625–49 (Index Libr.), 105–7; Hoare, *Mod. Wilts.* Branch and Dole, 46; *W.A.M.* xl. 394.
50 Hist. MSS. Com. 55, *Var. Colln.* v, p. 246; B.L. Add. Ch. 15124.

51 G.E.C. *Baronetage,* iii. 123; Hoare, *Mod. Wilts.* Branch and Dole, 49; W.R.O. 530/1.
52 W.R.O. 530/1.
53 *Complete Peerage,* iii. 156–7.
54 W.R.O. 2057, deeds, Wishford, box 1, Wilson to Pembroke, 1808.
55 *Complete Peerage,* x. 427–30; *Debrett's Peerage* (1976), 897–8.
56 Inf. from the agent, Wilton Estate Off., Wilton.
57 *Wilts. Inq. p.m.* 1242–1327 (Index Libr.), 85.
58 *Tax List, 1332* (W.R.S. xlv), 83.
59 *W.A.M.* xlviii. 274; W.R.O., D 1/2/7, ff. 111, 146v., where Welford may be given for Wishford in error.
60 *Taxation Lists* (W.R.S. x), 7, 110.
61 Hoare, *Mod. Wilts.* Branch and Dole, 46, 49; W.R.O. 753/1, *passim.*
62 *Complete Peerage,* iii. 159; *Andrews and Dury, Map* (W.R.S. viii), pl. 5.
63 MS. notebook of Geo. Petty, in possession of Lady (Marjorie) Paskin, Chequers Cottage.
64 W.R.O. 2057/P 1/11; ibid. tithe award; O.S. Map 6", Wilts. LIX (1889 edn.).
65 Kidston, *Bonhams,* 7; *Cal. Inq. p.m.* ii, p. 232; iii, p. 197.
66 Kidston, *Bonhams,* 7; *Cal. Chanc. Wts.* 99.
67 *Cal. Inq. p.m.* vi, p. 414; viii, p. 376; Phillipps, *Wilts. Inst.* i. 48, 75.

moiety was held by John Brent (d. c. 1413), probably Robert's grandson.[68] John was succeeded in turn by his son Sir Robert (d. 1421) and daughter Joan, whose husband John Trethek held the moiety in 1428.[69] With Ford manor in Bawdrip (Som.) it presumably passed to Robert Brent (d. 1508); from Robert's son John[70] (d. 1524) it passed in the direct line to William[71] (d. 1536) and Richard.[72] In 1564 Richard (d. 1570) settled the moiety for his life on his daughter Anne and her husband Thomas Paulet and thereafter on his wife Dorothy for life with reversion to Anne and Thomas.[73] It was reunited with the other moiety in 1576 when Anne and Thomas Paulet sold it to Walter Bonham.[74]

At her death in 1281 Edith, daughter of John Humphrey, held in Great Wishford an estate of 2 yardlands, later QUINTIN'S: 1½ yardland was held by serjeanty of keeping the north bailiwick of Grovely forest. The estate passed to Edith's son Henry Quintin (d. 1284) and from him in the direct line to William (d. by 1290), William[75] (d. by 1341), William[76] (d. 1351), and Richard (fl. 1373).[77] Thomas Stabber held it at his death c. 1416 and it passed in moieties to his daughters Elizabeth (d. c. 1419) and Joan, wife of John Wilton (alias John at the end). Elizabeth's moiety was inherited by Joan (d. 1421), whose heirs were Thomas's sisters Edith (d. 1433), wife of John Stone, and Agnes (d. 1433), wife of John Dykeman. Dykeman apparently held both moieties until 1445. John Cooper and his wife Maud, granddaughter and heir of Agnes and evidently Edith's eventual heir,[78] in 1466 conveyed what was probably the whole estate to Maurice Berkeley.[79] By 1597, when the lord of Great Wishford was forester of the northern part of Grovely forest, the whole had evidently been absorbed by the manor.[80]

Bolle held 3 yardlands in Great Wishford in 1066: Robert held them of Waleran the huntsman in 1086.[81] The overlordship apparently descended like Steeple Langford manor and was held by John of Monmouth in 1242–3 and by Oliver de Ingham, Lord Ingham, in 1343 or 1344. In 1242–3 the estate, ⅒ knight's fee, was held of Monmouth by John de Camp and of John by Warin of Wishford. By 1344 it had been added to Great Wishford manor.[82]

Arnulf Bisset gave to Margery or Margaret Bisset 8 yardlands in Great Wishford which by 1243 she had given to the hospital and priory of Maiden Bradley.[83] The estate passed to the Crown at the Dissolution. In 1544 it was granted to Edward Seymour, earl of Hertford,[84] and sold by him to Nicholas Bonham:[85] thereafter it passed with Bonham's moiety of Great Wishford manor.

Tithes from the demesne of Great Wishford manor were c. 1191 an endowment of South Newton prebend in the conventual church of Wilton abbey;[86] they were confirmed to the abbey in 1208.[87] By 1291 they had been replaced by a pension paid by the rector of Great Wishford, of 13s. 4d. in 1291,[88] 6s. 8d. at the Dissolution.[89]

The tithes of the first cut of part of Asserton mead, 12 a. in Great Wishford, belonged to Asserton chapel in Berwick St. James parish.[90] The endowment of the chapel passed to the Crown c. 1547, from 1615 belonged, like Great Wishford manor, to Sir Richard Grobham,[91] descended with the manor, and was devised by Sir Richard Howe (d. 1730) to Great Wishford school.[92] In 1840 the tithes were valued at 30s. and commuted.[93]

ECONOMIC HISTORY. In 1086 Great Wishford had land for 2½ ploughteams. Although not expressly mentioned there may have been demesne with 1 team or more on it; 3 villani and 2 bordars had 1 team, and there were 2 other bordars. There were 12 a. of meadow.[94]

In 1273 the demesne of Great Wishford manor was said to comprise 500 a. of arable, 33 a. of meadow, and pasture for 32 beasts and 400 sheep: what may have been a roughly equal amount of land was held by 18 customary tenants.[95] Between c. 1278 and 1576, while the manor descended in moieties, the demesne may have been worked in two parts. In 1326 one of the moieties was said to include in demesne 100 a. of arable and 8 a. of meadow; on the moiety were 2 free tenants, 4 customary tenants who held 32 a. and had to wash and shear sheep and to mow, and 6 cottagers.[96] In 1545 on the other moiety 145 a. of arable with pasture rights for 274 sheep was in 5 copyholds and 1 leasehold.[97] The other holdings in Great Wishford in the Middle Ages were evidently small. In 1284 that held for keeping part of Grovely forest and comprising 54 a. of arable, 2½ a. of meadow, and presumably pasture rights, may have been the largest:[98] in 1341 houses on it were in disrepair and of its 60 a. of arable 15 a. had

68 Feud. Aids, vi. 627; V.C.H. Som. vi. 187.
69 Feud. Aids, v. 243; V.C.H. Som. vi. 187; P.R.O., C 138/56, no. 25.
70 V.C.H. Som. vi. 187; Cal. Inq. p.m. Hen. VII, iii, pp. 309–11. 71 P.R.O., C 142/44, no. 140.
72 Ibid. C 142/58, no. 68.
73 Ibid. C 142/156, no. 14.
74 B.L. Add. Ch. 15107.
75 Cal. Inq. p.m. ii, pp. 232, 307, 466.
76 Ibid. viii, p. 220.
77 Ibid. ix, p. 445; xiii, pp. 258–9.
78 Cal. Fine R. 1413–22, 185, 306–7, 369–70; 1445–52, 26–7; Cal. Pat. 1429–36, 497; P.R.O., C 139/57, no. 7; C 139/118, no. 16.
79 Feet of F. 1377–1509 (W.R.S. xli), p. 145.
80 V.C.H. Wilts. iv. 433; W.A.M. xxxv. 312–14.
81 V.C.H. Wilts. ii, p. 151.
82 Bk. of Fees, ii. 735; Cal. Inq. p.m. vii, p. 376; above,
Steeple Langford, manor.
83 Sir Chris. Hatton's Bk. of Seals, ed. L. C. Loyd and D. M. Stenton, pp. 222–3; for the woman's forename cf. V.C.H. Wilts. iii. 296. 84 P.R.O., E 318/13/574.
85 L. & P. Hen. VIII, xix (2), p. 261.
86 Sar. Chart. and Doc. (Rolls Ser.), p. 52.
87 Hoare, Mod. Wilts. Branch and Dole, 47–8.
88 Tax. Eccl. (Rec. Com.), 181.
89 P.R.O., SC 6/Hen. VIII/3985, rot. 15d.
90 Endowed Char. Wilts. (S. Div.), 909; P.R.O., C 2/Eliz. I/G 56. 91 Above, Berwick St. Jas., manors.
92 Below, educ.
93 W.R.O., tithe award.
94 V.C.H. Wilts. ii, pp. 151, 168.
95 Wilts. Inq. p.m. 1242–1326 (Index Libr.), 85–6.
96 Ibid. 444–5; above, manor (Great Wishford).
97 B.L. Add. MS. 23152, pp. 1–3.
98 Cal. Inq. p.m. ii, p. 307.

evidently gone out of cultivation.[99] The 8 yard-lands given to Maiden Bradley priory by 1243 were held by 13 tenants,[1] in 1544 apparently by 8 tenants.[2] From the later 16th century, when the moieties of the manor were reunited,[3] most of the demesne was in a single farm, later called Manor. In 1606 the farm was apparently in hand except for fishing rights in the Wylye, small areas of meadow, and a warren: from 1659 it was leased.[4]

Common husbandry prevailed at Great Wishford until 1809. In 1326, when three different values were set on arable, there may have been three open fields, as there were later.[5] Some or all of the downland was used in common,[6] and from 1252 or earlier men of Great Wishford had a right of pasture in Grovely forest.[7] Quintin's estate had pasture there for all animals except sheep and goats,[8] and c. 1356 the lord of a moiety of Great Wishford manor claimed common there both for his demesne and his tenants.[9] In 1603 all men of Great Wishford had common of pasture throughout the forest for all beasts except 'cattle of two teeth', perhaps cattle over a year old, and, during the fence month, goats and pigs over a year old.[10]

In 1802 Great Wishford had c. 852 a. of arable, nearly all in open fields. The three fields were of roughly equal size, and each holding with land in them had about the same amount in each. South field was c. 279 a., Middle field c. 282 a., West field c. 265 a. Between the fields and the Wylye there were c. 98 a. of meadows, of which c. 61 a. were in five common meadows. Between the fields and Grovely forest were 543 a. of downland: East End down, north of Heath wood, and, about twice as large, West End down, south-west of Ebsbury Hill, 278 a. in all, were tenantry downs; Farm down, 265 a., was south-west of the village between the tenantry downs. Manor farm, 595 a., included commonable and several land. Its downland, Farm down, was several, and by 1802 c. 9 a. of it had been burnbaked and 61 a. planted with trees. The farm included 29 a. of several meadows and rights in the common meadows, and it had 247 a. in the open fields, mostly in parcels much larger than those of the other holdings. There were 28 other holdings of Great Wishford manor with land in the open fields: some were small and some tenants had more than one. They included c. 555 a. of arable with feeding for 1,027 sheep on the downs and for cattle in the common meadows: the largest holding, later called Wishford farm, was of c. 190 a. with grazing for 344 sheep. In 1806 Manor farm no longer included

the 61 a. of new woodland, and c. 17 a. more of Farm down had been ploughed.[11]

Common husbandry was ended in 1809 by an agreement which also extinguished pasture rights in Grovely forest. Lands already several were among those allotted; Farm down was taken from Manor farm which, worked from the buildings near the manor house, was thenceforth restricted to a compact area in the west part of the parish. The other farms were worked from South Street and West Street and the lands allotted to them were intermingled in the centre and east parts of the parish.[12] The parish contained 862 a. of arable and 649 a. of grassland in 1839, when there were four principal farms. Manor farm was 497 a.; Wishford farm, worked from Wishford Farmhouse and with most of its land in the south-east part of the parish, was 429 a.; a farm of 187 a. was worked from Wishford House, and one of 108 a. was worked from South Street.[13] About 1863 Manor farm included 289 a. of arable, 159 a. of downland, and 13 a. of water meadow, Wishford farm 250 a. of arable, 177 a. of downland, 20 a. of lowland pasture, and 9 a. of water meadow.[14] An additional farmstead for each of those farms was built outside the village between 1839 and 1886.[15] By 1910 the smaller farms had been absorbed: Wishford farm was c. 800 a. in 1896, Manor farm 569 a. in 1910.[16] Sheep-and-corn husbandry predominated until c. 1920; thereafter more dairy cattle were kept.[17] In the 1930s there was much less arable than there had been in the 1830s, and Wishford farm was nearly all pasture.[18] More land on Wishford farm was ploughed during the Second World War, but it remained principally a beef and dairy farm. In 1993 it included 450 a. of arable on which cereals were grown and 435 a. of pasture: there was a dairy herd of 150, beef cattle were kept, and 75 a. were set aside.[19] Manor farm, 570 a., then included c. 460 a. on which cereals were grown and 100 a. of permanent grassland: a flock of 450 breeding ewes was kept, and the farm had 180 a. of additional sheep pasture in South Newton parish.[20]

Like others in the Wylye valley[21] meadows at Great Wishford may have been watered from the 17th century. Three common meadows, King's mead, Broad mead, and Little mead, a total of c. 30 a. north-west of the village, were being watered in 1782, when two parishioners were appointed at the manor court to oversee the watering.[22] The inclosure agreement of 1809 provided for King's mead, thereafter used in severalty, to be watered between 1 November

99 *Wilts. Inq. p.m.* 1327–77 (Index Libr.), 141–2.
1 *Sir Chris. Hatton's Bk. of Seals*, p. 222.
2 P.R.O., E 318/13/574.
3 Above, manor (Great Wishford).
4 B.L. Add. Ch. 15119; W.R.O. 2057, deeds, Wishford, box 1, Howe to Lawes, 1659.
5 *Wilts. Inq. p.m.* 1242–1326 (Index Libr.), 444; below, this section.
6 Cf. B.L. Add. MS. 23152, pp. 1–3.
7 *Close R.* 1251–3, 434.
8 *Cal. Inq. p.m.* ix, p. 445.
9 B.L. Add. Ch. 15082.
10 *V.C.H. Wilts.* iv. 432.
11 W.R.O. 317/12; 861/13; 2057/P 1/11.
12 Ibid. EA/81.

13 Ibid. tithe award.   14 Ibid. 2057/S 128.
15 Ibid. tithe award; O.S. Maps 6", Wilts. LIX (1889 edn.); LXV (1890 edn.).
16 W.R.O. 2057/R 106; ibid. Inland Revenue, val. reg. 145.
17 P.R.O., MAF 68/493, sheet 11; MAF 68/1063, sheet 14; MAF 68/1633, sheet 17; MAF 68/2203, sheet 7; MAF 68/2773, sheet 16; MAF 68/3319, sheet 16; MAF 68/3814, no. 241; MAF 68/4182, no. 241; MAF 68/4452, no. 241.
18 [1st] Land Util. Surv. Map, sheet 122.
19 Inf. from Mr. S. Thatcher, Wishford Farmhouse.
20 Inf. from Mr. R. Huntley, Manor Farm; above, S. Newton, agric. (Stoford).
21 Cf. below, Wylye, econ. hist. (Wylye).
22 W.R.O. 2057/M 75.

and 5 April each year.[23] From 1812 until 1842 or later two overseers and a common drowner were appointed at the manor court.[24] There were 50 a. or more of water meadows in the parish c. 1863[25] but by 1877 watering of some had probably ceased. Drowners were recorded in the 1930s, when the Wilton Fly Fishing club held dinners for them, but not thereafter.[26]

Great Wishford had no woodland in 1086,[27] and later the men of the parish had rights to take wood from Grovely forest.[28] One of the coppices of the forest, Heath wood, 59 a., is in the parish,[29] and new woodland was planted on 61 a. of Farm down (Hadden Hill) evidently not long before 1802. There was little other woodland in the parish in 1802[30] or the later 20th century.[31]

There was a mill in 1086 on what became Great Wishford manor.[32] A mill at Great Wishford in 1273 was, as part of the manor, held in moieties from c. 1278 and was in poor repair in 1326.[33] It may have stood beside Stoford bridge, where a mill standing in 1773[34] had been demolished by 1802.[35] There was a mill in 1243 on Maiden Bradley priory's estate.[36] It may have stood south of the village on the site of Cobbs Mill, so called in the earlier 19th century.[37] Cobbs Mill is unlikely to have been used for grinding in 1773[38] and there is no evidence that it was later.

A weaver lived in the parish in 1699, as did a clothier in 1729 and 1741: the weaver was associated with the Wilton cloth industry, and the clothier may have been.[39] There was a malthouse in the village in the early 19th century,[40] and a foundry near the church in 1839.[41] From the 1850s, presumably after the opening of Great Wishford station, until the 1930s, coal merchants traded in the parish.[42]

In 1298 rights to hold an annual fair on 31 August and 1 September and a weekly market on Mondays were granted to Adam de la Ford, the lord of a moiety of the manor:[43] the holding of neither fair nor market is recorded.

LOCAL GOVERNMENT.

Although Great Wishford was held before 1127 with rights including sac and soc, toll and team, and infangthief,[44] Roger de Hales, sheriff of Wiltshire 1226–7, distrained men of Great Wishford to do suit at Branch hundred court: they were summoned as two tithings, said to correspond to a fee of Daubeney and, inexplicably, to a fee of Fancourt. In 1268, however, it was confirmed that Great Wishford manor was held free of suit of shire and hundred and with a gallows and an ordeal pit, and then and thereafter Great Wishford was apparently a single tithing.[45]

A court may have been held for Adam de la Ford (d. by 1326) as lord of a moiety of the manor,[46] but none held for his successors is recorded. View of frankpledge passed with the Bonhams' moiety: there are records of a view and a manor court held, usually together and probably twice yearly, in 1391, 1404, and 1454. Cert money was paid and a tithingman presented defaulters from the court, strays, infringements of grazing rights, and affrays. Tenurial business was transacted, and orders were made to repair a bridge, probably one over the Wylye, and for fishing the river. In 1454 a jury found on the presentments.[47] A court of survey was held in 1545. A view or law day and a manor court are recorded for 1560 and for most of the years 1579–87; some of the records consist only of lists of presentments. The view and the manor court were usually held on the same day as each other and twice a year. In 1579 the tithingman presented at the view, the homage at the manor court. Matters presented at the view included breaches of the assize of ale, the taking of stray animals, the dilapidation of bridges, the butts, and the pound, and, in 1582 and 1586, the playing of unlawful games of bowls. In 1586 the tithingman was presented for allowing a traveller suspected of felony to escape. Business before the manor court included defaulters from the court, vacant tenements, and breaches of grazing customs; orders were made to maintain ditches and headlands, in 1584 to destroy rabbit burrows, and to regulate the gathering of wool from fields.[48]

A court leet and a manor court were held together, usually in October, from 1782 to 1842, annually until the mid 1830s, less frequently thereafter. In 1782 the homage and jury presented customs of the manor, that the stocks needed repair, and the death of a copyholder; a tithingman, a hayward, two sheeptellers, and the overseers of the water meadows were appointed. The business of the court was similar until c. 1830; in 1801 it was recorded that swans on the manor had been destroyed, apparently unlawfully. From the 1830s most non-tenurial business concerned watercourses and water meadows. Between 1782 and 1887 a court for the transaction only of tenurial business was held occasionally.[49]

23 Ibid. EA/81.
24 Ibid. 2057/M 79.
25 Ibid. 2057/S 125.
26 V.C.H. Wilts. iv. 363; Hatcher Review, ii. 180–6.
27 V.C.H. Wilts. ii, pp. 151, 168.
28 Above, intro.
29 Ibid. intro. [boundaries].
30 Andrews and Dury, Map (W.R.S. viii), pl. 5; W.R.O. 2057/P 1/11.
31 O.S. Map 1/50,000, sheet 184 (1979 edn.).
32 V.C.H. Wilts. ii, p. 168.
33 Wilts. Inq. p.m. 1242–1326 (Index Libr.), 85, 444–5; above, manor.
34 Andrews and Dury, Map (W.R.S. viii), pl. 5.
35 W.R.O. 2057/P 1/11.
36 Sir Chris. Hatton's Bk. of Seals, p. 222.
37 Hoare, Mod. Wilts. Add. 36; Meeting Ho. Certs.

(W.R.S. xl), p. 130.
38 Andrews and Dury, Map (W.R.S. viii), pl. 5.
39 V.C.H. Wilts. vi. 26; Wilts. Apprentices (W.R.S. xviii), pp. 64, 132.
40 W.R.O. 317/12.
41 Ibid. tithe award.
42 Kelly's Dir. Wilts. (1859 and later edns.); above, intro.
43 Cal. Chart. R. 1257–1300, 473.
44 Reg. Regum Anglo-Norm. ii, no. 1517.
45 W.A.M. iii. 194; Cal. Inq. Misc. i, pp. 120–1; Cal. Chart. R. 1257–1300, 93–4.
46 Wilts. Inq. p.m. 1242–1326 (Index Libr.), 445.
47 B.L. Add. Ch. 15085–6; 15091.
48 Ibid. Add. Ch. 15105; 15109–10; ibid. Add. MS. 23152.
49 W.R.O. 2057/M 75–6; 2057/M 79; above, econ. hist. [water meadows].

The parish[50] spent £81 on poor relief in 1775–6 and an average of £87 a year in the three years to 1785; £209 was spent in 1802–3, when the poor rate was about the average for the hundred, 19 adults and 34 children were regularly relieved, and no occasional relief was given.[51] In 1806 the parish held houses in the village on lease to accommodate some of the poor.[52] Spending was at a peak of £830 in 1813, when 237 of a population of c. 300 received relief, 51 regularly, 186 occasionally.[53] It fell to £313 in 1816, but rose to £712 in 1817. It was usually between £250 and £350 in the 1820s[54] and averaged £242 between 1833 and 1835. Great Wishford became part of Wilton poor-law union in 1836,[55] and of Salisbury district in 1974.[56]

CHURCH. The church may have been standing in the 12th century or earlier.[57] It was first recorded in 1207, when it was served by a rector.[58] In 1952 the area served by Grovely Wood chapel was added to the ecclesiastical parish,[59] and in 1992 Great Wishford rectory became part of the benefice of Lower Wylye and Till Valley.[60]

In 1207 the advowson of the rectory was disputed between the abbess of Wilton and Henry Daubeney, lord of Great Wishford manor.[61] The abbess surrendered her claim in 1208,[62] and the advowson presumably passed with the manor to Henry Daubeney (d. c. 1278). A right of presentation at alternate turns descended with each moiety of the manor from c. 1278 to 1576. Thereafter the advowson passed with the manor,[63] and from 1992 Lord Pembroke shared the patronage of the new benefice.[64] Six presentations other than by owners of the manor or a moiety of it are recorded. Hugh le Despenser, Lord le Despenser (cr. earl of Winchester 1322), keeper of the estate of William Bonham, a minor, presented between 1302 and 1305;[65] the bishop collated by lapse in 1391; trustees of John Brent, probably the half-brother of Joan Brent (fl. 1421), presented in 1430; in 1637 trustees of John Bower, a former rector, presented his son Robert by grant of a turn; Dorothy, relict of John, Lord Chedworth (d. 1742), presented in 1770 and 1774.[66]

The rectory was valued at £5 in 1291, a little below the average for Wylye deanery;[67] at £17

10s. 6d. in 1535 and c. £342 in 1830 it was about the average.[68] Between 1609 and 1705 the rector's income included rent from 2 a. in South Newton parish: no later reference to the rent has been found.[69] The rector was entitled to all tithes from the parish, from 1291 or earlier including those from the demesne of Great Wishford manor, but excluding those from part of Asserton mead:[70] they were valued at £437 in 1838 and commuted in 1840.[71] In 1609 the glebe comprised 20 a. of arable, 1½ a. of meadow, and feeding for 5 cattle, an unlimited number of pigs, and, in autumn, 4 horses;[72] some of the grazing may then as later have been in Grovely forest.[73] After inclosure the glebe measured 18 a.;[74] c. 2 a. were sold in 1961,[75] and c. 13 a. remained glebe in 1993.[76] There was a house on the glebe in 1513.[77] In the early 17th century a new house was built of stone; its north–south range survives in the present house. In the early 18th century the house was extended to the south and east and mullioned windows were used in the new walls. A north-east wing was built, probably later in the century and possibly as a replacement. Between c. 1825 and c. 1850 the inside of the house was altered. The west front was refaced in brick probably in the same period, and c. 1850 bay windows were added to the north-east wing. In 1976 the house was sold and a new rectory house built north of the church.[78]

In 1386 St. Mary was invoked at the altar in the north part of the church; the lights of St. Nicholas, St. John, and Holy Cross in the church may have been on separate altars.[79] In 1305 Richard of Langtoft, the rector, was licensed to leave the parish for a year's study, and a curate was appointed.[80] Richard Burleigh, rector 1468–93, Alexander Hody, rector 1493–1518, and Thomas Hulse, rector 1518–31, were all pluralists.[81] In 1553 the church had no copy of Erasmus's *Paraphrases* or covering for the communion table:[82] in 1556 the rector, William Hardy, was said to have been guilty of simony.[83] Robert Bower, rector from 1637 and a canon of Salisbury, was ejected in 1645 or 1646; he was charged with keeping fasts appointed by the king, using prayers against parliament, and using the Book of Common Prayer. He was restored to the rectory in 1660.[84] In 1648 and 1650 the living was served by Robert Parker, a signatory of the *Concurrent Testimony* and a regular

50 For the par. fire engine, above, intro.
51 *Poor Law Abstract, 1804,* 558–9.
52 W.R.O. 317/12.
53 *Poor Law Abstract, 1818,* 492–3.
54 *Poor Rate Returns, 1816–21,* 186; *1822–4,* 225; *1825–9,* 216. 55 *Poor Law Com. 2nd Rep.* App. D, 560.
56 O.S. Map 1/100,000, admin. areas, Wilts. (1974 edn.).
57 Below, this section [architecture].
58 *Cur. Reg. R.* v. 44; Hoare, *Mod. Wilts.* Branch and Dole, 48.
59 *Lond. Gaz.* 18 Apr. 1952, p. 2105; below, this section.
60 Ch. Com. file, NB 34/209B/2.
61 *Cur. Reg. R.* v. 44.
62 Hoare, *Mod. Wilts.* Branch and Dole, 47–8.
63 Phillipps, *Wilts. Inst.* i. 36, 48, 66, 75, 95, 107, 158, 176, 193, 201, 214, 227; ii. 18, 27, 50, 65, 68–9, 85, 87; M. Paskin, *Church of Wishford Magna,* 73–9; above, manor (Great Wishford).
64 Ch. Com. file, NB 34/209B/2.
65 *Reg. Ghent* (Cant. & York Soc.), ii. 878; *Complete Peerage,* iv. 262–4; B.L. Add. Ch. 15084.

66 Phillipps, *Wilts. Inst.* i. 76, 121; ii. 18, 85, 87; *V.C.H. Som.* vi. 187; *Complete Peerage,* iii. 157.
67 *Tax. Eccl.* (Rec. Com.), 181.
68 *Valor Eccl.* (Rec. Com.), ii. 103; *Rep. Com. Eccl. Revenues,* 854–5.
69 W.R.O., D 1/24/228/1; D 1/24/228/4.
70 Ibid. D 1/24/228/1–2; above, manor.
71 W.R.O., tithe award.
72 Ibid. D 1/24/228/1.   73 Ibid. 861/13.
74 Ibid. EA/81; ibid. tithe award.
75 Ch. Com. deeds 576007; 576206.
76 Inf. from Lt.-Col. C. Ross, Wishford Ho.
77 B.L. Add. Ch. 15303.
78 Paskin, *Church of Wishford Magna,* 72; Ch. Com. deed 62572.   79 *W.A.M.* xlviii. 274–5.
80 *Reg. Ghent* (Cant. & York Soc.), ii. 878.
81 Phillipps, *Wilts. Inst.* i. 158, 176, 193, 201; *Cal. Papal Reg.* xvi, pp. 336, 553; *W.N. & Q.* ii. 114.
82 W.R.O., D 1/43/1, f. 117v.
83 Ibid. D 1/43/2, f. 6v.
84 *Walker Revised,* ed. Matthews, 370–1.

preacher.[85] James Birch, rector 1773–1823, also served Burcombe chapel in 1783. At Great Wishford he then held two services every Sunday and services on Christmas Day, Good Friday, the Monday and Tuesday after Easter, and the Monday after Whit Sunday. Communion was celebrated at Christmas, Easter, Whitsun, and Michaelmas: there were c. 20 communicants.[86] In 1851 on Census Sunday 66 people attended morning service, 149 afternoon service: numbers were said to be lower than usual because of an outbreak of measles.[87] In 1864 three services were held each Sunday; there were also services at the great festivals, on Ash Wednesday, on Fridays in Lent and Advent, and every evening in Holy Week. In the Wiltshire part of Salisbury diocese Great Wishford was one of only five parishes in which communion was celebrated weekly: there were 40–50 communicants at the great festivals, 20–30 at other times. The rector, T. B. Buchanan, regretted that the liturgy was too inflexible to make possible brief daily services which agricultural workers might have time to attend.[88] Between 1926 and 1973 the rectors also served Little Langford. From 1926 they presumably served Grovely Wood chapel,[89] which had been built in Grovely forest in 1867,[90] was in Barford St. Martin civil parish from 1934,[91] and was demolished probably in the 1940s.[92] From 1973 until 1992 Great Wishford was served by a priest-in-charge, and from 1992 the benefice of Lower Wylye and Till Valley was served by a rector resident in Great Wishford.[93]

In 1681 Philip, earl of Pembroke and of Montgomery, gave £6 a year to Great Wishford church in return for the surrender by the parish of rights to take wood from Grovely forest. Payments were irregular until 1712 when Thomas, earl of Pembroke and of Montgomery, compounded with Sir Richard Howe, lord of Great Wishford manor. Howe charged his estate in Stapleford with a payment to the church of £10 a year,[94] which was made until 1981.[95] From 1714 and probably earlier the right to cut hay from the Monday before Ascension day to 12 August from 6 a. in Great Wishford was auctioned each year and the money paid for it given to the church. From the late 18th century the grass was called the Midsummer Tithe. The auction raised c. £3 yearly in the early 18th century, c. £11 in the early 19th and early 20th.[96] Grass from part of the meadow was not auctioned after 1945: that from the remainder raised

£85 in 1993.[97] Agnes Kennedy (d. 1941) gave by will to the church three cottages:[98] they were sold in 1945 and the income from the proceeds, £176 in 1993, has since been used for the church's upkeep.[99]

The church of *ST. GILES*, so called in 1386[1] and possibly in 1298,[2] is built of irregularly chequered chalk ashlar and flint and has a chancel with north vestry, an aisled and clerestoried nave with south porch, and a west tower. The narrowness of the nave, which was rebuilt in the 19th century, suggests that its predecessor may have been of the 12th century or earlier. The chancel was probably rebuilt in the 13th century, when a stepped-lancet east window was inserted. The south aisle and the lower stages of the tower were built in the 14th century. Possibly in the 15th or 16th century the upper stages of the tower were built, and the porch was probably built in the 16th. In the 17th the chancel was largely rebuilt to accommodate a monument to Sir Richard Grobham (d. 1629). In the early 18th the north wall of the nave was raised and given a clerestory of oval windows, the south wall of the aisle was raised, the arcade was removed, and the roof of the aisle was merged with that of the nave.[3] In 1863–4 the chancel arch, the nave with north and south aisles and a clerestory of rectangular windows, and the porch were rebuilt in a 14th-century style to designs by T. H. Wyatt; the chancel was reroofed, the upper part of the tower rebuilt with elaborate crenellation and pinnacles, and the vestry added.[4] The vestry was rebuilt in 1955.[5] Stone figures of the 14th century, representing a man and a woman, each in an arched recess in the north aisle, probably commemorate members of the Bonham family, as does a 15th-century brass.[6]

John Bonham (d. 1411) gave to the church a crucifix, a paxbred, and a cup, all of silver.[7] In 1553 a chalice weighing 10 oz. was left in the parish and 2 oz. of plate were confiscated. The chalice was replaced by a tazza-shaped cup of silver gilt, hallmarked for 1576 and probably of secular origin. A flagon of 1637, a chalice with paten cover of 1679, a paten of 1711, and an almsdish converted in 1864 from a flagon, all of silver gilt, were, with the cup, held by the church in 1993.[8]

Two bells hung in the church in 1553. The ring was increased to five, presumably in 1751 when five new bells were cast by James Burrough of Devizes. The fourth was recast by

85 *Calamy Revised*, ed. Matthews, 557; *W.A.M.* xl. 394.
86 Paskin, *Church of Wishford Magna*, 77; *Vis. Queries, 1783* (W.R.S. xxvii), pp. 241–2.
87 P.R.O., HO 129/265/1/5/12.
88 *V.C.H. Wilts.* iii. 67; W.R.O., D 1/56/7.
89 Paskin, *Church of Wishford Magna*, 72; above, Little Langford, church.   90 W.R.O., D 1/4/2/143.
91 *V.C.H. Wilts.* iv. 340.
92 Inf. from Mr. E. F. Huntley, Manor Farm.
93 Paskin, *Church of Wishford Magna*, 78; Ch. Com. file, NB 34/209B/2.
94 *Endowed Char. Wilts.* (S. Div.), 913, 920; W.R.O. 2057, deeds, Wishford, box 1, Howe to Pembroke, 1712; above, intro. [Grovely forest].
95 Inf. from Lt.-Col. Ross.
96 *Endowed Char. Wilts.* (S. Div.), 913, 920; *Vis. Queries, 1783* (W.R.S. xxvii), p. 242; W.R.O. 1160/11.

97 Paskin, *Church of Wishford Magna*, 66; inf. from Lt.-Col. Ross.
98 Princ. Regy. Fam. Div., will of A. E. Kennedy, 1941.
99 Paskin, *Church of Wishford Magna*, 66; inf. from Lt.-Col. Ross.
1 *W.A.M.* xlviii. 274.
2 *Cal. Chart. R.* 1257–1300, 473.
3 Hoare, *Mod. Wilts.* Branch and Dole, 47–9; J. Buckler, watercolour in W.A.S. Libr., vol. iii. 23; see above, plate facing p. 235; for the mon., see above, p. xxii.
4 W.R.O. 2007/43/1–2.
5 Ibid. 2007/49.
6 Paskin, *Church of Wishford Magna*, 33–45; E. Kite, *Wilts. Brasses*, 33–4.
7 *W.A.M.* xlviii. 280–1.
8 Nightingale, *Wilts. Plate*, 77–9; inf. from Lt.-Col. Ross.

Mears & Stainbank in 1887.[9] Those five bells and a sixth, bought from Queenhill (Worcs.) in 1978, hung in the church in 1993.[10]

Registers of baptisms, marriages, and burials survive from 1558: those of baptisms and burials are largely complete, that of marriages lacks the years 1747–54.[11]

NONCONFORMITY. In 1662 four parishioners, presumably dissenters, were regularly absent from divine service: one had not had his child baptized.[12] There was no dissenter in the parish in 1676 or 1783.[13] In 1797 a house was certified for nonconformist meetings. One was certified for Independent meetings in 1817[14] and converted to a chapel in 1839. An evening service held there on Census Sunday in 1851 had a congregation of 22.[15] The chapel is said to have stood in West Street.[16] A house was certified in 1832 for Primitive Methodist meetings,[17] and in 1864 c. 12 Wesleyans and Independents met in a small room.[18]

EDUCATION. The foundation stone of a school, of red brick with stone dressings and standing in 1993, was laid in 1722. Sir Richard Howe (d. 1730) by will endowed the school with tithes from Asserton mead and from Asserton, all valued at £30 c. 1730. A master and a mistress were to receive £10 each for teaching subjects including the church catechism to 20 boys and 20 girls respectively. The school's remaining income was for fuel and repairs. The income was £63 5s. annually between 1810 and c. 1830, £51 in 1903,[19] and the interest on c. £1,000 in 1993.[20] The school had two rooms and accommodation for a teacher in 1846.[21] Another classroom was built in 1896,[22] and the school was further extended in 1962.[23] In the 1830s there were difficulties in filling the school until children under five and more girls than boys were admitted.[24] There were 21 boys and 22 girls in 1846:[25] the total had risen to 70 by 1859.[26] Average attendance was 62 in 1906,[27] 60 in 1911–12, and 50 in 1935–6;[28] in 1993 there were 51 pupils, principally from Great Wishford and South Newton parishes.[29]

In 1833 a boarding school in Great Wishford was attended by seven girls.[30]

CHARITIES FOR THE POOR. Sir Richard Grobham (d. 1629) gave by will lands in South Newton to endow an almshouse in Great Wishford. The almshouse, a range of banded flint and stone, was built probably in the mid 17th century and survived in 1993. It was built as four cottages, each for a single parishioner, and the services of a nurse or housekeeper were to be provided. Rents from the lands were £60–£80 from the mid 18th century to the early 20th.[31] The lands were sold in 1948;[32] the income from the proceeds was between £250 and £500 in the 1960s.[33] Men and women were nominated to places in the almshouse until c. 1790: in most cases in the 1790s and in the 19th century the nominee was a married man whose wife shared his accommodation. In 1904 two couples and a single man occupied three of the cottages: the fourth was leased and from the rent another parishioner was given money. Each almsman received c. 30s. monthly in the mid 19th century. A housekeeper was appointed 1870–85 but probably not at other times. By a Scheme of 1898 the almshouse was managed with Oland's, Williams's, and Smokem's charities.[34] It was converted to two dwellings in 1969–70, and thereafter occupants paid rent according to their means. The income from endowments and rent, £1,396 in 1991, was used to maintain the building.[35]

David Oland (d. 1737) by will gave the income from £200 to apprentice boys from Great Wishford school and, on their apprenticeship, to give each £5 for tools. He also gave the income from £50 to buy bread and meat on Christmas Eve for 10 poor families not receiving poor relief. No payment was made until 1762; thereafter the income, c. £10 yearly in total, was used as Oland directed. The Revd. F. de V. Williams (d. 1863) by will gave £70, and Mary Smokem by will proved 1888 gave £100, to augment the doles provided by Oland. In 1888 and 1903 bread and beef were given to 30 families.[36] Apprenticeship premiums and grants for tools were occasionally paid until the 1930s or later,[37] but in the 1980s and in 1992 the charities' whole income of c. £10 was distributed in cash at Christmas.[38]

The poor of Great Wishford were entitled to a third share of a charity set up by the Revd. E. B. Hill (d. 1925) and governed by a Scheme of 1926. In the 1960s the income of the charity was c. £1 10s. yearly and occasional grants were made to the needy.[39]

9 Walters, *Wilts. Bells*, 239–40, 316.
10 Inf. from Lt.-Col. Ross.
11 W.R.O. 1160/1–8; bishop's transcripts for missing years are ibid.
12 Ibid. D 1/54/1/4, no. 42B.
13 *Compton Census*, ed. Whiteman, 125; *Vis. Queries, 1783* (W.R.S. xxvii), p. 242.
14 *Meeting Ho. Certs.* (W.R.S. xl), pp. 46, 82.
15 P.R.O., HO 129/265/1/5/13.
16 Inf. from Lady (Marjorie) Paskin, Chequers Cottage.
17 *Meeting Ho. Certs.* (W.R.S. xl), p. 130.
18 W.R.O., D 1/56/7.
19 *Endowed Char. Wilts.* (S. Div.), 909–10, 919; see above, plate facing p. 267.
20 Inf. from the head teacher, Great Wishford sch.
21 Nat. Soc. *Inquiry, 1846–7*, Wilts. 12–13.
22 P.R.O., ED 21/18431.
23 Wilts. Cuttings, xxii. 105.
24 *Endowed Char. Wilts.* (S. Div.), 911.

25 Nat. Soc. *Inquiry, 1846–7*, Wilts. 12–13.
26 *Acct. of Wilts. Schs.* 51.
27 *Return of Non-Provided Schs.* 23.
28 *Bd. of Educ., List 21, 1913* (H.M.S.O.), 550; *1936*, 422.
29 Inf. from the head teacher.
30 *Educ. Enq. Abstract*, 1052.
31 *Endowed Char. Wilts.* (S. Div.), 907–8, 917; W.R.O. 1160/16; see above, plate facing p. 267.
32 W.R.O. 2007/78.
33 Char. Com. file.
34 *Endowed Char. Wilts.* (S. Div.), 907–8, 918; W.R.O. 1160/16; 2007/71; below, this section.
35 Paskin, *Church of Wishford Magna*, 63; Char. Com. file.
36 *Endowed Char. Wilts.* (S. Div.), 911, 915–16; W.R.O. 1421/21.
37 W.R.O., L 2, Great Wishford.
38 Char. Com. file; inf. from the rector.
39 Char. Com. file; Princ. Regy. Fam. Div., will of E. B. Hill, 1925.

WYLYE

WYLYE village is half way between Salisbury and Warminster, 15 km. from each.[40] The parish, 2,314 a. (936 ha.) until 1934, lies north–south across the Wylye valley with the river flowing from west to east across its middle. It contains the land of Wylye and of Deptford, that of each forming a strip, Deptford's to the north and, twice as wide, Wylye's to the south.[41] In 1934 the half of Fisherton de la Mere parish containing Fisherton de la Mere village but not Bapton village was transferred to Wylye parish,[42] thereafter 1,608 ha. (3,974 a.).[43]

The boundaries of Wylye's land were defined c. 940 and have evidently been little changed; the east boundary of Deptford's land was apparently defined c. 977 and possibly its whole boundary in 988. For much of its length the parish boundary crosses downland and ignores relief and man-made features, but in the extreme south it is marked by an ancient ditch, in the south-east crosses a prehistoric earthwork and follows a coomb and an ancient track,[44] in the north-west follows another coomb for 800 m., and in the extreme north is marked by a road. In the centre of the parish the river is the boundary with Steeple Langford and for a short distance was with Fisherton de la Mere.

Chalk outcrops over the whole parish. Deposits of clay-with-flints cover it in the extreme south, and wide bands of gravel and alluvium have been deposited across the middle where the Wylye falls no more than 5 m. On each side of the river a tongue of gravel projects into a coomb. The chalk downs reach 198 m. in the south-east, 163 m. on the north boundary. Where it marks the boundary to the east the Wylye is below 70 m. Although they are broken by coombs the downs to both north and south have some flat land on them.[45]

Land use in the parish was characteristic of the Wylye valley with meadow land on the alluvium, watered from the 17th century to the 20th, settlement sites on the gravel, open fields on the gravel and on the chalk nearer the villages, and extensive pastures on the steeper and further chalklands. Wylye village had more land than most other villages in the Wylye valley and two distinct sets of open fields developed on it, each perhaps of average size for the valley. Some of

Wylye's downland was ploughed from the 18th century, some of Deptford's from then or later.[46] In 940 Wylye was allotted limited rights to take timber from Grovely forest and elsewhere,[47] suggesting that it then had little woodland of its own; in 1086 Wylye had only 10 a. of coppice wood, Deptford no woodland;[48] there was no extensive woodland in the later 16th century.[49] The parish had only 1 a. of woodland c. 1840,[50] c. 15 a. c. 1918.[51] Several coverts were later planted on Deptford's downs. Despite having little woodland the part of the parish south of the Wylye and east of the Wylye–Dinton road was in Grovely forest as defined in 1219: it was disafforested in 1300.[52] The west lodge of the forest may have been in the parish.[53] The Wylye has long been valued for its fish, and in the later 15th century or early 16th cygnets were reared on an island in it.[54]

Three short stretches of a Roman road from Winchester and Old Salisbury to the Mendips possibly crossed the extreme south of the parish;[55] the Grovely ridge way on the Wylye–Nadder watershed may also have crossed the parish there; the ancient Harrow way, thought to have linked Kent and Somerset, may have kissed the south-east corner;[56] a downland road between Wilton and Mere kissed the south-west corner; and the road along the northern parish boundary branched from what was until the 18th century the main Salisbury–Bath road and led to Chitterne.[57] The downland road between Amesbury and Mere crosses the parish from north-east to south-west through both Deptford and Wylye: it was called the London roadway c. 1600,[58] London way in 1669,[59] and was apparently an important route long before it was turnpiked in 1761.[60] The parish was ordered to repair it in 1736.[61] At the north end of Wylye village it forded the Wylye at Wylye water east of the mill as late as 1742;[62] a bridge was built west of the mill before 1773,[63] presumably when the road was turnpiked. That bridge was replaced in 1964.[64] A statue in Wylye water allegedly commemorates the drowning of the conductor of a coach which crashed when fording the river there.[65] South-west of the village a hollow way beside the road[66] may have marked its pre-1761 course, and in 1856 a new section,

40 This article was written in 1991. Maps used include O.S. Maps 6", Wilts. LIII, LIX (1889 and later edns.); 1/25,000, ST 93, SU 03–04 (1958 edns.); 1/50,000, sheet 184 (1974 edn.).   41 W.R.O., tithe award.
42 V.C.H. Wilts. iv. 361; viii. 34.
43 Census, 1971.
44 Arch. Jnl. lxxvi. 261–6; Cart. Sax. ed. Birch, iii, pp. 237–8; R. Forsberg, Old Eng. Place-Names, 215–16.
45 Geol. Surv. Map 1/50,000, drift, sheet 298 (1976 edn.).
46 Below, econ. hist.
47 Finberg, Early Wessex Chart. p. 86.
48 V.C.H. Wilts. ii, pp. 130, 138.
49 W.R.O. 212B/7190H.   50 Ibid. tithe award.
51 Ibid. 475/40–1.   52 V.C.H. Wilts. iv. 456–7.
53 W.R.O. 212B/7190H.
54 First Pembroke Survey, ed. Straton, i. 284; cf. above, Bathampton, manors.

55 W.A.M. xxxiii. 324; I. D. Margary, Rom. Roads in Brit. (1973), 101–3.
56 H. W. Timperley and E. Brill, Anct. Trackways of Wessex, 64, 134, and map 6; W.R.O. 212B/7190H.
57 Andrews and Dury, Map (W.R.S. viii), pls. 4–5; above, Steeple Langford, intro. [roads].
58 W.R.O., D 1/24/234/2.
59 Ibid. 1332, box 22, deed, Mompesson to Ash, 1669.
60 W.A.M. lxxxiv. 94; V.C.H. Wilts. iv. 257, 270; L.J. xxx. 138.   61 Q. Sess. 1736 (W.R.S. ix), pp. 6–7.
62 W.R.O. 628, map of Fisherton de la Mere, 1742.
63 Andrews and Dury, Map (W.R.S. viii), pl. 5.
64 Inf. from Dept. of Planning and Highways, Co. Hall, Trowbridge.
65 W.A.M. xxxiv. 235; Pevsner, Wilts. (2nd edn.), 601.
66 O.S. Map 6", Wilts. LIX (1889 edn.); personal observation by R. B. Pugh, May 1963.

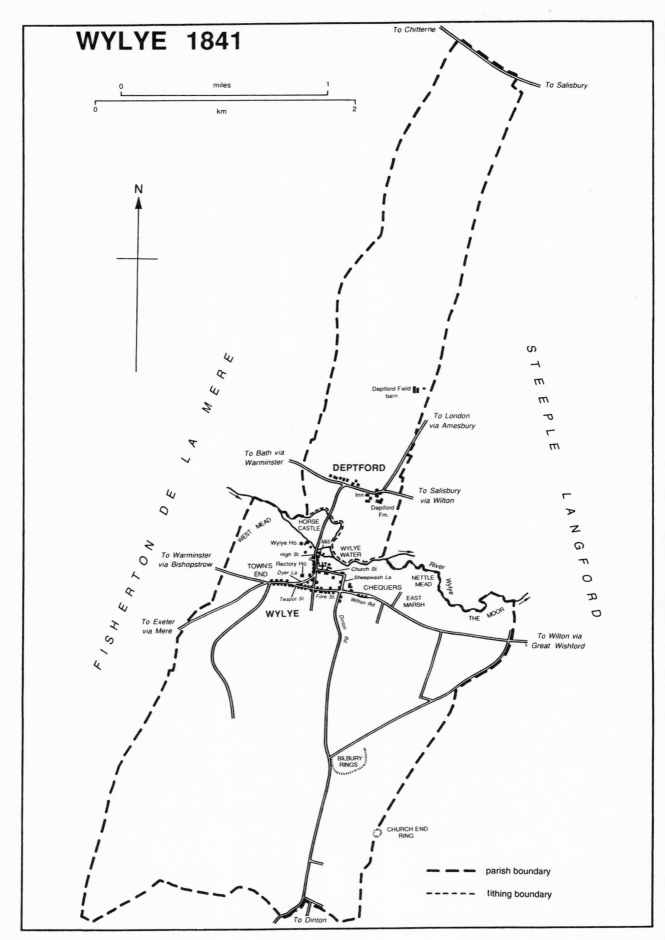

WYLYE 1841

FISHERTON DE LA MERE

STEEPLE LANGFORD

To Chitterne

To Salisbury

To London
via Amesbury

Deptford Field
barn

To Bath via
Warminster

DEPTFORD

To Salisbury
via Wilton

Inn

Deptford
Fm.

HORSE
CASTLE

Wylye Ho.

Mill

WYLYE
WATER

High St.

To Warminster
via Bishopstrow

Rectory Ho.

Church St.

TOWN'S
END

Dyer La.

Sheepwash La.

WEST MEAD

River

Wylye

NETTLE
MEAD

CHEQUERS

EAST
MARSH

To Exeter
via Mere

Teapot St.

Fore St.

Wilton Rd.

THE MOOR

To Wilton via
Great Wishford

WYLYE

Dinton Rd.

BILBURY
RINGS

CHURCH END
RING

To Dinton

parish boundary

tithing boundary

with a sharp bend, was made to bridge the new railway.[67] The road was disturnpiked in 1871. The Wilton–Warminster road on the left bank of the Wylye crosses the Amesbury–Mere road at Deptford: as part of a Salisbury–Bath road it was turnpiked in 1761, disturnpiked in 1870, and in the 20th century it was the main Southampton–Bristol road.[68] For 300 m. the two roads shared a course. Both were designated trunk roads, the Amesbury–Mere road in 1958 as part of the main London–Exeter road, the Southampton–Bristol road in 1946, and in 1975 their junction was reconstructed:[69] both were remade as dual-carriageway roads, the Southampton–Bristol road to bridge the London–Exeter road which was diverted away from Wylye village, and several slip roads were made. The parish is also crossed by the Wilton–Warminster road linking the villages between Great Wishford and Bishopstrow on the right bank of the Wylye, turnpiked between Little Langford and Stockton in 1761 and disturnpiked in 1871.[70] In the south-west part of Wylye village that road too shared a course with the Amesbury–Mere road until in 1975 it was bridged by the new road. A toll house[71] survives in the shared section. A road leading south from Wylye to Dinton was apparently on its present course in 1219:[72] a straight section was made across the downs at inclosure c. 1843.[73] The road on part of the south-east boundary led across Wylye's downs towards Chilmark but went out of use between the late 18th century and the late 19th.[74]

In 1856 the Salisbury–Warminster section of the G.W.R. was opened across the parish, parallel to and a little south of the minor Wilton–Warminster road, with a station west of Dinton Road. New sidings and loading platforms were built east of that road in the First World War.[75] The station was closed in 1955.[76]

Artefacts from the Mesolithic and Neolithic periods and from the Bronze Age have been found in the parish, and there are barrows on the downs of both Wylye and Deptford. To the south Bilbury rings and, on the south-east boundary, Church End ring are Iron-Age settlements which remained in use in the Roman period: nearby field systems of 80 a. and 250 a. were in use as long as the settlements. Along the south boundary Grim's ditch is probably later than the Roman road.[77]

In 1377 the parish had 112 poll-tax payers (Wylye 86, Deptford 26).[78] The population was 352 in 1801. It rose rapidly to reach 466 in 1821, was over 500 in 1841 (Wylye 421, Deptford 87), 1851, and 1871, but from 1871 declined. In 1931 it was 313. The decline apparently continued:

the enlarged parish had 400 inhabitants in 1951,[79] 311 in 1981. New housing in the 1980s caused a rise, to 409 in 1991.[80]

WYLYE. Its name suggests that Wylye was one of the earliest settlements in the valley. It presumably originated where the church, the site of the demesne farmstead east of it, and the demesne mill are in the north part of the village near the river.[81] Other settlement was in a small grid of streets. North–south are High Street and east of it Sheepwash Lane and Dinton Road; east–west are Church Street and Fore Street. None of the names seems to be older than the 19th century. The development of the grid can be conjectured. The first lands assigned to customary tenants, possibly before 940, were in the west part of the tithing, and evidence from the 16th century and later suggests that they were worked from tenements built on the line of High Street. Lands assigned later were in the east and evidence suggests that some were worked from tenements on the line of Sheepwash Lane.[82] Each line may have tended to assume an identity as a separate settlement, possibly those alluded to by the names Abbess Wylye and Wylye by Langford c. 1567:[83] the church was to the west, and the cross which stood in the village from before 1219 to after 1589 was to the east, apparently at the north end of Sheepwash Lane.[84] The west-end holdings were larger than those of the east end,[85] and several substantial farmhouses stood in High Street. About 1626 the demesne farmstead was replaced by or converted to a row of eight small farmhouses east of the church on the line of, but set back from, Church Street.[86] The division of the demesne between eight equally sized farms, each with a farmhouse in the row, adds weight to the conjecture as to how the village developed earlier. Also in the 17th century farmhouses were built, perhaps for the first time, in Fore Street, where long and narrow plots on the north side suggest a subdivision.[87] By the mid 18th century settlement had extended west of Fore Street into Teapot Street, and cottages had been built on the waste there and further west at Town's End;[88] east of Fore Street in Wilton Road cottages had been built on the waste at Chequers by 1773,[89] and a farmstead had been built by 1794.[90] High Street was the course of the Amesbury–Mere road, and Fore Street that of the minor Wilton–Warminster road:[91] the two roads may have shared Teapot Street until, before 1742,[92] Dyer Lane was made to take the Amesbury–Mere road away from it to the west.

In High Street 6–8 substantial farmhouses survive, some having been used as inns. The

67 For the railway, below, this section.
68 V.C.H. Wilts. iv. 257, 270; L.J. xxx. 77; cf. above, Steeple Langford, intro. [roads].
69 W.R.O. 2472/12; ibid. F 4/200/3; F 4/200/21.
70 V.C.H. Wilts. iv. 257, 270; L.J. xxx. 138.
71 W.R.O., tithe award.
72 V.C.H. Wilts. iv. 456–7.
73 W.R.O., EA/187; ibid. tithe award.
74 Ibid. 2057/I 6; Andrews and Dury, Map (W.R.S. viii), pl. 5; O.S. Map 6", Wilts. LIX (1889 edn.).
75 V.C.H. Wilts. iv. 284, 291.   76 Ibid. xi. 213.
77 Ibid. i (1), 129–30, 204, 251, 271, 278–9; i (2), 431, 436, 440; W.A.M. lviii. 416.   78 V.C.H. Wilts. iv. 306–7.

79 Ibid. 361.   80 Census, 1981; 1991.
81 For the demesne, below, this section; econ. hist. (Wylye); for the mill, econ. hist. (Wylye).
82 Below, econ. hist. (Wylye).
83 First Pembroke Survey, i. 104.
84 V.C.H. Wilts. iv. 456–7; W.R.O. 212B/7190H.
85 Below, econ. hist. (Wylye).
86 Pembroke Manors, 1631–2 (W.R.S. ix), pp. 86–8; W.R.O. 2057/I 6; 2057/S 106.   87 W.R.O. 1553/125.
88 Ibid. 628, map of Fisherton de la Mere, 1742.
89 Andrews and Dury, Map (W.R.S. viii), pl. 5.
90 W.R.O. 1553/125.   91 Above, this section [roads].
92 W.R.O. 628, map of Fisherton de la Mere, 1742.

oldest is apparently that at the junction with Dyer Lane, which is partly timber-framed, partly of ashlar, and late 16th- or early 17th-century in origin. Alehouses were kept at Wylye in the 16th century,[93] presumably on the main road in High Street, where later there were four inns. The Green Dragon was built shortly before 1631:[94] it was later on the west side near the north end in Down House, which was extensively altered in the earlier 18th century. The Bull, which had a malthouse, was on the east side at the north end, was open in 1696[95] and 1736,[96] and, like the Green Dragon, was apparently closed before 1796.[97] The White Lion, opposite the west end of Church Street, was open in 1782 and 1796[98] but was replaced by a pair of cottages, of brick and flint in bands, dated 1838. The Bell, in a building of the earlier 17th century immediately west of the church, was first mentioned in 1684[99] and was open in 1991. The other surviving farmhouses in High Street are mainly 17th- and 18th-century, and one has chequered walling. In the south part of the street a large house was built in the early 19th century; in the middle on the east side, all of red brick, a school and a schoolhouse were built in the later 19th century, two substantial houses in the early 20th.[1] Behind High Street to the north-west a new farmstead was built before 1742,[2] probably in 1709.[3] Wylye House, a new farmhouse with banded flint and limestone walling and with a Tuscan porch in a symmetrical south front, was built there in the early 19th century: east of it in 1991 were farm buildings and cottages of the 18th and 19th centuries. At the north end of High Street the Wyvern Hall was built c. 1890.[4] From 1918 to 1957 it belonged to the Order of Oddfellows; from 1957,[5] altered and extended 1963–4,[6] it has been a village hall.

In Sheepwash Lane stands an early 17th-century cottage, thatched and of banded flint and stone. In Church Street stand a late 17th-century house with chequered walling and another, probably 18th-century, with some similar walling, but in the earlier 20th century all but one of the houses in the row east of the church were demolished.[7] The survivor adjoins the churchyard and retains some 17th-century features. A church house near the church in 1567[8] has not survived. In Fore Street stand several small houses of the later 17th century or early 18th, some thatched and some with chequered or banded walling. A new farmstead, East Farm,

was built in the west angle of Fore Street and Dinton Road 1862–4.[9] In Teapot Street stand two apparently 18th-century cottages, one with chequered walling, and at Town's End stand a thatched cottage of the 17th or 18th century and the toll house of the later 18th century, but in the 19th century other cottages were replaced in both places and a nonconformist chapel was built in Teapot Street.[10] There was a public house at Town's End in 1796,[11] and the Swan, sometimes called the White Swan, was open in 1840.[12] It was rebuilt, apparently after a fire in 1923,[13] extended in 1936,[14] and closed c. 1975 when the village was bypassed.[15] To the east the farmhouse at Chequers was replaced in the early 19th century. The cottages on the waste there in 1794[16] were replaced in the 19th century: of three standing in 1991 two, of which the newer was dated 1832, were derelict. On the south side of the line near the station the G.W.R. built a house and four cottages between 1886 and 1899.[17] On the downs Wylye Down Buildings was built between c. 1840 and 1864, Bilbury Farm 1862–4: the farmsteads included three and four cottages respectively.[18] The cottages at Wylye Down Buildings had been demolished by 1991.

Only a few private houses were built in the earlier 20th century. In 1933 four council houses were built in Fore Street, in 1935 four in Wilton Road, and in 1952 four in Church Street and six in Fore Street; in Teapot Street four old people's bungalows were built in 1964,[19] four c. 1971. Private houses built since then include 9 in and off Church Street and 18 in terraces between Teapot Street and Town's End. The whole village was designated a conservation area in 1975.[20]

DEPTFORD. A manor house possibly stood at Deptford in 1267, when 10 cartloads of fencing from Grovely forest were granted to the lord of the manor[21] and there was probably a small village.[22] There was almost certainly an inn in 1686,[23] and one stood there in 1714.[24] In 1773 buildings stood on both sides of the Wilton–Warminster road, with the principal farmstead and, west of it, the inn on the south side. Those on the north side included, from c. 1840 or earlier to the mid 20th century, a post office[25] and, in the mid 20th century, a police house[26] and a commercial garage. The new sections of road built in 1975 made an island of Deptford Farm and caused the demolition of five cottages.[27] In 1991 all 11 houses on the north side

93 *Sess. Mins.* (W.R.S. iv), 81, 91, 111.
94 *Pembroke Manors, 1631–2* (W.R.S. ix), p. 89.
95 W.R.O. 2057/I 6; 2057/S 27; 2057/S 106.
96 *Q. Sess. 1736* (W.R.S. xi), p. 6.
97 W.R.O. 2057/S 106.
98 Ibid.; 2057/I 6; 2057/S 27, f. 46.
99 Ibid. 2057, deeds, Wylye, Pembroke to Hillman, 1684.
1 Ibid. tithe award; O.S. Maps 6", Wilts. LIX (1889 and later edns.); below, educ.
2 W.R.O. 628, map of Fisherton de la Mere, 1742.
3 Reset date stone in Wylye Ho.
4 O.S. Maps 6", Wilts. LIX (1889 edn.); LIX. SW. (1901 edn.); W.R.O. 2472/1. 5 W.R.O. 475/40; 2505/2.
6 Ibid. 2499/400/3; 2505/2.
7 O.S. Maps 6", Wilts. LIX. SW. (1901, 1926 edns.).
8 *First Pembroke Survey*, i. 281.
9 W.R.O. 2057/E 2/4.
10 Below, nonconf.   11 W.R.O. 2057/S 106.

12 Ibid. 2057/S 186; ibid. tithe award.
13 D. Howell, *Remember the Wylye Valley*, 30.
14 W.R.O., G 11/760/240.
15 Inf. from Major M. D. Burroughes, Wylands Cottage.
16 W.R.O. 1553/125.
17 Ibid. Inland Revenue, val. reg. 143; O.S. Maps 6", Wilts. LIX (1889 edn.); LIX. SW. (1901 edn.).
18 W.R.O., tithe award; ibid. 475/40; 2057/E 2/4; 2057/S 186.   19 Ibid. G 11/602/1–2; G 11/603/1.
20 Inf. from Dept. of Planning and Highways, Co. Hall, Trowbridge.   21 *Close R.* 1264–8, 296.
22 Cf. below, econ. hist. (Deptford).
23 *W.A.M.* lxxxiv. 87.
24 W.R.O. 1332, box 3, lease, Walker to Warne, 1756.
25 Ibid. tithe award; *Andrews and Dury, Map* (W.R.S. viii), pl. 5; *Kelly's Dir. Wilts.* (1939).
26 W.R.O., G 11/505/6.
27 Inf. from Lt.-Col. H. G. Cassels, Deptford Farm Ho.

of the road were 20th-century except an early 19th-century stone house with a symmetrical south front of five bays, a small stone house of similar date, and an apparently 19th-century cottage. A pair of cottages was built at Deptford Field barn in the early 19th century[28] and rebuilt in the later 20th.[29]

Deptford Farm is an early 18th-century stone farmhouse altered and extended in red brick c. 1810. Near it a building of banded stone and flint now used as a barn may also be of the early 18th century, a long stone stable and hay loft may also be of c. 1810, and a pair of cottages, formerly three, is 19th-century. From 1810 to 1817 the pamphleteer and proponent of reform Robert Gourlay (1778–1863) was tenant of Deptford farm. Gourlay quarrelled with his landlord Edward Seymour, duke of Somerset, before he entered on the farm in 1810 and was at law with him for many years; he persuaded parishioners of Wylye to petition against the poor law and proposed to abolish pauperism in parishes of fewer than 1,000 inhabitants by assigning to the poor 50 a. for a common cow pasture and 50 a. for division into ½-a. plots on each of which a cottage was to be built. In 1817 Gourlay emigrated to Canada and was later influential as the author of *Statistical Account of Upper Canada*.[30]

The Deptford inn, which may have been called the Black Lion in the mid 18th century,[31] was the meeting place of the Deptford club, in the 18th century and early 19th an informal political association of the gentry of south Wiltshire.[32] The first cricket club in Wiltshire was formed there in 1798, the first coursing club in 1819.[33] The inn was demolished in the mid 19th century.[34]

MANORS AND OTHER ESTATES. An estate of 10 *mansae* which became *WYLYE* manor was granted by King Edmund to his thegn Ordwold in 940: it was held with detached land which later may have been in Baverstock parish and with a 'haw' at Wilton, meadow land called Duttenham, hedgebote in Grovely forest, and one tree in three in a wood apparently near the Wylye.[35] By 1086 it had been acquired by Wilton abbey,[36] which held it until it passed to the Crown at the Dissolution.[37] The manor was granted to George Howard, the brother of Queen Catherine, in 1541[38] and sold by him in 1547 to Sir William Herbert[39] (cr. earl of Pembroke 1551). It descended with the Pembroke title[40] until 1918 and included all but c. 150 a. of Wylye tithing.[41] By 1567 it had lost the appendages recorded in 940 except for the first cut of hay from 10 a. of Duttenham mead in Little Langford,[42] which it retained until c. 1860.[43]

Ernest Courtney bought Manor farm and Wylye Down farm, 628 a., in 1918:[44] in 1920 he owned only Wylye Down farm, 509 a.,[45] which in 1929 belonged to H. F. Roberts.[46] That farm, 434 a., had become part of the Bapton Manor estate by 1955, when it belonged to E. Leigh Pearson. As part of that estate it was sold by Leigh Pearson in 1959 to R. H. Heywood-Lonsdale, who in 1975[47] sold it to Mr. J. C. Lyall, the owner in 1991.[48] The remainder of Wylye Down farm, 77 a., was with land in Hanging Langford in Steeple Langford part of a 292-a. holding which belonged to Mr. W. Helyar until 1991.[49] Manor farm belonged from 1920, when it was 143 a.,[50] to Charles Lush (d. 1956); it passed to his brother Sidney (d. 1957) and to their nephew Mr. E. H. Lush and to his son Mr. J. A. E. Lush, the owner in 1991.[51] East farm, 588 a., was bought by S. J. Blyth c. 1918[52] and belonged to him in 1939. Between 1939 and 1945 he sold part of it as Bilbury farm, which, at 300 a., was bought in 1946 by Barrett Bros., the owners in 1991.[53] In 1978 the Nature Conservancy Council bought 34 ha. of Bilbury farm.[54] The remainder of East farm was divided after 1945.[55]

In 1334 Simon of Wylye was licensed to grant a small estate in Wylye to St. John's hospital, Wilton, for service in Wylye church. The hospital apparently entered on it c. 1336,[56] but later evidence of the holding has not been found.

Five *mansae* at Wylye, formerly held by Ethelwold and his brother Aelfhelm, were granted by King Ethelred to his thegn Aelfgar in 988: the estate may have been the land of Deptford.[57] Osward and Godwin each held 1 hide at *DEPTFORD* in 1066. Edward of Salisbury held both hides in 1086 and Azelin held them of him.[58] The overlordship descended to Edward's heirs with his Shrewton estate and with the earldom of Salisbury and the overlordship of Shrewton:[59] the earls of Salisbury were overlords in the late 14th century and the early 15th.[60]

28 Ibid. tithe award; O.S. Map 1", sheet 14 (1817 edn.).
29 Inf. from Lt.-Col. Cassels.
30 L. D. Milani, *Rob. Gourlay, Gadfly*; R. Gourlay, *Address to the Jurymen of Wilts.* (copy in W.A.S. Libr.); R. Gourlay, *Village System* (copy in W.A.S. Libr.).
31 Eton Coll. Mun. 43/162.
32 *V.C.H. Wilts.* v. 200–1.   33 Ibid. iv. 378, 382.
34 O.S. Map 6", Wilts. LIX (1889 edn.); W.R.O., tithe award.
35 Finberg, *Early Wessex Chart.* p. 86; *Arch. Jnl.* lxxvi. 261–7; *V.C.H. Wilts.* ii, p. 16; other pre-Conquest doc. dealing with land identified by the name Wylye referred to Bathampton, Stockton, and possibly Deptford: *V.C.H. Wilts.* xi. 214; Forsberg, *Old Eng. Place-Names*, 215–16; above, Bathampton, manors; below, this section (Deptford).
36 *V.C.H. Wilts.* ii, p. 130.
37 *Valor Eccl.* (Rec. Com.), ii. 109.
38 *L. & P. Hen. VIII*, xvi, p. 424.
39 Ibid. xxi (2), p. 408; P.R.O., CP 25/2/65/531, no. 9.
40 *Complete Peerage*, x. 405–30.
41 W.R.O. 475/40; 2057/S 106.

42 *First Pembroke Survey*, ed. Straton, i. 276–84.
43 Above, Little Langford, econ. hist.
44 W.R.O. 475/40.   45 Ibid. G 11/500/4.
46 Ibid. G 11/505/2.
47 Ibid. G 11/505/5; ibid. 1844/43; *V.C.H. Wilts.* viii. 40.
48 Local inf.   49 Ibid.; sale cat. 1991.
50 W.R.O., G 11/500/4.
51 Inf. from Mr. J. A. E. Lush, Riverside Cottage.
52 W.R.O. 475/40; ibid. G 11/500/4.
53 Inf. from Miss D. Barrett, Bilbury Farm.
54 Nature Conservancy Council, *Wylye Down* (1980).
55 Local inf.
56 *Wilts. Inq. p.m.* 1327–77 (Index Libr.), 96–7, 118; *V.C.H. Wilts.* iii. 365.
57 *Cart. Sax.* ed. Birch, iii, pp. 237–8; Forsberg, *Old Eng. Place-Names*, 215–16.
58 *V.C.H. Wilts.* ii, p. 138.
59 Above, Shrewton, manors; cf. *Bk. of Fees*, ii. 708, 720; *Feet of F. 1272–1326* (W.R.S. i), p. 132.
60 *Cal. Inq. p.m.* xvii, p. 321; xix, p. 233; P.R.O., C 139/41, no. 57, rot. 39.

In 1242–3 Roger son of Pain held ½ and ⅒ knight's fee in Deptford, and John of Deptford held ½.[61] Roger's estate was later held by Robert son of Pain, who settled it on his sister Margery and her husband Walter Burgess; Walter held it in 1267. The Burgesses' heir was their daughter Margery, whose husband Ralph Chenduit held the estate in 1316 and son John Chenduit in 1321.[62] John of Deptford's estate may have been that held by Robert of Deptford in 1346,[63] but by 1386 had apparently been merged with the Chenduits' as Deptford manor.[64]

From 1386 to 1919 the manor passed with Little Bathampton manor. In 1386 it was settled for life on Elizabeth and John Knottingley with reversion to Catherine, wife of Thomas Bonham; it descended in the Mompesson family 1420–1751, was held by Thomas Walker (d. 1782) and by John Drummond, and from 1783 belonged to the dukes of Somerset.[65]

In 1919 Algernon St. Maur, duke of Somerset, sold Deptford farm, 733 a., to James Hooper,[66] whose son C. L. Hooper sold it in 1955 to F. W. N. Jeans (d. 1972), owner of the adjoining Fisherton de la Mere manor. In 1982 Jeans's executors conveyed it to his stepson Lt.-Col. H. G. Cassels, the owner in 1991.[67]

In 1403 Richard Pitts, rector of Wylye, was licensed to grant an estate at Deptford including 30 a. of arable to Wells cathedral for masses in the cathedral for John Manston.[68] If Manston was a form of Mompesson, Pitts may have been an agent of the Mompesson family. The cathedral held the estate in 1473[69] but, probably before 1498 and certainly before 1553, it was acquired by a Mompesson and added to Deptford manor.[70]

ECONOMIC HISTORY. WYLYE. In 1086 Wylye had land for 5 ploughteams: 5 hides were demesne with 2 teams and 2 *servi*, and 9 *villani* and 10 bordars had 3 teams; there were 12 a. of meadow and 100 a. of pasture.[71] Almost certainly by 940 and until *c.* 1860 Wylye had additional meadow in Duttenham mead at Little Langford.[72] Evidence from the 16th century suggests that early in the history of Wylye, perhaps before 940 when some land of farm servants (*hina*) was to the west, the eastern half of its land was assigned as demesne, the western half to customary tenants. Small parts of each half were later granted freely, and in the eastern half, presumably before the 14th century, new customary holdings were apparently taken from the demesne.[73] Other later evidence suggests that the demesne was worked from buildings immediately east of the church, some of the eastern copyholds from farmsteads roughly on the line

of Sheepwash Lane, and the western copyholds from farmsteads in High Street and Fore Street.[74]

In the 16th century the east end of Wylye and the west end each had its own largely separate system of common husbandry, an arrangement probably of long standing. The *c.* 600 a. of arable were divided roughly equally between the two ends, the east having slightly more arable, the west more meadow. The only inclosed lands were the home closes around the village and the Moor, a 10-a. pasture which was part of the demesne. The east end had three open fields and the west end had two. The east-end fields were of roughly equal size: later evidence suggests that East field and Middle field were in the east part of Wylye tithing and that West field was in the west. Of the west-end fields West was the larger: both were apparently in the west part of the tithing. The strips in the east-end fields were apparently a little larger than those in the west-end fields. On the downs the east and west ends had separate common pastures for sheep, each almost certainly much more extensive than the 100 a. at which it was estimated in 1567, but they shared the common cattle pastures, East marsh and Horse castle near the Wylye, and Cow down. The west end had two common meadows of its own, West mead and Nettle mead. There were *c.* 36 yardlands in all. In the east end there were the 8 demesne yardlands, with 170 a. of arable apparently in scattered strips, some freeholders' land and glebe, and 6½ copyhold yardlands. The copyholds apparently originated as ½ yardlands and were small. They were poorly stinted, at 20 sheep and 4 beasts to 1 yardland, while the demesne, on which 600 sheep could be kept, was generously stinted. In the west end there were some freeholders' land and glebe and 14 copyhold yardlands. Each copyhold apparently originated as 1 yardland, and 10 were still of 1 yardland in 1567: each yardland was *c.* 20 a. of arable with 1 a. in West mead, ½ a. in Nettle mead, and feeding for 60 sheep and 8 beasts. In the whole tithing *c.* 2,100 sheep and *c.* 215 horses and cattle could be fed in common.[75]

The demesne farm, which in the late Middle Ages was leased for rent mainly in the form of produce,[76] was in 1626 divided into eight equal portions: each had 1 yardland with a small farmstead east of the church, and was separately leased on lives. Each new holding had 21 a. in the three east-end fields, the hay from 1¼ a. of Duttenham mead, and feeding for 1 cow and 100 sheep; the Moor, *c.* 24 a., was divided into small closes. Also between 1567 and 1631 a third west-end field, Middle, was created from land of the other two, and West mead, East marsh, and

61 *Bk. of Fees*, ii. 708, 720.
62 *Close R.* 1264–8, 296; *Feud. Aids*, v. 211; P.R.O., CP 40/240, rot. 113.
63 *Feet of F.* 1327–77 (W.R.S. xxix), pp. 80–1.
64 *Feet of F.* 1377–1509 (W.R.S. xli), p. 20.
65 Above, Bathampton, manors.
66 W.R.O. 475/41; Wilts. Cuttings, xiv. 120.
67 Inf. from Lt.-Col. H. G. Cassels, Deptford Farm Ho.
68 *Cal. Pat.* 1401–5, 262; Phillipps, *Wilts. Inst.* i. 75, 100.
69 Hist. MSS. Com. 12, *Wells*, ii, p. 95.
70 Le Neve, *Fasti, 1300–1541, Bath and Wells*, 5; P.R.O., C 142/104, no. 123.
71 *V.C.H. Wilts.* ii, p. 130.
72 *Arch. Jnl.* lxxvi. 264; above, manors (Wylye); Little Langford, econ. hist.
73 *Arch. Jnl.* lxxvi. 262–3; below, this section.
74 W.R.O. 1553/125; 2057/P 1/8; 2057/S 27; 2057/S 106.
75 Ibid. 1553/125; 2057/P 1/8; *First Pembroke Survey*, ed. Straton, i. 276–84; the name Horse castle was derived from the chart. of 940: *Arch. Jnl.* lxxvi. 264.
76 W.R.O. 2057/S 1, pp. 186–7.

Horse castle were divided, allotted, and inclosed: in East marsh the west-end copyholders were allotted 2 a., the east-end copyholders 2½ a., for each yardland. Of the riverside grassland only Nettle mead remained commonable.[77] By an agreement recorded in 1632 the Moor, East marsh, and Nettle mead were adapted so that they could be watered: the work was paid for by the tenants,[78] and Wylye manor court prohibited individual tenants from interfering with the activities of the paid drowners thereafter appointed.[79]

The east and west ends kept separate systems of husbandry until 1796, but in the 17th and 18th centuries, especially after the demesne and some copyholds were fragmented, holdings were increasingly accumulated and it became normal for those holding the most land to have arable in all the tithing's six fields. It is also clear that in the 18th century many of the copyholders sublet, and likely that the number of farmsteads in the village was reduced. In 1794 the tithing had 587 a. of arable, all in the open fields and divided into c. 1,060 strips of c. ½ a. West of the village and at the eastern parish boundary the arable extended north of the Great Wishford to Bishopstrow road. Also between the road and the river were most of the home closes, West mead, 28 a., Horse castle, 17 a., the Marsh, c. 21 a., the Moor, c. 24 a., and Nettle mead, 6½ a. South of the arable fields were 800 a. of common down.[80]

In 1796, by an agreement of 1794, the northernmost arable, that north of the Great Wishford to Bishopstrow road and a greater amount in a strip across the tithing south of the road, 173 a. in all, was divided, allotted, and inclosed, as was Nettle mead. The remaining arable, c. 414 a., was rearranged into four equally sized open fields, the strips were rearranged as c. 140 parcels, and all but the smallest holdings were allotted land in each field. At the south-east and south-west corners of the tithing 171 a. of downland were ploughed to make four new open fields, two at each corner: each field was of c. 43 a., there were 72 parcels in all, and each holding with new arable had an equal amount in each field. Cattle pasture on the downs was ended, and thereafter 2,115 sheep could be fed in common. In 1796 four composite holdings were over 100 a., the largest 165 a., with rights to feed a total of 1,060 sheep;[81] in 1803 there were only five farms, one of which exceeded 300 a.[82] By 1840 a further 50 a. of downland may have been ploughed.[83]

In 1840 it was agreed to inclose the arable and downland and to exchange existing closes. The death of a commissioner delayed a formal award, which was made in 1861 under a general Act, but the allotments had been entered on by 1843 and were thenceforth occupied without dissent. South of the Great Wishford to Bishopstrow road the land was worked as large fields,[84] and in the mid or later 19th century more pasture was converted to arable.[85] After inclosure there were three principal farms. The largest, later called Manor, was worked from buildings at Wylye House and from Wylye Down Buildings.[86] East farm was 248 a. from inclosure, 399 a. in 1863: a new farmstead in the village and a new downland farmstead, Bilbury Farm, were built for it.[87] Court farm, 112 a., was worked from the farmstead at Chequers.[88] By the early 20th century most of Manor farm had been added to East farm, then 1,111 a.; Court remained a separate farm and there were two other small farms.[89] There were c. 900 a. of arable in 1918, when much meadow land was still watered.[90]

From 1918 to the Second World War East was a mixed farm of c. 575 a. From it 300 a. were taken as Bilbury farm, which from 1946 has been solely pasture: in 1991 sheep and Ayrshire and Herefordshire cattle were kept on Bilbury farm, including the 34 ha. which became a nature reserve in 1978.[91] Most other land of what had been East farm was arable in 1991. Manor farm was 628 a. when sold in 1918 but was split into Manor farm and Wylye Down farm soon after.[92] From 1955 or earlier most of Wylye Down farm, 434 a. including 279 a. of arable in 1975, was worked from Bapton.[93] Another part of it, 77 a., mostly arable, was worked from Hanging Langford until 1991.[94] In the mid 20th century Manor, 143 a., and Court, 166 a., were mixed farms: in the late 20th neither was worked as a farm and their lands were leased.[95]

There was a mill at Wylye in 1086,[96] and one was part of Wylye manor until 1919.[97] It stands at the north edge of the village and was driven by the Wylye. Apparently in the mid 16th century it was enlarged or converted to be both a corn and fulling mill,[98] and fulling continued until between 1677 and 1705. The tenants of Wylye manor were required to use the corn mill, and in 1677 the manor court ordered fulling racks erected on waste land to be removed because they were detrimental to the fulling mill. The building housed two corn mills in 1705.[99] Until 1872 the machinery was incorporated in a T-shaped 17th- or early 18th-century house,

77 Ibid. 2057/P 1/8; 2057/S 106; *Pembroke Manors, 1631–2* (W.R.S. ix), pp. 86–97.
78 *Pembroke Manors, 1631–2* (W.R.S. ix), pp. 138–40; *W.A.M.* lv. 114.
79 W.R.O. 2057/M 8; 2057/M 12; 2057/M 15; 2057/M 54.
80 Ibid. 1553/125; 2057/P 1/8; 2057/S 5; 2057/S 27; 2057/S 106.
81 Ibid. 2057, deeds, Wylye, art. of agreement, 1794; deed of conf. 1797; 2057/I 6; 2057/P 1/8; 2057/S 106.
82 Ibid. 529/218, abstr. of Wylye parsonage, 1803.
83 Ibid. 2057/P 1/8; 2057/S 106; ibid. tithe award.
84 Ibid. EA/187.
85 Ibid. tithe award; ibid. 475/40.
86 Ibid. tithe award; ibid. 2057/S 186.
87 Ibid. tithe award; ibid. 2057/E 2/4; 2057/S 186.

88 Ibid. tithe award; W.A.S. Libr., sale cat. xxviii (E), no. 67.
89 W.R.O., Inland Revenue, val. reg. 143.
90 Ibid. 475/40.
91 Ibid.; Nature Conservancy Council, *Wylye Down*; inf. from Miss D. Barrett, Bilbury Farm.
92 W.R.O. 475/40; above, manors (Wylye).
93 W.R.O. 1844/43; above, manors (Wylye); local inf.
94 Sale cat. 1991; local inf.
95 W.R.O., G 11/500/4; inf. from Mr. J. A. E. Lush, Riverside Cottage.
96 *V.C.H. Wilts.* ii, p. 130.
97 W.A.S. Libr., sale cat. xxxiv, no. 63.
98 *First Pembroke Survey*, i. 278; W.R.O. 2057/S 1, p. 188.
99 W.R.O. 2057/M 13; 2057/M 16; 2057/S 27.

most of which survives: the house was extended north twice in the early 19th century, the first time in 1812. In 1872 a new three-storeyed red-brick mill was built, partly on the site of the south part of the house, and from then the mill was powered by turbine.[1] It was used by C. Carpenter & Son from 1946, and was closed in 1962 when the firm moved to Station Mill, in the buildings of East Farm, where new electrically powered machinery was installed.[2] The machinery was removed from the old mill in 1963.[3] In 1991 C. Carpenter & Son continued to prepare animal foodstuffs at Station Mill.[4]

There were two tanners at Wylye in 1379,[5] a weaver in 1583, two tailors in 1586,[6] a tobacco seller in 1637,[7] and a linen weaver in 1841.[8] There was fulling in the later 16th century and the 17th,[9] and malting in the 18th and 19th.[10] Until 1975 trades and commercial enterprises in Wylye, particularly innkeeping, catered for travellers on the main road through the village.[11]

Yarnbury castle fair, formerly held on the downs of Steeple Langford, was held on the south side of Wilton Road in Wylye from 1917 to c. 1929.[12]

DEPTFORD. In 1086 Deptford had land for 2 ploughteams and 2 were there: 1½ hide was demesne, on other land there were 1 *villanus*, 3 bordars, and 2 cottars, and there were 8 a. of meadow and 16 a. of pasture.[13] From the 13th century there is evidence of open field and common pasture at Deptford,[14] and in the 14th century it is likely that there was both demesne and customary land.[15] Wells cathedral's estate in 1429 included 60 a. of arable and feeding in common for 12 beasts and 160 sheep.[16] A reference to Deptford marsh in 1567 suggests that grassland near the Wylye was for use in common.[17]

In the late 17th century Deptford apparently had only inclosed meadow and pasture near the river; north of that lay three open fields, in which some cultivation was in parcels of 10–20 a., and further north lay common downland pasture for sheep. A holding which may have been the demesne of Deptford manor had 7 a. of meadow, c. 10 a. of pasture, 108 a. of arable, and feeding for 240 sheep. In 1687 the demesne, Deptford farm, was held by Tristram Biggs, who held other farms nearby.[18]

The arable and downland were inclosed between 1714 and 1756, presumably by agreement,[19] and by the 1780s nearly all Deptford land had apparently been absorbed by Deptford farm.[20] The making of Robert Gourlay tenant in 1810 may have been part of an attempt by Edward, duke of Somerset, to improve the farm, and the subsequent disputes between the two were largely over the cost of repairs and improvements.[21] The farm, 688 a. c. 1840,[22] 732 a. in 1919, continued to be worked from Deptford Farm and to be for sheep and corn, but in the 19th century, possibly when downland pasture was ploughed, new farmsteads were built incorporating Deptford Field barn and Deptford Down barn. In 1919 the farm had 91 a. of lowland meadow and pasture, of which 60 a. were watered meadows, 480 a. of arable, and 151 a. of downland pasture.[23] From 1955 to 1982 it was worked with Fisherton de la Mere farm, from 1982 as a single arable and dairy farm by its owner. A new dairy was built at Deptford Field barn in 1958 and enlarged in 1972. In 1991 Deptford farm was c. 670 a. and had a dairy herd of 110 cows.[24]

There was a mill at Deptford in 1086.[25]

LOCAL GOVERNMENT. Wylye tithing, which excluded Deptford,[26] evidently attended the tourn of Chalke hundred, a private hundred of Wilton abbey.[27] In the later 16th century and earlier 17th Wylye manor court was held twice yearly. The homage presented through a foreman: female tenants were listed among the homage but not sworn. The rules of husbandry in common were enforced and new ones sometimes made, and the court transacted manorial business, hearing reports that tenants had died or buildings were dilapidated, witnessing surrenders and admittances, and choosing a hayward.[28] In the later 17th century such matters were dealt with once a year at a court held in autumn until c. 1678, thereafter in spring, and the court also met at need to transfer copyholds. The court required tenants to use Wylye mill and appointed additional officers such as overseers of drowning and tellers of sheep. Little business was recorded 1692–1714. Later, common husbandry was again regulated by the court but from the 1720s the orders became stereotyped; copyhold business continued to be enrolled. The court was held yearly until 1817, and four times between then and 1841.[29]

[1] W.R.O. 1553/125; inf. from Mr. D. H. Thomas, Mill Ho.; dates on bldg.
[2] Inf. from C. Carpenter & Son, Station Mill.
[3] W.A.S. Libr., sale cat. xxxiv, no. 63.
[4] Inf. from C. Carpenter & Son.
[5] *V.C.H. Wilts.* iv. 234.
[6] *Sess. Mins.* (W.R.S. iv), 81, 111.
[7] *Early-Stuart Tradesmen* (W.R.S. xv), p. 101.
[8] P.R.O., HO 107/1167.
[9] Above, this section.
[10] W.R.O. 2057/S 106; ibid. tithe award.
[11] *Kelly's Dir. Wilts.* (1848 and later edns.); above, intro. [roads; inns].
[12] Howell, *Remember the Wylye Valley*, 24; above, Steeple Langford, econ. hist. (fair); inf. from Major M. D. Burroughes, Wylands Cottage.
[13] *V.C.H. Wilts.* ii, p. 138.
[14] *Feet of F.* 1327–77 (W.R.S. xxix), p. 34; P.R.O., CP 25/1/250/2, no. 31.
[15] *Feet of F.* 1327–77 (W.R.S. xxix), pp. 80–1.
[16] Hist. MSS. Com. 12, *Wells*, ii, p. 669.
[17] *First Pembroke Survey*, i. 284.
[18] W.R.O. 1332, box 22, deeds, Mompesson to Ash, 1669; Mompesson to Russell, 1687; above, Little Langford, econ. hist.
[19] W.R.O. 1332, box 23, lease, Walker to Warne, 1756.
[20] Ibid. 1332, box 3, lease, Som. to Thring, 1789; 1332, box 22, lease, Dampier to Som., 1785.
[21] Gourlay, *Address to the Jurymen of Wilts.*; above, intro. (Deptford). [22] W.R.O., tithe award.
[23] Ibid. 475/41; O.S. Maps 6", Wilts. LIII, LIX (1889 edns.).
[24] Inf. from Lt.-Col. H. G. Cassels, Deptford Farm Ho.
[25] *V.C.H. Wilts.* ii, p. 138.
[26] Below, this section.
[27] *First Pembroke Survey*, i. 104.
[28] B.L. Add. Ch. 24440–1; W.R.O. 2057/M 4–5.
[29] W.R.O. 2057/M 8; 2057/M 12–17; 2057/M 34; 2057/M 54; 2057/M 81.

Deptford and Bathampton together consti-
tuted a tithing, usually called Bathampton, in
Heytesbury hundred.[30] Records of a court baron
for Deptford manor survive for 1828–50. Most
business was tenurial, but a dilapidated building
was reported in 1828, and in 1841 a new building
was declared to be part of the manor.[31]

From 1775–6, when £94 was spent, to 1802–3,
when 9 adults and 34 children were regularly
and 12 adults occasionally relieved for £207, the
cost of poor relief in Wylye parish was apparently modest.[32] The parish owned four cottages
at Town's End presumably to be lived in by
paupers.[33] Expenditure on the poor reached
peaks of £507 in 1812–13, when 30 adults were
regularly relieved, and £538 in 1817–18, but
averaged c. £335 between 1813 and 1836.[34] The
parish joined Wilton poor-law union in 1836,[35]
and became part of Salisbury district in 1974.[36]

CHURCH. Wylye church may have been standing in the 12th century and had a rector in
1249.[37] A proposal of 1650 that Deptford should
be transferred from Wylye to Fisherton de la
Mere parish was not put into effect.[38] Wylye
rectory was united with Fisherton de la Mere
vicarage 1929–57, additionally with Stockton
rectory 1957–73, and with the benefice of the
Langfords in place of Stockton 1973–9: all those
benefices, including Stockton, were merged as
Yarnbury benefice in 1979. Wylye and Fisherton
de la Mere parishes were united in 1974.[39]

The lords of Wylye manor were patrons of the
church.[40] In the 1370s and early 1380s the
rectory was disputed between John Batecombe,
whom the king presented in 1377, and John
Aspull, the rector before 1377, whose estate as
rector the king ratified in 1383 and 1384.[41] The
king presented twice in 1389,[42] and the archbishop of Canterbury collated by lapse in 1774.[43]
In 1953 Reginald Herbert, earl of Pembroke and
of Montgomery, transferred the advowson to the
bishop of Salisbury, who from 1957 shared the
patronage of the united benefices.[44]

Valued at £10 in 1291,[45] £22 in 1535,[46] £140
c. 1620[47] and in 1650,[48] and £492 c. 1830,[49] the
living was of above average wealth. The rector

was entitled to all tithes from the parish, except
from the wool of 300 sheep kept on the demesne
of Wylye manor, and to the hay tithe of 10 a. of
Duttenham mead.[50] In the late 18th century the
wool tithes from all sheep kept in the parish were
claimed by the lord of Wylye manor.[51] In 1842,
when they evidently included the wool tithes but
no tithe from Duttenham mead, the rector's
tithes were valued at £540 and commuted.[52] In
1249 the rector claimed all of 1 hide, except 17
a., as glebe, but the land was found to be part
of Wylye manor.[53] In 1341 the glebe was ½
yardland with 2 a. of meadow and feeding for 6
cattle and 62 sheep,[54] a holding which in 1567
included 12 a. of arable.[55] The rector had 11 a.
c. 1840.[56] The rectory house was probably on its
present site c. 1600, when the tiles or slates on
its roof were replaced by thatch.[57] In 1783 the
house was of stone and flint with two storeys and
attics.[58] A new house was built in 1827 to designs
by John Peniston.[59] The house was sold in 1957,
other glebe in the 1960s and 1970s.[60]

Deptford had a chapel in the 16th century. It
retained a chalice of 7½ oz. and a bell when 13
oz. of plate were taken for the king in 1553,[61]
apparently went out of use between 1583 and
1587, and by 1587 had been profaned.[62] Its exact
site is unknown.

Many rectors of Wylye, including John of
Crauford (1253),[63] Richard Pitts (1390–1411),
Henry Mompesson (1480–1509), and Thomas
Martin (from 1509), were either pluralists, prebendaries, or both.[64] Henry Willoughby was
rector from 1535 or earlier to 1582:[65] in 1553 the
parishioners complained that no quarterly sermon was preached,[66] and in 1556 the church had
no lamp to burn before the sacraments.[67] In
1585, while Thomas Bower was rector,[68] the
church was served by a curate who could not
read the chapters.[69] From 1619 to 1759 most
rectors were resident.[70] John Lee (1619–34),
treasurer of Salisbury cathedral from 1624,[71]
sought strict religious observance, celebrated
communion frequently, and required all to hear
the catechism regularly. Lee and his successor
Alexander Hyde employed curates, and Lee was
assisted by the schoolmaster and Latinist
Thomas Crockford,[72] vicar of Fisherton de la

30 e.g. ibid. A 1/345/252; *W.A.M.* xxxvii. 375; P.R.O.,
SC 2/208/65; SC 2/208/68; above, Bathampton, local govt.
31 W.R.O. 1332, box 22, rec. of ct. baron.
32 *Poor Law Abstract, 1804*, 558–9.
33 W.R.O. 521/17; 2057/S 106; ibid. tithe award.
34 *Poor Law Abstract, 1818*, 492–3; *Poor Rate Returns,
1816–21*, 186; *1822–4*, 225; *1825–9*, 216; *1830–4*, 209; *Poor
Law Com. 2nd Rep.* App. E, 400–1.
35 *Poor Law Com. 2nd Rep.* App. D, 560.
36 O.S. Map 1/100,000, admin. areas, Wilts. (1974 edn.).
37 Below, this section [architecture]; *Civil Pleas, 1249*
(W.R.S. xxvi), p. 73.   38 *W.A.M.* xl. 299.
39 *V.C.H. Wilts.* viii. 44; xi. 220; Ch. Com. file, NB
34/412C.
40 Phillipps, *Wilts. Inst.* (index in *W.A.M.* xxviii. 235).
41 *Cal. Pat. 1377–81*, 75; *1381–5*, 310, 315, 377–8, 405.
42 Ibid. *1388–92*, 114, 127.
43 P.R.O., E 331/6/35, rot. 695.
44 Ch. Com. file, NB 34/412C.
45 *Tax. Eccl.* (Rec. Com.), 181.
46 *Valor Eccl.* (Rec. Com.), ii. 101.
47 P.R.O., C 2/Jas. I/L 18/35.
48 *W.A.M.* xl. 393.
49 *Rep. Com. Eccl. Revenues*, 854–5.
50 W.R.O., D 1/24/234/1; D 1/24/234/3.
51 Ibid. 2057/S 106.
52 Ibid. tithe award; Little Langford tithe award.
53 *Civil Pleas, 1249* (W.R.S. xxvi), p. 73.
54 *Inq. Non.* (Rec. Com.), 177.
55 *First Pembroke Survey*, ed. Straton, i. 277.
56 W.R.O., tithe award.
57 Ibid. D 1/24/234/2; P.R.O., C 2/Jas. I/L 18/35.
58 W.R.O., D 1/24/234/4.   59 Ibid. D 1/11/57.
60 Ch. Com. deeds 536214; 578504; 621716.
61 *W.A.M.* xii. 365.
62 P.R.O., C 66/1289, m. 1; ibid. PROB 11/66, ff. 52–4.
63 *Cal. Papal Reg.* i. 286.
64 Phillipps, *Wilts. Inst.* i. 75, 100, 168, 187; Le Neve,
Fasti, 1300–1541, Salisbury, 31, 40, 97, 102; *Reg. of Wylye*,
ed. G. R. Hadow, pp. viii–ix.
65 *Valor Eccl.* (Rec. Com.), ii. 101; Phillipps, *Wilts. Inst.*
i. 231.   66 W.R.O., D 1/43/1, f. 118.
67 Ibid. D 1/43/2, f. 8.
68 Phillipps, *Wilts. Inst.* i. 231; ii. 10.
69 W.R.O., D 1/43/6, f. 17A.
70 Ibid. bishop's transcripts, bdles. 1–3.
71 Phillipps, *Wilts. Inst.* ii. 10, 17; Le Neve, *Fasti,
1541–1857, Salisbury*, 12.
72 M. Ingram, *Church Cts., Sex and Marriage in Eng.
1570–1640*, 118–23; W.R.O., bishop's transcripts, bdle. 1.

Mere from 1613, who kept Wylye's registers as elaborately as he did those of Fisherton and Stockton.[73] Hyde was subdean of Salisbury from 1637, a royalist, sequestrated in 1645, and bishop of Salisbury 1665–7.[74] Thomas Hill was the minister in 1650: he or his curate preached every Sunday and there were two sermons when both were present, but the curate was charged with failing to read parliamentary orders.[75] Hill was instituted in 1660.[76] In 1662 the church had no Book of Homilies nor Jewell's *Apology*.[77] Neither Thomas Dampier, rector 1759–74, lower master at Eton College (Bucks.) and from 1774 dean of Durham,[78] nor his son John, rector 1774–1826, rector of West Meon (Hants) and a canon of Ely, was resident.[79] From 1760 to 1792 John Eyre was resident curate, and his successors included William Moody, 1792–1801, lord of Great Bathampton manor from 1798, and John Seagram, 1801–9, curate of Steeple Langford from 1810.[80] In 1783 Eyre held two services every Sunday, held weekday services, catechized, and celebrated communion six times a year: he considered the sale of the *Salisbury Journal* on Sundays to be profane.[81] From 1826 the rectors resided. J. S. Stockwell, rector 1840–69, held several livings in the gift of the earl of Pembroke and of Montgomery[82] but in 1864 only Wylye. He then held services thrice on Sundays and celebrated communion c. 15 times a year.[83]

In 1678 Christopher Willoughby endowed yearly gifts of 10s. to the rector for a sermon, 10s. to the churchwardens, 10s. to the parish clerk, and 10s. to the minister to keep the accounts and a register of his charities for the parish. The sums were still being given in the early 20th century but the sermon was not then preached.[84] In 1931 the whole £2 was spent on upkeep of the churchyard,[85] and in 1991 with Willoughby's eleemosynary charity.[86]

The church of *ST. MARY*, so called in 1333,[87] is built of coursed limestone and consists of a chancel with north vestry and organ chamber, a nave with north aisle and south porch, and a west tower. Of the church before it was largely rebuilt the nave, which had thick walls, may have been of 12th-century origin, the chancel, from which the triple-lancet east window survives, was added in the later 13th century, the tower was built in the early 15th century, and the porch

may also have been 15th-century.[88] In the later 16th century and early 17th the rector was accused of neglecting and damaging the chancel.[89] The church was reseated in 1665[90] and had a west gallery in 1774.[91] Apart from the tower and some walling of the chancel the church was rebuilt 1844–6 to designs by T. H. Wyatt and D. Brandon. In 1876 the vestry, built 1844–6, was enlarged to incorporate an organ chamber,[92] and in 1902 the four pinnacles on the tower were taken down. Both the new font given in 1765 and that which replaced it in 1846[93] were in the north aisle in 1991. Fittings brought from St. Mary's church, Wilton, 1844–6, when Wilton's church was replaced and Wylye's rebuilt, include the pulpit dated 1628, the lectern, the reading desk, and two candelabra given to Wilton in 1814:[94] Wilton and Wylye had the same patron, and the rector of Wylye from 1840 had until then been rector of Wilton.[95] There was a clock in the tower in 1678: it was replaced in 1775.[96] In the churchyard a large railed 18th-century tomb is reputed to have been built for, but not occupied by, one Popjay.[97] The lych gate was erected in 1885.[98]

The king took 7½ oz. of plate in 1553 and left a high quality silver-gilt chalice, hallmarked for 1525, which belonged to the parish in 1991. A tankard hallmarked for 1674 and an almsdish hallmarked for 1661 were given in 1686, a silver basin for baptisms was given in 1781, a silver-gilt paten in 1864, a silver-gilt flagon probably in 1865, and a wafer box in 1945. After c. 1890 a communion cup hallmarked for 1562 and a paten dated 1570 were given. All that plate also belonged to the parish in 1991.[99]

Of the three bells in 1553 one, cast in Salisbury c. 1425, remained in the church in 1991 as the fourth bell in a ring of six. The tenor was cast by John Wallis in 1587, another bell by William and Robert Cor in 1697. In 1897 the ring was increased from four to five by a bell cast by Mears & Stainbank, in 1898 a bell of 1755 cast by James Burrough was recast by Mears & Stainbank, and in 1975 the ring was increased to six by a bell brought from Fisherton de la Mere church.[1]

The registers date from 1581 and are nearly complete. Entries to 1629, those to c. 1600 being transcripts, were written by Thomas Crockford.[2] An earlier register was burnt c. 1568.[3]

73 *V.C.H. Wilts.* viii. 45; xi. 221; W.R.O. 521/2.
74 *D.N.B.*; *W.N. & Q.* vi. 388–9.
75 *W.A.M.* xl. 393.
76 Phillipps, *Wilts. Inst.* ii. 22.
77 W.R.O., D 1/54/1/4, no. 36B.
78 Phillipps, *Wilts. Inst.* ii. 78; *D.N.B.*
79 *Alum. Oxon. 1715–1886,* i. 335; *Reg. of Wylye,* p. vii; *W.N. & Q.* viii. 504; *Clerical Guide* (1822).
80 *Reg. of Wylye,* p. vii; W.R.O., bishop's transcripts, Steeple Langford, bdle. 3; Wylye, bdle. 3; above, Bathampton, manors.
81 *Vis. Queries, 1783* (W.R.S. xxvii), pp. 14, 247.
82 *Reg. of Wylye,* p. ix; *Tithe Apportionments* (W.R.S. xxx), pp. 28, 67, 80, 94.   83 W.R.O., D 1/56/7.
84 *Endowed Char. Wilts.* (S. Div.), 925, 927.
85 W.R.O., L 2, Wylye.
86 Inf. from Major M. D. Burroughes, Wylands Cottage; below, charities.
87 *Wilts. Inq. p.m. 1327–77* (Index Libr.), 97.
88 W.R.O., D 1/61/6/9; J. Buckler, watercolour in W.A.S. Libr., vol. iii. 22; see above, plate facing p. 235.

89 P.R.O., C 2/Jas. I/L 18/35; W.R.O., D 1/43/6, f. 17A.
90 W.R.O., agreement concerning seats in Wylye church, 1665.
91 Ibid. 521/4; Buckler, watercolour in W.A.S. Libr., vol. iii. 22.   92 W.R.O., D 1/61/6/9; D 1/61/27/4.
93 Ibid. 521/4; 521/17.
94 *W.A.M.* xxxvi. 141; *V.C.H. Wilts.* vi. 29–30; Pevsner, *Wilts.* (2nd edn.), 601.
95 W.R.O., D 1/2/33, f. 96v.
96 Ibid. 521/4; S. F. Buxton, *Church of St. Mary the Virgin, Wylye* (W.R.O. 2505/3), 5.
97 Hoare, *Mod. Wilts.* Branch and Dole, 7.
98 Date on lych gate.
99 Nightingale, *Wilts. Plate,* 79–80, from which dates of hallmarks are taken; Buxton, *Church of St. Mary,* 10–11, where different dates are given for some hallmarks; inf. from Major Burroughes; for the chalice, see above, plate facing p. 187.
1 Walters, *Wilts. Bells,* 244–6, 262, 309; inf. from Major Burroughes.
2 *Reg. of Wylye,* p. v; W.R.O. 521/2–9.
3 W.R.O., D 1/43/5, f. 30v.

NONCONFORMITY. A papist lived in the parish in 1780.[4] Between 1662 and 1686 Henry Ingram, reputedly a Quaker, failed to attend church and to have children baptized.[5] Wylye's two nonconformists in 1676[6] were presumably Ingram and his wife. A former malthouse in Wylye was licensed for worship by Independents in 1813:[7] in 1851 the afternoon service was attended by 118 on Census Sunday.[8] It was superseded by a Congregational chapel built in 1860 at the east end of Teapot Street.[9] That chapel was opened as a branch of the church at Codford,[10] was registered for the solemnization of marriages in 1872,[11] and remained open in 1991.

EDUCATION. In 1818 there was no school,[12] and in 1833, although a total of 54 children were in three day schools, more than half the children of the parish were not taught.[13] About 1840 a schoolroom stood at the west end of Teapot Street;[14] the school was united to the National society and in 1846–7 was attended by 31 boys and 30 girls.[15] In 1858 it was attended by only 20–30, the room and the teaching were considered poor, and children left at 10 or 11.[16] A winter evening school was being held in 1863–4,[17] and a new National school and a teacher's house were built near the church in 1873.[18] From 1860 or earlier the Congregationalists had a school,[19] the teaching at which was also poor; the school was open until 1877 or later.[20] The National school was enlarged in 1893;[21] average attendance, 78 in 1902,[22] gradually declined from 93 in 1906 to 60 in 1938,[23] and the school was closed in 1973.[24]

CHARITIES FOR THE POOR. Shortly before her death in 1583 Susan Mompesson built an almshouse at Deptford.[25] Nothing more is known of it.

Wylye parish shared with Steeple Langford parish the 4 qr. of wheat, 25 ells of canvas, and 25 yd. of blue cloth given yearly by will of Elizabeth Mervyn (d. 1581). Bread and, by the early 19th century, £3 6s. 8d. instead of cloth were given to the poor. From 1875 Wylye's share of the charity was a yearly payment of £8 5s.; the money was spent on bread which was given away, 495 loaves in 1903,[26] 86 loaves in 1953.[27] From c. 1960 the number of recipients was reduced and money was given instead of bread. The payment was compounded for in 1990, and in 1991 two gifts of money were made.[28]

In 1678 Christopher Willoughby endowed life pensions of £3 a year for each of two aged parishioners who were to be badged.[29] The charity has apparently never lapsed, and two payments of £3 were made in 1991.[30] In 1681 Willoughby gave a further £20 to the poor of the parish, and the parish added £10 and in 1688 Robert Hyde £10 to the endowment. In the late 1680s and early 1690s the income was spent on clothes given to four people. There is no later evidence of such gifts, and in 1833 the endowment was supposed to have been used in 1793 to buy a house at Chequers to be lived in by the poor: a stone inscription to record the charity was erected c. 1833. The house was occupied in the 1860s but in 1904 was uninhabitable.[31]

By will proved 1865 William Perrior gave the income from £500 as yearly pensions to five old men of the parish, excluding beneficiaries of Willoughby's pension charity and giving preference to servants of himself, his father, and his brother. The income was £15 in 1904,[32] and in 1953 £2 10s. was given to each of five old men.[33] In 1991 the five recipients were given £15 each.[34]

4 V.C.H. Wilts. iii. 96.
5 Williams, Cath. Recusancy (Cath. Rec. Soc.), 313; W.R.O., D 1/54/1/4, no. 36B; D 1/54/6/5, no. 15; D 1/54/10/5; D 1/54/11/5, no. 39.
6 Compton Census, ed. Whiteman, 125.
7 Meeting Ho. Certs. (W.R.S. xl), p. 73.
8 P.R.O., HO 129/265/1/10/21.
9 Kelly's Dir. Wilts. (1939).
10 S. B. Stribling, Wilts. Congregational Union, 51–2.
11 Lond. Gaz. 1 Mar. 1872, p. 1271.
12 Educ. of Poor Digest, 1041.
13 Educ. Enq. Abstract, 1052.
14 W.R.O., tithe award.
15 Nat. Soc. Inquiry, 1846–7, Wilts. 12–13.
16 Acct. of Wilts. Schs. 52.
17 W.R.O., D 1/56/7.
18 P.R.O., ED 7/131, no. 336.
19 Stribling, Wilts. Congregational Union, 51; above, nonconf.
20 P.R.O., ED 21/18632.
21 W.R.O., F 8/320, Wylye; F 8/600/305/1/22/1.
22 Ibid. F 8/220/1.
23 Bd. of Educ., List 21, 1908–38 (H.M.S.O.).
24 W.R.O., list of primary schs. closed since 1946.
25 P.R.O., PROB 11/66, ff. 52–4.
26 Endowed Char. Wilts. (S. Div.), 924, 927; above, Steeple Langford, charities.
27 W.R.O., L 2, Wylye.
28 Inf. from Major Burroughes.
29 Endowed Char. Wilts. (S. Div.), 925.
30 W.R.O., L 2, Wylye; inf. from Major Burroughes.
31 Endowed Char. Wilts. (S. Div.), 925–6, 928; Char. Don. H.C. 511 (1816), xvi (2), 1338–9; W.R.O., tithe award.
32 Endowed Char. Wilts. (S. Div.), 928.
33 W.R.O., L 2, Wylye.
34 Inf. from Major Burroughes.

INDEX

NOTE. Page numbers in bold-face are those of the chapter on the hundred, parish, or township. A page number in italics refers to a map or illustration on that or the facing page. A page number followed by *n* is a reference only to the footnotes on that page.

INDEX

woodland, 184, 197
Batho, G. B., 22
Bavaria, duke of, *see* William
Baverstock, 299
Bawdrip (Som.), 289
Baxter:
  Anne, *see* Trenchard
  Ric., 87
Bayeux (Calvados), bp. of, *see* Odo
Baynton, Wal. de, 269
Beach:
  Henrietta Maria, m. Mic. Hicks, 112
  Wm. 112
  Wm., *see* Hicks Beach
Beaches (in Wokingham, Berks.), 3
Beacon Hill (in Amesbury, Bulford, and Cholderton), 13, 63–6, 68, 70
beagles, 48, 97
Beauchamp:
  Alice, *see* Tony
  Anne, 180
  F. B., 172, 257, 278
  Guy de, earl of Warwick, 146
  John, Ld. Beauchamp, 146
  Thos., earl of Warwick, 146
  Sir Wm., 146
  Wm., Ld. Bergavenny, and his w. Joan, 257
Beauchamp, Vct., *see* Seymour, Sir Edw.
Beaufort:
  Hen., Cardinal, bp. of Winchester, 31
  John, earl of Somerset, 139
  Marg., *see* Holand
Beaufort, dukes of, *see* Somerset
Beaumont:
  Amice de, styled ctss. of Leicester, m. 1 Sim. de Montfort, 2 Wm. des Barres, 277
  Hugh, 172, 177
  Isabel, *see* Willington
  Marg. de, m. Saier de Quency, earl of Winchester, 36, 277
  Phil., 172
  Rob. de, count of Meulan, 98
  Rob. de, earl of Leicester (d. 1168), 98
  Rob. de, earl of Leicester (d. 1190), 277
  Rob. de, earl of Leicester (d. 1204), 277
  Sir Thos. (d. 1450), 172, 177
  Thos. (d. 1488), 172
  Waleran de, count of Meulan, 98
  Wm., 172
  Wm. (d. 1453), 172
Bec-Hellouin (Eure), abbey of, 98
Beckington:
  Gilb. (d. 1527–8), 36
  Gilb. (d. c. 1615), 36
  Gilb. (fl. 1654), 36
  Gilb. (fl. 1662–4), 36
  John, 36
  Mellor, 36
Beckington (Som.), 272
Bedford:
  duke of, *see* John
  earls of, *see* Coucy, Ingram de; Russell; Tudor, Jasper
beech (trees), 175
Belgium, *see* Louvain
bell foundries, *see* Aldbourne; Devizes; Loughborough; Salisbury
Bellême, Rob. de, 138
bellfounders, *see* Bilbie; Boulter; Burrough; Cockey; Cor; Danton; Florey; Lott; Mears, C. & G.; Mears & Stainbank; Purdue; Rudhall; Taylor; Tosier; Wallis, John; Warner; Wells, John
Bellham, Rog., rector of Newton Tony, 151
Bemerton (in Fugglestone), 165–6
benefit society, *see* friendly societies
Benett, *see* Bennett

Benger, John, 261
Bennett (Benett):
  Fred., curate of Maddington and vicar of Shrewton, 212, 250
  Lucy, m. Arthur Fane, 238
Benson:
  Sir Wm. (fl. 1710), 147
  Wm. (d. 1754), 147
Bentley wood (in West Dean), 13, 30
Beresford-Peirse, Sir Noel, and his w. Camilla, 66
Bergavenny, Ld., *see* Beauchamp, Wm.
Berkeley:
  Cath., m. 1 John Stourton, Ld. Stourton (d. 1485), 2 Sir John Brereton, 219
  Cath., w. of Thos., Ld. Berkeley (d. 1361), *see* Veel
  Eve, *see* Zouche
  John, 139
  Maur., Ld. Berkeley (d. 1326), 138–9
  Maur. (d. 1347), 138, 237, 257
  Maur. (d. 1400), 139, 141
  Sir Maur. (d. 1464), 139, 141
  Maur. (d. 1474), 219, 289
  Thos., Ld. Berkeley (d. 1361), 110, 138–9, 141
  Thos., Ld. Berkeley (d. 1417), 139, 141
  Wm. (d. 1485), 219
  Sir Wm. (d. c. 1500), and his w. Anne, 139
Berkshire, 4; *and see* Appleton; Ashridge; Ashridge or Hertoke hundred; Beaches; Buckhurst; Burghfield; Diddenham; Farley; Hinton, Broad; Hinton Hatch; Hinton Odes; Hinton Pipard; Hungerford; Hurst; Reading; Sheepbridge, Great *and* Little; Twyford; Wallingford; Windsor
Aldworth, vicar, *see* Hetley, Hen.
Aston Tirrold, rector, *see* Scrope, Ric.
Bermondsey priory (Surr.), 140
Bernard (fl. 1086), 73
Bernard:
  John s. of, *see* John
  Wal. s. of, *see* Walter
Bernard:
  Eudes, 57, 73
  Mabel, 57
  Rog., 57, 60, 73, 76
  fam., 73
Berry, fam., 129
Berwick St. James, 16, 165–6, *168*, **169–77**, 252–3, 259, 275
  adv., 175–6
  agric., 169, 173–4
  Asserton, *q.v.*
  boundaries, 169
  bridges, 169
  char., 177
  ch., 169–70, 172, 175–7, *176*
    chalice, *187*
  common meadow, 169, 173–4
  common pasture, 169, 173, 175
  cts., 175
  curates, 176, 262
  cust. tenants, 173
  dom. archit., 170, 174
  farms, 171, 174, 188–9, 197, 257, 259, 281
  field systems, 169, 276
  glebe, 174–6
  inc., 174
  inn, 170
  man., 73, 166, 169–76, 288
    Bonham's, 171, 173, 257
    Rectory, 172–6
  mill, 170, 174
  place name, 169
  poor relief, 175
  pop., 169–70
  prehist. rem., 169; *and see* Yarnbury castle

prot. nonconf., 177
rectors, 173–5
rectory, 173, 175
roads, 169–70
Romano-Brit. rem., 169; *and see* Yarnbury castle
sch., 170, 177, 263
tithes, 172–3, 175–6
vicarage, 175, 177, 261–2, 283
vicarage ho., 176
vicars, 175–6; *and see* Powell, Rog.; Sadler, Ant.
woodland, 169
Yarnbury castle, *q.v.*
Bessin:
  John de, 98
  Thos., and his w. Agnes, 99
Beuseval, Geof. de, rector of Sherrington, 240
Bevis:
  Rob., 149
  Thos., 149
Biddesden (in Ludgershall), 4–5, 119, 126, **133–5**
  adv., 135
  agric., 134–5
  Biddesden Ho., *74*, 119, 134, *135*
  ch., 130, 133, 135
  common pasture, 127, 134
  cts., 135
  cust. tenants, 134
  dom. archit., 133–4
  farm, 134–5
  man., 130, 133–4
  pk., 134–5
  pop., 121, 133
  rectors, 135; *and see* Purbrook; Tonge
  roads, 119
  tithes, 131, 135
  woodland, 134–5
Biddesden estate, 135
Bigge:
  Anne, m. Jos. Bates, 110
  Geof., 110
Biggs:
  Chris., and his w. Alice, 263
  H. G., 207
  Harry, 172–3, 207–8
  Hen., 172–3, 207
  Jane, *see* Miles
  John, 261
  Tristram (fl. 1681–7), 180, 302
  Tristram (fl. later 18th cent.), 207
  fam., 180
  and see Yeatman-Biggs
Bigod, Rog. le, earl of Norfolk, 157
Bilbie, Thos., 273
bioscope, 27
Birch:
  Jas., rector of Great Wishford, 293
  Peter, 130
  —, 177
birds (less common), *see* cygnets; partridges; swans; *and see* cockfighting; cockpit; fowling; hawking; rook hawking; rook nets; shooting
Birmingham, Hen. of, 159
Birmingham (Warws.), 160
Bishop:
  Beatrice, m. John Everard, 83
  John (fl. 1191–2), 83
  John (d. c. 1324), and his w. Alice, 83
  Jordan (fl. 1242–3), 83
  Jordan (fl. 1344), 83
Bisset:
  Arnulf, 289
  John, 158
  Margery or Marg., 289
Blacker, Wm., 151
Blackett, Sir John, 83
Blagden:
  Anne, 188
  Edw., and his w. Anne, 188

INDEX

diseases, *see* gaol fever; measles; plague; smallpox
disseisin, 261
disturbing the peace, 151
Ditchampton (in Burcombe and Wilton), 165, 167
Ditcheat (Som.), 52
Dole hundred, 1, 165–7, 271
  meeting place, 165
domestic architecture, *see under places*; *and see* bungalows; council houses; dovecot; flats; folly (archit.); hotels; model farm buildings; oast house; pigeon house; police houses
doorkeeper, John the, *see* John
Dorset, 233; *and see* Marnhull; Shaftesbury
  Iwerne Courtney, rector, *see* Wotton
  Steepleton Iwerne, rector, *see* Moore, Thos.
Douglas:
  Archibald, Ld. Douglas, 31
  Cath., *see* Hyde
  Chas., duke of Queensberry, 22, 28, 31, 33–5, 37, 40–1, 43–4
  J. A., 70
  Wm., duke of Queensberry, 31, 33
dovecot, 238
Dowling, Hen., 95
Downe:
  Edw., 230
  Nic., 230
  Rob., 230
Downing, Edm., 126
Downton, *see* Woodfalls, Upper
dramatist, *see* Gay
Drax:
  Edw., 206, 231, 268
  Eliz., *see* Ernle
  Hen., 206
  Sarah, m. Ric. Erle-Drax-Grosvenor, 206, 231, 268
  Thos., 206–7, 231, 268
Draycot, Wm. of, and his w. Susan, 8
Dredge:
  Anne, m. Wm. Blake, 188
  John, 188
  Mary, m. Geo. Smith, 188
  Solomon, 188
dressage training, 76
driveller, Godwine the, *see* Godwine
drowners (of water meadows), 223–4, 291, 301–2
Druid's Lodge estate, 172, 256–7, 259, 278
Drummond, John, 196, 300
drunkenness, 102
Dugdale, Jas., 87
Duke:
  And. (d. 1633), 65–6
  And. (d. 1678), 66, 112
  And. (d. 1727), 66
  And. (d. 1730), 66–7
  Anne, m. Ant. Southby, 66
  Avice, w. of John (d. 1671), 112, 176
  Edw. (d. 1705), 279
  Edw. (fl. 1809), 86
  Geo. (d. 1618), 65, 86
  Geo. (fl. 1627), 66
  Geo. (fl. 1647), 66
  Geo. (d. 1655), 86
  Geo. (d. 1690), 86
  Geo. (fl. 1675–99), 87, 112, 114, 172
  John (d. 1657), 86, 90
  John (d. 1671), 87, 112, 114, 172
  John (another, d. 1671), 66, 86–7, 114, 172
  John (d. 1743), 87
  John (fl. 1756), 87
  Mary, dau. of And. (d. 1730), 66
  Mary, w. of And. (d. 1678), 66
  Rebecca, m. Geo. or Gorges Hely, 279
  Ric., 66–7, 70
  Rob. (d. 1725), 86
  Rob. (d. 1749), 86

Rob. (d. 1793), and his w. Jane, 86
fam., 67
Dun:
  Aubrey, w. of Geof., m. 2 Ellis the huntsman, 139
  Geof. le, 139
  Sir John (fl. 1312), 8, 11
  John le (?another, d. c. 1331), 139
  Sim. le, 139
  Wm. le (d. 1286), 139
  Wm. (fl. 1388), 179
Dunham:
  Anne, m. Francis Meverell, 37
  Eliz., *see* Bowet
  John (d. 1524), 37
  Sir John (d. 1533), 37
Dunsany, Baroness, *see* Plunkett-Ernle-Erle-Drax, Ernle
Dunstanville:
  Adelize, *see* Lisle
  Parnel de, m. John de la Mare, 194
  Reynold de, 194
  Reynold de, earl of Cornwall (d. 1176), 194–5
  Sibyl, w. of Wal., m. 2 Ingram de Pratell, 194
  Wal. de (d. 1194), 194
  Wal. de (d. 1241), 194
Dunworth hundred, 166
Durford abbey (in Rogate, Suss.), 110, 248
Durham:
  bp., *see* Tunstall
  dean of cath. ch., *see* Dampier, Thos.
Durnford:
  John of, 74
  Wal. of, and his w. Joan, 57
  Wm. of (fl. 1242–3), 83–4
  Wm. of (?the same, fl. 1268), 4
  Wm. of (?another, fl. 1286), 84
Durnford, 3–5, 78, **79–93**, 213
  adv., 91
  agric., 79, 88
  boundaries, 18, 40, 79, 81
  bridges, 79
  ch., 80, 87, 91–3, *92*
  common meadow, 88
  common pasture, 88
  curates, 92
  cust. tenants, 88
  Diamond bottom, 79–80
  Durnford, Great, *q.v.*
  Durnford, Little, *q.v.*
  field systems, 18, 80
  High Post, 79, 81, 90
  ind., 90
  man., 80, 82–8
    Rectory, 4–5, 87–8, 91
  mills, 90
  Netton, *q.v.*
  Newtown, *q.v.*
  Normanton, *q.v.*
  pks., 80, 83, 85, 88–9
  poor relief, 91
  pop., 80
  prebend and prebendaries, *see* Salisbury, cath. ch.
  prebendal ho., 80
  prehist. rem., 80
  prot. nonconf., 81, 93
  roads, 79
  Romano-Brit. rem., 80
  Salterton, *q.v.*
  schs., 81–2, 93
  tithes, 87–8, 91
  vicarage, 91
  vicarage ho., 80, 91
  vicars, 91–2; *and see* Hinxman, J. N.; Parr, J. O.; Selby; Squire; Walter
  woodland, 79, 88–90
Durnford, Great (in Durnford), 5, 15–16, 79, 81, 91
  agric., 80, 88, 90
  airfield, 79, 81, 88, 90
  common meadow, 88

common pasture, 88
cts., 90
cust. tenants, 88, 90
dom. archit., 80–1, 83, 90–1
Durnford Manor, 80, 83, 93
farms, 84, 88–9
inc., 84, 88, 91
ind., 81
inn, 81
man., 82–4, 88, 91
  Southend, 4, 82–4, 86
mills, 81, 90
Ogbury camp, 80, 88
pop., 80
Durnford, Little (in Durnford), 5, 79, 81, 91
  agric., 80, 88–9
  bridge, 81
  common meadow, 88–9
  common pasture, 88–9
  cts., 90–1
  cust. tenants, 89
  dom. archit., 81, 84–5
  farms, 81, 89
  Little Durnford Manor, 81, 84–5, *186*
  man., 4, 80, 84–6, 91
  mill, 90
  pop., 80
  roads, 81
Durrington, 1, 3–4, 29 *n*, 38, 44, 61, **93–105**, *94*, 117
  adv., 102
  agric., 93, 95, 99–102
  army camp, 97; *and see* Larkhill camp
  boundaries, 15, 29, 93
  bridges, 96
  chaplains, 101–2; *and see* Marris
  char., 105
  ch., 95, 102–3
    cross, *251*
  common meadow, 93
  common pasture, 93, 100
  cts., 101–2, 116
  curates, 102–3, 117, 142; *and see* Fowle, Hen.; Head, Hen. *and* Ric.; Maton, Leonard; Owen; Ruddle, C. S.; Webb, Ric.; Westcombe
  cust. tenants, 99–102
  dom. archit., 95–6
  Durrington Walls, 95
  Fargo camp, 97
    hosp., 97
  farms, 44, 99–101, 115
  field system, 95
  fire, 96
  inc., 98–100
  inns, 95–6, 101
  Lark Hill, 93, 95
  Larkhill camp, *q.v.*
  man., 97–9, 141
    Bessin's, 98–100
    East End, 4, 93, 98–100, 102, 113
    Ingram's, 99–100
    Lawes, 99–100
    Marsh's, 98, 100
    Rectory, 99–100, 102
    West End, 4, 93, 97–102
  military activity, 93, 95, 101
  mill, 96, 101
  police sta., 97
  poor relief, 102
  pop., 95
  prehist. rem., 95; *and see* (both s.v. Durrington) Durrington Walls; Woodhenge
  prot. nonconf., 95, 103, 105
  public libr., 97
  rectors, 96, 102–3; *and see* Ruddle, A. G. *and* C. S.
  rectory ho., 102
  roads, 63, 95
  Rom. Catholicism, 103
  Romano-Brit. rem., 95
  schs., 95–6, 105, 143

315

Hinxman (*cont.*)
Edw. (d. 1855), 84
Edw. (d. 1896), and his w. Charlotte, 84
J. N., vicar of Durnford, 91–2
Hippisley:
Frances, *see* Trenchard
John, 87
Wm., 87
Hiredman, Thos., 98
Hoare, Hen., 74, 147
Hobbes:
Anne, *see* Saucer
John, vicar of Tilshead, 273
Thos. (fl. 1428), 34–5
Thos. (another), 35–6, 42
Wm., rector of Sherrington and of Boyton, 241
Hody, Alex., rector of Great Wishford, 292
hoe manufacture, 116
Holand:
Edm. de, earl of Kent, 139
Joan, w. of Thos., Ld. Holand (d. 1360), *see* Joan
Marg. de, m. John Beaufort, earl of Somerset, 139
Maud, *see* Zouche
Sir Rob. de, Ld. Holand, 158, 277
Thos. de, Ld. Holand (d. 1360), 139
Thos. de, earl of Kent (d. 1397), 139
Thos. de, earl of Kent (d. 1400), 139
and see Holland
Holcombe:
Agnes, *see* Sturmy
John, 109, 256, 261
Holden, F. S., *see* Rendall
Holland:
Sir Nat., Bt., and his w. Harriett, 248
Thos., curate of Amesbury, 51
Thos. (another), curate of Amesbury, 51
and see Holand
Hollyman, Lionel, rector of Sherrington and of Boyton, 240–1
Holstein Friesian cattle, 181
Homanton (in Maddington), 166, 201, 211, 277
agric., 208, 210
bridge, 244
common meadow, 208, 210
common pasture, 208, 210
cts., 211
dom. archit., 204
farms, 206, 210
inc., 210
man., 206–7, 210
pop., 204
honors and liberties, *see* Everleigh; Leicester; Sherrington; Shrewton; Trowbridge; Wallingford
Hooker, Ric., rector of Boscombe, subdean of Salisbury, 60, 75
Hooley, E. T., 171, 187, 205, 257, 278
Hooper:
C. L., 300
H. W., 268
Jas., 300
Hopper, Thos., 33
Hopton:
Cath., m. John Wyndham, 270
Mary, m. Sir Thos. Hartop, 270
Ralph, Ld. Hopton, 270
Rob., 270
hopyards, 209, 231
Horne:
Jas., 9
Rog., 9
horse mill, 128
horse trials, 194
horses, *see* Cleveland Bays; dressage training; equestrian centre; Grand National; horse mill; horse trials; hunter trials course; hunting; polo and polo ground; racecourses; racehorse training; racing stables

Horton:
Edw. (d. 1603), 269
Edw. (d. 1605), 269
Sir John, 269
Thos., 269
Toby, 269
Wm., 269
Hospitallers, 85
hospitals, 133; *and see* Bulford, Bulford camp; inoculation hospital; Netheravon camp; nursing and rest homes; Tidworth camp; *and* (*for cross references*) health and medical centres
hospitals and colleges (charitable), *see* Arundel college; Wilton, hosp. of St. Giles and St. Ant. *and* hosp. of St. Jas.; Winchester, hosp. of Holy Cross *and* hosp. of St. John; *and see* (*for cross references*) almshouses
hotels, 22, 29, 81, 245
Houlton:
Jos. (d. 1720), 269
Jos. (d. 1731), 269
Nat., and his w. Mary, 269
Howard:
Bernard, 257
Cath., *see* Catherine
Geo., 299
John, duke of Norfolk, 230, 278
Howe:
Dorothy, w. of John, Ld. Chedworth (d. 1742), 288, 292
Hen., Ld. Chedworth, 187, 207, 257, 278, 288
Sir John, Bt., 187, 288
John (d. 1721), 207, 278
John, Ld. Chedworth (d. 1742), 187, 207–8, 257, 278, 288
John, Ld. Chedworth (d. 1762), 187, 207, 257, 278, 288
John, Ld. Chedworth (d. 1804), 171, 187, 207, 257, 278, 288
Mary, 187
Mary, w. of Sir Ric. (d. 1730), 288
Sir Ric. Grobham, Bt. (d. 1703), 187, 257, 259, 288
Sir Ric., Bt. (d. 1730), 173, 187, 190, 257, 288–9, 293–4
fam., 171, 258–60
Huddelstone:
Joan, *see* Stapleton
Sir John, 187
hue and cry, 48, 90, 260
Hugall, J. W., 103, 118
Hugh (fl. 1086), 229
Hughes:
Ann, *see* Brickenden
John, 159
Hulbert, W. D., 268
Hull:
Ellis of, 269
Eustace of, 269
Hulse, Thos., rector of Great Wishford, 292
Hume, J. H., vicar of Calne, of Figheldean, and of Hilmarton, 117
Humphrey, duke of Gloucester, 198
Humphrey:
Edith, m. — Quintin, 289
John, 289
Humphreys:
Frances, *see* Webb
Thos., 126, 134
fam., 134
hundred courts, 116, 188, 250
quittance from suit at, 4, 116, 165–6, 201, 250, 260, 272, 291
hundreds, *see* Alderbury; Amesbury; Ashridge or Hertoke; Branch; Branch and Dole; Cadworth; Cawdon; Cawdon and Cadworth; Chalke; Dole; Dunworth; Elstub; Elstub and Everleigh; Heytesbury; Mere; Rowborough; Underditch; Whorwellsdown

Hungerford:
Ant., 205, 278
Cecily, w. of Sir Edw. (d. 1607), m. 2 Francis Manners, earl of Rutland, 282
Sir Edm., 83
Edw. (d. by 1507), 83
Sir Edw. (d. 1521), 278
Sir Edw. (d. 1607), 205, 278
Sir Edw. (d. 1648), 205, 212, 278
Edw. (d. by 1667), 83
Edw. (fl. 1673), 205, 207, 278
Eleanor, *see* Arundel
Sir Geo., 83
John, and his w. Eliz., 83
Marg., w. of Sir Edw. (d. 1648), 205
Marg., w. of Rob., Ld. Hungerford (d. 1459), *see* Botreaux
Rob. (d. 1352), 74, 220
Rob., Ld. Hungerford (d. 1459), 206, 278
Rob., Ld. Hungerford and Moleyns (d. 1464), 278
Rob. (d. 1517), 83
Rob. (d. *c.* 1558), 83
Sir Thos. (d. 1397), 8, 11, 57
Thos. (fl. 1564), 205, 208
Wal., Ld. Hungerford (d. 1449), 83, 206–7, 238, 278
Sir Wal. (d. 1516), 278
Sir Wal., Ld. Hungerford (d. 1540), 278
Sir Wal. (d. 1596), 205, 207–8, 278–9, 282
Wal. (d. 1601), 83
Wal. (d. 1754), 83
fam., 207, 280
Hungerford (Berks.), 15, 55, 63, 71, 137, 143, 155
Hunt:
Hen., 275
Jas., 128
fam., 47
hunter trials course, 108
hunting, 18, 119
Huntingdon, Hen. of, 17
Huntingdon, earl of, *see* Hastings
Huntingdonshire, *see* St. Neots priory
huntsman, Croc the, *see* Croc
huntsman, Ellis the, *see* Ellis
huntsman, Waleran the, *see* Waleran
Hurst, R. A., 172, 257, 278; *and see* Hearst
Hurst (Berks.):
woodland, 13
and see Hinton, Broad; Hinton Hatch; Hinton Odes; Hinton Pipard; Twyford
Hussey:
Agnes, w. of Sir Hen. (d. 1290), m. 2 Peter de Breuse, 158
Edm., and his w. Joan, 113
Geof. (fl. 1166–7), 256
Geof. (fl. 1198), 4, 109–10, 112, 256, 258, 260–1
Geof. (d. *c.* 1218), 109–13, 256
Geof. (fl. 1242–3), 113
Gundreda, w. of Geof. (fl. 1198), m. 2 — Warenne, 261
Hen. (fl. later 12th cent.), 109–10, 112, 256, 258
Hen. (fl. 1201), 97
Hen. (d. *c.* 1213), 112
Hen. (d. by 1235), 112, 158
Hen. (d. *c.* 1260), 109–10, 112–13, 256
Sir Hen. (d. 1290), 97, 112, 158
Hen., Ld. Hussey (d. 1332), 112, 158
Hen., Ld. Hussey (d. 1349), 158
Sir Hen. (d. 1383), 158
Hen. (fl. 1503), 246
Sir Hubert, 109, 113, 256–7, 261
Hugh (fl. 1135), 97
Isabel, m. John of Thorney, 109, 256, 261

A HISTORY OF WILTSHIRE

Knighton (*cont.*)
common meadow, 106, 115
common pasture, 106, 115
cts., 102
cust. tenants, 115
dom. archit., 108–9
farms, 101, 112–16
field system, 95, 106
inc., 113, 115
man., 4, 109, 112–14, 116
military activity, 109
mill, 116
pop., 109
Knottingley, John, and his w. Eliz., 195, 300
Knowles, Geo., 110, 113
Knoyle, Upton (in East Knoyle), 158, 194

Lacock:
abbess, *see* Salisbury, Ela
abbey, 36, 242, 248, 250
Lacy:
Alice de, ctss. of Lincoln and of Salisbury, m. 1 Thos. of Lancaster, earl of Lancaster, 2 Ebles Lestrange, Ld. Strange, 28, 30, 36–7, 246
Hen. de, earl of Lincoln, 30, 36, 246, 250
Hugh de, 158–9
Joan, w. of Hen., 28, 36
Marg., *see* Longespée
Lamb, Ralph, 37
Lambert:
Anne, 242
Aylmer Bourke, 238
Edm. (d. 1493), 36
Edm. (d. 1608), and his w. Anne, 238
Edm. (d. 1734), 238, 241–2
Edm. (d. 1751), 238, 241–2
Edm. (d. 1802), 238
Edm. (d. by 1878), 242
John, 248
Nic., 195
Ric., 238
Thos. (d. 1509), 36
Thos. (d. 1638), and his w. Anne, 238
Thos. (d. 1692), 238
Thos., rector of Sherrington and of Boyton, archdeacon of Salisbury, 241
Thos. (another), rector of Sherrington and of Boyton, 241
Wm. (d. 1504), 36
Wm. (fl. 1569), 36
Wm. (fl. 1570), 248
fam., 238
Lancashire, *see* Altcar
Manchester, bp., *see* Fraser, Jas.
Lancaster:
Alice, *see* Lacy
Hen. of, earl of Lancaster and of Leicester (d. 1345), 30, 171, 288
Hen. of, *see* Henry IV
Jos., 53
Maud, *see* Chaworth
Thos. of, earl of Lancaster, 30, 36, 246
Lancaster:
dukes of, 73; *and see* Henry; John (of Gaunt)
duchy, 30, 73, 146, 166, 171
dukedom, 288
earls of, 73; *and see* Edmund; Henry; John (of Gaunt); Lancaster, Hen. *and* Thos.
earldom, 288
Landford, rector of, 91
landscaping, 33, 74, 85, 147–8; *and see* gardens
Lane, Anselm, 257
Langford:
Alan, 179
John (fl. 1242), 179
John (fl. 1329), 179, 182

John (fl. 15th cent.), 100
Ric., 247
Steph. of, 179–80
Thos., 179
Turbert, 179
Wm. of, 179
fam., 179
Langford, Hanging (in Steeple Langford), 165–6, 181, 183, 190, **197–201**
agric., 183, 197, 199–201
A.-S. rem., 192, 197
chap., 191, 197
common meadow, 183, 197, 199–200
common pasture, 183, 197, 199–200
cts., 201
cross, 197
cust. tenants, 199–201
dom. archit., 197–8
farms, 197–200, 299, 301
inc., 183, 199–200
inn, 198
man., 182, 191, 197–201
mill, 189, 197, 200
place name, 184
pop., 198
prot. nonconf., 192, 197–8, 201
rly. sta., 178, 184, 198
roads, 184
tithes, 191, 199
woodland, 183
Langford, Little, 165–6, **178–83**, 184, *185*, 190, 201
adv., 181
agric., 178, 180–1
almshos., 183
boundaries, 178, 183
chant., 182
char., 183
ch., 178, 181–3, *182*
common meadow, 178, 180, 299–300
common pasture, 178, 180
curates, 182, 191
dom. archit., 178–9, 181–2
farms, 180–1, 183
field system, 178
glebe, 180–2
man., 178–80, 182
Langford Dangers, 36, 179–81
mill, 181
place name, 184
poor relief, 181
pop., 178
prehist. rem., 178
rectors, 181–3, 293; *and see* Green, Thos.; Hawes; Hyde, Alex.; Lee; Moody, Wm.; Wilson
rectory, 181–2
rectory ho., 178–9, 181–2
roads, 178
Rom. Catholicism, 182–3
sch., 183
tithes, 181
woodland, 178, 180–1
Langford, Steeple, 165–6, 178, 181, **183–93**, *185*
adv., 190–1
agric., 183, 188–9
Bathampton, *q.v.*
boundaries, 183
bridges, 184
char., 191, 193, 305
ch., 184, 190–2, 199
ch. ho., 186
common meadow, 183, 188–9
common pasture, 183, 188–9
cts., 189–90
curates, 191, 193
cust. tenants, 188
dom. archit., 184, 186, 189, 191
East End, 186
fair, 190, 302
farms, 174, 187–9, 196–7, 259
field systems, 184
glebe, 191
inc., 183, 189, 191

inns, 186
Langford, Hanging, *q.v.*
Langford, Tucking, *q.v.*
man., 186–90, 193, 246, 289
Kingston's, 188–9, 192
mills, 184, 188–90, 200
place name, 184
poor relief, 190
pop., 184
prehist. rem., 183–4; *and see* Yarnbury castle
prot. nonconf., 192
rectors, 182, 188–91, 201; *and see* Coates; Collier; Giles; Harrison, Mic.; Jessop; Mompesson, Hen.; Parham, John; Tunstall; Weller; Winchester, John of *and* Nic. of
rectory ho., 184, 191
roads, 184
Rom. Catholicism, 192
Romano-Brit. rem., 184
sch., 186, 192–3
tithes, 191
woodland, 183–4
Yarnbury castle, *q.v.*
Langford, Tucking (in Steeple Langford):
dom. archit., 186
farms, 186
mill, 189
place name, 189
pop., 186
Langfords, the, benefice, 181, 190, 303
Langtoft, Ric. of, rector of Great Wishford, 292
Langton, Geof., 87
larderer, 205
Larkhill camp (in Durrington), 1, 16, 18, 23, 47, 93, 97, 101, 245
architt., 97
chs., 97, 103
fire, 97
inn, 97
medical centre, 97
police sta., 97
R.A.F. sta., 109
Rom. Catholicism, 103
sch., 97, 105
streets, 97
Larkhill light military railway, 16, 97
laundering, 129; *and see* Shrewton laundry
Laverstock, 79
Lavington, Alice, *see* Lawes
Lavington, Market, 167, 184
Gore, *q.v.*
Lavington, West, *see* Littleton Pannell
Lawes:
Alice, m. — Lavington, 99
Christian, 99
Jane, 99
Leonard, 99
Susanna, m. — Amor, 99
Thos., 99
Layham, Rob. of, 111
Le Sueur, L., 87
Lee, John, rector of Little Langford and of Wylye, treasurer of Salisbury cath., 182, 303
Leicester:
earls of, *see* Beaumont; Edmund; Lancaster, Hen. of; Montfort, Sim. de
honor, 3, 111
Leicestershire, *see* Loughborough
Leighton:
Sir Edw., 37
Eliz., *see* Meverell
Lesley, C. M., 208
Lestrange:
Alice, *see* Lacy
Ebles, Ld. Strange, 30, 37, 246
Joan, *see* Ingham
Sir Rog., Ld. Strange, 37, 187
Letard (fl. 1086), 179

A HISTORY OF WILTSHIRE

Nadder, riv., 165, 183, 213, 215–16, 218
Nail, Wm. (?two of the name), 74
Nairn, John, rector of Boscombe and of
Pertwood, 60
Naish:
    Thos. (fl. 1654), 268–9
    Thos. (fl. 1694), subdean of Salis-
        bury, 52
National society, 192, 241, 284, 305;
    and see schools
National Trust, 17, 35, 37, 44, 265
Nature Conservancy Council, see
    English Nature
nature reserve, 301; and see Parsonage
    Down national nature reserve
Navarre, Joan of, see Joan
Neate:
    Anne, see Cowper
    John, 111
Nelson:
    (formerly Bolton), Frances, ctss.
        Nelson, 73
    Sir Maur., 73
Netheravon, 95, 116
    man. (Cormayles; Netheravon Lam-
        bert), 112
Netheravon camp (in Figheldean and
    Fittleton), 108
    airfield, 108
    hosp., 108
Netton (in Durnford), 5, 79, 81–2, 90–1
    agric., 80, 88–9
    common pasture, 88–9
    cust. tenants, 89
    dom. archit., 81–2
    farms, 81–2, 88–9
    inc., 89
    ind., 82
    inn, 81
    man., 84–6
    Netton Elm, 81
    Netton Green, 81–2, 93
    pop., 80
    prot. nonconf., 81, 93
    roads, 81–2
    sch., 81–2, 93
Netton (in Shrewton), 166, 204, 242,
    244, 248, 250
    agric., 248–9
    common pasture, 248–9
    dom. archit., 244
    pop., 244
Neville (Nevill):
    Alan de, 97
    Eliz. de, m. 1 Sim. Simeon, 2 John
        la Warre, Ld. la Warre, 97
    Ernis de, 97
    Gilb. de (d. 1294), 4, 97
    Gilb. de (d. 1359), 97
    Gillian, w. of Alan de, m. 2 Steph.
        Chamber, 97
    Hugh de (fl. 1124), 124, 131
    Hugh de (d. c. 1229), 97–8
    Isabel, m. Geo. Plantagenet, duke of
        Clarence, 31
    Isabel, see Waleran
    Joan de, m. Jordan de St. Martin,
        186–7
    John de (fl. 1179), 148
    John de (fl. 1242–3), 148
    John de (d. 1334), 97
    Ralph de, rector of Ludgershall, bp.
        of Chichester, 131
    Ric., earl of Salisbury and of War-
        wick, 31, 111
    Wm. de, 186
New:
    John, 146
    Rog., 146
New Zealand, 63, 65
Newcastle, duke of, see Pelham-
    Clinton-Hope
Newdick, Rob., 35–6
Newman:
    J. H., 77
    John, 86

Newnton, Long (now Glos.), 252
Newnton, North, 216
    rector, 199
Newport (in Maddington), 201, 204
Newsham, Ric., 287
Newton, South, 165–6, **213–27**, *214*,
    292, 294
    adv., 225
    agric., 215, 220–1
    almshos., 227
    boundaries, 215
    Burden's Ball, q.v.
    char., 226–7
    Chilhampton, q.v.
    ch., 216, 225–6
    common meadow, 215, 220–1
    common pasture, 215, 220–2
    cts., 224
    cust. tenants, 220–2, 224
    dom. archit., 216–17, 224–5
    farms, 216–17, 221, 223, 290
    field systems, 216
    fire, 216
    inc., 221
    ind., 224
    inns, 216
    man., 217–25
        Prebendal, 220–1, 225
    mills, 216, 223–4
    place name, 216
    poor relief, 224–5
    pop., 216
    prebend and prebendaries, see Wil-
        ton, abbey
    prehist. rem., 216
    prot. nonconf., 226
    rly., 216
    rector, 225
    roads, 215
    Romano-Brit. rem., 216
    sch., 216, 226
    Stoford, q.v.
    tithes, 220, 225
    trades, 224
    Ugford, North, q.v.
    vicarage, 225
    vicarage ho., 216–17, 225
    vicars, 225; and see Dickenson;
        Hetley
    Wishford, Little, q.v.
    woodland, 215
Newton Tony, 3–4, 6, 10, 16, 56,
    143–53, *145*
    adv., 151
    agric., 143, 148–50
    boundaries, 143
    bridges, 144–5
    cemetery, 145
    char., 153
    ch., 144, 151–3, *152*, *235*
    common meadow, 149
    common pasture, 149–50
    cts., 150
    curates, 151–2
    cust. tenants, 149–50
    dom. archit., 144–7, 151
    farms, 10, 147, 150
    field systems, 71, 144
    glebe, 151
    inc., 150–1
    inns, 144, 146–7
    man., 143, 146–51, 153
        Norris's, 148–50
    military activity, 143, 150
    mill, 150
    place name, 143
    poor relief, 150
    pop., 144
    prehist. rem., 143–4
    prot. nonconf., 12, 144, 151, 153
    rly. sta., 144
    rectors, 150–2; and see Bellham;
        Chitterne, John; Cliff; Ekins,
        John; Kelsey; Peill; Price; Riley;
        Watts; White, Jas.
    rectory, 77, 151–2

    rectory ho., 144, 151
    roads, 71, 143–4
    Rom. Catholicism, 147, 153
    Romano-Brit. rem., 143
    sch., 12, 61, 144, 153
    tithes, 149, 151
    Tower Hill, 143–4, 147, 150
    Wilbury Ho., 32, 74, 145, 147, *148*,
        153
        lodges, 145
        pk., 71, 143, 145, 147–8, 150
    woodland, 150
    workho., 150
Newtown (in Durnford), 5, 79–80, 82
    agric., 89
    bridge, 82
    cust. tenants, 89
    dom. archit., 82
    farms, 82, 89–90
    inc., 89
    mission hall, 82, 91
    pop., 80
    roads, 82
Nicholas son of Ellis, and his w. Alice,
    35
Nicholas:
    Edw., 207, 278
    Sir John, 207, 278
Nine Mile river, 63–5, 68, 106, 137
Noble, Rob., 148
Norfolk:
    duke of, see Howard, John
    earl of, see Bigod
Norman (fl. 1066), 198
Normanton (in Durnford), 3, 5, 35, 44,
    49, 79, 82, 91
    agric., 90
    boundaries, 40, 79
    chap., 82, 91
    common pasture, 90
    cts., 91
    cust. tenants, 90
    dom. archit., 82
    farms, 42, 82, 90
    man., 4, 36, 87, 90
    mill, 90
    pop., 18, 80, 82
    prehist. rem., 79–80
    roads, 79–80
    Romano-Brit. rem., 80
Norris:
    Joan, m. Rob. Craford, 87
    Ric., 266, 269
    Thos. (fl. 14th cent.), 87
    Thos. (d. 1489), 148
    Wal., 87
    Mrs., 269
Northampton, earls of, see Bohun,
    Humph. de; Compton, Wm.
Northcote:
    John, 257
    Wm., 257
Nottingham, Wm., 130
Noyes, Nat., rector of Cholderton, 76
Nubold (fl. 1086), 170
nursery (horticultural), 128, 260
nursing and rest homes, 22, 34, 122,
    217, 266

oast house, 47
obits, 51, 151, 233, 258
occupations and professions, see
    alehouse keepers; bacon factor;
    bakers; breeches maker; brewers;
    building contractors; butchers;
    camp furnishers; chandlers;
    clothiers; clothmakers; coal dealers
    and merchants; corn dealer;
    curriers; engineer; glazier; glider
    pilots; glovers; goldsmith; gravel
    merchant; handle manufacturer;
    haulier; innkeepers; linen weavers;
    millers; motor cycle dealer; pastry
    cook; pets' undertaker; pipe
    makers; railway workers; road
    contractors; roper; serge weaver;

326

INDEX

dom. archit., 276–9, 283
farms, 44, 174, 257, 259, 276–82
field systems, 276
glebe, 279–80, 283
inc., 281, 283
inns, 276–7
man., 207, 277–82
   Rectory, 279–80, 282–4
   Winterbourne Mautravers, 279–81, 283
mills, 174, 281
place name, 275
poor relief, 282
pop., 276
prehist. rem., 275–6
prot. nonconf., 283–4
rectors, 279–80, 282
rectory, 282
roads, 275–6
Romano-Brit. rem., 276
sch., 284
tithes, 279–80, 282–3
vicarage, 279, 282–3
vicarage ho., 276, 283
vicars, 176, 208, 282–4; and see Harward; King, Mark; Maton, Rog.; Tomkinson; Wells, Neville
woodland, 275
Winterslow, 6
Ramshill wood, 13
Winterslow, East, 3–5
Wiseman, Jas., see Parham
Wishford, Warin of, 289
Wishford, Great, 165–6, 174, 177, 217, **284–94**, *286*
adv., 292
agric., 285, 289–90
almsho., 219, *267*, 285, 294
boundaries, 284–5
bridge, 291
char., 294
ch., *235*, 258, 285, 287, 292–4
common meadow, 221, 285, 289–90
common pasture, 259, 285, 290
cts., 291
curate, 292
cust. tenants, 289, 291
dom. archit., 285, 287–8, 292, 294
fair, 291
farms, 181, 222, 285, 287, 290
field systems, 285
fire engine, *219*, 287
glebe, 292
inc., 290, 292
inn, 287
man., 171, 173, 177, 187, 219, 257, 278, 287–9, 291–3
   Quintin's, 289–90
mkt., 291
mill, 285, 291
Oak Apple club, 287
poor relief, 292
pop., 285
prehist. rem., 285
prot. nonconf., 294
rly. sta., 178, 285, 287, 291
rectors, 285, 289, 292–3; and see Birch, Jas.; Bower, John and Rob.; Buchanan; Burleigh; Hardy; Hody; Hulse; Langtoft; Parker
rectory, 182, 292
rectory ho., 285, 292
Romano-Brit. rem., 285
sch., 173, 263, *267*, 285, 289, 294
tithes, 285, 289, 292
woodland, 285, 290–1
Wishford, Little (in South Newton), 165–6, 213, 215, 224
agric., 221–2
ch., 217, 225
common meadow, 221
common pasture, 221–2
cust. tenants, 221–2
dom. archit., 217

farms, 217, 222
man., 219–20
mills, 223
pop., 216
Wistan (fl. 956), 220
witan, 19
Wokingham (Berks.), see Ashridge; Beaches; Buckhurst
Wolverton:
Alice of, m. Rog. Champion, 148
Joan of, 148
Rob. of, 148
Woodfalls:
Joan of, 194
Joan of, m. 1 Sir Hugh Cheyne, ?2 John Dauntsey, 3 Sir Thos. Blount, 4 Thos. Linford, 194
Sir Steph. of, see Milford
Sir Wm. of, see Milford
Woodfalls, Upper (in Downton), 194
Woodford:
Jeremiah, 86
Ric., 111
Thos., 99
Woodford, 79, 89, 91, 213, 215
bridge, 79, 82
Druid's Head, 256
Heale Ho., 82
Heale man., 139
sch., 93
Woodford, Little, 82
Woodford Valley benefice, 91
Woodhenge, see Durrington
Woodhill:
Agnes, m. 1 Ric. Chetwood, 2 Sir Geo. Calvely, 83
Ant., 83
Eliz., w. of Sir Thos., m. 2 Thos. Ludsop, 83
Fulk, 83
Isabel, w. of John (d. 1367), m. 2 Sir Gerard Braybrooke, 84
(or Wahull), John (d. 1336), 84
John (d. 1348), and his w. Eleanor, 84
John (d. 1367), 84
John (d. 1490), 84
Nic. (d. 1410), 83–4
Nic. (d. 1531), 83
Ric., 84, 91
Sir Thos., 83
woodland, see under places
Woodroffe:
Geo., 74
Rob., 74
Thos., 74
Wm., 213
Woodshaw, Jas., 206
wool carding, 189
wool sorter, 90
wool trade, 128
Woolfe, John, 257
woollen cloth manufacture, 116
woollen mills, 116
woolstaplers, 47, 90
Worcester, bp. of, see Thornborough, John
Worcestershire, see Queenhill
workhouses:
parish, see Newton Tony
union, see Amesbury; Wilton
working men's clubs, 57, 64, 107, 124
World Heritage Site, 1, 17
Wormstall (alias Tyler), Anne, 35
Wort:
J. H., 31, 247
John, 31, 247
fam., 37, 247
Wort & Way, 31–2, 37, 247
Worthen, Thos., vicar of Shrewton, 251
Worting (Hants), rector of, see Bradley
Wotton, John, chaplain of Asserton, rector of Iwerne Courtney, 177
Wrey, Bouchier, 87
Wriothesley, Thos., earl of Southampton, 8

Wroe, John, 232
Wroth, John, 177
Wulfgar (fl. 943), 218
Wulfheah (fl. c. 950), 179
Wulfthryth (fl. 10th cent.), 219, 237
Wyatt, T. H., 72, 77, 152, 182, 212, 225, 251, 273, 293, 304
Wylye:
Agace, w. of John (fl. mid 12th cent.), m. 2 Nic. of Merriott, 195
Joan of, 198
John of (fl. mid 12th cent.), 195
John of (fl. 1270), 195
Maud, ?w. of John (fl. 1270), 195
Nic. of (fl. earlier 13th cent.), 195, 198
Nic. of (fl. 1300), 198
Nic. of (fl. 1339), and his w. Isabel, 139
Sim. of, 299
Thos. of, 194
fam., 198
Wylye, 165–6, 178, 193–4, **295–305**, *296*
adv., 303–4
agric., 295, 300–1
boundaries, 183, 295
bridge, 295
char., 193, 304–5
ch., *235*, 297, 299, 303–5
chalice, *187*
ch. ho., 298
common meadow, 178, 180, 300–1
common pasture, 300–1
cts., 301–2
cross, 297
curates, 303–4
cust. tenants, 297, 300
Deptford, q.v.
dom. archit., 297, 301–3
fair, 190
farms, 297–301
field systems, 297
glebe, 300, 303
inc., 297, 301
inns, 297–8
man., 299–301, 303
mill, 297, 301–2
place name, 297
poor relief, 303
pop., 297
prehist. rem., 295, 297
prot. nonconf., 298, 305
rly. sta., 184, 297
rectors, 303–4; and see Aspull; Batecombe; Bower, Thos.; Crauford; Dampier; Hill, Thos.; Hyde, Alex.; Lee; Martin; Mompesson, Hen.; Pitts; Stockwell; Willoughby, Hen.
rectory, 303
rectory ho., 303
roads, 295, 297
Rom. Catholicism, 305
Romano-Brit. rem., 297
sch., 298, 305
tithes, 303
trades, 302
woodland, 295
Wylye deanery, 175, 232, 250, 261, 272, 283, 292
Wylye and Fisherton de la Mere benefice, 181, 190
Wylye, riv., 1, 165, 178, 183–4, 189, 197, 200, 213, 215–17, 222, 234–5, 237, 239, 253, 259–60, 285, 287, 290–1, 295, 299, 301–2
Wylye Valley hunt, 267
Wyndham:
Caroline, m. John Campbell (later Campbell-Wyndham), 8
Caroline, w. of H. P., see Hearst
Cath., see Hopton
John, 270
Wadham, 8
Wm. (d. 1841), 199–200
Wm. (d. 1862), 199

337